Fodor's

INDIA

6th Edition

Where to Stay and Eat for All Budgets

Must-See Sights and Local Secrets

Ratings You Can Trust

Fodor's Travel Publications New York, Toronto, London, Sydney, Auckland

www.fodors.com

FODOR'S INDIA
Editor: Maria Teresa Burwell

Editorial Production: Evangelos Vasilakis, Tom Holton
Editorial Contributors: John Rambow, Douglas Stallings
Writers: Harpeet Anand, Vaihayasi Pande Daniel, Barbara Floria, Prashant Gopal, Alison Granito, Monica Mercer, John Rambow
Maps & Illustrations: David Lindroth, *cartographer*; Bob Blake, Rebecca Baer, William Wu, *map editors*
Design: Fabrizio LaRocca, *creative director*; Guido Caroti, Siobhan O'Hare, *art directors*; Tina Malaney, Chie Ushio, Ann McBride, *designers*; Melanie Marin, *senior picture editor;* Moon Sun Kim, *cover designer*
Cover Photo: (Taj Mahal, Agra, Uttar Pradesh): Livia Corona/Stone/Getty Images
Production/Manufacturing: Matthew Struble

COPYRIGHT

6th Edition

ISBN 978–1–4000–1912–0

ISSN 1079–6444

SPECIAL SALES

This book is available at special discounts for bulk purchases for sales promotions or premiums. Special editions, including personalized covers, excerpts of existing books, and corporate imprints, can be created in large quantities for special needs. For more information, write to Special Markets/Premium Sales, 1745 Broadway, MD 6-2, New York, New York 10019, or e-mail specialmarkets@randomhouse.com.

AN IMPORTANT TIP & AN INVITATION

Although all prices, opening times, and other details in this book are based on information supplied to us at press time, changes occur all the time in the travel world, and Fodor's cannot accept responsibility for facts that become outdated or for inadvertent errors or omissions. So **always confirm information when it matters,** especially if you're making a detour to visit a specific place. Your experiences—positive and negative—matter to us. If we have missed or misstated something, **please write to us.** We follow up on all suggestions. Contact the India editor at editors@fodors.com or c/o Fodor's at 1745 Broadway, New York, NY 10019.

PRINTED IN THE UNITED STATES OF AMERICA
10 9 8 7 6 5 4 3 2 1

Be a Fodor's Correspondent

Your opinion matters. It matters to us. It matters to your fellow Fodor's travelers, too. And we'd like to hear it. In fact, we need to hear it.

When you share your experiences and opinions, you become an active member of the Fodor's community. That means we'll not only use your feedback to make our books better, but we'll publish your names and comments whenever possible. Throughout our guides, look for "Word of Mouth," excerpts of your unvarnished feedback.

Here's how you can help improve Fodor's for all of us.

Tell us when we're right. We rely on local writers to give you an insider's perspective. But our writers and staff editors—who are the best in the business—depend on you. Your positive feedback is a vote to renew our recommendations for the next edition.

Tell us when we're wrong. We're proud that we update most of our guides every year. But we're not perfect. Things change. Hotels cut services. Museums change hours. Charming cafés lose charm. If our writer didn't quite capture the essence of a place, tell us how you'd do it differently. If any of our descriptions are inaccurate or inadequate, we'll incorporate your changes in the next edition and will correct factual errors at fodors.com immediately.

Tell us what to include. You probably have had fantastic travel experiences that aren't yet in Fodor's. Why not share them with a community of like-minded travelers? Maybe you chanced upon a beach or bistro or B&B that you don't want to keep to yourself. Tell us why we should include it. And share your discoveries and experiences with everyone directly at fodors.com. Your input may lead us to add a new listing or highlight a place we cover with a "Highly Recommended" star or with our highest rating, "Fodor's Choice."

Give us your opinion instantly at our feedback center at www.fodors.com/feedback. You may also e-mail editors@fodors.com with the subject line "India Editor." Or send your nominations, comments, and complaints by mail to India Editor, Fodor's, 1745 Broadway, New York, NY 10019.

You and travelers like you are the heart of the Fodor's community. Make our community richer by sharing your experiences. Be a Fodor's correspondent.

Happy traveling!

Tim Jarrell, Publisher

CONTENTS

MAPS

CONTENTS

CLOSE UPS

ABOUT THIS BOOK

Our Ratings

Sometimes you find terrific travel experiences and sometimes they just find you. But usually the burden is on you to select the right combination of experiences. That's where our ratings come in.

As travelers we've all discovered a place so wonderful that its worthiness is obvious. And sometimes that place is so experiential that superlatives don't do it justice: you just have to be there to know. These sights, properties, and experiences get our highest rating, **Fodor's Choice,** indicated by orange stars throughout this book.

Black stars highlight sights and properties we deem **Highly Recommended**, places that our writers, editors, and readers praise again and again for consistency and excellence.

By default, there's another category: any place we include in this book is by definition worth your time, unless we say otherwise. And we will.

Disagree with any of our choices? Care to nominate a place or suggest that we rate one more highly? Visit our feedback center at www.fodors.com/feedback.

Budget Well

Hotel and restaurant price categories from ¢ to $$$$ are defined in the opening pages of each chapter. For attractions, we always give standard adult admission fees; reductions are usually available for children, students, and senior citizens. Want to pay with plastic? **AE, D, DC, MC, V** after restaurant and hotel listings indicate if American Express, Discover, Diners Club, MasterCard, and Visa are accepted.

Restaurants

Unless we state otherwise, restaurants are open for lunch and dinner daily. We mention dress only when there's a specific requirement and reservations only when they're essential or not accepted—it's always best to book ahead.

Hotels

Hotels have private bath, phone, TV, and air-conditioning and operate on the European Plan (aka EP, meaning without meals), unless we specify that they use the Continental Plan (CP, with a Continental breakfast), Breakfast Plan (BP, with a full breakfast), or Modified American Plan (MAP, with breakfast and dinner) or are all-inclusive (including all meals and most activities). We always list facilities but not whether you'll be charged an extra fee to use them, so when pricing accommodations, find out what's included.

Many Listings

- ★ Fodor's Choice
- ★ Highly recommended
- ⊠ Physical address
- ✣ Directions
- Mailing address
- Telephone
- Fax
- On the Web
- E-mail
- Admission fee
- Open/closed times
- M Metro stations
- Credit cards

Hotels & Restaurants

- Hotel
- Number of rooms
- Facilities
- Meal plans
- ✕ Restaurant
- Reservations
- Smoking
- BYOB
- ✕ Hotel with restaurant that warrants a visit

Outdoors

- Golf
- Camping

Other

- Family-friendly
- ⇨ See also
- Branch address
- ☞ Take note

Experience India

A festival in Jaipur

WORD OF MOUTH

"India is just like a big, juicy fruitcake, and you must limit yourself to a slice at a time. It is killing, trying to tick off all the places [that] people and guidebooks talk about."

–FanofIndia

www.fodors.com/forums

WHAT'S NEW

Shantaram on the Silver Screen

In 2009, the sweeping, big-budget movie Shantaram, directed by Mira Nair (*The Namesake, Vanity Fair*) and co-produced by Johnny Depp and Brad Pitt, hits theaters. The international cast includes Johnny Depp as well as the Indian actors Bipasha Basu and "Big B" himself, Bollywood god Amitabh Bachchan. Adapted from Gregory David Roberts's semi-autobiographical bestseller, the film follows a drug addict who escapes from an Australian prison to start a new life in Mumbai.

India's First Madame President

In the summer of 2007, India's parliament and state legislators elected the country's first female president, 72-year-old Pratibha Patil, who replaced the grandfatherly missile scientist Dr. A.P.J. Abdul Kalam. Although the post is by and large ceremonial, many people are anxious to see what Patil does with her new position and prominence.

60 Years of Freedom

India and Pakistan celebrated their 60th year of Independence in August 2007 with parades, speeches, and lots of soul-searching: what will the future hold for them both? For these long-term rivals and often bitter enemies, there is some justified hope that they might be willing to mend at least some of their long-simmering arguments over borders and work together to confront terrorism, money laundering, and other cross-border crimes.

Artist in Exile

Perhaps India's most famous living artist, and almost certainly its most controversial, M.F. Husain has been living a self-imposed exile in Dubai and London for the past few years. Now in his nineties, Husain has angered right-wing Hindu fundamentalists and received death threats because of several paintings that include stylized and sometime sexual images of naked Hindu deities. Some accuse him of hypocrisy, given that the Islamic and familial subjects in his paintings are not nearly as racy. One of the most recent major flame-ups occurred in early 2006 when the newsmagazine *India Today* reprinted his *Bharat Mata* (Mother India), a personification of India as a nude goddess that some Hindus considered blasphemous.

Southern Splendour

By 2009 Indian Railways plans to launch *Southern Splendour,* luxury train tours modeled on the Palace on Wheels trips in the north. The line will most likely depart and return to Hyderabad, making stops at major locations in Tamil Nadu, Kerala, and Karnataka. At the same time, an additional Palace on Wheels tour is planned for the desert cities of the north, and Karnataka aims to launch its own *Golden Chariot* line of luxury trains in early 2008.

A Boom Year for Flights to India

As domestic airlines go international, more options for getting to India keep rolling out. In August 2007, the national carrier Air India launched a nonstop flight between New York and Mumbai (a nonstop between New York and Delhi is coming in 2008). The 16-hour flight is aboard brand-new Boeing 777s. Also in August, the popular private carrier Jet entered the U.S. market for the first time, debuting a flight from Newark aboard Boeing 777s that makes a stop in Brussels before flying on to Mumbai. Jet also has similar flights heading from Toronto to Delhi and Chennai.

Doing Away with Double Standards?

For over three decades, many middle- and high-end hotels in India have had a dual-tariff system, in which Indian residents were quoted a price in rupees and foreigners were quoted a dollar price that could be up to 25% higher once it was re-converted back to rupees. In the fall of 2007, the Taj luxury group announced it was doing away with the system, and charging everyone the same rupee rate for the same room. Other major chains are following their lead. Although it's unlikely that this will lower luxury-hotel charges significantly for the average tourist, it is a sign of India's new confidence and the strength of its currency.

Sanjay Dutt Faces the Music

Known for the anti-heroes and gangsters he has frequently played in movies, Bollywood star Sunjay Dutt's off-screen life has become just as dramatic. In July 2007 Dutt was sentenced to six years in jail for his involvement in the 1993 Mumbai bomb blasts that killed 250 people and injured 750. The blasts were widely believed to have been ordered by the international gangster Dawood Ibrahim as payback for the destruction of the Babri Mosque a year before. Sentenced to six years for possessing illegal firearms and ammo that may have been involved in the blast, Dutt was first arrested for this crime a month after the bombings, and subsequently served 18 months in jail before being released on bail. At the moment it's uncertain if he'll have to serve out all of this new sentence, or will manage to have it overturned.

Bollywood's Brangelina

In April of 2007, a much-hyped union of two major Bollywood stars occurred, when Aishwarya Rai, the stunningly beautiful former Miss World, married Abhishek Bachchan. The two, who have starred in at least five movies together, were already superstars before the marriage, but this certainly kicked things up a notch. And Aishwarya didn't just gain a husband; she also gained Bollywood royalty for in-laws. Ab's dad is Amitabh, also known as Big B and quite possibly the biggest Hindi film star of all time. At first there was some question of whether Aish would return to acting after her marriage, but the announcement of several upcoming projects with her name attached put those fears to rest. One of the biggest is a movie about the Taj Mahal, set to begin shooting in 2008. Ben Kingsley of *Gandhi* fame will play the Moghul emperor Shah Jehan, and Aish will be his third wife, Mumtaz Mahal, for whom the Taj was built as a tomb.

Booze King Heads for the Scotch

The larger-than-life billionaire Vijay Mallya, whose company owns Kingfisher Airlines as well as Kingfisher beer and many other brands of Indian liquor, stepped outside of the country in 2007 to buy Whyte & Mackay, Scotland's best-selling whisky, in a deal worth 595 million pounds ($1.2 billion). Because Scotch can only be made in Scotland (but can be bottled outside of it), Mallya's purchase ensures that his company will have ample supplies in the future. Whisky is very popular among Indians who drink, and the increase in disposable income among the middle classes means there's no shortage of the bottled spirits.

WHAT'S WHERE

The following numbers refer to chapters in the book.

2 Delhi. Delhi can seem like a world in itself. In a city whose present and future are so tied up with its Moghul past, the top sights are mostly Islamic. These include the enormous Red Fort, the stately Humayun's Tomb, and the mysterious Qutub Minar, the tallest stone tower in India.

3 Agra & North Central India. A sort of Hindi heartland, the country around Delhi contains superlative sites such as Agra's incomparable Taj Mahal and Khajuraho's provocative Hindu temples. Varanasi, Hinduism's holiest city, draws a constant stream of pilgrims to bathe in the Ganges.

4 Rajasthan & Gujarat. Travelers come from all over the world to visit the "Land of Kings," whose storied attractions include the Pink City of Jaipur, the Jain temples in Ranakpur and Mount Abu, tiger-spotting at Ranthambhore National Park, the enchanting lake-city of Udaipur, and Jaisalmer Fort, which rises dramatically out of the desert. Gujarat, to the south and west, is noted as the birthplace of Gandhi. Its capital, Ahmedabad, is famed for bazaars and the Indo-Islamic lines of its buildings.

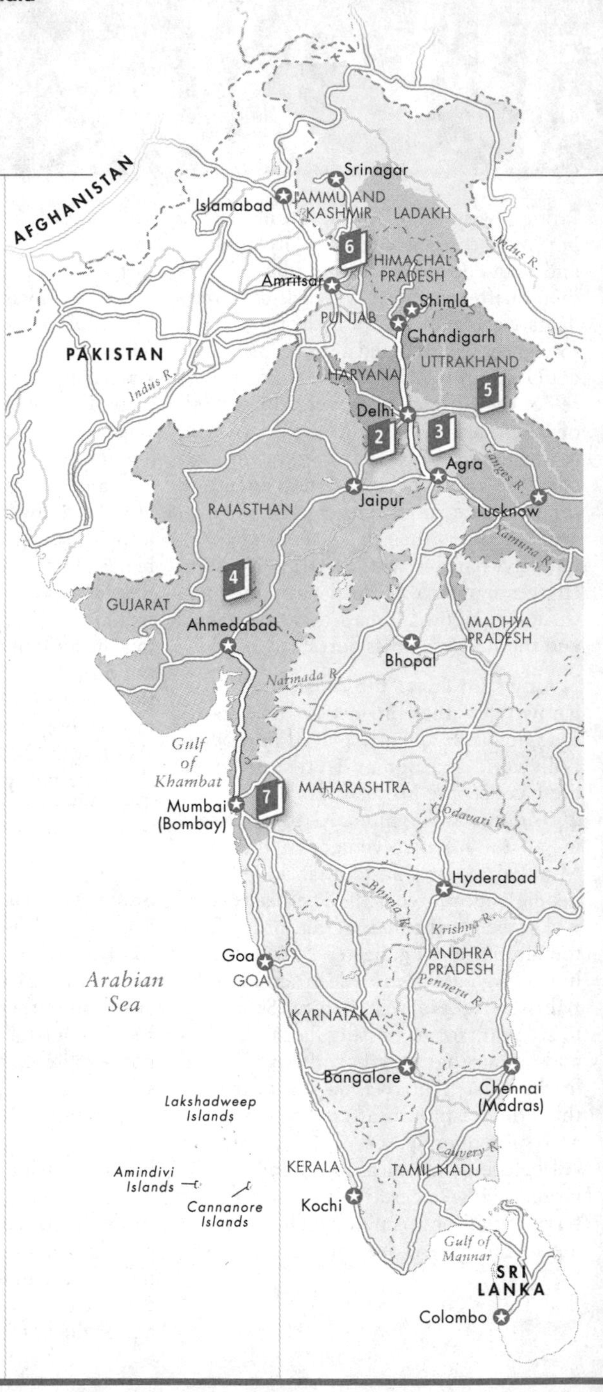

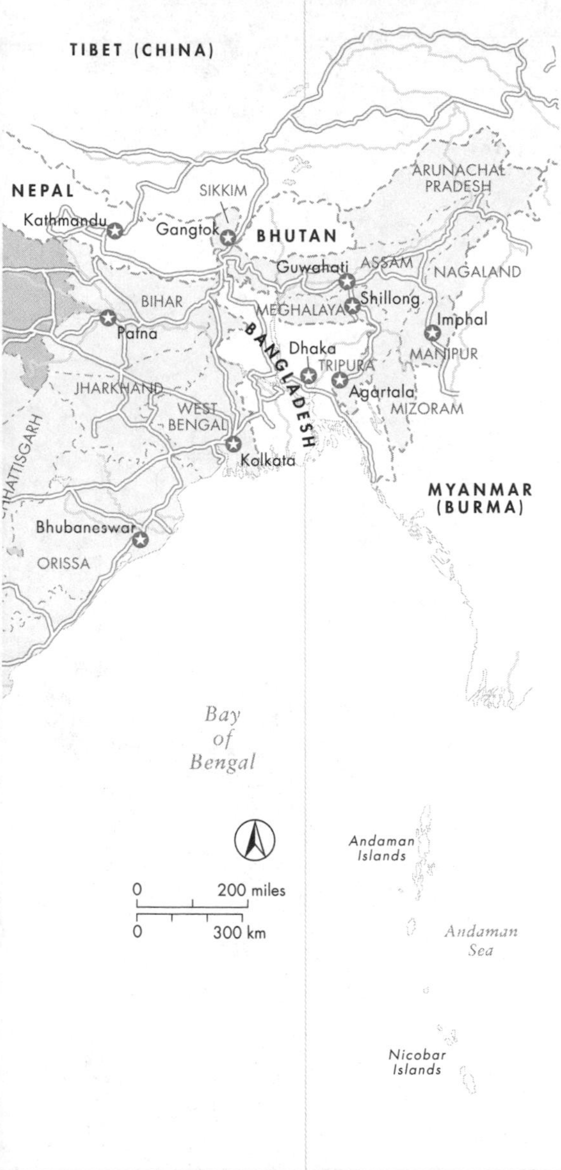

TIBET (CHINA)
NEPAL
Kathmandu
SIKKIM
Gangtok
BHUTAN
ARUNACHAL PRADESH
ASSAM
Guwahati
NAGALAND
BIHAR
Patna
MEGHALAYA
Shillong
Imphal
BANGLADESH
Dhaka
TRIPURA
MANIPUR
Agartala
MIZORAM
JHARKHAND
WEST BENGAL
CHHATTISGARH
Kolkata
MYANMAR (BURMA)
Bhubaneswar
ORISSA
Bay of Bengal
Andaman Islands
0 200 miles
0 300 km
Andaman Sea
Nicobar Islands

5 Uttarakhand. It's best known in the west for its hippie-and-ashrams HQ at Rishikesh, but the state of Uttarakhand has a wealth of natural as well as spiritual riches. Sharing a border with Nepal and Tibet, it's an other-worldly land that's made for adventure sports, including river rafting, paragliding, or tiger spotting from elephant back at Corbett National Park.

6 Himachal Pradesh & Ladakh. The awe-inspiring Himalayas run through the north and east of Himachal Pradesh. Its capital, Shimla, is the largest hill station in India, and Dharamshala is home to the Dalai Lama and thousands of other Tibetans in exile. Amritsar, just a few dozen miles from the Pakistan border, is synonymous with the stunning Golden Temple, holy to the Sikh. Ladakh is a draw for its glorious trails and ancient Buddhist monasteries.

7 Mumbai & Maharashtra. The country's most important urban center, the former Bombay is India at its most modern and contradictory—here the most glamorous and wealthy bump up against the millions that are barely getting by. As the center of India's bustling Bollywood movie factory, Mumbai embraces both traditional values and Western styles.

WHAT'S WHERE

8 Goa. This former Portuguese colony and trade center for spices, silk, and pearls is blessed with a bright blue coastline stretching down to sparkling, palm-lined beaches along the Arabian Sea. As popular for its laidback values as its legendary seafood and beautiful views, Goa holds picturesque wide inland rivers that meander around small pastel houses and churches.

9 Karnataka & Hyderabad. Karnataka is known for three things: the tech capital of Bangalore; nature parks and jungles; and religious and political monuments, including the ruined city of Hampi. Hyderabad, in Andhra Pradesh state, is Bangalore's rival in software and IT. Head here for its Islamic forts and palaces, and shopping—bangles, textiles, and pearls are where it's at.

10 Kerala. The best way to see the central parts of this splendid region is to float through backwater villages on a wooden houseboat. Lush forests cover the cool hillsides inland, where elephants, wildlife sanctuaries, and plantations abound. To the south are beach resorts famous for their ayurvedic massages.

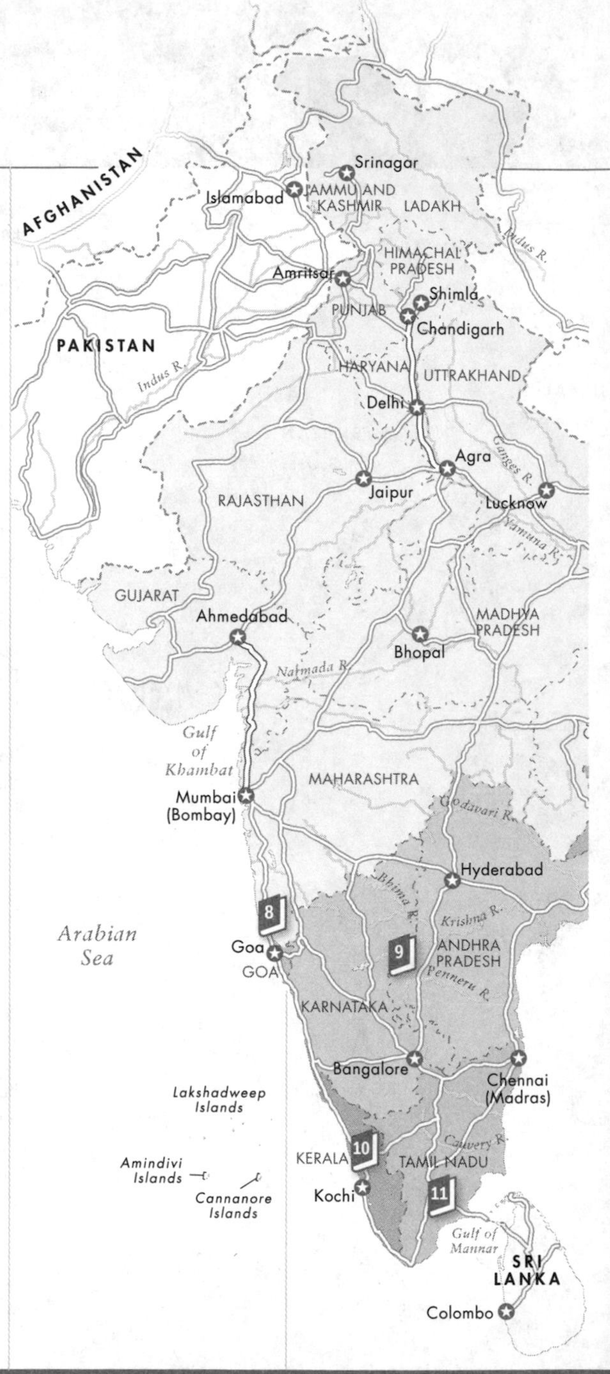

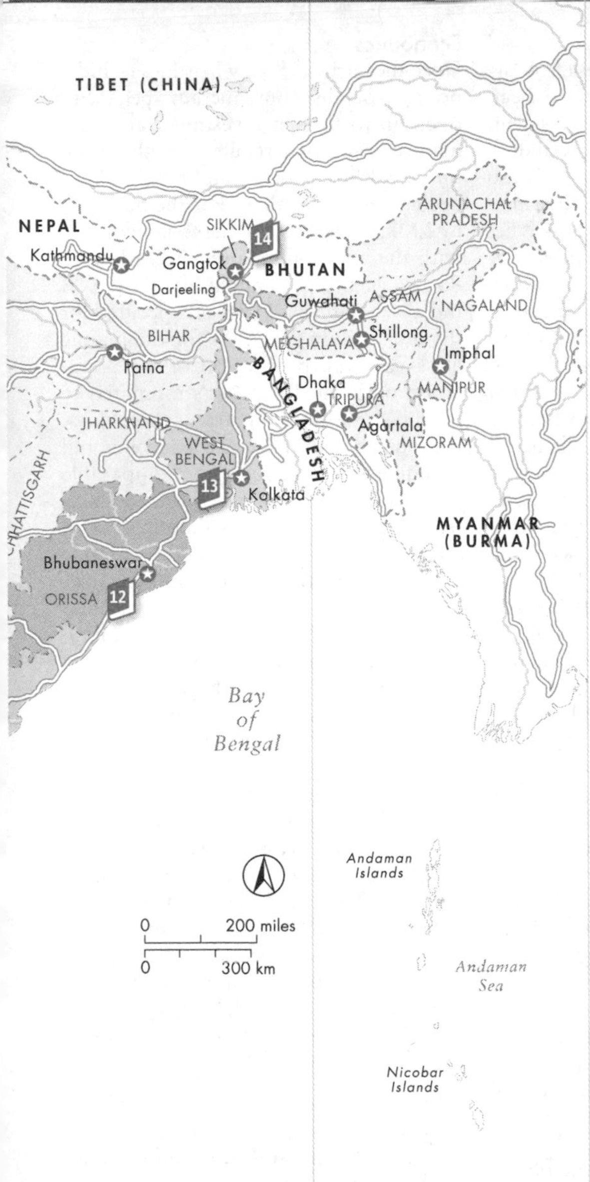

11 Tamil Nadu. Tropical Tamil Nadu stretches between the Eastern Ghats and the Bay of Bengal, down to the southernmost tip of the subcontinent. Here, age-old temples endure on coastal sands and rice fields, and colonial architecture graces the cities.

12 Orissa. If you come to this often overlooked agrarian state, you'll find a different version of India: a tropical countryside, villages and settlements peopled by animist "tribals" and miles of unpopulated coastline. In addition there's the temple-filled capital of Bhubaneswar and the ancient kingdom of Kalinga.

13 Kolkata. Close to the Bay of Bengal and perched on the eastern bank of the river Hooghly, Kolkata (Calcutta) is the gateway to eastern India. It's also the artistic and literary soul of India, with an intellectual heritage beyond that of Mumbai or Delhi.

14 Sikkim & Darjeeling. Wedged between Nepal and China, Sikkim was annexed by India in 1975. A mountainous region, it's popular for its beauty and the many challenges it offers trekkers. Darjeeling, in a corner of West Bengal, is the most famous of the Raj-built hill stations, and it makes a good stop before tackling Sikkim to the north.

INDIA TODAY

Politics

Right now the secular, center-left India National Congress is the party to beat. Congress's somewhat unlikely president, Sonia Gandhi (no relation to *the* Gandhi), is Roman Catholic and an Italian. She's also the widow of Rajiv Gandhi, the prime minister assassinated in 1991, which makes her head of a political dynasty that goes back to independent India's first prime minister, Jawaharlal Nehru, and his daughter, Rajiv's mother, Indira Gandhi. Sonia could have been prime minister: the post was hers to take after Congress won enough votes in the general elections of 2004 to become head of the United Progressive Alliance, a newly formed coalition of left-leaning and centrist political parties. To the surprise of just about everyone, Sonia obeyed what she described as "her inner voice" and declined the job of PM. Instead, she recommended Manmohan Singh, who won the nomination. As a finance minister in the early 1990s, Singh was instrumental in liberalizing India's economy, helping open it up to foreign investment. With no one party able to get enough votes to rule by itself in contemporary India, coalitions of political parties are essential—but they're also unstable. In the summer of 2007 the romance between Congress and its more lefty friends cooled in the face of a proposed agreement with the United States that would give India access to nuclear technology and fuel, even though it never signed the Nuclear Non-Proliferation Treaty. Coalition members object strongly to the possibility that the deal would limit India's sovereignty or right to develop its own nuclear program. Although general elections are not due until 2009, the breakup of the coalition may lead to elections being held even earlier, which could bring Singh's term to an untimely end.

Economics

Since the early 1990s, when India's hidebound socialist bureaucracy began to open up to foreign investment and ease many cumbersome regulations, the country's wealthiest citizens and families have become even wealthier. For the first time in 2007, India became the Asian country with the most billionaires, according to *Forbes* magazine's annual list. Of the 36 Indians included, 14 of them appeared for the first time in 2007. As for the middle class—a small proportion of the population until the 1990s—it's estimated to be about 300 million strong these days. Although the middle class's earning and spending power here is not comparable to its counterparts in the west, the heftier wallets haven't gone unnoticed, with credit cards, shopping malls, mobile phones, cosmetics, cars, foreign name-brand clothes, and pricey organic and convenience foods all seeking—and finding—a bigger audience every day. India's energized economy has also helped entice back well-educated Indians who left for the U.S., Britain, and other foreign lands, and kept others from straying. Driven by the desire to be where the action is, as well as by the post-9/11 hassles of emigrating to many western countries, highly skilled Indians are often choosing to either return to "Mother India" or never leave in the first place. It's a good time to be a skilled employee here: the relatively small number of Indians equipped to take on those much-vaunted IT and service-sector jobs means that salaries for this sliver keep going higher and higher.

All this growth, of course, has come at a price. Roads in major metro areas are saturated with cars and motorbikes, other kinds of infrastructure are also going from

QUINTESSENTIAL INDIA

Riding the Rails

The large rise in domestic airline flights has made it easier to get to many big and mid-size cities fast, but jets are unlikely to ever overtake trains as the most popular—and most scenic—way to get from point A to B. When riding these rails, the journey's the thing. Most routes cover countryside that would otherwide be tedious to reach, passing through fields, over rivers, and along and across hills. You might see people walking along the tracks, oxen at the plow, and crops irrigated through streams running through ditches. And trains aren't just worthwhile for the scenery. The often leisurely trips mean that there's ample opportunity to strike up a conversation—and also to get your fill of tea and regional snacks sold by the wandering sellers who step on at stations along the way.

A Sport and a Pastime

It's cricket that holds the highest place in the typical Indian sport-lover's heart, with soccer only a distant second. Major games are treated like international events, and a loss can cause more than just disappointment—especially when the other team is from Pakistan, India's nemesis and rival in so many things. Even if all the talk of sticky wickets, centuries, leg-spinners, and long hops goes right over your head, a game can still be diverting, and it's a great way to see India at play. If visiting a cricket stadium for an official game seems like too much, just keep your eyes peeled for city *maidans* (open fields). When the weather's fine (or even if it isn't), chances are good that you'll catch some boys working on their game.

bad to worse, and there's been no let-up in India's longstanding problems with corruption. Worst of all, this economic liberalization has done little for the poorest 75%, who still live on less than 40 rupees ($1) a day. Poverty is endemic in rural areas, beset as they are with failing crop prices and the greedy eyes of companies and government agencies anxious to turn farmlands into factories and suburbs. If India is to keep itself stable in the future, it will have to find a way to take its poorest citizens along for the ride.

Movies

Many of India's English-language novelists get a fair amount of attention outside India, but in the country itself, it's all about the movies, especially the Hindi films of Bollywood. Unfortunately, they don't seem to export to a world audience quite as well. With their operalike length (3+ hours) and tendency to throw together low comedy, romance, violence, crying and tears, and copious singing and dancing in a *masala* of storytelling, these creations are at best an acquired taste for many non-Indians.

By the same token, Indians have little taste for most foreign movies, although exceptions are made for global (i.e., American) blockbusters such as the latest action movie or Harry Potter installment. But there have been some small signs of cross-fertilization between Hollywood and Bollywood. Cinema legend Amitabh Bachchan has dipped his toe into movies for Westerners, most notably the prison-break pic *Shantaram*. In addition, the English-language Bollywood movie *The Last Lear,* in which Bollywood actor "Big B" plays a Shakespearean actor, debuted at the Toronto Film Festival.

Technology and Science

India has many riches, but fossil fuels are not among them. About 75% of all petroleum must be imported, and that's a big drag on a poor country's economy. To help cut down on these imports, India has been at the forefront of the use of biogas (fuel created by breaking down organic matter) and wind energy (keep an eye out for wind farms in rural areas, especially in Tamil Nadu and Gujarat). Solar energy, especially for heating water and for lighting, has also made inroads, and it's common to see small solar panels atop houses and light poles. India's government estimates that there are some 25,000 villages that still have not been electrified, and it hopes that solar energy will finally allow the current to reach these settlements. India has also been investing in biodiesel factories that manufacture fuel from a kind of shrub called the jatropha; in 2007 Indian Railways began trials using biodiesel as part of the mix fueling its long-haul trains.

If you want to get a sense of India culture and indulge in some of its pleasures, start by familiarizing yourself with the rituals of daily life. These are a few highlights—things you can take part in with relative ease.

Time for Tiffin

Indians want variety and big flavor in their food, and the tiniest Podunk as well as the biggest megapolis always has its share of tiny restaurants and stalls for buying *tiffin* (small meals or snacks) throughout the day. In the late afternoon, *chaat* (Indian street snacks) stalls set up to sell offerings that are tangy, sour, sweet, crunchy, and delicious all at once. Along the road are the *dhabas* (roadside eateries), so popular that even big-city restaurants attempt to imitate their skill with hearty North Indian dishes. But the best place for India's culinary riches doesn't involve carts or menus or even money. If you find yourself invited to someone's house for dinner, you're in for the full experience. The *chapati* (flatbread) being rolled out, the spices being "tempered" (fried in oil), and conversation at the table—memories of all these will linger on long after you've returned to your own home.

"Is That Your Final Price?"

Many newcomers find bargaining a nuisance, at least at first, but it can also be entertainment. Waiting for an offer, reacting with polite surprise, countering with a much lower offer, and then repeating the process until someone either gives up or gives in—it's a mini-drama as old as civilization and as new as a boy selling not-exactly-name-brand T-shirts in the middle of Bombay traffic. First, keep in mind is that it's impossible to bargain well if you don't know what things ought to cost. Spend a little time visiting shops with fixed prices. When you're ready for a haggle, don't be the first to name a price—yours will be too high and most likely quickly accepted. Wait for an offer, and then counter with something more reasonable. And don't be afraid to walk away and come back tomorrow—it's all part of the game.

IF YOU LIKE

Regal Grandeur

Everyone knows about the Taj Mahal, but India, especially its north, is chock-a-block with many other impressive palaces, mausoleums, and memorials that serve as reminders of its periods of Hindu, Moghul, and Raj rule. Although few are in pristine shape, they all retain some of the magic of the past.

- **Lake Palace (Jag Niwas), Udaipur.** Rising out of Lake Pichola like a mirage, the Lake Palace is a real-life wonder. Now that it's a hotel, you'll need to either get a room or have a pricey dinner here to inspect the courts and fountains up close, but even if you remain admiring it from afar, you'll still find it a memorable part of the scenery. Some of the best views are from the sprawling, equally stunning City Palace.
- **Fort, Jaisalmer.** More than 5,000 people still live in this spectacular 12th-century citadel, which ascends strikingly out of Rajastan's Thar Desert. Inside is a network of temples, palaces, mansions, and tiny winding lanes.
- **Marble Palace, Kolkata.** Everything about this oddball palace, built by a raja in 1855, is baroque: sculptures of animals and religious figures, strutting peacocks, and an interior filled with urns, chandeliers, strange lamps, and striking paintings.
- **Humayun's Tomb, New Delhi.** Ornate and yet calm, this complex of tombs in southern Delhi was a precursor of the Taj Mahal as well as a stunning Moghul artifact in its own right.

Spiritual Wonders

In a country so old and so full of distinct, often competing religions, it's no wonder that India has some of the most impressive and glorious religious monuments in the world. Some sites are still in heavy use for religious purposes, while others are visited far more by travelers and curiosity seekers than they are by religious pilgrims. Either way, most still possess a spiritual quality that's distinctly Indian.

- **Churches of Old Goa.** The ultrabaroque 16th- and 17th-century churches of this Portuguese colony contain the final resting place of St. Francis Xavier, Goa's patron saint, and intricate chapels and carvings.
- **Hampi.** Within the 8 square mi (20 square km) of the ruined city of Vijayanagar are the still-beautiful structures of the graceful Lotus Mahal, a Queen's bath, and the elegant domed stables that once housed 11 elephants. It's easy to imagine the city's heyday in the 1500s.
- **Sanchi, northwest of Bhopal.** This major Buddhist pilgrimage destination, begun in the 3rd century BC and worked on for 1,000 years, includes a serene group of *stupas* (Buddhist memorials) and monastery and temple ruins on a remote hilltop. Gates are elaborately carved with scenes from the life of Buddha.
- **Sun Temple, Konark.** Built to honor the Sun God, this richly carved temple in the shape of a chariot is decorated with images of erotic scenes and as well as magisterial statues of the Surya himself.

- **Meenakshi Temple, Madurai.** The old part of town was laid out around this South Indian temple par excellence. Within its walls and beyond its multihued, iconic *gopurams* (entrance gates) are a hall with nearly a 1,000 unique and elaborate pillars, a large temple tank (pool), and thousands of sculptures.
- **Golden Temple, Amritsar.** Rivaling the Taj in beauty and serenity, the most important site for the world's Sikhs is covered in gilt and surrounded by a lake that's over 500 feet long.
- **Jama Masjid, New Delhi.** India's largest mosque is made of deep red sandstone and still manages an aura of calm and beauty, despite the crowds covering it and the timeworn streets surrounding it.

Natural Escapes

Smooth-sandy beaches, sultry jungles, wind-swept desert horizons, ice-topped mountains—-India's huge size and complicated geography mean that its landscapes are as diverse as its people. Although India will always have to balance nature preservation against the needs of its burgeoning population, there have been signs of increased concern for the environment in recent years. Among the Indian middle-class, it's trendy to be green, and with luck this will encourage even more efforts to keep India's natural beauty as pristine as possible.

- **Lakshadweep Islands, west of Kerala.** The Indian government allows foreigners access to just three of these picture-perfect islands, which have soft-sand beaches, lots of water sports, and an unspoiled feeling that's hard to find elsewhere.
- **Keoladeo Ghana National Park, Bharatpur.** This sanctuary between Agra and Jaipur holds 400 species of waterfowl, which come from as far as Siberia, Afghanistan, and the Himalayas. Birdwatching at dawn here is an unforgettable experiences for "twitchers" (bird-watchers), many of whom come from very far away.
- **The Himalayas.** With their distinct species, towering mountains, windswept hills, and many lush valleys, the Himalayan regions of India seem like another country—if not another world. One especially stunning area is Ladakh, in India's northernmost tip. This cold desert area contains elaborate Buddhist monasteries that first emerged as long as 1,000 years ago but still very much in operation.
- **Backwater Cruises, Kerala.** An escape down Kerala's sultry backwaters on a houseboat has become justly famous for the beautiful scenes that float past—gleaming green rice fields, waving coconut palms, and tiny waterfront villages are all part of the show.

GREAT ITINERARIES

NORTH INDIA'S GREATEST HITS

16 days

India's Golden Triangle, which links Moghul and Rajput sites in Delhi, Jaipur, and Agra, is well traveled, but it's well traveled for a reason. What you see—the Taj Mahal, the impressive palace-fort and Islamic monuments in Delhi, and the timeless Pink-City fairytale that is Jaipur—are some of the most splendid edifices that India has to offer. This tour expands on the Golden Triangle to include the holy city of Varanasi and the village of Khajuraho, with temples that are world-famous for their erotic (some would say explicit) carved scenes.

DELHI

3 days. Fly to Delhi to explore the old and new capitals. Hit the ground running with a little light touring on the first day, perhaps doing a little shopping or taking in the lovely, pre-Moghul Lodi Gardens. Over the next two days, visit Old Delhi's Moghul remnants, such as the Red Fort, Jama Masjid, and Chandni Chowk, now a hodgepodge market. New Delhi has the Moghul Humayun's tomb as well as the imperial buildings of the Raj-era buildings. Pay a visit to the excellent collections at the National Museum as well, but also save lots of time for getting acquainted with Delhi weather, crowds, and food. ⇨ *Delhi, in Chapter 2.*

JAIPUR

2 days. Take an overnight train or set out early to be chauffeured the six or so hours from Delhi to Jaipur. Alternately, set out a day earlier and make an overnight stop at the Neemrama Fort Palace, built in the 15th century and now a luxury hotel. Once in Jaipur, head out to explore the city's unforgettable bazaars and monuments, as well as the Amer Fort and Palace, just beyond city limits. ⇨ *Rajasthan, in Chapter 4.*

FATEHPUR SIKRI & AGRA

3 days. On the way to Agra, tour the splendid royal remnants of the ancient Moghul capital Fatehpur Sikri. (Or take a train to Agra and rent a car and driver to visit it from there.) In Agra you'll encounter the world-famous Taj Mahal and the less famous, but almost equally impressive, Agra Fort and the tomb of Itmad-ud-Daulah. ⇨ *Rajasthan, in Chapter 4, and Agra & North Central India, in Chapter 3.*

GWALIOR & ORCHHA

3 days. Leave Agra to head south 120 km (75 mi) to Gwalior's spectacular pre-Moghul Hindu fort and palace, built on a high plateau and with a wall that's 2 mi long. From here head farther south to Orchha, which means "hidden place." This former seat of Hindu rajas is filled with palaces, temples, monuments and a small, picturesque river. ⇨ *Agra & North Central India, in Chapter 3.*

KHAJURAHO

2 days. Drive farther south down to Khajuraho and spend two days absorbing the exuberant, occasionally X-rated carvings that adorn the town's 10th- and 11th-century Hindu temples. ⇨ *Agra & North Central India, in Chapter 3.*

VARANASI

3 days. Fly from Khajuraho to Varanasi. Take a peaceful early-morning cruise on the Ganges River to witness Hindus receiving blessings and worshipping on the steps of, and in, the sacred waters. Wander among Varanasi's winding streets, full of food stalls and temples, and also make time for the

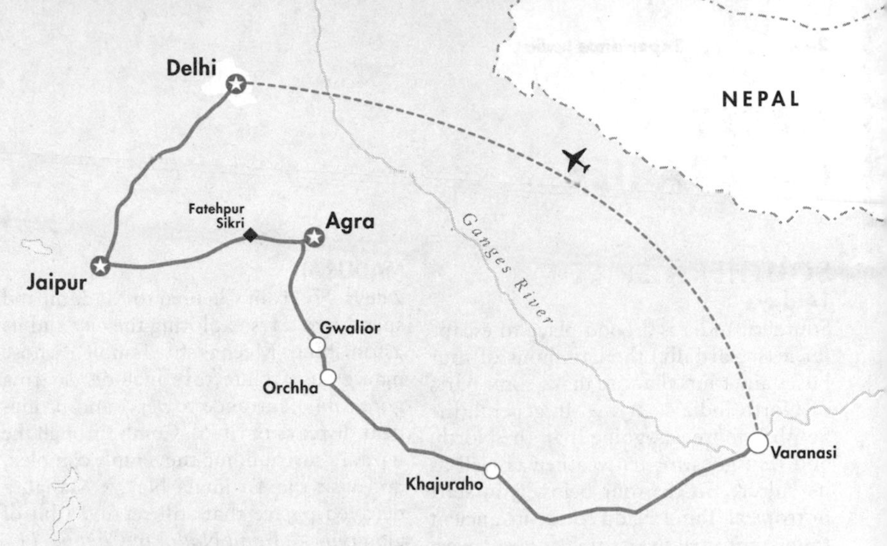

impressive Bharat Kala Bhavan Museum. Nearby Sarnath, full of Buddhist ruins from the time of the great king Ashok, makes for a very good day trip. ⇨ *Agra & North Central India, in Chapter 3.*

DELHI

1 day. Fly back to Delhi to get ready for your flight back home. If there's time for some last-minute shopping, the Central Cottages Industries Emporium and Khan Market are both good bets for silks, rugs, wood and metal idols, stationery, and other small, eminently packable souvenirs. ⇨ *Delhi, in Chapter 2.*

Transportation

The itinerary above suggests when to fly, take a train, or hire a car and driver, but in the end it will depend on your own circumstances. To decide on the method of transportation, consider the time you have available, your budget, and the amount of flexibility you need. Although you give up some flexibility with a train, the countryside views are at least partial compensation, as is being able to avoid the generally manic and loud Indian driving style. Domestic flights can be a good way to make up for some lost time, but be sure to have back-up plans—last-minute flight cancellations are hardly unknown.

TIPS

If this is your first time in India, it may seem normal to rent a car and drive it yourself, but this is actually an unusual choice. India's traffic is fierce and should only be tackled by seasoned drivers familiar with Indian roads and traffic conditions. Most visiting Westerners opt to hire a car and driver. You'll find this isn't as expensive as it sounds.

Delhi is one of the most expensive places to stay in India. Agra and Jaipur are a close second. If you want to make your trip less expensive, try spending time visiting some of the places a little less congested with foreigners, like Gwalior or Khajuraho.

These destinations are among the most popular spots in India for visitors, which means hotels book up quickly along this route, particularly in high season. If you have your heart set on a specific hotel, book early.

Northern India is also a popular circuit for guided tours. If you like the comfort of a knowledgeable guide and the structure of a set plan, consider a package tour. (See the Essentials chapter in the back of this book for recommendations.)

GREAT ITINERARIES

SOUTHERN SPICE

14 days

Southern India is a good place to escape (at least partially) the battalions of tour buses and touts that can make some parts of North India so trying. In general, the South is more easygoing than the North, and that goes for its weather as well as its culture. In the tour below, you start in tropical Tamil Nadu to see its ancient towns and massive temples. Head west to search for wildlife at Kerala's excellent Lake Periyar Wildlife Sanctuary, and set aside time to relax at seaside resorts and on small boats as you cruise through that state's lush backwaters. On the way, add one more cultural dimension—say, a Kathakali dance performance—and perhaps a soothing ayurvedic massage.

CHENNAI & MAHABALIPURAM

4 days. Spend two days in Chennai, whose Fort St. George was once the first headquarters of the British East India Company. After wandering through the fort, soak up Chennai's traditional South Indian culture of crowded bazaars, bustling Hindu temples, and spicy vegetarian dishes. Head west for a leisurely two-day excursion to Mahabalipuram via the silk-weaving center of Kanchipuram, which holds more than 200 temples. Mahabalpuram, on the Bay of Bengal, holds exquisite cave sculptures as well as a shore temple left behind by the Pallava dynasty (4th–8th centuries). Catch some sun and surf at a relaxing resort along the way, and return to Chennai. ⇨ *Tamil Nadu, in Chapter 11.*

MADURAI

2 days. Fly from Chennai to Madurai and spend two days exploring the city and its astonishing Meenakshi Temple, whose marvelous architecture includes soaring *gopurams* (entrance towers) and prominent displays of ritual. Comb through the bazaars surrounding the temple complex, and visit the Tirumala Nayak Mahal, a decayed palace that still retains a bit of glamour. ⇨ *Tamil Nadu, in Chapter 11.*

LAKE PERIYAR WILDLIFE SANCTUARY

2 days. Drive about four hours west from Madurai across the Western Ghats to Kerala's Thekkady, at 3,000 feet above sea level. Visit the Lake Periyar Wildlife Sanctuary, where boat rides provide the leisurely means for a safari: wild elephants and other animals roam the banks of this lovely preserve. ⇨ *Tamil Nadu, in Chapter 11, and Kerala, in Chapter 10.*

KOCHI

2 days. Proceed northwest by car to the ancient port city of Kochi, and take two days to see its 16th-century synagogue and palace while poking in curio shops. After eating dinner at one of impressive restaurants in town, try to attend a Kathakali dance performance, where the complicated makeup is as much part of the show as the hard-honed talent on display. ⇨ *Kerala, in Chapter 10.*

BACKWATER CRUISE

2 days. Drive to Alleppey early in the morning and cruise through some of Kerala's backwaters, past palm trees, shaded villages, and bright-green rice fields. If you get hooked, take an overnight houseboat cruise. Back in the car, head to Kovalam, at Kerala's southern tip, and relax at one of its impressive beach resorts. ⇨ *Kerala, in Chapter 10.*

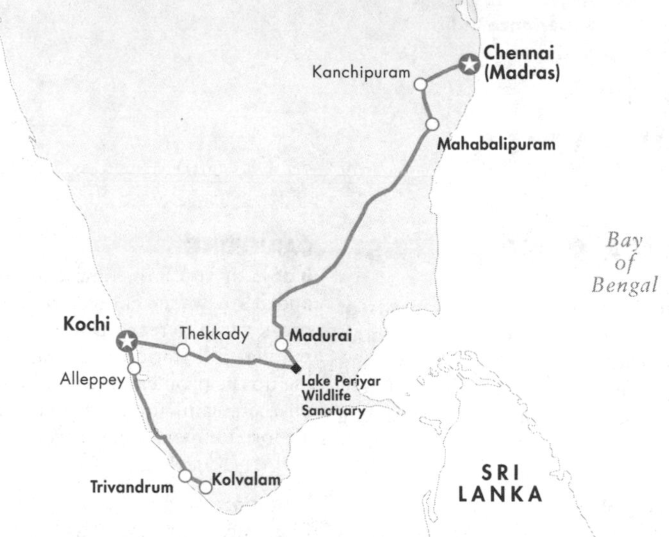

KOVALAM & TRIVANDRUM

2 days. Spend two nights at a beach resort lolling about and eating seafood; you might want to look into having an ayurvedic massage or taking classes in yoga and meditation here. You can fly out from nearby Trivandrum; if you have the time to spare, visit the atmospheric Horse Palace, whose many striking works of art include life-size Kathakali figures. ⇨*Kerala, in Chapter 10.*

Transportation

Hire a car and driver for excursions from Chennai, then fly or take the train from Chennai to Madurai. Hire another car and driver for the trip west to Lake Periyar in Thekkady; continue to Kochi and then pause for a slow cruise on the backwaters near Alleppey. Drive on to Kovalam and wind up at Trivandrum, where you can catch flights to other major cities.

TIPS

Bus travel is not always advisable in this area. Although the cheap prices can be a temptation, buses are often crowded, uncomfortable, and badly in need of repair. Typically, train travel or private car and driver are the way to go.

If you'd like to add a little je ne sais quoi to your trip, consider traveling south from Chennai to Pondicherry. This little town still retains a certain French flavor of its former colonizers. The white-washed villas, quaint churches, and French cuisine offer an interesting contrast to neighboring regions.

Another option in this itinerary would be to extend your time and stay a few days in Bangalore, a modern city-on-the-move with an impressive restaurant scene.

For a chance to dwell in Karnataka's natural surroundings without being divorced from the creature comforts of a typical hotel, consider staying in a Jungle Lodge. (See the Karnataka Chapter Planner.)

GREAT ITINERARIES

KOLKATA & INDIA'S EAST

7–10 days

Beginning in a town with hundreds of elaborate temples and ending in a modern city heavily identified with the Raj, this tour concentrates on the Bay of Bengal coast. Continuing on to Darjeeling will give you a chance to ride its world-famous toy train.

BHUBANESHWAR

2 days. Fly into the capital of Orissa to see the magnificent 10th- and 11th-century structures that have helped earn it the title "City of Temples." Set aside some time for perusing the area's distinctive handicrafts. ⇨*Orissa, in Chapter 12.*

KONARK & PURI

1 day. Head 90 minutes south to Konark's unearthly Sun Temple, dedicated to the Vedic god Surya. After lunch, drive to Puri's Jagannath Temple, with a spire that's over 21 stories tall. Allow enough time to walk through the hubbub of bazaars selling Jagannath paraphernalia. ⇨*Orissa, in Chapter 12.*

RAGHURAJPUR & DHAULI

1 day. Pay a visit first to Raghurajpur, a village of carvers and fabric painters, and then Dhauli, to see ancient Buddhist carvings. Push on to Bhubaneshwar to catch a plane or an eight-hour train to Kolkata, 480 km (298 mi) to the northeast. ⇨*Orissa, in Chapter 12.*

KOLKATA

3 days. Spend three days exploring the former center of British imperial power, where once-grand buildings are still impressive. Save some time for shopping at the massive New Market. ⇨*Kolkata, in Chapter 13.*

DARJEELING

3 days. If you have time and ambition—and it's a warm enough time of year—break camp to reach Darjeeling, the most popular hill station in India. After soaking up the promenade and hitching a ride on the steam-run toy train, head to the airport for your next adventure. ⇨*Sikkim & Darjeeling, in Chapter 14.*

Transportation

Bhubaneshwar is a long way from the major cities, and flying into it and then onto Kolkata will be most practical for most travelers. To get to Darjeeling, either fly (the nearest airport is a three-hour drive away) or take an overnight train from Kolkata.

THE HIMALAYAS

11 days

Whether you're hankering to head out on a hike, tour monasteries, or kick back in a hill station, the awe-inspiring Himalayas have a seductive attraction. This ambitious tour—only possible in summer when highways aren't filled with snow—takes you from Shimla upward to Manali and higher still to the even more forbidding heights of Leh. If you want to cut to the chase, you can fly directly to Ladakh, but be sure to allow time to acclimate to the thin air.

SHIMLA

4 days. From Delhi, set out on the Shatabhi Express that connects with the Himalayan Queen, another toy train, which makes the final journey to this storied hill station. After a rest, head outside for some short hikes that take in the decayed grandeur of Shimla's Raj-era buildings. ⇨*Himachal Pradesh & Ladakh, in Chapter 6.*

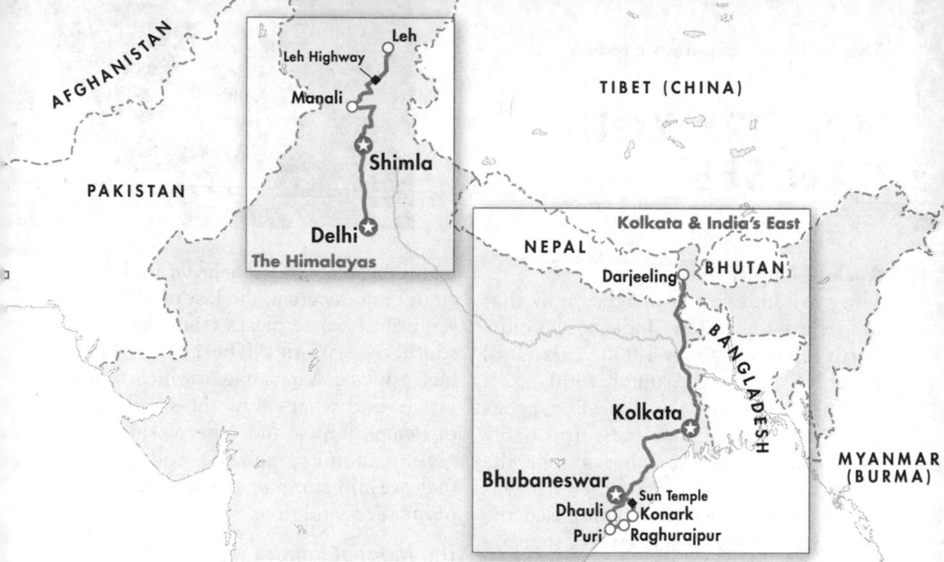

MANALI

3 days. Hire a car to drive you up to Manali, 260 km (160 mi) to the north, a six-hour drive through waterfalls and remote villages (⇨ CloseUp: Eye-Popping Drive: Shimla–Manali). Spend some time in Manali shopping—and mentally preparing for one of the best road trips in the world. ⇨ *Himachal Pradesh & Ladakh, in Chapter 6.*

MANALI—LEH HIGHWAY

2 days. This (in)famous, nail-bitingly twisty road takes two days to reach the mountain town of Leh. For the most comfortable experience, hire and car and driver, and be sure to make frequent stops to catch your breath, and to get some shots of the astonishing scenery. ⇨ *Himachal Pradesh & Ladakh, in Chapter 6.*

LEH

3 days. Head out for short hikes in and around town, and then take some day trips to visit the outstanding Buddhist monasteries in the area. From here there is also some great river rafting and trekking. When it's time to return to a reasonable altitude, catch a flight from Leh's airport back to Delhi. ⇨ *Himachal Pradesh & Ladakh, in Chapter 6.*

Transportation

Although you can drive or fly to Shimla, the train route gives you a better chance to soak in the scenery. Flights from Leh to Delhi fill up quickly; be sure to reserve ahead and re-confirm.

HISTORY YOU CAN SEE

Ancient Empires

The vast Indus Valley civilization that flourished in western India and points north lasted for about 1,000 years, until roughly 1700 BC. Around 1500 BC, a group known as the Indo-Europeans began to migrate into India (probably from central Asia) and live among the peoples who were already there. It was the Indo-Europeans who composed the Vedas and other Sanskrit texts that are the underpinnings of Hinduism. In this period, Kashi, the area that includes modern-day Varanasi, was founded, and India began to be cut up into various monarchies and republics. India's first empire was begun by the Hindu Mauryans in 321 BC and extended throughout the majority of the subcontinent as well as to parts of Afghanistan. Soon after, the great empires of South India, the Andhras, the Cholas, the Cheras, and Pandyas arose. Because the Indo-Europeans did not make it to these southern areas, they retained a great deal of the local culture, called Dravidian, and to this day southern languages such as Telagu, Kannada, and Tamil are grammatically separate from the Indo-European languages of the north.

What to See: Varanasi may very well be the oldest continuously occupied city in the world. **Sarnath,** north of Varanasi, is where Buddha preached his first sermon. Here, as well as at **Sanchi,** near Bhopal, great Mauryan king Ashok built several Buddhist shrines and temples, whose extensive ruins remain. Sarnath is also the location of Ashok's famous pillar with a three lions at the top—post-Independence India uses it as its national emblem. To see some stellar examples of southern Indian art at its most impressive, head to the temple towns of Tamil Nadu, including **Madurai, Thanjavur,** and (especially) **Kanchipuram,** the last of which has sculptural masterpieces from three great southern dynasties. The ancient Hindu metropolis of Vijayanagar, which sprawls far beyond what's now the small village of **Hampi,** is vast and otherworldly, with granite temples, palaces, and carvings that are still stunning despite the ravages of invaders and time.

The Moghul Empire

The Moghul period begins in 1526 AD, when Babur, who traced his ancestry back to the Moghul warrior Genghis Khan, wrested control of Delhi and Agra from an earlier group of Muslim conquerors, called the Delhi Sultanate. The Moghuls' rule would contain most of the subcontinent at its height, and it would last through 1761. During their reign, many of the landmarks we associate with modern-day India were created.

What to See: Moghul traces are thick on the ground throughout North India, especially in the capitals of Agra and then Delhi. The **tomb of Babur's son, Humayun,** is one of Delhi's treasures. Probably the greatest Moghul, Shah Jehan, left some amazing trinkets behind, most notable of them the **Taj Mahal.** The biggest mosque in India, Delhi's **Jama Masjid,** was finished in 1656 after six years of work by 5,000 laborers working under Shah Jehan's orders. Both it and the stunning **Red Fort** remain landmarks of Chandni Chowk, Old Delhi's ancient avenue.

Colonial Despots: the East India Company and the Raj

The British East India Company, arguably the world's first corporation, was chartered by Queen Elizabeth I. Soon it began opening up trading posts and spreading out from bases in Madras, Calcutta, and Bombay (now Chennai, Kolkata, and Mumbai). In 1699, the company's strongest and fiercest enemy, Tipu Sultan, was defeated on the battlefield near his palace at Srirangapattana. In 1857, the Indian Rebellion, or First War of Independence, as it's also known, began with the East India Company's Indian troops. The Indians were finally conquered, but the uprising also brought an end to the Company's control of India. Fed up with the way the Company's was run, he British Government revoked its charter, and instead began direct rule of India itself. Thus began the 90-year-long era of the Raj.

What to See: The first British fort in India, Chennai's **Fort St. George,** contains a museum with many portraits and other leftover evidence of the East India Company and the Raj. Kolkata can sometimes seems like one long holdover of the Raj, including most notably the enormous white-marble **Victoria Memorial. New Delhi,** which succeeded Calcutta as the Raj's capital, is packed to the gills with imperial buildings, especially in the seat of government, which can be seen from west from the India Gate. As for Mumbai, it contains buildings that swirl together Indian and Muslim architecture with Victorian Gothic, with entertaining results: two must-sees are the **Prince of Wale Museum** and the **Mahatma Jyotiba Phule (aka Crawford) Market.**

From Independence On

India gained its independence in 1947 after a history of agitation that went back to and beyond the mutiny of 1857. Integral to the movement, of course, was Mohandas K. Gandhi, also known as the Mahatma (Great Soul), and his policy of nonviolent resistance. You can remember the Mahatma and others who worked for India's freedom at many museums and memorials throughout the country.

What to See: Gandhi was put under house arrest in Pune's **Aga Khan Palace** for nearly two years, until May 1944. During that time both his wife and his secretary, imprisoned there as well, passed away. New Delhi's **National Gandhi Museum,** the **Gandhi Smriti** (the site of his assassination in 1948), and the Nehru Memorial Museum are three other important places to pay homage and learn more about the Independence movement. Mumbai's **Gateway of India,** built in the 1920s to honor the king and queen of England, also had a place to play in Independence: British soldiers passed through it when leaving India for the last time.

INDIA'S TOP EXPERIENCES

Majestic Taj Mahal

The Taj Mahal gets top billing. Very few people would want to take a first trip to India without making it to this tremendous landmark. Sure it's a hassle—the aggressive touts nearby are in a class of their own. But all that melts away once you're within the formal garden in sight of its four minarets. Try for an overnight stay—you'll be able to see the Taj at sunrise, when its dazzling beauty, on a scale of 1 to 10, gets cranked up to 11.

Durga Puga in Kolkata

The carnival-like days of Kolkata's Durga Puja, held near the fall equinox, are devoted to the 10-armed warrior goddess Durga, slayer of the buffalo demon Mahishasur. During the celebration, large unbaked clay idols of Durga and other gods, each more colorful and elaborate than the one before, are sculpted and taken to *pandals* (stages) throughout the city to be worshipped. On the final day, the idols are thrown into the Hooghly River or other bodies of water—a sign that nothing is permanent but that Durga will return next year.

Boating the Backwaters

Over the past few years, touring some of Kerala's hundreds of miles of sultry backwaters on a houseboat, has become a must-do experience. As the boat glides past tiny villages and rice fields, with palms moving slowly above, you can lounge in the shade taking in one of the most beautiful regions in India.

The Temple That's a Village

The largest temple in India, Sri Ranganathaswamy, is enormous enough to hold an entire village within its seven rings of walls. Its grounds include 22 stunning *gopurams* (highly decorated entrance towers) and a hall with 1,000 ornate granite pillars—there's enough in here to take up an entire day.

Treks in India's "Scotland"

The mountainous terrain of Coorg, in Karnataka, full of plantations raising coffee, cardamom, and other plants best adapted to the cool, wet climate, has earned it the endearing, if slightly misleading, nickname of the "Scotland of India." Many of the plantations are now also homestays, opening their doors (and grounds) to those attracted by the lush surroundings and rewarding hikes.

Darjeeling Himalayan Railway

More commonly called the "toy train" for its miniature dimensions, the DHR is as popular with many old India hands as it is with first-time tourists. During its laborious, incredibly scenic run from Siliguri up to the once-elegant hill station nicknamed the "Queen of the Hills," its wheezing, coal-fired steam engines must gain some 6,900 feet (2,100 meters) in elevation. The blue-and-off-white train—which began operation in 1881—is also a sort of time machine back to the Raj.

Varanasi, the City of Light

The major Hindu pilgrimage city of Varanasi is as ancient (it dates back to at least the 6th century BC) as it is holy (it was founded by Shiva). A walk along the 70-odd stone *ghats* (flights of stairs) that lead down into the Ganges means an encounter with fakirs, beggars, backpackers, a plenitude of goats and cows, and just maybe a bit of the sanctity that brings so many here to make offerings, obtain blessings, and, sometimes, to die. (A peaceful death in Varanasi means bringing to an end the cycle of reincarnation.)

Delhi

Old Delhi, Jama Masjid (the Great Mosque)

WORD OF MOUTH

"Don't miss Humayan's tomb—it was my favorite monument in Delhi. Perhaps people say it is like the Taj because of its perfect symmetry—[but] it's not like the Taj at all."

—Craig

www.fodors.com/forums

WELCOME TO DELHI

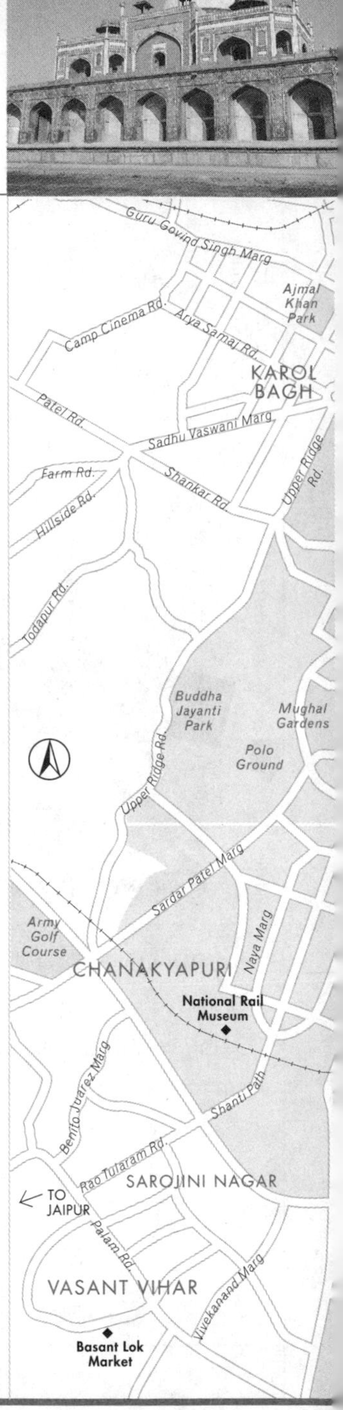

TOP REASONS TO GO

★ **Moghul Masters:** Lal Qila (the Red Fort), Humayun's Tomb, and the Jama Masjid—the monuments left behind by the Muslim emperors who ruled Delhi for hundreds of years are stunning.

★ **Remnants of the Raj:** The British may be long gone, but the buildings of Lutyens' Delhi still cast an imperial shadow.

★ **The Crowded Capital:** Old Delhi's twisting, narrow lanes and packed bazaars provide unparalleled people watching.

★ **Shopper's Paradise:** Whether it's custom-made clothes at bargain-basement prices, silk saris, or crafts from around the country to take home as souvenirs, you can't beat Delhi's selection.

★ **Taste of India:** Street-side stalls, traditional kebab houses, lounges serving contemporary Indian with a twist—dining in Delhi doesn't disappoint.

1 Old Delhi. Anchored by the Red Fort and Jama Masjid, Old Delhi provides the best glimpse into the city's Moghul past. Amid the crumbling *havelis,* grand old homes line Chandni Chowk and the narrow lanes that branch off. Crowds rush past bustling bazaars selling everything from gold jewelry to used batteries.

2 Connaught Place. Its inner and outer rings are a central tourist hub. This was also once the city's financial heart, but most businesses have decamped from "C.P." for gleaming suburban office towers.

3 Lutyens' Delhi. This manicured group of buildings was to be the seat of the British Empire in India, and it remains the center of independent India's government.

4 South Delhi. In these residential colonies, markets and commercial districts spread over dozens of miles. Life here varies from neighborhood to neighborhood with everything from modest apartment blocks with packs of motorcycles parked outside to the palatial gated villas of Delhi's uber-wealthy. Many of Delhi's can't-miss sites (including Humayun's Tomb and the Qutub Minar) are found here.

GETTING ORIENTED

India's wild, sprawling capital is divided into two major parts, with the cramped alleys of Old Delhi in the north giving way to the broad avenues of New Delhi in the center and farther south. Major roads radiate out from the circles of Connaught Place, Delhi's central hub and main business district. Nearly impossible to classify, the city proper packs almost 15 million people within its borders and even more if you count its suburbs, which seem to gobble up more land by the day. Luxury high-rises dot the landscape of sprawling satellite cities in the neighboring states of Uttar Pradesh and Haryana.

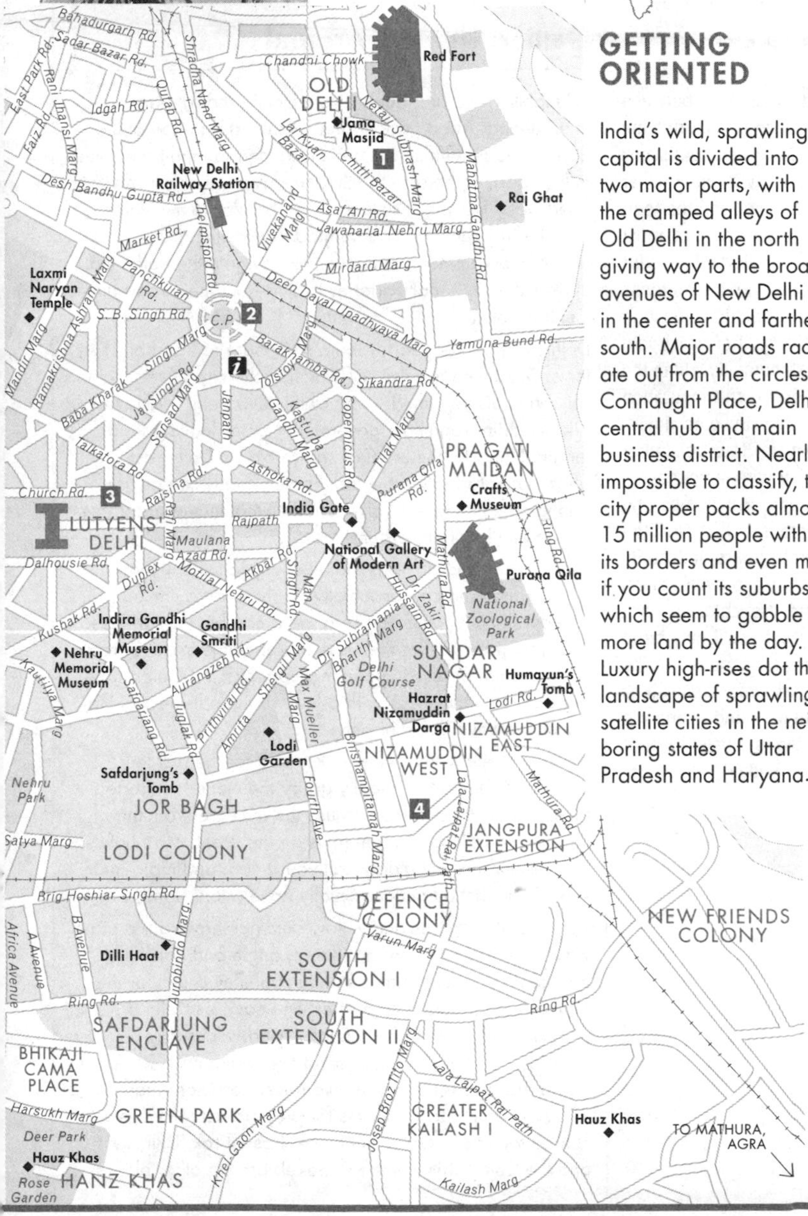

DELHI PLANNER

When to Go

It's best to visit Delhi between mid-October and March. Autumn and early spring yield mild, sunny days. The crowds are thinner than in the winter, and the temperatures are such that most people are comfortable in shirt sleeves. The heat is intense from April until the monsoon arrives in July, after which rain and intense humidity add to the misery. Despite the reputation for heat, the city gets downright cold in late-December and January, with temperatures near freezing. But homes and hotels here are built for the heat: marble floors and drafty interiors don't provide much relief from the cold, so pack accordingly. If you'll only be in Delhi a few days, note that the Red Fort and most museums are closed on Monday, and the Jama Masjid is closed to non-Muslims on Friday.

Getting There & Around

All flights arrive and depart from Delhi's Indira Gandhi International Airport, along the southwestern edge of the city. Its two terminals (domestic and international) are some miles apart, so be sure to tell your driver which airport you need when leaving. The airport is about a 45-minute drive from Delhi's center in light to moderate traffic. During rush hours, allow an hour, minimum, to navigate the traffic that chokes the city's main arteries to and from the airport and Central Delhi.

Delhi is the major hub for India's northern rail and bus systems. Determine in advance which of the city's three main rail terminals you need: New Delhi, Old Delhi, or Hazrat Nizamuddin. Long-haul government buses leave from a terminal near Kashmere Gate north of Old Delhi, but are often uncomfortably crowded. Travel agents can advise on the air-conditioned Volvo coaches that leave and arrive from many locations around the city.

Hiring a car and driver is the best way to see the most of this sprawling city, especially for those on a limited schedule. Most hotels can arrange a car, but they will also charge a premium for the service. Reputable travel agents do the same for much cheaper (budget Rs. 1,000 or more per day for a basic car with a/c and an English-speaking driver, for travel in Delhi only).

Black-and-yellow taxis charge Rs. 350 for the first four hours or 40 km and typically go by the meter for shorter trips. If your driver refuses to use the meter, get another cab. Avoid hailing random taxis on the street. Most hotels and restaurants will gladly call you a cab, and major markets and tourist attractions usually have a taxi stand.

The ubiquitous green-and-yellow auto-rickshaws are a good way to see the city from a different angle and catch the breeze during hot summer months. But they aren't for the faint of heart. Negotiating fares isn't easy, as Delhi drivers usually speak only minimal English and will usually refuse to go by the meter. A trip around the corner costs Rs. 20, and a trip across the city should never cost more than Rs 100. Government-run booths for prepaid auto-rickshaws can be found at Connaught Place, Basant Lok, Dilli Haat, and the Community Centre in Saket, among other places.

Shopping, Dropping & Dining

The city's shopping options are virtually inexhaustible. Handmade crafts and fabrics from all over India are sold in a pleasant outdoor setting at Dilli Haat, and in government-run emporiums featuring typical items from India's many states. Various neighborhood markets are a chance to join Dilli-wallahs (Delhiites) in their quest for the latest fashions and sportswear (Greater Kailash I, South Extension, Hauz Khas Village, Connaught Place); jewelry, curios, and antiques (Sundar Nagar); books (Khan Market); and cheap apparel of every kind (Sarojini Nagar). The INA Market is a true Eastern experience, bursting with fresh produce, spices, salty snacks, and squawking chickens. In Old Delhi, endless holes-in-the-wall sell brassware, curios, and silver jewelry. And if all that shopping makes you hungry, head for one of the various stand-out North Indian restaurants, many of which rank with the best in the world. If you only splurge on one really expensive meal in India, do it here.

Arts & Culture

This is the center of politics, but to a large extent it's also the center of culture. Delhi has the richest arts scene in the country. If you love dance, music, theater, or painting you'll have plenty of opportunities to experience the Indian versions: the dazzling footwork of Kathak dance, the otherworldly sounds of Hindustani music, the freshness of contemporary Hindi plays, cleverly curated group art shows, and much more. Pick up the bi-monthly *Time Out* or the monthly *First City* for citywide listings.

What It Costs In Rupees

	¢	$	$$	$$$	$$$$
Restaurants	under Rs. 100	Rs. 100–Rs. 300	Rs. 300–Rs. 500	Rs. 500–Rs. 700	over Rs. 700
Hotels	under Rs. 2,000	Rs. 2,000–Rs. 4,000	Rs. 4,000–Rs. 6,000	Rs. 6,000–Rs. 10,000	over Rs. 10,000

Restaurant prices are for an entrée plus bread or rice. Hotel prices are for a double room in high season, excluding a tax of up to 20%.

Planning Your Time

The best way to cover a lot of ground in Delhi is to hire a car, especially for those on a limited schedule. Avoid tackling Old Delhi on your first day, especially if you've never been to India before—its chaos can be overwhelming. Starting with New Delhi will also give you a better idea of the aesthetic and cultural dichotomy between the two cities. A drive through the graceful avenues of Lutyens' imperial city will ease you gently into the capital. Depending on your interests, visit some Independence sites (the Nehru Museum or Gandhi Smriti), a museum, or a temple or *gurdwara* (Sikh temple). When you're ready, plunge into Old Delhi—explore the Lal Qila (Red Fort) and the stunning Jama Masjid, then venture into Chandni Chowk. After a breather, visit Humayun's Tomb and the Hazrat Nizamuddin Darga, two pockets of Old Delhi in New Delhi. At some point, head south to the Qutub Minar, then check out some museums or galleries, do some shopping, and, before sunset, stroll through the Lodi Garden. Those with a lot of time in Delhi should consider side trips outside the city as part of their plans. An overnight excursion to the Neemrana Fort Palace outside the Shekhavati region of Rajasthan lets you unwind in Rajput splendor. Alternatively, head northwest to Corbett National Park in Uttarakhand (⇨ chapter 5), where wildlife (and tiger-spotting tourists) reigns supreme.

2

Updated by
Alison Granito

OF ALL OF INDIA'S MAJOR CITIES, only Delhi was already ancient when the British arrived. Smack in the middle of the northern plains, the city has always been prized by South Asia's rulers—their dwellings and forts still stand in clusters, testaments to a long imperial cycle of sacking and rebuilding. The Moghuls, with their exalted Persian aesthetic, left the most striking legacy, but now, in modern-day India, even they compete for attention with bustling cafés and sleek designer boutiques.

In Delhi, the different versions of modern India all coexist, and its contradictions become abundantly clear. Newly minted junior executives ride in chauffered, air-conditioned comfort as the millions of children on the capital's streets beg for change and hawk magazines. To feed the consumer craze of India's rapidly expanding middle class, gleaming mega-malls on the rise in some parts of the city tower over splendid Moghul monuments, some of which stand crumbling and forgotten in residential areas. It is entirely possible to find your own corner of the capital and feel like you've disovered a secret thanks to its rich, multilayered history.

The ancient epic *Mahabharata* places the great town of Indraprastha on the banks of the Yamuna River, perhaps in what is now Delhi's Old Fort. Late in the first millennium AD, Delhi became an outpost of the Hindu Rajputs, warrior kings who ruled what's now Rajasthan. However, it was after 1191, when Mohammad Ghori of Central Asia invaded and conquered, that the city acquired its Islamic flavor. Other Afghan and Uzbek sultanates handed Delhi back and forth over the next 300 years, until the mighty Moghuls settled in. Beginning with the invasion of Babur in 1526, the Moghuls shifted their capital between Delhi and Agra until 1858, leaving stunning architecture at both sites, including the buildings at what's now known as Old Delhi.

The fall of the Moghul empire coincided with the rise of the British East India Company, first in Madras and Calcutta and eventually throughout the country. When several of Delhi's Indian garrisons mutinied against their Company employers in 1857, the British suppressed them, moved into the Red Fort, and ousted the aging Moghul emperor. In 1911, with anti-British sentiment growing in Calcutta, they moved their capital from Calcutta to Delhi—the ultimate prize, a place where they could build a truly imperial city that would dwarf the older ones around it. Architect Sir Edwin Lutyens was hired to create New Delhi, a majestic sandstone government complex surrounded by wide, leafy avenues and roundabouts, in contrast to Old Delhi's hectic lanes.

When India gained independence on August 15, 1947, with Jawaharlal Nehru the first prime minister, the subcontinent was partitioned into the secular republic of India and the Muslim nation of Pakistan, which was further divided into West Pakistan (now Pakistan) and East Pakistan (now Bangladesh). Trapped in potentially hostile new countries, thousands of Muslims left Delhi for Pakistan while millions of Hindu and Sikh refugees streamed in—changing Delhi's cultural overtone almost overnight from Persian to Punjabi.

Since Prime Minister Rajiv Gandhi (grandson of Nehru) and his successor, Narasimha Rao, began to liberalize India's planned economy in the late 1980s and early '90s, Delhi has experienced tremendous change. Foreign companies have arrived and hired locals for white-collar jobs, residential enclaves and shopping strips have sprouted in every crevice, and land prices have skyrocketed. Professionals seeking affordable living space now move to the suburbs and drive into town, aggravating the already substantial pollution problem. At the same time, North Indian villagers still come here in search of work and build shanties wherever they can, sometimes in the shadows of forgotten monuments. It is they—Rajasthani women in colorful saris digging holes with pickaxes, men climbing rickety scaffolds in sarong-like lungis—who build new homes for the affluent. Many Delhiites say, with a sigh, that their city is in a perpetual state of flux.

Precisely because of its cheek-by-jowl mixture of Old Delhi's Moghul glory, Central Delhi's European grandeur, and South Delhi's boutiques and lounge bars, Delhi is a profoundly Indian place. In the Delhi Golf Course, Islamic monuments share the fairways with peacocks; in Lodi Garden, they're interspersed with young lovers and families out for a stroll. Hindu temples, Sikh *gurdwaras* (temples), and secular discos are packed with their respective devotees. Yet, even as private enterprise transforms its business climate and social life, the capital remains a bureaucracy, with political big shots the talk of the town. Delhi is not the most beautiful city in India, but it is in many ways the grandest.

EXPLORING DELHI

Delhi's commercial and geographic hub used to be Connaught Place, a fact reflected in the area's hub-and-spokes layout. Connaught Place (commonly referred to as just "C.P.") remains popular with tourists, particularly backpackers—hence its abundance of beggars, money changers both legitimate and illegitimate, and drug dealers—but it's no longer the capital's nerve center. As development sprawls south, spilling over into suburbs, South Delhi has become the center of social and, to a large extent, commercial life.

Central Delhi, between Connaught Place and South Delhi, is also known as Lutyens' Delhi. Designed by the British architect Sir Edwin Lutyens (1869–1944) for the ruling British government of the early 20th century, Lutyens' Delhi remains the home of the Indian government, including Rashtrapati Bhavan (the Presidential Palace), the North and South Secretariats, Sansad Bhavan (Parliament House), and India Gate, a massive monument to British Indian Army soldiers killed in World War I and the Afghan wars. Most of Delhi's museums are nearby, and the surrounding area is filled with tree-lined boulevards, lovely old bungalows, and affluent residential neighborhoods.

Sprawling New Delhi is best navigated on wheels—hire a car, taxi, or auto-rickshaw to get around. In contrast, the narrow lanes of Old Delhi are a walker's delight.

Note that brochures, maps, floor plans and annotation are nonexistent at most sights; you must be guided by your own inclination. Be prepared to remove your shoes when visiting religious institutions, including the Charity Birds Hospital; women should bring a scarf to cover their heads. Shorts are not appropriate attire for adults at any religious sites and may also be inappropriate at some bars and restaurants and cultural performances.

GETTING ON BOARD WITH THE METRO

The city's new metro service is air-conditioned, reliable, and state-of-the-art. Service is expected to expand rapidly through 2010, when the Commonwealth Games arrive in town. With new stations and lines opening for service every few months, subway service is rapidly changing the face of the city. It's a cheap (starting at Rs. 8 per one-way trip) and convenient way to move between Connaught Place (Rajiv Chowk station) or Lutyens' Delhi (Central Secratariat station) and Old Delhi (Chandni Chowk station). Ask your hotel for a map.

ABOUT THE RESTAURANTS

Restaurants are generally open daily 12:30 to 3 for lunch and 7:30 to 11 for dinner. Delhi's liquor laws have loosened in recent years and all restaurants serve alcohol unless we indicate otherwise. However, imported liquor is extremely expensive—inquire before you imbibe. Expect a 20% tax on your food and beverage bill.

ABOUT THE HOTELS

Unless we note otherwise, all the hotels we list have air-conditioning, bathrooms with tubs, currency exchange, and room service. Most have a doctor on call. In addition, all hotels have wireless or broadband Internet access and deluxe hotels have executive floors with special lounges and services for business travelers. You *must* reserve in advance for stays between October and February, as even the largest hotels fill up.

OLD DELHI

Old Delhi (6 km [4 mi] north of Connaught Place), once known as Shahjahanabad, for the emperor who built it, lies in a perpetual state of decay. Havelis that line the *galis* (lanes; origin of the word "gully") are architecturally stunning but irreversibly crumbling. Old Delhi's monuments—the Jama Masjid and Red Fort—are magnificent, and the main artery, Chandni Chowk, is great fun to explore.

Old Delhi is crowded and hectic, and the roads and footways are poorly maintained. Fast-moving carts and overloaded laborers plow through whatever comes in their way. If you find the throng too daunting, or just need a break after a few hours, try a cycle-rickshaw tour: For about Rs. 100, you can be carted around in a cycle-rickshaw (which seats two slim people) for about an hour. The rickshaw-wallahs (rickshaw drivers) in front of the Red Fort are serious bargainers, but they know the city well, and many can show you places you wouldn't discover on your own.

Numbers in the text correspond to numbers in the margin and on the Old Delhi map.

A GOOD WALK

Start in Old Delhi with a morning tour of the **Lal Qila** ❶, or Red Fort, Emperor Shah Jahan's sprawling 17th-century capital. When you emerge, set your sights on the red Jain temple across the boulevard, and walk around to its left side. Inside the gate, remove your shoes and proceed into the **Charity Birds Hospital** ❷, a one-of-a-kind institution.

After leaving the hospital, return to the main road and walk back around the temple (keeping it on your left) to enter the famous strip known as **Chandni Chowk** ❸. Chaos reigns supreme here, so gather your wits and watch your feet lest they be flattened by a cart or cycle-rickshaw. You'll pass a short but fragrant row of flower-sellers. About four blocks down the street on the left, identifiable by its small gold dome, is the marble **Sisganj Gurdwara** ❹, a Sikh shrine. After seeing it, continue down Chandni Chowk and cross three more lanes (galis); then, at Kanwarji's sweet shop (across the street from the Central Bank of India), turn left on **Gali Paranthe Wali** ❺. Stop for a snack if you need fortification; then continue down the lane, following its jogs to the right, until the road hits a T at the Sant Lal Sanskriti sari shop. Turn left into Kinari Bazaar, a sparkling bridal-trimming market where Hindu families can buy every item required, and then some, for their wedding festivities. Scooters and rickshaws can mess things up in this narrow thoroughfare, so don't be in a hurry.

At 2130 Kinari Bazaar (a bric-a-brac shop called Krishna & Co.), turn right into one of Chandni Chowk's most beautiful lanes, Naughara Gali, where a community of Jains lives in some old havelis painted in aquas, pinks, and yellows. At the end of this peaceful alley is the **Svetamber Jain Temple** ❻. Even if the temple is closed, Naughara Gali is a temporary escape from the bustle of the bazaar.

Return to Kinari Bazaar and turn right. If it suits your fancy, stop in a glitzy wedding shop called **Shivam Zari Palace** (2178 Kinari Bazaar) and spend half an hour dressing a tiny brass statue of Gopal (baby Krishna) in an outfit of your choice, including a headpiece, necklace, and bangles. The cost of your finished memento is Rs. 750, more for a larger statue.

Continue down Kinari Bazaar until it intersects with **Dariba Kalan**, or "Silver Street." If you're in the market for jewelry or curios, check out the shops to the left; if not, turn right and head down Dariba Kalan to its end. Turn right again and you'll find yourself on a broad street in the brass and copper district. Take the next right, then an immediate left under a stone arch. Now head up Chah Rahat, a typical narrow lane with old wooden balconies and verandas.

When Chah Rahat opens into a courtyard, take the hairpin turn to the left and follow the arrow on the sign for "Singh Copper and Brass Palace." After about 30 feet, a second sign directs you down an alley on

Chandni Chowk 3
Charity Birds Hospital 2
Gali Paranthe Wali 5
Jama Masjid 7
Lal Qila 1
Sisganj Gurdwara 4
Svetamber Jain Temple 6

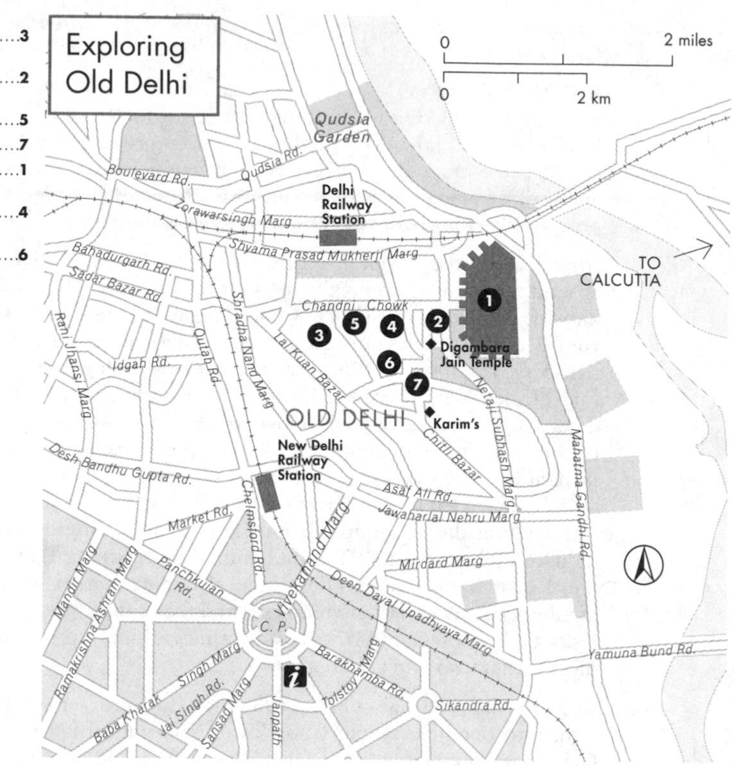

the right. Singh's emporium is filthy, but every floor has an interesting collection of miscellany.

From Singh's, return to the courtyard on Chah Rahat and take the short, narrow lane to the left. You'll emerge to see the splendid **Jama Masjid ❼**, preceded by a somewhat incongruous tool bazaar. To reach the mosque's entrance, head right, then follow the bazaar to the left.

At the end of this long tour, you'll probably be ready for a proper Muslim meal. Walk out of the Jama Masjid to Karim's, conveniently located on the colorful lane heading away from the mosque's entrance, or take a cycle-rickshaw to the Chor Bizarre restaurant.

TIMING Allow a full day for this tour, and don't attempt it on a hot day. Avoid Friday, when entrance to the mosque is tricky for non-Muslims; Sunday, when most shops in Old Delhi are closed; and Monday, when the Red Fort is closed. (If you have to choose between Sunday and Monday, go for Monday. The bazaars are crucial to Old Delhi's flavor.) Note, too, that the Jain temple—near the end of the walk—is closed between 12:30 and 6:30 each afternoon, so if art and architecture make your heart sing, try to start very early *or* right after lunch.

WHAT TO SEE

3 **Chandni Chowk.** This was Delhi's former imperial avenue, where the Moghul emperor Shah Jahan rode at the head of his lavish cavalcade. That scene is hard to picture today, as bullock carts, bicycles, taxis, freight carts, cows, auto-rickshaws, horse-drawn tongas (two-wheeled carts), and pedestrians create a constant, breathtaking bazaar. As in the days of the Moghuls, commerce is everywhere: astrologers set up their charts on the pavement; shoemakers squat and repair sandals; sidewalk photographers with old box cameras take pictures for a small fee; medicine booths conceal doctors attending to patients; and oversize teeth grin from the windows of dentists' offices. Peer through a portico and you might see men getting shaved, silver being hammered into paper-thin edible sheets, or any other conceivable form of commerce, while outside a goat blithely chews vegetables from a merchant's cart. ✉*East–west artery from Red Fort 1.5 km (1 mi) west to Fatehpuri Masjid, Old Delhi* ⏲*Most shops closed Sun.*

2 **Charity Birds Hospital.** Across from the Red Fort is a delightful and unusual attraction: a hospital for birds and rabbits. Founded by Jains in 1956, the hospital is modest, but it shows how tender loving care can stretch limited funds. Go all the way upstairs to see the "general ward," a feeding frenzy; there's even an intensive-care ward and a research laboratory. Bathed, fed, and given vitamins, the healthy birds refuse to leave, and that's how you can spot the building—flocks of birds swirl around its roof. The hospital is attached to a Jain temple that is also worth a quick visit. ✉*Netaji Subhash Marg, opposite Red Fort, Old Delhi* 🎫*Donations accepted* ⏲*Daily 8–8.*

5 **Gali Paranthe Wali.** This narrow, festive lane is filled with shopkeepers selling fabric and saris, including the well-known Ram Chandra Krishan Chandra's, where young brides choose their red-and-gold finery. The lane is named for its other industry: the fabulous *paranthas* (fried flatbreads) that are sold here in no-frills open-air eateries. Stuffed or served with a variety of fixings, such as radishes, soft cheese, and seasonal vegetables, parathas are delicious. A few kitchens have seating, making them excellent places to refuel, even if the staff doesn't speak English. ✉*South off Chandni Chowk, Old Delhi.*

7 **Jama Masjid.** An exquisite Islamic statement in red sandstone and marble, India's largest mosque was the last monument commissioned by Shah Jahan. Completed in 1656 after six years of work by 5,000 laborers, it's arguably one of the loveliest houses of worship in the world. Three sets of broad steps lead to two-story gateways and a magnificent courtyard with a square ablution tank in the center. The entire space is enclosed by pillared corridors, with domed pavilions in each corner. Thousands gather to pray here, especially on Friday.

Fodor's Choice ★

With its onion-shaped dome and tapering minarets, the mosque is characteristically Moghul, but Shah Jahan added an innovation: the stripes running smartly up and down the marble domes and minarets. The whole structure exudes peace and harmony—climb the south minaret to see the domes up close, complete with swarms of pigeons, and to see how finely the mosque contrasts with the commercial streets around it. (Women cannot enter the minaret without a man; if you're a woman traveling solo, enlist a man to help you, as the beauty of the architecture is best appreciated from above.) Look into the prayer hall (you can only enter after a ritual purification at the ablution tank) for the pulpit carved from a single slab of marble. In one corner is a room where Shah Jahan installed the marble footprints of the Prophet Mohammed. ✉ *6 km (4 mi) north of Connaught Pl., across from Red Fort, Old Delhi, 110006* ☎ *11/2326–8344* 🎫 *Free, Rs. 10 to climb minaret, Rs. 100 for permission to use camera or camcorder* ⏲ *Non-Muslims: winter, daily 8:30* AM*–12:15* PM *and 1:45–½ hr before sunset; summer, daily 7* AM*–12:15 and 1:45–½ hr before sunset. Closed for prayer ½ hr each afternoon. Muslims: daily 5* AM*–8* PM.

❶ ★ **Lal Qila** *(Red Fort).* Named for its red-sandstone walls, the Red Fort, near the Yamuna River in Old Delhi, is the greatest of Delhi's Moghul palace-cities, outdoing even Lutyens' Delhi in majesty. Built by Shah Jahan in the 17th century, Lal Qila recalls the era of Moghul power and magnificence—imperial elephants swaying by with their *mahouts* (elephant drivers), a royal army of eunuchs, court ladies carried in palanquins, and other vestiges of Shah Jahan's pomp. At its peak, the fort housed about 3,000 people. After the Indian Mutiny of 1857, the British moved into the fort, built barracks, and ended the grand Moghul era; eventually the Yamuna River changed course, so the view from the eastern ramparts is now a busy road. Still, if you use your imagination, a visit to the Red Fort gives an excellent idea of what a fantastic city Shahjahanabad was.

The view of the main entrance, called **Lahore Gate,** flanked with towers facing Chandni Chowk, is unfortunately blocked by a barbican (gatehouse), which the paranoid Aurangzeb added for his personal security—to the grief of Shah Jahan, his father. From his prison, where he was held captive by his power-hungry son, Shah Jahan wrote, "You have made a bride of the palace and thrown a veil over her face."

Once you pass through Lahore Gate, continue down the **Chhatta Chowk** (Vaulted Arcade), originally the shopping district for the royal harem and now a bazaar selling rather less-regal goods. From the end of the arcade, you'll see the **Naubat Khana** (Welcome Room), a red-sandstone gateway where music was played five times daily. Beyond this point, everyone but the emperor and princes had to proceed on foot. Upstairs, literally inside the gateway, is the Indian War Memorial Museum (Tues.–Sun. 10–5; free), with arms and military regalia from several periods.

An expansive lawn leads to the great **Diwan-i-Am** (Hall of Public Audience)—you have now entered the Delhi of Shah Jahan. Raised on a platform and open on three sides, the hall is studded with some of the most emblematic arches in the Moghul world. In the center is Shah Jahan's royal throne, once surrounded by decorative panels that sparkled with inlaid gems. (Stolen by British soldiers after the Indian Mutiny, some of the panels were restored 50 years later by Lord Curzon.)

Watched by throngs of people from the courtyard below, the emperor heard the pleas of his subjects; the rest of the hall was reserved for rajas and foreign envoys, all standing with "their eyes bent downwards and their hands crossed." High above them, wrote the 17th-century French traveler François Bernier, under a pearl-fringe canopy resting on golden shafts, "glittered the dazzling figure of the Grand Moghul, a figure to strike terror, for a frown meant death."

Behind the Diwan-i-Am, a row of palaces overlooks the now-distant river. To the extreme right is the **Mumtaz Mahal** (*Tues.–Sun. 10–5* *Free*) now the Red Fort Museum, with numerous paintings and relics from the Moghul period, some in better lighting than others. Heading back north, you'll come next to the **Rang Mahal** (Painted Palace), once richly decorated with a mirrored ceiling that was dismantled to pay the bills when the treasury ran low. Home of the royal ladies, the Rang Mahal contains a cooling water channel—called the Canal of Paradise—that runs from the marble basin in the center of the floor to the rest of the palace and to several of the others. You can't enter this or any of the palaces ahead, so you must peer creatively from the side.

The emperor's private **Khas Mahal** has three sections: the sitting room, the "dream chamber" (for sleeping), and the prayer chamber, all with lavishly carved walls and painted ceilings still intact. The lovely marble screen is carved with the Scale of Justice—two swords and a scale that symbolize punishment and justice. From the attached octagonal tower the emperor Muthamman Burj would appear before his subjects each morning or watch elephant fights in the nearby fields.

The **Diwan-i-Khas** (Hall of Private Audience) was the most exclusive pavilion of all. Here Shah Jahan would sit on his Peacock Throne, made of solid gold and inlaid with hundreds of precious and semiprecious stones. (When Nadir Shah sacked Delhi in 1739, he hauled the famous throne back to Persia. It was destroyed a few years later after Nadir Shah's assassination.) A Persian couplet written in gold above a corner arch sums up Shah Jahan's sentiments about his city: IF THERE BE A PARADISE ON EARTH—IT IS THIS! IT IS THIS! IT IS THIS!

The **Royal Hammam** was a luxurious three-chamber Moghul bath with inlaid-marble floors. The fountain in the center supposedly had rose-scented water. Sometimes called a Turkish bath, the *hammam* is still used in many Muslim cultures. Peek through the windows for a look.

Next door to the hammam is the **Moti Masjid** (Pearl Mosque), designed by Aurangzeb for his personal use and that of his harem. The building is now closed, but the prayer hall is inlaid with *musalla* (prayer rugs) outlined in black marble. Though the mosque has the purity of white marble, some critics say its excessively ornate style reflects the decadence that set in late in Shah Jahan's reign.

Beyond the mosque is a typical Moghul *charbagh*, or four-section garden. Stroll through this quieter part of the fort to see some small pleasure palaces including the Zafar Mahal, decked out with carved sandstone *jalis* (screens) and once surrounded by water. ✉ *Eastern end of Chandni Chowk, Old Delhi* 🎫*Rs. 100; sound-and-light show, weather permitting, Rs. 50, purchase tickets 30 mins in advance* ⏲*Tues.–Sun. sunrise–sunset. Show times: Nov.–Jan., daily 7:30* PM–*8:30* PM; *Feb.–Apr., Sept. and Oct., daily 8:30* PM–*9:30* PM; *May–Aug., daily 9* PM–*10* PM.

❹ **Sisganj Gurdwara.** Old Delhi's most famous Sikh shrine is a restful place to see one of North India's emblematic faiths in practice. Built at various times between 1784 (when the Sikhs conquered Delhi) and the 20th century, it marks the site where the Moghul emperor Aurangzeb beheaded Guru Teg Bahadur in 1675, when the guru refused to convert to Islam. As in any gurdwara (Sikh temple), sections of the *Guru Granth Sahib* scripture are chanted continuously; depending on the season, you might also find decorations of tinsel, colored foil, and blinking lights. Leave your shoes at the opening about 30 feet to the right of the entrance, and cover your head before entering. Women: if you don't have a head covering, climb the stairs and ask the man on the left to lend you one (it's free). If you have any questions about Sikhism or the shrine after your visit, stop into the friendly information office to the left of the entrance to hear legends and symbols unfold. ✉*Chandni Chowk, Old Delhi* ⏲*Daily 24 hrs.*

❻ ★ **Svetamber Jain Temple.** Properly called the Indraprastha Tirth Sumatinatha Jain Svetamber Temple, this splendid house of worship is painted head to toe with finely rendered murals and decorations covering the walls, arches, and ceilings. Reflecting the building's surroundings, some of the artwork shows Moghul influence. Look inside the silver doors of the shrine to Sumatinatha—the 5th of Jainism's 24 *tirthankaras* (perfect souls)—to see some incredible original painting finished with gold leaf. ✉*End of Naughara Gali, Old Delhi* ☎*11/2327–0489* ⏲*Daily 5:30* AM–*12:30* PM *and 6:30* PM–*8* PM.

NEW DELHI

New Delhi, which begins in Connaught Place and extends about 6 km (4 mi) south, is the city the British built when they moved their capital from Calcutta to Delhi in 1911. South Delhi, the southern part of New Delhi, ironically has even older monuments, such as the Qutub Minar, Hauz Khas, and numerous Muslim tombs that lie abandoned in the midst of contemporary houses and apartments.

Numbers in the text correspond to numbers in the margin and on the New Delhi map.

A GOOD TOUR

Hire a car or taxi and head to **Humayun's Tomb** ❶ in the early morning. Created by the wife of the Moghul emperor, the 16th-century tomb is relatively peaceful at this time of day. Proceed north to see where Humayun actually died—in the **Purana Qila** ❷, or Old Fort—and check out the white tigers in the adjacent **National Zoological Park** ❸. Go north one more block to the **Crafts Museum** ❹ for a taste of India's artisanal heritage. From here, head west to Dilli Haat and the INA Market, two wonderful shopping-and-eating bazaars.

After lunch, proceed to the **India Gate** ❺ and drive along Rajpath to see the grandeur of **Lutyens' Delhi** ❻. If you're interested in art, visit the **National Gallery of Modern Art** ❼ or the ancient sculptures and artifacts at the **National Museum** ❽.

Choose one or two of the following sights—all within a few kilometers of one another—to occupy the rest of your afternoon. If you're interested in politics and the Independence movement, visit **Gandhi Smriti** ❾, the **Nehru Memorial Museum** ❿, and the **Indira Gandhi Memorial Museum** ⓫. A good alternative, especially for railroad enthusiasts and children, is to continue south and visit the **National Rail Museum** ⓬ near Nehru Park. Drive northwest to the Sikh temple **Bangla Sahib Gurdwara** ⓭ to listen to hymns; then drive a few streets west to check out the colorful and ornate **Laxmi Naryan Temple** ⓮.

Around 5 PM, drive to the Old World Muslim bazaar in Nizamuddin West, about 3 km (2 mi) east of Lodi Garden, and walk down the winding lanes to **Hazrat Nizamuddin Darga** ⓯, the tomb of a Sufi saint. It's a lovely place to linger at dusk, and if you're lucky, singers will perform *qawwali,* songs of devotion sung by Sufi muslims,as the sun sets.

If you have an extra afternoon, chill out in **Lodi Garden** ⓰ amidst the tombs of the 15th- and 16th-century Lodi rulers. Walk a few blocks west of the garden to see **Safdarjung's Tomb** ⓱. Drive south and wander through **Hauz Khas Village** ⓲, and head farther south to see the towering **Qutub Minar** ⓳. Another option, especially in the early evening, is to visit the **ISKCON Temple** ⓴ of the Hare Krishna sect or the lotus-shaped **Bahai House of Worship** ㉑, both in southeastern New Delhi. The Swaminaryan Akshardam complex, on Delhi's outskirts, is an amazing sight worth the long lines and somewhat hard-to-get-to location.

TIMING Divide this itinerary into two or three days. Choose a monument and museum (or the zoo) for morning and midday, then punctuate it with a visit to a temple at sunset. Traffic and heat will slow you down considerably—especially between April and October, when the sun is intense. Lodi Garden is a good place to take a break. Note that museums are closed on Monday, and that Sunday is the traditional family day out in India, so many sights, particularly outdoor sights such as the Bahai House of Worship and the zoo, are more crowded then.

WHAT TO SEE

㉑ **Bahai House of Worship.** The lotus flower is a symbol of purity throughout India, and Delhi's Bahai Temple celebrates this in a unique architectural way. Designed by Fariburz Sahba, an Iranian-born Canadian architect, and completed in 1986, the building incorporates the number nine—the highest digit and, in the Bahai faith, a symbol of unity. The sleek structure has two layers: nine white marble-covered petals that point to heaven, and nine petals that conceal the portals. From a short distance, it looks like a fantastic work of origami. The nine pools outside signify the green leaves of the lotus and cool the starkly elegant,

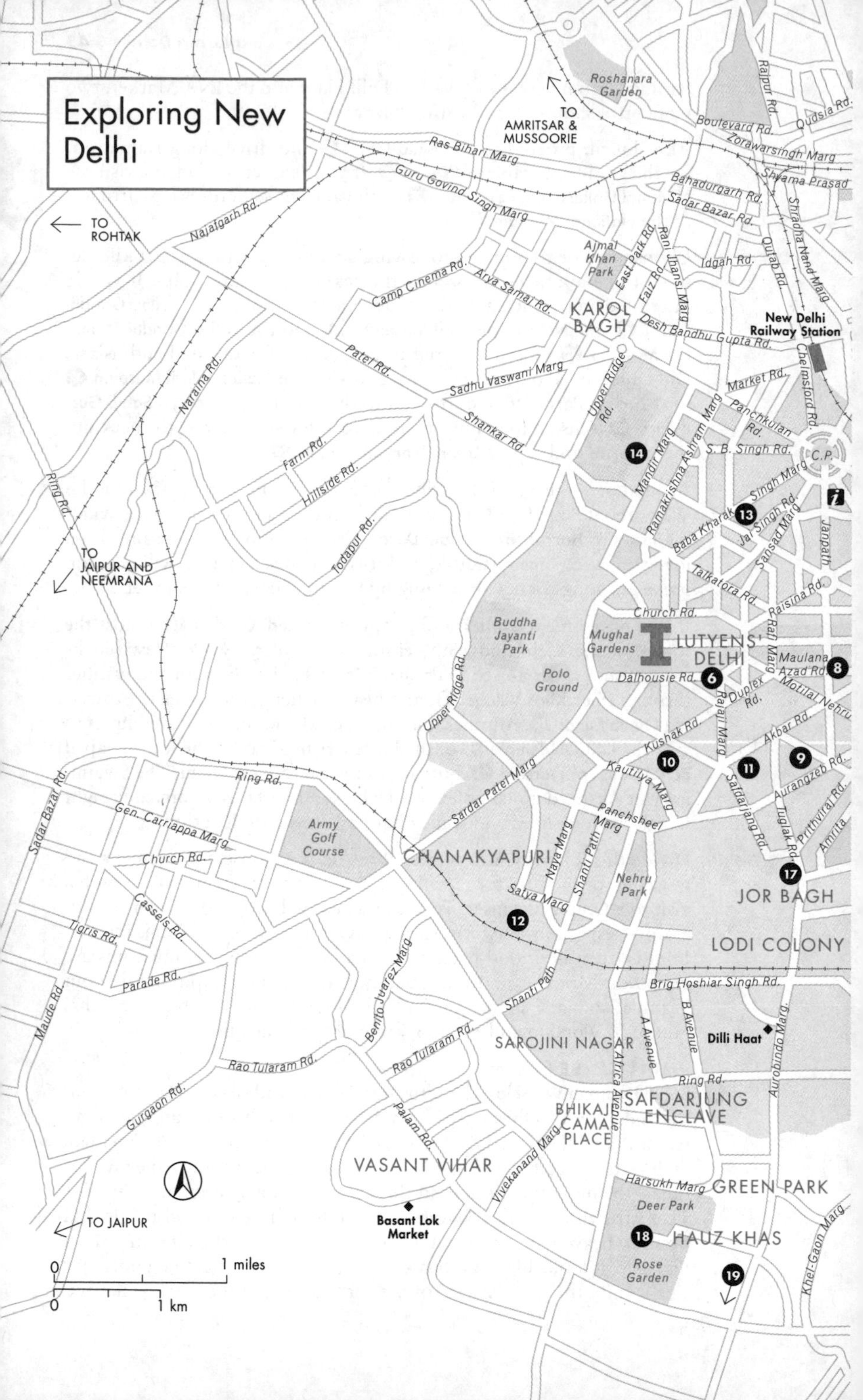
Exploring New Delhi
TO AMRITSAR & MUSSOORIE
TO ROHTAK
TO JAIPUR AND NEEMRANA
TO JAIPUR
Roshanara Garden
Ajmal Khan Park
KAROL BAGH
New Delhi Railway Station
C.P.
Buddha Jayanti Park
Mughal Gardens
Polo Ground
LUTYENS' DELHI
Army Golf Course
CHANAKYAPURI
Nehru Park
JOR BAGH
LODI COLONY
SAROJINI NAGAR
Dilli Haat
BHIKAJI CAMA PLACE
SAFDARJUNG ENCLAVE
VASANT VIHAR
Basant Lok Market
GREEN PARK
Deer Park
HAUZ KHAS
Rose Garden
0
1 miles
0
1 km

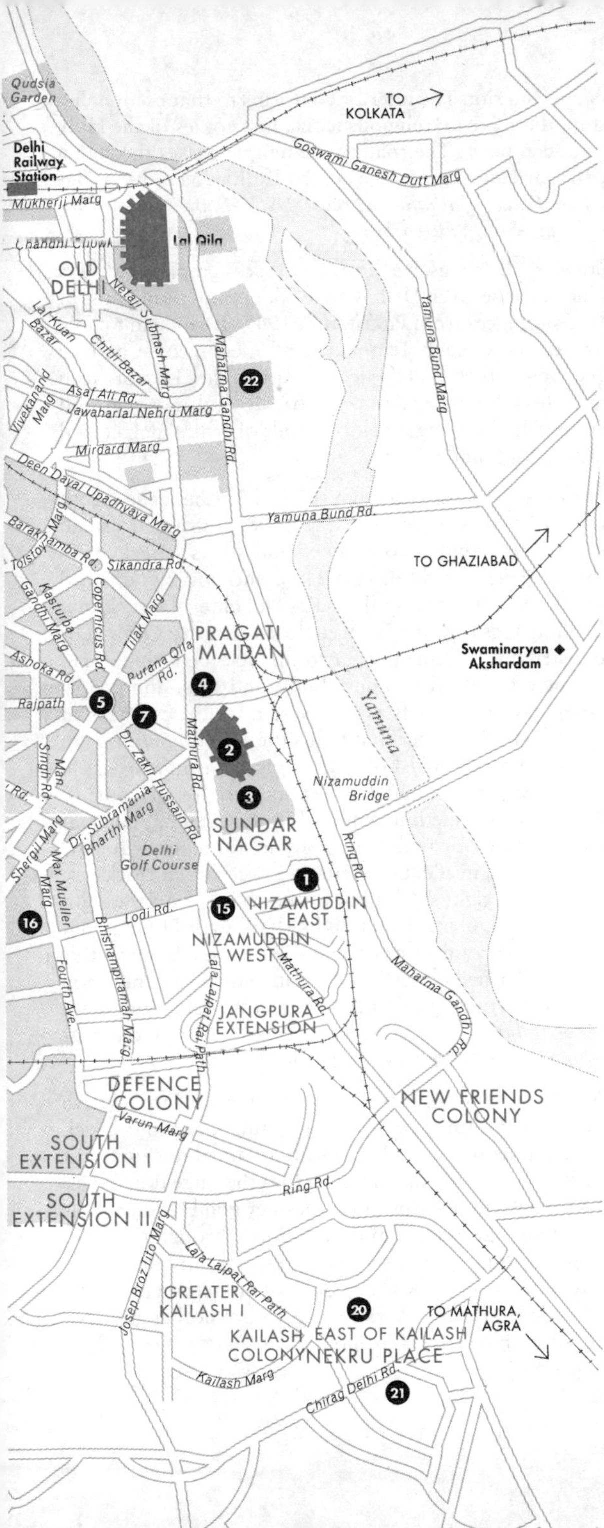

Bahai House of Worship	21
Bangla Sahib Gurdwara	13
Crafts Museum	4
Gandhi Smriti	9
Hauz Khas	18
Hazrat Nizamuddin Darga	15
Humayun's Tomb	1
India Gate	5
Indira Gandhi Memorial Museum	11
ISKCON Temple	20
Laxmi Naryan Temple	14
Lodi Garden	16
Lutyen's Delhi	6
National Gallery of Modern Art	7
National Museum	8
National Rail Museum	12
National Zoological Park	3
Nehru Memorial Museum	10
Purana Qila	2
Qutub Minar	19
Raj Ghat & National Gandhi Museum	22
Safdarjung's Tomb	17

usually silent marble interior. The interior conforms to that of all Bahai houses of worship: there are no religious icons, just copies of the Holy Scriptures and wooden pews. The road to the temple passes through a colorful temple bazaar connected to the nearby Kalkaji Mandir. ✉ *Bahapur, near Nehru Place, Kalkaji* 🎫 *Free* ⏲ *Apr.–Sept., Tues.–Sun. 9–7; Oct.–Mar., Tues.–Sun. 9:30–5:30.*

13 **Bangla Sahib Gurdwara.** This massive *gurdwara* (Sikh temple) is always full of activity—no surprise given Delhi's huge Sikh population, most of whom came here as refugees from Pakistan in 1947. If you can't make it to Amritsar to see the Golden Temple, by all means come here to admire the distinctively ostentatious style of their temples. Like Sikhism itself, gurdwaras reflect both the symmetry of Moghul mosques and the chaos of Hindu temples. Bangla Sahib is built of white marble and topped with a shiny, gold onion dome.

The gurdwara stands on the site where Guru Hari Krishan, the eighth of ten Sikh gurus who lived between 1469 and 1708, performed a small miracle. Before entering, remove your shoes and socks (check them at the counter on the left), get rid of cigarettes, and cover your head with a piece of cloth. As you walk up the stairs and enter the sanctum, you'll see people filling jugs of water from enclosed cisterns. Guru Hari Krishan used to distribute sanctified water to the sick, believing it had a miraculous healing effect on their mind, body, and soul, and people still treat the contents of these pools as holy water. Inside, devotees sit facing a small pavilion in the center that holds the *Granth Sahib* (Sikh scriptures). Hymns from the holy book are sung continuously from well before sunrise until approximately 9 PM, and you're welcome to sit and listen; if you fancy something cultural in the evening, come at about 9 to see the ceremony by which the book is stored away for the night. As you walk around inside, be careful to proceed in a clockwise direction, and exit on the right side in back. Out the door to the right a priest distributes *prasad,* a ritual that Sikhs share with Hindus that resembles the Christian sacrament of communion: take a lump of this sugar, flour, and *ghee* (clarified butter) concoction with both hands, pop it into your mouth with your right hand, then rub the remaining ghee into your hands. ✉ *Baba Bangla Sahib Marg, across from Gole Post Office, Connaught Place* 🎫 *Free* ⏲ *4 AM–9 PM.*

OFF THE BEATEN PATH

Chattarpur Temples. If you're on your way south to Agra or Jaipur, drive a few miles beyond the Qutub Minar on Mehrauli Road and check out this massive Hindu temple complex. It's an untamed mishmash of architectural styles, but the unifying factor—from the huge dome over the Shiva lingam to the 92-foot statue of the monkey god Hanuman—is the ostentatious Punjabi Baroque architecture. Enter through the sanctum with the devotees, stop at the idols to pay respects, and take some prasad on the way out. Many gods and goddesses are represented, but the inner sanctum is dedicated to Adhya Ma Katyan, a mother goddess. Hymns are sung all night during full moons. ✉ *Chattarpur* 🎫 *Free* ⏲ *Daily sunrise–sunset.*

4 **Crafts Museum.** Designed by the Indian architect Charles Correa, this charming complex near the Purana Qila houses thousands of artifacts and handicrafts. You're greeted outside by playful terra-cotta sculptures from Tamil Nadu. Inside, the annotations are sketchy, but the collection is fascinating. Items in the Folk and Tribal Art Gallery, including some charming toys, illustrate village life throughout India. In one courtyard you'll see a giant wooden temple car (cart), built to carry deities in festive processions; one of the adjacent buildings contains a lavishly decorated Gujarati haveli. The Courtly Crafts section suggests the luxurious lives of India's erstwhile royalty, and the entire upper floor is a spectacular showcase of saris and textiles. In the village complex out back, craftspeople demonstrate their skills and sell their creations in replicas of village homes. The museum shop is the best in Delhi, with high-quality art books and crafts, and there's a small snack bar. ✉ *Pragati Bhavan, just off Mathura Rd., Pragati Maidan* ☎ *11/2337–1817* 🎟 *Free* 🕓 *Tues.–Sun. 10–5.*

9 **Gandhi Smriti.** Mohandas K. Gandhi, better known as Mahatma (Great Soul), lived a life of voluntary poverty, but he did it in some attractive places. It was in this huge colonial bungalow, designed by a French architect for Indian industrialist G. D. R. Birla, that Gandhi was staying as a guest when he was assassinated in the back garden on his way to a prayer meeting. Gandhi's bedroom is just as he left it, with his "worldly remains" (only 11 items, including his glasses and a walking stick) mounted on the wall. Pictures and text tell the story of Gandhi's life and the Independence movement; there's also a collection of dioramas depicting events in Gandhi's life. In the theater, 10 different documentaries are available for viewing, on request. Take off your shoes before entering the somber prayer ground in back; an eternal flame marks the very spot where Gandhi expired. This, not the National Gandhi Museum at Raj Ghat, is the government's official museum dedicated to the Mahatma. ✉ *5 Tees January Marg, Central Delhi* ☎ *11/2301–2843* 🌐 *gandhismriti.nic.in* 🎟 *Free* 🕓 *Tues.–Sun. 10–5.*

18 **Hauz Khas Village.** The road south to the urban village of Hauz Khas is lined on both sides by ancient stone monuments, and the entire village is dotted with domed structures—the tombs of minor Muslim royalty from the 14th to the 16th centuries. At the end of the road is the tomb of Firoz Shah Tughluq, who ruled Delhi in the 14th century. Hauz Khas means "Royal Tank," referring to the artificial lake visible from Firoz Shah's pillared tomb. The tank was actually built a century earlier by Allauddin Khilji as a water source for his nearby fort, then called Siri (the second city of Delhi). Back in the village, wander through the narrow lanes to experience a medley of old and new structures—expensive shops and art galleries in a medieval warren. ■ **TIP→ Find your way to the gardens near the ruin of a *madrassa* at the back of the village. The kindly old gentleman often playing cards can sometimes be coaxed into an impromptu Urdu lesson.** In the 1980s Hauz Khas was designated an upscale tourist destination, but (perhaps fortunately) the process of redevelopment was never completed, so some of the village character persists. After exploring, stop for a meal at one of the village's restaurants, particularly Park Balluchi (in the Deer Park), Naivedyam, or the Village Bistro.

15 ★ **Hazrat Nizamuddin Darga.** One of Delhi's greatest treats is hearing devout Sufis sing *qawwalis,* ecstatic devotional Muslim songs with a decidedly toe-tapping quality. To get here, follow the twisting lanes in the bazaar section of Nizamuddin West—you'll pass open-air restaurants serving simple meat-based meals, tiny shops selling Urdu-language books and cassettes (some by famous qawwali singers), and probably a number of beggars appealing to the Muslim tradition of alms for the poor. When you see vendors selling flowers and garlands, you're getting close to the *darga* (tomb) of Hazrat Nizamuddin Aulia, who was born in Bukhara (now in Uzbekistan) in 1238 and later fled with his family to Delhi, where he became an important Sufi mystic and attracted a dedicated following. He died in 1325.

The saint's tomb, built in 1562 in the center of a courtyard, is topped with an onion-shaped dome. It's also covered with intricate painting and inlay work, best viewed on the carved parapet above the verandas. Men can enter the shrine to pay their respects; women must peer in from outside. The tomb is flanked by a mosque and the graves of other important Muslims, including the great Sufi poet Amir Khusro and Jahanara, a daughter of the Moghul emperor Shah Jahan. Evenings from around 5 to 7, especially Thursday, the saint's male followers often sing in front of the darga. ⚠ **Crowds can be dense and it's easy to lose your wallet or purse before you notice. Keep money and valuables secured when you're in and around the darga.** ✉ *Old Nizamuddin Bazaar; enter bazaar from Mathura Rd., Nizamuddin West* 🎫 *Free, donations to shrine and musicians accepted* ⏲ *Daily 24 hrs.*

1 Fodor's Choice ★ **Humayun's Tomb.** Built in the middle of the 16th century by the widow of the Moghul emperor Humayun, this tomb launched a new architectural era of Persian influence, culminating in the Taj Mahal and Fatehpur Sikri. The Moghuls brought to India their love of gardens and fountains and left a legacy of harmonious structures, including this mausoleum, that fuse symmetry with decorative splendor.

Resting on an immense two-story platform, the tomb structure of red sandstone and white marble is surrounded by gardens intersected by water channels in the Moghuls' beloved *charbagh* design: perfectly square gardens divided into four (*char*) square parts. The marble dome covering the actual tomb is another first: a dome within a dome (the interior dome is set inside the soaring dome seen from outside), a style later used in the Taj Mahal. As you enter or leave the tomb area, stand a moment before the beveled gateway to enjoy the view of the monument framed in the arch.

Besides Humayun, several other important Moghuls are buried here, along with Isa Khan Niyazi, a noble in the court of Sher Shah—who lies in the fetching octagonal shrine that precedes the tomb itself. The site's serenity belies the fact that many of the dead buried inside were murdered princes, victims of foul play. To see where Humayun actually died, combine this visit with a trip to the Purana Qila. ✉ *Off Mathura Rd., Nizamuddin East, 110003* 🎫 *Rs. 250* ⏲ *Daily sunrise–sunset.*

5 **India Gate.** Anchoring a traffic circle near the far end of Rajpath from the Indian government, this massive sandstone arch was designed by Lutyens in 1931, in memory of the 90,000 soldiers of the British Indian Army who fell in World War I and the third Afghan War of the late 19th century. In the 1970s, the government of India added a memorial to India's unknown soldier, the Amar Jawan Jyoti, beneath the arch. While traffic speeds neatly around the outer circle, vendors occupy the inner circle, and people amble and socialize on the lawns. Come in early evening and you'll find all sorts of activity, from men offering to make monkeys "dance" for a fee to impromptu cricket matches to youngsters splashing in the decorative stream nearby. ✉ *East end of Rajpath, Central Delhi.*

11 **Indira Gandhi Memorial Museum.** On October 31, 1984, Prime Minister Indira Gandhi was shot outside her home by two of her Sikh bodyguards in retaliation for her violent suppression of a violent Sikh independence movement in Punjab, which included a military operation that entered Amritsar's Golden Temple. The murder sparked gruesome anti-Sikh riots in Delhi, and political turmoil ensued. The simple white bungalow in which Mrs. Gandhi lived from the 1960s to 1980s is now a small museum with endless photographs, quotations, and newspaper articles, plus a few rooms preserved as they were used. The photos get more interesting as you progress, and the museum ends with displays on Indira's son, Rajiv, himself prime minister from 1984–91 before he, too, was assassinated. Displays include the sari, handbag, and shoes Mrs. Gandhi was wearing when she was killed, and the sneakers Rajiv was wearing during his even more grisly demise at the hands of a female suicide bomber who was retaliating for India's support of the Sri Lankan government during a civil war. Outside, the spot where Indira fell is marked and preserved. Popular with Indian tourists, the museum can get very crowded; allow extra time if you want to peruse things carefully. ✉ *1 Safdarjung Rd., Central Delhi* ☎ *11/2301–0094* 🎫 *Free* ⏲ *Tues.–Sun. 9:30–4:45.*

20 **ISKCON Temple.** The International Society for Krishna Consciousness is better known as the Hare Krishna sect, and despite the 1960s association they are very much alive and kicking. In the 1990s ISKCON erected enormous, gleaming Krishna temples in several Indian cities, and these offer a unique glimpse into the remaining pockets of international Hinduism, with shaven-headed foreigners in saffron robes mingling with Indian colleagues, devotees, and tourists. Built impressively on a rock outcropping near a residential market, Delhi's temple is an amalgam of architectural styles: Moghul, Gupta, and the flashy Delhi style jokingly called Punjabi Baroque. The sanctum contains three idols—Balram Krishna, Radha-Krishna, and Laksman (along with Ram and Sita)—each representing a different incarnation of Lord Krishna. The art gallery behind the idols must be viewed in a clockwise direction, as this *parikrama* (revolution) is the only appropriate way to move around the gods. To learn more about Krishna, pop into the "Vedic Expo," where an upstairs collection of dioramas illustrate his life in the incarnation of Lord Chaitanya, and various sound-and-light shows (even a robotics display) enact the Bhaga-

vad Gita scriptures and the ancient epic, the *Mahabharata,* from which the scriptures come. It's all a bit Southern California, but ISKCON's temples are by far the cleanest in India, and very welcoming to visitors. Finish with a meal at Govinda's, the on-site restaurant, where a vegetarian buffet goes for Rs. 150. ⊠*Hare Krishna Hill, Sant Nagar Main Rd., East of Kailash* ☎*11/2623–5133 or 11/2623–3400* 🎫*Free* ⏲*Daily 4:30* AM*–1* PM *and 4* PM*–9* PM.

22 **Laxmi Naryan Temple.** This large, red-and-yellow temple (known as Birla Mandir) west of Connaught Place is an excellent example of a reformist Hindu temple—both architecturally and in terms of temple practices. It was built in 1938 by Indian industrialist G.D.R. Birla—the same man whose house is now the Gandhi Smriti—as a nondenominational temple. (The sign outside welcomes all "Hindus," including Jains and Sikhs.) The temple is colorful and ornate: note the lotus patterns at the top of each phallic steeple and the inlaid lotus pattern on the floor in front of the main *murti* (idol) of Laxmi Narayan. Although the temple exhibits many of the gaudier elements of Hindu design, overall it's relatively subdued. This is a common feature of reformist, 20th-century Hindu architecture, which was influenced by European architecture. ⊠*Mandir Marg, Connaught Place.*

16 ★ **Lodi Garden.** After Mughal warrior Timur ransacked Delhi at the end of the 14th century, he ordered the massacre of the entire population—acceptable retribution, he thought, for the murder of some of his soldiers. As if in unconscious response to this horrific act, the subsequent Lodi and Sayyid dynasties built no city, only a few mosques and some mausoleums and tombs, the latter of which stand in what is now a delightful urban park. Winding walks cut through landscaped lawns with trees and small flowers, past schoolboys playing cricket, politicians taking some air, friends and lovers relaxing in the greenery, and parrots squawking. Near the southern entrance on Lodi Road is the dignified mausoleum of Mohammed Shah, third ruler of the Sayyid dynasty, and some members of his family. This octagon, with a central chamber surrounded by verandas carved with arches, is a good example of the architecture of this period. Near the road is the open-air National Bonsai Park, with some nice specimens of the trees. The smaller, equally lovely, octagonal tomb of Sikandar Lodi, surrounded by a garden in the park's northwestern corner, has an unusual double dome. ⊠*Lodi Rd., across from Jor Bagh* 🎫*Free* ⏲*Daily sunrise–sunset.*

6 ★ **Lutyens' Delhi.** Rajpath—the broadest avenue in Delhi—leads to Delhi's eighth capital: Sir Edwin Lutyens' imperial city, built between 1914 and 1931 in a symbolically imperialistic design after the British moved their capital from Calcutta to Delhi in 1911. (While the British were building, they hit marshy land prone to floods, so they reversed direction and put the bulk of their capital, the imperial city, a few miles to the south.) Starting from India Gate at the lowest and eastern end of Rajpath, nearby land was allocated to numerous princely states, which built small palaces, such as the **Bikaner House** (now the Rajasthan tourism office) and **Jaipur House** (now the National Gallery of Modern Art). It might be said that this placement mirrored the British

sentiments toward the princes, who lost much of their former power and status during the British Raj. Moving up the slowly inclining hill at the western end of the avenue, you also move up the British ladder of power, a concept inherent in the original design. First you come to the enormous **North and South Secretariats,** facing each other on Rajpath and reflecting the importance of the bureaucracy, a fixture of Indian society since the time of British rule. Identical in design, the two buildings have 1,000 rooms and miles of corridors.

Directly behind the North Secretariat is the Indian parliament house, **Sansad Bhavan,** a circular building in red and gray sandstone, with an open colonnade that extends around its circumference. Architecturally, the Indian design is meant to mirror the spinning wheel that was the symbol of Mahatma Gandhi, but the building's secondary placement, off the main avenue, may suggest the attitude of the British toward the Indian legislative assembly.

At the top of the hill is the former Viceroy's House, now called **Rashtrapati Bhavan,** where the President of India (not the prime minister) resides. It was built in the 20th century, but the building's daunting proportions seem to reflect an earlier, more lavish time of British supremacy. The Bhavan contains 340 rooms and its grounds cover 330 acres. The shape of the central brass dome, the palace's main architectural feature, reflects that of a Buddhist *stupa* (shrine).

The execution of Lutyens' design has a flaw: the entire palace was supposed to fill the vista as you approach the top of the hill, but the gradient is too steep, so only the dome dominates the horizon. And in a nicely ironic twist, a few years after the imperial city was completed, the British packed up and went home, and this lavish architectural complex became the grand capital of newly independent India. Permission to enter Rashtrapati and Sansad Bhavan is almost impossible to obtain; unless you have contacts in high places, satisfy yourself with a glimpse from outside. ■ **TIP→ However, for several weeks each Feburary, the extensive gardens are open to the public. Heavy security is in place (no bags or cell phones, for instance), but a rare view of the impressive gardens is worth the hassle.** ⊠ *Central Delhi.*

7 **National Gallery of Modern Art.** Facing India Gate, this neoclassical building was built by the British in the early 20th century as a palace for the maharaja of Jaipur. With its small dome and large, open rooms, the structure makes a fine space for this art museum, established in 1954 to preserve Indian art forms (mainly painting) that developed after 1850. The displays are attractive by local standards but distinctly uneven and unexplained. They also hold only a fraction of available works—thousands are in storage due to lack of gallery space. Highlights are the colorful paintings of Amrita Sher-Gil (the Frida Kahlo of India) and, upstairs, the myth-inspired works of Raja Ravi Varma and the Bengali Renaissance oils and watercolors of the Tagore family, Jamini Roy, and Nandalal Bose. There are a few representative works by contemporary masters such as M. F. Husain and Ganesh Pyne. Documentaries, shown daily at 11 and 3, explain Indian art. ⊠ *Jaipur House, India Gate, Central Delhi* ☎ *11/2338–2835* 🎟 *Rs. 150* 🕓 *Tues.–Sun. 10–5.*

8 **National Museum.** The facade of this grand building imitates Lutyens' Presidential Palace: a sandstone dome is supported by classical columns of brown sandstone on a red-sandstone base. When you enter, you'll see a 13th-century idol—from the Konark Sun Temple in Bhubaneswar—of Surya, the sun god, standing beneath the dome. Such a statue is emblematic of the National Museum's strength—it showcases ancient, mainly Hindu, sculptures. An entire room is dedicated to artifacts from the Indus Valley Civilization, circa 2,700 BC; others display works from the Gandharan, Chandela, and Chola periods. Besides sculpture, also on exhibit are jewelry, painting, musical instruments, coins, carpets, and weapons, including Shah Jehan's sword. Be sure to pick up a brochure to help you navigate, and also consider grabbing the audio guide, included in foreigner ticket rates, which is also worth a listen. No cameras are allowed. ✉ *Janpath and Rajpath, Central Delhi* ☎ *11/2301–9272* 🎟 *Rs. 150* ⏲ *Tues.–Sun. 10–5.*

12 **National Rail Museum.** This large, mostly outdoor, museum is a glimpse into the largest railway system in the world. The 10-acre grounds are home to 75 authentic engines, bogies (railway cars), and even a working roundabout (a device that spins rail cars). Parked behind glass is the Fairy Queen; built in 1855, it's the oldest running steam engine in the world. It still takes nine trips a year to Sariska National Park and back for a weekend trip (contact the Director of the Museum if you're interested, but it's not worth the outrageous price). Inside the museum are displays that discuss the history of the India rail system. The museum is good not only for train buffs but also children, who love riding the tiny train that circumambulates the grounds. ✉ *Near Nehru Park; from Ring Rd., turn left onto Nyaya Marg, then left again, Chanakyapuri* ☎ *11/2688–1816 or 11/2688–0939* 🎟 *Rs. 10* ⏲ *Oct.–Mar., Tues.–Sun. 9:30–5, Apr.–Sept., Tues.–Sun. 9:30–7.*

3 **National Zoological Park.** White tigers are the draw at Delhi's zoo, which was designed in the late 1950s by the German designer Carl Hagenbeck. There are many noteworthy animals roaming about, such as emu, gazelle, Indian rhino, and a great many deer, not to mention some smart-looking water birds. Animals in cages, including the famous white tigers and Asiatic lions, are part of the national collection. The zoo is spacious and leafy, a virtual botanical garden for peaceful walks, and the central lake hosts numerous Central Asian migratory aquatic birds (pelicans, storks, and cranes) pausing on their way to Keoladeo National Park in Bharatpur, Rajasthan, for the winter. If you don't have time to make it to Bharatpur or a tiger reserve, this is a pretty good alternative. ✉ *Mathura Rd., behind Sundar Nagar* 🎟 *Rs. 50* ⏲ *Mid-Oct.–Mar., Sat.–Thurs. 9:30–4; Apr.–mid-Oct., Sat.–Thurs. 9–4:30.*

10 **Nehru Memorial Museum.** This colonial mansion, also known as Teen ★ Murti Bhavan, was originally built for the commander of the British Indian Army. When the Viceroy's residence, Rashtrapati Bhavan (at the other end of South Avenue), became the home of India's president, India's first prime minister, Jawaharlal Nehru, took up residence here. Those interested in the Independence movement should not miss this landmark or the nearby Gandhi Smriti. Nehru's yellow mansion is

fronted by a long, oval-shaped lawn; out back, there's a tranquil flower garden. Inside, several rooms remain as Nehru left them, and extensive displays chronicle Nehru's life and the Independence movement. Move through the rooms in order: one by one, photographs, newspaper clippings, and personal letters tell the breathtaking story of the birth of the world's largest democracy. On your way out, stop and see the 14th-century hunting lodge next to the Nehru Planetarium. (The latter, good for children, has shows in English at 11:30 AM and 3 PM.) ⊠ *Teen Murti Marg, Central Delhi* ☎ *11/2301–3765* 🎫 *Free* 🕓 *Tues.–Sun. 9–5:30.*

2 **Purana Qila** *(Old Fort)*. India's sixth capital was the scene of a fierce power struggle between the Afghan Sher Shah and Humayun, son of the first Moghul emperor, Babur, in the 16th century. When Humayun started to build his own capital, Dinpanah, on these grounds in the 1530s, Sher Shah forced the emperor to flee for his life to Persia. Sher Shah destroyed what existed of Dinpanah to create his own capital, Shergarh. Fifteen years later, in 1555, Humayun returned and seized control, but he died the following year, leaving Sher Shah's city for others to destroy.

Unfortunately, once you enter the massive Bara Darwaza (Main Gate), only two buildings are intact. The **Qila-i-Kuhna Masjid,** Sher Shah's private mosque, is an excellent example of Indo-Afghan architecture in red sandstone with decorative marble touches—walk around to the "back" to see the beautiful front of the building. The nearby **Sher Mandal,** a two-story octagonal tower of red sandstone and white marble, became Humayun's library and ultimately his death trap: hearing the call to prayer, Humayun started down the steep steps, slipped, and fell to his death. On pleasant afternoons, every bush on these grounds hides a pair of young lovers in search of a little privacy. ⊠ *Off Mathura Rd., near Delhi Zoo, Pragati Maidan* 🎫 *Rs. 150* 🕓 *Daily sunrise–sunset.*

19 ★ **Qutub Minar.** Named for the Muslim sultan Qutub-ud-din Aibak, this striking tower is 234 feet high, with 376 steps, and the tallest stone tower in India. Qutub-ud-din-Aibak began construction in 1193; his son-in-law and successor, Iltutmish, added the top four stories. The result is a handsome sandstone example of Indo-Islamic architecture, with terra-cotta frills and balconies. At its foot lies the **Quwwat-ul-Islam Masjid,** the first Muslim mosque in India. The Muslims erected the mosque in the 12th century after they defeated the Hindu Chauhan dynasty—they built it on the site of a Hindu temple and used pillars and other materials from 27 demolished Hindu and Jain shrines. (Which explains why you see Hindu and Jain sculptures in the mosque.) The mosque is also famous for a 24-foot-high, 5th-century iron pillar, inscribed with six lines of Sanskrit. According to legend, if you stand with your back to the pillar and can reach around and touch your fingers, any wish you make will come true. (Unfortunately, it's now fenced off.) ⊠ *Aurobindo Marg, near Mehrauli* 🎫 *Rs. 250* 🕓 *Daily sunrise–sunset.*

22 **Raj Ghat and National Gandhi Museum.** After Mohandas K. Gandhi was shot and killed by a Hindu fanatic on January 30, 1948, his body was cremated on the banks of the Yamuna River. His *samadhi,* or cremation site, is now a national shrine, where Indian tourists and pilgrims stream across the peaceful lawn to pay their respects to the saintlike Father of the Nation. At the center of a large courtyard is a raised slab of black marble adorned with flowers and inscribed with Gandhi's final words, HAI RAM! (Oh, God!). An eternal flame burns at its head. The sandstone walls enclosing the shrine are inscribed with passages written by Gandhi, translated into several tongues including Tamil, Malayalam, Nepali, Urdu, Spanish, Arabic, and Chinese. Near Raj Ghat are the cremation sites of two other assassinated heads of state, Indira Gandhi and her son Rajiv (no relation to Mohandas). Back across the boulevard is the **National Gandhi Museum,** run by a private foundation, which houses a great many photographs, a display of spinning wheels with some information on Gandhi's *khadi* (homespun cotton) crusade, and some of the Mahatma's personal effects, including the blood-stained dhoti he was wearing at the time of his murder. The tiny art gallery has a poignant wooden sculpture, made by a South African, of Gandhi in a pose suggesting Jesus's Crucifixion. A film on Gandhi's life is shown on weekends at 4. ✉ *Mahatma Gandhi Marg (Ring Rd.), Old Delhi, 110006* 🎟 *Free* ⏲ *Raj Ghat daily sunrise–sunset, museum Tues.–Sun. 9:30–5:30.*

Fodor'sChoice ★

17 **Safdarjang's Tomb.** Delhi's last great garden tomb, built in 1754 for the prime minister of the emperor Mohammad Shah, is pleasantly located in the center of town. With its oversize dome and minarets, it can't compete with Humayun's resting place, but the finials and other details have a distinctly Moghul fineness, and the *charbagh* (four-section garden) is a peaceful place to listen to the birds chirp. The site would be lovelier if water still ran through the four large channels in the gardens, but you have to imagine that part to complete the 18th-century scene. ✉ *Aurobindo Marg at Lodi Rd., Jor Bagh* 🎟 *Rs. 150* ⏲ *Daily sunrise–sunset.*

OFF THE BEATEN PATH

Fodor'sChoice ★

Swaminaryan Akshardam. Rising over the traffic jams of National Highway 24 on the way to the eastern suburb of Noida lies a massive, 100-acre temple complex where religion and commerce meet. Completed in November 2005, the pink-stone religious emporium pays tribute to Bhagwan Swami Narayan (1781–1830), the founder of a worldwide spiritual movement that claims a million devotees. An architectural marvel built over five years and without using steel, the elaborate main temple and its soaring domes and 20,000 carved figures only appear ancient. This gleaming complex includes a giant movie theater and a 14-minute boat ride. Whisking the visitor through 10,000 years of Indian culture, the ride could be mistaken for something straight out of Disney World. Don't miss the Yagnapurush Kund & Musical Fountain, India's largest, which has an entertaining show echoing the Vedic sentiments of creation. Just viewing the exhibits takes at least two hours, and admission lines can be lengthy, so allow plenty of time. Security is airtight. ⚠ **All bags and purses, electronics (including mobile phones and cameras), and tobacco**

products are banned, so check them in or leave them at the hotel or in the car before you get in line. But don't forget your wallet. While donations are voluntary, marketing is persistent. Exhibitions tend to shut an hour before the complex itself; the food court provides decent, cheap vegetarian meals and snacks for those who opt to spend the day. ✉*Akshardam Setu, N.H. 24 New Delhi* ☎*11/2201–6688* *Free* *Daily 9–7.*

WHERE TO EAT

NORTH INDIAN

$$$$ ★ ✕**Bukhara.** Served amid stone walls, rough-hewn dark-wood beams, copper urns, and blood-red rugs, Bukhara's menu hasn't changed in years, and the groups of tourists and businesspeople who eat here—and eagerly pay the princely sums required—wouldn't have it any other way. The cuisine of the Northwest Frontier, now the border between Pakistan and Afghanistan, is heavy on meats, marinated and grilled in a *tandoor* (clay oven). The *murgh malai kebab* (boneless chicken marinated with cream cheese, malt vinegar, and green coriander) is very good; red-meat lovers find the tender *sikandari raan* (leg of lamb marinated in herbs) equally memorable. Bukhara's *dal* (black lentils simmered overnight with tomatoes, ginger, and garlic) is so famous it's now sold in grocery stores. Vegetarians can opt for a tandoori salad of vegetables, pineapple, and *paneer* (a soft cheese), but this isn't really a good place for them. In addition, service can sometimes be perfunctory, especially for smaller groups. ✉*ITC Maurya Sheraton Hotel, Sardar Patel Marg, Diplomatic Enclave, Chanakyapuri 110021* ☎*11/2611–2233* ▭*AE, DC, MC, V.*

$$$$ Fodor'sChoice ★ ✕**Dum Pukht.** Like the *nawabi* (princely) culture from which it's drawn, the food and style at this restaurant are subtle and refined. Chef Imtiaz Qureshi, descended from court cooks in Avadh (Lucknow), creates delicately spiced meals packed with flavor: *dum ki khumb* (button mushrooms in gravy, fennel, and dried ginger), *kakori kabab* (finely minced mutton, cloves, and cinnamon, drizzled with saffron), and the special *raan-e-dumpukht,* a leg of mutton marinated in dark rum and stuffed with onions, cheese, and mint. The formal room is white, blue, and hushed. ✉*ITC Maurya Sheraton Hotel, Sardar Patel Marg, Diplomatic Enclave, Chanakyapuri 110021* ☎*11/2611–2233* ▭*AE, DC, MC, V.*

$$$–$$$$ ✕**Punjabi by Nature.** What was once one of the most cutting-edge eateries in town is now advertised on campy billboards around the city. Though the hip factor may have faded, top-notch versions of hearty Punjabi classics like *murgh Punjabi masala* (the house chicken curry), *dal makhni* (black lentils with butter and cream), and *raan-e-Punjab* (a tender whole leg of lamb grilled just so) make up for it. In true Punabi style, the over-the-top purple and gold decor remains, as does the most popular gimmick: *golgappas* (fried dough containers) filled with vodka instead of traditional spicy water. The upstairs lounge, which favors loud house and trance music, is a fun place to have a drink while waiting for a movie at the nearby PVR Priya. ✉*11 Basant Lok, Vasant Vihar* ☎*11/5151–6669* ▭*AE, DC, MC, V.*

Where to Eat & Stay in Delhi
KAROL BAGH
Arya Samaj Rd.
Desh Bandhu Gupta Rd.
Market Rd.
Sadhu Vaswani Marg
East Park Rd.
Upper Ridge Rd.
Shankar Rd.
Panchkuian Rd.
S.B. Singh Rd.
Mandir Marg
Ramakrishna Ashram Marg
Baba Kharak Singh Marg
Jai Singh Rd.
Sansad Marg
Talkatora Rd.
Farm Rd.
Hillside Rd.
Todapur Rd.
Church Rd.
Raisina Rd.
Rafi Marg
Buddha Jayanti Park
Polo Ground
Dalhousie Rd.
Duplex Rd.
Rajaji Marg
Kushak Rd.
Akbar Rd.
Tughlak Rd.
Kautilya Marg
Safdarjang Rd.
Ring Rd.
Sardar Patel Marg
Panchsheel Marg
Army Golf Course
Gen. Carriappa Marg
Church Rd.
Naya Marg
Shanti Path
Nehru Park
Satya Marg
Cassels Rd.
Parade Rd.
Benito Juarez Marg
Brig Hoshiar Singh Rd.
Shanti Path
A Avenue
B Avenue
Sri Aurobindo Marg
Rao Tularam Rd.
Olof Palme Marg
Gurgaon Rd.
Rao Tularam Rd.
Africa Avenue
Ring Rd.
TO JAIPUR
Vivekanand Marg
Harsukh Marg
HAUZ KHAS
Deer Park
Rose Garden
0
1 miles
0
1 kms
4
5
16
19
20
21
25
26
27
28

Restaurants ▼

Azzurro **28**
Baan Thai **15**
Basil and Thyme **16**
Bukhara **20**
Chilli Seasson **18**
China Fare **12**
Chor Bizarre **2**
Coconut Grove **7**
Dum Pukht **20**
Fire **5**
Karim's **1**
Khan Chacha **11**
Moti Mahal Delux **31**
Naivedyam **26**
Park Balluchi **27**
Punjabi by Nature **25**
Sagar **23**
San Gimignano **6**
Smokehouse Grill **29**
Spice Route **6**
Swagath **22**
Taipan **15**
The Big Chil **32**
Yellow Brick Road **13**
Zaffran **30**

Hotels ▼

Ahuja Residency **14**
Ambassador **13**
Claridgges **10**
Connaught **4**
Hyatt Regency **21**
The Imperial **6**
ITC Maurya Sheraton Hotel & Towers **20**
Jor Bagh 27 .... **17**
Maidens **3**
The Manor **24**
The Oberoi **15**
Shervani New Delhi **9**
Taj Mahal **8**
Taj Palace **19**

$$–$$$ ✕ **Chor Bizarre.** Delhi's only Kashmiri restaurant is also one of
Fodor'sChoice
★ its most beautiful, an art deco enclave with a tile floor, a spiral staircase leading nowhere, lamps in pinks and yellows, and a mixture of antique furniture and mirrors from various *chor* ("thieves'") bazaars. The bar is all dark wood and stained glass, and the salad bar is a 1927 Fiat roadster. Kashmiri food uses milder spices than many Indian cuisines, exemplified by mutton *yakhni* (simmered in a sauce of yogurt, cardamom, and aniseed), mutton *mirchi korma* (in a gravy of cardamom and cloves), and *haaq* (Kashmiri spinach cooked in its own juice). Try a *tarami* platter to sample several dishes, and punctuate your meal with *kahwah,* fragrant Kashmiri tea. ✉ *Hotel Broadway, 4/15A Asaf Ali Rd., just outside Old Delhi, near Delhi Gate* ☎ *11/2327–3821* ▭ *AE, DC, MC, V.*

> **NO RESERVATION?**
>
> Tables fill up fast in Delhi. If reservations are proving hard to get, try one of the multi-restaurant complexes. The Moets building in Defence Colony Market holds decent seafood at Shack and a laid-back lounge with tasty Mediterranean at Stone. The Kasbah complex in Greater Kailash I's N-Block Market has knockout North Indian at Zaffran, but if that's busy, French, Italian, and a lounge with bar snacks are all downstairs. Main courses run an average of Rs. 350–Rs. 500, and all places set tables aside for walk-ins.

$$ ✕ **Moti Mahal Delux.** This old-fashioned family restaurant serves North Indian comfort food. It's a knock-off of an Old Delhi classic, Moti Mahal, but some say the food here is even better. The meal of choice is butter chicken, otherwise known as chicken *makhni,* a tomato-based Punjabi classic that sticks to your ribs. The basic chicken curry is also good. There's no plain rice here; the so-called "plain *pulao,*" zesty rice made with cumin and a kick of its own. All meals are served with spicy little pickled onions. ✉ *M-30 Greater Kailash I* ☎ *11/2628–0480* ▭ *No credit cards* ⊙ *Closed Tues.*

$$ ✕ **Park Balluchi.** No, the name isn't Italian; it refers to Baluchistan, part of present-day Pakistan. Tucked away in Hauz Khas Deer Park, this kabab house serves some very good barbecue dishes. The building is glass on three sides, the better to enjoy the greenery; stone floors, cast-iron furniture, and traditional dress complete the lush environment. The amazing victuals include *nawabi kesri kabab* (chicken marinated in a saffron mixture, stuffed with chopped chicken, and grilled), *murg potli* (marinated chicken breast wrapped around minced mutton and served flambéed), and *mewa paneer tukra* (soft cheese stuffed with nuts, currants, and mushrooms, marinated in cream and grilled). Kababs are served all day; other dishes are not served between 3:30 and 6. Unfortunately, service can be extraordinarily slow and poorly informed. ✉ *Deer Park, Hauz Khas Village* ☎ *11/2685–9369* ▭ *AE, DC, MC, V.*

$$ ✕ **Zaffran.** Classic presentations of simple Punabi fare such as butter
★ chicken, *shahi paneer,* and *dal makhni* draw top marks here thanks to fresh ingredients and a light hand with the oil (not the case at most Punjabi joints). Where other restaurants will leave you sopping up the film

on your plate with the last piece of *naan* (flatbread), this place understands that more grease doesn't always mean more flavor. The refreshingly quiet dining room is clean and minimalist with blond wood and cream accents. Service is friendly, knowledgable, and content to leave you alone if you ask. If you want to have a quiet conversation over excellent North Indian fare, head here and recharge after a long day touring the city. ✉*Kasbah Building, N-Block Market, Greater Kailash I* ☎*11/4163–5000* ▭*AE, DC, MC, V.*

¢ ✕**Karim's.** A popular addition to the Jama Masjid tour, Karim's is an Old Delhi institution. Mutton, which generally means goat in India, is king here, especially in thick, rich gravies; try *mutton Mughlai* or *badaam pasanda* ("almond delight," mutton in a slightly sweet gravy) for the full experience. To get here, walk down the street that runs out from the mosque's main entrance, Gate 1, and about four shops down on the left, walk through the passageway into a small courtyard—you'll see smoking kababs on spits and several indoor seating areas. The newer Karim's, **Dastar Khwan-e-Karim,** near Hazrat Nizamuddin Darga, is more of a restaurant proper. Alcohol is not served. ✉*Matiya Mahal, opposite Hotel Bombay Orient, Old Delhi* ☎*11/2326–9800* ✉*168/2 Jha House Basti, Nizamuddin West* ☎*11/2469–8300* ⏲*Daily 7 AM–midnight; closed during daylight hrs of Ramadan* ▭*No credit cards.*

¢ ✕**Khan Chacha.** You can recognize this no-frills stall in the service lane in Khan Market by the crowd of people, usually four or five deep, clamoring for the kebabs hot off the grill. There isn't anywhere to sit or even to stand really, but you won't notice once you bite into your first chicken *tikka* or *paneer tikka roomali* roll (spiced chicken or soft cheese grilled and wrapped in a thin, flatbread). Eat the succulent *seekh kebabs* (minced mutton rolls) before they get cold. For those who don't like to walk and eat, take your food to nearby Lodi Garden for a picnic. Cans of soda are available. No alchohol is served. ✉*Khan Market, 75 Middle La.* ☎*No phone* ▭*No credit cards* ⏲*Daily noon–10.*

Fodor'sChoice ★

SOUTH INDIAN

$$ ✕**Coconut Grove.** Malayali cuisine (from Kerala) is inspired by the coconut and the sea, as exemplified by the delicious *konju theng*—prawn curry in a mild, turmeric-colored coconut sauce—and the coconut-based mutton stew. Coconut Grove also features spicy Chettinad cuisine from Tamil Nadu, which you can sample in a mixed platter served on a banana leaf. Order any other main course with *appams,* Kerala's inimitable fluffy rice-based flatbreads, and use the bread to scoop up the morsels. The restaurant is cavernous and plain, with green tablecloths the only real nod to South India. ✉*Hotel Janpath, Janpath, Connaught Place* ☎*11/2336–8553* ▭*AE, DC, MC, V.*

$$ ★ ✕**Swagath.** Delhi's only Mangalorean restaurant—specializing in fish and seafood from the western coast between Goa and Kerala—is outstanding. Choose your sauce, then decide whether you want fish, prawns, or crab. Anything served *sawantwadi* (in a spicy mint-and-coriander sauce) is unforgettable, as is *gassi,* a mild coconut-flavored gravy, and the butter-pepper-garlic sauce. Another specialty is Chetti-

nad food from Tamil Nadu, cooked in a very spicy black-pepper sauce. Mop up your food with an *appam* or *neer dosa,* soft South Indian rice breads. The prim dining rooms, stacked vertically, are softly lit, and service is excellent. Doors are open all day. ✉ *14 Defence Colony Market* ☎ *11/2433–0930* ▭ *AE, DC, MC, V.*

$ ✕ **Naivedyam.** This dark, soothing restaurant with gold-embossed paintings was designed by artisans from the Tamil Nadu town of Thanjavur. The food is Udupi, a vegetarian cuisine from a temple town near Mangalore. All meals begin with a *rasam* (peppery soup) that must be the best in Delhi, and the rice dishes, served with coconut chutney and *sambar* (tomato-based accompaniment), are great introductions to South Indian home cooking. To plunge into a *dosa*—a giant semolina or lentil-flour crepe filled with spicy potatoes—consider the *maharaja sajjige masala dosa,* which also includes vegetables. At night, look for the stained-glass entrance; by day, follow signs for the SOUTH INDIAN EATING PANORAMA. Alcohol is not served. ✉ *1 Hauz Khas Village* ☎ *11/2696–0426* ▭ *AE, DC, MC, V.*

¢ ✕ **Sagar.** This no-frills, three-story vegetarian family joint bustles nonstop from 8 AM to 11 PM. The dosa is king, and you can choose from 20 varieties, including some made with *rava* (semolina) rather than lentil flour. The vegetable *uttapam* (rice-flour pancake) is also good, and there's a North Indian menu with delicious *bhindi masala* (spicy okra). The wonderful *thalis,* or combination platters, are served from 11 to 3 and 7 to 11. ✉ *18 Defence Colony Market* ☎ *11/2433–3110* ▭ *No credit cards.*

CHINESE

$$$$ ✕ **Taipan.** The formal Taipan is the finest Chinese restaurant in Delhi. The food is authentic, luscious, and artfully presented, and the view from the top of the Oberoi—over the Delhi Golf Course toward the high-rise buildings of Connaught Place—is grand. The menu highlights Cantonese and Szechuan cooking, including salt-and-pepper prawns, minced prawns with asparagus, Calcutta beckti fish in a *nonya* (spicy lemon) chilli sauce, and various duck dishes. The best-loved house specialty is dim sum, available in a daily fixed-price lunch—reserve in advance for this feast. ✉ *The Oberoi, Dr. Zakir Hussain Rd., next to Delhi Golf Club* ☎ *11/2436–3030* ▭ *AE, DC, MC, V.*

$ ✕ **China Fare.** Chinese food in Delhi tends to be five-star or takeout, with little in between. China Fare is an exception, with delicious meals at modest prices in attractive (if cramped) faux-Tuscan surroundings. The menu is basic, with strengths in poultry and noodles: options include crispy honey chicken, chicken with mushrooms and baby corn, the devilishly spicy Chicken Singapore, and "chilly garlic" noodles, an Indo-Chinese classic. The crispy lamb dishes are also good, and you don't have to be vegetarian to make a meal of the mixed vegetables in hot garlic sauce. Alcohol is not served. ✉ *27-A Khan Market* ☎ *11/2461–8602* ▭ *AE, DC, MC, V.*

CONTEMPORARY

$$$$ ★ **Fire.** Seasonal ingredients and unexpected flavor combinations update Indian classics and form new ones altogether, making the flagship eatery at the Park Hotel a real standout. Recent stunners included a savory banana stem salad (it uses all parts of the fruit) and a surprisingly light, tomato-infused *dal* (stewed lentils). Regional classics with a twist, such as the fiery hot chicken chettinad from Tamil Nadu, are menu mainstays and consistently delicious. A vegetarian or non-vegeterian taster's menu lets you sample the season's goods. It will cost you roughly 50% more than ordering individual dishes, but foodies will find it well worth it. The carefully chosen wine list here a winner and the service staff is knowledgable enough to make informed recommendations, a rarity in Delhi. Expect unsolicited inquiries to be met with a haughty raise of the eyebrow. *Park Hotel, 15 Parliament St., Connaught Place 11/2374–3000 Reservations essential AE, D, MC, V.*

$$$$ Fodor'sChoice ★ **Smokehouse Grill.** The fashionable crowd clamours to get into this Delhi cousin of Mumbai's acclaimed Saltwater Grill, where the food is delicious and the drinks are desirable. Order anything with "smoke" in the name—from the smokehouse chicken (two perfectly cooked smoked chicken breasts served with impeccably seasoned green beans and roasted potatoes) to the smoked apple and rosemary pie. The award-winning smoked melon martini defies words and the smoked apple mojito is even better. Unlike most see-and-be-seen places, the service is unpretentious and friendly. The space, accented with contemporary comic book panels on blood-red walls and a gleaming chrome staircase leading to the upper level, feels industrial. It's odd, but it works. For those who turn up without reservations, management keeps some tables aside (but expect a long wait). The generous fruit and cheese spread at the bar helps dull the hunger pangs. *North Wing, VIPPS Center, LSC Masjid Moth, Greater Kailash II 11/4143–5530 AE, D, MC, V.*

$$ Fodor'sChoice ★ **Basil and Thyme.** Celebrity chef Bhicoo Manekshaw is now in her eighties, but that doesn't stop her from creating daily specials and seasonal menus. There's no telling what she'll come up with, but you can bank on fresh flavors, such as carrot-and-orange soup, pita triangles with garlic butter, roast chicken stuffed with black mushrooms, or a "filo parcel" stuffed with vegetables and glazed with a coriander hollandaise. The room is a minimalist warm white, with stone floors and large windows that look onto the greenery of Santushti Market. Alcohol is not served, but this lunch spot is beloved of Delhi's upper crust and the embassy crowd. *Santushti Shopping Complex, Chanakyapuri 11/2467–3322 Reservations essential AE, DC, MC, V Closed Sun. No dinner.*

$$ **Yellow Brick Road.** Delhiites love this super-bright, tiny 24-hour coffee shop. The blinding-yellow striped wallpaper, vintage French-colonial posters, and distressed-yellow tables are a perfect cure for jet lag. The menu wears several hats, mainly North Indian and European, and everything is cheerfully presented. Vegetarian options are many, including tasty paneer dishes, ravioli *calabrese* (with spinach and basil), mushroom crepes, and sweet corn soup. The *chote miya biryani* (lamb in seasoned rice) is rich and filling. *Ambassador Hotel, Cornwallis Rd., Sujan Singh Park 11/2463–2600 AE, DC, MC, V.*

$ ✕ **The Big Chill.** For those looking to beat the summer heat by cooling off with Delhi's best ice cream, make haste to this casual café that takes its name from the movie and its decor from Hollywood classics. The pizzas and pastas are hearty and tasty, if not terribly authentic, and Middle Eastern and Lebanese choices are usually a good bet. However, leave room for dessert, the real standout. The Mississippi Mud Pie (mocha, chocolate, and peanut butter ice cream with a chocolate crust) is extraordinary. It's an ideal place to linger over lunch or catch an early dinner, and the ■ TIP→ **East of Kailash branch is a convenient stop before or after the Lotus or ISKCON temples.** But if you're in a hurry, keep in mind that service can be painfully slow and sometimes even rude. Alcohol is not served. ✉ *F-38 East of Kailash* ☎ *11/2648–1020 or 11/2648–1030* ✉ *Middle La., 32 Khan Market, Sujan Singh Park* ☎ *11/5175–7588* ▭ *MC, V.*

ITALIAN

$$$ ✕ **San Gimignano.** Chef Ravi Saxena uses his Tuscan training to create playful, sensuous dishes in Delhi's most rarefied Italian restaurant. The three-course regional menu changes periodically, but you might find such fancies as a "flan" of spinach, black olives, and risotto with fresh basil-and-tomato sauce; tagliatelle with a fresh herb sauce of minced duck and Parmesan cheese; sliced grilled tenderloin with grilled polenta and marsala sauce; or grilled milk-fed baby lamb chop with grilled balsamic vegetables. The wood-paneled rooms are small and inviting, accented by ceramics and large sepia photos of the town of San Gimignano. In winter you can dine in the fabulous garden, complete with terra-cotta tile floor. Service is excellent. ✉ *Imperial Hotel, Janpath, Connaught Place* ☎ *11/5111–6634* ✍ *Reservations essential* ▭ *AE, DC, MC, V.*

$$ ★ ✕ **Azzurro.** Fresh ingredients and attention to detail place the cuisine this unpretentious neighborhood spot way ahead of most of the other casual Italian eateries in town, which charge double its prices. The menu keeps it simple, and that's a good thing. Crisp, thin-crust pizzas hot from the wood-fired oven make generous use of top-shelf buffalo mozzarella and fresh basil: they're easily the best in Delhi. The main courses, which travel beyond Italian, are based on the cuisine of the "olive oil belt" in the Mediterranean. For dessert, the chocolate fondant (gooey, bubbling chocolate in a cookie shell with a dollop of fresh cream) is divine. ■ TIP→ **After a visit to the nearby Qutb Minar, come for the half-price pizza at lunch and in the afternoon catch the latest Bollywood hit next door at PVR Anupam.** ✉ *1st Fl., 15 Community Centre, Saket* ☎ *11/4166–4275* ▭ *AE, MC, V.*

PAN-ASIAN

$$$$ Fodor'sChoice ★ ✕ **Spice Route.** Designed by the flamboyant Rajeev Sethi and seven years in the making, Spice Route is known internationally as an aesthetic experience. Each section focuses on a different stage in life (relationships, wealth, etc.), and every inch of the walls and ceiling is hand painted with corresponding scenes from ancient epics. Antique rose-

wood and teak columns add to the enchantment. The clever menu gathers cuisines from the lands of the ancient spice route—Kerala, Sri Lanka, Myanmar (the former Burma), Malaysia, Indonesia, Thailand, and Vietnam. The Sri Lankan curries are surprising and delicious; you might also find Kerala-style prawns stir-fried with coconut, curry leaves and black tamarind and flavored with mustard seeds, or Thai-style lobster stir-fried with ginger and black Thai mushrooms. ✉*Imperial Hotel, Janpath, Connaught Place* ☎*11/5111–6634* ▭*AE, DC, MC, V.*

THAI

$$$$ ✕**Baan Thai.** The city's first Thai restaurant, modeled on a traditional Thai *baan* (house), remains arguably the best. The entrance corridor is an Asian art gallery, and the formal dining room is partitioned by Burmese-teak latticework. Sit at a table, adorned with an orchid, or on a traditional Thai *khantok* (floor cushion) on the raised platform. The husband-and-wife chefs create traditional cuisine, from *thod man koong* (crisp golden cake of Thai-spiced prawns, served with plum sauce) to *kai phad med mamuang* (diced chicken stir-fried with cashews, mushrooms, and sun-dried chillis), all served on sage-green crockery. The lunch buffet is popular. ✉*The Oberoi, Dr. Zakir Hussain Rd., next to Delhi Golf Club* ☎*11/2436–3030* ▭*AE, DC, MC, V.*

$$ ★ ✕**Chilli Seasson.** This chic Southeast Asian place gets just about everything right. The rooms are airy and cheerful, with cream-color walls and blond-wood furniture, and the contemporary artwork is often for sale. The tangy papaya salad is delicious, and it looks fantastic on the restaurant's contemporary yellow and coral-color dishes. The Thai curries are equally divine, and best of all, the vegetable dishes are intriguing and delicious, from pad thai to stir-fried Tibetan zucchini to eggplant with white mushrooms. There are plenty of salads and noodles to distract you as well. It's hard to have a bad meal here, especially at these relatively reasonable prices. ✉*18 Lodi Colony Market* ☎*11/2461–8358 or 11/2464–3362* ▭*AE, DC, MC, V.*

WHERE TO STAY

$$$$ ★ **Ambassador.** Service is heart-warmingly friendly in this quiet hotel, which is run by the Taj Group but costs a bit less than its glamorous siblings. The building is a converted section of Sujan Singh Park, an exclusive 1930s neighborhood dripping with late-Raj charm. The small marble lobby has comfortable banquette seating; upstairs, the hallways are windowed and bright. Most rooms have carpeting, basic teak furniture, and a modern bathroom with window; a few have tile floors, area rugs, and old-style bath fixtures. ■**TIP→ Try to get a room in front, with a balcony overlooking the garden, as rooms in back can be noisy.Pros:** excellent value for money, next door to Khan Market and close to Lodi Garden. **Cons:** on a busy street, so don't attempt to walk to the market. ✉*Cornwallis Rd., Sujan Singh Park, 110003* ☎*11/2463–2600* 🌐*www.tajhotels.com* *76 rooms, 12 suites* *In-room: safe, refrigerator. In-hotel: 2 restaurants, room service, bar, laundry service, concierge, public Internet.* ▭*AE, DC, MC, V.*

$$$$ **Claridges.** In 1950, three years after Independence, an Indian family was talked into building a hotel with a British aesthetic, and the result was a winner: tasteful yet unpretentious, in a central yet quiet location. The old-fashioned charm reveals itself on the front lawn—unusual in Delhi—where cane chairs invite you to take a breather, and in the lobby, where two swing staircases suggest a way up. Standard rooms are medium-size, but all rooms facing the pool have either a window seat, terrace, or balcony. Rooms in the newer wing have plasma televisions, marble floors, and immaculately turned out designer furnishings. **Pros:** Sevilla, the Meditteranean eatery, gets high marks; excellent pool. **Cons:** some rooms in the old wing sport musty, hideous plaid carpeting; rooms near the nightclub can be noisy. ✉ *12 Aurangzeb Rd., Central Delhi, 110011* ☎ *11/2301–0211* 🌐 *www.claridges.com* *112 rooms, 26 suites* *In-room: safe, refrigerator. In-hotel: 3 restaurants, bar, pool, gym, spa, laundry service, concierge, public Internet.* 💳 *AE, DC, MC, V.*

$$$$ ★ **Hyatt Regency.** The Hyatt has a surprisingly homey feel, with the mirror-spangled cream-color lobby suffused with light from the pool-facing pastry shop at the back—where you can relax at a marble-top window table with one of the best European desserts in town. A clay waterfall spills past this aerie to the ground-level coffee shop. Guest rooms have cream-color walls and parquet floors, a rarity in India; views on the pool side are superior. **Pros:** the shopping arcade is easily the best in Delhi, with dozens of shops selling jewelry, handicrafts, and Kashmiri carpets and shawls; the pool may take top honors, too. **Cons:** service can be impersonal; pricier than the competition. ✉ *Ring Rd., Bhikaji Cama Place, 110066* ☎ *11/2679–1234* 🌐 *www.delhi.hyatt.com* *508 rooms, 29 suites* *In-room: safe, refrigerator. In-hotel: 3 restaurants, room service, bars, tennis courts, pool, gym, spa, laundry service, concierge, public Internet.* 💳 *AE, DC, MC, V* *BP.*

$$$$ **ITC Maurya Sheraton Hotel and Towers.** A favorite with executives and dignitaries, the Maurya works hard to style itself as the swankest hotel in Delhi, and the whole place has the buzz of importance. The lobby soars, yet somehow creates intimacy in reds, browns, and a three-tiered, wood-beamed dome painted with a fantastic technicolor mural. Fountains outside the picture windows add a natural touch. Rooms are essentially Western, in masculine color schemes, but they take many forms; the more money you spend, the more wood paneling, plush carpeting, and pampering you receive. **Pros:** knockout restaurants draw as many locals as travelers, especially the famous Bukhara and Dum Pukht; pool and gym are best-in-class; business services get top marks. **Cons:** far from most major sites, chattering tour groups can dominate the atmosphere. ✉ *Diplomatic Enclave, Chanakyapuri, 110021* ☎ *11/2611–2233* 🌐 *www.welcomgroup.com* *515 rooms, 44 suites* *In-room: safe, refrigerator. In-hotel: 4 restaurants, room service, bar, tennis courts, pool, gym, spa, laundry service, concierge, public Internet.* 💳 *AE, DC, MC, V.*

$$$$ Fodor'sChoice ★ **The Imperial.** This landmark luxury hotel was designed by Edward Lutyens' associate D. J. Bromfield in a unique mixture of colonial, Victorian, and art deco styles. Opened in 1931, it was restored in the 1990s

and is easily the most appealing hotel in Delhi, with twisting hallways and small-pane windows. The driveway is lined with 24 soaring king palms, and the terrace of the Royal Imperial Suite peeks out from above the entrance. Inside, the entire building is lit and decorated in warm creams and taupes, and hung with original lithographs and engravings from the hotel's enormous collection. Guest rooms continue the Raj look with quilted bedspreads, wardrobes, and marble or parquet floors; "Heritage" rooms have sitting areas and are significantly more sumptuous than the cheapest rooms. **Pros:** unparalleled service and location, top-notch restaurants, especially the other-worldly Spice Route and the garden section of the 1911 bar. **Cons:** extremely expensive, standard rooms are on the small side, pool is lackluster. ✉*Janpath, south of Tolstoy Marg, Connaught Place, 110001* ☎*11/2334–1234* 🌐*www.theimperialindia.com* *185 rooms, 45 suites* *In-room: safe, refrigerator. In-hotel: 3 restaurants, room service, bars, pool, gym, laundry service, concierge, public Internet.* *AE, DC, MC, V.*

$$$$ **Maidens.** It opened in 1907, before New Delhi even existed, and it's the oldest hotel in the city. Now run by the Oberoi group, the hotel remains a classic Raj building, with high-arched windows, deep verandas, grand old trees, pleasant lawns, and a quirky interior. Thanks to the building's age, the rooms and bathrooms are huge. Service is friendly and close to flawless. With the adjacent Civil Lines Metro Station just 50 meters away, the hotel is now a speedy, air-conditioned subway ride from both Old Delhi and Connaught Place. **Pros:** coffee shop has a nice patio and an English feel, enhanced by the British tour groups that often stay here; nearly finished renovations have brightened up what were formerly dark and outdated rooms, though a few still sport faded silk bedspreads and worn carpets. **Cons:** even with the metro, you are far removed from the rest of the city; food and beverage options are limited. ✉7 *Sham Nath Marg, Civil Lines, 110054* ☎*11/2389–0505* 🌐*www.oberoihotels.com* *53 rooms, 3 suites* *In-room: safe. In-hotel: restaurant, room service, bar, tennis courts, pool, laundry service, concierge.* *AE, DC, MC, V.*

$$$$ ★ **The Oberoi.** Delhi's first modern luxury hotel, built in 1965, is distinguished by its calm—even when the hotel is packed, the sleek, black-marble lobby is peaceful. You're welcomed by a small, marble lotus fountain strewn with rose petals, and the windows opposite reception look down on the zig-zag pool. Rooms have Western furnishings with pleasant sitting areas and Indian accents; deluxe rooms have more amenities, such as DVD players. All rooms have 24-hour butler service. Pool-facing rooms take in the greenery of the Delhi Golf Club; those on the other side face Humayun's Tomb. **Pros:** Thai and Chinese restaurants are among Delhi's finest, top-flight spa. **Cons:** extremely expensive, the bar is best described as sedate. ✉*Dr. Zakir Hussain Rd., next to Delhi Golf Club, 110003* ☎*11/2436–3030* 🌐*www.oberoihotels.com* *258 rooms, 31 suites* *In-room: safe, DVD (some), refrigerator. In-hotel: 5 restaurants, room service, bar, pool, gym, spa, laundry service, concierge.* *AE, DC, MC, V.*

$$$$ **Taj Mahal.** The Taj Mansingh, as it's locally known, is Delhi's premier social hotel, with nightly cocktail affairs, cultural events, and the occasional society weddings drawing the glitterati. The lobby has Mughal-inspired decorative domes, a giant Oriental rug, and a general feeling of bustle, so you won't feel like you're off in a tourist enclave. Rooms have simple Western furnishings; those on the pool side overlook plenty of greenery. **Pros:** centrally located in prestigious Lutyens' Delhi; popular with business travelers and celebrities, and the service is correspondingly slick. The coffee shop, Machan, throws frequent food festivals and hosts Delhi's best Sunday brunch. **Cons:** rooms on the small side, flagship restaurants are overpriced, and lag behind other hotels in this class in quality. ✉ *1 Mansingh Rd., Central Delhi, 110011* ☎ *11/2302–6162* 🌐 *www.tajhotels.com* *275 rooms, 19 suites* *In-room: safe, refrigerator. In-hotel: 3 restaurants, room service, bar, gym, spa, laundry service, concierge, public Internet.* 💳 *AE, DC, MC, V.*

$$$$ **Taj Palace.** Facilities are top-notch in this giant, boomerang-shaped business hotel. The teak-paneled business center provides the online Knight-Ridder service and laptops for hire, the health club is amply outfitted, the beauty salon has a range of treatments, and the outdoor pool overlooks manicured lawns. There's even a putting green. Giant traditional lanterns serve as chandeliers in the sprawling marble lobby, but the rest of the building is Western, designed for corporate convenience. Half the rooms face the pool and a swath of greenery; the rest have city views. **Pros:** business services are best-in-class; the romantic Orient Express is one of India's finest European restaurants, with dishes from the fabled old train route. **Cons:** far from some tourist sites; in high season, you will battle the package-tour crowd. ✉ *2 Sardar Patel Marg, Chanakyapuri, 110021* ☎ *11/2611–0202* 🌐 *www.tajhotels.com* *421 rooms, 40 suites* *In-room: safe, refrigerator. In-hotel: 3 restaurants, room service, bar, pool, gym, spa, laundry service, concierge, public Internet.* 💳 *AE, DC, MC, V.*

$$$ **The Connaught.** About 1 km (½ mi) from Connaught Place, this mid-size hotel is close to the center of things yet far enough away from the hubbub. The cream-and-rust lobby is large yet cozy, with a few wooden beams overhead, and filled with sunlight in late afternoon. Guest rooms are adequately clean, but the furnishings are worn and some carpets stained. If location and value are more important, this hotel remains a decent bet. Discounts of up to 30% can be negotiated between April and August. **Pros:** rooms on the east side directly overlook a field-hockey stadium, which is more appealing than it sounds; attached RBS Travels agency provides round-the-clock service. **Cons:** small rooms; some travelers report extremely poor service here. ✉ *37 Shaheed Bhagat Singh Marg, Connaught Place, 110001* ☎ *11/2336–4225* 📠 *11/2334–0757* *72 rooms, 9 suites* *In-room: safe. In-hotel: restaurant, room service, bar, laundry service, public Internet.* 💳 *AE, D, MC, V* 🍽 *CP.*

$$$ ★ **Shervani New Delhi.** The understated and elegant guest rooms here come with clean white cotton duvets, silk accents in muted colors, and gleaming white marble bathrooms. From electronic keys and wall safes to flat-screen televisions, everything is updated after complete renovations in 2006. Some "premium" rooms have partial views of the Purana Qila across the street. The buffet dinner, Rs. 250 per per-

son, is decent though not delicious. **Pros:** staff is efficient, friendly, and willing to go out of its way for guests; quiet but central setting. **Cons:** in-house food options are limited; taxis at the neighborhood stand can be slow to arrive. ✉ *11 Sunder Nagar* ☎ *11/4250–1000* 🌐 *www.shervanihotels.com* *19 rooms, 3 suites* *In-room: safe, Wi-Fi. In-hotel: restaurant, laundry service.* 💳 *MC, V.*

$$–$$$ ★ **The Manor.** Next door to a country club in one of Delhi's wealthiest residential neighborhoods, this is Delhi's premier boutique hotel. It's the perfect place to come home to at dusk, with lanterns highlighting the greenery and softening the building's sharp lines. The interior is ultramodern but in soft tones—taupes and creams as well as white. Some walls are paneled in wood or stone; otherwise the guest rooms are fairly stark, accented by a fresh flower or two. Bathrooms are in dark marble, and all but suites have showers only. **Pros:** the restaurant, which serves Indian and Mediterranean food, is beautifully candlelighted at night; ultraprivate grounds and garden are stunning. **Cons:** off the beaten path, and extremely difficult for drivers to locate; far from most sites and restaurants. ✉ *77 Friends Colony W, 110065* ☎ *11/2692–5151* 🌐 *www.themanordelhi.com* *12 rooms* *In-room: safe, refrigerator. In-hotel: restaurant, bar, laundry service, concierge, public Internet.* 💳 *AE, DC, MC, V* *CP.*

$ Fodor's Choice ★ **Ahuja Residency.** This little-known guest house is a jewel, Delhi's only combination of style and affordability. It's in a converted house in a quiet, leafy, upper-class neighborhood, so it's a great way to get a feel for residential life. Rooms are simple but cozy, with bright-color fabrics, blond-wood furniture, gleaming floors, and large windows. Bathrooms have showers only. The restaurant is delightful, with terra-cotta floors and yellow-and-orange plaid fabrics and crockery; and the rooftop terrace, with flowering plants and wrought-iron furniture, is unbeatable on a winter day. Reserve early, and if all rooms are booked, ask about the sister facility in Defence Colony. (A third property for overflow, Golf Apartments, trails the main house and Defence Colony in atmosphere, but is slightly cheaper.) **Pros:** immaculately clean—from fresh squeezed juice to organic bath products, Mrs. Ahuja's attention to detail is flawless. **Cons:** reservations difficult to get. ✉ *193 Golf Links, 110003* ☎ *11/2462–2255* 🌐 *www.ahujaresidency.com* *12 rooms* *In-room: safe. In-hotel: laundry service, public Internet.* 💳 *AE, MC, V.*

$ **Jor Bagh 27.** Peace, proximity, and price are the benefits at this whitewashed guest house, which is popular with visiting UN and World Bank staffers. With plenty of greenery and excellent markets, and several major monuments a short hop away, Jor Bagh is one of Delhi's most desirable residential neighborhoods. Rooms are very simple and bathrooms have showers only. **Pros:** five minutes from the shopping and restaurants of Khan Market; serene neighborhood opposite Lodi Garden, an excellent choice for a morning stroll or afternoon picnic. **Cons:** some rooms are shabby; look at what's available before you settle in; breakfast is served in the dining room, but other meals must be ordered in; generator cannot run all air-conditioners for very long, so this isn't your best bet in summer. ✉ *27 Jor Bagh, 110003* ☎ *11/2469–8647* 📠 *11/2469–8475* *guesthouse27@hotmail.com* *18 rooms* *In-room: refrigerators (some). In-hotel: laundry service.* 💳 *MC, V* *CP.*

NIGHTLIFE & THE ARTS

THE ARTS

Delhi is India's cultural hub, if only because performers from all over the country come to the capital at least once a year to cultivate their national audience. Painting, music, dance, theater, and, of course, film are all well represented. The India Habitat Centre, a large, modern cultural center, has the best combination of all of the above; on any given evening, it hosts several good programs. The only problem is that hype is nonexistent, so you must be persistent to find out what's happening—pick up the bi-weekly *Time Out* or the monthly magazine *First City* for details. Failing that, the daily newspapers, especially the *Indian Express* and the *Hindustan Times,* are also good sources. The staff at your hotel may be able to help, too.

ART GALLERIES

Delhi's art scene is extremely dynamic. Contemporary Indian painting—which often blends traditional Indian motifs with Western techniques—is blossoming. But bargains are getting harder to come by. Private galleries have mushroomed and art prices have skyrocketed. Most galleries are quite small, so if you want a broad view of what's happening, hire a car or taxi for an afternoon of gallery-hopping. Authenticating any major purchases is advisable. Pick up the latest *Time Out* or *First City* for exhibit details and profiles of featured artists. Galleries are closed on Sunday.

Art Heritage (✉*Triveni Kala Sangam, 205 Tansen Marg, Connaught Place* ☎*11/2371–9470*), part of a government-run cultural institute with several galleries, has some of the finest exhibits in town. **Dhoomimal Art Centre** (✉*A-8 Connaught Pl.* ☎*11/2332–4492*) is a bit chaotic but often has good shows. **Gallery Espace** (✉*16 Community Centre, New Friends Colony* ☎*11/2632–6267*) is a tiny but remarkable space featuring both new and canonical artists, sometimes mixed together in interesting theme shows. The various exhibition spaces at **Habitat World** (✉*India Habitat Centre, Lodi Rd., Lodi Institutional Area* ☎*11/2468–2222*) showcase painting, sculpture, Indian craft, and creativity of every kind. The main Visual Arts Gallery is just inside Gate 2. The government-run **Lalit Kala Akademi** (✉*Rabindra Bhavan, Copernicus Marg, Connaught Place* ☎*11/2338–7243*) is a large 1950s building showing several exhibits at once, usually of varying quality. **Vadehra Art Gallery** (✉*40 Defence Colony* ☎*11/2461–5368*) is respected for its permanent collection of 20th-century masters.

Hauz Khas Village has a cluster of galleries. **Art & Deal** (✉*23 Hauz Khas Village* ☎*11/2652–3382*) has a large contemporary collection. **Art Konsult** (✉*12 Hauz Khas Village* ☎*11/2652–3382*) hangs some accomplished contemporary work. **Delhi Art Gallery** (✉*11 Hauz Khas Village* ☎*11/2656–8166*) has a substantial collection of paintings by old masters and contemporary artists; for major purchases, try to verify authenticity. **Navratana** (✉*2A Hauz Khas Village* ☎*11/3101–0846*) is a tiny but spirited hoard of old paintings, photographs, and movie posters, with a few contemporary works thrown in. The **Village Gallery** (✉ *14 Hauz Khas Village* ☎ *11/2685–3860*) has tasteful, relatively small-scale contemporary work.

FILM

India's Bombay-based film industry, known as Bollywood, produces more films annually than any other country in the world. Most Bollywood films are in Hindi, but anyone can understand them—most are romantic musicals, with dollops of family drama and occasionally a violent villain. Delhi cinemas show all the latest Hindi movies plus a few current Hollywood films, the latter tending toward action and young romantic comedy. To find out what's playing, check listings in the magazine section of any daily newspaper. If your movie of choice is a hot new release, consider buying tickets a day in advance; your hotel can help, and tickets can often be bought online. **Chanakya** (✉ *Yashwant Pl., off Vinay Marg, Chanakyapuri*). **Priya** (✉ *Basant Lok, Vasant Vihar*). **PVR Anupam** (✉ *Community Centre, Saket*).

Art films from all over the world are shown at various cultural institutes; the monthly magazines *First City* and *Time Out* have listings.

MUSIC & DANCE

Great musicians and dancers are always passing through Delhi. Incredibly, most performances are free, but tickets ("passes") are sometimes required for high-demand performers. The **India Habitat Centre** (✉ *Lodi Rd., Lodi Institutional Area* ☎ *11/2468–2222*) has several events every evening. **India International Centre** (✉ *40 Lodi Estate* ☎ *11/2461–9431*) is an established performance space near the Habitat Centre. **Kamani Auditorium** (✉ *Copernicus Marg, Connaught Place* ☎ *11/2338–8084*) is a long-standing venue for Indian classical music and dance. The Chamber Theatre at **Triveni Kala Sangam** (✉ *205 Tansen Marg, Connaught Place* ☎ *11/2371–8833*) is well known.

THEATER

India has an ancient dramatic tradition, and *nautanki* plays, which combine drama, comedy, and song, are still held in many villages. Delhi has an active theater scene in both English and Hindi, with many shows locally written, produced, and acted. Most run only for one weekend and don't travel afterward, so they can seem a bit unpolished even when they're fundamentally good. For all the options, pick up *Time Out* or *First City* magazine. The **India Habitat Centre** (✉ *Lodi Rd., Lodi Institutional Area* ☎ *11/2468–2222*) is Delhi's biggest and best theater venue, with several different shows each week. **LTG Auditorium** (✉ *Copernicus Marg, Connaught Place* ☎ *11/2338–9713*) is a veteran theater. **Shri Ram Centre** (✉ *Mandi House, Safdar Hashmi Marg, Connaught Place* ☎ *11/2371–4307*) stages a constant stream of plays, some for one day only.

NIGHTLIFE

Delhi's nightlife is in a constant state of flux. Though it doesn't rival more exciting towns such as Mumbai or Bangalore, it seems as if a new lounge opens here every week. That said, the city's somewhat stodgy reputation is still partly deserved: bars still shut by midnight and many nightclubs close not much later. Those in search of late-night dancing and drinking sometimes head for the suburbs: watering holes and dance floors in neighboring Noida and Gurgaon packed until the wee hours.

BARS & PUBS

Among the growing set of youngsters who can afford it, Delhi's nightlife is intense. Various forms of the watering hole are now on offer, with the lounge bar and the British pub emerging as the most successful formulas. **Blues** (✉ *N-18 Outer Circle, Connaught Place* ☎ *11/2331–0957*) is vaguely Chicagoesque. The music is live on Thursday. Brick-walled **DV8** (✉ *13 Regal Bldg. Outer Circle, Connaught Place* ☎ *11/2336–3358*) is a casual place to kick back. **Q'Ba** (✉ *E-42/43, Inner Circle, Connaught Place* ☎ *11/4151–2888*) has a cavernous space, a pleasant terrace with wonderful views, and well-mixed drinks that all add up to a pleasant nightspot.Slick **Rick's** (✉ *Taj Mahal Hotel, 1 Mansingh Rd., Central Delhi* ☎ *11/2302–6162*) is a magnet for Delhi's beautiful people, with as many voices yelling into their cell phones as talking to each other. The booze selection is hard to beat, and the snacks are Southeast Asian. Go before 9 PM if you want a seat. **Shalom** (✉ *N-18 Greater Kailash I* ☎ *11/4163–2280*), the granddaddy of Delhi's lounge bar scene, is unlikely to fade anytime soon. It remains one of the best options for Middle Eastern food in town. Reservations are recommended.**Stone** (✉ *Moets Restaurant Complex, 50 Defence Colony Market, Defence Colony* ☎ *11/6569–7689*) is a laid-back lounge with plenty of low-slung couches. Expats head here for quiet drinks and conversation over wood-fired pizza.

DISCOS

Nightlife in Delhi has undergone a transformation in recent years. Select places attract top international DJs and charge cover prices to match. But, you're still more likely to hear drunk renditions of classic rock and Bollywood favorites than cutting edge fare at most places. Overly casual attire (shorts, T-shirts, sandals on men) is typically frowned upon, and closing times tend to vary with the mood of the city government that month. *Time Out* magazine is your best bet to find the current hotspot. Named for the Vedic fire god, the swanky **Agni** (✉ *The Park Hotel, 15 Parliament St., Connaught Place* ☎ *11/2374–3000* ⊙ *11 AM–1 AM*) attracts Delhi's A-list party crowd, playing electronic interspersed with pop, hip-hop, and Bollywood hits. The door staff can be selective.At the dark and publike **Dublin** (✉ *ITC Maurya Sheraton, Sardar Patel Marg, Diplomatic Enclave* ☎ *11/2611–2233*), you're sure to hear cheesy pop and rock hits from the '80s onward (think wedding reception). It's one of the few places where people dance instead of pose. **Ministry of Sound** (✉ *The Pyramid, LSC Sector C, Pockets 6&7, Vasant Kunj* ☎ *98/7380–0060* 🌐 *www.ministryofsound.in* 🎫 *Rs 2,000* *minimum, with two free drinks* ⏲*After 10* PM), a branch of the London stalwart, is set in a giant glass pyramid. Electronic music reigns supreme here, as do high cover and drink prices.

Soho (✉*Ashok Hotel, 50-B Channakyapuri* ☎*11/2611–1066* ⏲*After 10* PM) attracts a strange mix of traveling businessmen and the very young and well-heeled, but it remains one of the few places that favors hip-hop, R&B, and funk with its Bollywood hits.

HOTEL BARS & LOUNGES

All the major hotels have bars, but most are better suited for a collective nap with a few tired foreigners than a night of Indian camaraderie. Richly decorated, often aiming for a British Raj look, these bars attract an older, quieter crowd than those listed above, and drink prices come close to those in London and New York. The large bar in **1911** (✉*Imperial Hotel, Janpath, Connaught Place* ☎*11/2334–1234*) is a classic watering hole decked out the way it looked during the Independence movement in the 1940s. The drink menu is massive, and lounge music keeps the vibe contemporary. Casual little **H2O+** (✉*Ambassador Hotel, Sujan Singh Park* ☎*11/2463–2000*) is ideal for quiet conversation; the whimsical underwater theme, complete with soft blue lighting and Western pop music, is oddly soothing. There's a small menu featuring fish, meat, and a few vegetable dishes. The **Patiala Peg** (✉*Imperial Hotel, Janpath, Connaught Place* ☎*11/2334–1234*) is an intimate, masculine old-world bar with an extensive cocktail menu. The **Polo Lounge** (✉*Hyatt Regency, Ring Rd., Bhikaji Cama Place* ☎*11/2679–1234*), while very much a hotel bar, can be very lively. The wood-paneled room has a curved bar, a leather sofa, a library with newspapers, an oddball collection of books, and sports channels playing on TV.

SPORTS & THE OUTDOORS

PARTICIPANT SPORTS

GOLF

Call well in advance if you want to play on a weekend in winter. The **Army Golf Club** (✉*Delhi Cantonment* ☎*11/2569–1972*) is close to Delhi. To play against a backdrop of ancient monuments, try the 27-hole **Delhi Golf Club** (✉*Dr. Zakir Hussain Rd.* ☎*11/2436–0002 Ext. 227 or 98100–03064*) in the center of town.

SWIMMING

The top hotels have excellent pools, but most are open only to guests. City pools should be avoided, as there's no way to judge the water quality.

TENNIS

If your hotel doesn't have a tennis court, reserve one at the **Delhi Lawn Tennis Association** (✉*Africa Ave., next to Safdarjung Enclave* ☎*11/2617–6140*).

YOGA

The international **Sivananda Yoga Vedanta Nataraja Centre** (✉*A-41 Kailash Colony* ☎*11/2648–0869*) holds several classes daily.

SPECTATOR SPORTS

Check any newspaper or ask your hotel about **cricket** and **football** (soccer) matches. Rivalries are intense, so these games are popular; see if your hotel can get you tickets. Delhi's polo games (October–February) are another crowd-pleaser—contact the **Delhi Polo Club** (✉*61st Cavalry, Cariappa Marg, Delhi Cantonment* ☎*11/2569–9777*), maintained by the Army Polo and Riding Club.

SHOPPING

Delhi is a shopping center for goods from all over India, making it the best place to stock up on gifts and souvenirs. Bargaining is often appropriate—and almost mandatory. A good rule of thumb: When the price is written down, it's probably fixed. When you have to inquire about the price, it's negotiable.

In shops where foreign customers are uncommon, the staff is likely to follow your every move with great interest. If this bothers you, simply state your objective or emphasize that you're just looking; they'll cooperate if you indicate nicely that you don't need to be followed around.

Most shops are open six days a week, as each neighborhood's market area closes one day a week, usually Sunday, Monday, or Tuesday. Most shops in Old Delhi are closed on Sunday.

BAZAARS & MARKETS

Connaught Place, open every day but Sunday from about 10 to 7:30, is the former commercial district of the British Raj. Pillared arcades and a wheel-shaped layout make it a pleasant place to stroll, especially the inner circle, though you have to get used to the intermittent entreaties of hawkers and beggars. Shops run the gamut from scruffy to upscale. Beneath the green park at the center of Connaught Place is **Palika Bazaar,** a cheap underground market with all the charm of a Times Square subway station. Avoid it: it's a favorite haunt of pickpockets and many shopkeepers are dishonest.

Fodor's Choice ★ **Dilli Haat** (✉*Aurobindo Marg* ☎*11/2611–9055*) is a government-run food and crafts bazaar that invites artisans from all over the country to sell their wares directly. More than 60 do so at any given time; the vendors rotate every two weeks according to changing themes such as handicrafts, textiles, or Rajasthani goods. Constants include Kashmiri shawls, Lucknavi *chikan* (white embroidery on pastel cotton), woodwork, pottery, and cotton dhurries. At the back of the bazaar, 25 stalls serve regional food from around the country, a rare opportunity to sample Goan fish curry, Bengali fish in mustard sauce, and Kerala chicken stew outside their states of origin. Best of all, doors are open daily from 10 to 9 (10 to 10 in summer). Admission is Rs. 15.

In the narrow medieval alleys of South Delhi's **Hauz Khas Village,** boutiques and shops in converted old homes sell crafts, curios, jewelry, artisanal furniture, and clothing (mostly glitzy Indian wear). Most stores are open every day but Sunday from 10:30 to 6 or 7.

INA Market (✉ *Aurobindo Marg*), across the street from Dilli Haat, is a colorful stop open every day but Monday. This is one of Delhi's most exciting food bazaars, with shops full of imported packaged foods giving way to a covered fruit-and-vegetable market complete with coolies (porters) ready to carry your choices in a basket while you shop. Dry-goods merchants sell spices, nuts, and Indian salty snacks, and meat is prepared and sold on a muddy lane in back.

Khan Market is one of the capital's most pleasant and popular markets, with dozens of fine shops selling books, CDs, cameras and film processing, drugs, ayurvedic cosmetics, clothing, home decorations, imported magazines, and imported foods. The shops are open roughly 10 to 7 every day but Sunday; some of the cafés and restaurants stay open for dinner. The crowd is thick with Delhi intelligentsia and expats.

Lajpat Nagar Market is a lively market where middle-class locals stock their households. Several Western brand names have outlets here, but Lajpat is best known for cheap kitchenware, curtains, Indian clothing, raw fabric, and shoes. A good place to take in the chaos and sample some street food, it's open every day but Monday from about 10:30 to 8.

Old Delhi is an endlessly interesting place to shop, admittedly more for the experience than for what you'll take away. The sidewalks of Chandni Chowk are lined with clocks, baby clothes, tacky toys, blankets, and much else; the shops on Dariba Kalan are filled with silver and gold jewelry. Stalls behind the Jama Masjid sell metalware and utensils, and one street specializes in stationery, especially Indian wedding invitations. Kinari Bazaar glistens with Hindu wedding paraphernalia. Khari Baoli, west of Chandni Chowk toward Lahori Gate, is renowned for its wholesale nuts, spices, and Indian pickles and chutneys. Shops are closed on Sunday.

The **Santushti Shopping Complex** in Chanakyapuri, open every day but Sunday from 10 to 6 or 7, is a collection of posh and arty boutiques scattered around a small, quiet garden across from the Ashok Hotel in the Diplomatic Enclave. Prices match those in the West, but this is a relaxing place to stroll and browse. Clothing is the main draw, followed by home furnishings, jewelry, leather, and ayurvedic beauty products. The restaurant Basil and Thyme serves excellent contemporary Euro-American food.

Sarojini Nagar Market is popular with locals for its endless array of cheap clothing, from Indian nightgowns and flashy kurtas to rejected Western export apparel. Note how much is charged for brand-name T-shirts and sweats compared with what you pay back home. The fruit and vegetable bazaar is great fun, especially at night. The market is open every day but Monday from about 10:30 to 8.

CLOSE UP

Classic Chaats

No trip to India is complete without some Indian snack food. The most popular street foods are *papri chaat* (fried wafers piled high with potatoes, chick peas, yogurt, and chilli powder), *chole bhatura* (also known as chana bhatura—spicy chick peas with fried, airy *puri* bread), and *golgappas* (fried dough in a hollow golf-ball shape, which you fill with a spicy mixture of potatoes, chick peas, tamarind, and coriander sauce), *pakoras* (battered and fried vegetables, cheese, or chicken), and the Bombay delicacy known as *bhel puri* (spicy rice with bits of onion). The best places to nosh on these snacks are in neighborhood markets.

Near Connaught Place, the **Bengali Sweet House** (✉ *27–37 Bengali Market, Connaught Place*) is a classic spot for evening *golgappa* outings. **Evergreen Sweet House** (✉ *S-30 Green Park Market*) has a charming tin ceiling under which a large crowd stuffs itself with *chole bhatura* and vegetarian thalis (combination platters). **Nathu's** (✉ *2 Sundar Nagar Market*) is the perfect place to kick back after shopping for high-end souvenirs, with its robust Indian sweets and pleasant seating area. The nearby Sweets Corner supplies the fried stuff outdoors. **Prince Paan Box** (✉ *M-Block Market, eastern corner, Greater Kailash I*) has one of Delhi's most popular chaat-wallahs (snack vendors), with a crowd at all hours. They're also known, of course, for their *paan* (betel nut leaves that include various ingredients). There's no seating. At the **Bikanerwala** (✉ *Hauz Khas Village*) you can sample Gujarati snacks—ask for *khandvi* (a delicious pan-fried snack made from a seasoned batter of chick-pea flour and buttermilk, then cut into rolls and sprinkled with coconut and coriander) or *dhokla* (a savory, fluffy, steamed cake made with chick-pea flour, mustard seeds, and a pinch of sugar and topped with coriander leaves).

SPECIALTY STORES

BOOKS

As the center of India's English-language publishing industry, and, arguably, India's intellectual capital, Delhi has something of a literary scene. For those with hard currency, Indian books are great bargains, including lower-price local editions of titles published abroad. If you'll be in Delhi for a while, hunt down the elusive but excellent *Old Delhi: 10 Easy Walks,* by Gaynor Barton and Laurraine Malone (New Delhi: Rupa, 1997)—these painstakingly detailed routes are fascinating and manageable. The top hotels have small bookshops, but Khan Market has several of the capital's best.

A candy store for history lovers is the cramped showroom for **Asian Educational Services** (✉ *31 Hauz Khas Village* ☎ *11/2656–0187* ⊙ *Closed 2nd Sat. each month*). This enterprising publisher reproduces old histories and travelogues on Asia, with hundreds of books on India. **Bahri Sons** (✉ *Opposite main gate, Khan Market* ☎ *11/2469–4610*) is stuffed to the ceiling with dusty nonfiction, particularly academic history, politics, and Indian heritage. **The Bookshop** (✉ *14A Khan Market*

2

☎11/2469–7102) is strong on literary fiction, including hot new titles from abroad. In Connaught Place, **Bookworm** (✉*B-29 Connaught Pl.* ☎*11/2332–2260*) has general fiction and Indian nonfiction, including academic social-science books. In South Delhi, **Fact and Fiction** (✉*39 Basant Lok, Vasant Vihar* ☎*11/2614–6843*) caters to the diplomatic community with books on international affairs, history, science, and language study. **Faqir-Chand** (✉*15A Khan Market* ☎*11/2461–8810*) carries a fair number of coffee-table books. **Full Circle** (✉*5B Khan Market* ☎*11/2465–5641*) is known for its spirituality, self-help, and coffee-table books. Geared toward travelers, **Mascot's** (✉*6 Sundar Nagar Market* ☎*11/2435–8808*) has sundry books on India.

NEED A BREAK?

Two flights up, in the Full Circle bookshop, Café Turtle (✉*5B Khan Market* ☎*11/2465–5641* ⏲*Mon.–Sat. 10–7:30*) serves light bistro food, exotic fruit juices, and excellent Western desserts in a smart contemporary setting, with music from the record shop below. The terrace is very pleasant in winter.

CARPETS

India has one of the world's foremost Oriental-rug industries, and there are carpet vendors all over Delhi. Unfortunately, carpet sellers are a notoriously dishonest crowd. In addition to being obnoxiously pushy, they are likely to sell you inauthentic merchandise at colossally inflated prices and then deny it later. There are some exceptions to this rule, but they tend to sell out of their homes rather than upscale showrooms—so call before you go. Jasim Jan, of **Janson's Carpets** (✉*A-14 Nizamuddin East* ☎*11/2435–5615, 98111–29095 cell phone*), delivers exactly what he describes—carpets old and new, silk and wool, Persian and tribal—and at fair (not cheap) prices. The family that runs **Novel Exports** (✉*D-23 Jangpura Extension* ☎*11/2431–2226*) comes from Kashmir, and they have stunning Kashmiri carpets, shawls, jewelry, and lacquered papier-mâché items.

CLOTHING

Clothes shopping is one of Delhi's great pleasures. *Khadi,* the handspun and -woven cotton that Gandhi turned into a nationalist symbol during the Independence movement, has made a roaring comeback and is now worn by many Delhi women during the long, hot summer. You can experience khadi in a salwar-kameez—the classic North Indian ensemble of long tunic and loose pants, also popular in a variation called the kurta-churidar—and in Western-style tops and skirts. Some Indian fabrics can fade or bleed easily, so it's always a good idea to wash clothes first before wearing.

WOMEN'S FABRIC & SALWAR-KAMEEZ SETS

Fodor's Choice ★

Stylish Delhiites, expats, and tourists rub shoulders at **Anokhi** (✉*Khan Market* ☎*11/2460–3423* ✉*Santushti Shopping Complex, Chanakyapuri* ☎*11/2688–3076*) for stylish kurtas, dupattas, and Western separates in boldly colored block-printed cottons. **Daman Choli** (✉*V-1 Green Park Main* ☎*11/2656–2265*) has bright, tastefully decorated cotton salwar-kameez and a convenient while-you-wait alteration service. The outdoor market **Dilli Haat** (✉*Aurobindo Marg* ☎*11/2611–9055*) usually has the capital's largest selection of cheap, distinctive cotton kurtas and raw salwar-kameez fabric. Designs vary widely, from Rajasthani mirror work to gossamer Maheshwari cotton to *ikat* weaves from Orissa. **Fabindia** (✉*N-14 Greater Kailash I* ☎*11/2646–5497* 🌐*www.fabindia.com* 🕒*Closed Sun.*) is a Delhi institution—an emporium stuffed with block-printed kurtas, salwars, churidars, dupattas, Western tops, and skirts in subtle colors for trendy Delhiites, their mothers, expats, and tourists. Quality can vary. Avoid Saturday, when the place is a madhouse and it's difficult to get your hands on the stock. There are also branches in Khan Market and Connaught Place. **Kanika** (✉*M-53 Connaught Pl.* ☎*11/2341–4731*) has beautiful, if somewhat pricey, salwar-kameez in contemporary cuts of traditional fabrics. **Khanna Creations** (✉*D-6 Connaught Pl.* ☎*11/2341–1929*) sells handsome salwar-kameez, some hand-embroidered, and raw fabric sets in great colors and patterns at good prices. Their in-house tailor can create a salwar-kameez in as little as four hours for Rs. 300. **Kilol** (✉*Upstairs, N-6 Greater Kailash I* ☎*11/2924–3388*) has some of the most stunning salwar-kameez fabric sets in India, with color-drenched crêpe dupattas topping off soft, block-printed cottons. They're stacked on shelves upstairs. **Tulsi** (✉*Santushti Shopping Complex, Chanakyapuri* ☎*11/2687–0339*) sells supple garments and home furnishings of handwoven silk, linen, and cotton.

NEED A BREAK?

Upstairs from Anokhi's home store, the Market Cafe (✉*32 Khan Market* 🕒*Mon.–Sat. 10–7:30*) serves light Western salads, pastas, and desserts and refreshing cold drinks in an airy contemporary setting.

SARIS

If you find yourself shopping for a sari, savor the experience of learning about this amazing handicraft. Silks and attractive cotton saris are sometimes sold at Dilli Haat market, depending on which vendors have set up shop that week. Silks are sold en masse at upmarket stores in South Extension, Greater Kailash I, and Connaught Place, but the highest thumbs-up go to Kalpana and Padakkam. **Banaras House** (✉*N-13 Connaught Pl.* ☎*11/2331–4751*) sells the rich brocaded silks of Varanasi. **Kalpana** (✉*F-5 Connaught Pl.* ☎*11/2331–5368*) is like an upscale version of Dilli Haat, with exquisite traditional saris from all over India plus gorgeous Kashmiri shawls. **L'Affaire** (✉*M-59 Greater Kailash I* ☎*11/2641–9977*) has flamboyant party wear at prices to match. **Nalli** (✉*F-44 South Extension I* ☎*11/2462–9926* ✉*P-7/90 Connaught Pl.* ☎*11/2336–7334*) is a Chennai-based chain specializing in gold-trimmed silks from the Tamil town of Kanchipuram. The South Extension location is larger. **Padakkam** (✉*Santushti Shopping Complex, Chanakyapuri* ☎*11/2465–4695*) has incredible one-of-a-kind saris—mostly South Indian silks, but also interesting cottons—and Kashmiri shawls. In Old Delhi, the venerable **Ram Chandra Krishan Chandra** (✉*Gali Parante Wali* ☎*11/2327–7869*) has several rooms full of traditional silks.

MEN'S FABRIC & TAILORS

The oldest and finest men's tailors are in Connaught Place. The venerable **D. Vaish & Sons** (✉*17 Regal Bldg., Connaught Place* ☎*11/2336–1806*) has a huge selection of fabric and can tailor both men's and women's Western suits, not to mention Indian outfits, for about US$80 plus fabric. **Mohanlal & Sons** (✉*B-21 Connaught Pl.* ☎*11/2332–2797*) whips up men's Western and Indian suits at very low prices. **Vedi Tailors** (✉*M-60 Connaught Pl.* ☎*11/2341–6901*) has a good reputation.

CLOSE UP

Dressing the Part

Many traveling women (and a few traveling men) are inspired to buy an Indian outfit to wear for the duration of their trip. Here's a primer:

The traditional North Indian women's ensemble of a long tunic over loose pants is known as a salwar-kameez. Today, it is equally common in a variation called the kurta-churidar. The word *kameez* is a general term meaning "shirt," whereas *kurta* specifies a traditional Indian tunic worn by both women and men. The pants worn beneath women's kurtas take two forms: the *salwar,* which is very loose, with only a slight gather at the ankle, and the *churidar,* which is loose in the thigh but tight along the calf, bunched up near the ankle like leggings. Presently the churidar is in greater vogue than the salwar, and true fashionistas now wear very short (above the knee) kurtas over thigh-tight churidars, a look with a Western element: it favors skinny women. Most women opt for knee- or calf-length kurtas.

The outfit is usually finished with a matching *dupatta* or *chunni,* a long scarf draped over the chest with the ends dangling in back, traditionally two meters long and one meter wide. These days you're free to drape the dupatta however you like; slinging it back from the neck, or even forward from the neck (Western-style), gives the outfit a modern twist. Just beware of dupattas made of stiff or starchy fabric—no matter how beautiful they look, you will probably find them unwieldy. A dupatta is particularly useful in places like Old Delhi and Nizamuddin, where you can pull it over your head as a kerchief if you feel too conspicuous.

You won't have to invest much in any of these items; at Fabindia or Dilli Haat you can buy a smart trio of kurta, churidar or salwar, and dupatta for US$25. Another option at Dilli Haat and some fabric stores is to buy uncut "suit fabric," a smartly matched set of three pieces of fabric meant to be sewn into the full regalia. If you buy suit fabric, simply take it all to a tailor (ask any market merchant to suggest one; most are holes-in-the-wall), allow him to measure you, tell him what kind of neckline you fancy and whether you want a churidar or salwar, and come back for your custom-made "suit." This can take a few days, but the tailoring costs about US$10 and these ensembles are very attractive.

Men's kurtas are traditionally paired with a churidar or with loose, straight-legged "pyjamas." Most urban Indian men wear Western shirts and trousers, but Delhi's politicians keep the white cotton kurta-pyjama and the more formal *dhoti* (a loose, bunchy men's skirt) alive and kicking. Formal silk kurta-churidars are trotted out only for weddings.

Many Western women who buy salwar-kameez choose muted colors, perhaps on the premise that light skin tones need light fabric tones. Unfortunately, muted colors often make Westerners look washed-out and even more "foreign." Be bold! Women of all complexions are flattered by the jewel tones of many Indian clothes.

CRAFTS & CURIOS

Delhi's fixed-price government emporiums, near Connaught Place, offer good values to travelers with limited time. They're also conveniently open seven days a week. The best market for fine curios and antiques is in the exclusive leafy neighborhood of Sundar Nagar. In addition to the shops listed here, a few shops on the southern (right-hand) side of the market have collections of old optical instruments.

★ **Art Bunker** (✉*24/2 Hauz Khas Village* ☎*98103–88804 mobile*) has lovely picture frames and other gifts in wood, cane, and jute. **Bharany's** (✉*14 Sundar Nagar Market* ☎*11/2435–8528*) sells rare old shawls and wall hangings from all over India. The **Central Cottage Industries Emporium** (✉*Jawahar Vyapar Bhavan, Janpath, opposite Imperial Hotel, Connaught Place* ☎*11/2332–6790*) has crafts from all over the country. The subterranean **Cottage of Arts & Jewels** (✉*50 Hauz Khas Village* ☎*11/2696–7418*) is a musty jumble of old prints, photos, maps, curios, and junk. **Curio Palace** (✉*17 Sundar Nagar Market* ☎*11/2435–8929*) has an overwhelming array of silver and brass curios, with much of the brass oxidized for an antique look. Among the bizarre, kitschy miscellany at **Friends Oriental Arts** (✉*15 Sundar Nagar Market* ☎*11/2435–8841*) are Kashmiri lacquerware, antique glassware, and old optical instruments. **India Arts Palace** (✉*33 Sundar Nagar Market* ☎*11/2435–7501*) is an absolute hurricane of Indian ephemera, with dangling colored lanterns, Hindu icons, cute animal curios, drawer pulls, and so forth. **La Boutique** (✉*20 Sundar Nagar Market* ☎*11/2435–0066*) pleases the eye with painted wooden items from Rajasthan, plus Hindu and Buddhist icons and other curiosities. **Ladakh Art Gallery** (✉*10 Sundar Nagar Market* ☎*11/2435–8679*) has distinctive silver items and small, tasteful Hindu icons. Exclusive **Natesan's** (✉*13 Sundar Nagar Market* ☎*11/2435–9320*) has elaborate Hindu sculptures in bronze and teak. In Old Delhi, **Shivam Zari Palace** (✉*2178 Kinari Bazaar* ☎*11/2327–1464*) and its neighbors sell inexpensive Hindu wedding paraphernalia such as turbans, fabric-covered boxes, *torans* (auspicious door hangings), tiny brass gods, and shiny bric-a-brac. **Singh Copper & Brass Palace** (✉*1167 Chah Rahat Gali, near Jama Masjid, Old Delhi* ☎*11/2326–6717*) has several dusty floors filled with brass, copper, and wood artifacts. The many **state emporiums** (✉*Baba Kharak Singh Marg, Connaught Place*) strung out over three blocks, can keep you busy for hours: the Kashmir store specializes in carpets, Karnataka in sandalwood, Tripura in bamboo, and so on.

HOME FURNISHINGS

Anokhi (✉*32 Khan Market* ☎*11/2462–8029* ✉*Santushti Shopping Complex, Chanakyapuri* ☎*11/2688–3076*) is loved for its block-print cotton home furnishings and gifts, including tablecloths, bedcovers, makeup bags, bathrobes, and cloth-bound journals. **Fabindia** (✉*N-5, 7, and 9 Greater Kailash I* ☎*11/2646–5497*) has cheap, attractive cotton tablecloths, placemats, bedcovers, curtains, and rugs. The upscale **Neemrana Shop–Kotwara Studios** (✉*Middle lane, upper fl., 12 Khan Market* ☎*11/2462–0262*) has some beautiful India-inspired women's clothing, men's kurtas, and household gifts at Western prices. **Noor Jehan**

(✉ *Santushti Shopping Complex, Chanakyapuri* ☎ *11/2611–2971*) is all about color, with blinding combinations of jewel tones on silk pillow covers, bedspreads, handbags, and dupattas.

WHERE'D IT GO?

If you have a favorite little shop or restaurant, don't be surprised if you find its sign swinging in the breeze and the building falling down. Since 2005, an ongoing crackdown on zoning has seen some of South Delhi's most upscale and popular shopping and eating complexes to shut their doors and fall to the wrecking ball. More may follow in advance of 2010's Commonwealth Games. The M.G. Road, South Extension and parts of GKI have seen many shops move to suburban malls. It's best to check before you head out of your way.

JEWELRY

India consumes more gold annually than any other country in the world, mainly because gold is an essential part of a bride's trousseau. With Delhi's upper middle class spending ever more money, and now chasing such Western fancies as diamonds and platinum, jewelry is big business here. The flashiest jewelry stores are clustered in South Extension, Greater Kailash I, and Connaught Place, offset by a handful of older shops in Sundar Nagar. Indian gold is 22-karat, and some Westerners tend to find its bright-yellow tone a bit too flashy. For a gold Indian piece in a subtler antique style, stroll through the market in Sundar Nagar. Hit the glitzier stores for the princess look. Indian jewelers as a group have been accused of adulterating their gold, but alas, you as a consumer will have no way to determine the content of each piece. Old Delhi is packed with jewelry and curio shops, though you have to search harder for fine designs. Stroll Dariba Kalan for the best selection of silver and gold.

Aakaar (✉ *5-L Shahpur Jat* ☎ *11/2649–7632*) is hard to find, but its arty silver baubles are hard to resist. Enter from Khel Gaon Marg and park near the electricity plant behind Siri Fort. **Bharany's** (✉ *14 Sundar Nagar Market* ☎ *11/2435–8528*) has traditional gold earrings and beaded necklaces in muted colors and styles. **Cottage Gallery** (✉ *Claridges Hotel, 12 Aurangzeb Rd.* ☎ *11/2301–4658*), in business for more than 30 years, has necklaces, bracelets, and earrings, including some antiques. **Ethnic Silver** (✉ *9A Hauz Khas Village* ☎ *11/2696–9637*) has supremely elegant pieces, especially earrings, and is open daily till 9 PM. **Hazoorilal** (✉ *M-44 Greater Kailash I* ☎ *11/2646–0567*) carries relatively modern designs. **Ivory Mart** (✉ *F-22 Connaught Pl.* ☎ *11/2331–0197*) has a huge selection of smashing necklaces in updated traditional styles. Reproductions of antique *kundan* jewelry, in which several gems are set in a gold-outlined design, are a specialty. **Lotus Eaters** (✉ *Santushti Shopping Complex* ☎ *11/2688–2264*) has interesting chunky silver and a few gold pieces, all very expensive. **Mehrasons** (✉ *E-1 South Ext. II* ☎ *11/2625–3138*) is a bit of a factory—service is surly, but the selection is immense. **Multan Enamel Mart** (✉ *No. 246–247 Dariba Kalan, Old Delhi* ☎ *11/2325–5877*) sells old and new silver jewelry and curios by weight. **Roopchand** (✉ *C-13 Connaught Pl.* ☎ *11/2341–1709*) has some eye-popping regal pieces in antique styles. **The Studio**

(✉4 *Sundar Nagar Market* ☎*11/2435–9360*) has beautiful silver and gold jewelry, especially necklaces, in tasteful traditional styles, including gemstone wedding sets.

MUSIC

South Delhi is best for discriminating music lovers. **Dua** (✉*F-27/2 Connaught Pl.* ☎*11/2335–4283*) is a hole-in-the-wall with a small but representative selection of Indian music. **Mercury** (✉*20 Khan Market*) looks ordinary but is strong on Indian classical music and *ghazals* (Urdu-language love songs). **The Music Shop** (✉*18AB Khan Market* ☎*11/2461–8464*) has a good selection of Bollywood, Bombay lounge, Indian classical, and Western rock music and a helpful staff. **Music Street** (✉*B-29 Connaught Pl.* ☎*11/2332–1171*) has mostly Hindi-film pop and DVDs. Delhi's largest music store is **Music World** (✉*Ansal Plaza, Khel Gaon Marg, near South Extension II* ☎*11/2625–0411*), where uniformed youngsters help you find your heart's desire in any category, Indian or international.

TEA & COFFEE

Fodor's Choice ★ At **Mittal** (✉*12 Sundar Nagar Market* ☎*11/2435–8588* ✉*8A Lodi Colony Market* ☎*11/2461–5709*), stuffed to the ceiling with Indian teas, herbs, and spices, charming owner Vikram Mittal will tell you everything you ever wanted to know about tea. **Regalia** (✉*12 Sundar Nagar Market* ☎*11/2435–0115*), next door to Mittal, sells fine teas and tea paraphernalia.

DELHI ESSENTIALS

To research prices, get advice from other travelers, and book travel arrangements, visit www.fodors.com.

AIR TRAVEL

International airlines fly into Indira Gandhi International Airport (⇨*Air Travel in India Essentials*). Most flights from the West arrive close to midnight.

On domestic routes, the top private carriers are Jet Airways, Indigo, and Sahara Airlines. Air India is the national carrier.

Airlines & Contacts Indian Airlines (☎*11/2462–0566 or 11/2331–0517* 🌐*http://indian-airlines.nic.in*). **Jet Airways** (✉*N-40 Connaught Pl.* ☎*11/5164–1414* 🌐*www.jetairways.com*). **Jetlite** (✉*N-41 Connaught Pl.* ☎*11/2331–0860 or 11/2332–3695* 🌐*www.jetlite.com*).

AIRPORTS & TRANSFERS

Delhi's two airports are close together, about 23 km (14 mi) southwest of Connaught Place. Be sure to tell your taxi driver whether you're going to the international or domestic airport. The domestic airport has two terminals, but they're far apart and your driver isn't likely to know which one you need—so when you buy or reconfirm a domestic ticket, *find out which terminal to use.*

The trip between either airport and Delhi itself should take about 45 minutes if you arrive before 9 AM or after 8 PM. During the day, traffic can increase the time to an hour. Every major hotel provides airport transfers for Rs. 500–Rs. 1,000, depending on the hotel's location.

Taking a cab is the easiest way to reach your hotel. A taxi from the international airport to the city center should cost Rs. 250–Rs. 300; from the domestic airport, Rs. 200–Rs. 250. To avoid being overcharged, use the prepaid taxi service in either airport, run by the Delhi Traffic Police from a counter near the exit. Unfortunately, hucksters have set up similar services, so ignore the men shouting at you and press on toward the door. In the domestic airport, the counter is just inside the exit; at the international airport, leave the building altogether and use the outdoor counter with the yellow sign. Your destination determines the fare, to which a small fee for each piece of luggage is added. Pay in advance at the counter, then take the receipt and exit. When you get outside, people might try to help you with your luggage; ignore them, and make sure they do not touch your things. Wheel your luggage down the ramp toward the black taxis with yellow tops, at which point the drivers will appear. If your receipt contains a taxi number, use that cab; if not, the drivers will decide among themselves who should take you. Tell the driver where you're going, and hold on to the receipt until you arrive. Tips are not expected unless they help with your luggage.

Be aware that people at the airports, and even at hotel-reservation counters, may try to trick you into booking a hotel room by claiming that your prior reservation is invalid, perhaps even saying that your hotel burned down. Ignore them. If you do need a room, go to the Government of India Tourist Office counter or phone a hotel directly.

BUS TRAVEL WITHIN DELHI

Avoid public buses, which are filthy, crowded, unpleasant for women, and notoriously dangerous to pedestrians—stay far away from them generally.

CARS & DRIVERS

Driving is not recommended for newcomers to India, as traffic takes highly unfamiliar forms here. If you're not on a tight budget, let an experienced driver take you around Delhi and outside town. Cars and drivers are available for half a day (four hours, 40 km [24 mi]) at about Rs. 350 or a full day (eight hours, 80 km [50 mi]) at about Rs. 700. Ask about different prices for different cars. The cheapest car is usually an Ambassador without air-conditioning; newer, bigger, or more comfortable cars cost more.

For out-of-town journeys, you'll pay upward of Rs. 3,000 per day for an air-conditioned car with an English-speaking driver, based on mileage and hours. If you're staying in a deluxe hotel, note that arranging a car through the travel desk costs significantly more than arranging one yourself through a travel agent, which is easy to do.

EMBASSIES

The consular-service branch of the U.S. embassy is open weekdays from roughly 8:30 to 1 and 2 to 5. Call to confirm hours before you go.

Contacts United States Embassy (*✉ Shanti Path, Chanakyapuri ☎ 11/2419–8000*).

MONEY

ATMS ATMs are common in India, especially in large cities like Delhi. Machines on the Cirrus and NYCE networks can now be found in every major market in Delhi, including Connaught Place, Khan Market, Defence Colony, Greater Kailash, Basant Lok, and so forth. Your hotel can point you to the closest one. AmEx machines are for cardholders only.

Locations American Express (*✉ A-Block, Connaught Place*). **ANZ Grindlays Bank** (*✉ E-Block, Connaught Place*). **Bank of America** (*✉ 16 DCM Bldg., Barakhamba Rd., Connaught Place*). **Citibank** (*✉ Jeevan Bharati Bldg., Outer Circle, Connaught Place ✉ Archana Shopping Centre, W-Block, Greater Kailash I ✉ New Delhi Railway Station, back side, near Platform 12*). **HSBC** (*✉ Khan Market*).

CURRENCY EXCHANGE Most hotels have foreign-exchange facilities for their guests and will cash traveler's checks with twice the speed and half the hassle of banks, albeit at inferior rates. The Central Bank of India in the Ashok Hotel is open 24 hours (except national holidays), but hours for the other banks vary; the Bank of America cashes traveler's checks only weekdays 10 to 2 and Saturday 10 to noon. Note that American Express and Thomas Cook cash only their own traveler's checks.

If you want to change money at the international airport, be sure to do it at the Bank of India counter—on the left as you exit Immigration, *before* you go through Customs. Thomas Cook runs a 24-hour exchange booth at the back side of New Delhi Railway Station, near Platform 12.

Exchange Services American Express (*✉ Wenger House, A-Block, Connaught Place ☎ 11/2371–2513 or 11/2332–4119*). **Thomas Cook** (*✉ Imperial Hotel, Janpath, Connaught Place ☎ 11/5111–6328 ✉ International Trade Tower, 717–718 Nehru Pl., 7th fl. ☎ 11/2646–7484 ✉ New Delhi Railway Station, back side, near Platform 12 ☎ No phone*).

Banks Central Bank of India (*✉ Ashok Hotel, Chanakyapuri ☎ 11/2611–0101 Ext. 2584*). **Bank of America** (*✉ 16 DCM Bldg., Barakhamba Rd., Connaught Place ☎ 11/2372–2332*). **Citibank** (*✉ Jeevan Bharati Bldg., Connaught Place ☎ 11/2371–4211*).

TAXIS & RICKSHAWS

Apart from a hired car, the best way to get around New Delhi is by taxi. Black-and-yellow metered taxis are available at every major hotel and at taxi stands in every shopping area and residential neighborhood and shopping area, and most drivers speak a little English. **■ TIP→ Tell the driver where you want to go and make sure he turns on the meter before you set off.** If he insists the meter is broken, get out of the car and find another cab. Most taxi drivers are honest, so it's not worth dealing with one who isn't.

Three-wheeled auto-rickshaws, known locally as "autos," are half the price of taxis and roughly half as comfortable—except in summer, when the open-air breeze keeps you cool while taxis trap the heat horrendously. The problem is that auto drivers refuse to use their meters (here they really often are broken, as the drivers deliberately break them), and if you look even remotely new to Delhi they will quote absurdly high fares. A trip around the corner costs Rs. 20; most longish trips cost Rs. 40–Rs. 60. A very long trip from one end of Delhi to the other might cost Rs. 100; under no circumstances pay more than that. Try to have exact change, as many drivers will claim to have none, and discussion is difficult, as most do not speak English.

In Old Delhi and other neighborhoods, you can still hire a cycle-rickshaw. It's a great way to cruise Chandni Chowk, explore the maze of narrow lanes, and get from one sight to the next. A short one-way trip costs Rs. 20; work out a higher fare, perhaps Rs. 100, if you want to ride around for an hour. **■TIP→Don't bargain too aggressively—these guys pedal hard for a living, and many are kindly old gentlemen.**

TRAIN TRAVEL

Delhi's main train stations are New Delhi Railway Station, Delhi Railway Station (usually called Old Delhi Railway Station), and Hazrat Nizamuddin. The name of the station you need is printed on your ticket; if you can't find it or read it, check with someone in your hotel to be absolutely sure. New Delhi station can be particularly chaotic and consumer-unfriendly, so keep your wits about you.

For information and tickets, try to save time and energy by using your hotel's travel desk or a travel agent. Otherwise, you must present yourself at the International Tourist Bureau on the upper floor of New Delhi station, open Monday through Saturday from 8 to 8 and Sunday from 8 to 2 for the use of foreigners with tourist visas only. Unless you've saved the ATM or encashment slip from a recent currency exchange, you must purchase tickets in U.S. dollars or pounds sterling. If you don't have an encashment slip *or* dollars or pounds, you can purchase a ticket in rupees at the general ticket counter, open daily 9:30 to 8 on the ground floor, but this can be a long and complicated process. Tickets can also be purchased online. Before you board any train, you must have a confirmed ticket and a reservation, including a reservation for your sleeping berth if you're traveling overnight *(⇨Rail Travel in India Essentials)*. When you arrive at the train for your journey, find your car—the coach number is printed on the ticket—and then find your name on the printout posted on that car.

⚠Upon arrival in Delhi, if hotel touts approach you at the station to offer you a room or claim that your hotel is closed or full, ignore them.

Train Information International Tourist Bureau (✉*New Delhi Railway Station, 1st fl.*).

TRAVEL AGENTS & TOURS

Travel agencies offer varying rates for cars and drivers, tours, excursions, and even hotel rooms, so shop around, and use only government-recognized agents (ask to see a license if necessary). RBS Travels offers extremely competitive rates, has a huge fleet of cars, and is open 24 hours. American Express has travel services for card members only.

Contacts **American Express** (✉ *A-1 Hamilton House, inner circle, Connaught Place* ☎ *11/2331–1763*). **Cox and Kings** (✉ *Indira Palace, H-16 Connaught Pl.* ☎ *11/2373–6031*). **RBS Travels** (✉ *Shop A-1, Connaught Palace Hotel, 37 Shaheed Bhagat Singh Marg, Connaught Place* ☎ *11/2336–4603*). **Sita Travels** (✉ *F-12 Connaught Pl.* ☎ *11/2331–1122 or–1133*). **Thomas Cook** (✉ *Imperial Hotel, Janpath, Connaught Place* ☎ *11/5111–6328*).

VISITOR INFORMATION

The Government of India Tourist Office south of Connaught Place is open weekdays 9 to 6 and Saturday 9 to 2, but it doesn't have anything a decent hotel can't offer. Its airport counters are open for major flight arrivals, and its train-station counters are open 24 hours.

Tourist Information **Government of India Tourist Office** (✉ *88 Janpath, Connaught Place* ☎ *11/2332–0005*).

North Central India

Wading through the shallow water of the Yamuna River in Agra

WORD OF MOUTH

"[Then] we went back out into the city with our driver to photograph the Taj Mahal from the other side of the Yamuna River. [They were] some of the best pictures of my entire trip. Children playing cricket with the Taj in the background, camels walking with the setting sun in the background, girls gathering sticks for fuel. It was mesmerizing."

—BostonHarbor

www.fodors.com/forums

WELCOME TO NORTH CENTRAL INDIA

Khajuraho Temples

TOP REASONS TO GO

★ **Front and Center on the World Stage:** With 7 out of India's total of 27 UNESCO World Heritage Sites, North-Central India has more sites than any other region in the country.

★ **A Religious Magnet:** A trip to Varanasi is essential for experiencing Hinduism's power in the lives of millions of believers.

★ **There's Always a Celebration:** Stunning cultural and religious festivals happen in North-Central India throughout the year.

★ **Legendary Skill at Work:** Discover how some of India's most-admired art forms—marble inlay in Agra, silk weaving in Varanasi—are created by generations of artisans.

★ **You Won't Miss the Flight Home:** The must-sees of the region are relatively short, no-hassle trips from Delhi, and easily reached by car, plane, or train for those with limited travel time.

1 Agra and Environs. Full of squalor and magnificence alike, this is the architectural heart of North-Central India, with over-the-top creations left by Moghuls. There's lots of walking and gazing to be done here, especially at the Taj Mahal and the abandoned city of Fatehpur Sikri.

2 Khajuraho. In contrast to Agra's chaos, Khajuraho projects extreme calm amid equally impressive temples built by the Chandelas. It's also a good base for exploring the wildlife of Madhya Pradesh, with the Panna National Park just 19 miles away.

Varanasi

3 Bhopal and Environs. Bhopal, the capital of Madhya Pradesh, is the least touristy of all the cities here. Nearby are two lesser-known World Heritage sites, Sanchi and the Bhimbetka Caves.

4 Varanasi. This cornerstone of Hinduism is a maze of nameless lanes and corridors, making it well suited to getting blissfully lost amid its constant din.

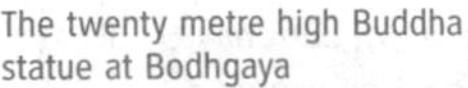

The twenty metre high Buddha statue at Bodhgaya

5 Lucknow. The capital of Uttar Pradesh, Lucknow is distinctly different, with wide roads and European architectural elements. Because of its history of Muslim rule, it remains an important center for Shiites.

6 Bodhgaya. A detour to the state of Bihar leads to the Buddhist center of Bodhgaya, one of the country's main pilgrimage spots for the religion.

GETTING ORIENTED

North-Central India may be the most awe-inspiring region of this tremendous country, and if you plan to visit India only once in your lifetime, this is the place to go, tourist traps and all. With a sprawling population, North-Central India is composed of the states of Uttar Pradesh (Northern Province in English), Madhya Pradesh (Central Province) and, to a lesser extent, Bihar to the east. It's fairly easy to move from one place to another, and each area has its own unique offerings.

Vishwanath Temple, Khajuraho

NORTH CENTRAL INDIA PLANNER

When to Go

If you decide to go to Agra from April to early July, even Indians might look at you as if you're crazy. There's no denying this region is at its hottest then, making sightseeing in Agra and Khajuraho, which involves hours in the sun, borderline unbearable. December and January are ideal, but it can get chilly in the evenings. (That said, it could be argued that December at the Taj Mahal is actually the worst, since you're simply trading the sun for sky-high prices and unbelievable amounts of foot traffic.) The weather from early February to mid-March is wonderfully temperate, and the mid-monsoon period (late July through early August) is good: temperatures are in the 80s, rain is intermittent, and hotel rates go down. As for Orchha, it's at its best during the monsoon, when the river is in full flow and the surrounding scrubland is green.

Getting There & Around

At this writing, domestic airlines are considering re-starting service to Agra's airport—in the past, companies had found it unprofitable to fly here, since Agra is so close to Delhi and people can sometimes get there faster (and more enjoyably) by car (four hours) or train (three hours). A few airlines may begin service again by early 2008. The airports in Bhopal, Khajuraho, Lucknow, and Varanasi are all connected by air from Delhi and other cities, and the airport in Patna, the capital of Bihar, can be used to access Bodhgaya on a bumpy two-hour drive. Train service is superb, as the region is connected by several local and express trains originating in Delhi and other major cities. Traveling this way offers great views of the countryside, but keep in mind that if you travel in an air-conditioned car, the views will be obstructed by dirty, sealed windows. A few of the offerings include the *Shatabdi Express,* India's fastest train, which runs daily along the Delhi–Agra–Gwalior–Jhansi–Bhopal route. You can get off at Jhansi for the short drive to Orchha. The *Marudhar Express* travels the Jodhpur–Jaipur–Agra–Lucknow–Varanasi route daily, which comes in handy for those coming off a trip to Rajasthan. There are tons of other options, some of wich are much slower but more convenient if you want to go directly from Delhi to Varanasi, for example. The Indian Railways Web site has a complete itinerary 🌐 *www.indianrail.gov.in.* Your best bet is to arrange your tickets through an Indian travel agent before you land in Delhi and then pick them up at the office *(⇨ Tours, North Central India Essentials)*. If you're going to be traveling during the peak season, make reservations well in advance. Train service is not currently available to Khajuraho, but a railway is being constructed.

Bus travel is probably the cheapest option, but it's only for the truly adventurous, since local schedules are difficult to come by and service is spotty. You can book a seat on a private, air-conditioned bus for travel between the cities through any local travel agent.

Auto-rickshaws and taxis are a cheap, convenient option for getting around in all the big cities, and can also be hired for an entire day of sightseeing. The only form of public transportation is the local bus lines, which are not recommended.

Dance, Drums & Art

North Central India provides ample opportunities to experience Indian classical music and dance. Agra, Khajuraho, Gwalior, and Lucknow host annual festivals that gather the best talents; Khajuraho's include performances in front of the Western Group of temples. Varanasi, home of Ravi Shankar, also maintains a vibrant local tradition of music and dance and is noted particularly for its *tabla* (drum) players. Many hotels throughout the area offer live classical music in the evening.

The visual arts are strong as well. Khajuraho's archaeological museum displays sculptures that once graced the niches of the town's temples, and its tribal–arts museum has superb folk pieces from all over Madhya Pradesh. Varanasi's Bharat Kala Bhavan has many collections of miniature paintings and locally discovered classical sculpture.

Shopping

Agra is known for marble inlay, jewelry, and leather; Varanasi, for exquisite silk (particularly brocade) and rug weaving. Lucknow is known for a traditionally white-on-white straight-stitch embroidery style called *chikan*. You'll find shops selling Kashmiri pashminas, embroidered shawls, and other attractive goods just about everywhere.

What It Costs In Rupees

	¢	$	$$	$$$	$$$$
Restaurants	under Rs. 100	Rs. 100–Rs. 300	Rs. 300–Rs. 500	Rs. 500–Rs. 700	over Rs. 700
Hotels	under Rs. 2,000	Rs. 2,000–Rs. 4,000	Rs. 4,000–Rs. 6,000	Rs. 6,000–Rs. 10,000	over Rs. 10,000

Restaurant prices are for an entrée plus bread or rice. Hotel prices are for a double room in high season, excluding a tax of up to 20%.

Planning Your Time

A good way to see North Central India is to mix up your transportation. If you go only by air, you'll miss the Indian train experience, practically a destination unto itself. Try taking the express train to Agra to avoid Delhi traffic, and plan to spend one or two days before heading out with a car and driver on a two-day, ten-hour road trip to Khajuraho. Along the way, you can overnight in Gwalior and Orchha—the sights here require less than a day each. Set out early for Khajuraho. Here you can settle up with your driver and spend two days exploring the Chandela temples on your own before flying to Varanasi. For a detour to Bhopal, catch an express train to Khajuraho (a downside to this is you'll have to backtrack: there are no flights or trains from Bhopal to Khajuraho). Varanasi requires at least two days. From there you can take a six-hour train ride to Lucknow. The Uttar Pradesh capital is a good place to decompress—consider spending two days before flying back to Delhi. A trip east to Bodhgaya will add a couple of days, and to get there you can take the train or hire a car and driver. To see every significant point in the region, plan on two weeks. If you have a week or less, fly first to Varanasi, then catch a plane to Khajuraho. From there, head to the Jhansi railway station where you can catch an express train to Agra for a magnificent ending to your trip. The same train can get you back to Delhi within two hours.

Updated by Monica Mercer

ANCHORED BY AGRA, KHAJURAHO, AND VARANASI, this section of the traveler's trail heads southeast of Delhi into the state of Uttar Pradesh, detouring into Madhya Pradesh and Bihar. This Hindi heartland has long held the balance of power in North India, from the ancient Gupta kingdoms through the Moghuls and the British Raj to the present day. Sometimes disparaged as the Cow Belt, North Central India has often been slow to advance economically, but it remains a vital part of India's heritage and contemporary culture.

Agra was a seat of Moghul power. Dominated by Muslim influences in culture, art, architecture and cuisine, the city is a testament to the beauty and grandeur of Moghul aesthetics, most notably in the form of the Taj Mahal, but also some exquisite smaller Muslim tombs and monuments.

Southeast of Agra, in the northern part of Madhya Pradesh, the sleepy village of Khajuraho predates the Moghuls. Khajuraho was founded at the end of the classical age of Hindu civilization—its stunning temples celebrate an eroticized Hinduism that flourished when Hindu kings adopted mystical beliefs. Excavations here have also uncovered a previously unknown complex of Buddhist temples.

In many ways, Varanasi, in southwestern Uttar Pradesh, is the antithesis of Khajuraho. The holiest city in Hinduism and one of the oldest continuously inhabited cities in the world, Varanasi teems with pilgrims, hospice patients, ascetics, priests, Hindu pundits, and international citizens of many religions. Unlike those of Khajuraho, Varanasi's temples are squeezed into the city itself, and the *ghats* (wide stone stairways leading down to the Ganges) are both key religious sites and secular promenades.

The popular Agra–Khajuraho–Varanasi route has plenty of worthwhile arteries. From Agra, it's an hour's drive southwest to Fatehpur Sikri and 30 minutes more to Keoladeo Ghana National Park—a bird sanctuary in Bharatpur, across the Rajasthan border. A separate day trip takes you from Agra to the Moghul-influenced Hindu provincial capital at Gwalior. The magical town of Orchha, a two-hour drive southeast of Gwalior toward Khajuraho, is riddled with 16th- and 17th-century ruins built by the Hindu Bundela rulers, including underground chambers and passageways. Buddha preached his first sermon in Sarnath, just outside Varanasi. Superb sculpture and the peaceful resonance of stupas and monastery ruins at Sanchi draw Buddhists from all over Asia, and the international Buddhist center of Bodhgaya is east of Varanasi in the state of Bihar. Lucknow, capital of Uttar Pradesh, was once the seat of an elegant Muslim province on a northern route between Varanasi and Delhi.

EXPLORING NORTH CENTRAL INDIA

Agra and Varanasi are at opposite ends of India's largest state, Uttar Pradesh. Both lie on the Gangetic plain, and the countryside around each is similar: a dry landscape planted with sugarcane, mustard, and

NORTH CENTRAL'S FESTIVALS

Agra's cultural festival, Taj Mahotsav (10 days in February), and the Khajuraho Festival of Dance (a week between late February and March) are geared primarily to visitors. During Gwalior's Tansen Music Festival (5 nights in November or December), renowned singers come to perform classical ragas near the tomb of the greatest classical singer of them all, Tansen. At the Lucknow Mahotsav (December), the evening music and dance performances are excellent.

In Varanasi there's a major religious festival practically every week, but festival dates shift every year (check www.incredibleindia.org for upcoming dates). Varanasi's great bathing days, when thousands stream down the ghats into the Ganges, include Makar Sankranti (January), the full moon of the Hindu month Kartik (October or November), and Ganga Dussehra (May or June). Durga Puja (September or October) ends with the city's large Bengali community marching to the river at sunset to immerse large mud-daubed images of the goddess Durga.

Buddhists from Tibet and all over Asia celebrate their festivals in Sarnath, Bodhgaya, and Sanchi.

wheat in winter and inhabited by poor peasants and well-off landowners. The landscape of Madhya Pradesh morphs into a more dramatic scene, with rolling hills and fertile valleys. Especially in Khajuraho and the state capital Bhopal to the southwest, you'll get a better sense of the natural environment because of less congestion and more open spaces. The monsoon hits harder to the east, around Varanasi and Bodhgaya, so the terrain there is a little more lush. The Yamuna River—backdrop to the Taj Mahal—joins the Ganges at Allahabad, about 161 km (100 mi) west of Varanasi.

ABOUT THE RESTAURANTS

Restaurants on this route generally serve kebabs and other grilled meats, *birianis* (rice casseroles), and the rich almond-and-saffron-scented concoctions of Mughlai cuisine. Most hotels offer a menu of Indian (with choices from various regions), Continental, Chinese (sort of), and sometimes Thai or Japanese dishes; Khajuraho has several Italian restaurants. Small places in villages along the way have simple local vegetarian dishes that are often delicious and cheap. Also keep an eye out for South Indian joints, where a delicious spiced-potato-filled *dosa* (crisp rice crepe) will fill you up for a 20 rupees or less and is tremendously satisfying. Most restaurants are open from 7 to 10 for breakfast, noon to 3 for lunch, and 7:30 to 11 for dinner; hotels often have a 24-hour or all-day coffee shop.

Hotels in Agra serve particularly good Mughlai dishes. Varanasi, with its abundant "food for the soul," is extremely light on restaurants—orthodox Hindus do not eat meat and prefer to keep food preparation a family affair. Out of respect, most spots near the holy river will not only be "pure vegetarian," but also will be geared toward observant Brahmins by avoiding onions, garlic, and other ingredients thought to be overly stimulating. However, the city is known for its sweets, mostly based on distillations of milk and cream, such as *lavan lata,* a kind of supercharged baklava. Lucknow, too, is known for excellent sweets (and without the swarms of flies that swirl around the wares in Varanasi's famous shops), as well as for Avadhi cuisine. Developed at a time when high Muslim nobles called "nawabs" ruled the Mughal empire, Avadhi food is characterized by subtle blending of flavors and aromas of Avadh.

ABOUT THE HOTELS

India's main hotel groups are represented in this region, providing increased amenities and efficiency at increasing prices. More and more good, air-conditioned hotels cater to India's upper-middle class and businesspeople, but such places are often quite generic. Outside the old British cantonment areas, where most top hotels are clustered, and often closer to the center of town, you'll find clean, well-run guest houses and small Heritage Hotels. Unless otherwise noted, all hotels listed have air-conditioning and private baths.

AGRA & ENVIRONS

The journey from Delhi to Agra follows the Grand Trunk Road—a royal route established by India's Moghul emperors in the 16th and 17th centuries, when their capital alternated between Delhi, Agra, and Lahore (now in Pakistan). If you get an early start, you can see Agra's sights in one very tiring day: turn off the Grand Trunk Road 10 km (6 mi) north of Agra to visit Akbar's Tomb, then move on to Itmad-ud-Daulah's Tomb, the Taj Mahal, and Agra Fort.

Excursions make the trip to Agra more interesting. Many find Akbar's deserted dream city at Fatehpur Sikri as rewarding as the Taj Mahal; a short drive farther, toward Jaipur, brings you to Rajasthan's Keoladeo Ghana National Park, winter home of the Siberian crane. Another day trip takes you to the Moghul-influenced Hindu provincial capital at Gwalior. If you drive on to Khajuraho, Orchha makes an excellent place to spend the night amid temple and palace ruins.

AGRA

200 km (124 mi) southeast of Delhi.

Under the Moghul emperor Akbar (1542–1605) and his successors Jahangir (1605–1627) and Shah Jahan (1628–1658), Agra flourished. However, after the reign of Shah Jahan's son Aurangzeb (1658–1707), and the gradual disintegration of the empire, the city passed from one invader to another before the British took charge early in the 19th century. The British, particularly Governor General Lord Curzon (in office 1898–1905), did much to halt and repair the damage inflicted on Agra's forts and palaces by raiders and vandals.

Agra today is crowded and dirty. Although some of the Moghul buildings are irrevocably scarred, the government has taken steps to protect the city's most important site from pollution, closing the streets

CLOSE UP

"'Wonder' Wallows in Filth"

That was an unflattering headline describing the Taj Mahal in the Indian national newspaper *Mid-Day*, in July of 2007, and the sentiment came from none other than P.R.S. Oberoi, the chairman of India's luxury Oberoi Hotel chain. Even bigwigs in the hospitality industry aren't inclined to let Agra rest on its laurels anymore. Despite the draw of a beautiful monument and top hotels—Agra's Oberoi Amarvilas Hotel is consistently ranked among the best in the world—the city is popularly considered one of India's dirtiest. Corporate initiatives to clean it up are a new trend, given that government projects begun in the 1990s haven't shown much progress. A "social responsibility project" begun by the Taj View Hotel in 2007, for example, was to educate shopkeepers and baggage porters on the negative effects of trashing the Agra railway station. Baby steps may be all that can be hoped for in the near future.

around the Taj Mahal to gas-fueled vehicles (visitors are ferried from a remote parking lot by battery-powered buses) and relocating small factories and fire-burning shops away from the area. Still, Agra's monuments remain strewn like pearls in ashes, evoking that glorious period in Indian history when Agra was the center of the Moghul empire, and the empire itself was the focus of political, cultural, and artistic evolution.

■ TIP→ Opening hours change constantly; inquire in advance at your hotel or the Uttar Pradesh State Tourist Office.

Numbers in the text correspond to numbers in the margin and on the Agra map.

GETTING AROUND AGRA

It's a good idea to spend a night in Agra and start tackling the sights early in the morning, if only because you'll get a couple of hours in before the hot sun begins to bear down. If you happen to sleep in, don't worry. Although hotels and tour guides tend to make a big deal about the best times of day to see the Taj Mahal, this legendary mausoleum is spectacular whenever you choose to visit, so you shouldn't feel despondent if you arrive at noon as opposed to sunrise or sunset. (A mid-day visit, however, *would* be the worst time to forget your sunglasses.) Another thing to remember is that the Taj Mahal is extremely crowded at all hours of the day, so don't assume that an early start necessarily will save you from the relentless foot traffic.

Assuming you see the Taj Mahal first (and that's certainly not mandatory), it's easy to take leisurely drives to the rest of the sights and be ready to unwind by early evening. Drive 5 km (3 mi) north of the Taj Mahal—about a 20-minute drive on a congested road—to **Itmad-ud-Daulah's Tomb** ❷ and then 8 km (5 mi) northwest—about a half-hour drive, with traffic—to **Akbar's Tomb** ❸. From here it's a 12 km (7 mi), or 45-minute, drive northeast to **Agra Fort** ❹, where it's easy to spend

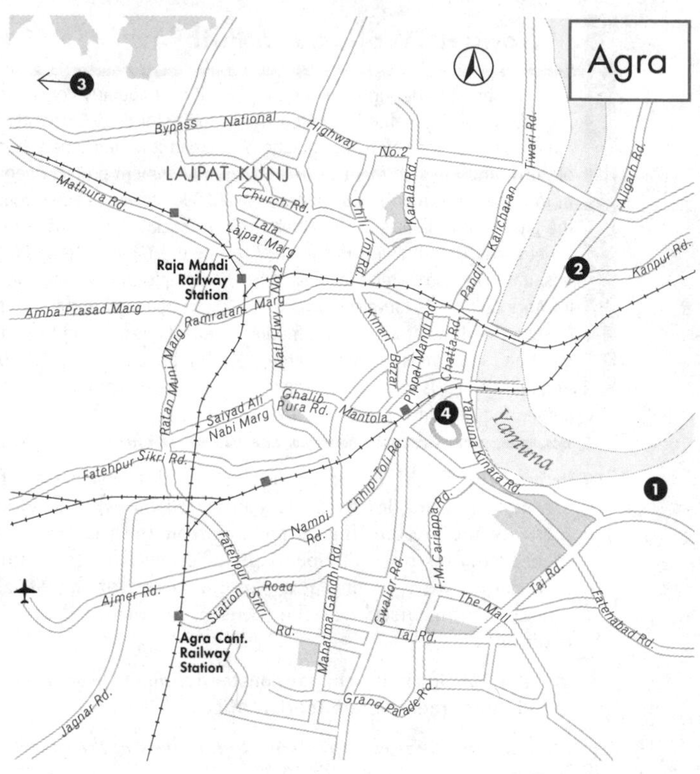

an hour or more. If you have the time and energy, drive southwest for an hour (37 km or 23 mi), to **Fatehpur Sikri**.

However, if you're day-tripping from Delhi with a car and driver, it's a must to leave by 5 AM to avoid terrible traffic. You can see Akbar's Tomb and Itmad-ud-Daulah's Tomb on the way to the Taj Mahal, at which you'll easily arrive before noon. Spend the afternoon visiting the Agra Fort or Fatehpur Sikri, then hit a good restaurant before heading back to Delhi.

TIMING If you try to pack all of Agra's sights into a day that starts in Delhi, you'll have quite a long, tiring day; starting fresh in the morning from Agra will make for a full, but fairly easy day. Consider staying a second night at your hotel and dividing your excursions between two days to eliminate that constant hectic feeling that Agra's crowds and sights seem to impart.

WHAT TO SEE

4 ★ **Agra Fort.** The architecture of this fort—one of the area's 7 World Heritage Sites (and India's 27), along with the Taj Mahal and Fatehpur Sikri—reflects the collective creative brilliance of Akbar, and his son Jahangir and grandson Shah Jahan. The structure was built by Akbar on the site of an earlier fort. As with similar Moghul facilities in Delhi

and Lahore, the word "fort" is misleading: the complex is really a fortified palace, containing royal apartments, mosques, assembly halls, and a dungeon—the entire cityscape of an imperial capital. A massive wall 2½ km (1½ mi) long and 69 feet high surrounds the fort's roughly triangular shape. With the Yamuna River running at its base, the fort was also protected by a moat and another wall, presenting a daunting barrier to anyone hoping to access the treasures within.

The fort's entrance is easily accessible through the Amar Singh Gate. North of this entrance sits the fort's largest private residence, the **Jahangiri Mahal,** built as a harem for Jahangir. (Akbar's own palace, closer to the entrance, is in ruins.) Measuring 250 feet by 300 feet, the Jahangiri Mahal juxtaposes *jarokhas* (balconies) and other elements of Hindu architecture with pointed arches and other Central Asian influences imported by the Moghuls—a mixture foreshadowing the stylistic synthesis that would follow at Fatehpur Sikri. The palace's central court is lined with two-story facades bearing remnants of the rich, gilded decoration that once covered much of the structure.

After Jahangir's death in 1628, Shah Jahan assumed the throne and started his own buildings inside the fort, often tearing down those built by his father and grandfather in the process. The **Anguri Bagh** (Grape Arbor) shows the outlines of a geometric garden built around delicate water courses and chutes. The 1637 **Khas Mahal** (Private Palace) is an early masterpiece of Shah Jahan's craftsmen. The central pavilion, made of white marble, follows the classic Moghul pattern: three arches on each side, five in front, and two turrets rising out of the roof. Of the two flanking pavilions where Shah Jahan's two daughters resided, one is of white marble and was supposedly decorated with gold leaf; the other is made of red stone. The arched roofs of all three pavilions are stone translations of the bamboo architecture of Bengal. In one part of the Khas Mahal, a staircase leads down to the palace's "air-conditioned" quarters—cool underground rooms that were used in summer.

The octagonal tower of the **Mussaman Burj** has fine inlay work and a splendid view down the river to the Taj Mahal. This is where Shah Jahan is said to have spent the last seven years of his life, imprisoned by his son Aurangzeb but still able to look out on his greatest monument, the Taj Mahal. On the northeastern end of the Khas Mahal courtyard stands the **Sheesh Mahal** (Palace of Mirrors), built in 1637 as a bath for the private palace and dressing room for the harem. Each of the two chambers contained a bathing tank fed by marble channels.

The emperor received foreign ambassadors and other dignitaries in the **Diwan-i-Khas** (Hall of Private Audience), built by Shah Jahan in 1636–37. Outside, the marble throne terrace holds a pair of black and white thrones. The black throne, carved from a single block of marble, overlooks the Yamuna and, according to the inscription, was used by Shah Jahan; the white throne is made of several marble blocks and was his father's seat of power. Both thrones face the **Machhi**

Bhavan, an enclosure of fountains and shallow pools, and a number of imperial offices.

To the empire's citizens and to the European emissaries who came to see these powerful monarchs, the most impressive part of the fort was the **Diwan-i-Am** (Hall of Public Audience), set within a large quadrangle. This huge, low structure rests on a 4-foot platform, its nine cusped Moghul arches held aloft by rows of slender supporting pillars. Here the emperor sat and dispensed justice to his subjects.

Northeast of the Diwan-i-Khas is the **Nagina Masjid,** a private mosque raised by Shah Jahan for the women of his harem. Made of white marble and walled in on three sides, it has typical cusped arches, a marble courtyard, and three graceful domes. Nearby is the lovely **Moti Masjid,** a perfectly proportioned pearl mosque built in white marble by Shah Jahan. ✉ *Yamuna Kinara Rd.* 🎫 *Rs. 300 (Rs. 250 with a ticket to Taj Mahal)* ⏲ *Daily sunrise–sunset.*

3 **Akbar's Tomb.** Akbar's resting place was begun by the emperor himself in 1602 and completed after his death by Jahangir. Topped with white marble and flanked by graceful minarets, this mausoleum of rough red sandstone sits in a typical Moghul garden—four quadrants separated by waterways. The garden, however, is not well tended, and Jat raiders (who invaded Agra after the fall of the Moghul empire) destroyed much of the gold work that once adorned the tomb, though the British partially restored it. In a domed chamber three stories high, the crypt is inscribed with the 99 names of Allah, plus the phrases *Allah-o-Akbar* (God is great) at the head and *Jalla Jalalahu* (Great is His glory) at the foot. You can actually see the tomb's enormous gateway, topped with bright tilework, from the train from Delhi—look out the left window 10 or 15 minutes before the train is due to reach Agra. ✉ *Sikandra, 10 km (6 mi) north of Agra on Grand Trunk Rd. to Delhi* 🎫 *Rs. 110* ⏲ *Daily 6–5:30.*

2 ★ **Itmad-ud-Daulah's Tomb.** The empress Nur Jahan (Jahangir's favorite wife) built this small but gorgeous tomb for her father, a Persian nobleman who became Jahangir's chief minister. The monument, one of Agra's loveliest, was supposedly built by workers from Persia. The tomb incorporates a great deal of brown and yellow Persian marble and marks the first use of Persian-style marble inlay in India—both features that would later characterize the style of Shah Jahan. Particularly in its use of intricate marble inlay (known in Italy as *pietra dura*), this building was a precursor of, and very likely an inspiration for, the Taj Mahal (for this reason it has earned the somewhat goofy nickname of the "Baby Taj"). The roof is arched in the style of Bengali terra-cotta temples, and the minarets are octagonal, much broader than the slender cylinders of the Taj Mahal—in its fine proportions this mausoleum almost equals that masterpiece. Inside, where the elegant decoration continues, the central chamber holds the tombs of Itmad-ud-Daulah and his wife; other relations are buried in adjacent rooms. Most travelers to Agra never see this place, but its beauty and tranquillity are extraordinary, and its well-maintained gardens make it a wonderful

place to pause and reflect. ✉ *5 km (3 mi) north of Taj Mahal on left bank of Yamuna River* 🎫 *Rs. 110* ⏲ *Daily sunrise–sunset.*

NO MORE SPARKLE

Around 2001 it became illegal to shine flashlights inside the dark mausoleum of the Taj Mahal because of the damage it can do to the stones used in the delicate inlay work. Until then it had been a popular gimmick to illuminate stones such as the red carnelian, which sparkles with transluscence when exposed to light. Unfortunately employed guards of the mausoleum still carry small flashlights and try to charge a fee for this surreptitious service.

❶ Fodor's Choice ★ **Taj Mahal.** The haunting tale of love and loss that supposedly sparked the existence of the Taj Mahal sometimes seems as incredible as the monument's beauty. It is said that Shah Jahan fell in love with his favorite wife, Arjuman Banu, at first sight, and went on to revere her for her generosity, intelligence, and the 14 children she bore. She rightly became his *Mumtaz Mahal* (the Exalted of the Palace), and her love for him was apparently just as great—on her deathbed, or so the legend goes, she begged the king to build a monument so beautiful that the world would never forget their love. Five months later, a huge procession brought Mumtaz Mahal's body to Agra, where Shah Jahan began the process of honoring her request.

Indeed, it's difficult to imagine a grander gesture throughout history, but the design, execution and end result is what truly makes the Taj Mahal a must-see. Begun in 1632, it took 20,000 laborers a period of 17 years to complete the vast tomb of white marble on the banks of the Yamuna River, making it the most stunning example of the elaborate aesthetic world that the Moghuls created in India.

The Taj Mahal stands at the end of a large, four-quartered garden, or *charbagh,* symbolizing paradise, extending about 1,000 feet in each direction from a small central pool. You enter the grounds through a huge sandstone gateway boldly emblazoned with an inlaid Koranic inscription. Ahead, facing the long reflecting pool, the Taj Mahal stands on two bases, one of sandstone and, above it, a marble platform measuring 313 square feet and worked into a chessboard design. A slender marble minaret stands at each corner of the platform, blending so well into the general composition that it's hard to believe each one is 137 feet tall. The minarets were built at a slight tilt away from the tomb so that, in case of an earthquake, they'd fall away from the building. Facing the Taj Mahal from beneath its platform are two majestic sandstone buildings, a mosque on the left and its mirror image (built purely for symmetry) on the right. Behind the tomb, the Yamuna winds along its broad, sandy bed.

The tomb's central archway is deeply recessed, as are the smaller pairs of companion archways along the sides and the beveled corners of the 190-square-foot structure. The Taj Mahal's most extraordinary feature is its onion dome, crowned by a brass finial mounted in a scalloped ornament, which is an inverted Hindu motif of the lotus. The dome uses the Central Asian technique of placing a central inner dome, in this case 81 feet high, inside an outer shell to attain the extraordinary exterior height of 200 feet; between the two is an area nearly the size of the interior hall itself. Raising the dome above the minarets was the builders' great stroke of genius. Large *chattras* (umbrellas), another feature borrowed from Hindu design, balance the dome.

Inside the mausoleum, the changing light creeps softly in through marble screens that have been chiseled like silver filigree. Look closely at the tiny flowers drawn in inlaid semiprecious stones and the detailed stonework on each petal and leaf. The work is so fine that not even a magnifying glass reveals the tiny breaks between stones, yet a single one-inch flower on the queen's tomb has 60 pieces. Directly under the marble dome lie the tombs of Mumtaz Mahal and Shah Jahan, surrounded by a jali screen carved from a single block of marble, with latticework as intricate as lace. In the center of the enclosure, diminishing rectangles lead up to what looks like a coffin; in fact, both Mumtaz Mahal and Shah Jahan are buried in a crypt below these tombs in deference to the Islamic tradition that no one should walk upon their graves. After his death, Shah Jahan was buried next to his wife by his son Aurangzeb, upsetting the perfect symmetry, most likely a cost-cutting measure that forms an ironic postscript to the munificence of Shah Jahan. But it's fitting that the emperor lies in perpetuity next to his favorite wife.

GET THE BEST GUIDE

Most hotels have reputable, government-approved guides on hand, which are crucial for understanding the Taj Mahal in the correct context. Prices start at Rs. 450 for a group of up to five people. One of the city's best is Yogesh Sharma. You can make an appointment with him by calling him at ☎ 98/3788–5558 or 98/9705–8885, or e-mailing him at yogi.agra@gmail.com

In early morning, the pale rays of the sun give the marble of the Taj Mahal a soft pink luster, while at sunset the west side of the monument turns lemon yellow, then pumpkin orange. Once the sun goes down, the marble is pure white against a black sky.

The small **Taj Mahal Museum** stands near the mosque to the left of the Taj. It holds Moghul memorabilia and provides some historical background to the Taj, as well as paintings of the famous couple, manuscripts, letters, and a display of precious stones used in the construction of the Taj. ✉ *Taj Ganj, Taj Rd. 282001* ☎ *562/233–0498* *Taj Mahal Rs. 750; museum Rs. 5* ⏲ *Taj Mahal Sat.–Thurs. sunrise–sunset; museum Sat.–Thurs. 8–5.*

WHERE TO EAT & STAY

$$$$ ✕ **Esphahan.** Through the Amarvilas' illuminated Moghul courtyard and grand marble lobby, you'll arrive at this intimate den with decorations celebrating local craftsmanship—from square pillars of alternating red sandstone and white marble to carved wooden screens. Through the glass wall of the display kitchen, you can watch the chefs cook breads and meats in the tandoori ovens. The Indian menu emphasizes Avadhi cuisine (from the Lucknow area). Specialties include *Esphahani raan,*

leg of lamb marinated for 24 hours, roasted for 6 to 8 more, deboned, then cooked in the tandoor until it's crisp. Another good choice: tiger prawns marinated in citrus yogurt. Live instrumental music adds to the mood. ✉*Oberoi Amarvilas, Taj East Gate Rd.* ☎*562/223–1515* ▭*AE, DC, MC, V.*

$$$$ ★ ✕**Peshawri.** This premier restaurant's design is one obvious draw: rustic wood tabletops resting on tree-trunk bases, plush, bright-orange seat cushions, hammered copper plates and goblets. The dark, romantic mood it creates is complemented by the simple, delicious barbecue cuisine of India's North West region—all kinds of meats freshly prepared over open flames and served with rich, aromatic gravies. The ultra-rich *dal bukhara,* a combination of whole black lentils, tomatoes, ginger, and garlic along with plentiful ghee and cream, is slow-roasted for hours and makes a perfect choice for any vegetarians in the group. Reservations are a good idea here. ✉*ITC Mughal Hotel, Taj Ganj* ☎*562/233–1701* ▭*AE, MC, V.*

$$$–$$$$ ★ ✕**Mughal Room.** A ceiling of faux twinkling stars floats over this top-floor restaurant, done in rich reds, with brass trays hanging on walls and tables set with silver goblets. During daylight hours, the panoramic view from a wall of windows takes in both the Taj Mahal and the fort—the cream of Agra in one fell swoop. At night live *ghazals* (Urdu-language love songs) set the mood for Mughlai cuisine. At a display window, a chef at a tandoori oven makes delicious *bajari tikka,* boneless chicken cubes marinated with cream and yogurt, coated with spices, and topped with cashews; and *kabuli naan,* bread stuffed with dried fruits and cheese and sprinkled with black cumin seeds. ✉*Clarks Shiraz, 54 Taj Rd.* ☎*562/222–6121 to 32* ▭*AE, DC, MC, V.*

$$–$$$ ✕**Jhankar.** Occupying an elegant, airy space open to the lobby of the Taj View Hotel, the chefs at Jhankar cook up excellent Indian dishes that include the house specialty, *aloo dum chutneywale* potatoes with dried fruits and herbs simmered in a mint and coriander sauce. Also terrific is the Agra delicacy *magazi murgh korma,* chicken in yogurt, cashews, and poppy seeds, garnished with rose petals and melon seeds. Flavors are subtle and distinct; many herbs and vegetables come from the kitchen garden. ✉*Taj-View Hotel, Taj Ganj, Fatehabad Rd.* ☎*562/223–2400 to 18* ▭*AE, DC, MC, V.*

$ ★ ✕**Dasaprakash.** The light and spicy South Indian vegetarian dishes served here are a nice change from Agra's usual rich Mughlai fare. The Formica tables and fake Tiffany–style lamps evoke an American pizza joint. The food is excellent and service is fast. The *thali* (a sampler combination plate) may include crisp *appam* (fried bread made from rice flour) and *rasam* (thin, spicy lentil soup), as well as fluffy *idlis* (steamed rice cakes) and *dosas* (rice crepes). Also available are an unusual selection of fresh juices and a great dessert menu with ice creams and floats. (There's another, unaffiliated Dasaprakash in the city, but locals prefer this one.) ✉*1 Meher Cinema Complex, Gwalior Rd.* ☎*562/246–3368* ▭*No credit cards.*

$$$$ ★ 🏨**ITC Mughal.** Formerly the WelcomHotel Mughal Sheraton, this complex of brick and marble is one of Agra's largest hotels. Its size can be overwhelming—there's a lot of walking between one section and another.

Within the 36 acres of lush gardens there's even a miniature lake. Most of the big, bright rooms have modern furnishings, window settees, marble-top desks and headboards upholstered in a light floral-print fabric. Chamber of Emperors deluxe rooms have lots of green and cream-color marble, light woods, and silky deep-green and gold bedspreads. There's also an overwhelming activities program, including Saturday-night dancing, a mock Indian village complete with cycle-rickshaws and mock marriage ceremonies where couples can dress up like an Indian bride and groom. **Pros:** you'll never be bored at this hotel. **Cons:** so huge you may need a map to find everything. ✉ *Taj Ganj, Fatehabad Rd., 282001* ☎ *562/402–1700* 🌐 *www.itcwelcomgroup.in* *268 rooms, 5 suites* *In-room: refrigerator. In-hotel: 3 restaurants, room service, bar, tennis courts, pool, gym, spa, no elevator, laundry service, public Internet, no-smoking rooms.* 💳 *AE, DC, MC, V.*

$$$$ Fodor's Choice ★ **Oberoi Amarvilas.** One of India's best resorts brings to life the opulent lifestyle of the Moghul emperors. At this Moorish fantasy of sandstone arches and glistening pools, each spacious room—understatedly elegant, with teak floors and rich fabrics—has a breathtaking view of the Taj Mahal over a sea of green treetops. Agra's culture and heritage are celebrated in details taken from the Taj Mahal, from the colonnade with its floral frescoes to the guest rooms' marble-inlay tables. Standards of service from staff, including your own butler, are high. If you don't stay here, come to dine, or stop at the bar for a drink and a terrace view of the Taj Mahal and, in the evening, the Rajasthani dancers performing on the roof of the pool pavilion. **Pros:** gorgeous views, flawless service, free rides to the Taj Mahal. **Cons:** extremely expensive, constant attention from staff can become annoying. ✉ *Taj East Gate Rd., 282001* ☎ *562/223–1515 or 800/562–3764* 🌐 *www.oberoihotels.com* *106 rooms, 7 suites* *In-room: safe, refrigerator, DVD, ethernet, Wi-Fi. In-hotel: 2 restaurants, room service, bar, pool, gym, spa, laundry service, concierge, public Internet, public Wi-Fi.* 💳 *AE, DC, MC, V.*

$$$ **Clarks Shiraz.** Set on 8 acres with lush green gardens, this 1961 property has an all-deluxe-room Tower Wing. The sweeping marble lobby leads you to comfortable rooms with standard contemporary furnishings. There are many Taj Mahal–facing rooms; the best are from the Taj Mahal end of the tower's top floors. There's also an excellent restaurant, and a bevy of travel conveniences: a post office, bank, travel agencies and airline offices are all on-site. **Pros:** little extras like an astrologer on-hand and ayurvedic massages that won't gouge the wallet make it a good value. **Cons:** small pool, and the public spaces are a bit dark. ✉ *54 Taj Rd., 282001* ☎ *562/222–6121 to 32* 🌐 *www.hotelclarksshiraz.com* *235 rooms, 2 suites* *In-room: refrigerator, Wi-Fi. In-hotel: 2 restaurants, room service, bar, pool, gym, spa, laundry service, public Internet, public Wi-Fi, no-smoking rooms.* 💳 *AE, DC, MC, V.*

$$$ **Mansingh Palace.** A mix of Rajasthani and Moghul styles decorate this hotel in the middle of Agra, popular with Indian and foreign tourists. The large lobby features several generously sized seating areas. Rooms have green marble floors strewn with Persian carpets and

accented with dark wood furniture, and all have large bathtubs, rare in Indian hotels. Cultural shows such as folk dancing from different regions in India can be arranged on request. **Pros:** a travel counter and a 24-hour money exchange service. **Cons:** a typical hotel with no unique details setting it apart; a bit overpriced considering limited amenities. ✉*Fatehabad Rd., 282001* ☎*562/233–0202* 🌐*www.mansinghhotels.com* *100 rooms* *In-hotel: 2 restaurants, room service, bar, pool, gym, laundry service.* ▭*AE, MC, V.*

3

$$$ **Taj-View.** Many rooms at this fine Taj Group hotel do, in fact, have good views of the Taj Mahal, though it is a kilometer away. The best are from suites 522, 422, and 322, where daybeds are placed so you can sit before the huge windows and enjoy a dead-on frontal view of the palace (albeit across a bit of unsightly Agra). The lobby is an elegant expanse of marble opening onto an excellent restaurant. Room furnishings include headboards in red sandstone with marble inlay and dressing alcoves set off by screens of inlaid white marble. A blue-tile pool is fringed with palm trees and surrounded by acres of landscaped lawn. **Pros:** the upscale amenities for a decent price—and two-for-one drinks at happy hour—make it the best choice for those seeking luxury without outrageous prices. **Cons:** the hotel's popularity coupled with its small lobby make it seem extremely crowded. ✉*Taj Ganj, Fatehabad Rd., 282001* ☎*562/223–2400 to 18* 🌐*www.tajhotels.com* *95 rooms, 5 suites* *In room: refrigerator, ethernet. In-hotel: restaurant, room service, bar, pool, gym, laundry service, public Internet.* ▭*AE, DC, MC, V.*

$$$ ★ **Trident Hilton Agra.** The lobby of the Trident Hilton, which was redecorated in 2006, is perhaps the most inviting part of the hotel: bright yellow chairs, dark wood accents, and modern chandeliers made of glass tubes are infused with sunlight, making it an ideal spot to lounge and take everything in. Built around a large garden courtyard with fountains, water spilling over rocks, a soothing expanse of green lawn, and a pool, this place is a real oasis in Agra. The spacious rooms are tastefully done in soft greens and browns, with terra-cotta-like tile floors, large desk-areas, and coffeemakers. Rooms facing the courtyard offer the best views. Live Indian classical music accompanies dinner at the poolside barbecue. **Pros:** a thoughtful feature—rare in India—is two handicap-accessible rooms, and kids have their own kids' club. **Cons:** rooms are close to the lobby. ✉*Fatehabad Rd., 282001* ☎*562/233–1818 or 800/774–1500* 🌐*www.hilton.com* *136 rooms, 2 suites* *In-room: safe, ethernet. In-hotel: 2 restaurants, room service, bar, pool, gym, no elevator, laundry service, public Internet, no-smoking rooms.* ▭*AE, DC, MC, V.*

$$ **Hotel Yamuna View.** As part of a property-wide upgrade in 2005, the former Agra Ashok became Hotel Yamuna View, adding expensive touches like black granite bathrooms, some of which have hot tubs. The lobby is bright and airy with a small fountain, and all rooms are spacious and modern with standard furnishings and 25-inch TVs. A floor of deluxe rooms has been created, and the hotel's Mandarin Restaurant has been decked out with Chinese-style woodwork and a fountain. When you make a reservation you can buy an ayurvedic package,

taking advantage of the hotel's upgraded Kerala massage center. **Pros:** everything still feels new, and it's probably the best price you'll find in Agra for a mid-size, modern hotel. **Cons:** a bit far from the Taj Mahal, most rooms have twin beds. ✉ *6-B, The Mall, 282001* ☎ *562/246–2990* 🌐 *www.hotelyamunaviewagra.com* *56 rooms, 2 suites* *In-room: dial-up (some). In-hotel: 2 restaurants, room service, bar, pool, laundry service, no-smoking rooms.* *AE, MC, V.*

¢ ★ **Col. Lamba Indian Home Stay.** Get a lesson in North Indian cooking, or learn how to play cricket with the neighborhood teams. Whatever you've been missing at large Indian hotels, Retired Indian Army Col. Lamba and his family want you to experience in their real Indian home in the heart of residential Agra. In 2007 they modified their home per government standards to create eight guest rooms, each with separate bathrooms and unique family furnishings. Such intimate accommodations are a first for the city, but so is the family's brand of hospitality—the gracious owners will gladly give you lessons in everyday life, from how the Indian military works to where the milk comes from. Short of already knowing someone living in Agra when you get here, you won't find anything else like it. **Pros:** service is personalized, and you could learn some genuine aspects of Indian culture. **Cons:** you're literally staying in someone's house, so expect everyday noises from people going about their business. ✉ *58 Gulmohar Enclave, Shamshabad Rd., 282001* ☎ *562/329–8921* *lambaindianhomestay@yahoo.co.in* *8 rooms* *In-hotel: no elevator, laundry service, public Internet.* *No credit cards* *CP.*

¢ **Hotel Atithi.** The low rates at Hotel Atithi will no doubt be most attractive to visitors more interested in the grandeur of the Taj Mahal than fancy hotel rooms. But even if the accommodations are no frills, the staff is unusually warm and friendly, and seems genuinely glad to see you check in. The spiral staircase in the small lobby leads to four levels of clean, simple rooms that have tiled floors—much better than the old musty carpeting prevalent at other Indian budget hotels. Additional perks include a pool and a public Internet connection, making for a comfortable stay that won't completely drain your wallet. **Pros:** affordable, sincere service, other like-minded travelers in abundance. **Cons:** views from rooms are of back alleys or dirty Agra streets. ✉ *Tourist Complex Area, Fatehabad Rd., 282001* ☎ *562/233–0878* 🌐 *www.hotelatithiagra.com* *44 rooms* *In-room: refrigerator (some). In-hotel: restaurant, room service, pool, laundry service, public Internet.* *AE, DC, MC, V.*

¢ **Priya Guesthouse.** Opened in 2007, this charming guesthouse hopes to help fill Agra's dearth of affordable accommodations. The bright pink walls and crystal wall sconces of the small lobby are an indication of the overall use of cheery colors, which can make you forget you'll be sleeping in cheap digs. The stairwell, surrounded by cream and yellow tiled mosaic designs, leads to small rooms, which are all painted in different pastel colors and furnished with simple beds and dressers. The large rooftop balcony features a great view of the Taj Mahal at sunset, although the room windows don't. **Pros:** friendly staff, very affordable. **Cons:** showers are Indian-style, with no curtain or divider to hold water in. ✉ *Opposite Priya Restaurant near Big Bazaar, Fatehabad Rd., 282001* ☎ *562/223–1350* 🌐 *www.priyagroupofhotels.com* *18 rooms* *In-hotel: restaurant, room service, no elevator, laundry service.* *No credit cards.*

SHOPPING

Tourist shops are generally open daily 10 until 7:30. Many Agra shops sell hand-knotted dhurries and other carpets, jewelry made from precious and semiprecious stones, brass statues, and marble inlays that continue the form and motifs seen in the city's great monuments. Resist drivers and touts who want to take you to places offering special "bargains"; they receive big commissions from shopkeepers, which you pay in the inflated price of the merchandise. Beware, too, of soapstone masquerading as marble: this softer, cheaper stone is a convincing substitute, but you can test it by scraping the item with your fingernail—Indian marble won't scrape. Finally, for what it's worth, local lore has it that miniature replicas of the Taj Mahal bring bad luck.

3

Cottage Industry (✉ *18 Munro Rd.* ☎ *562/222–6019*) sells good dhurries and other carpets. **Cottage Industries Exposition** (✉ *39 Fatehabad Rd.* ☎ *562/222–6813*) carries a good selection of high-quality rugs (mostly Kashmiri), silks, gemstones, and, like everyplace else in Agra, marble inlay. Prices are high. **Ganeshi Lall and Son** (✉ *ITC Mughal, Fatehabad Rd.* ☎ *562/233–0181* ✉ *13 Mahatma Gandhi Rd.* ☎ *562/246–4567*), a reliable, family-owned jeweler since 1845, specializes in older pieces and also creates new ones; the Mahatma Gandhi Road location, adjacent to the owner's home and open only by appointment, is a museum-like gallery of very fine old textiles, paintings, wood carvings, and some jewelry. Past clients have included major museums and Jacqueline Kennedy Onassis. **Kohinoor** (✉ *41 Mahatma Gandhi Rd.* ☎ *562/236–4156 or 562/236–8855*) has been designing jewelry using cut and uncut emeralds and other precious stones since 1862; a special connoisseur's room is open by appointment. Don't miss the little museum of fantastic 3-D *zardoji* (embroidered paintings). Some paintings, known as Shams, have been encrusted with gems by the master of the technique, Shamsuddin (some are for sale). **Oswal Exports** (✉ *30-B Munro Rd.* ☎ *562/222–5710 or 562/222–5712*) has excellent examples of inlaid white, pink, green, and black marble; you can watch as the artisans do their work and learn the technique. **Sanjay Cottage Industry** (✉ *1A Jasoria Enclave, Fatehabad Rd.* ☎ *562/309–0828 or 562/233–4209*), near the Taj-View hotel, is the larger showroom of Cottage Industry, with workmen at looms demonstrating weaving techniques. It has a great collection of tribal, Moghul-design, Kashmiri silk, and Agra rugs. **Subhash Emporium** (✉ *18/1 Gwalior Rd.* ☎ *562/222–5828 to 30*) was the first store to revive Agra marble work in the 1960s; today you'll find perhaps the finest, best-priced examples of it here. Ask to see some of the incredible pieces in the private gallery to give you a better perspective on quality.

FATEHPUR SIKRI

★ *37 km (23 mi) southwest of Agra.*

In 1569, so the story goes, the mystic Salim Chisti blessed the Moghul emperor Akbar with a much-wanted male heir. Two years later, Akbar began building a new capital in Chisti's village of Sikri, later renaming it Fatehpur Sikri (City of Victory) after a great triumph in Gujarat. Standing on a rocky ridge overlooking the village, Fatehpur Sikri, in the state of Uttar Pradesh, originally had a circumference of about 11 km (7 mi). Massive walls enclosed three sides, and a lake (now dried up) protected the fourth. When the British came to Fatehpur Sikri in 1583 to meet Akbar, they were amazed to see a city that exceeded contemporary London in both population and grandeur—with more rubies, diamonds, and silks than they could count. What remains is a beautiful cluster of royal dwellings on the top of the ridge, landscaped with lawns and flowering borders. The remarkably preserved buildings, mostly of local red sandstone, elegantly blend architectural styles from Persia as well as Akbar's various Indian holdings, a reflection of the synthesizing impulse that characterized the third and greatest of the Moghul emperors. Akbar ruled here for only 14 years before moving his capital—perhaps in pursuit of water, but more likely for political reasons—to Lahore and then eventually back to Agra. Because it was abandoned and never resettled, the city was not modified by later rulers and thus is the best reflection of Akbar's aesthetic and design philosophies. Fatehpur Sikri now stands as an intriguing ghost town, reflecting a high point in India's cultural history.

> **THE MARBLE MECCA**
>
> It's believed the Taj Mahal's marble may have come from the mines of Makrana, a small Rajasthani village 250 miles to the east that's renowned for its marble supply. The artisans creating marble inlay in Agra today are likely using Makrana marble, and they're believed to be descendants of those who mined the marble or did the inlay work on the Taj.

The usual starting point for exploring is the **Buland Darwaza** (Great Gate, built to celebrate the Gujarat victory) at the city's southwestern end. Unfortunately, the hawkers and guides who crowd the parking lot can be unrelenting. If you arrive by car, you can avoid this minor annoyance by asking to be dropped at the subsidiary entrance at the northeastern end of the city, where the following tour begins. Coming from Agra, bear right just after passing through Agra Gate, the main one in Akbar's day.

Approaching the complex, you'll walk through the **Naubat Khana,** a gate that was manned by drummers and musicians during imperial processions. Just ahead on the right is the **Mint,** a workshop that may have minted coins. Across the road is the **Archaeological Survey of India (ASI) Museum** (☎ *562/228–2248* *Free* *Sat.–Thurs. 9–6*), in the reconstructed old Treasury building. One section has dioramas replicating the area's painting-decorated prehistoric rock shelters. Another section is devoted to 11th-century Jain sculptures that were excavated nearby. The third section is devoted to the history of Akbar, with exhibits on

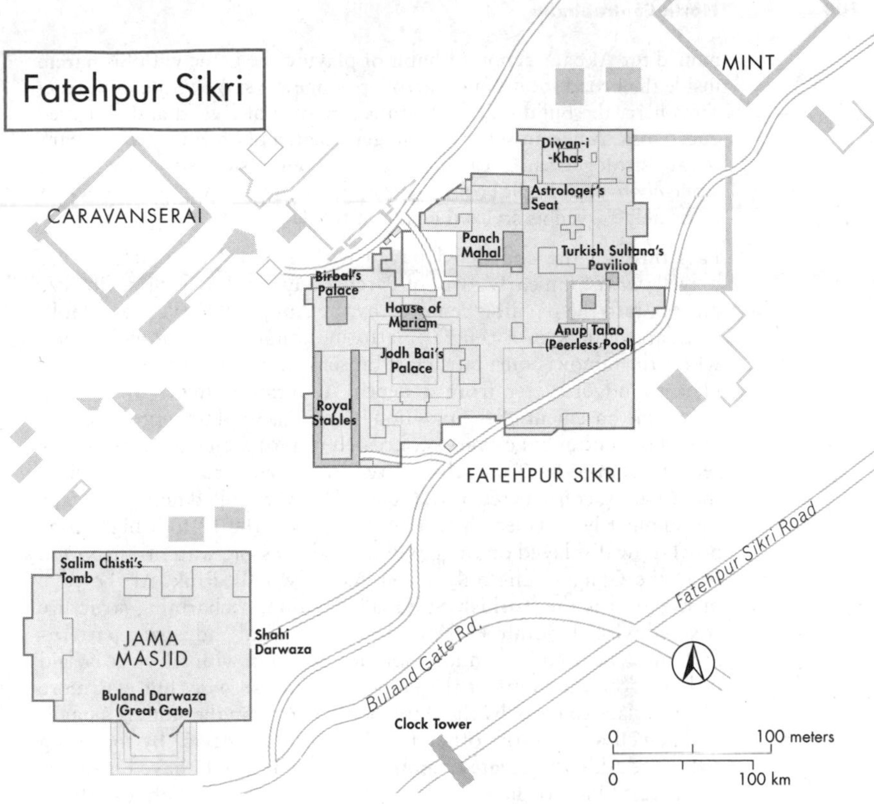

the material culture of his time, such as coins, miniature paintings, tiles, and costumes, as well as near life-size models of Akbar and his ministers—the Nine Jewels. A few steps from the museum is the **Diwan-i-Am** (Hall of Public Audience), a large courtyard 366 feet long and 181 feet wide, with colonnades on three sides. Ahead is the balcony where the emperor sat on his throne to meet subjects or observe celebrations and other spectacles. Through chiseled marble screens, the women of the court would watch discreetly as Akbar, the empire's chief justice, handed down his decisions: those condemned to die were reportedly impaled, hanged, or trampled under the feet of an elephant. What looks like a square two-story building with domed cupolas at each corner is the **Diwan-i-Khas** (Hall of Private Audience). Inside it's actually one tall room where Akbar sat on an elaborate elevated platform and, it's thought, conducted meetings with his ministers. Supported by a stone column topped with a giant lotus flower intricately carved in stone, it's connected by causeways to four balconies with window seats on which the ministers sat. The throne's position is thought to have symbolized the center of the world or, alternatively, the one god sought by several major religions; it also may have shielded the emperor from would-be assassins. Across from the hall is the **Ankh Michauli** (Hide and Seek), named for Akbar's reported habit of playing the game with his harem inside the broad rooms and narrow passageways. As with many structures here, the building's function is a matter of legend and educated guesswork. Adjacent is the **Astrologer's Seat,** a platform where Akbar's royal astrologer sat. Surrounding it is a whimsical structure whose stone *chattri* (umbrella) roof is supported by pillars joined by brackets intricately carved as stylized elephant trunks.

Pass through the courtyard paved with a board on which Akbar played *pachisi* (an early form of Parcheesi using slave girls as life-size pieces), into the pavilion centered by the **Anup Talao** (Peerless Pool), a square pool with a central platform, connected by four bridges, where the famous court musician Tansen would sing for the emperor. (The sound of water from a nearby fountain softened the echo.) Below the basement of the pavilion is an excavated underground palace whose entrances cleverly concealed it until archaeologists, led by reports from Akbar's day, discovered it. The emperor would come to these rooms, constructed at the center of a water-filled tank, to escape the summer heat. Unearthed within them was the 12-foot-high stone bowl (now displayed on the pavilion) used to store water transported from the Ganges—the only water Akbar would drink. At the edge of the pool is the **Turkish Sultana's Pavilion,** a charming structure covered with elaborate Persian carvings in floral and zigzag patterns and once enclosed by sandalwood doors plated with silver. It is said to have been the home of the emperor's Turkish wife, but was more likely a place to relax by the pool. Separated from the sultana's pavilion as well as from the official buildings of the palace by the Anup Talao are **Akbar's private chambers,** where he would have his favorites read to him, or he would converse with courtiers, philosophers, and close advisers.

The Imperial Harem, where the women of Akbar's household resided, consists of several buildings connected by covered passages and screened from view of the more public areas. The **Panch Mahal** is a breeze-catching structure with five arcaded stories (*panch* in Hindi), each smaller than the one below. Its 176 columns are carved with tiny flowers or other motifs (no two of the first floor's 56 columns have the same design). Fatehpur Sikri's tallest building, it affords grand views of the city and the surrounding landscape from its upper stories. When the women wished to pray, they did so behind the screened arches of the **Nagina Mosque,** behind the Panch Mahal across a small garden. The largest residence in the complex is the Gujarati-influenced **Jodh Bai's Palace,** more properly called Principal Haram Sara, says the Archaeological Survey, because behind its eunuch-guarded entrance lived a number of the emperor's wives rather than just that of his Hindu wife Jodh Bai. The **Hawa Mahal** (Palace of the Winds) is a cool vantage point from which women could peek out at the court unseen from beautifully carved stone screens. The **House of Maryam** (on a diagonal between Jodh Bai's Palace and the Panch Mahal), the home of either Akbar's Christian wife or, more likely,

> **NEED A BOY?**
>
> Many people believed that Salim Chisti, the famous Muslim saint, could perform miracles. Women of all faiths still come to his tomb to cover it with cloth and tie a string on the marble latticework in hopes of giving birth to a son.

3

his mother, is said to suggest the wooden architecture of the Punjab at that time. Look for the faded paintings of horses and elephants on the exterior walls. Some of the brackets supporting the eaves are carved with scenes from mythology. **Birbal's Palace,** which sits a few yards northwest of Jodh Bai's Palace and the Hawa Mahal, was named for the emperor's playfully irreverent Hindu prime minister. Because it's unlikely that he would have lived inside the harem, the ASI ascribes it to Akbar's two senior wives. The palace's ornamentation makes use of both Hindu and Islamic motifs.

The big open colonnade behind the harem is known as the **Royal Stables** because the stalls were once thought to have housed elephants and horses; however, according to ASI it is more likely that it was the quarters of the serving women, and that the open stalls were enclosed by curtains tied to the stone rings once thought to have tethered the animals. Follow the path down to the east gate of the **Jama Masjid** (Imperial Mosque); built around 1571 and designed to hold 10,000 worshipers, it's still in active use. Note the deliberate incorporation of Hindu elements in the design, especially the pillar decorations.

In the courtyard of the Jama Masjid (opposite the Buland Darwaza) lies **Salim Chisti's tomb,** surrounded by walls of marble lace, each with a different design. Begun upon the saint's death in 1571 and finished nine years later, the tomb was originally faced with red sandstone but was refinished in marble by Jahangir, the heir Akbar's wife conceived after the saint's blessing. From here you can cross the courtyard and exit through the imposing Buland Darwaza. With its beveled walls and inset archways, the southern gate rises 134 feet over a base of steps that raise it another 34 feet, dwarfing everything else in sight. Akbar built it after conquering Gujarat, and it set the style for later gateways, which the Moghuls built habitually as symbols of their power. Directly ahead is the parking lot, where you can prearrange to have your driver meet you.

To reach Fatehpur Sikri from Agra, hire a car and driver or join a tour. Plan to spend two or three hours wandering the grounds. *Rs. 260* *Daily sunrise–sunset.*

NEED A BREAK?

The simple Indian restaurant at the Gulistan Tourist Complex (*561/3288–2490*), just down the road (toward Agra) from Fatehpur Sikri, is a convenient lunch stop.

GWALIOR

120 km (75 mi) south of Agra.

Now a busy commercial city in Madhya Pradesh, Gwalior traces its history back to a legend: the hermit saint Gwalipa cured a chieftain named Suraj Sen of leprosy. On the hermit's advice, Suraj Sen founded his city here and named it for his benefactor. The city changed hands numerous times, and each dynasty left its mark. Gwalior was also the home of the classical singer Tansen, one of the Nine Jewels (ministers) of Akbar's court, whom many regard as the founder of North Indian classical music. The annual Tansen Music Festival, held here in late November or early December, is one of the best in India.

The huge **Gwalior Fort** sits on a high, rocky plateau, and its 2-mi-long, 35-foot-high wall dominates the skyline. (Take a taxi up and have the driver wait for you—auto-rickshaws can't make it up the steep hill.) The first Moghul emperor, Babur, admired the structure, which may explain why it's the only pre-Moghul Hindu–palace complex to survive in this region. The fort was often captured and achieved its greatest glory under the Tomar rulers in the 15th century. At **Man Mandir,** or Mansingh Palace, bands of gilded and enameled blue, green, and yellow mosaic tiles wrap the vast structure, giving a glimpse of its former splendor. Bring a flashlight to explore the underground dungeons where the Moghuls kept their prisoners after finally capturing the fort in Akbar's time in the late 16th century. Don't miss the beautifully carved 11th-century **Sas-Bahu** or the 9th-century **Teli ka Mandir** temple. The state museum in the **Gujari Mahal,** at the base of the fort, displays an excellent collection of sculptures and archaeological treasures dating as far back as the 2nd century BC. Ask to see the statue of the goddess Shalbhanjika, an exquisite miniature kept in the curator's custody. ✉ *Gwalior Rd.* ☎ *751/248–0011* 🎫 *Fort Rs. 100, museum Rs. 2, sound-and-light show Rs. 250* ⏲ *Fort: daily sunrise–sunset; museum: Sat.–Thurs. 10–5; sound-and-light show: Oct.–Feb., daily 7 PM, Mar.–Sept., daily 8:30 PM.*

An opulent structure with Tuscan and Corinthian architecture, the **Jai Vilas Palace** belonged to the Scindias, Gwalior's rulers up through Indian Independence (the current titular maharaja now has a palace adjacent to this one). Lots of photographs throughout depict the maharajas' past glories, including many of shooting parties where Brits and Indian royals stand over tigers they shot. At this writing, Jai Vilas is going through a much-needed renovation, with no end date yet announced. There's a gallery of miniature paintings, a few tatty royal costumes, furniture galleries, an arms room, a pretty marble courtyard centered by an unusual marble-and-cut-glass fountain, and a large pull-no-punches sculpture of Leda and the swan. Enormous chandeliers hang from the coffered and gilded ceiling of the massive **Durbar Hall** (look for the photo with Bill Clinton). In a case in the dining room below is a crystal train that carried liqueurs along the maharaja's banquet table. ✉ *Jayandra Gang* ☎ *751/232–1101* 🎫 *Rs. 175* ⏲ *Thurs.–Tues. 10–6.*

Sarod Ghar is an elegantly designed museum with a collection of musical instruments and photographs from the family of the late Amjad Ali

Khan (d. 1979), the greatest sarod player of his day. Cases are arranged in rooms off the leafy interior courtyard of a pretty house. ✉*Jiwaji Ganj, Ustad Hafiz Ali Khan Marg, Lashkar* ☎*751/242–5607* *Free* ⏲*Tues.–Sun. 10–4.*

WHERE TO STAY

$$$ Fodor'sChoice ★ **Usha Kiran Palace.** Since it was built just down the drive from the Jai Vilas, this white palace trimmed with filigree sandstone has served as a royal guest house, a royal residence, and the grandest hotel in town. In 2003 the Taj group took it over and closed it for a total, much-needed renovation. Now the property is truly stunning, easily one of the best of the Taj group. An illuminated fountain and dual-staircases lead to a light, airy lobby swathed in baby-blue and silver paints. No two rooms are alike, but each has luxurious jewel-toned bedding, jewel-toned floors with marble inlay, and bathrooms intricately detailed with mosaics made of glassy blue and peach tiles. A beautiful art-deco bar and a spa with signature treatments might make you ask yourself why you even need to leave the hotel. **Pros:** all the luxury of a Taj hotel without the big city price. **Cons:** small corridors throughout the property make it difficult to find your way. ✉*Jayandraganj, Lashkar, 474009* ☎*751/244–4000* *www.tajhotels.com* *40 rooms, 6 suites* *In-room: refrigerator, Wi-Fi. In-hotel: restaurant, room service, bar, pool, gym, spa, laundry service, public Wi-Fi, public Internet.* *AE, DC, MC, V.*

$ **Central Park.** Despite its name, this hotel is not on a park but on a busy road. It is central, however—about 2 km (1.2 mi) from both the railway station and Jai Vilas. Everything here is modern and comfortable. Hallways and stairways are long sweeps of marble with cheerful art on the walls. A concierge on each floor, a big bright gym with lots of equipment, evening barbecue by the pool bar, and a bake shop make this a nice place to stay. **Pros:** gimmick-free hotel for a good price. **Cons:** largely a business hotel, it may seem uninspired to the romantically inclined traveler. ✉*2-A City Centre, Side No. 1, 474009* ☎*751/223–2440* *www.thecentralpark.net* *72 rooms, 6 suites* *In-room: refrigerator, dial-up. In-hotel: restaurant, room service, bar, pool, gym, laundry service, concierge, public Internet.* *AE, MC, V.*

$ **Tansen Residency.** You'll get a preview of the famous temples in Khajuraho walking into this government-run hotel, as several columns in the lobby are carved in the Khajuraho style. When they remodeled it in 2006, Madhya Pradesh State Tourism made significant upgrades and added distinctive details that include bright floral paintings along the whitewashed open-air halls. They also installed air-conditioning and a refrigerator in every room, and replaced carpet with shiny white-tile floors. A price increase price reflects these changes, and the hotel is no longer an ultra-cheap option, but it's still very affordable, with basic room amenities. **Pros:** state tourism office on-site with government officials who can accurately answer questions. **Cons:** open-air halls give a slight cheap-motel feel. ✉*6-A Gandhi Rd., 474009* ☎*751/234–0370* *www.mptourism.com* *24 rooms, 12 suites* *In-room: refrigerator. In-hotel: restaurant, room service, bar, no elevator, laundry service, public Internet, some pets allowed.* *AE, MC, V.*

ORCHHA

119 km (74 mi) southeast of Gwalior, 16 km (10 mi) east of Jhansi, 170 km (105 mi) northwest of Khajuraho.

In the 16th and 17th centuries the Hindu Bundela rulers, allies of the Moghuls, built up Orchha as a provincial capital on the banks of the winding Betwa River. They were great patrons of the arts, and the palace became a magnet for artists and craftsmen who left their mark on it in the form of beautiful stonework and murals. Orchha also attracted poets, including the Hindi poet Keshav Das. In 1783 the Bundela capital was moved from this isolated location, and today Orchha is little more than a sleepy village crowded with palaces, temples, and *chattras,* or funerary monuments of the Hindu rulers. The structure resemble Muslim tombs but contain no remains—the rulers were cremated on the riverbanks.

Orchha, in the state of Madhya Pradesh, is a great place to explore in peace, without the crowds you'll find at other sites. Orchha's isolation proved useful to nationalist leader Chandrashekhar Azad, who hid from the British here in the 1920s, and even today you may feel you've entered a sort of benignly protected corner of the world. Take a flashlight so you can explore the rooms and passageways that were constructed under the town's buildings as escapes from the hot summer. Most of the sites are accessible around the clock, but some are open only daily from 10 to 5. Unless otherwise indicated, all sites are free.

Fifteen sandstone **chattras** (also known as "cenotaphs"), built in honor of the former rulers, sit serenely on the bank of the rock-strewn Betwa River—an especially fine place to catch the sunset. The arches of these chattras and their placement in a garden setting evoke Islamic architecture; the spires, or *shikharas,* recall North Indian Hindu temples. ⊠*5-min walk south of the Ram Raja Temple.*

The four-story, many-arched **Chaturbhuj Temple,** next to the Ram Raja Temple on a rise facing the Raja Mahal, towers over Orchha. It was built in the 16th century to house an image of the Hindu god Rama that would be brought back from Ayodhya, capital of Rama's mythic kingdom, by Kunwari, wife of Madhukar Shah (1554–92), the third and greatest of Orchha's kings. According to local lore, however, the temple was incomplete when she returned, so she installed the icon in her own nearby palace, the Rani Mahal—now the Ram Raja—from which it refused to move. The temple was rededicated to Krishna and Radha. *Free with ticket from fort-palace complex ⏲Daily 9–5.*

★ Perched on a slight rise on a small seasonal island where the river splits as it passes through town, Orchha's **fort-palace** complex is approached by a multiarch granite bridge leading to a broad courtyard with historic buildings on three sides. To your left as you arrive is the 16th-century **Raja Mahal** (Royal Palace), which has beautiful murals in 15 rooms, including the bedrooms of the king's seven wives (find a watchman or a guide to unlock the rooms for you). The paintings, all done with natural pigments on walls prepared with a wash of lime and shell powder, include scenes from Hindu mythology, such as the 10 incarnations of Vishnu and the life of Rama. Adjacent is the **Sheesh Mahal,** built in 1763 as a Raja's country house and today a government-run hotel. Close by is the 17th-century **Jahangir Mahal** palace, which is constructed around a large, fountain-centered courtyard in five terraced stories, and has wide-open views of the countryside and the river below. Built for a visit from the Moghul emperor Jahangir—who married the sister of an Orchha king—the palace elegantly blends Hindu and Moghul themes. At the entrance is a small museum whose collection includes pillars built to commemorate kings' wives who committed *sati* (self-immolation) upon their husbands' death. *Jahangir Mahal Rs. 30; museum free Jahangir Mahal and Raja Mahal, daily sunrise–sunset; Jahangir Mahal museum Tues.–Sun. 10–5.*

★ The **Laxminarayan Temple,** on a hilltop about 1 km (½ mi) west of town, is a 17th-century mix of temple and fort architecture (with renovations from 1793). Vibrant, well-preserved murals on the walls and ceilings depict mythological and historical subjects. The drawings etched in a red wash are from the 19th century. *Rs. 30 Daily 9–5.*

Scattered among agricultural fields on the floodplain below the fort-palace complex are a number of other buildings, including a Turkish bath, stables, and several royal chattras, all within walking distance. Nearest to the complex, at the base of the hill, is the **Rai Praveen Mahal,** a two-story brick palace named for the dancer-poet consort of King Indramani (1672–76); her praises were sung in many of Keshav Das's poems. On the upper floor are paintings of *nayikas* (mortal women) and a warrior on horseback. The underground rooms, where the lovers took refuge from the hot summer sun, can be explored. A short walk leads to the **Panchmukhi Mahadeva** (Shiva with Five Faces Temple), a group of three temples accompanied by three cenotaphs.

Facing the bridge to the fort-palace complex is the **Ram Raja Temple,** a large low-rise palace building fronted by a tidy, pleasant plaza that is the center of community life as well as the center of town. It is especially vibrant in the early evening, when the sellers of snacks and religious items in the illuminated plaza peddle their wares to the locals who've come to worship and the few tourists who've discovered there's nothing else to do in town. In late November, a reenactment of Rama's marriage, complete with elephants and big crowds, takes place here. *Free Daily 8–12:30 and 7–9:30.*

WHERE TO STAY

$ ★ **Amar Mahal.** One of Orchha's most beautiful hotels is just up the hill from the river and the cenotaphs, and there are some good views of the water and monuments. Built in the style of the Bundela monuments, with rooms off a colonnade that surrounds a bright, green garden courtyard, the hotel has floral-painted arches echoing those in the palaces. Most striking about the marble-floor guest rooms are the elaborately carved Rajasthani beds and the hand-painted walls, again in the Rajasthani style, making it a treat to go to sleep. The restaurant, with a coffered ceiling painted with enamel and gilt flowers, is just as beautiful. **Pros:** the perfect hotel for lounging while admiring its many facets of Indian architecture and design. **Cons:** a bit of a walk up hill from the center of this small village. ✉*District Tikamgarh, 472246* ☎*768/025–2102* 🌐*www.amarmahal.com* *31 rooms, 3 suites* *In-room: refrigerator. In-hotel: restaurant, room service, pool, gym, no elevator, laundry service, public Internet.* *AE, MC, V.*

$ **Orchha Resort.** Tired of sleeping on the traditional, rock-like Indian mattress? The mattresses at this fine resort arguably are the softest in the country, though management probably wouldn't consider them first on its list of defining characteristics; that honor probably would be reserved for the hand-carved marble-inlay beds provided by Oswal, noted Agra inlay maker and owner of the Orchha Resort. These special touches may make you feel like you're a guest at the Taj Mahal. On the riverbank, literally butting up against one of the cenotaphs, the rest of the resort is pointedly Indian, from the lobby's brightly colored wall panels of scenes from Hindu epics to the other marble inlay in floors and tables. The ex-Taj general manager is constantly adding polish, from a beautiful lotus-shaped pool to stylish bathroom accessories you'd expect at an expensive city hotel. **Pros:** modern, air-conditioned tents available from October to March provide a half-price alternative to the marble-heavy rooms. **Cons:** halls are long and dark, making it difficult to navigate. ✉*Kanchana Ghat, Tikamgarh District, 472246* ☎*768/025–2222* 🌐*www.orchharesort.com* *34 rooms, 11 tents* *In-room: refrigerator. In-hotel: restaurant, room service, tennis court, pool, gym, laundry service, public Internet, no-smoking rooms.* *AE, MC, V.*

¢ **Betwa Cottages.** These cute cottages for two, each on its own lawn near the river and the cenotaphs, have simple wood furnishings with small paintings, plus phones and TVs. Cottage No. 5, on slightly higher ground, has a view of the well-maintained gardens and a bit of the river. For Rs. 4,990 you can rent the heritage suite, which is like your own little house, with a gorgeous, high-domed ceiling over the four–poster bed that's draped in red silks and surrounded by bright Tiffany-style lamps. The establishment's lobby, decked out with large Hindu murals in muted tones, leads to a dining hall surrounded by window walls—it's a sun-infused spot to take in the delicious Indian meals or stop for a snack while visiting the cenotaphs. **Pros:** quiet and very private. **Cons:** a bit buggy, with lots of little lizards running around. ✉*Tikamgarh District, 472246* ☎*768/025–2618* 🌐*www.mptourism.com* *10 cottages, 1 suite* *In-hotel: restaurant, room service, laundry service, public Internet, some pets allowed.* *MC, V.*

¢ ★ **Sheesh Mahal.** The rough facade of this royal guesthouse built in 1763 might literally make you feel like you're stepping back in time. Part of the fort-palace complex, the government-run Sheesh Mahal can't be beat for the historical location and pure novelty of staying in its rooms, many of which have full views of every monument in town. After climbing one of the open-air staircases made of the original stone, you can take ones of the small, romantic rooms with hidden entryways, white-washed walls and plush beds, making it easy to imagine being cloistered in the presence of royalty. Or try the more expensive suites, starting at around Rs. 4,000, which still have the original, unbelievably huge marble-slab bathtubs. Candlelit dinners are served on the roof as musicians entertain—another reason this hotel definitely becomes something worth writing home about. **Pros:** great historical significance and an expert staff. **Cons:** access is difficult for anyone with mobility problems. ✉ *Tikamgarh District, Orchha, 472246* ☎ *768/025–2319* 🌐 *www.mptourism.com* *8 rooms* *In-room: refrigerator (some). In-hotel: restaurant, room service, no elevator, laundry service, public Internet.* 💳 *AE, MC, V.*

SHOPPING

Taragram (✉ *1077 Civil Lines, Jhansi* ☎ *768/025–2866*), 8 km (5 mi) outside Orchha, is an innovative development program that focuses on the revival of traditional papermaking methods. A little shop sells handmade notebooks and other items; walk around back and you can observe the papermaking process in its various stages The small local **market** has less hard-sell pressure than more touristy areas and sells an abundance of inexpensive mixed-metal objects, from votive *diyas* (prayer lamps) to *kum-kum* boxes with tiny compartments to separate colored powders. For inexpensive, beautifully crafted plaster sculptures of Hindu and Jain gods, stop at the small, nameless **shop** just inside the entrance gate to the Raja Mahal.

KHAJURAHO

This small Madhya Pradesh village, with the Vidhya hills as a backdrop, is very rural, and being 395 km (245 mi) southeast of Agra, it seems far removed from any substantial economic activity. Yet Khajuraho was the religious capital of the Chandelas, one of the most powerful Rajput dynasties of Central India, from the 10th- to 12th-century. They built 85 temples here, 25 of which remain to give a glimpse of a time when Hindu art and devotion reached its apex. When the dynasty eventually succumbed to invaders, Khajuraho's temples lapsed into obscurity until their rediscovery by the British explorer Captain T.S. Burt in 1838.

During the Chandelas' rule, the temples' royal patrons were rich, the land was fertile, and everyone lived the good life, trooping off to hunts, feasts, and theater, music, and dance performances. This abundance was the perfect climate for creativity, and temple-building emerged as the major form of expression. There were no strict boundaries between the sacred and the profane, no dictates on acceptable deities: Shiva, Vishnu, Brahma, and the Jain saints were all lavishly honored here. Excavations have also uncovered a complex of Buddhist temples. Despite the interest in heaven, the real focus was Earth, particularly the facts of human life. Here, immortalized in stone, virile men and voluptuous women cavort and copulate in the most intimate, erotic, and sometimes bewildering postures. Khajuraho represents the best of Hindu temple sculpture: sinuous, twisting forms, human and divine, pulsing with life, tension, and conflict.

The temples—designated a World Heritage Site—have more to offer than erotic sculpture. Their soaring *shikharas* (spires) are meant to resemble the peaks of the Himalayas, the abode of Lord Shiva: starting with the smallest, over the entrance, each spire rises higher than the one before it, as in a range of mountains that seems to draw near the heavens. Designed to inspire the viewer toward the highest human potential, these were also the builders' attempts to reach upward, out of the material world, to *moksha,* the final release from the cycle of rebirth. One scholar has suggested that Khajuraho's temples were in effect chariots of the kings, carrying them off to a heavenly world resembling an idealized view of courtly life. Their combination of lofty structure and delicate sculpture gives them a unique sense of completeness and exuberance.

Of the extant temples, all but two were made from sandstone mined from the banks of the River Ken, 30 km (19 mi) away. The stone blocks were carved separately, then assembled as interlocking pieces. Though each temple is different, all observe precise architectural principles of shape, form, and orientation and contain certain essential elements: a high raised platform, an *ardh mandapam* (entrance porch), a *mandapam* (portico), an *antrala* (vestibule), and a *garbha griha* (inner sanctum). Some of the larger temples also have a walkway around the inner sanctum, a *mahamandapam* (hall), and subsidiary shrines at each corner of the platform, making a complete *panchayatana* (five-shrine complex).

A number of sculptural motifs run through the temples. Certain gods, for instance, have directional positions: elephant-headed Ganesh faces north; Yama, the god of death, and his mount, a male buffalo, face south. Other sculptures include the *apsaras* (heavenly maidens), found mainly inside, and the Atlas-like *kichakas,* who support the ceilings on their shoulders. Many sculptures reflect everyday activities, such as a dance class, and there are sultry *nayikas* (mortal women) and plenty of *mithunas* (amorous couples). The scorpion appears as an intriguing theme, running up and down the thighs of many female sculptures as a kind of erotic thermometer.

No one knows why erotic sculptures are so important here, though many explanations have been suggested. The female form is often used as an auspicious marker on Hindu gateways and doors, in the form of temple sculptures as well as domestic wall paintings. In the late classical and early medieval periods, this symbol expanded into full-blown erotic art in many places, including the roughly contemporary sun temple at Modhera, in Gujarat, and the slightly later one at Konark, in Orissa. Khajuraho legend has it that the founder of the Chandela dynasty, Chandravarman, was born of an illicit union between his mother and the moon god, which resulted in her ostracism. When he grew up to become a mighty king, his mother begged him to show the world the beauty and divinity of lovemaking. A common folk explanation is that the erotic sculptures protect the temples from lightning; and art historians have pointed out that many of the erotic panels are placed at junctures where some protection or strengthening agent might be structurally necessary. Others say the sculptures reflect the influence of a Tantric cult that believed in reversals of ordinary morality as a religious practice. Still others argue that sex has been used as a metaphor: the carnal and bestial sex generally shown near the bases of the temples represent uncontrolled human appetites, whereas the couples deeply engrossed in each other, oblivious to all else, represent a divine bliss, the closest humans can approach to God. The mystery lives on, but it's clear that the sculptors drew on a sophisticated and sensual worldly heritage, including the *Kama Sutra*. Some of the far-out positions recommended in that classical Hindu love manual are in fact illustrated here.

Khajuraho holds an annual, weeklong **dance festival,** set in part against the backdrop of the temples. If you'll be in India in late February or early March, try to catch this superb event, which attracts some of the country's best performers. Contact the head office of **Madhya Pradesh Tourism** (*755/255–3006 www.mptourism.com*).

From August through mid-April, for Rs. 350 you can see folk dances from all over India performed nightly at 7 and 8:30 PM at **Kandariya** (*Bamitha Rd. near Jhankar hotel*), a theater attached to the shop **Shilpgram.**

For Rs. 50 you can **rent a bicycle** for the day from one of the many stands near the town center; it's a great way to get around this relatively traffic-free town and to explore the small streets of Khajuraho village, the old residential area near the Eastern Group of temples that teems with shops, animals, and children. Entrepreneurial boys will gladly guide you around for Rs. 50.

The popular 50-minute **sound-and-light show,** which runs in Hindi and English every evening (except during the summer monsoon season) at the Western Group of temples, traces the story of the Chandela kings and the temples from the 10th century to the present. Showtime varies based on sunset, so confirm it with your hotel or the tourist office. *Rs. 300 English-language show: Oct.–Mar. 6:30; Apr.–June and Sept. 7:30.*

WESTERN GROUP OF TEMPLES

Numbers in the text correspond to numbers in the margin and on the Khajuraho map.

Most of the Western Group temples are inside a formal enclosure whose entrance is on Main Road, opposite the State Bank of India. Although the rest of the town's temples are always accessible and free, these are open daily from sunrise to sunset and have an admission charge of Rs. 250.

The first three temples, though considered part of the Western Group, are at a slight distance from the enclosure.

11 The **Chausath Yogini Temple,** on a granite outcrop southwest of the Shivsagar Tank, a small artificial lake, is the oldest temple at Khajuraho, possibly built as early as AD 820. It's dedicated to Kali (a form of

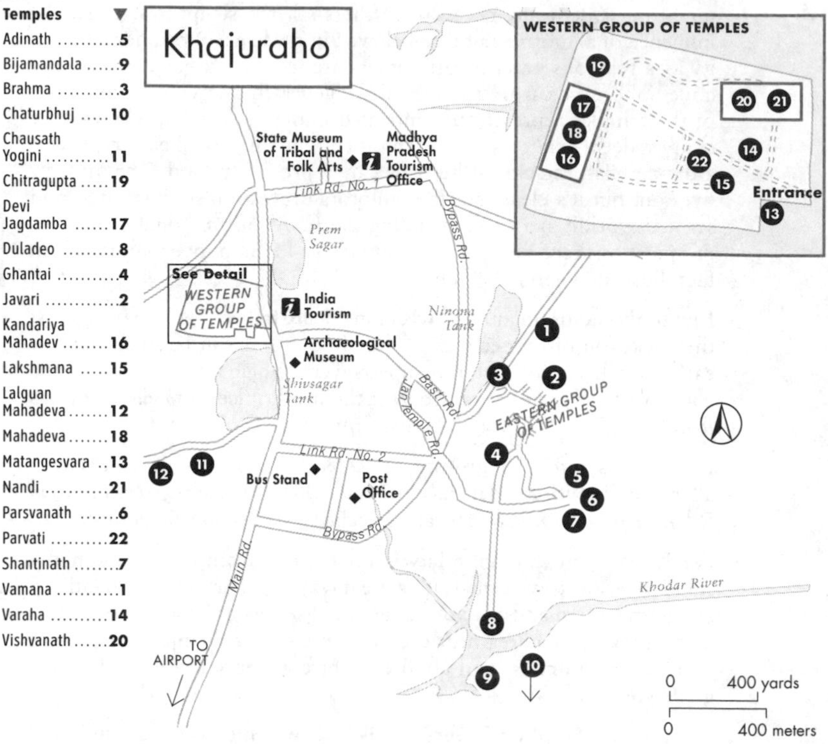

the Goddess Durga, Slayer of Demons), and its name refers to the 64 (*chausath*) female ascetics who serve this fierce goddess in the Hindu pantheon. Unlike its counterparts of pale, warm-hue sandstone, this temple is made of granite.

12 **Lalguan Mahadeva**—600 meters west of Chausath Yogini—lies in ruins and the original portico is missing. This Shiva temple is historically significant because it was built of both granite and sandstone, marking the transition from Chausath Yogini to the later temples.

13 Just outside the boundary of the Western Group (there's a separate gate to the left of the entrance) stands the **Matangesvara Temple,** the only one still in use here; worship takes place in the morning and afternoon. The lack of ornamentation, the square construction, and the simple floor plan date this temple to the early 10th century. It has large bay windows, a projecting portico, and a ceiling of overlapping concentric circles. An enormous lingam (a phallic symbol associated with Shiva), nearly 8½ feet tall, is enshrined in the sanctum.

The **Archaeological Museum,** across the street from Matangesvara Temple, displays exquisite carvings and sculptures that archaeologists have recovered from the temple sites. The three galleries attempt to put the works into context according to the deities they represent. ✉ *Main Rd.* ☎ *768/627–2320* *Rs. 5* ⏲ *Mon.–Sat. 10–5.*

14 Just inside the main entrance gate, to your left, next to a small Laxmi temple, is the **Varaha Temple** (circa 900–925). It's dedicated to Vishnu's Varaha avatar, or Boar Incarnation, which Vishnu assumed in order to rescue the earth after a demon had hidden it in the slush at the bottom of the sea. In the inner sanctum, all of creation is depicted on the massive and beautifully polished sides of a stone boar, which in turn stands on the serpent Shesha. The ceiling is carved with a lotus relief.

15 ★ Across from the Varaha Temple is the **Lakshmana Temple,** dedicated to Vishnu and the only complete temple remaining. Along with Kandariya Mahadeva and Vishvanath, this edifice represents the peak of achievement in North Indian temple architecture. All three temples were built in the early to mid-10th century, face east, and follow an elaborate plan resembling a double cross, with three tiers of exterior sculpture on high platforms. The ceiling of the portico is carved with shell and floral motifs. The support beam over the entrance to the main shrine shows Lakshmi, goddess of wealth and consort of Vishnu, with Brahma, Lord of Creation, on her left and Shiva, Lord of Destruction, on her right. Around the exterior base are some of Khajuraho's most famous sculptures, with gods and goddesses on the protruding corners, erotic couples or groups in the recesses, and apsaras and *sura-sundaris* (apsaras performing everyday activities) in between. Along the sides of the tall platform beneath the temple, carvings depict social life, including battle scenes, festivals, and more X-rated pursuits.

16 Fodor's Choice ★ The **Kandariya Mahadev,** west of the Lakshmana, is the tallest and most evolved temple in Khajuraho in terms of the blending of architecture and sculpture, and one of the finest in India. Probably built around 1025–50, it follows the five-shrine design. Its central spire, which towers 102 feet above the platform, is actually made up of 84 subsidiary towers built up in increments. The feeling of ascent is repeated inside, where each succeeding portico rises a step above the previous one, and the inner sanctum is higher still; dedicated to Shiva, this inner sanctum houses a marble lingam with a 4-foot circumference. Even the figures on this temple are taller and slimmer than those elsewhere. The rich interior carving includes two beautiful *toranas* (arched doorways). Outside, three bands of sculpture around the sanctum and transept bring to life a whole galaxy of Hindu gods and goddesses, mithunas, celestial handmaidens, and lions.

17 The **Devi Jagdamba Temple** was originally dedicated to Vishnu, as indicated by a prominent sculpture over the sanctum's doorway. It now honors Parvati, Shiva's consort, but because her image is black—a color associated with Kali—it's also known as the Kali Temple. From the inside, its three-shrine design makes the temple appear to be shaped like a cross. The third band of sculpture has a series of erotic mithunas. The ceilings are similar to those in the Kandariya Mahadev, and the three-headed, eight-armed statue of Shiva is one of the best cult images in Khajuraho.

18 Sharing the platform with the Kandariya Mahadev and the Devi Jagdamba is the small, mostly ruined **Mahadeva Temple.** Now dedicated to Shiva, it may originally have been a subsidiary temple to the Kandariya, probably dedicated to Shiva's consort. In the portico stands a remarkable statue of a man caressing a mythical horned lion.

19 The **Chitragupta Temple** lies just north of the Devi Jagdamba and resembles it in construction. In honor of the presiding deity, the sun god Surya, the temple faces east, and its cell contains a 5-foot-tall image of Surya complete with the chariot and seven horses that carry him across the sky. Surya also appears above the doorway. In the central niche south of the sanctum is an image of Vishnu with 11 heads; his own face is in the center, and the other heads represent his 10 main incarnations. Sculptural scenes of animal combat, royal processions, masons at work, and joyous dances depict the lavish country life of the Chandelas.

20 Two staircases lead up to **Vishvanath Temple**: the northern flanked by a pair of lions and the southern by a pair of elephants. The Vishvanath probably preceded the Kandariya, but here only two of the original corner shrines remain. On the outer wall of the corridor surrounding the cells is an impressive image of Brahma, the three-headed Lord of Creation, and his consort, Saraswati. On every wall the female form predominates, portraying women's daily 10th-century occupations: writing a letter, holding a baby, applying makeup, or playing music. The nymphs of paradise are voluptuous and provocative, the erotic scenes robust. An inscription states that the temple was built by Chandela King Dhanga in 1002. The temple sits on a terrace to the east of the Chitragupta and Devi Jagdamba temples.

21 The simple **Nandi Temple,** which faces Vishvanath, houses a monolithic statue of Shiva's mount, the massive and richly harnessed bull Nandi.

22 The small and heavily rebuilt **Parvati Temple,** near Vishvanath, was originally dedicated to Vishnu. The present icon is that of the goddess Ganga (a representation of the river Ganges) standing on her mount, the crocodile.

NEED A BREAK?

Exit the gate, and smack across the street from Vishvanath and Nandi temples is Blue Sky (☎ *768/627–4647*), a café on the main road, open for all meals. It has a great view of the entire Western Group from its second-floor and rooftop terraces. The view's the thing, but the food's not bad. You can just stop by for a *lassi* (a yogurt-based drink; they serve five flavors) or tea, or try the breakfast menu of omelets, porridge, and Indian items; at lunch, there are soups and salads, plus Indian, Chinese, Italian, and Japanese choices. At dinner you can watch the sound-and-light show from your table.

★ The **State Museum of Tribal and Folk Arts** has an excellent collection of more than 500 artifacts of terra-cotta, metal, and wood crafts, paintings, jewelry, and masks from all over Madhya Pradesh and the Bastar region (known for tribal crafts) in the neighboring state of Chhattisgarh. ✉ *Chandela Cultural Complex, Rajnagar Rd.* ☎ *768/627–4051* 🎫 *Rs. 50* ⏲ *Tues.–Sun. noon–8.*

EASTERN GROUP OF TEMPLES

Scattered around the edges of the old village of Khajuraho, the Eastern Group of temples includes three Brahma and four Jain temples, whose proximity attests to the religious tolerance of the times in general and the Chandela rulers in particular.

DON'T MISS THE DETAILS

The number of carvings can seem overwhelming, but keep an eye out for work into which the carvers injected their own views of life, often with a sense of humor. In the Western Group there is an elephant turning his head and laughing at the couple having sex beside him. In another carving a man has covered his face in embarrassment, but he's still peeping through his fingers at what's going on nearby. It's well worth hiring a guide, for the Western group at least, who can point out the more quirky aspects.

3

1 Northernmost is the late-11th-century **Vamana Temple,** dedicated to Vishnu's dwarf incarnation (though the image in the sanctum looks more like a tall, sly child). The sanctum walls show unusual theological openness, depicting most of the major gods and goddesses; Vishnu appears in many of his forms, including the Buddha, his ninth incarnation. Outside, two tiers of sculpture are concerned mainly with the nymphs of paradise, who strike charming poses under their private awnings.

2 The small, well-proportioned **Javari Temple,** just south of the Vamana and roughly contemporary, has a simplified three-shrine design. The two main exterior bands of sculpture bear hosts of heavenly maidens.

3 The granite-and-sandstone **Brahma Temple,** one of the earliest here (circa 900), is probably misnamed. Brahma, a titular member of the triad of Hinduism's great gods, along with Shiva and Vishnu, rarely gets a temple to himself. It differs in design from most of the other temples, particularly in the combination of materials and the shape of its spire.

4 All that's left of the **Ghantai Temple** are its pillars, festooned with carvings of pearls and bells. Adorning the entrance are an eight-armed Jain goddess, Chakreshvari, riding the mythical bird Garuda and a relief illustrating the 16 dreams of the mother of Mahavira, the greatest religious figure in Jainism and a counterpart to the Buddha. The temple sits south of the Vamana, Javari, and Brahma temples, toward the Jain complex.

5 The late-11th-century **Adinath Temple,** a minor shrine, is set in a small walled compound southeast of the Ghantai temple. Its porch and the statue of the Tirthankara (literally, Ford-Maker, a figure who leads others to liberation) Adinatha are modern additions. Built at the beginning of the Chandelas' decline, this temple is relatively small, but the spire and base are richly carved.

6 The **Parsvanath Temple,** built in the mid-10th century, is the largest and finest in the Eastern Group's Jain complex and holds some of the best sculpture in Khajuraho, including images of Vishnu. In contrast to the intricate calculations behind the layout of the Western Group, the plan for this temple is a simple rectangle, with a separate spire in

the rear. Statues of flying angels and sloe-eyed beauties occupied with children, cosmetics and flowers adorn the outer walls. The stone also conveys even the texture of the women's thin garments.

7 The early-11th-century **Shantinath Temple** has been remodeled extensively but does contain some old Jain sculpture.

SOUTHERN GROUP OF TEMPLES

8 Though built in the customary five-shrine style, the 12th-century **Duladeo Temple** (about 900 yards south of the Eastern Group's Ghantai) looks flatter and more massive than most Khajuraho shrines. Probably the last temple built in Khajuraho, the Duladeo lacks the usual ambulatory passage and crowning lotus-shaped finials. Here, too, in this temple dedicated to Shiva, eroticism works its way in, though the amorous figures are discreetly placed.

9 As part of continuing explorations, the largest temple yet—4 meters longer than the Kandariya Mahadeva—has been partially unearthed since 1999 between the Duladeo and the Chaturbhuj. At the **Bijamandala Temple,** you can see multiple tiers of beautifully carved moldings and a Shiva lingam placed on a marble pedestal. Archaeologists surmise that the temple, begun in the late 10th or early 11th century, may never have been completed, judging by the remains and unfinished statues found on the site.

10 The small, 12th-century **Chaturbhuj Temple,** nearly 3 km (2 mi) south of Duladeo, has an attractive colonnade entrance and a feeling of verticality thanks to its single spire. It enshrines an impressive four-hand image of Vishnu that may be the single most striking piece of sculpture in Khajuraho. With few exceptions, the temple's exterior sculpture falls short of the local mark (a sign of the declining fortunes of the empire), but this temple is definitely the best place in Khajuraho to watch the sun set.

WHERE TO EAT & STAY

$$$ ✕ **Apsara.** This hotel restaurant is decorated with lattice screens of teak and bird paintings on silk. The Indian and Continental dishes are both good. Try the tandoori kebabs or the *sarsonwala machli tikka* (fish cubes marinated in yogurt, flavored with mustard and cooked in a clay oven). If you're aching for some red meat, you can even get a tenderloin steak here. ⊠*Jass Radisson, Bypass Rd.* ☎*768/627–2344* ▭*AE, DC, MC, V.*

$ ✕ **Mediterraneo.** Eat on the rooftop or in a small dining room at this Italian restaurant near the Western Group. Like most of the restaurants in Khajuraho that aren't connected to a hotel, there are no frills here. The pizzas, one of the many pasta dishes (the carbonara has actual bacon), or standbys like eggplant Parmigiana or lamb cacciatore may just do the trick when you're tired of the Indian-Continental-Chinese menu popular in tourist areas throughout India. At breakfast, you can order crepes and omelets. ✉*Jain Temple Rd., opposite Surya Hotel* ☎*768/627–2246* ▭*No credit cards.*

$$ ★ **Chandela.** Though without the usual sparkle of a Taj Hotel, the Chandela is a fine property with every amenity, and each comfortable room has a balcony or patio facing the pool or the gardens (if you come in summer, request one of the rooms with the extra air conditioner). The junior suites have a small room with a TV so you can watch without disturbing anyone. Worriers will be glad to know that all rooms have sprinklers and smoke detectors, more the exception than the rule in India. A camel and a bullock cart are on standby for rides around the property; there's also a jogging track. **Pros:** warm and friendly service; managers are concerned about safety. **Cons:** restaurant is small, occupying a windowless area behind the lobby. ✉*Airport Rd., Chhatarpur District, 471606* ☎*768/627–2355 and–2364* ⊕*www.tajhotels.com* *89 rooms, 5 suites* *In-room: refrigerator, Wi-Fi. In-hotel: restaurant, room service, bar, tennis court, pool, gym, laundry service, public Internet, public Wi-Fi, some pets allowed, no-smoking rooms.* ▭*AE, DC, MC, V.*

$$ **Ken River Lodge.** Near Panna National Park, about a half hour from Khajuraho, this lodge is well suited for a nature-lover, with basic mud huts and cottages with hot water and private baths, but no phones, TVs, or air-conditioning. You might feel like Robinson Crusoe eating at one of the lodge's restaurants, a platform built in a tree on a bank of the picturesque Ken River, or barbecuing over a campfire. If you plan to see Panna, you may want the Rs. 7,000-per-person-daily package, which includes all home-style Indian meals and two jeep trips into the park with an experienced guide and the lodge's own naturalist. The owner has two other properties in the area: a night-safari camp and a jungle wildlife camp reached by boat. **Pros:** very secluded and quiet, with no tourist traps in sight. **Cons:** a substantial ride from town, making transport expensive, and monkeys regularly (and loudly) run across the roofs. ✉*Near Madla Village, Panna District, 488001* ☎*7686/275–235 at the lodge, 098/1002–4711 for reservations* ⊕*www.kenriverlodge.com* *10 cottages, 10 huts* *In-room: no a/c, no phone, no TV. In-hotel: 2 restaurants, room service, beachfront, laundry service.* ▭*No credit cards* *Closed June–Sept.* *FAP.*

$$ **Radisson Hotel Khajuraho.** For an extra Rs. 40 per night, the Radisson contributes money to a well-known charity called Plan India, which develops programs for poor children across the country. It's refreshing to encounter a hotel that openly encourages philanthropy of its guests. There's still no shortage of amenities here, with a large modern lobby strewn with plush geometric carpets in creams and off-whites. The dark-wood winding staircase leads to room, which have an eclectic array of Indian art, flat screen TVs, and balconies overlooking either the pool or the hills. **Pros:** impeccably kept; feels fresh. **Cons:** feels like a big city hotel, with no intimate charms. ✉*Bypass Rd., 471606* ☎*768/627–2344* ⊕*www.radisson.com/khajurahoin* *90 rooms, 3 suites* *In-room: refrigerator. In-hotel: restaurant, room service, bar, tennis court, pool, gym, no elevator, laundry service, public Internet.* ▭*AE, DC, MC, V.*

$ ★ **Ramada Khajuraho.** At this Ramada, the friendly owner seems enthusiastic about constantly trying to give his hotel the grandest look in town. It's all cool white-marble elegance: chandeliers, curving white staircases, and well-chosen Indian antiques throughout. The rooms (some with king beds) are decorated in soft cream shades and rich fabrics and have large bay windows, some with temple views. Other more spacious rooms have 18-carat gold fittings and carved teak headboards from Rajasthan. At this writing, 20 rooms were under renovation, and plans include adding a ladies-only floor with security guards, cubicle showers, and plasma screen TVs. Thirty suite rooms (to be added by late 2008) will come with large bath tubs and private sauna and steam facilities. There's a poolside puppet show and classical music in the lobby every evening. **Pros:** a lot of bang for your buck compared with others in town, and discounts are possible. **Cons:** despite its grandeur, the ambience is predictable, and you might wonder why you need such luxury in a sleepy Indian village. ✉ *Airport Rd., 471606* ☎ *768/627–2301 to 03* 🌐 *www.ramadahotelkhajuraho.com* *76 rooms, 6 suites* *In-room: refrigerator. In-hotel: restaurant, room service, bar, tennis court, pool, laundry service, public Internet, no-smoking rooms.* *AE, DC, MC, V.*

$ **Usha Bundela.** You'll find the biggest rooms in Khajuraho in this nice hotel with a friendly staff. The large atrium lobby swathed in marble greets you with traditional portraits of Indian royalty, while the rooms with standard furnishings have quirky little details like pink phones in the bathrooms and purple hair dryers. French doors lead to balconies overlooking the gardens, and at this writing, management was planning on replacing all carpeting with wood floors—the second floor of rooms already has this much-needed upgrade. **Pros:** puppet shows are held on the lawn in the evenings, and yoga and meditation classes can be arranged. **Cons:** pool looks very worn and has a green tinge. ✉ *Temple Rd., 471606* ☎ *768/627–2386* 🌐 *www.ushalexushotels.com* *68 rooms, 2 suites* *In-hotel: restaurant, room service, bar, pool, no elevator, laundry service, public Internet.* *AE, DC, MC, V.*

¢ **Jhankar.** The lobby feels a bit like that of a college dorm, complete with plaid furniture and an Internet room in plain sight, but government-run Jhankar does have comfortable accommodations for a reasonable price. Two long hallways on either side lead to the rooms, each with potted flowers outside the doors. Eclectic art decorates the walls; beds have cotton covers in bright oranges and reds. **Pros:** small and easy to navigate, taking you less than a minute to get to your room to relax. **Cons:** some walls are moldy and riddled with chipping paint; staff isn't very friendly. ✉ *Airport Rd., 471606* ☎ *768/627–4063 or 768/627–4194* *19 rooms* *In-hotel: restaurant, room service, bar, laundry service, public Internet.* *MC, V.*

SHOPPING

Numerous shops around the Western Group of temples sell curios, including humorous knockoffs of Khajuraho's erotic sculptures, as well as tribal metalwork. **Kandaryia Shilpgram** (✉ *Bamitha Rd., near Jhankar* *hotel* ☎*768/627–2243* ⏲*Oct.–Feb., daily 11–9*) is a large crafts shop owned by the Agra marble-inlay maker Oswal. It's associated with a government project that hosts craftspeople from all over India for residences during peak travel season; you can watch the artisans at work as you shop. **Tijori** (✉*Ramada Khajuraho, Airport Rd.* ☎*768/627–2302*) is a two-story shop with fine, beautifully displayed crafts, such as new and antique silver and gold jewelry, diamonds from a local mine, silver boxes and vases, enameled silver elephants, sandalwood carvings, small and very large brass statues, Varanasi and Kashmiri carpets, papier-mâché, and silk and paper paintings.

SIDE TRIPS

If you have time, take an extra day to explore and picnic in the beautiful countryside around Khajuraho.

Backed by the distant mountains, **Khajuraho Village**—the old residential part of town near the Eastern Group of temples—is a typical Indian village.

Drive or bike to the **Gharial Sanctuary** on the Ken River, 28 km (17 mi) away; the park was set up to protect the slender-snouted crocodile and has some lovely waterfalls.

October through June, hire a jeep and driver to take you to **Panna National Park,** 31 km (19 mi) from Khajuraho, to see wildlife that includes antelope, deer, and a lot of monkeys; if you're lucky (and arrive very early in the morning or in late afternoon and hire a guide at the park or come with Ken River Lodge), you'll see one of the 35 elusive tigers. Sign on for the elephant safari for Rs. 300. The best viewing season is January through March. (Sightings are said to be better at Bandhavgarh Park, a five-hour, 237-km [147 mi] drive from Khajuraho).

BHOPAL & ENVIRONS

Bhopal, the capital of Madhya Pradesh, blends natural beauty—it's known as the City of Lakes—ancient history, and modern comforts. Fine mosques, palaces, and markets take you back to the city's 18th- and 19th-century roots (little remains of the original 11th-century settlement), yet much of the city is new and modern. With two superb hotels, Bhopal is an ideal base for day trips to places like Sanchi.

BHOPAL

744 km (461 mi) south of Delhi, 383 km (237 mi) southwest of Khajuraho.

Bhopal is best known for the 1984 toxic-gas leak at a Union Carbide chemical plant, which killed an estimated 20,000 people and injured thousands more. Perhaps for this reason, the city has been slow to develop as a tourist destination. It's a pretty city centered by two tree-fringed lakes—as evening approaches, a string of little sunken fountains around the edges of the lakes spout flumes into the air, adding whimsy to the scene while aerating the water. Bhopal is also a nurturing ground for the study, composition, and performance of Urdu poetry; readings draw the kind of crowds you'd expect at a pop concert.

Indian architect Charles Correa designed Bhopal's center for visual and performing arts, **Bharat Bhawan,** to harmonize with its surroundings as it spills down the hillside toward the lake. Various gallery spaces house excellent collections of modern and tribal arts (which you can appreciate but not learn anything about, since it's all labeled only in Hindi—here's where a guide will come in handy), a theater, indoor and outdoor auditoriums, libraries of Indian poetry and music, and a café. ✉*Shamla Hills* ☎*755/266–0239 or 755/266–0353* 🎫*Rs. 10* ⏲*Tues.–Sun. 2–8.*

The small **Birla Museum,** attached to the Lakshmi Narayan Temple, houses a good collection of ancient sculpture from various districts of Madhya Pradesh. ✉*Arera Hill* ☎*755/255–1388* 🎫*Rs. 50* ⏲*Tues.–Sun. 9:30–8.*

The **Government Archaeological Museum** has 10th- to 12th-century temple sculptures from all over Madhya Pradesh nicely displayed indoors and out in the garden. Among the other exhibits are 87 Jain once-lost wax bronzes found in a single hoard, and copies of paintings from the Bagh Caves near Mandu. ✉*2 Banganga Rd., opposite Ravindra Bhavan* ☎*755/266–0239* 🎫*Rs. 100* ⏲*Tues.–Sun. 10–5.*

The only way into the 1837 **Jama Masjid,** with its gold-crown minarets, is on foot through the bustling narrow lanes of the Chowk (central market). Consider combining a visit to the mosque with a shopping excursion; after an hour of negotiating prices, you may appreciate the spiritual respite.

Madhya Pradesh tourism's **Boat Club,** on the road to the zoo, rents motor-, paddle-, sail-, and rowboats as well as kayaks, canoes, and windsurfers for exploration of the Upper Lake. Fees are nominal; with notice, the club staff can arrange for a guide to go with you. ✉*Lake View Rd.* ☎*755/329–5043* ⏲*Daily sunrise–sunset.*

Manav Sangrahalaya *(National Museum of Mankind)* celebrates the many cultures of India past and present. One part of the 200-acre campus is the open-air Tribal Heritage Park, which exhibits some 40 tribal houses and other structures transported from their original locations. The houses are grouped together—sometimes with such additions as farm implements or surrounded by typical grass fences—to give a picture of life in villages. Those from Gujarat's Kutch area, for instance, have whitewashed, mirror-studded sculpted-mud furnishings, and the beautiful, shady wood houses of coastal Kerala elegantly screen out the hot southern sun. Avoid venturing off the path into the long grass, the authentic natural habitat of snakes. Aside all this tradition is a very modern-looking building that houses a museum with a permanent collection of 12,000 costumes, arts and crafts, agricultural and household implements, and other objects. ✉ *Shamla Hills* ☎ *755/266–1319* 🎫 *Rs. 10* ⏲ *Tues.–Sun. 10–6.*

The **Taj-ul-Masajid** *(Crown of Mosques)*, one of India's largest mosques, is a striking red sandstone building with white marble onion-shaped domes, octagonal minarets, and a vast main prayer hall noted for its massive pillars. Construction began during the reign of Shah Jehan Begum (1868–1901), third in a line of powerful woman rulers of Bhopal, but wasn't completed until 1971. Come just before dusk, when the sun sets over the nearby lake and small boys play cricket in the spacious courtyard. Note that the mosque is closed to non-Muslims during worship hours: 6:30 to 7:30 AM, 1 to 2 PM, 4 to 5 PM. ✉ *Airport Rd.* ⏲ *Daily 6:30 AM–8 PM.*

3

Van Vihar *(Bhopal National Park)*, on the Upper Lake, is really a glorified zoo, but makes for a pleasant walk. Park stations allow you to observe tigers, leopards, lions, bears, and crocodiles from the safe side of a fenced ravine. The best time to view wildlife is just before feeding times (usually 7 AM and 4:30 PM). ✉ *Lake View Rd.* 🎫 *Rs. 100, cars Rs. 30* ⏲ *Sat.–Thurs. 7–11 and 3–5:30.*

WHERE TO EAT & STAY

$$ ✕ **At Home in Bhopal.** Tour guide Rekha Chopra of Radiant Travels shares her home and family with you as she serves her delicious, eggless vegetarian cooking—generally dal, rice, roti, and cheese and vegetable dishes. After eating, you're welcome to try your hand at rolling and making fresh roti, or for about Rs. 600 you can eat and receive a full cooking lesson. Before you leave, she'll wrap you in wedding garb (male or female) so you can have a picture of yourself decked out in regal Indian fashion. ✉ *24 Ahmedabad Rd.* ☎ *755/254–0560* *Reservations essential* *No credit cards.*

$$ ★ **Jehan Numa Palace.** At this graceful former royal guest house convenient to the New Market area, most of the pleasant rooms, simply decorated in Indian fabrics, open off a garden courtyard filled with flowers. Forty rooms in a wing built in 2004 are a third larger, face the huge, palm-fringed pool, and have Internet access. There's lots to do here, thanks to a good health club with ayurvedic massage, a spa, a pub with dancing on weekends, a bakery/café for when you need a cappuccino fix, and a backyard area where children can ride horses. In addition to four restaurants, an evening outdoor dining area is built around an open-fire kitchen. **Pros:** no shortage of activities. **Cons:** the hotel is about twice as large as it used to be, and feels too busy at times. ✉ *157 Shamla Hills, 462013* ☎ *755/266–1100 to 04* 🌐 *www.hoteljehanumapalace.com* *98 rooms, 6 suites* *In-room: dial-up (some), Wi-Fi (some). In-hotel: 4 restaurants, room service, bar, tennis court, pool, gym, spa, public Internet, public Wi-Fi.* *AE, DC, MC, V.*

$$ ★ **Noor-Us-Sabah Palace.** Built in the 1920s for the daughter of a nawab, the "Light of Dawn" palace is an elegant Heritage Hotel near the old city's mosques and market. It sits high up on a hill, with a wonderful view of the Upper Lake from the lawn (where you can take your meals) and from the balconies of all guest rooms. Reception areas are resplendent with Italian white marble, crystal chandeliers, and such antiquities

as a silver-clad royal wedding palanquin. Guest rooms are beautifully done with carved-wood furniture, gilt-frame art, and marble baths; rooms on the first floor (especially the Nazir ud-Daulah Suite) have the best views and furnishings. At this writing, renovations were ongoing, with plans to add an unspecified number of rooms. **Pros:** unique charms make it a good antidote to the average hotel room in the rest of the city. **Cons:** an open-ended renovation may make for construction headaches. ✉ *VIP Rd., Koh-e-Fiza, Bhopal, 462001* ☎ *755/422–3333* 🌐 *www.noorussabahpalace.com* *57 rooms, 11 suites* *In-room: refrigerators, dial-up, Wi-Fi. In-hotel: 2 restaurants, room service, bar, pool, gym, laundry service, public Internet, public Wi-Fi.* 💳 *AE, MC, V.*

$ **Hotel Lake View Ashok.** At this government-run hotel right on the lake, each room has a tiny private balcony overlooking the water. The style is simple and functional, but it's all very clean—new curtains and bathroom tiles were added in 2007. Suites have mini–refrigerators; third-floor rooms have tubs. One of the multi-cuisine restaurants, with wraparound windows, takes full advantage of the lake view. **Pros:** the government employees are extra knowledgable about Bhopal, and there's a full-service travel desk on site for last-minute arrangements. **Cons:** an average city hotel that caters mainly to domestic travelers. ✉ *Shamla Hills, Bhopal, 462013* ☎ *755/266–0090 to 93* 🌐 *www.lakeviewashok.com* *39 rooms, 4 suites* *In-room: dial-up. In-hotel: 2 restaurants, room service, bar, laundry service, public Internet.* 💳 *AE, DC, MC, V.*

SHOPPING

Shops are generally open from 10:30 to 8; those in the New Market close on Monday, and those in the old town around Jama Masjid close on Sunday. At the **Chowk,** the market in the heart of the old city, you can spend hours wandering or bargaining for all manner of Bhopali crafts and specialties, including silver jewelry, saris, and ornately beaded and embroidered purses and pillows. **Mrignayani** (✉ *23 Shopping Centre* ☎ *755/255–4162*), in the shop-filled New Market area, carries gold- and silver-embroidered saris, ready-to-wear clothing, silk and other yardgoods, and lots of kitschy crafts.

SIDE TRIPS FROM BHOPAL

The 11th-century **Bhojeshwar Temple** is a simple square in which a huge Shiva lingam—a cylinder of stone 7½ feet tall with an 18-foot circumference—rises from a stone pedestal. An apparatus of ropes and pulleys "feed" the lingam with offerings of fresh milk, and devotees dress it with fresh flowers. The temple was never completed, and the earthen ramp used to raise it still stands. There are carvings on the dome, doorway, and pillar brackets. This isn't essential viewing unless you're already going to visit the nearby Bhimbetka Caves. ✉ *28 km (17 mi) southeast of Bhopal, in Bhojpur* *Rs. 10* ⏲ *Daily sunrise–sunset.*

The **Bhimbetka Caves** are actually naturally formed open rock shelters, with well-preserved prehistoric painting. Fifteen of them are accessible along a marked path. (About 500 others are scattered throughout this

World Heritage site, but you're advised to stick to the paths—there are animals, including a boar, that you might not want to meet up with.) The paintings, in white, red, green, or yellow, date from the Paleolithic era (huge bison, tigers, and rhinos) to the Mesolithic (small, stylized figures hunting with weapons or dancing with hands joined) to the cruder efforts of medieval times. In the paintings you'll also spy musical instruments, monkeys, hunters on horseback, and a big, yellow vase of flowers. You can combine a visit here with a trip to Bhojeshwar Temple, about 1 km (½ mi) away, for a half-day excursion. ✉ *46 km (29 mi) southeast of Bhopal on Rural Rd.* 🎟 *Rs. 10* ⏲ *Daily sunrise–sunset.*

Fodor's Choice ★ One of India's most important Buddhist sites, as well as a World Heritage Site, serene **Sanchi** consists of a group of stupas (large, mound-shape reliquary shrines), and monastery and temple ruins on a hilltop. The famous domed stupa, was built in the 2nd century BC over a damaged brick stupa built a century earlier by the Mauryan emperor Ashoka. Its four amazing gates, or *toranas,* opening into a ground-level path by which devotees may circumambulate the stupa, were added in the 1st century BC. The toranas are elaborately and beautifully carved with stories from the life of Buddha and even erotic scenes (at odds with Buddhism). An inscription on the west gateway identifies the sculptors as ivory workers, an explanation for the carvings' precision. The north gate is the best preserved, fully displaying the carvers' artistry in its natural, supple forms and movement. Against the walls facing the gates are four images of a haloed Buddha seated under a pillared canopy; these images date to Gupta rule in the 5th century AD. Just before the entrance to Sanchi, the Archaeological Survey of India Museum displays some of India's earliest known artworks, found during excavation of the site, including the superb capital from the Ashoka Pillar by the south gate. Restoration and excavation are ongoing. ✉ *46 km (29 mi) northeast of Bhopal on Rural Rd.* 🎟 *Sanchi Rs. 250; museum Rs. 5* ⏲ *Site: Sat.–Thurs. sunrise–sunset; museum: Sat.–Thurs. 10–5.*

★ A 13-km (8-mi) detour from Sanchi takes you to the remarkable **Udaygiri Caves,** a group of sanctuaries carved into caves and rock faces on a sandstone hill. Some of the sculptures—distinctive examples of Gupta art—date to the 4th and 5th centuries AD. A few not to miss: in cave 5, by the road, a beautifully carved giant Vishnu in his boar incarnation stands, victorious, dangling the goddess Prithvi from his tusk as rows and rows of sadhus thank him for saving her. (Prithvi, a representation of the earth, had been held captive under the sea.) In cave 12, another giant image of Vishnu reclines on a bed of snakes, having given birth from his navel to the god Brahma to again save the earth (the Brahma has unfortunately disappeared). In cave 3, the face of Shiva appears on a lingam, his third eye prominent on his forehead. ✉ *60 km (37 mi) northeast of Bhopal* 🎟 *Free* ⏲ *Daily sunrise–sunset.*

VARANASI, LUCKNOW & BODHGAYA

Spread out along the Ganges, Varanasi's interior lanes and ghats (staircases leading down to the river) throb with religious and commercial energy like no other place in India. Sarnath, just north of Varanasi, is the historic center of the Buddhist world, and Bodhgaya, east of Varanasi in the state of Bihar, is an international center of Buddhist worship. European-flavored Lucknow, the capital of Uttar Pradesh, is an easy diversion between Varanasi and Delhi.

VARANASI

676 km (419 mi) northeast of Bhopal, 406 km (252 mi) east of Khajuraho, 765 km (474 mi) southeast of Delhi, 677 km (420 mi) northwest of Kolkata.

Varanasi, in Uttar Pradesh, has been the religious capital of Hinduism through all recorded time. No one knows the date of the city's founding, but when Siddhartha Gautama, the historic Buddha, came here around 550 BC to deliver his first teaching he found an ancient and developed settlement. Contemporary with Babylon, Nineveh, and Thebes, Varanasi has been called the oldest continuously inhabited city on earth.

Every devout Hindu wants to visit Varanasi to purify body and soul in the Ganges River, to shed all sin, and, if possible, to die here in old age and achieve *moksha,* release from the cycle of rebirth. Descending from the Himalayas on its long course to the Bay of Bengal, the Ganges is believed by Hindus to hold the power of salvation in each drop. Pilgrims seek that salvation along the length of the river, but their holiest site is Varanasi. Every year, the city welcomes millions of pilgrims for whom these waters—physically fouled by the pollution of humans both living and dead—remain spiritually pristine enough to cleanse the soul.

Formerly called Banaras or Benares—or, by devout Hindus, Kashi ("resplendent with light")—Varanasi has about 1 million inhabitants. About 70 ghats line a 6-km (4-mi) stretch of the Ganges, effortlessly wedding the great Hindu metropolis to the river. At the heart of the city is a maze of streets and alleys, hiding a disorderly array of at least 2,000 temples and shrines. Domes, minarets, pinnacles, towers, and derelict 18th-century palaces dominate the river's sacred left bank. The streets are noisy and rife with color, and the air hangs heavy, as if in collaboration with the clang of temple gongs and bells. Some houses have simply decorated entrances; other buildings are ornate with lacy, Indian-style gingerbread (filigreed ornamentation) on balconies and verandas. You're likely to encounter funeral processions, cows and goats munching on garlands destined for the gods, and, especially near the Golden Temple (Kashi Vishvanath) and centrally located Dashashvamedh Ghat, assertive hawkers and phony guides.

Its variety of shrines notwithstanding, Varanasi is essentially a temple city dedicated to Shiva, Lord of Destruction. Shiva is typically said to live in the Himalayas, but myths say he was unable to leave Kashi after manifesting himself here. Exiling the earthly maharaja to Ramnagar, across the river, Shiva took up permanent residence here. (As a popular song has it, in Varanasi "every pebble is a Shiva linga.") The city itself is said to rest on a prong of Shiva's trident, above the cycles of creation, decay, and destruction that prevail in the rest of the world.

The maze of lanes may seem daunting, but you're never far from the river, where you can hire a boat for a quiet ride. Banarasis, as the locals call themselves, typically hire boats at sundown for twilight excursions, sometimes with tiny candlelit lamps made of leaves and marigolds, which they leave on the water as offerings. The Ganges turns sharply at Varanasi to flow south to north past the city, so the riverbank aligns perfectly with the rising sun. In sacred geography the city is demarcated by the Ganges to the east and two small rivers—the Varana, to the north, which winds by the cantonment area and joins the Ganges near Raj Ghat, and the Asi, a small stream in the south.

Traditionally, Varanasi is seen as a field divided into three sections named after important temples to Shiva. Omkareshvara is the namesake temple in the northern section, which is probably the oldest area but is now impoverished and seldom visited by pilgrims. The central section is named after Kashi Vishvanath, the famous "Golden Temple." Vishvanath itself means "Lord of the Universe," one of Shiva's names, and there are many Vishvanath temples. The southern area, the Kedar Khand, is named for Kedareshvara, a temple easily picked out from the river thanks to the vertical red and white stripes painted on its walls, a custom of the South Indian worshipers who are among the temple's devotees. The ghats stretch along the river from Raj Ghat in the north to Asi Ghat in the south; beyond Asi is the university, across the river from Ramnagar Fort and Palace. The city itself spreads out behind the ghats, with the hotels in the cantonment area about 20 minutes from the river by auto-rickshaw.

It's wise to hire a guide in Varanasi on your first day to orient you with this complicated city. For one to four people, India Tourism's licensed guides cost Rs. 450 for one to four hours, Rs. 600 for up to eight hours (if your block of time starts before 7:30 AM or finishes after 8:30 PM, add Rs. 75); cars and boats can be hired from the office as well—a way to avoid haggling on the streets or the ghats. Also, many temples and mosques are open only to their own sects, so a government guide may help get you in.

Numbers in margins correspond to numbers on the Varanasi map.

WHAT TO SEE

4 **Alamgir Mosque.** From a dramatic high point, the Alamgir Mosque overlooks the Ganges River. Destroying the 17th-century temple Beni Madhav ka Dharehara, which had been dedicated to Vishnu, the Moghul emperor Aurangzeb built this mosque with an odd fusion of Hindu (lower portions and wall) and Muslim (upper portion) designs. Panchganga Ghat, down below, is an important bathing point, particularly on Makar Sankranti (January 14), when the sun crosses the tropic of

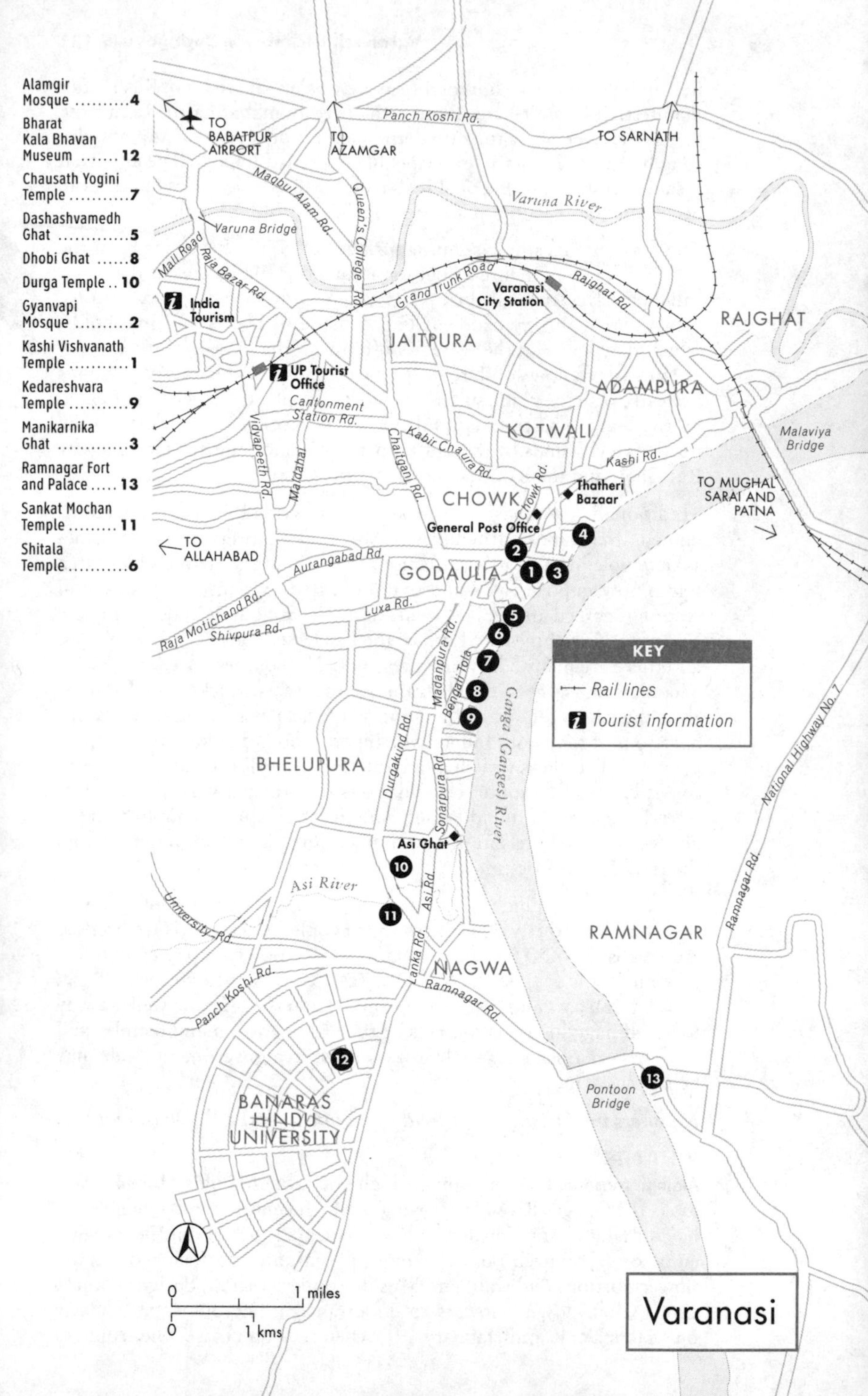
Alamgir Mosque 4
Bharat Kala Bhavan Museum 12
Chausath Yogini Temple 7
Dashashvamedh Ghat 5
Dhobi Ghat 8
Durga Temple .. 10
Gyanvapi Mosque 2
Kashi Vishvanath Temple 1
Kedareshvara Temple 9
Manikarnika Ghat 3
Ramnagar Fort and Palace 13
Sankat Mochan Temple 11
Shitala Temple 6
TO BABATPUR AIRPORT
TO AZAMGAR
Panch Koshi Rd.
TO SARNATH
Maqbul Alam Rd.
Queen's College Rd.
Varuna River
Varuna Bridge
Mall Road
Raja Bazar Rd.
Grand Trunk Road
Varanasi City Station
Rajghat Rd.
India Tourism
RAJGHAT
JAITPURA
UP Tourist Office
ADAMPURA
Cantonment Station Rd.
Malaviya Bridge
KOTWALI
Kabir Chaura Rd.
Chaitganj Rd.
Vidyapeeth Rd.
Maldahai
Kashi Rd.
Chowk Rd.
Thatheri Bazaar
CHOWK
TO MUGHAL SARAI AND PATNA
General Post Office
TO ALLAHABAD
Aurangabad Rd.
GODAULIA
Raja Motichand Rd.
Luxa Rd.
Shivpura Rd.
Madanpura Rd.
Bengali Tola
KEY
Rail lines
Tourist information
Ganga (Ganges) River
Durgakund Rd.
BHELUPURA
Sonarpura Rd.
National Highway No. 7
Asi Ghat
Asi River
Asi Rd.
Ramnagar Rd.
University Rd.
RAMNAGAR
Lanka Rd.
NAGWA
Panch Koshi Rd.
Ramnagar Rd.
Pontoon Bridge
BANARAS HINDU UNIVERSITY
0
1 miles
0
1 kms
Varanasi

Capricorn as the earth shifts on its axis following the winter solstice. The mosque is closed to non-Muslims. ✉ *From Dashashvamedh or Manikarnika Ghat, head north along the river; the mosque towers above Panchganga Ghat* ⏲ *Daily sunrise–sunset.*

12 ★ **Bharat Kala Bhavan Museum.** No one interested in Indian art should miss this museum on the campus of Banaras Hindu University. The permanent collection includes brocade textiles, excellent Hindu and Buddhist sculptures, and miniature paintings from the courts of the Moghuls and the Hindu princes of the Punjab hills. One sculpture with particular power is a 4th-century Gupta-dynasty frieze depicting Krishna (an incarnation of Vishnu) holding up Mt. Govardhan to protect his pastoral comrades from the rain. Have your car or rickshaw wait for you, as transport can be hard to find on the university's sprawling campus. ✉ *Banaras Hindu University, Lanka* ☎ *542/230–7621* *Rs. 40* ⏲ *Mon.–Sat. 11–4:30.*

7 **Chausath Yogini Temple.** One of the interesting temples between Prayag and Asi ghats, Chausath Yogini is at the top of a particularly steep set of steps by the ghat of the same name. Originally devoted to a Tantric cult that is also associated with an important ruined temple at Khajuraho, it's now dedicated to Kali (the goddess most popular with Bengalis), known here simply as "Ma"—Mother. The worshippers are mainly white-sari-clad widows from Varanasi's Bengali quarter; in the early morning you'll see them coming for the *darshan* (vision) of Kali after bathing in the Ganges. The temple is closed to non-Hindus. ⏲ *Daily sunrise–sunset.*

5 Fodor's Choice ★ **Dashashvamedh Ghat.** If you decide to hire a boat, an essential Varanasi experience, come to this unofficial "main" ghat for most purposes. The best time to see the ghats is at sunrise, when a solemn group of people and even animals—lit by the sun's darkly golden first rays—hover on the water's edge, bent on immersion in the holy stream. As you float on the river, you'll see young bodybuilders, members of the city's many wrestling clubs, exercising. Older men sit cross-legged in meditation or prayer. A corpse may even float by. ✉ *Head east to the water from Godaulia Crossing, the central traffic circle in the Chowk area.*

8 **Dhobi Ghat.** At this ghat south of Dashashvamedh, dhobis (washer men and women) do early morning laundry by beating it against stones in the river while their donkeys bray disconsolately on the bank. This may be the sight that moved Mark Twain to declare that "a Hindu is someone who spends his life trying to break stones with wet clothes."

10 **Durga Temple.** This 18th-century shrine, dedicated to the goddess Durga, Shiva's consort, stands beside a large, square pool of water due west about a kilometer from Asi Ghat. The spire is formed on top of five lower spires, a convergence symbolizing the belief that all five elements of the world (earth, air, water, fire, and ether) merge with the Supreme. This shrine is also called the Monkey Temple, for good reason: the pests are everywhere, and they'll steal anything. Keep all food and water safe and out of sight. The temple is closed to non-Hindus. ✉ *Durgakund Rd.* ⏲ *Daily sunrise–noon and 2–sunset.*

NEED A BREAK?

The Vaatika Café, an easygoing, inexpensive second-floor outdoor eatery with tables looking out on Asi Ghat, serves excellent thin-crust pizza made in an Italian oven with real mozzarella, as well as pasta dishes, bona fide espresso, and other unlikely delicacies.

❷ **Gyanvapi Mosque.** Moghul emperor Aurangzeb pulled down Vishveswara Temple to erect this mosque, and the building's foundation and rear still show parts of the original temple. The tallest of the mosque's minarets, which dominated the skyline of the holy city, collapsed during a flood in 1948. The surrounding area—next to Kashi Vishvanath—has been the focus of Hindu revivalist attempts to reconsecrate the site of the former temple, and is staffed with police and fenced with barbed wire. It's normally very sedate, however, and is an important starting point for Hindu pilgrims. The mosque is closed to non-Muslims. ⏲*Daily sunrise–sunset.*

❶ **Kashi Vishvanath Temple.** Dedicated to Shiva, whose pillar of light is said to have appeared on this spot, this temple in the old city is the most sacred shrine in Varanasi, but it is generally off-limits to non-Hindus. To get here, walk from Dashashvamedh Road down the relatively broad, shop-lined lane (Vishvanath Gali, the main sari bazaar) to Vishvanath Temple. The lane turns sharply right at a large image of the elephant-head god Ganesh, then passes the brightly painted wooden entrance to the 1725 temple of Vishvanath's consort, Annapurna, on the right. On the left, look for the silver doorway and the policeman ready to pat you down before you enter—this is the entrance to the Kashi Vishvanath Temple. Known as the Golden Temple for the gold plate on its spire—a gift from the Sikh maharaja Ranjit Singh in 1835—the temple is set back from the Ganges between Dashashvamedh and Manikarnika ghats. Because non-Hindus can't enter, your best bet is to glimpse it from the top floor of the house opposite (pay the owner a few rupees). You'll see men and women making offerings to the lingam in the inner shrine. The present temple was built by Rani Ahalyabai of Indore in 1776, near the site of the original shrine, which had been destroyed by Aurangzeb. Various forms of the *arti* prayer ceremony are performed outside at 3:30 AM, noon, and 7:30 and 11 PM. ✉*Vishvanath Gali* ⏲*Daily 4 AM–11 PM.*

❾ **Kedareshvara Temple.** You can recognize this temple, the most important Shiva temple in this part of town, by its red-and-white candy-stripe walls. Take off your shoes at the small rear door at the top of the ghats before entering. The lingam here is an unsculpted stone and is said to have emerged spontaneously when a pure-hearted but feeble devotee of Shiva prayed for a chance to visit Kedareshvara Shiva temple in the Himalayas. Shiva, the god of destruction, is sometimes fierce in aspect, but he is famously kind to his devotees, or *bhaktas*. In this myth, Shiva was touched by his bhakta's piety, so instead of bringing him to the mountain, Shiva brought his own image to the bhakta. The lingam emerged out of a plate of rice and lentils, called *kichiri,* which believers see in the rough surface of the lingam's natural stone. ✉*Bengali Tola at Kedar Ghat* ⏲*Daily 5 AM–11 PM.*

CLOSE UP

The Economics of Burning

It's difficult to find a more curious aspect of Varanasi than the public cremations of those who came to die on the bank of the Ganges. Although public cremation is the norm for Hindus throughout India, the act as it's performed in this holy Hindu city is more emotional because of its important spiritual implications. But most Hindus do not experience this ultimate release for many reasons, money being the most common.

A proper wood cremation ceremony, even in one's hometown, involves basic expenses that much of India's poor majority simply cannot afford. The most expensive supply is the wood itself, costing about Rs. 150 for 40 kg. With a minimum requirement of about 300 kg., the price of wood cremation starts at Rs. 1,125. Other supplies include ghee (an oily, clarified butter), sandalwood powder and cloth to prepare the body, and there's a tax to be paid, too. The total price for the ritual usually comes to a minimum of Rs. 2,000. Add to that the cost of traveling to Varanasi, and the prospect of honoring the dead at the bank of the Ganges becomes financially daunting—many of the poorest people in India make only Rs. 2,000 a month or less.

To help with cost, traditional funeral pyres share space at the burning ghat with Varanasi's one electric cremation center. Burning a body here costs just Rs. 500, a fraction of the cost of wood cremation, though still expensive by Indian standards. A lack of money, in fact, is probably the best explanation for a body drifting by during a boat ride on the Ganges. It's unlawful to offer dead bodies to the river now, except in the case of a pregnant woman, a child younger than five, someone with smallpox, someone who has been bitten by a cobra, or a holy man—Hindus believe that gods live inside these bodies, so they can't be burned. But in the absence of money for a cremation, poor relatives often have no other choice but to break the law if they want to honor the dead in the holiest of waters.

3 ★ **Manikarnika Ghat.** Thin blue smoke twists up to the sky from fires at Varanasi's main burning ghat. Day and night, bodies wrapped in silk or linen—traditionally white for men, red or orange for women—are carried through the streets on bamboo stretchers to the smoking pyres. After a brief immersion in the Ganges and a short wait, the body is placed on the pyre for the ritual that precedes the cremation. Funeral parties dressed in white, the color of mourning, hover with their deceased. Photographing funeral ghats is strictly forbidden, but you are allowed to watch. At the top of Manikarnika's steps is a small, deep pool, or *kund,* said to have been dug by Vishnu at the dawn of creation and thus to be the first *tirtha*—literally, "ford," and figuratively a place of sacred bathing. Shiva is said to have lost an earring (*manikarnika*) as he trembled in awe before this place, one of the holiest sites in Varanasi.

13 **Ramnagar Fort and Palace.** Across the Ganges is the 17th-century palace of the Maharaja of Varanasi, who still lives here (if the flag is up, he's in residence) and performs ceremonial and charitable functions. It's for his sake

that there are guards sleeping in open rooms off the entranceway. The Durbar Hall (Public Audience Chamber) and Royal Museum have good collections, but the place is sadly rundown and the objects are not well maintained. A case full of beautiful black musical instruments, for example, is so completely white with dust and the case so covered with grime that it's almost impossible to see anything, and the royal costumes are ratty. Still, there are palanquins and howdahs in ivory, goldplate, or silver (completely tarnished); old carriages and cars; furniture; portraits of maharajas; and arms from Africa, Burma, and Japan. The palace was built to resist the floods of the monsoon, which play havoc with the city side of the river. (Official taxi rate for four hours from the Cantonment area to here: Rs. 400.) Note that the site is closed some days during monsoon season. ✉*End of Pontoon Bridge, off Ramnagar Rd.* ☎*542/233–9322* *Rs. 7* ⏲*Daily 10–5.*

> **A VERY GOOD GUIDE**
>
> **Ashok Kumar Sharma** (☎*542/220-4963 Pradeep Hotel, 93/3691-4387 mobile*), who is associated with the Pradeep Hotel, is full of humor and humility, presenting Varanasi with fascinating detail as only a local can. All the boat operators know him, and he'll negotiate the proper price for boat rides, too. Contact the hotel to book a tour with him.

11 **Sankat Mochan Temple.** Sankat Mochan (Deliverer from Troubles) is one of Varanasi's most beloved temples, as well as one of its oldest—it was built in the late 16th century. Though the city has encroached all around it, the building still stands in a good-size, tree-shaded enclosure, like temples elsewhere in India. (Most temples in Varanasi are squeezed between other buildings.) Although most of the city's major shrines are dedicated to Shiva or various aspects of the mother goddess, Sankat Mochan belongs to Hanuman, the monkey god, revered for his dedicated service to Rama, an incarnation of Vishnu whose story is told in the *Ramayana.* The best time to see Sankat Mochan is early evening, when dozens of locals stop for a brief visit at the end of the workday, and on Tuesday and Saturday—days sacred to Hanuman—when worshippers come in large numbers to pay their respects. The temple is closed to non-Hindus. ✉*Durgakund Rd.* ⏲*Daily 5 AM–11 PM.*

6 **Shitala Temple.** This unassuming but very popular white temple near Dashashvamedh Ghat is dedicated to Shitala, the smallpox goddess. Despite the eradication of smallpox, Shitala is still an important folk goddess in North India. Here, as in many Shitala temples, a shrine has been added in honor of Santoshi Mata, the "Mother of Contentment"—a goddess who gained popularity in the 1970s when a Hindi movie was made about her. The temple is closed to non-Hindus. ✉*Shitala Ghat* ⏲*Daily 5 AM–11 PM.*

WHERE TO EAT & STAY

$ ✕ **Amrapali.** At this big wood-paneled restaurant lit by crystal domes and overlooking a garden full of palm trees, the lunch and dinner buffets—including several soups, steamed vegetables, and a great dessert section—are excellent. Or you can choose from four separate menus, including kebabs, tandoori dishes, and thalis (served with superbly soft, warm naan), plus Chinese dishes, Continental choices, and snacks. ✉*Clarks Varanasi, The Mall* ☎*542/250–1011* ▭*AE, DC, MC, V.*

¢ ✕**Haifa.** Connected to Hotel Haifa, which offers rooms starting at Rs. 550, this restaurant's specialty is Middle Eastern food. It's basically a long room with non-descript tables and lots of tourists flowing in and out—and no wonder, since it's incredibly cheap and the only place in town to sample freshly made Middle Eastern treats. An entire Middle Eastern "thali" consisting of hummus, babaganuj, labaneh (strained yogurt), falafel, and potato costs only Rs. 70. In case you're sticking to Indian, there's plenty of that, too, along with Chinese and Continental, also at rock-bottom prices. ✉*B. 1/107 Assi Ghat, Varanasi* ☎*542/231–2960* ▭*No credit cards.*

¢–$ ✕**Bread of Life Bakery.** There's an abundance of tourists in this café which is lined with wood walls and close to the Asi Ghat—it's an impressive haven for homesick Western palates. It also makes a great place for breakfast after a morning boat ride, because here the pancakes are real and so is the maple syrup—something that anyone who's lived in India for any length of time will tell you is rare. Stop in anytime to write postcards over coffee and sweets, which include chocolate-chip cookies, apple strudel, eclairs, and Black Forest cake. Simple lunches and dinners include omelets, quiches, sandwiches, soups and stews, pastas, and some Chinese dishes. All profits of the café and the art gallery upstairs go to charities or are used for employees' education. ✉*B 3/322 Shivala* ☎*542/227–5012* ▭*No credit cards.*

¢ ✕**Kerala Cafe.** As the name implies, South Indian food is on the short menu at this no-frills, popular little diner that's lined with narrow, dingy booths and filled with mostly Indian pilgrims. The specialty is dosas—specifically masala dosas—and they're terrific, full of juicy chunks of potatoes, onion, and peas. In addition to choices like plain, tomato, or coconut *uttapams* (Indian-style pancakes), *idlis* (steamed bread made of rice flour), and *vadas* (deep-fried savory "doughnuts"), they do a great lemon rice with peanuts and a sprinkling of coriander leaves, and beautiful puffy pooris (fried bread) as big as your head. It's open for breakfast. ✉*Bhelupura Crossing* ☎*No phone* ▭*No credit cards.*

$$$ ★ **Taj Ganges.** Although its spacious lobby bustles with large tour groups, rooms are cozy and quiet at this Taj property, particularly if you get an upper-story room facing the adjacent Nadesar Palace, once the maharaja's palace but long abandoned. (Taj owns the palace and is planning to turn it into a boutique hotel.) Rooms are spacious and modern, done in soft colors with brass-accent furniture, and service is superior. Hop a horse-drawn carriage to tour Taj's 40 acres of grounds, featuring rose and peacock gardens. Weekend nights there's an hour of dancing on the lawn. **Pros:** lots of space to take peaceful walks without fear of being run over in this crowded city. **Cons:** a tour group magnet. ✉*Nadesar Palace Grounds, Varanasi, 221002* ☎*542/250–3001 to 19* 🌐*www.tajhotels.com* *120 rooms, 10 suites* *In-room: safe, refrigerator (some), Wi-Fi. In-hotel: 2 restaurants, room service, bar, tennis court, pool, gym, spa, concierge, laundry service, public Internet, public Wi-Fi, no-smoking rooms.* ▭*AE, DC, MC, V.*

$$ **Clarks Varanasi.** The best thing about staying here may be the restaurant, Amrapali, with its beautiful spreads of Indian food. Guest rooms at this fine hotel in the relatively quiet Cantonment area, where the upscale properties are located, have lots of natural light and cheery floral bedcovers and wood laminate floors amid other standard furnishings. The best rooms overlook the palm-fringed pool or lawn. A unique amenity is the *haveli,* a traditional Rajput mansion, that the hotel maintains at Raja Ghat for evening cultural programs and morning demonstrations of Hindu rituals; trips are arranged for groups, but you can sign on individually if space is available. **Pros:** a 24-hour coffee shop and a well-stocked shopping arcade are amenities not present in other local hotels. **Cons:** a bit far from the unique hustle and bustle of Varanasi. ✉*The Mall, Varanasi, 221002* ☎*542/250–1011 to 20* 🌐*www.hotelclarks.com* *113 rooms, 2 suites* *In-room: dial-up. In-hotel: restaurant, room service, bar, pool, laundry facilities, public Internet.* *AE, DC, MC, V.*

KARMA SEEKERS AT THE GHATS

There's definitely a spirit of give and take in Varanasi. From your boat you'll likely see locals at every ghat feeding a special raw wheat dough to the fish, since in Hinduism it's considered good karma to feed any living thing in need. But as your boat is preparing to leave the dock, you may also see a lone man who looks pretty busy in the water. He's collecting the coins from the bottom that are regularly tossed in by those seeking good karma.

$$ **Palace on Ganges.** At this comfortable hotel created from a century-old building on Asi Ghat, rooms recall Gujarat (with brightly colored quilted drapes studded with mirrorwork), Rajasthan (elaborately carved doors and furnishings), Assam (lots of bamboo), or other states while delivering all the modern comforts of home. Rooms at the front have a great view of the ghat, but others are quieter. The long lobby hall seems to be infused with air floating off the Ganges, and it's a great place to relax with tea. The vegetarian meals are prepared in a way meant to appeal to especially strict Brahmins, meaning that no plant parts that grew underground, such as onion or garlic, are used in preparation. **Pros:** magnificent view from the rooftop is a panorama of the entire city; a well-stocked library with countless cultural and history books. **Cons:** you'll have to climb a flight of stairs to even get in the front door, making it pretty difficult for those with disabilities. ✉*B-1/158 Asi Ghat, Varanasi, 221001* ☎*542/231–5050, 542/231–4304 to 05* 🌐*www.palaceonganges.com* *42 rooms* *In-hotel: 2 restaurants, room service, no elevator, laundry service, public Internet.* *MC, V.*

$ ★ **Hotel Ganges View.** Still the residence of a well-to-do Varanasi family, this guest house has small, beautiful rooms with quirky charm—for example, there's a jungle painting and stone shrine (with goddess) you sleep under in Room 13—and a great veranda with tables overlooking the river and Asi Ghat. (The Rs. 1,200 rooms without air-conditioning are closest to the ghat's noises and are best avoided unless you're a heavy sleeper.) The hotel still feels homey, but you're also likely to come across one of the classical Indian concerts or lectures that are often held here. The dinners served under a galaxy of lamps and chandeliers are Brahmin-style vegetarian, but so delicious you won't miss a thing that's been left out. Book months ahead for peak season. **Pros:** the veranda is the best place in town to sit for hours and watch an endless stream of pilgrims and tourists. **Cons:** it's pretty noisy, and the narrow stairs leading to the front door make it difficult to access. ✉ *Asi Ghat, Varanasi, 221006* ☎ *542/231–3218* 🌐 *www.hotelgangesview.com* *11 rooms* *In-room: no a/c (some), no phone, no TV. In-hotel: restaurant, room service, no elevator, laundry service, public Internet.* ▭ *No credit cards.*

$ **Hotel India.** For a less expensive option in the Cantonment area, try this hotel. The rooms are unfortunately nothing special, with tan being the drab color of choice, and the bathrooms are tiny. Executive rooms have king beds, marble floors, and big marble baths, but you'll pay more. There are five restaurants in all here, including a multicuisine and Chinese–Thai restaurant, a rooftop Punjabi spot with a stone fountain, and a bar–restaurant on a lower rooftop that's good for a drink and a kebab. **Pros:** affordable, with plenty of dining options. **Cons:** halls are dark, with worn green carpet that makes things look a bit shabby overall. ✉ *59 Patel Nagar, Varanasi, 221001* ☎ *542/250–7593 to 97* *70 rooms, 2 suites* *In-room: refrigerator. In-hotel: 5 restaurants, room service, bar, gym, laundry service, public Internet.* ▭ *AE, MC, V.*

¢ ★ **Pradeep.** There's a huge portrait of Mahatma Gandhi in Pradeep's small, bustling lobby, along with the words "A customer is not an interruption on our work—he is the purpose of it." Staff members embody this sentiment through warm and sincere service. The simple rooms are attractively furnished in browns and golds against cream walls (ask for one away from the busy road). But the rooftop restaurant, Eden, is the true asset here: with its white wrought-iron garden furniture amid tidy plots of green lawn, flowers, and fountains, you might not believe you're actually on a rooftop in the middle of Varanasi. There are great views of all the chaos below, just in case you forget. **Pros:** a shining example of inexpensive lodging in an expensive tourist town. **Cons:** some of the rooms don't have windows, and it's usually pretty crowded. ✉ *Jagatganj, 221002* ☎ *542/220–4963, 542/220–4594, or 542/220–7231* 🌐 *www.hotelpradeep.com* *45 rooms* *In-room: refrigerator. In-hotel: 2 restaurants, room service, bar, no elevator, laundry service.* ▭ *AE, DC, MC, V.*

SHOPPING

The city's shops are open generally from 10 to 8; the larger shops close on Sunday, but the street sellers and smaller shops are open daily. One of India's chief weaving centers, Varanasi is famous for its silk-brocade saris, which start at around Rs. 2,000. Some saris are still woven with real gold and silver threads, though in most noncustom work the real thing has been replaced by artificial fibers. (You can see the fabric being woven by entire families in Muslim neighborhoods like Qazi Sadullahpura.) Most hotels sell silk-brocade saris in their shops, but the main bazaars for saris are in **Vishvanath Gali**—the lane leading from Dashashvamedh Road to the Kashi Vishvanath Temple, where the customers are mainly pilgrims and tourists.

Among the brass vendors in **Thatheri Bazaar** *(Brass Market)*, on a small lane 50 meters north of the Chowk, some shops sell silks and woolens to a local crowd. **Banaras Art Culture** (✉ *Shri Krishna Kunj, B–2/114 Bhadhaini, near Bread of Life Bakery* ☎ *542/231–3615 or 542/231–1715*) displays regional and other Indian art, folk art, and crafts—bronzes, terra-cottas, marble sculptures, wood carvings, paintings—in many rooms of an old home. **Cottage Industries Exposition** (✉ *Mint House, Nadesar, across from the Taj* ☎ *542/250–0814*) has excellent Varanasi weaves in silk and cotton, a vast rug room, plus brass wares and Kashmiri embroidered shawls. Everything is expensive. **Dharam Kumar Jain & Sons** (✉ *K 37/12 Sona Kuan* ☎ *542/233–3354*), operating out of their home near Thatheri Bazaar, have an extraordinary private collection of old brocade saris, pashmina shawls, and other textiles. **Mehta International** (✉ *S 20/51 Varuna Bridge* ☎ *542/234–4489 or 542/250–7364*), in the Cantonment area around the corner from the Radisson, is a large showroom with a wide selection of fine saris, scarves, bed covers, fabric, and some elaborately worked tapestries.

NIGHTLIFE & THE ARTS

Ganga Arti is an *arti* (prayer ceremony) performed at Dashashvamedh Ghat every night at sunset. The steps fill with people singing Vedic hymns, lighting lamps, and praying along with the priests, but it's perhaps best appreciated from a boat so you can take in the whole scene without the crush on the ghat. **Gyanpravaha Institute for Indological Learning** (✉ *east side of Pontoon Bridge* ☎ *542/236–6326*) holds seminars and cultural shows, and has a **museum and library** (⊙ *Tues.–Sun. 11–5*). **Nagari Natak Mandal** (✉ *Kabir Chowra*) presents infrequent concerts of some of Varanasi's—and India's—best musicians. There are also numerous music festivals. Ask your hotel to check the local Hindi newspaper, *Aj*, for events while you're in town, or check the English-language papers yourself.

SARNATH

11 km (7 mi) north of Varanasi.

In 528 BC Siddhartha Gautama, having attained enlightenment at Bodhgaya, preached his first sermon (now called Dharma Chakra Pravartan, or Set in Motion the Wheel of Law) in what is today Sarnath's Deer Park. Here he revealed his Eightfold Path leading to the end of sorrow and the attainment of enlightenment. Three hundred years later, in the 3rd century BC, the Mauryan emperor Ashoka arrived. A zealous convert to Buddhism, he built in Sarnath several stupas (large, mound-shaped reliquary shrines) and a pillar with a lion capital that was adopted by independent India as its national emblem. The wheel motif under the lions' feet represents the *dharma chakra,* the wheel (*chakra*) of Buddhist teaching (*dharma*), which began in Sarnath. The chakra is replicated at the center of the national flag. Sarnath reached its zenith by the 4th century AD, under the Gupta dynasty, and was occupied into the 9th century, when Buddhist influence in India began to wane. By the 12th century, Sarnath had more or less fallen to Muslim invaders and begun a long decay. In 1836 Sir Alexander Cunningham started extensive excavations here, uncovering first a stone slab with an inscription of the Buddhist creed, then numerous other relics. It was then that the Western world realized the Buddha had been an actual person, not a mythical figure. Most of the sites are in a well-manicured park behind a gate (admission is Rs. 100). Any taxi or auto–rickshaw will take you to Sarnath from Varanasi; India Tourism also arranges a three-hour trip (giving you two hours to explore) from Cantonment area hotels or its office for Rs. 300.

In the 16th century, the Moghul emperor Akbar built a terraced brick tower on top of the 5th-century **Chaukhandi Stupa** to commemorate his father's visit some years earlier. It's the first monument you come to in Sarnath, on the left-hand side of Ashoka Marg on the way to the park.

Legend has it that the Buddha was incarnated as King of the Deer in the **Deer Park,** north of Dhamekh Stupa. Before you leave Sarnath, take a short walk here, pay a few rupees for some carrots, and feed the current denizens.

Dappled with geometric and floral ornamentation, the stone-and-brick **Dhamekh Stupa** is the largest surviving monument in Sarnath at 43.6 meters (143 feet) in height and 228 meters (748 feet) in diameter at the base. Built around 500 AD, Dhamekh is thought to mark the place where the Buddha delivered his sermon, though excavations have unearthed the remains of an even earlier stupa of Mauryan bricks of the Gupta period (200 BC).

The **Mulagandha Kuti Vihari Temple,** built in 1931, joins the old foundations of seven monasteries. The walls bear frescoes by a Japanese artist, Kosetsu Nosu, depicting scenes from the Buddha's life, and relics of Sakyamuni Buddha are enshrined here. On the anniversary of the temple's foundation—the first full moon in November—monks and devotees from all parts of Asia assemble here. The temple is behind a separate gate just outside the park.

★ At the entrance to the excellent **Sarnath Archaeological Museum** is Ashoka's Lion Capital, moved here from its original location in the park. The museum represents the oldest site in the history of India's Archaeologial Survey. Other beautiful sculpture is here as well, including lots of Buddhas; still more of Sarnath's masterpieces are in the National Museum, Delhi, and the Indian Museum, Kolkata. ✉*Ashoka Marg at Dharmapal Marg* ☎*542/259–5095* 🎟*Rs. 100* ⏲*Sat.–Thurs. 10–5.*

BODHGAYA

266 km (165 mi) east of Varanasi.

In central Bihar, one of the poorest and most corrupt states in India, is one of the four main pilgrimage centers of Buddhism: Bodhgaya. Here, sometime around 520 BC (or later—the commonly accepted dates are in dispute), Prince Siddhartha Gautama meditated under a pipal tree and achieved enlightenment. A descendant of that tree, grown from a cutting, still stands, and in recent decades Buddhists from around the world have built monasteries and temples nearby, each in the style of their own country. Today the so-called Buddhist Circuit (including Lumbini, his birthplace, in Nepal; and in Uttar Pradesh, Sarnath, where he preached his first sermon, and Kushinagar, where he died) brings the faithful by the busload—and an airport outside of town brings them by the planeload from Thailand, Singapore, and elsewhere, particularly when the Dalai Lama comes to lecture, usually in late December. In the temples and while wandering the village—which can be seen by foot or bicycle-rickshaw—you'll encounter lay Buddhists from Maharashtra (center of a 20th-century Buddhist revival); Tibetan monks in maroon robes, some prostrating themselves repeatedly as they approach the temple; Sri Lankan and Thai *bhikkus* (monks) in yellow robes; and a small number of Westerners, believers as well as the merely curious.

Many of India's other Buddhist centers are primarily archaeological monuments, but Bodhgaya gives you an idea of how Buddhism thrives as a contemporary faith. The monasteries have tried to be good neighbors: most run a school, clinic, or other project for the benefit of the local people. And other Buddhist institutions here provide charitable assistance as well. The Mahabodhi Society, a Sri Lankan organization that played a key role in reviving the practice of pilgrimage to Buddhist centers in India, runs a clinic and ambulance service from its complex on the main road. The Maitreya Project (🌐*www.maitreyaproject.org*)—whose grander mission includes building a 500-foot-tall bronze Buddha in Kushinagar as an enduring symbol of "loving kindness"—has a free school for more than 200 children. The Root Institute for Wisdom Culture (☎631/220–0714 🌐*www.rootinstitute.com*), which runs residential workshops on Buddhism and meditation, also has a clinic with a polio-rehabilitation center.

It's a pleasure to wander among the town's temples and monasteries (most close for an hour or two at lunchtime). Many have ornately decorated interiors, including beautiful, wildly colorful wall frescoes that usually depict scenes from the life of the Buddha. The tourist office has a hard-to-read map of town; the Mahayana Guest House, on the one main road, has a better map, which they may give you if you ask nicely.

Bodhgaya's **Archaeological Museum** holds some of the Mahabodhi Temple's original railing—6-foot pillars and cross-bands of granite and sandstone, carved with themes from the *Jatakas* (Buddhist parables that tell tales of Buddha's previous lives), zodiac signs, folk scenes, and inscriptions—which have been arranged like a Buddhist Stonehenge in a courtyard. Also here is some good classical sculpture, including a beautiful black stone four-sided Buddha pillar. ✉*South side of town, off the short road leading to the Lotus Nikko hotel* ☎*631/220–0739* 🎟*Rs. 2* ⏲*Sat.–Thurs. 10–5.*

The physical and symbolic center of Bodhgaya is the **Mahabodhi Temple,** in a large, tree-shaded compound you enter through a gateway off a tidy but crowded pedestrian plaza. Here, as on each of the village's few streets, vendors sell sandalwood beads, prayer bells, Buddha statues, CDs, Tibetan blankets, and snacks. Built before the 7th century, possibly as early as the 2nd century, and remodeled several times, the Mahabodhi is one of the earliest examples of the *nagara* (North Indian) temple style, which emphasizes the spire; rising some 160 feet, the spire can be seen far and wide from the surrounding flat country. At the top is a stone stupa, a representation of the reliquary mounds the first Buddhists built all over the subcontinent, topped by a series of stone chattras, symbols of both the Buddha's princely lineage and the shelter provided by the faith he founded. The temple's four flat sides are tiered with niches that hold Buddha images offered by pilgrims (the small stone stupas that dot the grounds are also offerings). The temple is enclosed on three sides by a stone railing, which opens under a high *torana* (archway) on the east side. Much of the original railing has been carted away to museums (including Bodhgaya's) and replaced by less elaborately carved reproductions. Pilgrims typically circumambulate the temple before entering the tall central chamber that houses a large gilt image of the Buddha in meditation. The sanctum is strung with colored lights, and the surrounding space is enlivened by the obvious emotion of pilgrims. The **Bodhi Tree,** in an enclosed courtyard, gives a more visceral feeling of sanctity. Pilgrims place flowers on the stone slab representing the **vajrasan** ("diamond seat") where the Buddha meditated, and tie bits of colored cloth to the tree. Contemporary Buddhists often sit in emulation of his practice along the railing surrounding the tree. The carved-stone path next to the north wall is said to mark the track of the Buddha's walking meditation, and he is thought to have bathed in the lotus pond on the southeast side. *Free* *Outer gate: daily 4* AM*–9* PM*; temple: daily 5* AM*–9* PM.

3

Near the Tourist Bungalow on the main road is the **Thai Monastery,** with gilded "sky tassels" curling up from the eaves, two giant guardian *yakshas* keeping evil spirits from entering the temple, and a big gold Buddha in the elegant, chandelier-lit interior. (The largest Buddha of all is found behind the nearby Japanese Daijekyo Temple—it's about three stories high.)

The main **Tibetan Monastery,** representing the Dalai Lama's *gelugpa* (Yellow Hat) tradition, is on the north side of town behind the Mahabodhi Society building; inside are wall paintings and a big gold Buddha surrounded by hundreds of little gold Buddhas. When the Dalai Lama visits, he teaches under a large tent in an adjacent field.

On the opposite side of the street from the Tibetan Monastery and next to the Mahayana Guest House is the lovely **Shechen Gompa,** where every surface has been brightly painted with murals, dragons, flowers, and all manner of ornament.

OFF THE BEATEN PATH

Rajgir & Nalanda. These two towns are 85 km (53 mi) and 101 km (63 mi), respectively, northeast of Bodhgaya, a four-hour train ride on the *Budhpurnima Express,* which leaves Gaya three afternoons a week, arriving in Nalanda at 5:30 and Rajgir 20 minutes later. (The timing of this requires an overnight stay.) Alternatively, you can take a three-hour taxi ride on rough roads. Rajgir is the capital of the 6th-century BC kingdom of Magadha and the site of the first Buddhist Council in Buddha's time. Today the town, encircled by remnants of a pre-Mauryan cyclopean wall and known for its hot springs, is a winter health resort. A chairlift leads to an impressive contemporary Peace Pagoda erected by Japanese Buddhists on the hilltop where the Buddha preached each year during the rainy season. Treks lead to 26 Jain temples. If you have time, visit the redbrick ruins of the great 5th-century Buddhist university at **Nalanda,** but don't go on Friday, when the archaeological museum, with Buddhist and Hindu bronzes and statues of the Buddha found in the area, is closed. Middle Way Travels *(⇨ Tours, North Central India Essentials)* can organize a trip for you. You can also get information at the Bodhgaya tourist office.

WHERE TO STAY

$$$ **Royal Residency.** Surrounded by farmland and palm trees, about 1.5 km (1 mi) from the Mahabodhi Temple, this hotel has grand aspirations, evidenced in the elegant white-marble lobby. Though it opened in February 2002, at this writing the place still had a bit of a deserted feel and a too-spare look (no wall art or bedspreads). The rooms are large, with green-and-gold marble floors and marble baths with large showers and separate tubs. Nine Japanese-style rooms have wood floors and mattresses on tatami mats (the owners are Japan-based). **Pros:** none of Bodhgaya's hotels have extras like pools, but the Residency does have big men's and women's marble Japanese-style group baths with blue mosaic-tile ceilings. **Cons:** with such little design, it feels a bit institutional, high price for the area. ✉ *Domuhan Rd., Gaya District, Bodhgaya, 824231* ☎ *631/220–1156 or 631/220–1157* 🌐 *www.theroyalresidency.net* *64 rooms, 5 suites* *In-room: refrigerator, Wi-Fi. In-hotel: restaurant, room service, bar, laundry service, public Internet, public Wi-Fi.* 💳 *AE, MC, V.*

$$ **Lotus Nikko.** At what was once a government-owned hotel, the lobby is spotless and bright with shiny marble floors and sunlight from all directions. All rooms are fresh and pleasant, but not fancy: cream walls, blue carpet and fabrics, and woven leather headboards. Suites are simply very large rooms. **Pros:** close to all the sights. **Cons:** a bit pricey for the basic accommodations. ✉ *Gaya District, Bodhgaya, 824231* ☎ *631/220–0789* 🌐 *www.lotustranstravels.com* *60 rooms, 2 suites* *In-room: refrigerator, dial-up. In-hotel: restaurant, room service, bar, laundry service, no elevator, public Internet, no-smoking rooms, some pets allowed.* 💳 *AE, MC, V.*

$ **Sujata.** The large rooms in this well-liked hotel are decorated with Formica-esque furniture in the sitting areas, and gold satin covers on the beds. Like other hotels in town, Sujata has separate marble Japanese group baths for men and women in place of an actual pool. **Pros:** on-site restaurant is probably the best choice in a town of limited reliable dining options—try the delicious *kaju kanthi kababs,* boneless chunks of chicken marinated in cashew paste and cream. **Cons:** don't expect a romantic evening: every bed in the hotel is a twin, with the exception of larger beds in the two suites. ✉ *Gaya District, Bodhgaya, 824231* ☎ *631/220–0761* 🌐 *www.hotelsujata.com* *43 rooms, 2 suites* *In-room: refrigerator. In-hotel: restaurant, room service, laundry service, public Wi-Fi* 💳 *AE, MC, V.*

¢ **Hotel Siddhartha Vihar.** This government-run property in the Bihar Tourist Bungalow complex provides clean, basic private-bath, twin-bed rooms (more pleasant than some at this price) with phones and small TVs. There's a railway counter on the campus, which is shared with the Bihar tourist office and two rock-bottom state hotels. **Pros:** get good inside information on what to see from state tourism employees. **Cons:** absolutely no frills. *For reservations contact B.S.T.D.C., Paryatan Bhawan, Beer Chand Patel Path, Patna 612/222–5411 Gaya District, Bodhgaya, 824231 http://bstdc.bih.nic.in 25 rooms In-room: no a/c (some). In-hotel: restaurant, room service, no elevator, laundry service, public Internet. No credit cards.*

¢ **Mahayana Guest House.** Operated by Tibetan monks from the nearby Namgyal monastery, this sprawling guesthouse is laid-back and friendly. But don't come if you expect snappy service; what you'll find is inexpensive, clean, and pleasantly furnished rooms arranged around an open-air atrium. All but the 10 shared-bath rooms have phones and TVs; suites have mini-refrigerators and bathtubs. The vegetarian restaurant serves Tibetan, Chinese, and Indian food, and the bookshop can help fill any gaps in your knowledge of Buddhism or Tibet. **Pros:** staying here means a chance to meet and chat up real Buddhist monks. **Cons:** you'll need to be vigilant about your reservation if you don't want to end up sharing a bathroom with a stranger. *Box 04, Gaya District, Bodhgaya, 824231 631/220–0675 631/220–0676 mahayanagt@yahoo.com 67 rooms, 6 suites In-room: no a/c (some), no phone (some), refrigerator (some). In-hotel: restaurant, room service, laundry service, some pets allowed. No credit cards.*

LUCKNOW

300 km (186 mi) northwest of Varanasi, 516 km (320 mi) southeast of Delhi.

The capital of Uttar Pradesh, Lucknow is—in its lingering self-image, anyway—a city of ornate manners, inherited from the last significant Muslim court to hold sway in North India. Settled on the banks of the Gomti River in the earliest period of Indian history, it came to prominence in 1775, after Moghul power had declined in Delhi, as capital of the independent kingdom of Avadh. The nawabs of Avadh were members of the Shia sect of Islam, and the city remains an important center for that minority. Shia *imambaras*—gathering places used during Muharram, the month of mourning for Hussain, the martyred third imam of Islam—are Lucknow's most important monuments. Wajid Ali Shah, the last nawab and a legendarily impractical aesthete, was deposed by the British, who annexed Avadh in 1856. Resentment over that act, combined with the decades of indirect control that preceded it, contributed to Lucknow's strong support for the rebels during the Sepoy Mutiny of 1857 (also known as the Indian Rebellion), with members of Avadh's disbanded army manning the barricades against the British. British residents and troops, and an equal number of Indian troops and servants, were besieged for almost five months. After the Mutiny, the British drastically altered the city's plan in the name of safety: many congested, easily defensible older parts of the city were razed, and narrow alleyways became broad avenues where troops could move safely and smoothly.

Today Lucknow is a pleasant city—less crowded, dirty, and hassle-ridden than Agra and Varanasi, though without Agra's killer monuments or Varanasi's fascination. For a few days here you can relax in good hotels, dine extremely well on the elegant cuisine of the nawabs, shop in markets—modern and medieval–visit the few tourist sites at leisure, and just pedal or be pedaled around the back streets past remnants of the town's past as a cultural and royal capital, including 18th- and 19th-century nawabi palaces.

Driving along the Gomti River at the eastern end of the city, just past the Rumi Dawaza, or Turkish Gate, you'll see the **Bara Imambara.** Preceded by a wide plaza and set at an oblique angle to its accompanying mosque, Lucknow's largest imambara is noted for its great vaulted hall with a vast roof unsupported by pillars. Guides will pester you to use them, and you may need them when you climb up to the top floor: here a labyrinth of identical doorways (supposedly 489 of them), passages, and stairways, with hidden routes and many dead ends, make up the *bhul bhulaiya*—roughly, "place of forgetting"—leading back down to the ground level. You can go through the warren solo, but it takes time and patience, and with dark stairways and broken pavement in some places, it can be slightly hazardous. The imambara's raison d'être is the **tomb of Nawab Asaf-ud-Daulah,** who built his own resting place in 1784. The excellent views from the top floor take in a deep step well on the opposite side of the plaza from the mosque. ✉ *Husainabad Rd.* 🎫 *Rs. 300* ⏲ *Daily sunrise–sunset.*

The **Chota (or Husainabad) Imambara,** built in 1838, is about half a kilometer west of the Bara Imambara. At the end of a courtyard with a large ornamental pool is this elegant white building with calligraphy etched across the facade and a gilded onion dome. Inside is a hanging garden of chandeliers from China, Japan, everywhere; a fantastic pair of German torcheres about 8 feet high, with gold accents and cranberry glass bowls; a huge stepped throne of heavily embossed silver; an intricately inlaid-marble floor; and the tombs of Muhammad Ali Shah, third nawab of Avadh, and his mother. ✉ *Husainabad Rd.* 🎫 *Free* ⏲ *Daily sunrise–sunset.*

Part of the fun of visiting Lucknow is exploring its markets. The oldest is the **Chowk,** dating from the medieval period. You enter via the Akbari or the Gol Gate. Once the street of highly accomplished courtesans patronized by wealthy men and even nawabs, later a red-light district off-limits to British soldiers, today it's a run-down but teeming market with temples, madrasas, and the odd merchant's haveli thrown in here and there with scooters, people, and cows wandering around. In workshops you'll see men pounding silver into edible, whisper-thin foil (called *vark*) that will grace the tops of sweet confections. At night, here and in Aminabad market and in Nakkhas, which meets the Chowk at Akbari Gate, food stalls set up in front of closed shops send good smells wafting through the lanes, and locals mill about, sipping tea and catching up with one another. ⏲ *Shops Fri.–Wed. 10:30or 11* AM*–8* PM*, food stalls daily 10* AM*–10:30* PM.

NEED A BREAK?

There are three prime snacking stops in the Chowk (aside from the delicious nuggets of water-buffalo liver cooked in the evening on skewers, over charcoal made from the wood of tamarind trees). Prakash Kulfi is renowned for its version of *kulfi,* a rich almond-, cardamom-, and saffron-flavored ice cream that's sometimes served with *faluda,* a creamy rosewater-flavored kind of pudding with the surprising addition of vermicelli. Radhey-Lal Misthan Bhandar (Gol Gate ☎522/225-6087) has a wonderful selection of Indian sweets, such as *barfi,* a dense "milk sweet" topped with edible silver foil; the shredded-carrot treat *gajer halwa,* redolent of cardamom and spiked with cashews and dried fruit; and another milk sweet, the Lucknow specialty *malai gilori.* Tunday Kebabi (near the Akbari Gate)—the city's most famous hole-in-the-wall eatery, which has been in the same family for a century—continues to be thronged with devoted fans of its *gelawat* ("melt in your mouth") kebabs, small fried patties made from twice-minced lamb mixed with more than 100 spices. Its street-front stoves make only these and *parathas*; for more choices, try Grandson of Tunday Kebabi, the family's newer spot near Ghari Wali Masjid in Aminabad.

The 221-foot-high gunmetal **Clock Tower,** with components transported from London's Ludgate Hill, is a striking Victorian structure. Reminiscent of that other British clock tower, Big Ben, it was built in 1887 to mark the arrival of the first lieutenant governor of Avadh. ✉ *Husainabad Rd., between Bara Imambara and Chota Imambara.*

The Saturn-shaped **Indira Gandhi Planetarium,** built in 2003, has a 40-minute show in English at 2 PM. Unlike most places in India, the building is accessible to people with disabilities. ✉ *9 Mabiullah Rd., Suraj Kund Park* ☎ *522/262–9176* 🎟 *Rs. 25* ⏲ *Tues.–Sat. 2–6.*

At the eastern edge of the city, on the banks of the Gomti, is **La Martinière,** the most outlandish building in town. Built in the late 18th century as a palace by Major-General Claude Martin, a French adventurer who profited handsomely from his military service to the nawabs and happily spread his epicurean tastes, it's now a school for boys of any religion, as provided by Martin in his will. The lower floors were designed to flood in summer—an innovative, if malarial, cooling system. From the outside you can get a good sense of the place, with its oddly angled wings, four octagonal towers that rise from basement to roof, and four stone lions growling down from the parapet. With advance notice, Uttar Pradesh State Tourism (☎522/263–8105) can arrange a tour.

The **Picture Gallery** is a small room with life-size oil paintings of the nawabs of Avadh. ✉ *Husainabad Rd., near Satkhanda Palace* ☎ *No phone* 🎟 *Rs. 100 or free with ticket from Bara Imambara* ⏲ *Daily sunrise–sunset.*

About 1½ km (1 mi) toward the city center from the Bara Imambara is the **Residency** compound, where the British garrison was besieged on June 30, 1857. A relief force entered (as you will) through the **Baillie Guard Gate** on September 25, only to end up besieged themselves. On the right is the **Treasury** building, and behind that a large **Banquet Hall** that served as a hospital. (About 2,000 people died in the siege, more from disease than from gunfire.) Up a slight rise is a large open green, with an active shrine to a Muslim *pir* (holy man) under a tree to the left and an obelisk on the right commemorating Henry Lawrence, the chief commissioner who gathered his people here only to fall to gunfire on July 4. The Residency itself lies largely in ruin. Part of the building has been converted into a museum, called the **Model Room,** displaying a model of the compound under siege as well as cannonballs, arms, photographs, and other artifacts. Belowground are the chambers where many of the women and children escaped intermittent fire from the rooftops of surrounding buildings. Down the slope on the far side of the Residency is a **cemetery** for the many who were lost before the siege was finally broken on November 17. The wording of pre- and post-Independence markers and signs indicates the differences in how events here have been viewed. (Until August 15, 1947, a Union Jack flew over the compound.) Other buildings are scattered throughout, and you'll want at least an hour and a half to absorb the Residency's melancholy significance. Come back in the evening for the sound-and-light show, but have your hotel call before you set out to check the time for the English version, which depends on the time of the sunset; also, be aware that shows generally won't run unless there are at least 15 people. *Grounds, Rs. 100, museum Rs. 5, sound-and-light show Rs. 25* ⌚ *Grounds daily 7–7, museum Mon.–Sat. 10–4:30.*

WHERE TO EAT & STAY

$$–$$$ ★ ✕ **Oudhyana.** The Taj's formal restaurant, an elegant, seafoam-green room lit by gorgeous chandeliers, with a floral Persian carpet in deep maroon, green, and gold, features specialties of the nawabs. A banquet of superb Avadhi dishes, served nawabi-style with heavy pounded-brass tableware and goblets, may include *kakori kabab,* here made with finely minced lamb, saffron, rose petals, and cardamom; *gelawat kababs,* pan-fried finely minced spiced lamb; *nahari gosht,* lamb on the bone, cooked in lamb stock with herbs and spices; and *sheermal,* an orange Lucknow flatbread made with milk, fat, and saffron. ✉ *Taj Residency, Vipin Khand, Gomti Nagar* ☎ *522/239–3939* ▭ *AE, DC, MC, V.*

$–$$ ★ ✕ **Falaknuma.** Lunchtime at this rooftop restaurant shows the city and the river spread out below you beyond a wall of windows and a vaguely tropical themed decor of white-lattice planters and green plants. At night the scene is more romantic, especially with the musicians singing soft ghazals. The food is an excellent introduction to local Avadhi cuisine, characterized by meats stuffed with spices that are then removed so only the aromas remain. Try the meat sampler, an array of tender kebabs like *lasooni kebab,* boneless chicken marinated with garlic, yogurt, mint, and spices. Other selections such as *naushai jaan,* a drumstick marinated with spices and herbs and cooked in a tandoor, and the Lucknow specialty *kakori kabab,* a cigar-shaped lamb kabab cooked on a skewer, are also delicious. ✉*Clarks Avadh, 8 Mahatma Gandhi Marg* ☎*522/262–0131* 💳*AE, DC, MC, V.*

$$$ **Clarks Avadh.** With its prime location on the river, Clarks is ideally situated for good views—especially from the rooftop restaurant, Falaknuma—and easy sightseeing. Some rooms have wood flooring, while others have carpet, and all seem to be dimly lit. For more light, ask for a room overlooking the beautiful lawn. The hotel caters heavily toward business clientele, and the lobby shows it with suits mingling and relaxing in all the common areas. There's a Privilege Club floor, with rooms done in rich fabrics, a lounge with a computer, and a small chandelier-lit room for private meetings, parties, or lunch. The green-and-gold suites have miles of silk drapes and expansive river views. **Pros:** in the center of town, you're close to all the sights. **Cons:** you might feel a bit out of place as a carefree tourist who isn't hurrying off to the next meeting. ✉*8 Mahatma Gandhi Marg, 226001* ☎*522/262–0131 to 33, 522/261–6500 to 09* 🌐*www.hotelclarks.com* *94 rooms, 3 suites* *In-room: Wi-Fi. In-hotel: 2 restaurants, room service, bar, pool, gym, laundry service, public Internet, public Wi-Fi.* 💳*AE, DC, MC, V.*

3

$$$ Fodor'sChoice ★ **Taj Residency.** The pristine, pale turquoise pool here, centered by a fountain and landscaped with big palm trees, may be one of the largest in India. This fabulous Taj business hotel is in a British colonial-style building, with an expansive lobby of white marble and one of the restaurants in plain view. The spacious guest rooms have queen or king beds, rich fabrics, artwork depicting the life and architecture of the Moghuls, and a welcome fruit basket. Come and visit even if you're not staying here to have a drink at the Mehfil bar, which has ghazals and soft music playing every evening. **Pros:** some of the best dining in town, and a well-stocked bookstore with good maps of the city. **Cons:** far from the center of town; the unusually hard mattresses are due for an upgrade. ✉*Vipin Khand, Gomti Nagar, 226010* ☎*522/239–3939* 🌐*www.tajhotels.com* *106 rooms, 4 suites* *In-room: safe, refrigerator, Wi-Fi. In-hotel: 2 restaurants, room service, bar, pool, gym, spa, laundry service, public Internet, public Wi-Fi, no-smoking rooms.* 💳*AE, DC, MC, V.*

$$ **La Place Park Inn.** Built in 2000, this Hazratganj area inn targeting business travelers has spacious rooms with green or cream marble floors and marble-top bedside tables, rich fabrics in greens, reds, and golds, hand-colored prints and large baths. The rooftop restaurant and bar serves tandoori and barbecue dishes; the main restaurant has candlelit dinners on weekends with pop or jazz bands. **Pros:** close to the Hazratganj shopping center, and discounted rates at a nearby fitness center are available. **Cons:** as with many Lucknow hotels, it's heavy on business travelers. ✉*6 Shahnajaf Rd., 226001* ☎*522/400–4040, 800/670–7275 in North America* 🌐*www.parkinnlucknow.com* *49 rooms, 1 suite* *In-room: refrigerator, Wi-Fi. In-hotel: 2 restaurants, room service, bar, laundry service, public Internet, public Wi-Fi.* 💳*AE, DC, MC, V* *BP.*

$ **Arif Castles.** The lobby is small and covered in dull-gray marble at this modest hotel in central Lucknow. Standard guest rooms are comfortable, but are beginning to show signs of wear, with tattered covers on the twin beds; in addition, the bathrooms are so small that they feel a bit like cubbyholes. Consider springing for an executive room, which has a double bed. **Pros:** convenient location, about 1½ km (1 mi) each from Clarks, Hazratganj, and the Botanical Gardens (a good place for morning walks); decent price. **Cons:** the bare-bones accommodations may still have you thinking you paid too much. ✉ *4 Rana Pratap Marg, 226001* ☎ *522/261–1313 to 17* 🌐 *www.arifcastles.com* *52 rooms* *In-hotel: restaurant, room service, laundry service.* ▭ *AE, MC, V.*

¢ **Sagar International.** In the Butler Palace area, where visiting bureaucrats stay (about 2½ km [1½ mi] east of Hazratganj and 5½ km [3½ mi] from the Residency), Sagar offers plenty of amenities at a fairly low price. There's classical Indian music playing in the lobby and the typical expanse of marble and red furniture. Rooms on the Executive Floor have better furnishings (such as ornate wooden headboards) and face greenery instead of the city; all rooms, done mostly in shades of red, have bathrooms with large windows, something rare even for top hotels. The rooftop restaurant has wraparound windows, which make for a great view. **Pros:** very affordable. **Cons:** a musty smell in some rooms, and the carpet needs to be replaced. ✉ *14A Jopling Rd., 226001* ☎ *522/220–6601 to 05* 📠 *522/220–6644* *60 rooms, 1 suite* *In-room: refrigerator. In-hotel: 2 restaurants, room service, bar, laundry service, public Internet, no-smoking rooms.* ▭ *MC, V.*

SHOPPING

Shops in Lucknow are generally open daily from 10 to 7, except those in Hazratganj, which close on Sunday, and in Aminabad and the Chowk, which close on Thursday.

Lucknow is famous for a style of straight-stitch embroidery on fine cotton cloth known as *chikan,* found in great variety and at bargain prices in the old **Chowk** and **Aminabad** markets, as well as at more upmarket shops in the modern **Hazratganj** area. Also in the markets is another characteristic Lucknow product, *attar,* the essential oils used in perfumes, made from aromatic herbs, spices, flowers, and leaves. The attar merchant with the longest pedigree is **Asghar Ali Mohammed Ali and Sons** (✉ *Gol Darwaza La., Chowk, near the Medical College* ☎ *No phone*), begun in 1830 by a perfumier brought to Lucknow to create his fragrances for the nawab. **Chhangamal Ramsaran Garg** (✉ *87 Hazratganj* ☎ *522/222–3252*) specializes in chikan work; you'll find both very fine and inexpensive pieces here. **Ram Advani** (✉ *Mayfair Bldg., Mahatma Gandhi Rd., Hazratganj* ☎ *522/227–3789*) is a bookshop with a well-edited general selection and works on Lakhnavi history by scholars from around the world. The eponymous gracious owner has run the place since 1948.

NIGHTLIFE & THE ARTS

The courtly cultivation of singing, dancing, and poetry that characterized Lucknow in earlier eras has waned, but efforts are on to revive it. Each December 1 through 5, the Lucknow Mahotsav festival hosts excellent musicians and dancers for nightly performances; some events begin on November 25.

NORTH CENTRAL INDIA ESSENTIALS

To research prices, get advice from other travelers, and book travel arrangements, visit www.fodors.com.

AIR TRAVEL

The major domestic airlines servicing North Central India are Air India, Deccan, Jet Airways, Jet Lite, Kingfisher Airlines, and Spice Jet. There is no service to Gwalior.

Air India and Jet Airways provide the most options, with daily direct flights from Delhi to Bhopal, Khajuraho, Lucknow, Patna (two hours from Bodhgaya), and Varanasi. Both airlines also operate flights between Khajuraho and Varanasi.

Deccan flies daily from Delhi to Bhopal and Lucknow. Jet Lite flies daily from Delhi to Lucknow. King Fisher Airlines flies daily to Khajuraho (via Varanasi) and Varanasi. At this writing, they were planning on adding service to Agra. Spice Jet flies daily only to Varanasi.

AIRLINES & CONTACTS **Air India** (☎ *180/022–7722 toll-free in Delhi, 800/625–6424 toll-free in U.S.* 🌐 *www.airindia.com*).

Deccan (☎ *080/4114–819–099 in Bangalore* 🌐 *www.airdeccan.net*).

Jet Airways (☎ *180/022–5522 toll-free in Delhi, 877/835–9538 toll-free in U.S.* 🌐 *www.jetairways.com*).

Jet Lite (☎ *180/022–3020* 🌐 *www.jetlite.com*).

King Fisher Airlines (☎ *226/649–9393, 866/435–9532 toll-free in U.S.* 🌐 *www.flykingfisher.com*).

Spice Jet (☎ *0987/180–3333 toll-free in Delhi* 🌐 *www.spicejet.com*).

AIRPORTS

Agra's Kheria Airport is roughly 7 km (4 mi) from the Taj Mahal. Provided there is current service there, your hotel can usually send a car for around Rs. 250. You can also take a fixed-rate taxi or auto-rickshaw from the airport to the city center for less than Rs. 200.

Bhopal's Raja Bhoj airport is 10 km (6 mi) from town. The taxi ride costs about Rs. 300.

From the Patna Airport, it's a 125-km (78-mi) drive to Bodhgaya, and prices for transport by car start at Rs. 1,000 one-way.

Khajuraho Airport is 5 km (3 mi) from town; the taxi ride costs about Rs. 150.

Lucknow's Amausi Airport is about 22 km (14 mi) or 30 minutes by car from most hotels; a taxi costs around Rs. 200.

The nearest airport to Varanasi, Bhabatpur, is 22 km (14 mi), or a 45-minute drive, from most hotels. A taxi costs about Rs. 350 or Rs. 500 (air-conditioned) to the cantonment area, or from Rs. 400 to Rs. 600 into the city proper.

AUTO-RICKSHAWS

Be prepared to negotiate the rate for an auto-rickshaw, which is the most common mode of transportation throughout the region. Three exceptions are Orchha, Khajuraho, and Badhgaya, which are so small that bicycles, cycle-rickshaws, and/or walking (aside from vehicles) are the best available options. Especially in Agra, auto-rickshaw fares depend on several factors, including how wealthy you look, how far you want to go, how many times you want to stop, the time of day, and whether it's raining. You can generally expect to pay about Rs. 100 for a half day, Rs. 200 for a full day. If you're not comfortable with the price you're given, look for another auto-rickshaw, and if you don't want to haggle, take a metered taxi or book a car.

Auto-rickshaws are a fast way to scoot through Varanasi's crowded streets, but the fumes from other automobiles can be horrendous at busy times. When traffic is heavy, take an air-conditioned taxi with the windows closed, especially if you're coming from one of the hotels far from the ghats. Ask your hotel or the tourist office for the going rate, and agree on a fare in advance. Note that from 9 AM to 9 PM these and other motor vehicles are not allowed beyond Godaulia Crossing, the traffic circle near the central bathing ghat, Dashashvamedh; they'll drop you off a short walk from the river if that's where you're headed.

BICYCLE & CYCLE-RICKSHAW TRAVEL

Renting a bike in Khajuraho costs about Rs. 50 per day and is one of the most popular ways to get around this tranquil town. You can rent bikes across from the bus stand, behind the museum, and from some hotels.

You can get the latest rate estimates for cycle-rickshaws from the local India Tourism office. Cycle-rickshaws should cost no more than Rs. 30 per hour in Agra or Khajuraho. They're a particularly pleasant way to get around Khajuraho, especially to the outlying temples. Distances are long in Varanasi, so a cycle-rickshaw is better for a leisurely roll through the old city (it frees you from fighting the crowds) than for cross-town transport. A trip from the cantonment to the ghats should cost about Rs. 50. If you hire a cycle-rickshaw for the day, agree on the price in advance and expect to pay about Rs. 150. Though Lucknow has plenty of traffic on the main tourist route, the back streets are pleasant viewed from a cycle-rickshaw, and short hops cost about Rs. 10.

BOAT TRAVEL

Boat rides on the Ganges in Varanasi should cost Rs. 50 for an hour for a small boat; the bigger, sturdier boats fit more people and cost Rs. 100 per hour. At Dashashvamedh Ghat, however, touts will demand as much as Rs. 600 for the typical round-trip along the shoreline that takes about two hours. If you just show up at the popular sunrise hour, you'll have limited time to shop around; for a reasonable rate, chat with some boatmen the previous evening and arrange to meet one by the river the next morning. A boat from the main ghats to Ramnagar should cost about Rs. 250 round-trip.

CAR & DRIVER

Hire a car and driver only through your hotel or tour operator; UP Tours, the government of Uttar Pradesh's tour arm *(⇨ Tours)*; the Madhya Pradesh State Tourism Development Corporation *(⇨ Visitor Information)*; or a recommended local travel agent.

For trips to Agra from Delhi, contact Dhanoa Tours and Travels. Rates start around Rs. 3,600 and go up to Rs. 10,000 for a day trip, depending on the size of the vehicle and whether there's air-conditioning. The price includes tax and a driver. Expect to pay about Rs. 500 extra for a worthwhile detour to Fatehpur Sikri.

Prices in Agra are generally Rs. 6–Rs. 8 per kilometer. A non-air-conditioned car for four hours or 40 km should cost about Rs. 500—the minimum charge. For overnight excursions, add a halt charge of Rs. 200. The standard charge for a trip to Fatehpur Sikri is Rs. 650, but prices are always negotiable. You can hire a taxi at the train station under a fixed-rate system. If you'd prefer not to be taken to the driver's choice of stores, restaurants, or hotels (where he gets a commission), say so firmly up front.

In Khajuraho, a hired car can be convenient if you want to wander outside town or can't walk the 3 km to the most distant temples. A non-air-conditioned car should cost about Rs. 200 for two hours or 30 km. You can hire a taxi for about Rs. 6 per km.

In Bhopal, a car is essential for side trips into the countryside. Rates depend on how much you want to see and the mileage involved. For sightseeing in town, expect to pay Rs. 400 for a half-day, Rs. 650 for a full day, for a non-air-conditioned car; Rs. 500 for a half-day, Rs. 800 for a full day, for an air-conditioned car.

In Lucknow, the recommended rates are Rs. 110 for less than 5 km; Rs. 160 for 5 to 10 km; Rs. 450 for 40 km; and Rs. 800 for 80 km. Again, prices are negotiable.

To reach Orchha from the Jhansi railhead 16 km away, you can hire a car from Touraids for about Rs. 400 for the half-hour drive.

In Varanasi, a four-hour car excursion should cost Rs. 350 in a non-air-conditioned car, Rs. 450 with air-conditioning. For eight hours (90 km) a car should cost you about Rs. 600. A taxi from Varanasi will drop you in Sarnath and wait about three hours for Rs. 300. (Auto-rickshaws will make the round-trip for about Rs. 200.) The Grand Trunk Road (NH 2) east of Varanasi passes south of Bodhgaya. The local connecting roads, for which you turn off just east of Aurangabad, are in poor condition and sometimes beset by robbers.

Contacts Dhanoa Tours and Travels (✉ *Hara Marg, near Malcha Marg Market, Chanakyapuri, New Delhi* ☎ *112/688–6051*). **Touraids Travel Service** (✉ *46 Gopichand Shivhare Rd., Agra Cantonment, Agra* ☎ *562/222–5029 or 562/222–5074* *touraids@sancharnet.in* ✉ *Moti Mahal, Moti Palace, Gwalior* ☎ *751/232–4354 or 751/232–0758* *touraidsi@yahoo.com* ✉ *Jai Complex, Civil Lines, Jhansi* ☎ *517/233–1760* *tourjhs@sancharnet.in* ✉ *Kandariya Campus, Khajuraho* ☎ *768/627–4060* *tourhjr@sancharnet.in*).

CAR TRAVEL

For a scenic five- or six-day trip covering Agra, Gwalior, Orchha, Khajuraho, Bhopal, and Sanchi, hire a car in Delhi or Agra from a tour operator or travel agency.

Agra is 200 km (124 mi) south of Delhi on roads built by the Moghul emperors to connect their two capitals. The roads are good but heavily used—don't expect to travel much above 50 kph (30 mph). The trip should take 3½ to 4 hours. The best route is National Highway 2 (NH 2).

Lucknow is connected to Delhi by National Highway (NH) 2, the Grand Trunk Road, which runs through Agra and the industrial city of Kanpur before NH 25 turns north to Lucknow. This is one of the most heavily used truck routes in India, and is for the most part devoid of lanes. An alternate route is NH 24 through Bareilly and central Uttar Pradesh. NH 56 links Lucknow with the Grand Trunk Road at Varanasi and allows a stop in little-visited Jaunpur, capital of an early Muslim sultanate.

To reach Varanasi by car, take NH 2 or NH 56 from the northwest, NH 29 from Gorakhpur (if you started in Kathmandu), NH 2 from Kolkata, or NH 30 and NH 2 from Patna.

MONEY

ATMS There are ICICI Bank ATMs, which accept all foreign cards, in Agra, Bhopal, Gwalior, Lucknow, and Varanasi. Ask your hotel or taxi driver for one close to you. Definitely have enough cash on hand before arriving in Orchha, Khajuraho, and Bodhgaya, as most ATMs here only accept domestic cards.

CURRENCY EXCHANGE Your hotel is the easiest place to change currency, but you can also do so at the State Bank of India in Agra, Bhopal, Bodhgaya, Khajuraho, Lucknow, and Varanasi. Other banks may change money as well, but note that not even all State Bank branches will accept foreign travelers' checks.

TOURS

Outbound Travels in Delhi can arrange flights and coordinate flights with train or car travel to help you make the most of limited travel time. UP Tours (Uttar Pradesh's tour agency) has a vast offering of tours, including Buddhist circuit tours and a daily guided bus tour of Fatehpur Sikri, Agra Fort, and the Taj Mahal for Rs. 1,700 per person (this covers transport, guide, and admission fees, including the Rs. 750 admission to the Taj); a half-day tour of Fatehpur Sikri alone is Rs. 550. For a personal guide, ask your hotel or contact the nearest India Tourism office.

Middle Way Travels runs multiday pilgrimage tours and will organize tours of Bodhgaya's temples and other sights as well as day trips to Rajgir and Nalanda. Radiant Travels has one of the region's few female tour guides, who gives a feminine perspective on Bhopal. Tornos specializes in Lucknow's Avadhi culture, crafts, and cuisine, as well as the history of the British in India, and can really make a visit to the city fun and enlightening. Offerings include a visit or a traditional royal meal (*dastarkhwan*) with the nawab, who has a wonderful collection of antique chikan garments; a tour of chikan workshops; transport by horse cart; picnics in a traditional village with singing and dancing; and theme events.

Contacts **Middle Way Travels** (✉ *7/11 Main Rd., near Mahabodhi Temple, Bodhgaya* ☎ *631/220-0648 or 631/220-0668* ✉ *middleway2001@yahoo.com*). **Outbound Travels** (✉ *216A/11 Gautam Nagar, 3rd fl., New Delhi* ☎ *114/164-0565* 🌐 *www.outboundtravels.com*). **Radiant Travels** (✉ *243-B, Mezzanine Fl., Krishna Palace, M.P. Nagar, Zone 1, Bhopal* ☎ *755/255-4411 or 755/255-5800, mobile 942/530-3572* ✉ *24 Ahmedabad Rd., Bhopal* ☎ *755/254-0560*). **Tornos** (✉ *Tornos House, C-2016, Indira Nagar, Lucknow* ☎ *522/234-9472 or 522/234-6965* 🌐 *www.tornosindia.com*). **UP Tours** (✉ *Hotel Taj Khema, near Taj Mahal's eastern gate, Agra* ☎ *562/233-0140* ✉ *Tourist Bungalow, Parade Kothi, Varanasi* ☎ *542/220-8545* ✉ *Central Reservations Centre, Hotel Gomti, 6 Sapru Marg, Lucknow* ☎ *522/221-4708, or 522/261-4284*).

3

TRAIN TRAVEL

The Indian Railways Web site (🌐 *www.indianrail.gov.in*) provides comprehensive train information. It lets you buy and print out tickets in advance, but takes a fair amount of time to figure out. Every main station has a tourist reservation office. Reservations can be made there in person at the last minute provided there's space, but try to reserve as far in advance as possible during peak times of year.

The *Shatabdi Express*, India's best train, runs daily on the Delhi–Agra–Gwalior–Jhansi–Bhopal–Mumbai route, offering frequent meals and snacks en route; from Delhi to Agra takes 2 hours, from Agra to Gwalior 1 hour and 15 minutes, from Gwalior to Jhansi (a major rail junction and the nearest to Orchha, 16 km [10 mi] away) 1 hour, and from Jhansi to Bhopal 3½ hours. The slower *Bhopal Express* and *Lakshadweep Express* run the same route daily. The daily *Taj Express* connects Delhi, Agra, and Gwalior.

The *Marudhar Express* travels the Jodhpur–Jaipur–Agra–Lucknow–Varanasi route daily; the Jaipur–Agra leg takes 13 hours, the Agra–Lucknow 6 hours, and the Lucknow–Varanasi 6½ hours.

The *Rajdhani Express*, India's other premier train, passes through Bhopal frequently, including twice a week in each direction on the Delhi–Chennai route and four times a week on the Delhi–Bangalore route. The Delhi–Bhopal leg takes about 8 hours; two routes have late-night departures from Bhopal with arrival in Delhi at 5:30 the next morning, saving a night's hotel fare in Delhi.

Gaya is served by the *Rajdhani*, which connects it daily with Delhi (12 hours) and with Mughal Serai (about 9 hours), an hour's drive from Varanasi. The slower *Poorva Express* connects Gaya with Delhi (16½ hours) and Varanasi (3½ hours) three days a week. The *Budhpurnima Express* leaves Gaya three afternoons a week, arriving in Nalanda (4 hours) at 5:30 and Rajgir 20 minutes later (the same train connects Sarnath with Varanasi and Gaya).

Lucknow is connected to Delhi by many trains, including the 7½- to 8-hour *Rajdhani* twice a week in each direction and the 6¼-hour *Shatabdi* on weekdays. The *Lucknow Express* makes the 15½-hour trip between

Lucknow and Agra daily, and the 12½- to 14½-hour trip between Lucknow and Bhopal five days a week. The *Jan Shatabdi* makes the 5½-hour trip between Lucknow and Varanasi every day but Sunday.

Varanasi is 12½ hours from Delhi on the daily *Shiv Ganga Express,* 5½ hours from Lucknow on the *Jan Shatabdi,* 17 hours from Bhopal on the daily *Varanasi Kamayani Express* and from Gwalior on the daily *Bundelkhand Express,* and 4 hours from Gaya on the weekly *Ranchi Express.*

VISITOR INFORMATION

You can pick up maps and information on approved guides at India Ministry of Tourism offices in Agra, Khajuraho, and Varanasi's cantonment, and at an information desk at Varanasi's airport. If you are planning your trip from New Delhi, the India Ministry of Tourism's office on Janpath is worth a visit.

The Madhya Pradesh State Tourism Development Corporation, one of India's better state tourist offices, has friendly staff and information on Khajuraho, Gwalior, Orchha, Bhopal, and Sanchi.

The Uttar Pradesh State Tourism Development Corporation arranges tours and cars in Agra and Lucknow. The New Delhi office (centrally located near the Imperial Hotel) has maps, brochures, and information on approved guides. The best information at Varanasi's Uttar Pradesh State Tourism office is in Hindi, but the staff can still help you, and there's a satellite desk at the train station.

Tourist Offices **Bihar State Tourism Development Corporation** (*✉ Tourist Bungalow, Bodhgaya ☎ 631/220-0672 🌐 http://bstdc.bih.nic.in*). **India Ministry of Tourism** (*✉ 88 Janpath, New Delhi ☎ 112/332-0005 to 0008 ✉ 191 The Mall, Agra ☎ 562/222-6378 ✉ Opposite Western Group of temples, Khajuraho ☎ 768/6242-0347 ✉ Sudama Palace, Kankar Bagh Rd., Patna ☎ 612/234-5776 ✉ 15B The Mall, Varanasi ☎ 542/250-1784 🌐 www.incredibleindia.org*). **Madhya Pradesh State Tourism Corporation** (*✉ Room No. 12, Hotel Janpath, Ground Floor, Palash Residency, Near 45 Bungalow T. T. Nagar, Bhopal ☎ 755/255-3006 or 755/255-3066 ✉ Chandella Cultural Center, Rajnagar Rd., Khajuraho ☎ 768/627-4051 ✉ At airport and bus station ✉ Tansen Residency, 6 Gandhi Rd., Gwalior ☎ 751/234-0370 ✉ Railway station, Jhansi ☎ 510/244-2622 🌐 www.mptourism.com*). **Uttar Pradesh Tourist Office** (*✉ 36 Janpath, Chandralok Bldg., New Delhi ☎ 112/332-2251 ✉ 64 Taj Rd., Agra ☎ 562/222-6431 ✉ Parade Kothi, opposite train station, Varanasi ☎ 542/220-6638 ✉ Hotel Mrigdava Campus, Sarnath ☎ 542/259-5965 ✉ 10 Station Rd., Lucknow ☎ 522/263-8105 ✉ At railway station and airport 🌐 www.up-tourism.com*).

Rajasthan & Gujarat

4

Rajasthani dancing in Jaipur

WORD OF MOUTH

"I loved Jaisalmer, but it is the farthest away, and therefore the easiest to cut from a trip. The stone carving there is just beautiful, but unless you're planning to do a camel safari it might be hard to justify the extra travel after seeing Jodhpur and Jaipur. If you have a car and driver you could also visit the Shekhawati region, known for its painted havelis. It's north of Jaipur, and much less visited than the rest of Rajasthan."

—thursdaysd

www.fodors.com/forums

WELCOME TO RAJASTHAN & GUJARAT

TOP REASONS TO GO

★ **Pretty in Pink:** Dusty-pink Jaipur is your gateway to Rajasthan's beautiful palaces, forts, culture, and food.

★ **From the Thar Desert to the Lush Aravalis:** Travel from the golden sand dunes in Jaisalmer to the lovely Lake Pichola in Udaipur set against the Aravali mountains; don't miss the lush post-monsoon green in Ranakpur to its north.

★ **Head Back in Time at the Mehrangarh Fort:** Standing dramatically on a hill, this massive fort is one of Jodhpur's most imposing treasures.

★ **Royal for a Night:** Stay in one of the many opulent palaces and forts converted into Heritage Hotels.

★ **A Shopper's Dream:** Pack light and fill up your suitcase with jewelry, clothes, fabric, carpets, leatherbound journals, silver, and anything else that catches your eye.

1 Jaipur. The modern and ancient worlds collide in this bustling capital. Highlighted by the Hawa Mahal and the City Palace, this town is both an architectural delight and a shopping hotspot for textiles and jewelry.

2 Udaipur. With the Lake Palace floating in the middle of Lake Pichola, the White City is charming and serene. If you're feeling adventurous, you can hike up to Monsoon Palace or Neemach Mata for stunning birds-eye views.

3 Jodhpur. The blue houses in the old city here contrast with the desert landscape and the imposing Mehrangarh fort. The congested old city is fun to explore, and the fort is a short rickshaw ride away.

4 Jaisalmer. The Golden City is synonymous with its majestic fort, and a visit here is incomplete without a jeep or camel safari on the Sam Sand Dunes or near Khuri in the heart of the Thar Desert.

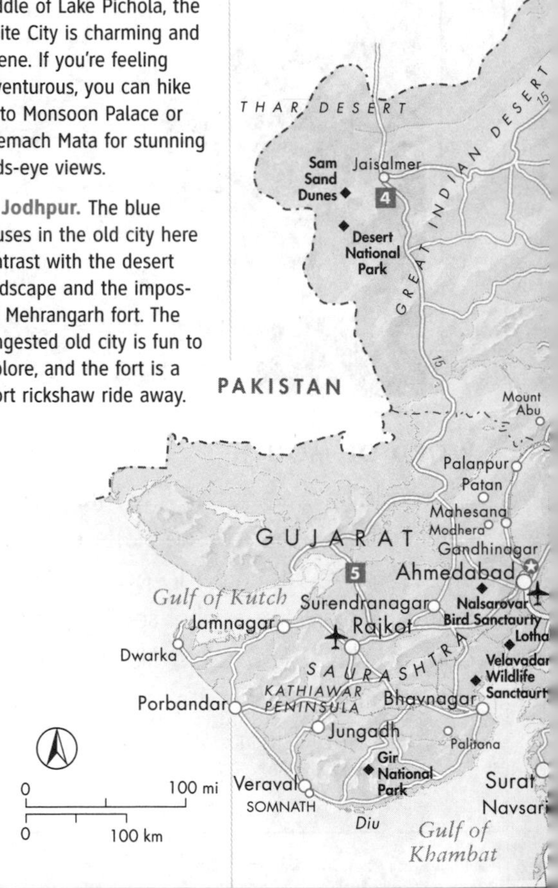

PUNJAB
Ganganagar
Sopron
Pamhagen
Pamhagen
HARYANA
DELHI
Delhi
NEW DELHI
Churu
Jhunjhunu
Mandawa
Mukandgarh
Bikaner
Fatehpur
Lachhmangarh
Nawalgahr
Neemrana
UTTAR PRADESH
AJASTHAN
SHEKHAVATI
Alwar
Sikar
Nagaur
Sariska N.P.
Agra
Jaipur
1
Bharatpur
Khimsar
sian
Sanganer
Jodhpur
Pushkar
Ajmer
Beawar
Guda Vishnoi
Rohet Garh
Ranthambhore National Park
Pali
ARAVALLI HILLS
Bhilwara
umbhalgarh
Castle Bijaipur
Bassi Fort Palace
Ranakpur
athdwara
Eklingji
Chittaurgarh
Udaipur
2
MADHYA PRADESH
adodara (Baroda)
MAHARASHTRA

5 Gujarat. Much less visited by tourists than Rajasthan, its neighbor to the north, Gujarat has many treasures. Its capital, Ahmedabad, is hectic and full of culture, and its rural districts contain some gorgeous wildlife sanctuaries and parks. A major draw for pilgrims throughout India are Gujarat's magnificent Jain shrines and temples, found throughout the state.

GETTING ORIENTED

The largest state in India, Rajasthan is in the northwestern part of the country, sharing a border with Pakistan. The Aravalli mountain range runs north–south almost the entire length of the state. The hot, dry northwest region is dominated by the Thar Desert while the milder south is known for its lakes and greenery. Jaipur, the state capital, is an hour's flight from New Delhi—travel options for getting farther afield include air, train, and road. To the south of Rajasthan is Gujarat, India's westernmost state.

Lake Palace Hotel on Pichola lake, Udaipur

RAJASTHAN & GUJARAT PLANNER

When to Go

The best time to visit Rajasthan and Gujarat is from October to March. Unfortunately, everyone knows this, so Rajasthan sights are packed and hotel tariffs are at their highest. If you're planning your Rajasthan vacation during the peak season, do so in advance. (Because Gujarat gets a fraction of the tourists that Rajasthan does, this advice is less important if you're heading there.)

If you want to get away from the hordes and can bear the heat of a desert summer, go to Rajasthan in April. By May and June, it's brutally hot. The monsoon season (July–September) is fine unless you want to see the wildlife parks, which tend to flood. Southern Rajasthan, especially Udaipur, is lovely at the tailend of the monsoons: everything is fresh and green after the rains.

Getting There & Around

There are domestic airports in Jaipur, Jodhpur, and Udaipur in Rajasthan and Ahmedabad, Vadodara, and Rajkot in Gujarat. The Union Territory of Diu also has its own airport.

Use a travel agent for advice on getting around. Popular domestic airline carriers to and around Rajasthan and Gujarat, include Jet Airways, Indian, Deccan, and Kingfisher Airlines. All these airlines now have Web sites, so searching for tickets is easier than ever.

There are daily trains to all major destinations in Rajasthan and Gujarat. Because of Jaisalmer's closeness to the Pakistan border, there are no commercial flights, and a train is the best method of getting there. Trains get crowded during peak season, and you may want to investigate special "tourist quotas" that set aside seats for foreign travelers. Check with your travel agent.

Renting private taxis with drivers is another option—though not cheap, it's a fast and easy way to cover regions like Shekhawati. Roads in Rajasthan can be bumpy, so allow for delays. The Delhi–Jaipur Highway (NH–8) is good, but once you're off the highway, the roads are full of potholes and it will take a long time to travel even short distances. Car rental prices are around Rs. 8–Rs. 10 per kilometer, and these can be cheaper if you opt out of air-conditioning. Get in touch with your hotel's travel desk or an independent travel agent for car rental options—the latter is more likely to give you a reasonable rate.

If convenience and a cheap price are more important to you than a super-comfortable journey, travel by bus—but keep in mind that the quality of buses in India varies widely. Some "tourist" buses end up picking up hitchhikers, so by the time you reach your destination, people are sitting in the aisles and sometimes even on the roof. If you don't mind an adventure, or if you have no other choice, by all means take a bus. Otherwise take a train or rent a car and driver. The easiest way to get a bus ticket in advance is not from the bus stations, but from many of the private vendors in tourist areas.

Rajasthani Razzle Dazzle

Rajasthani women adorn themselves with bangles; tinkling anklets; armbands; and finger, nose-, toe-, and earrings. Men are also fond of wearing gold hoops in their ears and amulets around their arms. In Jaipur, look for gold settings of *kundan* (a glasslike white stone) and *mina* (enamel) work. Udaipur, Nathdwara, and Jaisalmer are all known for antique and contemporary silver jewelry. Decorated *lac* (lacquer) bangles are worn for good luck. Rajasthani artisans also specialize in cutting precious and semiprecious stones. Jaipur is a trade center for precious stones, and one of the emerald capitals of the world.

The Common Camel

It's not unusual to see a single-humped camel drawing a cart on a dusty highway or through traffic in crowded Jaipur. These awkwardly assembled animals are an indispensable part of the local landscape and economy, and you'll see them wherever you go in the state. Apart from pulling loads (and that includes tourists), camels are also highly valued for their milk, meat, hair, leather, and even their droppings (used for manure).

But camels are best seen against their natural backdrop, the shifting dunes of the Thar Desert, which covers the northwest and extends into Pakistan. Here you can see caravans crossing the sands, sidestepping the odd shrub with an elegance that indicates they're on home ground. However, camel owners choose to dress their animals with a bit more flair: red, green, and gold saddle covers and tasseled bridles are signs of the well-dressed camel. The many camel fairs in the state are always a riot of colorful finery, wandering folk singers and musicians, merrymaking villagers, and preening, belching camels.

What It Costs In Rupees

	¢	$	$$	$$$	$$$$
Restaurants	under Rs. 100	Rs. 100–Rs. 300	Rs. 300–Rs. 500	Rs. 500–Rs. 700	over Rs. 700
Hotels	under Rs. 2,000	Rs. 2,000–Rs. 4,000	Rs. 4,000–Rs. 6,000	Rs. 6,000–Rs. 10,000	over Rs. 10,000

Restaurant prices are for an entrée plus bread or rice. Hotel prices are for a double room in high season, excluding a tax of up to 20%.

Planning Your Time in Rajasthan

The ideal way to see Rajasthan is to first fly to Jaipur, Jodhpur, or Udaipur and then tackle nearby towns by train, bus, or private car. Overnight train journeys between major towns in comfortable sleeper coaches are a cheap way to travel without wasting too much time or money on hotel stays. For instance, you could start in Jaipur and work your way to Udaipur, then to Jodhpur, Jaisalmer, and back to Delhi.

Depending on how much time you have, there are plenty of sights and day trips to be taken from each of these major destinations. Don't miss the Jain temples in Ranakpur and the Kumbalgarh fort, both of which are fantastic day-trip options from Udaipur. One day and night in Jodhpur is plenty, but make sure you give yourself at least two nights in Jaisalmer—spend one night in town and the second night on an overnight desert safari on camelback. If you're an art lover, consider renting a private taxi from either Delhi or Jaipur and heading to Shekhawati—base yourself in Mandawa or Nawalgarh and then head out to explore the region's beautifully frescoed *havelis* (mansions with interior courtyards). Ranthambhore National Park, reachable from Jaipur, is the place to get away from the hustle and bustle of Rajasthani cities and lose yourself in nature.

4

Updated by Harpreet Anand and Vaihayasi Pande Daniel

STEEPED IN TALES OF CHIVALRY and romance, and famous for its striking desert landscape and colorful festivals, Rajasthan is one of India's best-loved regions. From its legendary cities of Jaipur, Jodhpur, Udaipur, and Jaisalmer, built by the mighty Rajput warriors, to its indigenous tribal and artisan communities, Rajasthan is a unique combination of royal and tribal India. The variety of its landscape is unparalleled: the region is packed with awe-inspiring forts, sparkling palaces, soothing lakes and gardens, and exquisite temples and shrines. The crafts and folk art produced here are world-renowned. Once called Rajputana ("abode of kings"), this vast land consisted of more than 22 princely states before they were consolidated into modern Rajasthan in 1956. Each state was ruled by a Rajput, an upper-caste Hindu warrior-prince, and the Rajputs were divided into three main clans: the Suryavanshis, descended from the sun, the Chandravanshis, descended from the moon, and the Agnikuls who had been purified by ritual fire. When they were not fighting among themselves for power, wealth, and women, the Rajputs built the hundreds of forts, palaces, gardens, and temples that make this region so enchanting.

For centuries, many Hindu Rajputs valiantly resisted invasion, including attempts by the Muslim Moghuls. Their legendary codes of battle emphasized honor and pride, and they went to war prepared to die. When defeat on the battlefield was imminent, the strong Rajput women of Chittaur would perform the rite of *jauhar,* throwing themselves onto a flaming pyre en masse rather than live with the indignity of capture. With the prominent exception of the princes of Mewar, major Rajput states such as Jaipur, Bikaner, Bundi, and Kota eventually stopped fighting and built strong ties with the Moghuls. The Moghul emperor Akbar was particularly skilled at forging alliances with the Rajputs; he offered them high posts in his *darbar,* or court, and sealed the deal with matrimonial ties. (He himself married two Rajput princesses.) Those kingdoms who sided with Akbar quickly rose in importance and prosperity.

Maharaja Man Singh of Jaipur was the first to marry his sister to Akbar. As the emperor's brother-in-law and trusted commander-in-chief, Man Singh led Moghul armies to many a victory. Both rulers benefited immensely, as a traditional saying indicates: "*Jeet Akbar ki, loot Man Singh ki*" ("The victory belongs to Akbar, the loot to Man Singh").

In addition to securing wealth, these marriages opened the gates of the royal Rajput households to the Moghuls' distinctive culture. The same people who initially sacrificed their lives to resist the Moghuls quickly adapted themselves to Moghul domination and started borrowing heavily from Moghul aesthetics. Skilled craftsmen from the Moghul courts were enticed to Rajasthan to start craft schools, fomenting what would become a golden age of Indian art and architecture. The Moghuls' influence in Rajasthan is still visible in everything from food to palace architecture, from intricate miniature paintings to new musical styles, and from clothing to the tradition of *purdah* (the seclusion of women from males or strangers, or the act of covering the head and face with a veil).

CLOSE UP

Festivals in Rajasthan and Gujarat

The Pushkar camel fair is in November, the Shekhawati art festival in December, the Jaisalmer desert festival in January, Jaipur's Gangaur festival and Udaipur's Mewar festival are in April, and Mount Abu's summer festival in May.

Makar Sankranti—the point when the sun reaches the Tropic of Capricorn after the winter solstice—is celebrated on January 14 with a tremendous kite festival in Ahmedabad. A dance festival is organized immediately afterward at Modhera's sun temple, about 100 km (62 mi) north of Ahmedabad.

Navaratri, the goddess festival, in late September or early October, is celebrated throughout the state with performances of Ras Garba, Gujarat's folk dance, nowadays often embellished with disco moves and amplified music. Rhythmic dances, often using sticks and graceful movements, by young and old in extraordinarily colorful and elaborate costumes makes Garba, also called Dandiya and Ras Garba, a treat to watch. Tarnetar, northeast of Rajkot in the center of the Kathiawar Peninsula, is the site of a large folk fair in October or November. Diwali—end of the year festival of lights (falling sometime between October–December) marking the return of the epic hero Rama from exile with his wife, Sita—is celebrated distinctively here by the Jains, as is the birthday of their founder, Mahavira, in April.

The beginning of the 18th century marked the decline of the Moghul period, and with it came the decline of the Rajputs. The incoming British took advantage of the prevailing chaos. Not only did they introduce significant administrative, legal, and educational changes in Rajasthan, they also exposed the Rajputs to new levels of excess. The British introduced polo and other equestrian sports, the latest rifles and guns, *shikar* (hunting) camps, Belgian glass, English crockery, French chiffons, Victorian furniture, European architecture, and—eventually—fancy limousines. The influence extended to Rajput children: sons were sent to English universities, and daughters to the best finishing schools in Switzerland.

While the rest of India launched their struggle for independence, many Rajput princes ended up defending the Raj. Unwilling to give up their world of luxury and power, they did their best to suppress rebellion outside their own kingdoms by sending their soldiers to help the British forces. When India won independence, the Rajput princes and kings were forced to merge their kingdoms into one state as part of the new nation, but they were allowed to keep the titles to their palaces, forts, lands, jewels, and other sumptuous possessions. Since then, however, the government has taken over much of their land and many of their palaces and forts. Stripped of feudal power, many of the maharajas became hotel owners, while others have turned their properties over to leading hotel chains. A few have become paupers or recluses.

Rajasthan's heritage goes well beyond the maharajas, however. The Marwari trading community is known far and wide for its dynamic entrepreneurial spirit and its ornate havelis (mansions with interior courtyards). Seminomadic indigenous tribes, such as the Bhils, Meenas, Garasias, and Sahrias, create a rich canvas of folk life and folklore, their art, dance, music, and drama contributing much to Rajasthan's vibrant, festive culture. The exquisite craftwork of the state's rural artisan communities—leatherwork, textiles, puppetry, and miniature painting—is admired in India and around the world. The presence of saints and spiritual leaders from a variety of religious communities has also, over the years, made Rajasthan a trove of shrines, temple art, and religious architecture.

Cultures within Rajasthan vary in everything from the colors of their sandstone buildings to the languages they speak. Though five principal Rajasthani dialects are spoken here (Marwari, Mewari, Dhundari, Mewati, and Hadauti), a local saying has it that you hear a new language every 4 km. And despite the overwhelming spread of both English and Hindi, villagers continue to maintain the rich literary traditions, both oral and written, of their local tongues. Also regionally significant—and more noticeable to the average traveler—are the brilliant colors of the women's *lehangas* (long skirts with separate veils), designed to stand out against the starkness of the desert. Women also wear elaborate jewelry, and Rajasthani men are famous for their turbans—called *saafas*—which vary in style from region to region and caste to caste; the style of wearing high turbans with a tail is preferred by Rajputs, for instance, while *pagris* (compact turbans, often orange) are worn by businessmen. Even facial hair is unique in these parts: Rajputs, in particular, sport long, Salvador Dali–like handlebar moustaches. Although Rajasthan has many social problems, most notably widespread rural poverty and low literacy rates, its cities and people remain lively. Cultural festivals, crafts fairs, and religious gatherings take place throughout the year. With its bright colors and rich folk traditions, and the sheer variety of experiences it has to offer the traveler, Rajasthan easily earns its place as one of India's most popular tourist destinations.

The region's natural variety is also compelling. The Aravalli Hills are a natural divider between northwest and southeast Rajasthan. Arid sand dunes characterize the northwest: the sizzling Thar Desert is referred to in the ancient Hindu epic *Mahabharata* as the Maru-Kantar, "the region of death." The landscape of the southeast, however, belies Rajasthan's image as a desert state: craggy hills, lush forests, and shimmering lakes are typical. A rich array of birds, animal life, and insect species makes its home in each environment, and these may be seen in the several wildlife preserves of the state.

EXPLORING RAJASTHAN

You could easily spend a month in Rajasthan alone. The state's southwestern corner centers on Udaipur, a hilly town of palaces and artificial lakes. Central Rajasthan is anchored by Jodhpur, home to a glorious fort and the eye-catching blue houses of the Brahmin caste. Jaipur, the state capital, is in the east, toward Delhi. Western Rajasthan, largely given over to the Thar Desert, can best be explored via camel or jeep from the golden city of Jaisalmer. In the northeast, between Jaipur and Delhi, the Shekhawati region is home to lovely painted havelis, the mansions of prosperous merchants. The southern and eastern regions also have a number of first-rate wildlife parks.

RAJASTHAN IS BIG

Very big—with long stretches between the most popular destinations. If you have limited time, stay in one place and explore the surrounding area rather than rushing through all the highlights.

Numbers in the text correspond to numbers in the margin and on the chapter maps.

ABOUT THE RESTAURANTS

Rajasthan's culinary traditions are heavily influenced by its desert setting. Food tends to be highly spiced, perhaps for preservation. Instead of the rice and vegetables that are popular in regions with more rainfall, Rajasthani cuisine includes a lot of lentils and corn. Both posh, pricey restaurants and local dives are bound to serve regional food, so try some local delicacies, such as *dal baati churma* (lentils with wheat-flour dumplings) and *gatte ki subzi* (dumplings made out of chickpea flour, also known as *besan*). Breads include *bajra ki roti* (millet bread), *makki ki roti* (corn bread), and *missi ki roti* (chickpea-and-wheat-flour bread). *Mirchi badas* (spicy green pepper fritters) and *kachoris* (fried stuffed pastries) make hearty appetizers. Dessert is a highlight here—in some parts of the state, sweets open the meal. Favorites include *ghevar* (funnel cake), *laddoo* (balls of sugar, flour, clarified butter, and spices), *malpuas* (syrupy pancakes), and *diljani* (mini sugar balls).

ABOUT THE HOTELS

The most opulent hotels in India—and perhaps in the world—are in Rajasthan. You can literally live like a king in one of several converted palaces, surrounded by glittering mirrored walls, tiger skins, and stained-glass windows. The best-known of these lush lodgings are Udaipur's Lake Palace and Udaivilas, Jodhpur's Umaid Bhawan Palace, and Jaipur's Taj Rambagh Palace and Oberoi Rajvilas. Rajasthan is also famous for Heritage Hotels, a group of castles, forts, and havelis that have been converted to elegant accommodations. Samode Haveli (Jaipur), Castle Mandawa (Shekhawati), Rohet Garh (near Jodhpur), Fateh Prakash Palace (Udaipur), Jagat Niwas Palace Hotel and Kankarwa Haveli (Udaipur), and Laxmi Vilas Palace (Bharatpur) are among the finest. Ranthambhore has the Oberoi Vanyavilas, the finest tented hotel in India.

JAIPUR & ENVIRONS

Jaipur, the state capital, is worth a couple days' visit until you find your bearings; it's a delightful mixture of modernity and folk tradition. Don't be surprised to see camels pulling carts on the main streets, mingling ill-temperedly with vehicular traffic. With its towering forts and

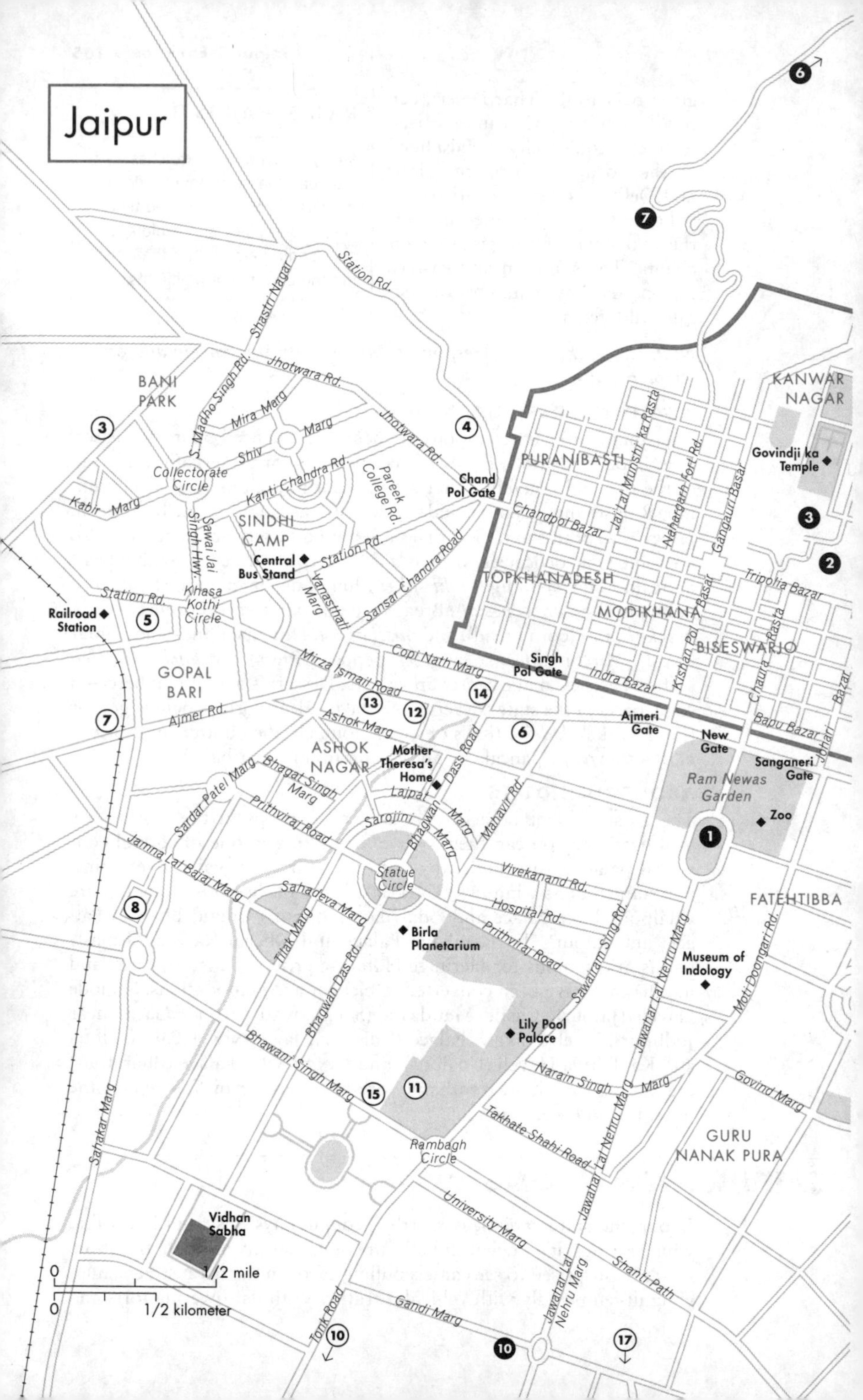

Jaipur
Station Rd.
Shastri Nagar
Jhotwara Rd.
BANI PARK
S. Madho Singh Rd.
Mira Marg
Shiv Marg
Collectorate Circle
Kanti Chandra Rd.
Pareek College Rd.
Jhotwara Rd.
Chand Pol Gate
Kabir Marg
Sawai Jai Singh Hwy.
SINDHI CAMP
Central Bus Stand
Station Rd.
Sansar Chandra Road
Vanasthali Marg
Station Rd.
Khasa Kothi Circle
Railroad Station
GOPAL BARI
Mirza Ismail Road
Copi Nath Marg
Ajmer Rd.
Ashok Marg
ASHOK NAGAR
Mother Theresa's Home
Dass Road
Sardar Patel Marg
Bhagat Singh Marg
Lajpat
Prithviraj Road
Sarojini
Bhagwan Marg
Marg
Mahavir Rd.
Jamna Lal Bajaj Marg
Sahadeva Marg
Statue Circle
Vivekanand Rd.
Hospital Rd.
Tilak Marg
Birla Planetarium
Prithviraj Road
Bhagwan Das Rd.
Sawairam Sing Rd.
Jawahar Lal Nehru Marg
Lily Pool Palace
Bhawani Singh Marg
Narain Singh Marg
Takhate Shahi Road
Rambagh Circle
Sahakar Marg
University Marg
Vidhan Sabha
0
1/2 mile
0
1/2 kilometer
Tonk Road
Gandi Marg
Jawahar Lal Nehru Marg
Shanti Path
PURANIBASTI
Jai Lal Munshi ka Rasta
Nahargarh Fort Rd.
Gangauri Basar
Chandpol Bazar
TOPKHANADESH
MODIKHANA
Kishan Pol Basar
BISESWARJO
Chaura Rasta
Tripolia Bazar
Singh Pol Gate
Indra Bazar
Ajmeri Gate
New Gate
Bapu Bazar
Johari Bazar
KANWAR NAGAR
Govindji ka Temple
Sanganeri Gate
Ram Newas Garden
Zoo
FATEHTIBBA
Museum of Indology
Moti Doongari Rd.
Govind Marg
GURU NANAK PURA
1
2
3
6
7
10
3
4
5
6
7
8
10
11
12
13
14
15
17

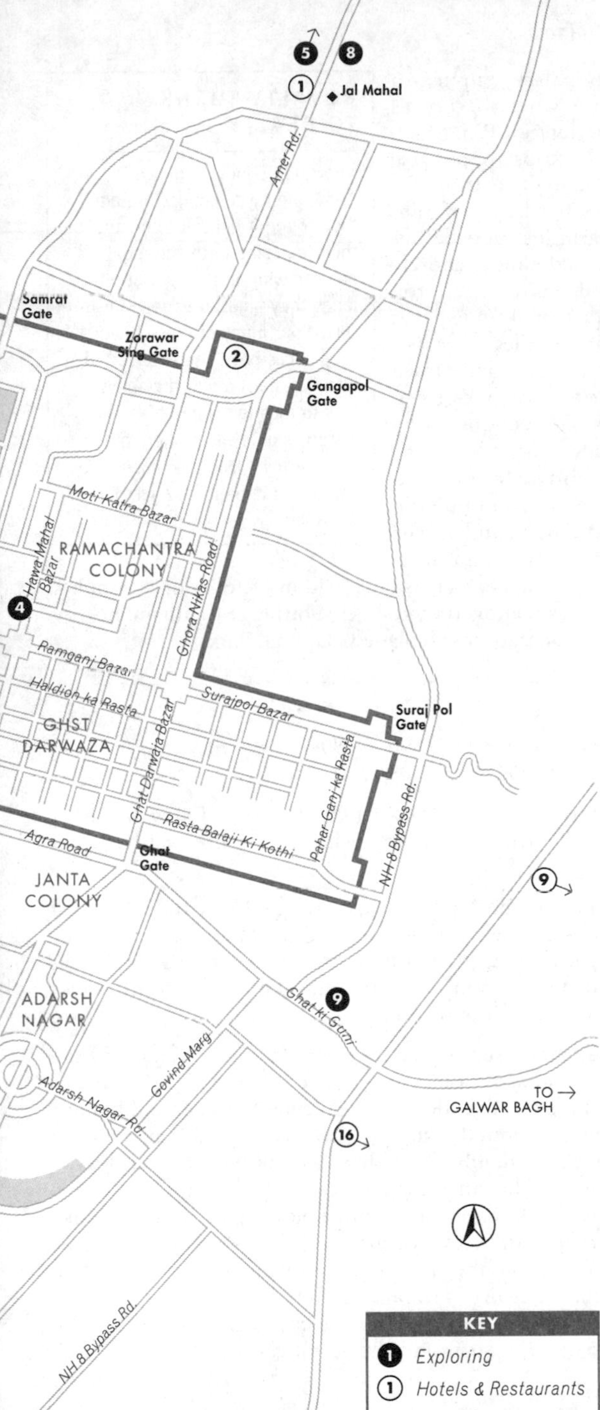

Exploring ▼

Albert Hall Museum	1
Amer Fort and Palace	5
City Palace	3
Hawa Mahal	4
Jaigarh Fort	6
Jantar Mantar	2
Jawahar Kala Kendra	10
Kanak Vrindavan Gardens	8
Nahargarh Fort	7
Sisodia Rani ka Bagh	9

Hotels & Restaurants ▼

Alsisar Haveli	17
Bissau Palace	4
Chokhi Dhani	10
Copper Chimney	12
Handi	13
Jasvilas	3
Natraj	14
Niros	6
Oberoi Rajvilas	9
Raj Mahal Palace	8
Rajputana Palace Sheraton	5
Samode Haveli	2
Samode Palace & Samode Bagh	16
Suvarna Mahal	11
Taj Jai Mahal Palace	7
Taj Rambagh Palace	15
Trident Hilton	1

impressive city palace, Jaipur is a good indicator of what to expect as you progress to interior Rajasthan. A number of day trips are possible around the countryside from the capital. The craft villages of Sanganer and Bagru, just outside Jaipur, are populated almost entirely by artisans, and you're free to stop in and watch them make fine paper and block-print textiles by hand. You may want to check out the town of Ajmer, a one-time Rajput stronghold that was later conquered by the Muslims, and which houses one of the most important shrines to a Sufi saint (Khwaja Mu'in-ud-din Chisti, 1142–1236) in India. The Hindu pilgrimage town of Pushkar is known for its annual camel festival, held in October or November. To escape civilization altogether, go tiger-spotting at Ranthambhore or bird-watching at Bharatpur's Keoladeo National Park.

ROYALTY TURNS TO REALTY

After India's independence in 1947, the royal families of Rajasthan found it difficult to maintain their imposing forts and regal palaces without the special privileges they enjoyed under British rule. Now, many of these beautiful palaces have been converted into five-star hotels—a creative way to maintain some of these historic sights while offering a taste of royal living to those who can afford it, be it even just for one night.

JAIPUR

261 km (162 mi) southwest of Delhi, 343 km (213 mi) east of Jodhpur, 405 km (252 mi) northeast of Udaipur.

A Rajasthani proverb asks, "*Je na dekhyo Jaipario, To kal men akar kya kario?*" ("What have I accomplished in my life, if I have not seen Jaipur?").

Surrounded on three sides by the rugged Aravali Hills, and celebrated for the striking, if somewhat run-down pink buildings in the old part of the city, Jaipur is the capital of Rajasthan, and a fine starting point for a trip through the region. The city is also known for being one of the few planned cities in the world.

Jaipur takes its name from Maharaja Sawai Jai Singh II, an avid scientist, architect, and astronomer, and is said to epitomize the dreams of the ruler and the creative ideas of his talented designer and builder, Vidhydar. Jaipur was founded in 1727, when Sawai Jai Singh moved down from Amer (commonly misrendered as Amber), the ancient rock-bound stronghold of his ancestors. Rectangular in shape, the city is divided into nine blocks based on the principles of the ancient architectural treatise *Shilp Shastra*. Every aspect of Jaipur—streets, sidewalks, building height, and number and division of blocks—was based on geometric harmony, environmental and climatic considerations, and the intended use of each zone. Part of the city is still enclosed in 20-foot-high fortified walls, surrounded by eight gates.

Timelessly appealing bazaars full of colorful textiles and trinkets—*lac* bangles (imitation fashion jewelry), steel utensils, copper ornaments—and *mehendi* (henna) artists form an integral part of the city center and its outlying villages. Another cultural highlight of Jaipur is its mouth-watering cuisine, particularly desserts: *ghevar* (lentil paste), *pheeni* (strawlike sweets), *jalebis* (fried, twisty orange sweets), *malpua* (deep-fried wheat flour rolls), and *churmas* (tasty wheat-flour dumplings). The sensory whirl and jumble of colorful *ghagharas* (skirts), complex turbans, and sturdy *jutis* (pointed shoes), of sidewalk shops overflowing with pottery and dyed or sequinned fabric, and of streets packed with camel carts, cycle-rickshaws, and wandering cows make Jaipur a dazzling, spirited city like no other.

A GOOD TOUR

Start outside the walled old city, at the **Albert Hall Museum** ❶, then walk north on Chaura Rasta into the old city. Pass through the Atishpol Gate to reach the **Jantar Mantar** ❷ observatory and the **City Palace** ❸. A walk "around the block" through Sireh Deorhi Bazaar takes you to the **Hawa Mahal** ❹ (you can see the back of the facade from the observatory). After a break for lunch, take a taxi north of town to the **Amer Fort and Palace** ❺. Continue to **Jaigarh** ❻ and **Nahargarh** ❼ forts, and watch the sun set at the nearby **Kanak Vrindavan Gardens** ❽ and admire the Man Sagar with its Jal Mahal, a lake palace not open to the public.

The next day, visit **Sisodia Rani ka Bagh** ❾ and, if you'd like to meet some local artists, **Jawahar Kala Kendra** ❿.

TIMING This tour can be done in one very exhausting day, as long as you start early; the Amer Fort closes at 4:30. You're better off saving the Amer Fort and Palace, Jaigarh, and Nahargarh for Day 2, however, because these involve a lot of walking.

WHAT TO SEE

❶ **Albert Hall Museum.** Worth a visit just for its architecture, this sandstone-and-marble building was built in the late 19th century in the Indo-Saracenic style. The collection, which unfortunately is not well-maintained or well-organized, includes folk arts, miniature paintings, traditional costumes, unexpected exhibits of yoga postures, and visual explanations of Indian culture and traditions. Photography is not allowed. ✉ *In Ram Niwas Gardens* 🎫 *Rs. 30* ⏲ *Sat.–Thurs. 10–4:30.*

❺ **Amer Fort and Palace.** Surrounded by ramparts, this marvelous fortress
★ is perched on a hill near Maota Lake. Raja Man Singh began building it in 1592; Mirza Raja Jai Singh and Sawai Jai Singh continued the construction over a period of 125 years. For centuries the fortress was the capital of the Kachhawah Rajputs, but when the capital shifted to Jaipur in the early 18th century, the site was abandoned. Although the fort is in ruins, the interior palaces, gardens, and temples retain much of their pristine beauty. Both the art and the architecture combine Rajput and Moghul influences in felicitous ways.

You approach the palace complex by walking or riding an elephant up a sloping incline to the **Singh Pole** gate and **Jaleb Chowk,** the preliminary courtyard. If you choose to come up on an elephant, keep in mind that these animals are not native to Rajasthan and are often in poor health because of the arid climate and overuse by owners. An effort is being made to increase awareness about the condition of the Amer elephants and you could contribute by questioning the *mahout* (driver) and keeping an eye open for sores and abscesses. The more tourists express concern, the greater the chance of something actually being done about the problem.

Two flights of stairs lead up from Jaleb Chowk; for now, skip the one leading to the Shila Mata Temple and take the one leading to the palace itself. In the next courtyard, the pillared **Diwan-i-Am** (Hall of Public Audience) contains alabaster panels with fine inlay work—the kind of craftsmanship for which Jaipur is famous. Typical of the Moghul period, the rooms are small and intimate, whereas the palace's successive courtyards and narrow passages are characteristically Rajput.

One elaborately carved and painted gate is known as **Ganesh Pol,** after the elephant god Ganesh. From a latticed corridor above it, the queen—always in purdah, or hiding—would await the King's return from battle and sprinkle scented water and flowers down upon him. Each room shows some vestige of its former glory, especially the **Sheesh Mahal** (Palace of Mirrors), with glittering mirror-work on the ceiling. Narrow flights of stairs lead up to the lavish royal apartments, and beyond the corridors and galleries here you'll find the small, elegant **Char Bagh** garden. Take in the views of the valley, the palace courtyards, the formal gardens abutting the octagonal pool next to the lake, and the vast **Jaigarh Fort,** the ancient fortress on the crest of the hill above you. Also on the upper floor is **Jas Mandir,** a hall with filigreed marble *jalis* (screens) and delicate mirror and stucco work.

On your way out, peek into the 16th-century **Shiladevi Temple** to the goddess Kali, with its silver doors and marble carvings. Raja Man Singh installed the image of the goddess after bringing it here from lower Bengal (now Bangladesh). Exit the palace by the gate near the temple, and just a few minutes down the road is the 450-year-old **Jagat Shiromani** temple. Dedicated to Krishna, this exquisitely carved marble-and-sandstone temple was built by Raja Man Singh I in memory of his son. ⊠*Delhi Rd., 11 km (7 mi) north of Jaipur, Amer* 🎫*Fort and palace Rs. 50, camera fee Rs. 75, video-camera fee Rs. 150* ⏲*Daily 9–4:30.*

❸ ★ **City Palace.** This complex of pavilions, courtyards, chambers, and palace was begun by Jai Singh II in 1727, with additions done by later maharajas. Once you're in the outer courtyard, the marble-and-sandstone building directly in front of you is the **Mubarak Mahal** (Guest Pavilion), built by Maharaja Madho Singh in the late 19th century. Now a museum, it's an ideal place to admire at close range some of the royals' finest brocades, silks, and hand-blocked garments and robes, many made in nearby Sanganer and some dating from as far back as the 17th century. The collection also includes musical instruments. The **armory** in the northwest corner of the courtyard has one of India's best collections of arms and weapons, including an 11-pound sword belonging to Akbar's Rajput general. Some of the paints on the beautiful, 18th century ceiling are said to be made of crushed semiprecious stones.

In the inner courtyard, through the gateway guarded by two stone elephants, is the art gallery housed in the cavernous **Diwan-i-Am** (Hall of Public Audience). Built in the late 18th century, the building has rows of gray marble columns, the second-largest chandelier in India, and a magnificent, vintage-1930s painted ceiling. The art includes scores of miniatures from the Moghul and various Rajput schools, rare manuscripts, and 17th-century carpets from the Amer Palace. From the inner courtyard, enter the Zenana courtyard on the left to see the seven-story **Chandra Mahal** (Moon Palace). Built by Jai Singh II, this attractive cream-hue building is still the official residence of the present maharaja, "Bubbles"—Lieutenant Colonel Sawai Bhawani Singh—who lives on the upper floors. The ground floor has sumptuous chandeliers, murals, and a painting of an old maharaja. Photography is not allowed in the gallery area, and there's a Rs. 500 fine for using a video camera without a special ticket, which should be purchased with your admission ticket. Note that some official-looking people near the entrance may claim that you must get a guide here. This isn't true: ignore them. ✉ *Center of the old city, enter the complex at the Virendra Pole gate, Pink City* 🎫 *Palace Rs. 180, camera free, video-camera Rs. 200* ⏲ *Daily 9:30–5.*

WHAT'S WITH THE PINK?

Originally colored yellow (a color you can still see on the backs of the buildings), the capital was painted pink when Prince Albert, consort of Queen Victoria, visited India in 1883. This explains why Jaipur is commonly referred to as the Pink City. The tradition stuck: by law, buildings in the old city must still be painted pink.

4 **Hawa Mahal.** Jaipur's photogenic Palace of Winds was built by Maharaja Sawai Pratap Singh in 1799 so that the women of the courtcould discreetly take some air and watch the activity on the street below. Every story has semi-octagonal overhanging windows, and each has a perforated screen. This curious five-story structure, named after the westerly winds that blow cool breezes through the windows, is just one room thick. The wind easily passes through the building and works like a cooler. (Traditionally, servants also threw water on the lattice, so any breeze would be cooled by the water, and would lower the temperature.) The building facade has a delicate honeycomb design with close to 1,000 windows, and is fashioned from pink sandstone. ✉ *Sireh Deorhi Bazaar, Pink City* 🎫 *Palace Rs. 5, camera fee Rs. 30, video-camera fee Rs. 70* ⏲ *Sat.–Thurs. 9–4:30.*

NEED A BREAK?

Known affectionately as LMB, Laxmi Misthan Bhandar (✉ *Johari Bazar, Pink City* ☎ *141/256–5844* 💳 *MC, V*) is famous all over Rajasthan for fresh and sumptuous sweets, including *ghevar* (lentil paste), *mave ki kachori* (a milk-base pastry), and other savory snacks and meals. The rest of the food is average, though the *shahi* (rich) thali has an impressive 15 items. This is a great

CLOSE UP

Palace on Wheels

If you only have a week, the most exciting and convenient way to see Rajasthan is to board the Palace on Wheels. This train, which runs September through April, takes you on one of the most luxurious rail journeys in the world, through a region well known for its historical architecture, varied wildlife, and heady culture. Your eight days aboard this locomotive begin at Delhi, from where you travel to Jaipur, the capital of Rajasthan, with its "pink" city, forts, palaces, and caparisoned elephants. From there, you travel across the desert to Jaisalmer, whose fort is a vision in sandstone, and to Jodhpur with its magnificent and well-preserved Meherangarh Fort. Then you continue on to Ranthambhore, where you can spot tigers in the wild, and Chittaurgarh—at the heart of chivalrous Mewar state. At Udaipur, the city of lakes, you have a chance to lunch at the famous Lake Palace hotel (the James Bond movie Octopussy was filmed here). The last leg of the journey takes you to Bharatpur, which you'll appreciate if you're a bird-watcher. You'll also go to Fatehpur Sikri, chosen capital of the Moghul emperor Akbar, and finally Agra, where the stunning, ethereal Taj Mahal is the crowning experience of a breathtaking week.

The destinations, however, are only half the fun. The train's 14 splendid coaches are replicas of those once owned by the rulers of the erstwhile princely states of Rajputana, Gujarat, and Hyderabad, and the Viceroy of colonial India. The plush accommodation allows you to sink blissfully into an unforgettable experience of India's sophisticated royal past while watching rural scenery through elegant, wood-framed picture windows. Bedchambers have private baths, whereas shared facilities include two dining cars and a lounge coach with a bar and library. Service is warm and attentive; each coach has a captain and an attendant. Your ticket on board this opulent train—$295 to $350 per person per night for double occupancy—covers all meals, including those taken off the train, entrance fees to every monument and national park, and cultural entertainment. Liquor is not included. If your time in India is limited, this train's well-planned route and thoughtful itinerary allows you to take in as much as you can in a week—and this is possibly more than you might have accomplished if you tried to reach the same destinations on your own.

(For reservations, contact **TravBuzz, Inc., USA** at ☎ *609/683-5018*, **Rajasthan Tourism Development Corporation [RTDC]** ✉ *Bikaner House, New Delhi* ☎ *11/2338-1884*; or **RTDC** ✉ *Swagatam Complex, Jaipur* ☎ *141/220-2586*.)

place to pick up gifts for Indian families, or sweets to donate at an evening *aarti* (prayer ceremony). Prices for sweets range from Rs. 95 to Rs. 600 per kilogram, but you'll probably spend about Rs. 200 on sweets here (for the average half a kilo).

6 **Jaigarh Fort.** The middle fort of Jaipur's three, both in position and altitude, Jaigarh Fort—originally the royal treasury—has large water-tanks meant to store rainwater channeled down the hill from imposing Nahargarh. There's a fantastic view from the watchtower, and an air

of ruin and abandonment. A large monkey population now provides endless entertainment and a certain amount of annoyance in the center of the fort, while the largest wheeled cannon in the world draws visitors to its periphery. It's possible to drive from Jaigarh to Amer; you might need a driver who knows the way through the narrow lanes. Guides are also available at the entrance, an English-speaking person will charge about Rs. 100. ✉ *About 7 km (4 mi) from Jaipur, off Amer Rd.* 🎫 *Fort Rs. 35, camera fee Rs. 35; video-camera fee Rs. 150, vehicle Rs. 50* ⏲ *Daily 9–4:30.*

2 ★ **Jantar Mantar.** Jai Singh II was well aware of European developments in the field of astronomy, and wanted to create the world's finest observatories. He supervised the design and construction of five remarkable facilities in northern India, of which this is the largest and best preserved. Built in 1726 of masonry, marble, and brass, it's equipped with solar instruments called *yantras,* which look like large, abstract sculptures, and are remarkably precise in measuring celestial data. Such accuracy was desired for creating astrological predictions. If you don't have a guide with you, try to recruit one to explain how these devices work, as they're fascinating and, for nonscientists, somewhat complicated. Avoid the observatory at noon, as it can be very hot. ✉ *Tripoliya Bazaar, near entrance to City Palace, Pink City* 🎫 *Observatory Rs. 10, camera fee Rs. 50, video-camera fee Rs. 100* ⏲ *Daily 9–4:30.*

10 **Jawahar Kala Kendra.** Jaipur's center for arts and crafts was founded by the state government with a specific vision: to create a space for understanding and experiencing culture and folk traditions amid the chaos and traffic of urban life. It's also becoming a venue for theatrical and musical performances. You can drop in to meet some of the locals who exhibit and perform here, or just to collect information on cultural events. ✉ *Jawaharlal Nehru Marg, opposite Jhalana Institutional Area, Moti Dhungri* ⏲ *Daily 10–6; concerts some evenings.*

8 **Kanak Vrindavan Gardens.** This picturesque set of gardens and temples is just below the majestic Amer and Nahar Garh forts. From here you can take a good look at the Jai Mahal Palace in Man Sagar Lake. The gardens also make a great picnic spot, especially if you like to people-watch. If you're lucky you might even catch a glimpse of Bollywood's brightest filming a Hindi movie. ✉ *Amer Rd., Man Sagar* 🎫 *Rs. 5* ⏲ *Daily sunrise–sunset.*

7 **Nahargarh Fort.** You can get a breathtaking view of Jaipur and its natural defenses from Nahargarh Fort's scenic hilltop location. Initially built by Sawai Jai Singh in 1734, it was enlarged to its sprawling, present-day glory in 1885 by Sawai Madho Singh, who commandeered it as a lookout point. Cannons placed behind the walls recall the days when artillery was positioned against potential attackers below. The Rajasthan tourist board runs a snack bar at the fort, and indeed it's a great place for a picnic. The palace of nine queens—with nine separate apartments for the wives of Maharaja Ram Singh—within the fort is also worth a short visit. Interestingly, massive channels (which can still be seen from the approach road) carried rainwater from Nahargarh to

nearby Jaigarh Fort, where it was stored in large tanks. ✉ *10 km (6 mi) north of Jaipur off Amer Rd.* 🎫 *Rs. 5, camera fee Rs. 30, video-camera fee Rs. 70, vehicle Rs. 5* ⏲ *Fort daily sunrise–sunset, palace daily 10–5:30.*

9 **Sisodia Rani ka Bagh.** On the road to Bharatpur stands one of many palaces built for the *ranis,* or queens, of Sawai Jai Singh II. Built in 1779, the palace still looks lovely against the backdrop of the hills. Its terraced garden is punctuated with fountains, and the palace itself is furnished with murals illustrating hunting scenes and the romantic legend of Krishna and Radha. From the terrace, you can see dancing peacocks and plenty of monkeys. Come during the day, as the site is often reserved for weddings and parties at night. ✉ *8 km (5 mi) east of Jaipur on road to Bharatpur* 🎫 *Rs. 5* ⏲ *Daily 8–6.*

OFF THE BEATEN PATH

Galwar Bagh. Known by locals and rickshaw-wallahs simply as Monkey Temple, Galwar Bagh is a popular pilgrimage site and temple complex on the outskirts of town. The temple itself is called **Gulta Ji Mandir**; it's a 30-minute walk from the ceremonial gate called Gulta Pol, located at the far eastern edge of the city, off Ajmer Road—about five minutes from the Muslim quarter. The walk leads you over a small mountain pass and past, inevitably, at least a few Hindu *sadhus* (holy men) and small temples. Jaipuri Hindus believe that at the site of the Gulta Ji Mandir, a local saint named Gala Rishi—nicknamed Gulta Ji—brought forth a spring of holy water from the Ganges and filled a tank (water reservoir 18 feet deep. The waters here are said to be spiritually connected to the Ganges—if you bathe here, you get the same benefits as a pilgrimage to the Ganges. The temple, which venerates Lord Brahma, Creator of the Universe, is in violation of a curse by Brahma's wife Savatri; she confined his temples to Pushkar. ✉ *Outside Suraj Gulta Pol, near Agra Rd. on the east side of town* 🎫 *Free.*

WHERE TO EAT

$$$$ ✕ **Suvarna Mahal.** Once the maharaja's royal banquet hall, this room is so grand—with a soaring, painted ceiling, handsome drapes, tapestry-covered walls, and gold-plated silverware—that it's hard to concentrate on the regional Indian menu. This fancy restaurant, open for lunch and dinner, specializes in regional cuisine from Hyderabad, Punjab, Awadh, and, of course, Rajasthan and includes *murgh tikka zaffrani* (chicken marinated in yogurt and saffron and cooked in a tandoor) and *dahi ka mass* (lamb cooked in a yogurt-base curry). ✉ *Taj Rambagh Palace, Bhawani Singh Rd., Rambagh* ☎ *0141/221–1919* 💳 *AE, DC, MC, V.*

$$–$$$ ✕ **Niros.** This Jaipur institution is probably the most popular restaurant with the city's upper middle class. Amid mirrors and marble floors, it serves good Indian and Chinese food, as well as Continental dishes. Specialties include *reshmi* kebab (skewered boned chicken), *paneer tikka* (soft Indian cheese with skewered tomatoes, onions, and green peppers), and mutton *tikka masala* simmered in a spicy tomato-and-butter sauce). Niros also has the best cold coffee in town, topped with a scoop of ice cream. It also serves beer and wine. ✉ *M. I. Rd., Panch Batti* ☎ *141/237–4493 or 141/221–8520* 💳 *AE, DC, MC, V.*

$ ✕ **Chokhi Dhani.** Come hungry to this village complex, where you'll sit on the floor in a lantern-lit hut and enjoy Rajasthani vegetarian dishes Indian-style (with your hands, no silverware). Be prepared to consume a large quantity of *shuddh desi ghee* (pure clarified butter) as it's poured on practically every dish. Around the compound, you'll see traditional dances, including the dramatic fire dance, folk singing, *katputli* (puppet shows), and juggling. A mehendi-wali may offer to apply intricate designs on your palms while a persistent wallah urges you to keep yourself warm with a traditional *rabdi,* a spicy, sweet, milk-based drink, served hot. Entertainment is included in the cost of the meal, and tipping is discouraged. The temples here are real. If you're here at sunset, you'll see the traditional village aarti (prayer ceremony). Camel rides are also available. ✉ *Tonk Rd., 19 km (12 mi) south of Jaipur via town of Vatika* ☎ *141/277–0555 or 0141/514–2122* 💳 *AE, MC, V.*

Fodor's Choice ★

$ ✕ **The Copper Chimney.** Jaipur's jet set needs some place to go for a night on the town, and this restaurant is often the evening's start. It takes its name from a copper chimney that's displayed center stage. Diners sit behind beautiful etched glass and look out onto the street below. Although the menu has Continental, Chinese, and Indian selections, it would probably be best to avoid some of the odd hybrids such as *paneer Manchurian* (deep-fried soft cheese in a spicy, thick sauce). However, the *palak paneer* (peas with cheese) and the sweet-and-sour lassis are exceptional. This is also a good place to try the traditional *lal mas* (mutton gravy) and Rajasthani-style *kadai* chicken (cooked in a heavy wok, and spicy). ✉ *Mirza Ismail Rd., near G.P.O. Panch Batti* ☎ *141/237–2275* 💳 *MC, V.*

$ ✕ **Handi Restaurant.** This no-frills restaurant with bamboo walls and a thatch roof has some of the best kebabs and nonvegetarian Mughlai food in town. One bite of the *kathi* kebab (garlicky mutton wrapped in thinly rolled bread with onions and tomatoes) and you'll forget all about the plastic chairs. Other specialties include a tangy butter chicken (chicken marinated in yogurt and baked in a tandoor, then cooked in a tomato curry) and the specialty, *handi* meat (a spicy mutton dish cooked in a handi, or clay pot). ✉ *M.I. Rd., opposite G.P.O., Panch Batti* ☎ *141/236–4839* 💳 *MC, V.*

$ ✕ **Natraj.** This all-vegetarian restaurant is a terrific place for coffee and dessert, although the setting is a little rough around the edges. It's one of the few places open for breakfast—if you're in the mood for stuffed *parathas* (whole-wheat flatbread). The house specialty is *bundi ki laddu* (sugary, deep-fried chickpea-flour balls), and the *rasgulla* (cheese balls in a sugary syrup) and *ras malai* (sweet cheese dumplings smothered in cream) melt in your mouth. The silver thali has a good assortment of vegetables and breads, and is one of the best on M.I. Road. ✉ *M.I. Rd., Panch Batti* ☎ *141/237–5804 or 141/510–2804* 💳 *AE, MC, V.*

WHERE TO STAY

$$$$ ★ 🏨 **The Oberoi Rajvilas.** Twenty minutes outside Jaipur, Rajvilas is a destination unto itself. Marble-and-stone carving and handmade brass doors have created a hotel that's luxurious and blends well with the arid environment. You arrive into a lovely scene: pastel-color buildings, orchards, and fountains. Rajvilas's standard double rooms are spacious

4

and minimalist in concept, but the real standout is the marble-and-glass bathtubs, which look out over private gardens. The separate villas with private pools have been favorites with bigwigs—they're available for a hefty price tag. Luxury tents are also available. **Pros:** ayurvedic spa treatments have a reputation as some of the most comprehensive available; excellent food; impeccable service: don't be surprised if the staff knows your name when they greet you in the hallways. **Cons:** expensive; outside Jaipur, so although a great retreat, not ideal if you want to be close to the town. ✉ *Goner Rd., Babaji-ka-Mod, 18 km (11 mi) from Jaipur, 303012* ☎ *141/268–0101* 🌐 *www.oberoihotels.com* ➪ *71 rooms, 3 villas with private pools, 13 luxury tents, 1 tented villa* ♨ *In-room: refrigerator, DVD, dial-up. In-hotel: restaurant, room service bar, tennis courts, pool, gym, spa, no elevator, airport shuttle.* ▭ *AE, DC, MC, V.*

$$$$ **Rajputana Palace Sheraton.** This sprawling brick structure designed as a haveli (mansion) has four courtyards and numerous fountains, but it's more chic than it is traditional. The Western-style rooms are plush and comfortable. The pool, set in the main courtyard along with an outdoor bar, is beautifully designed, and the nightclub is one of the central meeting points for the city's upper-class youth. This is the place to be if you value comfort over nostalgia. **Pros:** suites have balconies. **Cons:** despite the name, it's not very palatial or architecturally interesting. ✉ *Palace Rd., Bani Park, 302006* ☎ *141/510–0100, 888/625–4988 in U.S.* 🌐 *www.welcomgroup.com* ➪ *198 rooms, 20 suites* ♨ *In-room: refrigerator. In-hotel: 3 restaurants, room service, bar, pool, gym, spa.* ▭ *AE, DC, MC, V* 🍴 *CP.*

$$$$ ★ **Taj Jai Mahal Palace.** This palace built in 1747 was once the residence of the chief minister of the state. It's away from the city center, and the elegant white structure is extremely romantic. The lavish, Moghul-style garden has a row of fountains and an enormous chessboard with life-size pieces. The interior has been restored with Rajasthani handicrafts and heirlooms: the suites are sumptuous, with priceless antiques and artwork, and the other rooms are comfortable with ornate furnishings. Rooms look out over the lawns or the solar-heated pool. On-site entertainment includes puppet shows and folk dances. Soft strains of live Indian classical music waft over the lawn at breakfast time. The three restaurants here are Indian, Italian, and multicuisine. **Pros:** relatively good value for the money and the services you get, beautifully maintained lawns. **Cons:** the pool is just okay. ✉ *Jacob Rd., Civil Lines, 302006* ☎ *0141/222–3636* 🌐 *www.tajhotels.com* ➪ *94 rooms, 6 suites* ♨ *In-room: safe, refrigerator, Wi-Fi. In-hotel: 3 restaurants, room service, bar, pool, spa, laundry service.* ▭ *AE, DC, MC, V.*

$$$$ ★ **Taj Rambagh Palace.** Once home to the maharaja of Jaipur, this airy, cream-color palace is relaxing and wistfully romantic, down to the peacocks strutting across the lawns and the arcaded back patios. One of the first palaces to be converted into a Heritage Hotel, the standard rooms are spacious and largely contemporary. Superior and luxury rooms have traditional furnishings and colorful Shekhawati-style frescoes on the walls. Most higher-end rooms have original furnishings. The suites are opulent and an aesthically appealing blend of luxuriously

modern comforts and intricate old-world detailing. **Pros:** newly added wing with luxurious suites offers plush window seats and flat-screen TVs; lovely original indoor pool as well as a newer outdoor pool area. **Cons:** walking distance to the tourist sites (auto-rickshaws are available right outside hotel gates). ✉*Bhawani Singh Rd., Rambagh, 302005* ☎*141/221–1919* 🌐*www.tajhotels.com* *79 rooms, 31 suites* *In-room: refrigerator, safe, Wi-Fi. In-hotel: 2 restaurants, room service, bar, tennis courts, pool, gym, spa.* 💳*AE, DC, MC, V.*

$$$–$$$$ **Trident Hilton.** This rose-color, modern hotel benefits from a superb location between the Pink City and Jaipur's three forts, with wonderful views of Man Sagar and the Jal Mahal as well as of the Aravali hills. Rooms, furnished in earth tones, have *jharokhas* (balconies) that offer one or the other of these views. The Jal Mahal restaurant serves both Indian and Continental cuisine. **Pros:** Man Sagar bar has one of the loveliest views in the city; nonsmoking rooms available. **Cons:** not close to city sights. ✉*Opposite Jal Mahal Palace, Amer Rd., Man Sagar, 302002* ☎*141/267–0101* 📠*141/267–0303* 🌐*www.tridenthotels.com* *136 rooms, 2 suites* *In-room: safe, refrigerator. In-hotel: restaurant, room service, bar, pool, laundry service, no-smoking rooms.* 💳*AE, DC, MC, V.*

$$–$$$$ **Samode Palace and Samode Bagh.** In a narrow valley between red-and-green hills 45 km (28 mi) from Jaipur, this 18th-century palace, built in the shadow of a small fort, towers over its little village. The palace has splendidly painted and enameled public rooms. Guest rooms, which have pillars and arches, are furnished with traditional Rajasthani-style chairs and beds with mosquito-net canopies. The rooms are not regal, but they're charming, clean, and comfortable. Three kilometers (2 mi) from the palace is Samode Bagh, a luxurious tented camp, or "garden retreat"—all tents have attached bathrooms. **Pros:** staff can arrange horse, camel, and jeep safaris; both Samode Bagh and Palace have a swimming pool. **Cons:** outside Jaipur and city sights; no Internet at Samode Bagh. ✉ *Gangapol, Jaipur, 302002* ☎*142/324–0014 or 142/324–0023, 142/324–0235 Palace, 142/324–0236 Bagh* 🌐*www.samode.com* 🌐*www.reservations@samode.com* *Palace: 25 rooms, 18 suites; Bagh: 44 tents* *In-room: refrigerator. In-hotel: restaurant, bar, pool, gym, no elevator.* 💳*AE, DC, MC, V* *CP.*

$$–$$$ ★ **Samode Haveli.** Off in a corner of the Pink City, this lemon-yellow haveli is now a Heritage Hotel. Built for a prime minister of the royal court in the mid-19th century, and arranged around two courtyards, the haveli still has an air of stately grace and some original frescoes. Rooms are spacious and simply furnished. For opulence, stay in one of the two Sheesh Mahals, the luxurious quarters of the local Rajput himself; their walls, antique furniture, and pillars are all inlaid with mirror work. Low arches and mazelike corridors add to its Rajasthani style. The best views are of the elegant palace gardens. The hotel can arrange camel and elephant rides. The haveli also runs the Samode Palace and Samode Bagh (⇨*above*). You can reserve for both through the Jaipur haveli. **Pros:** main dining room with ornamented walls is charming, huge rooms, hotel's park has swings for kids. **Cons:** fancier rooms are expensive. ✉*Gangapol, Pink City, 302002* ☎*141/263–*

2407, 141/263–2370, or 141/263–1942 🌐www.samode.com ⇨29 rooms In-room: safe, refrigerator. In-hotel: restaurant, room service, bar, pool, gym, spa, no elevator, laundry service. ▭AE, DC, MC, V CP.

$$ **Chokhi Dhani.** Separated by a wall from the restaurant and ethnic village of the same name, this little hotel south of Jaipur offers a village setting plus modern conveniences. Although its distance from the city is a little inconvenient, the setting is delightful enough to make it worthwhile, plus transportation is arranged to and from town. Opt for a room in one of the mud huts, with wooden doors and carved furniture—unless you prefer to live like a landowner in the large painted haveli, with marble floors and modern bathrooms. The complex mirrors a village, right down to the swimming pool—designed to look like a village water tank—and the lobby, with a sunken sitting area and hookahs. The vegetarian restaurant does, however, have Western-style tables and chairs. **Pros:** kids enjoy the carnival atmosphere in the evenings at the traditional restaurant. **Cons:** rooms are basic and probably not worth the tariff. *⊠Tonk Rd., 19 km (12 mi) south of Jaipur via Vatika, 303905 ☎141/277–0555 to 56 🌐www.chokhidhani.com ⇨65 rooms, 8 suites In-room: safe, refrigerator, Wi-Fi. In-hotel: 2 restaurants, bar, tennis court, pool, gym, spa, no elevator, laundry service, airport shuttle. ▭AE, DC, MC, V.*

$–$$ **Bissau Palace.** This two-story 1919 bungalow, now a Heritage Hotel, is on the outskirts of the old city, Chandpol. There's a small museum with weapons from the 17th century. Guest rooms in the old wing have original furniture, cotton *dhurries* (rugs), and murals; those in the new wing are furnished with four-poster beds, divans, and pieces from the armory. Rooms aren't fancy, but are neat and clean, and have ethnic touches. The family also has a beautiful retreat (visited by British royalty) 27 km (19 mi) outside town, from where you can take a camel ride through the surrounding villages. The retreat charges the same price as the palace. **Pros:** beautiful building and nice rooms. **Cons:** service is indifferent; food unimpressive. *⊠Outside Chandpol, near Sarod Cinema, 302016 ☎141/230–4371 or 141/230–4391 🌐www.bissaupalace.com ⇨20 rooms, 22 suites In-room: no phone, no TV. In-hotel: restaurant, bar, tennis court, pool, no elevator. ▭AE, MC, V.*

$ ★ **Alsisar Haveli.** This gorgeous, cheerful yellow haveli—one of the most popular Heritage Hotels in the state—is close to the Pink City, but its large lawn distances you from urban noise, and there are numerous courtyards and alcoves to chill in. Built in 1892 as the city residence of Shekhawati Rajputs, the bungalow has elegant rooms with carved antique furniture, restored frescoes, bedspreads with traditional Rajasthani prints, rug-covered tile floors, and brass-frame bathroom mirrors. In the public areas are crystal chandeliers, hunting trophies, and various weapons. **Pros:** reasonably priced, jeep and camel safaris can take you to a nearby village and fort for an extra price. **Cons:** some rooms are dark, and the lighting is depressing. *⊠Sansar Chandra Rd., Chandpol, 302001 ☎141/236–4685, 141/510–7167, or 141/510–7157 🌐www.alsisar.com ⇨29 rooms In-hotel: restaurant, bar, pool. ▭AE, MC, V.*

$ **Jasvilas.** If you stay at this guest house, you forgo the facilities of a larger hotel for the comfort of a home away from home. Built during colonial times, the residence retains the traditional haveli shape of a mansion built around a courtyard. It also has a private pool in the courtyard. The Western-style rooms have marble floors, two sinks, and bathtubs. The Rajput family who runs it are happy to give tourist advice about Jaipur, and do their best to cater to the needs of foreigners. **Pros:** homey atmosphere; friendly staff, clean rooms. **Cons:** far from the action (need to take a rickshaw or taxi to get to the old city), swimming pool is small. ✉ *C-9 Sawai Jai Singh Hwy., Bani Park, 302016* ☎ *141/220–4638 or 0141/220–4902* 🌐 *www.jasvilas.com* *10 rooms, 1 suite* *In-room: W-Fi. In-hotel: restaurant, pool, no elevator.* 💳 *MC, V.*

4

$ **Raj Mahal Palace.** Built in 1729 by Sawai Jai Singh II, this small palace has a world-weary air. Now a Heritage Hotel, the palace offers spacious, if modest, rooms with high ceilings and few windows. **Pros:** decent price, Maharaja Suite doesn't cost much more than the somewhat lackluster standard rooms. **Cons:** rooms vary quite a bit (ask to see available rooms before you choose). ✉ *Sardar Patel Marg, C-Scheme, Civil Lines, 302001* ☎ *141/510–5667 or 141/510–5666* 📠 *141/222–1787* *24 rooms, 6 suites* *In-hotel: restaurant, bar, pool, no elevator.* 💳 *AE, DC, MC, V.*

NIGHTLIFE & THE ARTS

Your best bet for a night out is one of the hotel bars, which are usually open from about 11 AM to 3 PM and 7 PM to 11:30 PM. Hotel discos kick in at about 7 until 11:30.

Many hotels stage cultural programs for their guests, such as the dance performances with dinner in Panghat, at the Rambagh Palace. In addition, some restaurants, including Apno Gaon and the Chokhi Dhani village complex, combine excellent performances of Rajasthani folk dance with traditional regional meals. **Ravindra Rang Manch** (✉ *Ram Niwas Gardens* ☎ *141/261–9061*), a cultural organization, hosts occasional dinner-and-dance programs.

To experience a contemporary Indian institution, head to the movies. **Rajmandir Movie Theatre** (✉ *16 Bhagwandas Rd., near Panch Batti* ☎ *141/237–9372*) plays song-and-dance Bollywood films only. It has a beautifully ornate interior and is known as the best movie hall in Asia. The theater disperses different blends of incense at occasional points in the film. Widely visited by Indian and foreign tourists, Rajmandir is still constantly flooded with locals, who sing, cheer, and whistle throughout each film. Shows are at 3, 6:15, and 9:30. Buy tickets in advance.

SPORTS & THE OUTDOORS

Polo is a passion in Jaipur. In season (late March and late October), matches are held at the **Rajasthan Polo Club** (☎ *141/238–3580*). You can also call the Taj Rambagh Palace (☎ 141/238–1919) for information about polo matches in the city. The **Rajasthan Mounted Sports Association** (☎ *141/221–1276*) gives polo lessons for $350 a day (includes accommodation, all meals, and lessons twice a day.

To play golf, phone the **Taj Rambagh Palace** (☎*141/238–1919*) to reserve access to a driving range.

SHOPPING

Rajasthan's craftspeople have been famous for centuries for their jewel settings, stonework, blue pottery, enamel, lacquer, filigree work, tie-dye, and block-printed silk and muslin. You'll find all this and more in Jaipur, but watch out: your drivers and/or guides are likely to insist that they know the best shops and bargains in the city. (They get a commission on whatever you purchase.) If you have a specific shop in mind, be firm. Don't rely on the phrase "government-approved." Easily painted over a shop door, it's essentially meaningless. The following shops are reliable, and you're bound to find others in your explorations. Note that many shops are closed on Sunday.

A CARNIVAL OF COLORS AND THREADS

Rajasthan is famous for its dyed and hand-blocked printed fabric, often further embellished by embroidery and mirror work. Some hand-blocked patterns are familiar in the West, but the range of colors here is stunning. Of particular note are the *bandhani* (tie-dye), embroidered-mirror. Appliqué work is also stunning.

ARTS & CRAFTS If you have limited time and lots of gifts to buy or don't relish bargaining, head to the enormous, government-run **Rajasthali** (✉*Government Hostel, M.I. Rd., Panch Batti* ☎*141/237–2974*). This emporium is always flooded with crafts and textiles, though you might have to sift through a bewildering variety before you find what you want. **Tharyamal Balchand** (✉*M.I. Rd., Panch Batti* ☎*141/237–0376 or 141/236–1019*) sells a variety of authentic, good-quality crafts, including jewelry, brasswork, textiles, blue pottery, and woodwork. Here you'll get a good sense of the diversity of crafts and textiles from the different parts of Rajasthan. **Manglam Arts** (✉*Durgapura Station Rd., off the Tonk Rd.* ☎*141/272–1428*) is filled with exquisite antique and contemporary fine art, including Hindu *pichwais* (cloth paintings depicting Lord Krishna in various moods), Jain temple art, tantric and folk art, terracotta sculptures, silver furniture, handwoven *dhurries,* wood carvings, and wonderful old fabrics.

For specialty shops, wander through the **Khazana Walon ka Rasta** (✉*Pink City*), a lane in the old city (accessible through Chandpol gate), and watch stone-cutters create artworks in marble. For brass or other metalwork, visit **P.M. Allah Buksh and Son** (✉*M.I. Rd., Panch Batti*), established in 1880, which still sells the finest hand-engraved, enameled, or embossed brassware—including oversize old trays and historic armor. The tiny, unpretentious **Bhorilal Hanuman Sahar** (✉*Shop 131, Tripoliya Bazaar, Pink City*) has burlap bags full of old brass, copper, and bronze pieces that are sold by weight at bargain prices. The **Popular Art Palace** (✉*B/6 Prithviraj Rd., C-Scheme* ☎*141/229–2541 or 141/229–2571*) is great for both brass and wooden furniture, as well as miniature crafts and antiques.

For demonstrations of hand-block printing and other craftsmanship, visit **Rajasthan Cottage Industries** (✉*Shilpgram Complex, Golimar Garden, Amer Rd.* ☎*141/267–1853 or 141/267–1184*). It offers a fine variety not only of textiles, but also of other handicrafts and gems. Purchases are fair priced. **Rajasthan Small Scale Cottage Industries** (✉*Jagat Shiromani Temple Rd., Amer* ☎*141/253–0519*) sells textiles, gems, and handicrafts, including hand-block printing.

A special treat for lovers of miniature paintings is a trip to the home of award-winning artist **Tilak Gitai** (✉*E-5 Gokhle Marg, C-Scheme* ☎*141/237–2101*), who creates exquisite miniatures in classic Moghul, Rajput, Pahari, and other styles. Using antique paper, Gitai applies colors made from semiprecious stones, then real gold and silver leaf, in designs so fine he'll give you a magnifying glass to admire them. This is not a quick visit, but it's a great way to spend a few hours with a friendly Rajasthani family and learn about Indian art. **Juneja Art Gallery** (✉*Lakshmi Complex, M.I. Rd., Panch Batti* ☎*141/236–7448*) is Jaipur's leading gallery of contemporary art.

4

NEED A BREAK?

No visit to Jaipur is complete without a stop at Lassiwallah (✉*M.I. Rd., across from Niros, Panch Batti*), the most famous vendor of its kind in all of India. Located on the periphery of a long chain of imposters, the real thing can only be found under the sign KISAN LAL GOVIND NARAYAN AGRAWAL. Expect a long line. The *lassi* (yogurt-drink) wallah himself wears a *tilak* (an auspicious dot on the forehead) and *moti mala* (beaded necklace) to demonstrate his devotion to God and good service, and sits elevated above a large bowl of yogurt and cream (lassis cost Rs. 10–Rs. 20). Served in disposable red-clay cups with a dash of hard cream on top, drinks come only in medium and large sizes.

JEWELRY **Gem Palace** (✉*M.I. Rd., Panch Batti* ☎*141/237–4175*) has Jaipur's best gems and jewelry, a small collection of museum-quality curios, and a royal clientele; prices range from US$2 to US$2 million. **Amprapali Jewels** (✉*M.I. Rd., Panch Batti* ☎*141/237–7940 or 141/236–2768*) has some great silver and ornamental trinkets, as well as semiprecious stone artifacts. For precious jewels, including gold ornaments, find the **Bhuramal-Rajmal Surana Showroom** (✉*368 J.L.N. Marg, Moti Dhungri* ☎*141/257–0429 or 141/257–0430*), known worldwide for its *kundan* (a glasslike white stone) and *mina* (enamel) work. If you want something that's not so expensive and you're willing to bargain, you'll find your niche on **Chameli Valon ka Rasta** (✉*Off M.I. Rd., Panch Batti*). Walk among the shops on this lane for silver and semiprecious jeweled ornaments, trinkets, and small toys.

POTTERY **Jaipur Blue Pottery Art Center** (✉*Amer Rd., near Jain Mandir* ☎*No phone*) sells a broad selection of Rajasthan's fetching blue pottery. Clay pots are thrown, or made, on the premises. Blue pottery from the kiln of Kripal Singh can be bought at **Kripal Kumbh** (✉*B-18A Shiv Marg, Bani Park* ☎*141/220–1127*). The blue pottery at **Neerja Internationals** (✉*S-19 Bhawani Singh Rd., C-Scheme Extension, Bais Godam* ☎*141/238–*

0395 or 141/238–3511) is particularly funky—the designer, owner Lela Bordie, has exhibited all over the world, and she runs this shop for a discriminating crowd.

TEXTILES For fine hand-block fabrics, go south to the nearby towns of Sanganer and Bagru *(⇨ below)*.

Channi Carpets and Textiles (✉*Mount Rd. opposite Ramgarh Rd.* ☎*141/267–2231 or 141/267–2214*) has an excellent selection of hand-woven merino wool carpets, cotton dhurries, and hand-block cottons and silks. The staff can also tailor clothes on short notice.

Anokhi (✉*C-11, 2nd fl., KK Square, Prithviraj Rd., C-scheme* ☎*141/400–7244 or 141/400–7245* ⊕*www.anokhi.com*) is a leading shop for designer and ethnic wear, mostly in cotton. The selection includes beautiful bedspreads, quilts, cloth bags, saris, and other clothing—both Indian and casual Western. It has the prettiest *lehengas* (skirts) in the state. Stop for a bite to eat at the Anokhi café outside the swanky store. You can also visit the new Anokhi museum in Jaipur to learn more about block printing and textiles. Run and managed by women, the boutique **Cottons** (✉*4 Achrol Estate, Jacob Rd., Civil Lines*) carries simple, attractive clothes for men and women, as well as little bags, quilts, and other decorative household items. Catering to the ultra-elegant crowd, **Soma** (✉*5 Jacob Rd., Civil Lines* ☎*141/222–2778*) is a second-floor shop filled with vibrant colors. Here you'll find chutneys, clothing, and decorative fabrics—including fabulous, hand-painted white cloth lamp shades.

OFF THE BEATEN PATH

Apno Gaon. If you don't have time to visit a small village, here's your chance to get a feel for Rajasthani folk culture. Like the state's half-dozen simulated villages, Apno Gaon offers camel rides, playground swings, traditional music, and puppet shows. The food is so good even locals feast here. You'll get farm-fresh, organically grown vegetables, and *bhajra* (corn) delicacies and milk products. Be prepared to sit on the ground and eat with your hands. Apno Gaon is open from 11 AM to 11 PM, but is better at night. The street signs are in Hindi, so ask your driver for directions. ✉*Sikar Rd., past Vishwa Karma Industrial Area* ☎*141/233–1802* ▭*No credit cards.*

SANGANER

16 km (10 mi) south of Jaipur up Tonk Rd., near the airport.

Watch artisans in action throughout this well-known craft town, where nearly every family is involved in the production of block- and screen-printed textiles, blue pottery, or handmade paper.

Whatever handmade paper you've seen back home may well have come from **Salim's Paper** (✉*Gramodyog Rd.* ☎*141/273–0222*). In this factory you can see each step of the process. Some of the thick, beautiful papers are made with crushed flower petals; it's fun to see them thrown into the mixture of cotton and resin.

Shri Digamber Jain Temple, roughly 1,000 years old and covered with amazingly ornate carvings from its piled spires on down, is a highlight of Sanganer. The temple is right in town. The inner shrine has no roof, yet somehow the space seems to achieve total tranquillity. On your way into or out of town, check out the line of blue potters on Tonk Road.

OFF THE BEATEN PATH

Bagru. This small Rajput township, 35 km (22 mi) southwest of Sanganer on Ajmer Road, is famous for its hand-printed cloth industry. Bagru's simple, popular designs feature earthen colors of green, brown, black, and blue.

MARRIAGE BETWEEN THE EAST AND WEST

There was a time when only American teenagers wore ethnically inspired clothing, but now shops like Anokhi and Cottons (headquartered in Jaipur) are blending beautiful Indian hand-block printed fabrics with a Western sense of style. Not just limited to Indian clothing, these stores sell fashionable Western attire with an ethnic touch to upper-middle-class Indians and foreigners thirsting for unique clothing.

RANTHAMBHORE NATIONAL PARK

Fodor's Choice ★ *161 km (100 mi) south of Jaipur.*

Now incorporating several nearby sanctuaries in its borders, the spectacular Ranthambhore National Park encompasses 1,334 square km (515 square mi). The rugged Aravalli and Vindhya hills, highland boulder plateaus, and lakes and rivers provide homes for hundreds of species of birds, mammals, and reptiles. Ranthambhore is noted for its tiger and leopard population, although you still have only a 30% to 40% chance of seeing a large cat on any given expedition. The best time to see tigers is right before the monsoon, in summer, when the tigers emerge to drink from small water holes. (When it's dry and the water table is low, the tigers are forced out of hiding to quench their thirst.) What you will definitely see are numerous peacocks, sambar (large Asian deer), *chital* (spotted axis deer), *chinkara* (gazelle), wild pigs, jackals, crocodiles, and often sloth bears.

Sighting a wild tiger in Ranthambhore is an exciting experience: if you're lucky, open jeeps sometimes take you as close as 10 feet away from an animal. Before that, of course, you will hear the jungle sounds that warn of a tiger's presence. Monkeys and peacocks scream loudly and the deer in the area become agitated and nervous. Despite conservation efforts, the tiger population in Ranthambhore is small: there are less than 40 of the great amber-eyed cats in the reserve. Sighting a leopard is much more difficult, as these cats live on high, inaccessible slopes and are extremely shy.

The park is run by the Indian government, and the rules are inflexible: you can only enter the park in an official government jeep, and the jeeps keep strict hours, daily from 6:30 AM to 9:30 AM and 3:30 PM to 6:30 PM. Book a jeep two months in advance—there's heavy demand for them. (If you make bookings through your hotel, expect a service charge.) In the off-hours, you can explore the surrounding region; the 10th century **Ranthambhore Fort,** perched on a nearby hill, is one of Rajasthan's more spectacular military strongholds. You could also visit Dastkar, a craft-and-textile shop on the Ranthambhore Road, run by a nongovernmental organization.

Within the park is a government-run hotel called **Jhoomar Baori** (12 rooms, Rs. 650–Rs. 800) offers the chance to spend a night near the animals, but little else. A better option is to stay at one of the hotels along Ranthambhore Road. The neighboring town of Sawai Madhopur has numerous hotels, but most are extremely basic. ☎ *7462/220–808 Sawai Madhopur Tourist Information Center* 🌐 *www.rajasthantourism.gov.in* 🎫 *Rs. 391 per person; up to 6 people per jeep* ⏲ *Oct.–June.*

WHERE TO STAY

$$$$ Fodor'sChoice ★ **Oberoi Vanyavilas.** Ideal for those who want to "camp" in luxury, this is one of the best resorts in all India. In landscaped gardens on the edge of the national park, its ceremonial gateway (complete with welcoming elephants) leads to a magical lobby with beautiful frescoes and a splendid residential area, where luxury tents evoke all the magnificence of the former royal lifestyle. The air-conditioned tents have teakwood floors, walled gardens, private decks, and charming bathrooms with stand-alone bathtubs. The sand-tone resort blends with the hills and the forest. You can also take advantage of the excellent spa facilities and swimming pool here, or take an elephant picnic into the countryside. A renowned conservationist, Fateh Singh Rathore, delivers a lecture every evening. **Pros:** organically grown vegetables from the resort's own garden contribute to the fresh flavors at the restaurant; staff is young, warm, ever ready to go the extra mile to ensure your comfort. **Cons:** expensive. ✉ *Ranthambhore Rd., Sawai Madhopur, 322001* ☎ *7462/223–999* 📠 *7462/223–988* 🌐 *www.oberoihotels.com* *25 tents* *In-room: DVD, refrigerator. In-hotel: restaurant, bar, pool, spa, no elevator, laundry service.* 💳 *AE, DC, MC, V.*

$$$$ **Sawai Madhopur Lodge.** This laid-back property, run by the Taj group, may give you the impression that you're still in the old hunting-lodge days as you sit on the veranda and look out on the lawn. The colonial building that houses the lobby occupies the site of the royal tented camp, which was once a regular hunting event. A railway line once extended right up to the camp; you can see old photographs of the days when the railway line brought royalty and their guests here. **Pros:** just a 20-minute drive to the park, all meals included. **Cons:** extremely expensive, meals are buffet style and often unexciting. ✉ *Ranthambhore Rd., Sawai Madhopur, 322001* ☎ *07462/220–541, 07462/223–500* 📠 *07462/220–718* 🌐 *www.tajhotels.com* *30 rooms, 8 suites, 6 tents* *In-room: refrigerator. In-hotel: restaurant, bar, tennis court, pool, laundry service, no elevator.* 💳 *AE, DC, MC, V* 🍴 *FAP.*

$$$ **Ranthambhore Regency.** This is definitely the most comfortable mid-price place on the Ranthambhore Road. A long line of rooms is set against a rectangular courtyard with a pool, and a restaurant serves buffet meals (all are included in rates). There's also a barbecue outside.

The rooms are spotless, with bright Rajasthani furnishings. The helpful owner, Ravinder Jain, is committed to making your Ranthambhore experience pleasant, and is a mine of local information. **Pros:** friendly staff, clean rooms. **Cons:** meals are buffet-only. ✉ *Ranthambhore Rd., Sawai Madhopur, 322001* ☎ *7462/223–456 or 7462/221–176* 🌐 *www.ranthambhor.com* *32 rooms, 21 cottages, 7 suites* *In-hotel: restaurant, pool, no elevator, laundry service.* *MC, V* *FAP.*

SARISKA NATIONAL PARK

4

110 km (68 mi) northeast of Jaipur, 110 km (68 mi) southwest of Delhi, 40 km (25 mi) southwest of Alwar.

Sariska was once the exclusive game preserve of the rulers of the princely state of Alwar. Today, this sanctuary in the hills of the Aravalli Range makes a great weekend escape from Delhi. Traditionally a tiger reserve, Sariska is now better populated with other carnivorous animals, including the leopard, jackal, caracal, and jungle cat (though the cats' nocturnal habits make sightings rare). The terrain—mostly scrub and lush clusters of forest and grasslands—also provides an excellent habitat for herbivores. Peacocks abound here, as do monkeys, blue bulls, spotted deer, and wild boars. You do have a good chance of seeing langurs and other monkeys, porcupines, hyenas, and numerous species of deer (including the *chowsingha,* a four-horned deer unique to India), and all kinds of birds.

Forest officials have created water holes for the animals, which help you catch glimpses of otherwise elusive wildlife. The best times to view animals at Sariska are early morning and evening from November through June (though it starts getting hot by March). Jeeps are available at the hotels. Wear neutral colors to avoid scaring the animals away, and take a jacket in winter.

In Sariska you can also find a number of historic monuments. Within the park is the **Pandupol,** a huge hole in the rock supposedly made by Bhim, one of the five Pandava brothers who are celebrated in the ancient Hindu epic, the *Mahabharata.*

Outside the sanctuary, but still close by, is the **Neelkanth Mahadev,** an ancient ruin that includes pieces from about 300 Hindu and Jain temples. Among these ruins are some beautiful sculptures and an entire temple devoted to Shiva, as well as the ruins of the Kankwari Fort perched high on a hill (a good picnic spot).

WHERE TO STAY

$$$ **Sariska Palace Hotel.** This former palace and royal hunting lodge was built in 1892 by the Maharaja of Alwar for the visit of Queen Victoria's son, the Duke of Connaught. Animals often find their way into the flower-speckled grounds, so you may see wildlife while relaxing on the terrace. In addition, horse, camel, and jeep safaris are easily arranged. **Pros:** high-ceiling rooms and suites are gigantic and clean, lots of animal photo ops. **Cons:** no TV in rooms, fairly expensive. ✉ *Alwar district, 301022* *Reserve through 1/1-B Mohammedpur, Bikhaji*

Cama Pl., New Delhi, 110066 ☎144/284–1322 to 25, 11/2615–4388 to 89 reservations ⇨96 rooms, 5 suites ♁In-room: no a/c (some). In-hotel: restaurant, bar, tennis court, pool, no elevator. ▭AE, DC, MC, V.

BHARATPUR

150 km (93 mi) east of Jaipur, 55 km (34 mi) west of Agra, 18 km (11 mi) west of Fatehpur Sikri.

Fodor'sChoice ★ Founded by the Jat ruler Suraj Mal in 1733, the city of Bharatpur is famous for the **Keoladeo National Park** (also known as the Ghana Bird Sanctuary), once the duck-hunting forest of the local maharajas. The park is home to mammals and reptiles—blue bulls, spotted deer, otters, and Indian rock pythons—but birds are the main attraction. This famous waterbird haven is an ornithologist's dream—29 square km (10 square mi) of forests and wetlands with 400 species, more than 130 of which are resident year-round, such as the Saras crane, gray heron, snake bird, and spoonbill. In winter, birds arrive from the Himalayas, Siberia, and even Europe.

The best way to see the park is on foot or by boat (Rs. 75), but there are plenty of other options. The park's main artery is a blacktop road that runs from the entrance gate to the center. Surrounded by marshlands but screened by bushes, this road is the most convenient viewpoint for bird-watching, and is also traveled by cycle-rickshaws (Rs. 50 per hour), a horse and buggy, and the park's electric bus (Rs. 25 per person). The rickshaw drivers, trained by the forest department, are fairly good at finding and pointing out birds. You can also rent a bicycle and head into more remote areas; just remember that most roads are unpaved. The excellent guides at the gate (Rs. 120 per excursion) are familiar with the birds' haunts, and can help you spot and identify them.

Try to bring a bird guidebook: former royal-family member Salim Ali's *The Birds of India* is a good choice. The best time to see the birds is early morning or late evening, November through February; by the end of February, many birds start heading home. Stick around at sunset, when the water takes on a mirrorlike stillness and the air is filled with the calls of day birds settling down and night birds stirring. *For information, contact the park staff. ✉5 km (3 mi) south of city center 321001 ☎5644/222–777 ⊠Park Rs. 200, camera fee Rs. 10, video-camera fee Rs. 200 ⊙Park daily 6 AM–6:30 PM.*

In Bharatpur's Old City is the **Lohagarh Fort,** also known figuratively as the Iron Fort. Built of mud, the structure might seem fragile, but it was tested by a British siege in 1805: armed with 65 pieces of field artillery, 1,800 European soldiers and 6,000 Indian sepoys did manage to win the battle, but they failed to break the invincible fort. *⊠Rs. 5 ⊙Daily 10–5.*

The town of **Deeg,** 34 km (21 mi) north of Bharatpur, is known for its graceful palaces and gardens, complete with swings and ancient fountains. (The latter now serve as musical fountains—their waters dance to the rhythm of taped classical music.) Built in the 1730s, Deeg was the first capital of the Jat state.

WHERE TO STAY

$–$$ ★ **Laxmi Vilas Palace Hotel.** Still home to the descendants of the former maharaja's younger brother, this cozy Heritage Hotel is a two-story haveli built in 1887. Rural and old-fashioned, it's certainly the best place to stay in Bharatpur. The palace, on a 40-acre estate covered with mustard and wheat fields, blends Moghul and Rajput styles. Each room is different, but many contain old brass beds and antique furniture. Pricier rooms have original tiles and painted walls and fireplaces; the others are smaller and have newer furniture, but they're still pleasant. Deep Raj, the owner, is happy to organize jeep safaris or excursions to surrounding areas, such as Deeg, Agra, and Fatehpur Sikri, and is a great source of local information. **Pros:** a variety of cuisines are served in the dining room, cultural programs in the evening. **Cons:** lacks the luxury available at fancier Heritage and five-star hotels. ✉*Kakaji Ki Kothi, Bharatpur, 321001* ☎*5644/231–199 or 5644/223–523* 🌐*www.laxmivilas.com* *14 rooms, 16 suites* *In-hotel: restaurant, bar, pool, public Internet, no elevator.* *AE, MC, V.*

4

AJMER

131 km (81 mi) southwest of Jaipur.

Roughly three hours' drive from Jaipur, the town of Ajmer has a typically Indian past—with Hindu, Muslim, and colonial influences. Founded by Raja Ajay Pal Chauhan in the 7th century, the town was a center of Chauhan power until 1193, when Prithvi Raj Chauhan lost the kingdom to Mohammed Ghori. From then on, many dynasties contributed to making it the fascinating blend of Hindu and Islamic culture is it today. Demographically, Ajmer is primarily a Muslim town, but its proximity to Pushkar gives it a Hindu feel—it has a famous mosque as well as temples, and all pilgrims to Pushkar pass through Ajmer. It also has remnants of colonial-era architecture.

Accommodation options in Ajmer are somewhat limited; most travelers pass through on their way to Pushkar, where there are comfortable places to stay. Ajmer makes a convenient half-day halt, as it's the nearest rail station to Pushkar. The two places are separated by Nag Pahar mountain, across which an 11-km (7-mi) ghat, or mountain pass, traverses.

In the heart of the city is **Dargah Sharif,** the tomb of the Sufi saint Khwaja Moin-ud din Chisti. This site is comparable to Mecca in significance for South Asian Muslims, and is frequented by Muslims and non-Muslims alike, especially during Urs (a death anniversary celebration that takes place during six days in the Islamic month of Rajab—around September or October). Be prepared to deal with aggressive beggars on the street leading to the dargah.

A peaceful place of worship worth visiting, the 19th-century **Nasiyan Temple** is sacred to the Jains.

If you have enough time in Ajmer, take a guide with you to the **Dhai din ka Jhonpra,** a ruined 12th-century mosque, which, according to legend, was built in 2½ (*dhai*) days.

PUSHKAR

★ *11 km (7 mi) northwest of Ajmer.*

With more than 500 temples, Pushkar is one of Hinduism's holiest sites and an interesting place to visit even when the famous camel fair is isn't being held. In its narrow traffic-free main bazaar, sadhus, tribals, hippies, and five-legged cattle (such birth deformities are considered lucky) vie for space, while shops selling implements of the ascetic lifestyle rub shoulders with the Pink Floyd café and other such establishments selling porridge and pancakes to backpackers. Although goods from all over Rajasthan find their way to the bazaar, no alcohol or meat can be sold anywhere in Pushkar because of its religious significane.

Pushkar's religious significance derives from the Vedic text, *Padma Purana,* which describes how the town was created. Lord Brahma, Creator of the Universe, was looking for a place to perform the *yajna*—a holy ritual that involves placing offerings into a sacrificial fire for Agni, the fire god—that would signify the beginning of the human age. He dropped a lotus from his hand and Pushkar was the place it struck the ground.

The most important temple, in the center of town, is **Brahma Temple,** supposedly the only temple dedicated to Brahma in the world (if there are others, they number very few). Pilgrims visiting the temple climb a long stairway into the walled area of the temple to take the blessings of the god—in the form of small sweets. There are varying versions of legend concerning the temple, but most have to do with Brahma's wife Savitri, who refused to attend the ceremony. Impatient, Brahma married the goddess Gayatri (some say she was a milkmaid), and when Savitri found out, she put a curse on Brahma, declaring that the earth would forget him completely. She then relented, and said that Brahma could only be worshipped in Pushkar.

Before you visit the Brahma Temple, make an early start to check out the **Saraswati Temple** on a hill overlooking Pushkar Lake. It's a short walk: it only takes between a half-hour and an hour, and the view at sunrise is worth it. You could also go up in the evening.

During auspicious pilgrimage times, tens of thousands of people swarm the **holy bathing ghats** *(flights of steps)* on Pushkar Lake and get blessings from local Brahmins. Make sure you spend some time at these ghats. Many of the marble ghats were constructed for pilgrims by royal families who wanted to ensure power and prosperity in their kingdoms throughout Rajasthan by appeasing the gods. Even the British Raj built a ghat for Queen Elizabeth. When you pass an entrance to a ghat, be prepared for a priest to solicit you—he'll want you to receive a blessing, the "Pushkar Passport." He'll lead you to the water's edge, say a prayer, and will ask you to recite a blessing in Sanskrit (you'll repeat after him). Then he'll paste a tilak (rice and colored powder dot) on your forehead and tie a *raki* (a string bracelet, denoting a blessing) to your wrist. After the ceremony, you're expected to give a donation: don't give much more than Rs. 100.

If you really want an experience, go to Pushkar during its famous annual **Camel Fair.** Every October or November—depending on the lunar calendar—people flock here to see the finest camels parade around the fairground in colorful costumes. People come to buy, sell, and trade camels, and to race one camel against another. A good male camel goes for about US$250. The town gets packed during festival time, so make sure you reserve a room at least several weeks—if not longer—ahead of time. Several tented camps with modern conveniences also mushroom during the fair. Contact a travel agent for details. You could also directly ask the Pushkar Palace (Pushkar), the Balsamand Palace (Jodhpur), or Rajasthan Tourism Development Corporation (RTDC) in Jaipur (☎141/220–2586 🌐www.pushkar-camel-fair.com).

4

WHERE TO STAY

$–$$ **Pushkar Palace.** This small palace sits above its own ghat—private stairs leading down to the lake—with fabulous, panoramic views of Pushkar. Built by the Maharaja of Jaisalmer in the 15th century, the Pushkar Palace was later presented to the Maharaja of Kishangarh. All the rooms are outfitted with antique furniture from Rajputana's heyday. Horse, camel, and jeep safaris are available. **Pros:** great views, private, restaurant is on a terrace overlooking the lake and is one of the best in Pushkar. **Cons:** room rates skyrocket during the Pushkar festival, no pool. ✉*Chhoti Basti, southeast corner of Pushkar lake, off Pushkar Bazaar (the main street), 305022* ☎*145/277–3001 or 145/277–2401* 🌐*www.hotelpushkarpalace.com* *28 rooms, 25 suites* *In-room: refrigerator. In-hotel: restaurant, bar, no elevator.* *AE, MC, V.*

$–$$ **Pushkar Resorts.** The spirit of the maharajas blends well with the comforts of resort living here. Relax poolside under the shade of a palm tree and escape from Pushkar's chaotic main bazaar, a 15-minute jeep ride away. The restaurant, only for guests, serves nonvegetarian food. The hotel's regal camel cart rides are famous—you journey through nearby sand dunes while watching the sun set. **Pros:** European-style rooms (in cottages) have views of the Savitri temple that crowns a mountain near the resort, great camel rides. **Cons:** outside Pushkar, need a car to get around. ✉*Village Ganhera, Motisar Rd., outside Pushkar* ☎*145/277–2944 or 0145/277–2945* 🌐*www.pushkarresorts.com* *40 rooms* *In-room: refrigerator. In-hotel: restaurant, bar, golf course, pool, no elevator.* *AE, DC, MC, V.*

SHEKHAWATI

This region in northeastern Rajasthan is renowned for its painted havelis and old forts. Shekhawati (literally "garden of shekha") takes its name from Rao Shekhaji, a Rajput king of this region, who was born in 1433. He was named after a *fakir* (Muslim holy man) named Sheikh Burhanby, who granted a boon to his parents that they would bear a son. In another unwitting contribution to history, the sheikh had come to India with the Mongol invader Tamerlane in 1398, dressed in a blue robe—hence the color of Shekhawati's flag. The region has had a turbulent history ever since, experiencing the conquests and defeats of Rajput princes, alliances with the Moghuls after Akbar, and finally suzerainty under the British Raj. The region is made up of smaller principalities, including Sikar, Lachhmangarh, Churi Ajitgarh, Mukundgarh, Jhunjhunu, Mandawa, Fatehpur, and Churu.

A regional center of trade between the 18th and 20th centuries, Shekhawati is now known as Rajasthan's open-air art gallery, thanks to the frescoes painted on the walls of ornate havelis throughout the region. Influenced by the Persian, Jaipur, and Moghul schools of painting, Shekhawati's frescoes illustrate subjects ranging from mythological stories and local legends to hunting safaris and scenes of everyday life. You'll even find illustrated experiences with the British and cars or planes. The introduction of photography in 1840 gave Shekhawati's painters still more to work with. The painters themselves were called *chiteras* and belonged to the caste of *kumhars* (potters). Initially, they colored their masterpieces with vegetable pigments; after mixing these with lime water and treating the wall with three layers of a very fine clay, the chiteras painstakingly drew their designs on a last layer of filtered lime dust. Time was short, as the design had to be completed before the plaster dried, but the highly refined technique ensured that the images would not fade.

The havelis that contain these masterpieces are themselves spectacular. These havelis have courtyards, exquisitely latticed windows, intricate mirror work, vaulted ceilings, immense balconies, and ornate gateways and facades. They date from the British Raj, during which traditional overland trading routes to Central Asia, Europe, and China were slowly superseded by rail and sea routes. In the 19th century, Marwari traders (Hindus from the *vaisya,* or trading, caste) who had once profited from the overland trading system, then migrated to Calcutta, Bombay, and Madras (modern-day Kolkata, Mumbai, and Chennai) to seek new fortunes. The wealthy Marwaris maintained connections with their ancestral homes, sending remittance from their new enterprises. Often this money was used to build lavish havelis, adorned with elaborate frescoes. Many of the havelis, as well as some old Rajput forts, are now open to the public. Some have been converted to Heritage Hotels. Stay in a few if you can, and take a day or two to explore the towns around them.

The golden age of fresco painting came to an end by the 1930s with the mass exodus of the Marwaris, who had left to resettle in the commercial centers. Since then, many of these beautiful mansions and their paintings have fallen into disrepair. Only a handful have survived—some have been restored by their owners, and a few have been converted into hotels. In **Sikar,** formerly the wealthiest trading center, look for the Biyani, Murarka, and Somani havelis. **Lachhmangarh** features the grand Char Chowk Haveli, particularly evocative of the prosperous Marwari lifestyle. A planned city like Jaipur, Lachhmangarh is home to a popular ayurvedic center, **SPG Kaya Kalp and Research Center** (✉Tara Kung, Salasar Rd. ☎1573/64230), which teaches yoga, meditation, and various therapies. In the village of **Churi Ajitgarh**, unusually erotic frescoes are painted behind doors and on bedroom ceilings in the Shiv Narain Nemani, Kothi Shiv Datt, and Rai Jagan Lal Tibrewal havelis. The frescoed temples of **Jhunjhunu** make for interesting comparisons: visit Laxmi Nath, Mertani Baori, Ajeet Sagar, and Qamrudin Shah Ki Dargah Fatehpur. **Mukandgarh** has an excellent craft market, known especially for textiles, brass ware, and iron scissors, in addition to the Kanoria, Ganeriwala, and Bheekraj Nangalia havelis. Warrior-statesman Thakur Nawal Singh founded **Nawalgarh** in 1737, and the town boasts some of the best frescoes in Shekhawati in its Aath, Anandilal Poddar, Jodhraj Patodia, and Chokhani havelis, as well as in the Roop Niwas Kothi hotel.

You need at least two days to explore Shekhawati even perfunctorily; it cannot be accomplished en route between Jaipur and Delhi in a single day. Jhunjhunu, for instance, is 180 km (112 mi) northwest from Jaipur and 240 km (149 mi) west from Delhi. You would need to stop two nights in Shekhawati, perhaps one at Jhunjhunu and one at Dundlod, Mukandgarh, or Mandawa (55 km [34 mi], 45 km [28 mi], and 30 km [19 mi] southwest, respectively, from Jhunjhunu) or Nawalgarh (35 km [22 mi] southwest from Jhunjhunu). Alternatively, spend one night at Jhunjhunu and one at Neemrana if you're en route to Delhi.

Between Shekhawati and Delhi, just off the main Jaipur–Delhi highway (100 km [62 mi] southwest of Delhi, off NH–8, in Village Neemrana in the Alwar district) is the beautiful **Neemrana** Fort Palace, now a hotel and an outstanding example of imaginative restoration.

WHERE TO EAT & STAY

$ ✕**Garden Organic Restaurant.** This hotel restaurant serves mostly Indian cuisine prepared with organic vegetables grown on the farm just behind the restaurant. A buffet lunch and dinner is served daily, but à la carte dishes aren't a problem at this homey eatery run by a local woman entrepreneur. Don't miss this unpretentious and simple food—it's a nice change given that there are hardly any stand-alone restaurants in Shekhawati that aren't in hotels. ✉*Shekhawati Guesthouse, near Roop Niwas Kothi, Nawalgarh* ☎*1594/224–658* ▭*No credit cards.*

$$–$$$ Fodor's Choice ★ **Neemrana Fort Palace.** This 15th-century fort, now a Heritage Hotel, is one of the finest retreats in India. The fort is perched on a plateau in the Aravali Hills. The rooms, which vary in size and price, are masterpieces. The architecture is characterized by wooden jalis (latticework screens), cusped arches, gleaming pillars, and niches. Forget about phones and TVs, because there are none. Just relax and watch preening peacocks and swooping parrots from the countless terraces, balconies, and courtyards. The restaurant serves fixed Rajasthani and Continental menus. The pool area has spectacular views of the town and beyond because the fort itself is on the hill. If you get a chance, do go check out the dilapidated yet charming stepwell (a well with steps for water

collection) a 20-minute walk from the hotel (ask hotel staff for directions). Otherwise, the fort itself is fun to explore with all the stairways and pathways leading to stunning views and hidden alcoves. **Pros:** even some of the bathrooms have lovely views of the valley below, morning and afternoon tea with cookies included in room rate, sunsets are stunning. **Cons:** the just-okay buffet-style meals are served at fixed times, fort is full of stairs and steep ramps at every turn (watch your step), can get crowded on weekends. ✉ *Village Neemrana, Alwar district, 301705* ✣ *100 km (60 mi) southwest of Delhi, off NH–8 (3-hour drive from Delhi)* *Reserve through 13 Nizamuddin East Market, New Delhi, 110013* ☎ *1494/246–007 to 8, 11/2435–6145, 11/4182–5001, or 11/4182–5002 reservations* 🌐 *www.neemranahotels.com* *37 rooms, 13 suites* *In-room: no a/c (some), no phone, no TV. In-hotel: restaurant, bar, pool, gym, spa, no elevator.* *AE, DC, MC, V.*

$–$$ **Castle Mandawa.** Towering high above the town of Mandawa, this rugged, amber-color fort has been converted to a luxury Heritage Hotel. Sword-bearing guards welcome you at the gate; inside, the walls display 16th-century portraits of the Mandawa family. The spacious, airy rooms are furnished with period furniture. Check out the panoramic view from the canopied balconies and turreted battlements. Dinner is an enchanting candlelit affair in an open-air courtyard with live local entertainment. Camel, horse, and jeep safaris are available. It all makes for an ideal place to stay for a night and explore the enchanting town of Mandawa. **Pros:** beautiful pool with cascading waterfall, brand-new gym. **Cons:** overpriced buffet lunch; in a town with limited options. ✉ *Jhunjhunu district, 168 km (109 mi) northwest of Jaipur (6-hour drive from Delhi), Mandawa, 333704* *Reserve through Mandawa Haveli, Sansar Chandra Rd., Jaipur, 302001* ☎ *159/222–3124 or 159/222–23480 to 82, 141/510–6081 reservations* *159/222–3171* 🌐 *www.mandawahotels.com* *64 rooms, 10 suites* *In-room: no TV, refrigerator. In-hotel: restaurant, bar, pool, gym, spa, no elevator.* *AE, MC, V* *EP.*

$–$$ **Desert Resort.** On a sand dune in Mandawa, this eco-friendly hotel is influenced by traditional desert living. The rooms are stand-alone clay-colored "village huts" decorated with tribal handpainted art and inlaid glass work on the interior walls. The bedding and furniture radiates the warmth of Rajasthani fabrics and handicrafts. Even the main lounge is made of mud, and the dining room gleams from the bits of glass and shells in its walls. The suites are luxurious and elegantly designed. Sit by the pool or in the garden, and enjoy the striking desert panorama. Camel cart rides along with camel safaris are available. **Pros:** as close as you are going to get to the desert from Delhi, park with swings for children on-site. **Cons:** the pool is small, the hotel is slightly out of the way from the main parts of Mandawa. ✉ *Mandawa district, Jhunjhunu, 333704* ☎ *0159/222–3151, 0159/222–3514, or 0159/222–3245, 0141/5106081 or 0141/5102510 reservations (Mandawa Haveli, in Jaipur)* *0159/222–3171, 0141/237–2084 reservations* 🌐 *www.mandawahotels.com* *61 rooms 13 suites* *In-room: refrigerator (some), no TV. In-hotel: restaurant, room service, bar, no elevator.* *AE, MC, V.*

$–$$ **Mukandgarh Fort.** Founded in the mid-18th century by Raja Mukand Singh, this picturesque fort in the town of Mukandgarh, famous for its artisans, is now a Heritage Hotel. A bar overlooks the courtyard, where at an outdoor barbecue you can get kebabs and curry in the evening. Guest rooms have painted walls and ceilings, tie-dye curtains, and patchwork bedspreads. **Pros:** a five-minute walk from the Babali Baba Mandir, the main temple in town. **Cons:** some rooms in the new wing don't have windows, so check your room before you book it; cash only. ✉ *Jhunjhunu district, 250 km (155 mi) southwest of Delhi., Mukandgarh, 333705* ☎ *1594/252–398 or 1594/252–397, 11/4176–4324 or 11/4176–4325 reservations* *45 rooms, 5 suites* *In-room: no TV (some). In-hotel: restaurant, bar, pool, no elevator.* *No credit cards.*

4

$ **Dera Dundlod Kila.** In the heart of the Shekhawati region, this Heritage Hotel was built in 1750 and is still owned by the descendants of the former *thakur* (landowner). Surrounded by a moat, it has a mix of Moghul and Rajput architecture. Inside, the stunning Diwan-i-Khas ("hall of private audience") has original wall frescoes, European-style portraits, Louis XIV furniture, and a well-stocked library. The clean, simple bedrooms have painted walls. Horse safaris (and camel and jeep trips) are available. **Pros:** impressive interiors, swimming pool. **Cons:** no Internet. ✉ *Jaipur, Dundlod, Jhunjhunu district, 333702* ✧ *250 km (155 mi) southwest of Delhi, 165 km (103 mi) from Jaipur* *Reserve through Dundlod House, Hawa Sadak, Civil Lines, Jaipur, 302019* ☎ *1594/252–519* ☎ *141/221–1276 or 141/221–1498* 🌐 *www.dundlod.com* *22 rooms, 5 suites* *In-room: no a/c (some), no TV. In-hotel: restaurant, bar, pool, no elevator.* *AE, DC, MC, V.*

$ **Roop Niwas Kothi.** The only decent place to stay in Nawalgarh combines Rajput and European architecture in its beautiful gardens and private cottages. It's far from grand, but the owners, descendants of the former *thakur* (landowner), aim to please. The circular driveway upon entering the gates is impressive and the surrounding gardens are an oasis full of chirping birds and cool breezes. The rooms, with Victorian furniture, are modest but clean. The dining room is quaint. The restaurant contains an eclectic assortment of antiques of both Rajput and British origin, and some firearms, including six-shooters and a blunderbuss. It serves vegetarian and nonvegetarian cuisine and has a bar license. **Pros:** very affordable, ideal base to explore Nawalgarh's hundreds and havelis and the surrounding area. **Cons:** hotel is in one corner of town, so you'll need a car to get around. ✉ *Jhunjhunu district, Shekhawati, Nawalgarh, 333042* ✧ *250 km (155 mi) southwest of Delhi* ☎ *1594/222–008 or 1594/224–152* *1594/223–388* *22 rooms, 1 suite* *In-room: no a/c (some), no TV, In-hotel: restaurant, bar, pool, no elevator.* *AE, MC, V.*

¢–$ **Piramal Haveli.** Among the grandest of the traditional homes, this one in the village of Bagar has three courtyards enclosed by colonial pillared corridors. Originally built as the home of Seth Piramal Chaturbhuj Makharia (1892–1958), who made his fortune trading cotton, opium, and silver in Bombay, the frescoes here allude to Makharia's wealth—they depict flying angels and gods in motorcars. The hotel is run by the Neemrana Group, and although it's nothing like the Neemrana Fort Palace, its simple rooms are good-looking. **Pros:** intimate, without the hotel feel; a short car ride from the sights of Shekhawati. **Cons:** no pool. ✉ *Village Bagar, Jhunjhunu district* ✣ *250 km (150 mi) southwest of Delhi* ✉ *Reserve through No. 13 Nizamuddin East Market, New Delhi, 110013* ☎ *1592/221–220 or 11/2435–6145, 11/4182–5001 or 11/4182–5002 reservations* 🌐 *www.neemranahotels.com* ⇨ *8 rooms* ♨ *In-room: no a/c (some), no TV. In-hotel: restaurant, no elevator.* ▭ *AE, DC, MC, V.*

¢–$ **Hotel Mandawa Haveli.** Oozing with nostalgic charm, the small but splendid haveli is over 170 years old. The central courtyard is lovely—you can enjoy a cup of tea while gazing at the ancient frescoes that surround you on all sides. The food is simple and fresh in a homemade way. The rooftop restaurant is open for buffet dinners—if you have a special craving, let the hotel know in advance and they will do their best to make it happen. **Pros:** a budget hotel that's quite a steal, beautiful rooms have period furniture and not one is like the other, great personalized service. **Cons:** no Internet service; precarious steps leading up to the restaurant. ✉ *Near Sonthaliya Gate, Mandawa* ☎ *1592/223–088* 🌐 *http://hotelmandawa.free.fr* ⇨ *18 rooms* ♨ *In-room: no a/c (some), no phone, no TV. In-hotel: 2 restaurants, spa, no elevator, laundry facilities.* ▭ *MC, V.*

JODHPUR & ENVIRONS

Jodhpur is rich in fort and palace treasures and a great base for side trips to Guda Vishnoi, home of the gentle Vishnoi community and a haven for wildlife, or the temple town of Osian in the Thar Desert. Nagaur Fort also entices—you can camp here in splendid tents during the town's winter cattle fair.

JODHPUR

343 km (215 mi) west of Jaipur, 266 km (165 mi) northwest of Udaipur.

Jodhpur is known as the Blue City for it azure-painted houses, especially impressive when viewed from the ramparts of Mehrangarh Fort. A bird's-eye view of the town makes it resemble a sea on the fringe of the Thar Desert. Jodhpur is encircled by a wall 9 km (6 mi) around, which keeps out the desert sands. The city, at the base of a sandstone ridge, was the capital of the Marwar kingdom for five centuries. It was named after its 15th-century founder, Rao Jodha, chief of the Rathore clan of Marwar. The clan traces its lineage to Lord Rama, hero of the ancient Hindu epic, *The Ramayana.*

Getting around Jodhpur is relatively easy. Take an auto-rickshaw up the hillside and walk through the massive, impeccably maintained Meharangarh Fort, saunter through the Umaid Bhawan Palace Museum, and wander through the chaotic and colorful markets full of fruit, textile, and handicraft stalls near the city's clock tower. Take special note of

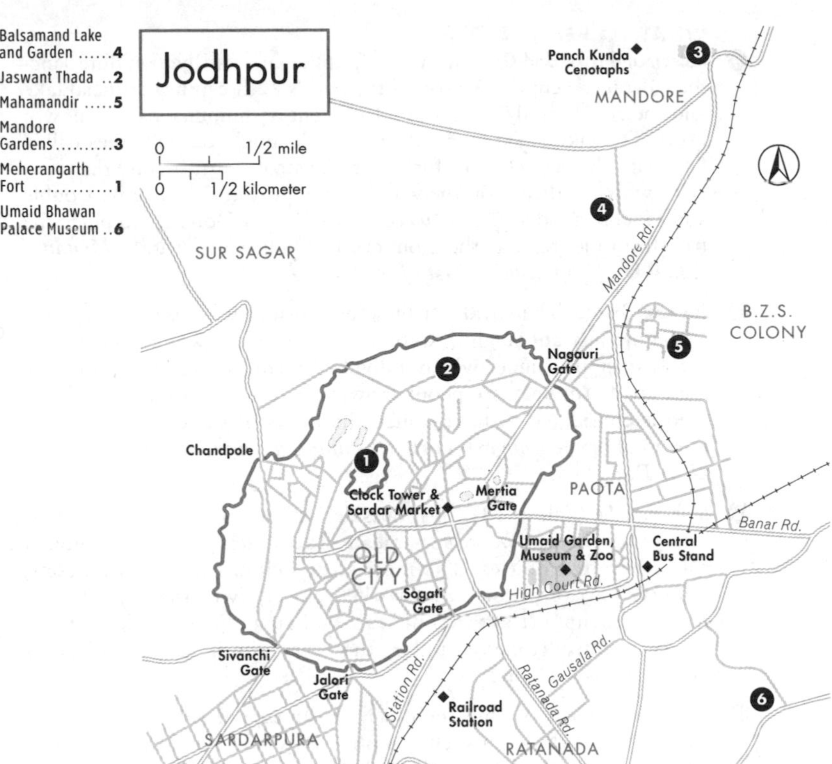

Jodhpuri *pathar*, peach-color stone that makes Jodhpur's houses and buildings stand apart from others in Rajasthan. If you have extra time, take a desert safari on camelback.

A GOOD TOUR

Start your day early, and spend a few hours at the majestic **Meherangarth Fort** ❶. Take one of the waiting rickshaws down the mountain and north to the **Jaswant Thada** ❷ memorial. After a break for lunch, hire a car and driver for the short drive 9 km (6 mi) north of Jodhpur to the **Mandore Gardens** ❸. From there, it's just a short drive to **Balsamand Lake and Garden** ❹. If you have a little extra time, visit **Mahamandir** ❺. End your day at the **Umaid Bhawan Palace Museum** ❻—walk through the museum before it closes at 5, then linger for a drink and dinner and enjoy the fabulous sunset views.

TIMING

With this plan you can tour Jodhpur in a day, covering the essentials first. If you have three days here, drive 25 km (16 mi) south of Jodhpur once again to see the wildlife-loving town of **Guda Vishnoi,** where deer and birds feed at water holes early in the morning. If you're very lucky, you might spot the elusive barasingha deer or blackbuck antelope. Return to Jodhpur for lunch and a bit of shopping. The next day, make a pilgrimage 58 km (36 mi) north to the temple town of **Osian.**

WHAT TO SEE

4 **Balsamand Lake and Garden.** At this public park (really a wildlife sanctuary) you can enjoy the view of the park's 12th-century artificial lake and the royal family's beautiful 19th-century summer palace, now a hotel. The lake is surrounded by a thick jungle of fruit trees called *badis*. It's the perfect place for a tranquil stroll—just beware the monkeys, who are always on the watch for opportunities to cause trouble and to score good vegetable *pakoras,* or fritters. Don't try to pluck the fruit from the trees, as the monkeys will fight you for it. ⊠ *Mandore Rd., 9 km (5½ mi) northeast of Jodhpur.*

2 **Jaswant Thada.** The royal marble crematorium was built in 1899 for Maharaja Jaswant Singh II. Capping the enormous white structure are marble canopies under which individual members of the royal family are buried. You may see people bowing before the image of the king, who is considered to have joined the ranks of the deities. ⊠ *½ km northeast of Mehrangarh Fort (10-minute walk from the fort)* 🎫 *Rs. 20* ⏲ *Daily 9–5.*

5 **Mahamandir.** Built in 1812 just outside Jodhpur, this old, walled monastery complex (*mahamandir* means "great temple") still contains a few hundred houses. The monastery belongs to the Nath community, warrior-priests who worked closely with the royal family to arrange support in times of war. Mahamandir is best known for the 84 beautifully carved pillars that surround it. ⊠ *4 km (2½ mi) northeast of Jodhpur.*

3 **Mandore Gardens.** Within the old Marwar capital at Mandore, these gardens house the exquisitely sculpted red-sandstone *davals* (memorials) to former rulers. The Hall of Heroes depicts 16 colorfully painted heroes and deities carved from a single piece of stone. The small **museum** on the grounds has sculptures from the 5th to the 9th centuries as well as ivory and lacquer work. There's even a **cactus nursery.** Lots of picnics and dal baati churma feasts held here, but unfortunately the gardens have grown dirty and are not well-maintained. ⊠ *Mandore, 8 km (5 mi) north of Jodhpur* 🎫 *Free* ⏲ *Gardens daily sunrise–sunset, museum Sat.–Thurs. 10–4.*

1 **Mehrangarh Fort.** On the top of a hill, this enormous fort was built by Rao Jodha in 1459, when he shifted his capital from Mandore to Jodhpur. Looking straight down a perpendicular cliff, the famously impregnable fort is an imposing landmark, especially at night, when it's bathed in yellow light. Approach the fort by climbing a steep walkway, passing under no fewer than eight huge gates. (If you're not up for the 40-minute hike, you can take auto-rickshaw instead for about Rs. 30–Rs. 40.) The first, the Victory Gate, was built by Maharaja Ajit Singh to commemorate his military success against the Moghuls at the beginning of the 18th century; the other seven commemorate victories over other Rajput states. The last gate, as in many Rajput forts, displays the haunting handprints of women who immolated themselves after their husbands were defeated in battle.

Fodor's Choice ★

Inside the rugged fort, delicate latticed windows and pierced sandstone screens are the surprising motifs. The palaces—**Moti Mahal** (Pearl Palace), **Phool Mahal** (Flower Palace), **Sheesh Mahal** (Glass Palace), and the other apartments—are exquisitely decorated; their ceilings, walls, and even floors are covered with murals, mirror work, and gilt. The palace museum has exquisite rooms filled with lavish royal elephant carriages (howdahs), palanquins, thrones, paintings, and even a giant tent. It also has an interesting weapons gallery. From the ramparts you can get an excellent city view; the blue houses at sunset look magical. The fort is possibly the best maintained historic property in all Rajasthan, and offers an audio tour with headphones (included in the admission price, for foreigners) with recorded commentary in six languages, including English. *⊠Fort Rd. ☎291/254–8790 or 291/254–9790 🌐www.mehrangarh.org 🎫Rs. 250 (including audio tour), cameras free, video-cameras fee Rs. 200 ⏲Daily 9–5.*

JODHPUR'S SWEETNESS

Jodhpur's famed tradition of hospitality, known as *mithi manuhar*, frequently takes the form of offers of food. Such items, especially *mithai* (sweets), are not to be missed. When you're offered a *mave ki kachori* (milk-based pastry) or *besan ki barfi* (a fudgelike sweet made of chickpea flour), along with *mirchi bada* (fried, breaded green peppers) and *kofta* (deep-fried balls of potatoes or vegetables), don't resist: the offer will be repeated until you take some.

4

NEED A BREAK?

In the highly competitive world of lassi wallahs, only the strong survive. Standing in the shadow of Jodhpur's famous clock tower in Sadar Market, Shri Misrilal Hotel, a lassi shop misleadingly called a hotel, is an age-old favorite among locals and foreigners. Look past the simple interior and neon lighting, and settle down on one of the long wooden benches. Then sit back and take in the rosewater flavors; lassis here are consumed with a spoon. Note to sweet-lassis lovers: they serve salty lassis here.

6 **Umaid Bhawan Palace Museum.** Built between 1929 and 1942 at the behest of Maharaja Umaid Singh during a long famine, this public-works project employed 3,000 workers. Now part museum, part royal residence, and part Heritage Hotel, its art-deco design makes it unique in the state. Amazingly, no cement was used in construction; the palace is made of interlocking blocks of sandstone, something to admire when you stand under the imposing 183-foot-high central dome. The museum's collection includes royal finery, local arts and crafts, miniature paintings, stuffed big cats, and a large number of clocks. You may catch a glimpse of the titular Maharaja of Jodhpur, who still lives in one large wing of the palace, but in any case you won't miss the magnificent peacocks that strut around the palace's marble *chattris* (canopies) and lush lawns. Photography is allowed on the lawns but not in the museum. *⊠Airport Rd., Umaid Bhawan Palace ☎291/251–0101 🎫Rs. 50 ⏲Daily 9–5.*

WHERE TO EAT & STAY

All the hotels listed below can arrange camel and jeep safaris and usually other excursions, on request.

$$$$ ✕**Risala.** If you are looking to splurge and wine and dine like royalty, head to this elegant dining room adorned with portraits from the royal collection or, or to a balcony overlooking luscious gardens. The à la carte restaurant serves contemporary European and unique Indian dishes, a welcome change from the usual Indian and Rajasthani fare. If you are craving seafood, this is the place to try it—don't miss the prawn curry in a tomato cream sauce. The ambience is formal to the point of being a bit stuffy, but the food is delicious and the service is impeccable. The drinks menu is extensive and includes wines from all around the world. ✉*Umaid Bhawan Palace, Airport Rd., Jodhpur* ☎*291/251–0101* ▭*AE, DC, MC, V.*

$$$–$$$$ ✕**Marwar.** One of the better attempts at upscale cuisine in Jodhpur, this buffet and à la carte restaurant serves Continental and Indian food, with a few Rajasthani specialties. Try Jodhpuri *gatta* curry (steamed chickpea flour dumplings in yogurt-base gravy); the Jodhpuri *maas* (lamb) curry is also typical of this region. You can head to the pasta dishes for a break from the usual Indian fare: the penne *arrabiata* is particularly tasty. The restaurant is built in neo-Moghul style, and every night, live classical Indian music plays in the background. ✉*Taj Hari Mahal, 5 Residency Rd.* ☎*291/243–9700* ✍*Reservations essential* ▭*AE, DC, MC, V.*

$–$$$ ✕**Mehran Terrace.** Sip a chilled beer and enjoy spectacular views of Jodhpur city at this romantically lit restaurant high up within Mehrangarh Fort. Notable more for its ambience than the food, this touristy outdoor eatery is as good an option as any within the old city, and it's especially fitting after an evening tour of the fort. Try the traditional Rajasthani food (veg and non-veg thalis, or combination platters), as well as standard tandoori favorites like paneer tikka. ✉*Mehrangarh Fort* ☎*291/255–5389* ▭*No credit cards* ⏲*No lunch.*

$–$$ ✕**Indique.** After a long day of sightseeing, stop here at sundown for a drink or dinner and take in stunning views of the nearby lake, the fort, the clock tower, and the Umaid Bhawan Palace. This good, basic rooftop hangout is at Pal Haveli in the old city. The mostly Indian menu includes a couple pasta dishes. Note that there are steep steps leading to the restaurant. ✉*Pal Haveli, Gulab Sagar* ☎*291/329–3328 or 291/263–8344* ▭*No credit cards.*

$–$$ ✕**On the Rocks.** This jungle-theme restaurant is aptly named, not because it has a well-stocked bar, but because the ground inside the mostly outdoor restaurant is gravel. On the same road as Ajit Bhawan hotel and close to numerous shopping boutiques, it's an ideal rest stop for a quick drink or lunch. The standard Indian fare is famous with the local upwardly mobile. The smoky and dark bar has happy hour daily from 4 to 6. ✉*Circuit House Rd.* ☎*291/251–0410* ▭*MC, V.*

¢ ✕**Sukh Sagar.** This place specializes in South Indian food, but also serves North Indian and Chinese dishes. Try the *rava idli* (steamed semolina-and-rice cakes) and *vada sambar* (deep-fried lentil doughnuts served with spicy lentil stew). If you're sensitive to heat, either be sure to order something bland or head elsewhere. Down some South Indian filter coffee for an extra kick. ✉ *Ratanada Bazaar* ☎ *291/251–1450 or 291/262–1450* ▭ *No credit cards.*

$$$$ **Taj Hari Mahal.** Outside the old city, this is a respite from its hustle and bustle. Of the tastefully decorated and spacious rooms, some overlook the pool and have their own small balcony. The modern rooms and bathrooms are well-equipped but ordinary. However, what this hotel lacks in excitement, it makes up in friendly service and subdued charm. The Chinese restaurant opens only for dinner, but a good multicuisine restaurant is open all day. For special occasions, ask for a demonstration of the elaborate chess dance, during which women in Rajasthani dress swirl across a life-size chessboard. **Pros:** large closets in rooms, nightly puppet show for kids. **Cons:** very expensive, far from the sights; the lobby is noisy, with way too much going on. ✉ *5 Residency Rd., Jodhpur, 342001* ☎ *291/243–9700* 🌐 *www.tajhotels.com* *In-room: safe, refrigerator, Wi-Fi. In-hotel: 2 restaurants, room service, bar, pool, gym, spa.* ▭ *AE, DC, MC, V.*

4

$$$$ ★ **Umaid Bhawan Palace.** Live like royalty for a night in this magnificent fort palace, one of the grandest hotels in Rajasthan. Still home to the titular Maharaja of Jodhpur, it has served as a backdrop for many Indian and foreign films. Walking into the massive circular domed lobby is an awe-inspring experience. The public rooms are lavish, and filled with objects d'art; many of the rooms, though not opulent, are designed in art-deco style. There's a beautiful, blue indoor pool and an exclusive spa in the basement. **Pros:** a haven away from the city, impeccable service, the massive lawn area is great for walks. **Cons:** rack rates for basic rooms start around $900, subterranean pool is lovely but no good for tanning; stone architecture, high ceilings, and marble flooring are a bit stuffy and echo-filled. ✉ *Airport Rd., Jodhpur, 342006* ☎ *291/251–0101* 📠 *291/251–0100* *64 rooms, 40 suites* *In-room: safe, refrigerator. In-hotel: 2 restaurants, room service, bar, tennis courts, pool, gym, no elevator.* ▭ *AE, DC, MC, V.*

$$$–$$$$ **Fortune Ummed.** This luxurious, character-filled hotel is outside the city on the Jodhpur–Jaipur Highway. Once you're here it's a pleasant retreat, among peaceful, landscaped gardens. Rooms are uncarpeted, with gleaming marble floors and cream-color drapes, and have traditional Rajsthani paintings on the walls. You can choose between garden, courtyard, or pool views. **Pros:** big windows and high ceilings in the rooms, inviting pool, architecturally interesting. **Cons:** outside of the city and a bit inconvenient, no other restaurants nearby so you have to eat at the hotel or go into Jodhpur. ✉ *Banar Road, Jodhpur–Jaipur Hwy., Jodhpur, 342027* ☎ *291/226–3430 to 39* 🌐 *www.fortuneparkhotels.com* *80 rooms, 8 suites* *In-room: refrigerator. In-hotel: restaurant, bar, tennis court, pool, gym, spa, no elevator, children's programs (all ages), public Internet.* ▭ *AE, DC, MC, V.*

$$–$$$$ Fodor's Choice ★ **Ajit Bhawan.** This small but enchanting palace and village complex has a garage full of royal vintage cars (they're available for hire). Not one of the big rooms is alike: each is decorated with traditional Rajasthani fabrics and artifacts, and some even have trees growing inside. The hotel's centerpiece, the pool has built-in waterfalls and caves. There is

one all-day dining restaurant; in peak season nightly outdoor dinners feature live entertainment. Horse-riding, village, and camel safaris can be arranged. **Pros:** warm and inviting—the bar is especially cozy, the gravel paths and tiny lanes connecting the rooms give the hotel a spacious outdoor vibe, the rooms are big. **Cons:** not close to the old city, some of the rooms may smell a bit earthy from mud walls. ✉*Circuit House Rd., 342006* ☎*291/251–3333 or 291/251–1410* 🌐*www.ajitbhawan.com* *75 rooms, 4 suites* *In-room: safe (some), refrigerator, Wi-Fi. In-hotel: restaurant, bar, pool, gym, spa, no elevator, public Internet.* 💳*AE, MC, V.*

$$–$$$$ **Ranbanka Palace.** Stay in this affordably priced Heritage Hotel without compromising on modern comforts. Overall, the somewhat anonymous rooms are spacious, and many overlook a central courtyard with a fountain where outdoor buffet meals are served during peak season. The rooftop restaurant has views of Umaid Bhawan Palace and the fort, and the loungey trophy bar is a good place to smoke a fruit-flavored hookah or enjoy a drink. **Pros:** close to boutique shops down the street; spacious, newly renovated rooms. **Cons:** not near the old city, lobby feels a little institutional, some rooms are charming but a little run down. ✉*Circuit House Rd., 342006* ☎*291/251–2801 or 291/251–2802* 🌐*www.ranbankahotels.com* *70 rooms, 5 suites* *In-room: safe (some). In hotel: 2 restaurants, room service, bar, pool, spa.* 💳*AE, MC, V* *BP.*

$$–$$$ **Park Plaza.** Surprisingly, this hotel on the main road that opened in 2006 is even more impressive than it looks from the exterior. Popular among business travelers, it may also work for vacationers looking for homelike convenience away from home. There's nothing "heritage" here: what it lacks in feudal charm, it makes up in modern comforts. The lobby is small and inviting, with spotless marble interiors and a well-dressed staff. The rooms are tastefully designed with hardwood floors and have comfy beds with immaculate white sheets and plush pillows. The bathrooms are pristine and modern. **Pros:** room rate includes breakfast; spotless rooms; good, well dressed staff. **Cons:** not right fit for those looking for a typical Rajasthani experience, away from the old city, small pool. ✉*Airport Rd., Ratanada, 342001* ☎*291/510–5000 or 1800/111–222 (toll-free) reservations* 🌐*www.sarovarhotels.com* *45 rooms* *In room: safe, refrigerator, Wi-Fi. In hotel: 2 restaurants, room service, bar, pool, gym, spa.* 💳*AE, MC, V* *BP.*

$$ **Balsamand Lake Palace.** A fine example of Rajput architecture, this red sandstone Heritage Hotel is surrounded by lush, expansive green gardens on the outskirts of Jodhpur. On the banks of Balsamand Lake, an artificial lake built in the 12th century, the palace has long been a dreamy setting for royal R & R. The park around the lake contains a small bird sanctuary; just watch out for aggressive monkeys. Meals are prepared for guests only. **Pros:** palace living at a reasonable price, quiet retreat on the outskirts of Jodhpur, ideal for nature lovers. **Cons:** a bit remote and out of the way, "deluxe" rooms are ordinary, no Internet. ✉*Mandore Rd., 9 km (5½ mi) northeast of Jodhpur, 342006* ☎*291/257–1991* 📠*291/257–1240* *36 rooms* *In-hotel: restaurant, bar, pool, spa, no elevator.* 💳*MC, V.*

$$ **Rohet Garh.** This 17th-century desert fortress 40 km (25 mi) south of Jodhpur is both a Heritage Hotel and the home of its Rajput family, whose members are your hosts. It's a great place to experience the lifestyle of Rajput nobility. The public rooms are decked out in original paintings, family photographs, and weapons. Guest rooms have traditional carved furniture and colorful hand-blocked prints, and some even have swings. Horseback safaris are a specialty, as there are plenty of bird species and other animals nearby—keep an eye out for the peacocks strutting on the hotel lawn. Trips can be organized to Bishnoi (tribal villages). **Pros:** rooms are spacious and the suites are exceptionally large with tons of character, the bar area is like a semi-outdoors living room and has lovely views of the gardens. **Cons:** small pool, not much to do at the hotel unless you venture out on an organized village safari. ✉ *Pali district, Rohet Garh Village* 📫 *Reserve through Rohet House, P. W. D. Rd., 342001* ☎ *2936/268–231, 291/243–1161 reservations* 📠 *291/264–9368* 🌐 *www.rohetgarh.com* ⇆ *28 rooms, 2 suites* 👍 *In-room: no TV. In-hotel: restaurant, bar, pool, gym, no elevator, laundry service.* 💳 *MC, V.*

$$ **Sardarsamand Lake Resort.** The hunting lodge of Jodhpur's former Maharaja Umaid Singh is now a resort. Built in 1933, the verandas of this pink sandstone-and-granite building have fabulous views of an artificial lake that attracts birds migrating between October and March. Just beyond the lake are the sands of the Thar Desert. Rooms are decorated in their original fittings, though they also have some art-deco furnishings. Reserve through Balsamand Lake Palace (the phone line is more likely to be working there). **Pros:** beautiful setting, good spot for bird-watchers. **Cons:** far from Jodhpur, and not much else around. ✉ *66 km (41 mi) southeast of Jodhpur, 20 km (12 mi) from Pali District, Sardarsamand, 306103* ☎ *296/024–5001 to 03, 291/257–2321 reservations (Balsamand Lake Palace)* 📠 *291/257–1240* ⇆ *22 rooms* 👍 *In-room: no a/c (some), safe, no TV (some). In-hotel: restaurant, bar, tennis court, pool, no elevator.* 💳 *MC, V.*

$–$$ **Fort Chanwa.** This century-old, somber red fort in the dusty village of Luni is now a Heritage Hotel getaway with spacious courtyards and delightful rooms that have small, arched windows called *jharokhas*, Rajasthani-style furniture and fabrics, and old photographs. Many of the small rooms have stairways leading to an alcove or to the bathroom. The waterwheel—now a fountain in the bar—was originally used to channel water around the fort. The restaurant has a fixed-price Indian menu. **Pros:** charming fort stay, good value. **Cons:** far from anything. *Reserve through* 📫 *Dilip Bhawan House 1, P. W. D. Rd., 342001* ✉ *58 km (36 mi) south of Jodhpur, Luni* ☎ *293/128–4216, 291/243–2460 reservations* ⇆ *55 rooms* 👍 *In-room: no TV. In-hotel: restaurant, pool, gym, no elevator.* 💳 *MC, V.*

$ **Jhalamand Garh.** Run and managed by the extremely hospitable Jhalamand family, this small Heritage Hotel is an ideal setting for a peaceful holiday. In addition to making sure you're comfortable, the Jhalamands can help you plan your stay. By the end of your time here, you'll feel like a member of the family. Rooms have ethnic furnishings, and the terrace has stunning views of Jodhpur. Fifteen rooms and a pool are planned for 2008. **Pros:** friendly haveli living. **Cons:** no pool. ✉ *Village and Post Jhalamand, 342005* ✣ *10 km (6 mi) outside town* ☎ *291/272–0481* 🌐 *www.heritagehotelsindia.com* *15 rooms* *In-hotel: restaurant, bar, no elevator, laundry service.* ▭ *AE, DC, MC, V.*

$ **Karni Bhavan.** This homey hotel is famous for its personalized service. The colonial-style bungalow's interior is much larger than it seems from the outside. The rooms are simple but clean, and each is decorated in the theme of local festivals. The rooftop restaurant serves Indian and Continental cuisine (the Rajasthani food is exquisite). Evening entertainment and dinner are organized in and around traditional thatched huts in the garden area. **Pros:** large airy rooms; fabulous hospitality. **Cons:** away from action in the old city, no gym or spa, ordinary pool. ✉ *Palace Rd., 342006* ☎ *291/251–2101 to 03* 🌐 *www.karnihotels.com* *26 rooms, 5 suites* *In-room: no a/c (some). In-hotel: restaurant, pool, no elevator.* ▭ *AE, MC, V.*

¢ **Devi Bhawan.** One of the most moderately priced hotels in Jodhpur, Devi Bhawan is run by a friendly young couple, Prithviraj and Rambha Singh. The hotel is in a pleasant garden, and the homey rooms here are spotless and tastefully furnished. A small restaurant serves thalis to guests only. Jeep, horse, and camel safaris around Jodhpur can be arranged. **Pros:** on a quiet street away from the city; good service, clean rooms, excellent value. **Cons:** not as many facilities are other places. ✉ *1 Ratanada Circle, Defence Lab. Rd., 342001* ☎ *291/251–1067* 📠 *291/251–2215* *15 rooms* *In-room: no a/c (some). In-hotel: restaurant, pool, no elevator, public Internet.* ▭ *MC, V.*

¢ **Haveli Guesthouse.** This is a good budget option for those interested in staying in the heart of the old city. This family-run guesthouse offers hospitable service. The vegetarian rooftop restaurant has excellent views of the city, and you'll be close enough to hear evening *aarti* (a Hindu prayer service) at the temples near the clock tower. The rooms are basic and unpretentious, and don't have bathtubs: but what the hotel lacks in facilities it more than makes up for in convenience by being so close to the sights. Excursions for village and camel safaris can be arranged. The hotel provides a handy map in English that includes non-auto-rickshaw fares to common sights—a good tool to avoid getting ripped off. **Pros:** enterance on quiet street in the otherwise bustling old city, impressive facade, Internet on site. **Cons:** no pool, multistory building with no elevator. ✉ *Makrana Mohalla, behind clock tower, opposite Toorji Ka Jhalra (a stepwell)* ☎ *291/261–4615 or 291/264–7003* 🌐 *www.haveliguesthouse.com* *25 rooms* *In-room: no a/c (some), no TV (some). In-hotel: restaurant, no elevator.* ▭ *No credit cards.*

NIGHTLIFE & THE ARTS

Your best bet for Jodhpur nightlife is one of the hotel bars, which are usually open from 11 AM to 2:30 PM and 6 PM to 11 PM.

The **Trophy Bar** (✉ *Umaid Bhawan Palace* ☎ *291/251–0101*), with richly paneled walls and carpeted floors, is regal, but still feels intimate.

Geoffrey's (✉*Park Plaza, Airport Rd., Ratanada* ☎*291/510–5000* 🌐*www.sarovarhotels.com* ⏲*Daily noon–11* PM) is a fully equipped bar reminiscent of an Engish pub. It's popular among the upwardly mobile Jodhpuri crowd as well as with hotel guests.

Mehrangarh Fort stages festivals and exhibits throughout the year; inquire at the **Tourist Information Center** (☎*291/254–5083*) or your hotel to see if anything is going on.

SPORTS & THE OUTDOORS

Many hotels offer excursions to outlying villages.

If yours doesn't, try one of the horse or camel trips offered by **Rohet Safaris** (☎*291/243–1161*). Also try **Princy Holidaymakers** (✉*Nayabas, Killikhana* ☎*291/320–0254, 291/694–0654, or 992/881–9979* ✉*princy.holidaymakers@rediffmail.com*) for tailor-made itineraries, including half- and full-day tours of Jodhpur and village stays and safaris.

4

SHOPPING

Jodhpur's vibrant bazaars are among the city's key sights, particularly **Sadar Bazaar** and the **Girdikot Bazaar,** near the clock tower. Wandering among the tiny shops dotting narrow lanes in the heart of town, you'll get a real feel for the life and color of Marwar. Jewelry, underwear, steel utensils, kitchenware, leather shoes, trinkets, wedding clothes—they're all sold here. Local spice merchants deal in saffron and other spices from all over India. Beware of tourist markups and young men guiding you to their "uncle's store." There are also plenty of stores to shop in if you don't like haggling in bazaars—most notably the government-run emporium.

M. V. Spices (✉*Shop 209B, near clock tower, Sadar Market*) has a wide selection of spices clearly marked and packed in plastic for travelers with a passion for cooking Indian food. There's also an outlet (really a tent pitched on the sidewalk) at the entrance to Mehrangarh Fort.

For boutique shopping, don't miss out on Rani Bagh, a cluster of high-end retail shops just outside Ajit Bhawan hotel that sells antiques, silver jewelry, and clothing.

At the local outlet of the popular **Anokhi** (✉*Circuit House Rd.* ☎*291/251–7178 or 291/251–7179* 🌐*www.anokhi.com* ⏲*Daily 11–8*) brand, you can shop for Western clothing with an Indian flair. **Tulsi** (✉*Circuit House Rd.* ☎*291/510–2583* ⏲*Daily 11–8:30* PM) is worth a stop for classic and contemporary textiles and home furnishings.

Amarpali (✉*Circuit House Rd.* ☎*291/325–0544* ⏲*Daily 11–8*) for traditional and contemporary silver and gold jewelry. **Gems & Jewels Palace** (✉*Circuit House Rd.* ☎*291/251–6666* ⏲*Daily 11–8*) is another good local jewelry store.

Lalji Handicrafts Emporium (✉*Opposite Umaid Bhawan Palace* ☎*291/251–1378*) has woodwork, antiques, leatherwork, and brass furniture. The collection includes unique painted boxes and *jharokhas* (carved doorways or windows) made of dark wood with brass decoration. This place is a joy if you love antiques. **Bhandari Handicrafts** (✉*Old Police*

Line, Raika Bagh ☎*291/251–0621*) sells wood items and antiques. For textiles, including cotton dress fabric, and other handicrafts, check out the four-story emporium **National Handloom Corporation** (✉*Nayi Sadak* ☎*291/506–1103 or 291/503–1198*). For a vast selection of cushion covers, bedspreads, handicrafts, and authentic hand-stitched jodhpurs (these riding trousers are priced at Rs. 1,800 and can be tailored to order), visit **Shree Govindam** (✉*Opposite Circuit House, A163 Ajit Colony Rd.* ☎*291/251–0519 or 291/251–6333*) and don't forget to look at the range of wholesale textiles in the basement.

Roopraj Dhurry Udyog (✉*4 km [2½ mi] from the village, Salawas* ☎*291/289–6658*). Local artisan Roopraj learned the art of weaving dhurries (carpets) from his father, who learned it from *his* father—the tradition goes back to the early 19th century. His cotton carpets were originally reserved for the village thakur, or landowner, but once Indira Gandhi enacted the Integrated Rural Development Project (IRDP), his carpets were finally able to reach a wider market. The Roopraj Dhurry Udyog co-op cottage industry employs weavers from the village and keeps the tradition alive. It's as rewarding to watch the weaving process as it is to come with a purchase in mind, or just to shop for souvenirs. Salawas is near the railway crossing on the way to the town of Kakani; you'll definitely need a guide to help you get here.

OFF THE BEATEN PATH

Guda Vishnoi. This is one of several immaculately kept villages of the Vishnoi community, a Hindu caste that takes its name from the 29 edicts its members agree to follow. In 1520, during a 20-year drought, the saint Jamboji came to the Vishnoi to ease their troubles by finding new water sources for them, and creating natural springs. Jamboji made a pact with the Vishnoi that if they accepted his commandments, they would never experience a water shortage again. The next year, the drought ended. The Vishnoi, who have faithfully kept to the teachings of Jamboji for almost 500 years, are one of Jodhpur's most distinct scheduled castes. Part of their pact was to respect the land and treat animals like their family—they are staunch believers in plant and animal life. The Vishnoi are very protective of their environment, and look harshly on anyone who appears to hurt their sacred deer and antelope populations, which they look on as members of their family. Notable are the rare migratory birds, such as the godavan and sara cranes, that pass through here. The Vishnoi are extremely outgoing and hospitable—they will invite you into their home for a cup of chai or *amala,* a mixture of opium and water traditionally reserved for special occasions and lazy days. Remember to bring your camera—you might just see a barasingha or blackbuck at dusk. One word of advice: this area is difficult to navigate, as there are no real landmarks. Ask at your hotel for transport arrangements and make sure you come with a tour guide. ✉*25 km (16 mi) south of Jodhpur.*

OSIAN

58 km (36 mi) north of Jodhpur.

The ancestral home of the Oswal Jains, Osian was one of the strongholds of Jainism in India. Many invasions and several hundred years later, Osian is now a popular Hindu pilgrimage site, with . . . no significant Jain community remaining. It's worth coming here just to see the temples, or to take a camel safari.

On a hill in the center of town is the **Sachiya Mata Mandir,** a temple where the (Jain) Naga Snake god reliefs and etchings of Jain saints are readily apparent. Built around 1177 AD, some of the older statues were damaged during the reign of Moghul emperor Aurangzeb (1658–1707).

An older, and arguably more important, 7th-century temple is said to be the first Jain temple in the world. Hidden in the twisting alleys of the city, the **Mahavira Jain Temple** is venerated from all over India. The feet of one particular statue of Bharu on the outside of the temple are often covered with bright paper, oil, coconuts, and even human hair. Hindus (not just Jains) believe that if they make offerings here before they get married, their union will be blessed, and they'll be able to produce a child. To invoke the powers of the god Bharu, devotees must make two pilgrimages to the temple. During the first pilgrimage they leave traditional offerings of coconuts and oil to ask the god for fertility, they must also promise to return after the child's birth to offer the newborn's hair to the god.

Just outside town is the home of **Chuna Ram**—he carves new statues to help temple renovations, does all sorts of restoration work using old techniques, and encourages people to watch him work. He's lives in Osian, but right on the outskirts; call to make sure he's home. ✉ *Near Kushi Mundi, toward Jodhpur* ☎ *2922/274–577.*

WHERE TO STAY

$$$ **Reggie's Camel Camp.** Atop a sand dune, this base of operations for camel safaris in the Thar Desert is run by Reggie Singh; it's a great alternative to the more touristy camps that operate around Jaisalmer. All costs are included in the price of camp. Every route takes you through several different types of terrain and into the homes of local craftsmen. Make sure you watch the sunset from the dunes—it's truly breathtaking. Camel races and camel polo are also available. **Pros:** accommodation throughout the trip is in deluxe tents with carpets and running hot and cold water, and you are well taken care of; the outfit even has its own musicians. **Cons:** open only between October and April. ✉ *Near railway station* 📫 *The Safari Club, High Court Colony, Jodhpur, 342001* ☎ *291/243–7023, 291/261–0192 reservations* 🌐 *www.camelcamposian.com* *51 permanent tents, 50 mobile tents* *In-room: no a/c, no phone, no TV. In-hotel: restaurant, bar, pool.* *FAP.*

4

KHIMSAR

90 km (56 mi) northeast of Jodhpur.

The 16th-century fort at Khimsar, a three-hour drive from Jodhpur, was once the province of one of Rao Jodha's sons. His descendants still live in the palace. Surrounded by a small village, green fields, and sand dunes, it's now a Heritage Hotel, and a delightful place to relax. The building is gorgeously floodlit at night.

WHERE TO STAY

$$$ **Welcomgroup Khimsar Fort.** A two-hour drive from Jodhpur takes you to rural Khimsar in the Thar Desert. At this graceful palace and fort, the best rooms are in the original structure; some with furniture from the 1920s. Dinner is served by candlelight in the crumbling ruins of one of the original fort towers. Relax and enjoy the fine service, as well as the peace and quiet. If you feel like exploring, you can take a horse, camel, or jeep safari or tea on the nearby sand dunes. For the complete desert experience, stay in luxury tents in Khimsar village 7 km (4½ mi) from the fort. **Pros:** retreat from city life and take day trips to Jodhpur and Bikaner. **Cons:** self-contained oasis offers a lot, but it's in the middle of nowhere. ✉ *Khimsar, Nagaur district, 341025. Reserve through* *Welcomgroup Khimsar Fort, 27 Shivaji Nagar, Civil Lines, Jaipur, 302006* ☎ *1585/262–345 Jaipur, 141/222–9700 reservations* *www.khimsarfort.com* *64 rooms, 16 tents* *In-room: refrigerator. In-hotel: restaurant, bar, tennis court, pool, gym, no elevator.* *AE, MC, V.*

NAGAUR

150 km (94 mi) northeast of Jodhpur.

Try to visit Nagaur during its colorful cattle fair, in late January or early February. Make sure you check out the remnants of beautiful frescoes on the fort's crumbling walls. The complex has an amazing engineering system, which supplied enough water for the fountains and royal baths. The system also functions as a kind of air-conditioning in this otherwise arid land. Nagaur and its surrounding area are famous for making clay toys.

WHERE TO STAY

$$$ **Nagaur Fort.** Built between the 4th and 16th centuries, this enormous fort serves as backdrop to a royal camp of spacious tents, decorated inside with hand-blocked designs. Conveniently, the tents also have electric lanterns and attached bathrooms with flush toilets (hot water is hand-carried via bucket). To signal for service, you hang a little red flag outside the door of your tent. The camp is open between March and October and functions with an additional 50 tents during the cattle fair. Meals are served in a marble pavilion, in what was once a Moghul garden; in the evening, you can sip cocktails and sit back on cushions, in front of a bonfire, to watch a performance of traditional folk dances. **Pros:** unique experience in an extraordinary place. **Cons:** a lot of money to live in a tent, you must reserve at least 60 days in advance for the

cattle fair. ✉*Ahhichatragarh Fort, Gandhi Chowk, Nagaur, 341001* ☎*01582/242–082* ✉*reservations@jodhpurheritage.com* *10 tents* *In-room: no a/c, no TV. In-hotel: restaurant, no elevator.* *AE, MC, V* *Closed Apr.–Sept.* *FAP.*

UDAIPUR & ENVIRONS

Expect to see marble palaces, elaborate gardens, serene temples, lush forests, and sparkling lakes as you explore Mewar, Rajasthan's southern region, in the marvelously green Aravali Hills. Mewar also has several famous temples and religious sites attended yearly by thousands of pilgrims.

The region is perhaps most famous for having a rich military history—the chivalry and courage of its Rajput warriors are legendary. The Sisodia rulers of Mewar, who claim descent from the divine Lord Rama, are considered the most senior and respected members of all Rajput clans. The Mewar rulers were among the most determined foes of the Moghuls: long after other Rajput rulers conceded defeat, they alone resisted. The name Maharana Pratap (the word *maharana,* rather than "maharajah," is used in Rajasthan) still inspires pride in Mewar—Pratap resisted Emperor Akbar's reign through several guerilla wars. His struggle against Akbar is celebrated in murals and ballads all over Rajasthan, and it has been said that "As a great warrior of liberty, his name is, to millions of men even today, a cloud of hope by day and a pillar of fire by night." Udaipur's airport is named after him.

Mewar is also famous for the vibrant festivals that take place in its cities and villages, and its motto—"*Saat vaar, aur nau tyauhaar,*" which means "Seven days, nine festivals"—is apt. The biggest festival of the year is Gangaur, held in April in honor of the goddess Parvati, and observed primarily by girls of marriageable age. In the villages, the ancient tradition of *raati jagga*—all-night singing of mainly devotional songs by saint-poets, such as Kabir and Mirabai—takes place after weddings, childbirth, and sometimes even mourning, as a form of thanksgiving to a particular deity.

Mewar has two major indigenous tribal groups, the Bhils (also called *van putras,* or "sons of the forest") and the Garasiyas. The lively songs, music, art exhibits, and dances of the tribes' festivals are a compelling reason to visit the region. Particularly memorable is the Ghoomer dance, in which hundreds of women dance in a giant circle. If you're here during a festival, try to see the *terahtal* dance, in which women dance—from a seated position—with *manjiras* (little brass discs) tied to their wrists, elbows, waists, arms, and hands. For added effect, the women may hold a sword between their teeth or balance pots or even lighted lamps on their heads.

To get a real feel for the spirit of the Mewar region, plan at least two or three days here, if not an entire week. Mewar is best seen at a somewhat leisurely pace: whether you see the area by taking quiet walks, long treks, or bike rides, you'll find lots of cultural variety, and you'll see some stunning sights. Romantic Udaipur, the major city here, warrants at least several days. From Udaipur, you can explore the ornately carved Jain temples of Ranakpur and Mount Abu, or see the medieval citadel of Chittaurgarh. West from Chittaurgarh, it's worth a stop to see the remarkable fort at Kumbalgarh. You can also take a wildlife safari or learn more about pichwai paintings at Nathdwara's Krishna temple.

UDAIPUR

Fodor's Choice ★

335 km (207 mi) southeast of Jodhpur.

The jewel of Mewar is Udaipur, the City of Lakes. Some have dubbed it the Venice of the East. In his *Annals and Antiquities of Rajasthan,* Colonel James Tod described the valley of Udaipur as "the most diversified and most romantic spot on the sub-continent of India." The city of Udaipur was founded in 1567, when, having grown weary of repeated attacks on the old Mewar capital of Chittaur—Chittaur is the historic name of the area, and Chittaurgarh literally means "the fort of Chittaur"—Maharana Udai Singh asked a holy sage to suggest a safe place for his new capital. The man assured Udai Singh that his new base would never be conquered if he established it on the banks of Lake Pichola, and thus was born Singh's namesake, Udaipur.

Despite being one of Rajasthan's largest cities, with a population of over a half-million people, modern Udaipur still feels like a small town; its weather is balmy year-round except for the summertime heat between April and July, and the locals are friendly. Udaipur's city center is the old city, a labyrinth of winding streets, which borders Lake Pichola's eastern side. Five main gates lead into Udaipur's old city: Hathi Pol (Elephant Gate) to the north; Kishan Gate to the south; Delhi Gate to the northeast; Chand Pol (Moon Gate) to the west; and Suraj Pol (Sun Gate) to the east.

Anchoring Udaipur's old city are the famed City Palace and Lake Palace; the latter is in the middle of Lake Pichola, and is now a Taj hotel. The old city itself is built on tiny hillocks and raised areas, so its lanes are full of twists and turns, leaving plenty of charming little niches to be discovered. Many lanes converge on the Jagdish Temple area, near the northeastern corner of Lake Pichola. The major landmarks in the new section are Chetak Circle, Sukhadia Circle, and Sahelion Ki Bari gardens.

The Mewar region is famous for its silver jewelry, wooden folk toys, miniature paintings, tribal arts, *molela* (terra-cotta work), appliqué, and embroidery. The landscape around Udaipur is dotted with crafts villages; the unique creations of the villages are sold in the city itself. Udaipur is also one of Rajasthan's great centers of contemporary art, as well as of miniature paintings. Mewar gastronomy features *diljani* (mini sugar balls) and *imarti* (pretzel-shaped pastries dipped in sugary syrup), dal baati churma, *chaach* (buttermilk with masala), various *makhi* (corn) products, and the guava.

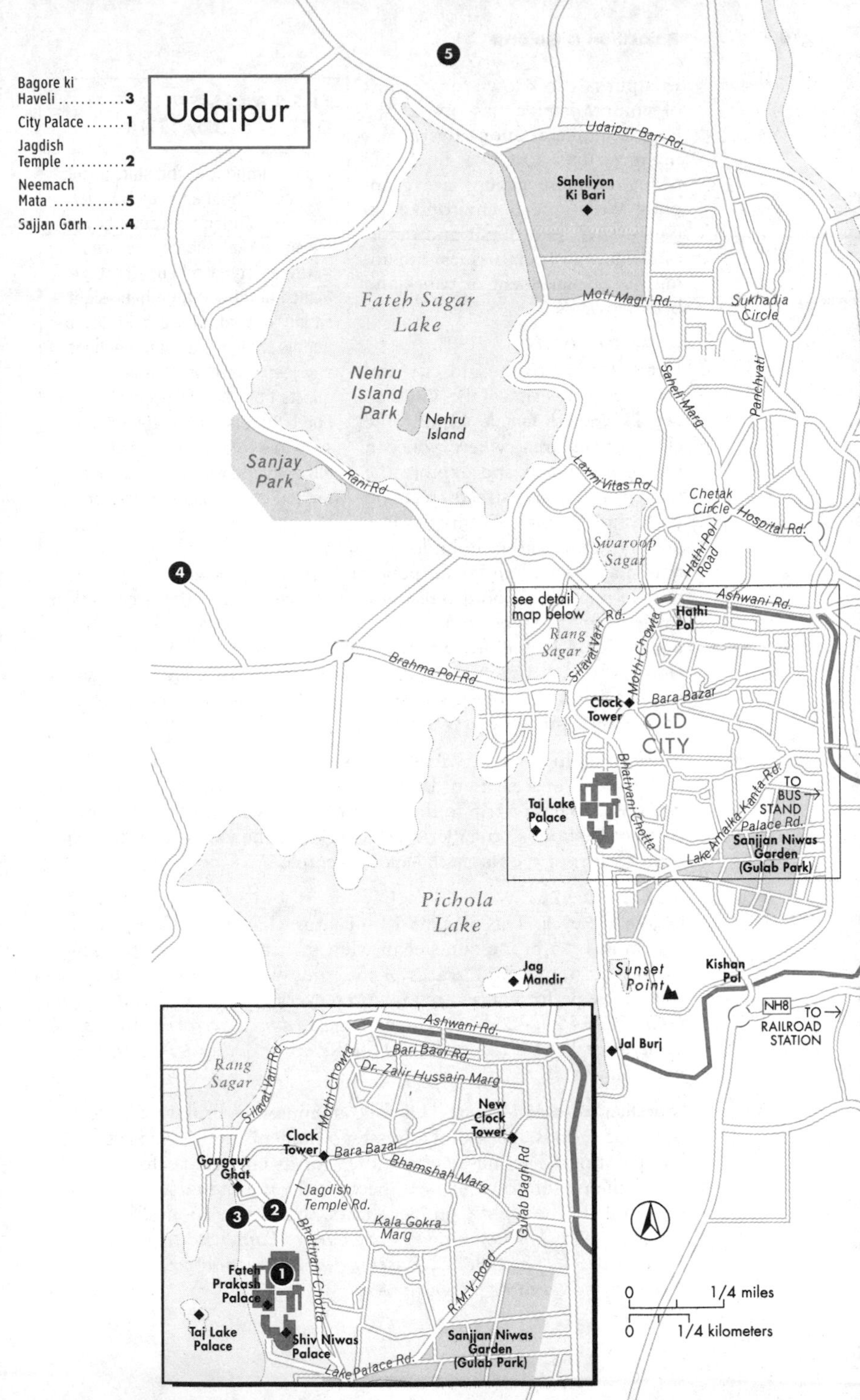

Udaipur
Bagore ki Haveli 3
City Palace 1
Jagdish Temple 2
Neemach Mata 5
Sajjan Garh 4
Udaipur Bari Rd.
Saheliyon Ki Bari
Fateh Sagar Lake
Moti Magri Rd.
Sukhadia Circle
Saheli Marg
Panchvati
Nehru Island Park
Nehru Island
Sanjay Park
Rani Rd
Laxmi Vilas Rd.
Chetak Circle
Hospital Rd.
Swaroop Sagar
Hathi Pol Road
see detail map below
Ashwani Rd.
Hathi Pol
Rang Sagar
Silavat Vari Rd.
Mothi Chowta
Brahma Pol Rd
Clock Tower
Bara Bazar
OLD CITY
Bhatiyani Chotta
TO BUS STAND
Taj Lake Palace
Lake Amalka Kanta Rd.
Palace Rd.
Sanjjan Niwas Garden (Gulab Park)
Pichola Lake
Jag Mandir
Sunset Point
Kishan Pol
NH8
TO RAILROAD STATION
Jal Burj
Ashwani Rd.
Bari Badi Rd.
Dr. Zalir Hussain Marg
Rang Sagar
Silavat Vari Rd.
Mothi Chowta
New Clock Tower
Clock Tower
Bara Bazar
Gangaur Ghat
Bhamshah Marg
Jagdish Temple Rd.
Gulab Bagh Rd
Kala Gokra Marg
Bhatiyani Chotta
Fateh Prakash Palace
R.M.V. Road
Taj Lake Palace
Shiv Niwas Palace
Sanjjan Niwas Garden (Gulab Park)
Lake Palace Rd.
0 1/4 miles
0 1/4 kilometers

Udaipur is also known for its spirit of voluntarism: it has one of the largest numbers of non-government organizations (NGOs) in India. Many of these groups are grappling with crucial environmental issues, such as drought and deforestation, and social issues, including the displacement of tribes and bride dowries.

THE LAKES SPILL OVER IN UDAIPUR

After a drought at the start of this decade, Pichola and Fateh Sagar lakes both dried up: young boys played cricket and cows grazed in the empty lake beds. The Lake Palace hotel was a pathetic sight, sitting in what looked more like a puddle than a lake, and elephants and jeeps were used to ferry guests from the "lakeshore" to the hotel. But during the 2005 monsoon, the skies opened. The lakes filled up in days, and locals and the tourism industry heaved great sighs of relief.

A GOOD TOUR

Head straight to the old city and start with a visit to the **City Palace** ❶, **Jagdish Temple** ❷, and the clock tower area, where you can have some lunch and explore the windy and hilly streets teeming with shops selling clothing, silver jewelry, and leather-bound journals made with handmade paper. Stop at one of the rooftop restaurants for coffee and the breathtaking sunset over the lake; from the old city's ghats you can take a leisurely boat ride on **Lake Pichola,** and admire the old city's lovely lakeshore from a distance. Catch an evening folk-dance performance at **Bagore ki Haveli** ❸ and then finish your day with dinner at the legendary Lake Palace hotel (make reservations).

TIMING You can cram these activities into one very full day, but you should really spend at least two days in this glorious city, especially if you want to also fit in a trip to the arts-and-crafts village of Shilpgram, see some of Udaipur's art galleries, or check out the views from the **Sajjan Garh** ❹ fort or the **Neemach Mata** ❺ temple.

WHAT TO SEE

❸ **Bagore ki Haveli.** This elegant 18th-century haveli on Gangaur Ghat was built by a prime minister of Mewar. It takes a while to explore the many rooms and terraces of this roomy old mansion. One-hour folk-dance performances are organized every evening at 7. ✉ *Gangaur Ghat* ☎ *294/242–2567* 🎫 *Haveli Rs. 25, dance performance Rs. 60, camera fee Rs. 10, video-camera fee Rs. 50* ⏲ *Daily 10–5:30, performance at 7* PM.

Bharatiya Lok Kala Mandal. This folk-art museum displays a collection of puppets, dolls, masks, folk dresses, ornaments, musical instruments, and paintings. The museum is known for its cultural performances—this is the reason to come here, because the museum itself is not well maintained. The nightly puppet shows, which run about 15 minutes, are cute. ✉ *½ km north of Chetak Circle, Panch Batti, near Mohta Park* ☎ *0294/252–9296* 🎫 *Museum Rs. 25, evening program Rs. 50* ⏲ *Daily 9–7, evening program 6–7.*

1 **City Palace.** The sprawling maharana's palace—the largest in Rajasthan—stands on a ridge overlooking the lake. Begun by Udai Singh and extended by subsequent maharanas, the sand-color City Palace rises five stories, with a series of balconies. Cupolas crown its octagonal towers, which are connected by a maze of narrow passageways. The City Palace is one of a complex of palaces—two have been converted to hotels and one houses the current titular maharana, Arvind Singh of Mewar. Part of the palace is also a museum; the museum's entrance is near the Jagdish Mandir and the entrance to the City Palace Hotel is at the bottom of the hill, to the south. The rooms inside the City Palace Museum contain decorative art: beautiful paintings, colorful enamel, inlay glasswork, and antique furniture. This is one place to have a full-fledged site publication (buy one in the book shop) or a guide (hire one at the gate, for no more than Rs. 100). ✉ *City Palace Complex* ☎ *0294/252–8016* *Palace Rs. 50, camera fee Rs. 100, video-camera fee Rs. 300* ⏲ *Daily 9–4:30.*

4

NEED A BREAK?

Overlooking Lake Pichola from a gallery adjoining the magnificent Durbar Hall in Fateh Prakash Palace, Gallery (✉ ***Fateh Prakash Palace, City Palace Complex*** ☎ ***294/252–8016 to 19*****) serves high tea only between 3 PM and 7 PM. There's a full tea (cakes and scones with jam and cream, tea or coffee) as well as sandwiches. If you're visiting the crystal gallery above the restaurant, your Rs. 350 ticket also includes a soft drink, plain tea, or coffee at the restaurant. (The crystal gallery houses the palace's early 19th-century collection of Birmingham crystal, with everything from wine decanters to beds.)**

Lake Pichola. You can't leave Udaipur without seeing the stunningly romantic **Lake Palace** (Jag Niwas), which seems to float serenely on the waters of Lake Pichola. A vast, white-marble fantasy, the palace has been featured in many Indian and foreign films, including the James Bond film, *Octopussy.* Unfortunately, the palace's apartments, courts, fountains, and gardens are off-limits unless you're a guest at the Lake Palace hotel or you have reservations at the restaurant (well worth it). The equally isolated, three-story **Jag Mandir** palace occupies another island at the southern end of the lake and at the end of 2007 was turned into an elegant restaurant. You can take a boat there during daylight hours. Built and embellished over a 50-year period beginning in the 17th century, Jag Mandir is made of yellow sandstone, lined with marble, and crowned by a dome. The interior is decorated with arabesques of colored stones. Shah Jahan, son of the Moghul emperor Jahangir, took refuge in Jag Mandir after leading an unsuccessful revolt against his father. Legend has it that Shah Jahan's inspiration for the Taj Mahal came from this marble masterpiece. ✉ *Motorboat cruises leave from the jetty at the base of City Palace* *½-hr cruise Rs. 100 per person; 1-hr cruise Rs. 200 per person, including stop at Jag Mandir Island* ⏲ *Boats run daily 10–5.*

MLV Tribal Research Institute. Stop in here if you're curious about Mewar's tribal communities. The institute has a compact museum of tribal culture and a good library on tribal life and issues. ✉ *University Rd., Ashok Nagar* ☎ *294/241–0958* *Free* ⏲ *Mon.–Sat 10–5.*

5 **Neemach Mata.** This hilltop temple in the new part or town is dedicated to the goddess of the mountain, has a good view of Udaipur. Because no taxis or cars are allowed, you must make the steep 20-minute climb up (on a paved path that zigzags up the hill) on your own, so have comfortable shoes ready. ✉*North of Fateh Sagar Lake.*

Sahelion Ki Bari. Udaipur's famous Garden of the Maidens was founded in the 18th century by Maharana Sangam Singh for the 48 young ladies-in-waiting who were sent to the royal house as dowry. Back then, men were forbidden entrance when the queens and their ladies-in-waiting came to relax (though the king and his buddies still found their way in). The garden is planted with exotic flowers and theme fountains—with carved pavilions and monolithic marble elephants. The fountains don't have pumps: designed to take advantage of gravity, the fountains run on water pressure from the lakes. If the fountains are not on, ask one of the attendants to turn them on. The pavilion opposite the entrance houses a small **children's science center.** For some touristy fun, you can dress up in traditional Rajasthani garb and have your picture snapped by a local photographer. ✉*Saheli Marg, north of the city, near Bharatiya Lok Kala Mandal* 🎫*Rs. 5* ⏲*Daily 8–7.*

4 **Sajjan Garh.** High in the Aravali Hills just outside Udaipur, this fort–palace glows golden orange in the night sky, thanks to the lights that illuminate it. Once the maharana's Monsoon Palace, it's now dilapidated, and serves as a radio station for the Indian Army. The panoramic view is spectacular from the fort's lofty tower, and locals claim you can see distant Chittaurgarh on a clear day. The winding road to the top of Sajjan Garh, surrounded by green forests, is best covered by car (you can take an auto-rickshaw, but the ride will be a lot longer and bumpier). A small fee is required for cars at the gate leading up the hill.

OFF THE BEATEN PATH

Shilpgram. This rural arts-and-crafts village 3 km (2 mi) west of Udaipur includes a complex with 26 recreations of furnished village huts (authentic right down to their toilets) from Rajasthan, Gujarat, Maharashtra, Goa, and Madhya Pradesh. The town comes alive in December with the **Shilpgram Utsav,** when artists and craftspeople from around India arrive to sell and display their works. Puppet shows, dances, folk music, and handicrafts sales take place year-round, however. You can see all of the compound on a slow camel ride. ✉*Rani Rd.* ☎*294/242–2567* 🌐*www.wzccindia.com* 🎫*Rs. 25, camera fee Rs. 10, video-camera fee Rs. 50* ⏲*Daily 11–7.*

WHERE TO EAT & STAY

$$$$ ✕**Jharokha.** The Lake Palace hotel's informal all-day dining restaurant is worth a visit especially for the views of Udaipur. The food isn't bad, either: the menu of Italian, Thai, Indian, and other crowd-pleasing cuisines makes it ideal for a stop during a day of frantic sightseeing—or if you're craving a juicy burger. The desserts are delicious: definitely save room for the homemade warm apple pie with vanilla ice cream. ✉*Lake Palace* ☎*294/252–8800* 💳*AE, DC, MC, V.*

$$$$ ✕**Neel Kamal.** This fancy restaurant in the Lake Palace hotel focuses on regional cuisine. The interior is ethnic. The elegant dinner is by candle-

light, and includes great service. Sit close to the clear glass window separating the chef from the guests and watch him at work. All dishes are cooked over a wood fire and in clay pots. Try the deliciouus *macchli jaisamandi* (fish fillets cooked in mint and coriander gravy), *kurkuri bhindi* (deep-fried okra), *mathania laal murg* (traditional Rajasthani chicken curry spiced with red chillies) or the *sikandari raan* (whole leg of lamb marinated overnight, and slow roasted). Seafood is flown in fresh every day and includes tandoori pink salmon and *tawaa jhinga* (freshwater prawns marinated in cider vinegar, ginger, and mint). The restaurant has one of the largest wine lists in India, with more than 120 wines. ✉*Lake Palace hotel* ☎*294/252–8800* ✍*Reservations essential* ▭*AE, DC, MC, V.*

$$$$ ✕**Sunset Terrace.** Overlooking Lake Pichola from the mainland, this café benefits from a constant breeze and first-rate service—sitting on the terrace feels as if you've joined the aristocracy and have unlimited leisure. The menu includes Indian, European, and Chinese dishes, with fixed-price as well as à la carte options available. The favorite orders at this restaurant are the *paneer lababdar* (cottage cheese in an onion and tomato gravy) and the *safed maas,* a Rajasthani lamb dish cooked in cream sauce. ✉*Fateh Prakash Palace, City Palace Complex* ☎*294/252–8016 to 19* ▭*AE, MC, V.*

$$ ✕**Jagat Niwas Palace Terrace Restaurant.** The open-air restaurant at this converted haveli on Lal Ghat has retained the mansion's lovely design, and has spectacular views of the Lake Palace. The vista, especially at night, captures the almost unbearably romantic essence of the city. To watch the brilliantly illuminated Lake Palace float like a mythological castle on the water from a bolstered and cushioned alcove is a signature Udaipur experience. Here you'll get a decent range of Continental and Indian food. The haveli is at the tail end of one of Lal Ghat's labyrinthine lanes, but getting there is easy—everybody knows where it is. ✉*Lal Ghat* ☎*294/242–2860 or 294/242–0133* ▭*MC, V.*

$$ ✕**Palki Khana.** Inside the City Palace Complex, this casual café makes a perfect post-museum stop—it's good relaxing and people-watching. The menu emphasizes standard dishes that include salads, sandwiches, pizza, and pasta. Try the yummy "mochachillo" (espresso shake) for a caffeine kick. This restaurant also serves beer and has an extensive international and Indian wine menu. Dinner is also served on the patio for the nightly sound-and-light show, which runs from 7 to 8 in the winter and 8 to 9 in the summer. ✉*Shiv Niwas Palace, City Palace Complex* ☎*294/252–8016 or 294/252–8017* ▭*AE, MC, V.*

$–$$ ✕**Ambrai.** On the bank of Lake Pichola opposite Lal Ghat, this pleasant and popular outdoor restaurant gets stunning views of the City Palace complex and the Lake Palace. It serves Continental and Chinese dishes as well as Indian: the standards include *paneer do piaza* (soft white cheese in an onion gravy) and mutton *rajputana* (spicy, Mewari-style). There's beer, and the restaurant is open for all three meals. If you're here at dinner, be sure to bring the mosquito repellant. ✉*Opposite Lal Ghat* ☎*294/243–1085* ▭*No credit cards.*

$ ✕**Savage Garden.** This midnight-blue-and-white three-story restaurant is in the heart of Udaipur's old city in Chandpole. The staff is trained by an Italian chef, and the place feels Mediterranean, with minimal decorations, inside and outside seating, and lots of white and blue. The menu, just a page long, is a refreshing change from sheafs of standard Indian, Chinese, and Continental options available elsewhere. Owned by a German, the restaurant specializes in homemade pastas, and all dishes are prepared with filtered water. Beer and wine are available, and there are also baked goods available. There's even free Internet for guests. ✉*22, inside Chandpole* ☎*294/242–5440* 🌐*www.savagegardenindia.com* ▭*No credit cards.*

¢–$ ✕**Café Edelweiss German Bakery & Coffee Shop.** Take a break from sightseeing at this tiny bakery, famous in town for its delectable chocolate desserts. A minute's walk up the hill from Gangaur Ghat, this café is popular among backpackers and locals alike. Try the chocolate balls, made with coconut, or the delicious apple pie. Seating is limited, so grab an empty chair when you see one. ✉*73 Gangaur Ghat* ☎*941/423–3573* ▭*No credit cards.*

$$$$ **Fateh Prakash Palace.** Small but grand, and with suitably excellent views of Lake Pichola, this palace was built by Maharana Fateh Singh at the turn of the 20th century. The suites are elegantly furnished with period furniture (some of it was once used by the royal family), heavy drapes, and brass fixtures. **Pros:** in the midst of the action—it's right next to the City Palace. **Cons:** very expensive, standard rooms are luxurious, but lack the main palace's sense of history. ✉*Next to City Palace Complex* *Reserve through City Palace, 313001* ☎*0294/252–8016 to 19 reservations (City Palace)* 🌐*www.hrhindia.com* *21 rooms, 9 suites* *In-room: safe, refrigerator, Wi-Fi. In-hotel: restaurant, room service, bar, pool, gym, no elevator.* ▭*AE, MC, V.*

$$$$ Fodor's Choice ★ **Lake Palace.** Managed by the Taj Group, this 250-year-old white-marble palace—the main setting for the James Bond film *Octopussy*—floats like a vision in the middle of Lake Pichola. You arrive, of course, by boat. The standard rooms are contemporary but elegant, featuring plush beds but small bathrooms; the suites are much larger and more opulent and come with your own private butler. The bathrooms are modern and spotless—the ones in the suites have both showers and bathtubs; the water pressure in the showers is fabulous and the housekeeping has thought of your every need. Most rooms have lake views, though some look onto the lily pond or the courtyard, where nightly folk dances are performed. The interiors have numerous inviting public alcoves and balconies for hanging out in. Nonguests can't visit the palace unless they have a reservation to dine at the restaurant or on the hotel's wooden barge, *Gangaur.* **Pros:** exemplary service to match the palatial setting, boat service from the jetty to the palace available at all hours. **Cons:** astoundingly expensive (and watch out for the hidden luxury and service taxes not included in the base price), the outdoor pool is nice but not massive. ✉*Lake Pichola, 313001* ☎*294/252–8800* 🌐*www.tajhotels.com* *83 rooms, 17 suites* *In-room: refrigerator, DVD, Wi-Fi. In-hotel: 2 restaurants, room service, bar, pool, gym, spa, no elevator, laundry service.* ▭*AE, DC, MC, V.*

$$$$ **Laxmi Vilas Palace.** Built in 1933 on a hillside above the banks of Fateh Sagar Lake, this former royal guesthouse is filled with nostalgia.

From the hotel's verandas and gardens you can get a lovely view of the lake and the nearby Sajjan Garh fort. The maharana's hunting trophies line the entranceway. The restaurant serves Indian food. Rooms in the new wing are modern; the old wing, though not lavish, has original architecture and Rajput relics. **Pros:** nice views of the lake, quiet area, good service. **Cons:** expensive. ✉ *Opposite Fateh Prakash Lake, Sagar Rd., 313001* ☎ *0294/252–9711* 🌐 *www.thegrandhotels.net* *55 rooms, 14 suites* *In-room: safe, refrigerator. In-hotel: restaurant, room service, bar, pool, no elevator, laundry service.* *AE, MC, V.*

$$$$ **Oberoi Udaivilas.** Built on the edge of Lake Pichola with a sublime
Fodor's Choice ★ view of the Lake Palace, the City Palace Complex, and the ghats, the Oberoi Udaivilas is one of the most luxurious—and expensive—hotels in India. Given the grand architecture with numerous domes and elegantly furnished rooms, this is a contemporary palace in its own right. For the ultimate experience, splurge on the suite with semiprivate pool (shared with other suites in the same row) that seems to ripple over onto serene Pichola, while deer come up to the edge of the hotel's private wildlife reserve. Traditionally dressed staff have an unusual old-world courtesy and genuine concern for the welfare of guests. The restaurants serve delicious Continental and Indian food. **Pros:** great service and surroundings, airport or railway pickup is free and luxurious, expansive garden and sanctuary area are ideal for spotting free roaming peacocks up close. **Cons:** extremely expensive, a bit out of the way from the old city by road (you can take a boat shortcut). ✉ *Haridasji ki Magri, 313001* ☎ *94/243–3300, 800/562–3764 reservations from U.S. and Canada* 🌐 *www.oberoihotels.com* *87 rooms, 5 suites* *In-room: safe, DVD, ethernet. In-hotel: 2 restaurants, room service, bar, pool, gym, spa, laundry service, airport shuttle.* *AE, DC, MC, V.*

$$$$ **Shiv Niwas Palace.** Laid out like a white crescent moon around a large pool, this was once a royal guesthouse. The regal suites are gorgeous, with molded ceilings, elaborate canopied beds, and original paintings and furniture. The Paneera Bar is styled with Victorian furnishings. Dine poolside for a romantic experience. Some of the rooms have private terraces; all have excellent views of Lake Pichola. **Pros:** doesn't get more central than this (you're within walking distance of the lake, old city, City Palace Museum, and shopping). **Cons:** fairly expensive, the standard rooms are set apart from the main building and have contemporary furnishings. ✉ *City Palace Complex* *Reserve through City Palace, 313001* ☎ *294/252–8016 to 19* 🌐 *www.hrhindia.com* *19 rooms, 17 suites* *In-room: safe, refrigerator. In-hotel: restaurant, bar, pool, no elevator, public Internet.* *AE, DC, MC, V.*

$$$–$$$$ **Trident Hilton.** This property sits at the end of a long and solitary road,
★ on acres of beautiful gardens. On the shore or Laka Pichola, it's totally removed from the bustle of downtown Udaipur. The hotel's architecture is striking, but the interior is somewhat lacking in aesthetic sensibility; rooms, facing either the garden or pool, are well equipped and modern, but nondescript. The pool is heated and thus pleasant day or night. The smiling and attentive staff aims to please. Bada Mahal, the adjoining hunting lodge, offers the opportunity to watch deer and wild boar being fed every evening by a caretaker. The restaurant, Aravalli,

serves Indian and Continental buffet and à la carte dishes at lunch and dinner. **Pros:** one of the relatively affordable options among luxury hotels in Udaipur, peaceful location. **Cons:** uninspiring rooms are a bit on the small side, the location is not central. ✉ *Haridasji Ki Magri, Mulla Tulai, 313001* ☎ *294/243–2200* 🌐 *www.hilton.com* *139 rooms, 4 suites* *In-room: safe, refrigerator, Wi-Fi. In-hotel: 2 restaurants, room service, bar, pool, gym.* 💳 *AE, DC, MC, V.*

$$ **Hilltop Hotel Palace.** On a hill overlooking Fateh Sagar Lake, this hotel comes with splendid views. It's modern, with a spacious marble lobby, a glass elevator, an elegant garden, and a number of rooftop terraces. The hotel may not take you back in time, but it's an excellent value. **Pros:** Western-style rooms are simple but clean, and each has a balcony. **Cons:** 2 km (1 mi) from old city. ✉ *5 Ambavgarh, Fateh Sagar, 313001* ☎ *294/243–2245* 🌐 *www.hotelhilltoppalace.net* *62 rooms* *In-hotel: 2 restaurants, room service, bar, pool, no elevator.* 💳 *MC, V.*

$$ **Paras Mahal.** This modern, non-fancy hotel is only ½ km (¼ mi) from Udaipur's train station, and it's also close to a Bollywood theater. The main feature is a glass elevator that shoots up through the hotel's central atrium. Rooms have low-lying beds, with lavish, colorful bedspreads; the walls are hung with Rajasthani paintings. All rooms have sofas and desks. **Pros:** reasonable price. **Cons:** not an ideal location to get the true feel for Udaipur. ✉ *Near Paras Cinema, Hiran Magri, Sector 11, NH–8, 313001* ☎ *294/248–3391 Ext. 4* 🌐 *www.hotelparasmahal.com* *60 rooms* *In-room: refrigerator, safe. In-hotel: restaurant, bar, pool, laundry service.* 💳 *MC, V.*

$$ **Udai Kothi.** Who can pass up regal accommodations at cut-rate prices? From the rooftop and its pool you get spectacular views of the Udaipur skyline—the hotel is across Lake Pichola from the City Palace. Every room is themed, with antique furniture and art and other furnishings that relate to a specific region and group of people in Mewar history. **Pros:** probably the best hotel for the money in all of Rajasthan, renovated bathrooms in all rooms. **Cons:** no Internet, only the suites have lake views. ✉ *Outside Chandpol on Hannuman Ghat, 313001* ☎ *294/243–2810 to 12* 🌐 *www.udaikothi.com* *17 rooms, 9 suites* *In-room: safe, refrigerator (some). In-hotel: restaurant, bar, pool, laundry service.* 💳 *MC, V.*

¢–$$ **Jagat Niwas Palace Hotel.** With a stunning location on the Lake Pichola at Lal Ghat, a whitewashed interior, and simple but elegant furnishings, this converted 17th-century haveli is one of the best medium-budget places in the city. The charming restaurant has romantic open-air alcoves overlooking the lake and a stunning view of the Lake Palace Hotel. Twelve of the rooms have lake views; some suites have window seats directly overlooking the lake. **Pros:** unsurpassed views of the lake and the Aravalli hills, one of the best values in town, short walk from nearby shopping and restaurants. **Cons:** no pool. ✉ *23–25, Lal Ghat, 313001* ☎ *294/242–2860 or 294/242–0133* 🌐 *www.jagatniwaspalace.com* *25 rooms, 4 suites* *In-hotel: restaurant, bar, no elevator, laundry service, public Internet.* 💳 *MC, V.*

¢–$$ **Lake Pichola Hotel.** Not to be confused with the Lake Palace on Lake Pichola, this hotel is run by a Rajput family and benefits both from an excellent location on Lake Pichola and friendly service. Two suites have a Jacuzzi and another has a steam room. The rooms are full of artifacts and colored glass panes. **Pros:** deluxe rooms and suites have a terrace with beautiful city views, great location, and good service. **Cons:** no pool or Internet. ✉ *Outside Chandpol, on western side of Lake Pichola, 313001* ☎ *294/243–1197* 🌐 *www.lakepicholahotel.com* *26 rooms, 4 suites* *In-room: a/c (some), refrigerator (some). In-hotel: restaurant, spa, no elevator.* *MC, V.*

¢–$ **Kankarwa Haveli.** Next door to the Jagat Niwas Palace on Lal Ghat, in the old city, this haveli has a homey feel. The staff is family servents, and members of the family supervise the kitchen, which serves home-style Rajasthani food—a relief from the Punjabi and Mughlai cuisines that seem to dominate menus through the state. Ask for the rooms on the upper floor, since lower-floor rooms, closer to the water, can let in more smells. Rooms are large, simple, and lovingly restored. You will have to shout down the stairs for room service and there's a chance you'll be answered by a bark from the family dog that guards the courtyard. **Pros:** a decent budget option in the old city. **Cons:** no five-star frills or legions of staff, might be a little too homey for some. ✉ *26 Lal Ghat, 313001* ☎ *0294/241–1457* 🌐 *www.indianheritagehotels.com* *15 rooms* *In-room: no phone, no TV. In-hotel: restaurant, no elevator, laundry service, public Internet.* *MC, V.*

SHOPPING

Udaipur's main shopping area spans the area around the **Jagdish Temple.** You'll discover interesting nooks and crannies around here, but watch out for would-be guides. There are plenty of stores to explore and items to buy: along with leather-bound journals, wooden toys, silver, and Udaipuri and Gujarati embroidery, you'll find miniature paintings in the Moghul and Rajput styles. Most of these paintings are machine-made prints, a fact reflected in the wide disparity in prices. If you want to buy original art, ask the proprietor to show you what's in the back room—and plan to bargain.

ART Serious art collectors should know that Udaipur has many galleries that exhibit original work by internationally renowned and burgeoning artists. The **B.G. Sharma Art Gallery** (✉ *3 Saheli Marg* ☎ *294/256–0063*) has 45 years of work by B.G. Sharma himself, one of the most eminent painters in India. Unlike most artists of miniature paintings, Sharma doesn't copy traditional pictures, but makes his own—and has made huge contributions to advancing the Moghul, Kishangarh, and Kangra painting styles. **Ganesh Art Emporium** (✉ *152 Jagdish Chowk* ☎ *294/242–2864*) is a trendy little shop focusing on a gifted young artist, Madhu Kant Mundra, whose oeuvre includes more than 125 funky representations of Lord Ganesh. Don't miss the artistic refrigerator magnets, sculptures, and antique photographs. **Pristine Gallery** (✉ *6 Kalapi House, Bhatiyani Chohatta, Palace Rd.* ☎ *294/241–5291*) specializes in both contemporary and folk art, with many small pieces by Shail Choyal, a guru of contemporary Indian painting. Other highlights

CLOSE UP

Rajasthani Paintings

Rajasthan is famous for paintings in the phad and pichwai styles. The phad is a red, green, and yellow scroll depicting the life of a local hero; the dark and richly hued pichwais, hung in temples, are cloth paintings depicting Lord Krishna in different moods.

Equally popular are reproductions of mandana art, designs traditionally drawn by women on the walls and floors of rural homes using a chalk solution on a crimson cow-dung background. These unique works are ritual decorations for festivals and ceremonial occasions. Udaipur has the biggest and best selection of miniature paintings, and is considered a center for this traditional art. Whether on paper, silk, marble, or bone, these astonishingly intricate works depict wildlife and courtly scenes, and illustrations of religious stories and mythological themes. Originally created by the chittrekar (artist) community, miniatures now usually blend both Rajput and Moghul styles. Building on the Rajputs' bright colors and courtly themes, the Moghuls added more detail to the faces and the landscapes.

include the stylized work of Shahid Parvez, a very fine local artist. At the **Sharma Art Gallery** (✉*15-A New Colony, Kalaji-Goraji* ☎*294/242–1107*), Kamal Sharma paints mainly birds and animals on paper, marble, silk, and canvas—all are for sale. Apart from being the chief resident artist at Udaipur Medical College, **S. N. Bhandraj** (✉*Studio 70, Moti Magri Colony* ☎*294/256–1396*) has been creating sculpture out of sea foam for more than 20 years; he demonstrates this unique craft in his home studio. At the **Traditional Art Gallery** (✉*13 Bhatiyani Chohatta, Jagdish Mandir* ☎*No phone*), you can see the watercolor tribal portraits and village scenes of the talented artist Anil Sharma.

CRAFTS & CURIOS If your time is limited, you'll find everything under the sun at an emporium, and you won't have to bargain. The **Manglam Arts** (✉*Sukhadia Circle* ☎*294/256–0259*) emporium deals in Rajasthani handicrafts, including rugs, block-printed textiles, knickknacks, and furniture. The government-run **Rajasthali** (✉*Chetak Circle* ☎*294/241–5346*) emporium sells high-quality Rajasthani arts and handicrafts. This is also a good place to pick up a wool-stuffed washable quilt covered with a Rajasthani motif.

Sadhna (✉*Seva Mandir Rd., Fatehpura* ☎*294/245–1041 or 294/245–4655* 🌐*www.sadhna.org*) has two shops. The first is at Seva Mandir, one of the oldest NGOs in India, working for the advancement of the village poor, and the other is near the clock tower in the old city. Sadhna works with rural women in Udaipur district and trains them to produce traditional appliqué work on cushion covers and bedspreads (along with silk stoles, bags, kurtas, light quilts, and jackets). Sadhna has gained popularity over the years and the women are involved in touring around the country at exhibitions in major cities during festivals.

While you're in the Jagdish Temple area, make sure you check out the collection of more than 500 handmade wooden puppets at the **University of Arts** (✉*166 Jagdish Marg, City Palace Rd.* ☎*294/242–2591*).

Ask the proprietor, Rajesh Gurjarjour, an excellent puppeteer, for a private demonstration. Embroidered jackets are also for sale.

JEWELRY From Jagdish Temple, stroll down to **Ganta Ghar** (literally "clock tower") and the area around it, a base for silver jewelry. Browse freely, but take care not to purchase items that are merely coated with silver-tone paint. **Gehrilal Goverdhan Singh Choudhary** (✉ *72 Jagdish Marg, clock tower* ☎ *294/241–0806*) has a good selection of fixed-price, antique jewelry, and contemporary designs with stonework. Choudhary has been in the business more than two decades, and has exhibited several times abroad.

Silver Corner (✉ *17 Lal Ghat, opposite Jagat Niwas Palace Hotel* ☎ *294/510–0660*) carries unique designs in silver- and stonework. The friendly owner can also design jewelry to your liking and resize rings if they don't fit. **Silver Moon** (✉ *117 Bhattiyani Chouhtta* ☎ *294/137–52765*) is yet another treasure trove for contemporary and antique silver jewelry.

4

NEED A BREAK?

Right next door to Gehrilal Goverdhan Singh Choudhary is a sweet stall, Lala Mishtan Bhandar, where you can satisfy your sweet tooth and refuel with the best *gulab jamun* (fried milk balls in syrup) and imarti (pretzel-shaped pastries dipped in sugary syrup) in town.

RANAKPUR

★ *96 km (60 mi) northwest of Udaipur.*

Legend has it that this town's 15th-century **Jain temple,** dedicated to Lord Rishabadeva, was built after it appeared in a dream to a minister of the Mewar king. One of the five holiest places for India's Jains, the three-story temple is surrounded by a three-story wall that contains 27 halls supported by 1,444 elaborately carved pillars—no two carvings are alike. Below the temple are underground chambers where statues of Jain saints were hidden to protect them from the Moghuls. The way the white marble complex rises up from the fertile plain will easily inspire your awe—the relief work on the columns are some of the best in all of India. As you enter, look to the left for the pillar where the minister and the architect provided themselves with front-row seats for worship. Another pillar is intentionally warped, to separate human works from divine ones—the builders believed only gods could be perfect, so they intentionally added imperfections to some of the columns to avoid insulting the gods. Outside are two smaller Jain temples and a shrine adorned with erotic sculptures and dedicated to the sun god. ■ **TIP→ Although there are a couple of hotels for an overnight stay in Ranakpur, this town is best approached as a day trip from Udaipur.** *Temple free, camera fee Rs. 40, video-camera fee Rs. 150* ⏲ *Non-Jains, daily 11:30–5.*

WHERE TO STAY

$$$ **Fateh Bagh.** A short drive from the Jain temple, this hotel offers traditionally decorated rooms. The traditionally decorated rooms are spacious: some of the suites have Jacuzzis. The honeymoon suite has a traditional wedding swing-bed hung from the ceiling. The hotel also arranges jeep and horse safaris and vintage car rides. **Pros:** serene setting. **Cons:** in the middle of nowhere: probably only worth staying here if you don't want to take on the topsy-turvy round-trip between Ranakpur and Udaipur in one day. ✉*Ranakpur Rd., Pali district* ☎*293/428–6186* 🌐*hrhindia.com* *11 rooms, 7 suites* *In-hotel: restaurant, bar, public Internet.* ▭*MC, V.*

MOUNT ABU

185 km (115 mi) west of Udaipur.

High in the Aravalli Hills, Mount Abu has long been the site of one of Hinduism's most sacred rites, the *yagya* (fire ritual). Legend has it that the clan of the mighty Agnikula Rajput warriors rose from this mystical fire. Today, Mount Abu is Rajasthan's only hill station, and a pilgrimage center for Jains, who come here to see the famous Dilwara Temples. Mount Abu is also a great place to stop if you like taking long walks. **Nakki Lake,** resting between green hills, is believed to have been carved out by the gods' fingernails. The far side of the lake is quieter and cleaner. At **Sunset Point** you can imbibe a romantic Mount Abu sunset, but you can't avoid the crowds here.

Mount Abu's ashram-cult hotspot, **Brahma Kumaris Spiritual University,** attracts thousands of followers from all over the world. Members of the Brahma Kumari sect don white robes or saris, and study spiritual knowledge or Raja yoga meditation. (Potential devotees beware: their services don't come cheap.)

The Brahma Kumaris have also designed the **Peace Park,** which includes a series of beautiful gardens.

Beyond Peace Park, on Guru Shikhar Road, is **Guru Shikhar,** the highest point between South India's Nilgiri Hills and the Himalayas, in the north. From here you can enjoy excellent views of the countryside.

The stunningly carved, unforgettably beautiful **Dilwara Temples,** dedicated to Jain saints, were built of marble between the 11th and 13th centuries.

WHERE TO STAY

$–$$ **Palace Hotel (Bikaner House).** Besides once being the summer residence of the Maharaja of Bikaner, this was for decades also the center of Mount Abu's aristocratic social life. Built in 1893 and now a Heritage Hotel, it still feels something like a hunting lodge, and is a good place to retreat and relax for a few days. **Pros:** service is excellent, hotel is in the middle of 20 acres of lawns and woods. **Cons:** no pool or Internet. ✉*Delwara Rd., Mount Abu, 307501* ☎*2974/235–121 or 2974/238–673* 📠*2974/238–674* *32 rooms, including 16 suites* *In-room: refrigerator. In-hotel: restaurant, bar, tennis court, no elevator, laundry service.* ▭*AE, MC, V.*

$ **Cama Rajputana Club Resort.** Cradled in the Aravalli hills, this late-19th-century club is where British officers and royalty from Gujarat and Rajputana came to escape the summer heat, and now it combines modern amenities with country style. The main building is a rambling old bungalow with a tiled roof; the hotel itself has 18 acres of gardens, with waterfalls and an artifical lake. **Pros:** rooms belonging to the old club property are old-world. **Cons:** new blocks have modern rooms with nondescript furnishings;. ✉ *Adhar Devi Rd., Mount Abu 307501* *Reserve through Cama Hotel Ltd., Khanpur Rd., Ahmedabad, Gujarat, 380001* ☎ *2974/238–205, 2974/238–206, 079/560–1234 reservations* *www.camahotelsindia.com* *40 rooms, 2 suites* *In-room: refrigerator. In-hotel: restaurant, bar, gym, tennis court, pool, gym, no elevator.* *MC, V.*

CHITTAURGARH

★ *112 km (69 mi) northeast of Udaipur.*

If any one of Rajasthan's many forts had to be singled out for its glorious history and chivalric lore, it would be Chittaurgarh. This was the capital of the Mewar princely state from the 8th to the 16th centuries, before Maharana Udai Singh moved the capital to Udaipur. The sprawling hilltop fort occupies about 700 acres on a hill about 92 meters (300 feet) high. It was besieged and sacked three times: after the first two conquests, the Rajputs recovered it, but the third attack clinched it for the Moghuls for several decades.

The first attack took place because of a woman: the beauty of Rani Padmini, wife of the then-current ruler, so enamored the Sultan of Delhi Allauddin Khilji that he set out to attack the fort and win her in battle. Thirty-four thousand warriors lost their lives in this struggle, but the Sultan did not get Padmini: she and all the women in the fort committed *jauhar,* mass self-immolation in anticipation of widowhood and assaults by invading armies. Frustrated, Khilji entered the city in a rage, looting and destroying much of what he saw. Chittaurgarh was also the home of the saint-poet Mirabai, a 16th-century Rajput princess and devotee of Lord Krishna who gave up her royal life to sing *bhajans* (hymns) in his praise.

The massive fort encompasses the palaces of **Rana Kumbha** and **Padmini** Rana Kumbha's palace is a fine 15th-century ruin, whereas Padmini's tranquil palace sits beside a small, still body of water. Also worth visiting in the fort are the victory towers—the ornate **Vijay Stambh** and **Kirti Stambh**—and a huge variety of temples, including **Kunbha Shyam, Kalika Mata,** and the **Meera temple** associated with the devotional poetess Mirabai. The **Fateh Prakash Mahal** displays some fine sculptures. Spend at least half a day in Chittaurgarh; a vehicle helps, because the sights are spread out and the sun can be very sharp on the unprotected hill.

At present there are no exciting accommodation options in Chittaur town, but Heritage Hotels in the nearby villages offer wonderful retreats and good bases from which to explore rural Mewar.

WHERE TO STAY

$ **Bassi Fort Palace.** You'll find this 16th-century fort 20 km (12 mi) from Chittaurgarh. It was converted into a Heritage Hotel by descendants of the Chundawat royals. The approach road to the fort goes through the unspoiled village of Bassi. You can also visit the family's former hunting lodge overlooking Bassi and Orai lakes. Government plans are afoot to reintroduce tigers to the wild in the Bassi Wildlife Sanctuary. The hotel organizes tented safaris near the lake, and trips into the nearby Bhil villages. **Pros:** common areas are large and elegant, with period furniture, and the rooms spacious and comfortable. **Cons:** no pool or Internet. ✉ *On Udaipur Chittaurgarh-Bundi-Kota NH–76, Bassi, Chittaurgarh, 312022* ☎ *1472/225–321 or 1472/225–606* 🌐 *www.bassifortpalace.com* *17 rooms, 2 suites* *In-room: no a/c (some), TV (some). In-hotel: restaurant, bar, no elevator.*

KUMBHALGARH

84 km (52 mi) north of Udaipur.

Isolated and serene, this formidable **fort** was a refuge for Mewari rulers in times of strife. Built by Maharana Kumbha in the 15th century, the fort ramparts run 4 km (2½ mi) and the outer wall encloses an area of 83 square km (32 square mi). At one time its ramparts nearly encircled an entire township, self-contained to withstand a long siege. The fort fell only once, to the army of Akbar—whose forces had contaminated the water supply. The fort was also the birthplace of Maharana Pratap. The **Badal Mahal** (Cloud Palace), at the top, has an awesome view of the surrounding countryside.

Surrounding the fort, the modern-day **Kumbalgarh Sanctuary** is home to wolves, leopards, jackals, nilgai deer, sambar deer, and various species of birds, and makes for great treks. Have a leisurely lunch at the open-air restaurant of the Aodhi Hotel.

NATHDWARA

48 km (30 mi) north of Udaipur.

The town of Nathdwara is completely built around the **Shrinathji Temple,** visited by thousands of pilgrims each year. Built in the 18th century, this simple temple is one of the most celebrated shrines to Lord Krishna: it houses a unique image of the deity sculpted from a single piece of black marble. Nathdwara is known for its *pichwais,* large cloth paintings depicting legends from Krishna's life, and for its special style of devotional music.

A few minutes outside Nathdwara is **Rajsamand Lake,** which attracts a large number of migratory birds. Maharana Raj Singh ordered the construction of the lake in 1662 as a famine-relief work project, so a workforce of 60,000 people brought it into being over the course of 10 years. The architecture of its main dam, **Nauchowki** (Nine Pavilions), combines Rajput and Moghul styles; interestingly, the Rajaprashasthi (Rajput Royal Eulogy) is engraved on 25 of the dam's niched slabs. Locals come here early in the morning to learn to swim, in the pool behind the dam.

Also near Nathdwara is the village of **Molela,** where artisans craft and paint fine terra-cotta images of gods, goddesses, and animals, as well as more functional pots and utensils.

4

EKLINGJI & NAGDA

22 km (14 mi) north of Udaipur.

A pleasant drive from Udaipur through the Aravallis, Eklingji village is famous for its 15th-century **Shiva Temple** (some parts date back to the 8th century). There's a unique four-sided, four-faced black marble image of Shiva here, miniature replicas of which will be eagerly offered to you in the village bazaar. Every Monday evening, the Udaipur maharana visits the temple privately. The temple is closed at various times of the day; it's best to ask your hotel for the prevailing admission schedule.

At nearby Nagda, 1 km south of Eklingji, 10th-century Jain temples make for an interesting detour from the highway. The chief attractions are the ruins of **Adbudji Temple** and the beautifully sculpted **Sas Bahu Temple.**

A few kilometers north up the road, the towering 18th-century **Devi Garh Palace** (✉*off NH–8, near Eklingji, Rajsamand district, Delwara*), beautifully restored and now run as a luxury hotel, merits an hour's exploration (nonguests are charged a fee).

WHERE TO STAY

$$$$ ★ **Devi Garh.** Rising from the middle of the Aravali hills, this yellow-ocher hotel is one of the loveliest palaces in Rajasthan. It's been carefully restored, and is beautifully maintained. The rooms, however, are modern, and though very attractive, have little of that fairy-tale palace feel that some visitors want. The heritage look and feel is deliberately missing, creating a sharp contrast between the ancient exterior and the contemporary interiors. Marble predominates; even some beds are made of marble. Furniture is sleek and contemporary. Windows look out on terrific views of the Aravalis—the palace was positioned to command one of the three passes into the Udaipur Valley. Walk west from the palace at sunset and look back at it, or relax on the terrace or explore the surrounding hills. **Pros:** all rooms have private balconies, beautiful location close to sites in Eklingji and not too far from Udaipur. **Cons:** quite expensive. ✉*NH–8, near Eklingji, Rajsamand district, Delwara, 313202* ☎*295/328–9211 to 20* 🖷*02953/289–357* 🌐*www.deviresorts.com* *39 suites* *In-room: safe, refrigerator, DVD, Wi-Fi. In-hotel: restaurant, bar, pool, gym, spa, bicycles.* 💳*AE, MC, V.*

JAISALMER & ENVIRONS

The stark, compelling beauty of the Thar Desert draws travelers to far-western Rajasthan—for good reason. Jaisalmer, resplendent with golden buildings and a towering citadel, is a good base for camel safaris into the desert, and photogenic Sam Sand Dunes and Desert National Park are a short distance from this striking medieval city.

JAISALMER

Fodor'sChoice ★ *663 km (412 mi) northwest of Udaipur, 285 km (177 mi) northwest of Jodhpur, 570 km (354 mi) west of Jaipur.*

Jaisalmer seems like a mirage: its array of sandstone buildings are surrounded by the stark Thar Desert and illuminated in a gold hue by the penetrating sun. The ancient medieval city is defined by its carved spires and palaces, and the massive sandcastlelike fort that towers over the imposing wall that encircles the town. Jaisalmer is a remote and unusual city; it's out of the way, but it's worth it if you want to see a different side of India, and definitely if you want to take a camel safari.

Founded in 1156 by Rawal Jaisal, a descendent of the Yadav clan and a Bhatti Rajput, Jaisalmer lies near the extreme western edge of Rajasthan, about 160 km (about 100 mi) east of the Pakistan border. It began as a trade center: from the 12th through the 18th centuries, rulers amassed their wealth from taxes levied on caravans passing through from Africa, Persia, Arabia, and other parts of Central Asia. Smugglers were also known to frequent Jaisalmer to work the profitable opium trade. The rise of Bombay (modern-day Mumbai) as a major trading port in the 19th century, however, eclipsed Jaisalmer's role as a staging post.

Today Jaisalmer attracts travelers attracted by the mystery and harsh, remote charm of the desert. A welcome change from crowded, polluted cities, the city is an architectural masterpiece that never fails to amaze. At night the fort is bathed in golden light, which illuminates the seemingly impregnable walls; most of the buildings inside are made out of yellow sandstone. Jaisalmer is also known for its ornate 19th-century havelis—mansions with facades so intricately carved the stonework looks like lace. It's also worth wandering through the mazelike alleys and bazaars, though the markets have a bad reputation among tourists. ⚠ **Expect some harassment, especially if you're a woman traveling solo.** With clean lanes, no traffic, and few crowds, Jaisalmer is easily covered on foot. Camel safaris are a good way to see the desert. These are great fun, but choose one carefully—don't skimp and choose a cheap outfitter. Take a light scarf to protect your face in case of a sandstorm.

Spend at least two nights in Jaisalmer. Nothing is more romantic than a Thar Desert sunset, and the city's cultural festivities—the heart and soul of its people—begin at night. For the traveler, these can reach intoxicating levels of passion: around blazing bonfires, dancers and musicians gather together and re-create the ancient traditions of Rajasthan. To get an even bigger dose of it, visit during the Desert Festival,

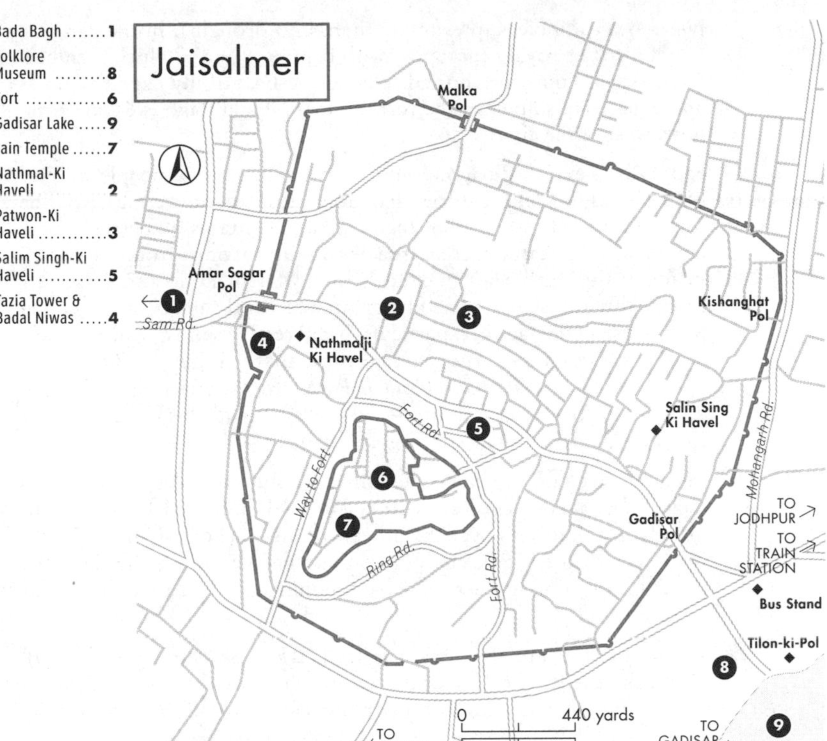

4

in late January and early February. You'll see music, dance, camel races, turban-tying contests, and craft bazaars with regional traders.

A GOOD TOUR

In Jaisalmer, it's next to impossible to follow a straight path: it's a maze of streets and passageways. Trust your instincts and don't be afraid to ask the locals for directions. You may have fun getting a little lost—especially because Jaisalmer isn't big enough to get hopelessly turned around. The major landmark is the **fort** ❻, which is every bit as labyrinthine as the rest of the city; allow several hours to explore the attractions within. From here, walk north to the **havelis.** Finally, hop a camel—you must arrange this with a local travel agent a day in advance—and head southeast toward **Gadsisar Lake** ❾ and the nearby Folklore Museum.

TIMING You can do this tour in a day. If you spend a second day in town, visit the **Bada Bagh** garden and then drive northwest from there to the **Ludarva Temples.**

WHAT TO SEE

❶ **Bada Bagh.** Much of the city's vegetables and fruits are grown at Bada Bagh, which is more like a giant orchard than a garden. On the banks of an artificial lake, and with so much lush greenery, the garden resembles a beautiful oasis (presuming there's no drought). In the gardens, you'll also see royal cenotaphs, with canopies under which members of the royal family are buried. Notice the beautifully carved ceilings and equestrian statues of the former rulers. Bada Bagh is 6 km (4 mi) northwest of the city.

6 **Fort.** What's extraordinary about this fort is that 5,000 people still live
Fodor's Choice ★ here, just as they did centuries ago. Some 250 feet above the town, the fort is protected by a 30-foot-high wall and contains 99 bastions. Several great *pols* (gateways) approach and jut outward from the battlements of this 12th-century citadel. Built of sandstone and extremely brittle, the fort is rumored to be an architectural time bomb, destined to collapse in the face of a particularly aggressive sandstorm. So lovely is this structure that the poet Rabindranath Tagore (1861–1941) composed *Sonar Kila* (*The Golden Fort*) after seeing it, and inspired another creative Bengali in turn—Satyajit Ray made his famous film by the same name after reading Tagore's work.

Inside the web of tiny lanes are Jain and Hindu temples, palaces, and charming havelis. The seven-story **Juna Mahal** (Old Palace), built around 1500, towers over the other buildings. The **Satiyon ka Pagthiya** (Steps of the Satis), just before the palace entrance, is where the royal ladies committed *sati,* self-immolation, when their husbands were slain.

7 Within the fort are eight **Jain temples** (*Free Daily 7 AM–noon*), built from the 12th to 16th centuries, which house thousands of carved deities and dancing figures in mythological settings. No photography is allowed here, and you'll have to leave your leather items at the gate (Jains worship life in all forms, so leather is sacrilegious). The **Gyan Bhandar** (*Free Daily 10 AM–11 AM*), inside the Jain temple complex contains more than 1,000 old manuscripts—some from the 12th century, written on palm leaf, with painted wooden covers—and a collection of Jain, pre-Moghul, and Rajput paintings. The historic
4 **Tazia Tower** is a delicate pagoda rising five tiers from the **Badal Mahal** (Cloud Palace), each tier designed to include an intricately carved balcony. Muslim craftsmen built the tower in the shape of a *tazia*—a replica of a bier carried in procession during Mohurram, a Muslim period of mourning. ⊠*Juna Mahal* *Rs. 5* *Daily 8–5.*

9 **Gadsisar Lake** *(Gadi Sagar Tank).* Built in the 12th century, this freshwater lake surrounded by numerous golden-hue shrines is frequented by a spectacular and diverse avian community. Plan for a camel ride, a picnic, and perhaps a short paddle-boat excursion. Near the shrines
8 and behind the main bus stand is a charming **Folklore Museum,** built in the style of a traditional home. Filled with memorabilia, it's the perfect place to ground yourself in local history and culture. ⊠*About 1 km southeast of Jaisalmer's fort* *Rs. 2* *Daily 8–7.*

Havelis. Outside the fort, about 1½ km (1 mi) from the Gopa Chowk entrance, is a string of five connected havelis built by the Patwa brothers in the 1800s. The Patwas were highly influential Jain merchants back when Jaisalmer was an independent principality. The Patwa brothers forbade the repetition of any motifs or designs between their mansions, so each is distinctive.

Two of the five havelis are now owned by the government and open to the public, and you can explore the interiors of the others by offering a small fee (not more than Rs. 50) to the residents. Three havelis
3 are noteworthy in this area. One, **Patwon Ki Haveli**, is arguably the most elaborate and magnificent of all Jaisalmer's havelis; in addition to exquisitely carved pillars and expansive corridors, one of the apartments in this five-story mansion is painted with beautiful murals. The
2 19th-century **Nathmal Ki Haveli** was carved by two brothers, each working independently on his own half; the design is remarkably harmonious, though you can spot small differences. The interior of the
5 **Salim Singh Ki Haveli,** built in about 1815, is in sad disrepair, but the mansion's exterior is still lovely—it has an overhanging gallery on its top floor. Note the havelis' ventilation systems: the projecting windows and stone screens keep them cool even in the searing summer months.

Ludarva Temples. The founder of Jaisalmer, Rawal Jaisal, lived here before shifting to his new capital. Here you can still see the ruins of his former city. The Jain temple complex is known for its *nag devta* (snake god), a live snake that appears on auspicious days and nights. The snake is worshiped because, as legend goes, it has been protecting this temple for thousands of years. The temples are famous for their graceful architecture and detailed carving. ⊠ *16 km (10 mi) northwest of Jaisalmer.*

WHERE TO EAT & STAY

There are few decent restaurants in Jaisalmer. The good hotels are your best bet for a savory meal.

$–$$ ✕ **Trio.** Serving Indian food and some Continental dishes, this rooftop restaurant is an old favorite with travelers. ⊠ *Near Amar Sagar Gate, Mandir Palace, Gandhi Chowk* ☎ *2992/252–733* ▭ *MC, V.*

¢–$ ✕ **8 July Restaurant.** Run by an eccentric Indo-Australian, this restaurant serves simple snacks, pizzas, vegetable dishes, and wonderful coffee milk shakes throughout the day. It also stocks marmite and baked beans imported from Australia. The restaurant is just inside the fort, up a staircase. It has a breathtaking view of Jaisalmer and is open for all three meals. ⊠ *Fort* ☎ *2992/252–814* ▭ *No credit cards* ⊙ *Closed May and June.*

$$$ **Gorbandh Palace.** Built of golden sandstone, this popular hotel is spacious and elegant. Rooms are arranged in haveli-style blocks around a series of small interior courtyards with skylights and fountains. Interiors are Western-style, with some Rajasthani touches and large, lovely windows. This expansive retreat is popular with foreign tour groups looking for a break from the city center. **Pros:** palace's pool is the deepest in Jaisalmer. **Cons:** food is decent but nothing special. ⊠ *1 Tourist Complex, Sam Rd., 345001* ☎ *2992/253–801 to 7* 🌐 *www.hrhindia.com* *64 rooms, 3 suites* *In-room: refrigerator. In-hotel: restaurant, bar, pool, no elevator.* ▭ *AE, MC, V.*

$$ ★ **Fort Rajwada.** The luxurious hotel in Jaisalmer blends French interior design with historic Marwari touches. The entranceway once belonged to a 16th-century haveli from the fort. Standard rooms are Western, with contemporary furnishings; suites are far more extravagant, with frescoes and antique beds with pure silver bedposts. The restaurant, Sonal, serves à la carte Indian, Chinese, and Continental food. The buffet is good but expensive. **Pros:** nice architecture. **Cons:** plain rooms. ✉*No. 1 Hotel Complex, Jodhpur-Barmer Link Rd., 345001* ☎*2992/253–233* 🌐*www.fortrajwada.com* *90 rooms, 4 suites* *In-room: refrigerator, safe. In-hotel: restaurant, bar, pool, no elevator, laundry service.*

$$ **Jawahar Niwas Palace.** This elegant sandstone palace to the west of the fort was built in 1899. Still owned by the Maharaja of Jaisalmer, the palace has large rooms with old-style furniture and views of the fort. The restaurant serves multicuisine food. **Pros:** elegant setting. **Cons:** there's no bar, but beer can be served on request. ✉*1 Bada Bagh Rd., 345001* ☎*2992/252–208 or 2992/252–288* *2992/250–175* *20 rooms* *In-room: refrigerator (some). In-hotel: restaurant, pool, gym, no elevator, laundry service, public Internet.* *AE, MC, V.*

$$ **Rawalkot.** This cozy Taj hotel on the edge of town has a great view of the fort. Small sandstone rooms, tasteful old-style furniture, pebbled courtyards, and stained-glass windows lend this hotel more character than most of the other modern hotels in Jaisalmer. Some of the rooms face the fort. **Pros:** one of the best hotels in Jaisalmer, good service. **Cons:** a bit inconveniently located away from the main sights in Jaisalmer. ✉*Jodhpur Rd., 345001* ☎*2992/252–638, 2992/251–874, or 2992/254–610* 🌐*www.tajhotels.com* *32 rooms* *In-room: safe, refrigerator, dial-up. In-hotel: restaurant, bar, pool, gym, spa, no elevator, laundry service.* *AE, MC, V.*

$ **Rang Mahal.** This mid-level sandstone complex has an austere interior. Frescoes decorate some of the walls, many of which are otherwise whitewashed. Standard rooms are spacious and furnished with Western amenities—but include Rajasthani bed frames. There are occasional pleasant surprises, such as a traditional puppet hanging on the bathroom wall. Definitely get a room with a balcony and a fort view, and take a dip in the pool—it's the largest in Jaisalmer. **Pros:** basic, decent rooms; good views. **Cons:** not luxurious. ✉*5 Hotel Complex, Sam Rd., 345001* ☎*2992/250–907 to 09* 🌐*www.hotelrangmahal.com* *63 rooms, 3 suites* *In-room: refrigerator. In-hotel: restaurant, bar, pool, no elevator, laundry service.* *AE, MC, V.*

$ **Himmatgarh Palace.** Opposite the royal cenotaphs, this hotel is about 1 km (½ mi) from the city, The standard rooms are modern and comfortable, but the small, circular *burj* (tower) rooms are more charming, with marble beds and lights concealed in the nooks of the stone walls. The hotel sponsors performances of folk dance and music. **Pros:** a good deal; one of the best views in town, especially at sunset. **Cons:** food is mediocre—dine elsewhere. ✉*1 Ramgarh Rd., 345001* ☎*2992/252–002 Ext. 4* *2992/252–005* *40 rooms* *In-hotel: restaurant, bar, pool, no elevator.* *AE, MC, V.*

$ **Killa Bhawan.** The fort is a UNESCO heritage site and the plumbing is an issue so the hotel apparently takes special care about water usage.This gem is inside the fort but the management is very responsible about waste and water management. The hotel is tastefully decorated in traditional Rajasthani style. **Pros:** location couldn't be better, fabulous views from the terrace; room rate includes breakfast. **Cons:** plumbing can be problematic; some of the rooms have shared bathrooms; no bar but alcohol available on request. ✉*On fort, Kotri Para, 345001* ☎*02992/251–204* 🌐*www.killabhawan.com* *8 rooms, 1 suite* *In-room: no a/c (some), no TV.* *MC, V.*

4

CAMEL SAFARIS

Safari prices vary dramatically depending on the itinerary and the level of tourist crush. Your hotel should also be able to book or arrange safaris for you—but make sure you check exactly what you're going to get for the price asked. Camel safaris are slow; if you're pressed for time, try combining them with jeep travel. One option is contact the Rajasthan Tourism Development Corporation in the Hotel Moomal (☎2992/252–392), or the Indian Tourism Development Corporation at the Dhola Maru hotel (☎2992/252–863), for reservations. **Royal Safaris** (✉*Gandhi Chowk* ☎*2992/252–538*) is the best agent around, tailoring trips to nearby villages or overnight sojourns in the desert. **Sahara Travels** (✉*Fort Gate* ☎*2992/252–609*) is a reliable agent for camel safaris.

SHOPPING

Jaislamer is famous for its mirror work, embroidery, and woolen shawls. Local artisans also make attractive, good-quality wooden boxes, silver jewelry, and curios. The main shopping areas are **Sadar Bazaar, Sonaron Ka Bas, Manak Chowk,** and **Pansari Bazaar,** all within the walled city, near the fort and temple areas. Sonaron Ka Bas, in particular, has exquisite silver jewelry. Avoid solicitors dispensing advice, take time to browse carefully, and bargain hard.

Damoder Handicraft Emporium (✉*Fort, near Rang Prol*) has an excellent selection of local handicrafts, especially old textiles.

Khadi Graamudyog (✉*Dhibba Para, near fort, in the walled city*) has *khadi* (hand-spun cotton) shawls, Nehru jackets, scarves, and rugs. The government emporium **Rajasthali** (✉*Gandhi Chowk*) has fair prices and some good shopping (though you can't bargain here). Coming here is also a good way to gauge the prices of other stores.

SAM SAND DUNES

★ *42 km (26 mi) west of Jaisalmer.*

No trip to Jaisalmer is complete without a visit to Sam Sand Dunes, a photographer's feast. Although the dunes have become somewhat touristy in recent years, the ripples of these wind-shaped dunes still create fantastic mirages, and it's still a magical place to be. Take a camel safari to the dunes, if you can cope with the heat and the time it takes to get here (all day). Alternatively, look for "parked" camels a few kilometers before you reach Sam, and take a short ride to the dunes. Expect some amount of heckling from persistent camel owners and girls offering to dance or sing for you, but don't let it put you off staying for the sunset, which is often spectacular. A peculiar sort of peace descends on the dunes in the late evening, when the icy cold desert wind begins to blow, and this is the most enjoyable part of the dunes experience. Just note there are no hotels here so you must return to Jaisalmer at night.

An alternative to crowded Sam is the more remote village of **Khuri,** 40 km (25 mi) southwest of Jaisalmer, to which fewer tourists find their way. This is closer to the real thing, and you'll sense some the isolation of life in a desert village.

DESERT NATIONAL PARK

45 km (28 mi) southwest of Jaisalmer.

The desert birds here include birds of prey (vultures, desert hawk) as well as sandgrouses, doves, shrikes, bee eaters, and warblers. The rarest, most remarkable bird is the great Indian bustard, a large, majestic crane said to be found only in the Thar Desert. It's not a good idea to visit the park in summer, as the heat is unbearable.

GUJARAT

There's no dearth of sights in Gujarat: age-old temples and mosques, deserted beaches, wildlife, ancient but buzzing urban quarters, palaces and monuments. Bordering the Arabian Sea as well as the Pakistan and Rajsthan, Gujrarat has long relied on trade to make it prosperous. In pre-Aryan days it exchanged goods with Sumer and the Persian Gulf. The Hindu Solanki dynasty produced a flowering of architecture late in the classical period, and some of India's earliest Muslim kingdoms were founded here a few centuries later. Today Gujarat is the country's most industrialized state, contributing about 20% of India's manufacturing productivity. Culturally and economically, it's one of India's richest states and the arts flourish in its cities and artisanship thrives in its villages.

Ahmedabad, the state's capital and one of the largest cities in India, is a repository of architectural styles: from the early Indo-Saracenic forms of the 15th-century Muslim sultans to the modern forms of Le Corbusier, the contemporary Indian architect Charles Correa, and the American Louis Kahn. Historical records and accounts of travelers indicate that in the Middle Ages and afterwards Ahmedabad was larger than London. Today the city is congested and hectic, but it has a wealth of museums, performing-arts centers, galleries and opportunities to shop. In Ahmedabad and elsewhere in western India, you'll find decorated stepwells, or *vavs* as they're known in Gujarat that plunge fathoms down into the earth's water table.

Southwest of Ahmedabad, the Saurashtra region has remarkable wildlife preserves and the palaces of the dozens of princes who ruled here before Independence. Southeast of the capital, the pretty college town Vadodara (a Sanskrit name commonly anglicized as Baroda) is the former headquarters of an important princely state; today it has a vibrant cultural life, with good art museums and bookstores. Scattered about the state are pilgrimage centers of the Jains, members of an ancient religion that practices strict nonviolence.

Previous neglect of tourism in Gujarat means that the hard-sell approach is fairly rare among guides, touts, and taxi drivers. And yet, Gujaratis are relatively unfazed by visitors from overseas: they themselves are India's greatest travelers, composing about a quarter of Indian immigrants around the world. Even their most famous son, Mahatma Gandhi, began his adult life as a lawyer in South Africa. Welcoming but not overly touristy, Gujarat is a glimpse into workaday Indians' India.

AHMEDABAD & ENVIRONS

Gujarat's richness and variety are apparent in the immediate region of its capital. The ruins at Patan and Modhera bear testament to the classical Hindu period, and Ahmedabad itself shows how a sense of style persisted through eras of Muslim rule and the modern period. Ahmedabad is a lively, clean and growing city with plenty of excellent places to eat cheaply at and large malls and sleek shops, and is a relatively simple city to get around, with good roads and easy traffic. The people are kind, courteous, and ready to offer help.

AHMEDABAD

545 km (339 mi) north of Mumbai.

Founded in AD 1411 by the Muslim sultan Ahmed Shah, Ahmedabad flourished under the Gujarat dynasty and became the seat of the Moghul governors of Gujarat—Jehangir, Shah Jahan, and Aurangzeb—all of whom later became emperors. It was said that Ahmedabad hung on three threads: gold, silk, and cotton. The city's present prominence is due largely to one family of textile magnates, the Sarabhais, who were patrons of the arts (they invited Le Corbusier to build here) and supporters of Mahatma Gandhi. Family members are still active in the city's cultural life. Although textiles remain a principal industry in Ahmedabad, the city is also a booming national and international center for the mineral, power, agribusiness, petrochemical, IT, and pharmaceuticals industries.

Ahmedabad is divided into old and new by the Sabarmati River, which is lined with built-up banks and is a mostly dry riverbed in summer; much of the new development is on the river's west side. The pace and scope of the development has been amazing: towering office complexes, designed by well-known Indian architects and shiny, attractive shopping complexes and showrooms are up everywhere, particularly along C. G. Road, the business and shopping strip where real-estate prices can even challenge some areas of Mumbai.

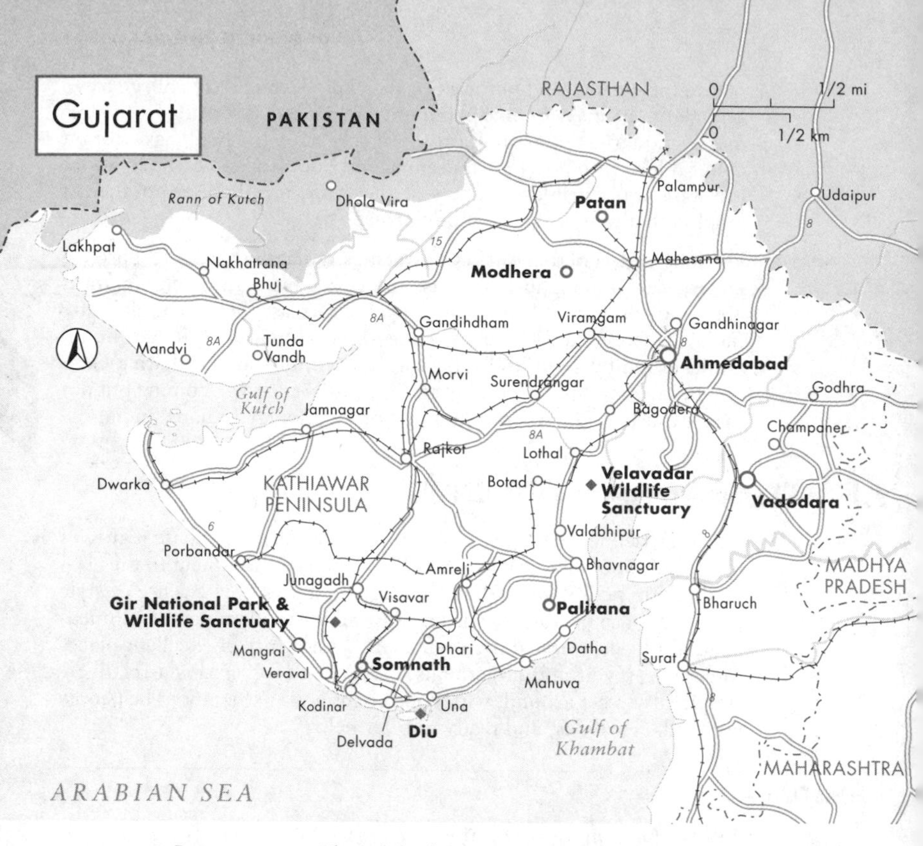

In some ways, Ahmedabad doesn't quite look the part of a major international business hub. It is a large city with the pace and culture of a smaller town. The friendly nature of the locals seems to confirm this. And unlike India's other metropolises, Ahmedabad seems to function smoothly, with wide roads and several leafy neighborhoods.

Ahmedabad is a self-confident, accessible, and welcoming city full of history (the Archaelogical Survey of India lists 65 ancient monuments within its urban limits).

A GOOD TOUR

Traffic in Ahmedabad is chaotic in the old city: lanes exist, but largely in theory. Getting around on foot in busy areas of even the new city can be tricky. Sometimes there are no sidewalks to speak of, just dirt, and traffic hurtles toward you from every direction. To see the main sights in a day, arrange for a car and driver. Head first to the **Jama Masjid,** then to **Ahmed Shah's Tomb** and the **Sidi Saiyad Mosque,** all in the central, walled part of town. Then proceed north to the **Hathisinh Jain Temple.** After lunch, trek a few kilometers farther north to the **Calico Museum of Textiles**—take the tour, which starts at 2:45 PM. If you prefer, skip the second (religious) part of the Calico tour and go directly on to **Sabarmati Ashram,** just across the river to the west.

One or more of the next three stops can be shoehorned into your first day, but it's probably best to save them for the next. Get on the highway to Gandhinagar and the **Adalaj Stepwell**; then travel a few minutes farther on the highway for a quick look at the **Vaishnavadevi Temple.** These two stops should take you less than an hour. If time permits, end your day by heading north on the highway to **Akshardham**, where you can relax in the peaceful gardens, participate in the evening prayers, and have a Gujarati thali dinner in the Premvati Restaurant. To fully tour Akshardham, you'll need a few hours to view all the exhibitions and temples.

TIMING If you visit all the sights, it will take you from sunup to sundown. It's better to either be choosy or to divide the tour into two days. You'll probably spend the biggest chunks of time in the Hatheesing Jain Temple, the Calico Museum, and the Sabarmati Ashram.

WHAT TO SEE

OFF THE BEATEN PATH

Adalaj Stepwell *(Adalaj Vav).* Stepwells, also called vavs or *baolis,* are unique, ornate wells, where the water can be reached by steps, found mainly in western India and have been built since around AD 600. The intricate carvings and decorative structures around the wells—all below ground—were used as cool resting places for nomads and traveling merchants. The steps allow maintenance and access to the water in the dry season. Richly carved pillars and friezes lead down 200 feet to this 15th-century five-story, octagonal, narrow-mouthed well. The surrounding gardens make a lovely respite from the dry environs. ✉ *Gandhinagar Hwy., Chharodi, 17 km (10½ mi) north of Ahmedabad* 🎫 *Free* ⏲ *Daily, sunrise to sunset.*

Ahmed Shah's Tomb. The grave of Ahmedabad's founder (and his queens and sons) is venerated with incense, flowers, and colorful cloths called *chadars,* in the manner of a Muslim saint. Women are not allowed in the central hall. ✉ *Gandhi Rd.* 🎫 *Free* ⏲ *Daily, sunrise to sunset.*

Akshardham. This 23-acre, exquisitely well-maintained cultural and religious complex is dedicated to the Lord Swaminarayan, a 19th-century saint believed by his followers to be an incarnation of god. He founded the Swaminarayan faith, which preaches nonviolence, peace, and love. To build it, it took 13 years and thousands of devoted volunteers interested in preserving Indian heritage and the religious legacy of the Swaminaryan Sanstha, a group who keeps alive the thoughts and vision of Lord Swaminarayan. The whole complex at Akshardham, finished in 1992, is made of 6,000 tons of intricately carved pink sandstone and reflects the creativity of modern India. It includes three temples, four exhibition halls, gardens, a game area, an amusement park, a restaurant, and a bookstore. The largest of the three temples, Hari Mandapam, houses a 7-foot gold-leaf-covered statue of Lord Swaminarayan. Behind the Hari Mandapam is the Vibhuti Mandapam, a temple dedicated to the revelations of Swaminarayan, which are etched in brass and glass structures. At the Hari Smruti, an *aarti* (prayer or mass) takes place at 7 PM daily. The section titled Sanskruti Vihar showcases India's culture through an interesting 12-minute boat ride. The temple is very popular with locals who flock here for the boat excursion and the rides in the amusement park. Because of a terrorist attack in 2002, security is tight here. No cell phones, cameras, electronic items, video recorders, bags/purses, or food are allowed into the temple—they must all be left at a special holding center (no charge) at the entrance. Shoes must be taken off outside the temple and kept in a shoe checkroom (no fee). ✉*J Rd., Sector 20 (on NH–8C), Gandhinagar* ☎*79/2326–0001 or 79/2326–0002* 🌐*www.akshardham.com/gujarat* 🎫*Temple free, exhibitions Rs. 125* ⏲*Oct.–Mar., Tues.–Sun. 9:30–6; Apr.–Sept., Tues.–Sun. 9:30–7. Exhibitions Oct.–Mar., Tues.–Sun. 10–5:30; Apr.–Sept., Tues.–Sun. 10–6:30.*

★ **Calico Museum of Textiles.** Visiting this vast collection is a rich way to experience the lavish colors and textures of Ahmedabad's age-old primary industry. Housed in a composite haveli (a traditional carved mansion) brought from another site, the museum buildings are connected by paths through lovely peacock-populated gardens. The museum is filled with beautiful examples of embroidery, dyeing, weaving, and other textile traditions from all over India—heavy royal costumes with gold brocade, battle scenes embroidered on silk, silver gilt, 12-foot-long Banarasi silk cummerbunds, 17th-century painted prayer cloths, and so on. For reasons of security and preservation, you must go on a rigid guided tour, which includes fascinating historical tales about the origin and use of these tapestries and garments. The two-hour tour, conducted in two parts, covers first the larger historical exhibit and then goes on to cover religious textiles. Call ahead, since the museum closes for several different holidays. No electronic items (including cell phones, cameras, and video recorders), bags or purses, or food are allowed into the museum; leave them at the holding center at the entrance. Children under 10 are not allowed. ✉*Retreat Bungalow, near Shahibag overpass* ☎*79/2286–8172 or 79/2286–5995* 🎫*Free* ⏲*Tours in winter (roughly Nov.–Feb.), Mon.–Tues. and Thurs.–Sun. at 10:30 and 2:45. Tours in summer (roughly Mar.–Oct.), Mon.–Tues. and Thurs.–Sun. at 10:30.*

Hathisinh Jain Temple. The finest of Ahmedabad's beautiful Jain temples is this elaborate white-marble structure. Established by a merchant named Hathee Singh Jain and dedicated to Dharmanath, the 15th Jain apostle, it took 25 years to complete in the mid-19th century. Every surface of every pillar and arch is intricately carved with figures and ornaments; just pick a spot and allow yourself to get lost in the details. The main structure is surrounded by 52 miniature temples representing India's holiest Jain sites. The magnificent stone lattice screens of the second-floor windows look as if they're woven of stone threads. Photography of gods or goddesses is prohibited, and menstruating women are theoretically banned from entry. ✉*Balvantrai Mehta Rd., by Delhi Gate* 🎫*Free* ⏲*Daily 5:30–1 and 3:30–7:30.*

Jama Masjid. The Friday Mosque, as it is also known, is the city's largest. It was built in 1424 by Ahmed Shah as part of a larger urban plan—it was aligned with the Teen Darwaza, an entranceway into the walled city. The prayer hall, with its niche facing Mecca, is covered by five domes held up with 260 pillars, carved in a style evocative of Hindu and Jain temple architecture. The mosque is best seen before business hours congest the surrounding streets of the old city; also avoid Fridays, the Muslim day of prayer. Shoes must be taken off and left at the entrance (women are there to keep them safe, for a small tip). A large open courtyard, 245 feet long, in the middle of the mosque becomes burning hot by midday. Jami Masjid is not accessible by car—take an auto-rickshaw into the old city to get here. ✉ *Gandhi Rd.* *Free.*

Sabarmati Ashram. Born in Gujarat, Mahatma Gandhi established his simple retreat, called the Satyagraha (literally, "seizing truth"), here when he returned from South Africa in 1915. In those days, it was close to a British-run jail from which Gandhi hoped to seek inspiration to motivate his struggle (he was imprisoned there as well). The ashram, which eventually became the nerve center of the Indian independence movement, occupies a tranquil spot on the bank of the Sabarmati River just outside the city center. From here, in 1930, Gandhi and 79 followers began the 24-mi march to the seacoast at Dandi to protest the British salt tax, galvanizing the movement that brought India independence after World War II. After the salt march, Gandhi swore never to return to Sabarmati until India gained independence. The main, open-air building houses exhibits, including a photo display documenting Gandhi's life and work (the archives here contain some 30,000 letters written by Gandhi and 6,000 photographs). The grounds also give a deep, if less tangible, impression of Gandhi's legacy: under shade trees on the lawns, students and others come to talk quietly or reflect on the history of this place and on modern India. When you sign the register in the humble cottage where Gandhi lived, your name will share the pages with those of Nelson Mandela and other dignitaries and peace workers who come to pay homage to the father of modern India. ✉ *Ashram Rd. and Sabarmati River, 7 km (3 mi) north of city center* ☎ *79/2755–7277* *Free* *Daily 8:30* AM*–6:30* PM.

Sidi Saiyad Mosque. Named for a slave in Ahmed Shah's court, this inviting mosque stands at a busy intersection in the heart of Ahmedabad, but the chiseled stone friezes on its western wall, depicting the tree of life, will transport you out of the hubbub. Built in the late 1500s by Sidi Saiyad, the mosque is a masterpiece: its stonework has the delicacy of filigree (though the full effect is reduced, as the central screen is now in Delhi's National Museum). Women are not allowed under the dome, but you can also see the friezes from a small garden outside it. ✉ *Relief Rd.* *Free* *Daily, sunrise to sunset.*

OFF THE BEATEN PATH

Vaishnadevi Temple. This temple, dedicated to the goddess Vaishnadevi (whose incarnations include Lakshmi, Saraswati, Kali, and Durga), was built as a replica of a larger, original Vaishnavadevi temple set in a mountain cave in Jammu. Five thousand years ago Vaishnadevi herself is said to have meditated in the cave, waiting for Krishna to incarnate on earth. The temple here resembles a chunk of limestone rock and is crowded with Hindu devotees who are forgoing a pilgrimage to Kashmir for fear of terrorist attacks. Walk up the winding path to the top and crawl through the narrow, cavelike passage to the main chamber to pay homage to Lakshmi, the goddess of wealth and prosperity. The three avatars you see are, from left to right, Saraswati, Vaishnavadevi, and Kali. Encircling the room are nine idols of Durga (a fierce version of the mother goddess) representing her nine different incarnations on earth. Ring the bell and accept the coin from the priest as a blessing of good fortune. ✉ *Gandhinagar Hwy., Chharodi* 🎫 *Free* 🕒 *Daily, sunrise to sunset.*

OFF THE BEATEN PATH

Magen Abraham Synagogue. India has just a handful of synagogues, and this modern, attractive synagogue is probably the only one in the entire state of Gujarat. Built in 1934 and named after the man who established it, Dr. Abraham Erulkar, it serves the very tiny Gujarati Bene-Israeli community of Indian Jews. It's famous for its collection of *sefer* (handwritten) Torahs. ✉ *Bukhara Mohallah, opposite the Parsi Agiary, Khamsa* ☎ *79/533–0981.*

WHERE TO EAT & STAY

$$ ★ ✕ **Agashiye.** At what's easily the most elegant address to dine at in Ahmedabad, an elevator takes you up to a rooftop restaurant that spreads across a covered, open-air terrace and overflows into a kind of a sunporch. Stained glass, old-style Gujarati furniture, overstuffed comfy low seating, marble tables, vividly hued puppet mobiles, and super-polite waiters clad in traditional clothes all contribute to a colorful and memorable dining experience. The sumptuous vegetarian thali—about 50 types of tiny dishes that include a variety of *papads* (lentil crisps) and other Indian breads, dozens of snacks, and a selection of sweets—is especially tasty and not to be missed. A sister restaurant next door, the Green House, serves *dosas* (crisp, thin lentil and rice pancakes) and other snacks. ✉ *The House of Mangaldas Girdhardas Hotel, opposite Sidi Saiyad Mosque, Lal Darwaja* ☎ *79/2550–6946* ▭ *MC, V.*

$ ★ ✕ **Govaradhan.** Famous for serving diners meals off "silver thalis" (platters), what's more interesting here is the lightly cooked, wholesome vegetarian food. The excellence of the food is confirmed by the number of diners who crowd this not-very-well-lit restaurant, which has a dark and overbearing decor. Warm, soft rotis, carefully spiced dal, green vegetables, interesting *farsan* (snacks), *basundi* (milk pudding), and sweets tumble onto your thali, one after the other, courtesy the friendly waiters. ✉ *Ground fl., Sapat building, opposite Rajpath Club* ☎ *79/2687–8905* ▭ *MC, V.*

$ ★ ✕ **Jacaranda.** The Taj's multicuisine restaurant and coffee shop, near the airport, is a bit far to come for a meal but if you're heading out, are tired of the city's bustle, and have sampled enough Gujarati thalis, come here to relax in luxury. The restaurant's dishes—Continental, pasta, a slice of Indian, sandwiches, cakes—are well-cooked and flavorsome. Overlooking the pool, the restaurant is pleasant and peaceful, with good service. The buffet lunches and dinners (Rs. 500), which include Indian, Continental, and a bit of Chinese, and Gujarati, are sumptuous and a good value. It's open from 6 AM until 2 AM. ✉ *Next to the army cantonment, Hansol* ☎ *79/6666–1234* ▭ *AE, D, MC, V.*

CLOSE UP

An Intro to the Famous Vegetarian Thali

The rich sauces and meats of North India are foreign to Gujarat, though many hotel restaurants do have classic Mughlai cuisine on the menu. But when in Gujarat, eat like the locals do and tuck into their vegetarian version of easy-on-the-pocket thalis (combination platters).

You will encounter thalis in all parts of India, but none are as sumptuous and vast as the Gujarati thali. So numerous and varied are the offerings—30 dishes—that they often spread across your entire table. Gujarati cuisine, slightly sweet and rich, is in a class of its own, and the sheer variety of vegetables and vegetarian preparations will astonish you.

At top thali places you may be presented with a rose and offered water to freshen up before beginning with a dozen Indian-style salads (often mixed with lentils, chickpeas, paneer, and a blend of spices called *chaat masala*) and some thin salty buttermilk, called *chaas*. Course after course follows, served by a flotilla of waiters, so eat sparingly if you want to sample the thali's full range. The next course is usually a snack called a *farsan—dhoklas*, or *handvo* (steamed lentil cakes), or *wadas* (batter-fried potato-and-pea fritters) may be offered, or perhaps a similar delicacy, to be eaten by daubing with a chutney.

Finally, a choice of pickles, condiments, chutneys, *raitas* (vegetables in yogurt), lightly pickled vegetables (like shredded green papaya) and papads (lentil crisps) will be placed on your table along with the main course on a large thali (platter). The platter will contain numerous *katoris* (small bowls) of lightly stir-fried and spiced vegetables, lentils, and yogurt- or vegetable-based curries, another small farsan, and a sweet dish. You will be initially expected to eat this course with a variety of flatbreads—some made from millet and some from wheat, and often lathered with ghee or butter. You can request multiple helpings of anything on your platter. A rice dish follows—it may be *khichdi* (a lentil-rice dish), a *pulau* (special rice preparation) or plain, steamed rice—and it is to be eaten with the vegetables, lentils, and curries already on your platter.

The final course is another sweet dish or ice cream and sometimes masala chai. You will be given a small bowl of warm water with a slice of lime to wash your hands in. First give the lime a squeeze to help cut the grease and make your hands smell good. If you have done justice to your thali, the best plan of attack may very well be a strategic retreat to your hotel for a small nap to help with digestion. And maybe by evening you'll be ready for another round.

4

$ ★ ✕ **Mirch Masala.** Done up colorfully in imitation of a roadside truck stop, with painted murals of rural scenes, Bollywood stars, and crazy signs, this cheerful basement restaurant on Ahmedabad's main shopping strip draws a congenial, affluent crowd of young people and families. Specialties include well-cooked tandoori meat dishes and kebabs as well as some Jain-inspired vegetarian dishes, made without onions or garlic. You can also sample some *chaats* traditional street snacks, prepared in a cleaner environment than the street. Expect to wait for a table. ✉ *Chandan Complex, C. G. Rd., near Swastik Char Rasta, Navrangpura* ☎ *79/2640–3340* ▭ *AE, MC, V.*

$ ✕ **Rajwadu.** Like the better-known Vishala, this outdoor restaurant in a residential suburb serves traditional vegetarian Rajashtani and Gujarati meals in faux-rural surroundings. The menus are only in Gujarati, so you're best off asking for help. ✉ *Jivaraj Tolanaka, near Ambaji Temple, Malar Talav* ☎ *79/2664–3845* ▭ *No credit cards* ⊙ *No lunch.*

$ ✕ **Seasons.** This 24-hour coffee shop is in a vastly overpriced luxury hotel. Come here for a flavor of the more modern Ahmedabad. Sandwiches, pastas, fast food, and quick meals are available in sleek and cheerful surroundings. ✉ *Pride Hotel, Judges Bungalow Rd., off S. G. Rd.* ☎ *79/3011–5555 or 79/3011–5556* ▭ *AE, D, MC, V.*

$ ✕ **"10."** As its numerical name implies, this restaurant strives for perfection. Heated plates, free bottled water, and linen napkins embroidered with the names of restaurant regulars reflect management's mission of personalized service. The chef prepares top-notch Punjabi, Continental, and Chinese fare. Try the *paneer khada masala* (cheese chunks in a spicy clove and nutmeg gravy) with some floppy garlic naan. ✉ *Urja House, Swastik Char Rasta* ☎ *79/642–5703* ▭ *AE, MC, V.*

$ ✕ **Tomato's.** Resembling a 1950s-style American diner, this eatery is crammed with American pop paraphernalia. The menu mixes Mexican, Chinese, Punjabi Indian, and Continental food, and tacks on coleslaw and apple pie. The decor outdoes most of the food, which is fresh but far from the real thing; stick with the Indian offerings. That said, the Tex-Mex food is popular with the locals. ✉ *Mardia Plaza, off C. G. Rd.* ☎ *79/2646–1998* ▭ *No credit cards.*

$ ★ ✕ **Vishala.** Try to make time for this famous 30-year-old restaurant, a re-created Gujarati village outside Ahmedabad that may serves the city's best food. Place your order at the entrance, and then try a sugarcane aperitif from the thatch-roof hut, where a boy cranks a giant cog-and-wheel contraption that squeezes juice out of the cane. Stroll on dirt paths lit by candles and lanterns toward an especially interesting kitchen-and-utensil museum and a Rajasthani puppet show performed under a palm tree, or wander into a clearing where musicians sing folk songs. When your order is ready, you sit at low, rough wood tables while turbaned waiters serve an authentic thali on *dona* and *pattals,* plates and bowls, made out of dried sal-tree leaves. Come hungry and prepared to eat with your hands. ✉ *Vasana Tol Naka* ☎ *79/660–2422, or 79/644–6554* ▭ *No credit cards.*

¢ ✕ **Gopi Dining Hall.** This busy sit-down lunchroom in the center of town is a good place to restore yourself after a morning's sightseeing. Serving hundreds of hungry office workers at once, it specializes in large Gujarati thalis. The setting is hectic, with service to match, but you'll have a tasty and filling vegetarian meal. In the evening you can try Kathiawar thali, with regional dishes from Gujarat's Kathiawar Peninsula. ✉ *Opposite Town Hall, Ashram Rd., Ellis Bridge* ☎ *79/2657–6388* ⊙ *Open 10 AM–3 PM and 6 PM–10:15 PM* ▭ *MC, V.*

¢ ✕ **South-Indian Restaurant.** Tucked into the hotel pocket on the east side of the Sabarmati River, this tiny, simple restaurant fills up at lunchtime with businesspeople and hotel staff enjoying large portions of tasty, inexpensive vegetarian fare. Choose from nearly 30 different dosas, or try the fixed thali menu, available for lunch and early dinner. Service is snappy. ✉ *Opposite Ministry Chambers, near Cama Hotel, Khanpur* ☎ *79/2560–1343* ▭ *No credit cards.*

¢ ★ ✕ **Toran Dining Hall.** Barefoot waiters dressed in plain gray uniforms swarm around the dining room of this Ahmedabad institution, tossing handfuls of chapati and puri bread and spooning refills of the various vegetarian concoctions, chutneys, and condiments into stainless-steel thali bowls. Each waiter carries just one garnish or type of food and will hover over you throughout the meal, replenishing your tray before you can eat the last bite (wave him off if you don't want more). The large, simple room is air-conditioned and dark, with pale-gray walls and mirrors set into pillars. ✉ *Opposite Sales India, Ashram Rd.* ☎ *79/2754–2197* ▭ *No credit cards* ⊙ *No dinner Mon.*

4

$$$ **Le Méridien Ahmedabad.** Glass elevators glide up and down in the soaring atrium of one of Ahmedabad's classiest hotels. Gleaming with glass and polished marble, the lobby is a hushed bustle of businesspeople. Rooms are especially elegant, with crisp white bedclothes, shiny rich wood floors, cotton rugs, and heavy silk drapes in subdued hues; beige marble bathrooms have tubs. On the east bank of the Sabarmati River, the hotel is slightly removed from the city center, a short trip across the Nehru Bridge. Rooms facing west have river views that also take in part of India's paradox: just below the towering white hotel, a dense stretch of slum housing lines the shore. **Pros:** elegant, comfortable, conveniently located. **Cons:** tiny hotel, expensive. ✉ *Near Nehru Bridge, Khanpur, Ahmedabad, 380001* ☎ *79/2550–5505* 🌐 *www.lemeridien.com* *63 rooms, 2 suites* *In-room: Wi-Fi safe, refrigerator, Wi-Fi. In-hotel: restaurant, room service, pool, gym, laundry service, parking (no fee).* ▭ *AE, DC, MC, V.*

$$$ **Taj Residency Ummed.** The Taj chain's Ahmedabad branch is upscale, low, sprawling and done in dull brown stone. A few minutes from the airport and 9 km (5½ mi) from the city, it lacks a spectacular location or exteriors. The medium-size rooms, done in rich colors such as dark green and orange silk and with mahogany-colored, heavy wood furniture, are attractive and rather comfortable, with views of either the pool or into the garden. Excellent food is served at the coffee shop and at its Indian cuisine restaurant, Narmada; service, too, is above average. **Pros:** comfortable rooms, very good restaurants, great pool. **Cons:** uninteresting location, expensive, ugly building. ✉ *Next to the army cantonment, Hansol, Ahmedabad, 382475* ☎ *79/6666–1234* 🌐 *www.tajhotels.com* *91 rooms, 2 suites* *In-room: safe, refrigerator, Wi-Fi. In-hotel: 2 restaurants, room service, pool, laundry service.* ▭ *AE, DC, MC, V.*

$–$$$ **The House of Mangaldas Girdhardas.** One of Ahmedabad's top textile-mill-owning families has converted a circa-1900 Gujarati haveli into a exceedingly charming hotel, giving each room a different character and size. Furnished with rare antique pieces, giant beds with voluminous mosquito nets and lots of colorful fabric each room is a surprise. Although the feel is decidedly old fashioned, the facilities are not—they include high-pressure showers and satellite radio. What the hotel suffers in location (it's in a busy area with not much in the way of views) it makes up with impeccable service and excellent restaurants. The Green House serves piping-hot snacks and Indian fast food, and you won't forget its attached restaurant, Agashiye thalis in a hurry. **Pros:** lovely rooms, excellent dining options, comfortable. **Cons:** no view, expensive. ✉ *Opposite Sidi Saiyid Mosque, Lal Darwaja, Ahmedabad, 380001* ☎ *79/2550–6946* 🌐 *www.houseofmg.com* *12 rooms, 2 suites* *In-room: refrigerator, safe, Wi-Fi. In-hotel: 3 restaurants, pool, gym, laundry service, parking (no fee).* *MC, V.*

$$ ★ **Cama.** The upscale, 40-year-old Cama has the city's loveliest gardens and best views of the Sabarmati. The lawns, palm trees, chirping birds, and small swimming pool grant respite after a hectic, hot day. The reception area has an elegant art-deco motif, and the lobby is decorated with Gujarati handicrafts, antiques, and has large white-marble *jalis* (intricately carved window frames). Rooms, slightly faded, are large, comfortable, and have an old-style feeling, with pale walls, dark bedspreads, and huge tubs. Request a room facing the river. The hotel has a liquor store and can get a liquor permit for you, a valuable item in this dry state. **Pros:** pretty location, large, atmospheric rooms, great garden area in back. **Cons:** aging hotel, expensive. ✉ *Khanpur Rd., Khanpur, Ahmedabad, 380001* ☎ *79/2560–1234* 🌐 *www.camahotelsindia.com* *49 rooms, 5 suites* *In-hotel: 2 restaurants, room service, pool, gym, laundry service.* *AE, DC, MC, V.*

$$ **The Grand Bhagwati.** High off the road a few kilometers from the city center, at the top of about 50 steep steps, this bright-white hotel is one of the newest in town. Its seven floors mix nouveau-riche style with modernity and sleekness, but it's also a practical and decent choice. Guest rooms, medium in size, with wood floors, have a somewhat over-jazzy decor but are clean and neat. The public spaces are slightly less tidy. **Pros:** modern and therefore comfortable, conveniently located. **Cons:** uninteresting views, inelegant decor and not very classy. ✉ *S. G. Rd., Bodakdev, Ahmedabad, 380054* ☎ *79/2684–1000* 🌐 *www.thegrandbhagwati.com* *rooms, suites* *In-room: refrigerator, Wi-Fi. In-hotel: 3 restaurants, laundry service.* *AE, DC, MC, V.*

$ **Comfort Inn Sunset.** This comfortable business hotel, part of the Choice chain, is convenient to the airport. Rooms are spacious, bright, and well appointed; they include work areas but don't have any sort of spectacular views. Bathrooms, tiled in green granite, are neat. Service is prompt and friendly, and the food served here is appetizing. Day-use rooms are available for three-fourths of the tariff. **Pros:** good service and value for money, efficient. **Cons:** no pool, far from city. ✉ *Airport Circle, Hansol, Ahmedabad, 382475* ☎ *79/2286–2200* 🌐 *www.choicehotels.com* *36 rooms, 4 suites* *In-room: refrigerator, Wi-Fi. In-hotel: restaurant, room service, laundry service, airport shuttle.* *AE, DC, MC, V* *CP.*

$ **Hotel Klassic Gold.** Because this four-story business hotel sits across the Ellis Bridge, away from the Khanpur hotel district, its room rates are better. There's a trim courtyard in front of the sleek, modern building. The large rooms have busy, mildly ugly decorations, white marble tile floors, and low beds with dark bedspreads. **Pros:** good value for money,

CLOSE UP

Gujarat's Hotels and Restaurants

Ahmedabad and some other cities have some good business hotels, and in the countryside some formerly state-run tourist facilities have been refurbished under private ownership. Several of the modest palaces of former princes have been converted to Heritage Hotels in charming rural locations. Prices are generally fairly reasonable at most hotels in Gujarat and service more than adequate. But Gujarat does believe in checking in its hotel guests bright and early, and as a result you may have to check out as early as 9 AM.

Note that Gujarat is a dry state in more ways than one. Its citizens are not allowed to consume alcohol. Alcohol is available only in a few hotel shops and hotel restaurants. Ask your hotel how to obtain a permit from the Excise Department to purchase from these stores.

North Indian and Punjabi food is widely available, and is the standard fare at most hotels and restaurants. Many dishes tend to be vegetarian here, and the local dish is the over-the-top Gujarati take on the pan-Indian thali, or combination platter. In Muslim areas of Ahmedabad and elsewhere in the state you will find excellent kebabs, *biryanis* (rice cooked with meat), and *boti* rolls (rotis stuffed with meat and rolled up).

4

close to city's main drag, comfortable and adequately sized rooms. **Cons:** unthrilling decor, no grand view, small hotel. ✉ *42 Sardar Patel Nagar, behind Navrangpura, Ahmedabad, 380006* ☎ *79/2644–5508, 79/2644–5595, or 79/2644–5578* 🖷 *79/2656–9195* *35 rooms, 1 suite* *In-room: refrigerator, Wi-Fi. In-hotel: restaurant, room service, laundry service, airport shuttle.* 💳 *MC, V.*

$ ★ **Rock Regency.** A giant, red neon sign blazes above this white, four-story hotel, very conveniently located off C. G. Road. The lobby is stylish and contemporary, with polished granite floors and twisting white pillars; in the rooms, wood paneling and pea-green-floral-upholstered chairs and headboards with white wooden frames create a garden look. **Pros:** excellent value, handy location, nice rooms. **Cons:** no view, few facilities, bathrooms are a little grubby. ✉ *Law Garden Rd., Navrangpura, Ahmedabad, 380006* ☎ *79/2656–2101 to 07* *36 rooms, 2 suites* 🌐 *www.hotelrockregency.com* *In-room: refrigerator. In-hotel: restaurant, laundry service, public Internet.* 💳 *AE, MC, V.*

$ **Sarovar Portico.** On the Sabarmati River, this eight-story business hotel with polished marble floors, manicured lawns at the back, and contemporary, typically Indian decor is an excellent value. The standard single rooms, though economical, are rather tiny and do not offer much of a view or character. The deluxe rooms, slightly more expensive, are spacious and have a large sitting area with white couches and rich blue curtains and a desk. Black shiny floors and attractive wood furniture lends the room a graceful style. Bathrooms, done in gray granite, are sparkling clean. **Pros:** great bang for your buck, comfortable rooms, nice views. **Cons:** single rooms too small and characterless. ✉ *Bhavan's College Rd., Khanpur, Ahmedabad, 380001* ☎ *79/2560–1111* 🌐 *www.*

sarovarhotels.com ⇆ *69 rooms, 12 suites* ⚲ *In-room: safe, refrigerator, Wi-Fi. In-hotel: restaurant, laundry service.* ▭ *AE, MC, V.*

NIGHTLIFE & THE ARTS

You won't find discos in this dry city, but you may well discover a new master of the sitar or the next great Indian painter. The **Darpana Academy of the Performing Arts** (☎ *79/2755–1389* 🌐 *www.darpana.com*) is in Usmanpura, a neighborhood just north of the Khanpur hotel district. Managed by renowned dancer Mallika Sarabhai, the academy has regular performances that include classical dance and folk puppet shows. The complex, which has an arts bookstore, offers training in dance, drama, music, and puppetry.

Arts performances are held in the **Tagore Auditorium** (✉ *Sanskar Kendra municipal complex, Bhagtacharya Rd.*), designed by Le Corbusier. The Sanskar Kendra complex also houses an intriguing kite museum.

The **Amdavad-ni-Gufa** (✉ *Gujarat University*) is an eccentric collaboration between the famed and controversial painter M.F. Husain and the prominent local architect Balkrishna Doshi, who collaborated with Le Corbusier. It displays contemporary arts and crafts in a cave-like space.

The **Lalbhai Dalpatbhai Institute of Indology Museum** (✉ *L.D. Institute of Indology, opposite Gujarat University, Navrangpura* 🌐 *www.namami.nic.in/mrc/LalbhaiDalpatbhaiInstituteofIndology.htm*) houses a library with a famous collection of Jain manuscripts. Its museum has an admirable collection of sculpture and pre-Moghul classical miniature painting. Also at the insitute is the **N.C. Mehta Gallery,** with an excellent collection of medieval sculpture.

The **National Institute of Design** (✉ *Paldi* ☎ *79/2662–3692*) holds regular exhibitions. Call in advance to see what's on. The **Archer Art Gallery** (✉ *Archer House, Gurukul Rd., Paldi* ☎ *79/2741–3634 or 79/2741–3872* 🌐 *www.archerindia.com*) is a leading gallery for modern and contemporary art.

SHOPPING

Ahmedabad is a great place to buy authentic Gujarati handicrafts, famous throughout India. The outstanding textiles include finely woven silk *patola* fabrics and *bhandej* (tie-dyed) materials, embroidered vests, purses, wall hangings, slippers, and bedspreads from the Kutch desert and Saurashtra. Look also for *moti-kaam* (beadwork) textiles and figures, and for copper, brass, and bronze metalwork. Mobiles and chains of small stuffed parrots, horses, and other figures of various sizes make inexpensive decorative accents and great gifts for kids. Most shops are open Monday through Saturday, 10 to 6 or 7. Some stores accept credit cards.

Banascraft (✉ *8 Chandan Complex, near Mirch Masala Restaurant, C.G. Rd., Swastik Char Rasta, Navrangpura* ☎ *79/2640–5784* 🌐 *www.banascraft.org*) is a boutique featuring embroidery and other high-quality, very attractive craftwork, including bedspreads, tablecloths, wall hangings for kids' rooms, door panels, eyeglass cases and cell-phone holders, cushion covers, clothes, purses, and tote bags. The items are made by members of the Self-Employed Women's Association (SEWA), a highly successful women's cooperative that works with slum dwellers in Ahmedabad.

Gurjari (✉ *Opposite La-Gajjar Chamber, Ashram Rd.* ☎ *79/2658–9505*), also known as the Gujarat State Handicrafts Emporium, is a fixed-price government shop with low prices and guaranteed quality. It sells an impressive variety of brightly embroidered dresses, handwoven wall hangings, beaded tribal jewelry, brass figures, traditional silver and brass *pataris* (jewelry boxes), and other examples of Gujarati craftwork.

Kapasi Handicrafts Emporium (✉ *Jitendra Chambers, R.B.I. Lane, Income Tax Square* ☎ *79/2754–1092 or 79/2754–1986*) has a very wide selection of handicrafts, particularly brass and other metalwork.

Law Garden Market (✉ *Netaji Rd.*) gets going only at around 7 or 8 each night, when the road is transformed into a vibrant, chaotic scene. Vendors drape their stalls with exquisitely embroidered wall hangings, shirts, vests, bedspreads, and more, studded with tiny mirrors. Bargain like mad.

Manek Chowk (✉ *Off Ramanlal Jani and Desai Rds.*) is a colorful bazaar in the old city where crowded, narrow streets are packed with stalls and shops selling excellent fabrics and ready-made clothes.

Honeycomb International (✉ *Cama Hotel, Khanpur Rd., Khanpur*), in the basement of the hotel, is an expensive boutique selling women's garments and some interesting antique bedspreads and home furnishing items.

4

PATAN & MODHERA

Modhera is 100 km (62 mi) northwest of Ahmedabad. Patan is 30 km (20 mi) northeast of Modhera.

Northwest of Ahmedabad, these two groups of ancient cities can be combined in a day trip or worked into a longer road trip to or from Rajasthan.

Patan was capital of the Hindu Solanki dynasty from the 8th to 12th centuries. The ornate **Rani-ka-Vav**, built in 1050, is Gujarat's most stunning baoli (stepwell), set within enormous manicured gardens. A great flight of steps leads down into the well, halting at a covered colonnade just above the waterline; the walls are covered in fine sculptures of Vishnu, Ganesh, and other Hindu gods—the entire effect is captivating. The nearby **Sahasra Linga Tank** once housed a thousand *lingas* (stone icons of the god Shiva, usually characterized as phallic symbols). Little remains of the shrines today, but the outlines of the extensive water tanks are impressive. ⏲ *Daily, sunrise to sunset* 🎟 *Entry fee Rs 100.*

On the way into town from the Sahasra Linga Tank, you can see the very modest workshop of the last makers of patola saris, who use a weaving technique called double ikat—threads used for both warp and weft are tie-dyed with costly organic dyes before they're woven into saris. Ikat is only produced in a few locations in the world, including Japan, Indonesia, Guatamala, Mexico, Uzbekistan as well as in the India states of Orissa and Andhra Pradesh. In the very uncommon double ikat variation, hand-dyed threads are precisely matched along their width as well as their length. Double ikat is produced in Indonesia as well as Patan, and it's believed that as the cloth traveled from Gujarat to Indonesia for the royal family there, the craft was passed on, too. It can take up to seven months for two weavers to produce a single 6-yard-long sari (they get orders one to two years in advance for wedding saris); the slightly blurred but intricate pattern recalls an impressionist painting. The prices match their efforts its rarity—a small stole which you can purchase on the spot will set you back Rs 25,000. Saris cost upwards of Rs. 75,000 and must be ordered. The process is fascinating to watch—ask for directions to the Salvi family's shop, **Patolawala** (✉*Salviwado, Patolawala St.* ☎*2766/232–274 or 2766/231–369* 🌐*www.patanpatola.com*). The clan will be happy to demonstrate their art in detail if you are interested. They have plans to start a museum tracking ikat art through swatches of cloth. This humble family have won innumerable awards and traveled the world with their art, once holding an exhibition at the Smithsonian Insitute. The sleepy contemporary town of Patan is famous actually for its innumerable Jain temples. In its center is the attractive temple complex called Panchasara Parasvanath, known for the beauty of its idols. Next to the temple is a Jain Gyan Mandir, or temple of knowledge, with an important collection of illuminated manuscripts. Mornings from 8 to 10 and afternoons from 2 to 4, young monks come to study the manuscripts. The caretaker has a photo album of the collection, and upon request he'll bring out a few of the original works, which are masterpieces of miniature painting. Make a small donation in return for his help.

★ The 11th-century sun-temple complex at **Modhera** is the Solanki dynasty's most striking architectural achievement. The main temple sits on a moderately high plinth, which is now missing its spire, or *shikara*. Fronting this is the *ranga mandapa,* or hall for dance and other entertainments, and a large stone bathing tank, which contains some 108 small shrines. The temple, mandapa, and tank were lined up so that on the fall and spring equinoxes, the sun rose to shine directly on the temple's main image of Surya, the sun god. All three structures are embellished with high-quality sculpture reminiscent of the better-known temples at Khajuraho, which date from the same period. The temple is much regarded by the locals, and villagers in colorful traditional clothes pour in and out of the shrine. A guide can point out scenes of the Hindu epics *Mahabharata* and *Ramayana,* as well as images of the sun god and numerous erotic scenes. On the east side of the bathing tank, a shrine houses a fine relief of Vishnu reclining on the serpent Anant Nag, preparing for the sleep that follows the cosmic dissolution and precedes the rejuvenation of the universe. ⏲*Daily, sunrise to sunset; entry fee Rs 100.*

NEED A BREAK?

Hotel New Janapath, on the highway near Radhanpur Char Rasta, Mahesana, 80 km (50 mi) north of Ahmedabad, has an excellent air-conditioned vegetarian restaurant where you can break your journey between Ahmedabad and Patan or Modhera.

WHERE TO STAY

¢ **Balaram Palace Resorts.** If you plan to enter or leave Gujarat via Rajasthan, this Heritage Hotel at the edge of the Aravalli Hills and close to two smaller wildlife sanctuaries makes an ideal base. Patan and Modhera are 73 km and 112 km (45 mi and 70 mi) away, respectively, and Mount Abu, in Rajasthan, is even closer. Once a princely mansion, it's well restored and professionally run. Accommodation is available in tents and grand-looking rooms, and there's also camel- and horseback riding on request. Palanpur, a stop on the main rail line between Ahmedabad and Delhi, is 15 km (9 mi) away. **Pros:** palace setting, historical feeling, large rooms. **Cons:** remote location. ✉ *Chitrasadni Village, off Abu-Palanpur Hwy. No. 14* ☎ *2742/284–278 to 80, 79/2657–5286 or 79/2657–6388 in Ahmedabad* 🌐 *www.balarampalace.com* *17 rooms* *In-room: refrigerator (some). In-hotel: restaurant, room service, pool, gym, laundry service.* *MC, V.*

4

KATHIAWAR PENINSULA

Gujarat's Kathiawar Peninsula, fanning out west of Ahmedabad and bounded by the Gulf of Kutch to the north and the Gulf of Khambat to the south, was once made up of dozens of small princely states, lending the region the name Saurashtra, or the "Hundred Kingdoms." Mahatma Gandhi's father was an official in Porbandar, on the coast, and the grandfather of former Pakistani prime minister Benazir Bhutto was a minister in Junagadh, near the center of the region. The landscape is dry, flat, but fertile, and dotted with hills, many of which hold temples on their summits.

Krishna, the incarnation of Vishnu whose story is told in the epic *Mahabharata,* is believed to have lived his last years in the legendary kingdom of Dwarka, at the peninsula's northwest tip. Somnath, site of one of India's most famous Shiva temples, is also on the Saurashtra coast, and just off it is Diu, an island settled by the Portuguese in the 16th century that's a Union Territory and run separately from Gujarat. Though cities such as Rajkot and Surat are booming industrial centers, Saurashtra is entirely rustic. Men and women both wear traditional costumes: an all-white ensemble of turban, jodhpurs, and a pleated shirt for men, backless embroidered blouses, called *cholis,* for women. The land supports limited agriculture, which has inadvertently led to the preservation of two excellent wildlife preserves. Good hotels, including Heritage Hotels, are gradually being established here. The easiest and most interesting way to get around is by hired car and driver; trains are slow, and air connections are few.

GIR NATIONAL PARK & WILDLIFE SANCTUARY

60 km (37 mi) southeast of Junagadh via Visavadar, 400 km (249 mi) southwest of Ahmedabad, 110 km (68 mi) north of Diu, and 160 km (99 mi) south of Rajkot.

The Gir National Park and Wildlife Sanctuary (it and its entrance town are both informally known as Sasan Gir) is a remarkable success story. The park was established in 1965 to protect a dwindling population of Asiatic lions here, then numbering just 11. This royal beast, which once roamed territories as far west as Persia and Arabia, now only has the Gir to call home. Encompassing about 1,400 square km (540 square mi) of unusual-looking hill country, the area is covered in teak forest, dotted with pools of water, languid streams, giant termite hills, grassy knolls, and shady groves. Within the forest, 16 square km (6 square mi) of land has been fenced off at Devaliya, 12 km (7 mi) from Sasan. Within this area, the movements of lions are closely monitored, and tourists coming here are guaranteed a lion viewing. Asiatic male lions are smaller and have sparser manes than their African relations, and they're used to the presence of humans. You can roll right up to them in a jeep and view them close if you do spot one; they are beautifully camouflaged in the cool, dry Gir Forest.

GUJARAT'S WILDLIFE

Viewing the rare and magnificent Asiatic lion, in addition to leopards, deer, and crocodiles, makes the Gir Forest one of Gujarat's biggest draws. Even if you don't see lions in the Gir Wildlife Sanctuary, Gujarat's hilly landscape teems with deer and other animals, giving a sense of the natural landscape celebrated in Indian art and literature. At Velavadar Wildlife Sanctuary (in southeastern Gujarat 140 km/84 mi south of Ahmedabad), you're likely to glimpse great herds of blackbuck on a large, grassy plain.

This jungle, because of its aridity, is quite different from other Indian wildlife parks. About 350 lions live here, along with an adequate population (around 300) of leopards, hordes of chitals (axis deer; 45,000), nilgai (a member of the antelope family), sambar (large Asian deer; 25,000), king cobras, langur monkeys, jackals, hyenas, mongoose, wild boars, monitor lizards, crocodiles, and hundreds of peacocks and other birds. A recent project to augment the population of *makara* (crocodiles) in the reservoir in the park was successful: many crocodiles can be seen on the Hiran river and at the Kamaleshwar reservoir inside the park.

The lion population here has bounced back enough that in one instance a pride was exported to an adjoining sanctuary. This exporting has not met with much success, however, because the Asiatic lion prefers a dry, slightly grassy habitat found at Gir rather than lusher onces found elsewhere. The forest department, refreshingly, keeps a very watchful eye of the park, ensuring the safety of the wildlife by having nearly 400 personnel roam the area, making sure park rules are enforced. Despite this, 11 lions were lost in a rare incident of poaching in 2007.

Lions are more easily encountered in dry weather (practically on every jungle safari). It's then that they tend to take jeep roads to water points in the park. The park is most beautiful, however, from October to March, when the forest is green and teeming with life. Lion-spotting is more challenging then, but the chase can be as fun as the actual sighting. Tours are restricted to open jeeps.

There is one more beast one must break for whilst inside the park: trains. The narrow gauge railway line to Junagadh makes its picturesque journey through the park in daytime.

To tour the park, have your hotel organize a jeep and a park guide or approach the orientation center. There are about 20 guides, and in high season they have to be shared. Trips to the park are organized from 6 to 11 AM and 4 to 6 PM only. Matches, lighters, and food are not allowed into the sanctuary, and you are not allowed to disembark from your vehicle.

✉Junagadh district, Sasan, 362135 ☎2877/285–541 ⊕www.girnationalpark.com 🎫Tours Rs. 2,200 (per person), tours Rs. 3,300 during fall festivals of Diwali (10 days) and Navratri (15 days), and Dec. 25–Jan. 2. Rs. 1,200 for a vehicle, payable to your hotel (you can also use your own vehicle if it runs on gasoline rather than diesel). Tipping encouraged ⏲Oct. 15 (or Nov. 15, depending on rainfall)–June 15, sunrise–sunset.

WHERE TO STAY

$$ ★ **Lion Safari Camp.** This 21-tent facility is run by Camps of India, which has campsites across the country. Come to this pretty and peaceful site and you can stay in a comfortable tent with the best address at Gir. The tents are simple but attractive, with comforts that include air-conditioning, a fan, mosquito netting, electrical outlets, bamboo mats, a seating area, a little porch outside the tent, and a cute, clean attached bathroom. They're about 1 km from Sasan town along the Hiran River, near the colorful, tiny Hiraneshwar Temple. A fixed menu of simple, predictable Indian buffet meals is included in the room rate; Continental fare and seafood are also available, and you can request for local food; they will eagerly oblige. Attached to the camp are knowledgeable safari drivers who will take you and an official park guide into the forest. Fewer tents are available in the off-season, from June 15 to October 15. Camps of India also has tent hotels at Bhuj and at the Wild Ass Sanctuary in the Little Rann of Kutch (saline desert–wetlands area) in Gujarat. **Pros:** beautiful location, unique tents, good service, all meals included. **Cons:** remote, hot in summer, no Internet. *✉Junagadh district, Sasan, 362135 ☎2877/295–507, 2877/295–508 to 04 and 011/4151–4120 in New Delhi and 022/2203–1554 in Mumbai 📠2877/285–920 ⊕www.campsofindia.com 21 tents In-room: no TV. In-room: laundry service. No credit cards FAP.*

$ **Gir Birding Lodge.** Edging Gate 2 of the Gir Sanctuary, this cozy, small, two-story lodge has an enviable location and is an economical option. Simply furnished with camouflage prints, verandas, swings, the decent, modest rooms are either within cottages or are part of the main

CLOSE UP

The Maldharis & the Siddis

Living deep inside the Gir National Park and Wildlifie Sanctuary is an unusual group of tribal people (known as "tribals" in India): the traditional cattle-herding group known as the Maldharis. *Maal* means "possessions," in this case cattle, so their name loosely and ironically translates as "those who have enough possessions." Numbering about 1,000, this group coexists fearlessly with the lions and leopards, tending their buffalo and never straying far from this extremely primitive environment—no electricity, phones, or formal education. They are not comfortable in an urban environment; the older folk do not like using public transport, and prefer camels or walking when they venture out of the park. Belonging to a mixed bunch of castes, their style of life unites them into a group who make good earnings from selling buffalo milk. (As they are vegetarian, they do not sell their buffalo for meat.) Living in the park, their costs are low and they invest much of their money in gold jewelry. The Maldharis are generally skilled at protecting their buffalos from lions, but in the event that one is killed, the Indian government gives them compensation.

About 15 km (9 mi) and 35 km (22 mi), respectively, from Sasan town are two isolated villages—Shirvan and Jhambuwaria—where Siddis (also called Hashbis) live. Siddis, who live in large numbers in the Junagadh district, trace their ancestry to East Africa. Though they speak Gujarati, dress in Indian style, are Muslim, and eat local Muslim-style food, they have marked African features that make them stand out in this countryside. The small numbers of Siddis that live in Sasan and other parts of Junagadh are aware of their roots, but the Shirvan and Jhambuwaria Siddis are less conscious of this, and merely believe themselves to be local tribals. These Africans, it is documented, were sold to India by Arab and Portuguese traders and arrived in the subcontinent between the 11th and 19th century. They were well known for their musical and dancing skills, and a large population of Siddis worked for the Nawab of Junagadh. Even today they have distinctive dances and play the *dhol* (a traditional style of drum) with great verve. A few of them are famous for their tantric or shaman powers, and the terminally ill, mentally disadvantaged, and those believed possessed are brought to them for cures. If you are interested in an excursion to meet either the Maldharis or Siddis, your hotel or a local travel agent ought to be able to set one up.

building. **Pros:** conveninetly located at the park gates, cozy, reasonably priced. **Cons:** small resort with basic furnishings. ✉*Bhambafod Naka, Junagadh district, Sasan, 362135* ☎*2877/295–5140* *2 rooms, 2 tents, 10 cottages* *In-room: no a/c (some), no phone, no TV. In-hotel: restaurant.* *No credit cards* *FAP.*

$ **Maneland Jungle Lodge.** This small lodge at Bhalchul Village, about 2 km (1 mi) from Sasan town is a slight distance from the road. The stone rooms, with Gujarati touches, are simple and well appointed, with either two or four rooms per building. Bathrooms, however, could be cleaner and service improved. Jeeps are available for trips to the park. **Pros:** peaceful location, pretty rooms. **Cons:** not clean enough, poor service, very remote. ✉*Near Bhalchul village, Junagadh district,*

Sasan, 362135 ☎2877/285–555 or 2877/285–690, 22/2618–4014 or 22/6693–8230 reservations (Juhu Hotel, Mumbai) 🌐www.maneland.com ☎2877/85555 16 rooms In-room: no a/c (some), no TV. In-hotel: pool. No credit cards FAP.

¢ **Sinh Sadan Guest House.** This forest-department guesthouse has large, sparsely furnished rooms, with grim-looking bathrooms. However, they surround a British-style flower garden next to the park orientation center, so the place gets full marks for the atmosphere and the price—but not much else. Breakfast and thali lunch and dinner are served for an additional charge. Reserving in advance requires sending a fax and then a demand draft from your bank for the first day's fee. **Pros:** attractive garden location, very economical. **Cons:** dirty rooms, poor service, dull surroundings. ✉*Deputy Central Forest Service Superintendent, Wildlife Division, Junagadh district, Sasan, 362135 ☎2877/285–540 2877/285–641 14 rooms, 1 dormitory In-room: no TV. In-hotel: restaurant, laundry service. No credit cards.*

JUNAGADH AND THE LION-AND-TIGER TRAIN

The Gir sanctuary lies southeast of the town of Junagadh, an important religious center since at least the time of Ashoka in the 3rd century BC. Once a Muslim princely state, it was one of the few states to throw in its lot with Pakistan at the time of India's independence. For the very adventurous there is a 36-hour train, the Veraval–Jabalpur Express, chugging from Junagadh to Jabalpur in the neighboring state of Madhya Pradesh. The train takes you from Gir sanctuary to India's most popular tiger sanctuary, Bandhavgarh, a short distance from Jabalpur.

SOMNATH

45 km (28 mi) southwest of Sasan Gir and 90 km (56 mi) from Diu.

The Gujarati coastline has attracted traders and invaders for centuries.

The **Shiva temple** at Somnath, which is believed to hold a naturally occurring Shiva linga, was a landmark to mariners from time immemorial until it was broken in bits in the 11th century by Mahmud of Ghazni, an invader from Afghanistan who raided India 17 times and stole away Somnath's idol jewels. Since then the temple has been rebuilt seven times, most recently in 1950 under the patronage of Sardar Patel, a Gujarati minister in Jawaharlal Nehru's government.

The modern structure is not architecturally spectacular, but its beach setting is. Devotees stream in—through metal detectors and past watchful security guards (all purses, bags, cameras, and cell phones must be checked in at a secure locker at the entrance). They come to pay homage to one of the country's most sacred Shiva shrines. At dawn, noon, and sunset, kettle drums are beaten and conch shells blown while a large oil lamp is circled around the icon. This ceremony, known as *aarti,* is meant to summon the god's presence in the temple. The small Prabhas Patan museum, in a tiny lane leading off from the right of the temple, five minutes away, holds remnants of the temple's earlier incarnations. Walk out of the temple complex and around the back to get great pictures of the temple rising next to the ocean. The beach is popular with local tourists, who arrive here to take rides on colorfully decorated camels and horses, buy knickknacks, munch snacks, and sip coconut water. A kilometer or two ahead is the bustling fishing town of Veraval, which supplies much of western Indian with seafood. The fisherfolk here wear extra-bright traditional costumes. ⏲ *Thurs.–Tues., 9–noon and 3–6; closed 2nd and 4th Sat. of each month.*

DIU

90 km (56 mi) southeast of Somnath and 110 km (68 mi) from Sasan.

Diu, a narrow island measuring 11 by 3 km (7 by 2 mi), is an early Portuguese enclave that was taken over by the Indian government in 1961 and is now administered as a federal Union Territory, separate from Gujarat. Today it's popular with budget travelers as well as Gujaratis taking advantage of its free-flowing liquor laws, a stark contrast with the officially sober state of Gujarat. Once you cross the short causeway that separates Diu from the mainland, you'll feel as though you've entered a sleepy Mediterranean market town. The streets are lined with two- and three-story buildings bearing the names of similar towns in Portuguese Africa.

If you come to Diu expecting a Goa, you will be disappointed. Or relieved. Anonymous Diu has none of the happy-go-lucky, hyper-partying, carefree air of its former sister colony, but it is a lovely, sunny, cheerful, and rather drowsy spot with great beaches. This former colony has not changed much with the times. It hasn't suffered the commercialization that much of Goa has undergone, and neither has it suffered an invasion of mangy, trance-happy beach bums. At this very tiny outpost the sights are few and can be covered in hours. For the rest of your time, be prepared to settle down on the beach and sunbathe and enjoy the calm.

An enormous **fort**, built after the Portuguese conquered, is open daily usually 9–5. Dominating the island's seaward end, it offers great views of Diu. When you walk along its ramparts you'll understand just how tenuous the colonists felt their hold on India was. Toppled gravestones alongside the fort's chapel date from as early as 1608.

The churches of St. Paul, St. Thomas, and St. Francis of Assisi, all with whitewashed, baroque facades, hold faded paintings from the Portuguese era. St. Thomas's church, perched high at the market square's north end, is now a small **museum** with some interesting artifacts. These include statues of Christ and the Virgin Mary collected from churches nearby: some of them are carved from 400-year-old petrified wood, and a few of them are pretty ghastly looking. The museum is free and open daily from 9–9. You must take off your shoes before entering.

A walk around the small ocean-side market can be appealing. Everything from clothing to cheap, made-in-China toys is on sale. Close to the airport at Nagoa Beach is a small seashell museum run by a former ship caption. Its 2,000 shells from around the world are worth a *chota* (small) peep. Hop over to the fishing village of Vanakbara in western Diu also near Nagoa to catch a flavor of the life of the traditional fisherfolk.

THE BATTLE OF DIU

In 1509 about 2,000 Portuguese won this island in a naval battle against a motley group of opponents that included the Sultan of Gujarat Mahmud Begada (whose capital was Champaner), Zamorin of Calicut, the Ottomans, and the Sultanate of Egypt. After victory, the Portuguese army brutally executed the remaining Turkish and Egyptian soldiers in retaliation for the killing of the Portuguese Viceroy's son in an earlier skirmish. The Muslim forces retaliated with two more battles until Portugal took control in 1535 and ended the Ottomans' aspirations of advancing farther in the Indian Ocean.

WHERE TO EAT & STAY

There are many small beer halls in town, but in general the island's restaurant food is disheartening. Diu has just a few regular restaurants. The town's best is Radhika Resort's Rivera, where quality North Indian fare is available. Hop over to Deepee Fast Food near the main taxi stand for a Gujarati thali or pizzas and dosas.

$ **Cidade de Diu.** The splashy, light-purple-and-red exterior of this modern hotel adds color to the neighborhood. The rooms, some of them sea-facing, are simply furnished but cheerful and tidy; bathrooms could be nicer. **Pros:** clean, neat rooms, good setting, reasonable. **Cons:** simple decor, dull bathrooms, not on the beach. ✉*Near vegetable market, 362520* ☎*2875/254–595, 2875/254–695, or 2875/254–443* 📠*2875/252–754* *31 rooms* *In-room: In-hotel: restaurant, room service, bar, laundry service.* *MC, V.*

$ **Radhika Beach Resort.** Across the road from Diu's most popular beach, Radhika's two-story white villas with red shingle roofs encircle a courtyard and pool area that has Grecian statues, flying dolphins, and other kitschy touches. The large rooms are attractive and fronted by a veranda. They're furnished with floral Indian bedspreads and matching curtains, white-marble tiles, and large, clean bathrooms. Private cottages are available for honeymooners and others seeking seclusion and romance. Its neatly decorated Rivera restaurant offers hearty north Indian specialties like *nans* (oven-baked Indian-style breads), tandoori chicken, chicken curry, *paneer* palak (spinach with cottage cheese) and more, as well as a few Continental choices, offering an air-conditioned, relaxing place to have a meal, even if you are not staying in the hotel. **Pros:** pretty, comfortable, close to the beach and airport, good food. **Cons:** some may find it cheesy, a tad expensive, far from town. ✉*Nagoa Beach, 362520* ☎*2875/252–553 to 2875/252–555* *www.radhikaresort.com* *40 rooms, 4 cottages* *In-room: refrigerator. In-hotel: restaurant, bar, pool, gym.* *MC, V.*

¢–$ ★ **Magico do Mar Beach Holiday Resort.** Diu has several newish hotels and older Portuguese-style lodgings, but none are as attractive as this complex of rooms and cottages about a ½ km (¼ mi) over the border in Gujarat, within striking distance of the town of Diu. The plain reception room was constructed in 1937 by the Maharaja of Junagadh. Opt for the slightly more expensive beach-facing cottages, which are a more upscale version of typical, Gujarati village homes. They have large wooden swings on the front porches but the bathrooms are slightly messy. The resort looks out over the clean and private Ahmedpur Mandavi Beach, where meals are served under a thatch canopy. It's possible to go parasailing, rent a speedboat or water scooter, and ride a camel here. **Pros:** idyllic setting, full of character, pretty cottages. **Cons:** far from town, could be cleaner. ✉*Diu Checkpost, Ahmedpur Mandvi, Una district, Junagadh, 362510* ☎*2875/252–567* 🌐*www.magicodomar.com* *24 rooms, 15 cottages* *In-room: no a/c, no TV (some). In-hotel: restaurant, laundry service, airport shuttle.* *No credit cards* *MAP.*

DIU'S BEACHES

The beaches of Diu, offer plenty of solitude and beauty. Unlike many of Goa, these strips of sand are pristine and relatively free of stalls selling soda pop and handicrafts and armies of hawkers. Nagoa Beach is close to the tiny airport (it only gets six flights a week). Horseshoe-shaped Nagor is fringed by branching African hoka palms and is ideal for swimming. Ghoghla Beach, a little farther away, has a variety of water sports.

¢ **Hotel Kohinoor.** Designed to resemble a Portuguese villa—an all-too-modern one at that—this hotel has the best (and technically the only) disco in the Gujarat region. Guest rooms are modern and very clean with modest, unremarkable furnishings and upholstery, but shiny marble floors. Each has a small sitting area and views of either the trim flower garden or the large pool and open-air hot tub. A few buildings away is an ayurveda treatment center belonging to the hotel. The resort is close to the city center and overlooks the Arabian Sea. Try a Manchow soup, a spicy thick vegetable noodle soup, and the Hyderabadi *biryani* (meat cooked with rice) at the restaurant. **Pros:** quiet, well priced, garden location. **Cons:** ersatz feel, location is neither in town nor at the best beach, boring decor. ✉*Fofrara-Fudam, 362520* ☎*2875/252–209, 2875/253–575 to 2875/253–577* 🌐*www.hotelkohinoordiu.com* *50 rooms* *In-room: refrigerator (some). In-hotel: restaurant, room service, pool, laundry service.* *No credit cards.*

¢ **Hotel Samrat.** A few blocks from the tourist office and town square, this is the best and most hospitable budget hotel in town. The functionally decorated, slightly dull rooms, housed in a modern building and some with balconies, have beautiful views of the city. They're also clean and comfortable. Larger family rooms offer accommodations for 4 or 6 people. Hefty discounts are possible in the off-season. **Pros:** cheap, functional, clean, well located. **Cons:** no beach, little atmosphere, dull, modern look. ✉*Near vegetable market, 362520* ☎*2875/252–354, 2875/254–554, or 2875/252–514* 🌐*www.cidadedediu.com* *30 rooms, 2 family rooms.* *In-room: no a/c (some). In-hotel: restaurant, bar, laundry service.* *MC, V.*

¢ **Hotel São Tomé Retiro.** You'll stay on top of an old Portuguese church if you check in here. Basic, reasonably decent, no-frills rooms come with the atmospheric surroundings. The Portuguese-style food and barbecue food are both recommended. **Pros:** cool surroundings, great home-style food, cheap, hospitable. **Cons:** basic rooms, small hotel, no beach. ✉ *Next to Diu Museum, 362520* ☎ *2875/253–137* *8 rooms* *In-room: no a/c, no TVs. In-hotel: restaurant* *No credit cards.*

PALITANA

150 km (93 mi) northeast of Diu, 277 km (172 mi) southwest of Ahmedabad.

★ Hilltop pilgrimage sites are a common feature in Saurashtra, but none is quite so expansive and beautiful as **Shatrunjaya.** Its 863 temples were built by Jains on a 600-meter-high (1,969-foot-high) hill overlooking the ocean. Near the modern-day city of Palitana, it's about 50 km (31 mi) from the town of Bhavnagar. (The actual temple count varies from 800 to more than 2,500, depending on the area under scrutiny: beyond the main hill of temples, shrines continue to abound on other hills, for an area of 20 acres or more.)

A prosperous, small-merchant community, the Jains have maintained and refurbished the temples over the centuries; so while many of the temples here date from the 1600s, the attraction is not that of an ancient ruin but that of a living faith. In fact the temples were rebuilt some 16 times over, especially after they were attacked by Muslim king Alauddin Khilji. This temple city is one of the 100 *tirthas,* or holy spots, of the Jains. High above the surrounding floodplain, the place has an eerie calm about it. The temples are only open to the public during the day; at night, the gates are closed, and the temples' only inhabitants are their figures: white marble sculptures that each represent a Jina, one of the extremely few human souls who, the Jains believe, have been able to liberate themselves from the cycle of rebirth. This hill marks the spot where, according to myth, such a Jina was liberated; he's worshiped in Shatrunjaya's largest temple as Adinath, the original master; called Lord Rishabha, he is the first Tirthankar or mortal to achieve salvation.

You reach the temples by climbing the mountain—an exhausting mile-long stretch of 4,000 steps rising some 2,000 feet to the summit. This can take two hours although there is an option to use a *doli* (palanquin) carried by two bearers. Accompanying you will be lay pilgrims, white-garbed monks, and *sadhvis* (female sadhus). Jains hold visiting Palitana once in their life very important and one of the means towards reaching salvation. The central tenet of Jain philosophy is nonviolence, or *ahimsa,* and Jain practice is believed to have influenced Mahatma Gandhi. Some of the ascetics here wear gauze filters over their mouths so as not to harm microorganisms with their breathing; and before they prostrate themselves at the shrines, they take care to sweep the ground of any tiny creatures beneath them. There is a small fee for both still and video cameras within the temple complex, and photography is not allowed inside the individual temples. Put aside two hours to have a good look at this extraordinary hill of temples. *Rs. 100 for camera* *Daily, sunrise to sunset.*

4

WHERE TO STAY

$ **Nilambag Palace.** The sumptuous palace (built in 1869) of Bhavnagar's former maharaja, once the ruler of a fairly prestigious state, is now a Heritage Hotel and the most upscale lodging in the area. The elegant rooms are furnished with striking, old pieces of furniture, and the main sitting areas of the palace include such decorations as a stuffed cheetah, oil paintings of former rajas, and other trappings of a royal life. Chinese, Indian, and Continental food is served. This palace hotel makes the most comfortable base for excursions to Palitana, 50 km (31 mi) southwest of here, and to Velavadar. **Pros:** elegant living at a historic location, close to a sanctuary (60 km [37 mi]). **Cons:** a little expensive. *50 Km (31 mi) Northeast of Palitana Bhavnagar, 364001 278/242–9323, 278/242–4241, or 278/243–2295 www.nilambagpalace.com 20 rooms, 1 suites, 8 cottages In-room: refrigerator. In-hotel: restaurant, room service, pool, laundry service. MC, V.*

¢ **Sumeru.** Run by the Tourism Corporation of Gujarat, this hotel is the best place to stay in Palitana itself, and its dining room is the only restaurant in town. The rooms are no more than basic (five are air-conditioned), and the dining room keeps an erratic schedule. Checkout is at 9 AM. **Pros:** very low rates, decent food, close to Shatrunjaya. **Cons:** basic rooms, service unexceptional. *Station Rd., Palitana Reserve through Tourism Corporation of Gujarat, Ltd., H.K. House, Ashram Rd., Ahmedabad, 364002 2848/252–327 79/2658–9172 reservations 79/2656–8183 16 rooms, 2 dormitories In-room: no phone, no a/c (some), no TV. In-hotel: restaurant. No credit cards.*

VELAVADAR WILDLIFE SANCTUARY

65 km (40 mi) north of Bhavnagar, 85 km (53 mi) north of Palitana, 140 km (87 mi) south of Ahmedabad.

Once a hunting reserve for the maharaja of Bhavnagar, this small *vidi* (grassland) sanctuary is home to large herds of graceful Indian blackbuck. Often depicted in miniature paintings, this elegant and fast-running, wholly Indian antelope has ringed, spiral horns and black, brown, and white coloring. Although it's been hunted almost to extinction elsewhere, here its only predator is the Indian wolf, also an endangered species. The park, edging the Gulf of Khambhat, is only 34 square km (13 square mi) but it's home to about 1,000 blackbuck, with more coming in from surrounding areas when foraging is plentiful. The terrestrial and rare bustard bird, as well as wild pigs, jackals, foxes, wild cats, cobras, and porcupines are also here. The park is open all year round, but chances of seeing the wolf and the blackbuck are best from October through November and February through March, its mating and foaling seasons, respectively. *10 km (6 mi) off main Bhavnagar–Ahmedabad hwy.; turnoff is between the towns of Vallabhipur and Barvala 0278/242–8644 Sanctuary $5, guide $10, vehicle entry fee $10, camera fee $5, video-camera fee $200 Daily 6:30–8.30 and 4:30–6:30.*

VADODARA

112 km (70 mi) south of Ahmedabad, 419 km (260 mi) north of Mumbai.

Vadodara—commonly called Baroda—was, until recently, a laid-back garden city and college town on the banks of the Vishwamitri River. It's now an urban hub with a population of just over 1.5 million. The city dates back to the days of legend, and before Independence it was (along with Mysore) the capital of one of the largest and best-administered princely states of the British period; its kings, called Gaekwads, were honored with the highly prestigious 21 rounds of cannon fire on arrival anywhere. The Gaekwads helped their people prosper and accumulated for themselves a great many artistic treasures from all over India and the world. The city retains a pleasant civic atmosphere, with some fine old buildings, though much of its greenery has been overwhelmed by city sprawl. Vadodara's limited sights are not particularly compelling and do not warrant a special place on your Gujarat itinerary, but if you happen to be passing through this city on your way to Champaner or Daman, you might want to pop into the Baroda Museum and Picture Gallery at the pretty Sayaji Bagh. Vadodara has loads of shops but not too many handicrafts on sale. Try Raj Handicrafts, 5 B.N. Chambers, opposite Welcomgroup Vadodara, R.C. Dutt Road, for interesting brass ornaments and Gujarati crafts. Or head to the government craft emporium, Gurjari, at 415 G-2/3 Vantage Point, opposite Masonic Hall Productivity Road, Alkapuri (☎265/357–575). Vadodara is just one hour from Ahmedabad and connected by an excellent highway.

The blue-domed, ancient-looking **College of Fine Arts** at Maharaja Sayajirao University is known as the finest in India, and its graduates include India's best-known contemporary painter, M.F. Husain. Stopping by just to take in the attractive exterior of this building is worthwhile—definitely a Vadodara photo op. The university's **Archaeology Faculty** has a small display area with an excellent rendition of life and crafts in the ancient Indus Valley Civilization.

Many graduates stay in town, exhibiting their work at the **Nazar Arts Gallery** (☎*265/322–945*).

The large, attractive park known as Sayaji Bagh, on University Road, contains the **Baroda Museum and Picture Gallery,** open daily except Monday 10:30–5:30 (*Rs 200*). The former royal collection is housed in a eye-catching Indo-Saracenic palace in the center of the peaceful park and showcases a very interesting assortment of artifacts (some from Japan, Nepal and China), historical objects, weapons, art and paintings as well as rare Hindu and Jain sculpture and miniature paintings. There are also some zoological specimens. Giant, beautifully carved doors unearthed from former Gujarati havelis can be seen here, too. There is also a surprisingly large collection of pictures attributed to international artists like Cezanne, Van Gogh, and Matisse. Sayaji Bagh also has a floral clock; a wee, boring zoo; and an interesting mini train that chugs about the park.

The former royal collection is housed in the **Maharaja Fateh Singh Museum** on the run-down, once-gorgeous grounds of the maharaja's palace. Just taking a peek at the ornate gates of this palace and its exterior is an experience—a peep into how some of India's top royalty once lived. The palace now houses a museum that's popular with the locals but does not have that much to look. However, there is an excellent assembly of work by the important 19th-century painter Raja Ravi Verma, as well as those of Titian, Poussin, and Raphael. ⊠*Nehru Rd.* ☎*265/ 2426372* *Rs. 100* *Tues.–Sun. 10:30–5.*

Better-maintained examples of the maharaja's architectural taste are the **Naya Mandir,** or Law Courts, and the **Kothi Building,** or Secretariat, both in the center of town. Both structures display the mixture of Moghul and Gothic elements common to the public works of British India.

The **Kirti Mandir,** a memorial or cenotaph to the Gaekwad family, is decorated with murals painted by Nandalal Bose, a leader in the Bengal school of painting that launched contemporary art in India early in the 20th century. ⊠*Old City, near Vishwamitri Bridge.*

The **Makarpura Palace,** near GIDC in the southern outskirts of the town, is designed in an Indo-Italianate style, now houses a training school for the Indian Air Force; take an auto-rickshaw through the campus to get a glimpse of the grounds.

If you stay in Vadodara, you can make side trips to some truly out-of-the-way medieval sights. World Heritage site **Champaner,** 47 km (29 mi) northwest of Vadodara in the Girnar Hills, was an 8th-century Rajput capital and later Muslim capital. The capital moved to Ahmedabad in the 1500s, so Champaner is now—like Mandu or Fatehpur Sikri (in North Central India)—an intriguing ghost town full of wonderful architecture. Preservation groups are working to spruce it up, but the place is not yet on many travelers' itineraries. Most of the buildings date from the 15th century and blend Muslim and Jain influences; a few Hindu temples date from as early as the 11th century. Check out the beautifully built Jama Masjid.

On the way back to Vadodara you can stop at **Pawagadh Fort,** just a few kilometers outside Champaner, for an impressive view. The fort is mostly in ruins, but the Hindu and Jain temples here remain active pilgrimage centers. Its history is touching: once a Rajput fortress, it was overcome at the hands of Mahmud Begada, a Muslim king of Gujarat, in 1484 after a siege. This defeat led to the *johar* or self-immolation. Overshooting Vadodara brings you to **Dabhoi Fort** (30 km, or 19 mi, southeast of town), built by the Raja of Patan in the 13th century. The fort's four ornate gates are early masterpieces of the Solank Rajput style. Dabhoi town is a center of one of the oldest narrow gauge lines and home to some impressive steam engines.

Nearby, the town's **Kali temple** also has beautiful carvings. Dabhoi is also home to the world's largest collection of steam locomotives.

To make travel arrangements or change money in Vadodara, ask your hotel or contact **Narmada Travels** (⊠*19–21 Panorama, 2nd floor, R. C. Dutt Rd.* ☎*265/235–8062*).

WHERE TO EAT & STAY

Excellent Gujarati thalis are a bit harder to find in Vadodara, but head to Sayajigunj for some interesting eateries. Near the Sardar Patel statue you can also find sandwiches, cappuccinos, and desserts at Café Coffee Day or Subway (a branch of the international chain), and pizzas at Uncle Sam's Pizzas.

¢ **Haveli.** You can sample a scrumptious and enormous traditional vegetarian thali at this restaurant, within a small old-style bungalow. At Vadodara's best restaurant, the food is first-class and the typical Gujarati surroundings run to white Warli murals (tribal stick-figure art) on red walls interspersed with mirrors. *Opposite B.B.C. Tower, Sayajigunj 265/324–8585 Closed 3 PM–7 PM.*

Fodor's Choice ★

¢ **The Rajputana.** Bead curtains, bright copper utensils, and Gujarati knickknacks hanging on daubed white walls decorate this sunny, second-floor restaurant. Head here for typical North Indian fare, vegetarian and nonvegetarian. Highlights include naans, paneer dishes, and more. *Opposite Sardar Patel Statue, Sayajigunj 265/662–2799.*

$$ **Taj.** An ugly, modern and drab exterior conceals some comfortable, attractive rooms with wooden floors and a lot of emphasis on white and black. The public areas in this sprawling hotel lack style but not luxury. Though it's away from the center of town in a not-very-pleasant neighborhood, the Taj is nevertheless one of the city's best hotels. **Pros:** alluring pool area, efficient and luxurious. **Cons:** ugly, expensive for the area, poor location. *Akota Gardens, Vadodara, 390020 265/661–7676 or 265/235–4545 www.tajhotels.com 86 rooms In-room: safe, refrigerator, Wi-Fi. In-hotel: restaurant, room service, laundry service.* AE, DC, MC, V.

$$ **Welcomgroup Vadodara.** An excellent place to relax after the rigors of traveling, this is the city's most upscale hotel. An attractive mural by the prestigious painter Anjolie Ela Menon lights up the lobby, and the rooms are classy, with marble floors, rich blue furnishings, and comfortable, stylish wood furniture. The Ruchika restaurant serves good North Indian Mughlai food; the Cascade serves interesting Western and Chinese dishes. **Pros:** well located, elegant rooms. **Cons:** expensive, far from airport. *R. C. Dutt Rd., Vadodara, 390005 265/233–0033 www.itcwelcomgroup.in 134 rooms, 6 suites In-room: safe, refrigerator, Wi-Fi. In-hotel: 4 restaurants, pool.* AE, DC, MC, V.

¢ **Aditi.** Centrally air-conditioned, Aditi is within walking distance of the university and a short auto-rickshaw ride from the train station and most of Vadodara's sights. Guest rooms are on the small side, slightly musty and have not much of a view but are fairly clean. Furnishings are of the busy and shudderingly bold variety, but the hotel's prices are very difficult to beat. One restaurant serves a range of North Indian dishes, and Gujarati food is available at its Pearl eatery. **Pros:** cheap, in the city center. **Cons:** dull rooms lacking maintenance. *Opposite Sadar Patel Statue, Sayajigunj, Vadodara, 390005 265/236–1188 265/236–2259 53 rooms, 8 suites In-hotel: 2 restaurants, room service, laundry service.* MC, V.

¢ **Surya.** In a modern, white building block, this popular mid-range business hotel offers good comforts. The clean guest rooms have shiny white tile floors and dark not-so-pretty furnishings, a small sitting area and not much in the way of views; bathrooms are not super-clean but passable. A mild medicinal smell pervades the hotel. Vegetarian food and Gujarati thalis are offered at the two in-house restaurants. **Pros:** conveniently located, good food, easy airport transfer. **Cons:** room bathrooms could be cleaner. ✉*Sayajigunj, Vadodara, 390005* ☎*265/236–1361* 🖷*265/236–1555* *76 rooms* *In-room: Wi-Fi. In-hotel: 2 restaurants, room service, laundry service.* 💳*MC, V.*

RAJASTHAN & GUJARAT ESSENTIALS

To research prices, get advice from other travelers, and book travel arrangements, visit www.fodors.com.

AIR TRAVEL

There are domestic airports in Jaipur, Jodhpur, and Udaipur. Although there's an airport in Jaisalmer, civilian flights no longer operate for security reasons. Indian Airlines flies among the three and connects Rajasthan with Delhi, Bombay, and Aurangabad. Ask your travel agent about service on private airlines and remember that flights to and within Rajasthan fill up—reserve well in advance. The Udaipur–Jodhpur sector is particularly difficult as there's no rail connection between the two cities. Private carriers such as Jet Airways and Kinfisher offer some connections in Rajasthan, including daily flights from Delhi to Jaipur, Udaipur, and Jodhpur.

Air India, Air France, Air Alitalia, British Airways, KLM, and Lufthansa have offices in Jaipur.

Several airlines fly to Ahmedabad from Mumbai, Delhi, Bangalore, and Chennai daily, and often twice a day. You can also fly to Vadodara from Mumbai or Delhi. Four flights a week connect Mumbai with Bhavnagar, and five flights a week leave Mumbai for Diu. There are also daily flights to Rajkot, and both this and Diu are well located for accessing Sasan Gir.

Airlines & Contacts **Deccan** (☎*city code plus 3900–8888* 🌐*www.airdeccan.net*). **Go Air** (☎*79/1/800/222-111 or 9223/222-111* 🌐*www.goair.in*). **Air India** (☎*1407* 🌐*http://indian-airlines.nic.in*). **Indigo** (☎*99/1038–3838 or 1/800/180–3838* 🌐*www.goindigo.in*). **Jet Airways** (✉*Ratnanabh Complex, 1st fl., opposite Gujarat Vidyapith Income Tax, Ashram Rd., Ahmedabad* ☎*79/2754–3304 to 10, 265/233–7051 or 265/233–7052 in Vadodara, 2875/255–030 in Diu, 281/247–9623 or 281/247–9624 in Rajkot, 278/243–3371 or 278/243–3372 in Bhavnagar* 🌐*www.jetairways.com*).

Kingfisher (☎*20/2729–3030 in Mumbai* 🌐*www.flykingfisher.com*). **SpiceJet** (☎*1800/180–3333 or 987/180–3333* 🌐*www.spicejet.com*).

AIRPORTS & TRANSFERS

Jaipur's Sanganer Airport is about 13 km (8 mi) south of town; a taxi into town costs about Rs. 150. Jodphur's airport is 5 km (3 mi) from the city center; a taxi into town costs about Rs. 150. Udaipur's Dabok Airport is 25 km (16 mi) from the city center; the ride costs about Rs. 250.

Ahmedabad Airport is 15 km (9 mi) from the city center. You'll find plenty of taxis plus a booth selling prepaid fixed-price rides. The trip should cost roughly Rs. 150–Rs. 200. Vadodara Airport is 8 km (5 mi) from town, Rajkot Airport is 4 km (2½ mi) from town and Diu Airport is 2 km (1 mi) from most hotels and 8 km (5 mi) to the town.

CARS & DRIVERS

It's not cheap, but having a car and driver to yourself is highly efficient if you're short on time. In Rajasthan, hire a car through your hotel or a recognized travel agent, the latter of which will be cheaper. It should cost about Rs. 10–Rs. 12 per km (½ mi). If you organize a car directly through the driver, it will be cheaper but check the vehicle and driver out properly the day before you start.

Expect to spend about Rs. 3,200 from Delhi to Jaipur in an air-conditioned car, or about Rs. 2,500 in a non-air-conditioned alternative. Know that because the driver has to return to his port of origin, you pay the round-trip fare even if you're going one-way.

Rajasthan's roads are not in good shape, and the going is slow—when calculating driving time, plan to cover 40 kph–50 kph (25 mph–31 mph) at best. That said, driving is an excellent way to see the Indian countryside and glimpse village life.

Jaipur is a 5½-hour drive from Delhi on National Highway (NH) 8. This is a congested industrial road with a high accident rate, so prepare for a trying experience.

The Shekhawati region is usually a five to six hour drive from Delhi, and in this case driving is much quicker and smoother than train travel. Hire a car and driver through a Delhi travel agency and plan to pay about Rs. 10 per km, with a halt charge (for stopping overnight) of Rs. 200–Rs. 250 per night. A thorough tour of the region should cost about Rs. 4,000.

Roads are rough in and out of Jodhpur, and the going is slow. Don't expect to average more than 40 km (25 mi) per hour. Udaipur is on National Highway 8, which links Bombay and Delhi. Again, expect your road speed to top out at 40 km (25 mi) per hour.

In Gujarat, rates for cars without air-conditioning start at Rs. 5–Rs. 8 per km (½ mi), usually with a minimum of 250 km (155 mi) per day. Additional charges apply to overnight stays and the driver's return trip. A driver needs to be tipped and given time off and money for lunch. Arrange for a car and driver through a travel agency or tourist office—your hotel can do it for you, but you'll pay more.

Contacts **Camarro Travels** (*✉ Lal Darwaja, Ahmedabad ☎ 79/2550–3565 or 79/2550–2661 ✉ camarro@satyammail.com*). **Deepak Travels** (*✉ 23/33 New Jaganath Plot, Rajkot ☎ 281/248–3469 or 98/2420–8487*). **Oceanic Travel** (*✉ Main market, Diu ☎ 2875/252–180*). **Umeru Travels** (*✉ Sasan, Gir ☎ 997/906–5101*).

MONEY

ATMS ATMs are easily avialable in Rajasthan. In major cities it's possible to at least get a credit card advance from a bank (which works for MasterCard and Visa), if not actually withdraw money from a machine. Most machines do take foreign credit cards—but do not rely on ATMs as a source of cash in Rajasthan. The Bank of Baroda in Jaisalmer offers credit card advances weekdays 10–2 and Saturday 10:30–11:30. Most Bank of Baroda's are open 9–1 and 2–3:45.

Ahmedabad is probably the best place to find an ATM in Gujarat. C. G. Road is the city's major financial center, home to Citibank, HSBC, and other banks. The State Bank of India at Lal Darwaja (the bus stand) and the Bank of Baroda on Relief Road on the eastern bank of the Sabramati River also have ATMs.

CURRENCY EXCHANGE Nearly all hotels exchange foreign currency for their guests. You might get better rates at state banks, but the hassle of waiting in line may defeat the purpose.

TAXIS & AUTO-RICKSHAWS

Taxis are unmetered in Jaipur, Jodhpur, and Udaipur, so ask your hotel for the going rate and negotiate with the driver before you set off. For sightseeing within Jaipur and Jodphur, hire a cab through your hotel or the RTDC's Tourist Information Center (Visitor Information). Depending on the distance to be covered, a taxi for half a day will cost about Rs. 600, and for a full day about Rs. 1,200.

Auto-rickshaws in Jaipur are metered, but the meters are often ignored. Insist on adhering to the meter or set the price in advance. The rate should be no more than Rs. 4.50 per km (½ mi), with a minimum total of Rs. 10. Auto-rickshaws in Jodphur and Udaipur are unmetered, so you must agree on a price before departing. You can also hire an auto-rickshaw by the hour, for about Rs. 30 per hour. Note that all of these rates go up by about 50% after 11 pm.

In Gujarat, savvy auto-rickshaw driver can reach your destination faster than a cabbie or a driver. At this writing, fares in Ahmedabad are about Rs. 10 per km, with a starting charge of about Rs. 4; but rates change as fuel prices increase, and fares are theoretically calculated by matching the meter amount to the adjusted rate on the driver's tariff card. If the driver refuses to show you the card, get another rickshaw or agree on a fare in advance (ask a hotel staffer or a passerby what the fare should be). You can catch a taxi at the Ahmedabad airport or call one through your hotel. They're not plentiful, however, so you may have to hire a car and driver for the day.

TRAIN TRAVEL

In Rajasthan, if you want to travel overnight, it's safer and more comfortable to take the train than a bus or car. Trains offer classes of service for all budgets (seats and sleepers, air-conditioning and nonair-conditioning, reserved and unreserved).

The Shatabdi Express, an air-conditioned chair-car train, travels every day but Sunday from New Delhi to Jaipur, roughly a five-hour trip.

The Pink City Express covers the same ground in about six hours. The Shekhavati Express runs daily from Delhi to Jaipur, stopping at Jhunjhunu, Mukungarh, and Sikar. The Shekavati Express runs overnight and arrives in Jaipur around 7 am.

The daily Bikaner Express from Delhi passes through Shekhavati en route to Bikaner. The overnight Superfast Express leaves New Delhi at 8 pm and reaches Jodhpur at 5:30 am. A separate Superfast Express connects Jodhpur with Jaipur in four hours; contact the Tourist Information Center in either city for more information.

Daily trains connect Udaipur with Jaipur, Ajmer, Chittaurgarh, Ahmedabad, and Delhi; for more information, call the Tourist Reception Center. Trains also run out to Jaisalmer from Jodhpur but they're significantly slower than the road routes.

There are also trains leaving from Jaipur that pass through the wildlife destinations of Ranthambhore and Bharatpur. Of course, for the ultimate rail experience in Rajasthan, you would have to take the famous Palace on Wheels, a luxury train that runs across the state, connecting its major sights.

In Gujarat, Ahmedabad and Vadodara are connected to Mumbai, Delhi, and Rajasthan by good, fast trains, including the Rajdhani Express. The air-conditioned Shatabdi Express connects Ahmedabad with Vadodara in 1½ hours every day except Friday, and Vadodara with Mumbai's Central Station in 5½ hours. It is possible to reach Junagadh, near Sasan, by overnight train from Ahmedabad.

Because Gujarat was ruled separately from British India (by various local princes), its rail network has yet to be fully integrated into the Indian grid—many lines are on slow, meter-gauge tracks. You can book train tickets on the Internet or through your hotel. A comfortable but expensive way to see Ahmedabad, Sasan Gir, Diu, and Palitana is the Royal Orient luxury train. It makes a seven-night round-trip from Delhi, stopping for sightseeing in both Rajasthan and Gujarat. Rates in season are US$200 per person per night for a double-occupancy berth, $175 for triple occupancy.

Two express trains run daily between Bhavnagar and Ahmedabad, and there is slower service on the meter-gauge line between Palitana and Ahmedabad. The station nearest Diu is at Veraval, near Somnath, on the Gujarati mainland 90 km (56 mi) to the northwest. Overnight trains connect Ahmedabad with Veraval and Junagadh, and taxis outside the Junagadh station can take you the final 60 km (37 mi) to Sasan Gir for about Rs. 500 if you haven't arranged to be picked up by your hotel.

Train Information **Palace on Wheels** (✉ *Rajasthan Tourism Development Corp., Palace on Wheels Division, Bikaner House, Pandara Rd., near India Gate, New Delhi 110011* ☎ *11/2338–1884 in Delhi, 888/463–4299, 609/683–5018 U.S. and international* 🌐 *www.palaceonwheels.com).*

Royal Orient Train (*Tourism Corporation of Gujarat, Ltd. ✉Ashram Rd., Ahmedabad ☎132 train information, 132, 131, or 135 ticket information 🌐www.gujarattourism.com*). **Shatabdi Express** (*☎131 for inquiries, 135 reservations anywhere in Rajasthan*). **Superfast Express** (*☎291/131, 291/132 in Jodhpur*). **Jodhpur Tourist Information Center** (*☎291/244–010*). **Udaipur Tourist Reception Center** (*☎294/241–535, 294/131 general train information*).

TRAVEL AGENTS & TOURS

Alternative Travels organizes terrific stays in artisan villages; trips focusing on music and dance; treks; and bike, jeep, horse, and camel safaris. The Rajasthan Mounted Sports Association gives riding and polo lessons in Jaipur; runs elephant, horse, and camel day trips in Shekhawati; and leads horse and jeep safaris, which may include stays at palaces and forts. Rajasthan Safaris and Treks offers less luxurious but more authentic camel, camel-cart, and jeep safaris out of Bikaner. Food (traditional desert food) and water are provided, but you're on your own when it comes to toilet facilities.

Roop Nivas Safaris leads a Shekhawati Brigade Horse Safari around the colorful painted towns of this region, and offers longer safaris from Nawalgarh to Pushkar or Bikaner. You'll be sleeping in tents with bathroom facilities or at palace and fort hotels. Royal Safari administers treks, camel safaris, and nights in the desert around Bikaner, Jodhpur, and Jaisalmer, as well as visits to traditional villages, craftspeople's homes, little-known fairs, and ashrams.

Karwan Tours in Jaipur and TGS Tours and Travels (an American Express representative) in Jaipur and Udaipur can also help with general travel arrangements, including a hired car with driver to any location in Rajasthan. Le Passage to India offers custom tours as well as reliable cars and drivers in all major Rajasthan towns. Rajasthan Tourism Development Corporation also leads tours.

Twice daily, at 9 AM and 1:30 PM, the Ahmedabad Municipal Transport Service offers tours of the city in English for Rs. 75. The tour departs from the local bus stand at Lal Darwaja and lasts four hours.

Contacts **Ahmedabad Municipal Transport Service** (*✉0 Number Bus Platform, opposite State Bank of India, Lal Darwaja, Ahmedabad ☎79/255–7739 🌐www.amts.in/html/tourist.html*). **Alka Travel Service** (*✉Ashish Complex, C. G. Rd., near Swastik Cross Rd., Ahmedabad ☎79/2642–1197 or 79/2643–1700 🌐http://alkatravel.com*). **Alternative Travels** (*✉Shekhawati, Nawalgarh P1594/222–129*). **Green Channel Travel Services** (*✉576 Sun Complex, Navrangpura, Ahmedabad ☎79/656–8457*). **Karwan Tours** (*✉Bissau Palace Hotel, outside Chand Pol, Jaipur ☎141/230–8103* ✉karwantours@usa.net). Le Passage to India (*✉Ganpati Plaza, M.I. Rd., Jaipur ☎141/511–5415 or 982/905–1387 🌐www.lepassagetoindia.com ✉Quality Inn, Vishnu Priya, Udaipur ☎294/510–0075 ✉Gandhi Chowk, Jaisalmer ☎2992/252–722 ✉Ghoomar RTDC, High Court Rd., Jodhpur ☎291/255–4934*). Meera Tours and Travels (*✉14 Badu Ji, Udaipur ☎0294/241–5249*). Parul Tours and Travels (*✉32, Lal Ghat, Udaipur ☎0294/2421697 🌐www.rajasthantravelbycab.com*). Rajasthan Mounted Sports Association (*✉c/o Dundlod House, Hawa Sarak, Civil Lines, Jaipur ☎0141/221–1276*). Rajasthan Safaris and Treks (*✉Birendra*

Singh Tanwar, Bassai House, Purani Ginani, Bikaner ☎ *0151/228-557).* Rajasthan Tours (✉ *Garden Hotel, Udaipur,* ☎ *294/252-5777* ✉ *Airport Rd., Jodhpur* ☎ *0291/236-942 or 0291/262-8265).* Roop Nivas Safaris (✉ *c/o Roop Nivas Palace, Jhunjhunu district, Shekhawati, Nawalgarh* ☎ *01594/222-008).* Royal Safari (✉ *Royal Safari, Box 23, Nachna Haveli, Gandhi Chowk, Jaisalmer* ☎ *02992/252-538 or 02992/253-202).* Sana Travels (✉ *Nehru Nagar, Hasanpura C, Plot No. 607, behind Jai Mahal Palace, Jaipur* ☎ *098/2801-7814* ✍sanatravels@mail.com). **TGS Tours and Travels** (✉ *Tholia Circle, Mirza Ismail Rd., Jaipur* ☎ *0141/236-7735* ✉ *Chetak Circle, Udaipur* ☎ *0294/229-661).* **Travel Corporation of India** (✉ *Ashram Rd., behind Handloom House, Ahmedabad* ☎ *79/2642-1981 79/2644-6001).*

VISITOR INFORMATION

Many hotels provide regional information and travel services. In Jaipur, Jodhpur, Udaipur, and Jaisalmer, the Tourist Information Centers of the Rajasthan Tourism Development Corporation provide information, travel assistance, and guides. Jaipur Vision and the Jaipur City Guide, available in most hotels, are periodicals with visitor information and up-to-date phone numbers.

Based in Ahmedabad, the Tourism Corporation of Gujarat provides information, organizes tours, and arranges cars and drivers.

Tourist Offices **Tourism Corporation of Gujarat, Ltd.** (✉ *H.K. House, Ashram Rd., Ahmedabad* ☎ *79/2658-9683, 79/2658-9172, or 79/2658-7217* 🌐 *www.gujarattourism.com).* **Rajasthan Tourism Development Corporation** (✉ *Swagatam Complex, Jaipur* ☎ *0141/255-4970* 🌐 *http://www.rajasthantourism.gov.in).* **Union Territory's Office of Tourism, Information, and Publicity** (✉ *Marine House, Bunder Rd., near market square, Diu* ☎ *28758/252-653 or 2875/252-212* 🌐 *www.diuindia.com).*

4

Uttarakhand

The Dhanolti Temple, near Mussoorie

WORD OF MOUTH

"There is also a great, great spa in the state of [Uttarakhand] you can consider . . . It is not far from Rishikesh. It is called Ananda Spa [and it's] gorgeous!"

—Bonita

www.fodors.com/forums

WELCOME TO UTTARAKHAND

Ganges river. Rishikesh

TOP REASONS TO GO

★ **From Dusk till Dawn:** Watch the Himalayan peaks turn purple, gold, red, and everything in between as the sun rises and sets over the mountains.

★ **Just Say Om:** Drop into a Rishikesh ashram for a yoga class and follow in the footsteps of rock-and-roll royalty or grab a massage at one of the world's top ayurvedic spas.

★ **The Great Ganges:** Join Hindu pilgrims as they launch thousands of bouquets of flowers on a journey down the sacred river during the holy city of Haridwar's sunset *aarti* (prayer).

★ **Call of the Wild:** Search for the elusive tiger in the picturesque Corbett National Park.

★ **Get Moving:** Ride some of Asia's best white-water rapids, trek to a mountain paradise or just stroll by waterfalls and orchards in the fresh air.

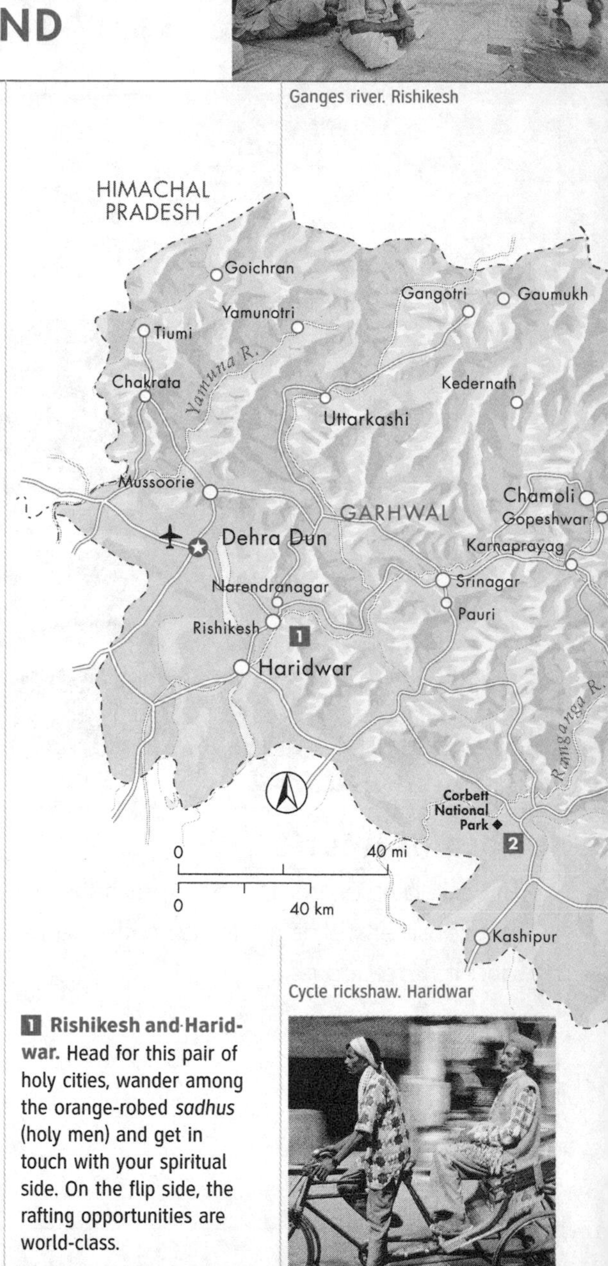

Cycle rickshaw. Haridwar

1 Rishikesh and Haridwar. Head for this pair of holy cities, wander among the orange-robed *sadhus* (holy men) and get in touch with your spiritual side. On the flip side, the rafting opportunities are world-class.

Corbett National Park

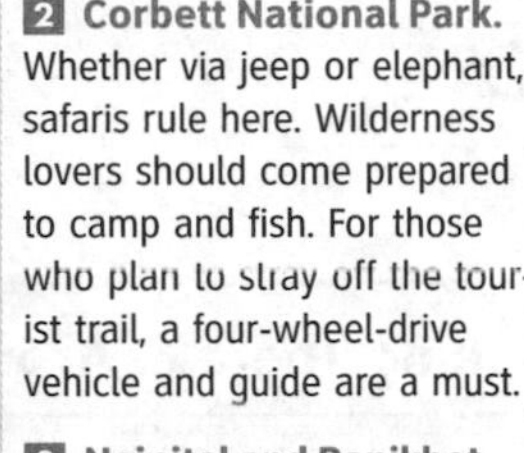
2 Corbett National Park. Whether via jeep or elephant, safaris rule here. Wilderness lovers should come prepared to camp and fish. For those who plan to stray off the tourist trail, a four-wheel-drive vehicle and guide are a must.

3 Nainital and Ranikhet. From mountain lakes ringed with remnants of the Raj to splendid alpine temples, the Himalayan foothills around the area's old British hill stations (hillside shelters) reward the curious explorer. Leave time to adjust to the altitude, take a sturdy vehicle and motion sickness medicine.

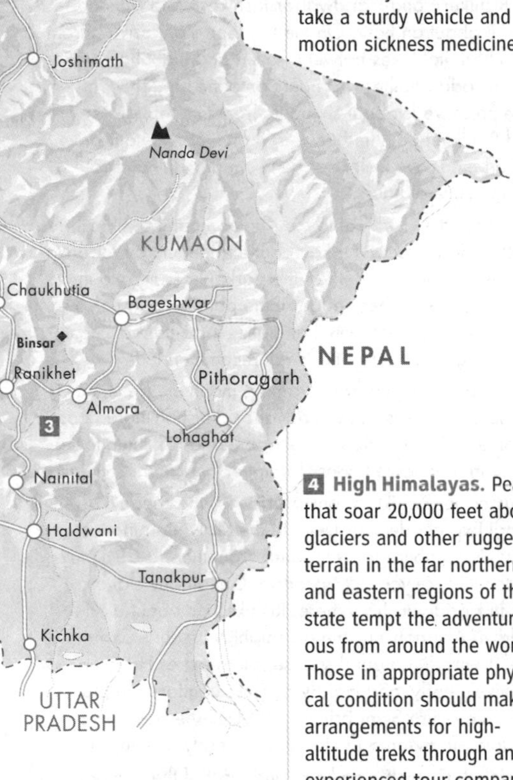

4 High Himalayas. Peaks that soar 20,000 feet above glaciers and other rugged terrain in the far northern and eastern regions of the state tempt the adventurous from around the world. Those in appropriate physical condition should make arrangements for high-altitude treks through an experienced tour company. The less hearty should enjoy the phenomenal views from the foothills.

GETTING ORIENTED

Uttarakhand, formerly Uttaranchal, is divided into two main regions, the Garhwal in the west and the Kumaon in the east. The plains of the Uttar Pradesh to the south give way the foothills that eventually rise to the high Himalayas. The peaks in the northern part of the state are some of the highest in the world (rising 15,000 to 20,000 feet) and tower over rugged terrain such glaciers as you reach the eastern region along the border with Nepal and Tibet. The source of many rivers, including the Ganges, tumble down from the mountains while the central part of the state boasts rich, biodiverse forests and wildlife preserves.

UTTARAKHAND PLANNER

When to Go

March through June and mid-September through December are the ideal windows to visit Uttarakhand. Unlike other mountainous regions, the monsoon tend to hit full force here turning the hills a beautiful verdant green during July and August but bringing landslides that can make trekking tough and driving on narrow, winding mountain roads difficult to impossible. Although the weather is clear and the vistas of the high Himalayan ranges are breathtaking during the winter, the temperature can dip to uncomfortable levels and road travel can be difficult during and after snow storms at higher altitudes. When the kids are on holiday from school, crowds of Indian families make tracks to the hills, particularly to Nainital and Mussoorie in the weeks following the middle of April. Reserve well in advance during this time, as well as around Diwali in November and around the New Year.

Getting There & Around

For extended trips in Uttarakhand, most people prefer to hire a car and driver. However, even the highways here are often narrow, crumbling roads that slowly wind their way through the mountains, making even trips that are short on distance long on time.

On the Garhwal side of the state, the drive from Delhi to Haridwar takes about six hours. Driving to Rishikesh takes about seven hours; Mussoorie close to eight. The drive between Rishikesh and Haridwar or Rishikesh and Mussoorie both take about an hour. On the Kumaon side, driving from Delhi to Nainital takes between seven and eight hours—Ranikhet will add another two hours onto the trip. The Corbett wildlife preserve is about six hours from the capital. Nainital and Ranikhet both lie between a one- or two-hour drive from Corbett. Leave Delhi before 6 am or rush-hour traffic could add several hours.

Moving from the Garhwal to the Kumaon can be difficult. Corbett to Haridwar will take about eight hours by road via the highway that runs south of the park. Crossing into the Garwhal by the northern edge of the park is via a narrow state road in bad condition that makes for a hair-raising drive in rugged territory and is not recommended.

The train can save you from draining mountain drives but it books up early, so reserve in advance. For non-Indian passport holders, check with a travel agent and ask them to see if tickets are available under "foreigner" or "tourist quota."

For Mussoorie, Rishikesh, and Haridwar, the speedy Shatabdi Express departs Delhi in the early morning for the roughly six-hour trip Dehradun. From there a 50-minute taxi ride will take you to Mussoorie. Get off one station earlier in Haridwar; from there, Rishikesh is about a one-hour drive. Alternatively, the overnight Mussoorie Express reaches Dehradun around sunrise, but reaches Haridwar prohibitively early, and Haridwar lacks comfortable places to wait. The return Shatabdi train for Delhi leaves Dehradun in late afternoon and Haridwar in early evening.

For Nainital, Corbett, Ranikhet, and most of the Kumaon, the overnight Ranikhet Express leaves Delhi in the late evening to reach the railhead at Kathgodam by the early morning.

Planning Your Time

The Garhwal Circuit

It takes about six days to connect the Garhwali dots: **Mussoorie, Rishikesh,** and **Haridwar.** You can drive the entire way, or go partially by train. By road the trip is more expensive and tiring, but you can set your own pace and enjoy slightly better views—just don't drive at night. There are trains from Delhi and Dehra Dun (for Mussoorie) and Delhi and Haridwar. Catch the early morning Shatabdi (express) from Delhi to Dehra Dun, where your hotel can pick you up or you can hire a taxi for the 50-minute ride to Mussoorie. After two nights, hire another car to take you to Rishikesh, a journey of no more than three hours. Spend two or three days around Rishikesh and Haridwar, perhaps including some rafting and hiking, then catch the six-hour evening train from Haridwar to Delhi.

The Kumaon Circuit

This route is a gentle but colorful introduction to the region. Hire a car or jeep through a Delhi travel agency. Start by driving northeast from Delhi to Ramnagar, site of **Corbett National Park.** The drive takes six hours *if* you leave Delhi by 6 AM; after that, traffic near Delhi will extend the trip by several hours. When you've had your fill of Corbett, drive east to **Nainital** for a taste of modern Indian culture with a Raj flavor. From Nainital, go north to **Ranikhet** for golf or peaceful walks through the pine forests; from here you can make side trips to some important **Hindu temples.** Finish by looping back at the north end of Corbett, and perhaps by fishing on the Ramganga River. The trip takes from seven days to two weeks, depending on how long you want to linger over such diversions as searching for tigers.

What It Costs In Rupees

	¢	$	$$	$$$	$$$$
Restaurants	under Rs. 100	Rs. 100–Rs. 300	Rs. 300–Rs. 500	Rs. 500–Rs. 700	over Rs. 700
Hotels	under Rs. 2,000	Rs. 2,000–Rs. 4,000	Rs. 4,000–Rs. 6,000	Rs. 6,000–Rs. 10,000	over Rs. 10,000

Restaurant prices are for an entrée plus bread or rice. Hotel prices are for a double room in high season, excluding a tax of up to 20%.

Rafting Rush

White-water rafting is a major industry in Uttarakhand. At this writing there are close to 50 rafting camps between Rishikesh and Kudiala, set up by tour companies to provide Delhi's well-heeled with relaxing adventure vacations. People now drive up for weekends of rafting and horseplay on a sandy beach by the upper Ganges. It's highly recommended if you want to escape the city and do some rafting without committing to a long, strenuous adventure trip. The season runs from October to June, and you choose from several swift rivers—the Alakananda, Bhagirathi, Tons, Kali, and Ganges. Contact Aquaterra Adventures, Himalayan River Runners, Snow Leopard, or Outdoor Adventures India ⇨ *Travel Agents & Tours in Uttarakhand Essentials.* Outdoor Adventures India stands out, with its focus on safety, ecology, and good food. Aquaterra, led by a team of experienced, enthusiastic, fun-loving river guides, is recommended for its hearty spirit and campfire barbecues.

5

Updated by Alison Granito

FIGURING PROMINENTLY IN THE HINDU EPICS, Uttarakhand (formerly called Uttaranchal), is the mythological abode of the Hindu pantheon. Every year thousands of pilgrims make *yatras* (Hindu pilgrimages) to the mountain temples considered the homes of the Hindu gods Vishnu and Shiva and source of the holy Yamuna and Ganges rivers.

With more than 100 peaks towering above 20,000 feet, Uttarakhand's Garhwal mountains (especially Mt. Nanda Devi, at 26,056 feet) inspire climbers from all over the world. Trekkers are drawn to its natural sanctuaries, such as Nanda Devi (surrounding the peak of the same name) and the Valley of Flowers, strewn with blossoms and surrounded by glaciers and white-capped mountains.

In the Garhwal foothills, next to the Nepali border, is Uttarakhand's second major region, the Kumaon (pronounced koo-mow, to rhyme with "cow"). A relatively peaceful, underdeveloped corner of the country, the Kumaon is a wonderful place to begin a love affair with India. Ceded by Nepal to British India in 1815, it remains an area of forests, mountains, farmland, temples, and tigers. Life here is on a smaller scale—the topography is gentler, the forests thicker, and you can enjoy it all without the effort of a full-blown trek. Far from the frenzy of Garhwal's Hindu pilgrims and Mussoorie's honeymooners, the Kumaon has a relaxed vibe, and the animal-rich Corbett National Park makes it a must-see destination.

Coming to Uttarakhand in summer lets you avoid the crowds of foreigners that descend on Himachal Pradesh and Ladakh. Aside from a few routes frequented by Hindu and Sikh pilgrims (the road to Rishikesh can get very busy), you'll be alone with the villagers and shepherds. Given the great rafting on the headwaters of the Ganges and its tributaries, tour companies recommend combination trips, which include trekking and rafting in addition to, say, fishing and mountain biking.

EXPLORING UTTARAKHAND

ABOUT THE RESTAURANTS

Few people come to Uttarakhand to experience India's many culinary delights. German bakeries and falafel shops aimed at backpacking Europeans and Israelis abound around budget hotels. Larger hotels typically serve fair to middling set menus. Lunch and dinner buffets often include passable Indian standards with a little bit of Chinese and Continental thrown in for variety. The area around Nainital, however, is orchard country, so more likely than not the jam for your toast will be fresh and locally sourced here. Meat and alcohol are rare commodities in the holy cities of Rishikesh and Haridwar.

ABOUT THE HOTELS

Standout hotels such as Ananda and Kalmatia Sangam place unerring focus on details such as fresh, organic food coupled with top-flight spa and health services and an overall "green" atmosphere. However, the large majority of upscale hotels in and around Corbett, Nainital, and Mussoorie, while doing a big foreign trade, are squarely aimed at making traveling Indian families comfortable with amenities for the kids and large rooms with multiple beds. Many properties have well preserved Raj-era architecture and decor, calling back to the days when British civil servants took to the hills to escape the blistering heat on the plains.

GARHWAL REGION

RISHIKESH & HARIDWAR

★ *Rishikesh is 238 km (148 mi) northeast of Delhi and 67 km (42 mi) southeast of Mussoorie; Haridwar is 214 km (133 mi) northeast of Delhi and 91 km (57 mi) south of Mussoorie.*

Yoga, ayurvedic healing, spiritual retreats...the resurgence of Western interest in the mind-body-spirit connection has put the ancient holy city of **Rishikesh** on the map in recent years, revitalizing its appeal for the first time since the Beatles visited in the 1960s. The town's location on the Ganges is sacred, but its streets are anything but tranquil: you'll find them crowded with *sadhus* (holy men), Hindu pilgrims, con men, peddlers, monkeys, and hippies. Whether you come to check into an ashram or just to check out the scene, to "find" yourself or watch herds of others doing so, you'll encounter Rishikesh's slightly bizarre sometimes irresistible energy.

Only one side of Rishikesh is accessible by road. You have to cross one of the two suspension bridges or by boat to see the other half. The Ram Jhula bridge area is the most vigorous part of town, packed with shops, tiny eateries, and yoga ashrams. Fragrant sandalwood bead necklaces make nice souvenirs. **Shivananda Ashram** (☎135/243–0040 or 135/243–1190 🌐*www.divinelifesociety.com*) is the hub of ashram life in Rishikesh and organizes everything from yoga and meditation classes to overnight stays in spartan rooms. The visitor center is right next to Ram Jhula. A boat ride on the Ganges from Ram Jhula just after dawn will set you back Rs. 75–Rs. 400 depending on your bargaining skills and the length of time you want to spend on the river. About a kilometer from Ram Jhula, in a more peaceful part of town, is Rishikesh's older, more famous suspension bridge, the Lakshman Jhula. Stop into one of the nearby cafés to watch the world go by, or cross the bridge to find a relatively quiet spot along the bathing ghats (steps going down to the river, where people perform their ablutions or do laundry). This neighborhood is packed with craft emporiums and shops selling jewelry, shoes, spiritual music, and pipes.

About a half-hour's drive (24 km [16 mi]) from Rishikesh is **Haridwar,** which many feel is the holier town—the real thing. Visit Haridwar around sunset. Head to the heart of town to see the activity on one of the most sacred bathing ghats, Har-ki-Pairi (you may not be allowed to walk on the ghat itself), then visit some of the temples in this neighborhood. At sunset the Ganga Maha Aarti begins, a simple ceremony that beautifully distills the essence of Hinduism. Pilgrims from all over

India gather on the riverbank holding little leaf baskets of flowers and *diyas* (oil candle lamps). At nightfall, all the temples along the Ganges begin their evening *puja* (worship) and *bhajans* (hymns) at once, and the baskets holding lighted diyas are floated down the river to accompaniment of rousing music.

WHERE TO EAT & STAY

$ ✕ **German Bakery.** One of several German bakeries (usually run by Nepalis, as this one is) that invariably spring up in places hopping with budget European travelers, this Rishikesh version serves a variety of cakes, beverages (juices, lassis, and hot drinks) and simple Western meals. Located at a bit of a height off the road overlooking the Ganges at Lakshman Jhula, it's an ideal place for a break. ✉ *Lakshman Jhula* ☎ *135/244–2089* ▭ *No credit cards.*

$$$$ Fodor'sChoice ★ **Ananda in the Himalayas.** In the heart of the Tehri Garwhal region, at Narendra Nagar—a breathtaking 17-km (11-mi) ascent from Rishikesh through *sal* trees (tall trees that resemble black oak)—is this magnificent spa resort, a converted maharaja's palace that glows by night like a jewel on the mountain. Each room has a balcony that looks into the forest and down the Ganges and Rishikesh—and better still, you get the same view from your glass-pane bathroom. Furnishings are understated, with ivory-color hand-sewn quilts. In the restaurant, rich tandoori kababs are artfully balanced with tasty organic spa food and freshly baked bread and cakes. The 14-room spa offers massage, yoga, and sybaritic health treatments; if you're feeling vigorous, day-trek to the Kunjapuri Temple, visit the Rajaji National Park, or go river rafting. **Pros:** internationally acclaimed spa is second to none, impeccable service, delicious food. **Cons:** new-age atmosphere may make some uncomfortable; extras, such as excursions, can be pricey. ✉ *The Palace Estate, Narendra Nagar, 249175* ☎ *1378/227–500* 🌐 *www.anandaspa.com* *75 rooms, 5 suites* *In-hotel: 2 restaurants, bar, pool, gym, spa, bicycles.* ▭ *AE, MC, V.*

$–$$ ★ **The Glass House.** The crystal-clear Ganges flows auspiciously past the verandas in front of this charming, secluded Heritage Hotel, once a garden retreat of the maharajas of Tehri Garhwal. Spend the day at a nearby rafting camp, walk into the jungle or down to a river beach, visit a nearby ashram, or just read in the tropical garden packed with fruit trees. In the evening, you can stretch out by a log fire and fill up on plain but tasty Indian and Western buffet meals before retiring. Several quiet cottages are simply but uniquely decorated with hand-dyed fabrics and paintings. **Pros:** peaceful, remote location in the forest, excellent service. **Cons:** reaching Rishikesh will require a lengthy drive. ✉ *23rd Milestone, Rishikesh-Badrinath Rd., Village Gular Dogi, 23½ km (15 mi) or 45 min north of Rishikesh just before village of Byasi, 249303* ☎ *01378/269–224 or 01378/269–218, 11/435–8962 in Delhi* 🌐 *www.neemranahotels.com* *16 rooms, 12 suites* *In-room: no phone, no TV. In-hotel: restaurant, laundry service.* ▭ *AE, MC, V* 🍴 *FAP.*

$ ★ **Haveli Hari Ganga.** A few minutes' walk from the famous Har-ki-Pauri ghat is a *haveli* (royal home) built nearly a century ago by the maharaja of Jaipur and owned by the maharaja of Pilibhit. Now restored into a Heritage Hotel, the haveli is perched on a ghat on the shores of the Ganges. Rooms are done in the old-fashioned stately style, and the entire building feels like a royal lodge. One terrace serves as a river-view sitting area, and guest rooms open onto an atrium. **Pros:** architechture buffs won't be disappointed, top-notch service. **Cons:** some rooms can be slightly noisy. ✉ *Pilibhit House, 21 Ramghat, Haridwar, 249401* ☎ *1334/226–443* 🌐 *www.leisurehotels.co.in* *20 rooms* *In-room: No TV. In-hotel: restaurant, spa.* 💳 *No credit cards* 🍽 *CP.*

¢ **The Great Ganga.** The best hotel in the town sits on a hill a few minutes from Ram Jhula, overlooking the Ganges at some distance from the chaos. Ask for accommodations with a river view. Rooms are nondescript and modern, slightly overbearing in color and texture, but they're comfortable. The restaurant serves Indian, Chinese, and a few Western dishes, and on request in summer they offer Garhwali food, much of which is made with black lentils. **Pros:** the best choice in town for creature comforts, quiet location. **Cons:** set away from the action, which is what many come to Rishikesh for. ✉ *Muni-ki-reti, near Ram Jhula, 249201* ☎ *135/244–2243* 🌐 *www.thegreatganga.com* *21 rooms, 2 suites* *In-room: no TV, phone. In-hotel: restaurant, bar, tennis court.* 💳 *MC, V.*

TREKKING UTTARAKHAND

Uttarakhand offers everything from nature walks through forests with gently rolling hills to sheer snowcapped mountains. Experienced tour operator Ibex Expeditions (⇨ *Travel Agents & Tours in Uttarakhand Essentials)* consistently gets high marks. Allow at least five or six days for a trek into the stunning Valley of the Flowers, a World Heritage Site. For those who really want to get off the trail beaten path, consider joining a trek to one of the high-altitude Sikh or Hindu Temples in the upper Garhwal.

5

MUSSOORIE

278 km (173 mi) northeast of Delhi, 110 km (68 mi) northwest of Rishikesh.

As you approach Mussoorie, you'll encounter billboards advertising hotels and fleets of cars carrying young, middle-class Indians. Both are tip-offs: Mussoorie is no longer a peaceful mountain getaway. Still, this former British hill station at about 6,500 feet is a good place to escape Delhi's brutal summer heat, and makes an interesting break from the plains if you're on a short trip to India. The main part of town looks down on the plains, but the northern side of its hill has wonderful views of the Himalayas. Founded in 1823 by a British Army captain, Mussoorie has a few remnants of the Raj—churches, an old British library, the "Gun Hill," from which the noon cannon was fired, and a dilapidated grand hotel—but they're less extensive than those in Shimla or Nainital. The best way to experience the town, besides strutting your stuff on the main thoroughfare, is to take a long walk up the hill to its quieter sections.

Mussoorie has grown around its **Mall,** which extends 5 km (3 mi) from the library (Kithab Ghar, Gandhi Chowk) to Landour Bazaar, so almost everything is a short walk off it. There are four 19th-century churches on or near the Mall—Christ Church, Union Church, Central Methodist Church, and St. Paul's—all of which hold Sunday services at 10 or 11 AM.

The peaceful, 5-km (3-mi) **Camel Back Road** grants wonderful views of the Himalayas and valleys below while it winds past the British Cemetery (ask permission at Christ Church to enter; it's usually locked), the oddly shaped Gun Hill, and groups of mischievous black-faced langurs. A rickshaw can take you from end to end for Rs. 50 if you don't want to walk

The **Savoy Hotel,** a five-minute walk from the Library end of the Mall, is a must-see (though not a must-stay). Built in 1890, the hotel has gone to seed and is manned by an ancient watchman who presides over cinematic Edwardian ballrooms and dining rooms opening onto verandas, lounges, and a billiards room (where a sign notes that a leopard was once spotted under the table). A total of 121 rooms sprawl across an area as large as two football fields. You can technically still stay here, but it's not recommended. Visit after dark for an amazingly creepy experience—the hotel stays open but feels haunted, perhaps by the festive crowds who filled the rooms in years past.

On the other side of the Library, a road leads up to the majestic abode of the maharaja of Kapurthala's. You won't be allowed in, but you can have a look from the gates.

For the best impression of Mussoorie, set aside a full afternoon and walk up through Landour Bazaar, with its imperial clock tower, toward Sisters Bazaar and the exceedingly tranquil **Landour** area. This was the original settlement, and it's pleasantly dotted with old cottages and bungalows. Landour Bazaar has a few interesting shops selling antiques, probably from Raj-era homes. It's a long, uphill 7-km (4-mi) walk from Gandhi Chowk, in the Mall, to Char Dukhan, in the heart of Landour, so you may want to hire a taxi (Rs. 300) and consider walking down.

There isn't much to shop for in Mussoorie; wooden crafts and simplistic, gaudy Garhwali tapestries rule the bazaar. But several Mall emporiums sell artifacts from other states, especially Kashmir and, for some reason, Karnataka.

You only need two nights and one full day here, unless you want to spend more time walking in the wilderness. The most pleasant way to arrive is to take the five-and-a-half-hour Shatabdi Express train (departing Delhi 7:30 AM) to Dehra Dun, then take a 50-minute taxi ride (34 km [21 mi]) from the station to Mussoorie. Alternately, the road trip from Delhi to Mussoorie via Dehra Dun takes seven hours; leave early in the morning to reach Mussoorie by late afternoon. Make arrangements through a Delhi travel agency.

WHERE TO EAT & STAY

$ **Atul.** This tiny second-floor eatery serves good wholesome vegetarian food. The hot butter rotis with your choice of vegetable are a good bet. Decor is nonexistent, apart from the view of the Gandhi Chowk. *Gandhi Chowk, the Mall 135/263–2398 No credit cards.*

$ **Cafe Coffee Day/Le Chef.** A branch of the modern all-India chain, this is Mussoorie's sleekest coffee house. A giant picture window looks out on the street. Dig into the well-made cakes and sandwiches or just take a chai/coffee break. Alternately, climb up to the second-floor restaurant, Le Chef, and have a hot Indian meal—they serve curries and vegetables with rice and tandoori breads. *Nirmal Ashram Estate, the Mall, Kulri 135/263–0880 No credit cards.*

$ **The Rice Bowl.** Mussoorie's most popular Chinese restaurant is also famous for its Thai cuisine and Tibetan momos. *Amitash hotel, next to Kwality, Kulri 135/362–1684 No credit cards.*

$$$ ★ **Claridges Nabha.** Once the property of the maharaja of Nabha, this summer bungalow consciously maintains the aura of an old-fashioned hill station. Away from the crowded Mall, it lets you unwind in peaceful surroundings. The 1845 main bungalow has a typical red-tin roof and an enormous foyer. Guest rooms, created in the 1940s, have understated elegance; the best rooms open onto a veranda facing a courtyard. You can sit under a huge cypress on the front lawn and watch langurs jump through the trees; stroll through the terraced gardens; or walk in the nearby woods. The staff can drop you off at the Mall and pick you up free of charge. **Pros:** beautiful grounds, excellent service. **Cons:** pricey, some rooms are a little faded. *Airfield, Barlowganj Rd., 4 km (2½ mi) from Mall, toward Dehra Dun, 248179 135/263–1426 or 135/263–1427 www.claridges.com 22 rooms In-hotel: restaurant, bar, tennis court, gym. AE, DC, MC, V.*

$ **Kasmanda Palace.** High above the Mall, past Christ Church, is this snow-white lodge with red-roofed turrets. Built in 1836 by the Bengal Engineers, it later became the summer home of the local royalty. The public areas are decorated with old photographs, tiger and leopard skins, and stuffed trophies from yesteryear hunts. Rooms vary widely, so inspect a few; the largest rooms upstairs have chunky antique furniture, mementos, and valley views. Garhwali meals are prepared on request. **Pros:** the genial proprietor, Dinraj Pratap Singh of the erstwhile principality of Kasmanda, has a fund of stories on Mussoorie. **Cons:** service is lax, rooms can be chilly in winter, and the walk from town is very steep. *Above Mall next to Christ Church, a steep 5-min climb from Vasu Cinema, 248179 135/263–2424 www.indianheritagehotels.com 14 rooms In-room: no a/c, no TV. In-hotel: bar, no elevator. AE, MC, V.*

¢–$ **Padmini Nivas.** Built in the mid-19th century, Rushbrooke Estate, a cluster of rambling cream-color buildings with green roofs, was later acquired by the maharaja of Rajpipla. Now a hotel, it has numerous nooks and crannies converted into sitting and eating areas. Each room has its own interesting character and furniture. The staff can organize river rafting and trips to Rajaji National Park. All meals are vegetarian. **Pros:** easy to find your own private space in common areas. **Cons:** only vegetarian meals available. ✉*Library, the Mall, 2-min walk down from Vasu Cinema, 248179* ☎*135/263–1093* 🌐*www.hotelpadmininivas.com* *27 rooms, 5 suites* *In room: no a/c, no TV. In-hotel: 2 restaurants, no elevator.* 💳*MC, V.*

KUMAON REGION

CORBETT NATIONAL PARK

★ *Ramnagar is 250 km (155 mi) northeast of Delhi.*

India's oldest wildlife sanctuary, founded in 1936, Corbett National Park is named after Jim Corbett, the fearless hunter and author of a famous treatise on tigers, *Man-Eaters of Kumaon,* who later became a conservationist and photographer. Corbett grew up in these hills, and the local people—a number of whom he saved from tigers at the risk of his own life—revered him. Corbett hunted tigers, but later came to regret the sport as he saw the turn-of-the-20th-century population of up to 40,000 tigers drastically reduced. Upon his death in 1956, India honored Corbett by renaming Hailey National Park after this beloved man.

The park, with elephant grass, forests, and the Ramganga River slicing through its entire length, covers 1,318 square km (509 square mi) and its well-preserved ecological diversity makes it one of the finest parks in the world. You can explore it on the back of an elephant swaying quietly through the jungle brush; sit in an open jeep as it rolls along miles of tracks; or just take in the sights and sounds from the top of a watchtower. The park is extraordinarily peaceful and unspoiled, worthy of Corbett's memory: you'll see several species of deer, monkeys, and migratory birds (over 500 species have been spotted in the park), and, if you're lucky, wild elephants, leopards, foxes, jackals, jungle cats, black bears, wild boars, snakes (including pythons), and crocodiles. If you're so inclined, spend three or four days here and make eight or nine different safaris through the park's various gates. Fishing for the giant mahaseer river fish in the rivers of this area is another absorbing pastime.

Many people, however, come to Corbett to see a tiger, so you'll pass jeeploads of visitors wearing woebegone "Where's the tiger?" looks. Remember that there are about 123 tigers roaming through more than 1,300 square km, so this quest is like searching for a needle in a haystack. (Your chances improve radically in summer, especially May, since there are fewer watering holes to track.) Still, trying to track a tiger down generates plenty of excitement and adrenaline even if you fail, and it's fun to listen to tiger tales from the naturalists and guides.

The park can be accessed by several different gates, including Amdanda, Jhirna, Dhangari, Durga Devi, and Dhikala. The most popular entrance is Amdanda Gate, just 2 km (1 mi) from Ramnagar and about 10 km (6 mi) from Dhikhuli, where most hotels are located. Only 100 day-trippers are allowed into the park for six hours each day—from three hours after sunrise to three hours before sunset, and all gates except one (Jhirna) are closed from June 15 to November 15. To enter by Amdanda Gate for a day trip, you must get an entry permit from either the gate or the tourist office in Ramnagar—this allows you into the park's Bijrani area for morning and evening safaris. If you stay at a private lodge, the staff there will make your daily arrangements. Each vehicle must be accompanied by a guide, available at the park or through your hotel. A few advisories for cruising: You cannot get out of your vehicle in the park; matches, lighters, and firearms are not allowed; it is important to keep silent; and eating is not encouraged. A three-hour safari with a guide, organized by your hotel, costs about Rs. 800 by jeep, Rs. 1,000 by elephant. Don't forget to bring binoculars and, if you're coming in winter, warm clothes and a jacket.

Before leaving Corbett, you might want to stop at the small **museum** at Dhangarhi Gate, which houses some stuffed wildcats, or purchase a bottle of Corbett honey at one of the shops outside the park entrance.

5

Ramnagar is roughly six hours from Delhi via Moradabad, and the drive is pleasant—past fields of sugarcane or rice and quaint mud hut villages—though at times the road deteriorates into a bumpy pathway or grows severely narrow, squeezing the traffic. You can also take an overnight train from Delhi to Kathgodam and drive the last 63 km (39 mi) to Ramnagar, a 90-minute drive—hire a taxi at Kathgodam, or ask your hotel to pick you up (about Rs. 800). Or access Corbett from Ranikhet, and this three-hour drive (85 km [53 mi]) southwest into the park is breathtaking, both for its Himalayan views and for the sometimes frightening way the narrow road hugs the mountainsides. If you're prone to motion sickness, you might want to take medication before setting off; the road is almost deserted, so at least the drive is peaceful. After passing through a small town, the route meanders through hillsides and farmlands, then sinks into sal forests. (The Corbett Ramganga Resort is off this road, 34 km [21 mi] from Ramnagar.) Just before you reach Corbett, turn right at the town of Mohan, and climb over the heavily forested ridge that separates the Kosi from the Ramganga river valleys—this brings you to the north side of the park, which offers anglers a unique fishing experience and all travelers a rest stop en route back to Delhi. ✉ *Ramnagar* *Reservations: Kumaon Mandal Vikas Nigam Ltd., Indra Prakash, 21 Barakhamba Rd., 1st fl., New Delhi, 110001* ☎ *11/2371–2246 or 11/2851–9366* 🌐 *www.kmvn.org* *Park Rs. 200, video-camera fee Rs. 500, car Rs. 200, guide Rs. 200.*

WHERE TO EAT & STAY

Most hotels are grouped around Dhikhuli, 10 km (6 mi) from Amdanda Gate. The staff at each hotel can organize transport to the park, a guide or naturalist, and park-fee payment. Room prices are on the high side, but they often include all meals.

To bring costs down, ask about room-only tariffs and have some meals at other hotels, such as the glass-fronted restaurant at **Corbett Riverside Resort** (✉ *Next to the Corbett Hideaway* ☎ *5947/284–125*) on the Kosi River.

No trip to Corbett is complete without at least one night in the park itself. At the government-owned **Forest Rest Houses**—most of which were originally built as stopping points for British forest officers on their way to and from inspections deep in the jungle—you can beat the convoys of tourists entering the park in the morning to watch game until sunset, then fall to sleep amid a deep silence pierced only by the occasional cry of a wild animal. There are a total of 24 Forest Rest Houses in the park. Some, such as Dhikala, are quite large, with electricity and food service, but most are very basic, with four to six beds in two to three rooms, no electricity, bucket baths, and only seasonal access. Bring your own sleeping bags and sheets.

Although you can make personal arrangements to stay in a rest house, it's not advisable; their bureaucratic management is not attuned to customer service. Instead, stay at one of the lodges listed below, inform them of your wish to stay at a forest rest house in advance, and for a fee they'll make the necessary arrangements, including transport, bedding, meals, and housekeeping provisions. These resorts are very close to Amdanda Gate, and their package stays (Jungle Plans) include full board and jeep and elephant safaris with knowledgeable naturalists.

One independent guide recommended for wildlife tours is **Manoj Sharma,** who lives near the park—contact his agent in New Delhi, **Manoj Mehta** (☎ *11/2557–1489, 11/2557–3489, or 98101–11124*) several weeks in advance to book his services.

$$$ ★ **Infinity Resorts Corbett Lodge.** Still widely known by its old name, Tiger Tops, this popular resort sits on a high bank of the Kosi River, so you can listen to rushing water while looking across the foothills. Each spacious room has a large picture window, a wall of rough stone, a bamboo-and-tile ceiling, a modern bathroom with shower, and a large balcony overlooking the pool. The circular central lodge, with its vaulted timber dome, is where you can eat, drink, and relax in front of the fire in winter. The deck outside overhangs the river, with lush jungle on the opposite bank. **Pros:** the price includes all meals (delicious homestyle Indian food, plus Western options) *and* activities, such as safaris, hiking, rafting, and pony treks. **Cons:** can be noisy. ✉ *Dhikuli, Ramnagar, 244715* ☎ *5947/251–279, 5947/251–280, or 5947/284–157 In Delhi, contact Khatau International* 📫 *A-3 Geetanjali Enclave, New Delhi, 110017* ☎ *11/2669–1189 or 11/2669–1209* 🌐 *www.tigercorbettindia.com* *24 rooms* *In-room: no TV. In-hotel: restaurant, bar, no elevator.* 💳 *AE, DC, MC, V* *FAP.*

$$–$$$ **Corbett Ramganga Resort.** Other Corbett resorts allude to fishing opportunities, but this extraordinarily peaceful facility, smack on the clear Ramganga River in the absolute wilderness, specializes in helping the angler. The collection of casting rods is well maintained, and the successes of the fishing guide are documented with photos in the reception room. From September to December, you can also go rafting. Stay in a small, clean, yellow-brick cottage, an airy suite, or, best of all, a cozy "safari tent" with attached brick bathroom. The grounds are dotted with flower beds. Staff-planned safaris will take you to the park's less popular gates, not least since Amdanda Gate is an hour away. **Pros:**

excellent fishing, peaceful location, food included in price. **Cons:** very far off the beaten path, so tell your driver: Drive from Ramnagar to Dhikhuli 11 km (7 mi), then on to Mohan 10 km (6 mi). Turn left and drive 13 km (8 mi) to Marchula, over the forested ridge that separates the Kosi and Ramganga river valleys. *Reserve through Surbhi Adventures P. Ltd., New Delhi ✉ Village Jhumaria, Marchula, near Corbett National Park ☎ 05962/281–592 or 05962/281–692, 11/2652–2955, 11/26523722, or 11/26523744 in Delhi ⊕ www.ramganga.com 10 cottages, 10 tents, 6 suites In-room: no phone, no TV. In-hotel: restaurant, pool, no elevator. AE, DC, MC, V BP.*

$$ ★ **Claridges Corbett Hideaway.** On the banks of the Kosi River, this rustic resort has a snapshot-worthy setting. Pebble walkways lead to the ocher cottages, which have baked-tile roofs, stone-tile floors, bamboo-mat ceilings, and fireplaces. Rattan and jute furniture lend a rustic feel. Each cottage has a porch, indoor sitting area, and modern bathroom with shower. Tea and snacks are served poolside. Fixed-menu meals are served in the new lodge on the riverbank, or you can tuck into grilled meals at Jim's; these are followed by bonfires on the lawn. With advance notice, the staff can arrange mountain-biking trips and horseback safaris to Nainital. Five minutes away is the more economical **River View Retreat,** a sister establishment, which lags somewhat in service and facilities. **Pros:** professional management, old-fashioned ambience, and lush orchard setting. **Cons:** no river view. *✉ Zero Garjia, Dhikuli, Ramnagar, 224715 ☎ 5947/284–132 or 5947/284–134, 11/2641–3304, 11/2629–3905, 11/2629–3906 in Delhi 5947/284–133, 11/2641–3303 in Delhi corbett@ndf.vsnl.net.in 38 cottage rooms In-room: no TV. In-hotel: 2 restaurants, bar, pool, gym, no elevator. AE, DC, MC, V.*

NAINITAL

63 km (39 mi) east of Corbett National Park, 277 km (172 mi) northeast of Delhi.

The drive from Corbett to Nainital takes less than two hours, but is memorable for its solitude and scenery. East of Ramnagar the road leads you on a tour of unspoiled agrarian India: mud dwellings with grass roofs stand next to fields of sugarcane, wheat, and lentils. Interspersed with the fields are small stands of teak and sal, with the occasional banana plantation thrown in. In the distance glimpses of the Himalayan foothills that await you. Just before you turn up into the hills at Kaladungi, you'll pass Jim Corbett's old winter home, a small colonial bungalow with a museum. The road uphill begins in a sal forest, which occasionally gives way to terraced fields. As the trees thin out, the road gets steep and starts to wind. Toward the top you might be held up by troops of langurs sunning themselves on the road or children on their way home from school in the city. Suddenly the road turns downhill, and the congestion of Nainital begins.

Nainital is one of India's most popular hill stations. "Discovered" by the British in the 1840s, this one was later made the official summer capital of Uttarakhand (then known as the United Provinces). The town clutches steep slopes around a lake of the same name, and is one of India's few hill stations with this distinction to add to its beauty. It's easy to see why the British fell in love with this idyllic spot, yet development is beginning to take its toll in the form of congestion, pollution, and noise. Indian tourists, especially honeymooners, come to Nainital year-round to enjoy the cool air and mountain views. The school holidays, April 15–June 15, bring the largest crowds and should be avoided if possible.

SHOPPING WITH A CONSCIENCE

Stop by the outlets of the Panchauchuli women weaver's collective along the malls in Mussoorie, Nainital, or Almora. All the proceeds from the beautiful wool and pashmina shawls go to the artisans that make them. Unlike most tourist emporiums where you never know what you get, the pure pashmina shawls here are the real thing, and comparatively cheap at about Rs. 5,500. If you have time, make an appointment to stop by the factory in Almora and watch the handlooms at work. Vist the Web site at 🌐 *www.panchauchuli.com*.

The region is best known for its pretty woodlands and boating opportunities, but as a former colonial capital, it packs quite a bit of history. Those interested in colonial architecture are in for a treat—there's another British building, generally with a high-gable tin roof, around every corner, including the clock tower, the Boat Club, the Masonic Hall, the High Court, the library, and the Church of St. John of the Wilderness. Most of these buildings are, unfortunately, slowly tumbling down.

The northern end of town is built around the **Flats,** a large open field created by a landslide in the late 19th century. Facing the Municipal Office, this area has an air of perpetual carnival, with magicians and acrobats performing while tourists munch away on snacks purchased from the many vendors. Sit and watch a cricket game, or take in a Hindi movie at the old Capital Cinema Hall on the Flats.

Elusive to the eye but unavoidable to the ear is the busy **Sri Ma Naini Temple** on the Flats. Open sunrise to sunset, this lakeside shrine is dedicated to many gods, including Shiva, but Naina Devi (an incarnation of Parvati, the wife of Shiva) is its focus. Take off your shoes, wander around, and watch devotees make offerings to the large black Shiva lingam by the lake. For a classic Indian experience of the coexistence of faiths, you can also visit the *gurdwara* (Sikh temple) that faces the Flats, or the mosque across from the flats.

A fabulous place to take in Nainital's famous Himalayan views is **Cheena Peak** *(Chinese Peak)*. The highest point near Nainital, at 2,611 meters (8,566 feet), it was technically renamed Naini Peak after India's 1962 war with China. You can reach the peak on foot or rent a horse and ride over.

The outlook called **Snow View** can be reached on foot or horseback, and there's a Tibetan monastery on the way. Tourists commonly take a gondola ride (the "Ropeway") to Snow View from town, which runs roughly—read: not reliably—9:30 to 1 and 2 to 5 daily. At some point, do take a boat ride into the middle of this serene *tal,* or crater lake. Boatmen will approach you on the Mall; rates vary from Rs. 50 to Rs. 200 an hour, depending on the season, and you must bargain hard. A large number of boats are moored at Nainital Boat Club, next to the Flats, and you can organize a sailboat through the club.

WHERE TO EAT & STAY

¢–$ ✕**Ahar Vihar.** Located on the second floor above the Mall, looking over the lake, this simple, reasonably clean joint offers wholesome Gujarati vegetarian *thalis* (sampler platters). Even meat eaters appreciate this light, home-style, sweet-and-sour cuisine. ✉*The Mall* ☏*5942/223–5446* ▭*No credit cards.*

$ **Claridges Naini Retreat.** In this elegant retreat with a splendid view of the Mall, the new combines almost seamlessly with the old; the old being Hari Bhavan, built as a summer residence of the maharaja of Pilibhit in 1926. Set around a red-tile garden patio, the bluestone buildings have classic Kumaoni red-tin roofs with latticework windows and high gables. Rooms are simple, with hardwood floors and furniture; some look down past wrought-iron railings to Nainital and the lake. To get to the Mall, use the hotel's complimentary shuttle or stroll about 10 minutes down the hill from the hotel. **Pros:** lovely gardens, excellent night view of the lights on the facing slope, private setting. **Cons:** some furnishings are tired, rigid fixed menus (and unexciting culinary options) may find you eating out. ✉*Ayarpatta Slopes, 263001* ☏*05942/223–5105 or 05942/223–5108* 🌐*www.leisurehotels.co.in* *32 rooms, 1 suite, 6 duplex rooms, 3 cottages* *In-hotel: restaurant, bar, laundry service.* ▭*AE, DC, MC, V.*

5

$ **Manu Maharani.** One of Nainital's top hotels is a charming, rambling, bright-white building with a red roof, overlooking the Mall. The inviting rooms are stylishly furnished, almost plush. The bathrooms, with showers only, are neat and modern. Common areas are spacious and attractive. **Pros:** rooms have a sitting area looking out onto the garden, pickup and drop-off at the Mall is complimentary. **Cons:** bathrooms have no tubs. ✉*Grassmere Estate, Mallital, 263001* ☏*5942/223–7341 or 5942/223–7342* 📠*05942/223–7350* ✉*manumaharani@vsnl.com* *66 rooms* *In-hotel: restaurant, bar, gym, laundry service.* ▭*AE, DC, MC, V.*

$ **The Ramgarh Bungalows.** Perched in an orchard halfway up a mountain about an hour from Nainital, this ultraquiet getaway easily let you make day trips into town but fosters relaxation away from the noise and crowds. Overlooking the picturesque village of Ramgarh, its individually decorated cottages have attracted the likes of acclaimed Indian writer Rabindranath Tagore. Aspiring scribes may want to rent the aptly named Writer's Bungalow and see if inspiration hits. Prices fall to a third in the semi-peak season and as much as half in the off season. **Pros:** professional management and excellent service, hotel brochure and map on walks in the area is a gem, on-site jam and preserves factory adds an interesting touch. **Cons:** not the place for those who like to be in the thick of things, views from the cheaper room in the Old

Fodor'sChoice ★

Bungalow trail others. ✉ *Ramgarh (Malla), Kumaon Hills, District Nainital, 263137* ☎ *11/4182–5001 in Delhi for reservations.* 🌐 *www.neemranahotels.com* ⇨ *19 cottages* ♨ *In room: no a/c, no phone, no TV. In hotel: restaurant, room service, laundry service.* 💳 *AE, MC, V* ☞ *American Express accepted for booking only (not on site).*

SHOPPING

The **Mall** is dotted with shops selling wooden items—bowls, boxes, pencil holders, furniture—but none are of outstanding quality.

For quality Almora tweeds and woolens such as shawls and scarves, head out to **Ram Lal and Brothers** (✉ *Bara Bazaar* ☎ *5942/235–484*) at the Capitol Cinema end of the Mall.

RANIKHET

55 km (34 mi) north of Nainital.

As with Nainital, the drive here takes less than two hours but is an event in itself. After leaving the crowded confines of Nainital on a road that hugs the mountain, you'll quickly enter the town of Bhiwali—a grubby little place, with small shops and tea stalls that serve as the center of the local fruit industry. In season the roadside is crowded with men selling crates of apples, peaches, and plums to travelers and dealers, and for the next hour of your drive the bottom of the river valley is filled with small orchards. After crossing another small river, you'll head back up to Ranikhet, at which point the forests give way to some spectacular sections of terraced farmland.

Ranikhet itself is ensconced in evergreen confines on a Himalayan hilltop. Of all the British hill stations in India, only Ranikhet retains some of its original sylvan tranquillity. This may be because it's an army town, home of the Kumaon Regiment ever since the Raj, so development has been controlled. The spacious army cantonment stretches along the Mall, which winds along the top of hill, and many of the regiment's stone buildings, erected well before Independence, are still smartly maintained specimens of colonial architecture. Walk on the **Upper Mall Road** to see the Parade Ground or Regimental Headquarters. Ranikhet has at least six old colonial churches that are usually open to visitors.

Heading uphill (south) from the Westview Hotel, take the **Lower Mall Road,** almost completely abandoned now, for a peaceful stroll through a forest of pine and oak.

About 2 km (1 mi) up the road, it merges once again with Upper Mall Road and you come upon the small, relatively new **Jhula Devi Temple,** open sunrise to sunset. The temple is bursting with brass bells, as Hindu temple bells are traditionally rung to alert the god to the devotee's need.

If you keep walking, in a few more miles you'll reach the **Chaubatia Orchards,** a 260-acre fruit orchard run by the state government. Feel free to stroll among the trees.

WHERE TO EAT & STAY

$–$$ ✕▣ **Westview.** Perched on a small hill, the Westview's yellow-flagstone main building was designed as a home in the mid-19th century. It's now a Heritage Hotel, but renovations have not altered the unique design of each room; the Westview Suite and Suite 28 are large, bright, and quiet. The Western food is superior to the Indian: try the roast leg of lamb with mint sauce or fish meunière. Order meals an hour in advance. **Pros:** In winter you can drift off in front of your own fireplace or wood-burning exceptional. **Cons:** Indian food lovers may be disappointed by the culinary options. ✉ *Mahatma Gandhi Rd., 263645* ✆ *Reserve through C-16 Greater Kailash 1, New Delhi, 110048* ☎ *5966/220261, 11/5163–3692 or 11/2648–5981 in Delhi* ✎ *westviewhotel@hotmail.com* ⇨ *18 rooms, 7 suites* ♿ *In-room: no a/c. In-hotel: restaurant, no elevator.* ▭ *No credit cards* 🍽 *CP.*

SPOTTING THE SNOWCAPS

Nature lovers who want to skip Corbett's crowds head for the unsullied forests of the Binsar Wildlife Sanctuary, approximately two hours drive north of Ranikhet. Marvel at the rhododendrons in bloom, watch for spotted deer and rare birds and make the easy climb to the top of Zero Point, where you get breathtaking views of the peaks of the Nanda Devi Range in all their snowcapped glory.

5

SHOPPING

At the **Ranikhet Tweed and Shawl Factory,** a hand-loom production center of woolens, you can buy things to help shut out the cold mountain chill. This operation is run by the Kumaon Regiment for soldiers injured in the line of duty and for army widows. Let the clattering draw you inside for a look at how hand looms work, or visit the little store down by the field, housed in the regiment's old bank. The factory and store are open Monday through Saturday from 9 to 5.

AROUND ALMORA/HINDU TEMPLES

If you have an extra few days, take a side trip from Ranikhet to see several important temples dedicated to Lord Shiva. Many are old, dating from the Katyuri (8th–14th centuries) and Chand (15th–18th centuries) dynasties. The most significant temples northeast of Ranikhet are at **Baijanth, Bhageshwar,** and **Jageshwar.** Unlike temples on the North Indian plains, these are built from rough-hewn stone, and their alpine locations—such as the cedar forest in Jageshwar—give these temples a totally different feel. The hill at **Binsar** has both a nature sanctuary and some ruins of the Chand dynasty's capital.

WHERE TO STAY

$$$ Fodor's Choice ★ ▣ **Kalmatia Sangam.** Perched on a mountain high above Almora, this little oasis combines panoramic views of the high Himalayas with best-in-class service and facilities. If you are lucky, you may see all seven snowcapped peaks in the Nanda Devi Range from the private outdoor sitting area of the resort's tastefully appointed private cottages. Charm-

ing owners Geeta and Dieter Reeb, accomplished mountaineers, are sticklers for detail and for sustainability (they say not a single tree on the property fell for the hotel's construction) who believe in supporting the local community. The talented young Indian chef serves delicious Western and Indian (all organic and sourced locally) cuisine and an accomplished French massage therapist practices on-site, further blending East and West. The resort can be a destination on its own for those looking to unwind for a couple of days, or an excellent base for adventures further afield—it's convenient to the area's temples, the beautiful Binsar Wildlife Sanctuary, and more. **Pros:** the food is divine, the view is worthy of a postcard, the service is top-notch. **Cons:** reservations can be difficult to get in high season, off the beaten trail. *Kalimat Estate, Post Bag 002, Almora, Uttarakhand, 263601* *05962/231–572* *www.kalmatia-sangam.com* *8 rooms, 2 suites* *In room: woodburning stove, showers only, no a/c. In-hotel: spa, restaurant, laundry services* *AE, MC, V.*

VILLAGE VISITS

For a taste of day-to-day life in the Kumaon, stay overnight in a village. Take in traditional food and folk entertainment around a roaring fire to shut out the mountain chill. Kalmatia Sangam has renovated houses in nearby villages and takes guests on treks there, while some other hotels and tour companies, including Delhi-based Ibex Expeditions, can also arrange a look at local life. The accommodations are clean and comfortable, but very basic.

UTTARAKHAND ESSENTIALS

To research prices, get advice from other travelers, and book travel arrangements, visit www.fodors.com.

BUS TRAVEL

Bus fares are a tiny fraction of what it costs to travel by hired car, but non-air-conditioned (ordinary class, state-run) buses are not recommended. The handiwork of their drivers produces severe motion sickness, not to mention serious accidents, and they tend to make frequent stops and take unnecessary breaks. Air-conditioned deluxe buses are safer—opt for the most expensive category, such as a Volvo or picture-window coach with good suspension; check out the bus before buying a ticket, and travel only by day. (In Uttarakhand, so-called "luxury" buses sometimes turn out to be rattle traps with taped TV entertainment blaring up front.) Deluxe coaches usually depart from roughly the same stands as state buses, and seat reservations are usually not required; a travel agent or hotel can help you make arrangements.

CARS & DRIVERS

Most Himalayan drives involve endlessly winding, often bumpy, sometimes precarious roads on the edges of steep slopes. If you're prone to motion sickness, carry medication and eat light meals before and during your journey. Even more important, hire a heavy and powerful car. Ambassadors and jeeps (the Sumo or Qualis models) are sturdy but not that speedy; a solid sedan car such as a Cielo or Esteem moves faster. Do *not* take a Maruti van, as it's not heavy enough to be safe. Expect to pay as much as Rs. 16–Rs. 17 per kilometer for a non-air-conditioned Ambassador or a diesel Toyota jeep, a bit more for a better car. The cost is highest if the vehicle starts in Delhi or takes you from one state into another, which involves road taxes; if you hire a car and driver in the Himalayas for use only in that state, the rate will be slightly cheaper. If your driver will be staying with you the entire time, ask your hotels whether they have food and accommodation for drivers. If not, the daily tip you give the driver (over and above the initially agreed-upon charge) should cover these costs for him. If you're starting from Delhi, plan to leave the city early—before 6 AM—to avoid wasting hours in traffic.

Night driving in the hills is extremely dangerous because of poor lighting and steep drops and must be avoided at all costs.

RBS Travels (⇨ *Travel Agents & Tours)* maintains a large fleet of cars and offers reasonable rates and, more important, experienced and safety-conscious mountain drivers. Their Delhi office is open 24 hours.

MONEY

ATMS In areas of Uttarakhand outside of Nainital, Rishikesh, and Mussoorie, which are well served by India's major banks, carry enough cash and traveler's checks to cover your expenses, as you simply can't depend on withdrawing cash here. Both ICICI and HDFC banks have branches along the Mall in Nainital and Mussoorie. Check the banks' Web sites for a list of ATM locations.

Locations (Dehra Dun) **ICICI** (✉ *Rajpur Rd.* 🌐 *www.icicibank.com*). **Axis Bank** (✉ *56 Rajpur Rd.* 🌐 *www.axisbank.com*).

Locations (Mussoorie) **HDFC** (✉ *Library, the Mall*).

Locations (Rishikesh) **ICICI** (✉ *Bharat Bazaar, 16 Adarsh Gram, at Dehra Dun Rd.* 🌐 *www.icicibank.com*).

CURRENCY EXCHANGE Try to carry American Express traveler's checks, as you might have a problem cashing Thomas Cook checks in smaller towns. Checks can be cashed at your hotel or a local bank; just note that most banks keep short hours, 10–2 weekdays and 10–noon on Saturday. There's a State Bank of India in just about every town—count on branches in Mussoorie, Nainital, and Rishikesh. If you're curious about smaller towns, check the full list of branches on the bank's Web site.

Exchange Services **State Bank of India** (🌐 *www.statebankofindia.com*).

TRAIN TRAVEL

Shatabdi Express trains—India's fastest and most comfortable trains, with air-conditioned cars and minimal stops—can drop you at several gateways to the mountains. Reserve as far in advance as possible, as trains fill up early.

A **Shatabdi Express** departs New Delhi at 6:55 AM for the 4½-hour trip to **Haridwar** and the roughly six-hour trip to **Dehra Dun.** From there you can hire a taxi to **Rishikesh** or **Mussoorie,** respectively.

The best train from Delhi to **Corbett National Park** or **Nainital** drops you in Kathgodam—the Delhi–Kathgodam **Ranikhet Express** leaves New Delhi at 10:45 PM to reach Kathgodam at 6:15 AM. From here, you must still drive 90 minutes to Ramnagar (for Corbett) or an hour to Nainital. The night train from Delhi to Ramnagar is only for the adventurous, as it has no upper-class accommodations.

Train Information **Indian Railways** (*www.indianrail.gov.in*).

TRAVEL AGENTS & TOURS

Most of the outfits listed here offer treks and jeep safaris; some also lead rafting and angling expeditions. The Delhi-based firms Aquaterra Adventures India, Himalayan River Runners, Ibex Expeditions, and Outdoor Adventures India are highly recommended for trips anywhere in Uttarakhand (and elsewhere in the Himalayas), as is Snow Leopard Adventures for rafting on the Ganges. If you're planning your own itinerary, call Delhi's reliable RBS Travels to make driving arrangements and Outbound Travels for airline bookings.

UTTARAKHAND–GENERAL

Contacts **Aquaterra Adventures India** (*S-507 Greater Kailash II, New Delhi 11/2921–2641 or 11/2921–2760 www.treknraft.com*). **Great Himalayan Adventures** (*N-95 Sham Nagar, New Delhi 11/2546–5783 www.wildquestindia.com*). **Himalayan River Runners** (*N-8 Green Park Main, upper floor, New Delhi 11/2685–2602 or 11/2696–8169 www.hrrindia.com*). **Ibex Expeditions** (*G-66 East of Kailash, New Delhi 11/2691–2641 or 11/2682–8479 www.ibexexpeditions.com*). **RBS Travels** (*Shop A1, Connaught Palace Hotel, 37 Shaheed Bhagat Singh Marg, New Delhi 11/2336–4603 or 11/2336–4952 lateef@giasdl01.vsnl.net.in*).

UTTARAKHAND TOUR SPECIALIST

Contacts **Outbound Travels** (*216A/11 Gautam Nagar, 3rd fl., New Delhi 11/2652–6316 outbound@vsnl.com*). **Outdoor Adventures India** (*S-234 Panchsheel Park, 2nd fl., New Delhi 11/2601–7485 www.outdooradventuresindia.com*). **Skylark Travels** (*Alka Hotel Annexe, the Mall, Nainital 5942/235–165 or 5942/236–096*). **Snow Leopard Adventures** (*Sector C-9, Vasant Kunj, New Delhi 11/2689–8654 www.snowleopardadventures.com*).

VISITOR INFORMATION

Tourist Offices **Uttarakhand** (*102 Indra Prakash Bldg., 21 Barakhamba Rd., New Delhi 11/2332–6620 or 11/2335–0481*).

Himachal Pradesh & Ladakh

WITH AMRITSAR

A novice monk praying at the Likkir Monastery

6

WORD OF MOUTH

"In terms of Shimla in December, well, you can certainly go, but as you know, it does get pretty cold in Himachal Pradesh in winter. I would generally recommend a visit to this area May–October."

—Bonita

www.fodors.com/forums

WELCOME TO HIMACHAL PRADESH & LADAKH

TOP REASONS TO GO

★ **The Himalayas:** This massive mountain range is home to the planet's 100 or so highest peaks, and a journey to these regions provides great ringside views.

★ **Solitude and Silence:** Some of quietest and loneliest places on earth are in beautiful Ladakh.

★ **Amritsar's Pride:** One of the world's most precious and important Sikh shrines, the Golden Temple rivals the Taj Mahal in its beauty.

★ **Tibet in India:** It may be a tourist zoo, but the McLeod Ganj section of Dharamshala also holds 15,000 Tibetan refugees; in some ways the area is more Tibetan than modern-day Tibet.

★ **Timeless Monasteries:** The monasteries of Himachal Pradesh and Ladakh are a unique chance to see Tibetan Buddhism in practice, the way it's been for centuries.

1 Shimla. Once the summer capital of the British Raj, Shimla is the gateway into this mountainous region and a good jumping-off point to prettier, smaller hill towns like Mashobra or Kinnaur.

2 Manali and the Kullu Valley. Much deeper in the state of Himachal, these twin spots present an authentic flavor of the higher Himalayas, with their pagoda-style temples, alpine meadows and streams, ancient wooden palaces, and hill folk. The area is a good place for trekking, paragliding, and skiing, too.

3 Dharamshala. The home of the leader of the Tibetans, the venerable Dalai Lama, Dharamshala teeters at 4,780 feet atop the Dhauladhar Range. Upper Dharamshala, also known as McLeod Ganj, has been dubbed Little Lhasa: culturally it's a kingdom of its own.

Monks dance during Phyang Buddhist monastery festival

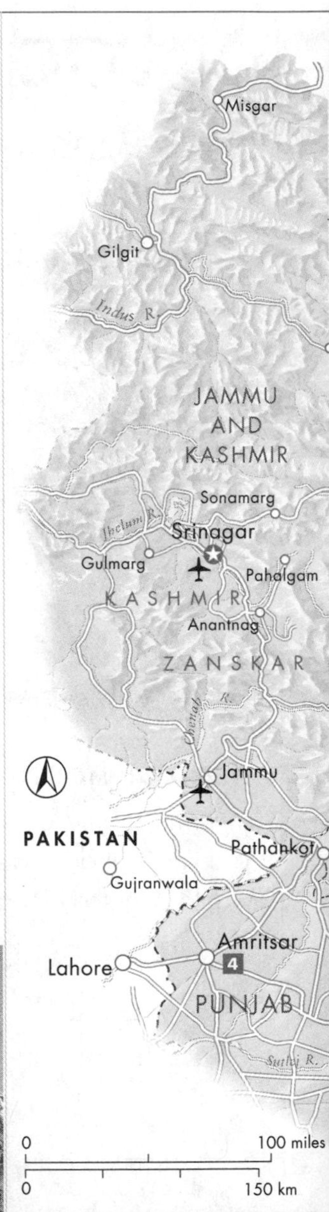

The Golden Temple, Amritsar

4 Amritsar. Located in the state of Punjab, this city makes a wonderful detour to a mountain excursion in Himachal Pradesh. The Golden Temple of the Sikhs here is an unforgettable sight.

5 Ladakh. One of the remotest and coldest desert kingdoms in the world, Ladakh now sees a fair number of tourists in summer. All the same it remains rooted to its isolated, colorful medieval past.

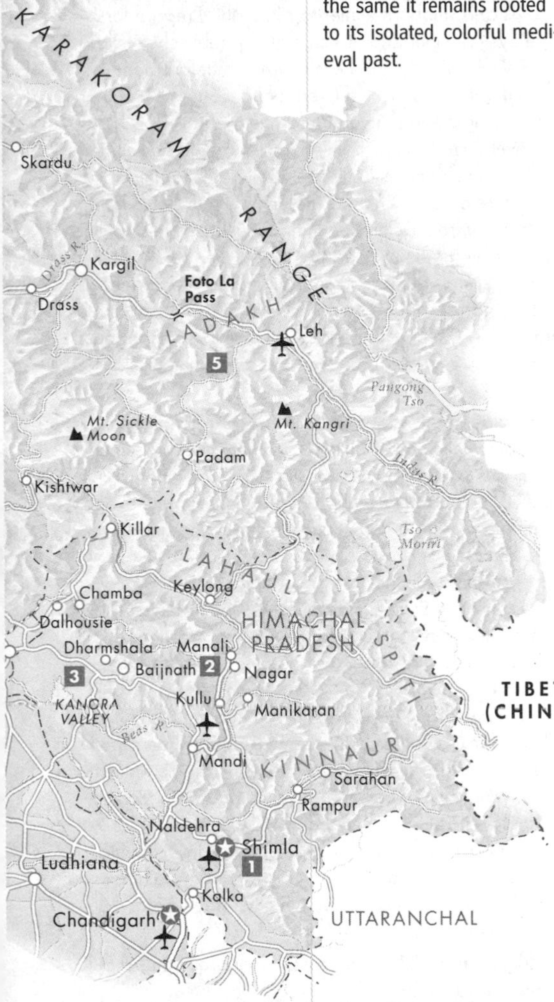

KARAKORAM RANGE
Skardu
Kargil
Drass R.
Drass
Foto La Pass
LADAKH
Leh
5
Pangong Tso
Mt. Kangri
Mt. Sickle Moon
Padam
Indus R.
Kishtwar
Killar
Tso Moriri
LAHAUL
Chamba
Keylong
Dalhousie
HIMACHAL PRADESH
SPITI
Dharmshala
Manali
Baijnath
2
Nagar
3
KANGRA VALLEY
Kullu
Manikaran
TIBET (CHINA)
Beas R.
Mandi
KINNAUR
Sarahan
Rampur
Naldehra
Shimla
1
Ludhiana
Kalka
Chandigarh
UTTARANCHAL

GETTING ORIENTED

Ladakh, part of the state of Jammu and Kashmir, occupies the northernmost part of India's territory. To its south is Himachal Pradesh, which literally means "land of the snowy mountains." A journey to either region is a chance to experience the towering western Himalayas at close quarters. Extremes in elevation here—from just 450 feet to 6,500 feet—lead to vast differences, from dry cold desert to steep lush countryside and snowy peaks. Amritsar, close to the Pakistan border in the breadbasket plains of the Punjab, is best approached as a detour on the way to Himachal Pradesh's peaks.

Chemrey Monastery, Ladakh

6

HIMACHAL PRADESH & LADAKH PLANNER

When to Go

May through August is the ideal window for a comfortable visit to the mountainous areas in this chapter. May and June, when the rest of the country is broiling, is an especially good time. And when torrential rains inundate most of North India in July and August, Himachal Pradesh and Ladakh make for great escapes, as the mountains usually hold back the monsoons. The Himalayas can be extremely cold in winter, and deep snow renders many mountain passes and valleys impassable, so summer is the best bet. If you do head for the hills in summer, reserve a hotel room well in advance. The best time to visit the plains city of Amritsar, however, is in the winter, somewhere between October and March—it is swelteringly hot in summer.

Getting There & Around

Flying is the quickest way to reach most of the Himalayas, and it's usually easiest and most convenient to book the tickets online. Keep in mind that flight schedules can be thrown off, especially in winter, by variable weather in the mountains and stubborn winter fog in Delhi. Prepare for long delays on either end. It's crucial to double-check the flight schedule with the airline a few hours before departure. If a flight gets canceled overnight because of weather, the airline is liable to put you up for the night. A good way to cut travel time to Himachal Pradesh and enjoy a scenic drive at the same time is to fly from Delhi to Chandigarh and then hire a car to Shimla. The drive is four hours as opposed to eight from Delhi. Reaching Shimla by the so-called Toy Train is by far the most scenic way to go, but it also takes a long time. The pint-sized train travels along a 95-km (62-mi) narrow-gauge track built in 1903, taking you to Shimla at 7,170 feet. It only goes about 9 to 15 mph, passing through 102 tunnels and over 845 bridges to make the journey in five or so hours.

Most Himalayan drives involve endlessly winding, often bumpy, sometimes precarious roads on the edges of steep slopes. If you're prone to motion sickness, carry medication and eat light meals before and during your journey. Even more important, hire a heavy and powerful car, and never drive yourself. Ambassadors and jeeps (Sumo or Qualis models) are sturdy but not that speedy; a solid sedan car such as a Cielo or Esteem moves faster. Don't take a Maruti van, as it's not heavy enough to be safe. Most journeys will cost at least Rs. 1,000 one-way. The cost is highest if the vehicle starts in Delhi or takes you from one state into another, which involves road taxes; if you hire the car in the Himalayas for use only in that state, the rate will be slightly cheaper. If your driver will be staying with you the entire time, ask your hotels whether they have food and accommodation for drivers. If not, the daily tip you give the driver (over and above the initially agreed-upon charge) should cover these costs for him. If you're starting from Delhi for Himachal Pradesh, plan to leave the city early—before 6 AM—to avoid wasting hours in traffic.

Night driving in the hills is extremely dangerous and should be avoided at all costs.

Toy Trains

The romance of riding wee trains that run on tracks a mere two-and-a-half feet apart can be enjoyed in few locales in the world. Himachal Pradesh has two such historic systems, running high into the snow-capped Himalayas—the Kalka-Shimla Railway and the Kangra Valley Railway.

These journeys take you past and to some of the most picturesque railway stations in the world. The miniature trains daintily meander in and out of forests and villages and around hillsides—they lend beauty to the countryside rather than detracting from it. But don't take one of these trains if you're pressed for time—they travel like snails, taking as much as three times longer to travel between points than a car does.

Tibetan Specialties

Lahaul, Spiti, Dharamshala, and Ladakh bring with them the prospect of sampling some of the finest Tibetan and Tibet-influenced food. *Thukpa,* a steamy soup of noodles, meat, and vegetables, parties a staple of Ladakhi and Tibetan cuisine. Fragrant and delicately steamed *momos,* dumplings stuffed with vegetables, cheese, or meat, are also a standby. Other interesting dishes to sample include salty yak-butter tea, dumplings and porridge made from *tsampa* (roasted wheat and barley flour), and *chhung* (barley beer).

What It Costs In Rupees

	¢	$	$$	$$$	$$$$
Restaurants	under Rs. 100	Rs. 100–Rs. 300	Rs. 300–Rs. 500	Rs. 500–Rs. 700	over Rs. 700
Hotels	under Rs. 2,000	Rs. 2,000–Rs. 4,000	Rs. 4,000–Rs. 6,000	Rs. 6,000–Rs. 10,000	over Rs. 10,000

Restaurant prices are for an entrée plus bread or rice. Hotel prices are for a double room in high season, excluding a tax of up to 20%.

Planning Your Time

To see Himachal Pradesh thoroughly—a life-changing experience—allow both time and money for a series of long, winding road trips in a car handled by a local driver (⇨ *Travel Agents & Tours in Himachal Pradesh & Ladakh Essentials*). Most trips between any two destinations take a full day, as daylight hours are short, and you don't want to drive in the dark. Even a basic, somewhat rushed tour covering Shimla (two days), Manali (two days), and Dharamshala (three days) requires 7½ days, including travel to and from Delhi. A longer itinerary—covering Shimla/Mashobra (four days), Kinnaur (three days), Spiti/Lahaul (six days), Manali (three days), Dharamshala (three days), Dalhousie (one day), and Pragpur, for Judge's Court (one day)—takes three weeks including travel to and from Delhi. Save money and energy on the first leg out of Delhi by taking a train to Shimla or to Pathankot, near Dharamshala. To make the a trip to Ladakh worth the effort, plan on visiting one of the area's impressive monasteries (Hemis, Thiksay, or Alchi), venture into the spectacularly attractive countryside for a small jaunt, and explore a few of the sights and bazaars, as well as the culture and food, of the district's main town, Leh. You should budget at the very least three days to accomplish this program, including a little time to acclimatize to the thin air and to get Inner Line Permits, if needed.

Updated by Monica Mercer and Vaihayasi Pande Daniel

THREADED WITH RIVERS AND DOTTED WITH LAKES, the lovely state of Himachal Pradesh spans five Himalayan mountain ranges—the Shivalik, Dhauladhar, Pir Panjal, Great Himalayas, and Zanskar. Except for the capital, Shimla, and the overpopulated towns of Dharamshala and Manali, Himachal is a land of alpine villages, speckled with thousands of Hindu and Buddhist temples and monasteries.

As for the former Himalayan kingdom of Ladakh, it's effectively cut off from the rest of the world, as it has been throughout history, by a formidable, 6,000-foot-plus boundary made up of the lofty Great Himalayas, the Karakoram Range, and the Kunlun Mountains. It's not surprise, then, that life on this 13,000-foot-high plateau, through which the Indus River meanders, has an almost celestial flow to it. Indeed when you fly into "the land of the high passes," across towering ranges, you are welcomed with a ringing, deafening silence. This soulful stillness is only an introduction to the charm of this beautifully stark and remote land. Even more alluring is the simple eternal rituals and rhythms of living in Ladakh. With the major exception of Leh, most of Ladakh has not changed much from medieval times and still peacefully revolves around Buddhism and the *gompas* (Tibetan monasteries), farming, and eking an existence, cheerfully and contentedly, in spite of terrific odds.

If you're headed for the mountains of Himachal Pradesh, you may find Amritsar a worthwhile cultural detour. The largest city in the predominantly Sikh state of Punjab, Amritsar is the holiest city to the Sikh religion, its massive Golden Temple is an inspiring destination in its own right. History buffs may also want to visit the site of the infamous Amritsar Massacre, a turning point in the fight for Indian Independence.

EXPLORING THE HIMACHAL PRADESH & LADAKH

Whatever your interest in the Himalayas, contact the recommended tour operators for details. Most will design a special trip just for you, whatever your budget or age. It's especially important to use a tour operator if you're keen on camping, trekking, or rafting. Smaller outings can also be organized through your hotel. Try to make arrangements at least two months in advance. If you're planning a trek, contact a tour operator who is familiar with the specific area you have in mind. Play it safe: don't embark on any route without a guide. Travelers in high-altitude areas should heed all warnings about sun exposure and high-altitude sickness—allow up to three days for full acclimatization. Even if you'll be ensconced in a jeep, bring powerful UVA/UVB sunblock, a wide-brim hat, and sunglasses that block ultraviolet rays. For travel to remote areas, bring a means of water purification, a quart-size canteen, and energy-producing snacks.

To visit the Nubra, Khaltse (Drokhpa area), Tso Moriri, Pangong Tso, and Nyoma subdivisions in Ladakh, foreigners must travel with at least three other people and a government-recognized tour operator; they must also obtain an Inner Line Permit, which most tour operators—and even better, most hotels—can secure (⇨ *Permits in Himachal Pradesh & Ladakh Essentials*).

ABOUT THE RESTAURANTS

Fast-food restaurants and coffeehouses in Shimla abound on the Mall—Devicos, Indian Coffee House, and Barista among them. They're good for quick fixes, but ambience is not a priority; for that you're better off driving to one of the fancier hotels for an authentic and delightful Himachali meal.

In summer, Manali attracts restaurant owners from all over, who set up shop for the season, and you have a chance of sampling good versions of Italian food or cheese fondues or, better still, fresh trout. Dharamshala also caters to international tourists with food that includes Indian favorites, Israeli cuisine, first-class Tibetan and Chinese food, and also pastas and excellent pastries. In smaller Himachal towns it's better to stick with regular Indian fare.

Almost all of Leh's restaurants are small and informal. Try the standards: momos and a noodle soup called *thukpa*. You may also have a chance to try *chang* (a local brew made from fermented barley) or, more likely, some *gur-gur cha*, yak-butter tea mixed with milk and salt. Competent Indian food is also available.

ABOUT THE HOTELS

Himachal Pradesh has some memorable luxury hotels at Mashobra and Shimla as well as notable hotels or bungalow lodges in Shimla, Dharamshala, Dalhousie, and in the Kangra Valley.

Ladakh has a number of family-run, traditional hotels memorable for their character; but very few luxury hotels. Rooms are generally simple, with heating provided in winter and during cold spells and hot water only in the mornings and evenings. Hotels are only of a few stories high and do not have elevators. Electricity can disappear at times because of "load-shedding," and hotels usually lack backup generators. Nearly all rooms come with televisions but not always with room phones.

AMRITSAR

Because of its proximity to the Pakistani border—Lahore is only 64 km (40 mi) away—Amritsar has not seen the development and overwhelming sprawl of other North Indian towns. The city is an important commercial hub: much of the aromatic and relatively expensive Basmati rice that's now an international staple is exported by Amritsar dealers, and dried fruits and woolens from hill regions are handled by wholesalers here. The robust rural culture of Punjab's farmlands permeates the city, with tractors on the roads and peasants making their way through the market centers and through the famous Sikh temple.

The Golden Temple is perhaps the best reason to take a detour through Amritsar as you're leaving the mountains of Himachal Pradesh. Even if you think you've had enough of India's religious pageantry, you shouldn't miss this main pilgrimage site of the Sikh faith. An argument could be made that the Golden Temple, with its Moghul-style architecture and gleaming copper detail, is just as grand as the Taj Mahal without all the government rules, hefty admission fees, and hordes of foreign tourists clamoring for photographs. As a living lesson of the Sikh faith, which teaches a welcoming attitude toward all, the Golden Temple's pristine grounds and lush golden details attract Indian citizens year-round regardless of social status or religion. It's also a popular setting for Bollywood films.

PASHMINA SHAWLS

The wool for fine pashmina shawls is sourced from the *pashm* (Persian for wool) of herds of special hairy goats and yaks found in the upper altitudes of an area stretching from Kashmir to Outer Mongolia. In India, they've been woven into shawls for many centuries. Himachal Pradesh and Ladakh are ideal places to purchase a reasonably priced, beautiful shawl—the best are said to be fine enough to pass through a wedding ring. Shops in Kullu, Manali, Dharamshal, Leh, and Shimla sell shawls with different regional textures and patterns.

The Sikh faith is a syncretic movement that was formed to combine Hinduism's bhakti (devotion to a personalized god) with Islam's monotheism and egalitarianism. Sikhism was founded by Guru Nanak around the turn of the 16th century, developing into a distinct new religion under the gurus who succeeded him. Amritsar (Pool of Nectar, in Punjabi and Sanskrit) takes its name from an ancient sacred pool that Nanak is said to have preferred for his meditation and teaching. In succeeding years, Sikhism gained increasing importance and Amritsar became its pilgrimage center. Gobind Singh, the tenth guru, consolidated the faith by establishing a distinctive appearance for his followers, most notably long hair kept in a turban for men, and braids for women. (Almost all Sikh men carry the last name of Singh, which literally means "tiger.") Upon his death in 1708, Singh's disciples announced his instruction that the Sikh faith would henceforth be centered on the teachings of the sacred book (now called the *Guru Granth Sahib*) rather than a human guru. To this day, life in the Golden Temple and all *gurdwaras* ("temple" or "door to the guru" in Punjabi) revolves around the *Guru Granth Sahib*. Before dawn, the book is taken out of a building called the Akal Takht and carried processionally across the huge, white marble compound—including a causeway over a square artificial pond—to Harmandir Sahib, the central temple whose gilded copper plating gives the complex its popular name. The temple's day ends late in the evening, when the book is brought back to its resting place.

During the time of the gurus, the Sikhs' development as a community often brought them into conflict with other forces in Moghul India. In 1761, as the Moghul empire declined, the temple was sacked by the Afghan raider Ahmad Shah Durrani. (It was rebuilt three years later.) In 1984 the Indian Army's Operation Bluestar brought tanks into the complex in a disastrous four-day firefight with heavily armed Sikh separatists who had virtually taken over the complex. India's Prime Minister Indira Gandhi was assassinated about five months later by two of her Sikh bodyguards, in what was widely believed to be retribution for the Army attack on the temple. Amazingly, the temple now shows few signs of this tragic event, or of the decade of separatist violence and state repression that plagued Punjab afterward.

All day long, while a select group of singers, or *ragis,* broadcast hymns throughout the complex, pilgrims from rustic Punjabi towns and villages—India's hugely productive breadbasket—make their way around it, some performing *seva* (voluntary service) by cleaning the marble or completing other tasks. The dignity that pilgrims invest in the Golden Temple, the grandeur of its design, and the hospitality extended to visitors transcend the turmoil of the past.

WHAT TO SEE

Fodor'sChoice ★ The train station and most hotels are near the British-built cantonment, about 15 minutes from the **Golden Temple.** You approach the temple through the Hall Bazaar, which leads to the **clock-tower** gate. (To symbolize an egalitarian welcome to all castes, all Sikh temples have four entrances, but this is the main one.) There is a counter where visitors leave their shoes—many of the attendants here are volunteers, and their handling of others' shoes is another illustration of the Sikh doctrine of caste equality. (A tip of a couple rupees is appreciated.) If you smoke, leave all tobacco products behind, as they're forbidden here. Cameras and mobile phones, however, are allowed. Pilgrims wash their feet at a spigot by the gate before entering the temple complex. Sikhs will already have their heads covered, with turbans for males and *chunnis* (large scarves) for women; if you haven't brought a head covering, make use of the bin of scarves by the stairs.

From the top of the gateway stairs, you'll see a wide pool of water—known as the *sarovar* (sea). Walking down the steps, you'll reach the white marble walkway, called the *parikrama* (circumambulation path), that surrounds the pool. Each side of the pool is 510 feet long, and pilgrims normally make a complete circuit before approaching the Harmandir Sahib. Doing so gives a good sense of the scale of the place. Various points around the parikrama are considered auspicious places to bathe; the bathing steps along the east length of the walkway are said to mark a spot that's especially potent. Just behind this is the entrance to a small garden that adjoins an assembly hall on the right and two pilgrims' hostels to the rear. On the left, under two tall minarets is the **Guru Ram Das Langar**—the temple's communal dining hall, named after the fourth Sikh guru. All Sikh temples have such a *langar* (the name of the place as well as the free meal served here): eating together and serving a meal to others is perhaps the most fondly practiced of all Sikh rituals. Don't hesitate to join in; meals are served daily from 11 to 3 and 7 to 11, and the food, usually a few thick chapatis and some dal, is simple and robust. In another kitchen at the southwest corner of the parikrama, pilgrims make a donation in return for a packet of halvah, a rich and sticky sweet usually made from farina, which they then take to Harmandir Sahib and present as an offering. A portion is given back to worshippers as *prasad,* which some translate as the "edible form of God's grace."

Halfway across the east side of the parikrama, the causeway out to Harmandir Sahib is on your right, and to the left is the five-story **Akal Takht,** topped by a gilt dome. This building, whose name means "timeless throne," represents Sikh temporal authority—day-to-day administration—as opposed to the spiritual authority of Harmandir Sahib. It was here that much of the heavy fire that met the Indian Army during Operation Bluestar originated; the first building was largely destroyed during the fighting, but has now been fully restored.

To reach **Harmandir Sahib** you go under an archway known as the **Darshani Deorhi** ("gateway of vision") and cross a 204-foot-long causeway. Take the left passageway. (Note that pilgrims sometimes arrive in large numbers for ceremonies, particularly at dusk. Access to the Harmandir Sahib is controlled at such times and pilgrims can back up the causeway, making a visit to the sanctum a lengthy undertaking.) Pilgrims typically bow down at the doorway after crossing the causeway, then circumambulate the central temple around a small parikrama. The exterior walls are decorated in beautiful *pietra dura* (marble inlaid with semiprecious stones) said to have been brought by Maharaja Ranjit Singh from Moghul monuments in Lahore.

On the temple's ground level, the *Guru Granth Sahib* sits on a special throne. Attendants wave whisks over it to keep flies away, and a *granthi* (lay specialist) sits reciting the text with harmonium players and other musicians off to one side. Feel free to enter the temple; just remember to keep your head covered and refrain from taking pictures. As you go back through the Darshani Deorhi, a temple priest or volunteer will usually be stationed under a small tree handing out servings of the halvah that previous pilgrims have offered. The ritual of receiving prasad is one that Sikhs share with Hindus. Just around the northwest corner of the parikrama stands an old jujube tree that is said to have healing powers.

The **Central Sikh Museum,** upstairs in the clock-tower entrance, contains graphic paintings depicting the tumultuous history of the Sikh gurus and their followers. Included are scenes from the British period and Operation Bluestar. *Free* *Temple daily (usually) 5 AM–10 PM, museum daily 10–6.*

Outside the temple's clock-tower entrance, about 500 yards north, a small plaque and narrow gateway mark the entrance to **Jallianwala Bagh.** Here, on April 13, 1919, occurred one of the defining moments in India's struggle for independence. The day was Baisakhi, celebrated by Sikhs as both the first day of the new year and the day that Guru Gobind Singh consolidated the faith under the leadership of the Khalsa ("God's own"; a fraternity of the pious) in 1699. The city was under curfew after reported attacks on some British residents, yet some 20,000 people had gathered here to protest the arrest of Indian nationalist leaders under the Rowlatt Act, a British legislation that allowed for detention without trial. Seeing this crowd, British Brigadier General Reginald E.H. Dyer positioned his troops just inside the narrow entrance to the small garden (which is surrounded on all sides by residential buildings) and ordered them to open fire. Some 1,200 people were wounded, and several hundred died. This massacre, chillingly reenacted in Richard Attenborough's film *Gandhi,* caused widespread outrage and contributed to the launch of Mahatma Gandhi's noncooperation movement. The British attempted to suppress news of the incident, and when an inquiry was finally held, such comments as "It was no longer a question of merely dispersing the crowd, but one of producing a sufficient moral effect" (Dyer) did nothing to assuage the worldwide response. Nobel Laureate poet Rabindranath Tagore renounced his English knighthood, and even Winston Churchill, himself no enemy of the empire, raised an uproar in Parliament (though a majority in the House of Lords approved of Dyer's actions). Jallianwala Bagh was subsequently purchased by Indian nationalists to prevent its being turned into a covered market, and it remains one of the most moving monuments to India's 20th-century history. Queen Elizabeth visited in 1997, after much negotiation over whether or not she should make a formal apology (she didn't, but she and Prince Philip did remove their shoes before entering the grounds). Today the garden is planted with a few rosebushes, but the bullet holes from the British fusillade remain. The well, into which some dove in a vain attempt to save themselves, is on the north side. A modern memorial occupies the east end, and a small display to the left as you enter the garden features contemporary newspaper accounts of the incident. *Free* *Dawn–dusk.*

6

Other sights in Amritsar include the 16th-century **Durgiana Temple** (opposite Gole Bagh, south of the train station), a Hindu shrine to the goddess Durga, which in its design replicates its more famous Sikh neighbor. *Free* *Dawn–dusk.*

The **Ram Bagh** gardens, northeast of the train station (enter on Mall Road), date from the period of Maharaja Ranjit Singh (1780–1839). At the center of the garden, the **Punjab Government Museum** displays weapons and portraits from the maharaja's era in a period building; *Free* *Tues. through Sun. 10–7.*

The **Wagah–Attari border crossing** about 30 km (19 mi) west of Amritsar is a well-known checkpost on the India–Pakistan border. The daily flag-lowering ceremony, in the evenings around 6 PM, is the draw here—with great pomp, Pakistani and Indian soldiers in full-dress uniform go through a sort of competitive ritual of winding up the day, and even shake hands at the end.

WHERE TO EAT & STAY

$ ✕ **Bharawan Dhaba.** Amritsar is famous for its cheap *dhabas* (roadside eateries), restaurants where the Punjabi love of good country cooking is exhibited in very basic surroundings. Try this one or Surjit's Chicken House on Lawrence Road. River fish are a special attraction, as is chicken, cooked dry in a tandoor (oven) or with a spicy sauce. In winter ask for *sarson ka saag*—mustard greens stewed in ginger with a dollop of *ghee* (clarified butter) and served with *makki ki roti* (delicious cornmeal chapatis). ✉ *Opposite Town Hall on way to Golden Temple* ☎ *No phone* ✍ *Reservations not accepted* ▭ *No credit cards.*

$ ✕ **Crystal.** Large, middle-class Punjabi families with rambunctious children in tow flood this popular restaurant in the middle of town every night of the week. But there's plenty of room for everyone else who might get a kick out of all the people-watching if not the menu, chock-full of the standard mishmash of cuisines that seems to be the prevailing wisdom at most large restaurants in India. Tired of Punjabi fare? Crystal's Italian dishes such as baked manicotti come close to the real deal. The art-deco style (dark hardwood floors, mirrored walls, plush table settings) gives off a five-star restaurant vibe without the high prices. ✉ *Crystal Chowk* ☎ *183/222–5555 or 183/222–9999* ▭ *No credit cards.*

$ **Mohan International.** Amritsar continues to lack upscale accommodations, but this large modern hotel, a short ride from the Golden Temple, remains a dependable choice for both Indians and foreign travelers. Don't expect luxury—the lobby is a bland shade of gray marble decked with a single chandelier. Rooms are a bit more colorful, with carpet and basic bedcovers in various shades of red. And the pool, a rare amenity in Amritsar hotels, is something to look forward to after a day in the blistering sun. The restaurant is a popular place for Amritsar families to have parties. **Pros:** largest pool in town, well-known locally, free breakfast. **Cons:** updates not a top priority, uninviting staff, mold issues in some rooms (ask to inspect any room before taking it) ✉ *Albert Rd., 143001* ☎ *183/222–7801 and 183/222–7802* 🌐 *www.mohaninternationalhotel.com* *76 rooms, 1 suite* *In-room: refrigerator. In-hotel: restaurant, room service, bar, pool, laundry service, public Internet, no-smoking rooms.* ▭ *AE, MC, V* *CP.*

¢ **Mrs. Bhandari's Guesthouse.** Run by the same family for more than 50 years, this sprawling set of cantonment bungalows harkens back to an earlier age of travel in India. The charming family matriarch, Mrs. Tahmi Bhandari, died in August, 2007, at 101 years old. But the intimate, eco-friendly establishment plans to press on, continuing to play up its large vegetable gardens and farm animals that you can help tend if you wish. The rooms are huge, with polished-wood furnishings, high ceilings and eclectic decorations from the family stash. Each has a fireplace (a fee is charged for lighting it), and most open onto a well-maintained lawn. Food will gladly be served in your room. **Pros:** an experience in real Indian living, home-cooked food, romantic rooms, good value. **Cons:** a bit out of the way, modern amenities lacking. ✉ *10 Cantonment Rd., Amritsa, 143001* ☎ *183/222–8509 or 183/222–5714* *183/222–2390* *15 rooms* *In-room: no phone, no TV. In-hotel: restaurant, pool, laundry service, room service, no elevator.* ▭ *AE, MC, V.*

Fodor's Choice ★

CHANDIGARH

Most of India's major cities emerged gradually, around ancient or colonial monuments. Chandigarh, in starkly modernist contrast, was designed in the 1950s, in the pink of India's new-found independence, by the French architect Le Corbusier. The capital of two bordering states, Haryana and Punjab, it's a refreshing stop on the long day's drive from Delhi to Shimla or other Himachal Pradesh destinations. Blessed with spacious avenues and plenty of green, including bright bougainvillea, the city has a downtown devoid of the usual scruffy chaos—sidewalk stalls, *paan* (betel-leaf) shops, slums, trash, and hawkers seem to be in shorter supply here. However, over time, Chandigarh's neglected areas, replete with barbed wire and garbage, have made Le Corbusier's trademark concrete buildings much less attractive.

It's easy to get around, as Chandigarh is organized on a grid, and you can see the main sights in a day. Hire an auto-rickshaw or cycle-rickshaw (Rs. 40 and Rs. 20, respectively, from one sector to the next) for short distances. Sector 17 is the hub of the city, where all the restaurants, banks, theaters, and shops are; much of this sector is pedestrian-only and easy to negotiate. Adjoining and surrounding 17, forming the rest of the city center, are Sectors 1, 8, 9, 10, 16, 18, 21, 22, and 23.

WHAT TO SEE

The innovative **Rock Garden,** three sectors from 17, near Sector 1, was designed by Nek Chand, an Indian artist who, despite his acclaim, still calls himself "an untutored former road inspector." This 6-acre fantasy is a maze of waterfalls and walkways through sculptures made from a mixture of oddly shaped stones from the Shivalik foothills, industrial waste, and discarded materials collected by the artist on his bicycle. There's also an open-air pavilion and a theater with giant swings. The artist is available to meet visitors; ask at the main reception area.

The modernist **Art and Picture Gallery** in Sector 10 is worth a look, especially for its outdoor sculpture gallery, open Tuesday to Sunday 10 to 4:30.

The 2-km (1-mi) walk around the well-kept, man-made **Sukhna Lake,** near Sector 1, is pleasant in early evening, when all of Chandigarh comes out to stroll; during the day you can rent pedal boats.

In Pinjore, 20 km (12 mi) northeast of Chandigarh, the 17th-century Moghul-style **Yadvindra Gardens** are laid out on a gentle slope, with seven terraces of pools and fountains.

WHERE TO EAT & STAY

$$$ ★ ✕ **Black Lotus.** It's common to see important government officials and other prominent Punjabi leaders sipping martinis and lounging on the sleek red cubes at the front bar of this modern Asian restaurant. Sprinkled with red teardrop light fixtures and sparse black tables, the Taj Chandigarh's main dining establishment has tried to

break the monotony of the city's standard food scene by employing a native Chinese chef. His Chinese-inspired dishes, thankfully, have no trace of Indian masalas, and standouts include crispy chilli garlic lobster and lightly-fried chilli corn. Even if you're not a hotel guest, it's well worth a visit. ✉ *Taj Chandigarh, Block No. 9, Sector 17-A* ☎ *172/651–3000* ▭ *AE, MC, V.*

$ ✕ **Mehfil.** Named for the gatherings once enjoyed by the Urdu-language poets, this no-frills restaurant-pub is popular for its Mughlai food, though it also serves sizzlers (steaming metal platters of meat and vegetables), kebabs, and Chinese dishes. It's in a shiny food-mall area of the city, with a variety of other restaurants nearby, so it's a fairly happening place to sample Chandigarh's nightlife and observe locals out with their friends and families. ✉ *Sector 17C, near Titan showroom,* ☎ *172/270–3539 or 172/270–4224* ▭ *MC, V.*

$$$ **Taj Chandigarh.** There was no modern business hotel in this increasingly important business center until the Taj Group arrived in 2005. Now it's easily the best hotel in town for all travelers who can afford it, especially those who wouldn't mind a dose of casual luxury before heading to the mountainous north. The large lobby is bright and inviting, with plenty of places to lounge next to a tall window wall that overlooks a series of inky-blue fountains. Plush, geometric-patterned area rugs are in all the rooms, which also come with modern blond-wood furniture and 42-inch plasma TVs. The hip Lava Bar and its bevy of classic lava lamps off the main lobby fills a void for Chandigrah's fashionable younger crowd. **Pros:** attentive service, casual vibe, good drinks. **Cons:** expensive, lots of "suits," un-cozy. ✉ *Block No. 9, Sector 17-A, Chandigarh, 160017* ☎ *172/651–3000* 🌐 *www.tajhotels.com* *148 rooms, 1 suite* *In-room: refrigerator, DVD, Wi-Fi. In-hotel: 3 restaurants, room service, bar, pool, gym, spa, laundry service, concierge, executive floor, public Internet, public Wi-Fi.* ▭ *AE, DC, MC, V.*

$$ **Hotel Mountview.** Transcending its inherent limitations as a government-run operation, the Mountview is a good choice, with all the amenities a private hotel would offer, at about half the price. The front entrance is busy with lots of tour groups constantly being unloaded from buses. The marble lobby is spacious, but a large fountain's echo can make conversation difficult. Still, the plush, tastefully decorated rooms overlook a manicured lawn with glittering silhouettes of palm trees. You're walking distance from the Art and Picture Gallery and a rose-garden park. The hotel's Chinese restaurant, the Wok, serves huge portions laced with fresh garlic and ginger, plus Indian and Western food. **Pros:** close to sights, free breakfast. **Cons:** old carpeting, noisy in common public areas. ✉ *Sector 10, Chandigarh, 160011* ☎ *172/274–0544, 172/274–0444, or 172/467–1111* 🌐 *www.citcochandigarh.com* *145 rooms, 10 suites* *In-room: refrigerator. In-hotel: 2 restaurants, room service, bar, pool, gym, laundry service, public Internet, public Wi-Fi.* ▭ *AE, MC, V* *CP.*

$ **Hotel Shivalikview.** Well known and usually full of tourists, Hotel Shivalikview is one of the least-expensive government-run hotels in town. Large picture windows decorate all the common areas, but the lobby is a bit dark with old plaid furniture and the subcontinent's ubiquitous florescent tube lights that can make your surroundings feel a bit institutional. The café serves a range of delicious South Indian snacks, and the bar, Indian restaurant, and rooftop Chinese restaurant are popular and lively. Rates include breakfast and dinner. **Pros:** good views of the Shivalik mountain range, walking distance from most sites, free food. **Cons:** cramped elevators hold only three people at a time, dingy lobby, noisy. ✉*Sector 17E, Chandigarh, 160017* ☎*172/270–0001* 📠*172/270–1094* *104 rooms, 4 suites* *In-room: Wi-Fi. In-hotel: 2 restaurants, room service, bar, laundry service, public Internet, public Wi-Fi.* ▭*AE, MC, V* *MAP.*

$ **Maya Palace.** Standard rooms in this tall, strip-mall hotel are quite small, but they're clean, comfortable, and have tidy bathrooms. Tiled floors are surrounded by wood-paneled walls and simple modern furniture. The equally small lobby has a coffee shop called Nibbles whose tables are just a couple of feet away from where you check in. Think no-frills boutique hotel with an identity crisis—the hotel also happens to come with a 100-person banquet hall despite its size. Because of the building's odd design, the cheaper rooms look out on the stairwell; all you can do is draw the curtain across. **Pros:** personal service, boutique feel, good selection of coffees. **Cons:** narrow, steep stairwells; no elevators; difficult to find. ✉*SCO 325–328, Himalaya Marg, Sector 35B, Chandigarh, 160022* ☎*172/260–0547* 🌐*www.mayahotels.in* *26 rooms* *In-room: refrigerator, Wi-Fi. In-hotel: restaurant, room service, bar, no elevator, laundry service, public Wi-Fi, parking (fee).* ▭*AE, DC, MC, V* *CP.*

6

HIMACHAL PRADESH

Threaded with rivers and dotted with lakes, Himachal Pradesh spans five Himalayan mountain ranges—the Shivalik, Dhauladhar, Pir Panjal, Great Himalayas, and Zanskar. Except for the capital, Shimla, and the overpopulated towns of Dharamshala and Manali, Himachal is a land of alpine villages, speckled with thousands of Hindu and Buddhist temples and monasteries.

Each of the various groups in this region has its own customs, clothing, religion, food, and lifestyles. Most Himachalis are Hindu, but the people of Lahauli and Spiti are Buddhist, and Kinnauris follow both Hindu and Buddhist traditions. Two seminomadic tribes, the Gaddi and Gujjar, also maintain many of their ancient customs here. The Gaddi, who travel with sheep, goats, and cattle, are Hindu, and generally believe in evil spirits that are appeased by animal sacrifices and animist rituals. Gaddi men traditionally wear a *chola* (white thigh-length woolen coat) over *sutthan* (tight woolen trousers) held in place by a *dora* (a black rope of sheep's wool) coiled around the waist. Women wear a *luanchari* (a long, colorful dress) with a woven dora tied around the waist and lots of jewelry, both for good luck and to indicate wealth. The Muslim Gujjar travel with buffalo, and make their living selling fresh milk and ghee. Gujjar men, usually bearded, wear turbans and long robes. Women wear the traditional Indian Muslim *salwar-kameez*, a long tunic over loose pants tapered at the ankle. Often somber in color, this outfit is accentuated by paisley scarves and chunky silver necklaces, bracelets, and dangling earrings.

Trekking, driving, fishing, and biking in Himachal Pradesh can take you through flowering alpine meadows, forests of pine, oak, fir, and ash, Buddhist monasteries, mountain wildlife, and generally unforgettable panoramas. Inquire with a tour company *(⇨ Himachal Pradesh & Ladakh Essentials)* about the following routes: Lahaul–Kinnaur (with a stop in Spiti), McLeod Ganj–Machhetar (through the Dhauladhar Range, from the Kangra Valley to the Ravi Valley), and Manali–Bir (from the Kullu Valley to the Kangra Valley). Jeep safaris are an easy option on the three-day stretch from Manali to Leh, or the longer, quieter stretch from Shimla into Kinnaur and on to Spiti. Mountain biking from Manali to Leh is another way to cover this popular route; avid bikers can complete the ride in eight days. There's plenty to see along the way, including spectacular views from towering passes including the impressive Rohtang Pass (13,130 feet long), the gateway to Lahaul and Spiti.

Fish for trout in the Pabar River near Rohru, a two-day trip from Shimla, or in the Larji River, at its confluence with the Tirthan River over the Jalori Pass. You can also catch trout in the Uhl River, near Barot, and in the Sangla. Try for *mahaseer*, an enormous river fish, in the Beas River near Dharamshala. Between July and September you can also go white-water rafting on the Beas.

The peak tourist season in Himachal Pradesh runs from May though September. June and September are dry and warm; July and August have monsoon rains and are not the best months to visit, as roads can deteriorate and landslides occur. In April and November, the days can be sunny enough for short sleeves, and hotel prices drop. In winter, temperatures hover around freezing and some hotels close from December through February; the others discount their rates up to 50% (except Christmas and the New Year). Only a few hotels have central heating; in the others you may end up worshipping your wee electric heater, for which the cheaper hotels charge Rs. 50–Rs. 100 extra per night.

SHIMLA

360 km (225 mi) north of Delhi, about 117 km (73 mi) northeast of Chandigarh.

The capital of Himachal Pradesh, Shimla is perhaps best perceived as a gateway to the district of Kinnaur. If it's fresh mountain air and serenity you seek, don't spend more time than you need to here. The charms of Rudyard Kipling's city have faded: paint peels on Victorian structures, and mortar is left to crumble. Garish, large developments now dot the surrounding hills, and traffic lines the road in high season, sometimes causing delays on miles of switchbacks en route. The town is often packed with Indian families on holiday, and also attracts

British travelers whose antecedents made an annual trip to this summer capital during the Raj.

The crowds that swarm Shimla's main plaza and thoroughfare, the pedestrian-only **Mall,** sweep you along at their pace, providing a gracious break from motor traffic. The Mall is well preserved, its old buildings pleasantly lighted at night. Chattering, yelping monkeys are about as common as tourists, so you'll see them vaulting off electricity polls and swinging from eave to eave chewing plants, potato chips, and whatever else they find in their path. **Scandal Point,** where the Mall meets the Ridge, offers a fascinating view not just of the town but of families shopping, strolling, buying treats from vendors, and riding ponies. It's a good place to rest and meet fellow travelers.

THE MONKEY MENACE

You know it's bad when hotels have to tell patrons to keep their windows closed or risk a visit from a monkey. The so-called "monkey menace" throughout India is as old as the hills, but the Himachal Pradesh government started taking it seriously in 2007 when farmers complained of mass crop devastation. But animal control in a country where many animals are often worshipped is impossibly complex—the government-backed operations to "scientifically cull" monkeys in the Himalayas continue to meet with resistance from animal-rights activists who call it "unscientific killing."

6

Christchurch, the **Gaiety Theatre,** the **Town Hall,** and the **General Post Office** are prominent architectural reminders of the Raj in the Gothic, Arts and Crafts, and timbered Tudor styles. Other less-famous examples in town have become worn and are not as well kept.

The **Oberoi Cecil** hotel makes a good stop for high tea or, better still, a superb Himachali dinner of vegetables or meat cooked in a yogurt-based curry, chickpeas sautéed with spinach and burnt walnuts, or lentils, potatoes, and other specialties spiked with aniseed.

Beyond the Cecil is the gigantic **Viceregal Lodge,** which houses the Indian Institute of Advanced Study and is well worth a visit just for its teak-panel library or the view from its well-tended gardens. Easily one of the grandest and haughtiest buildings in North India, it reeks of the days when the British ruled all they surveyed.

Take in the architectural and historical highlights with a walk through town and up to **Jakhoo Hill** (2 km [1 mi] uphill from the center of town). At 8,054 feet, it's the highest peak around, crowned with a temple dedicated to the monkey god Hanuman. The monkeys en route are notoriously aggressive, so don't walk around with food or beverages in plain sight.

If you're nervous about encountering monkeys, take a local guide along—the creatures all recognize **Sanjay Sood** (☎*177/280–5806 or 98170–16580*), who lives in Rothney Castle near the base of the hill, on Jakhoo Road, and visits the temple daily. Sood also leads walks to local heritage sites and temples.

The **Temple of Kamna Devi,** 5 km (3 mi) from Shimla on the way to Jutogh, perches on the top of Prospect Hill—accessible partly on foot and partly by car—and offers glorious views of the surrounding hills and the Toy Train from Taradevi to Jotogh.

The **Sankat Mochan Temple,** dedicated to Hanuman, is about 7 km (4 mi) outside town at 6,073 feet.

The town of **Chail** is built on three forested hills 45 km (28 mi) southeast of Shimla, just over an hour by car. Once the summer capital of the maharaja of Patiala, it's best known for having the highest cricket pitch in the world. It's an excellent spot for picnics.

Shimla is not a shopping destination, but the lack of car traffic in the Mall area makes it easy to wander and browse. There are bargains to be had on woolens (blankets, shawls, sweaters) and handwoven items from Kashmir and Tibet. The **Dewandchand Atmaram** (✉ *The Mall* ☎ *177/265–4455*) is rated the best in town for woolen clothing and shawls. Expect to pay Rs. 1,000 or less for a basic shawl.

Shezadi (✉ *The Mall* ☎ *177/281–3333*) sells designer salwar-kameez, shawls, and bathrobes.Fixed-price crafts are available at the state-run **Himachal Emporium** (✉ *The Mall* ☎ *177/280–1234*).**Lakkar Bazaar,** beyond the Ridge, sells a wide range of interesting and inexpensive wooden handicrafts.

There are several bookshops on the Mall, stacked with a mixture of best sellers and unexpected titles; **Maria Brothers** is recommended for rare books, old prints, and lithographs.

WHERE TO EAT & STAY

$ ✕ **Alfa.** After a stroll on the Mall, visit one of its popular mainstays, Alfa, for a fried Indian snack or full meal. The restaurant has a horde of both locals and tourists constantly coming and going, and the blond-wood furniture with bright green and red trimmings make it a cheerful, albeit hectic, break. The Indian fare is traditional—naan, black dal (lentils cooked with spices), your choice of meat or vegetable. You can also sample the Chinese and Western dishes. They also make a good cup of piping-hot Bournvita, the classic British malted milk. ✉ *The Mall* ☎ *177/265–7151* ▭ *No credit cards.*

$ ✕ **Baljees.** Owned by the local hotel of the same name, but located on the Mall, Baljees is one of Shimla's toniest places to dine, though admittedly this is not saying much. The second-floor air-conditioned dining room offers a wide range of Indian, Chinese, and Western food in simple, comfortable surroundings. ✉ *The Mall* ☎ *177/265–2313* ▭ *No credit cards.*

$$$$ ★ **Oberoi Cecil.** Fresh-squeezed juice served on arrival is standard at Oberoi properties, but the Cecil will even have personalized cookies waiting if you've got kids in tow. Expect to see lots of Indian kids, in fact, who are encouraged to run around and have a good time at the indoor heated pool, the activity center with games and movies, or the old-fashioned ice-skating rink in winter. There's some serious luxury going on, too. Rooms have hardwood floors, Kashmiri car-

pets, Victorian Raj–style furnishings, and luxurious bathrooms with oversized showerheads and plush robes. Follow a hard day of play with an ayurvedic massage at the hotel's signature spa, or have afternoon tea, pastries, or cocktails in the huge atrium. As the only hotel in Shimla with modern creature comforts and a high level of quality and efficiency, it's a magnificent retreat. **Pros:** kid-friendly, free DVDs on request, spectacular views of the Himalayas. **Cons:** monkey menace (guests are encouraged to keep windows closed), must walk through lobby after a visit to the spa or pool. ✉ *Chaura Maidan, Shimla, 171001* ☎ *177/280–4848* 🌐 *www.oberoihotels.com* *79 rooms* *In-room: refrigerator, DVD, ethernet. In-hotel: restaurant, room service, bars, pool, gym, spa, children's programs (all ages), laundry service, concierge, public Internet.* 💳 *AE, DC, MC, V.*

$$$$ ★ **Wildflower Hall.** Huge chandeliers hanging above the indoor heated pool set the tone for this majestic "destination spa" run by the Oberoi group—luxury with no expense spared. The Jacuzzi right outside feels like it's floating in the snow-capped panorama of the Himalayas, and your room balcony has an equally splendid view. Considered one of the best resorts in India, Wildflower Hall is a 45-minute drive from Shimla. At 8,250 feet above sea level and surrounded by a 12-square-km (31-square-mi) sanctuary protected by the government, it aims to please both beauty junkies and rugged outdoor types: there's a long menu of holistic spa treatments as well as treks lasting up to six hours (these are led by a staff environmentalist who can identify just about every plant along the way). **Pros:** no kids running around, emphasis on environmental appreciation, staff at your beck and call. **Cons:** extremely expensive, the numerous calls to see if you're OK may be a bit much. ✉ *Chharabra, Shimla, 171012* ☎ *177/264–8585* 🌐 *www.oberoihotels.com* *87 rooms* *In-room: refrigerator, DVD. In-hotel: 2 restaurants, room service, bar, tennis court, pool, gym, spa, bicycles, laundry service, concierge, public Internet, airport shuttle, no kids under 12.* 💳 *AE, DC, MC, V.*

$$$ **Chapslee.** Faded opulence surrounds you in this ivy-covered old manor house, built in 1835 and once home to the maharaja of Kapurthala. An eclectic mix of Gobelin tapestries, European wallpaper, Persian carpets, Indian pottery, and rare furnishings from the Doge's Palace in Venice cover practically every inch of the hotel. Each suite is uniquely decorated and named—ask for the "pink" room, which has a stunning pink glow by firelight, if you want an outrageously romantic experience. Little details like a hot-water bottle slipped into your bed at night and antique walking sticks for your strolls make you feel like a family member, not just a guest. The fixed-menu Indian and Western meals are excellent (nonguests can dine also if they reserve in advance; by reservation only). **Pros:** impeccable service, historic grandeur. **Cons:** rooms starting to show their age, screaming children at the school nearby. ✉ *Lakkar Bazar, Shimla, 171001* ☎ *177/280–2542* 🌐 *www.chapslee.com* *6 rooms* *In-room: no a/c, no TV. In-hotel: restaurant, tennis court, no elevator, laundry service.* 💳 *MC, V* *FAP.*

$$ **Springfields.** The former summer retreat of the royal family of Shekhupura has 10 Victorian rooms in a large period bungalow, set in a

garden about 5 km (3 mi) from the center of town in Chhotta Shimla. The spacious rooms have a 1920s air, with antique pieces, wood floors, fireplaces, and balconies. Located well away from the madness of the Mall, Springfields has lovely views of the valley. A one-way taxi ride to the Mall costs Rs. 100. **Pros:** good value for the money, special rates available on request, will arrange almost any activity in Shimla for you. **Cons:** getting to the pedestrian mall is a bit of a hassle. ✉*Opposite Tibetan school, Chhotta Shimla, 171002* ☎*177/262–1297 or 177/262–1298* 🌐*www.ushalex-ushotels.com* *10 rooms* *In-room: no a/c. In-hotel: restaurant, room service, bar, no elevator, laundry service, public Internet.* ▭*MC, V.*

ASCENDING TO THE MALL

You can't easily walk to the Mall, since the town is built layer upon layer into the mountainside. Instead, you'll need to use the Mall's public elevators (Rs. 10 round-trip). There's a long line to board the three lifts, which are too small to accommodate the crowds. Be careful during the time-consuming process—some people get aggressive while trying to get on.

$ **Woodville Palace.** Topped with a jumble of towers and red-roof turrets, the rambling Woodville Palace is perched on top of a hill in the midst of Indian cedars, but it's still close to the town center. Dating back to 1866 and still owned by descendents of local royalty, it's a popular backdrop for period Bollywood productions. In 2007 the hotel made significant changes, adding six new rooms with hardwood floors, unique color schemes and canopy beds draped in silk. Some of the older rooms feel a little tired—most noticeably with worn carpet—but the beautiful antiques and historical references throughout the public spaces make the palace a memorable place to stay. **Pros:** intimate feel, lots of arranged extras like pony rides for kids, cool bar in a 1930s style. **Cons:** no Internet, room quality varies, can get stuffy in summer months with no a/c. ✉*Raj Bhavan Rd., Shimla, 171002* ☎*177/262–4038* 🌐*www.woodvillepalacehotel.com* *31 rooms* *In-room: no a/c. In-hotel: restaurant, room service, bar, no elevator, laundry service, no-smoking rooms.* ▭*AE, MC, V.*

¢ **Baljees Regency.** A few minutes from the Mall, Baljees probably offers the best value for money in Shimla and its public spaces look much more expensive than the room rates suggest. The shiny marble lobby has ample sitting room, and there's a beautiful terrace with hanging greenery. Although not terribly imaginative, the rooms are neat and comfortable—with green carpets, simple furnishings, and small sitting areas—and have decent views. You may want to opt for a deluxe room, because they're somewhat more pleasant for just Rs. 200 extra. The bathrooms, done in red granite, are clean and modern. **Pros:** unfussy service, a reasonable antidote to Shimla's generally pricey, over-the-top homage to the British Raj. **Cons:** no frills beyond pleasant facade, old carpeting that doesn't look regularly cleaned. ✉*Circular Rd., Shimla, 171003* ☎*177/281–4054* 🌐*www.hotelbaljeesregency.com* *30 rooms* *In-room: no a/c. In-hotel: restaurant, room service, bar, laundry service, public Internet.* ▭*AE, MC, V.*

EN ROUTE

To access the Kinnaur region, which holds the wonderful Sangla Valley, head northeast of Shimla. Sangla is eight hours (227 km [140 mi]) from Shimla on a road that gets more precarious in the second half of the trip. You'll be on NH–22 until Karcham; at Karcham, turn right and drive the remaining 18 km (12 mi) south to Sangla. If you're approaching Kinnaur from Lahaul or Spiti, consider accessing Sangla from Tabo, a large Spiti town 47 km (29 mi) south of Kaza. This 185-km (115-mi) journey takes six to seven hours, and you can stay at the friendly Banjara Camps at both ends.

KINNAUR

Sangla is 227 km (141 mi) northeast of Shimla.

The Sutlej River runs through the eminently green district of Kinnaur, made up of the Baspa and Sangla valleys in the towering Kinnaur Kailash Range. Like Spiti, Kinnaur hides wonderful old Buddhist monasteries, but despite the proximity to Tibet, only the far eastern and northern, cold-desert parts of Kinnaur are Buddhist. The curved roofs of gompas reflect the transition of the landscape from Hinduism to Buddhism. Kinnauris are decked in green jackets, cummerbunds, hats teamed with shawls, and elaborate silver jewelry.

The Sangla Valley is magnificently dramatic, with orchards, burbling streams, and stupendous alpine landscapes. Day hikes, overnight treks, and jeep excursions are well worth the effort it takes to drive here from Shimla. Kinnaur was opened to travelers in 1992, and you still need an Inner Line Permit to travel beyond Rekong Peo to Puh en route to Spiti.

WHERE TO STAY

$ **Banjara Camp** The Sangla Valley's best lodging is a group of deluxe tents with full-size beds and attached cement-floor bathrooms (bucket bath only). At 8,850 feet the camp is smack on the banks of the Baspa River just 30 km (19 mi) shy of Chitkul, the last village on the Old Hindustan–Tibet Road (some 50 km from the China border). Relax in a clearing overlooking the water after a rousing day hike, and listen to the river rush by as you drift off to sleep. The price includes vegetarian meals, served three times a day in a mess tent. The friendly, attentive staff can take you on day hikes or drives, complete with a home-cooked Indian lunch. **Pros:** rugged camping with modern luxury tents, meet like-minded travelers in a small group setting. **Cons:** chilly in April, September and October, so pack carefully. *Reserve through ✉1A Hauz Khas Village, New Delhi, 110016 ☎11/2685–5153 ⊕www.banjaracamps.com ⇨18 tents ♨In-room: no a/c, no phone, no TV. ▭No credit cards ¶○|FAP.*

MANALI

280 km (174 mi) north of Shimla.

Until about 15 years ago, Manali was a small, relaxed place. On one side of town was a settlement of Tibetan refugees; on the other side, near the bus stop, Western backpackers smoked dope and swapped trekking stories. But in 1989, Kashmir descended into chaos following the kidnapping of the Indian Home Minister's daughter by separatist militants. Most of the Indian honeymooners and foreign travelers who would otherwise have vacationed in Kashmir detoured to the village of Manali. The subsequent explosion of development has ruined Manali's tranquility—concrete hotels keep rising, and today Manali is a resort town. The new Manali overshadows the original settlement, Old Manali, whose popularity with hippie Israeli backpackers is reflected in the many Hebrew shop signs. Unfortunately, many of the old homes are now gone, and the area is associated mainly with tourist traffic along its main strip of shops—and it's also known as a place to buy marijuana.

Manali is deep in the culturally rich Kullu Valley, in the shadow of some magnificent Himalayan peaks. The neighboring hillsides are cloaked in forests of towering deodar cedars. The friendly Kullu Valley people are known for their unique traditional dress, including men's pillbox caps with colorful geometric embroidery. Most of the town revolves around its main strip, the **Mall,** and you can negotiate small distances to and from there with auto-rickshaws (Rs. 20 for a few kilometers).

In the heart of town is a Tibetan monastery, the brightly colored **Gadhan Thekchhokling Gompa,** worth a visit if you don't plan to visit any Buddhist areas. The stalls outside sell Tibetan trinkets.

The Mall, Manali's main commercial strip, is lined with shops selling shawls, Kashmiri crafts, and woolens.

Sultaan Kashmir (⊠*Shop 1, City Heart Shopping Complex* ☎*1902/251–610*) has lovely embroidered shawls and jackets—but bargain hard. You shouldn't be paying more than Rs. 500 for any garment.

The **Bhutti Weaver Cooperative Society showroom** (⊠*Manu Market, off Mall*) sells pretty Kullu shawls, Himachali vests, and pashmina shawls and scarves.

Manali's main bazaar, **Manu Market,** occupies a network of lanes near the bus stand on the Beas side of the road. Vendors of wool, fresh local fruit and vegetables (the Kullu Valley is famous for its produce), and colorful Kullu lace, woolens, and caps do brisk business. Noodle kitchens and snack counters beckon as well.

There are several shops selling Tibetan artifacts; try **Samten,** near the taxi stand in one of the market's first lanes.

Make time for a walk to the Hadimba Temple (also called Dunghri Temple), nestled in the woods 20 minutes from the Mall. A cross between temple and pagoda, this ancient shrine has a wooden exterior

CLOSE UP

Eye-Popping Drive: Shimla–Manali

After spending two to four days in the Shimla area, consider driving on to Manali via Mandi and Kullu—this trip (260 km [160 mi]) takes about six hours and is one of the most enjoyable drives in the region. The route curves a fair bit for the first two hours, past bright-green terraced fields, but once it reaches the banks of the Beas River, near Mandi (156 km [100 mi]), the road straightens out and the scenery grows steadily more spectacular. As the road, NH–21, approaches the Kullu Valley it wanders beside the emerald-green Beas between impossibly steep mountains and gorges dotted with traditional mud-and-brick Himachali homes with slate roofs. The regions on the opposite side of the river, bordering Spiti, are incredibly remote—their only form of transport is the basket, a sort of manual cable car that runs from mountaintop villages down to the road. During the monsoon season (July and August), waterfalls drop from the peaks high above. This road was built largely with the labor of Tibetan refugees after their exodus in 1959; they were employed by the Indian government to pave the way north for army convoys.

As you approach Kullu, snow-covered peaks pop up on the horizon, and you start to pass apple orchards and traditional wooden dwellings. After March, the apple trees flower—apples are a major cash crop in this area, and apple-flavor liquor is popular with locals. You might see some Angora rabbit farms, too, as their hair is used to weave shawls. Locals are colorfully dressed in traditional *pattus* (robes) and Himachali *topis* (hats). Stop in Kullu, a thriving market town, to take in a bit of local color. Kullu shawls, in solid colors with distinctive borders, are cheap here and can be found in practically every shop in town. Nice examples are available for well below Rs. 1,000.

On the outskirts of town is the **Bhuttico** (✉ *Bhutti Colony, Bhuntar, Kullu* ☎ *1902/260–049*), the showroom for the work of the Bhutti Weavers Cooperative Society. **Gagan Shawl Industries** (✉ *Bhutti Colony, Bhuntar, Kullu* ☎ *1902/265–325*) sells shawls and more.

Manali is 42 km (26 mi) beyond Kullu. After 21 km (11 mi), turn right off the highway at Patlikuhl, toward Nagar. As the road ascends, the slopes are forested with pines and deodar, and herds of sheep graze on the mountains.

Ten kilometers (6 mi) before Manali, you'll reach the hamlet of Jagat Sukh, a cluster of typical Kullu Valley homes that gives you an idea of what Manali was like before tourists. In these two-story dark-wood houses, livestock is kept on the ground floor while the family lives upstairs. Handlooms whir in many homes, weaving colorful pattus. Have a look at the ancient-looking Shiva temple, with its age-old deity, in the heart of the village—according to a local, "It must be 500 years old, but don't ask the priest. He'll tell you it's over 1,000 years old."

6

decorated with deer antlers. It's dedicated to Hadimba Devi, a demoness who turned respectable when she married one of the noble Pandava brothers, Bhima. Animal sacrifices, usually chickens, take place here, as they do in many Himachali temples since local Hindus have a tradition of appeasing the *devi,* or fearsome goddesses. Yaks from Ladakh are parked outside for those who want joy rides on these giant beasts. Summer sees a carnival open up in the park behind the temple.

Fall—when the valley's many apple trees bear fruit—brings the famous Perahera Festival: a local variation of the Hindu festival of Dussehra, celebrated over most of India in October or November. Ten days after the new moon, villagers bring their local deities—more than 200—from their temples down to Kullu, at the head of the valley. Dragged by hand on palanquins or wheeled on carts known as *raths,* the idols are brought to pay respect to Raghunathji, Kullu's patron god. For three nights, people from all over the valley, including the descendants of local royalty, mill around a temporary market on the dusty fairgrounds next to the Beas River.

At the high end of the Kullu Valley, farther up toward the Rohtang Pass, 20,000-foot peaks loom on three sides. Day hikers will find endless exhilarating paths, often alongside Gujjar shepherds with flocks of goats. Manali is also the origin and endpoint for more serious adventures into the Himalayan wilderness—from here you can launch trekking, driving, and rafting trips into Lahaul, Spiti or, to the west, the Kangra and Chamba valleys. In addition, the road north from Manali over the Rohtang Pass is currently the only open road to Ladakh.

In winter Indian tourists head out from Manali to Snow Point for sledding, tobogganing, skiing, and snowmobiling.

WHERE TO EAT & STAY

¢ ✕ **Chopsticks.** With an odd mix of fake wood flooring, checked tablecloths, and Chinese lanterns—not to mention Western music blaring from a scratchy sound system—this well-known hole in the wall churns out a crowded menu of standard Japanese, Chinese, and Tibetan dishes. It's pretty popular with tourists, and you won't find too many locals here. But it does serve some of Manali's best Chinese food. ✉ *The Mall, opposite taxi stand, Manal* ☎ *1902/252–639* ▭ *No credit cards.*

¢ ✕ **Il Forno.** Only one member of the Italian couple that started this unique restaurant in a traditional wooden Manali home runs it now (the pair divorced right before this writing). Angelone, as the locals call her, plans to return every summer by herself to live upstairs and serve traditional Italian specialties on the ground floor. Her homemade pastas are famous for miles around, and a touch of Indian masala could be tasted in the Bolognese sauce. The homemade tiramisu is better than most versions in major Indian cities. Sadly, there's no wine. ✉ *Beyond the Log Huts next to Hadimba temple with a 15-min steep walk uphill, Manali* ☎ *981/692–2481 mobile* ▭ *No credit cards* ⏲ *Closed Nov.–Mar. No lunch.*

¢ ✕ **Mountview.** Booths and tables are crammed into this narrow space, and the walls hold photos of the Dalai Lama and Lhasa. The Tibetan chef creates Tibetan, Chinese, and Japanese dishes. Try the momos (dumplings), soups with homemade noodles, or spicy Szechuan fare. ✉*The Mall, opposite taxi stand, Manali* ☎*1902/253–617* ▭*No credit cards.*

¢ ✕**Sagar.** Don't let the ground-floor interior painted in an outrageous shade of green and decorated with mustard-color furniture turn you off—a vegetarian restaurant in India has to set itself apart somehow! Thankfully the upstairs room with a great view of Manali's main thoroughfare is more cozy, with dark wood paneling and simple table settings. The catch-all menu mixes Indian food, Chinese dishes, pizzas, pastas, and sizzlers, best enjoyed while cramming in some quality people-watching from above. ✉*The Mall, at taxi stand, Manali* ☎*1902/251–172* ▭*No credit cards.*

$$$ **Manu Allaya.** The front-facing rooms with large private balconies at the Manu Allaya probably have the best views in town of the raging Beas River. Built on several levels, this red-roof hotel bills itself as Manali's only spa retreat. Expect interesting designs like curved hallways lined in smooth wood and bathrooms decked out almost entirely in shiny black marble. If it seems like you're in a modern art museum, Persian rugs and other traditional accents in the rooms add an element of coziness. Rates include breakfast and dinner. **Pros:** it's on the less-populated side of the river so you won't feel like one of the crowd every time you leave your room. **Cons:** expensive, hard to get to, and a dizzying number of room categories and themes that can make you wonder what you're going to get. ✉*Sunny Side, Chadiyari, Manali, 175131* ☎*1902/252–235* 🌐*www.manuallaya.com* *50 rooms, 4 suites, 1 cottage* *In-room: refrigerator. In-hotel: 2 restaurants, room service, bar, pool, gym, spa, laundry service, public Wi-Fi, no-smoking rooms.* ▭*AE, MC, V* *MAP.*

$ **Johnson Hotel and Cafe.** The lush flower garden out front and melon-colored halls with yellow sponge-painted designs add a whimsical touch to this airy, rustic lodge. There are three large apartments in addition to the already huge rooms, making it perfect for families or groups of four. Some open onto the lawn and all are decorated in colorful cotton bedcovers and Persian rugs. Across the garden is the lodge's famous café (closed in winter) serving Indian and Western dishes. Fresh local trout, when available, is a house specialty, and locals rave about it. **Pros:** good bang for the buck with memorable food and a laid-back atmosphere. **Cons:** the chatter of the busy café permeates lawn-facing rooms. ✉*Circuit House Rd., Manali, 175131* ✣*At top of Mall Rd., turn left at Nehru Park and look for sign to Johnson's Restaurant* ☎*1902/253–023* 🌐*www.johnsonhotel.in* *12 rooms, 3 cottage rooms* *In-room: no a/c, no TV (some). In-hotel: restaurant, room service, no elevator, laundry service, public Wi-Fi, parking (fee).* ▭*No credit cards.*

$ **Retreat Cottages.** Coming face-to-face with the Dalai Lama is unlikely, but you can meet his niece at the Retreat Cottages in Manali. Chuki Mahant, whose father is the Dalai Lama's brother, runs the place with her Himachali husband. The large Swiss-style chalet has self-contained sections on different levels, each with a sitting area, kitchenette, and

6

dining area, as well as a little porch and a loft. Airy and well lighted, the units are sparsely but attractively furnished with Tibetan artifacts and carpets, small stoves, and simple wooden furniture. Call in advance in winter, as the hotel sometimes closes. **Pros:** staff leaves you to your own devices, and the location blots out all the tourists walking along the road. **Cons:** you're basically on your own, and there's no food on site—you have to tell them in advance if you want something to eat. ✉ *Log Huts Area, Manali, 175131* ☎ *1902/252–042 or 1902/252–673* ✍ *chukimahant@gmail.com* *8 rooms* *In-room: no a/c, kitchen, refrigerator. In-hotel: no elevator, laundry service.* ▭ *AE, DC, MC, V.*

$ ★ **Snowcrest Manor.** Just standing on the huge deck of this modest hotel overlooking the Kullu Valley and Rohtang Pass is probably the best way to appreciate the awesome beauty of the region. No wonder, since Snowcrest Manor sits on Manali's highest point, putting the entire town into perspective. The sparse lobby's window wall leading to the deck will probably entice you outside before you even check in. Guest rooms are below the lobby: the hotel is built into a cliff. At this writing, the hotel is in the process of replacing old, musty carpet with wood laminate, helping to give a more expensive feel, but furnishings—a simple bed and two floral chairs—remain basic. Regardless of the makeover, Snowcrest's charming staff and unequaled views make it a smart choice. **Pros:** despite being laid-back, the staff are wonderfully attentive without the usual obsequiousness prevalent on the Indian hospitality circuit. **Cons:** rooms are unusually difficult to access for people who can't handle stairs, and it's a long walk up from the center of town. ✉ *Beyond Log Huts, Manali, 175131* ☎ *1902/253–351 or 1902/253–352* ⊕ *www.ushaslexushotels.com* *32 rooms* *In-room: no a/c. In-hotel: restaurant, room service, gym, no elevator, laundry service, public Internet.* ▭ *AE, DC, MC, V.*

¢ **Mayflower.** The large, rustic, wood-paneled rooms with fireplaces next to the beds give the Mayflower a distinct log cabin feel. Soft cotton bedcovers, plush rugs, and separate seating areas add to the romantic coziness. Some of the bathrooms even have tubs, which aren't standard in such budget accommodations. Every room looks out onto the lush, green lawns. About a 10-minute walk uphill from the Mall, the Mayflower experience can't be beat for the money. **Pros:** close to sites, expensive feel, very affordable. **Cons:** no views of the mountains or town, lots of foot traffic nearby. ✉ *Club House Rd., Manali, 175131* ☎ *1902/252104* ⊕ *www.negismayflower.com* *19 rooms* *In-room: no a/c. In-hotel: restaurant, room service, no elevator, public Internet.* ▭ *MC, V.*

EN ROUTE

The districts of Lahaul and Spiti are best accessed from Manali. The Manali–Leh road, open in summer only, sweeps north into Lahaul across the Rohtang Pass, taking about five hours (114 km [70 mi]) to reach the town of Keylong, district headquarters of Lahaul.

Kaza, the district headquarters of Spiti, is 201 km (125 mi) northeast of Manali, a seven- or eight-hour drive. Follow the Manali–Leh highway north up to Gramphoo (62 km [38 mi]), then turn right and head east toward Kaza via Batal.

LAHAUL & SPITI

Keylong, Lahaul, is 114 km (70 mi) north of Manali; Kaza, Spiti, is 201 km (124 mi) southwest of Manali.

The district comprising Lahaul and Spiti (pronounced "piti") is the largest in the state of Himachal Pradesh. The pretty town of Kibber, in Spiti, is one of the highest settlements in the world, at 13,688 feet above sea level.

Beginning 51 km (32 mi) north of Manali on the far side of the Rohtang Pass, **Lahaul** is a heady place for treks and jeep safaris. It's much smaller than Ladakh and has fewer and simpler gompas (Tibetan monasteries), but the two share a general mingling of religion and landscape. Tibetan influences are all over this district. From the Spiti town of Tabo—famous in the Tibetan world for its gompa, which has some spectacular murals—Tibet is hardly 25 km (16 mi) away. Mountains bear in from all directions, and windswept passes overlook stunningly harsh, remote landscapes of stark mountains, boundless sky, and deserted spaces. Expect extremes of weather: mornings and evenings are freezing, but afternoons blaze. The glaciers look icy and somber, and an occasional lake sparkles under the hot sun. Prayer flags and the rare green valley pulse with color. At this writing, Lahaul continues to experience an influx of trekkers, so work with your tour operator to choose a route that avoids crowds.

6

You can raft, day-hike, trek, and tool around by jeep in the **Spiti Valley,** a sensitive border area southeast of Lahaul, on the other side of the Kunzum Pass (15,055 feet). Spiti's landscape is more arid than Lahaul's; its mountains, split by the raging Spiti River, are steeper; and the culture is more thoroughly Buddhist. Here you'll find the 11th-century **Tabo Gompa** (46 km [29 mi] east of Kaza), one of the holiest monasteries for Tibetan Buddhists. Foreigners need an Inner Line Permit to visit Spiti, though formalities are getting looser over time.

EN ROUTE

Two routes, both snowbound in winter, connect Lahaul and Spiti with the rest of the state. To reach southern Himachal Pradesh from Spiti, you can drive via Kaza and Tabo to Kinnaur; to access western Himachal Pradesh from Lahaul, you must go through Manali.

The drive from Manali to **Dharamshala** (253 km [146 mi]) takes six hours. The route is not as picturesque as the drive through the Kullu Valley, but once you enter the **Kangra Valley** (beyond Mandi) on the NH–20, you pass through an endless patchwork of vividly green fields sown with wheat, corn, rice, and bright-yellow mustard. At Baijnath, you'll see the ancient stone Vaidyanath Temple. Closer to Palampur, as the land begins to roll, is a large belt of tea plantations stretching out to the snowy Dhauladhar range—Kangra tea is a specialty here. Consider stopping at the Taragarh Palace Hotel *(⇨ below)* for a meal or an overnight stay. An hour beyond Palampur, the road climbs sharply to Dharamshala.

KANGRA VALLEY

References to the Kangra Valley date back 3,500 years to the age of the Hindu Vedas. Now densely populated, the valley climbs gently into Himachal Pradesh from the plains of Punjab, with the pine-covered Dhauladhar Range jutting out to the west like a Himalayan spur on the northern horizon. The upper part of the valley gave birth to the famous Kangra style of painting, featuring scenes from the life of Lord Krishna, often highly romantic, in a style heavily influenced by Moghul miniatures.

Aside from the Vaidyanath Temple in Baijnath, the Kangra Valley has no sights per se; it's just a pleasant place to wander around, and it has two lovely Heritage Hotels. With a heady mixture of tropical and alpine terrain backed by snow-topped mountains and intersected by rivers, the valley is a popular destination for trekking, fishing, and horseback riding. Experienced riders can take in impressive Himalayan views from spirited polo ponies. Wandering through meadows and forests, you can visit Kangra villages and a Tibetan monastery, spending each night in a tent at a different idyllic campsite. Given the relatively low elevation and lack of air-conditioning, try to come to Kangra before mid-April or after mid-September.

Much of the land here is cultivated.

Although local farmers grow mostly "winter" crops such as wheat and fruit, the plantations in **Palampur** contain the only tea gardens in this part of India. Take home a box of Kangra Green Gold tea to sip while remembering this gentle valley.

Up the road from Palampur is Baijnath, home of the **Vaidyanath Temple.** Dedicated to Lord Shiva, this 9th-century temple is well worth a visit for the intricate stone carvings of Surya (the Vedic sun god) and Garuda (the half-man, half-bird helper of the god Vishnu) on its interior and exterior walls.

WHERE TO STAY

$$ **Taragarh Palace Hotel.** This 1930s summer resort and its 15-acre forested estate now comprise a Heritage Hotel owned by a member of Kashmir's Hindu royalty. In 2005 the owners did something rare for a Heritage property, adding a completely new wing of rooms as well as a new dining hall in hopes of drawing more tourists. It still retains its charm—the open-air art-deco lounge is a pretty place to relax after a dip in the pool and the older rooms have stark royal-blue walls and eclectic furnishings from the family's estate. The long, wide hallways are filled with family photos, old and current. Request a room in the original structure for a more authentic experience. **Pros:** commune with nature and enjoy a relaxing stop on the way to Dharamshala an hour beyond. **Cons:** the new wing distracts slightly from its identity as a Heritage property. ✉ *Taragarh, Kangra Valley, 176081* ☎ *1894/242–034 or 1894/243–077, 11/2464–3046 in Delhi* 🌐 *www.taragarh.com* *26 rooms* *In-room: no a/c. In-hotel: restaurant, room service, tennis court, pool, no elevator, laundry service, public Internet.* ▭ *MC, V.*

$ Judge's Court. In a 12-acre orchard of mango, lychee, plum, persimmon, clove, and cardamom trees and fields of vegetables, this beautifully restored 300-year-old ancestral home of the Kuthiala Sood family includes the family's historic cottage and a country manor. In spring and fall you can sit on a shady veranda, smell the trees in the garden, and look out to the Dhauladhar range; in winter a fire can be arranged in the sitting room. The staff can organize angling, water sports, treks, and picnics. **Pros:** pure relaxation without any of the crowds in Himachal cities. **Cons:** not much to do other than walk around and appreciate nature. ✉*Jai Bhawan, Pragpur, 177107* ☎*1970/245–035 or 1970/245–335, 11/2411–4135 in Delhi* 🌐*www.judgescourt.com* *10 rooms, 3 cottages* *In-room: no TV. In-hotel: restaurant, room service, no elevator, laundry service, public Internet.* *AE, MC, V.*

DHARAMSHALA

253 km (157 mi) west of Manali, 248 km (154 mi) north of Chandigarh.

High above the floor of the Kangra Valley, Dharamshala is an old hill station, an area established in the 1800s for British families to escape the heat elsewhere in India. However, its main attraction is the cloistered upper part of town, McLeod Ganj. Here, 9 km (6 mi) uphill through the Indian Army cantonment, is the Tibetan Government in Exile and the home of the Dalai Lama, Tenzin Gyatso, and an entire Tibetan community.

6

On March 31, 1959, as the Chinese army took over Lhasa, the 24-year-old Dalai Lama, dressed as a soldier, crossed from Tibet into the safety of India via the Khenzimana Pass. After a 15-day, 800-mi trek, across the wide Brahmaputra river, from Lhasa with six cabinet ministers in tow, he reached the Tawang Monastery in the northeastern Indian state of Arunachal Pradesh. Some 80,000 Tibetans followed him into exile in the days that followed. Looking for a mountain home for his displaced people, His Holiness arrived in Dharamshala in 1960, and finally settled here.

Visiting Dharamshala is the best way to see Tibet without actually going there. A population of 15,000 Tibetans has turned McLeod Ganj into a miniature Tibet to the point where it feels anachronistic, like a phony Shangri-La (they call it Dhasa). The town attracts a strange mix of soul seekers and dope seekers, not to mention down-at-the-heel backpackers looking for a cheap extended holiday. Simply put, McLeod Ganj is a tourist zoo, with crowds of yuppies, hippies, Western Buddhists, honeymooners . . . and occasionally Richard Gere.

Thousands of Buddhists live here, as well as in the remote, high-altitude districts of Lahaul, Spiti, and Kinnaur. Most practice a Tibetan form of tantric Buddhism, whereby various spiritual techniques are used to achieve enlightenment in a short amount of time. Tibetan women twist their hair into numerous long pigtails held in place by a silver ornament, and wear a long robe outfit called a *chuba* with a colorful apron; many men wear long maroon or brown overcoats. As in most Buddhist communities, men and women share all tasks, from raising a family to working in the fields where they grow crops of barley, buckwheat, and potatoes.

Dharamshala now suffers from a profusion of travelers and ugly hotels, which seem to disturb the inherent tranquility of this hill station. The tourist office and many hotels are in lower Dharamshala, but there's no real reason to linger here.

Just before you reach the bus and taxi stands on your way up from Dharamshala, you'll see one of the few remaining structures from the British days, **St. John's Church in the Wilderness** (*Daily 10–5, Sun. service 11:30*), built in 1852. The headstones in the churchyard attest to the difficulties and diseases the British suffered; among them are the graves of David McLeod, lieutenant governor of Punjab, who founded Dharamshala in the mid-19th century, and Lord Elgin, Viceroy of India, who died in 1862 and asked to be buried here (his grave lies just behind the church, marked by a large monument). Lord Elgin was so fond of Dharamshala that, if he'd lived, it might have become the summer capital of the British Raj.

McLeod Ganj is at the center of Tibetan efforts to preserve and maintain their culture during their exile. Several sites devoted to this effort are worth checking out. The **Tibetan Institute of Performing Arts (TIPA),** on the road to Dharamkot, hosts wonderful evenings of music and dance, and an International Himalayan Festival every December.

The **Norbulingka Institute for Tibetan Culture,** 40 minutes (15 km [9 mi]) below McLeod Ganj in Sidhpur, and registered as a trust under the Dalai Lama, is committed to preserving Tibetan arts-and-crafts skills. Master artists train young apprentices in *thangka* (intricate Tibetan scroll painting depicting meditational deities), metalwork, appliqué, embroidery, and wood carving. You can visit the artists in their studios, pick up a sample in the gift shop, and pop into the **Losel Doll Museum** to see a wonderful collection of traditional Tibetan costumes.

The **Dalai Lama's private residence** and the **Thekchen Choling temple** (sometimes called the Central Cathedral) are on the east end of Temple Road, joined to each other by a footpath. The view across the valley from the temple balcony is magnificent, and the complex, run by 200 monks who assist the Dalai Lama, includes a bookstore and restaurant. Buddhist pilgrims come here from near and far, so you might see crowds of monks, urbanites, and devotees from Lahaul and Spiti arriving with packets of biscuits and chocolates to pay homage. The **Tibet Museum** (*Rs. 5* *Tues.–Sun. 9–5*) highlights the struggle for a Free Tibet and many Tibetans' escapes from the Chinese regime, including the blood-stained prison clothes of one victim. The Dalai Lama's birthday, July 6, is a festive occasion, with performances by students from the Tibetan Children's Village school. For more information on the Tibetan Government in Exile and the history of their struggle, see the Web site of the Department of Information and International Relations (www.tibet.com).

CLOSE UP

Everyday Holiness

The Dalai Lama waves from his vehicle when he's being driven through Dharamshala. He has a "delightful, infectious laugh, a little like a child," says one native resident who met him years ago. In fact His Holiness's "genuine love for humanity" is apparent in everything he does, says another, and it seems to have a trickle-down effect—Dharamshala might indeed be the only crowded place in India where a motorist is likely to yell a hearty "sorry!" if he accidentally cuts off a pedestrian. Such sentiments are common for those who make their homes in Dharamshala and who have witnessed firsthand how the Buddhist leader's celebrity has grown over the years. Even with all the change that this little mountain town has experienced, the Dalai Lama remains a positive, sincere force. However, the unbelievable amount of people wanting a piece of what he symbolizes that can often sour the scene, most surprisingly for the countless Kashmiri merchants who moved here to take advantage of Dharamshala's emergence as a tourist trap. "When the Dalai Lama is in town, it's totally crazy around here," says a young Kashmiri merchant. "Sometimes we forget to take people's money, our store is so filled with tourists."

The Dalai Lama's popularity has also meant greater concerns for his safety, so gone are the days when locals had easy access—now he does not routinely give public audiences in the town he calls home; such meetings used to be commonplace. As a result, the closest you might come to the Dalai Lama is during your visit to the temple, or when you see his image on a T-shirt, mug, or key chain, making Dharamshala spiritually enlightening and blatantly commercial in the same breath.

NEED A BREAK?

After navigating the crowds all day, try dabbling in soothing Tibetan massage and astrology. Partners Tsezin and Chootack administer astrology readings and acupuncture and give excellent massages at the Tibetan Traditional Himalayan Massage Center (***✉ House No. A, Dhensum House, near Green Hotel, Bhagsu Rd., McLeod Ganj ☎ 98/1685–1937*** **). Then head over to Moonpeak Espresso (** ***✉ Temple Rd., McLeod Ganj*** **) for good pressed sandwiches and coffee, as well as an outside patio perfect for watching the interesting foot traffic headed toward the Dalai Lama's residence.**

For educators and students, a trip to the **Tibetan Children's Village** (*TCV ☎ 1892/221–348 🌐 www.tcv.org.in*), on the road north to Naddi, is a memorable experience. Try to arrange a visit in advance. Established in 1960, the TCV boarding school is home to 2,400 Tibetan orphans and refugees supported by individual and agency donors from all over the world, primarily the SOS Kinderdorf International in Vienna. In all, the organization has more than 16,000 children under its care in branches extending from Ladakh down to Bylakuppe, near Mysore. The pleasant 30-minute walk to the school takes you through deodar cedars (follow the water pipe). The **Handicraft Centre** (*☎ 1892/221–592*) below the school has good crafts and carpets at reasonable prices.

Tibetan crafts, antiques, jewelry, and clothing are available in McLeod Ganj.

Tibetan Gallery (☎*1892/221–398*), near the bus stand, stocks a wide ranges of Tibetan-style blouses, skirts, shirts, kurtas, and T-shirts for adults and children.

The **Tibetan Handicraft Center** (*At the McLeod Ganj post office* ✉*Jogibara Rd.*) sells thick, reasonably priced Tibetan carpets.

Norling Designs (✉*Temple Rd., next to Little Lhasa bookshop*) has expensive but very fine crafts and clothing from the Norbulingka Institute. The local **wine shops** sell apple beer and apple wine.

A drive or trek into the countryside makes for a nice change. Don't linger after dark—muggings and other crimes have been reported on Bhagsu Road—and be sure to take an umbrella or raincoat, as Dharamshala's weather is variable.

A CALMER DHARAMSHALA

The best way to experience a more tranquil Dharamshala might be when the Dalai Lama is out of town. Check out his official Web site, 🌐www.dalailama.com, for a schedule of his whereabouts, listed months in advance. If you feel like you can't miss His Holiness, there is a schedule of teachings on the Web site. You'll need to register in person at the **security office** (✉*Bhagsunagh Rd., next to Hotel Tibet* ☎*1892/221–560*) and bring your passport and two passport photos. The teachings are on a first-come, first-served basis; you can't register in advance.

There's a **Shiva temple** below a waterfall at Bhagsunag, 2 km (1 mi) northwest of the McLeod Ganj bus stand.

The muddy Dal Lake is 3 km (2 mi) north of the Shiva temple. About 3 km (2 mi) further is **Talnoo,** where you can take in a pretty view that might include Gaddi shepherds and their flocks. Gaddis are a distinctive group of nomadic Himachalis, with fair skin and hazel eyes, who cover their heads with scarves. Some still move from place to place with their livestock. Near Talnoo is the large Gaddi village of Naddi.

On the spiritual and physical levels, there's lots to do at McLeod Ganj. You can enroll in yoga classes, have your long-term ailments considered by a doctor of Tibetan medicine, learn Buddhist philosophy, or study Tibetan art. Practically every hotel and Tibetan restaurant has literature detailing what's going on, and you'll also see flyers all over town.

WHERE TO EAT & STAY

$$ ✕**Snow Lion.** One of McLeod Ganj's more upscale dining venues is attached to a low-end hotel. Run by the Tibetan Administration Welfare Society, the restaurant has a parquet floor and basic decor. Unfortunately, its windows overlook garbage and slum dwellings. Concentrate instead on the distant Himalayas, the black-and-white Tibetan photos on the walls, or the food: Japanese, Chinese, Western (including grilled meats), and authentic Tibetan. ✉*Hotel Tibet, Bagsunagh Rd., McLeod Ganj* ☎*1892/221587* ▭*MC, V.*

¢ ✕**McLlo.** The hub of tourist life in Dharamshala is in the dimly lit McLlo in the middle of McLeod Ganj. It's a good place to nurse a beer and watch the crowds below: many of the tables line its two window walls. The restaurant has wall-to-wall old carpet, neon lights, and a jukebox—it's the diverse clientele that provides the interesting atmosphere. The menu is fairly predictable, swinging from Indian and Tibetan to Chinese, South Indian, Israeli, and Western—including Baskin-Robbins ice cream. Doors are open until 10:30 PM. ✉*Next to bus stand, McLeod Ganj* ☎*1892/221–280* ▭*No credit cards.*

¢ ★ ✕**Nick's Italian Kitchen.** If you need a break from Tibetan food, try this excellent vegetarian restaurant in the Kunga Guest House. Quiches, pizzas, lasagna, and other pastas are cooked by a Tibetan family whose skills were inspired by a benefit organized by a traveling Italian-American from New York. Richard Gere has been known to drop by occasionally, and they have a great selection of Italian cakes and pies. The outdoor concrete deck, probably five times larger than inside, has great views of McLeod Ganj on clear days. ✉*Kunga Guest House, Bhagsunag Rd., McLeod Ganj* ☎*1892/221–180 or 1892/221–569* ▭*No credit cards.*

¢ ★ ✕**Yak.** It's not much bigger than a small bedroom and has only two tables, but the Tibetan food at Yak more than makes up for its utter lack of pretense. The cook serves up the tastiest vegetarian momos and noodle soups, but also ask for a recommendation from the friendly owners. The menu often changes and you likely won't be familiar with the less-standard selections. There's a reason Yak is popular with locals, and you might walk away feeling like you've had a real experience in both Tibetan food and hospitality. ✉*Jogibara Rd., opposite Aroma and Ashoka restaurants, McLeod Ganj* ☎*No phone* ▭*No credit cards.*

$ ★ **Glenmoor Cottages.** Ajai Singh, the owner of this secluded group of cottages, will gladly tell you all the little secrets of Dharamshala beyond the countless tourist traps. That alone is worth a stay here. That said, the cottages have spectacular mountain and valley views, and their modest concrete-and-wood facades conceal charming interiors: crisp white walls contrast with modern spruce and pine furnishings. The centerpiece of the property is a spectacular Scottish bungalow where Mr. Singh and his wife live, always on hand for great conversation. Two simple rooms with a shared bathroom are available for just Rs. 750. **Pros:** bend the ear of a local and get a needed break from the town's chaos. **Cons:** hotel is a 20-minute walk up a steep hill and can't be seen from the road. ✉*First right turn (no sign) uphill after you exit Dharamshala on road to Dal Lake, also called Mall Rd., McLeod Ganj, 176219* ☎*1892/221–010* 🌐*www.glenmoorcottages.com* *2 rooms, 5 cottages* *In-room: no a/c. In-hotel: room service, laundry service.* ▭*MC, V.*

¢ Fodor'sChoice ★ **Chonor House.** Built and run by the Norbulingka Institute, this is the most beautiful, best-kept place to stay in McLeod Ganj. The pretty lounge and guest rooms are furnished with handmade furniture, carpets, and linens made by institute artists, and most rooms have balconies. But the special touch is the murals in each guest room that cover the Tibetan themes of myth, religion, and ecology. The restaurant serves excellent Tibetan cuisine, and you can take meals outdoors on a large balcony in season. **Pros:** stunning interiors for a stunning price. **Cons:** local Lhasa Apso dogs, which often set up a chain reaction of midnight yelping, are unfortunately beyond the staff's control. ✉ *Near Thekchen Choling, McLeod Ganj, 176219* ☎ *1892/221–468, 1892/221–006* 🌐 *www.norbulingka.org* *11 rooms* *In-room: no a/c, no TV. In-hotel: restaurant, room service, no elevator, laundry service, public Internet.* *AE, MC, V.*

¢ **India House.** The appeal of one of McLeod Ganj's more modern budget hotels is its excellent restaurant, with an menu offering Indian, Chinese, Western, and Tibetan food. Beer is served. Unfortunately the rooms at India House are nothing special, with furnishings heavy on velour, tattered bedcovers, and cold tile flooring. The small balconies with good views are one redeeming quality, and the staff is eager to answer questions and make you feel welcome. The front desk sells a good map of the town for Rs. 50. **Pros:** good value and good restaurant, attached to well-stocked grocery and pharmacy. **Cons:** dark bathrooms, steep stair climb to every room, crowded with other budget travelers. ✉ *Bhagsunag Rd., just beyond Tibet House, McLeod Ganj, 176219* ☎ *1892/221–457* 🌐 *www.hotelindiahouse.com* *18 rooms* *In-room: no a/c, refrigerator (some). In-hotel: restaurant, room service, no elevator, laundry service.* *MC, V.*

¢ ★ **Pema Thang Guest House.** Everything about this place is so sincere and unpretentious that long-term travelers often stay here for weeks and become life-long friends with the staff. At first glance the selling point of this Tibetan-run hotel is its simplicity—clean, unfussy rooms with wood floors, large glass windows, wood trimmings, and valley views. But the best aspect is the attitude at the front desk. With managers constantly looking out for you like you're a member of their family, this place is a living example of Tibetan hospitality—the best reason to visit Dharamshala in the first place. **Pros:** great room for a rock bottom price (around $20), with discounts available for extended stays. **Cons:** road leading up to the hotel is steep and chockfull of potholes, making it difficult to navigate by vehicle and on foot. ✉ *Opposite Hotel Bhagsu, a few minutes away from Chinar Lodge, McLeod Ganj, 176219* ☎ *1892/221–871* *12 rooms* *In-room: no a/c, no TV (some). In-hotel: restaurant, room service, no elevator, laundry service, public Internet.* *No credit cards.*

EN ROUTE

Allow two days for a trip from Dharamshala to Dalhousie, plus another two for a trip to Chamba. The drive to Dalhousie takes 4½ hours on a bumpy road. The landscape is unforgiving, with the road slicing through stark brown mountains. The quiet town of **Chamba**—which has a small art museum featuring Kangra miniature paintings and local embroidered pictures called *rumals*—is 2½ hours (50 km [31 mi]) beyond Dalhousie, accessed by a treacherous road that weaves past the Ravi River. Aim to see Chamba if you have a lot of time and can follow a relaxed pace.

DALHOUSIE

130 km (81 mi) northwest of Dharamshala.

The hill station of Dalhousie was fashionable with British administrators based in Lahore (now in Pakistan) in the mid-19th century. It was established by the Lord Dalhousie, who, as India's governor-general, founded the Indian rail system. Today Dalhousie draws crowds of Indian tourists in the summer, so try to see it between March and May or September and November. The setting that drew the British is still spectacular, with forested slopes, green valleys, and the snow-capped Pir Panjal peaks on the town's doorstep; here you really get a sense of being close to the great Himalayas.

There's not much to occupy you in this sleepy, two-rickshaw settlement. The main town is actually the nondescript Banikhot (6 km [4 mi] downhill), which you climb through on the way up. The best way to soak in the atmosphere is to take walks, and perhaps watch some migratory birds. Evidence of the colonial days is mostly gone, barring the two churches at each *chowk* (crossroads or marketplace). One of the prettiest, **St. Francis Church** on Subhash Chowk, was built in 1894. The town has pedestrian-only walkways between Gandhi Chowk and Subhash Chowk, and along Potryn Road. At Gandhi Chowk, in the Garam Sarak area, a few shops sell Himachal Pradesh handicrafts: walnut and oak-wood boxes and trays, and colorful jute Chamba slippers.

6

Before Tibetan exiles were directed to Dharamshala, Dalhousie housed them for a short time. A visit to the **Tibetan Handicraft Center** in Upper Bakrota, nearly 2 km (1 mi) from the Dalhousie's main square on the Khajjiar Road, is a must if you like hand-knotted Tibetan carpets.

WHERE TO EAT & STAY

$ ✕ **Davat.** The dining options in Dalhousie are nothing to write home about, but for a good, quick bite, try this restaurant in the Hotel Mount View. The noise from the nearby bus stand detracts somewhat from the experience, but the food—Mughlai, tandoori, and Chinese cuisine—is reliable. ✉ *Dalhousie St., Dalhousie* ☎ *1899/242–120* ▭ *MC, V.*

$ ✕ **Kwality.** Owned by the Grand View hotel, this branch of the Kwality chain is one of Dalhousie's fanciest restaurants. The menu centers on classic tandoori and North Indian food, with a few Chinese, South Indian, and Western options. The restaurant has a strongly woodsy look, with wooden tables, chairs, walls, and ceilings. ✉ *Gandhi Chowk, Dalhousie* ☎ *1899/242–194* ▭ *No credit cards.*

$ **Alps Resort.** About 2½ km from the center of town on the crest of a hill, this pretty, red-roof white resort commands a view of the valley. The two buildings are set in a lush garden with a tree house, a swing, and wrought-iron garden furniture surrounded by a picket fence. Guest rooms have soft beds with bright white linens and either wood or tile floors. Across from the hotel is a Tibetan colony with countless Buddhist prayer flags adorning the hillside. **Pros:** beautiful landscaped grounds, full service spa on premise, will do a round of your laundry for free. **Cons:** a bit far to walk everywhere, yelping dogs in the Tibetan colony. ✉ *Bakrotta Hills, Dalhousie, 176304* ☎ 📠 *1899/240–721 or 1899/240781* 🌐 *www.alpsdalhousie.com* ⇨ *19 rooms, 2 suites* ⓘ *In-room: no a/c. In-hotel: 2 restaurants, room service, gym, spa, no elevator, laundry service, public Internet.* 💳 *MC, V.*

¢ **Grand View.** Enter this charming hotel and you're in another age, full of Raj remnants. The long wooden building has a vast dining room, and each room opens onto its own garden and outdoor sitting area with valley views. The hotel has seen better days, and although its suites are still grand, the standard rooms are a bit shabby. Furnishings are modern except for the heavy wood furniture and red or blue carpets. **Pros:** in the center of town with gorgeous views. **Cons:** inaccessible by car, must climb steep stairs to property. ✉ *Thandi Sarak (Mall walkway), Dalhousie, 176304* ☎ *1899/240–760 or 1899/242–823* 🌐 *www.grandviewdalhousie.in* ⇨ *27 rooms, 5 suites* ⓘ *In-room: no a/c. In-hotel: restaurant, room service, laundry service.* 💳 *No credit cards.*

¢ **Guncha Siddhartha.** Each room in this budget hotel has a terrace overlooking the affable owner's apple orchard and residence, with a 180-degree panorama of the valley and mountains beyond. The rooms, tiered down the hillside, are comfortable but pretty shabby, with carpeting, heavy velour decor, and a sitting area. Take your meals on the terrace to soak in the best views in town. Rates drop 50% in winter, and Fodor's guests get breakfast on the house. The restaurant serves only vegetarian food. **Pros:** gorgeous scenery, laid-back atmosphere. **Cons:** somewhat run down, staff doesn't always seem like they try too hard. ✉ *Church Baloon Rd., Dalhousie, 176304* ☎ *1899/242–709 or 1899/240–620* 📠 *1899/240–818* ⇨ *13 rooms, 11 suites* ⓘ *In-room: no a/c, refrigerator. In-hotel: restaurant, no elevator, laundry service.* 💳 *No credit cards.*

¢ ★ **Silverton Estate Guest House.** Built in 1939, this small and gracious home has both charm and location—a hilltop in a forest where troops of langurs live. The estate, which includes a terraced garden, is run by the genial Vickram Singh, who will tailor your entire stay to your preferences in both food and activities. The cuisine is Indian and Western vegetarian. **Pros:** nice owner who treats you like family, free breakfast and dinner. **Cons:** closed in winter, driveway not accessible by vehicle. ✉ *Top of Moti Tibba, above Circuit House, off Mall Rd., Dalhousie, 176304* ☎ *1899/240–674 or 941/801–0674* ⇨ *5 rooms* ⓘ *In-room: no a/c, no TV. In-hotel: restaurant, room service, no elevator, laundry service.* 💳 *No credit cards* ⊙ *Closed Jan.–Mar.* 🍽 *MAP.*

EN ROUTE

The road from Dalhousie to Chamba has two pleasant stops for nature lovers. The first is **Kalatope Wildlife Sanctuary,** a forest preserve with beautiful mountain views. Leave your car at the entrance (unless you have a permit from the Forest Officer in Chamba) and stroll to the end of the 3 km (2 mi) paved road, which continues through mature deodar cedars and yews. Halfway to Chamba is **Khajjiar,** a spacious glade encircled by virgin forest and centered on a pond with a grassy island that seems to float. It's a good place to have a picnic and enjoy the beautiful surroundings.

LADAKH

> **HOW DID BUDDHISM COME TO LADAKH?**
>
> Buddhism arrived from Kashmir in the 2nd century, when Ladakh was part of the Kushana Empire. Until then, both Ladakh and Tibet followed the Bon religion, an early animistic faith.

Tucked between the two highest mountain ranges in the world—the Karakoram to the north and Greater Himalayas to the south—stunningly beautiful and remote Ladakh beckons you into the world of Mahayana Buddhism. The region is actually part of the state of Jammu and Kashmir, but bears little cultural resemblance to either; sometimes called Little Tibet, Ladakh is now more culturally pure than its namesake. Tourists in Leh, the capital of the former Ladakh kingdom, may be diluting the Buddhist culture, but Ladakh's gompas are still splendid, with gorgeous interior frescoes and statues as breathtaking as the landscape. With gray barren crags, an occasional green valley, jewel-like waterways, and mountains of different hues, this high-altitude desert is punctuated by colorful prayer flags and scattered stark white *chortens*—memorial stupas or shrines for relics. Initiate Ladakhi greetings of "*Ju-le*" (ju-*lay*) and you'll be pleased with the smiles and kindness you receive in return.

Outside Leh it's still possible to travel up and down Ladakh's windswept terrain without encountering many people. The region's 270,000 residents occasionally appear near the remnants of Buddhist culture scattered around the countryside. On even the most deserted stretch of road, you'll find stones stacked into little chortenlike piles and *mani* (walls of beautifully engraved stones) that Ladakhis have erected to protect the land from demons and evil spirits. The walls are enticing, but don't touch the stones—they're sacred to the people who put them there.

Ladakh offers world-famous trekking opportunities, such as Manali–Leh, Spiti–Tso Moriri, Lamayuru–Chilling, and the Nubra Valley. You can also raft on the challenging Zanskar and Indus rivers. Runs are best in July and August; just make sure your outfitter has all the right equipment and expertise. The Government of India oversees specified tour circuits here—foreign tourists in groups of four, sponsored by recognized tour operators, are allowed to visit the Nubra, Khaltse, and Nyoma subdivisions after obtaining a permit from the District Directorate in Leh. Ladakh's trekking season lasts from late May, after most of the snow has melted, until mid-October, with the biggest crowds appearing in July and August. Rafting is best from July to mid-September. June and September are the best months to come—if you come in early to mid-June, before the plows have opened the road from Manali, you'll have your pick of lodgings in Leh, and by September the crowds will thin out again. When you come, take all precautions against high-altitude sickness and bring a flashlight to see the paintings in poorly lit gompas.

Winter is an opportunity to see a tourist-free Ladakh, albeit in searingly cold conditions: temperatures can drop to -30°C. Since Ladakh is a cold desert, only the higher mountain roads get snowbound, and

CLOSE UP

Ladakh Shopping

On the prowl for handicrafts and other items? Ladakh has a wealth of good things to buy. You can pick up handwoven woolen carpets, with dragon or geometric motifs, for chairs, divans, and the floor, from any of the stalls at or at the Tibetan Handicrafts Centre on Leh's Main Road or at Choglamsar's Tibetan Refugee Handicraft Center showroom a few kilometers from Leh town at a reasonable price. Antique carpets available elsewhere are much more expensive.

Tibetan/Ladakhi-style silver, copper, and brass *diyas* (oil lamps) used in monasteries, some of them 3 feet high, are available at most handicraft shops. Also available are dragon masks, "singing" brass bowls, *thankas* (Tibetan tapestries depicting the stages of Buddha's life), and pashmina shawls. Also try the Tibetan market at the corner of Main Road.

At the fascinating and extensive Moti Market, five minutes by foot from the Main Road, you can hunt around for tea kettles, Ladakh-style samovars for brewing butter tea, long ornamental horns, prayer wheels, brass Kashmiri stoves, turquoise, lapis-lazuli, pearl, malachite, and coral (strung into jewelry as per your requested design). Try Himalayan Arts, Shop 48, for Tibetan locks, oil lamps, and samovars.

In the lanes behind the Main Road, accessed from a lane next to the less the more downmarket of the two Amdo Cafés going towards the old town, a number shops sell fine silk brocade smuggled in from China. Sonam Wangdus Chamday and Sons on the Main Road has some interesting Ladakhi/Bhutanese cotton typical of this area. Several tailors nearby can sew anything your heart desires.

Tall Ladakhi hats, *gonchas* (traditional woolen robes), raw silk sashes, and cross-buttoned short jackets are available in the main market.

The lanes leading up to the main bazaar near Lasermo Hotel and Khangri hotel are several shops selling low tables hand-carved with dragons and leaves, some done in blond wood and others colorfully lacquered, Ladakhi-style. Traditionally used by monks, the tables are collapsible. Lacquered bowls for serving nuts are also available in these shops.

The more expensive Kashmir handicraft shops on the Main Road offer a fine selection of antique brass items, breathtakingly beautiful turquoise-and-silver jewelry, carved almond-wood handicrafts, as well as craft bits and pieces sourced from other parts of India.

Apricot jam, dried apricots, and yak-butter are also are readily available. For interesting black and white postcards of Ladakh try Ali Shah's Postcard Shop near the mosque.

even some of those are cleared quickly. Many hotels and restaurants are closed, and those that stay open are fairly chilly (despite heaters) and have no running water because the pipes freeze. Even electricity is in short supply, since the frozen rivers affect local hydroelectric projects, so you must choose a hotel that has its own generator. Food is slightly more expensive, as fresh vegetables and chicken are hard to come by.

LEH

473 km (295 mi) north of Manali, 434 km (271 mi) east of Srinagar, 230 km (143 mi) east of Kargil.

Ladakh's major city is built into the base of the snow-covered Karakoram Range, at just over 11,500 feet. The two-day drive from Manali to Leh is a legendary ordeal, with rough, narrow, mountain-hugging roads prone to traffic jams and landslides. However, this mode of arrival is incredibly scenic, and a good way to acclimatize yourself to the altitude. The army convoys on the road increase the danger and the time involved, because they have immediate right-of-way over all traffic. The prudent and the less adventurous simply fly from Delhi if they can afford it: flights leave early in the morning, with the sun beginning to rise as you leave the plains and enter the Shivalik Hills. As the first snow-capped mountains appear, the plane seems to skim over the summits, and the ice fields stretch to the horizon before you reach the barren moonscape of the high Tibetan plateau; this is easily one of the most spectacular air journeys you can make in India. The flight attendant may instruct you to lower your window blind as you approach Leh, your first hint of military security, and you may be told not to take any photos from the plane. The 20th century turned Leh into an important Indian military base thanks to its proximity to Kashmir.

LEH'S JAMA MASJID

Ladakh's ties to Islam go back hundreds of years. The earliest mosque in the area, built in Leh, was small and functional, built to accommodate the needs of Muslim traders. Also old but much grander is the Jama Masjid, a centerpiece of Leh's Main Bazaar. In the 17th century, Ladakh received protection from the Mughals. In return, Ladakhi kings agreed to build the mosque and pay money to the Moghul emperor, Aurangzeb. Today Ladakh has about 110 mosques and a sizeable Muslim population, which is mostly based in the nearby Kargil district.

6

An afternoon in Leh's **Ecology Centre** (☎ *1982/252–5814 or 1982/253–221* ⏲ *Fall–spring, 10–4:30; winter Mon.–Sat. 10:30–4*), five minutes north of the main bazaar past Zangsti, may help distract you while you acclimatize; in addition to various exhibits, its excellent video, *Ancient Futures* (not shown in winter), illustrates how Ladakhi culture is threatened by a rapidly changing world. The Ecology Centre is a good place to head to for advice on trekking in an sustainable manner in Ladakh. There is a small store attached that sells eco-friendly items that include locally made apricot jam and handmade clothes.

An important Buddhist center since the 3rd century BC, Leh was also a hub on the ancient Silk Road of central Asia. Sadly, the city's 16th-century, nine-story **palace** with a grandeur reminiscent of Lhasa'a Potala Palace, and, above it, the **Temple of the Guardian Deities** are both in disrepair, but they're worth the steep walk uphill if you're a history buff or want to take in the astounding view from the palace roof.

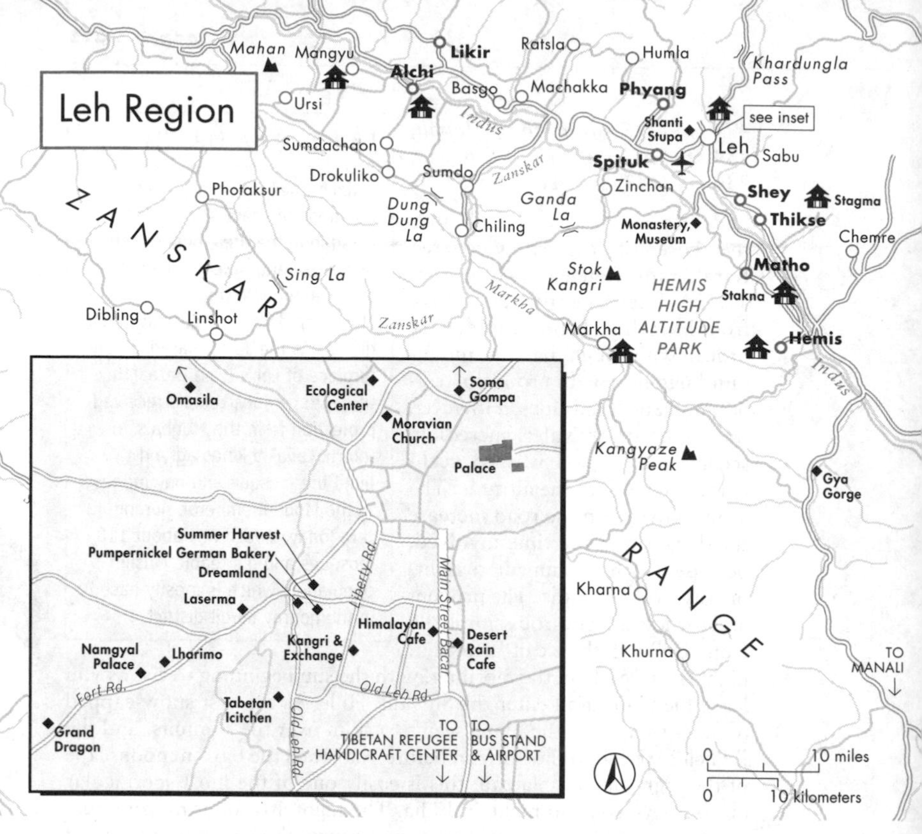

Handicraft shops and pavement stalls around Leh's **market** sell Tibetan antiques, Chinese silk, Buddhist ornaments, turquoise stones, woolens, and silver jewelry.

For a magnificent view of the valley, taxi to the **Shanti Stupa,** in the village of Changspa—then walk down the 500-plus steps leading up to it.

On your way south out of town to Thiksay monastery or Shey palace, stop at the **Tibetan Refugee Handicraft Center** (☎ *1982/244–131* ⏲ *Weekdays 9–5*) in the village of Choglamsar. The beautiful crafts here include handwoven rugs and mats meant for placing on chairs and other furniture, thick woolens, and an odd selection of trinkets.

If you don't have time to see any of Ladakh's fine monasteries, at least pop in to the colorful but less historic **Soma Gompa,** in the bazaar behind the new mosque and opposite the State Bank of India. At dusk, this large gompa, which houses the headquarters of the Ladakh Buddhist Association, shines quietly with the light of numerous oil lamps.

To take in an interesting snippet of history visit the very simple **Moravian Church.** There has been a mission in this area since 1885. The Moravian Mission brethren arrived in Ladakh from Bohemia in the

19th century while on the way to China. After China refused them entry, they settled in Ladakh with hopes of gathering a following in this Buddhist kingdom—they were not very successful. They took to translating Ladakhi texts and growing potatoes—the fathers can apparently be credited with introducing the vegetable's cultivation to Ladakh. Today membership at the Moravian Church stands at around 100 people, and their school has been in operation since 1889. Call the pastor Elijah Gergan to arrange a visit at 1982/252–295. The church is near the Leh police station.

LEH-AREA MONASTERIES AND PALACES

Before you leave Leh, arrange trips to area monasteries and nearby Shey Palace and get a festival schedule from the tourist office (or check *www.jktourism.org/cities/ladakh/festivals/cal.htm*); dates vary according to the Tibetan lunar calendar. Periodic dance-drama festivals called *chaams,* which bejeweled locals attend in droves in their finest costumes, are not to be missed; those held at the Hemis and Thiksay gompas are particularly colorful.

Ladakh's monasteries have custody of its ancient culture and age-old wisdom as well as its future. The tempo of daily life—festivals, spiritualism, education, leadership—revolves around the gompas. Nearly every Ladakhi family offers one of their sons to the monasteries to be educated as priests: they are home to Ladakh's monks of tomorrow as well as today.

Leh's taxi union has fares that are high but consistently applied. Roads are bumpy here, so request a Sumo or a Qualis (not a Maruti van) for a safe, reasonably smooth trip.

Gompas are the center of Ladakhi religion and culture—drive south to explore the Shey, Thiksay, Matho, and Hemis gompas; northwest are Spituk, Phyang, Likir, and Alchi Choskor—the jewel of Ladakh's religious sites. It's possible to get gompa-ed out, so choose one or two depending on your interests and schedule. Whichever you visit, be sure to respect religious customs: wear appropriate (non-revealing) clothing, remove your shoes, don't smoke, circle all chortens and spin prayer wheels clockwise, leave a small donation, and never take a mani stone. Most monasteries do not allow flash photography.

Seventeenth-century **Hemis** (45 km [28 mi]/1 hour south of Leh) is Ladakh's most popular gompa, but it's often swamped with tourists. The imposing **Thiksay** (19 km [12 mi]/½ hour south of Leh), built around the 15th century, is tiered down the side of a barren hillside like an ancient apartment building; it has a 14-foot golden statue of Buddha within and is one of Ladakh's prettiest gompas. Also attractive, the 15th-century **Spituk,** with 600-year-old paintings inside, sits on a hillside overlooking the Indus River and gives you a bird's-eye view of this expanding town. The 16th-century **Phyang** gompa 24 km [15 mi] northwest of Leh) is famous for its collection of thangkas and bronzes and its stunning location, overlooking the countryside.

CLOSE UP

The Ladakh Kingdom's Rise and Fall

Ladakh has existed as an independent kingdom off and on through its tumultuous history. In the 7th century an invading Tibetan warlord kept Ladakh for himself, Tibetanizing it and elevating it to a separate realm. Ladakh's sovereignty was under threat after the Islamic conquest of India and Central Asia in the 1200s. During this period the kingdom was periodically raided. Portions of its population embraced Islam. In the 15th century the Namgyal dynasty took control and for two hundred golden years its line of kings expanded their territory up to Nepal, keeping invaders at bay. In the 17th century the Tibetans were back at Ladakh's door. The kingdom's rulers brokered a deal with Kashmir and the Moghuls to stave off Tibetan invasion, but Ladakh lost much of its autonomy as a result. It was a downward slide after that. In the 19th century Ladakh was annexed into the Dogra kingdom, the original inhabitants of neighboring Jammu. The Namgyal monarchs were reduced to landholders in the area of Stok, where their palace still stands today.

Reaching the 17-century **Shey Palace** (15 km [9 mi]/½ hour south of Leh) requires a difficult 20-minute climb to reach its serene, three-storey statue of Buddha and a bird's-eye view of the countryside. The serene 19th-century **Ridzong** (127 km [78 mi]/five hours west of Leh) gompa, considered by locals to be Ladakh's finest, receives very few visitors. Inside a gorge, its sheer remoteness accentuates its purpose—isolation for a monastic life.

A tour of **Alchi Choskor** (70 km [43 mi]/2½–3 hours west of Leh) can be done in a day for about Rs. 2,000 if you don't combine it with anything else. The drive takes you through stark mountains, past the confluence of the serene, blue Indus and Zanskar rivers, appealing villages, willow groves, farms, and lonely monasteries. Your journey will be enlivened by the numerous road signs entreating you to be ALERT TODAY, ALIVE TOMORROW OR MILD ON MY CURVES, BECAUSE FAST WON'T LAST. The road goes via tiny **Nimmo**—the largest settlement you'll pass—and ancient **Basgo,** once a capital of Ladakh and an invincible fortress against Moghul and Tibetan invasion. The monastery here is a UNESCO World Heritage Site. Stop before Nimmo at the army-maintained **Pathar Sahib** *gurdwara* (25 km [16 mi] one hour northwest of Leh), built in 1964 to provide a place of worship for Sikh soldiers. If you happen to be traveling on a Sunday, stop here for lunch, known as *langar,* served free of charge from noon to 2. In summer as many as 600 come here to fortify themselves. *See Amritsar, above, for more on Sikhism.*

Alchi is one of the oldest monasteries in Ladakh, dating back to 1020 AD. This small, low-slung cluster of mud buildings on the banks of the Indus River shelters some of the oldest and finest Buddhist murals and wood carvings in the world. The murals are said to have been created by a specially hired group of Tibetan and Kashmiri artisans.

To visit Alchi Choskor, you might want to plan an overnight stay nearby. One of the better options is tent accommodation (open from May to Sept) at the **Uley Tokpo Camp** (☎ *1982/253–640* 🖷 *1982/252–735* ✉ *ulecamp@sancharnet.in*). Tents cost Rs. 2,970 for double accommodation, with all meals included. From here you can also access the gompa at **Lamayuru** (130 km [80 mi]/four hours northwest of Leh), one of Ladakh's most strikingly situated gompas—on top of an impossibly steep mountain. The monastery's age is uncertain, but it might date back to the 10th century.

AN ALTITUDE ADJUSTMENT

Take strong sunblock, aspirin, and a thick book to Ladakh; the altitude change and intense sunshine may require you to spend a few days relaxing and taking slow walks—at least 24 hours if you've flown in. The thin air will make you feel slightly breathless. Drink lots of water and avoid alcohol, excessive eating, and smoking.

On your return to Leh, turn left just beyond Saspol and drive 6 km (4 mi) to **Likir.** As you approach this 18th-century monastery, its giant golden Buddha rises out of the horizon against the craggy hills, overlooking green fields and sleepy hamlets. It's an unforgettable sight.

6

A visit to **Stok Palace** (✉ *Village of Stok, 17 km (a half-hour) from Leh* ☎ *No phone* 🎟 *Rs. 30* ⏲ *Daily 8–1 and 2–6*) is a small peek into the history of Ladakh. The former queen of Ladakh (now queen mother), Parvati Devi Deskit Wangmo, still lives in this interesting medieval fortress at Stok, about half an hour (17 km [11 mi]) away from Leh across the Indus River. Part of this tiny multiple-storied palace, which clings precariously to the craggy hillside, has been converted into a museum. You can view the royal *perag* (headgear), embedded with a priceless collection of coral and turquoise; the late king Chogyal Kunsang Namgyal's *chorten* (memorial); costumes of an earlier era; coins and seals; and an excellent collection of photographs documenting the queen's life as well as her meetings with Indira Gandhi, Jawaharlal Nehru, and Britain's Prince Charles.

The **Khardungla Pass,** which may be the world's highest motorable road, was built in 1976 and is 37 km (22 mi) from Leh, on the road to Nubra Valley. Its height (18,380 feet, or 5,602 meters) is a matter of dispute—Semo La in Tibet may be higher. Either way, this pass was once the route for livestock and Bactrian camels. Reaching it and its historic *chai* (tea) stop is a dramatic journey through steadily more austere and harsh countryside. Taking a motorbike up to this spectacular pass is a favored option. An Inner Line Permit is required for this journey.

WHERE TO EAT & STAY

The peak tourist season in Ladakh runs from early June to mid-September. During this period the largest number of visitors come in July and August, as well as for the Hemis Festival (late June–early July) and the Ladakh Festival (September 1–15). If you're planning on showing up at the same times, make your hotel and airline bookings well in advance. Hotels, restaurants, and even shops do not remain open all

CLOSE UP

Pangong Lake

A memorable 4½-hour, 150-km (93-mi) drive east from Leh across an unforgiving landscape takes you to a stunning jewel of a lake on India's border with China. The Pangong Lake, at 134 km (83 mi) long, one of the highest saltwater lakes in the world, stretches like a finger from India into China; only one-third of it in India.

To make this journey you need to plan ahead. The Inner Line Permit you must have to get to this border area takes one working day to be issued by the local government. It can be organized through your hotel or travel agent, and it requires that a group of four tourists make the journey. There are very limited eating and camping facilities by the lake, so it's best to plan on returning back to town the same day. An early start is therefore important. Take along a packed lunch, water, sunglasses, plenty of warm clothes, and toilet paper.

The journey to Pangong Lake, which begins on the Srinagar road, takes you past Shey Palace and Thikse monastery (36 km [22 mi] from Leh). If you get going early and have plenty of energy, you could take in either the monastery or the palace on your return. The driver will want some extra payment for these side trips.

About 45 km (28 mi) from Leh the road breaks away from the highway to meander through isolated countryside: little farms, a few villages, tiny monasteries. After a while habitation melts away and the road climbs through gray, monotonous boulder-ridden terrain to reach the third-highest pass in the world: the Chang La. The Indian army provides very welcome piping hot tea and a not-so-clean bathroom at this snowy outpost, where the thin air will leave you panting for breath. The lake is still two hours and three villages beyond.

During your descent from the snows of Chang La you pass herds of black-and-white yaks, flocks of sheep, nomadic herding communities living in tents, and, if you're lucky, some wild mountain goats. Sustenance is eked out around here from pashmina wool and from growing wheat and peas in the fertile patches. The land, often covered in a red lichen-like vegetation, is flat and harsh-looking—it's almost as if you're in the middle of central Mongolia rather than India.

As you turn the last few mountain corners you are treading pebbled riverbeds and icy slush and the road disappears. It's then that tantalizing glimpses of the shimmering sapphire-blue Pangong Lake first appear. The lake is sparkling, salty, and free of fish. Its white shores are actually strips of deposited sand. The iridescent, hypnotizing blue of the lake against the bleak brown, towering mountains is dazzling, as is the sheer solitude here.

Here on the India end of lake, there's little more than a tiny army station with a bathroom and a few huts offering tea (in summer) at Spangmik and an occasional donkey (known locally as *kiang*). Spangmik is the farthest point you can go on the shores of the lake; beyond is off limits.

The Indian Army has a large settlement 50 km (31 mi) ahead in the village of Chushul (off-limits to tourists). After that, China begins—or so that country claims. The area, called Aksai Chin by India, has been in dispute since China occupied this area in 1962.

year round in Ladakh. When the season tapers to an end in late September, and chilly weather sets in, more than half of Ladakh's hotels and restaurants close and the place hunkers down for the winter. By mid-October or the end of the month, most seasonal restaurants and hotels shut. When snow hits the high mountain passes on the Manali–Leh and the Srinagar–Leh highways, and road entry into Ladakh is cut off for the winter, Leh and the surrounding areas close down even further (the status of the highways is posted on Ladakh's official government site, 🌐 *http://leh.nic.in*). Very few shops and restaurants remain open, and winter hotels keep just a few rooms open, operating with a skeleton crew. Many Ladakhis use winter as a time to travel to someplace warmer. Hotels and restaurants start reopening in April. If you haven't made reservations, at least call ahead to find out if the hotel you plan to stay at is open.

$ ✕**Dreamland Hotel.** A popular spot with tourists, Dreamland serves hearty breakfasts and a mix of Tibetan, Kashmiri, and Chinese food. The Tibetan *thukpas* (hearty noodle soups) and the wonton-like momos should not be missed at this second-story eatery with very basic furnishings. The pastas are also good. In summer sample the trout fried in garlic butter. The restaurant closes from mid-October to June. ✉*Fort Rd.* ☎*No phone* ▭*No credit cards.*

$ ✕**Desert Rain Cafe.** At this modern but cozy café that opened in 2007 you can get what may be Ladakh's only espressos. The coffees here are creamy, frothy, and superb for the weather. Snacks include carrot cake and other baked good, noodle dishes, and sandwiches. In this cheerful, welcoming place, done in light-color wood, you can lounge on the rug-covered, low seating reading books (provided by the café) and listening to music. There are a movie club and special music evenings, as well as rooftop seating. ✉*Main Rd.* ☎*1982/256–426* ▭*No credit cards.*

$ ✕**Grand Dragon Coffee Shop.** At Ladakh's only upscale restaurant (they even have napkins!), the hearty Indian dishes are whipped up by the hotel's Himachali chefs and served in style. Try the *saag ghosh* (lamb simmered in spinach) or any of the *paneer* (Indian cottage cheese) dishes, with piping hot naans or rotis. Western and Chinese entrées are also available. In the elegant interior there are wood floors and Tibetan artifacts; giant glass picture windows look out onto the lawns outside. ✉*Grand Dragon Hotel, Old Road, Shyenam* ☎*1982/250–786 or 1982/255–866* ▭*MC, V.*

$ ✕**Pumpernickel German Bakery.** Just as in Goa and tourist hotspots elsewhere in India, the German Bakery quasi-chain has an outlet in Leh too, which is open only in summer. Head here for a great slice of apple pie or lemon tart. You can try their breakfast, lasagne and sandwiches as well, but pastries are their forte. ✉*Old Fort Rd.* ☎*No phone* ▭*No credit cards.*

$ ✕**Tibetan Kitchen.** Many locals feel that this summer-only joint serves some of the most authentic Tibetan food in Leh. Step in here for a full Tibetan meal called a *gyakok,* a heavy meat stock–based dish that also includes vegetables and dumplings. Also worth seeking out is the special soup called *gyakho (beef, pork and vegetable broth)*. The res-

6

taurant is closed from approximately October through May. ✉*Hotel Tsokar, Fort Rd.* ☎*No phone* ▭*No credit cards.*

¢ ✕**Himalayan Cafe.** A large painting of Lhasa's Potala Palace and other Tibetan artifacts, dim lights shaded with dark-red lampshades, and wooden tables keep things intimate at this spacious Tibetan-run café, which commands a good view of Leh's main thoroughfare from its upstairs perch. The menu is vast, with Indian, Chinese, Tibetan (including fragrant momos), and Western options. It's open from June through September. ✉*32 (6) A, Upstar, Main Market* ☎*1982/250–144* ▭*No credit cards.*

¢ ✕**Summer Harvest.** Sample Tibetan and Kashmiri food in this tiny shack tucked away off the main road and decorated with the plastic-tablecloth-and-flowers method. On the Tibetan side of the menu there are steamy, tasty Tibetan thukpas, momos, and noodles; on the Kashmiri side, there's mutton *yakhni* (simmered in a fragrant sauce of yogurt, cardamom, and aniseed) and *rogan josh* (lamb). It all attracts plenty of locals, attesting to the quality of the cooking. Summer Harvest also serves chow meins and fried rice, and other Chinese fare. ✉*Down Fort Rd. from taxi stand* ☎*1982/253–226* ▭*No credit cards.*

$$ **Grand Dragon.** Opened in 2007, this centrally heated hotel, famous for owning the first elevator in Ladakh, is probably the town's most luxurious. A giant and exotically hued Ladakhi gateway ushers you into a modern, low-slung building that spreads in a wide V shape. The lobby and public areas are airy and decorated with the best Ladakhi ornaments, including tea samovars and statues. The rooms, with picture windows and wood floors, may lack the traditional Ladakh feel, but they are plush and comfortable, with elegant furnishings and TVs on the walls; bathrooms are done in marble and have tubs. A 24-hour coffee shop serves Western, Indian, and local cuisine. Plans are afoot to add an indoor pool and more restaurants. **Pros:** international-standard luxury. **Cons:** lacks Ladakhi character, expensive for the area. ✉*Old Road, Shyenam Leh, 194101* ☎*1982/250–786 or 1982/255–866* 📠*1982/255–266* *53 rooms, 6 suites* *In-room: no a/c. In-hotel: restaurant, room service, laundry service.* ▭*AE, MC, V.*

$ ★ **Lha-Ri-Mo.** A short walk from the market, behind an attractive garden, Lha-Ri-Mo ("abode of the angels") is one of the loveliest, more traditional hotels in Leh. The hotel's three buildings, white with black-and-red trim, surround a courtyard garden, so rooms are secluded and quiet. They have plush carpeting, large, attractive bathrooms, and great views. The Ladakhi look continues in the lobby and the restaurant, which also has intricately hand-painted beams. Lha-Ri-Mo runs a camp at Gyamtsa, 6 km (4 mi) from Leh, as well as at Nubra 150 km from Leh, for those wishing to experience a rustic holiday in a place that very few tourists see. **Pros:** family run, comfy, cheerful. **Cons:** might be too secluded for some people. ✉*Old Fort Rd., Leh, 194101* ☎*1982/252–101 or 1982/252–177* 📠*1982/253–345* *lharimohotel@hotmail.com* *47 rooms* *In-room: no a/c. In-hotel: restaurant, no elevator.* ▭*AE* *Closed Oct.–Apr.*

$ ★ **Omasila.** Since 1980 a hospitable Ladakhi family has run this popular hotel below the Shanti Stupa. Brad Pitt and Angelina Jolie stayed here in 2006, as did Bollywood god Amitabh Bachchan years ealier. They may all have been lured by its views, cleanliness, colorful Ladakhi decor, privacy, and food (some ingredients are sourced from the hotel's own gardens). The cozy, centrally heated rooms have wood floors and a wall of multiple windows that allows for plenty of sun and warmth; rooms also contain a selection of Buddhist reading material. The spacious terrace looks south to a stunning vista, the grounds are planted with flowers, and a stream runs along the edge of the property. There are also a lounge and emergency oxygen supply for the breathless. Bathrooms have only showers and there are no room phones, but the front desk has a cordless phone. Only six rooms are heated in winter: ask for a room number in the 40s. Dinner is a buffet. **Pros:** warm, cozy, family run, great food, open all year. **Cons:** no room phones. ✉ *Changspa, Leh, 194101* ☎ *1982/252–119 or 1982/255–248* 🌐 *http://hotelomasila.com* *38 rooms, 9 suites* *In-room: no a/c, no phone. In-hotel: restaurant, no elevator, public Internet.* 💳 *MC, V.*

$ ★ **Shambha-La.** This family-owned, Ladakhi-style two-tier hotel sits in a shaded courtyard in an apple orchard, a little way outside town. Owner Mr. Pintoo Norbu, formerly the state's tourism minister, is often around to extend a personal welcome to his guests. Comforts include a rooftop deck, a traditional and attractive lounge and video library, and—in half the rooms—stove heaters in May and October. The rooms, which look out onto the garden, are pretty, with colorful rugs and elegant Ladakhi trimming; bathrooms, much less attractive, have showers only. Adjust to the altitude by relaxing in a hammock strung between poplar trees in the garden, or taking a walk through the surrounding meadows or to the nearby village. The manager will recommend local treks—his jeep drops you at one location and picks you up in another in time for the next meal—and organize camping at Nubra Valley. The motel is just south of Leh, off the airport road. **Pros:** charming looks, courtesy dropoffs in town. **Cons:** bathrooms need upgrading. ✉ *Skara, Leh, 194101 Reserve through K-40 Hauz Khas, 1st fl., New Delhi, 110016* ☎ *1982/252–607 or 1982/253–500, 11/2652–0970 in Delhi* 🌐 *www.hotelshambhala.com* *27 rooms, 3 suites* *In-room: no a/c. In-hotel: restaurant, no elevator, laundry service.* 💳 *AE, MC, V* *Closed Nov.–Apr.*

¢ **Hotel Namgyal Palace.** Modern but slightly characterless, this family-run hotel has an appealing pale green and wood facade. Its rooms are spacious, sunny and comfortable, with wall-to-wall carpeting, and attached bathrooms are clean and pleasing. The large hotel comes with oodles of lobby space decorated with intricate wood beams, a terrace and dining areas, and great views. What it lacks in coziness it makes up in cleanliness and cheer. **Pros:** large cheerful rooms. **Cons:** short on character. ✉ *Old Fort Rd., Leh, 194101* ☎ *1982/256–356* 🌐 *namgyalpalace.com* *30 rooms, 2 suites* *In-room: no a/c. In-hotel: restaurant, laundry service, no elevator.* 💳 *AE, MC, V.*

¢ **Lasermo.** One of Leh's older hotels, the Lasermo is centrally located and stays open year-round, aided by central heating. You can bask in the sun in a central courtyard. Rooms, which lack a view, are large and reasonably comfortable. True, the decor is a bit ugly, and the shabby

CLOSE UP

Padam

About 270 km (169 mi) southwest of Leh, Padam sits in the vast, high-altitude Zanskar Valley, ringed by mountains, with the Karsha Gompa perched on a nearby cliff. The valley's sweeping panoramas are framed by mountains, and the bases of the barren slopes are barricaded by sand and shaped by the wind and the water into oversize ramparts. Parts of the district consist of rocky desert punctuated by bits of green, with the Zanskar River racing along a deep gorge. Zanskar men in robes gallop by on handsome ponies.

In this sparsely populated district, the dominant sounds come from chattering birds or the wind, which grows intense by late afternoon, rustling the wheat, barley, and countless prayer flags. The arrival of tourists, especially trekkers, has begun to alter Zanskar's lifestyle: the men, who traditionally worked alongside the women in the fields and helped with the household chores and child-rearing, now look for jobs as porters while the women sell crafts. A growing attraction to money and Western goods is changing a society accustomed to bartering, and is threatening Buddhist traditions here.

bathrooms (showers only) need improvement, but you do have sun-drenched sitting areas in compensation. The newest rooms are the best, and from these you can access the rooftop terrace, with wonderful views of the countryside. **Pros:** open all year, convenient location. **Cons:** could be prettier. ✉*Chulung Old Rd., Leh, 194101* ☎*1982/252–313 or 1982/250–778* 📠*1982/252–203* ✉*lasermo@sancharnet.in* *38 rooms* *In-room: no a/c. In-hotel: restaurant, no elevator, laundry service.* 💳*AE.*

PANGONG & MORIRI LAKES, NUBRA VALLEY & DROGPA VILLAGES

Foreigners need an Inner Line Permit to visit any of these areas.

The brackish Pangong Tso and Tso Moriri (*tso* means "lake") in the eastern district of Changthang are astonishing alpine bodies of water. Both lakes are accessible by road from Leh between late May and late October. Road trips to Pangong Tso (159 km [99 mi]), which lies to the northeast, cost about Rs. 5,000, and those to Tso Moriri (225 km [140 mi]), which lies to the southeast, set you back Rs. 6,500.

Pangong Tso, at 14,018 feet, is more than 150 km (90 mi) long—and two-thirds of it lies in China.

Tso Moriri, 240 km (149 mi) southeast of Leh at 15,000 feet, is a pearl-shaped lake rich in mineral deposits, giving it a mysterious range of colors against the barren mountains.

North of Leh, Ladakh's "Valley of Flowers," the **Nubra Valley,** is sublime: a heady mixture of cultivated fields set in an arid desert that glows with white sand surrounded by the Karakoram Range and sliced by rivers. (*Nubra* means "garden.") Getting to this richly vegetated area around the Shayok and Siachen rivers requires a journey over the 18,383-foot-high Khardungla Pass, and takes about seven hours. From here you descend through the towering peaks to the villages of Nubra, which were important stops for rations along the Silk Road to Central Asia. Today's population is a mixture of Buddhists, Muslims, and the rare double-humped Bactrian camels once used for transport on the Silk Road. Local trekking routes go through virtually untouched territory, and you can explore by camel as well as on foot or by jeep. River rafting is also available, and hot springs warm weary travelers at Panamik Village. For the entire visit, budget at least two days and approximately Rs. 7,000.

In the **Drogpa villages** about 170 km (106 mi) west of Leh, the Dard people, numbering about 4,000, still inhabit the shimmering Indus Valley. Isolated from the modern world and racially different from other Ladakhis, they subsist on farming, eking a living from the rugged mountainsides. Their animist traditions set them apart from the firm Buddhists that surround them: has led to a belief that they have descended from the Indo-Aryans. You can arrange an overnight stay in Khaltse, where the main road forks off toward Kargil, 70 km (43 mi) from these villages or much closer at Dah. Arranging Inner Line Permit for this excursion takes a few days; the whole trip will set you back by about Rs. 7,000.

HIMACHAL PRADESH & LADAKH ESSENTIALS

To research prices, get advice from other travelers, and book travel arrangements, visit www.fodors.com.

AIR TRAVEL

Ladakh is accessible only by air in winter (October–May), as the roads are blocked by snow. Summer flights (until late September) tend to fill up, so reserve well in advance, and remember to confirm your seats with the airline 72 hours in advance. The fare is usually around US$100 one-way. On your return flight from Leh, check in about 1½ hours before, as security is strict—make sure your hand luggage is free of scissors, penknives, anything else sharp, and lighters, matches, and batteries.

Jagson Airlines flies Monday, Wednesday, and Friday from Delhi to Jubbarhatti Airport, an airstrip on a plateau created on top of a mountain 23 km (14 mi) south of **Shimla.** Roundtrip prices vary depending on when you book, and taxis into Shimla cost Rs. 500. The flight continues from Shimla to Kullu, whose airport is at Bhuntar, 9 km (5½ mi) from Kullu town and 50 km (30 mi) from **Manali.**

Deccan (formerly Air Deccan) has daily flights from Delhi to Amritsar, Chandigarh, Dharamshala, Kullu, Leh, and Shimla.

Air India flies from Delhi to Amritsar every day except Tuesday and Thursday. It also flies daily to Leh from Delhi.

Jet Airways flies daily from Delhi to Amritsar, Chandigarh, Jammu, and Leh. From Jammu it's roughly a four-hour drive to Dharamshala.

Spice Jet and Jet Lite also have daily flights to Jammu.

MDLR Airlines flies daily from Delhi to Chandigarh. At this writing, the airline is in the process of adding a daily flight to Kullu.

Airlines & Contacts Air India (aka Indian) (☎ *141, 11/2569–4070 in Delhi, 19/8225–2076 or 19/8225–1973 in Leh, 800/625–6424 toll-free in U.S.* 🌐 *www.airindia.com*). **Jagson Airlines** (☎ *11/2372–1593 in Delhi* 🌐 *www.jagsonairline.com*). **Jet Airways** (☎ *11/5164–1414, 11/2567–5404, or 11/3989–3333 in Delhi, 1982/250–999, 1982/250444, 1982/250–324, or 1982/250–638 in Leh, 877/835–9538 toll-free in U.S.* 🌐 *www.jetairways.com*). **Jet Lite** (☎ *1800/223–020* 🌐 *www.jetlite.com*). **MDLR Airlines** (☎ *124/451–0001* 🌐 *www.mdlrairlines.in*). **Simplifly Deccan** (☎ *98/1817–7008 or 11/2567–4679 in Delhi, 1800/425–7008 in Leh, 80/4114–8190 in Bangalore* 🌐 *www.airdeccan.net*). **Spice Jet** (☎ *1800/180–3333 toll-free in Delhi* 🌐 *www.spicejet.com*).

BUS TRAVEL

Bus fares are a tiny fraction of what it costs to travel by hired car, but non-air-conditioned (ordinary class, state-run) buses are not recommended, especially in the mountains. The handiwork of their drivers produces severe motion sickness, not to mention serious accidents, and they tend to make frequent stops and take unnecessary breaks. Air-conditioned deluxe buses are safer—opt for the most expensive category, such as a Volvo or picture-window coach with good suspension; check out the bus before buying a ticket, and travel only by day.

Deluxe coaches usually depart from roughly the same stands as state buses, and seat reservations are usually not required; a travel agent or hotel can help you make arrangements.

CARS & DRIVERS

Dharamshala, Dalhousie, Kullu, and Manali as well as more interior parts of Himachal such as Kinnaur, Spiti, and Lahaul can be reached by long journeys made by road from Shimla or Delhi. Dharamshala is 520 km (323 mi) and 12 hours or more from Delhi; Manali is 570 km (354 mi) from Delhi and 16 hours or less by road. Shimla is 260 km (162 mi and 8 hours) from Manali and 235 km (146 mi and 8½ hours) from Dharamshala.

You can book a car with driver through your hotel. In and around Leh the fares are fixed for most monasteries and other main tourist spots. The hourly rate, Rs. 100 per hour within and around Leh, is also fixed. Nor will you pay any extra fee by making the booking through your hotel.

Based in Delhi, RBS Travels (⇨ *Travel Agents & Tours*) maintains a large fleet of cars and offers reasonable rates and, more important, experienced and safety-conscious mountain drivers.

CELL PHONES

If you have a cell phone with an Indian service provider, you'll find that reception in Himachal Pradesh cities such as Shimla, Manali, and Dharamshala is pretty good. Reception in Amritsar and Chandigarh is also reliable. Otherwise, buy a calling card with roaming facilities before you leave Delhi. These cards can be found in any phone shop. Reception is spotty in Dalhousie and the more rural areas.

As for Leh, cell-phone reception is good but diminishes as you drive away from the town. Cell phone calling cards for local and long-distance use are widely available.

EMERGENCIES

In remote areas, the best emergency measures are your own caution—followed by an experienced and knowledgeable tour company, hotel manager, guide, and/or driver, who can get you quickly to the most appropriate doctor or emergency facility (not necessarily the nearest government-run hospital). Carry a good first-aid kit, including plenty of bandages for blisters if you're trekking. Take altitude precautions seriously—the waiting list for flights out of Leh is often filled with those who did not.

East–West Rescue, based in New Delhi, has an air ambulance for urgent evacuations from the remotest parts of India, Pakistan, Nepal, and Bhutan. The experienced staff in the 24-hour alarm center can recommend a network of medical centers, hospitals, and doctors throughout India.

Medical Care **East–West Medical Centre** (*✉ 38 Golf Links, New Delhi ☎ 11/2629–3701, 11/2629–3702, 11/2462–3738, 11/2464–1494, 11/2469–9229, 11/2469–0429, or 11/2469–8865 🌐 www.eastwestrescue.com*).

MONEY

ATMS If you're planning on skipping the Himachal Pradesh tourist hubs in favor of the rugged, rural areas of the Himalayas, it's a good idea to carry enough cash to cover your entire trip. In cities, ATMs are now abundant and accessible with foreign cards provided you use the right ones. Most ATMs are for local account-holders only, but at ICICI and Axis (formerly UTI) banks can you withdraw cash against your Visa or MasterCard—check the banks' Web sites for a complete list of ATM locations. In tourist towns, currency-exchange agents and banks might advance you cash against your Visa or MasterCard, but they usually charge a 10% commission.

When in Ladakh, carry enough cash or traveler's checks to cover your entire trip as you simply can't depend completely on withdrawing cash here. As always, cash is much preferable to checks. And don't count on using your credit cards for purchases.

Locations (Amritsar) **Axis** (*✉ 29 Kennedy Ave. 🌐 www.axisbank.com*). **ICICI** (*✉ ICICI, Hotel City Heart, Jallianwala Bagh 🌐 www.icicibank.com*).

Locations (Chandigarh) **Axis** (*✉ Booth 1, Sector 10D 🌐 www.axisbank.com*). **ICICI** (*✉ Accountant General Office, Sector 17 🌐 www.icicibank.com*).

Locations (Leh) **State Bank of India** (*✉ Main Bazaar 🌐 www.statebankofindia.com*).

Locations (Shimla) **Axis** (*✉ Trishool Tours and Travels, 53 The Mall 🌐 www.axisbank.com*). **ICICI** (*✉ Scandal Point, The Mall 🌐 www.icicibank.com*).

CURRENCY EXCHANGE Try to carry American Express traveler's checks, as you might have a problem cashing Thomas Cook checks in smaller towns. Checks can be cashed at your hotel or a local bank; just note that most banks keep short hours, 10–2 weekdays and 10–noon on Saturday. Sometimes banks don't open on the second Saturday of the month, and they definitely close on holidays.

There's a State Bank of India in just about every town—count on branches in Dalhousie, Darjeeling, Dharamshala, Leh, Manali, Mussoorie, Nainital, Rishikesh, Gangtok, Shimla. If you're curious about smaller towns, check the full list of branches on the bank's Web site.

Exchange Services **State Bank of India** (🌐 *www.statebankofindia.com*).

PERMITS

Because of diplomatic tensions with Pakistan and China, which have occasionally escalated into war, India's northern borders have been sensitive for decades and remain heavily guarded. Movement is restricted in these regions, which means foreigners need permits to enter some parts of Ladakh and Himachal Pradesh. It's generally easiest to apply for a permit in advance through a travel agent or tour operator or your hotel. Have two or three passport photographs and photocopies of your passport with proof of address and your Indian visa handy. Once you have the permit, keep several photocopies of it with you, and make sure you have it stamped at checkposts. Remember not to take pictures of bridges, airports, or military installations in restricted areas.

In Himachal Pradesh, permits are required for sections of the Spiti and Lahaul valleys and for upper Kinnaur. Groups of four foreigners can get permits from the Himachal Pradesh Tourism Development Corporation in New Delhi, which supposedly offers next-day service—but given the nature of Indian bureaucracy, we don't recommended this route. Whether you're traveling with a group or not, let your tour operator handle your permit in advance; just bring extra passport photos.

You do not need a permit to enter Ladakh, but you need a Inner Line Permit to visit parts of Ladakh that border on China, such as the Nubra Valley, Pangong Tso, and Tso Moriri. Have a tour operator process the application. For official information on Ladakh before you arrive, contact the Jammu and Kashmir Tourism office in New Delhi (⇨ Visitor Information).

TRAIN TRAVEL

There are several trains with air-conditioned cars and minimal stops that can drop you at several gateways to the Himalayas. You can buy tickets on line with Indian Railways—you must have a printer available to print such "iTickets" out. Reserve as far in advance as possible, as trains fill up early. Or skip the hassle by having a travel agent arrange your train tickets.

One of the Shatabdi trains departs New Delhi Railway Station at 7:20 AM for the nearly six-hour trip to Amritsar.

The Kalka Shatabdi departs at 7:40 AM for the 3½-hour trip to **Chandigarh,** from which buses go to Dharamshala, Kullu, and Manali. Spend the night in Chandigarh and start by car or bus the next day for the 12-hour trip to Kullu or the 14-hour trip to Manali. If you hire a driver to tour Himachal Pradesh, consider sending him ahead to Chandigarh and arranging for him to meet you as you arrive on the train from Delhi at 11 AM—this will save you three hours of a potentially tiring road trip.

The train is also the best way to get to **Shimla.** You're best off with the Himalayan Queen, which leaves Delhi at 5:55 AM daily to reach Kalka at 11:20 AM. From there, you'll connect to the famous Toy Train. First class on the Toy Train is extremely comfortable, with upholstered chairs to sink into as you marvel at the scenery and take refreshments; second class is crowded, with people pushing and shoving to sit on the wooden seats. It's a stiff uphill walk from the train station to the center of town. A taxi will take you to the pedestrian-only Mall for about Rs. 100. If you hire a porter, he'll expect at least Rs. 50, depending on the amount of luggage; just beware that porters double as hotel touts, so don't let them steer you away from your lodging of choice. The overnight Howrah–Kalka Mail leaves Delhi at 8:40 PM to reach Kalka at 4:45 AM, where you can catch the 5:30 AM departure of the Toy Train to Shimla. This departure, the Shivalk Express, is a little faster than other departures, but note that the Mail night train is often delayed.

The trip to **Dharamshala** and the **Kangra Valley** is also more pleasant by train than by car. The Jammu Mail, which leaves Delhi at 9:20 PM to reach Pathankot at 7:15 AM, has first- and second-class air-conditioned compartments; after a good night's sleep you can hop in a car and enjoy the remaining three hours to Dharamshala.

There is no train that's useful for travelers in Ladakh.

Train Information **Indian Railways** (*www.indianrail.gov.in*).

TRAVEL AGENTS & TOURS

Most of the outfits listed here offer treks and jeep safaris; some also lead rafting and angling expeditions. The Delhi-based firms Aquaterra Adventures India, Great Himalayan Adventures, Himalayan River Runners, and Ibex Expeditions are highly recommended for trips anywhere in the Himalayas. If you're planning your own itinerary, call Delhi's reliable and very efficient RBS Travels to make driving arrangements and airline bookings.

HIMALAYAS–GENERAL **Contacts** **Aquaterra Adventures India** (*S-507 Greater Kailash II, New Delhi 11/2921–2641 or 11/2921–2760 www.treknraft.com*). **Great Himalayan Adventures** (*N-95 Sham Nagar, New Delhi 11/2546–5783 or 981/011–1124 www.wildquestindia.com*). **Himalayan River Runners** (*N-8 Green Park Main, upper floor, New Delhi 11/2685–2602 or 11/2685–2604 www.hrrindia.com*). **Ibex Expeditions** (*G-66 East of Kailash, New Delhi 11/2691–2641, 11/2682–8479, or 11/2691–7829 www.ibexexpeditions.com*). **RBS Travels** (*Shop A1, Connaught Palace Hotel, 37 Shaheed Bhagat Singh Marg, New Delhi 11/2336–4603, 11/2336–4952, 11/2336–5766, or 11/2334–708 www.rbstravels.com*).

HIMACHAL PRADESH TOUR SPECIALISTS

Contacts **Band Box Heights and Valleys** (✉ *9 The Mall, Shimla* ☎ *177/265-8157 or 98160-61160*). **Himalayan Journeys** (✉ *The Mall, Box 15, Manali* ☎ *1902/252-365 or 1902/253-355* 🌐 *www.himalayanjourneysindia.com*). **Naresh Tours and Travels** (✉ *3 Chaura Maidan, Shimla* ☎ *177/265-6692 or 177/265-7445*). **Yeti Travels** (✉ *The Mall, Manali* ☎ *1902/253-135 or 1902/252-655*).

LADAKH TOUR SPECIALISTS

Contacts **Adventure North Tours and Travels** (*c/o Dragon Hotel, Old Leh Rd., Leh* ☎ *1982/252-720 or 1982/252-139* *advnorth@vsnl.com*).

Explore Himalayas (✉ *Box 45, Main Bazaar, Opp. State Bank of India, Leh* ☎ *1982/252-727 or 1982/252-403* 🌐 *www.explorehimalayas.com*). **Himalayan Home Stays** (✉ *Ibex Hotel Complex, Leh* ☎ *1982/250-953* 🌐 *www.himalayan-homestays.com*). **Overland Escape** (✉ *Raku Complex, Fort Rd., Leh* ☎ *1982/250-858* 🌐 *www.overlandescape.com*).

VISITOR INFORMATION

In Leh there's also a counter for visitor information in the main bazaar opposite the Jammu and Kashmir (J and K) Bank.

Punjab Development Corporation Office **Amritsar** (✉ *Pegasus Hotel, opposite railway station* ☎ *183/223-1452*). **Chandigarh** (✉ *1st fl., Interstate Bus Terminus, Sector 17* ☎ *172/270-4614*).

Himachal State Tourism Office **Himachal Pradesh** (✉ *Chandralok Bldg., 36 Janpath, New Delhi* ☎ *11/2332-5320* ✉ *Hotel Baghsu, McCleod Ganj* ☎ *1892/221-091* ✉ *Hotel Kunjum, near taxi stand, The Mall, Manali* ☎ *1902/253-197* ✉ *The Mall, Shimla* ☎ *177/281-2890*). **Jammu and Kashmir** (✉ *201-203 Kanishka Shopping Plaza, New Delhi* ✉ *19 Ashoka Rd., New Delhi* ☎ *11/2334-5373* 🌐 *www.jktourism.org*). **Ladakh** (✉ *Tourist Reception Center, 3 km (2 mi) outside town, Leh* ☎ *1982/252297*).

Mumbai & Maharashtra

A local train in Mumbai

WORD OF MOUTH

"Both Trishna and Mahesh Lunch Home feature food from the Malabar coast (west coast of India). In my opinion, the food from this general area is by far the best in India and certainly my favorite of any cuisine in the world (and no, I'm not from that area). Unfortunately many westerners believe that Punjabi food (while very good) is somehow the representative food of India, based on the ubiquity of Punjabi restaurants in the West. If you're in south Bombay, don't miss the opportunity to try one of these Malabari restaurants."

—krishnan

www.fodors.com/forums

WELCOME TO MUMBAI & MAHARASHTRA

TOP REASONS TO GO

★ **All of India in One City:** Mumbai is both modern and old-fashioned, rich and poor, beautiful and ugly—all of India concentrated in one metropolis.

★ **One Big Feast:** Whether it's down-home seafood joints or upscale temples to gastronomy, many of Mumbai's restaurants are the best in India.

★ **A Taste of India's Bazaars:** The buzz of a typical Indian bazaar is fascinating—Mumbai is packed with them. Time to get shopping.

★ **Look for Meditation and Peace:** Pune is famed for yoga and other ways to seek inner tranquility.

★ **The Astonishing Caves:** The carvings and paintings of the caves of Ellora and Ajanta have awe-inspiring beauty.

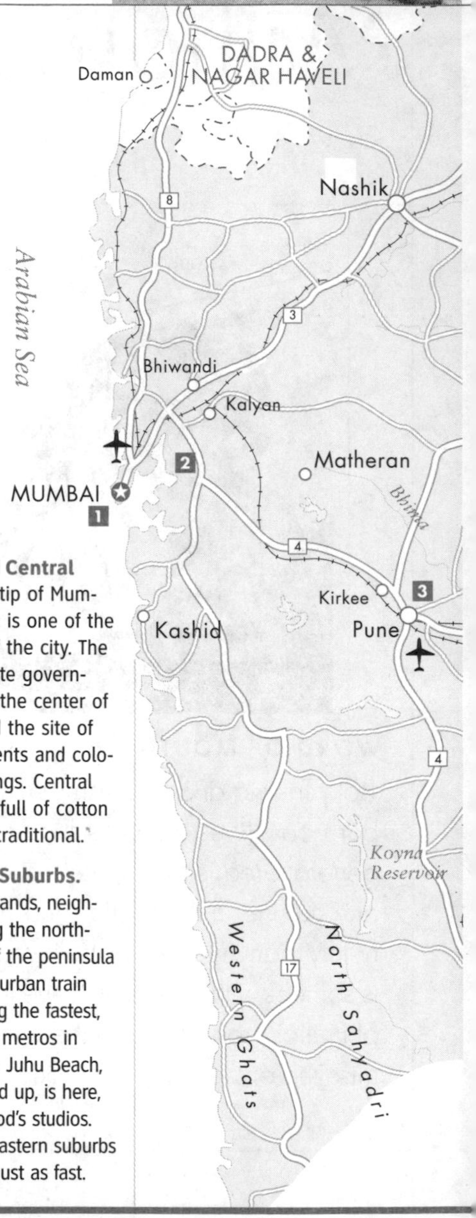

1 South and Central Mumbai. The tip of Mumbai's peninsula is one of the oldest parts of the city. The seat of the state government, it's also the center of commerce and the site of many monuments and colonial-era buildings. Central Mumbai, once full of cotton mills, is more traditional.

2 Mumbai's Suburbs. As Mumbai expands, neighborhoods along the northwestern side of the peninsula and on the suburban train line are growing the fastest, becoming little metros in their own right. Juhu Beach, recently cleaned up, is here, as are Bollywood's studios. The less-tony eastern suburbs are expanding just as fast.

DADRA & NAGAR HAVELI
Daman
Nashik
8
Arabian Sea
3
Bhiwandi
Kalyan
2
Matheran
MUMBAI
1
Bhima
4
Kirkee
3
Kashid
Pune
4
Koyna Reservoir
Western Ghats
17
North Sahyadri

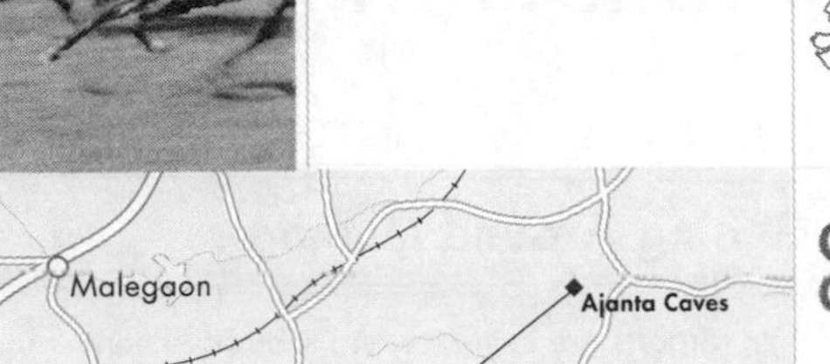

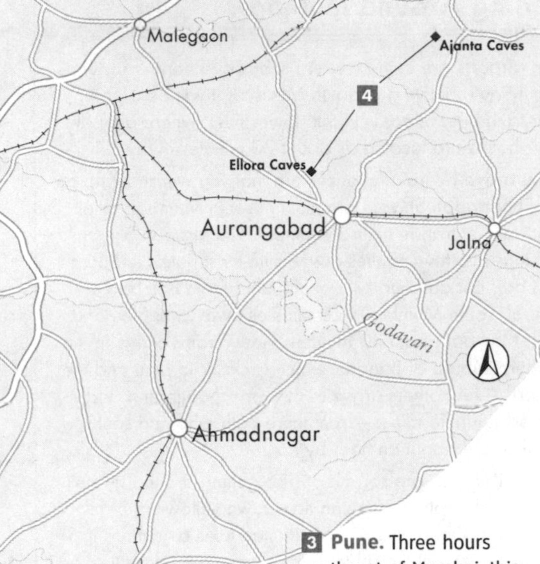

3 Pune. Three hours southeast of Mumbai, this rapidly expanding former hill station has its interest ing sights scattered throughout many neighborhoods. The main drag, where the shops and many restaurants are, is on the eastern end, near Mahatma Gandhi Road and East Street and a little beyond at Koergaon Park.

4 Aurangabad and the Caves. A base for exploring the astounding cave temples of Ellora and Ajanta, Aurangabad lies about 250 mi east of Mumbai. Its dusty, bustling, tree less downtown centers around a T-shaped area formed by Jalna Road and the road going to CIDCO.

GETTING ORIENTED

India's largest city is also one of the largest cities in the world, both in size and population. Nearly 20 million are crammed into an area of 1,600 square mi—that's about 11,000 people per square mi. On a peninsula jutting out of the western coast of India and facing the Arabian Sea, in the state of Maharashtra, Mumbai is roughly equidistant from the three other main Indian metros of New Delhi, Kolkata, and Chennai.

Beach vendors at Chowpatty Beach with Malabar Hill in the background

MUMBAI & MAHARASHTRA PLANNER

When to Go

Mumbai and Maharashtra are best explored between November and February, when the weather is warm but not unbearable, less humid, and free from monsoons. Ajanta and Ellora explode with greenery during and after the monsoon season (June to September), if the rains have been good; at Ajanta, a river springs into being at the bottom of the gorge into which the caves are cut. If the rains haven't been good, it can be quite hot—otherwise the rainy season is a good time to visit Aurangabad. Pune is very cool in winter (sweater required) but sunny and bright. Because most tourists arrive in Mumbai, Pune, and Maharashtra during winter, it's important to make hotel and transportation arrangements ahead of time.

Getting Around Mumbai

Both airports are in the western suburbs of northern Mumbai. If you're staying in South Mumbai, it will be a one-hour taxi, bus, or car ride into town. Juhu, where a lot of other hotels are located, is about 20 minutes away.

If you arrive by train, chances are that you will show up at the Chhatrapati Shivaji Terminus, in south Mumbai, or at Bombay Central, in central Mumbai. Chhatrapati Shivaji Terminus is a few minutes away from most hotels in South Mumbai, but an hour away from Juhu. From Bombay Central, south Mumbai is 20 minutes away and Juhu and north Mumbai about 40 minutes. A few trains arrive in the northern suburb of Bandra, which is closer to Juhu and the airport. A few others arrive at the very chaotic and oddly located Kurla Terminus—from there both Juhu and south Mumbai are about an hour by taxi.

Mumbai's sights are spread out, so getting around by taxi is a sensible option. You can flag down yellow-top black taxis or silver-and-blue air-conditioned taxis anywhere in the city. Insist that the driver turn on the meter, a rusty contraption on the hood of the car, before setting off. Because the meters haven't been adjusted for quite some time, it takes some arithmetic to compute the latest (higher) fares, based on the meter reading. Drivers must show you their revised tariff cards, but they sometimes "misplace" them, or whip out a chart for air-conditioned cabs, or show you fares chargeable after midnight. At this writing the legal fare was 14 times the total amount shown on the meter, based on roughly Rs. 13 for the first kilometer and about Rs. 1.5 for each additional kilometer. Air-conditioned taxi fares are 25% higher—the starting rate is Rs. 16.50 and Rs. 12 for each additional kilometer. If you are short of time you might consider hiring a car and driver.

Auto-rickshaws are permitted only in Mumbai's suburbs, beyond Bandra, where you can flag them down on the street. As with regular taxis, insist on paying by the meter and ask to see the tariff card. Mumbai has a good bus system; however, navigating long routes and big crowds is likely to turn trips into an uphill battle.

24-Hour Munchies

Looking for a bit of *hungama* (action) or something to eat at a crazy hour? Unlike most other Indian cities, that start snoozing as early as 8 PM, Mumbai buzzes around the clock. Food carts appear every few yards serving *chaats* (Indian street snacks). Even simple food is transformed into something impressive. The choices are enormous—hot, spicy vegetable sandwiches, slices of green mango peppered with masala, sizzling kebabs, Chinese noodles with vegetables, fresh strawberry milk shakes, carrot juice, *kulfi* (cream-based Indian ice cream), fresh slices of mangoes and cream, spicy boiled chickpeas, fried fish, potato turnovers, masala peanuts, coconut water, green chilli omelets in buns, and exotic snacks associated with Mumbai, such as *bhel puri* (puffed rice snack) and *wada paav* (savory potato snack stuffed in a bun and lathered with chutney).

Much of this snack food is created right at the side of the road on open grills and stoves and then assembled in front of you. As you would imagine, the hygiene may be a little suspect. But don't let that deter you, or you may miss out on some carnival-like happenings and some excellent local food. If you sample any of these streetside treats, follow some rules. Try food served hot on the spot. If the plates don't look clean, ask that food be either served or packed in a disposable container (a fresh plastic bag, a cup created from leaves, a paper plate, or newspaper) or bring your own little container. Carry your own spoon and paper or plastic cup, if possible. And don't worry—the vendors usually understand enough English to see the process through. Finally, those vendors who attract the biggest crowds and fame are likely to be safer than those who are ignored.

WHAT IT COSTS In Rupees

	¢	$	$$	$$$	$$$$
RESTAU-RANTS	under Rs. 100	Rs. 100–Rs. 300	Rs. 300–Rs. 500	Rs. 500–Rs. 700	over Rs. 700
HOTELS	under Rs. 2,000	Rs. 2,000–Rs. 4,000	Rs. 4,000–Rs. 6,000	Rs. 6,000–Rs. 10,000	over Rs. 10,000

Restaurant prices are for an entrée plus bread or rice. Hotel prices are for a double room in high season, excluding a tax of up to 20%.

Planning Your Time

India's most cosmopolitan city gives way to Maharashtra's rugged interior, which hides the spectacular Ajanta and Ellora caves, 370 km (229 mi) northeast of Mumbai, as well as the hill station of Pune to the southeast. Maharashtra's landscape fuses stark, semiarid mountains and rock formations with lush, green countryside. To see this state, spend the better part of a week here.

Mumbai, on the Arabian Sea, inhabited by 20 million and counting, can be ambitiously explored in about two days. Catching the flavor of colonial Mumbai is a must: this requires a walk around the Gateway of India, the Prince of Wales Museum and Victoria Terminus. To take in a bazaar, head to Crawford Market or stroll down Colaba Causeway to do some bargain hunting. Lunching at a seafood restaurant or snacking on Chowpatty Beach are both great experiences, as is a beer and some people-watching at Leopold Café in Colaba.

Pune, now one of India's ten largest growing cities, is a center of IT and outsourcing, but it's also famed for its culture and yoga center. Its sights will take you a little over a day to cover. Don't miss a visit to the Raja Dinkar Kelkar Museum and a walk through its environs, Pune's older quarter.

Aurangabad is the most common base for visiting the Ajanta and Ellora caves.

By Vaihayasi Pande Daniel

RAZZLE-DAZZLE, INDIAN-STYLE—THAT'S MUMBAI, THE FORMER Bombay, the country's seaside financial capital and trendsetting East–West nexus. India's greatest port and the capital of Maharashtra state, Mumbai perches on the Arabian Sea, covering an island separated from the rest of India by a winding creek. A world unto itself, Mumbai hits you with an intensity all its own. It is distinctly tropical, with pockets of palm trees and warm, salty breezes—and its culture is contemporary, vibrant, and often aggressive, reflecting both the affluence and poverty of the nearly 20 million people crowded onto this island. Behind all this, weathered Victorian mansions, some still privately owned, and grand public buildings, many beautifully lit at night, stand as lingering reminders of the British Raj.

In 1995 Bombay's name was officially changed to Mumbai, after Mumba Devi, the patron Hindu goddess of the island's original residents, the Koli fishermen. However, many residents still call their city Bombay. It's confusing, but just another chapter in the city's labyrinthine history.

Mumbai initially consisted of seven marshy islands—Colaba, Old Woman's Island, Bombay, Mazgaon, Worli, Mahim, and Parel—belonging to the Muslim kings of the Gujarat sultanate. The Muslims passed the parcel to the Portuguese (who occupied much of western India in the 16th and 17th centuries), who in turn passed it in 1661 to England's King Charles II as part of a dowry in his marriage to the Portuguese Princess Catherine de Braganza. The British established a fort and trading post that grew quickly in size and strength.

Soon enough, land reclamation joined the seven small islands into one, grafting a prototype for today's multifarious metropolis. The pride of the British in Bombay, and in their power over western India, is memorialized in the city's most celebrated landmark—the Gateway of India, built to welcome King George V to India in 1911. Ironically, it's now near a statue of the young 17th-century Marathi leader, Shivaji.

The Mumbai you see today is a city of mind-boggling contrasts: sometimes exciting, sometimes deeply disturbing. As your plane descends toward the runway, usually late at night, your first view of Mumbai takes in vast stretches of slums, stacked and piled onto each other like cardboard boxes—only a fleeting glimpse of the staggering poverty that coexists, invariably side by side, with the dazzling wealth flashed in trendy boutiques and deluxe hotels. In the neighborhoods of Churchgate or Nariman Point, Mumbai's slick hotel and business centers, a fleet of dark-suited executives may breeze by on its way to a meeting while a near-naked little girl with matted hair scavenges in the gutter beside them. A fancy department store is across the road from a group of shacks that a few hundred people call home—one customer in that store may spend more in an hour than all the people living in the shacks earn in a month. A journalist once pointed out that Mumbai is a city where the servant walking the pedigreed, handsomely groomed dog has no formal education, but his charge has been to an expensive training school.

It's important to view Mumbai in perspective. Mumbai can seem so different from the rest of India that it could be another country. It operates according to its own rules, and its pulse beats far more quickly than the rest of the country, which views it as the city of opportunity. Mumbai tantalizes millions with prospects of wealth and success. Every day, migrants arrive—be they business-school grads or laborers—to see if they too can make a life here. Apart from the city's original Maharasthrian population, every Bombayite, from the *hijra* (eunuch) to the taxi driver to the white-collar worker, *is,* as hard as it may be to believe, living out his or her dream—in a hovel or a palace. More often than not, Bombay is a place to build a better life.

SIDE TRIPS

If you have a few extra days, plan an escape from the city to the stunning Ajanta and Ellora caves, or head east to the town of Pune.

For the traveler, Mumbai is both disturbingly eye-opening and incredibly exciting. Here in the heady sun and breeze of the Arabian Sea you can feast in fabulous restaurants, bargain in street bazaars, browse in exclusive boutiques, take a horse-drawn ride past stately old Victorian buildings, get lost in the stone carvings of the 7th-century Elephanta Caves, watch the sun rise over the Gateway of India, and stroll at sunset along Marine Drive's endless waterfront promenade.

MUMBAI

There's plenty to see in Mumbai, but it's not generally in the form of stationary monuments like those in London, Paris, or Delhi. The art of experiencing Mumbai lies in eating, shopping, and wandering through strikingly different neighborhoods, and markets. Consider Mumbai a 30-mi-long open-air bazaar.

Colaba, headed by Gateway of India, is the fascinating tourist district and the main drag for visitors. From Gateway of India to Colaba Market, along the main road, is a walkable stretch of hotels, a few pubs, restaurants, and interesting shops; the quiet, leafy bylanes are residential, consisting of apartments and homes in ancient mansions and battered old buildings. Churchgate and Nariman Point are the business and hotel centers. Major bank and airline headquarters are clustered in skyscrapers on Nariman Point. The district referred to as Fort—which includes Mumbai's hub, Flora Fountain, in a square now called Hutatma Chowk—is the city's commercial heart, its narrow, bustling streets lined with small shops and office buildings, as well as colleges and other educational facilities. Farther north, Kemps Corner is a trendy area with expensive boutiques, exclusive restaurants, and high-price homes. Another upscale residential neighborhood, Malabar Hill, is leafy and breezy, with fine, old stone mansions housing wealthy industrialists and government ministers.

Shopping and people watching are most colorfully combined in Mumbai's chaotic bazaar areas, such as Chor Bazaar, Zaveri (jewelry) Bazaar, and Mahatma Jyotiba Phule Market (aka Crawford Market). More recently, Mumbai's suburbs have seen explosive business and residential development, as more and more people move out of the center to escape the soaring real-estate prices and lack of space. Many of the city's newest and trendiest shops and restaurants are now out in the suburbs. A number of travelers opt to stay in Juhu Beach, a popular coastal suburb between Mumbai and the airports (about 20 km [12 mi] north of the city center). Juhu's beaches are unsafe for swimming, and the place is scruffy, but staying out here is a good way to observe everyday Indian life outside the shadow of Mumbai's skyline. Sunday nights bring families down to the beach for an old-fashioned carnival, complete with small, hand-powered Ferris wheels, and lantern-lit snack stalls hawking sugarcane.

THE FOREIGNER TICKET TAX

As is common throughout India, admission to many of Mumbai's museums and sites is often ten times higher for foreign tourists than it is for locals. That can be annoying, but remember that in order for these sights to be accessible to the not-so-well-to-do general public, institutions and authorities need to make up revenues elsewhere.

Numbers in the text correspond to numbers in the margin and on the chapter map.

ABOUT THE RESTAURANTS

As Mumbai grows exponentially, so do its restaurants. Among Indian food you'll find kebabs and tandoori food—meat, bread, cottage cheese, and vegetables cooked inside a clay oven. These dishes, often found on menus and served with Mughlai (a variety of Muslim cuisine) and Punjabi cuisine, are by far the most popular food in town. Also popular, and closely related to Mughlai food are the typically meat-heavy dishes from the North-West Frontier, the area of undivided India that's partly in modern-day Pakistan. Another dish likely to pop up on menus is Gujarati vegetarian thalis—combination platters that are a little oilier than those from elsewhere in India. You may also encounter some Jain food, which is also vegetarian but cooked without root vegetables, such as onions and garlic. Jains try to avoid all destruction of life, and eating such vegetables destroys both the entire plant and any microorganisms that might be living on it. Seafood from the Konkan coast—from Maharashtra south through Goa all the way to Mangalore, in Karnataka—is also a favorite in Mumbai.

Authentic South Indian vegetarian food—*dosas* (fried, crepelike pancakes), *idlis* (steamed rice cakes), *wadas* (also spelled *vadas*; savory fried, and often flavored, lentil-flour doughnuts), and simple, light *thalis* (combination platters)—is a city staple. The city has hundreds of fast-food, piping-hot-idli-crispy-dosa restaurants run by the Manglorean Shetty community, which is known for their proficiency in this cuisine. Food in such restaurants is generally clean (the restaurants may be less so), quick, cheap, and tasty.

Even if you find yourself in one of the many average, cookie-cutter restaurants in town, you're unlikely to have a truly terrible meal. They tend to produce competently prepared, not overly authentic Punjabi dishes that taste the same wherever you go—chicken tikka, yellow dal, butter chicken, fried fish, vegetable *pulau* (a rice preparation). Sometimes such places throw in a few token Continental dishes, such as Russian salad (a sweet, mayo-heavy concoction) or vegetables in béchamel sauce, but these are rarely worth sampling.

Mumbai is also known for its chic restaurants and Western-style pubs. It is a city where you can get not only great meals, but can taste all sorts of cuisines—Continental, authentic Chinese, Italian, Thai, Lebanese, and Mexican. There is a wealth of Chinese eateries offering either lower-end, fiery Indian-Chinese, or fancier, more authentic Chinese. Such restaurants that focus on a particular cuisine tend to appear most to young spenders and tourists.

Many Bombay restaurants are pricey by Indian standards, but there are plenty of tasty bargains that will leave your taste buds and your wallet equally satisfied. Many hotels have good restaurants and all-night "coffee shops" that serve full meals. With Mumbai's approximately two-dozen upscale hotels are 24-hour coffee shops that serve simple meals from multicuisine menus in pleasing, but expensive (up to $50 per head per meal) rooms. Many of these hotels have Chinese, Continental, and Indian food restaurants, too. Some of the food is unremarkable and the stylings mildly repetitive—as they say in Hindi: *uchcha dukan, pheeka pakwan,* the loftier the establishment the more insipid the food. But the meals are hygienic and wholesome, and the service pleasant. The restaurants are comfortable, too; a refreshing break from Mumbai's humid, crowded streets or a hot afternoon of sightseeing. That said, a few of Mumbai's top hotels, among them the Hyatt, J. W. Marriott, and the Grand Maratha, put on exquisite buffet brunches that are a good value. The range and quality of the food makes dining at such places a memorable experience.

With Mumbai's traffic becoming more intolerable day by day it makes sense to explore the restaurant choices closer to your hotel. The geography of Mumbai is such that the concentration of hotels are in the northern suburb of Juhu as well as near the airport (Andheri) and in south Mumbai. These days there are loads of restaurants to choose from in Juhu and Andheri, and south Mumbai has always had plenty of compelling choices. On the other hand the northern suburb of Bandra has innumerable small restaurants offering many kinds of cuisine, including Japanese or Lebanese or great *biryanis* (rice cooked with meat). Menus are diverse and meal prices low. For the adventurous, a Bandra food expedition, about 45–50 minutes by taxi (outside traffic hours) from south Mumbai or Juhu and Andheri, can be worthwhile.

ABOUT THE HOTELS

In Mumbai, unlike elsewhere in India, even mid-range hotels can be shockingly overpriced and a hotel shortage means that good deals are few. Even hotels with the highest of prices can be full because of year-round demand; you are well advised to make your booking a few months in advance.

BOMBAY DRESS CODE

Bombay-*wallahs* (dwellers) generally dress for dinner. They aren't formal, but they are usually well-turned out. Shorts and a grungy look are not acceptable except at cafés.

Chains like the Taj, Oberoi, Hyatt, Marriott, Intercontinental, Hilton, and Sheraton run several massive lodgings, most of them deluxe; these cater to leisure and business travelers, and movie stars with money to burn. Whether you reserve with a hotel directly or through a travel agent, always ask for a discount. Tariffs quoted in this book and at hotels do not include 12% tax. Room rates at the luxury hotels fluctuate depending on occupancy, and they offer the rate of the day; the earlier you book the better rate you will get. If you are paying cash, convert your currency beforehand—most hotels give poor exchange rates. Most of Mumbai's hotels are collected around three locations: First in north Mumbai right near the airport; second, near Juhu Beach; and finally a majority of them are in south Mumbai, primarily in Colaba.

Mumbai's cheaper hotels, usually in south Mumbai, can be decent but are also overpriced. During the monsoon season (mid-June through late September), these hotels are overrun by large groups of vacationers from various Arab nations who come to Mumbai to enjoy the rain, during which time noise levels can be very high. Solo women travelers should probably stay elsewhere during this time.

Unless otherwise indicated, hotels have air-conditioning, room service, doctors on call, and currency exchange, and rooms have private bathrooms and cable television.

FORT DISTRICT & ENVIRONS

The most manageable, and probably the most colorful walks in Mumbai center on the Fort district. If Mumbai is the first stop on your first trip to India, remember that sightseeing here is nothing like touring, say, Europe—the streets are packed, some lack sidewalks, traffic takes many forms, crosswalks are a rarity, and people will stare or call out to you with sales pitches as you pass. Stopping to take a picture can make you feel terribly conspicuous. You'll get used to it soon enough, however, and will quickly learn to revel in the whirlwind.

A GOOD WALK

Start your walk by exploring the **Mahatma Jyotiba Phule Market** ❶, commonly known as Crawford Market, and the surrounding lanes. Abdul Rehman Street will take you north into **Zaveri Bazaar** ❷. ⚠ **At all bazaars, be sure to keep your eyes and hands on your wallet.** From Crawford or Zaveri you can either head south to the main Fort district or, if you're up for more narrow-lane navigation, detour to **Chor Bazaar** ❸, a bustling old antiques market.

To find Chor Bazaar, either walk or (far more preferably) cab it (a 15-minute ride) north from Crawford Market on Mohammed Ali Road, which joins Rahimtulla Road to bring you into South Mumbai's main Muslim quarter. After passing the Beg Muhammed School, Mandavi Telephone Exchange, and Mandavi post office on the left, you'll hit Sardar Vallabhbhai Patel Road: turn left and you can enter Chor Bazaar on Mutton Street. When you're almost bazaared out, retrace the route back down to Crawford Market, either on foot or by taxi.

To move south toward the center of the Fort district, follow A. Rehman Street until it becomes Dr. D. Naoroji Road: You are now in the heart of downtown, an area of broader streets and crowded sidewalks. On your right is the imposing, V-shaped, early Gothic–style Municipal Corporation Building, vintage 1893, with Indian motifs and a large dome; on your left is Mumbai's chief train station, the huge **Chhatrapati Shivaji Terminus,** also called by its old colonial name, Victoria Terminus, or just V.T. Push your way through the crowds of people and cars to cross the chaotic roundabout; rejoin Dr. D. Naoroji Road on the other side, and continue heading south. After about 15 minutes you'll arrive at the **Flora Fountain** ❹, the true center of Mumbai.

Take a right here onto Veer Nariman Road, pass the Central Telegraph office and its open-air book bazaars, and in a few minutes you'll hit K.B. Patil Marg. Turn left, keep heading south, and on your left you'll see the High Court, built in the early Gothic style in 1878. Farther south on the same street you'll see Mumbai University's 260-foot Rajabhai Clocktower, also Victorian Gothic. Turn left onto Mahatma Gandhi Road (better known as M.G. Road) and you'll soon reach a cluster of three major museums. The **Jehangir Art Gallery** ❺ will be on your left. Across the street from Jehangir, in the lane heading behind the music store Rhythm House (which has an excellent selection of music), is the Keneseth Eliyahoo Synagogue. On the other side is the fantastic looking Elphinstone College. Pause to absorb the Bombay that the British planned on a very grand scale. From Mahatma Gandhi Road, hang a left down K. Dubash Marg to the **Prince of Wales Museum** ❻. The **National Gallery of Modern Art** ❼ is across the street. From here, take C. Shivaji Maharaj Marg to the **Gateway of India** ❽, where you can relax among locals at the water's edge.

Right across the square from the Gateway of India is the historic Taj Mahal hotel. Even if you can't afford to stay here, it's a treat just to walk around the lobby and shopping areas (they don't mind) and perhaps have tea and snacks at the Sea Lounge.

TIMING This walk takes a full day: the going is slow and the bazaars eat up time in a stealthy manner. You'll probably want to spend close to an hour at both the Prince of Wales Museum and the Jehangir Art Gallery. Note that Crawford Market is closed Sunday, the Prince of Wales Museum is closed Monday, and Chor Bazaar shuts down on Friday. Early morning tends to be less humid, so you may want to set off then.

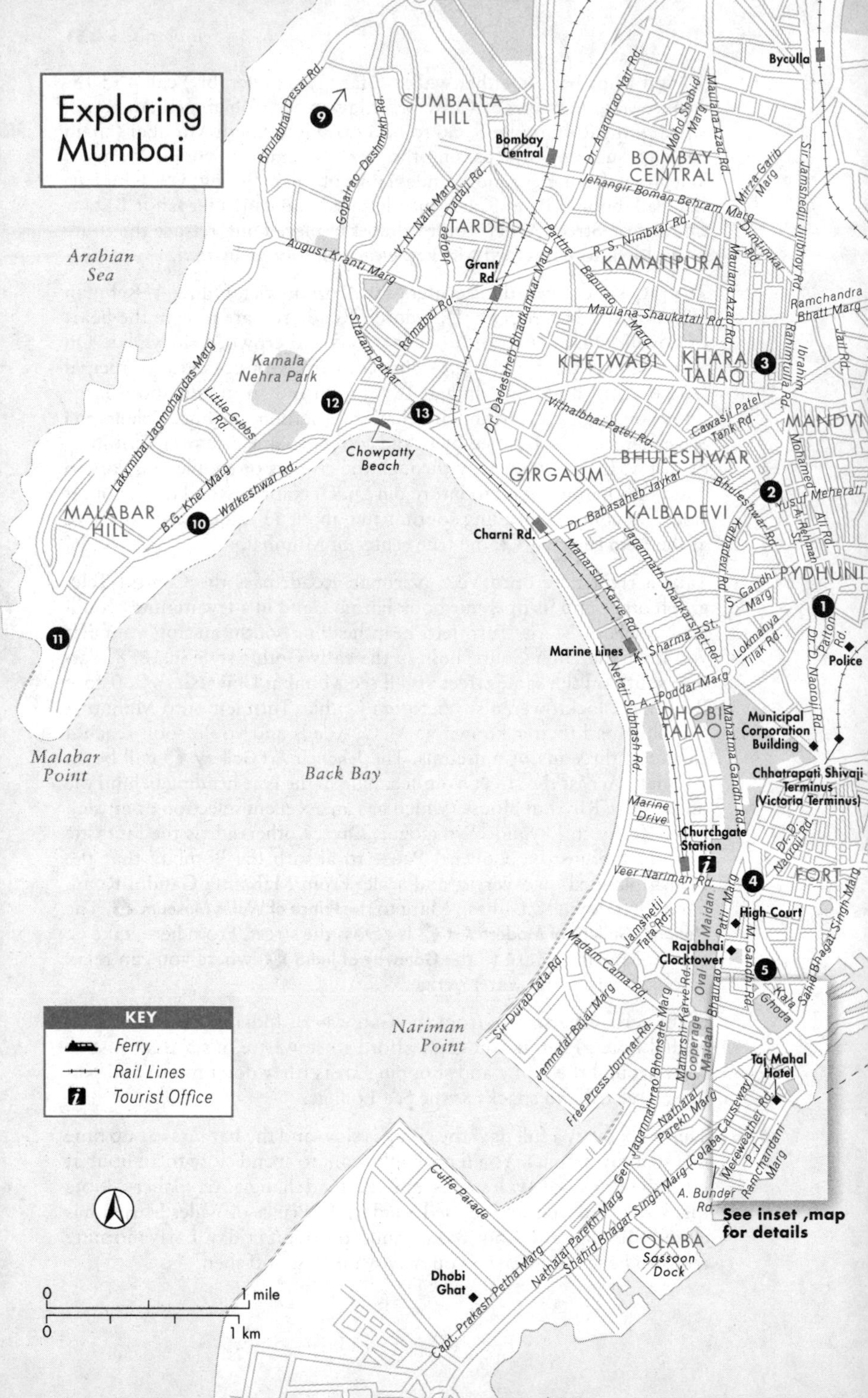

Exploring Mumbai
Arabian Sea
Malabar Point
Back Bay
Nariman Point
CUMBALLA HILL
TARDEO
BOMBAY CENTRAL
KAMATIPURA
KHETWADI
KHARA TALAO
MANDVI
BHULESHWAR
GIRGAUM
KALBADEVI
PYDHUNI
DHOBI TALAO
FORT
MALABAR HILL
COLABA
Kamala Nehru Park
Chowpatty Beach
Bombay Central
Grant Rd.
Charni Rd.
Marine Lines
Churchgate Station
Byculla
Police
Municipal Corporation Building
Chhatrapati Shivaji Terminus (Victoria Terminus)
High Court
Rajabhai Clocktower
Taj Mahal Hotel
Sassoon Dock
Dhobi Ghat
Marine Drive
Oval Maidan
Cooperage Maidan
Kala Ghoda
See inset ,map for details
KEY
Ferry
Rail Lines
Tourist Office
0
1 mile
0
1 km

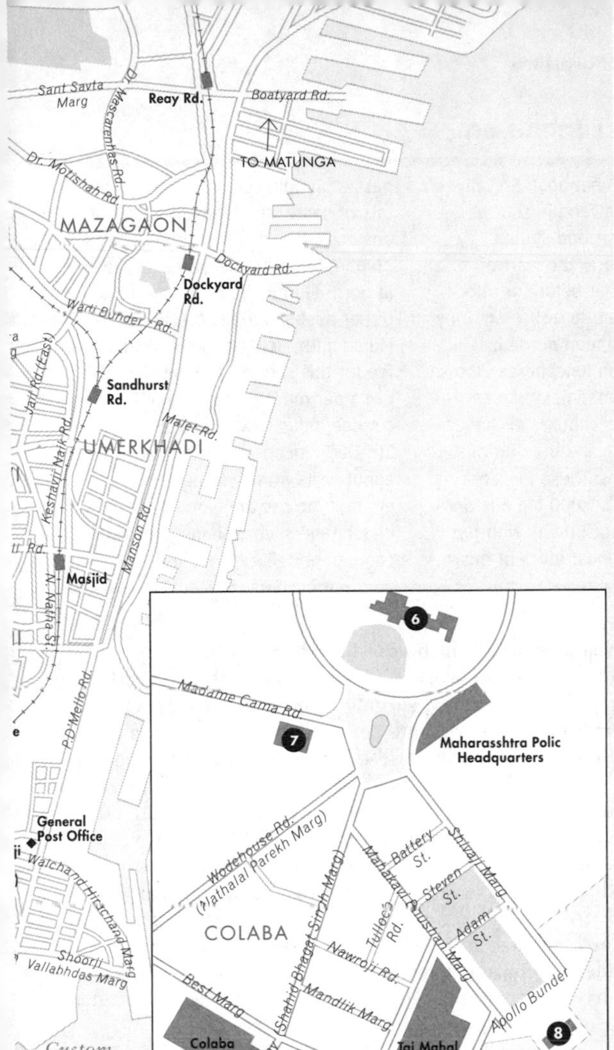

Babulnath Temple 12
Banganga 11
Chor Bazaar..........................3
Flora Fountain 4
Gateway of India......................8
Haji Ali Shrine.......................9
Jain Temple..........................10
Jehangir Art Gallery..................5
Mahatma Jyotiba Phule Market (Crawford Market).....................1
Mani Bhavan..........................13
National Gallery of Modern Art 7
Prince of Wales Museum 6
Zaveri Bazaar 2

7

CLOSE UP

Bombay's Lunchmen

If you stand at Chhatrapati Shivaji Terminus (Victoria Terminus) or at south Mumbai's second station, Churchgate, close to the start of Marine Drive, either before or after lunch, you are sure to notice an army of simply clothed men hurriedly shuffling flotillas of tin lunchboxes (known as *dabbas*, or sometimes *tiffin* carriers). Groups of lunchboxes exchange hands, are sorted, and then furiously loaded onto trains. These folks are some of Mumbai's 5,000 famous *dabbawallahs* (lunchbox men), who run one of the city's most efficient businesses. Simple coding procedures, lots of haste, and loads of hard work ensures every day that a hot lunch prepared mid-morning by a housewife in north Mumbai reaches the desk of her husband in his office in south Mumbai (or vice versa) still warm. The fee for this service is about Rs. 400 or so per month. The ingenuity of this cottage industry, which delivers some 200,000 lunches a day, has brought about visits from systems managers from across the world keen to understand such a simple but highly competent delivery system.

WHAT TO SEE

Chhatrapati Shivaji Terminus. Built by the British in 1888, this is one of Mumbai's—and probably the world's—busiest train stations, overflowing at rush hour with enormous, surging, scurrying crowds who use the suburban lines that also originate here (Mumbai's suburban trains carry eight million people a day). Still commonly called Victoria Terminus or just V.T., and bearing a hefty statue of Queen Victoria on its imposing dome, the haughty structure combines Indian and Victorian–Gothic architecture for an Eastern version of London's St. Pancras station. Why visit? To spend a few minutes admiring this enormous, incredible building, which is even more arresting lit up at night. If you are brave, walk around the corner to the modern suburban extension of the station around rush hour—9 AM or 5:30 PM—and experience Mumbai's maddening crowds. Even better, take a ride on a local train; many say you have not experienced Mumbai unless you have ridden one. ⊠*D. Naoroji Rd.*

3 **Chor Bazaar** *(Thieves' Bazaar)*. This narrow thoroughfare, smack in the heart of vintage Muslim Mumbai, is lined with 10 to 15 stores crammed with antiques and general bric-a-brac: clocks, old phonographs, brassware, glassware, and statues; some of it quite cheap. Over the years the value and breadth of much of this stock has dwindled, but there's still a chance that you'll find an unusual, memorable piece. Haggle. In the same lane a number of shops are engaged in the profitable business of constructing new furniture that looks old; many will openly tell you as much. Some shops do stock genuine antique furniture from old Parsi homes. Around the corner stolen cell phones and car stereo systems are being hawked. Getting here will take you on a tour of an interesting and very staunchly Muslim neighborhood, where life has a completely different flavor from elsewhere in the city. One street away is an interesting mosque belonging to the Bohri Muslims.

CLOSE UP

The Deccan Odyssey

Following the success of Rajasthan's luxury Palace on Wheels train, India introduced a Maharashtra counterpart, the Deccan Odyssey. Traveling first-class on Indian trains in the heyday of the British Raj was a comfortable, lavish experience, with chefs and bearers (waiters/attendants) taking care of your every need in royal surroundings as your train chugged through breathtaking countryside. This feeling is replicated aboard this train. Over seven nights and eight days you travel down the Maharashtra coast to Goa and then swing upwards to its cultural bastion Pune and then head to Ajanta and Ellora before returning to Mumbai. Such an excursion will set you back $285 per night in triple sharing accommodation, $350 in double-sharing accommodation and $485 for single occupancy rail cabins. The train has several restaurants, lounges, and even a gym. For more information visit 🌐 www.deccanodyssey.com and 🌐 www.irctc.co.in/deccanodyssey.html.

✉Mutton St., off Sardar Vallabhbhai Patel Rd., off Mohammed Ali Rd., Mandvi ⏲Sat.–Thurs. 11–7.

4 **Flora Fountain.** Standing tall in the middle of a major five-way intersection, this fountain marks the heart of Mumbai's Fort district. The ornately sculpted stone fountain was created as a memorial to one of the city's early governors, Sir Bartle Frere, who was responsible for urban planning in the 1860s. The square in which it stands is called Hutatma Chowk (Martyr's Square) in honor of those who died in the violence surrounding the establishment of Maharashtra in the 1960s (the Bombay Presidency was split into the states of Maharashtra and Gujarat). It's a hot spot for rallies, political and otherwise. Wander from Flora Fountain into the tiny lanes nearby to sample the business district or hit the roadside booksellers. *✉M. G. Rd., at Veer Nariman Rd., Fort.*

7

NEED A BREAK?

Status (*✉Regent's Chamber, Nariman Point ☎22/2287–2281*) is a convenient spot to have a long crispy dosa bathed in butter, crackling perfect. Weight-watchers can opt for an oil-free version. Equally good are the idlis and *rava* (semolina) dosas. Alternatively, you can try the various *pulaus* (rice dishes) and quick lunches on the menu.

8 ★ **Gateway of India.** Mumbai's signature landmark, this elegant 26-meter (85-foot) stone archway was hastily erected as a symbol of welcome to Queen Mary and King George V of England when they paid a visit to India in 1911. In the years following, artisans added decorative carvings and lovely *jharoka*-work (window carvings), finishing in 1923. Less than 25 years later, the last British troops departed India through the same ceremonial arch. The monument serves as a launching point for boats going to Elephanta Island; this is also where the *Queen Elizabeth 2* and other luxury liners dock on their cruises. The majestic Taj Mahal hotel, built before the Gateway of India, in 1903, now stands just behind it. Have tea at the Sea Lounge in the Taj afterwards and then walk from here towards the Prince of Wales museum and Jehangir

Art Gallery to get a flavour of classic old Bombay. ✉ *Peninsula at end of C. Shivaji Maharaj Marg, Apollo Bunder.*

NEED A BREAK?

For decades Bombayites have come to seedy Kalash Parbat Hindu Hotel (✉ *Sheela Mahal, 1 Pasta La., off Colaba Causeway, Colaba* ☎ *22/2287-4823 or 22/2284-1972* ⏲ *Daily 11-11*)—not actually a hotel—to indulge their craving for Indian-style vegetarian junk food, such as *chana bhatura* (giant *puris*, or puffed bread, served with spicy chickpea curry), *samosas* (stuffed vegetable turnovers), *sev puri* (deep-fried crackers layered with potato and chutney), *ragda pattice* (spicy potato cakes), *pani puri* (fried lentil-and-potato stuffed puffs), and other intricate snack food and kulfi (Indian-style ice cream). The place could be a tad cleaner, but the piping hot, tasty food makes it worth it. But go slow, the uninitiated may find the oily food difficult to digest.

5 **Jehangir Art Gallery.** Mumbai's chief contemporary-art gallery hosts changing exhibits of well-known Indian artists. Some of the work is lovely, and all of it is interesting for its cultural perspective. There's usually plenty of art outside as well—outside monsoon season the plaza in front of the building is full of artists selling their works and their talents for commission assignments. ✉ *M. G. Rd., Kala Ghoda, Fort* ☎ *22/2284-3989* 🎫 *Free* ⏲ *Daily 11-7.*

NEED A BREAK?

Cafe Samovar (✉ *M. G. Rd., Kala Ghoda, Fort* ☎ *22/2284-8000* ⏲ *Mon.-Sat. 10-7*), next to a bit of courtyard greenery in the Jehangir Art Gallery, is a popular, arty place for a fresh lime soda or a mutton samosa. Their meat-stuffed *parathas* (griddle-fried whole-wheat pancakes) and chicken rolls are also tasty.

1 ★ **Mahatma Jyotiba Phule Market.** Also known by its former name, Crawford Market, this building was designed in the 1860s by John Lockwood Kipling, father of Rudyard—who was born in this very neighborhood. Check out the stone relief depicting workers on the outside; the market's stone flooring supposedly came from Caithness, Scotland. Come here early one morning for a colorful walk through Mumbai's fresh-produce emporium, and if it's late spring or early summer, treat yourself to a delicious Alphonso mango, a food fit for the gods. Everything from cookies and party streamers to white mice and cane baskets are sold in other sections of the market—the meat section can be a bit hair-raising. Across the street from the market's main entrance on the west, spread across a trio of lanes, is the popular bazaar area Lohar Chawl, where the selection ranges from plastic flowers to refrigerators. Farther up the middle lane, Sheikh Memon Street, is the chaotic **Mangaldas Market** (closed Sunday), a covered, wholesale cloth market with a tremendous variety of fabrics at hundreds of indoor stalls. ✉ *D. Naoroji Rd., at L. Tilak Rd., Crawford Market* ⏲ *Mon.-Sat. 11:30-8.*

CLOSE UP

Dawn at the Docks in Colaba

Mumbai's budget-tourist district is often packed with vacationing Arabs in the rainy season and Western backpackers in the winter. Cheap boardinghouses, handicraft stalls, and eating places stand cheek-by-jowl on the southern tip of Mumbai's peninsula.

One of Colaba's most interesting sights is its fishing dock, built back in 1875. Extraordinarily smelly, mucky, and noisy, **Sassoon Dock,** on Shahid Bhagat Singh Marg, near the Colaba Bus Station, must be seen at dawn, when most of Mumbai's seafood catch is unloaded. Piles of pink prawns are sorted, and grisly looking fish are topped and tailed. The odor is severe, but you won't see this kind of chaos and color anywhere else. Out toward the ocean, the famously stinky Bombay duck, actually a fish unique to this coastline, dries on rack after rack in the sun.

Walk north for about 10 minutes toward Navy Nagar (the naval cantonment area) on Shahid Bhagat Singh Marg. Just beyond Colaba Post Office is the old **Afghan Memorial Church of St. John the Baptist**. Rather out of place in the heart of Colaba, this somewhat imposing structure honors British soldiers lost in the Afghan wars of the late 19th century. The plaques inside say things like, In the memory of Captain Conville Warneford of the Bombay Political Dept and the Gurkha Rifles who was born 13th October 1871 and was treacherously murdered by an Arab at Amrija in the Aden hinterland... If the church doors are closed look for the caretaker, who lives at the side of the church, in the church enclosure, and ask him to show you the church; give him a small something for his trouble.

From the church, retrace your steps on Shahid Bhagat Singh as far as the fork outside Colaba Post Office; on foot, take Wodehouse Road up to Panday Road, then turn left there. You'll see Capt. Prakash Petha Marg—take another left there, walk for five minutes (past the Taj President hotel), and just beyond the Colaba Woods (park) on your right on Cuffe Parade is a **dhobi ghat,** behind a facade of huts. (If you get lost, ask a local for help.) Another fascinating open-air sight, the *ghat* consists of a square half-kilometer of cement stalls where *dhobis,* or washermen, pound their garments to what seems like pulp to get them threadbare-clean. Rows of racks flutter with drying laundry, and in little huts nearby the incorrigibly dirty stuff is boiled with caustic soda.

NEED A BREAK?

Rajdhani (✉ *Sheikh Memon St., Lohar Chawl, near Crawford Market, Fort* ☎ *22/2342-6919* ⏲ *Mon.-Sat., noon-4 and 7-10:30; Sun. noon-3:15)* serves up hot Gujarati and Rajasthani *thalis* (combination platters; Rs. 169; Rs. 225 on Sun.) in spartan, clean surroundings. It's just a tiny bit north of Crawford Market. Eat sparingly: the restaurant uses a lot of ghee (clarified butter) in its dishes, which are also slightly (and authentically) sweet.

❼ **National Gallery of Modern Art.** This imposing, classical-looking circular building has interiors that bring to mind a shrunk-down version of New York's Guggenheim Museum. Built in 1911 by Gateway architect George Wittet, it was once the Sir Cowasji Jehangir Public Hall. The venue for the concerts of the violinist Yehudi Menuhin and the rallies

CLOSE UP

Indian Jews & Their Synagogues

Jews were once a prominent stream in Mumbai's population. There might have been three strains of Indian Jews—Maharashtrian (Bene Israel) Jews, Cochini Jews, and Baghdadi Jews. The Bene Israel Jews, considered by some to be the Lost Tribe of Israel, supposedly arrived (shipwrecked) in India in the early centuries of the Common Era (some say as far back as 500 BC), and settled along the Konkan coast south of Mumbai. The Cochini Jews, who were spice traders, arrived in approximately AD 1,000 and settled in Kerala, in the town of Cochin on the Malabar Coast; less than 20 Jews remain there. Jewish immigration began in earnest in India, however, in the 1800s. By the 1900s there may have been up to 50,000 Jews in India. These days there are about 5,000 left—most migrated to Israel in the 1950s. Baghdadi Jews, from Iraq and Syria, settled mainly in Mumbai and Kolkata; there's still a small but active population of Iraqi Jews in Mumbai.

Left behind by historic Jewish communities in Mumbai is an assortment of synagogues (closed daily from 1 to 4).

The old Baghdadi synagogue at the southern edge of Fort is the attractive and ornate, sky-blue **Keneseth Eliyahoo Synagogue** (✉ *V.B. Gandhi Rd., Kala Ghoda, Fort* ☎ *22/2283–1502*), across from Jehangir Art Gallery and behind Rhythm House. Built in 1884, it has compelling stained-glass windows and intricately constructed second-floor balconies. You can visit daily between 10 and 6:30, and are welcome for Sabbath prayers between 6:30 and 7:30 on Friday.

North of Crawford Market via P. D'Mello Road, past Carnac Bunder and right next to the Masjid train station) is the hard-to-find **Shaare Rahamim** (*Gate of Mercy* ✉ *254 Samuel St., Mandvi*), built in 1796. This sleepy, mildly dilapidated synagogue is still in use, and you're free to peek inside.

At Jacob Circle, a 20-minute taxi ride north of Shaare Rahamim, is **Tiphaereth Israel Synagogue** (✉ *Khare Rd., past Chinchpokli station, a few steps from Shirin Talkies, Mahalaxmi* ☎ *22/2305–3713*) home of the Bene Israel Jews—a still-thriving but tiny Maharashtrian Jewish community. Ask for the Jew *mandir* (temple). This small, shiny synagogue, tucked away on a side lane, is quite charming; unlike Shaare Rahamin, it seems well loved and well maintained. It is best to call before going: the synagogue is mostly open in the morning or evening.

The caretaker of Tiphaereth Israel Synagogue can also guide you a few streets away to the **Magen Hassidim Synagogue** (✉ *Morland Rd.–Maulana Azad Rd., near Fancy Market and Jula Maidan, Madanpura, Byculla* ☎ *22/2301–2685*). This Bene Israel shrine is in the Muslim area of Madanpura. Although the communities of Baghdadi and Cochini Jews have dwindled to just a few thousand, the Bene Israel community continues to modestly prosper. The congregation and caretakers at this well-attended shrine (with about 750 members) can lend insight into the future of this community: Magen Hassidim is the face of India's modern Jews, the ones who generally don't plan to migrate to Israel and who are now part of the nation's mainstream.

of Mahatma Gandhi, the hall still has the accoustics to match. Modern Indian art is displayed in an uncrowded, easy manner on four floors. It's not as spectacular as the Prince of Wales Museum across the street, but it's quiet, and worth a visit, especially if you're an art lover. On the top floor is Atul Dodiya's interesting interpretation of Bill and Chelsea Clinton's visit to India, hung side by side with portrait of Vladmir Putin's own visit. ✉*M. G. Rd., near Regal Cinema, Fort* ☎*22/2285–2457 or 22/2288–1790* 🎫*Rs. 150* ⏲*Tues.–Sun. 11–6.*

6 **Prince of Wales Museum.** Topped with Moorish domes, Mumbai's finest Victorian building and principal museum was completed in 1911 and named for King George V, who laid the cornerstone in 1905. It's divided into three sections: art, archaeology, and natural history. Unofortunately, its 30,000 artifacts, most of which are extremely interesting, are shown in a slightly dusty environment, with often poor lighting. The picture gallery contains scores of Mogul and Rajput miniature paintings, works by European and contemporary Indian artists, and copies of magnificent cave temple paintings from Ajanta. **■ TIP→ The museum was some time back renamed the Chhatrapati Shivaji Maharaj Vastu Sangrahalaya, but don't ask for directions to this—no one would have ever heard of it.** ✉*M. G. Rd., Fort* ☎*22/2284–4519 or 22/2284–4484* 🎫*Rs. 300* ⏲*Tues.–Sun. 10:15–5:45.*

NEED A BREAK?

Barista (✉*next to Regal Cinema, Colaba* ☎*22/663-6835 or 22/3201-4789* ⏲*Daily 9–1* AM**). This chic, casual espresso bar populated by youngsters and yuppies alike is part of a popular chain. You get a choice of 10 kinds of coffee, as well as sandwiches, pasta, croissants, calazones, wraps, and some good desserts.**

2 **Zaveri and Dagina Bazaars.** Zaveri and Dagina bazaars, a little beyond Fort in the neighborhood of Kalbadevi, are Bombay's crowded, 100-year-old jewelry markets, where the shops are filled with fabulous gold and silver in every conceivable design. At the Bhuleshwar end of Zaveri Bazaar is the six-century-old **Mumbadevi Temple** (☎*22/224–24974*), a noisy, busy structure that houses the mouthless but powerful patron goddess who is the city's namesake. *Aarti*, evening prayers, take place at 6:30. In front of the temple is the *khara kuan*, or saltwater well, an age-old water station funded by the jewelry bazaar from which free water is doled out to the thirsty from giant copper drums. One of the lanes leading off Zaveri Bazaar is called Khao Galli (literally "Eat Lane"): its endless food stalls feed most of the bazaar workers daily. ✉*Sheikh Memon St., a few blocks northwest of Crawford Market, a 10-min walk, Kalbadevi* ⏲*Mon.–Sat. 11–7.*

MALABAR HILL & ENVIRONS

Several of the attractions in this upscale residential area have stunning views of the city across Back Bay.

A GOOD TOUR

After checking the tides, take a taxi to the **Haji Ali Shrine** ❾, passing **Chowpatty Beach & Marine Drive** en route. At Haji Ali, have your taxi wait for you while you walk out on the jetty; then drive to **Kamala Nehru Park,** take some air, enjoy the views, and walk to the **Jain Temple** ❿. From here you can either walk or take a taxi along Walkeshwar Road to the **Banganga** ⓫ area. Finally, have your taxi take you to **Babulnath Temple** ⓬ and Gandhi's former home, **Mani Bhavan** ⓭. If you're interested in South Indian culture and have some extra time, drive out to **Matunga.**

TIMING This tour takes about two hours. The journey by taxi from Mani Bhavan to suburb of Matunga will take you half an hour—be sure to avoid rush hour. Spend half an hour seeing Matunga, or longer if you pop in for a dosa break at any of the restaurants we have suggested in Matunga.

WHAT TO SEE

⓬ **Babulnath Temple.** To get the flavor of a large, traditional Indian temple that's nevertheless jammed in the heart of a busy city, a visit to the Babulnath Temple is a must. Climbing the few hundred steps to reach the temple, perched on a hillside, will reward you with a panorama of south Mumbai. The first Babulnath Temple was apparently built by Raja Bhimdev in the 13th century and named after the *babul* trees that forested this area. The architecture of this imposing shrine, one of Mumbai's most important, is not remarkable, but it's interesting to watch the melée of worshippers coming, going, and milling about. Outside are rows of flower sellers hawking a temple-visitation kit—coconut plus flowers plus rock sugar—and a cluster of vendors concocting sweets in *karhais* (large woks) in the open air. Temple authorities are sometimes prickly about allowing foreigners into its innermost areas, but it's worth a try; more often than not they do not object. For Rs. 2 you can avoid the climb and take the elevator. ✉ *Babulnath Rd.*

⓫ ★ **Banganga.** This serene, under-visited temple complex in the Malabar Hill area is considered one of the city's holiest sites. It's also the oldest surviving structure in Mumbai. The small, sometimes dilapidated temples are built around a holy pool of water and surrounded by the ever-encroaching houses of Mumbai's newer residents. Cows and people mingle freely here, as do bathers who come to sample the "healing powers" of the water, and life around here harks back to earlier, more traditional times. A special musical festival takes place on its banks in winter. ✉ *At the end of Walkeshwar Rd., take the lane just beyond Ghanshyamdas Sitaram Poddar Chowk, Walkeshwar* 🎟 *Free.*

Fodor's Choice ★ **Chowpatty Beach & Marine Drive.** It's not much of a beach in the resort sense, but Chowpatty and the rest of long, spectacular, perfectly curved Marine Drive capture at once the mammoth, cheeky, beautiful seaside

CLOSE UP

Bombay Ice Cream

Give the predictable Kwality Walls and Baskin Robbins a miss and sample some traditional ice cream, made daily with fresh fruit. Delicious flavors on offer include include almond, coconut, and fig throughout the year, and the more seasonal custard apple (creamy and sweet), orange, *chikoo* (a bit like a pear), mango, strawberry, and mulberry.

Soam Sadguru Sadan (✉ *Ground fl., opposite Babulnath Mandir, Chowpatty* ☎ *22/2369–8080*).

Bachelorr (✉ *Opposite Thacker's restaurant, on Chowpatty Beach off Marine Drive* ☎ *22/2368–8107 or 22/2368–1408*).

Natural has outlets all over Bombay, including branches at Phoenix Mills, Marine Drive, and Juhu.

Swati Snacks (✉ *Opposite Bhatia Hopsital, near Ganga Jamuna Cinema, Tardeo* ☎ *022/5680-8405*). Excellent Gujarati snacks and minimeals are available, too.

beast that is Mumbai. Chowpatty is a taste of the bazaar and *mela* (festival) rolled into one. A hundred species of salesmen throng the beach in the evening, especially Sunday, selling everything from glow-in-the-dark yo-yos and animal-shaped balloons to rat poison. Men stand by with bathroom scales, offering complacent strollers a chance to check their heft. Hand-operated Ferris wheels and carousels are packed with children. A few stalls nearby distribute Mumbai's famously satisfying fast food—crunchy *bhel puris* (puffed-rice snacks), ragda pattices (spicy potato cakes), and *paav bhaji* (fried vegetable mash eaten with bread). From the beach, walk southeast down Marine Drive toward Nariman Point and you'll bump into flotillas of evening exercisers, cooing couples wandering past the waves in a daze, and dogs and kids being walked by their respective nannies. ✉ *Chowpatty, 400034.*

NEED A BREAK?

Cream Centre (✉ *Fulchand Niwas, 25B Chowpatty Seaface, opposite Chowpatty Beach, Marine Dr., Chowpatty* ☎ *22/2367–9222 or 22/2367–9333* ⏲ *Daily noon–midnight*), an old and very popular vegetarian eatery, is the best address in the city for delicious chana bhatura. Piping hot, football-size puris made from white flour and yeast are served up with a spicy chickpea concoction and raw onions and lemons. As good are the stuffed parathas, falafal, *lassis* (yogurt-based drinks), and hummus.

9 **Haji Ali Shrine.** Set far out on a thin, rocky jetty in the Arabian Sea, this striking, dilapidated white shrine was built in honor of the Muslim saint Haji Ali, who drowned here some 500 years ago on a pilgrimage to Mecca. When a coffin containing his mortal remains floated to rest on a rocky bed in the sea, devotees constructed the tomb and mosque to mark the spot. The shrine is reached by a long walkway just above the water. At high tide, the walkway is submerged, making the shrine unreachable. Walking there when the sea has completely receded, is not too romantic, because the exposed rocks smell of garbage. Choose a time in between. The walkway is lined with destitute families and beg-

gars ravaged by leprosy, some writhing, chanting, and (calling on the Muslim tradition of giving alms) beseeching you as you make your way down—a deeply discomfiting experience, but one that is unfortunately quintessentially Mumbai. Inside, the shrine is full of colored-mirror mosaics and crowded with worshippers praying over the casket, which is covered with wilted flower garlands. Men and women must enter through separate doorways. On many evenings a busker plays *quawalis* (a style of Muslim music) after the sunset prayers. There's no admission, but you may consider giving between Rs. 20 and Rs. 50 to the mosque charity box. The shrine closes at 10 PM. ✉ *Off Lala Lajpatrai Marg, near Mahalaxmi Race Course and Breach Candy.*

10 **Jain Temple.** What may be the most impressive temple in Mumbai belongs to the prosperous, strictly vegetarian Jains, the largely Gujarati followers of Lord Mahavira. The colorful interior is filled with marble but also understated and peaceful—check out the intricate work on the walls and ceilings. Worship at this shrine takes a somewhat different form than the *hungama,* or chaos, at Hindu temples. It's more introspective and humble in aspect—reflective of the Jain faith. At around 8 AM daily, freshly bathed Jain devotees in swaths of unstitched off-white cloth walk here barefoot from their nearby homes to pay homage to the splendid idol of Adinath, an important Jain prophet. (Jains show respect by arriving clean and without shoes—originally Jains used to wear only a silk cloth, the highest quality and hence most respectful material, but plenty now also wear cotton, and many others simply make do with ordinary clothes.) ✉ *B. G. Kher Marg, Teen Batti, near Walkeshwar, Malabar Hill.*

Kamala Nehru Park. Children love popping out of the "Old Woman Who Lived in a Shoe" structure here, at this small park on the eastern side of the top of Malabar Hill. It's primarily a children's playground, but also has gorgeous views of the city below that are worth checking out if you happen to be in the area. From the special viewpoint clearing, you can see all of Marine Drive and the Mumbai skyline, from Chowpatty Beach to Colaba Point—try to come up after dark to see why Marine Drive, sparkling with lights, is known as the Queen's Necklace. Just across the road, another park, the **Hanging Gardens,** (also known as the Pherozeshah Mehta Gardens) has pleasant views too, and a topiary garden. A few minutes north of here, heading down the hill, are the **Towers of Silence,** where Mumbai's Parsis—followers of the Zoroastrian faith—dispose of their dead. Pallbearers carry the corpse to the top of one of the towering cylindrical bastions, where it is left to be devoured by vultures and crows (a roughly two-hour process) and decomposed by the elements. None of this is visible to would-be onlookers, even relatives, and high walls prevent any furtive peeping. ✉ *B. G. Kher Marg, Malabar Hill* ⏲ *Daily* 6 AM–*9* PM.

13 ★ **Mani Bhavan.** This charming, old-fashioned three-story Gujarati house, painted brown and cream and in a quiet, tree-shaded Parsi neighborhood on Malabar Hill, was the home of Mahatma Gandhi from 1917 to 1934. Now overseen and lovingly maintained by the Gandhi Institute, it houses a library and an interesting and attractively presented

CLOSE UP

The Great Irani Café

Mumbai has a special breed of teahouse that's on the way out. Called "Irani joints" in local parlance, these corner shops were begun by the first waves of Zoroastrians, called the Iranis, who migrated to India in the 10th century from Persia to escape religious persecution. (Those who were part of later waves are referred to as Parsis.) In following centuries, thousands and thousands more Zoroastrians arrived in India. A community of about 70,000 remain today, a majority living in and around Mumbai.

Irani cafés probably arose out of need of a gathering place for Iranis to gather and exchange news. Simply furnished with solid wood chairs and cloaked in the appearance of yesteryear, they remain places where customers can tarry over endless cups of sweet tea for a couple rupees. Visiting these seedy, century-old cafés is a chance to glimpse a culture that has all but vanished. The clientele is usually very ordinary Bombaywallahs, more often than not old-timers who have been having the same chai and buns for the last 40 years in the same spot. Equally eccentric is the menu, an odd selection of chai, "cutting chai" (a half-cup of tea), *bun-maska* (a bun and butter), and typical Parsi cutlets, patties, rolls, fruitcakes, and confectionery. Amid the ancient mirrors, upright chairs, marble tables, elaborate balconies, and portraits of the Prophet Zarathustra is sometimes a sign acquainting you with the dos and don'ts of the particular establishment. Beer is sometimes served. But credit cards? Goodness, no. Early or mid-morning is a good time to visit.

As McDonald's and coffee-chain culture overtakes Bombay, Iranis cafés are dying. Overnight they are either being converted to fast-food joints or else are enclosed, air-conditioned, marbleized, and made more upmarket, with a little bit of Chinese food or spaghetti dropped onto their menus. Go have a peek at an authentic Irani café now. They may not be around forever.

Jimmy Boy (✉ *Vikas Building, 11 Bank St., near Horniman Circle, Fort* ☎ *22/266–2503 or 22/270–0880*) has been souped-up to house an asli Parsi cuisine eatery, but care has been taken to keep the Irani charm intact. Sample the Parsi staples here: mutton or chicken *dhansak* (Parsi style curry) and *patra ni machli* (fish steamed in green chutney).

Kyanis (✉ *Near Metro Cinema, Dhobi Talao*) is a great place to have chai and special *khari* (salty) biscuits. Their confectionary is popular. The Irani café ambiance is completely intact.

Yazdani (✉ *11/11-A, Cawasji Patel St., near Mahesh Lunch Home, Fort* ☎ *22/2287–0739*) is a good place to get "your daily bread," as their sign says. The little bakery café serves the freshest pav, *mava* cake (Parsi style pound cake), and mutton patties.

Café Military (✉ *Ali Chambers, Medouus, Street Fountain, Flora Fountain, behind Fountain Restaurant* ☎ *22/265–4181 or 22/265–7164*) is well suited for beer, chicken biryani, and a break.

Britannia and Co. (✉ *Ballard Estate* ☎ *22/2261–5264*) is legendary for this mutton, chicken, or vegetarian berry pulau. Or mutton dhansak, Sali-boti, or patra ni machli. Highly recommended.

small museum on Gandhi's life and work. Gandhi's simple belongings are displayed in his room, including his original copies of the Bible, the Koran, and the Bhagavad Gita (a famous discourse within the ancient Indian epic, the *Mahabharata*); other displays include spectacular colorful miniature dioramas of his life, photographs, and some important and moving letters from the fight for Indian independence. Don't miss the very humble and polite letter to Adolf Hitler asking him to not go to war. ✉ *19 Laburnam Rd., near Nana Chowk, Gamdevi, Malabar Hill* ☎ *22/2380–5864* *Rs. 10* *Daily 10–5:30.*

AT THE DHOBI GHATS

Dhobi ghats are where washermen (dhobis) pound clothes clean day and night in enormous open-air laundries. Mumbai actually has several, but the Cuffe Parade ghat is the most conveniently located for tourists. If you're feeling more adventurous, a visit to Mumbai's main Dhobi Ghat, near Mahalakshmi Station, a kilometer beyond the racecourse, may make for better photo ops. Here about 200 washermen are at work in an area covering 7 acres—it can best be viewed from the railway bridge leading into Mahalakshmi Railway Station.

Matunga. About 30 minutes west of Mumbai's business district, this suburb near King's Circle is home to a sizable chunk of the city's South Indian population. It's a little bit of Chennai up north—it even has a few South Indian temples complete with distinctive *gopurams,* or entrance towers (the **Asthika Samaj Temple** on Bhandarkar Road is a good example). Bazaars and shops sell banana leaves, Kanchipuram saris, and typical South Indian vegetables, flowers, 10-pound flower garlands, and pickles (bottled relishes); nearby eating houses serve clean, simple South Indian thali lunches on banana leaves or hot crispy dosas. **Shree Sunders** (☎ *22/2416–9216*) is known for having a large variety of excellent dosas, better and more authentic than anything you can find almost anywhere else in town. The legendary banana-leaf-lunch provider **A Ramanayak Udipi Shri Krishna Boarding** (☎ *22/2414–2422* *Tues.–Sun. lunch 10:30–3, dinner 7–10*) is near the train station. **Café Madras** (☎ *22/2401–4419*), one of the oldest South Indian restaurants in King's Circle, serves great dosas, vadas, *bise bele bath* (a spicy rice porridge), and fluffy idlis. Matunga's shops and restaurants are closed on Monday. ✉ *Telang Rd. near Matunga Central Railway Station.*

ELEPHANTA CAVES

★ *15 km from Gateway of India.*

Exactly who carved these 7th-century cave temples on Elephanta Island? No one knows. We do know, however, that the island was originally called Gharapuri; the Portuguese renamed it Elephanta after they found a large stone elephant near their landing place. (The figure collapsed in 1814 and was subsequently moved to the far-off Victoria Gardens and reassembled.) Shortly before these temples were created, Mumbai experienced the golden age of the late Guptas, under whom the talents of artists had relatively free range. By that time the Sanskrit language had been finely polished, and under the court's liberal patronage, Kalidasa and other writers had helped incite a revival of Hindu beliefs. It was Shivaism—the worship of Shiva—that inspired the building of these temples.

The outside of the main cave consists of a columned veranda 30 feet wide and 6 feet deep, which you approach on steps flanked by sculptured elephants. The entire temple, carved out of the basalt hillside, is 130 square feet. The principle sculptures are on the southern wall at the back. The central recess in the hall contains the most outstanding sculpture, the unusual Mahesamurti, the Great Lord Shiva—an 18-foot triple image. Its three faces represent three aspects of Shiva: the creator (on the right), the preserver (in the center), and the destroyer (on the left).

Other sculptures near the doorways and on side panels show Shiva's usefulness. Shiva brought the Ganges River down to Earth, the story says, letting it trickle through his matted hair. He is also depicted as Yogisvara, lord of Yogis, seated on a lotus, and as Nataraja, the many-armed cosmic dancer. The beauty of this stonework lies in the grace, balance, and sense of peace conveyed in spite of the subject's multiple actions.

In winter the Maharashtra Tourism Development Corporation (MTDC) organizes a top-notch dance festival in this memorable setting. The island itself is quiet and picturesque, with light-green foliage and monkeys scampering about. The MTDC leads an excellent daily tour and runs a tiny restaurant on the island for refreshments and beer. Elephanta Island is not a good location for a picnic lunch; avoid carrying food or snacks with you because the herds of street-smart monkeys will harass you. Motor launches, one hour each way, depart daily every half hour from 9 to 2:30 from the Gateway of India and from noon to 5 from Elephanta Island, unless the sea is very choppy. ⚠ **It's not advisable to visit Elephanta during monsoon season.** ✉ *Elephanta Island* 🎫 *Round-trip Rs. 100–Rs. 120 depending on type of seat or boat you choose; Rs. 250 tickets for entering the caves can be purchased at Mahesh Travels at the Gateway of India* ☎ *22/2282–0139.*

NEED A BREAK?

Down one of Colaba's cluttered back streets, near where ferries depart for the Elephanta Caves, little Basilico Bistro & Deli (✉ ***Sentinel House, Arthur Bunder Rd., next to Radio Club, Colaba*** ☎ ***22/6634–5670 or 22/6634–5671*****) offers fresh fruit drinks, lassis, desserts, sandwiches, soups, and pasta courses all day, and breakfasts from 7:30 to 11:30 AM. A glass cold case, stuffed with cakes, cheese, and cold meat, dominates this 11-table café. With its wood and glass and warm lighting, it's an inviting place to catch your breath.**

7

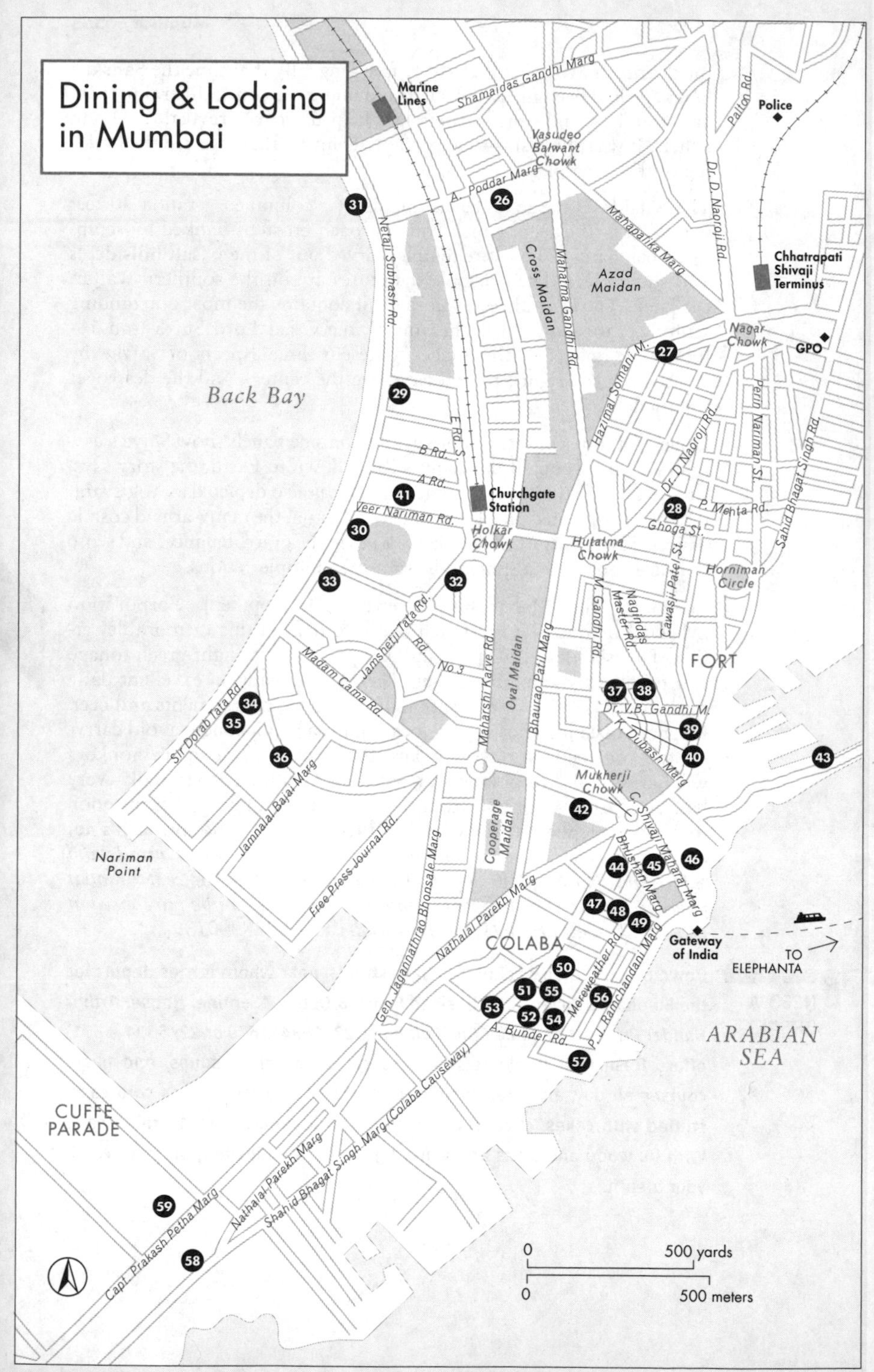

Dining & Lodging in Mumbai
Marine Lines
Shamaidas Gandhi Marg
Vasudeo Balwant Chowk
Police
Paltan Rd.
A. Poddar Marg
Dr. D. Naoroji Rd.
Mahapalika Marg
Netaji Subhash Rd.
Cross Maidan
Mahatma Gandhi Rd.
Azad Maidan
Chhatrapati Shivaji Terminus
Nagar Chowk
GPO
Hazimal Somani M.
Back Bay
Perin Nariman St.
Sahid Bhagat Singh Rd.
Dr. D. Naoroji Rd.
E. Rd.
S.
B Rd.
A Rd.
Churchgate Station
P. Mehta Rd.
Veer Nariman Rd.
Holkar Chowk
Hutatma Chowk
Ghoga St.
Horniman Circle
Jamshetji Tata Rd.
M. Gandhi Rd.
Nagindas Master Rd.
Cawasji Patel St.
Rd.
No.3
Madam Cama Rd.
Maharshi Karve Rd.
Oval Maidan
Bhaurao Patil Marg
FORT
Dr. V.B. Gandhi M.
K. Dubash Marg
Sir Dorab Tata Rd.
Jamnalal Bajaj Marg
Mukherji Chowk
C. Shivaji Maharaj Marg
Free Press Journal Rd.
Cooperage Maidan
Nariman Point
Gen. Jagannathrao Bhonsale Marg
Nathalal Parekh Marg
Bhushan Marg
Mereweather Rd.
P. J. Ramchandani Marg
COLABA
Gateway of India
TO ELEPHANTA
A. Bunder Rd.
ARABIAN SEA
CUFFE PARADE
Nathalal Parekh Marg
Shahid Bhagat Singh Marg (Colaba Causeway)
Capt. Prakash Petha Marg
0
500 yards
0
500 meters

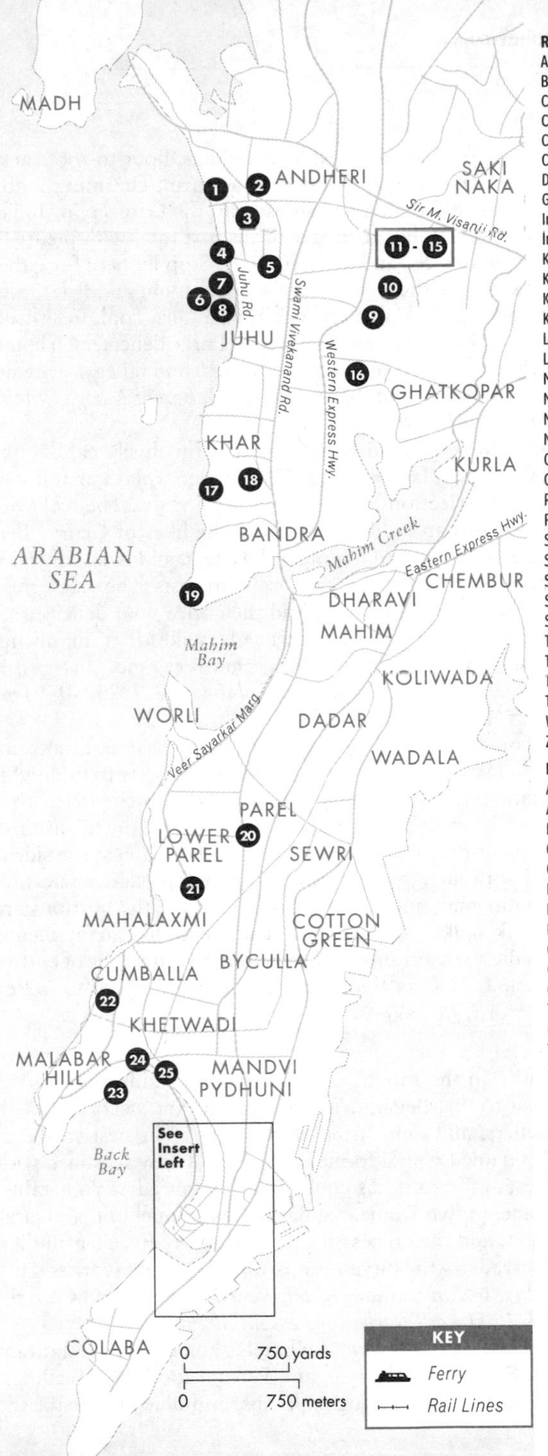

Restaurants ▼

All Stir Fry ... 45
Bombay Blue ... 39
Café Churchill ... 51
Café Mondegar ... 47
CG 83 ... 22
Chetana ... 40
Dakshin ... 12
Govinda's ... 1
Indigo ... 48
Indigo Deli ... 46
Kebabs and Kurries ... 20
Khyber ... 37
Kobe ... 23
Konkan Café ... 49
Leopold Cafe ... 50
Ling's Pavillion ... 44
Mahesh Lunch Home ... 28
Mainland China ... 2
Moshe's ... 58
Moti Mahal Delux ... 36
Oriental Blossom ... 33
Out of the Blue ... 17
Papa Pancho Da Dhaba ... 18
Royal China ... 27
Salt Water Grill ... 25
Sea Lounge ... 49
Soam ... 24
Society ... 41
Souk ... 49
Thai Pavilion ... 59
Theobroma ... 53
Trattoria ... 59
Trishna ... 38
Woodlands Garden Cafe ... 5
Zodiac Grill ... 49

Hotels ▼

Apollo ... 43
Astoria ... 31
Bawa International ... 9
Citizen ... 6
Cowie's ... 55
Eastern International Hotel ... 4
Fariyas ... 57
Four Seasons ... 21
Garden ... 54
Godwin ... 52
Gordon House ... 45
The Grand Central ... 20
Grand Hyatt ... 16
The Grand Maratha ... 12
Hilton Towers ... 34
Hyatt Regency ... 11
InterContinental ... 29
InterContinental The Grand Mumbai ... 15
JW Marriott ... 8
The Leela Kempinski ... 14
Marine Plaza ... 33
Ramada Plaza Palm Grove ... 7
Ramee Guestline ... 3
Ritz ... 32
Le Royal Meridien ... 13
Sea Green ... 30
Sea Palace Hotel ... 56
Taj Land's End ... 19
Taj Mahal Palace & Tower ... 49
Taj President ... 59
The Oberoi ... 35
The Orchid ... 10
West End ... 26
YWCA International Center ... 42

WHERE TO EAT

CAFÉS

$ ★ ✕**Indigo Delí.** Giant arched windows, high ceilings, floor-to-roof racks of wine, and an abundance of wood lend a warm, charming ambience to this two-year-old deli, a few steps from the Gateway of India. The food, like the welcoming environment, is first rate, with plenty of excellent vegetarian choices and daily specials. Stop by here for either a gourmet sandwich (try the Reuben or the mushroom and Brie), fish-and-chips, a burger, a salad, a pastry, pizza, or a long, cool, fresh-fruit drink. You also may like to sample their wine. Large delicatessen counters showcase cheese, cold meats, pastries, salads, and takeaway items. ⊠*C5 Pheroze Building, Chhatrapati Shivaji Maharshi Marg, Colaba* ☎*22/5655–1010* ▭*AE, MC, V.*

¢ ✕**Café Mondegar.** Next door to Regal Cinema, this lively café is one of South Mumbai's popular hangouts. The jukebox plays at full volume and has a wide selection of jazz and pop anthems. The walls are adorned with cartoons and glib quotes from the likes of George Bernard Shaw. The café is open 'til midnight, has beer, and is usually jam-packed and smoky with Mumbai preppies and tourists. The onion rings and french fries are good and greasy, and the coffee float delicious. A wide range of Continental and Chinese meals makes it to the menu, and breakfast (starting at 8, with waffles, pancakes, and sausages) is popular here, too. ⊠*Colaba Causeway, Colaba* ☎*22/2202–0591 or 22/2283–0586* ▭*AE, MC, V.*

¢ ★ ✕**Leopold Café.** Founded in 1871, this is one of the city's oldest Irani-run restaurants and a favorite tourist haunt, open from 8 AM to midnight. With an international, eclectic, sometimes outlandish clientele, it's a great place to people watch. The tables are well spaced, the furnishings simple, and the paintings and posters recall a French café; at the side is a fruit bar lined with mangos, oranges, and pineapples. The selection of tandoori, Continental, and Chinese food is broad, the portions are large, and the milk shakes are delicious. The menu, like many menus in Mumbai's smallest restaurants, has an astounding number of entries (319 in this case). ⊠*Colaba Causeway, Colaba* ☎*22/2287–3362 or 22/2202–0131* ▭*AE, MC, V.*

INTERNATIONAL

$$$$ ✕**Society.** If you're in the mood for Continental cuisine—or a good steak—pay a visit to this elegant Victorian restaurant, decorated with mirrors, chandeliers, and rich, striped furnishings. The best steak, "à la Fernandes," is named after a former maître d'. Richly seasoned with cinnamon, spices, and cream, it's cooked and flambéed at your table. The chicken Diane, prawn Diane, regular steaks, cannelloni, and lasagna are very good, and the crêpes Suzette delectable. Excellent Indian dishes are also served; try the biryani. A pianist plays old favorites daily except Wednesday. ⊠*Ambassador hotel, Veer Nariman Rd., Churchgate* ☎*22/2204–1131* ✍*Reservations essential* ▭*DC, MC, V.*

$$$$ ✕**Souk.** The top floor of the 19-floor Taj hotel is home to this restaurant serving Turkish, Egyptian, Lebanese, and Persian food. High ceilings, enormous pots, intricate giant hanging lamps, and blue light make the

restaurant mysterious and mystical. To add to its atmosphere, a Middle Eastern band croons mournful music while Bombay's lights twinkle at your feet. Like any good souk restaurant, the starters served with warm, fresh breads are delicious and filling. Go for the sampler platters, and make sure you have some hummus and an eggplant dish. For the main course try the *lahm bamia* (lamb stew), *d'jaj m'qualli* (stuffed chicken), and *tagine* vegetables (stew) with rice. Other good options include the kebabs and the *labneh bi zayt* (yogurt dumplings). Desserts are unusual: *bastilla* au lait (flaky pastry with almond cream) and baklavas spiked with honey and stuffed with dry fruit. ✉ *Taj Mahal Palace & Tower, Apollo Bunder* ☎ *22/6665–3366* ✍ *Reservations essential* ▭ *AE, DC, MC, V.*

$$$$ ✕ **Zodiac Grill.** This Continental restaurant in the legendary Taj Mahal hotel is one of the fanciest places to eat at in town. It's Western in style, with subdued lighting, handsome chandeliers, captains in black jackets, and waiters wearing white gloves. Specialties include Camembert *dariole* (soufflé) and a creamy Kahlua mousse for dessert. Entrées favor meat and seafood, such as steak, Cajun lobster, and grilled lobster. The Zodiac Grill offers a fixed meal for two for Rs. 5,500, with a glass of sparkling wine for each. ✉ *Taj Mahal Palace & Tower, Apollo Bunder* ☎ *22/6665–3366* ✍ *Reservations essential* ▭ *AE, DC, MC, V.*

$$$ ✕ **Salt Water Grill.** Mumbai has very few restaurants bang on the beach, but this is one of them. At what's one of the most romantic dining spots in the city, the decor runs to white twinkling lights, hammocks, white sand, palm trees, and the ocean. The food is equally stylish—try the grilled kingfish or pomfret, deep-fried Brie, and the pastas. You can dine on low wood tables on the sand or in white tented curtained alcoves slightly away from the water; there is adequate cover for rain. The selection of cocktails—lemongrass vodka, green-apple martinis, plum vodka, watermelon *caipiroskas* (a fruit flavored drink with a vodka and lemon base)—and wines is also a good draw. ✉ *H20 Water Sports Complex, Chowpatty* ☎ *22/2368–5459 or 22/2368–5485* ✍ *Reservations essential* ▭ *AE, MC, V.*

$$$ ✕ **Sea Lounge.** Innumerable marriages have been fixed and business deals struck over the years at the Taj Mahal hotel's best-looking restaurant. It's a very classy tea lounge—squishy sofas, simple glass tables, and upholstered chairs are scattered across a plush carpet, patterned in wavelike swirls; all in warm greens and blues. The backdrop is a technicolor view of the magnificent Gateway of India, the blue ocean, and a harbor full of bobbing sailboats. Make sure you take a window booth. The menu is not elaborate but the food is tasty. Dig into the selection of Bombay snacks. Don't miss the Viennoise coffee ice cream. The lounge opens at 7 AM and breakfast is a great idea. ✉ *Taj Mahal Palace & Tower, Apollo Bunder* ☎ *22/6665–3366* ▭ *AE, DC, MC, V.*

Fodor's Choice ★

$$ ✕ **Moshe's.** Owner and chef Moshe Shek, a Bombay Jew, worked in London and Israel before returning to India to open his own restaurant in 2004. Soon his a European-style café with dark-wood furniture and big glass windows become all the rage. The café offers some of the

7

best international food in Mumbai—pastas in creamy sauces, eggplant roulade, crusty cheese garlic bread (they bake their own breads and rolls), Israeli stuffed chicken, hearty soups, and the highly recommended char-grilled *rawas* (Indian salmon). A large delicatessen counter, overflowing with luscious cakes and cheese, occupies the back wall. There's seating outside on the patio, too. The restaurant also offers a selection of wines. ■**TIP→ Smaller branches of the restaurant have opened in the Kala Ghoda Fabindia in Fort and the Crossword bookstore at Kemps Corner.** ✉*7 Minoo Manor, Cuffe Parade, off Wodehouse Rd., Colaba* ☎*22/2216–1226* ✍*Reservations essential* ▭*AE, MC, V.*

$$ ✕ **Out of the Blue.** Mumbai's northern suburb of Bandra is an outpost that seems dedicated to dining and pubbing. This romantic and pretty hotel restaurant is one of Bandra's more popular and trendy hangouts, which is saying a lot. You can either sit outside in the simple, stylishly decorated courtyard to sample the live music, or lounge in the glassed-in, chic interior. What's hot? The fondues, the pastas, and the sizzlers (especially the one with smoked barbeque chicken) are delightful. Also try the Cajun fish, the barbecued prawns, chilli-lime prawns, and the stuffed mushrooms. Out of the Blue always has some side acts going in addition to the food, such as tarot readers, palmists, live music, magicians, pedicures, and art exhibitions. ✉*Hotel Pali Hill, 14 Union Park, Bandra* ☎*22/2600–3000 or 22/2600–3001* ▭*AE, DC, MC, V.*

Fodor's Choice ★

$ ✕ **Café Churchill.** Diners sitting at one of the six tables in this simple, no-frills place come for fresh, delicious pasta, pizza, and other Continental dishes; try the gnocchi and the steaks, too. Expect wholesome meals and first-rate desserts at this convenient spot. It opens at 10 for breakfast and stays open until late, and also provides any kind of take-out. It's also close to some of Colaba's popular budget hotels. ✉*103-B Colaba Causeway, opposite Cusrow Baug, Colaba* ☎*22/2284–4689* ▭*No credit cards.*

$ ✕ **Kobe.** Get delicious sizzlers, a Mumbai favorite, here. Burning hot metal platters piled high with fresh vegetables, fries, chicken or steak, and sauces arrive at your table wafting clouds of steam. You can ask the waiter to add your choice of topping, too—perhaps extra cheese or more mushrooms, pasta, or spice. Try the steak (or the garlic steak), *chicken shaslik* (masala chicken on a skewer), or vegetable *shaslik* with mushroom, cheese, and pasta. The place is simple—no frills and a bit dark and has been around and much loved for decades. No alcohol is served. Additional branches are at the Phoenix Mills mall and in Juhu. ✉*3 Sukh Sagar, Hughes Rd., Chowpatty* ☎*22/2363–2174* ✍*Reservations essential* ▭*AE, MC, V.*

$ ✕ **Theobroma.** The excellence of the brownies, pastries, chocolates, waffles, open-face beef, and marmalade sandwiches keeps this wee family-run café chock-full. Mainly a great address for exceptionally well-made desserts, the warm, cozy ambiance, with touches of wood accents, makes it an attractive place to come for breakfast (from 8:30 for eggs, banana-bread French toast, sandwiches), tea with cakes and snacks, or just for a break. It's open until midnight. ✉*Shop 24, Colaba Causeway, next to Cusrow Baug, Colaba* ☎*22/6529–5629 or 22/6529–2929* ▭*MC, V.*

CHINESE

$$$ ✕ **CG 83.** This restaurant is the third avatar of China Garden, which first began right at this spot. Like the original, this incarnation bustles with Mumbai's trendiest young VIPs and who's who. The spacious restaurant has maroon silk curtains, Chinese tapestries, a large Buddha, and a hushed, expensive look. It's easily the swishest Chinese eatery in town, with unusual Chinese artifacts decorating the room. The menu has a few pan-Asian dishes in addition to a wide selection of excellent Chinese food, some tailored to Indian tastes; including the *paneer* (cottage cheese) specialties and the numerous vegetarian choices. Hot favorites include prawns wrapped in bacon, crispy Peking chicken, crispy vegetable pancake, fried corn cream, sapo (cooked in banana leaves) chicken, Shantung prawns, gin chicken, and hakka fish. ✉*Om Chambers, 123 A.K. Marg, Kemps Corner* ☎*22/2363–0842* ▭*AE, MC, V.*

$$$ ★ ✕ **Royal China.** The menu is nearly 15 pages long at one of South Mumbai's more popular Chinese restaurants. But ordering a meal is actually rather simple. Be it braised wood-ear mushrooms with seasonal vegetables, dim sum, prawns in ginger chilli garlic, roasted pork, seafood dumplings, or vegetable noodles, all the food is lip-smackingly good. The place is plainly decorated but elegant nonetheless. Tall wooden screens of Chinese letters divide the main, dimly lit dining area into separate sections, and a few well-chosen Chinese items dot the room. ✉*Sterling, Hajarimal Somani Marg, behind Sterling Cinema, Fort* ☎*22/5635–5310 or 22/5635–5311* ▭*AE, DC, MC, V.*

$$ ✕ **Ling's Pavilion.** Baba Ling and his family have been providing Bombay film stars and yuppies alike with excellent Chinese food for two generations. Enter through the moon-shaped door and you'll find yourself on a bridge overlooking a gurgling, fish-filled stream. The tables are beyond; some tables are on a balcony. A testimony to Ling's popularity and authenticity is the number of Chinese tourists digging into their meals with gusto. Don't miss the barbecue platter, baby lobsters, mushroom pot rice, or steamed fish. The Chinese bread is soft and succulent—terrific with the ginger-garlic crab. ✉*19/21 Mahakavi Bhushan Marg, behind Regal Cinema, Colaba* ☎*22/2285–0023 or 22/2282–4533* ▭*AE, MC, V.*

$$ ✕ **Mainland China.** One of the best Chinese restaurants in the suburbs and close to Bollywood, this place attracts starry, as well as starry-eyed, customers. Try the selection of dumplings, the minced crab in salt and pepper, chicken-coriander soup, Shanghai chicken spring rolls. Large Chinese-style murals hang on the wall. ✉*Shalimar Morya Park, off New Link Rd., Andheri West* ☎*22/6678–0011* ✍*Reservations essential* ▭*AE, MC, V.*

$$ ✕ **Oriental Blossom.** Honey-glazed spare ribs, Chinese greens with black mushrooms, deep-fried corn curd, coconut pancakes, dim sum—the Chinese food at the Marine Plaza hotel's showcase restaurant is lightly spiced, a mixture of Cantonese and Szechuan, and very satisfying. The style is simple and chic—rich furniture, crisp white tablecloths, and subdued lighting—and the service unobtrusive. If you want seclusion, book a table in one of the semiprivate dining alcoves. ✉*Marine Plaza hotel, 29 Marine Dr.* ☎*22/2285–1212* ✍*Reservations essential* ▭*AE, DC, MC, V.*

CONTEMPORARY

$$$$ ✕ **Indigo.** This eatery and its laid-back lounge bar with an excellent selection of wines are a hit with foreigners and a haunt for Bombay's in-crowd: the narrow lane out front fills with a queue of cars at dinnertime. The small restaurant occupies an attractive, candlelit old mansion on a side street in Colaba; meals are also served on the terrace. A nouvelle Indian-Western fusion cuisine is served in simple, woodsy-but-elegant surroundings—much like dining in an old Goan home. Try the *rawas* (Indian salmon) pan-grilled, pepper tuna, filet mignon, lobster risotto, tandoori rosemary chicken, or the pumpkin ravioli—all pastas here are commendable. Save room for the tempting desserts. *⊠4 Mandalik Rd., near Cotton World, Colaba ☎22/6636–8980 or 22/6636–8981 ⚠Reservations essential ▭AE, MC, V.*

ITALIAN

$$$$ ✕ **Trattoria.** One of Mumbai's first Italian restaurants has always been famous for its crispy, light pizza, and it's easily one of the best 24-hour coffee shops here. Inside it's cheery: bright colors, comfy leather sofas and chairs, and warm lighting. A large mural of an ancient Roman scene stretches across one of the walls. The open-plan kitchen gives the place a casual feel. The pastas are delicious. Good menu choices include bruschetta, prawn cocktail, mushroom cocktail, primavera *al forno* (homemade vegetable pasta bake), canelloni, and penne *aglio eolio* (penne lightly tossed with olive oil). The tiramisu, chocolate mousse, signature cappuccino tart served with cashew ice cream, and *dolce tre latte* (sponge cake with cream) are all excellent. *⊠Taj President hotel, 90 Cuffe Parade, Colaba ☎22/6665–0808 ▭AE, DC, MC, V.*

MUGHLAI, PUNJABI & TANDOORI

$$$$ ✕ **Kebabs and Kurries.** The ITC Welcomgroup of hotels has always been praised for its food, and the Dakshin, Bukhara, and Dum Pukht "brand" restaurants in various hotels throughout India are favorites. In the chain's newest Mumbai hotel, which towers over central areas of the city, ITC serves dishes from all three restaurant menus, as well as a few more. In this airy and very large space, exotic Central Asian carpets and large mounted water pots decorate the walls. There's a view of the kitchen and of the chefs masterfully whipping up soft and flaky naans and rotis and grilling tender kebabs. The paneer tikka is exquisitely marinated and succulent, as are the *galouti* (literally, "melt-in-your-mouth") and *kakori* kebabs (from Kakori, near the kebab capital of Lucknow in north India). If you don't want to be forced to check into the hotel for a wildly expensive nap, take care to chomp in moderation or the heavy food will leave you comatose. *Grand Central Sheraton, ⊠287 Dr. B. Ambedkar Rd., Parel ☎22/2410–1010 ▭AE, DC, MC, V.*

$$$ Fodor's Choice ★ ✕ **Khyber.** Named for the Himalayan mountain pass between Afghanistan and northwestern India, Khyber and its three floor are done up in a modern versions of North-West Frontier style—white-marble floors, terra-cotta urns, carved stone pillars, low wooden rafters, and handsome fresco murals by Anjolie Ela Menon and M. F. Husain. The waiters, dressed in Pathan (North-West Frontier) garb, serve delicious and rich kebabs and naans. To see why this is one of Bombay's best restau-

rants, try the the pomfret green masala (fried pomfret fish stuffed with tangy green chutney), Khyber *raan* (leg of lamb marinated overnight, then roasted in a clay oven), egg biryani, black dal (lentils) or paneer *shaslik* marinated with spices and roasted). ✉*145 M. G. Rd., Fort* ☎*22/2267–3228* ✍*Reservations essential* ▭*AE, DC, MC, V.*

$$$ ✕**Moti Mahal Delux.** The standards of the legendary Moti Mahal of Delhi, known for the runaway popularity of its classic and plentiful Punjabi fare, have been reasonably well replicated in this branch, inside the upscale Nariman Point Inox cinema complex. The naans are hand tossed in front of you and lavishly topped with butter. The *seekh* (minced lamb) kebabs, *lasooni* (garlic) kebabs, and paneer tikkas are crisp and *khasta* (the right kind of soft). As for the chicken and mutton dishes, they're also well prepared, although they sometimes come with a little too masala; try the *murg bemisal* (tandoori chicken cooked in minced chicken and dal *ghost* (dal cooked with mutton). The Indian-boudoir decor—bead curtains, curtained alcoves, dark furniture—is a touch downbeat. Service is good. ✉*G102 Level 1, CR2 Mall, next to Inox, Nariman Point* ☎*22/3253–4134 or 22/6654–6454* ✍*Reservations essential* ▭*AE, DC, MC, V.*

$$ ✕**Bombay Blue.** Inside a large two-story complex behind Jehangir Art Gallery, Bombay Blue is brightly lit and cheerful, with a big glassy exterior, the complex looks like a swanky, upmarket version of a fast-food place. The menu is eclectic and tasty: choose between a meal of kebabs and naan, Chinese chicken noodles, very well executed chana bhatura, Thai curry and rice, pasta, nachos, sizzlers, or Lebanese food. The complex has two other restaurants: Copper Chimney serves standard but above average Mughlai/Punjabi food; Noodle Bar does great Chinese. If you're sensitive to noise, avoid weekends, when the place is invaded by loud families. ✉*K. Dubash Marg, Kala Ghoda* ☎*22/2202–2444 or 22/2202–2555* ▭*AE, DC, MC, V.*

$$ ✕**Papa Pancho Da Dhaba.** For some *asli* (authentic) and hearty Punjabi food, head out to this funky restaurant. Styled like a truckers' roadside *dhaba* (eatery) found along the highways of India, Papa Pancho has simple, clunky metal dishware and is decorated with bumper signs (for instance, OK HORN PLEASE) and lemon-and-green-chilli good-luck charms. The *dal makhani* (butter dal), *papdi chaat* (a cold snack), *baingan bharta* (roasted and spiced eggplant), mince parathas (stuffed meat whole-wheat pancakes), and the creamy lassi are delectable and could almost be homemade. Since the restaurant is in Bandra, a bit far from south or north Mumbai, it's a good idea to visit this place on a Sunday, when the commuter-free journey takes just half an hour. No alcohol is served. ✉*Shop 12, Gaspar Enclave, Dr. Ambedkar Rd., near Rupee Bank, Bandra* ☎*22/2651–8753 or 22/2651–8732* ▭*MC, V.*

NORTH INDIAN

$ ✕**Chetana.** Hand-blocked murals on the ceiling, traditional *toranas* (ornamental carvings above temple entrances) on the walls, and other Rajasthani decorations provide a cozy but simple setting for tasty vegetarian Rajasthani and Gujarati thalis. Chetana includes a variety of thalis to its repertoire—including low-cal Gujarati, mixed Gujarati and Rajasthani, and a traditional village version. Sample à la carte *dal bati* (lentils with wheat cakes), *kadhi* (curd curry), *dal dhokli* (a sweetish lentil-based pasta stew), *farsan* (snacks of the day), *theplas* (chickpea and fenugreek parathas), and mint *raita* (a spiced yogurt dish). If you're not enamored with Gujarati cuisine, there are also some standard Punjabi dishes. Service is excellent, and the owners' adjacent philosophy bookshop–craft store is worth a visit after your meal. Note that the restaurant is closed between 3 and 7. ✉ *34 K. Dubash Marg, Kala Ghoda, Fort* ☎ *22/2284–4968* ▭ *AE, MC, V.*

$ ✕ **Govinda's.** This Hare Krishna restaurant offers sumptuous 56-item vegetarian thalis for Rs. 230. Expect Lord Krishna's food—that is, Vedic meals, cooked without garlic and onions. The management in fact advertises a "transcendental dining experience," because the food served has already been offered to the gods, and *bhajans,* joyful devotional songs, liven up your meal. On weekends and Hindu holidays the restaurant often organizes food festivals. ✉ *ISKCON, Hare Krishna Mandir, Juhu Tara Rd., Juhu* ☎ *22/2620–0337 or 22/2620–6860* ▭ *MC, V.*

$ ✕ **Soam.** The authentic Gujarati food that's served all over Mumbai comes as a thalis (platter) and has a standard formula—a rice, a dal, several vegetables, hot rotis, *farsan* (snacks of the day), and a sweet. Soam is one of the first restaurants where one can sample, à la carte, a variety of unusual Gujarati food in pleasant surroundings. With typical Gujarati teatime snacks, breakfast items, and quick meals or desserts, it's a great place to start your adventure into this tasty, spicy, slightly sweet, and very filling, frequently vegetarian cuisine. Inside things are cheerful and simple, with yellow tones and wood, and a view of the ancient Babulnath temple across the street. Meals are served with traditional brass dinnerware. Try the farsan platter, *gatte ka sabzi* (a chickpea flour concoction) with *lachchedar* (flaky) paratha, *kachoris* (stuffed puris), *handvo* (spicy steamed snack), and homemade ice cream. ✉ *Sadguru Sadan, Ground Floor, across from Babulnath Mandir, Chowpatty* ☎ *22/2369–8080* ▭ *MC, V.*

PAN-ASIAN

$$ ✕ **All Stir Fry.** This popular Asian restaurant is minimalist and dark, with black-and-white benches and tables facing food stations in the back. At one island you choose the raw materials for an all-you-can eat meal—greens, cut vegetables, fish, prawns, beef, chicken—then, at a second station, a chef cooks it for you with the sauce of your choosing. Vegetarians take note: the restaurant offers meat-free soups and chefs use separate pans and utensils for veg dishes. You can also get à la carte items, Thai curries among them, and a small selection of desserts. The happening bar Polly Esthers upstairs is a good place to sample Mumbai nightlife. ✉ *Gordon House hotel, 5 Battery St., Apollo Bunder* ☎ *22/2287–1122* ▭ *AE, DC, MC, V.*

SEAFOOD

$$$$ ✕ **Konkan Café.** Seafood from the Konkan coast (which stretches from Maharashtra south through Goa to Mangalore, Karnataka) is extraordinarily popular in Mumbai, but for years it was only available in no-frills "lunch homes" in the business district. But here you can get

fish-curry rice-plate lunches in luxurious surroundings. Although crummy taverns and souped-up lunch homes may very well do it better, chef Ananda Solomon's food is tasty, and the coastal-home feel is appealing. Opt for the fried fish, *sukha* chicken (dry masala chicken), pepper chicken, red masala clams, *appams* (steamed dosas) steamed pomfret, coastal *maida* (white-flour) paratha, or the vegetarian thali. ✉ *Taj President hotel, 90 Cuffe Parade, Colaba* ☎ *22/6665–0808* ✍ *Reservations essential* ▭ *AE, DC, MC, V.*

$$ ★ ✕ **Mahesh Lunch Home.** One of the first Mumbai restaurants to popularize Konkan coast seafood, the formerly humble Mahesh, its two levels tucked away on a narrow street, has gone upmarket with marble walls and floors, giant fish tanks, and smartly clad waiters. (The diners have gone upmarket, too—no more leaving fish bones on the side of the table.) You'll get what may be Mumbai's freshest and best seafood, personally selected at the nearby Fort fish market every morning for the past few decades by the owner, Mr. S.C. Karkera, who lunches here himself. Local office workers, bankers, five-star hotel owners, and cricket and film stars come here for giant portions of exquisite crab, *rawas* (Indian salmon), prawn *gassi* (in a thick, tangy, spicy coconut gravy), fried kane (a bony Mangalorean fish), and pomfret dishes, all succulently tender and light and seasoned with tangy tandoori or Mangalorean spices. The seafood dishes prepared with butter, garlic, and pepper are also popular, but it's best to stick to the specials and to the authentic traditional Mangalorean dishes. ✉ *8-B Cawasji Patel St., Fort* ☎ *22/2287–0938* ✉ *Kings Apt., Juhu Tara Rd., Juhu* ☎ *22/5695–5554 or 22/5695–5559* ▭ *AE, DC, MC, V.*

7

$$ Fodor's Choice ★ ✕ **Trishna.** Once just another neighborhood lunch place, this small restaurant near busy M.G. Road has been very much discovered and it's now one of the hottest seafood restaurants in town. Yuppies and film stars crowd into the rows of benches and tables alongside Trishna's old-time regulars, all devouring fresh seafood or Indian and Chinese cuisine. Favorites include squid in green masala and butter-garlic crab (the latter is Rs. 800). Ask to see the crab before it's cooked: the creature's giant, still-snapping claws will dispel any doubts about freshness. Call in advance to find out the daily catch. ✉ *7 Rope Walk La., next to Commerce House, Kala Ghoda, Fort, 400023* ☎ *22/2270–3213 or 22/2261–4991* ✉ *3/A Crystal Plaza, opposite Infiniti Mall & Cinemax, New Link Rd., Andheri* ☎ *22/3266–1146 or 22/3266–1147* ✍ *Reservations essential* ▭ *AE, MC, V.*

SOUTH INDIAN

$$$$ ✕ **Dakshin.** South Indian eating places often rate high on taste but low on attention to decor, with functionality being the main theme. By contrast Dakshin makes a hullaballoo in the presentation of its delicious South Indian specialties, both vegetarian and non-vegetarian, serving dishes in gleaming brass bowls and thali platters on banana leaves with dozens of condiments. In this plush environment, fragrant with jasmine flowers and incense, soothing *nadaswaram* (a traditional South Indian wind instrument) hums in the background. The curd (yogurt) rice melts like butter in your mouth, and the platters of mini dosas offer an excellent chance to explore the possibilities of this addictive South Indian

CLOSE UP

Mumbai's Greatest Seafood Hits

Clams, squid, prawns, lobsters, crabs, and fish, rubbed with a spicy red masala or spiked with a green masala or simmered in a thick fragrant coconut gravy: that's the way seafood is eaten on the western Konkan coast of India, in seaside homes from Mumbai to Mangalore and Goa. Hole-in-the-wall restaurants across the city, offering typical homestyle Konkan fried fish or fish curry– or prawn *gassi*–and-rice meals, have always done the briskest business and have some of city's finest food. Everybody in Mumbai has their favorite seamy dive for gorging on seafood.

If you are a foodie and an avid seafood *wallah* (afficianado), help make your Bombay trip memorable by sampling the best of Konkan seafood cuisine.

First, here's a list of what to dig into:

Prawn gassi: small prawns simmered in a thick, tangy, spicy coconut gravy

Prawn curry: thinner than a gassi, with *kokum* (a sour berry)

Masala prawns: prawns marinated in garlic and spices and then pan-fried

Teesri masala: tiny clams cooked in a dry cocunut masala

Bombay duck *bombil*: this watery fish is first squeezed out and then batter-fried with semolina; it's light and flaky

Surmai, pomfret, and rawas: these three famous, fleshy fish of this region are either marinated and fried or popped into a curry

Masala crab: crab cooked in thick, almost dry, green or red masala

Neer dosa: a light crumpled soft-rice dosa meant especially for eating with seafood

Kori roti: a dry, crumbly rice roti

Appam: a Kerala-style steamed kind of dosa available in some Konkan joints

And here is a selection of good seafood restaurants, both low-down and ritzy:

Konkan Café (✉ *Taj President hotel, 90 Cuffe Parade* ☎ *22/6665–0808*). If you're not interested in hustling to find the best seafood in town, then the closest approximation of traditional Konkan curries and fried fish can be had at the swanky Konkan Café.

Gajalee (✉ *Hanuman Rd., Vile Parle East* ☎ *22/2616–6470*). Famous for their stuffed crab, fried bombil, surmai *kurkure* (crunchy fish), prawns *ambat tikhat* (dry masala); traditional Maharashtrian seafood can be found here. Another branch is at Phoenix Mills.

Apoorva (✉ *S. A. Brelvi Rd., off P. M. Rd.* ☎ *22/2287–0335*). This is a humble spot to stuff yourself silly with oyster curry, masala squid, fish curry, mackerel fry, bomil fry, and neer dosa.

Ananthashram (✉ *Kotachiwadi, Girgaum* ☎ *No phone*). This Mumbai culinary landmark is as traditional and authentic eatery as you can get. This staunchly "unfancy" comes with brusque service, but also some of the tastiest surmai curry, surmai fry, prawn curry, and teesri masala in Bombay. Its clientele is testimony to that—famous film stars and city notables hunt this place down to have an *asli* (real), satisfying seafood feed.

Hotel Bharat Excellensea (✉ *Ballard Estate* ☎ *22/2261–8991 or 22/2270–1284*). About 15 minutes due south of Victoria Terminus (V.T.) station and visited by the city's upwardly mobile. What you get here is good seafood, Mangalorean style. Try the crabs in red sauce, fried pomfret or surmai, Koliwada prawns, and the prawn gassi with idlis.

Ankur (✉ *Meadows House, Tamarind La., also known as M.P. Shetty Rd., enter via lane next to Kendeel Bar on M.G. Rd. and take a left, Fort* ☎ *22/2265–4194 or 22/2263–0393*). Once a downmarket fish house but now dressed up with wood and glass, Ankur is good at semolina-fried jumbo prawns, fried *kane* (ladyfish), tandoori crab, or *teesri* in pepper sauce—served with *sana* (fluffy rice cakes tempered with toddy, a wine made from palm sap) or neer dosa (lacy rice pancakes).

Mahesh (✉ *8-B Cawasji Patel St., Fort* ☎ *22/2287–0938*). Old faithfuls lament the drop in standards since Mahesh got a spot on the tourist map, but this king of fish joints still does a rare fried pomfret. Though tandoori is not the Konkan way, the tandoori pomfret is exceptional, too.

Trishna (✉ *7 Rope Walk La., next to Commerce House, Kala Ghoda, Fort* ☎ *22/2270–3213 or 22/2261–4991*). Easily reached from Regal Cinema, Trishna is one of the best addresses for crabs. Have them with butter and pepper, garlic and butter or done in a Konkan masala. Also tasty: butter pepper prawns and the pomfret fry.

Casa Soul Fry (✉ *M.G. Rd., next to Fabindia* ☎ *22/22671421*). Here you can tuck into Goan fish favorites and enjoy live music on weekends. Opt for prawn loncha spiced with a dry coconut, garlic masala, crab rechard, or clam masala.

Goa Portuguesa and Culture Curry (✉ *Milli Building, Dhananjay Keer Chowk, off Cadell Rd., near Hinduja Hospital, Mahim* ☎ *22/2444–0202*). There's good Goan food here—book ahead. Try the fried pomfret, prawns xacuti (Goan style curry), black-pepper prawns, stuffed bombil, or the stuffed crab, and the bibinca, an egg-heavy cake made out of layers of thin pancakes and coconuts, for dessert.

Highway Gomantak (✉ *44/2179, Gandhi Nagar, behind Apna Bazaar, Bandra* ☎ *22/2640–9692 or 22/2643–2472*). Good bets at this no-frills spot serving Gomantak-style seafood are mackerel, clams, crab, surmai fry, and oysters. Alternatively, go for one of thali lunches.

Sayba (✉ *Zarine Cooperative Society, S.V. Rd., opposite the Bandra mosque* ☎ *22/2643–6620*). The excellent fare here is typical of the Maharashtra coast. Try the prawn vindaloo and fish fry.

staple. *Kozi varuval* (spicy fried chicken tossed with onion) is excellent, as are the fish curries. To sample the whole gamut of south Indian food—especially those non-vegetarian dishes that are not available in more humble Southy eateries—opt for a thali. ✉*Grand Maratha Sheraton, Sahar Airport Rd., Sahar* ☎*22/2830–3030* ✍*Reservations essential* 💳*AE, DC, MC, V.*

$ ✕**Woodlands Garden Cafe.** The weekend line at this vegetarian restaurant is an unequivocal testimony to the quality of the food. This is the place for authentic South Indian fare—excellent dosas and Rs. 120 South Indian thalis in no-fuss but comfortable surroundings. *Bisi beli hule,* a spicy lentil and rice porridge that's hard to find elsewhere, is very tasty. ✉*Next to Kala Niketan sari shop, Vaikuntlal Mehta Rd., Juhu-Vile Parle Scheme, Juhu* ☎*22/2611–9119* 💳*AE, DC, MC, V.*

THAI

$–$$ ✕**Thai Pavilion.** The food served at this small, tastefully decorated dining room is exceptional, and portions are unusually generous. Start with a clay crock of *tom yum koong,* a spicy prawn soup aromatic with lemongrass and fiery with chillies (not for the faint of palate). Try this fabulous entrée: *kai haw bai toey,* sweet marinated chicken chunks wrapped in pandanus, or screwpine, leaves (don't eat them), then steamed and deep-fried. Knowledgeable, attentive waiters provide fantastic service. ✉*Taj President hotel, 90 Cuffe Parade, Colaba* ☎*22/6665–0808* ✍*Reservations essential* 💳*AE, DC, MC, V.*

WHERE TO STAY

$$$$ ★ 🏨**Four Seasons.** One of the newest and more opulent locations to stay at in Mumbai, this hotel is located in sleek, narrow skyscraper that soars over central Mumbai, about 25 minutes from the downtown business district. Rooms, appointed in starchy whites, mellow honey, and gold tones, have contemporary teak furniture, flat LCD-screen televisions, iPod docks, DVDs, and oodles of space. Each room and spacious bathroom has a view of the city skyline and the glittering Arabian Sea. A two-level vast and modernistic restaurant and pub, named San-qi offers food from across Asia; an Italian food restaurant is next door. The spa and a pool offer equally stunning sea glimpses. Elevators, lined with floor to ceiling panels of backlit onyx, shoot you up to the top floors. **Pros:** luxurious, well-located, since it poised between south and north Mumbai. **Cons:** expensive, opt for top floors lower floor views may be disappointing. ✉*114 Dr. E. Moses Rd., 400018* ☎*22/2481–8000* 🌐*www.fourseasons.com* ⇨*202 rooms, 24 suites* 🖒*In-room: safe, refrigerator, Wi-Fi. In-hotel: 4 restaurants, bar, room service, pool, gym, spa, laundry service, concierge, no-smoking rooms.* 💳*AE, DC, MC, V.*

$$$$ ★ 🏨**The Grand Central.** In central Mumbai, in an area that once bustled with cotton mills and industry, this 27-story palatial hotel brings exciting change to the horizon. The Grand Central, which incorporates a handsome old domed colonial building in its redstone facade, has style and a majestic appearance. Rooms on the upper stories have splendid views of the city and are sumptuously decorated with black marble, teak, elegant furnishings, and sepia photos of the Bombay of yesteryear.

Window seats in the balcony-like alcoves add charm to each room. **Pros:** one of the few hotels in central Bombay (it may suit those who have business in this area), good kebab restaurant. **Cons:** very expensive, in a business area that's dead after dark. ✉*287 Dr. B. Ambedkar Rd., Parel, 400012* ☎*22/2410–1010* 🌐*www.itcwelcomgroup.in* *242 rooms, 2 suites* *In-room: safe, refrigerator, Wi-Fi. In-hotel: 3 restaurants, room service, bar, pool, gym, laundry service, concierge, no-smoking rooms.* 💳*AE, DC, MC, V.*

$$$$ **Grand Hyatt.** Extraordinarily posh, this massive property rises incongruously from a bleak urban landscape. Cross through its ultra-contemporary, block facade and you'll feel like you're in a modern art museum (it has an excellent collection of Indian modern art) or a convention center (it also has giant pieces of sculpture, sweeping granite floors, and many harsh right angles). Once you get over the disconnect and overcome the lack of warmth in the hotel's architecture, you'll begin to take in the polite service, varied and tasty cuisine, and the rooms, elegant but sparse and done in cream-color soft furnishings with Scandinavian-style furniture. The luxurious bathrooms open out and become part of the room, making it spacious. **Pros:** near the domestic airport, luxurious, excellent dining choices. **Cons:** expensive, odd location, far from Bombay's attractions. ✉*Off Western Express Highway, Santa Cruz, 400055* ☎*22/6676–1234* 🌐*www.mumbai.grand.hyatt.com* *547 rooms, 38 suites, 112 apartments* *In-room: safe, refrigerator, Wi-Fi. In-hotel: 4 restaurants, room service, bar, pool, gym, spa, concierge, laundry service, no-smoking rooms.* 💳*AE, DC, MC, V.*

$$$$ ★ **The Grand Maratha.** This airport hotel is certainly grand, with attentive and efficient service to match. Rooms overlook a pleasant shrubbery-lined atrium where meals are served. The hotel is spacious and luxurious, with expanses of granite and marble. It's the only hotel in Mumbai that has a lovely Indian look: *jharokas* (windows carved from stone) and luxury reminiscent of an ancient palace. Opt for pool-facing rooms. The rooms are posh with colorful accents—light green silk curtains and plush patterned carpets—and fancy bathrooms (with tubs and glass shower cubicles and lots of marble). There are three excellent Indian food restaurants and a Continental restaurant—Peshawari serves North-West Frontier food, Dakshin serves South Indian food, Dum Pukht serves Mughlai food, and the coffee shop does an excellent buffet. **Pros:** very elegant hotel, excellent in-house restaurants, near international airport. **Cons:** extremely expensive, far from sightseeing spots. ✉*Sahar Airport Rd., Sahar, 400099* ☎*22/2830–3030* 🌐*www.welcomgroup.com* *386 rooms, 31 suites* *In-room: safe, refrigerator, Wi-Fi. In-hotel: 5 restaurants, room service, bar, pool, gym, laundry service, concierge, no-smoking rooms.* 💳*AE, DC, MC, V.*

$$$$ **Hyatt Regency.** This airport hotel resembles a slick, high-tech Far Eastern airport, with a control-tower kind of exterior: a vision of steel, chrome, and black glass. It's lit up in places by neon light, too, and the interiors look starkly modern but luxurious. Popular among high-powered executive types, its modernism spills over into the plush and airy rooms, which have wooden floors, marble walls, large mirrors, and minimalist contemporary furnishings. Bathrooms have sunken shower

7

areas in addition to tubs. **Pros:** great bathrooms, close to international airport, plush. **Cons:** far from downtown, expensive. ✉*Sahar Airport Rd., Sahar, 400099* ☎*22/6696–1234* 🌐*www.mumbai.regency.hyatt.com* *401 rooms, 20 suites* *In-room: safe, refrigerator, Wi-Fi. In-hotel: restaurant, room service, bar, pool, gym, laundry service, concierge, no-smoking rooms.* *AE, DC, MC, V.*

$$$$ **InterContinental.** The rooms at this boutique hotel on Mumbai's famous sea promenade at Marine Drive are gorgeous—spacious and ultramodern with polished wood floors, large comfortable beds, big desks in white marble, elegant furnishings in black, white and wood, and great views of the ocean. Hi-tech touches include built-in flat-screen TVs, touch-sensor lights, and electronic entry keys. In the large bathrooms, which are trimmed with oodles of white marble, you can watch televison or listen to music in the tub. The rooftop pool and open-air Dome bar, done in sparkling white and overlooking the ocean and Marine Drive, are excellent places to while away some time. **Pros:** breathtakingly lovely rooftop pool and lounge, ocean view, elegant and extra comfy rooms. **Cons:** breathtakingly expensive. ✉*135 Marine Dr., 400020* ☎*22/3987–9999* 🌐*www.intercontinental.com* *58 rooms, 112 suites* *In-room: safe, refrigerator, DVD, Wi-Fi. In-hotel: 3 restaurants, room service, bar, pool, gym, concierge, room service, laundry service, no-smoking rooms.* *AE, DC, MC, V* *BP.*

$$$$ **InterContinental The Grand Mumbai.** Another member of the airport hotel tribe, this spot has a curving, sand-color facade with an enormous lobby with high ceilings, but lacks a distinctive style. The fairly spacious rooms open out onto corridors that overlook the lobby, and are well appointed—wood floors, India-accents in the furnishings, and a comfy vibe. The views of rooms closest to the airport wasteland are not grand; opt for a pool view. The bathrooms are trimmed with marble and glass and have both tubs and shower cubicles. **Pros:** close to international airport and suburban malls. **Cons:** impersonal, far from civilization. ✉*Sahar Airport Rd., Sahar, 400059* ☎*22/6699–2222* 🌐*www.intercontinental.com* *369 rooms, 34 suites* *In-room: safe, refrigerator, Wi-Fi. In-hotel: 3 restaurants, room service, bar, pool, gym, laundry service, concierge.* *AE, DC, MC, V.*

$$$$ **JW Marriott.** The sheer size of this grand, sumptuous hotel may bowl you over. Walk beyond the vast lobby and you'll find a pair of flowing staircases that curve on either side down to a garden-level café. From the top of the stairs you'll see a giant wall of glass that by day looks out to an Olympic-size swimming pool and then out to sea, and by night looks out to a garden of flaming torches, flickering blue and orange in the breeze. Lotus ponds and sandstone statues dot the garden. The extremely elegant rooms have views of the ocean and tasteful, subdued furnishings that include large mirrors and striped bronze walls; bathrooms are especially luxurious. Airport transfers are included in rates. **Pros:** well-appointed rooms, stylish hotel, excellent meals to be had. **Cons:** expensive, far from city sights. ✉*Juhu Tara Rd., Juhu, 400049* ☎*22/6693–3000* 🌐*www.marriott.com* *322 rooms, 36 suites* *In-room: safe, refrigerator, Wi-Fi. In-hotel: 4 restaurants, room service, bars, pools, gym, spa, laundry service, concierge, no-smoking rooms.* *AE, DC, MC, V* *BP.*

$$$$ **The Leela Kempinski.** Close to both airports (it's a mile from the international airport) and 25 km (16 mi) outside the city, this stylish, posh property was once the only airport hotel used as a stopover for high-powered businesspeople and airline crew. Today there are four newer airport hotels, but the Leela is still a very good address. The cozy rooms are recently renovated with plush, ornate carpeting on rich wood floors, wall-mounted TVs, and Indian-style furnishings. Its 11 acres of gardens include lotus pools and a small waterfall. A popular Italian restaurant and an excellent Chinese restaurant, The Great Wall, are also here. **Pros:** attractive hotel and rooms, close to international airport. **Cons:** expensive, far from city center. ✉*Sahar, 400059* ☎*22/6691–1234* 🌐*www.theleela.com* *396 rooms, 40 suites* *In-room: safe, refrigerator, Wi-Fi. In-hotel: 4 restaurants, room service, bar, tennis courts, pool, gym, laundry service, concierge, no smoking rooms.* *AE, DC, MC, V.*

$$$$ **Le Royal Meridien.** This neat, small, luxury hotel doesn't have a fancy exterior, and its shining marble lobby is tiny, but the rooms have plenty of grandeur. It's only 5 minutes from Mumbai's international airport, in the thick of the city's neighborhood of airport hotels. Rooms are no less swanky for being comfy—they are decorated with lots of wood and crisp whites. Bathrooms are done in chrome and glass, and have shower cubicles, tubs, and bidets. Each room has DVD player. The hotel's restaurant, La Brasserie, serves a variety of meals around the clock; another restaurant on-site, Imperial China, serves Szechuan. **Pros:** close to international airport, plenty of dining options here and at nearby hotels. **Cons:** expensive, far from Mumbai's main sights, not a great view. ✉*Sahar Airport Rd., 400059* ☎*22/2838–0000* 🌐*www.lemeridien.com* *171 rooms, 6 suites* *In-room: safe, refrigerator, DVD, Wi-Fi. In-hotel: 3 restaurants, room service, bars, pool, gym, laundry service, concierge, no-smoking rooms.* *AE, DC, MC, V* *BP.*

$$$$ ★ **Marine Plaza.** The polished, smoky-glass exterior promises elegance, and inside it's delivered, with a modern, black-marble interior and clean, uncluttered sleekness. Glass elevators whiz you up to rooms that are small but very comfortable and fairly luxurious, and done elegantly in blue and black. Rooms have excellent sea views (no extra charge) and dressing rooms. The glass-bottom pool, outside on the roof of the hotel, has good vistas of the city. **Pros:** great views, well located, wonderful pool, good Chinese restaurant attached. **Cons:** expensive, rooms a little too compact. ✉*29 Marine Dr., 400020* ☎*22/2285–1212* 🌐*www.hotelmarineplaza.com* *68 rooms, 44 suites* *In-room: safe, refrigerator, Wi-Fi. In-hotel: 2 restaurants, room service, bar, pool, gym, laundry service, concierge.* *AE, MC, V* *BP.*

$$$$ ★ **The Oberoi.** At this elegant high-rise in the heart of the business district, just about everything is sleek and efficient. The beautiful, high-ceiling lobby and public spaces are punctuated with traditional craft pieces. Each floor is staffed with a butler for personal assistance, and each room has small, separate dressing and luggage areas to allow for clutter-free in-room meetings. The rooms are decorated in pastels, with rich dark-wood furniture. If possible, arrange for a room with a view of the Arabian Sea. **Pros:** excellent sea view, classy rooms. **Cons:**

7

expensive. ✉*Nariman Point, 400021* ☎*22/6632–5757* 🌐*www.oberoihotels.com* *327 rooms, 22 suites* *In-room: safe, refrigerator, Wi-Fi. In-hotel: 4 restaurants, room service, bar, pool, gym, spa, laundry service, concierge, no-smoking rooms.* *AE, DC, MC, V.*

$$$$ **The Orchid.** This small but intimate and quiet hotel has attractive green-and-cream rooms that are brightly lit, decently sized, and very comfortable. With a location right next to the domestic airport and a few minutes from the international, the Orchid is often full up. Boasting "eco-friendly waste-management and recycling policies," the hotel built its "green" rooms with a minimal amount of wood, plastic, and paper. The waterfall, which runs on recycled water, looks like falling glass—it lights up the lobby and provides humidity for the lustrous orchids that populate the hotel's interior. A rooftop barbecue restaurant provides interesting views of the airport. **Pros:** airport access, intimate, eco-friendly. **Cons:** smallish rooms, far from city sights, rather expensive. ✉*Nehru Rd., Vile Parle, 400099* ☎*22/2616–4040* 🌐*www.orchidhotel.com* *245 rooms, 18 suites* *In-room: safe, refrigerator, Wi-Fi. In-hotel: 2 restaurants, room service, bar, pool, gym, laundry service, concierge, no-smoking rooms, complimentary airport shuttle.* *AE, DC, MC, V* *BP.*

$$$$ **Ramada Plaza Palm Grove.** With its small entrance, squeezed driveway, and parking lot, this Juhu Beach high rise might seem small from the outside, but in fact it's fairly spacious. The lobby is lined with marble and etched glass. Rooms are airy, comfortable, and ordinary looking—each has a small sitting area—and have subdued contemporary furnishings with shades of cool green. Deluxe suites and executive salons face the water; other rooms have limited views. The pool is a pleasant, if not especially spacious, place to unwind. The fun Oriental Bowl restaurant, done in black marble, serves Thai and Chinese food. **Pros:** close to the buzz and color of Juhu Beach, spacious rooms, airport pickup. **Cons:** expensive, far from south Mumbai. ✉*Juhu Tara Rd., Juhu, 400049* ☎*22/2611–2323 or 22/6697–2323* 🌐*www.krahejahospitality.com* *114 rooms, 3 suites* *In-room: safe, refrigerator, Wi-Fi. In-hotel: restaurant, room service, bar, pool, gym, laundry service, concierge, complimentary airport shuttle.* *AE, DC, MC, V* *BP.*

$$$$ **Taj Land's End.** This opulent hotel faces the ocean in the suburb of Bandra. Its lobby seems like an acre of marble, with huge, sparkling chandeliers, fountains, and automatic revolving doors. Inside are some remarkably luxurious modern rooms, complete with bedside controls for the lights, curtains, and air-conditioning. Bathrooms have both showers and tubs. The Masala Bay restaurant serves Indian fusion food, and the elegant, super-expensive Pure restaurant serves Continental food with an Indian accent. **Pros:** beautiful rooms, close to the pubbing/dining zone in Bandra. **Cons:** expensive, far from city's historic sites. ✉*Land's End, Bandstand area, Bandra, 400050* ☎*22/5668–1234* 🌐*www.tajhotels.com* *368 rooms, 15 suites* *In-room: safe, refrigerator, Wi-Fi. In-hotel: 3 restaurants, bar, pool, gym, room service, laundry service, concierge, no-smoking rooms.* *AE, DC, MC, V.*

$$$$ **Taj Mahal Palace & Tower.** Looking past the Gateway of India to the Arabian Sea, the Taj's stunning brown stone exterior sports rows of jutting white balconies and Gothic windows. Onion domes on the corner turrets echo the high, central Italianate dome. The first hotel in what is now a pan-India luxury chain, this Victorian extravaganza was built in 1903. Foreigners and wealthy Indians choose this hotel over other fancy hotels in town because it's a beautiful and regal landmark—one worth visiting even if you don't plan to stay here. A less expensive 19-story modern wing ("the tower"), which throws in some Moorish elements, rises next to the older wing. Every corner of the older building is exquisitely decorated, often with antiques (for which the hotel's decorator scours India) and always with warm, tasteful colors. Rooms and suites in this building, some of which surround small, quiet interior verandas, retain their Victorian character with high ceilings, pastel colors, antiques, and cane furniture. Rooms facing the harbor are extremely attractive. Rooms in the the tower are slightly less expensive and spacious, but a bit unremarkable for their price. Furnished in maroon and subdued oranges, they have a tiny sitting area. **Pros:** location, location, location, and the city's best views. **Cons:** expensive, service can be disorganized. ✉ *Apollo Bunder, 400001* ☎ *22/6665–3366* 🌐 *www.tajhotels.com* *565 rooms, 45 suites* *In-room: safe, refrigerator, Wi-Fi. In-hotel: 5 restaurants, room service, bars, pool, concierge, laundry service, no-smoking room.* *AE, DC, MC, V.*

Fodor's Choice ★

$$$$ **Taj President.** In a residential neighborhood close to Afghan Church, this luxury hotel is a favorite of business travelers. The comfortable rooms have modern furnishings, polished wood floors, wall-mounted televisions, and massage showers. Women travelers can opt for special rooms with video phones and satin dressing gowns. Sea-facing rooms cost slightly more than a city-facing room, but the view of south Mumbai and the harbor beyond makes them worthwhile. Although the hotel is not as extravagant as others in its price range, service is outstanding. The hotel has good restaurants, and the bar, Wink, is a happening place. **Pros:** great in-house restaurants and popular bar, well located. **Cons:** expensive, compact rooms. ✉ *90 Cuffe Parade, Colaba, 400005* ☎ *22/6665–0808* 🌐 *www.tajhotels.com* *300 rooms, 20 suites* *In-room: safe, refrigerator, Wi-Fi. In-hotel: 3 restaurants, room service, bar, pool, gym, laundry service, concierge, no-smoking rooms.* *AE, DC, MC, V.*

$$$ **Bawa International.** For those looking for a quick-stay hotel near the airports, this place used to be a deal. Though it's not as good a deal as it once was, it's still one of the cheaper of the passable hotels near the airport. Bargain for a better rate, and maybe you'll be lucky. The standard rooms are carpeted in green, furnished with white furniture, and well lit; bathrooms are decent. It's all a bit short on atmosphere but reasonably cozy. The deluxe and fancier rooms aren't a great value for the money—rates escalate quickly. Top-floor rooms have a view of the airport. **Pros:** close to the domestic aiport. **Cons:** over-priced, expensive, shabby rooms. ✉ *Nehru Rd. Extension, near the domestic airport, Vile Parle, 400099* ☎ *22/2611–3636 or 22/2611–4015* 🌐 *www.bawahotels.com* *75 rooms, 4 suites*

7

In-room: refrigerator. In-hotel: restaurant, room service, bar, laundry service. *AE, DC, MC, V.*

$$$ **Eastern International Hotel.** Built in the 1970s, this Western-style high rise (formerally the Holiday Inn) has a spacious lobby, executive floors for business travelers, and rather attractive, large rooms uniformly decorated with standard contemporary furniture, floral wall-to-wall carpeting, and green-accented fabrics. The best standard rooms have limited views of the beach; only executive rooms face the sea directly. **Pros:** beachside location, airport pickup, close to suburban malls. **Cons:** far from downtown, expensive. *Balraj Sahani Marg, Juhu, 400049* *22/6693–4444* *www.eihlimited.com* *191 rooms, 13 suites* *In-room: safe, refrigerator, Wi-Fi. In-hotel: 2 restaurants, room service, bar, pool, gym, laundry service, concierge, complimentary airport shuttle.* *AE, DC, MC, V* *BP.*

$$$ **Hilton Towers.** Adjoining the Oberoi hotel, this enormous, 35-story high rise hosts a mixed international crowd of executives and tourists. Public spaces are many and varied, some overlooking the vast, gleaming, glass-wall lobby from smart mezzanines. Rooms are modern and classy, furnished with smooth, contemporary wood furniture and in subdued, elegant colors. Sea-facing rooms, more expensive, on high floors have stunning views of the Arabian Sea and Marine Drive, known as the "Queen's Necklace" because of its string of lights at night. The restaurant, Indiana Jones, serves superb Asian food. **TIP→ Because hotel room rates vary according to occupancy, it can be a great value for money in lean seasons.** **Pros:** ocean views, good value for money, tasteful rooms, easy access to restaurants at the Oberoi hotel. **Cons:** expensive. *Nariman Point, 400021* *22/6632–4343* *www.hilton.com* *553 rooms, 23 suites* *In-room: safe, refrigerator, Wi-Fi. In-hotel: 2 restaurants, room service, bar, pool, gym, laundry service, concierge, no-smoking rooms.* *AE, DC, MC, V.*

$$$ **Fariyas.** The shiny, small marble lobby of this modern hotel is filled with glass chandeliers and brass ornaments. The rooms, with contemporary furnishings and wood floors, are inviting—somewhat small but still worth its price tag. The location is terrific, just a few minutes by foot from the Gateway of India. Select a room with a sea-facing view. Only two suites have tubs; the rest of the rooms have showers. The swinging Tavern bar/pub, in the basement, plays a lot of classic rock and oldies. **Pros:** well-priced, well located, good views. **Cons:** smallish rooms. *25 Devshankar V Vyas Marg, at Shahid Bhagat Singh Marg, off Arthur Bunder Rd., Colaba, 400005* *22/2204–2911* *www.fariyas.com* *87 rooms, 6 suites* *In-room: refrigerator. In-hotel: 2 restaurants, laundry services, concierge, room service, bar, pool, gym* *AE, DC, MC, V.*

$$$ Fodor's Choice ★ **Gordon House.** The guest rooms, lobby, and restaurant in this boutique hotel are simply but fashionably decorated. The lobby is on the second floor, and room floors are designated either Mediterranean, Country, or Scandinavian. Rooms are no-fuss but chic—earth-color buffed tiles, bright white bedspreads, and blond-wood furniture. At All Stir-Fry, an excellent Asian restaurant here, you can construct your own meals and hand the raw ingredients to a chef who cooks them. The attached Polly

Esthers bar rocks. **Pros:** intimate hotel, great value for money, tasteful rooms. **Cons:** small hotel, no view. ✉ *5 Battery St., Apollo Bunder, 400039* ☎ *22/2287–1122* 🌐 *www.ghhotel.com* *29 rooms, 1 suite* *In-room: safe, refrigerator, Wi-Fi. In-hotel: restaurant, room service, bar, laundry service, concierge.* *AE, DC, MC, V* *BP.*

$$$ ★ **Ramee Guestline.** This small, compact, business hotel about 500 feet from the ocean in Juhu has reasonably attractive, neat, and plush but slightly dark rooms with standard amenities. It has a rooftop pool, an excellent place to sunbathe. The Ivy Club serves healthy breakfasts, salad lunches, and a cake buffet to executives and their clients in a quiet lounge area. Since the hotel isn't perched right on the sea and its rooms are small, it's slightly overpriced. Airport transfers are included. Ask for a discount if you're booking directly. **Pros:** close to the beach. **Cons:** expensive, small rooms, mildly pokey. ✉ *462 A. B. Nair Rd., Juhu Beach, 400049* ☎ *22/6670–5555 or 22/6693–5555* 🌐 *www.ramee-group.com* *91 rooms, 2 suites* *In-hotel: restaurant, bar, pool, gym, room service, laundry service.* *AE, DC, MC, V* *BP.*

$$ **Citizen.** Right on the beach and one of the cheapest of the more upscale hotels on the Juhu strip, Citizen is a deal in a city where you seemingly pay for every square inch. The hotel lacks style in its exteriors and interiors, as is illustrated by the rooms, with tile floors, mildly ugly furnishings, and none-too-pretty loud prints—but they are nevertheless quite comfortable, and there are beach views from the windows. Bathrooms are tiny, with just showers (no bathtubs). The open-air seaside restaurant is very pleasant and ideal for a beer and lazing around. **Pros:** good value for money, on the beach. **Cons:** unattractive rooms, far from south Bombay. ✉ *960 Juhu Tara Rd., Juhu Beach, 400049* ☎ *22/6693–2525 or 22/2660–7273* 🌐 *www.citizenhotelMumbai.com* *45 rooms 3 suites* *In-room: refrigerator, Wi-Fi. In-hotel: 2 restaurants, room service, laundry service.* *AE, DC, MC, V.*

$$ **Ritz.** This quaint 1930s hotel has a small lobby, somewhat shabby corridors, and pleasant but musty and worn rooms. The building is white, with green trim on the outside, and is centrally located on a peaceful, tree-lined side street off Marine Drive. Fifteen of the rooms have balconies, but not all have scenic views. The bathrooms, in tile and white stone, are a bit ancient and could be cleaner. **Pros:** decent value for money, in the city center, large rooms. **Cons:** faded charm, mildly shabby. ✉ *5 Jamshedij Tata Rd., Churchgate, 400020* ☎ *22/2285–0500 or 22/2282–0141* *22/2285–0494* *53 rooms, 10 suites* *In-hotel: 2 restaurants, room service, laundry service.* *AE, DC, MC, V.*

$ **Apollo.** It's steps from the Gateway of India (but utterly lacking a view of the magnificent monument). This budget hotel was once even more budget, but since renovation it has gained some respectability (and a place in this guide) but not more atmosphere. The tiny, cookie-cutter rooms are done in a bland cream. Rooms with twin beds are large than those with doubles. Choose a street-facing room. Bathrooms, tiled in a dull red, are quite clean and have tubs. **Pros:** cheap, well located, fairly good value. **Cons:** a tad seedy, no views, no atmosphere. ✉ *Lansdowne Rd., behind Regal Cinema, Colaba, 400039* ☎ *22/2287–3312 or 22/2202–0223* *22/2287–4990* *h.apollo@gmail.com* *41 rooms*

7

In-room: refrigerator, safe. In-hotel: restaurant, room service, bar, laundry service. *MC, V.*

$ **Astoria.** The Astoria, with a slightly servere 1930-ish art deco exterior, is a decent, reliable mid-range hotel. The brightly lit shiny glass and marble lobby is a cheerful welcome. The rooms, with wood floors and bland furnishings, are very neat, comfortable, and clean but somehow less that cheery—opt for a room with a decent view. The bathrooms, done in dull red tile, are also quite tidy. Although the Astoria is very well located, with Nariman Point, Marine Drive, and Regal Cinema all five minutes away, it's also away from the bustle, set in as it is from the road. **Pros:** good value and location, comfy hotel. **Cons:** less-than-cheery rooms. *Churchgate Reclamation, Jamshedji Tata Rd., Churchgate, 400020* *22/6654–1234 or 22/2287–1211* *www.astoriaMumbai.com* *65 rooms, 4 suites* *In-room: refrigerator. In-hotel: restaurant, room service, laundry service.* *AE, DC, MC, V.*

$ **Garden.** At this inexpensive place on a small side street in Colaba, minutes from major sights and shops, rooms are clean and comfortable, but gloomily furnished. Book a deluxe room; the standard rooms are not as nice. The only drawback is the lack of a pleasant view in many rooms, so check the room view before you make your decision and ask for a road-facing room on a higher floor. **Pros:** good location, reasonably priced. **Cons:** shabby, gloomy, no view. *42 Garden Rd., off Colaba Causeway, near Electric House, Colaba, 400039* *22/2283–1330, 22/2283–4823, or 22/2284–1476* *22/2204–4290* *gardenhotel@mail.com* *34 rooms, 3 suites* *In-room: refrigerator. In-hotel: restaurant, laundry service, room service.* *MC, V.*

$ **Godwin.** This nine-story, zero-atmosphere hotel is a decent, low-frills bargain. Accommodations vary widely, however—opt only for one of the 10 renovated deluxe rooms. These rooms, done in cream, have shiny tile floors and in-room amenities; the cheaper rooms are rather shabby. Most deluxe rooms have window air-conditioning units, but several are centrally air-conditioned. The bathrooms attached to the deluxe rooms could be cleaner, but are passable. Request an eighth-floor room with a distant view of the Taj Mahal hotel and Gateway of India—many rooms have either no view or views of something depressing. The restaurant serves Indian and Chinese food. Also ask about rooms at Godwin's sister hotel, Garden, next door. Some rooms have tubs, others only showers. **Pros:** cheap but not that cheap, well located. **Cons:** shabby rooms. *41 Garden Rd., off Colaba Causeway, near Electric House, Colaba, 400039* *22/2287–2050 or 22/2284–1226* *22/2287–1592* *hotelgodwin@mail.com* *52 rooms, 12 suites* *In-room: refrigerator. In-hotel: restaurant, room service, bar, laundry service.* *MC, V.*

$ **Sea Green.** The green trimmings on this five-story building have been weathered by the Arabian Sea during this hotel's more than 50 years of hosting guests. Beyond its friendly service, the hotel's main virtue is that it's a remarkable bargain for its price and location, if you don't mind the government-office look that implies that nothing has changed around here since Independence. Narrow hallways lead to surprisingly large rooms with window air-conditioners and clean but institutional furnishings, such as metal wardrobes and vinyl couches. All rooms but one have small balconies; a few look across Marine Drive to the sea and offer a splendid view of Mumbai's famous sea promenade. The bathrooms have only open showers, no stalls or tubs. Room service offers beverages and simple breakfasts only. Don't mistake this place for the hotel's twin—the Sea Green South Hotel—next door, where rooms are slightly less hospitable. **Pros:** good location, splendid sea view, large, clean rooms, reasonably priced. **Cons:** antiquated, worn. ✉*145 Marine Dr., 400020* ☎*22/2282–2294 or 22/6633–6525* 🌐*www.seagreenhotel.com* *34 rooms, 4 suites* *In-room: refrigerator. In-hotel: room service, laundry.* *MC, V.*

$ **Sea Palace Hotel.** Although this hotel is right on the waterfront near the Gateway of India, the rooms don't make great use of the view—they face the opposite direction. Bathrooms, however, have been fitted into the walls facing the sea, so most rooms have an abbreviated sea view in a far corner (cheaper ones don't). Recently renovated in 2007 with modern wood furnishings, the rooms are now attractive but still simple. The location is enough to make this a good choice, and the staff is attentive. **Pros:** cheap, well located, airy, pleasant rooms. **Cons:** could be classier. ✉*26 P.J. Ramachandani Marg, Apollo Bunder, 400039* ☎*22/2284–1828 or 22/2285–4404* 🌐*www.seapalacehotel.com* *50 rooms, 3 suites* *In-room: refrigerator. In-hotel: restaurant, room service.* *AE, MC, V.*

$ **West End.** More than half a century old, this simple, reliable place is especially popular with foreigners looking for a good deal. The very clean rooms—some more spacious than others—have private balconies, bathtubs, deep-blue carpets and outdated furniture; opt for one facing the street in front. The restaurant, the lobby, and even the bellboys still have a 1940s look. The old-style bar is charming, and the popular Gujarati thali restaurant Panchvati Gaurav is two minutes away. The building is near Bombay Hospital; you'll see doctors and visitors around until late at night. Around the corner is the Metro Cinema complex, where another outlet of Rajdhani, another Gujarati thali restaurant, is located. **Pros:** large rooms, decent location, mildly atmospheric, reasonable. **Cons:** a bit outdated, gloomy hallways. ✉*45 New Marine Lines, 400020* ☎*22/2203–9121* 🌐*www.westendhotelMumbai.com* *80 rooms, 15 suites* *In-hotel: restaurant, room service, bar.* *AE, DC, MC, V.*

¢ **Cowie's.** Minutes from the Gateway of India promenade, these cheap rooms are in an old, dilapidated, probably turn-of-the-20th-century building. The accommodation is simple and a bit dull, with red flooring and basic furnishings. Rooms are reasonably clean, the bathrooms less so; choose a room with air-conditioning. Two or three of the rooms have balconies, which is a good reason for staying here. **Pros:** decent and cheap, unlike other cheap hotels in Colaba, it's safe and not squalid. **Cons:** dull, could be cleaner. ✉*15 Walton Rd., off Colaba Causeway, near Electric House, Colaba, 400039* ☎*22/2284–0232 or 22/2284–5727* *22/2283–4203* *20 rooms* *In-room: no a/c (some), refrigerator. In-hotel: restaurant, room service, laundry service.* *MC, V* *CP.*

7

¢ **YWCA International Center.** About the cheapest you can go and still have decent, clean, and safe rooms is the Y. Rooms are in a colorless modern block and lack anything special, apart from bad decor. The air-conditioned rooms are more pleasant and less drab than the non-air-conditioned ones. You can expect just the basics, plus a shower; everything is at an average level of cleanliness and the hallways and stairwells could be spiffier. Try for a street-facing room; some have balconies. Rates include morning tea, breakfast, and a buffet dinner. It's essential to reserve a month or two in advance. Note that most rooms are singles or doubles, but they also have dormitory-style accommodation and "family" rooms. **Pros:** dirt cheap, decent, safe. **Cons:** institutional air, drab rooms. ✉*18 Madame Cama Rd., near Regal Cinema, Fort, 400039* ☎*22/2202–5053* 🌐*www.ywcaic.info* *31 rooms* *In-room: no a/c (some), no TV. In-hotel: room service.* 💳*MC, V* *MAP.*

NIGHTLIFE & THE ARTS

THE ARTS

The best source of arts information is *Time Out Mumbai*. Pick up the latest copy of this magazine from any corner newsstand for an excellent and informative lowdown on what's happening as well as special tidbits about the city. Another source is the fortnightly culture calendar "Programme of Dance, Music and Drama," available free at the Government of India Tourist Office. The daily *Times of India* usually lists each day's films, concerts, and other events and on Fridays brings out a guide to city events called *What's Hot* that can be purchased at any newsstand; the afternoon paper *Midday* publishes highlights of the coming week's events in its pullout *What To Do? Where To Go…*, also available online (🌐*http://wtdwtg.mid-day.com*). Program information and details usually appear on the Maharashtra Tourism Development Corporation's (MTDC) city-guide programs, shown regularly on hotels' in-house TV stations.

The **National Centre for the Performing Arts** (*NCPA* ✉*Nariman Point* ☎*22/2283–3737, 22/2283–3838, 22/2283–4500, or 22/2282–4567* 🌐*www.ncpamumbai.com*) posts its performance schedule on the bulletin board at the main entrance and at the entrances to its Tata and Experimental theaters and on its Web site. Note that many NCPA performances are open to members only; a year's membership is Rs. 2,500.

Other performance tickets in Mumbai are usually very inexpensive (from free to Rs. 500) and can be purchased from box offices or from the ticket counter at **Rhythm House Private Ltd.** (✉*40 K. Dubash Marg, Rampart Row, Kala Ghoda, Fort* ☎*22/2285–3963*), across the street from the Jehangir Art Gallery, one of Mumbai's main music stores and another source of information on what's happening.

DANCE The **National Centre for the Performing Arts** (✉*Nariman Point* ☎*22/2283–3737, 22/2283–3838, 22/2283–4500, or 22/2282–4567* 🌐*www.ncpamumbai.com*) houses the **Godrej Dance Academy Theater,** a main venue for classical Indian dance performances, as well as workshops and master classes, and the **Drama Opera Arts Complex,** a 1,000-seat auditorium, is Mumbai's ballet and opera theater.

FILM Mumbai, aka "Bollywood," is the center of the Indian film industry—the largest film producer in the world. Most of the epic Indian musicals shown in movie theaters are in Hindi. Every tourist should take in a Hindi film—three or so hours of song, tears, gun battles, and around-the-trees love dances, Indian films provide plenty of *tamasha,* or spectacle. To catch a Hindi film, one good options is the plush **Metro Adlabs** (✉*Metro House, M. G. Rd., Dhobi Talao* ☎*22/2403–6474*). Another good theater is the the upscale **Inox** (✉*CR2 shopping mall, opposite Bajaj Bhavan, Nariman Point* ☎*22/6659–5959*). At **Fame Adlabs** (✉*Andheri Link Rd., Andheri West* ☎*22/6699–1212*), you sit in reclining seats and are given a blanket, like in an airplane. The **Regal Cinema** (✉*Shaheed Bhagat Singh Rd., opposite Prince of Wales Museum, Colaba* ☎*22/2202–1017*) usually shows current English-language movies. The **Sterling Cinema** (✉*Tata Palace, Murzban Rd., off D. Naoroji Rd., near Victoria Terminus, Fort* ☎*22/2207–5187 or 22/6631–6677*) shows current English-language films. The first-rate **IMAX Adlabs** (✉*Anik Wadala Link Rd., Wadala* ☎*22/2403–6474*) is Mumbai's only IMAX theater. It shows a mixture of popular and documentary films in its main dome theater.

Nehru Centre Auditorium (✉*Dr. Annie Besant Rd., Worli* ☎*22/2496–4676* 🌐*www.nehru-centre.org*) sometimes shows interesting art films, some in English. If you're looking around for films, make sure to check listings for the **National Center for the Performing Arts** (✉*Nariman Point* ☎*22/2283–3737, 22/2283–3838, 22/2283–4500, or 22/2282–4567* 🌐*www.ncpamumbai.com*).

MUSIC & THEATER The **National Center for the Performing Arts** (✉*Nariman Point* ☎*22/2283–3737, 22/2283–3838, 22/2283–4500, or 22/2282–4567* 🌐*www.ncpa-mumbai.com*) complex includes the **Tata Theatre,** a grand 1,000-seat auditorium that regularly hosts plays, often in English, and classical concerts by major Indian and international musicians. The **Little Theatre** is the NCPA's smallest, hosting small-scale plays and Western chamber music. The **Experimental Theatre,** with 300 seats, is usually used for avant-garde drama and occasionally for concerts and small-scale dance performances.

The **Nehru Centre Auditorium** (✉*Dr. Annie Besant Rd., Worli* ☎*22/2496–4676* 🌐*www.nehru-centre.org*) is Mumbai's second major venue, where theater, music, and dance performances are regularly held.

The **Prithvi Theatre** (✉*Janaki Kutir, Church Rd., Juhu* ☎*22/2614–9546* 🌐*www.prithvitheatre.org*), run by the famous Kapoor acting family (the current Bollywood star Kareena Kapoor is one of them), stages a variety of plays each week, some in English, with reasonably priced tickets. They often stage special programs for children. It's a 45-minute drive north from downtown Mumbai or 20 minutes from the airport in nontraffic hours. An evening at Prtihvi, which has an arty café and bookstore, can be memorable.

CLOSE UP

Song & Dance, Bollywood Style

Nicknamed after its Hollywood exemplar, Bollywood, the famously spirited and wildly popular Indian film industry headquartered in Bombay, is one of the largest in the world. Its devoted Hindi-speaking patrons number in the tens of millions.

Most people don't realize that Bollywood is only one of India's film-production centers. There are also Tollywoods and Chollywoods and what have you—the Tamil, Telugu, Malayalam, Kannada, and Bengali film industries are nearly as prolific as their Mumbai chapter. But in Mumbai alone, several films may be produced in a given week.

For almost 40 years, the blueprint of Bollywood movies hasn't changed much: a little bit of *mirch* (spice), a little bit of *masala* (pungency), love, injustice, religion, violence, and a happy ending. Heroes rarely die in Bollywood, and joyous songs (at least six) are a must. The hero and heroine often frolic around trees at some exotic locale (the woods, the Himalayas, New Zealand, Switzerland). Dance sequences are essential and songs can make or break a film. Compelling fight scenes—the more improbable the better, the more fake blood the more appealing—also pique audiences. New films are often variants of tried-and-true plots—good cop vs. bad cop (often they turn out to be brothers), unrequited love, and one man anti-establishment wars.

Hindi films play a special role in the lives of the Indian people. For the poor, illiterate, and illusionless, paying a few rupees for three solid hours of fantasy is a terrific bargain. Middle- and upper-class Indians are no less attached to their movies and the filmy *bhagwans* (gods). The arrival of a Hindi star at a restaurant or a shooting attracts mobs; these actors and actresses are the demigods of India. The modest Amitabh Bachchan, one of India's favorite superstars, has a temple dedicated to him in West Bengal. "Big B," as he's known, was so popular that he was chosen to host the Indian equivalent of *Who Wants to be a Millionaire* on television for two seasons.

Watching the production of a film is a rare treat. Movie shooting extravaganzas bristle with pandemonium—hundreds of people shuffle between the arc lights while the star has one go after another at her lines. Staging can be schlocky, but fun to watch: a rain scene may consist of a showerhead attached to a hose held upside down over the hero's head, as cameras roll in for a close-up and crowds undulate. Like all things Indian, out of this chaos emerges a vague order that keeps the juggernaut moving.

On any afternoon, you can take in a Hindi film at a local theater. Better still, have a local accompany you to provide a translation.

NIGHTLIFE

Between couples strolling on the breezy promenade around the Gateway of India and fashion-forward twentysomethings dancing at Polly Esthers, a retro bar and club behind the Taj, Mumbai has what is probably the most vibrant nightlife in India. Because of astronomical real-estate prices and bullying by racketeers, however, only a few private groups have opened their own bars or clubs. Quite a few of the nightspots in Mumbai proper are in established hotels and restaurants; many of the rest are in wealthy suburbs like Juhu and Bandra, where the after-dark scene thrives on suburbia's young nouveau riche as well as city folk willing to travel for a good night out.

Note that many clubs and bars have "couples" policies, whereby a "stag" (lone man) is not permitted to enter without a woman—a circuitous attempt to prevent brawls, pick-up scenes, and prostitution. To avoid an unpleasant encounter at the door, check with your hotel staff if you can enter if you are a man traveling alone or in a group of men. Dress nicely and you'll probably get in; an advance call from your hotel concierge might also make your entry smoother. Most nightspots, even pubs that would otherwise be conducive to cozy talks over beers, tend to have extremely loud music and are very smoky. If you'd like to converse beyond a few shouts over blaring rock music, opt for the more reserved bars and lounges in hotels.

Revelry peaks from Thursday to Sunday nights, with an early-twenties-to-mid-thirties crowd. Pubs open daily at around 7 or 8 (except a few, which open in the afternoon) and close by midnight or a little later. Only few remain open longer, depending on current police rules in the area. Some places collect a cover charge at the door. As in any metropolis, the reign of a nightspot can be ephemeral; **■TIP→ask a young hotel employee to brief you on the current scene.**

BARS & LOUNGES The **Bay View Bar** (✉*The Oberoi hotel, Nariman Point* ☎*22/6632–4142*), facing the Arabian Sea, is elegant and more reserved than many of its peers, attracting a rather expensive clientele. It has live music Monday through Saturday. **Busaba** (✉*4 Mandlik Rd., near Cotton World, Colaba* ☎*22/2204–3779*) is an Asian restaurant (Burmese, Chinese, Vietanmese, Thai) with a relaxed but small and attractive bar-lounge. **Café Ivy** (✉*Indage House, Worli* ☎*022/6654–7939*) is wine bar that offers the opportunity to sample any of the wines produced by India's premium vintner from its vineyards in Maharashtra as well as a range of quick bites and desserts—sandwiches, pasta, onion rings. The sparkling-white **Dome** (✉*135 Marine Dr.* ☎*22/3987–9999*), an open-air bar-lounge on top of the Intercontinental hotel, is a superb location for a sundowner (a sunset-time drink); for half an hour you can be the King of the Arabian Sea. The mixed snacks available include Japanese bites.

Geoffrey's (✉*Marine Plaza hotel, 29 Marine Dr.* ☎*22/2285–1212*) draws a relatively staid yuppie crowd with golden oldies and a clubby setting. **The Ghetto** (✉*30 Bhulabhai Desai Rd., Breach Candy* ☎*22/2351–4725*) is a psychedelic-rave bar with a sometimes-grungy clientele, a strange combination of '60s and techno music, and convincingly graffitied walls. It can be fun late in the night. **Hard Rock Cafe** (✉*Bombay Dyeing Mills Compound, opposite Kamala Mills City Studio, Pandurang Budhkar Marg, Worli* ☎*22/2438–2888*), the global chain with the "love all, serve all" motto (sourced from India) has a spacious outlet in central Mumbai that plays '60s, '70s, and '80s. Get your Mumbai T-shirt here; it's open until 1:30 AM. Small but popular, **Hawaiian Shack** (✉*339 16th Rd., opposite Pal's Fish Corner, off Linking Rd., Bandra* ☎*22/2605–8753* ✉*Pipewalla Building, 4th Pasta La., Colaba* ☎*22/2202–0455*) resembles a Goa beach spot and plays retro music. The **Indigo** (✉*4 Mandlik Rd., near Cotton World, Colaba* ☎*22/6636–8980 or 22/6636–8981*) is more famous as a restaurant, but its comfortable, happy bar/lounge area and excellent wines make it a special place to have drinks too.

The **Koyla** (✉*Gulf Hotel, near Radio Club, Arthur Bunder Rd., Colaba* ☎*22/6636–9999*) is a rooftop hangout with hookahs, Arabian music, good breeze, and tasty barbecue bites. No alcohol is served. The stunning **Monza** (✉*Garden Court, Block No. 16, Unit 4, 5, 6, Phoenix Mills, Parel* ☎*22/2495–4856 or 22/2495–2879*) is a fancy spot to have expensive wine and Italian food. **Olive Bar and Restaurant** (✉*Pali Hill Hotel, Pali Hill Park, Bandra* ☎*022/26058228*) between bites of top-notch anti-pasta, risotto, seafood salad and sips of caipiroskas take in the Mumbai social whirl; Olive is a nightspot (candlelit and not open for lunch) where the city's who's who drops in. **Seijo and Soul Dish** (✉*206 Krystal, Waterfield Rd., Bandra* ☎*22/2640–5555*), a popular Asian restaurant, has a grooving bar that on certain days is very club-like. **Sports Bar** (✉*The Bowling Company, Phoenix Mills Parel* ☎*22/2491–4000, 2454–9130, or 2491–4401*) is great spot to watch a cricket or soccer match with a glass of beer. A pool table and punching bag are on hand. At **Sports Bar Express** (✉*Next to Regal Cinema, Shaheed Bhagat Singh Rd., Colaba* ☎*22/6639–6681*), a giant television screen, loud music, bowling, and pool tables next door are the attractions. **Six Degrees** (✉*Leela Kempinski, Sahar* ☎*22/6691–1234*) serves its drinks among palm trees in a beautiful garden environment.

Starters and More (✉*Cambata Building, 1st Fl. East Wing, M.K. Rd., Churchgate* ☎*22/6631–5871*) is a comfy, friendly spot for live music and snacks. It really swings on the weekend. **The Tendulkars** (✉*Next to Cottage Emporium, near Gateway of India, Apollo Bunder* ☎*22/2282–9934*) sports bar is named for India's cricketing legend. Come here to catch some F1 racing, cricket, or soccer with drinks and tasty quick bites. Dinner is served next door.

Visit **Tavern** (✉*Fariyas Hotel, 25 Devshankar V Vyas Marg, off Arthur Bunder Rd., Colaba* ☎*22/2204–2911*) for older dance numbers, a fun crowd, and a large television screen playing music DVDs. **Vie** (✉*102 Juhu Tara Rd., opposite Little Italy, Juhu* ☎*22/2660–2003*) has great food as well as great beats. Opt for the lounge on the beach. **Wink** (✉*Taj President hotel, 90 Cuffe Parade, Colaba* ☎*22/6665–0808*) is one of the more popular bars in south Mumbai. The main draw is its chill house music. **Zenzi** (✉*183 Waterfield Rd., Bandra* ☎*22/6643–0670*) is one of Bandra's edgy night spots. You can dine (great international cuisine), drink, and dance at this comfortable but trendy, happening restobar (restaurant/bar) with an attractive terrace.

CLUBS & DISCOS

Amnesia (✉*Leela Kempinski, Sahar* ☎*22/6691–1234*) is an elegant and posh lounge bar and nightclub. International bands and local acts play night after night at **Blue Frog** (✉ *Mathurudas Mills Compound, opp. Kamala Mills entrance, entrance from Tulsi Pipe Rd., Lower Parel, Mumbai* ☎ *022/4033–2300*), an extremely spacious, trendy nightclub, where the acoustics are top class. International cuisines—nibbly munchy stuff like onion rings, burgers, cheese platters as well as full meals, pasta, fried fish—are served. Entry per head Rs 300. **Club IX** (✉*Dr. Ambedkar Rd., Pali Hill, Khar* ☎*22/2646–5133 or 22/2646–5134*) is laid-back, with a penchant for golden oldies. **Enigma** (✉*J. W. Marriott, Juhu Tara Rd., Juhu* ☎*22/2693–3000*), in the swanky Marriott, is the hottest disco in the burbs. It's popular with rockers of all ages. **Lush** (✉*Phoenix Mills Compound, Parel* ☎*22/6663–3460*) is a small but tony nightclub-pub in the ever-expanding Parel shopping and entertainment complex.

Not Just Jazz by the Bay (✉*143 Marine Dr.Churchgate* ☎*22/2282–0883, 22/2285–1876, or 22/2282–0957*) is one of Mumbai's few jazz venues, with live music several nights a week. Its location by the sea is beautiful. It serves a buffet lunch, and it stays open until 1:30 AM. **Poison** (✉*001B Krystal, 206 Waterfield Rd., Bandra* ☎*22/2642–3006 or 22/2642–3007*) offers a bit of everything, including Bollywood numbers, depending on the day of the week. Weekends are all about dance tunes. **At Polly Esthers** (✉*Gordon House hotel, 5 Battery St., Colaba* ☎*22/2287–1122*), the retro music, large bar counter, and spacious dance floor attract hordes on the weekends. It's a great place to enjoy the oldies. Patterned on a London nightclub, **Prive** (✉*41/44 Minoo Desai Marg, near the Fariyas hotel, Colaba* ☎*22/2202–8700 or 22/2280–5175*) is one of Mumbai's snobbier lounges and a place to be seen. The entry is for members only unless you book a table: reserve in advance. **ProVogue Lounge** (✉*Phoenix Mills Compound, Parel* ☎*22/6662–4535 or 22/2497–2525*) is by day a shop for casual clothing and by night a casual-chic lounge bar with a cultivated scruffy, unpainted look. **Ra** (✉*Phoenix Mills compund, Lower Parel* ☎*022/6661–4343*) is an expensive, tony nightspot to shake a leg to Hindi favorites and the latest hits.

7

SPORTS & THE OUTDOORS

CRICKET

You can buy tickets, which range in price from Rs. 150 to Rs. 10,000, through the **Mumbai Cricket Association** (✉*D. Rd., Churchgate* ☎*22/2281–1795, 22/2281–7879, 22/2281–9910, or 22/2281–2714*). **Wankhede Stadium** (✉*D. Rd., Churchgate*) hosts Mumbai's major domestic and international cricket matches. In season—October through March—there are usually several matches a week.

CLOSE UP

After-Hours Traditional Dance Bars

Mumbai once had a category of rough-and-ready nightspots called dance bars. These were licensed bars that offered "cultural programs" and were frequented by men looking for an opportunity to watch—only watch—fully clad, but enticingly attired, dancing women gyrating to the latest Hindi film numbers. In 2005, after a lot of controversy and debate, Mumbai's moral police, headed by a top-level state minister, were finally successful in banning dance bars and throwing the city's 30,000 to 50,000 dance girls out of their jobs.

Two years later most of these bars have made a comeback in a diluted form. They are now bars with orchestras—the women stand near the orchestra but usually do not dance. These bars look like garishly furnished lounges. Sofas are arranged around an empty dance floor and the hottest Bollywood- and indie-pop music plays. Drinks, quite often made with low-quality liquor, are offered, usually at rather high prices. Tipping the women is the only interaction allowed with them. A visit to an orchestra bar—try Carnival at Worli, Topaz at Grant Road bridge, or Indiana at Tardeo—is eye-opening. It's unwise for women to go at all—women do not hang out at these places—and foreign men should not attempt to find or frequent orchestra bars unless they are chaperoned by a few local men who know the bar. The bars are generally open every night from about 10 PM to dawn.

GOLF

The **Willingdon Sports Club** (✉*K. Khadye Marg, Mahalaxmi* ☎*22/2494–5754*) has an 18-hole golf course. Nonmembers can usually play as "guests" of the secretary for $86 per week for a minimum of one week and a maximum of 12 weeks. Call ahead to make arrangements and see if you can work something out.

HORSE-AND-BUGGY RIDES

For a quick tour of Mumbai's illuminated sights by night, hop in one of the horse-drawn buggies parked at Nariman Point, next to the Hilton Towers, at the northern end of Marine Drive, or at the Gateway of India. Neither the carriages nor the horses are in particularly good shape, let alone elegant, but if you don't require luxury this can be an enjoyable jaunt. A spin from the Gateway of India to Churchgate and back, taking in key sights on the way, takes about an hour and should cost not much more than Rs. 300 (settle the price ahead of time).

HORSE RACING

Mumbai's **Mahalaxmi Race Course** (✉*Near Nehru Planetarium, Mahalaxmi* ☎*22/2307–1401*) is one of the finest courses in Asia. A visit here in season is a social experience—for a few months each year, this green patch in central Mumbai becomes an echo of London's Ascot racecourse in the 1950s, with posh accents, outfits that kill, and plenty of pomp and showiness. The season usually runs from November through April, with races on Thursday and Sunday. Right next door at the Amateur Riding Club you can rent horses for rides. Call

☎22/6600–5204 or 22/6600–5205 one day in advance. Half-hour riding sessions (Rs. 500) are from 6:15 to 7 AM and from 5 to 6:30 PM.

SAILING & WATERSPORTS

Members of any yachting association affiliated with the **Royal Bombay Yacht Club** (✉ *Chhatrapati Shivaji Maharaj Marg, Apollo Bunder400001* ☎ *22/2202–1880* 🌐 *www.royalbombayyachtclub.com*) can charter a boat for local sailing, October to June. The club also offers visiting memberships for a reasonable Rs. 281 per week.

With **Drishti Adventure Sports** (✉ *H2O Water Complex, Marine Drive, next to Chowpatty Beach* ☎ *22/2367–7546 or 22/2367–7584*) you can take a ride in a speedboat along Marine Drive (Rs. 175 for half an hour), a daytime bay cruise (Rs. 170), or a night cruise (Rs. 280). Boats can carry up to six people; small children are not permitted. The service is not open during the monsoon. Drishti also rents jet skis (Rs. 250 for 15 minutes), water skis, and motorboats (Rs. 60 boats, kayaks, row boats). Other options include pedal- and banana boats. A good option is to take a boat out to Knight's Wharf, a bar on a large boat in the ocean. It costs Rs. 150 to get onto the boat (children aren't permitted).

SHOPPING

From crowded street bazaars to exclusive air-conditioned boutiques, Mumbai can keep the enthusiastic shopper riveted for days. Colaba Causeway (technically now called Shahid Bhagat Singh Marg), Flora Fountain, Kemps Corner, and Breach Candy are all trendy shopping areas in South Mumbai; the latter two are chic and pricey. A walk down Colaba Causeway will probably take you past most things you want to buy in India: shoes, clothes, cheap knickknacks, *sasta* (cheap) cotton clothing, and wraps displayed at stalls lining the road, as well as more expensive items found in air-conditioned shops and boutiques on the same road. World Trade Center on Cuffe Parade, at the southern tip of Mumbai, looks discouraging from the outside but houses a cluster of government-run emporiums with fixed-price crafts from Madhya Pradesh, Kashmir, Maharashtra, Uttar Pradesh, and Mysore. Phoenix Mills and Atria Millenium Mall are south Mumbai's largest malls. Both unusually spacious and attractive, they're open daily, and until late. India's most fashionable clothing labels have stores here, and the rest of the shops sell everything from napkins to Rolls-Royces. Both are about 20 minutes from Colaba or Gateway of India area. Phoenix Mills, far larger, also has a far greater range of shops and restaurants.

The arcades in top hotels—those at The Oberoi/Hilton Towers (together called Oberoi Shopping Centre; but some shops are in The Oberoi and some in Hilton Towers) and Taj Mahal (smaller)—offer a little bit of everything for a lot more money than anywhere else, but the merchandise is beautiful and the pace unhurried (and it's climate-controlled). For lower prices and a more vibrant experience, throw yourself into the middle of one of Mumbai's famous bazaars.

Once you've exhausted Mumbai proper, you can venture out to the suburbs, where prices tend to be lower and the malls more numerous. Linking Road in Bandra is a trendy place to shop, and Juhu's main strip, Juhu Tara Road, is lined with trendy new boutiques, shops, art galleries, and restaurants. The enormous Inorbit Mall, close to Juhu and Andheri, is the city's top shopping destination. Note that each neighborhood has a different closing day for shops. In Colaba, up to Worli, shops are closed Sunday; in Worli, up to Bandra, they're closed Monday; and in Bandra, up to the suburbs, they're closed Thursday. Throughout Mumbai, many shops are closed on Sunday. Malls, however, are open on all days of the week. They are especially crowded on the weekend (mall-gazing has become a new Mumbai leisure activity).

Some good and cheap Bombay buys: silver jewelery, handicrafts, handloom cotton and silk clothing and household items, eyeglasses and contact lenses, DVDs, CDs, and books.

BAZAARS & MARKETS

Chor Bazaar (✉*Mutton St. near Kutbi Masjid, off Mohammed Ali Rd., Mandvi*) is a bustling but tiny flea market where you can find exactly what you don't need but have to have—old phonographs, broken nautical instruments, strange toys, dusty chandeliers, furniture, and brass objects ranging from junky knickknacks to valuable antiques and curios. Keep an eye on your purse or wallet and come relaxed—it can be chaotic. **Fashion Street** (✉*Stretch of M. G. Rd. opposite Bombay Gymkhana, Fort*) is a cotton bargain trove in a long row of open-air stalls, with mounds of colorful, cheap, mainly Western clothing for all ages. Come around 11 AM, when the crowds are thinner and the sun has not yet peaked—and bargain. **Zaveri Bazaar** (✉*Sheikh Memon St., a few blocks northwest of Crawford Market, Kalbadevi* ⏲*Mon.–Sat. 11–7*) is the place to go for diamond, gold, and silver *zevar* (jewelry). The tumultuous streets are lined with tiny, decades-old family jewelry businesses. Duck into one and sip a customary cup of tea or coffee while a salesperson shows you the merchandise. Most shops are authentic, but beware of false silver and gold; it's difficult to spot the fakes, so it might be best to buy primarily for appearance and make intrinsic value a secondary consideration.

DEPARTMENT STORES & MALLS

The Courtyard (✉*41/44 Minoo Desai Rd., Colaba*) is a tiny mall of ritzy designer shops that's one block from the Taj Mahal hotel. Indian designers are doing a brisk business these days, and the best address to get a flavor of their work is The Courtyard—silks, cottons, linens, garments rich with hand and machine embroidery and *zari* (gold-embroidered). Other clothes (Indian and Western), handbags, and knickknacks for the home are also sold here.

High Street Phoenix (✉*Phoenix Mills Compound, Senapati Bapat Marg, Parel*) is an ever-expanding shopping, entertainment, and dining area. This complex is an island of prosperity and chic modernity among slums and industry. A number of upscale shops, bars, and restaurants have come up at Phoenix Mills, and because of the almost unlimited space, everything is on a grand scale. Check out the international-looking and posh **Lifestyle** (☎*22/5666–9200*), a four-floor department store that stocks clothing, gifts, and household items. Try **Ritu** (☎*22/5666–9901*) for elegant, hand-embroidered silk, cotton, and chiffon formal wear, chic-casual, and household items.**Big Bazaar** is a warehouse shop selling brooms, pens, potato chips, and many other necessities. **Pantaloons** is a large outlet for casual wear for men, women and children. **Planet M** has all kinds of music. When it's time for a snack or dinner, Bombay Blue, Noodle Bar, Subway, Baskin Robbins, McDonald's, Lush, Natural Ice Cream, and Marroush (selling Middle-Eastern food) all await.

Inorbit Mall (✉*Link Rd., Malad West* ☎*22/5677–7999*), about 25 minutes from Juhu or the airport, is very popular with tourists. This enormous mall and the adjoining giant store Hypercity sells just about everything in its 100 or so shops. Available here is clothing from many major international brands as well as Indian-style garments, household items, purses, footwear and much more. Popular outlets include Shoppers' Stop (clothes), Tanishq and Titan (jewelry and watches), Biba (*kurtis,* or short tunics), Hidesign (leather goods), Ritu Kumar (exquisite embroidered Indian garments), Lifestyle, Planet M (music), Crossword (books), Hakoba (embroidered clothing), Fabindia, and plenty of designer boutiques. There are lots of good eateries, including the popular Gujarati thali spot Rajdhani, two dosa restaurants, Only Parathas, and a Moti Mahal for tandoori and Punjabi food.

Fabindia (✉*Jeroo Building, 137 M.G. Rd., Kala Ghoda, Fort* ☎*22/2262–6539* ⏲*Daily 10–7:45* ✉*F-2, First Floor, Inorbit Mall, Link Rd., Malad* ☎*22/5641–9989* ⏲*Daily 11–8:30* ✉*Navroze Apartments, Pali Hill, near HDFC bank, Bandra* ☎*22/2605–7780*) showcases the best of Indian fabrics—*khadis* (homespun cotton), muslin, vegetable-dyed, silks, and embroidered materials. You can find women's clothing—saris, *kurtas* (collarless or band-collar tunics), skirts, trousers, blouses, and kurtis—as well as men's shirts and kurtas, children's clothes, tablecloths, curtains, cushion covers, and napkins fashioned from these beautiful materials, some of which is also available by the meter. Also available are furniture. The Fort Fab India is the address to head to—it's in a high-ceilinged, period building, and there's a Moshe snack bar on the second floor that serves fresh fruit juices, yogurt drinks, excellent sandwiches, and pastries.

Shopper's Stop (✉*S. V. Rd., Andheri* ☎*22/2624–0451 or 22/2624–0453* ✉*Inorbit Mall, Link Rd., Malad West* ☎*22/5643–4700* ✉*Dynamix Mall, near Chandan Cinema, JVPD Scheme, Juhu* ☎*22/2625–6270* ✉*Suburbia Mall, Linking Rd., Bandra* ☎*22/2643–5454*) is a large and popular department store. It's a good place to buy trendy but reasonably priced Western clothes, especially men's clothing, and fine *salwar-kurta* (a loose long tunic with flowing pants) as well as kurtis. Across the road from the Andheri branch is Croma, a good stop for electronics, which are sometimes cheaper in India.

Westside (✉*158 M.G. Rd., Kala Ghoda, Fort* ☎*22/5636–0495* ⏲*Daily 10:30–8:30* ✉*39 Hughes Rd., Gwalior Tank* ☎*22/2384–1730* ✉*Infiniti, Raheja Classic Complex, Oshiwara Andheri Link Rd., Andheri* ☎*22/6702–1345*) stocks a decent range of Western wear, as well as interesting kurta sets and colourful kurtis for women. The menswear section includes a variety of office and casual cotton shirts. You'll also find reasonably priced household items such as bed linens, pottery, Indian handicrafts, and tablecloths. The Taj-run snack makes for a good break.

ART & ANTIQUES

The **Jehangir Art Gallery** (✉*Kala Ghoda, Fort* ☎*22/2284–3989*) has at least three art shows every week on the main floor or at the **Gallery Chemould** (☎*22/2283–3640*) or even on the pavement racks outside in fair weather. Prices vary vastly. The whole area adjoining Jehangir Art Gallery has become an art district, and exhibitions can be happening at adjoining buildings, too. Inquire at the gallery. **Natesans Antiquarts Ltd.** (✉*Basement of Jehangir Art Gallery, Fort* ☎*22/2285–2700* ✉*Taj Mahal Palace & Tower, Apollo Bunder* ☎*22/2202–4165*), which has branches in many Indian cities, sells magnificent but expensive curios, subcontinental antiquities, wood carvings, sculptures, and paintings as well as a few smaller items at better prices. **Phillips Antiques** (✉*Madam Cama Rd., opposite Regal Cinema, Fort* ☎*22/2202–0564*), begun in 1860, has the best choice of old prints, engravings, and maps in Mumbai. Phillips also sells many possessions left behind by the British—Staffordshire and East India Company china, old jewelry, crystal, lacquerware, and sterling silver. Salespeople here take a one-hour lunch break. The **Raj Company** (✉*Volga House, opposite the Turf Club, Khare Marg, near Mahalaxmi suburban railway station, Mahalaxmi* ☎*22/2494–1971*) sells colonial furniture and faithful reproductions.

BOOKS

Most large hotels have small bookshops, but Mumbai's best selection is at **Crossword** (✉*Ground Floor, Mohammed Bhai Mansion, Kemps Corner (below the flyover), N. S. P. Marg, Kemps Corner* ☎*22/2384–2001 or 22/2384–2002* ✉*Inorbit Mall, Link Rd. Malad* ☎*22/6645–0950* ✉*Dynamix Mall, Sant Dhyaneshwar Marg, next to Chandan Cinema, Juhu* ☎*22/2625–6316*), one of the largest book chains in India. The spacious Kemps Corner branch is a comfortable place to browse and has a branch of Moshe's serving sandwiches, cakes, and long cool drinks as well as steaming hot ones.

Danai (✉*Jain Arcade bldg., 14 Khar Danda Rd., Khar* ☎*22/2648–7123*), north of the commercial center between Bandra and Santa Cruz, is the largest suburban bookstore. It also sells CDs and DVDs. **Granth** (✉*30/A HM House, Juhu Tara Rd., Santa Cruz* ☎*22/2660–9327*) is a two-story bookshop, selling music and movies too, that offers a good browse. **Landmark** (✉*Infiniti Mall, New Link Rd., Oshiwara, Lokhandwala, Andheri* ☎*22/2639 6010 or 22/26396011*) has a superb collection that makes it ideal for bookworms.

Nalanda (✉ *Taj Mahal Palace & Tower, Apollo Bunder* ☎ *22/2202-2514*), open until midnight, has plenty of books on India, including travel guides and fiction, and the latest foreign newspapers and magazines. **Oxford Bookstore** (✉ *Apeejay House, 3 Dinsha Vachcha Rd., Churchgate* ☎ *22/5636-4477*) is a posh bookstore with books on India, magazines, children's books, and a modest café. The **Strand Book Stall** (✉ *Dhannur Sir P.M. Rd., Fort* ☎ *22/2266-1994 or 22/2266-1719*) has good discounts and will also inexpensively ship books home for you. The sidewalk book market on **M.G. Road,** opposite Flora Fountain, is a great source for secondhand books. You can score some rare finds here—bargain.

CARPETS

The government-run **Central Cottage Industries Emporium** (✉ *Narang House, 34 Shivaji Marg, 1 block north of Taj Mahal hotel, Colaba* ☎ *22/2202-6564 or 22/2202-7537*) stocks an excellent selection of traditional Kashmiri carpets at fixed, reliable prices. **CIE** (✉ *Electric House, Colaba* ☎ *22/2281-8802*) has a large selection of high-quality Indian crafts, from carpets to bronze art pieces. Prices are much steeper here than at the Central Cottage Industries Emporium with which this chain may wish to be confused. **Coir Board** (✉ *5 Stadium House, Veer Nariman Rd., Churchgate* ☎ *22/2282-1575* ⊙ *Mon.–Sat., except 2nd and 4th Sat. of each month*) has cheap jute and *coir* (coconut husk) matting. On **Colaba Causeway** between Regal Cinema and Cusrow Baug, and on lanes leading off the causeway, you'll find lots of carpet stores. You may find a genuine, well-priced carpet in any of these shops, but you're on your own vis-à-vis unscrupulous shopkeepers. A carpet's mix of silk, wool, and cotton determines its price; visit several shops, including the government emporiums, to get a sense of the market before cutting a deal in an independent shop. There are several Kashmiri-run carpet shops in the **Oberoi Shopping Centre** (✉ *Nariman Point*), where prices may be even higher than normal. A small, fixed-price outlet for the well-known brand **Shyam Ahuja** (✉ *Temptation 78, India House [stockist], under the flyover, Kemps Corner* ☎ *22/2386-7372* ✉ *C Wing, Gazdar Apartments, Juhu Tara Rd., Juhu* ☎ *22/2615-1749*) has cotton dhurries and wool carpets. **Shyam Ahuja's main showroom** (✉ *Opposite Murphy Radio, Hajuri Rd., off Eastern Express Hwy., Thane* ☎ *22/2582-2155 or 22/5624-6990*) for carpets is one hour from central Mumbai.

CHILDREN'S CLOTHING & TOYS

Tailoring children's clothes can be fun in India, given the variety of cloth available. For the best bargains in cheap cotton clothing head to Fashion Street *(⇨ Bazaars & Markets, above)*. **Bombay Store** (✉ *Sir Pherozeshah Mehta Rd., Fort* ☎ *22/2288-5048*) has cottons for children. The **Central Cottage Industries Emporium** (✉ *Narang House, 34 Shivaji Marg, 1 block north of Taj Mahal hotel, Colaba* ☎ *22/2202-6564 or 22/2202-7537*) has a small but imaginative assortment of Indian costumes for kids, and traditional Indian toys. Mirror-work elephants, Indian dolls, wood and cane doll furniture, tiny brass tea sets, stuffed leather animals, and puppets can all be found on the second floor, as can kurtas and long skirt ensembles in cotton and silk. **Colaba Causeway** is lined with pavement stalls selling various children's trinkets—leather animals, small drums, purses, beads, and peacock-feather fans—as well as Indian clothing. **Fabindia** (✉ *Jeroo Building, 137 M. G. Rd.Kala Ghoda* ☎ *22/2262–6539* ⏲ *Daily 10–7:45* ✉ *F-2, First Floor, Inorbit Mall, Link Rd., Malad* ☎ *22/5641–9989* ⏲ *Daily 11–8:30* ✉ *Navroze Apartments, Pali Hill, near HDFC bank, Bandra* ☎ *22/2605–7780*) sells attractive cotton, and some silk, clothing for children. Several shops in the **Hilton Towers section of the Oberoi Shopping Centre** (✉ *Nariman Point*) sell Indian children's clothes, including cool cotton dresses, and wooden dolls.

CLOTHING

Mumbai is an excellent place to shop for cotton, silk, rayon, and linen clothing. More and more designer boutiques sell expensive, well-tailored items by upcoming or top Indian designers. A clutch of boutiques is at Kemps Corner (Be and Melange), Breach Candy, Colaba, Phoenix Mills (in Parel), Bandra, and Juhu. But the best place to buy bargain cotton clothes is undoubtedly Fashion Street, across from the Bombay Gymkhana *(⇨ Bazaars & Markets, above)*. **Anokhi** (✉ *Rasik Niwas, Metro Motors Lane, Dr. A. R. Rangnekar Marg, Off Hughes Rd., Hughes Rd.* ☎ *22/2368–5761 or 22/2368–5308* ✉ *Govind Dham, 210 Waterfield Rd., Hughes Road.* ☎ *22/2640–8261 or 22/2640–8263*) has colorful clothes with block-print designs from Rajasthan. The small **Barefoot** (✉ *1st Floor, Anand Villa, Pali Mala Rd., Bandra* ☎ *22/2648–0423 or 22/2648–0424*) boutique has a tasteful selection of women's casual clothing and kurtis as well as shoes and accessories at decent prices. There are also some men's clothes and household items.

The large, attractive, and friendly **Bombay Store** (✉ *Sir Pherozeshah Mehta Rd., Fort* ☎ *22/2288–5048 or 22/2288–5049*) has men's shirts, kurtas, ties, women's *salwar-kameez* (a loose-fitting tunic over loose pants tapered at the ankle), blouses, skirts, shawls, saris, some silk by the meter, and cotton clothes for children. **Charagh Din** (✉ *64 Wodehouse Rd., Colaba* ☎ *22/2218–1375*) is one of the best-known Indian names for top-quality, pure-silk shirts for men in a tremendous variety of styles and patterns. **Christina** (✉ *The Oberoi hotel section of Oberoi Shopping Centre), Nariman Point* ☎ *22/2282–5069*) is a tiny, classy boutique with exquisite silk blouses and shirts, scarves, ties, *dupattas* (long, thin scarves for draping), and silk-edge purses and wallets. **Cotton World** (✉ *Ram Nimi bldg., Mandlik Rd., Colaba* ☎ *22/2285–0060 or 22/2283–3294* ✉ *Vipul Apartments, near Podar High School, Tagore Rd., [north of Bandra, and southwest of Sahar International Airport], Santa Cruz* ☎ *22/2649–6693 or 22/2605–1602*) is small but has some excellent Western cotton items at reasonable prices. The pricey **Ensemble** (✉ *Great Western Bldg., 130/132 Shahid Bhagat Singh Marg, Kala Ghoda, Fort* ☎ *22/2284–3227 or 22/2287–2882*) is not far from the Taj Mahal hotel. It has exclusive men's and women's Indian and Western fashions, and lovely costume jewelry, all by high-profile Indian designers. Ask to see the rare Banarasi silk saris, in rich colors woven with real gold and silver thread. **Fab India** (✉ *10 Sakar, opposite Jehan-*

CLOSE UP

Custom Tailors & Fine Fabrics

Mumbai's bazaars boom with some of the richest and widest varieties of cloth. The Mangaldas Cloth Market has enough bales of material to carpet all of South Mumbai.

Tailoring in Mumbai is not a particularly difficult proposition. A number of Mumbai tailors can turn splendid fabric into custom-made clothing—Indian or Western—in a matter of hours for both ladies and gents. The tailors are often armed with the latest catalogs and will faithfully copy a design from a picture. Tailors are fast and quite competent. If you have a blouse or shirt or trousers to give in as a sample they generally get it down pat. Make sure you personally shrink cotton material and its lining before you give it in for stitching (rinse for a few minutes and drip dry; colored cottons need to be rinsed by themselves for just a few seconds to prevent too much bleeding). Fix a rate beforehand and give an earlier deadline to allow for refittings if necessary. If the material needs a lining, buy it yourself.

Aamrapali Collections (⊠ *Shop 38, Ruki Mahal, near Standard Auto Petrol Pump, Colaba* ☎ *22/2288–5060*) are very prompt and efficient. They largely do Indian clothes, *salwar-kameez* (tunic and pants) outfits, and sari blouses, but if you give them a sample to copy they can make you a Western-style outfit, too. **Arjan Matching Centre** (⊠ *Ruki Mahal, near Standard Auto Petrol Pump, opposite Hanuman Mandir, Colaba* ☎ *22/2284–1516 or 22/2288–5767*) has brocade and plain silk, and is the best place to find material for linings. A reliable tailor (Aamrapalli) is next door at Shop 38. **Burlingtons** (⊠ *Taj Mahal Palace & Tower, Apollo Bunder* ☎ *22/2202–5593*) is a classy boutique. As such, prices are higher than some other places, but you'll get to choose from an enormous range of silk and embroidered material. **Hakoba Fabrics** (⊠ *Cusrow Baug, Shahid Bhagat Singh Rd., Colaba* ☎ *No phone*) is a tiny shop that offers a fine selection of *hakoba* material: pastel and deep-colored cottons, machine-embroidered with fine white thread designs or *selfed* (same color embroidery as the material), sold by the meter. Amrapalli Tailors is a few doors away. **Narisons Khubsons** (⊠ *49 Colaba Causeway, opposite Colaba police station* ☎ *22/2202–0614*) carries fine cotton and silk and can make excellent shirts, trousers, or women's outfits in one day if need be. They also sell ready-made women's clothing. There are two shops named Khubsons, back to back; make sure you have the right one (the one closer to Regal Cinema). **Raymond** (⊠ *Bhulabhai Desai Rd., opposite Breach Candy Hospital and Research Centre* ☎ *22/2368–2644*) is an outlet for Raymond Mills, which makes some of India's finest men's suits. They can tailor a first-rate suit for about Rs. 3,500 in about a week. Call ahead to ask about delivery time; during the wedding season (winter) they can get very busy. **Roop Milan** (⊠ *Maharshi Karve Rd., near Marine Lines Station* ☎ *22/2200–1257 or 22/2200–5951*) is primarily a sari shop, but they also sell a huge variety of fine silks at their upstairs counter.

gir Nursing Home, Sasson Rd. ☎*20/2612–4820*) is good for cotton clothing tailored from vegetable-dye prints—skirts, blouses, and kurtas for men and women. **Khazir Sons** (✉*The Oberoi section of the Oberoi Shopping Centre, Nariman Point* ☎*22/2204–9125*) is a great place to shop for pashminas of all hues and patterns. Bargain. The Mumbai branch of the famous Chennai store **Nalli** (✉*Trimurti Apartments, Bhulabhai Desai Rd., Breach Candy* ☎*22/2496–5577 or 22/2496–5599*) has a fair selection of classic silk saris. Have a look at the authentic gold-embroidered saris from Kanchipuram, in Tamil Nadu, as well as the Bangalore saris and the uncut silk sold by the meter. **OMO** (✉*204 Sagar Fortune, Waterfield Rd., Bandra* ☎*22/5698–1804*) has attractive women's clothing and earrings. **Premsons** (✉*Premsons House+, Breach Candy* ☎*22/2363–6600*) has tops, shirts, T-shirts, kurtis, and kurtas, but also perfumes, shampoo, accessories, household items, and cloth by the meter.

Ravissant (✉*131 August Kranti Marg, Kemps Corner* ☎*22/2368–4934*) was India's first haute-couture salon; it sells its own women's and men's clothing in exquisite patterns and fabrics, from rich silks to feather-light moiré. The branch in the Taj Mahal Palace & Tower (☎22/2281–5227) also sells unique silver housewares and furnishings. A few shops in the **Taj Mahal Palace & Tower** (✉*Apollo Bunder*) sell quality silks; try Burlington or the Indian Textiles Company. **Vama** (✉*72 Peddar Rd.* ☎*22/2387–1450*) looks like just another Benetton or Lacoste outlet, but it also has gorgeous, high-fashion Indian womenswear and menswear, and the nearly sacred Paithani saris, made from hand-woven silk with real gold-and-silver thread.

FRAMING

D. Kumar and Co (✉*79 Nagindas Master Rd., Fort* ☎*22/2265–4207*) can frame items cheaply, quickly, and attractively. Another framing option is **Picturesque** (✉*The Oberoi section of Oberoi Shopping Centre, Nariman Point* ☎*22/2283–5549*).

HANDICRAFTS & HOUSEHOLD FURNISHINGS

The **Central Cottage Industries Emporium** (✉*Narang House, 34 Shivaji Marg, 1 block north of Taj Mahal hotel, Colaba* ☎*22/2202–6564 or 22/2202–7537*) is packed with textiles, carvings, and myriad other traditional Indian handicrafts from all over the country. It's a wonderful place to buy souvenirs.

A number of stores that sell clothing *(⇨ Clothing)* also have good-looking handicrafts and furnishings on hand. Anokhi sells colorful tablecloths, cushion covers, and other items decorated with attractive block-print designs from Rajasthan. Bombay Store's classy collection of popular Indian handicrafts include metal work, sandalwood, china, marble, carpets, linens, and lamps. Prices are a tad higher here than at the government emporiums, but the store is enticingly laid out. At Fabindia, you can get brightly colored print tablecloths and linen.

Atmosphere (✉*Vaswani House, 7 Best Marg, Colaba* ☎*22/2283–1877 or 22/2283–1936*) has exotic home furnishings and fabrics for the home that are sold by the meter. There's lots of expensive silk, and they'll organize tailoring for you. **Colaba Causeway** sells a load of cheap trinkets, but it's possible to find some unusual items as well—brass items, beaded purses, wood handicrafts. **Contemporary Arts and Crafts** (✉ *19 Nepean Sea Rd., opposite Baskin-Robbins, Malabar Hill* ☎ *22/2363–1979*) has a small but representative selection of Indian handicrafts at reasonable prices.

Dhoop (✉ *101 Khar Sheetal Apartments, Dr. Ambedkar Road, Union Park, Khar* ☎ *22/2649–8646 or 22/2649–8647*) has a superb, unusual collection of handicrafts that includes upside-down incense holders and palm-leaf lampshades. It's worth traveling 45 minutes or so from Juhu or south Mumbai to buy gifts here. Maspar (✉ *Shop No. 2 and 3, ground fl., Sunny House, Mandlik Rd.* ☎ *22/2287–5619*) carries cushion covers, bed linen, tablecloths, and fabrics by the meters in excellent weaves, colors, and designs. **Mrignaynee** (✉ *World Trade Center, Cuffe Parade, Colaba* ☎ *22/2218–2114*) sells statues and clothing from the state of Madhya Pradesh. If you won't be traveling farther south, peruse regal Mysore silks at **Mysore Sales International** (✉ *World Trade Center, Cuffe Parade, Colaba* ☎ *22/2218–1658 or 22/2218–4952*).

Browse Maharashtra's own crafts and an outstanding collection of statues, sculptures, and idols at **Trimourti** (✉ *World Trade Center, Cuffe Parade, Colaba* ☎ *22/2218–6283*). The **World Trade Center** (✉ *Cuffe Parade, Colaba* ☎ *22/2218–9191*) gathers government-run handicrafts emporiums and boutiques from most of India's states under one air-conditioned roof. Fixed prices let you give your haggling skills a rest. **Tresorie** (✉ *60A Linking Rd., Santa Cruz* ☎ *22/661–2041 or 22/661–2042*) sells expensive, tasteful knickknacks for the home. **Yamini** (✉ *President House, Wodehouse Rd., Colaba* ☎ *22/2218–4143 or 22/2218–4145*) sells colorful cotton furnishings, cushion covers, and fabrics by the meter for the home.

INCENSE & PERFUMES

Ajmal (✉ *4/13 Kamal Mansion, Arthur Bunder Rd., Colaba* ☎ *22/2285–6976*) has a wonderful selection of rare Indian and French perfumes stored in huge decanters. It also stocks *agar* wood, a rare incense base, 1,000 grams of which costs as much as a night at the Taj Mahal hotel. Sandalwood oil is also another fragrance stocked by this shop.

JEWELRY

Exotic pieces of gold, platinum, rhodium, and diamond jewelry are often cheaper than you'd believe, and the range and workmanship is excellent here. Jewelers are often willing to create something for you in the space of a two weeks or less. India has some rare silver jewelry, too. When you're buying jewelry it's important to go to the right shop, or you can easily get duped.

Art Karat (✉ *Courtyard, 41/44 Minoo Desai Marg, Colaba* ☎ *22/6638–5474* ✉ *Shop 5, Fiona bldg., 176 Juhu Tara Rd., Juhu* ☎ *22/2660–2051*) stocks very attractive gold-plated jewelry with traditional Indian designs and stones. **Mangal Palace** (✉ *Colaba Market, Colaba* ☎ *22/2283–4333 or 22/2204–8928*) carries wonderful silver jewelry from all over India. Bargain. **Tanishq** (✉ *Brabourne Stadium,*

CLOSE UP

Street Food Favorites

Here's a list of some of Mumbai's street-food classics:

Bhel puri: Puffed rice tossed up with cubes of boiled potatoes, slices of tomatoes, peanuts, tamarind sauce, chopped onion, and *sev* (a savory, deep-fried treat made of chick pea flour).

Dahi puri: Tiny, flat, white-flour *puris* (deep-fried bread) layered with boiled potatoes, three types of chutney made from tamarind, dates, and cilantro, plus mung-bean sprouts and topped with curd and chopped cilantro leaves.

Sev puri: Tiny white-flour flat deep-fried puris or crackers layered with boiled potatoes, three types of chutney made from tamarind, dates, and cilantro.

Pani puri: Tiny, puffed white-flour, deep-fried globular puris, also known as *golgappas*, are cracked and filled with date water, tamarind sauce, mung-bean sprouts, and potatoes.

Ragda pattice: Spiced and mashed potatoes shaped into cutlets and fried on a griddle. These are served with hot chickpea curry and a few sauces.

Dahi bada: Large flat dumplings of white lentils, deep-fried to make *badas*, which are then dipped in water to soak out the oil. Badas are broken into pieces and served spiced with a variety of masala powders, tamarind sauce, cilantro chutney, and yogurt.

Pav bhaji: Potatoes are mashed and fried on a hot griddle for an hour with peas, tomatoes, and butter—until you have a juicy, spicy, potato mash. This is served with sliced onions, lemons, and butter-fried buns called *pavs*.

Wada pav: A cutlet—made from mashed potatoes, spice, cilantro, ginger, coated in chickpea flour and deep fried—is stuffed into a pav lined with hot garlic and red-chilli chutney.

Baida roti: White-flour dough is tossed by hand into thin sheets. Minced meat mixed with beaten egg is wrapped up into these sheets until you have a square, layered pancake that's fried on a hot griddle with oil.

Boti roll: Spicy pieces of grilled lamb kebab, chutney, and sliced onions are rolled into a *roomali* roti (a thin, hand-tossed and roasted white-flour pita).

WHERE IS IT SERVED?

The Canteena Juice Center on Shahid Bhagat Singh Road, next to Delhi Durbar and Titan Watch in Colaba, has excellent fresh juices. Their strawberry milk shakes are wonderful.

Bade Miya, next to Gokul Bar on Tullock Road, off Shahid Bhagat Singh Road (enter the lane next to Leopold's and take a left) is an open-air stall that has been supplying hungry Bombayites kebabs and *baida* (white flour) rotis since mid-century.

Delhi Darbar on Shahid Bhagat Singh Road (Colaba Causeway), five minutes from Regal Cinema, or Jafferbhai's Delhi Darbar near Metro Cinema (Shop 94, Big Three Building, opposite Metro Gol Masjid, First Marine Street, ☎22/2208–4613) are good addresses to sample first-class biryani. There is seating at both these outlets, or else pack up some takeaway.

Head to Kailash Parbat or Swati Snacks to sample bhel puris and sev puris. Also visit Shiv Shankar Tiwari's Dahi Puri stall on B. Road (aka Karmveer Pandit Shobhnath Mishra Marg) off Marine Drive, next to the InterContinental hotel.

Veer Nariman Rd., Churchgate ☎*22/2282–1621, 22/2282–6043, or 22/2283–8801*), run by the Tatas, a venerable and enormous Indian conglomerate whose founder built the Taj Mahal hotel, is a reliable place to buy gold jewelry. The prices, however, are a little higher here than elsewhere. In business since 1865, the **Tribhovandas Bhimji Zaveri** (✉*241 43 Zaveri Bazaar, Kalbadevi* ☎*22/2342–5001*) is said to be the largest jewelry showroom in India, with five floors of gorgeous 18-, 22-, and 24-karat gold, diamonds, and silver jewelry. The most cost-effective place to buy jewelry is from a smaller outfit, such as Naran-das and Sons, Zaveri Naran Das, or Ram Kewalram Popley, all on **Sheikh Memon Street** (which begins at Crawford Market and runs north-west through Zaveri Bazaar) in the Kalbadevi neighborhood. Insist on knowing how many karats you're buying and whether or not the store will stand by the piece's purity. For silver jewelry, try the **Bombay Store** (✉*Sir Pherozeshah Mehta Rd., Fort* ☎*22/2288–5048 to 49*). If you're a bargain-hunter or you're looking for more unusual silver jewelry, head for the heart of **Colaba Bazaar** (✉*Colaba*), a little south of the Taj Mahal hotel, where a series of tiny jewelry shops sells rings, earrings, necklaces, and more. Mangal Palace, in the heart of the bazaar, has an excellent selection. Haggling is a must here—try to knock off 10%, if not more. If you prefer calm, air-conditioned excursions and don't mind higher prices, look for silver jewelry in the lower-level arcade at **Oberoi Shopping Centre** (✉*Nariman Point*).

7

LEATHER & SHOES

Brave bargain-hunters should take an adventurous trip to **Daboo Street** (✉*Off Mohammed Ali Rd., a 5-minute walk south from Chor Bazaar, Kalbadevi*) for leather goods. The posh shopping arcade at **Oberoi Shopping Centre** (✉*Nariman Point*) includes leather and shoe shops with stylish goods priced lower (if expensive for India) than they would be in the West. Worth seeking out are the bags and wallets sold at the Hide-sign shop there. Wander down **Colaba Causeway,** from Regal Cinema (opposite the Prince of Wales museum) and you'll find leather items, money pouches, sturdy Indian-style Kolhapuri *chappals* (sandals), and other footwear.

MUSIC & MUSICAL INSTRUMENTS

If you want to take home some Indian recordings, especially classical music, head for **Rhythm House** (✉*40 K. Dubash Marg, Rampart Row, Kala Ghoda, Fort* ☎*22/2285–3963*). Along with pop, jazz, and everything else, the store has an excellent selection of *pacca gana* (classical vocal music), Indo-Western fusion music, Hindi film music, and Indian instrumental music, plus English and Hindi DVDs and VCDs (video compact discs).

For Indian musical instruments try **Bhargava Musical Enterprise** (✉*156 Khetwadi, Vallabhai Patel Rd., near Opera House, Prarthana Samaj*), a tiny, hard-to-find shop selling tablas (hand drums), harmoniums (a Western instrument with 42 black and white keys that has been adapted for Indian music), sitars (long-necked Indian lutes), and *tanpuras* (similar to sitars, but fretless). **Swami Music City** (✉*Sayani Rd., opposite Ravindra Natya Mandir, near Siddhi Vinayak Temple, Prab-*

hadevi ☎*22/2430–6024*) stocks traditional Indian instruments. The area is a few kilometers north of Haji Ali, in the suburbs

EYEGLASSES

Buying eyeglasses frames and having its lenses made does not seem like ideal holiday shopping. But in Mumbai making a pair of eyeglasses is very economical and quick. Try the upmaket **Gangar Opticians** (✉*62 Chinoy Mansions, Warden Rd., Kemps Corner* ☎*22/2361–0034 or 22/2361–0035*), which offers a wide selection of designer brand frames. **Ganko Optics** (✉*19 Tulsiani Chambers, ground fl., Nariman Point* ☎*22/2283–2335 or 22/2282–4692*) is a very old and trustworthy family-run optician with good frame choices. Another long-standing and reliable name in the business is **Lawrence and Mayo** (✉*8-B, Basera Co-Operative Housing Society Ltd., Lokhandwala Complex, Andheri West* ☎*22/2631–3376* ✉*Lawrence & Mayo House, 274 Dr. D.N. Rd., Fort* ☎*22/ 2207–6049 or 22/2207–6051*).

A conveniently located, reasonable and very efficient eyeglass outlet is **Lunettes** (✉*Ruki Mahal, near Kailash Parbat ground fl., Colaba* ☎*22/2283–3338*).

MUMBAI ESSENTIALS

To research prices, get advice from other travelers, and book travel arrangements, visit www.fodors.com.

AIR TRAVEL

Mumbai's international airport, Chhatrapati Shivaji International Airport—previously called Sahar International Airport—is 30 km (19 mi) north of the city center in Sahar. The domestic airport is at Santa Cruz, 4 km (2½ mi) away from the international airport. Arrive at the airport at least 75 minutes before takeoff for domestic flights, two to three hours before international flights (some airlines require three hours). ■ **TIP→ Mumbai airports are packed to their gills these days, and there are long queues for scanning luggage and checking in.** However, in recent years a huge effort has been put into renovating both airports (international and domestic), and things are finally looking up. The recently renovated domestic airport is now one of India's finest airports and is of international standard. Both airports have 24-hour business centers available to holders of major credit cards.

Most international flights arrive in the middle of the night. Be prepared: airports in Mumbai, like those in Delhi, Kolkata, or Chennai, may be among the shabbiest you encounter. Because airports typically run at or beyond capacity, many flights arrive at the same time, and luggage belts and trolleys are few. Your luggage may arrive after an interminable wait. ■ **TIP→ Make sure you secure a free baggage trolley first and send the touts (and assorted individuals posing as porters, luggage loaders, personal trolley pushers, hotel/taxi providers or customs clearance aids) packing.** Station yourself close enough to the right belt; check any stacks of luggage lined up against the wall in case your suitcases have come earlier.

CLOSE UP

Two Top Mumbai Getaways

KASHID

Four hours (about 134 km [83 mi]) out of Mumbai is one of the prettier beaches along the Maharashtra coast—Kashid, a shining strip of sand and palms that can give any of Goa's beaches a run for their money. The area is very peaceful and unspoiled, since day-trippers and picnickers prefer to continue on to neighboring Murud. There are two quiet hotels here that are perfect for spending a few days soaking in the sun and tranquility.

Prakruti Hermitage Resort (✉ *Kashid Beach, PO Nandgaon, District Raigad* ☎ *22/2404-2501 in Mumbai*) is set in the hillside across the road from the beach. Its cottages, with colorful roofs, are large, comfortable, and tastefully furnished. They offer a view of the ocean from the hillside. The cottages are designed for groups—two or three couples on vacation together—and the living room area is common. Rooms are around Rs. 3,000, and no credit cards are accepted.

Kashid Beach Resort (✉ *Kashid Beach, Taluka Murud, District Raigad* ☎ *21/4427-8501 or 21/4427-8502*) is at the top of a hill in a grove of coconut palms. KBR, as it's called, is not as upmarket as Prakruti, but it's much more authentic. The main hotel building is a row of identical rooms that extends up the hillside. Each room has its own veranda and a garden patio. Opt for the higher rooms—they have a better view of the sea. You can get some fresh seafood at the restaurant cooked in the local style. Book in advance: the hotel fills up on the weekends. Rooms cost around Rs. 3,000; credit cards are not accepted.

MATHERAN

The main attraction of this tiny town is the fact that it is car-free. Motorized vehicles of any variety are not allowed to enter Matheran: the main forms of transport are horses, hand-pulled rickshaws, and carts. Over the years this hill station has grown from a tiny hamlet to a tourist resort for budget Maharashtrian tourists. Riding horseback on the country paths beyond the town is a pleasant and popular pastime. Matheran is famed for its handmade shoes and stalls and stalls of footwear dot the town. Equally famous is its toy train.

Lords Central (☎ *2148/230-228, 22/2610-6978 or 22/3296-8614 in Mumbai* 🌐 *http://matheranhotels.com*) hasn't changed much in 20 years...thankfully. The late Jimmy Lord, a crusty Parsi gentleman who established this Raj-style hotel, was responsible for Matheran's drive to hang onto its heritage: he was at the forefront of campaigns to keep the hill station free of vehicles. The old-fashioned rooms here have antique furniture, tiled floors, and verandas. Request for a room in the old wing. Rooms cost around Rs. 2,400, and no credit cards are accepted.

The Verandah in the Forest (✉ *Near Charlotte Lake, Barr House, District Raigarh* ☎ *2148/230-296*), an old Parsi holiday bungalow, is surrounded by some six acres of greenery and plenty of solitude. Now a classy hotel run by the professional Neemrana group, the hotel has charm. Sweeping verandas, lounges stuffed with traditional furniture, and spacious bedrooms with heavy beds take you back to the days when British collector Hugh Malet founded this hill station. Rooms start at around Rs. 2,000.

If you have a lot of luggage, legitimate porters accelerate your journey out of the airport terminal. Ask for a porter as soon as you disembark—right at the plane gangway. A group of porters, identifiable by their uniforms, usually hang around the entrance, with wheelchairs. If you book one beforehand (get his name) he will meet you later at the baggage belt after you're done with immigration. Do not negotiate rates beforehand—if he tries to, hire someone else. Pay him between Rs. 100 and Rs. 300 depending on how helpful he has been.

Immediately after you exit the customs hall there are a row of tourist counters for hotels, taxi hire, car hire, tourist information, cell-phone-card counters, and currency exchange booths. If someone is meeting you at the airport, understand that he or she will have no idea when you will emerge from the airport, given the wait at immigration or at the baggage concourse, so don't panic.

CARRIERS Mumbai is served daily or frequently by Air France, Alitalia, Swiss International Airlines, Gulf Air, Lufthansa, Cathay Pacific, Emirates, Singapore Airlines, Air India, British Airways, Delta, and KLM/Northwest. Domestic carriers have multiplied and include Air India, Kingfisher, Go Air, SpiceJet, Simplifly Deccan, IndiGo, JetLite, and Jet Airways. Domestic flying has never been easier. Flights can very easily be booked online even with a foreign credit card.

Airlines & Contacts **Air France/Continental** (☎ *22/2202-5021*). **Air India** (☎ *22/2202-4142 or 22/2836-6767*). **Alitalia** (☎ *22/6663-0800*). **British Airways** (☎ *22/9892-577470*). **Cathay Pacific** (☎ *22/2202-9112*). **Delta** (☎ *22/2283-9712*). **Emirates** (☎ *22/4097-4097*). **Etihad Airways** (☎ *22/6610-7150*). **GoAir** (☎ *92/2322-2111*). **Gulf Air** (☎ *22/2202-1777*). **IndiGo Airlines** (☎ *99/1038-3838*). **Jet Airways** (☎ *22/3989-3333*). **JetLite (formerly Sahara)** (☎ *1800/223-020 or 1800/223-030*). **KLM/Northwest** (☎ *22/1600-114-777*). **Kingfisher Airlines** (☎ *1800/1800-101*). **Lufthansa** (☎ *22/5630-1933*). **Simplifly Deccan** (☎ *22/3900-8888*). **Singapore Airlines** (☎ *22/2202-2747*). **SpiceJet** (☎ *1800/180-3333 or 987-180-3333*). **Swiss International Airlines** (☎ *22/2287-0122*).

AIRPORTS & TRANSFERS

The trip from Chhatrapati Shivaji International Airport downtown to south Mumbai should take about 45 minutes if you arrive before 7:30 AM or after 11 PM (many international flights arrive around midnight). At other times, traffic near the city center can increase your trip as much as 90 minutes. Most hotels provide airport transfers starting at Rs. 900 and going up to Rs. 2,500, and some offer complimentary transfers if you're staying in a suite or on an exclusive floor or if the hotel is close to the airport.

The international airport has a prepaid taxi service. Head to the prepaid-taxi counter outside the baggage-and-customs area to hire a regular cab, either air-conditioned or non-air-conditioned. Your rate is determined by your destination and amount of luggage, and is payable up front; Rs. 500 should get you to the center of town (tips aren't necessary). If you want an air-conditioned taxi and do not spot one, call Group Mobile Cool Cab Service or Meru Cabs or Gold Cabs. Air-conditioned taxi fares are 25% higher than non-air-conditioned cabs—the starting rate is Rs. 16.50, then Rs. 12 for each additional kilometer. A trip to, for example, Colaba from the international airport will set you back Rs. 450 by day and Rs. 500 at night, and from the domestic airport Rs. 50 less.

At the domestic airport, metered taxis are available outside; a policeman notes the taxi's license plates before dispatching you on your way. A metered (not prepaid) taxi from the domestic airport to the downtown/south Mumbai area should cost about Rs. 300 and from the international airport about Rs. 350. This system has its problems, and the cabbies waiting at the domestic airport are often cheats with meters that run double-time. There is now a counter near the exit offering taxis driven by women for women passengers—the service is called Forsche. In any case, do not take a taxi that's outside the queue, or accept the offer of a taxi that's parked somewhere that requires you to walk out of the main airport area.

Airport Information Chhatrapati Shivaji International Airport (☎ *22/2682-9112*). **Forsche Cabs** (☎ *22/2432-4161 or 22/2432-4162*). **Gold Cabs** (☎ *22/3244-3333 or 22/3244-9999*). **Group Mobile Cool Cab Service** (☎ *22/2490-5151 or 22/2490-5152*). **Meru Cabs** (☎ *22/4422-4422*).

Mumbai Gold Cabs (☎ *22/3244-3333*).

Santa Cruz Domestic Airport (☎ *22/2615-6500*). **Taxi stand, international airport** (☎ *22/2682-9922 for booking regular taxis*).

7

BUS TRAVEL

The transport department of the India Tourism Development Corporation and the MTDC can organize, quite painlessly, bus tickets on reliable coaches to a variety of destinations, including Nasik, Aurangabad, and Pune, nearby. The Maharasthra State Road Transportation Corporation's Asiad (the best service) Raj National Express Volvo (can be booked online) and Metrolink Volvo buses, which depart from the Asiad bus stand, at the circle outside Dadar Train Terminus (better known as Dadar TT) in central Mumbai, offer the best service between Mumbai and Pune. Non-Volvo luxury coaches depart every 15 minutes (Volvo buses are usually by the hour); tickets can be purchased on the spot and you can hop right on.

Bus Information Asiad (✉ *Opposite Dadar post office, near Sharda Talkie, Dadar East* ☎ *22/2413-6835*). **Metrolink** (✉ *Next to Pritam Hotel, Dadar East* ☎ *22/2418-1273*).

Raj National Express (✉ *Aaram Hotel, Kalanagar, Near Chetna College, Bandra East* ☎ *22/2642—3373 or 22/26423374* 🌐 *www.rajnationalexpress.in/contact.htm*).

CARS & DRIVERS

In certain areas, such as bazaars, you really have to walk for the full experience. Aside from these, having a car at your disposal is the most convenient way to sightsee, as you can zip (or crawl, depending on the time of day) around town without the repeated hassle of hailing taxis and haggling over fares. To arrange a hired car, inquire at your hotel's travel desk or contact a travel agency. (You'll probably pay much more if you book through your hotel.) You'll get lower rates from private agents like Adarsh or Travel House: Rs. 800 to Rs. 1,000 for a full day (8 hours, or 80 km [50 mi]) in a car (Uno or Indica; small cars) with air-conditioning, and Rs. 1,500 or more for an air-conditioned sedan car like a Maruti Esteem. Rates go up for Toyotas, Mercedes, and other luxury cars.

Contacts Adarsh Rent a Car (✉ *Asmita Mogra Co-op. Soc., Bldg. No. 3, Shop No. 3, Jijamata Marg, Andheri East* ☎ *22/2837–7294 or 22/3096–9675*). **Euro Cars** (✉ *261 S. V. Rd., Bandra West* ☎ *022/2655–2424*). **Travel House** (✉ *Sterling Centre Kurla Rd., Andheri East* ☎ *22/6694–9753, 22/6694–9755*).

CAR TRAVEL

Fairly good roads connect Mumbai to most major cities and tourist areas. Hiring a car and driver gives you a chance to watch the often beautiful surroundings whiz by, but it can also be loud, hair-raising, and less than time-efficient. Drivers honk at anything, including birds, and many two-way "highways" are really one-lane roads with a little extra space for an oncoming car to swerve around you, and are flanked by steep ridges so the water can drain off the road during monsoon. So if you have the time and the nerves for a road trip, you'll experience what many people miss when they fly.

Some distances from Mumbai: Pune, 172 km (107 mi); Panaji (Goa), 597 km (371 mi); Ahmedabad, 545 km (339 mi); Hyderabad, 711 km (442 mi). Mumbai is 1,033 km (642 mi) northwest of Bangalore, 432 km (268 mi) northwest of Chennai, and 1,408 km (875 mi) southwest of Delhi.

CONSULATES

The U.S. Consulate is open weekdays 8:30–1 and 2–5 and the staff is on duty 24 hours in case of emergencies.

United States U.S. Consulate (✉ *Lincoln House, 78 Bhulabhai Desai Rd., Warden Rd., Breach Candy* ☎ *22/2363–3611*).

EMERGENCIES

Most hotels have house physicians and dentists on call, and pharmacies that are open daily until about 9 PM. The chemist at Nanavati Hospital and Royal Chemists are both open 24 hours. Your consulate can also give you the name of a reputable doctor or dentist. Otherwise, try the emergency room at Breach Candy Hospital and Research Center or Jaslok Hospital. Mumbai emergency services can't respond to an emergency as quickly as these services do in parts of the world with better roads and more manageable traffic.

Emergency Services Fire (☎ *101*). **Ambulance** (☎ *102, 105 for heart attacks only*). **Police** (☎ *100*).

Medical Care Breach Candy Hospital and Research Center (✉ *Bhulabhai Desai Rd., Breach Candy* ☎ *22/2367–1888, 22/2367–2888*). **Jaslok Hospital** (✉ *Dr. G. Deshmukh Marg, near Haji Ali, Peddar Rd.* ☎ *22/6657–3333*). **Lilavati Hospital** (✉ *Bandra Reclamation* ☎ *22/2642–1111*).

24-Hour Pharmacies **Bombay 24 Hour Chemist** (✉ *New Marine Lines, Dhobi Talao* ☎ *22/2206–7676*). **Dava Bazaar** (✉ *32, Kakad Arcade, opposite Bombay Hospital, New Marine Lines, Dhobi Talao* ☎ *22/6665–9079 or 22/6665–9557*). **Nanavati Hospital 24 Hour Chemist** (✉ *Swami Vivekanand (S.V.) Rd., Vile Parle, Juhu* ☎ *22/2618–2255*). **Royal Chemists** (✉ *Acharya Dhonde Marg, opposite Wadia Hospital, Vishwas Niwas Bldg. 8, Shop 3, Parel* ☎ *22/2411–5028*).

MONEY

ATMS ATM machines are widespread. You're likely to find an ATM machine a few steps from your hotel, especially if you're staying anywhere in South Mumbai. Any HDFC or ICICI ATM will let you withdraw cash with a Visa, MasterCard, Maestro, or Cirrus card. HDFC ATMs provide cash with an American Express card, too. If you're having difficulty locating an ATM ask anyone to direct you to the nearest HDFC or ICICI bank.

CURRENCY EXCHANGE Most luxury hotels will change money (albeit at poor rates) if you're a guest. American Express is open Monday–Saturday 9:30–6:30. Thomas Cook is open Monday–Saturday 9:30–6:30 and Saturday 9:30–6. The State Bank of India is open weekdays 10:30–4:30, as are most other banks.

Exchange Services **American Express Travel Services** (✉ *Regal Cinema bldg., Chhatrapati Shivaji Maharaj Rd., Colaba* ☎ *22/2204–8291*). **Nucleus Forex** (✉ *Nucleus House, Saki Vihar Rd., Tunga village, Andheri* ☎ *22/2857–4484*). **Thomas Cook India, Ltd.** (✉ *Thomas Cook Bldg., D. Naoroji Rd., near Flora Fountain, Fort* ☎ *22/2204–8556*). **Thomas Cook India Ltd.** (✉ *22/B Cusrow Baug, Colaba* ☎ *22/2282–0574*).

TAXIS

You may hire an air-conditioned taxi for a full day (8 hours or 80 km, whichever comes first) for Rs. 1,000, and a half day (4 hours) for Rs. 550. Ask your hotel what the going rates are in case they've gone up. You can also call Group Mobile Cool Cab Service (☎ 22/2490–5151 or 22/2490–5152; sometimes they take a while to answer the phone—do try again) for a cab with air-conditioning.

TRAIN TRAVEL

Mumbai has two train stations. Chhatrapati Shivaji Terminus, more commonly called Victoria Terminus, is the hub of India's Central Railway line. Mumbai Central Station is the hub of India's Western Railway line. Be sure to go to the right train station—check before you set out. To avoid the pandemonium at the stations, have a travel agent book your ticket; this costs a bit more but saves time and stress. Or do it on the Internet. If you do it yourself, head for the tourist counter established specially for foreign travelers. Eliciting information about trains on the telephone is rather impossible because the lines are busy more often than not and the interactive voice-response numbers are in Hindi. Instead, check out the decent Indian Railways site (🌐 *www.indianrailways.com*). For information on confirming a ticket or the arrivals and departures ask a local to make the phone call.

Train Information **Chhatrapati Shivaji Terminus** (✉ *D. Naoroji Rd.* ☎ *22/134 general information in English, including delays, 22/2263–5959 recorded informa-*

tion on reservation status in English). **Mumbai Central Station** (✉ *Mumbai Central, adjacent to Tardeo* ☎ *22/132 recorded information on arrivals and departures in English, 22/135 general information, including delays, in English, 22/2263–5959 recorded information on reservation status in English).*

TRAVEL AGENTS & TOURS

American Express and Ashoka Travels can help with general travel assistance and car hire; the former is open weekdays 9:30–6:30 and Saturday 9:30–2:30. The transport department of the India Tourism Development Corporation (ITDC) is also helpful with travel arrangements. For a complete list of travel agencies, pick up a copy of the ITDC's Mumbai brochure.

Contacts American Express Travel Services (✉ *Regal Cinema bldg., Chhatrapati Shivaji Maharaj Rd., Colaba* ☎ *22/2204–8291).* **Ashoka Travels** (✉ *Hindustan Bldg., Naushir Bharucha Rd., also called Slater Rd., near Grant Rd. post office, Tardeo* ☎ *22/2385–7622 or 22/2387–8639).* **Eurocars** (✉ *Behind Suburban Service Station, next to Hotel Siddharth, Swami Vivekananda Rd. or S.V. Rd., Bandra* ☎ *22/2645–2796).*

VISITOR INFORMATION

Don't count on hotels to stock general tourist information. The Government of India Tourist Office, near the Churchgate train station, has useful material; it's open weekdays 8:30–6, Saturday and holidays 8:30–2. There's information on trains and the office oversees knowledgeable, multilingual tour guides, available directly from the office or through the MTDC, or just about any travel agency. Rates are approximately Rs. 450 per half-day for groups of one to four, Rs. 600 for a full eight-hour day with no lunch break (he will have lunch when you do). Additional fees of Rs. 265 apply for trips beyond 100 km (62 mi) and for those involving overnight stays the rates could be still higher. Multilingual guides charge Rs. 300 extra, in addition to the regular fee.

The Maharastra Tourism Development Corporation (MTDC) is open daily 9–6. Both MDTC and the Government of India Tourist Office have 24-hour counters at the airports. The MTDC also has counters at Chhatrapati Shivaji Terminus (Victoria Terminus) and the Gateway of India (it's a booth right where the boats to Elephanta Island dock). MTDC phone numbers are not that useful as they are always busy—visit in person or check out their Web site.

Tourist Offices Government of India Tourist Office (✉ *123 Maharishi Karve Rd., Churchgate* ☎ *22/2207–4333, 22/2207–4334, 22/2203–3144, 22/2203–3145 recorded tourist background on Pune, Goa, Mumbai, Ahmedabad, and Aurangabad* ✉ *indiatourism@vsnl.com).* **Maharastra Tourism Development Corporation** *(MTDC* ✉ *Madame Cama Rd. opposite L.I.C. Bldg., Nariman Point* ☎ *22/2202–6713, 22/2202–7762, or 22/2202–7762* 🌐 *www.mtdcindia.com).*

PUNE

This hill station in the Sahyadris at 1,973 feet and three hours southeast of Mumbai, is a delightful town. Pune, or Poona, is also Maharashtra's second-largest city—with nearly 5 million people—and its proximity to

Mumbai has made it a cosmopolitan place. There are new restaurants, stores, pubs, and hotels opening all the time. The hottest fast-food chains and stores have their outlets in Pune. And Mumbai wannabes keep the pubs rocking.

Despite its modernity, Pune remains a cantonment town, with a distinct area once controlled by the British army. Raj touches (languid grace, fancy bungalows, wide boulevards, and some interesting architecture) remain. At 1 PM much of the city halts for a lunch break and a siesta. Markets and shops down their shutters until 4. The Indian army still has a major presence in Pune.

A conservative Maharashtrian town, Pune is steeped in Marathi culture. The older parts of the city—the *peths* (bazaars), *wadas* (homes), and Ganesh temples—are deeply Maharashtrian. You'll find Peshwa palaces and Maratha forts in Pune and nearby areas. This was the fierce, medieval Maratha warrior Shivaji's backyard, and his legendary battles with Mughal conquerors took place in this neighborhood. Lip-smacking Maharashtrian delicacies like *puran poli* (sweet lentil-stuffed pancakes), *shrikhand* (sweet yogurt), *batata wada* (savory fried potatoes), and *zunkhar bakri* (millet bread with spicy lentils) are widely available. Nowhere is Ganesh Chaturthi, the biggest festival of the state—a 10-day event in August and September that honors the elephant god Ganesh, or Ganpati—celebrated with more joy and *dhoom dham* (pomp) than in Pune.

Since the 1980s, Pune has become more international. In 1985 Bhagwan Rajneesh, aka "Osho, the captivating godman," who some call a sex guru, fled his commune in Oregon to set up shop here in 1985. His charisma was such that with him came a giant band of Western followers, who settled in Pune. Osho died in 1990, but the commune continues to thrive, even after a host of salacious controversies, still drawing hordes of seemingly drugged-out Westerners. As a result, an entire upscale neighborhood of Pune is inhabited by maroon-robe-clad, spacey foreigners seeking a new twist to their life. This has spawned an entire Osho tourist district, where everything from German bread to New Age meditation tunes to Kathmandu trinkets is available.

EXPLORING PUNE

Most of the sights in Pune are far flung, so you'd be wise to hire the services of an auto-rickshaw or a car to explore the town.

To experience the staunchly Maharashtrian quarters of the city, head to **Shaniwarwada Palace** in the heart of the old city. The palace, actually, no longer exists. Tall ramparts and imposing, two-story-high teak gates lined with enough spikes to ward off an army of elephants front an empty courtyard, once home to the beyond-your-wildest-imagination Shaniwarwada Palace. Built in the 18th century by the Maratha king Baji Rao I, the palace was destroyed less than 100 years later, after several fires. The premises aren't well maintained, but you can conjure your own images of the extravagant kingdom the Peshwas once ruled.

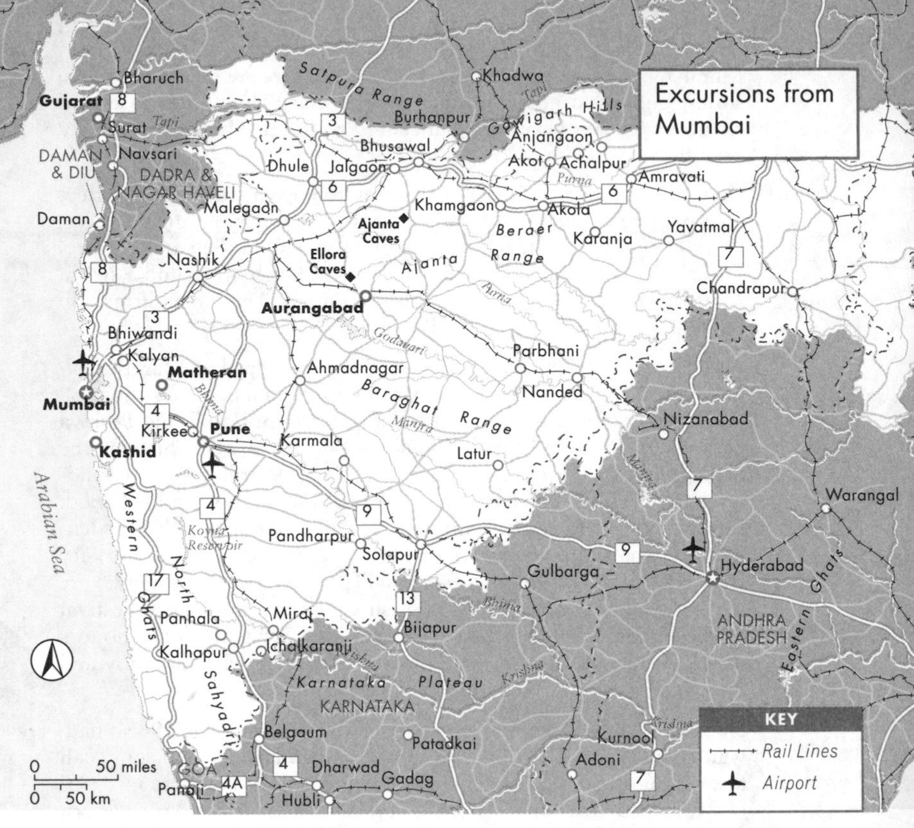

The view from the ramparts of the palace gates is intriguing. Rocky outcrops (once foundation stones) in endless lawns are the only remnants of this seven-story royal residence that once was famous, near and far, for its Shish Mahal (glass house), *hamam* (palace bathroom), and Mastani Mahal (dancers' wing). The Palace of Music, known as the Nagarakhana, still survives. The Maharashtra Tourism board holds an English-language sound-and-light show at the palace, on the history of the Peshwas and Shivaji; tickets are available on the premises. *✉Shaniwarwada, Bajirao Rd., Kasba Peth 🎫Palace Rs. 5, sound-and-light show Rs. 25 ⏲Palace Wed.–Mon. 8:30–6, sound-and-light show Wed.–Mon. 8* PM*–9* PM.

The little lanes leading away from the palace are narrow and populated with small temples, old homes, and vendors hawking their goods. Make sure you dive into some of these side lanes to sample typical *peth,* or Maharashtrian bazaar life. (The older, noncantonment sections of Pune were divided into *peths,* or areas, and named after the days of the week.) On your exit from the palace take a sharp right to arrive at a *chowk* or crossroads. If you continue walking and pass two more crossroads you'll be at **Shrimant Dagdu Sheth Halwai Ganpati Mandir.** This temple is a simple construction—essentially an idol under a roof, in an open-air shed—and worship proceedings are visible right from the road. The idol is cherished not just by locals but by all Maharashtrians. Dagdu Sheth was a *halwai,* or sweetmeat maker. He was also a good friend of Lokmanya Bal Gangadhar Tilak, a key figure in India's independence movement in the late 1800s. In order to disconcert the British rulers, Tilak gave the call for public or community celebrations of Ganesh Chaturthi (the state's biggest festival, held in late summer in honor of the elephant god). In 1893, Dagu Sheth became the first to institute a kind of "block" celebration of the festival. Unlike the idols made for Ganesh Chaturthi each year, which are immersed in bodies of water after the festival is over, the Dagu Sheth Halwai Ganpati (Ganesh) stays on, and over the years has been lavished with affection and prayers. Much of the idol has been embellished with gold by grateful devotees—solid-gold ears (a gift from a film star), as well as 8 kilos of gold decorating his garments. Visit this temple in the evening, around 8:30, if you want to be around when locals worship.

About 25 minutes due south on foot (better to take an auto-rickshaw) from Dagdu Sheth Halwai Ganpati, is the **Raja Dinkar Kelkar Museum.** This celebrated museum in the old city houses some 2,000 carefully catalogued daily utensils and objets d'art of metal, wood, stone, and earthenware from the remotest corners of India (18,000 items are still in storage). The range of items, accumulated over 60 years, is bewildering. The artifacts are illustrative of everyday life: coconut meat scrapers, hookahs, pots, and water containers; musical instruments, toys, lamps, locks, and ornate implements.

The household tools have been chosen on the basis of their utility and for their unusual form or design. The Chitrakathi paintings from Paithan, Maharashtra, are intriguing, as is the large Vanita Kaksha, or lady's parlor, devoted to personal and domestic objects women used. Equally fascinating is the room set up as a replica of the Mastani Mahal, which once existed at Shaniwarwada Palace, where Mastani, Baji Rao I's kept woman, lived. Do check out the poison testing lamp, a design that dates back to the Peshwa era; the lamp was used to check for poisoned food.

This collection was put together by a well-traveled Maharashtrian and award-winning poet Adnyatwasi, aka Dr. Dinkar Gangadhar Kelkar (1896–1990), who was a devoted collector of art, and his wife Kamlabai. What is most unusual about the museum is that Kelkar was an ordinary man of simple means—-not a wealthy maharaja with money to burn like most of the collectors of that era. Dinkar used most of his income and even money obtained by selling his wife's jewelry to collect the most unusual items that India had to offer. Late in life, Kelkar donated his collection of artifacts to the government for a museum in memory of his son, Raja, who died at the age of 12. The museum is housed in Kelkar's own home, a rambling *peth wadas* bungalow-courtyard complexes near Shaniwarwada Palace. Quite a bit off the beaten path, in somewhat dingy and dusty surroundings, the museum requires a bit of patience and real interest to make it worthwhile. If you have time, chat with Surendra Ranade, the grandson who runs the museum. He'll tell you all about the amazing poet, who was once offered a blank check for his collection by another collector, but refused. The museum's expansion plans are under way, and by about 2011 the entire collection, including the undisplayed items, will move to a 6-square-km (4-square-mi) location 10 km (6 mi) away in the village Bavdhan on the Mumbai–Bangalore highway. ✉ *1377–78 Natu Baug, off Bajirao Rd., Shukawar Peth* ☎ *20/2448–2101 or 20/2447–4466* 🎫 *Rs. 150* ⏲ *Daily 8:30–5:30.*

Built in the 1860s and called the Lal Deval (red temple) by locals, the **Ohel David Synagogue** is rather striking—it has beautiful stained-glass windows and an imposing 90-foot tower—and a bit out of place in Pune, which once had only a small Jewish population. The Jewish businessman and philanthropist David Sassoon, who divided his time between Mumbai and Pune, built this synagogue and the David Sassoon hospital. Sassoon is buried on the synagogue grounds. It's worth checking out the synagogue interior. To do so, however, it's advisable to call the number listed below to speak to David Solomon, the caretaker and organize a visit (for security reasons the synagogue is not open without an appointment). If you're here, it's a quick hop over to the trendy, up-and-coming area of town nearby, on M. G. (Mahatma Gandhi) Road and East Street. The area has lots of smart shops and restaurants. ✉ *9 Dr. Ambedekar Rd. Pune Camp, off M. G. Rd.* ☎ *20/2613–2048 only after 6* PM *on holidays.*

An air of secrecy and silence shrouds the **Osho Meditation Resort** *(OMR)*, commonly referred to as an ashram. The exterior of the ashram's buildings is well concealed by bamboo and tall walls. Started by Osho and sex guru, OMR was once described by a *Washington Post* correspondent as a cross between a college campus, Disneyland, and a resort. Lavishly constructed from white-and-black marble, and spread across 40 acres, the commune has wonderful greenery, pools, as well as cafés, shops, a pool, a basketball court, and tennis courts.

The deep-green pool, on the edge of a patch of greenery, is an odd shape, like a natural pond. A large shining steel kitchen and cafeteria supply inexpensive vegetarian food—freshly baked multigrain rolls and bread, organic fruit, Continental dishes, desserts, Indian-style *sabzis* (vegetables), dal, rotis, and more. Ashram members say its meditation hall is the largest in the world—a vast expanse (18,000 square feet) of black marble with a pyramid dome. This air-conditioned meditation hall is a phenomenon: a few maroon-robed devotees chill out here in a sea of serenity. The black floor is as large as a football field. Indeed, much of the resort has an otherworldly, anachronistic sensibility.

The meditation resort, or "Multiversity," offers meditation and self-knowledge or personal growth courses of all varieties, at moderate prices. Osho had no use for organized religion. He believed personal religion should be relatively painless—happy, not ascetic. He was famous for his rather opaque statements, such as: "I am here to seduce you into a love of life; to help you to become a little more poetic; to help you die to the mundane and to the ordinary so that the extraordinary explodes in your life." Meditation at Osho's kingdom takes many forms and he advocated release of tension by singing, dancing, and catharsis, often in group sessions. These "group sessions" have been the subject of much curiosity by locals. The commune, run by more than 500 "disciples," attracts rootless folks from India and all over—mainly Germans, Israelis, some Americans, and Japanese. For a fee, these disciples chill out, spring-clean their souls, and improve their morale. At any given time as many as 5,000 people from more than 100 countries may be floating in and out of the meditation resort.

The resort has its own guest house with 60 rooms; to reserve, call 20/6601–9900 or 20/6601 9911, or e-mail reservations@osho.com. It is austere, but very clean and well lit, and has a sleek Scandinavian look. Rooms ($78 per day for two, plus 10% tax) are accented in hues of white, blond, and black, and with materials such as granite, marble, and glass. Expect no televisions and no phones. No children under 15 are allowed. You can take a limited guided tour to see OMR's grounds—you have to wear a robe while inside. A day-long meditation pass, after you complete the compulsory HIV test, will set you back US$30 (Rs. 1,200).

Another reason to come here is to visit the neighborhood's interesting shops and watering holes. Hawkers sell Tibetan artifacts, Kashmiri crafts, jewelry, and cotton clothing nearby. The teahouses and restaurants are packed with Osho-ites. The ashram, in Koregaon Park, is across town, 4 km (2½ mi) east and slightly north of the Shaniwarwada area. For the general public, the ashram is only open during tour hours for very short half-hour tours. Purchase tickets at least one day in advance. Children under 15 are not permitted. ✉ *17 Koregaon Park* ☎ *20/6601–9999* 🌐 *www.osho.com* 🎫 *Tours Rs. 10* ⏲ *Tours daily at 9 and 2:30, ticket window open daily 9:30–1 and 2–4.*

7

NEED A BREAK?

For a taste of the strange world of Osho, park yourself at one of the rickety wooden benches at the German Bakery, where you can suck down a banana lassi, and eavesdrop on the flirting maroon robes (commune members) talking about the arcane—the meaning of life, the depth of the human soul, etc. You can also get some excellent eats here: fresh breads, herbal tea, fresh fruit juices, soy burgers, hummus and pita, pizza, salads, lasagne, and lemon cake. ✉ ***291 Vaswani Nagar, Koregaon Park*** ☎ ***20/2613–6532.***

After visiting the Osho ashram in Koregaon Park, head by car to the charming, tiny shrine **Shinde Chhatri** *(Shindechi Chhatri)*, about 15 minutes away. (A *chhatri* is a cenotaph or a monument to someone dead and revered.) From Koregaon Park, go past the civil lines (non-army areas) and the British landmarks, and right through the old-style cantonment or camp area. That journey will give you a feel of the old British cantonment Pune. The chhatri, with its striking gold-embossed roof, is the Hindu "chapel" of the Scindias, a famous royal family who once ruled Gwalior in Central India and who today are a political dynasty. The chhatri is a monument to one of the more famous Shindes (from whom the Scindias descended)—Mahadji Shinde, the commander of the Peshwa army. Give the gatekeeper a few rupees and he may allow you in to see the intriguing inner sanctum. Incidentally, one of their lesser palaces is across the street. ✉ *Off Prince of Wales Dr., Wanowrie, near Clover Apartments, 2 km (1 mi) from Pune racecourse* 🎫 *free* ⏲ *Daily dawn–dusk.*

Pune is as famous for its **Ramamani Iyengar Memorial Yoga Institute** as it is for the Osho commune. From this modest and serene three-story bungalow, the nearly 90-year-old grandmaster of yoga, the venerable Yogacharya (yoga teacher) B. K. S. Iyengar still runs a series of workshops along with his son and daughter. Iyengar's type of yoga was developed to be practiced by anyone and is a way of life. His numerous disciples come from all parts of the world; the specialized courses must be booked as much as two years in advance, and aspirants must also have eight years of familiarity with Iyengar Yoga. However, the institute does offer a monthlong beginner's course that is one hour, six days a week, starting at the beginning of each month (Rs. 4,500). ✉ *1107 B/1 Hare Krishna Mandir Rd., Model Colony, Shivajinagar* ☎ *20/2565–6134* 🌐 *www.bksiyengar.com.*

As you enter Pune from Aurangabad (northeast of the city), on the Ahmednagar Road—on the outskirts of the city, before the Mula River—the belching trucks and rushing traffic may distract you from noticing a tranquil patch of greenery on the right side of the road. This is the **Aga Khan Palace,** also known as the Gandhi National Memorial Society. During India's freedom movement, Mahatma Gandhi, his wife Kasturba Gandhi, the poet and patriot Sarojini Naidu, and Mira Ben spent periods of captivity here. Gandhi was imprisoned here from 1942 to 1944. The palace, which is both French and Muslim in design, once belonged to Prince Aga Khan, who donated it and seven of the 19 acres that surround it, to the government. Today it's a low-key national museum. You may wander through the palace and view the tiny rooms hung with photographs where these leaders were interred, or simply admire the pleasant gardens. Also on display are the few personal belongings of the Gandhis. You can even purchase some roughly woven cotton (khadi) cloth—khadi was a symbol of the independence movement; leaders donned the simple homespun garments to show they were shunning Western ways and to protest the taxes they had to pay for Indian cotton garments. A *samadhi* or cenotaph honors the Mahatma's wife, who died here during her imprisonment in 1944. The Aga Khan palace is a bit far from the city center—you need to make a special side trip, by car, to view this memorial. ✉ *Ahmednagar Hwy., also called Nagar Rd.* ☎ *20/2668–0250* 🎫 *Rs. 100 for foreigners* ⏲ *Daily 9–5:30.*

WHERE TO EAT

Pune has lots of reasonably priced restaurants, and you can get Mughlai, Chinese, Thai, and Italian food here. (To cater to Pune's transient foreign population, restaurants serving a variety of cuisines have opened, and a couple of foreigners have even started up their own restaurants.) If you wander over to Koregaon Park you're sure to find food that's tasty and affordable. Restaurants serve lunch noon to 3 and dinner 6 to 11 or 11:30; meals are not usually available outside those hours (though snacks may be). Don't expect alcohol in every restaurant, either.

For familiar fast food head out to Jungli Maharaj Road—McDonald's, Pizza Hut, Domino's, and Baskin-Robbins have all set up shop. The same area is also a good place for some Indian snacks—pav bhaji, sev puri, batata wada, idlis—are available hot and fresh off the griddle.

Nearby Vaishali (20/2553–1244; Fergussen College Rd., opposite college, open from 7 AM to 11 PM), a modest joint near Fergussen College, draws crowds for its dosas.

CHINESE & PAN-ASIAN

$$$ ✕ **Spice Island.** This restaurant at Pune's top hotel is the fanciest in town. Dining here is an extravagant affair—the restaurant is decorated with East Asian paintings and gold trim although it does not have a very Oriental look. You enter through a bar, a monument by itself, carved from glass and glowing with blue light. The dining room beyond, decorated with east Asian paintings and trimmed with gold, is intimate and classy, decorated in deep beige and dark reds. Tasty and innovative Chinese food is served, but it's the excellent Thai dishes that are recommended. Try the pan-fried river prawns, massaman platter, "jaded" fish (fish marinated with cilantro and then fried), Thai corn cakes, Konjy crispy lamb, or fried spinach. Dress nicely (no jacket and tie required, however). ✉ *The Meridien, Raja Bahadur Mill (RBM) Rd., near the main railway station* ☎ *20/2605–0505* ✍ *Reservations essential* ▭ *AE, DC, MC, V.*

$$ ✕ **The Chinese Room.** Owned by the old and popular Kwality chain, the posh, granite-and-glass restaurant is the place to go for Indian–Chinese, a culinary mash-up that leans heavily on cilantro, spices, and hot peppers. Try the crispy sesame chicken, honey-roast pork, steamed rice with vegetables, sesame prawns, three-treasure vegetable *hunani,* (Hunan style dish) or the litchis with ice cream. ✉ *2434 East St.* ☎ *20/2614–5613 or 20/2613–1336* ▭ *AE, MC, V.*

$$ ✕ **Mainland China.** At this branch of Mumbai's famous restaurant the dining room is bright and airy, the furniture wood, the floor marble, and the walls decorated with China-theme murals and wood-carved grilles. The restaurant has an attractive garden where you can dine. The lightly cooked, mildly spiced courses are full of flavor, and portions are large. Ask to have it spicy, with more chillies. Menu standouts include rice with woodear mushrooms and greens, sweet-and-spicy crispy chicken, chicken in sapo sauce, bean-curd dim sums, prawns in butter and garlic, seafood with crabmeat sauce, crackling spinach, steamed chicken with Chinese greens, and burnt-garlic fried rice. End your meal with *daarsaan,* crispy fried noodles with honey. ✉ *City Point, junction of Boat Club Rd. and Dhole Patil Rd.* ☎ *20/6601–3030* ✍ *Reservations essential* ▭ *AE, DC, MC, V.*

$$ ✕ **Malaka Spice.** This simple but cheerful restaurant's decor is provided by the art for sale that's hanging on its wall. The menu includes food from across Asia—Vietnam, Indonesia, China, Thailand, Japan,

7

Malaysia, and Korea. The place is managed by a husband-and-wife duo, Cheeru and Praful Chandawarkar. Try the flavorful pad thai, chicken satay, Thai green curry with chicken, coriander rice, chicken in pandanus leaves, or Singaporean *laksa* (a soup with noodles, prawns, chicken, and bean sprouts). ✉ *Vrindavan Apartments, N. Main Rd., Koregoan Park* ☎ *20/2613–6293 or 20/2614–1088* ▭ *AE, MC, V.*

$$ ✕ **Silk Route.** A variety of fairly authentic Far Eastern dishes—Vietnamese, Japanese, Chinese, Korean, Thai, Indonesian, Chinese—is whipped up in this small, popular restaurant. The purple-heavy interior is slightly gloomy but cozy all the same. Sample the *tom yum* (seafood soup), pad thai, green chicken curry, or the *gaeng massaman kai* (Thai-style lamb curry). ✉ *357/1 Pingle Corner, Cosmos Bank La, Koregaon Park* ☎ *20/2613–5793* ▭ *AE, DC, MC, V.*

INDIAN

$$ ✕ **The Great Punjab.** Head here for the more familiar naans, kebabs, and rich chicken *makhanis* (full of butter and cream) that are the backbone of hearty, utterly buttery Punjabi cuisine. Wine racks, lots of wood and glass and the shining granite floor all add character to the eatery. Stick to the well-made classics and you won't go wrong—chicken biryani (chicken cooked with rice), *kheema champ* (ribs cooked in minced meat), *paneer methi tikka* (paneer cheese grilled with fenugreek leaves), *seekh kabab* (grilled minced lamb), dal makhani (black lentils simmered with cream), and *rumali rotis* (a very thin soft type of roti). They also offer a weight-watcher's menu. ✉ *5 Jewel Tower, Lane 5, off North Main Rd, Koregaon Park* ☎ *20/2614–5060* ▭ *AE, MC, V.*

$$ ✕ **Mahesh Lunch Home.** The basement of 18 Dr. Ambedkar Road is the address of Pune's first—and probably only—proper seafood restaurant. A branch of the Mumbai landmark for seafoodies, Pune Mahesh offers pretty much the real thing, and that makes it some of the best seafood in the city. Tuck into their prawn gassis, lady fish fry, tandoori pomfret, or crab *sukka* (dry)—catch here is fresh and gussied up with traditional Manglorean coast *masalas* (spice mixes) composed of coconut, red chillies, *kokum* (a sour berry), and other condiments. The restaurant has a soothing, non-surprising Indian-restaurant vibe: green sofas, granite floors, etched glass, and Hindi film music playing in the background. ✉ *Ashok Pavilion, 18 Dr. Ambedkar Rd.* ☎ *20/2613–3091* ▭ *AE, MC, V.*

$ ✕ **Blue Nile.** Decoration in this popular Pune nonvegetarian restaurant is zilch, but you're in an established Muslim eating house with high ceilings and faded charm. In any case, it's the excellent chicken and mutton biryanis (spicy meat simmered with rice for hours), not the plastic chairs and paper napkins, that bring people in. No need to try the veg food; this is a place for carnivores. No liquor is served. ✉ *4 Bund Rd.* ☎ *20/2612–5238* ▭ *No credit cards.*

$ ✕ **Coffee House.** This established vegetarian multicuisine restaurant has gone upscale. Wood accents and busy upholstery contribute to its swanky new style. The total effect is reasonably pleasing to the eye. You can get Chinese, Mughlai, and South Indian food for breakfast, lunch or dinner, and snacks in the evening. Recommended are the crispy dosas, chana bhatura, vegetable biryani, and in the evening chats such as sev puri, bhel puri, and batata wada. ✉2 *Moledina Rd., Pune Camp* ☎*20/2613–8275* ▭*MC, V.*

$ ✕**Prem's.** This place in the heart of "Oshotown," a few minutes by foot from the ashram, has become something of a landmark. The open-air restaurant in a garden setting under tamarind trees, with its tinkling New Age meditation music, Christmas lights, and soothing vibe, largely exists for the ashram and its devotees. But its relaxing ambience and capable chefs are good incentive for others come here. Indian and Continental food—vegetable makhani, paneer butter masala, chicken garlic pasta, spinach with pasta—is served here. Opt for the pastas or the sizzlers—choose between chicken shaslik or the veg sizzler choices. Beer and wine are served. ✉*28/2 Koregaon Park* ☎*20/2613–0985* ▭*AE, MC, V.*

$ ✕**Ramakrishna.** *Pulaus,* sizzling dosas, soft idlis—this no-fuss air-conditioned restaurant serves excellent South Indian food. The place is simple and clean (lots of shiny granite) and the food arrives in minutes, hot and authentic. More than 30 varieties of dosas are served. Try the *rawa masala dosa* (semolina pancakes filled with potato stuffing), the table-length paper dosa (a light and crispy dosa with no filling), or the *mung dosa* (a dosa made using a green-lentil flour). The rasam-wadas (lentil fritters in spicy gravy) are superb but hot. ✉*Ramakrishna Resort, 6 Moledina Rd., Pune Camp* ☎*20/2636–3938 or 20/2633–0724* ▭*MC, V.*

¢ ✕**Nandu's.** Leave your bow ties and high heels at home, roll up your sleeves, and prepare for some typical *desi,* or Indian, dining. But Nandu's is not your conventional restaurant. This small vegetarian eatery sells amazingly good, fat, sizzling, vegetable-stuffed parathas served with yogurt and a dollop of butter. You can't go wrong here. Stuffings include peas, cauliflower, potatoes, onion, fenugreek, and paneer. The corn or *bajra* (millet) rotis are also worth a try. The shady outside seating area is a pleasant enough place to chomp down the divine food. Come either for lunch or for an early dinner—hungry locals pack the place by 9. No alcohol is served. ✉*Damodar Narain Dhole Patil Market, Dhole Patil Rd.* ☎*20/2634–728* ▭*No credit cards.*

¢ ✕**Shabree.** The queue of folks waiting for table on a weekend is a great testimony of the standard of food in this long-running vegetarian thali place. The simplicity of the decor (black-top tables, a picture window facing a patch of greenery) instantly attracts, as does the friendliness of the waitstaff. For Rs. 125 they offer a simple, not too oily and interestingly varied Maharashtrian thali with hot bajraand wheat rotis and a sweet at the end. It is easily one of the best Maharashtran thalis available. ✉*Hotel Parichay, FC Rd., near Fergusson College* ☎*20/2553–1511* ▭*MC, V.*

INTERNATIONAL

$$ ✕**ABC Farm.** Five simply furnished open-air restaurants, each under different management and each offering a different kind of cuisine, are spread over this spacious, shady garden property. Two of the restaurants, Soul and Curve the Dhabha, have live music every weekend, a rarity in Pune. It's therefore a good place to chill out over a few drinks and snacks—perhaps some garam-agaram Pune-style rosti, then some

7

fondue somewhere else, and then tandoori chicken at a third place. Rosti is a famous Swiss style of potatoes then some fondue somewhere else, and then tandoori chicken at a third place. The best restaurant here is the dark, cozy Swiss Cheese Garden, filled with red check and brick, with good raclette, goulash, and pizzas. One drawback: ABC Farm is a good 20 minutes from the city center. ☒*2 Moledina Rd., Pune Camp* ☎*20/2613–8275* ▭*MC, V.*

$$ ✕**Flag's.** The foods of a dozen-odd countries are served at this smart, large restaurant next to the Inox multiplex theatre center. Snacking is a better idea than filling yourself on one course. Hop like a dizzy lotus eater from a slice of zucchini flan to tempura prawns to Burmese *kaukswe* (a spicy, soupy chicken/vegetable noodle dish accented with coconut milk and eggs) to the Lebanese *shish taouk* (chicken marinated with tahini and then grilled) to the "crunchy munchy" (Manchurian dumplings with french fries). It will be a wild ride. No points for guessing what's decorating the restaurant's walls. Yup, flags of the world. ☒*G-2 Metropole, next to Inox, Bund Garden Rd.* ☎*20/2614–1617 and 20/2614–1718* ▭*AE, DC, MC, V.*

$$ ✕**La Pizzeria.** Freshly cooked pastas and pizzas are served up piping hot in this sunny, attractive eatery, with a garden sit out. The wood floors, wrought-iron furniture, and etched glass give the place quite some appeal. Like most restaurants in Koregaon Park the meals here are vegetarian, and here they are carefully and tastefully prepared. Go for the crostini (fresh bread topped with toppings like grilled bell peppers, eggplant, or sun-dried tomatoes), tortellini, lasagne, pasta al forno (baked pasta with white sauce and mushrooms), or the thin crust pizzas. ☒*Hotel Srimaan, 361/5B Bund Garden Rd., Bund Garden, Koregoan Park* ☎*20/2613–6565* ▭*AE, DC, MC, V.*

$$ ✕**Squisito.** In a quiet back lane is this Italian vegetarian eatery. Diners sit in front of a giant plate-glass window that looks out onto the road. To one side is a wine and beer bar; the Italian-themed mural on the wall opposite dominates the decor, but the place feels bright and airy. Good choices: ravioli in four cheeses, cream and sage tagliatelle, zucchini and thyme fritters, mushroom bites. ☒*1 Jewel Tower, Lane No. 5, off North Main St., Koregaon Park* ☎*20/2605–4005* ▭*AE, DC, MC, V.*

$ ✕**Mad House Grill.** At some point in your vacation you may get a huge craving for a giant steak. That's when you should head to this quaintly decorated, cozy Koregaon Park eating spot, with its white picket fence and drawing room furnishings (mirrors, curtains, green granite). They do very competent steaks—try the pepper steaks—as well as pepper-mustard chicken, grilled chicken, and grilled vegetables. ☒*Pingle's corner, near Cosmos Bank, 2 Lane No. 6, off North Main St., Koregaon Park* ☎*20/2612–4779* ▭*MC, V.*

WHERE TO STAY

Pune, which is slowly becoming a popular destination for business travelers, has its fair share of hotels. The city now has six luxury hotels and a number of business hotels. Luxury hotel prices are steep, though not as high as the prices in the larger cities, but standards are not exactly international. If you're booking directly, ask for a discount. Prices are more often than not negotiable, and hefty discounts may be available. Depending on the rate you get, breakfast and airport or railway station pickup may be included. Such deals tend to be available for long-term stays, and can be made on the spot.

Pune is fast growing into a very large and well-spread-out city and the hotels listed below are largely chosen for their central location. A variety of accommodations geared to tourists has always been available in the Koregaon Park area. Quite a few decent rooms, cheaper than those listed below, can be found there.

$$$$ **St Laurn.** This nine-story glass and chrome boutique business hotel makes up for what it lacks in views with comfortable, glossy modern rooms. Plenty of mirrors and glass, LCD wall-mounted televisions and wood floors accentuate the sleekness. Gray marble-tiled bathrooms have glass walls that offer views of your favorite television show from the bathtub. Rooms are done in muted tones of pale orange, beige, whites and matched with mahogany-hued furniture. The hotel's red and white accented Ebony restaurant serves Indian cuisine. **Pros:** intimate, restful rooms. **Cons:** rooms tad small, half the rooms face a noisy upcoming shopping center and the other half face another luxury hotel (Taj Blue Diamond). ✉ *15 A Koregaon Park, 411001* ☎ *20/4000-8000* 🌐 *www.stlaurnhotels.com* *63 rooms* *In-room: safe, refrigerator, Wi-Fi. In-hotel: 2 restaurants, bar, pool, gym, concierge, laundry service.* *AE, DC, MC, V* *BP.*

$$$ ★ **The Central Park Hotel.** As you enter this luxury hotel, the first thing that strikes you is its light, airy, modern look. The hotel staff is gracious and particularly helpful. The cozy rooms are comfortable and neat, with blue-green and brown furnishings and green granite bathrooms. Choose your room according to the view: the roadside view is more pleasant than the views in front or on the side of the hotel. Next door in a separate building, Central Park offers very sleek studio rooms for long-term stay. **Pros:** intimate, good service, airport pickup. **Cons:** expensive, small rooms. ✉ *Bund Garden Rd., near the Council Hall* ☎ *20/4010–4000* 🌐 *www.thecentralparkhotel.com* *73 rooms, 4 suites* *In-room: safe (some), refrigerator, Wi-Fi. In-hotel: restaurant, room service, bar, pool, gym, laundry service, no smoking rooms, complimentary airport shuttle.* *AE, DC, MC, V* *BP.*

$$$ **Le Meridien.** Glowing expanses of marble, shiny fittings, elegant furnishings, and no fewer than seven restaurants make this very large, Mumbai-class lodging a luxurious option. The large rooms are plush, but they are a bit uninspired in contrast to the exterior and lobby areas—they run to busy upholstery with red highlights, soft carpeting, and tile walls. By the windows are wrought-iron tables. Rooms have unexciting views of the railway station across the street. **Pros:** very plush, Pune's top hotel, airport pick-up, squash facilities. **Cons:** expensive, lacks view, not quite up to international standards. ✉ *Raja Bahadur Mill (RBM), near the main railway station* ☎ *20/2605–0505* 🌐 *www.starwoodhotels.com* *177 rooms, 15 suites* *In-room: safe, refrigerator, Wi-Fi. In-hotel:*

7

7 restaurants, room service, bars, pool, gym, concierge, laundry service, no-smoking rooms. ⊟*AE, DC, MC, V* 🍽*BP.*

$$$ **Sun-n-Sand.** There's no sand here, just sun. Glass elevators take you up and away from the shiny black granite-finished lobby. Of the luxury hotels in Pune, this is a bit less fancy than its counterparts. The comfortable rooms, furnished in blues and beiges, are overpriced and a tad small; they face the road and there's muffled traffic noise. Bathrooms are bright and reflectively clean. **Pros:** comfy, well-located, airport pick-up, good in-house Chinese and Indian restaurants. **Cons:** expensive, small rooms. ✉*262 Bund Garden Rd.* ☎*20/2616–7777* 🌐*www.sunnsandhotel.com* *137 rooms, 2 suites* *In-room: safe, refrigerator, Wi-Fi. In-hotel: 2 restaurants, room service, bar, pool, gym, laundry service, no-smoking rooms, concierge, complimentary airport shuttle.* ⊟*AE, DC, MC, V* 🍽*BP.*

$$$ **Taj Blue Diamond.** This is the only luxury hotel in Pune with rooms that have pleasant views (Koregaon Park). The cheerful, modern rooms have carpets, curtains, and bedspreads and are done in maroons and beiges. Bathrooms are tidy and shiny in brown marble. The hotel's 24-hour coffee shop serves excellent biryani; there's also an Indian restaurant and a popular Chinese restaurant. **Pros:** best luxury option in the city, good views and in-house restaurants, elegant rooms, sophisticated. **Cons:** expensive. ✉*11 Koregaon Rd.* ☎*20/6602–5555* 🌐*www.tajhotels.com* *109 rooms, 12 suites* *In-room: safe, refrigerator, Wi-Fi. In-hotel: 2 restaurants, room service, bar, pool, gym, laundry service, concierge, no-smoking rooms.* ⊟*AE, DC, MC, V* 🍽*BP.*

$ **Shrimaan.** This medium-budget hotel offers comfortable, simple, brightly furnished rooms at a fair price. All rooms are a reasonable size, with green and white accents and no carpets. The bathrooms are small. Air-conditioned rooms are slightly more expensive, but bigger and naturally preferable. None of the room have much of a view. The attached restaurant, La Pizzeria, serves Italian food, as well as a limited Mexican menu. Shrimaan is in a quiet area of town, a few minutes' walk from Koregoan Park. **Pros:** good value, nice location, Italian restaurant attached. **Cons:** could be cleaner, no view. ✉*361/5 Bund Garden Rd., opposite Bund Garden* ☎*20/2613–3535 or 20/2613–6565* 🌐*www.littleitaly-india.com* *28 rooms* *In-room: no a/c (some), safe, refrigerator. In-hotel: restaurant, room service, laundry service.* ⊟*AE, MC, V* 🍽*BP.*

$ **Sirona.** At this, the more attractive sister hotel of Shrimaan, which is just around the corner, the rooms are very clean, sleek, modern, and a bit more expensive. Done in Scandinavian style in cream and wood, each room is spacious and well-lit. There are flat-sceen televisions on the wall and microwaves in rooms. Bathrooms are black and have tubs. Views are nothing to write home about but this hotel most certainly offers value for money. **Pros:** very good value for money, sleek, well-located. **Cons:** no views. ✉*361/2–3 Bund Garden Rd., opposite Central Mall* ☎*20/2613–6565* 🌐*www.littleitaly-india.com* *30 rooms* *In-room: no a/c (some), televison, refrigerator. In-hotel: restaurant, room service, laundry service, public Internet.* ⊟*AE, MC, V* 🍽*BP.*

¢ ★ **Sunderban.** Once the home of Nepal royalty, this bungalow-hotel has old-style class, and is probably the most interesting place to stay in Pune. Popular with Osho *wallahs* (devotees), it's on a quiet street in the area of Koregaon Park. The more expensive air-conditioned studio rooms, renovated in 2007, are spacious with a contemporary look and a rich sepia tiles; they face green lawns and have an attached kitchenette with a microwave and refrigerator. Regular rooms are basic and small with a no-frills bathrooms (shower only) but very clean. Alcohol and meat are not permitted in the hotel. Off-season discounts are available April through September. **Pros:** tranquil rooms in a garden environment, in the prettiest neighborhood of Pune. **Cons:** tad expensive, only 16 air-conditioned rooms that get booked quick; need to book in advance. ⊠*19 Koregaon Park* ☎*20/2612–4949 or 20/2612–8383* ⊕*www.tghotels.com* *40 rooms* *In-room: no a/c (some), refrigerator. In-hotel: room service, no elevator, laundry service.* ▭*MC, V* *BP.*

NIGHTLIFE & THE ARTS

During **Ganesh Chaturthi,** celebrated in late August or September, the Maharashtra Tourism Development Corporation (MTDC) organizes a special cultural festival, during which top classical Indian dancers and musicians perform. Check out the MTDC Web site ⊕www.mtdcindia.com for details.

Pune has plenty of pubs where you can sample the city's nightlife.

Visit **10 Downing Street** (⊠*Gera Plaza, Boat Club Rd.* ☎*20/2612–8343*); it's a popular pub in Pune, open from 7:30 PM to 12:30 PM or later. There's a DJ, theme nights, and tasty snacks are served here. **Club Polaris** (⊠*Taj Blue Diamond, Koregaon Park* ☎*20/6602–5555*) is a popular nightclub open only on Saturdays from 9 PM onward. **11 East Street Café** (⊠*East St.,* ☎*20/2633–3711*) has a double-decker red bus parked square in the middle and this café/pub resembles a street in England. Cakes/pastries are available by day inside the bus and beer, drinks and more available from noon till nearly midnight. **Kiva Lounge** (⊠*opposite Symphony restaurant, Range Hills Rd., near E-Square Cinema* ☎*20/2553–8339*), opened in 2007, is the hottest address to head to in Pune especially popular for its music which is a bit of retro mixed with the latest—Mediterranean ambiance, good snacks. **Lush Lounge and Grille** (⊠*City Tower, Dhole Patil Rd* ☎*20/3094–4011*), with open-air seating and a dance floor inside, is one of the happening spots in town. Check out how Pune swings. **Scream** (⊠*Le Meridien, Raja Bahadur Mill (RBM), near the main railway station* ☎*20/2605–0505*) is quite posh. **Soho and Toscana** (⊠*Metro Traders Compund, next to Bishop's School, Kalyani Nagar* ☎*20/2668–1987*) is a very large garden bar and restaurant. The indoor seating area is decked out like an Indian-style barn. Weekends see this place busy with loud music and lots of Pune's young people. The attached Italian restaurant, Toscana, serves excellent pizza and ravioli.

SHOPPING

Shopping in Pune can be a thrill, given the immense variety and the good prices. Unlike other Indian cities, the shopping avenues are pretty much adjacent to each other. Comb M.G. (Mahatma Gandhi) Road, Moledina Road, and East Street for the best bargains, and visit the swank Magnum Mall to buy the best international brands and a quick bite. Remember, however, that Pune snoozes from 1 to 4.

The **Bombay Store** (✉ *302 M.G. Rd.* ☎ *20/2613–1891* ⏲ *Mon.–Sat. 10:30–8:30, Sun. 11–8*) has some of the best buys around on handicrafts, clothing, and artifacts.

Westside (✉ *1B Moledina Rd.* ☎ *20/2611–9395 or 20/2611–9920* ⏲ *Daily 10:30–8:30*), next to Dorabjees on Moledina Road, stocks casual wear and household goods.

Along **M.G. Road** you'll find plenty of shops, one after the next, selling cottons and salwar-kurta ensembles (a two-piece tunic and pants outfit). You'll even find roadside hawkers offering tops and skirts. Off of M.G. is a lane lined with open-air stalls; vendors here sell garments of all varieties.

At **Centre Street** you may find a good selection of jewelry.

Fabindia (✉ *10 Sakar, opposite Jehangir Nursing Home, Sassoon Rd.* ☎ *20/2612–4820* ⏲ *Tues.–Sun. 10–7:45*) sells great cotton clothing for adults and children. **Either Or** (✉ *Sohrab Hall, near Crossword Bookstore, Bund Garden Rd.*) sells interesting and sometimes funky Indian-style cotton casuals, plus jewelry and other gift items. On the shops and stalls at **Koregaon Park** you'll find Kashmiri handicrafts, silver jewelry, cotton garments, and Tibetan knickknacks.

Landmark (✉ *1B Moledina Rd.*, ☎ *20/4006–8888*), Pune's best bookstore, has three floors. There are lots of movies and CDs to look at, too.

PUNE ESSENTIALS

AIR TRAVEL

Pune and Mumbai are only 35 minutes apart by air. A one-way ticket costs about US$50. Jet Airways flies the route daily. Pune is also connected to New Delhi, Ahmedabad, Hyderabad, Indore, and Bangalore by daily or frequent flights on Jet Airways, Simplifly Deccan, Kingfisher Airlines, and Air India, the merged airline still partially operating under its older name of Indian.

Airlines & Contacts **Air India (Indian)** (☎ *20/1407, 20/2426–0932, 20/2668–9433, 20/2605–2147 20/2426–0938, 20/2426—0948 or at the airport 20/2669–0174*).

Jet Airways (☎ *20/2612–7524, 20/2613–7076 or for preferred passenger check in by phone or to call the Jet airport office dial 20/668–5591*). **Kingfisher** (☎ *1/800/2333—131 or 20/2729–3030* 🌐 *www.flykingfisher.com*). **Simplifly Deccan** (☎ *city code plus 3900–8888 or 20/3900–8888* 🌐 *www.airdeccan.net*).

BUS TRAVEL

Several competing companies run luxury buses from Pune to Mumbai; it's a four- or five-hour journey. But the Asiad buses run by the Maharashtra State Road Transport Corporation are the quickest and most efficient buses to take (no extra stops or waiting for more passengers); they go from Pune's main bus station close to the railway station. Raj National Express Volvo (can be booked online) and Metrolink Volvo bus services are also competent services; Raj is better among the two. Bus travel in Maharashtra does not involve overcrowded buses and "roof top bus travel" and such like and is relatively safer than other parts of the country. You can arrange such a ride through your Pune hotel or travel agent or easier still just head over to the bus station and catch the next bus. They go every half hour or even more frequently. Driving to Pune by car is an even better option, however. **Metrolink** (✉ *Opposite Hotel Aamir, Sadhu Vaswani Rd., near Pune Station* ☎ *20/2612–3137*).

Raj National Express (✉ *G7, Metro House, Mangaldas Rd., Opp Tata Management Training Centre, Behind Wadia College* ☎ *20/3058–1414 or 20/3058–1415* 🌐 *http://www.rajnationalexpress.in/contact.htm*).

CARS & DRIVERS

With the opening of the Mumbai-Pune expressway, one of India's first world-class highways, the driving to Pune from Mumbai takes under three hours if you avoid the Mumbai rush hour.

You can also arrange to hire a car and driver through your hotel travel desk or from an agency. Hiring a non-air-conditioned car for eight hours or 80 km (50 mi)—whichever comes first—will set you back Rs. 700; it's Rs. 850 for a car with air-conditioning. These are rates for a comfortable but small Maruti 800 or Indica, and depending on the type of car, prices go up. Tips and "lunch money" for the driver are additional, although the restaurant you eat at may feed him for free in return for your business. Travel House rates are much higher, and start at Rs. 1,500 for eight hours. Whoever you deal with, be sure to fix a rate beforehand.

Contacts Deccan Luxury (✉ *Fergusson College Rd., near Deccan Gymkhana and Champion Sports* ☎ *20/2553–2305*).

Travel House (✉ *City Point, Boat Club Rd.* ☎ *20/2611–3085*).

MONEY

CURRENCY EXCHANGE Most hotels will change money for guests. You can also change money at Thomas Cook Monday–Saturday 9:30–6. Or you could try American Express weekdays 9:30–6:30 and Saturday 9:30–1. If you want to advance cash against your MasterCard or Visa, you will have to head to any of the numerous ICICI or HDFC ATMs in the city center. HDFC offers cash against an American Express card. ATMs are open 24 hours.

Exchange Services American Express (✉ *c/o Kanji Forex, Ashoka Mall, opposite Sun-n-Sand hotel, Bund Garden Rd.* ☎ *9373031575*). **Thomas Cook** (✉ *13 Thacker House, 2418 G. Thimmaya Rd., off M.G. Rd.* ☎ *20/2634–8188* 🌐 *www.thomascook.co.in*).

TOURS

Pune Municipal Transport (PMT) (☎20/2444–0417) operates a daily six-hour Pune city tour that departs at 9, for Rs. 117 per person. Buses depart from the Pune bus station; you can purchase tickets there as well.

TRAIN TRAVEL

Several excellent fast trains run between Pune and Mumbai, including the Pragati Express, Deccan Queen, and Sahyadri Express. The Pragati and Deccan Queen are the fastest; the journey takes 3½ hours. There are daily connections between Pune and Chennai, Hyderabad, Bangalore, Trivandrum, and several other destinations. Ask a travel agent for details.

Train Information **Train Information Hotline** (☎*20/2612–6575*).

VISITOR INFORMATION

The Maharashtra Tourism Development Corporation (MTDC) office in Pune, near the main railway station, is open Monday–Saturday 10–5 (minus a 1:30–2 lunch break); every second Saturday, however, the office is closed. There are MTDC counters at the railway station and at the airport, too. The railway station counter is open daily 9:30–6. The airport office is open when the flights come in. In addition to these bureaus, most hotels have travel desks to help you plan your day—for a price.

Tourist Offices **Maharashtra Tourism Development Corporation (MTDC)** (✉*Block I, Central Bldg., Pune* ☎*20/2612–6867*).

AURANGABAD, AJANTA CAVES & ELLORA CAVES

Dating back more than 2,000 years, the cave temples of Ajanta and Ellora rank among the wonders of the ancient world. Here, between the 2nd century BC and the 5th century AD, great armies of monks and artisans carved cathedrals, monasteries, and entire cities of frescoed, sculptured halls into the solid rock. Working with simple chisels and hammers and an ingenious system of reflecting mirrors to provide light, they cut away hundreds of thousands of tons of rock to create the cave temples. These craftsmen inspire perpetual awe with the precision of their planning, their knowledge of rock formations, their dedication to achieve all this in isolation, and the delicacy and profusion of their artwork. Together, the cave temples span three great religions—Buddhism, Hinduism, and Jainism. For optimum absorption of these phenomenal caves, allow one full day for each site, and remember both are closed on Monday. To get to Ajanta and Ellora, take a train, bus, or plane to Aurangabad, the nearest major city. From Aurangabad you can hop on a tour bus or hire a car and driver for about Rs. 1,300 to the Ajanta caves (a two- to three-hour trip), Rs. 550 to the Ellora caves (30 minutes).

AURANGABAD

388 km (241 mi) east of Mumbai, 30 km (18 mi) southeast of Ellora, 100 km (62 mi) southwest of Ajanta

With several excellent hotels and a growing number of good restaurants, Aurangabad is a good base from which to explore the cave temples at Ajanta and Ellora. Its proximity to so many interesting, world-famous sights gives it a draw that no other place in Maharashtra has. Aurangabad has an intriguing old bazaar, and is known for its *himru* (cotton and silk brocade) shawls and saris, and its gorgeously and painstakingly decorated Paithani—*zari,* fine gold-embroidered saris. If you're interested, pop into the Aurangabad Standard Silk Showroom or Aurangabad Silk, both near the train station; Ajanta Handicrafts in Harsul, on the highway to Ajanta; or Himroo Saris, on the highway to Ellora. An even better option to view Himru saris being woven is to venture over to the Himru Cooperative Society at Jaffer (also spelled Zaffar) Gate, an area in the western part of Aurangabad; there you can see the entire process in action in a traditional environment. The saris (which incidentally can be cut up and tailored into other items) are more reasonable here.

More than a mere gateway, Aurangabad has a number of ancient sites of its own, such as the imposing **Daulatabad Fort** (✉*13 km [8 mi] west of Old Town, on the highway to the Ellora Caves* ⏲*Daily sunrise–6* 🎫*Foreigners US$2*), built in 1187 by the Hindu king and surrounded by seven giant walls more than 5 km (3 mi) long. Daulatabad was once called Deogiri, or "hill of the gods," but was changed to "city of fortune" when the sultan of Delhi overtook it in 1308. Devote at least half a day to this fascinating fort, considered one of India's most impressive. There is a wonderful view of the plains from the acropolis (fortified city) on the top. As you enter the fort you enter a labyrinth—note the moats, spikes, cannons, and dark maze of tunnels designed to make the fort as impregnable from enemies as possible. Equally interesting is the Jami Masjid (large mosque) inside; it was made from horizontal lintels and pillars taken from Jain and Hindu temples. Hindu folks around here put a lot of store in a *puja* (worship) done at the top of the fort and then down below, at the exit.

The 17th-century tomb **Bibi-ka-Maqbara** (✉*550 yards north of the old town, beyond Mecca Gate* ⏲*Daily sunrise–10* PM 🎫*Foreigners US$2*) is also known as the mini–Taj Mahal; you can usually see it from the plane when you're flying into Aurangabad. A pale but noble imitation of the original Taj Mahal, it is dedicated to the wife of the last of the six great Mogul emperors, Aurangzeb (founder of Aurangabad and son of the Taj Mahal's creator, Shah Jahan). It was supposed to be a shining, white-marble edifice but money ran out, so only the bottom 2 feet of the monument were built with marble; the rest is stone with a facade of plaster. Somewhat awkwardly proportioned, the structure can be said to illustrate the decline of Mogul architecture.

About 160 km (99 mi) and 3½ to 4 hours east of Aurangabad, beyond Jalna, *not* on the highway to either Ajanta or Ellora, is the **Lonar Crater.**

If you have a day free, or if you have an extra day because the caves are closed, visit this serene 50,000-year-old meteoric crater. Off the beaten path and away from postcard sellers, bead hawkers, and soft-drink-stall owners, the 1,800-meter-long crater lake—formed from a meteor—is one of India's more phenomenal sites. It's said to be Asia's largest and youngest crater. Lonar is a peaceful spot, full of wildlife and greenery. Maharashtra Tourism Development Corporation (MTDC) has a small, simple guest house here.

WHERE TO EAT & STAY

Aurangabad has few great restaurants. Most of them offer multiple cuisine options, including Indian (Mughlai and tandoori, or South Indian), Chinese, and the local variant of what passes for Continental food. Stick with Indian cuisine outside the luxury hotels—it's generally well prepared and tasty. Most Aurangabadi restaurants aren't big on decoration: a few plastic plants, jazzy upholstery, and darkened light bulbs serve as restaurant style. But they are comfortable and the meals well presented. Most restaurants here don't serve meals outside typical meal hours.

Most hotels in Aurangabad will discount their rates on request. If you book directly, push for 15% off—or more—and check if the rate you settle for includes breakfast and airport–railway station pickup. Unless otherwise noted, all hotels listed are fully air-conditioned.

$$ ✕ **Madhuban.** Dark furniture, large paintings of Indian scenes, an abundance of green granite, crisp white tablecloths, and a chandelier composed of multiple *diyas* (traditional Indian lamps) set a regal tone at one of Aurangabad's top restaurants. One wall of windows opens onto lovely tropical trees and flowers. The Indian menu choices are many, and the Chinese food is quite tasty. There's a popular buffet lunch. ✉ *Welcomgroup Rama International hotel, R-3 Chikalthana* ☎ *240/248–5441* ▭ *AE, DC, MC, V.*

$$ ★ ✕ **The Residency and the Garden Café.** The Taj Residency's two eateries adjoin one other and share the same menu, a mix of Indian and Continental. The choice is easy—if it's lunch you're after, have it at the Garden Café; for dinner head to The Residency. The café is easily the loveliest location around to have a light lunch. White cane garden furniture decorates a marble veranda that looks out over green lawns and flower beds; the place has old-world style. The Residency, done up in warm colors and lots of wood, is a classy place to have dinner. Try their multicuisine buffet or the local chicken curry. Desserts are good here, too. ✉ *8-N-12 CIDCO* ☎ *240/238–1106 to 10* ▭ *AE, DC, MC, V.*

$ ✕ **Angeethi.** It's one of Aurangabad's most popular restaurants, and gets packed on weekends. Named after a traditional Indian cooking vessel, this dark, cozy, slightly tacky place serves Punjabi, Continental, and Chinese food, and has a knack for tandoori items. Other specialties include chicken biryani, Afghani kebab *masala* (boneless chicken in a cashew sauce), and two-person *sikandari raan* (the leg portion of the mutton marinated). There are plenty of tasty vegetarian choices, too. Service is friendly but not terribly efficient. ✉ *6 Mehar Chambers, Vidya Nagar, Jalna Rd.* ☎ *240/244–1988 or 240/562–9038* ▭ *MC, V.*

$ ✕**China Town.** Indian-Chinese (packed with cilantro, garlic, red chillies and gooey sauces) is at its best at this well-favored Chinese restaurant, probably the city's best, not far from the Bibi-ka-Maqbara. Well-spaced tables and colorful patchwork pieces on the wall give China Town a happy buzz. Menu suggestions: chilli chicken, vegetable Manchurian (deep-fried and in a thick red sauce), spring rolls, hakka noodles, fried rice. ✉*Hotel Amarpreet, Jalna Rd.* ☎*240/662–1133, 240/233–2521* ▭*MC, V.*

$ ✕**President Park Semicircle Coffee Shop.** This is a great place to cool down. The airy, bright hotel coffee shop affords a view of the hotel's pool and gardens through it glass windows. The food, all of it vegetarian, is quite tasty. Try the South Indian items—hot dosas or *medu wadas* (deep-fried lentil fritters), and the fresh juices. ✉*R 7/2 Chikalthana, Airport Rd.* ☎*240/248–6201* ▭*AE, DC, MC, V.*

$ ✕**Tandoor.** The hospitality of manager Syed Liakhat Hussain is one good reason to visit this brightly lit, busy, cheerful restaurant that stays open very late. The kebabs are another reason, especially the *kasturi* (chicken) kebab. People come here for authentic and well-made tandoori food. It's become, indeed, a local landmark. Try the *murg tikka* (chicken kebabs), paneer tikka, biryani, black dal (lentils), and the fresh, fried local fish. Shoot for lunch instead of dinner if you're coming by auto-rickshaw, because later in the evening it's difficult to find transportation (this place is far from the main hotels). ✉*Shyam Chambers, Station Rd.* ☎*240/232–8481* ▭*MC, V.*

7

¢–$ ✕**Smile.** In the heart of the Nirala Bazaar, this may be a long way to venture from the city center (20 minutes from Jalna Road) for more authentic fast food. But as soon as you arrive, it becomes clear what a draw the food is (on weekends half of Aurangabad is waiting for a table). No fancy artifacts or mood lighting here, just a bunch of tables and white plastic chairs laid out in an open-ended courtyard. But those dosas are delicious. ✉*13/14 Nirala Bazar* ☎*240/232–4841* ▭*No credit cards.*

¢ ✕**Bhoj.** Both branches of this thali restaurant serve "unlimited" quick-and-tasty, light vegetarian Gujarati or Rajasthani platters—20 items for Rs. 70—for lunch (11 to 3) and dinner (7 to 10). It's a welcome change from the overdose of Mughlai and tandoori food available elswhere. The selection is wide, and the price is right. It's purely functional inside, however, and the din can be deafening; this is not a place for leisurely dining. Alcohol is not served, and there's no air-conditioning. ✉*Kamdar Bhavan, CBS Rd.* ☎*240/235–9438* ▭*No credit cards.*

¢ ✕**Laadli.** Five minutes away from most of the big hotels in the area, this simple vegetarian eatery, decorated with trying-to-be-modern flair, is just the place to head to for a crispy dosa, a lassi, chana bhatura, or some other Indian-style fast food that you may not find at your hotel restaurant. The geometrical shapes and plants all around make it a cheerful place. ✉*N2 Goodwill Complex, CIDCO* ☎*240/329–1819* ▭.

$$ **Taj Residency.** Inside and out, this gleaming Mogul palace is done in bright white marble and stone. The windows and doors arch to regal Moghul points, and the grand dome over the lobby is hand-painted in traditional Jaipuri patterns. The Taj has easily the best vibe

of the city hotels. The warm, Ajanta-esque rooms have good and solid furniture with matching headboards and mirror frames, and a small maroon-and-orange sitting area. All rooms look out onto the garden (but there's no access), and have balconies or patios with teak swings. Stone paths wind through 5 acres of beautifully landscaped lawns. Note that the hotel phones are sometimes very poorly manned, and you may have to dial repeatedly. **Pros:** city's most elegant hotel, lovely ambience. **Cons:** rather expensive, service disorganized. ⊠*8-N-12 CIDCO* ☎*240/2381–1106 to 10* ⊕*www.tajhotels.com* *66 rooms, 2 suites* *In-room: safe, refrigerator, Wi-Fi. In-hotel: restaurant, room service, bar, pool, gym, concierge, no elevator, laundry service.* *AE, DC, MC, V.*

$ **Ambassador Ajanta.** Next door to its rival, the Welcomgroup Rama International, this five-story marble hotel is surrounded by sweeping lawns, well-kept flower beds, and towering trees alive with singing birds. Filled with brass goddesses, marble elephants, wood carvings, and other Indian antiques, the hotel is decorated in that cluttered Indian-elegance look. The slightly gloomy rooms have an Indian feel, with local furnishings, red accents, and garden-view windows. Don't miss a dip in the pool, where you can imbibe mid-swim at the bar at the shallow end. **Pros:** nice view of sweeping lawns, hotel restaurant serves interesting food. **Cons:** not good value for money, gloomy rooms. ⊠*Jalna Rd., CIDCO, 431003* ☎*240/248–5211 or 240/248–5214* ⊕*www.ambassadorindia.com* *92 rooms, 12 suites* *In-room: refrigerator, Wi-Fi. In-hotel: restaurant, room service, bar, tennis courts, pool, laundry service, concierge.* *AE, MC, V.*

$ ★ **President Park.** In this attractive contemporary building, designed around a central garden, every room has a pool view. Ground-floor rooms are the best; they open directly onto the garden. You can walk out of your room and dive right into the pool. And what a pool: it's large, with a waterfall and a food pavilion. The rooms have balconies or patios and are cheerful inside, with teak-trim furniture, melon-color fabrics, and brass fixtures. Bathrooms, done in gray tile, are on the small side. Overall, this hotel is a great choice—it seems like a luxury hotel but has reasonable prices. **Pros:** well lighted, cheerful hotel, comfortable rooms, good value, serves excellent food. **Cons:** tiny bathrooms, restaurant serves vegetarian food only. ⊠*R 7/2 Chikalthana, Airport Rd., 431210* ☎*240/248–6201* ⊕*www.presidenthotels.com* *60 rooms, 4 suites* *In-hotel: restaurant, room service, bar, tennis court, pool, gym, no elevator, laundry service, concierge.* *AE, DC, MC, V.*

$ ★ **Quality Inn Meadows.** In this resort-style hotel, which has won architectural awards, the accommodations are in simple, carpet-free cottages, each with a private patio. Rooms here are a bit Spartan, but the hotel is wonderfully tranquil. The hotel uses a biotechnological system of plant roots to purify its air and waste water. The grounds, planted with trees and flowers, house rare birds. It's intensely quiet here, as the hotel is 5 km (3 mi) from the city center on the road to the Ellora caves. The hotel is ideal for kids—there are rabbits and parrots, and there's ample space to run around. The restaurant serves tasty Indian and Continental food. A courtesy bus goes to the city four times a day. Service is above average. **Pros:** green, spacious and peaceful location, good value, airport pickup, close to Ellora caves. **Cons:** far from the city. ✉ *Village Mitmita, Padegaon, Aurangabad–Mumbai Hwy., 431002* ☎ *240/267–7412 to 21* 🌐 *www.themeadowsresort.com* *48 rooms, 4 suites* *In hotel: restaurant, room service, bar, pool, gym, no elevator, laundry facilities.* 💳 *AE, MC, V.*

$ **Welcomgroup Rama International.** A long driveway takes you away from the main road and through spacious grounds to this not-very-majestic-looking hotel, decorated simply with red bands of elephants chiseled on its bleach-white facade. What the Rama lacks in external majesty is made up for by tasteful interiors. The efficient and friendly staff provide personalized service and create the kind of warm, intimate setting you'd normally associate with a smaller hotel. Standard rooms, in two wings around the pool, are spacious, plush, and comfortably elegant, with views onto the verdant garden of palms and bright flower beds. However, they open out into the garden. Corner suites are vast. **Pros:** very good value, intimate, good service, nice views, comfortable rooms. **Cons:** small pool. ✉ *R-3 Chikalthana, 431210* ☎ *240/248–5441 to 44 or 240/663–4141* 🌐 *www.welcomgroup.com* *90 rooms, 2 suites* *In-room: refrigerator, Wi-Fi. In-hotel: restaurant, room service, bar, pool, gym, laundry service, concierge.* 💳 *AE, MC, V.*

¢ **Amarpreet.** The cheerful, colorful rooms, with dark ochre-colored carpets, in this centrally located five-story hotel are above-average. The bathrooms could be cleaner, however. The simple, airy lobby opens out onto a small patch of lawn. Opt for a room with a view of the Bibi-ka-Maqbara, and check to see if your room is quiet enough. The hotel runs has a back-up generator because of frequent power cuts, but when the normal electricity disappears the elevators don't function. **Pros:** well located, city's top Chinese restaurant is here, cheap. **Cons:** slightly seedy, sparse furniture, no generator for elevators, rooms cleanliness lacking. ✉ *Jalna Rd.* ☎ *240/662–1133 or 240/233–2522* 🌐 *www.amarpreethotel.com* *30 rooms, 1 suite* *In-hotel: 2 restaurants, room service, bar, laundry facilities.* 💳 *AE, MC, V.*

¢ **Kailas.** If you're not the typical tourist and you don't intend to use Aurangabad as a base for day trips to Ellora and Ajanta, try this serene little hotel with a garden, a stone's throw from the Ellora caves. Its very clean, double-bed stone cottages are spartan, not uncomfortable, and have a rustic appeal. One huge bonus of staying here is that on days when the caves are open, you can visit them at 6 AM, experiencing them in the dawn light without the crowds. The hotel can organize transport to the city, and has a restaurant attached with a plentiful menu. Non-a/c rooms here are just Rs. 900. **Pros:** superb, quiet location, cheap. **Cons:** minimal furnishings, far from the city. ✉ *Ellora Caves, 431102* ☎ *2437/244–446 or 2437/244–543* 🌐 *www.hotelkailas.com* *5 rooms, 18 cottages* *In-room: no a/c (some), no phone, no TV. In-hotel: restaurant, room service, no elevator.* 💳 *No credit cards.*

7

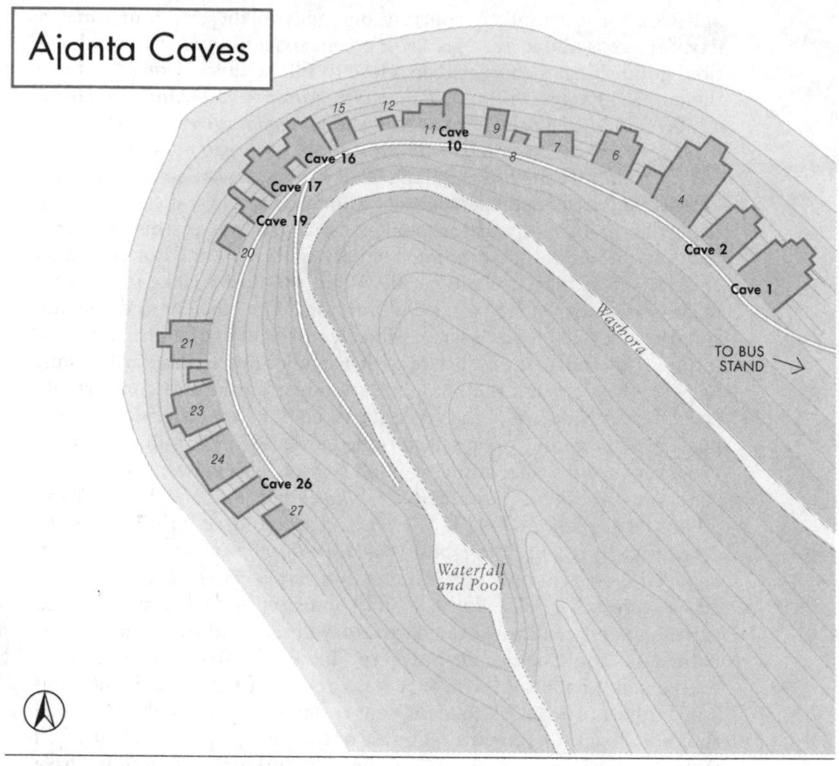

AJANTA CAVES

Fodor'sChoice ★ It's thought that a band of wandering Buddhist monks first came here in the 2nd century BC searching for a place to meditate during the monsoons. Ajanta was ideal—peaceful and remote, with a spectacular setting. It is a steep, wide, horseshoe-shaped gorge above a wild mountain stream flowing through a lush jungle below. The monks began carving caves into the greyrock face of the gorge, and a new temple form was born.

Over the course of seven centuries, the cave temples of Ajanta evolved into works of incredible art. Structural engineers continue to be awestruck by the sheer brilliance of the ancient builders, who, undaunted by the limitations of their implements, materials, and skills, created a marvel of artistic and architectural splendor. In all, 29 caves were carved, 15 of which were left unfinished; some of them were *viharas* (monasteries)—complete with stone pillows carved onto the monks' stone beds—others were *chaityas* (Buddhist cathedrals). All of the caves were profusely decorated with intricate sculptures and murals depicting the many incarnations of Buddha.

As the influence of Buddhism declined, monk-artists were fewer, and the temples were swallowed up by the voracious jungle. About a thousand years later, in 1819, Englishman John Smith was tiger-hunting on the bluff overlooking the Waghora River in the dry season and noticed the soaring arch of what is now dubbed Cave 10 peeking out from the thinned greenery in the ravine below; it was he who subsequently unveiled the caves to the modern world. Incidentally, tigers are not too far from this area (the thick forests from Ajanta to Kannad are the Gautala wildlife sanctuary). Today the caves at Ajanta and Ellora have been listed by UNESCO as World Heritage Sites.

At both Ajanta and Ellora, monumental facades and statues were chipped out of solid rock, but at Ajanta, an added dimension has survived the centuries—India's most remarkable cave paintings. Monks spread a carefully prepared plaster of clay, cow dung, chopped rice husks, and lime onto the rough rock walls, and painted pictures on the walls with local pigments: red ocher, burnt brick, copper oxide, lampblack, and dust from crushed green rocks. The caves are now like chapters of a splendid epic in visual form, recalling the life of the Buddha, and illustrating tales from Buddhist *jatakas* (fables). As the artists told the story of the Buddha, they portrayed the life and civilization they knew—a drama of ancient nobles, wise men, and commoners.

Opinions vary on which of the Ajanta caves is most exquisite: Caves 1, 2, 16, 17, and 19 are generally considered to have the best paintings; caves 1, 6, 10, 17, 19, and 26 the best sculptures. (The caves are numbered from west to east, not in chronological order.) Try to see all eight of these caves, at least. If you're not sightseeing with a guide, ask one of the attendants at each cave for help and tip them ten rupees for their kindness; keep some loose change with you.

Most popular at Ajanta are the paintings in **Cave 1.** These depict the Bodhisattva Avalokitesvara and Bodhisattva Padmapani. Padmapani, or the "one with the lotus in his hand," is considered to be the alter ego of the Lord Buddha; Padmapani assumed the duties of the Buddha when he disappeared. Padmapani is depicted with his voluptuous wife, one of Ajanta's most widely reproduced figures. When seen from different angles, the magnificent Buddha statue in this cave seems to wear different facial expressions.

Cave 2 is remarkable for its ceiling decorations and its murals relating the birth of the Buddha. For its sheer exuberance, the painting of women on a swing is considered the finest. It's on the right wall as you enter, and when you face the wall it's on the left side of it.

Cave 6 is a two-story cave with lovely detail. Climb the steep steps to the second floor. Here there are pillars that emit musical sounds when rapped. On the first floor is an interesting well/undergound tank just outside the cave.

The oldest cave is **Cave 10,** a chaitya dating from 200 BC, filled with Buddhas and dominated by an enormous *stupa* (a dome, or monument, to Buddha). It's only in AD 100, however, that the exquisite brush-and-line work begins. In breathtaking detail, the Shadanta Jataka, a legend about the Buddha, is depicted on the wall in a continuous panel. There are no idols of Buddha in this cave, indicating that idol worship was not in vogue at the time—but the fact that **Cave 19,** hardly nine caves later, contains idols of Buddha, shows the progression of thought and the development of new methods of worship as the centuries wore on. Guides and caretakers will enthusiastically point out the name of the Englishman, John Smith, who rediscovered the caves—his name, along with 1819 underneath, is carved on the 12th pillar on the right-hand side of this cave. (Incidentally, Cave 10 was the first cave Smith spotted because its domed arch made it quite visible from the bluff above.)

The mystical heights attained by the monk-artists seem to have reached their zenith in **Cave 16.** Here a continuous narrative spreads both horizontally and vertically, evolving into a panoramic whole—at once logical and stunning. One painting here is riveting: known as *The Dying Princess,* it's believed to represent Sundari, the wife of the Buddha's half-brother Nanda, who left her to become a monk. Cave 16 has an excellent view of the river and may have been the entrance to the entire series of caves.

Cave 17 holds the greatest number of pictures undamaged by time. Luscious heavenly damsels fly effortlessly overhead, a prince makes love to a princess, and the Buddha tames a raging elephant. (Resisting temptation is a theme.) Other favorite paintings include the scene of a woman applying lipstick and one of a princess performing *sringar* (her toilette). This cameo is on the right hand wall as you enter and as you face the wall on the farthest right pillar.

Cave 26 is the more interesting of the caves on the far end. An impressive sculpted panel of a reclining Buddha is on your left as you enter. it's apparently a portrayal of a dying Buddha on the verge of attaining nirvana. His weeping followers are at his side, while celestial beings are waiting to transport him to the land of no tomorrows or rebirths.

A number of unfinished caves were abandoned mysteriously, but even these are worth a visit if you can haul yourself up a steep 100 steps. You can also walk up the bridle path, a gentler ascent in the form of a crescent pathway alongside the caves; from here you have a magnificent view of the ravine descending into the Waghura River. There's a much easier way to reach this point. On your return by car to Aurangabad, 20 km (12 mi) from the caves, take a right at Balapur and head 8 km (5 mi) toward Viewpoint, as it's called by the locals.

A trip to the Ajanta caves needs to be well planned. You can see the caves at a fairly leisurely pace in two hours, but the drive to and from the caves takes anywhere from two to three hours. Come prepared with water, lunch or snacks (from a shop in Aurangabad, because you won't get that much here except packed items like potato chips at the visitor center, and nothing once you enter the caves), comfortable walking shoes (that can be slipped on and off easily, because shoes are not allowed inside the caves), socks to pad about the cave in and not get your feet dirty, a small flashlight, a hat or umbrella for the heat, and patience. Aurangabad can be hot year-round, and touring 29 caves tiring. The paintings are dimly lit to protect the artwork, and a number are badly damaged, so deciphering the work takes some effort. But the archaeological department has put a lot of effort into making the caves more viewable, including special ultraviolet lights to brighten up certain panels. Shades and nets installed at the mouth of each cave keep out excess sun and bats.

There's no longer direct access to the caves. All visitors are required to park their cars or disembark from their coaches at a visitor center 3 km (2 mi) from the caves. A Rs. 6 ticket (Rs. 10 for an air-conditioned coach, that go less frequently) buys you a place on frequently departing green Maharashtra Tourism Development Corporation (MTDC) coaches going to the caves. Remember to carry the most important (and just enough) possessions with you, because it's a long haul back to retrieve snacks, guide books, or hats, or to dump extra belongings. The visitor complex has stalls with people hawking souvenirs, film, sodas, water, and packaged and fresh hot snacks—plus lots of irritating hawkers and unknown guides that need to be assiduously ignored and firmly dismissed. *(To book a legitimate guide see Tours in Aurangabad, Ajanta Caves & Ellora Caves Essentials.)*

The caves are connected by a fair number of steps; it's best to start at the far end at Cave 26 and work your way back—or you'll have a hot trek back at the end. The initial climb up, before you reach the cave level, is also quite a climb at 92 steps. Palanquins carried by helpers are available for the less hardy, for Rs. 400. Flash photography and video cameras are prohibited inside the caves (shooting outside fine), but for an extra Rs. 5 added to your admission fee, lights are turned on in the caves as you enter. Right outside the caves, a shoddy MTDC-run restaurant, predictably called the Ajanta, offers simple refreshments; this is the only refreshment area or stall near the caves.

MTDC operates a small hotel (25 rooms, 15 with a/c; ☎2438/244–230) 5 km (3 mi) from the caves, at Fardapur. A cloak room is available at the caves to deposit bags for Rs. 5 per bag. ✉ *100 km (62 mi) northeast of Aurangabad* 💴 *Foreigners US$5, light fee Rs. 5 (includes all caves), video camera fee Rs. 25, parking Rs. 15* ⏲ *Tues.–Sun. 9–5; arrive by 3:30.*

ELLORA CAVES

In the 7th century, for some unknown reason, the focus of activity shifted from Ajanta to a site 123 km (76 mi) to the southwest—a place known today as Ellora. Unlike the cave temples at Ajanta, those of Ellora are not solely Buddhist. Instead, they follow the development of religious thought in India—through the decline of Buddhism in the latter half of the 8th century, the Hindu renaissance that followed the return of the Gupta dynasty, and the Jain resurgence between the 9th and 11th centuries. Of the 34 caves, the 12 to the south are Buddhist, the 17 in the center are Hindu, and the 5 to the north are Jain.

At Ellora the focus is on sculpture, which covers the walls in ornate masses. The carvings in the Buddhist caves are serene, but in the Hindu

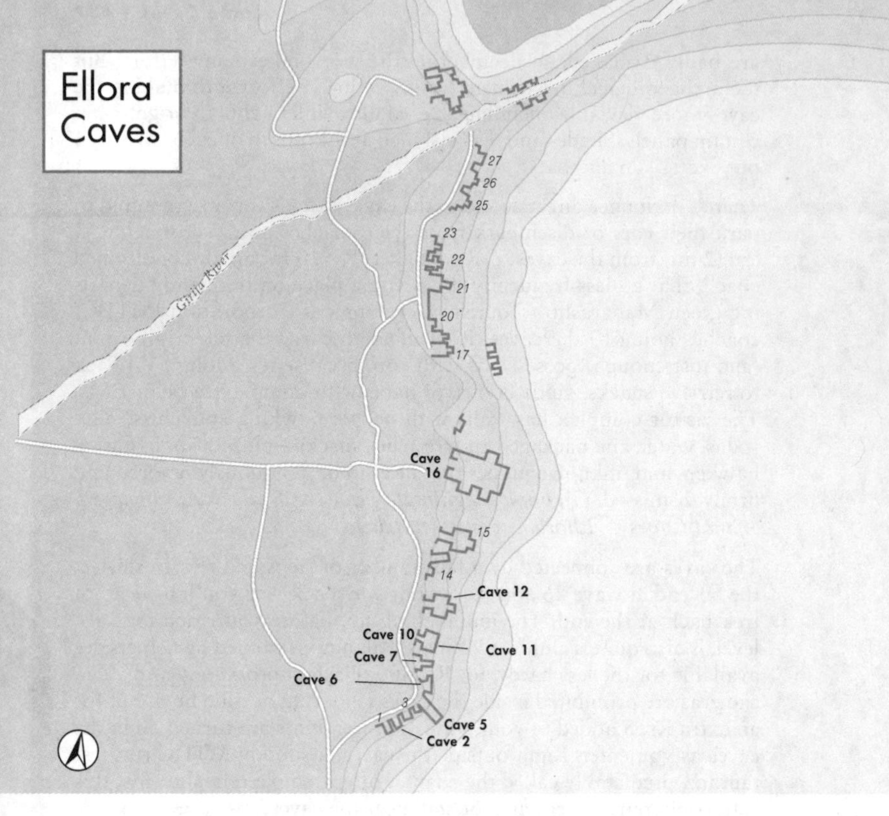

caves they take on a certain exuberance and vitality—gods and demons do fearful battle, Lord Shiva angrily flails his eight arms, elephants rampage, eagles swoop, and lovers intertwine.

Unlike at Ajanta, where the temples were chopped out of a steep cliff, the caves at Ellora were dug into the slope of a hill along a north–south line, presumably so that they faced west and could receive the light of the setting sun.

Cave 2 is an impressive monastery. The deceptively simple facade looms nearly 15 meters (50 feet) high; a lavish interior lies beyond. Gouged into this block of rock is a central hall with ornate pillars and a gallery of Buddhas and Boddhisattvas seated under trees and parasols.

The largest of the Buddhist caves is **Cave 5.** It was probably as a classroom for young monks. The roof appears to be supported by 24 pillars; working their way down, sculptors first "built" the roof before they "erected" the pillars.

Cave 6 contains a statue of Mahamayuri, the Buddhist goddess of learning—also identified as Saraswati, the Hindu goddess of learning—in the company of Buddhist figures. The boundaries between Hinduism and Buddhism are fuzzy and Hindus worship and recognize some Buddhist gods and goddesses as their own, and vice versa. For instance,

Hindus consider Buddha the avatar of Vishnu. **Cave 7**, an austere hall with pillars, is the first two-story cave. **Cave 10** is an impressive Chaitya Hall. Here the stonecutters reproduced the timbered roofs of their day over a richly decorated facade that resembles masonry work. Inside this chaitya—the only actual Buddhist chapel at Ellora—the main work of art is a huge sculpture of Buddha. Don't miss the high ceiling with stone "rafters" and note the sharp echo. The cave has been dubbed the Sutar Jhopdi or Carpenter's Cave and called a tribute to Visvakarma, the Hindu god of tools and carpentry. **Caves 11 and 12** rise grandly three floors up and are richly decorated with sculptural panels.

The immediate successors to the Buddhist caves are the Hindu caves, and a step inside these is enough to stop you in your tracks. It's another world—another universe—in which the calm contemplation of the seated Buddhas gives way to the dynamic cosmology of Hinduism. These caves were created around the 7th and 8th centuries.

Ellora is dominated by the mammoth Kailasa temple complex, or **Cave 16.** Dedicated to Shiva, the complex is a replica of his legendary abode at Mount Kailasa in the Tibetan Himalayas. The largest monolithic structure in the world, the Kailasa reveals the genius, daring, and raw skill of its artisans.

To create the Kailasa complex, an army of stonecutters started at the top of the cliff, where they removed 3 million cubic feet of rock to create a vast pit with a freestanding rock left in the center. Out of this single slab, 276 feet long and 154 feet wide, the workers created Shiva's abode, which includes the main temple, a series of smaller shrines, and galleries built into a wall that encloses the entire complex. Nearly every surface is exquisitely sculpted with epic themes.

Around the courtyard, numerous friezes illustrate the legends of Shiva and stories from the great Hindu epics, the *Mahabharata* and the *Ramayana*. One interesting panel on the eastern wall relates the origin of Shiva's main symbol, the lingam, or phallus. Another frieze, on the outer wall of the main sanctuary on the southern side of the courtyard, shows the demon Ravana shaking Mount Kailasa, from a story in the *Ramayana*.

The Jain caves are at the far end. If you have a car, consider driving there once you've seen the Hindu group of caves. These caves are attractive in their own right, and should not be missed on account of geography. The Ellora Caves are as complex as a rabbit burrow; it's marvelous to climb through the numerous well-carved chambers and study the towering figures of Gomateshvara and Mahavira.

Ellora is said to be the busiest tourist site in the state of Maharashtra. The Ajanta caves are a bit off the beaten track, but Ellora, a mere half an hour from Aurangabad, gets packed with crowds. Try to avoid coming here during school holidays from April to first week of June. Don't encourage hawkers and unknown guides; they can be a terrible nuisance. Viewing the Ellora caves, in contrast to the Ajanta caves, is an easier expedition—you can approach the caves laterally because the entire line of caves is parallel to the road and there are not many steps involved. The proximity to Aurangabad and the easy access makes seeing these caves a half-day's adventure. Choose either early morning or late afternoon. The winding drive to Ellora is very pleasant, through low-slung hills past old ruins as well as Daulatabad Fort (try to squeeze at least a half-hour stop there, too). *US$5, video camera fee Rs. 25 Wed.–Mon. 6–6.*

NEED A BREAK?

Ellora Restaurant (*Parking lot, Ellora Caves 2437/24441*) is a convenient place to stop for a cold drink and a hot samosa. The outdoor patio has fruit trees (home to many monkeys) and pink bougainvillea flowers. The restaurant closes before the caves. Walk straight out of the Ellora caves complex, past the umpteen souvenir stalls on your right, and you'll see the Hotel Kailas with its attached restaurant, Kailas (*Outside the Ellora Caves*). The menu, like so many Indian restaurants, is elastic—Chinese, Indian, Continental, snacks—Kailas has it all. Settle for a cool drink or some crisp *pakoras* (chick pea flour-and-vegetable fritters).

NIGHTLIFE & THE ARTS

Back in Aurangabad, the larger hotels have comfortable bars where you can while away time having a few drinks. Try the Taj Residency Garden Bar and Rama International's Madhuban.

The annual **Ellora Dance Festival,** held on one full moon night in December, draws top classical Indian dancers and musicians from around the country to perform outdoors against the magical backdrop of the Ellora Caves.

AURANGABAD, AJANTA CAVES & ELLORA CAVES ESSENTIALS

AIR TRAVEL

Aurangabad and Mumbai are about 45 minutes apart, and Aurangabad and New Delhi are 3½ hours apart by air. A one-way ticket costs about US$105 for foreign tourists between Mumbai and Aurangabad on Indian, Deccan, and Jet Airways and US$235 between New Delhi and Aurangabad on Indian. Indian, Jet, and Deccan fly to Aurangabad daily from Mumbai, and Indian flies daily to Aurangabad from Delhi. Make sure you ask a travel agent in advance about the current status and schedules, as there are links sometimes between Aurangabad and Jaipur and Udaipur in the winter. Schedules change every six months for these kinds of hop-and-a-skip flights.

Airlines & Contacts **Simplifly Deccan** (*240/3900-8888 www.airdeccan.net*). **Indian Airlines** (*240/248—5012 or 240/1407 or 240/248-1407 http://indian-airlines.nic.in*). **Jet Airways** (*240/244-1392 or 240/244-1770 office, 240/248-7076 or 248-4269 airport, 240/248-7076 Tele-Check-In www.jetairways.com*).

BUS TRAVEL

It's not the most comfortable option, but several competing companies run safe "luxury" overnight buses to Aurangabad from Mumbai, a 12-hour journey. You can arrange such a ride through Maharashtra Tourism Development Corporation (⇨ Visitor Information), or your Mumbai hotel or travel agent.

CARS & DRIVERS

A full-day trip in an air-conditioned Ambassador or Indica (sturdy but comfortable Indian cars that will give you a good ride) with a driver may cost around Rs. 2,000 to Ajanta and Rs. 950 to Ellora. A full-day trip in a non-air-conditioned Ambassador with driver may cost around Rs. 1,400 to Ajanta and Rs. 700 to Ellora. To hire an air-conditioned Ambassador, Uno, or Indica for use within the city for eight hours is Rs. 1,000 and in a non-air-conditioned Ambassador, Uno, or Indica Rs. 750. More luxurious cars are proportionately more expensive, but they are not necessary. You can arrange a car for hire through your hotel travel desk, one of the travel agencies below, or the Government of India Tourist Office; fix a price in advance and make sure you get a good rate.

If you hire a guide for the caves at Ellora or Ajanta, you are usually required to transport him there via a hired driver or your own rented car.

MONEY

ATMS You may withdraw cash against your Visa or Mastercard at either HDFC or ICICI Bank ATMs, and against American Express at HDFC ATMs. ATMs are farely common in major cities in this area, so ask your hotel or driver if you're having difficulty finding one.

CURRENCY EXCHANGE Most hotels will change money for you, as long as you're staying there. Aurangabad's State Bank of India is open weekdays 10:30–2:30 and 3–4 and Saturday 10:30–1. Trade Wings is open Monday–Saturday 9:30–6.

Exchange Services State Bank of India (✉ *Kranti Chowk, Aurangabad* ☎ *240/233-1386, 240/233-1872, or 240/233-4778*). **Trade Wings** (✉ *Near Bawa Petrol Pump, CBS Rd., Aurangabad* ☎ *240/235-7480 or 240/234-7480*).

TOURS

The Government of India Tourist Office in Aurangabad (⇨ Visitors Information *in* Aurangabad Essentials, *above*) oversees about 45 expert, polite, multilingual tour guides. You can hire one through the tourist office itself; the Maharashtra Tourism Development Corporation (MTDC) office, which is also in Aurangabad; and most travel agents. For parties of one to four, the fees are Rs. 1,000 for a full day visit to Ajanta caves and Rs. 750 for a full day visit to Ellora Caves and nearby sights. Hiring a half-day guide (four hours) will set you back Rs. 450. An extra Rs. 400 or so is charged for trips of more than 100 km (60 mi). It's best to book ahead. Ask for Al Mohammedi Abdul Nasser, a very knowledgeable, English-speaking guide, who comes recommended by the tourist office (they have a legitimate and qualified guide posted at the Ajanta caves, too). The archaeology department at the caves also has certain guides appointed, and although they are not as good as the tourist-office guides, they are satisfactory. Once you have a guide, you'll probably want to hire a car and driver.

Contacts **Aurangabad Tours and Travels** (*Aurangabad Transport Syndicate* ✉ *Welcomgroup Rama Hotel, Airport Rd., Aurangabad* ☎ *240/248–2423*). **Classic Travel Related Services** (✉ *MTDC Holiday Resort, Station Rd., Aurangabad* ☎ *240/233–5598 or 240/233–7788*).

TRAIN TRAVEL

Aurangabad is not very well connected by train to major hubs. Only a few trains run between Aurangabad and Mumbai. Tapovan Express is the best option; it departs from Mumbai at 6:10 AM and the journey takes just over seven hours. Aurangabad is also about seven hours away from Hyderabad by train; you can take the Mumbai-Nizamabad Devgiri Express there. It's possible to reach Aurangabad from New Delhi, but it's a tedious journey—you must change trains at Manmad after a five- to six-hour stopover. Alternatively, you can go up to Jalgaon—on the main Delhi–Mumbai route—and make the rest of the journey (108 km [67 mi]) by road. It's best to have your hotel organize transport from Jalgaon (ask them to arrange a car and driver; they will wait there for you). The journey takes three hours and will set you back about Rs. 1,650 for a non-air-conditioned car.

VISITOR INFORMATION

The Government of India Tourist Office, across from the train station, provides a warm and informative welcome to Aurangabad and is open weekdays 8:30–6 and Saturday and holidays 8:30–2. Ask for Mrs. I. R. V. Rao. The MTDC office in town (open Monday–Saturday 10–5:30; closed the second and fourth Saturday of the month) offers a variety of information about other destinations in Maharashtra, and they have a counter at the airport that's open when flights arrive.

Tourist Offices **Government of India Tourist Office** (✉ *Krishna Vilas, Station Rd., Aurangabad* ☎ *240/236–4999 or 240/233–1217*). **Maharashtra Tourism Development Corporation (MTDC)** (✉ *MTDC Holiday Resort, Station Rd., Aurangabad* ☎ *240/233–1513*).

Goa

The palm-tree grove at Vagator Beach

WORD OF MOUTH

"Besides Pänjim and Old Goa there is a whole array of things to see in Goa! Go to the hinterland of the Ponda district and see the Hindu temples . . . From Old Goa go to the island of Divar, and then proceed inland along the Mandovi River—it is quite magical and outside the main tourist circuit."

—agtoau

www.fodors.com/forums

WELCOME TO GOA

TOP REASONS TO GO

★ **World-Class Beaches:** The warm Arabian Sea and long sandy beaches create the perfect environment for sun worshipping.

★ **Portuguese Architecture and Influence:** Goa's history and Iberian influences are one of a kind within India.

★ **Relaxed, Friendly Locals:** Goans are outgoing, quick to smile, and not offended by less-than-modest Western clothing. In practical terms, men and women are free to wear shorts, tank tops, and sarongs both on and off the beach.

★ **Goan Trance Parties:** These are not as widespread or as wild as in years past, but the famed all-night beach parties continue to draw young and not-so-young people from around the world.

★ **Goan Cuisine:** Spicy fish and fresh seafood dominate area menus.

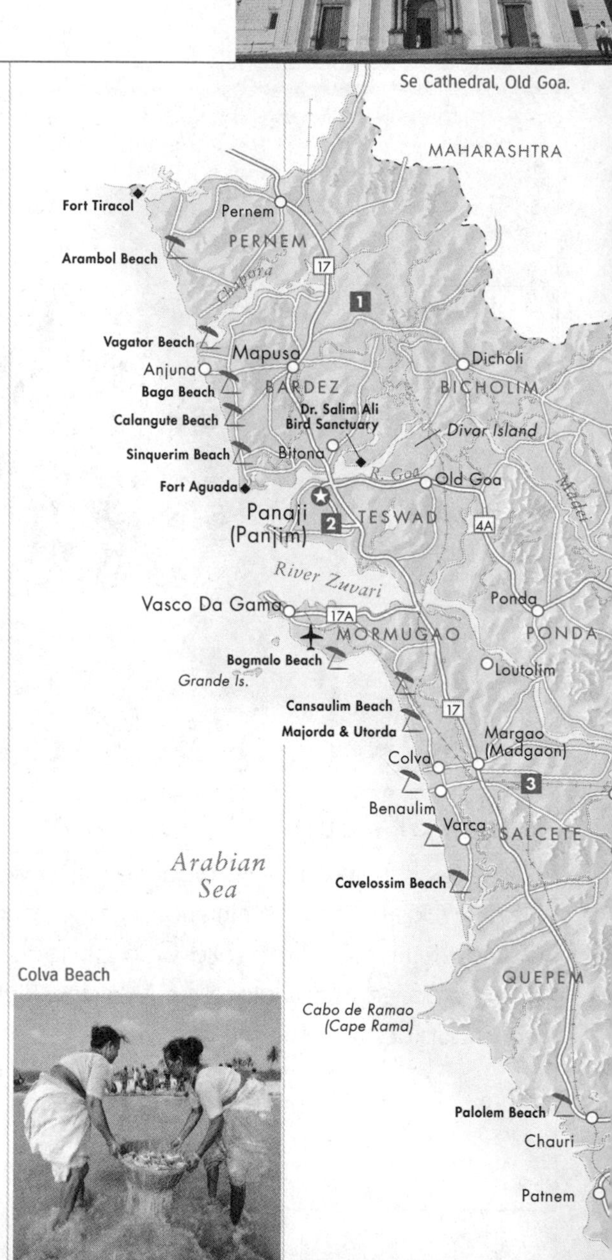

Se Cathedral, Old Goa.

Colva Beach

Shree Shantadurga Hindu temple, Northeast Ponda.

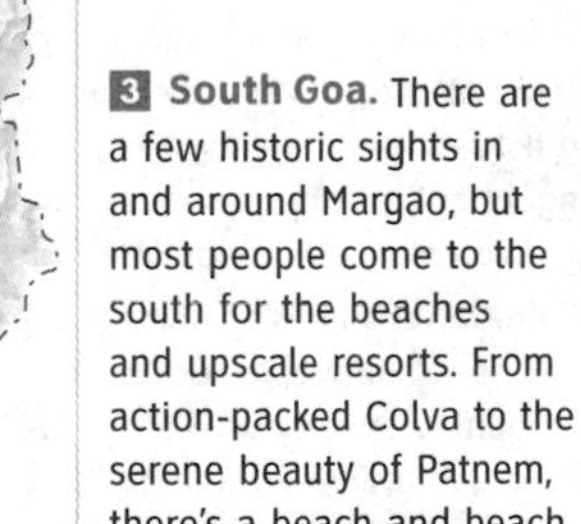

1 North Goa. For many visitors the heart and soul of Goa is found in the beaches and villages north of Panaji. Less Westernized than the overly developed southern part of the state, the classic Goan lifestyle can be attained in the beach towns of Baga and Anjuna.

2 Panaji and Central Goa. White-washed Catholic churches, palm-lined plazas, and the narrow streets of Panaji's historic Fontainhas district feel decidedly more European than Indian. The grandiose churches of Old Goa and the temples in Ponda are best accessed from here.

3 South Goa. There are a few historic sights in and around Margao, but most people come to the south for the beaches and upscale resorts. From action-packed Colva to the serene beauty of Patnem, there's a beach and beach town for every taste.

GETTING ORIENTED

Goa is best described as short (105 km/65 mi long) and sweet (full of friendly locals). The capital city Panaji divides the northern beaches from those in the south and is the regional transportation and cultural center of this diminutive territory. Though it's the smallest state in India, there's a wide diversity of terrain including sandy beaches, lazy backwaters, acres of emerald green rice paddies, thick palm forests, and steep, jungle-covered mountains. Unlike the enormous states to the north, Goa can be easily be explored from one end to the other.

Agonda Beach, South Goa

GOA PLANNER

When to Go

Most visitors come to Goa in mid-winter, and because December and January are popular months for scoring beach time and joining the party scene, lodging prices go sky-high and the beaches, roads, and restaurants are packed. Those who come in October, November, or early spring enjoy gorgeous weather and Goa's beauty without being part of a crowd. Early February visitors can join in the added excitement of Carnival. The monsoon stretches from the end of May to October, during which most beach-shack restaurants close due to torrential rains, heavy winds, and violent surf. On the plus side, those who venture to South India in August often find the cooler temperatures, rock-bottom prices, and lush countryside worth the occasional drenching.

Getting There & Around

Booking an international flight to Mumbai or Delhi, then hopping a domestic flight to Goa's Dabolim Airport, about 29 km (18 mi) south of Panaji is the way most travelers get to Goa. You can make online bookings with a number of airlines including Air India, Air Sahara, Indian Airlines, Jet Airways, and Kingfisher Airlines. From the centrally located airport it's easy to get a cab to your hotel or to Panaji for around Rs. 500.

You can take a train or bus to Goa from Mumbai, but be warned: such trips can be long—at least 12 hours by train, 17 hours by bus—crowded, and uncomfortable.

Goa is a small state, so everywhere is within a short drive of everywhere else and taxis are plentiful and fairly affordable, especially if you're sharing with other travelers. You don't really need to contact a tour operator, as there will always be a taxi stand outside your hotel, or the hotel can call one for you. Goa has a unionized taxi system with fixed rates from point A to point B. Fares are not supposed to be negotiable, but depending on the driver, you may be able to swing a deal. If you are visiting a number of places and covering a lot of ground, hire a taxi for a 4- or 8-hour stretch for a flat rate.

Auto-rickshaws, otherwise known as *tuk-tuks*, abound and cost considerably less than taxis. There are no fixed rates, so before climbing in ask a local or a knowledgeable visitor what the fare should be to your destination. Note: For safety and sanity reasons, tuk-tuks are best for short distances in town rather than for jaunts across the state.

You can rent motorbikes at bus stops, railway stations, markets, and beach resorts and cars at the airport. You'll need an international driver's license to drive anything larger than a 55-cc engine. However, Indian drivers and roads being what they are, think long and hard before renting any motorized vehicle you intend to drive yourself.

If you're in reasonable shape and confident riding on potholed, heavily traveled roads, consider renting a bicycle for a jaunt to save on taxi fares, especially if you simply want to get from your hotel to the beach and back. Don't expect more than one gear or anything resembling what you're used to; check the tires and brakes.

Choose Your Own Adventure

There are dozens of individuals and companies offering state tours, river cruises, and temple and spice plantation tours. Perhaps the best resource for up-to-date information is Find*All* Goa at www.findall-goa.com. This frequently updated site provides detailed calendars for live music, tours, cruises, hotel happenings and cultural and sporting events as well as useful information regarding arriving and departing flights and trains. Exceptionally detailed maps of Goa's districts and towns (they even include walking paths) can be downloaded.

The Goa Tourism Development Corporation ☎832/242–0779 🌐www.goa-tourism.com runs bus tours of both north and south Goa as well as river cruises from the Santa Monica pier in Panaji.

Lodging: Save vs. Splurge

Goa has plenty of luxury resorts and hotels in the north and south. In this category you have your pick of staying at a Western chain (Marriott, Park Hyatt, or Radisson) or an Indian-owned chain that equals or exceeds U.S. standards (Taj Hotels, the Leela).

For a sense of place stay at one of the Heritage Hotels, such as Siolim House, Marbella Guest House, Casa Anjuna or Casa Britona. You'll be treated like family, because you're one of perhaps a dozen guests, and most important you'll be staying at a distinctive property unique to the area.

If you're traveling light, can carry your valuables at all times, and are ready to really rough it (no indoor plumbing), check out a beach-shack. These can be fun to stay in when you're traveling in a group, but they are not advisable for women traveling alone.

What It Costs In Rupees

	¢	$	$$	$$$	$$$$
Restaurants	under Rs. 100	Rs. 100–Rs. 300	Rs. 300–Rs. 500	Rs. 500–Rs. 700	over Rs. 700
Hotels	under Rs. 2,000	Rs. 2,000–Rs. 4,000	Rs. 4,000–Rs. 6,000	Rs. 6,000–Rs. 10,000	over Rs. 10,000

Restaurant prices are for an entrée plus bread or rice. Hotel prices are for a double room in high season, excluding a tax of up to 20%.

Planning Your Time

Whether you have only a few days or a few weeks in Goa, you'll do well to spend most of them swimming in the warm waters of the Arabian Sea and enjoying the distinctive Goan cuisine. Base yourself either in the lively Bardez district in the north or at one of the more sedate southern resorts, depending on your style. If you have time, or simply want a break from the sun, spend a day walking around the historic Fontainhas and Sao Tome districts in Panaji, and at least a half day visiting Old Goa's grand churches built by the Portuguese in the 16th century. On Wednesdays, head for the lively market in Anjuna, held in a field not far from the beach. Here you'll find inexpensive jewelry, cotton sarongs, colorful shoulder bags, and handicrafts marketed by the beautiful women of Goa, Karnataka, and other Indian states. To find late-night beach parties follow the trance music to any of dozens of beach shacks on Baga, Calangute, Anjuna and Colva. Other not-to-be-missed pleasures include boat cruises on the Mandovi River, and day tours to the temples in Ponda and the rustic beauty of Dudhsagar Falls in the eastern part of the state.

Updated by Barbara Floria

THOSE WHO KNOW INDIA WELL will tell you that Goa, the smallest state in the Indian federation, is an anomaly—a territory that has Indian elements, but is decidedly its own entity, shaped by a unique set of circumstances and influences.

Goa's Hindu merchants flourished for centuries trading spices, silk, pearls, horses, and ideas with Arabs, East Africans, and Mediterranean cultures until its fortunes were profoundly altered by the arrival in 1510 of Affonso de Albuquerque, a Portuguese explorer and naval officer who wrestled the tiny realm from the hands of the Sultan of Bijapur. For the next 450 years the Portuguese exerted major pressures on Goan culture, language, and religion, not the least of which was converting the native Hindus and Buddhists to Catholicism by force. Ruling with an iron hand before, during, and after the rest of the Indian subcontinent was under the thumb of the British, they were finally driven out in 1961 in a land assault ordered by India's first Prime Minister, Jawaharlal Nehru.

The latest invaders to produce an undeniable influence on Goa's way of life, economy, and identity are the millions of foreign tourists who arrive year after year transporting contemporary lifestyles, Western values, and demands for ever more goods and services.

Accordingly, today's visitors find what some consider a paradise on earth: mile after mile of stunning beaches backed by palm forests and emerald green rice paddies; a distinctive cuisine forged by an exceptional blend of Indian and European traditions; and a local population who are generous to a fault and quick to return a smile, pat your arm, and offer assistance to anyone in need.

Although most Goans are poor by Western standards, they rank in the upper echelons of India's standards of living and literacy rates, prompting some travelers to refer to their experience here as "India Lite." Even so, the contrast between rich and poor, laborer and the middle class is still readily apparent. To wit: It's not uncommon to see houses made of plastic sheeting and palm fronds nestled in the shade of billboards advertising mutual funds, and the widening of major highways is likely to be accomplished by masses of barefoot men using pick-axes.

That said, Goa has more five-star resorts that match or surpass even the finest Western hotel chains in terms of comfort, amenities, and sheer indulgence than any other region in India. As a result, many tourists arrive at Goa's Dabolim Airport, are whisked to security-gated beach resorts and spend a week scarcely aware of being in India at all. Which is certainly a shame, because as a destination and an experience Goa has a lot to offer besides the sand and sea, including a rich Hindu heritage best seen at the temples in Ponda, striking Renaissance cathedrals in Old Goa, ancestral homes surrounding the ragtag southern city of Margao, and the capital city Panaji's Portuguese historic district, with its diverse shopping opportunities and urban energy.

Beach aficionados can happily chose from dozens of beaches that crowd the state's 35-mi coastline, depending on their mood or preferences.

Those looking for seclusion can head north to Arambol Beach, nestled below steep cliffs and home to Goa's remaining hippie enclave, or to the remote southern beaches in Agonda. For nonstop action—dance raves set to thumping Goan trance music are the norm at night—partygoers should head for Baga in the north or Colva in the south.

In the end, Goa's charisma resides in its ability to be all things to all people: a tranquil retreat from modern life or party central, a resort spot in which to perfect a tan or a destination in which to explore India's Hindu heritage. And whatever you come here looking for it's assured you'll encounter more than you expected.

MONSOON MASALA

Chances are you've never experienced anything like the monsoon in Goa. The downpours are heavy and sudden, and the drops so huge and close together it's as if someone is throwing buckets of water on you from a second floor window. The rain may last for days or a mere 30 minutes, disappearing as quickly as it came. Even so, if you're in Goa during a rainy spell, don't let it slow you down. Wear your flip-flops, bring an umbrella, and carry on as the Indians do.

ABOUT THE RESTAURANTS

If you like seafood and spicy food in general, you're in luck. You can spend all your time happily eating nothing but searingly hot (spicy) fish day in and day out, both in the best restaurants around (generally found at hotels) and at beachfront open-air shacks. But since Goa has such a huge tourist culture, food can be prepared to your liking—simply grilled or fried or with less spice, if you prefer. Goan food is big on flavor, whether it's chilli, tamarind, or coconut that dominate the dish. Make sure you order your meat (pork or beef) cooked through, and only order meat in the better-known larger restaurants, not at the beach shacks. Seafood is usually safe everywhere as long as it's fresh. If you're vegetarian, you'll get by fine, but vegetables are not as plentiful in the Goan diet as are fish, seafood, and meat.

ABOUT THE HOTELS

Make sure you reserve a room far in advance of December to February, when traveling hordes fill the hotels. During the monsoon season (June–October), prices drop by up to half and the resorts fill up with Indian visitors from the North. Unless noted otherwise, hotels have air-conditioning, TVs, and bathrooms with showers.

EXPLORING GOA

Goa's topography varies between beaches, jungle, and rich farmland. Much of the country's development is along the coast, where you'll find all the resorts Goa is famous for, plus the two major towns—Panaji in central Goa and Margao in the south. Also along the coast are scores of paddy fields, coconut groves, and small towns. Head inland for the natural sights, including waterfalls, bird sanctuaries, and temples ensconced in dense palm jungle, all easily navigated as long as you have a good guide.

IF YOU LIKE

ARCHITECTURE

Goa is best known for its grandiose churches, exquisitely sculpted temples, and mosques, all dating from the 16th to the 18th centuries. The most illustrious structures here include Old Goa's Sé (cathedral) and the Basilica of Bom Jesus, where the remains of St. Francis Xavier lie in a silver casket entombed in a Florentine-style marble mausoleum.

CARNIVAL

If you visit in February just before Lent, you'll see the Goans' zest for life in its finest form. Carnival time remains the official season for nonstop revelry, directed by King Momo ("King of Misrule"), a Goan appointed by his peers as the life of the party. Festivities include fanciful pageants (with some 50 floats depicting elements of Goa's folk culture, or more contemporary messages like preservation of the environment), hordes of musicians strumming the guitar or playing the banjo, and dancers breaking into the *mando* (a folk fusion of the Portuguese fado and the waltz)—all in streets spangled with confetti. This is prime time to have a beer or a *feni* and to savor Goa's legendary warmth.

HOT FISH & FENI

The Goans' legendary passion for seafood is borne out in the lines of the state's poet laureate, B. B. Borkar: "O, God of Death! Don't make it my turn today, because there's fish curry for dinner!" Portuguese dishes are generally adapted to Goan tastes with a healthy pinch of red chilli, tempered with coconut milk. Typical local dishes include zesty-sweet prawn-curry rice, *chouris pao* (sausage bread), chicken *cafreal* (amply seasoned with ginger, garlic, green chillies, and lime), and ultra-hot-vindaloo dishes. Goa's seafood is superb, especially fresh crabs, pomfret, squid, lobster, and prawns. Try pomfret in a red or green sauce, or tiger prawns *baffad* (spicy Goan style). For dessert, order *bebinca,* a rich, layered, dense pastry made of butter, egg yolk, and coconut. And no Goan experience is truly complete without at least a taste of *feni,* the potent local brew made of either coconut sap or cashew fruit.

Much farther west, toward Karnataka, are the mountains of the Western Ghats, and the lush rain forest that has developed from the rainwater that collects here from the monsoon that sweeps inland from the coast. Note that in addresses the terms *wadi, waddo,* and *vado* all mean "street."

NORTH GOA

You'll find most of the party beaches (and most of the foreigners) in the northern part of Goa. There's not much to see besides beaches, but you will find a few beautiful old forts built of the local red pitted stone. You may also want to take an excursion to one of the popular markets. The region is divided into several districts: Pernem at the far north, Bardez just below it, Bicholim directly east, and Satari still farther inland—to the mountains of the Western Ghats and the state of Karnataka. The Bardez district, where you'll find the beaches and most towns and hotels, is the most populated.

ARAMBOL BEACH

★ *48 km (30 mi) northwest of Panaji.*

Goa's northernmost beach, known as Arombol or Harmal, is rugged and lovely. You enter through a hippie colony where young foreigners live in small huts. The best stretch of beach is a 20-minute walk to the right, beyond the ragged food and drink shacks. Here, the scenery is spectacular: a freshwater pond nestles at the base of the hillside 50 yards from the crashing surf below, and the ocean foams around dark rocks rising offshore. The sea is rougher here than at other beaches—still good for swimming but a bit more fun for surf-seekers. To avoid crowds in season, walk past the pond and you'll find quieter tide-dependent inlets and rock ledges.

WHERE TO STAY

$$$$ ★ **Siolim House.** If you want to relax in style, stay at this small boutique hotel, which occupies a 300-year-old Portuguese villa on the south bank of the Chapora River. Beautifully restored in 1996, this old mansion has huge rooms, impeccably furnished with antiques and brightly colored linens, and plenty of comfortable common areas. A new bridge across the Chapora makes it easy to get to the beaches north of the river in Pernem, as long as you have a car or bicycle—it's about 6 to 7 km (4 mi) from Siolim House to the Pernem beaches. **Pros:** tranquil rural setting, sophisticated service, palacial rooms. **Cons:** inland location. ✉ *Casa Palaciao de Siolim, Wadi Siolim, Bardez district, 403517* ☎ *832/227–2138 or 833/227–2941* 🌐 *www.siolimhouse.com* *7 suites* *In-hotel: restaurant, pool, no elevator, laundry service, public Internet, airport shuttle.* *MC, V* *BP.*

$$$–$$$$ **Fort Tiracol.** This diminutive 18th-century Portuguese fort situated at land's end barely a stone's throw from Goa's northern border is now a striking heritage hotel. Each of the luxury rooms are furnished with exquisite antique furniture and accented by modern accessories and hand-detailed linens. Arambol, the closest town, is 8 km (5 mi) and a ferry-boat ride away, but if it's peace and quiet you want, you've come to the right place. You can visit the fort and have lunch or dinner on the terrace overlooking the rugged shoreline even if you're not staying at the hotel. **Pros:** optimum privacy, inspiring views of the Arabian Sea from every room. **Cons:** isolated, no beach access. ✉ *Tiracol, 403524* ☎ *832/652–9653* 🌐 *www.nilaya.com* *7 rooms* *In-hotel: restaurant, bar.* *MC, V* *BP.*

VAGATOR BEACH

25 km (16 mi) northwest of Panaji.

Little Vagator and Vagator come to life after dark with Goa's infamous raves. In the Bardez district, the beaches have secluded sandy coves with lots of palm trees, though they can be overrun during the day by busloads of tourists. To the north you can see the dark red walls of the old hill fort of Chapora, which was taken twice from the Portuguese by the Marathas. (The Marathas ruled a principality that covers much of the modern-day state of Maharashtra, north of Goa.) To the south, a striking white cross tops a rock jetty. The view from the ramparts is phenomenal, and farther up the shore are stretches of secluded sand. Vagator's gentle surf is good for swimming. This part of Goa is not as developed as the beaches farther south, and although there are plenty of shack restaurants they have a here-today-gone-tomorrow feel; indeed, many disappear from one season to the next, or take on a different name. The best way to find an eatery here is to ask fellow travelers for the name of the current favorite.

WHERE TO STAY

$$$$ **Casa Vagator.** From the time this contemporary hotel opened in September 2007, it's been packed with ultra-hip Indian guests and foreigners. Perched on a hillside high above the Arabian Sea, the property overlooks the wild beauty of Vagator Beach, which guests can reach by following a winding path that descends rather sharply. White leather sofas, glass tables, and designer lighting complete the look of the dining room and bar. The guest rooms have sleek built-ins, spare modern art on the walls, and comfortable beds. **Pros:** far from the hustle and bustle of Goa's beach scene, striking sea views. **Cons:** lots of stairs, small pool. ⊠*H. No. 594/4 Vozran, Vagator, 403507* ☎*832/652–9841* ⊕*www.casaboutiquehotelsgoa.com* *11 rooms, 1 penthouse suite* *In-hotel: restaurant, bar, pool, laundry service, public Internet, airport shuttle.* *MC, V* *BP.*

ANJUNA BEACH

Fodor'sChoice ★ *20 km (12 mi) northwest of Panaji.*

The Calangute Beach party seems to have shifted to Anjuna, and has spread farther north to Vagator Beach as well. Although Anjuna can get very crowded and the party scene become riotous, the beach is still not as commercial as Calangute, and does not have large-scale luxury resorts, such as those at Sinquerim Beach and those in the south. Drugs are all too easily available here, but are highly illegal—even if they seem to be part of the system. More happily, Anjuna is known for its **flea market** on Wednesday, a legacy of the '60s when hippies used to sell their belongings here to buy a few more weeks of love and peace. The Shore Bar is the place in Goa to watch the sunset and bond with the rest of Anjuna's laid-back population.

WHERE TO EAT & STAY

$ ✕**Biryani Palace.** American expats who favor the relaxed service, open-air setting, and good food claim this casual eatery is one of the best restaurants in Anjuna. The cook specializes in *biryanis* (Indian rice pilaf made with vegetables, spices and a choice of seafood, chicken or meat), of course, but also barbecued seafood, mixed seafood grills, and Goan specialties. Soft lighting, mat ceilings, rattan chairs on a sandy floor, and no a/c set the mellow mood that is enhanced by classic sitar music—instead of the driving Goan trance beat played in most area restaurants. ⊠*Anjuna Beach Rd. ¼ mi from beach, Anjuna* ☎*932/612–4699* *No credit cards.*

CLOSE UP

The Flea Market at Anjuna

Getting to the Wednesday flea market at Anjuna can be half the fun; you can take a bus or a motorcycle taxi, or a fisherman's boat from Baga, which is quicker (15 min by boat, 30 min by road). Although you will still find hippies there, it really isn't *their* market anymore. Now dominated by Lambani nomads in their striking clothes and jewelry, and craftspeople from elsewhere in India, the market is a splash of red and orange in a flat clearing above the rocky beach. Bead and white metal bangles, necklaces and earrings, silver toe rings, embroidered shoulder bags, silk and cotton sarongs, and ethnic footwear are among the more ordinary products on sale. If you look carefully, there are all sorts of other things here as well, from used motorbikes of uncertain age to do-it-yourself *mehendi* henna-tattoo kits. Buy a crochet bikini, tops and skirts embroidered with tiny mirrors top, or a tie-dye bandana to enhance your wardrobe for those really formal occasions, or just sit back at the market bar and down a ridiculously cheap beer while someone braids your hair deftly or offers to tattoo, pierce, or otherwise mutilate various parts of your anatomy. When your day's bargains have been struck (and getting things for a third or less of the quoted price is not uncommon), join the rest of Anjuna down at the shore. Be careful not to bargain unfairly, because you run the risk of a sarcastic "take it for free?" from one of the tribal women. The market only appears during the tourist season; during the monsoon there's a smaller market in Anjuna just above the main town beach.

8

$$$–$$$$ ★ **Casa Anjuna.** History, style, and attitude combine to make spending time in this 200-year-old Portuguese villa a rare pleasure. Each of the unique guest rooms (some of which have balconies overlooking the well-tended gardens or pool) are furnished with antique Goan and Balinese furniture, four-poster beds, and one-of-a-kind bedspreads. Artfully put together public and private spaces feature stenciled walls with whimsical architectural details throughout, and the open-air lobby has high ceilings and comfortable old-world upholstered couches. A rooftop bar and restaurant serves Goan and Continental dishes amid cool breezes and views of the countryside. **Pros:** beautiful setting, antiques-filled rooms, peace and quiet. **Cons:** 10-minute walk to the beach. ✉ *D'Mello Vaddo 66, Anjuna, 403509* ☎ *832/227–4123 to 25* 🌐 *www.casaboutiquehotelsgoa.com* *19 rooms* *In-hotel: restaurant, bar, pool, airport shuttle.* *MC, V* *BP.*

$$$ **Laguna Anjuna.** This upmarket place to stay is less than a kilometer from the beach in a tree-lined residential area. The elegant, minimalist cottages, each with one or two bedrooms, have soft lighting, entertainment areas with divans, and pretty blue bathrooms. The resort has an attractive pool, plenty of greenery, and a quiet restaurant if you don't want to trek to the eateries down the road. **Pros:** quiet, relaxed setting. **Cons:** a bit removed from the main attraction. ✉ *Soranto Vado, Anjuna Beach, 403509* ☎ *832/227–3248 or 832/227–4131* 🌐 *www.lagunaanjuna.com* *19 rooms, 6 suites* *In-hotel: restaurant, bar, pool, spa, no elevator, laundry service, public Internet, airport shuttle.* *MC, V* *BP.*

$ **Hotel Bougainvillea (Granpa's Inn).** This hotel occupies a 200-year-old restored Portuguese country house on an inland lane. Though granpa himself is long deceased and the place has changed management, the name has stuck as a mark of respect. A small pool, a lush garden, and simple, well-maintained rooms make this a well-priced place to stay in Anjuna. The multicuisine restaurant is a step up from the shack restaurants that line the beach. **Pros:** great value, funky vibe, rural setting. **Cons:** too far to walk to the beach. ✉ *Gaunwadi, Anjuna Beach, 403509* ☎ *832/227–3271, 832/227–3270, or 832/227–3271* 🌐 *www.granpasinn.com* *14 rooms* *In-room: no a/c (some), no TV (some). In-hotel: restaurant, bar, pool, public Internet, laundry service, airport shuttle.* ▭ *MC, V* *CP.*

NIGHTLIFE

The most popular place to down beer, watch the dramatic sunset over the Arabian Sea, and listen to loud music until the wee hours is the ★ **Shore Bar** on the beach. The steps of this place are usually packed with people, especially on Wednesday after the flea market. Walk north from the market for about a kilometer to get to the bar.

BAGA BEACH

15 km (9 mi) northwest of Panaji.

This small beach about 2 km (1 mi) north of Calangute in the Bardez district is a lively place known for its hopping "shack life." The many popular food and drink joints are headlined by St. Anthony's for seafood and Tito's Bar for nighttime revelry. The beach drops steeply to the shoreline, where fishing canoes make use of the easy boat-launching conditions to provide rides, often to the Wednesday market at Anjuna Beach just around the bend (the ride to Anjuna takes 15 minutes by sea, but significantly longer by road). A few hundred meters down the beach to the south of the entrance are more-open, less-crowded areas where you can spread out your towel and sunbathe. The beach gets its name from the Baga River, whose mouth is at the beach's northern end.

WHERE TO EAT & STAY

$ ✕ **St. Anthony's.** This seaside restaurant, which is a short step above Baga's many beach shacks, serves an astonishing variety of fish dishes in a casual setting that draws big crowds due to its location at the mouth of the river. The tuna steaks and pomfret dishes are particularly good. ✉ *Baga Beach, near the Baga River* ☎ *No phone* ▭ *No credit cards.*

$$$–$$$$ **Casa Baga.** Though this rambling hotel is far and away the best place to stay in Baga, it's still a bit on the funky side. However, the lively beach scene is only two minutes away, and the friendly staff treat you like family, making up for any upkeep deficits. Open-air public spaces, including the lobby and bar, have private seating areas sheltered by varying levels of lush landscaping. Each room is different in size and character, so see what is available at check in before settling in; choose a second floor room for more privacy and bet-

ter views. The restaurant specializes in Goan and Italian food. **Pros:** not on the noisy main road, exceptional staff. **Cons:** sketchy plumbing. ✉ *40/7 Saunta Vaddo, Baga* ☎ *832/227–6957, 832/228–2930, or 832/228–2931* 🌐 *www.casaboutiquehotelsgoa.com* *14 rooms* *In-hotel: restaurant, bar, pool, no elevator, laundry service, airport shuttle.* *MC, V* *BP.*

LOOK BOTH WAYS

India is second only to China in traffic fatalities, a high percentage of which involve pedestrians. When walking on Goa's country lanes or potholed city streets, beware of vehicles coming at you from every possible direction. Indian drivers pass on curves, head down the wrong side of the road, and swerve to miss stray dogs, cows, and the occasional wild pig.

NIGHTLIFE

Always packed, **Tito's** (☎ *832/227–9895 or 832/227–5028*) is the most happening bar and disco in Goa. Cafe Mambo, on the premises, is open 9:30 AM–3:30 AM daily, but the party crowd doesn't come in until close to midnight. Expect fashion shows, famous DJ mixers theme nights, and expensive drinks.

CALANGUTE BEACH

12 km (7 mi) northwest of Panaji.

Calangute Beach, between Sinquerim and Baga beaches in the Bardez district, is an open stretch of sand with occasional palm trees for patchy shade. The beach is accessible by cement steps. Note the sign warning that swimming is dangerous—there's a fairly strong undertow here. Calangute is bustling: the entrance area is crammed with restaurants, stalls, and shops. The mood is festive during the winter high season, when dozens of shacks serving inexpensive alcohol and seafood pop up on the beach.

WHERE TO EAT & STAY

$–$$ ✕ **Casandre.** TAVERNA, RESTAURANTE AND DIVERTIMENTO (tavern, restaurant, and fun)—the sign outside says it all. In an old house with a beautiful, high-beam bar, a pleasant style, and friendly service, this restaurant specializes in steaks, tandoori, and Continental cuisine, and the Goan food is decent. ✉ *Umta Vaddo, Calangute Beach Rd., Calangute Beach* ☎ *832/227–5934* *No credit cards.*

$–$$ ★ ✕ **Souza Lobo.** Established in 1932, and now managed by the third generation of the Lobo family, this restaurant on Calangute beach catches the exuberant sea breeze. The food is excellent, which means the place is always busy. The Goan masala fried prawns are exactly as they should be—with authentic red masala and fresh, perfectly deveined prawns. Other Goan specialties include the squid *amot tik* (a sour curry), kingfish steak *peri-peri* (in spicy, tangy red sauce), and prawn-stuffed pomfret. The restaurant also serves Western-style seafood with a good garlic butter sauce. There's live music every night. ✉ *Calangute Beach* ☎ *832/227–6463* *MC, V.*

8

CLOSE UP

Inner Peace

If there's anything that sums up the Goan attitude to life, it's *sussegado,* which means "take it easy." Even with the tourist influx exceeding the local population, the massive star resorts and hotels in the south, and the infamous rave and trance parties in the north, there's a certain peace in Goa that is unlikely to ever be disturbed, because it comes from within. A part of this state of daylong siesta can of course be attributed to a common love of excellent food and local alcohol—Goa brews its own *feni,* a potent and inexpensive concoction distilled from palm sap or cashew-fruit juice. If you're looking to imbibe the true spirit of Goa, try the coconut-palm feni—it smells less terrible than the cashew variety and goes down a little bit easier. You can buy the ridiculously cheap alcohol from just about anywhere in Goa (but make sure it's bottled properly) and down it with classic tender coconut water. A morning in the waves, tiger prawns at a seaside shack, and a couple of fenis, and you will come to discover why people come back to Goa year after year to rejuvenate, even as they complain that it's getting crowded and dirty. A week in the company of Goans, with their mellow attitude toward life and their legendary warmth—despite the heavy toll taken on their state by tourism—and you may find yourself, for better or for worse, not just a little intoxicated by the Goan way.

$$$$ **Pousada Tauma.** This boutique hotel is built of laterite—a local red pitted stone—and has an abundant, leafy garden. Stay here to be far enough away (less than a kilometer) from the beach but close enough to be part of the action when you want it. The rooms are well designed, with paintings, sculpture, and custom furniture. **Pros:** secluded setting, full ayurvedic treatmeats available. **Cons:** pricey compared to similar hotels in this range. ✉*Porba-Vaddo, Calangute* ☎*832/227–9061 to 63* 🌐*www.pousada-tauma.com* *13 rooms* *In-hotel: restaurant, bar, pool, spa, gym, no elevator, laundry service.* ▭*MC, V.*

$$$–$$$$ ★ **Casa Britona.** Set on the bank of a tributary of the River Mandovi, this boutique hotel 10 km (6 mi) from Sinquerim offers unique views of inland Goa, mangroves, and freshwater wildlife. The lobby features cozy seating areas and murals of country scenes and rooms are furnished with antique mirrors, dark hand carved rosewood wardrobes, and modern art. Goan seafood specialties are served around the pool, under a wooden gazebo in the garden or on a tranquil deck right above the river. **Pros:** private, tranquil hideaway. **Cons:** a taxi or scooter is needed to reach the beach. ✉*Near Charmanos Badem, Britona, 403101* ☎*832/241–0962* 🌐*www.casaboutiquehotelsgoa.com* *10 suites* *In-hotel: restaurant, bar, pool, airport shuttle.* ▭*MC, V* *BP.*

SPORTS & THE OUTDOORS

Hop aboard a dolphin- or crocodile-spotting tour, which winds past thick mangroves along the Zuari and Mandovi rivers, or take a ride on a banana boat. **Odyssey Tours** (☎*832/227–6941*) has a luxury yacht with a license to carry 27 passengers on deck, plus four crew members, including a captain and engineer. (Sorry, you can't rent the yacht and drive it yourself.) They offer half-day dolphin-spotting cruises (9:30 AM–1 PM) for about Rs. 1,000 per person, including lunch; reservations are necessary. The yacht leaves from Britona, where it has its own jetty. In the afternoon, it's available for private charter groups for Rs. 10,000 per hour.

MAPUSA

15 km (9 mi) north of Panaji.

Friday is the big market day in Mapusa (pronounced *map*-sa)—the main town in the Bardez district. People from adjoining villages and even transplanted hippies convene to sell everything from vegetables to blue jeans to handicrafts. It's an ideal place to buy souvenirs. Mapusa is not a place you'd want to stay for the night, and there's really nothing much to see here, but like Margao in the south, the town is good for brief forays to shop and take care of other necessities. Steer clear of it as much as possible if you want to maintain a cheerful mood—except for the lively Friday market, the town is a bit dreary.

REIS MAGOS FORT

5 km (3 mi) southeast of Sinquerim Beach.

Built by the Portuguese at the narrowest point of the Mandovi, Reis Magos is a good diversion before you get to the main fort in the area, which is Aguada. Although you cannot go into Reis Magos Fort, you can view the bastions from the church of the same name that stands below it. The church is one of the prettiest in Goa, standing on a bend in the road as it curves up the hill to the fort and skirts the Mandovi; you get here by taking very steep, mossy steps.

8

FORT AGUADA

Fodor'sChoice ★ *4 km (2½ mi) south of Sinquerim Beach.*

Perched high on a hill, with wonderful views west across the Arabian Sea and east across Aquada Bay to Panaji, Fort Aguada was built in 1612 and named for the natural springs that supplied not only the fort but also passing ships. Surrounded by wild grass, the fort is in excellent condition. Inside you can take a good look at the solid stone architecture and the old lighthouse. The fort's defenses actually enclosed a much larger area than the bastion at the top of the hill; a seaward bastion still juts into the Arabian Sea on Sinquerim beach, near the Taj cluster of hotels. If you only have time for one of Goa's many forts, hit Aguada—it's the best preserved and most magnificent. Hire a taxi if time is a constraint; it's not an easy walk, as it's 4 km (2½ mi) south of Sinquerim Beach and at least half the way is a fairly steep uphill.

SINQUERIM BEACH

10 km (6 mi) northwest of Panaji.

Sinquerim is the first beach you'll get to as you head northwest after crossing the Mandovi from Panaji. Along with Bogmalo, also in the Bardez district, it's one of the few beaches where you can rent windsurfers, water skis, and other water toys without having to be a guest at a hotel. It's much cheaper to rent equipment from these places, but check the condition of the equipment and make sure lifejackets are provided; also check, if possible, with others on the beach to verify adequate supervision. Stretching in front of the Taj resorts, this small, sandy beach can get fairly crowded with tourists and vendors. The water, however, is clean, and the consistent waves make for good bodysurfing.

WHERE TO EAT & STAY

$$$–$$$$ ✕**Morisco.** Goan specialties and the view of the historic fortification are the draws at this seafood restaurant at the Fort Aguada Beach Resort. The catch of the day is marinated in Goan spices and served along with local music. ✉*Fort Aguada Beach Resort, Sinquerim Beach* ☎*832/664–5858* ▭*AE, MC, V.*

$$$$ ★ **Fort Aguada Beach Resort.** Constructed within the boundary and adjoining the ramparts of an old Portuguese fort built in 1612, this hotel has gorgeous views of the fort, sea, and beach. Most of the rooms face the ocean and are furnished with contemporary Goan-style dark wood and cane furniture. If you crave seclusion stay in the exclusive (and expensive) villas tucked into the hillside behind the resort, which used to be a separate property known as the Aguada Hermitage. The restaurants, recreational facilities, and spa at the Taj Holiday Village next door are open to Fort Aguada guests as well. **Pros:** stunning location, beautifully furnished rooms. **Cons:** could be too formal for some guests. ✉*Bardez district, Sinquerim Beach, 403519* ☎*832/247–9123 to 36* 🌐*www.tajhotels.com* *144 rooms, 24 suites, 42 cottages, 15 villas* *In-hotel: 4 restaurants, bars, golf course, tennis court, pools, gym, spa, beachfront, water sports, children's programs (ages 4 to 11), laundry service, airport shuttle.* ▭*AE, DC, MC, V.*

$$$$ Fodor'sChoice ★ **Taj Holiday Village.** The guest rooms at this resort are housed in charming Goan-village style cottages and villas that face lush gardens or the broad expanse of Sinquerim Beach. All the rooms have been newly renovated and include private terraces, luxurious bedding, marble bathrooms, and flat-screen TVs. The freeform pool affords both views and access to the beach, and it's adjacent to the children's program facility. Three full-service restaurants specializing in Thai, Goan, and Continental cuisine ensure there is something for every palate. Myriad recreational activities are offered for adults and children and a world-class spa has ayurvedic treatments, yoga, and therapeutic massage in a serene setting. Guests are welcome to dine at and use the facilities of the adjacent Fort Aguada Beach Resort. **Pros:** spectacular setting, sophisticated yet friendly service. **Cons:** lots of kids can mean lots of noise. ✉*Sinquerim Beach, 403519* ☎*832/664–5858* 🌐*www.tajhotels.com* *142 rooms, 9 villa suites* *In-hotel: 4 restaurants, bars, golf course, tennis courts, pool, gym, spa, beachfront, water*

sports, no elevator, children's programs (ages 4 to 11), laundry service, airport shuttle. ▭*AE, MC, V* 🍽*BP.*

$ 🏨 **Marbella Guest House.** This heritage guest house is on one of north Goa's narrowest lanes, behind the massive Taj resorts. A restored Portuguese villa with clean rooms and antique furniture, it's a popular place among those who know Goa well, and it's only about a half of a kilometer from here down to Sinquerim Beach. **Pros:** great value, oozing with charm. **Cons:** no phones in room. ✉*Between Sinquerim and Candolim beaches, Bardez district, 403515* ☎*832/247–9551* 🌐*www.marbellagoa.com* *3 rooms, 3 suites* *In-room: no phone. In-hotel: restaurant, no elevator, laundry service.* ▭*MC, V* 🍽*BP.*

SPORTS & THE OUTDOORS

John's Boat Tours (✉*Candolim Beach* 🌐*www.digitalgoa.com/johnsboattours* ✉*johnsboattours@rediffmail.com*) has dolphin watching, snorkeling at Grand Island, crocodile spotting in the river backwaters and sea fishing.

PANAJI & CENTRAL GOA

Panaji, the capital of the former Portuguese realm and the present state capital, lies between the Zuari and Mandovi rivers in central Goa. Apart from its own considerable charms, the small city is a good base from which to explore Goa's history, particularly the imposing churches of Old Goa, an abandoned Portuguese capital upriver, and the river islands of Divar and Chorao. Although in eastern Goa, Ponda, with its temples and wildlife sanctuaries, is closer to the town of Margao in the south, it's easier to access from here.

8

PANAJI

600 km (372 mi) south of Mumbai.

Panaji has whitewashed churches, palm-lined plazas, and less of the poverty and hustle and bustle of India's other state capitals. The unhurried attitude of the residents adds to the city's charms and reminds you to take it easy. The best way to see the older parts of the city is on foot. In fact, if you leave without having explored the back streets at leisure, you haven't really seen Panaji at all. For diehard sun-and-sand lovers, there's the city beach at Dona Paula, but, Panaji isn't recommended for its beaches, as they tend to be dirty and crowded.

Church of Our Lady of Immaculate Conception. This grand shrine was a mere chapel before 1541. Soon after, in 1600, it became a parish, and its structure was rebuilt entirely. Now the church almost entirely presides over one of Panaji's squares. The building's distinctive zigzag staircases are a 19th-century addition, and the church's large bell was originally in the Church of St. Augustine in Old Goa. An annual December festival here draws huge crowds. At the other times of the year, the square is a peaceful place to linger. ✉*Near Municipal Gardens* 🎫*Free* ⏲*Mon.–Sat. 9–6, Sun. 10–6.*

Fontainhas. The shady, narrow streets of this largely residential neighborhood do not really belong to India—they are clearly still Portuguese at heart. From tiny *balcaos* (colonnaded porches), inhabitants watch as their quiet, unchanging world goes by, and through the old windows, you can hear people practicing the piano and violin. At the heart of Fontainhas is the little whitewashed Chapel of St. Sebastian, which dates only to the late 19th century—new by Goan standards. Its claim to fame is an old crucifix that was once housed in the infamous Palace of the Inquisition in Old Goa. ✉*Between Ourem Creek and Altinho.*

Sao Tome. This crumbling old neighborhood contains the General Post Office, once a tobacco trading house, and a maze of extremely narrow streets behind it. The tiny bars of this district are full of old-world character, and indeed you might need that drink to help banish the more grisly images of Goa's past. The area opposite the post office was once the site of Panjim's town executions. ✉*Between M. G. Rd. and Emidio Gracia Rd.*

The Secretariat. This heritage building occupies a pleasant spot by the Mandovi River and has several important associations. The palace of the Sultan of Bijapur, to whom Goa belonged at the time of the Portuguese invasion, was the first building on this site. The building that the Portuguese erected in its place served as temporary quarters for the viceroys of Goa upon their arrival or departure from the territory until it became their permanent residence in the mid-18th century, when the capital at Old Goa was abandoned. In the early 20th century, the Secretariat became a government office. ✉*Mandovi riverfront.*

WHERE TO EAT & STAY

$–$$ ✕ **Riorico.** The formal staff of this somewhat somber, dining hall serve tasty Goan specialties including *rawa* (semolina)-fried fish and prawns and Portuguese-influenced seafood *caldeirada* (poached fish layered with potatoes and tomatoes and cooked with white wine). ✉*Hotel Mandovi, D.B. Marg* ☎*832/242–6270 to 73, 832/222–4405 to 09* ▭*AE, MC, V.*

$ ✕ **Panjim Inn.** The veranda of the Panjim Inn provides a quaint location for those in the market for great food, casual dining, and fair prices. Friendly waiters serve Goan and Continental food from 7 AM to 10 PM. ✉*E-212 31st January Rd., Panaji* ☎*832/222–6523* ▭*MC, V.*

$ ★ ✕ **Ritz Classic.** You're likely to be the only foreigner in this Panaji family favorite—that is if you can find it. The restaurant is hidden away on the second floor of an anonymous block, but is certainly worth looking for. Goan specialties, including grilled kingfish and chicken *xacuti* (coconut and tamarind curry), are prepared to perfection. ✉*Wagle Vision, 18th June Rd., Panaji* ☎*832/564–4796* ▭*MC, V.*

$ ✕ **Viva Panjim.** A walk down a narrow alley will bring you to one of the best restaurants in Panaji. Featuring the award-winning cuisine of chef Linda De Souza, this cheery hideaway is crowded in with locals, tourists, and friends of the chef. The maître d' is happy to make recommendations to anyone unfamiliar with Goan specialties such as kingfish vindaloo, and chicken *cafreal* (marinated and cooked fresh coriander, green chillis and ginger). Indoor and outdoor seating is available, and the service is friendly and attentive without being overbearing. Great food, conviviality, and bargain prices are the rule. ✉ *H. No. 178 31st January Rd., Panaji* ☎ *832/224–2405* ▭ *MC, V.*

¢ ✕ **Sher-e-Punjab.** Locals and foreigners hungry for North Indian food from the Punjab seek this diner out for lunch, dinner, or a quick snack while taking a break from the intense shopping of the Bombay Bazaar across the street. Try the *affogato*—a scoop of vanilla ice cream drowned in espresso. ✉ *18th June Rd., Panaji* ☎ *832/222–7204* ▭ *MC, V.*

$$$$ ★ **Goa Marriott Resort.** Anyone with a keen interest in Panaji will appreciate the city location of this upscale Western chain hotel. Rooms are tasteful and the staff of the deluxe spa and fitness center provide excellent service. It's just a few minutes by foot to the beach—though this is very much a city hotel, not a beach resort. **Pros:** well located if Panaji is your main interest. **Cons:** not the cleanest beach, a bit pricey. ✉ *Miramar Beach Rd., 403001* ☎ *832/246–3333* 🌐 *www.marriott.com* *165 rooms* *In-hotel: 3 restaurants, bars, tennis court, pool, gym, spa, children's programs (ages 5–12), laundry service, airport shuttle.* ▭ *AE, MC, V.*

$$$ **Panjim People's** Four-poster beds, carved rosewood dressers, and plenty of windows grace each of the four spacious rooms in this historic annex of the Panjim Inn. The mosaic tile floors and walls of the bathrooms resemble a crazy quilt and were designed by local artists. Guests at the Panjim People's share the restaurant, amenities, and public rooms of the Panjim Inn, which is just across the street. **Pros:** old-world charm, plenty of space, neighborhood views. **Cons:** a steep outdoor staircase is the only way to reach the rooms, no room phones. ✉ *E-212, 31 January Rd., Fontainhas, Panaji* ☎ *832/222–6523* 🌐 *www.panjiminn.com* *4 rooms* *In-room: no phone. In-hotel: restaurant, no elevator.* ▭ *MC,V* *BP.*

$–$$ **Hotel Fidalgo.** The modern rooms of this business hotel are generically furnished, but clean. (Ask to see a few before unpacking your bags—some rooms are definitely better than others.) The spacious lobby looks out on a busy downtown street corner, but the colorful pool in the center courtyard offer a place to retreat from its hectic pace. **Pros:** good value for the money. **Cons:** noisy commercial part of town. ✉ *18th June Rd., Panaji, 403001* ☎ *832/222–6291* 🌐 *www.hotelfidalgo-goa.com* *103* *In-hotel: restaurant, bar, pool, laundry service.* ▭ *MC, V* *BP.*

¢–$ **Panjim Inn.** Backpackers and other travelers who appreciate a sense of place love the home-away-from-home warmth of the Panjim Inn. This unique hotel in the center of the historic Fontainhas district has 24 rooms—12 in the original inn, which was once the family home of the owner, Ajit Sukhija, the rest in an adjoining newly opened wing which offer a bit more space and river views. The new airy lobby/dining area is decorated in sleek black and white; it's the perfect place to enjoy the inn's Goan seafood specials, read the paper, or simply escape from the madness of Panaji's traffic. If you've stayed here in the past, not to worry: the original restaurant on the second-floor veranda hasn't changed a bit. The smaller, basic rooms in the old building are priced a bit lower than the larger deluxe and superior rooms in the annex.

8

Pros: great location in the center of the historic district, friendly staff, relaxed atmosphere. **Cons:** traffic noise, no phones in rooms. ✉*E-212, 31 January Rd., Fontainhas, Panaji* ☎*832/222–6523* 🌐*www.panjiminn.com* *24 rooms* *In-room: no phones. In-hotel: restaurant, no elevator.* *MC, V* *BP.*

IT'S A STAKEOUT

Goan taxi drivers stake out tourists by waiting outside hotels and restaurants. As soon as you walk out the door three or four of them are at your side asking you if you want a cab, and where you are going. They find it hard to believe you'd want to walk when you can afford to pay for a ride.

¢–$ ★ **Pousada Panjim.** Travelers who crave a private, quiet, stylish place to stay in noisy, chaotic Panaji stay at this historic inn tucked into a quiet street several blocks from the street noise of Rua de Ourem. The pousada's rooms are in a renovated Hindu-style home built around a central garden courtyard. Guests can dine and take advantage of the services of the Panjim Inn, which is a two-minute walk away. **Pros:** quiet refuge in a noisy city, memorable one-of-a-kind setting, exceptional value. **Cons:** no restaurant on premises. ✉*E-212, 31 January Rd., Fontainhas, Panaji* ☎*832/222–6523* 🌐*www.panjiminn.com* *9 rooms* *In-hotel: restaurant, no elevator.* *MC,V* *BP.*

BOAT CRUISES

Gambling, food, and drink can be enjoyed every night from 5 PM until 6 AM onboard the **Casino Caravela** (☎*832/223–4044 to 47*), a floating luxury casino that also has a TV/game room for those under 18, a toddlers' room with babysitters, and an open-air swimming pool. The dress code is smart–casual, which in India means no shorts, bikinis, or swimming trunks are allowed outside the pool area.

Department of Tourism (☎*832/243–8750* 🌐*www.goatourism.org*) as well as several private operators organize river cruises some with a Goan cultural show, music, and dinner. Most cruises depart from the Panaji jetty on the River Mandovi.

SHOPPING

Stores are open 10 am to 7 pm.

Bombay Bazaar (✉*18th January Rd.* ☎*832/222–1985*), a department store with a twist, is a gathering of dozens of vendors, each competing for your business in the confines of a jam-packed two-story building. Wares include Indian- and Western-style clothing, saris and handicrafts, plus basic needs including suitcases, shoes, and watches. Everything is well priced.

Sosa's (✉*E-245 Rua de Ourem* ☎*832/222–8063*) supplies Indian designer clothes for the fashionista in all of us. Even if your style is on the conservative side, consider visiting this shop just for the fun of it.

Barefoot (✉*H. No. 1/26, 31st January Rd.* ☎*832/243–6815* ⏲*Close Sunday*) sells trendy house wares, silk, and cotton men's and women's clothing in updated styles. **Sinari's** (✉*Padmavati Towers, 18th June Rd.* ☎*832/222–4842*) is the place to buy Indian music of all sorts including Goan trance, devotional Hindi, Indian pop, and rap. It's in an arcade next to Bombay Bazaar.

CLOSE UP

Take Home the Taste of Goa

If you haven't found your share of slippers and sarongs, and bags and bangles at Anjuna or the shack-shops near the main beaches, pay a visit to a local grocery. Look carefully and you'll find some great stuff to take home as a reminder of your stay in Goa or to give away as unusual "back from India" gifts. There's export quality *bebinca* (a rich, layered, dense pastry made of butter, egg yolk, and coconut) that has a long shelf life and make for easy packing; feni (Goan liquor) in fancy bottles (though it smells the same as the stuff in the downmarket bottles) which you'd be well-advised to transport only in your carry-on baggage; *prawn balchao* (in a red chilli sauce) and *mackerel reicheado* (pickled prawns and mackerals soaked in red masala, which have to be fried once you get home) with clearly marked expiration dates; a variety of dried and wet masalas (spice mixes) from *cafreal* (green masala) and *vindaloo* (hot red masala) to *xacuti* (a masala with coconut and ground spices, and sachets of *tendlim* (a pickled green vegetable). Chances are the storeowner will wrap it for you with a grin that acknowledges that you know a bit about Goa after all.

OLD GOA

Fodor'sChoice ★ *10 km (6 mi) east of Panaji.*

Numbers in the text correspond to points of interest on the Old Goa map.

8

Gorgeous Old Goa, with foliage creeping in around the ruins of old churches, served as the capital of the Portuguese colony until repeated outbreaks of cholera forced the government to move to Panaji in the 1843. The shift out of Old Goa, however, had begun as early as 1695. It was a slow desertion—first the viceroy, then the nobility, then the customs. So by the time the official declaration came, it was already a deserted ruined city.

1 Dedicated to the worship of the infant Jesus, the **Basilica of Bom Jesus** is also known throughout the Christian world as the tomb of St. Francis Xavier, patron saint of Goa. The saint's body has "survived" almost 500 years now without ever having been embalmed, and lies in a silver casket well out of reach of visitors. Built from local red stone around the turn of the 17th century, the basilica took the Florentine sculptor Giovanni Batista Foggini 10 years to complete. Once every 10 years the missionary's body is exposed to the public at close quarters, drawing thousands of pilgrims. The next such event is scheduled for November 2014. *Free Mon.–Sat. 9–6:30, Sun. 10–6:30.*

3 The imposing white **Sé (St. Catherine's) Cathedral**—the largest church in Old Goa—was built between 1562 and 1652 by order of the King of Portugal. Fine carvings depict scenes from the life of Christ and the Blessed Virgin over the main altar, which commemorates St. Catherine of Alexandria. Several splendidly decorated chapels are dedicated to St. Joseph, St. George, St. Anthony, St. Bernard, and the Holy Cross.

The Archeological Museum 2
Basilica & Professed House of Bom Jesus 1
St. Catherine 3
The Museum of Christian Art 4

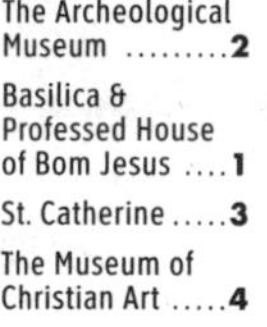

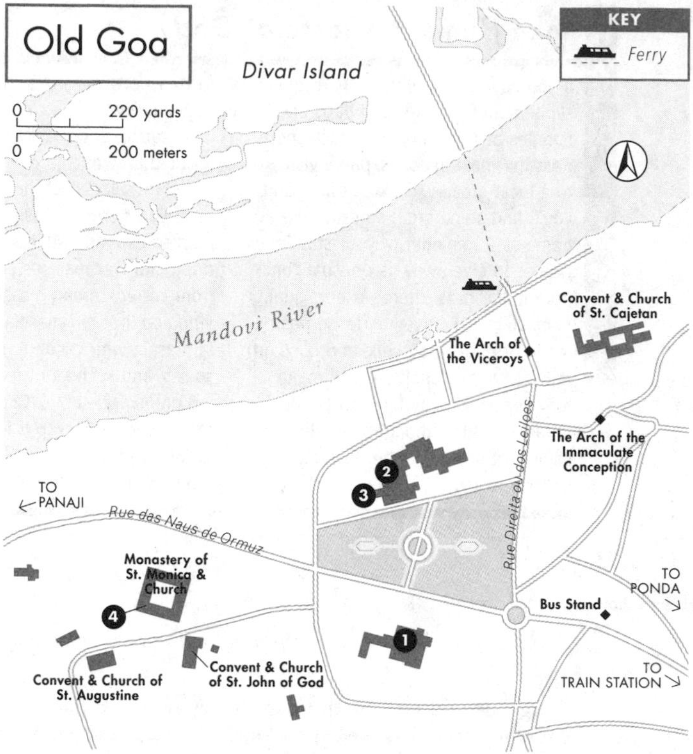

Only one of the cathedral's two original majestic towers remains; the other collapsed in 1776. ✉*Across the road from Basilica of Bom Jesus* 🎫*Free* ⏲*Mon.–Sat. 9–6:30, Sun. 10–6:30.*

Next to the cathedral stands the Church of St. Francis of Assisi, with its intricately gilded and carved interior. Behind the cathedral is the

2 **Archaeological Museum.** The museum's collection is not entirely devoted to Catholic objets d'art; it also has bits and pieces from Goa's early Hindu history. It's worth a quick look around, if only to peruse the portrait gallery of Goa's viceroys. ✉*Across the road from Basilica of Bom Jesus* ☎*832/228–6133* 🎫*Rs. 5* ⏲*Sat.–Thurs. 10–5.*

Housed until the late 1990s in the great but remote seminary at Rachol

4 in South Goa, the **Museum of Christian Art** now resides in the Convent of St. Monica in Old Goa. The museum has a number of objects of Christian interest including paintings and religious silverware, some dating back to the 16th century. The historic Convent of St. Monica was once a nunnery, the first of its kind in the East, and functioned as one until the late 19th century. ✉*Holy Mount Hill* 🎫*Rs. 5* ⏲*Tues.–Sun. 10–5:30.*

DR. SALIM ALI BIRD SANCTUARY

3 km (2 mi) northeast of Panaji.

Visit this delightful bird refuge on the tip of Chorao, an island in the Mandovi. The ferry jetty for Chorao is on Ribander jetty on the southern bank of River Mandovi, between Panaji and Old Goa, and boats travel regularly to the island and back. The Forest Department in Panaji (☎832/222–4747) organizes guided tours to Chorao. The tiny sanctuary is a mangrove paradise and is named after the dedicated Indian ornithologist Dr. Salim Ali.

DIVAR ISLAND

10 km (6 mi) northeast of Panaji.

The ferry jetty for Divar Island, Chorao's twin in the Mandovi, is in Old Goa. Protected by the river and somewhat isolated from mainstream Goa, Divar makes for a very pleasant day out. Piedade, its main village, is serene. The Church of Our Lady of Compassion, on a hill, is in good condition and worth a visit; it also has excellent views of the river and the countryside.

DUDHSAGAR FALLS

50 km (31 mi) southeast of Panaji.

★ With a name that means "sea of milk," the **Dudhsagar Waterfalls** are spectacular and imposing, with water cascading almost 2,000 feet down a cliff to a rock-ribbed valley. Pack refreshments and bath towels, and plan to spend a morning here. Monkeys, birds, bees, butterflies, and thick foliage complete the wild experience. The ideal time for a trek here is October–April; during the monsoon, the road that approaches it is inaccessible. The Goa Tourism Development Corporation runs tours to Dudhsagar from Panaji and Calangute. Tours include the waterfall and the nearby Tambdi Surla temple built by the Kadambas (9 AM–6 PM). The price for tours varies depending on whether your bus has a/c or not. You could also take a train to Dudhsagar from Margao and get there in an hour and a half. ✉*Sanguem district.*

8

PONDA

29 km (18 mi) southeast of Panaji.

Ponda itself is an uninteresting town, but it has a number of temples in the hills that surround it that shouldn't be missed. The area came under Portuguese control relatively late, in 1764, about 250 years after the Portuguese conquered Goa—which explains why the temples were not destroyed. One of the chief attractions here is the **Manguesh temple** in Priol, 7 km (4 mi) before you reach Ponda. With its domes and other eccentric, un-Hindu architectural features, the temple has evidence of Islamic and Christian influences. Other temples in the vicinity include the always-crowded Shantadurga temple with its distinctive tower, the

Mahalsa temple with its gargantuan (41-foot-high) oil lamp, and the Lakshmi Narasimha and Naguesh temples with their lovely temple tanks (large pools accessed with steps, where the faithful bathe).

BEACH BLANKET BINGO

Head straight to the beaches if you're looking for nightlife. On Sunday night, all of southern Goa seems to descend on Colva for drinking, eating, dancing, and playing *housie*, a local version of bingo. Dancing and partying also happen at Baga, Anjuna, and many of the more remote beaches.

SOUTH GOA

Margao is the main town in South Goa. It's about 7 km (4 mi) inland from the coast, has a bustling market, and is worth exploring for its old buildings and shopping areas, but there's no reason to stay here. If you want to check out the sights, make Colva or Benaulim your base, and get the benefit of the beach and the nightlife after your day out. Excursions include the villages of Loutolim and Chandor, which have beautiful ancestral homes, some of which date from the early 1600s. The beaches of the south are more relaxing than those of the north, and people here are less prone to partying. Although there is more shack life in the south now than there used to be. Some of the state's most luxurious and expensive resorts are in this area.

BOGMALO BEACH

24 km (15 mi) north of Margao, 25 km (16 mi) south of Panaji.

This tiny crescent of fine sand is perfect for swimming and sunning. It's near a low, verdant hill topped by a few modern buildings on one side and the Bogmallo Beach Resort on the other. Two tiny islands sit about 10 km (6 mi) out to sea. For the most privacy, walk down the beach to the far right—fewer fishing boats, shacks, and people. Another of Bogmalo's assets is its boating and water-sports facilities (diving, jet skiing). For a lunch break, try the **Seagull**, a simple, thatched-roof shack right on the beach—they serve some of the best prawn-curry rice in Goa.

WHERE TO STAY

$$$ **Coconut Creek.** On a dense coconut plantation, just a two-minute walk (about ½ km) from Bogmalo beach and a 3-km (2-mi) drive from Dabolim Airport, this charming little resort with spotless, airy rooms, and a small swimming pool is run by a friendly staff. Unlike many of Goa's midrange resorts, it succeeds in creating a mellow vibe. **Pros:** private jungle setting, one of the nicest mid-range resorts in South Goa. **Cons:** only half the rooms have a/c, the rest have fans. ✉*Bogmalo, 403806* ☎*832/253–8100* 🖷*832/253–8880* *coconutcreek@dataone.in* *20 rooms* *In-rooms: no a/c (some). In-hotel: restaurant, bar, pool, airport shuttle.* ▭*MC, V.*

$$–$$$ **Bogmallo Beach Resort.** This six-story high-rise hotel seems to have ignored all the rules about being close to the beach. Its chief assets are its reasonably priced rooms with a fantastic view of San Diego Island

and rolling ocean. **Pros:** close to the airport. **Cons:** very low on character. ✉*Bogmalo, 403806* ☎*832/253–8222 to 235* 🌐*www.bogmallobeachresort.com* *123 rooms* *In-hotel: restaurant, bar, pool, gym.* *MC, V* *BP.*

SPORTS & THE OUTDOORS

Trips to the islands are run by the experienced young staff at the **Sandy Treat** snack shack (the first one jutting out on the right); reserve in advance.

You can rent equipment from **Watersports Goa,** which operates out of a shack on the beach. They provide instruction in various sports and excursions to nearby islands.

CANSAULIM BEACH

10 km (6 mi) northwest of Margao.

This quiet, clean stretch of beach between Bogmallo and Colva has a fine location—close to both Dabolim Airport and Margao, and yet away from the crowded north and the congested beaches around Colva. The chief signs of life in these parts are the hotels and resorts in the vicinity, and a couple of sleepy villages.

WHERE TO EAT & STAY

$$$–$$$$ ✕**The Village Plaza.** The Hyatt's food "village" adjacent to the expansive lobby has a number of interconnected restaurants: Da Luigi serves wood-fired pizzas and pasta; the Market Grill offers charcoal-grilled prime cuts and seafood; the Juice Bar has light refreshments and health drinks; Masala is an Indian restaurant serving tandoori and Goan cuisine; and Sambar offers South Indian food. ✉*Park Hyatt Goa Resort and Spa, Arossim Beach* ☎*832/272–1234* *AE, MC, V.*

$$$$ **Heritage Village Club.** Popular with tour groups, this small, crowded resort has simple, comfortable rooms. Rates include all meals, and a few unlimited local beverages. There's also an ayurvedic spa. The resort operates largely on an all-inclusive package basis, with a three-night/four-day package costing between Rs. 36,500 and Rs. 51,000. **Pros:** ideal for those wanting all-inclusive deals. **Cons:** dark rooms, little privacy. ✉*Arossim Beach, Cansaulim, 403712* ☎*832/269–4444* *832/275–4324* *98 rooms, 2 suites* *In-hotel: 2 restaurants, bar, tennis court, pool, spa, airport shuttle, no elevator.* *AE, MC, V* *FAP.*

$$$$ Fodor'sChoice ★ **Park Hyatt Goa Resort and Spa.** Clearly in the very top bracket of the Goa resorts, the modern and sleek Hyatt has spacious rooms with unusual pebble-floor and glass-wall bathrooms. It also has great dining, an excellent spa, and the largest swimming pool in India (21,527 square feet). The library has 1,500 titles and there's a mini-theater where you can watch movies. A thoroughly luxurious spa houses body scrub and massage suites, hydrotherapy facilities, steam rooms, and well-trained staff; it offers a full range of ayurvedic treatments. A sprawling food village has every sort of restaurant, from Goan specialty and South Indian vegetarian to Italian and seafood. Praia de Luz, a

wine and tapas bar overlooking the Arabian, is one of the highlights here. All of this, of course, comes at a considerable price. **Pros:** ultra luxurious, impeccable service, world-class spa and restaurants. **Cons:** very spread out, very expensive. ✉*Arossim Beach, Cansaulim, 403712* ☎*832/272–1234* 🌐*www.goa.park.hyatt.com* *238 rooms, 13 suites* *In-hotel: 6 restaurants, bars, tennis court, pool, spa, laundry service, airport shuttle.* *AE, MC, V.*

MAJORDA & UTORDA

10 km (6 mi) from Margao.

Just north of Colva Beach, Majorda and nearby Utorda, which have a number of resorts, are rapidly sacrificing peace and quiet to larger volumes of tourists. However, they are cycling distance from Colva and Betalbatim (5 km [3 mi] from Colva, 3 km [2 mi] from Betalbatim), which are known for restaurants and shack life. If you stay here you'll have yourself a good base from which to explore the sights around Margao.

DRESS CODE REVISION

Almost anything goes at Western-style resorts and in beach towns even Indian women visiting from Bombay and Delhi wear shorts and spaghetti strap tops. As a rule, Indians don't wear bathing suits—too immodest—they just wade right in, the men wearing baggy pants and Western-logo T-shirts, the women wearing saris or salwar-kameez—long pants with a flowing tunic that hits below the knees.

WHERE TO EAT & STAY

$ **Martin's Corner.** This famous family-run restaurant in the village of Betalbatim near Majorda grew out of a small shop. With its cane lamps and cane bar, it still retains the shack feel. Its prices, however, are well above the average shack, and with good reason. Pleasant retro music and the aromas of Goan cooking fill the air at lunch and dinnertime. Try the Tiger prawns in garlic sauce. ✉*Bin Waddo, Betalbatim* ☎*832/288–0061* *MC, V.*

$$$$ **Majorda Beach Resort.** An old favorite with tourists from Bombay and Gujarat, this resort has an ayurvedic ashram and spacious rooms. It also feels lively, given all the families that come to stay here. **Pros:** good beach access. **Cons:** dark lobby. ✉*Majorda, Salcete, 403713* ☎*832/288–1111 to 13* 🌐*www.majordabeachresort.com* *100 rooms, 10 cottages, 10 suites* *In-hotel: 2 restaurants, bar, tennis court, pools, gym, laundry service.* *AE, MC, V* *BP.*

$$$ **Kenilworth Beach Resort.** Lacking the same frantic-to-please service typical of some other hotels in Goa, this large resort has a marble lobby with lots of quiet corners where you can relax. The staff here is experienced and calm, and the lobby and guest rooms were remodeled in 2007. There's an expansive swimming pool with a swim-up bar, an open-air Jacuzzi, a waterslide, and a 10-foot-deep area for beginning scuba divers. **Pros:** all rooms have private balconies. **Cons:** sprawling and crowded at times. ✉*Utorda, Salcete, 403713* ☎*832/275–4180* 🌐*www.kenilworthhotels.com* *104 rooms, 3 suites* *In-hotel: 2 restaurants, bar, pool, gym, spa, water sports, laundry service, public Internet.* *AE, MC, V* *BP.*

COLVA

7 km (4 mi) west of Margao.

Colva Beach, in the Salcete district, is the most congested beach in south Goa. Its large parking and entrance areas are crowded with shacks selling snacks and souvenirs and young men offering up mopeds for rent. The first 1,000 feet of the beach are hectic—stuffed with vendors, cows, and fishing boats—but the sand, backed by palm groves, stretches in both directions, promising plenty of quieter spots to settle down. The water is good for swimming, with only nominal waves. Restaurants and bar shacks are the hub of nightlife for this entire region.

WHERE TO STAY

$–$$ **Longuinhos Beach Resort.** This old Colva favorite is about a kilometer from the crowded village, and right on the beach. Rooms are comfortable and reasonably priced. You can eat at A Tartaruga, the in-house restaurant, or take your pick from dozens of shack restaurants close by. **Pros:** great beach access, one of the best mid-range resorts in Colva. **Cons:** a bit down-at-the-heels. ✉*Salcete, Colva Beach, 403708* ☎*832/278–8068 to 69* 🌐*www.longuinhos.net* *50 rooms* *In-room: no a/c (some). In-hotel: restaurant, pool, airport shuttle, no elevator.* *AE, MC, V* *CP.*

SHOPPING

You can find the best bargains in Colva in the small shacks along the main street leading to the beach, where you can get sarongs, bags, T-shirts, and jewelry of all kinds.

8

MARGAO

33 km (20 mi) south of Panaji, 7 km (4 mi) east of Colva beach.

Use Margao, a busy commercial center and one of the busiest towns in Goa to do your shopping for basic essentials if you plan to stay for a while at the secluded southern beaches. Check out the Golden Heart bookstore off Abade Faria Road, which carries English-language books, including quite a few about Goa. The town has a few attractions of its own as well; there are historic houses and churches, and a lively seafood market where you can also buy fresh fruit and vegetables. Near the railway station there's plenty of fabric for sale if you're so inclined.

LOUTOLIM

10 km (6 mi) northeast of Margao.

Loutolim village is good for a morning's outing; visit the somewhat overrated Big Foot Museum and an ancestral house across the road, explore the old village on foot, and stop to admire Miranda House—a well-preserved example of a Goan country house. Stopping to have lunch at one of Goa's most delightful restaurants, Fernando's Nostalgia, in the courtyard of the chef's house on the Ponda-Margao road, finishes the day trip perfectly.

Also known as the Ancestral Goa Museum, the **Big Foot Museum** re-creates a 19th-century Goan village in miniature. Guides explain the utility and significance of every object and article on display; highlights are the fishermen's shack, a mock feni distillery, and the spice garden. Within the museum's sprawling confines is an enormous, canopied dance floor, used for open-air private parties. But keep your expectations grounded; while some visitors are satisfied with the experience, many feel it's more of a tourist trap than a real attraction. ✉*Near Saviour of the World Church, Loutolim* ✣*10 km (6 mi) north of Margao* ☎*834/277–7034 or 834/273–5064* *Rs. 20* ⏲*Daily 9–6.*

WHERE TO EAT

$–$$ Fodor'sChoice ★ ✕**Fernando's Nostalgia.** In the tranquil, slow-paced old village of Raia is one of the best restaurants in the state. If you sit at certain tables you can catch glimpses of household life in the chef's country home. Fernando's serves classic Goan dishes such as salted ox tongue, *fofos* (fish cutlets mixed with mashed potatoes and spices, rolled in breadcrumbs and egg, and shallow-fried), *sopa de bretalha* (spinach soup), and *prawn almondegas* (prawn meat cakes), which are rarely found in restaurants; that probably explains why Fernando's is where Goans go. As most of the day's specials are listed in Portuguese, you might need a waiter's help to decipher the menu. The restaurant comes to life in the evening, when the alcohol begins to flow and the band starts to play. ✉*608 Uzro, Raia* ☎*832/277–7098* ▭*MC, V.*

CHANDOR

15 km (9 mi) east of Margao.

This small, sleepy village occupies the site of Chandrapur, ancient capital of the region from 375 AD to 1053 AD. Today, the chief reason to ★ come here is for the 400-year-old **Braganza House** (☎*832/278–4201 or 832/278–4227* ⏲*No regular visiting hours, call ahead for an appointment*); two wings are occupied by two branches of the Braganza family—the Menezes Braganzas and the Braganza Pereiras. You can see the style in which the wealthy landed gentry must have lived until the land reformation that followed Independence in 1947; the great rooms are filled with treasures, including beautiful period furniture and Chinese porcelain. Although some parts of the house have been renovated and are in reasonably good shape, it takes a lot of effort to maintain the two wings, and contributions toward upkeep are expected.

BENAULIM

9 km (6 mi) southwest of Margao.

Just 2 km (1 mi) south of Colva is the first of the beautiful, secluded beaches of South Goa—completely unlike the action-packed beaches of the north. Head to Benaulim and farther south only if you want to get away from it all, which comes at a price because the resorts are more expensive here. Benaulim village has a small supermarket and is centered around a crossroads called Maria Hall. The beach is less than a kilometer from the village.

WHERE TO EAT & STAY

$$$$ Fodor'sChoice ★ **Alegria.** This Goan specialty restaurant is reminiscent of an old-fashioned landlord's drawing room, with sepia photographs on the walls and carved wooden furniture. The variety of menu items makes an excellent introduction to local cuisine. Try the *kulliamchem mass kotteanim* (gratinated crabmeat with onions, coriander, and garlic), and *sannas* (delicately flavored, sweetish, steamed rice cakes) with an assortment of curries, such as classic pork vindaloo, pork *sorpotel* (curry simmered with Goan vinegar), and boneless chicken xacuti. If you want to be adventurous with dessert, try the *adsorachem merend,* a feni-infused coconut mousse with saffron sauce. Live singing accompanied by guitar and mandolin adds to the scene. ✉ *Taj Exotica, Calwaddo, Benaulim, Salcette* ☎ *832/277–1234* *Reservations essential* *AE, DC, MC, V.*

$ **Joecons.** The highlight of this open-air restaurant, a short walk for the Taj Exotica and less than a kilometer from the village, is the well-prepared fresh seafood specialties including exceptional grilled garlic prawns. ✉ *Near Taj Exotica, Benaulim* ☎ *832/277–0077.*

$$$$ ★ **Taj Exotica.** Beside tranquil Benaulim beach you'll find one of the most attractive places to stay in south Goa. The lobby has gleaming marble floors and spotless white sofas. Spacious rooms with shady verandas look out onto the golf course and Arabian Sea. You can opt for a villa with an outdoor private pool, or one with a hot tub overlooking the sea. Although all of this luxury takes you well away from the mass-tourist clutter of Colva, the resort remains close to the heart of Goa—with the exemplary warmth and good humor of its staff. In addition to four full-service restaurants there's a lobster shack just above the beach. The spa offers ayurvedic treatments as well as Western massage therapies. **Pros:** great restaurants, gorgeous setting. **Cons:** very spread out. ✉ *Calwaddo, Benaulim, Salcette, 403716* ☎ *832/277–1234* *www.tajhotels.com* *136 rooms, 4 suites* *In-hotel: 5 restaurants, bar, golf courses, tennis courts, pool, gym, spa, children's programs (ages 5 and up), airport shuttle.* *AE, MC, V* *BP.*

VARCA

14 km (8.7 mi) southwest of Margao.

The scenery at Varca is rural: there are deep fields on either side of the road, and you may get the distinct feeling that you're heading nowhere in particular. This is an illusion. There are a number of resorts close to Varca village that take advantage of its perfect, unspoiled stretch of beach. Stay at Varca for the beach and for the opportunity to take long walks through the green Goa countryside.

8

WHERE TO EAT & STAY

$$$–$$$$ ★ **Carnaval.** Low-hung black lamps light a woven bamboo ceiling, and Mario Miranda cartoons enliven the walls at this restaurant with excellent fusion food. Try the jerk potatoes *peri peri* (with hot chilli peppers), the tandoor-grilled tiger prawns with lemon mustard sauce, and the naan with pesto. After all this the dessert, crepes filled with *gajar ka halwa* (carrot sweetmeat), seems almost ordinary. *Ramada Caravela, Varca 832/274–5200 to 14 AE, MC, V No lunch.*

$$$–$$$$ ★ **Flavors.** If you're in the mood for something other than Goan cuisine, come here for great North-West Frontier food (from Pakistan to the Afghan border). You can dine indoors or on a terrace overlooking the Radisson's pool. The kebabs and tandoori breads are wonderful but filling; make sure you have enough room for some unusual and extremely good spiced ice cream at the end. *Radisson White Sands, Pedda, Varca 832/272–7272 AE, DC, MC, V No lunch.*

$$$$ ★ **Radisson White Sands.** This family-friendly hotel contains a massive free-form pool with a swim-up bar, as well as an indoor entertainment center complete with a small bowling alley and mini movie theater. A good health club, spa, a lively bar on the beach, and a water-sports center offer a smorgasbord of activities. The rooms are modern, if somewhat generic, but the service is warm and helpful. **Pros:** the pool forms a fun centerpiece for the resort. **Cons:** considerably overpriced compared to other hotels in this price range. *178–179 Pedda, Salcete, Varca Village, 403721 832/272–7272 www.radisson.com/goain 150 rooms, 4 suites In-room: dial-up. In-hotel: 2 restaurants, bars, pool, gym, spa, airport shuttle. AE, MC, V CP.*

$$$$ **Ramada Caravela.** The lobby of this beachfront resort is an odd mix of cathedral and piazza, with wrought iron garden benches and huge arches and beams. A casino, a fusion Indian-Mediterranean restaurant, and a Polynesian eatery on the beach add to the eclectic mix of this spread-out resort. The beach restaurant, Polynesian Hut, is perfect for seafood and an evening out; you can order a variety of grilled meat, fish and chicken with your choice of marinade, and Chinese and Thai food. **Pros:** refurbished rooms are a plus. **Cons:** public spaces could use a sprucing up. *Varca Village, Varca Village, 403721 832/274–5200 www.caravelabeachresort.com 192 rooms, 4 suites, 6 villas In-hotel: 4 restaurants, bars, golf course, tennis courts, pool, gym, laundry service. AE, MC, V CP.*

$$$ **Club Mahindra.** This primarily timeshare-apartment resort has a comfortable if unimaginative hotel block for walk-in guests. There's a three-tier swimming pool; one level is a hot tub. **Pros:** two bedroom units are good for families. **Cons:** not on the beach. *Survey No. 176/1 Varca Village, 403721 832/274–4555 www.clubmahindra.com 23 rooms In-hotel: restaurant, bar, tennis courts, pool, gym, airport shuttle. AE, MC, V CP.*

CAVELOSSIM

20 km (12 mi) southwest of Margao.

The last of the villages before the mouth of the Sal River, and the end of the coastal road southward from Bogmalo is Cavelossim. If you want to continue down the coast, you have to head back inland and take the national highway south, or take a country road up the river and use a ferry. Given that this is a rural area, Cavelossim is a surprisingly developed little place, complete with a shopping arcade; this is chiefly because of the presence of the Leela, arguably the most luxurious of the southern Goa resorts. The beach is clean and striking because it's at the mouth of the Sal River—serene and flanked by fields and coconut plantations. This part of South Goa is an end in itself, and not a good base from which to explore the rest of the state (if you're keen on beach hopping and other touristy activities, stay up north). It's the place to come when you want to relax, take up residence on the beach, and forget about everything, including trips to town.

WHERE TO EAT & STAY

$$$–$$$$ ✕**Jamavar.** This formal and stylish Indian restaurant overlooking the pool at the luxurious Leela hotel has dishes you're unlikely to encounter elsewhere in Goa: *cocum* (tamarind) marinated chicken with wild fig yogurt dressing, lobster tikka with cherry tomato chutney, and tamarind-glazed rack of lamb. ✉*Mobar, Cavelossim* ☎*832/287–1234* ▭*AE, MC, V.*

$$$$ Fodor'sChoice ★ **The Leela Goa.** For flat-out, over-the-top luxury and sophistication nothing in Goa can top this well-planned 75-acre resort that includes a secluded beach and a magnificent view of cliffs and coves. The open-air lobby is reminiscent of a Hampi temple, complete with panel carvings and a sculpted *nandi* (sacred bull), and is a wonderful place to spend a cool and quiet afternoon. The two-story, salmon-color villas are arranged along a winding artificial lagoon. Rooms or suites have tile floors, dark-wood furniture, well-appointed bathrooms, and private balconies. Some villas have private swimming pools. The restaurants offer diverse menus and beautiful settings. **Pros:** the best accommodations rupees can buy. **Cons:** pricey to say the least. ✉*Mobar, Cavelossim, 403731* ☎*832/287–1234* 🌐*www.ghmhotels.com* *54 rooms, 74 suites* *In-room: dial-up. In-hotel: 4 restaurants, bar, golf course, tennis courts, pool, spa, water sports, children's programs (ages 5 to 12), laundry service, airport shuttle.* ▭*AE, MC, V.*

$$$–$$$$ **Holiday Inn.** The chief advantage of this friendly place is its cozy vibe. It has a pleasantly large pool, and comfortable, if basic rooms. **Pros:** well priced for its location on a lovely beach. **Cons:** could use an update. ✉*Mobor Beach, Cavelossim, 403731* ☎*832/287–1303 to 310* 🌐*www.holiday-inn.com* *168 rooms, 2 suites* *In-hotel: 2 restaurants, bar, pool, gym, laundry service, airport shuttle.* ▭*AE, MC, V* *CP.*

$$$ **Royal Goan Beach Club (Haathi Mahal).** Primarily a timeshare resort, the RGBC at Haathi Mahal offers hotel rooms as well. Ask for a room that overlooks the riverside plantations. The hotel has a small pool and an ordinary restaurant. **Pros:** nice inland views. **Cons:** a good distance

8

(1-km walk) from the beach, considerable traffic noise. ✉ *Cavelossim, 403731* ☎ *832/287–1101 to 110* 🌐 *www.haathimahal.com* *66 rooms, 77 villas* *In-hotel: restaurant, bars, pools, gym, spa, laundry service.* 💳 *AE, DC, MC, V* 🍽 *CP.*

PALOLEM BEACH

37 km (23 mi) southwest of Margao.

Until recently, Goa's southernmost sandy stretch—nicknamed Paradise Beach—was like a dream. Palolem, in the Canacona district, received only those nature lovers and privacy seekers. Even so, despite the influx of shacks, hotels, restaurants, and discos, this gently curved stretch of white sand backed by the palm groves and low, green mountains remains one of the most beautiful beaches in India.

GOA ESSENTIALS

To research prices, get advice from other travelers, and book travel arrangements, visit www.fodors.com.

AIR TRAVEL

All flights go in and out of Goa's Dabolim Airport. Schedules and destinations are subject to change, and prices vary widely from airline to airline and season to season. For the most up-to-date information check the airlines' Web sites.

Airlines & Contacts

Air India (☎ *832/243–1100 to 04* 🌐 *www.airindia.com*). **Air Sahara** (☎ *832/223–0247* 🌐 *www.airsahara.net*). **Indian Airlines** (☎ *832/242–8181* 🌐 *www.indianairlines.in*). **Jet Airways** (☎ *832/243–8792* 🌐 *www.jetairways.com*). **Kingfisher Airlines** (☎ *1800/233–331 or 1800/180–0101* 🌐 *www.flykingfisher.com*). **SpiceJet** (☎ *1800/180–3333* 🌐 *www.spicejet.com*). **Simplify Deccan** (☎ *832/243–8950* 🌐 *www.flyairdeccan.net*).

AIRPORTS & TRANSFERS

Goa's Dabolim Airport is 29 km (18 mi) from Panaji. Buses are infrequent, so it's usually best to take a taxi from here to your destination. You can arrange for a prepaid taxi service at a counter inside the airport, or go straight outside and hire a private cab. Either way, the fare to Panaji should not exceed Rs. 500.

Airport Information **Dabolim Airport** (☎ *832/245–0723*).

BUS TRAVEL

The cheapest but least-comfortable way to reach Goa from Bombay over land is by bus, a grueling 17-hour trip if you're lucky, which will take you to the bus station in Panaji. Make this a last resort if you haven't planned several weeks ahead and booked a flight or train. Buses within Goa are cheap, frequent, and overcrowded—be prepared to fight your way on and off.

MAIL & SHIPPING

The General Post Office in Panaji is open weekdays 9:30–5:30.

Post Office General Post Office (✉ *Patto Bridge, Panaji* ☎ *832/222-3706*).

MONEY

Most hotels will change money for their guests as will bank offices. A safer option is to bring a Visa or MasterCard (Americans Express cards rarely work) and pull rupees directly from the many ATMs throughout Goa.

TAXIS

Goa has a unionized taxi system with fixed rates from point A to B. This is the best way to get around in Goa if money isn't a constraint. You don't really need to contact a tour operator, as there will always be a taxi stand outside your hotel. If not, the hotel will call one for you from the nearest stand. Fares are not negotiable (in theory) and drivers charge a fixed rate displayed on a board at every taxi stand. If you are visiting a number of places and covering a lot of ground, it makes more sense to hire a taxi for a 4- or 8-hour stretch (Rs. 1,500) and pay an additional rate for every kilometer above 80 km. Taxis levy a surcharge when they operate at night.

TOURS

There are dozens of private tour operators in Goa. The most reliable are run by the Goa Tourism Development Corporation, which runs bus tours of both North and South Goa—departing from Panaji, Madgaon, and Colva Beach—as well as river cruises from the Santa Monica Pier in Panaji, and the Goa Department of Tourism.

Contacts Department of Tourism (✉ *Tourist Home, Patto Bridge, Panaji* ☎ *832/243-8750* 🌐 *www.goatourism.org*). **Goa Tourism Development Corporation** (✉ *Trionara Apartments, Dr. Alvares Costa Rd., Panaji* ☎ *832/242-0779* 🌐 *www.goa-tourism.com*).

TRAIN TRAVEL

For complete train schedules and fares, and to book tickets online go to the Web site for the **India Railways Reservation Inquery** at 🌐 *www.indianrail.gov.in*. This complete and surprisingly easy-to-navigate site lets you purchase and upgrade tickets, determine the kind of train you want, and review the rather extensive list of rules.

Train Information Karmali station (☎ *832/228-5798*). **Margao station** (✉ *2 km (1 mi) from the main shopping area, Margao* ☎ *832/271-2790*).

VISITOR INFORMATION

In Panaji, the Directorate of Tourism fields general inquiries. For assistance with reservations, including bus tours, contact the Goa Tourism Development Corporation (GTDC). There's also a 24-hour "Hello Information" number for Goa (☎ 832/241-2121), which is extremely useful for finding out-of-date phone numbers. Another great resource is Find*All* Goa, at 🌐 *www.findall-goa.com*. This site provides detailed calendars and contact information for live music, tours, cruises, hotel happenings, and cultural and sports events as well as useful information air and train travel.

Tourist Offices **Department of Tourism** (✉ *Government of Goa, Tourist Home, Patto Bridge, Panaji* ☎ *832/243–8750* 🌐 *www.goatourism.org*). **Goa Tourism Development Corporation** (✉ *Trionara Apartments, Dr. Alvares Costa Rd., Panaji* ☎ *832/242–0779* 🌐 *www.goa-tourism.com*).

Karnataka & Hyderabad

Vittala Temple in Hampi

9

WORD OF MOUTH

"Of all the cities in India, Bangalore would be my first choice of a place to live. The climate is fantastic; it's never too hot or too cold. It's a very green city, low rise for the most part; although the amount of construction going on is quite amazing. It is the 'pub city,' with lots of restaurants and bars—kind of reminds me of Europe in that sense."

—Cicerone

www.fodors.com/forums

WELCOME TO KARNATAKA & HYDERABAD

Golconda Fort, Hyderabad

TOP REASONS TO GO

★ **So Long, Crowds:** Karnataka has many treasures. What it doesn't have are the bands of tourists that hit the Golden Triangle and Kerala.

★ **Monumental Art:** The ruins of Hampi and the soapstone temples of Belur and Halebid are some of the most stunning examples of Hindu art in all of India.

★ **Modern India:** Bangalore and Hyderabad are both great places to take in and gawk at the hotels, malls, nightclubs, art galleries, and other attractions that make up the "New India."

★ **Amazing Nature:** Karnataka's parks and nature preserves hold leopards, huge bison-like creatures, and wide expanses of green.

★ **So Easy to Get Away:** Coorg plantations, nature camps, and high-end resorts—Karnataka has ample means and methods of escape.

1 Bangalore. A buzzing tech capital as well as the capital of Karnataka, Bangalore lies in the state's southeast corner on a plateau that keeps its weather moderate. To its west are the temple towns of Belur and Halebid as well as the port city of Mangalore.

2 Mysore. Three hours by train to the southwest of Bangalore, the state's pomp-filled former capital draws crowds to its palace and major temple. Mysore's also a good stop before heading west to the coffee plantations and nature preserves of Coorg.

3 Hampi. These stunning ruins lie near the center of Karnataka, part of an alien landscape of boulders and small ravines. To reach the nearby base town of Hospet, it's a long night's train ride north from Bangalore.

4 Hyderabad. Roughly 300 mi north of Bangalore in the neighboring state of Andra Pradesh, this city brings travelers as much for its high-tech, big-business present as for the reminders of the past, including the stunning Golconda Fort.

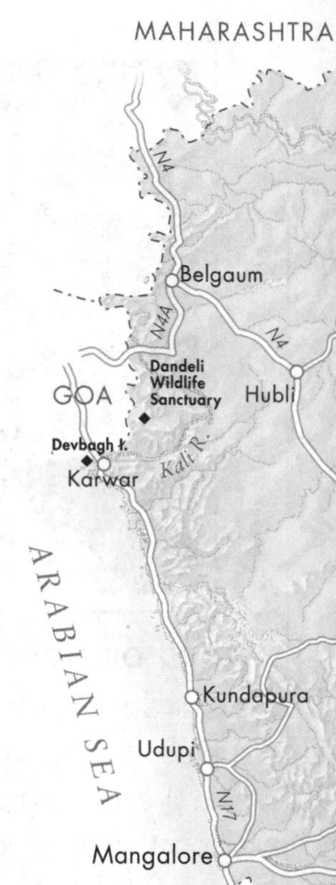

Lotus mahal of Zanana enclosure at ancient town of Hampi

Charminar, Hyderabad

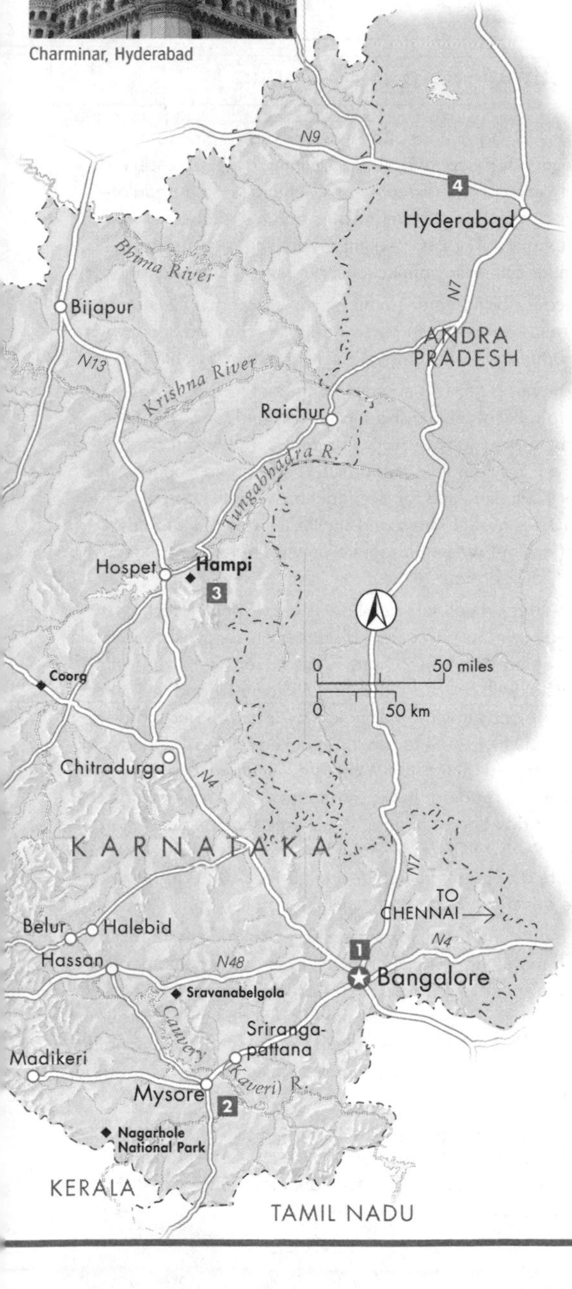

GETTING ORIENTED

The large state of Karnataka lies in India's southwest quadrant. Roughly the size of New England, it has a west coast that runs from just below Goa to south of Mangalore, and its interior is even longer, making it a kind of transitional state between India's lower center and its extremely southern states. Because its northern sections are difficult and time-consuming to reach, most travelers concentrate their journey in southern Karnataka, starting out from the main hub of Bangalore.

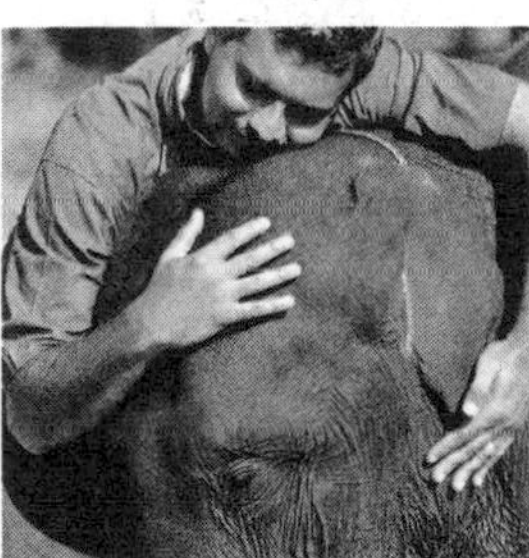

A baby elephant in Coorg

KARNATAKA & HYDERABAD PLANNER

When to Go

Like most of India, Karnataka and Hyderabad is nicest between October and February, when the weather is sunny and dry but not unbearably hot. With the exception of Bangalore, March through May is very hot, particularly in Hampi, with the temperature soating up to and beyond 104°F (40°C) but cooling down during the monsoon rains that fall June through September and periodically make everything wet, especially along the coast. If you can bear the heat, however, main attractions are much emptier in the hot months, and many hotels offer major discounts; but try to visit places like the Hampi ruins in the early morning or late afternoon to avoid the hot sun. Many towns hold long religious festivals just prior to the monsoon.

Getting There and Around

In 2008, Bangalore and Hyderabad both plan to open larger international airports. Until then, their over-served but well located current ones will have to do. Bangalore has connections to every major city in India as well as international flights. Begumpet Airport, in Hyderabad, has similar domestic connections, but fewer international ones.

Because Bangalore is a major rail center, it makes sense to take a train between here and Mysore or Hampi. *For more information, see Karnataka & Hyderabad Essentials.*

National highways connect Bangalore to Chennai, the Kerala coast, Hyderabad, Mumbai, and Goa. The best way to see many parts of Karnataka is to hire a car and driver. For journeys outside city limits, figure about Rs. 8.25 per kilometer, and for overnight trips a halt charge of Rs. 150 per night to feed and shelter the driver. Flat rates to get around within Bangalore or Mysore run approximately Rs. 150 per hour.

The three-wheel auto-rickshaw is a convenient, fast, and cheap way to travel short distances on congested streets. In Bangalore the metered rate is Rs. 12 for the first two kilometers, with Rs. 6 per additional kilometer, and unlike most other places in India (including Hyderabad), most drivers will actually agree to use those meters, at least during the day. From 10 PM to 5 AM the fare is theoretically 1½ times the meter reading, but in most cases you'll have to agree on a price ahead of time. (Most trips shouldn't cost more than Rs. 50.) Often, you can hire an auto-rickshaw for the entire day (eight hours) for around Rs. 500; bargain with the driver, and don't pay until the day is done.

In major cities, call taxis are also popular. They're faster and more expensive than auto-rickshaws but cheaper than hiring a car and driver. Taxies charge more or less according to their meters (usually more), with an initial charge of about Rs. 80 for the first 5 km (3 mi), with an additional Rs. 12 for each additional kilometer. Rates usually increase by 50% after 10 PM.

In Hyderabad, auto-rickshaws tend to go the long way to your destination unless you know—or pretend to know—where you're going. Spotting landmarks and an extra dose of patience will serve you well.

Karnataka's Adventure Trail

Karnataka's lovely, diverse terrain includes an emerald green coastline across the Western Ghats as well as the stark Deccan Plateau. Dense forest or lush plantations cover many parts of Karnataka. With its relatively mild weather, this country is ideal for adventure sports of several kinds—from rock climbing and trekking to white-water rafting, canoeing, and angling. The coast offers scuba diving off the island of Devbagh and water sports in the backwaters of the Sharavati River. Near Bangalore, the rock formations at Ramnagaram and Savanadurga have long attracted serious rock climbers, as have the moonscapes at Hampi. Treks through forested areas around Bangalore, Mysore, Coorg, and in the Western Ghats—along mountain paths or railway tracks, and through rolling plantations—can be very rewarding, not only for their spectacular scenic beauty but also for the chance to spot various wildlife. The trekking season is just after the rains, from September to January. White-water rafting is possible on some stretches of the Cauvery and the Kalinadi, and fishing for *mahseer* in the Cauvery is a popular sport (the massive fish are returned to the water after being caught). Guides, equipment, and advice are available from many adventure tour promoters (⇨ *Karnataka & Hyderabad Essentials*).

Another popular, less strenuous option would be a stay of a couple days in a Jungle Lodge. Staying at these camps, run by the state of Karnataka, is hardly roughing it—all meals are provided and rooms have their own bathroom and electricity and hot water for at least part of the day. Along with the frills they are usually in beautiful surroundings that include a beach-filled island and a maharaja's forming hunting lodge, up in the hills. Various Jungle Lodges are mentioned throughout this chapter, but for the entire range, visit *www.junglelodges.com*.

What It Costs In Rupees

	¢	$	$$	$$$	$$$$
Restaurants	under Rs. 100	Rs. 100–Rs. 300	Rs. 300–Rs. 500	Rs. 500–Rs. 700	over Rs. 700
Hotels	under Rs. 2,000	Rs. 2,000–Rs. 4,000	Rs. 4,000–Rs. 6,000	Rs. 6,000–Rs. 10,000	over Rs. 10,000

Restaurant prices are for an entrée plus bread or rice. Hotel prices are for a standard double room in high season, excluding approximately 12% tax.

Planning Your Time

If you only have a few days in Karnataka, skip Bangalore and head straight to **Mysore,** whose highlights are the sprawling Mysore Palace and the temple atop **Chamundi Hill.** The breathtaking temples at **Belur** and **Halebid,** 2½ hours away, can be visited as a (long) day trip from Mysore. **Bangalore** doesn't have a huge number of sights, but it can be a good place to recharge before moving on to less plush pastures. The ruins of **Hampi,** best reached via the overnight train from Bangalore to Hospet, deserve at least two days to see effectively. From Hospet you can make train connections to Guntakal, and from there to most major cities in India. As for Hyderabad, you could cover all of its major sights in one exhausting day, but it's best if you can spend at least two nights. The must-sees here are **Golconda Fort** and the **Qutab Shahi Tombs,** both several miles outside of the city and reachable by taxi or auto-rickshaw; Old Town's **Charminar,** a four-story arched, minaret topped gateway; and the impressive **Salar Jung Museum.** If you have a lot of stamina and intend to head south to Chennai, in Tamil Nadu, consider a 12-hour detour to the temple town of Tirupati, which is within the state of Andhra Pradesh but only four hours from Chennai. But be warned: it's much easier to go from Chennai to Tirupati than from Hyderabad to Tirupati.

9

Updated by John Rambow

KARNATAKA IS A MICROCOSM of the most colorful and fascinating aspects of India, presented at a comfort level that is efficient as well as sumptuous. The place has probably hosted human civilization as long as any place on earth. Throughout the state (in such places as Belur, Halebid, and Hampi) are some of the greatest religious monuments in India. The climate is as varied as the culture, ranging from humid to dry and cool, the result of a geography that combines sea coast with tropical uplands and arid zones.

Most of Karnataka's 53 million people are called Kannadigas after their language, Kannada, and they are often intensely proud of their heritage. Of Dravidian stock, as are most people in the South, the Kannadigas tend to be darker than the Hindi-speaking Indians to the north. In villages, women wait with their jugs at the well, which doubles as the social center. Men, often wearing *lungis* (colorful saronglike wraps), work in the rice fields, walking slowly behind oxen dragging plows. The climate makes it possible to live partially outdoors—village huts are often of rudimentary construction, and people frequently set up their beds outside.

The simplicity of Karnataka's countryside is balanced by the grand palaces and formal gardens of Mysore, the youthful cosmopolitanism of Bangalore, and the relics—both Hindu and Muslim—of centuries of royal living. Even the outdoors is impressive if you spend a few days on safari in Nagarhole National Park or trek between jungle camps along the banks of the Kaveri River.

Although Bangalore and Mysore are well connected by express trains and comfortable buses, there are advantages to traveling by car: the countryside along the way is verdant with palms and rice fields (known as paddies), and you'll often see colorfully dressed women washing clothes in the roadside streams. On the flip side, timid passengers may be put off—at least at first—by the Indian driver's way of roaring around tight curves on roads crowded with giant buses, plodding oxcarts, and men pushing bicycles laden with bunches of coconuts.

Hyderabad, to the north in the neighboring state of Andra Pradesh, is in some ways a twin sister of Bangalore, over 500 km (311 mi) away. It's known more for the technological businesses that have sprung up here in the past decade than for its often-dramatic history, which have nevertheless left some wonderful, impressive Muslim monuments in its wake.

EXPLORING KARNATAKA

Karnataka is packed with fascinating places and historic sights. The main transport hub is Bangalore, an inland city in the southeastern corner of the state, so it's easiest to start your trip here. Both Bangalore, which considers itself the Silicon Valley of India, and Mysore (2½ hours to the southwest by train) are worth exploring. Bangalore is a boomtown, with a population that now exceeds 5 million; huge municipal gardens and a teeming old commercial district are interspersed with lively pubs, restaurants, and boutiques. Mysore, in contrast, is an elegant old royal town, center of the princely state that existed from the mid-19th- to the mid-20th centuries. It's small in scale, tropical in appearance, and has India's finest zoo.

The northern Karnataka, including the town of Bijapur, isn't easily accessible by train, and would otherwise take a two-day road journey to get there. It's far easier to explore the southern region, from Hampi (in the east-central part of the state) south. From Mysore, you can make two-day trips to Nagarhole National Park, on the Kerala border, home to elephants and tigers; or to the 11th- and 12th-century temples at Belur and Halebid, which between them hold more than 30,000 intricately carved sculptures; or to Sravanabelagola, with its awesome monolithic statue of the Jain saint Gomateshwara. For a refreshing outdoor stint, try the fishing camp on the banks of the Cauvery River or spend a day or two at a coffee plantation in Coorg district. If you have time and stamina to spare, venture out from Bangalore to the spectacular abandoned city of Hampi. Although this ancient city is not as easily accessible as most other destinations in this guide, it's the single most rewarding historical destination in the state.

ABOUT THE RESTAURANTS

Bangalore has an impressive restaurant scene, but options for dining out in the rest of Karnataka are less varied, with tasty food but limited menus. You'll almost always find delicious, vegetarian southern favorites like various kinds of *dosas* (filled, crepelike pancakes), and *idlis* (steamed rice cakes), both served with coconut chutney and other condiments. A popular rice dish is *bisi belebath,* spicy lentil curry and mixed vegetables topped with wafers. Karnataka is truly famed for its *thali,* a combination platter done South Indian style—with rice surrounded by several bowls of vegetables and sauces. The thali is cheap, filling, and good. Also, unlike most parts of India, Karnataka brews a fine cup of coffee.

ABOUT THE HOTELS

Mysore, Hyderabad, and the affluent state capital of Bangalore have sumptuous hotels set in verdant tropical gardens. Since 1954, when the princely state of Mysore was incorporated into India, some of the maharaja's numerous summer palaces have been converted to luxury accommodations for travelers, including elegant restaurants in former grand ballrooms. All three cities also have some excellent hotels with more moderate rates. Options in smaller towns are fewer.

Unless we indicate otherwise, all hotels have central air-conditioning. In addition, many luxury hotels have floors with higher-priced rooms that come with special privileges or facilities.

Karnataka lodgings sometimes charge a 10% service fee, and the Indian government tacks on another 12% or so "luxury tax," depending on the facilities. But make sure you look into discounts, because you can often get reductions on the rack rate, especially in the off-season; alternatively, opt for a package deal.

IF YOU LIKE

ARCHITECTURE

Karnataka is best known for its Hindu temples and Indo-Saracenic palaces: the Hoysala-dynasty temples of Belur and Halebid in the south, the enormous ruined town of Hampi in the center of the state, and the Maharaja's Palace in Mysore.

KONKAN RAILWAY

For a scenic panorama of India's Western coast from Mumbai clear down to Kochi, there's no topping the Konkan Railway, which stretches 760 km (470 mi) across the states of Maharashtra, Goa, Karnataka, and Kerala. In its spectacular travels, it uses 170 major bridges, 1,800 minor bridges, and 92 tunnels to pass through the imposing Western Ghats (a chain of highlands covered with tropical evergreen forests). To make the most of the Konkan Railway in Karnataka, take a ride on the Mangalore–Margao passenger train, which runs every day. It isn't plush, but the sights and sounds outside will absorb you. The train chugs across bridges—the longest on this route is the 2-km (1-mi) stretch over the river Sharavathi—and past rice paddies, sleepy villages, fishermen's backyards, hills, and marshy stretches where children play and cattle wander. Keeping you company inside is a mixed crowd: traders, nuns, students, laborers, fishermen, hawkers of snacks and beverages, and fellow travelers staring happily into the distance.

Numbers in the text correspond to numbers in the margin and on the chapter maps.

BANGALORE

1,040 km (645 mi) southeast of Mumbai, 140 km (87 mi) northeast of Mysore, 290 km (180 mi) west of Chennai.

Bangalore exudes modernity, albeit with touches of a long-standing culture clash. Brigade Road, St. Marks Road, Fraser Town, Cubbon Road, and Queen's Circle have all retained their names from the British days, and there's a divide (although it's one that's fading) between the fairly cosmopolitan Cantonment area, the upscale Kormangala section to the south, and the more traditional City area near the city's main market. The yuppies and expats in Kormangala and in gated communities outside of town lead a semi-Western lifestyle, and the Cantonment retains a military flavor, with barracks and a parade ground contrasting with luxury hotels and large international banks and offices. At the other side of Cubbon Park from the Cantonment, the City's more traditional inhabitants guard middle-class values and a section once ruled by the princely state of Mysore. M. G. Road and Brigade Road constitute the center of the Cantonment, where quaint old buildings sit opposite latter-day shopping malls. In contrast, the K. G. Road area, also known as Majestic for the major movie theater there, has offices, shops, hawkers, travelers, and the city's main train and bus stations.

It was the feudal lord Kempegowda who founded the city in AD 1537, and his son, Kempegowda II, developed it. Both paid allegiance to the Vijayanagar empire, and after the fall of that empire in 1638, the city came under the rule of the Sultan of Bijapur, Mohammed Adil Shah. Shah, who was pleased with the services of his trusted lieutenant Shahji Bhonsle (father of the Maratha King Shivaji), gave him the city as a gift. Between Shahji Bhonsle and his son King Shivaji, the Marathas ruled Bangalore for 49 years until they lost it to the Moghuls, who in turn (supposedly) leased it to the Wodeyars of Mysore (though another version of the story maintains that the Wodeyars bought the city for the relatively small sum of 3 lakh (300,000 rupees).

BOILED BEANS AND BACK AGAIN

There's an odd anecdote about how Bangalore was named: in the 13th century King Ballala of the Hoysala dynasty lost his way in the forest and chanced upon a poor old woman who could only offer him boiled beans. Pleased with her hospitality, the king christened the place Bendakaluru (the "town of boiled beans"). Over the centuries, the name became Bengaluru, which eventually became anglicized to Bangalore. In 2006 the state government started plans to change the city's name back to Bengaluru. The old-new name hasn't caught on yet.

In 1759, the city was taken over by Hyder Ali. Bangalore flourished during his reign. Remembered as a brave warrior, his son Tipu Sultan fought against the British; Tipu's exceptional military tactics and valiance earned him the title of the Tiger of Mysore, as Mysore was the city from which he ruled. After Tipu died during the British siege of his island fortress, Srirangapattana, the British took over his territory and (nominally) reinstated the Hindu Wodeyars on the Mysore throne—though the British maintained a large presence in Mysore city to oversee the administration. Shortly after, they built Bangalore's Cantonment. In 1881 the British returned much of Mysore to the Wodeyars, who held great influence over the region until independence in 1947 and the eventual abolition of princely rule. After Independence, Bangalore became the capital of Karnataka (the new name for Mysore state).

Thanks to its pleasant climate and green environs, Bangalore was often called the "Pensioners' Paradise" and the "Garden City." However, in the 1980s it began to attract the telecommunications and technology industries, and it became India's fastest-growing city. This boom attracted multinational corporations, and, aided by the cantonment's long-standing Western identity, the city is now extremely cosmopolitan (some would say materialistic), with trendy boutiques, pizza parlors, coffee shops, and pubs. Indeed, beer is imbibed with gusto in nearly 200 establishments, though local authorities now enforce an 11 or 11:30 PM closing time. All this growth hasn't come without a price—the traffic snarls and under-maintained roads here are some of the worst in India, frequent power outages are a near daily event for some locals, and galloping housing costs have priced out more and more of the poor and middle class.

Bangalore Palace 6
Bull Temple 1
Cubbon Park 5
Lal Bagh Botanical Gardens...........2
Tipu's Palace 3
Vidhana Soudha 4

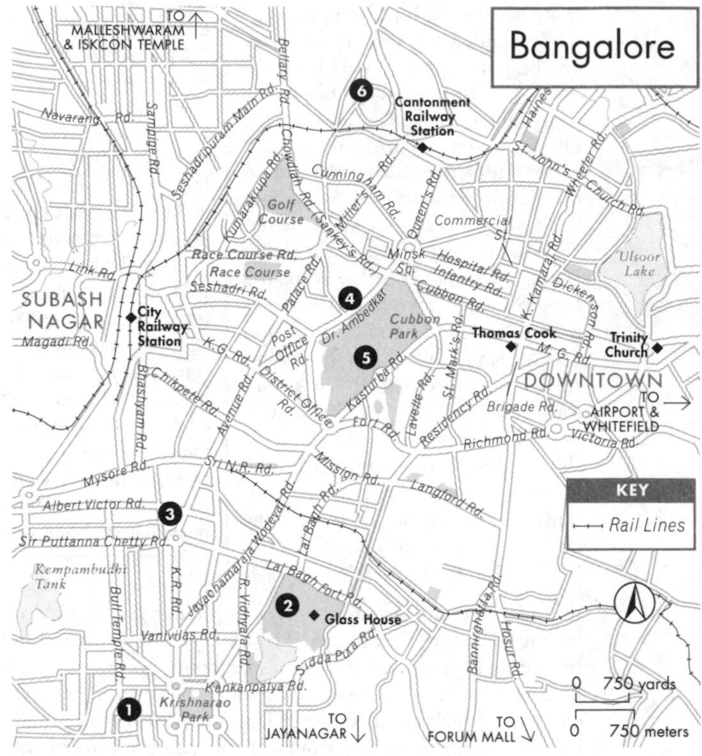

Numbers in the text correspond to numbers in the margin and on the Bangalore map.

A GOOD TOUR

This tour begins in one of the older parts of Bangalore and then proceeds to its current seat of government. Start by taking a taxi or auto-rickshaw to the **Bull Temple** ❶. Walk 2 km (1 mi) east for about 20 minutes on the crowded but basically flat Bugle Rock Road, later B.P. Wadia Road. This brings you to the southwestern corner of the tropical **Lal Bagh Botanical Gardens** ❷. Head north through the gardens and come out on the northern exit. Take a left as you leave, walking along Marigowda Road, which becomes Lal Bagh Fort Road. Walk to a large intersection with K.R. (Krishnarajendra) Road. Turn right onto K.R., which is also named Avenue Road. Shortly, on your left, where Avenue Road is intersected by Albert Victor Road, you'll come to **Tipu's Palace** ❸.

After the palace, the urban scenery is rather dull, so you might want to skip it and take an auto-rickshaw north on K.R. (Avenue) Road to Mysore Bank Circle. From here take a left, walking west along K.G. (Kempegowda) Road for 10 minutes to get a feel for this busy area. Alternatively, follow the narrow, busy Avenue Road for about 2 km (1 mi) north to reach Mysore Bank Circle and K.G. Road. From some point on K. G. Road, take an auto-rickshaw to **Vidhana Soudha** ❹, on Dr. Ambedkar Road, the spectacular building that houses the state legislature. To your right is the red-brick High Court. From here you can walk north (with the court on your left) to the nearest entrance to leafy **Cubbon Park** ❺. When you're done with your nature break, take an auto-rickshaw to the **Bangalore Palace** ❻, modeled on Windsor Palace and still used by the direct descendents of the last Maharaja.

TIMING You'll need the better part of a day for this tour; though taking auto-rickshaws on the plainer stretches can save some time. The Lal Bagh Gardens deserve at least 45 minutes, Tipu's Palace half an hour, and the Bangalore Palace perhaps another 45 minutes. It's best to set off fairly early in the morning, as the gardens are most pleasant then (and in the early evening). Beware of sunburn: Bangalore is cool but at 3,000 feet, the penetrating sun can be deceptively strong.

TIME FOR A WALK?

Bangalore's Cantonment, which includes M. G., Brigade, and Residency Roads, is full of office buildings, hotels, restaurants, schools, and some gorgeous bungalows. The bustling streets around the train station and Race Course Road are also well worth getting lost in for a couple of hours. Other good areas for wandering include the neighborhood of Malleswarum and the city markets (⇨ *Shopping*).

WHAT TO SEE

❻ **Bangalore Palace.** Opened to the public in early 2007, Bangalore's Palace isn't built on the same scale or with the same amount of grandeur as that of Mysore, but it's still an impressive, beautiful sight. Built in 1887 by the Maharaja of Mysore after a visit to England, the castle owes a debt to Windsor Castle and its Tudor architecture—turrets, arches, and peaks abound. During the short tour, led by a guide, you walk through brightly painted and tiled halls as well as dusty, junk-filled rooms that have seen better days. One highlight, in the entrance hall, is the mounted head of a good-sized tusker (male elephant)—he killed nine people before finding his way to the palace's wall. The other stops on the tour include the run-down room that was once the maharani's bedroom (the wallpaper was imported from Japan) as well as receiving halls and a curious "secret" passageway that has a mirror in its center, preventing anyone from seeing who might be at the other end. The current head of the Mysore royal family and his wife live in another section of the palace. Note that unless you're a big fan of palaces and their decorations, it's probably not worth paying the excessive extra fee for taking photos. ✉ *Palace Grounds, Vasanthnagar* ☎ *80/2336–0818 or 80/2331–5789* 🎫 *Palace Rs. 200, camera fee Rs. 500, video camera fee Rs. 1000* ⏲ *Daily 10–6.*

❶ **Bull Temple.** This small temple houses the enormous 1786 monolith of Nandi, the sacred Hindu bull that carries Shiva. The temple's front yard bustles with activity: peddlers sell coconuts, bananas, and jasmine blossoms for offerings. Dating from the 1980s, the *gopuram* (gateway), painted in cream and white, has fewer figures than many others in the south. Inside, Nandi lies in a traditional position, leaning slightly to one side with his legs tucked beneath him. The bull's hefty black bulk is beautifully carved and ornamented with bells, and glistens with peanut oil that priests apply weekly. Unfortunately, the temple can be a bit of a tourist trap, so don't be surprised if a self-appointed guide attaches himself to you, or if a priest offers you a *puja* (blessing) that turns out to be costly. Don't pay more than Rs. 50 for the guide's services, and ask about the puja before buying. Down a flight of strairs and near the street is another temple. ✉ *Bull Temple Rd., Basavanagudi* 🎫 *Free* 🕒 *Daily 6* AM*–8* PM.

5 **Cubbon Park.** At nearly 200 acres, Cubbon Park provides some much-needed greenery and quiet in the center of Bangalore. In addition to lots of trees and plants, there are also some interesting and old buildings here and there, most notably the Raj reminder at the intersection of Kasturba and M.G. roads; here you can see a rather haughty 1906 take on Queen Victoria, holding the world in her hands. It's rare to see such a statue of Queen Victorica in modern-day India, because most similar statues were, understandably, taken down after Independence. ✉ *Between Kasturba and Dr. Ambedkar Rds.* 🌐 *www.horticulture.kar.nic.in/cubbon.htm.*

ISKCON Temple. More commonly known as the Hare Krishna group in the West, the International Society for Krishna Consciousness was founded in 1966 by Swami Prabhupada, who based his religion on ancient Hindu writings such as the Bhagavad Gita. To visit the temple, you must first wait in line to deposit your camera in one area and your shoes in another, and then pass through a security check. After looking at several preliminary shrines devoted to aspects of Vishnu, you reach the the main temple, with three large idols of Krishna and some very vivid and entertaining paintings on the ceiling. In a room below, a multimedia show tells the story of Krishna, an avatar of Vishnu whose spiritual discourse with the warrior Arjuna makes up the Bhagavad Gita. There are also many (perhaps too many) opportunities to buy souvenirs, religious articles, and food. Go on weekdays during off-hours to minimize the line to get in, which can be astounding. ✉ *Hare Krishna Hill, 1R Block, Chord Rd., Rajaji Nagar* ☎ *80/0700–1300 or 80/1615–2030* 🌐 *www.iskconbangalore.org* 🎫 *Free; no cameras allowed* 🕒 *Daily 4:15* AM*–5* AM*, 7:15* AM*–12:50* PM*, 4* PM*–8:20* PM.

2 **Lal Bagh Botanical Garden.** This 240-acre park, popular with young lovers, is one of the remaining reasons for Bangalore's increasingly obscure nickname, "The Garden City." The park's paths contain more than 100 types of trees and thousands of varieties of plants and flowers from all over the world. Most of the flora is in fullest bloom between October and December. Some trees date from the time of Tipu Sultan, who continued to develop the park in the late 18th century after the death of his father, Hyder Ali, who designed the grounds in 1760. Marking the heart of Lal Bagh is the **Rose Garden,** a square, fenced-in plot blooming with some 150 different kinds of roses. Just beyond, near the north gate entrance, is the **Glass House,** a cross-shaped pavilion built in 1881 with London's Crystal Palace in mind. Twice a year, around

Independence Day (August 15) and Republic Day (January 15), weeklong flower shows are held here, attracting huge crowds. ✉*Lal Bagh Fort Rd., Lal Bagh* 🌐*www.horticulture.kar.nic.in/lalbagh.htm* 🎫*Rs. 7* ⏲*Daily 9–6:30.*

Shiva Temple. Unusual and over-the-top, this open-air temple is in back of the large department store Kemp Fort, both of which make for a convenient stop either coming or going to the airport. The temple, built in 1995, draws as many as 10,000 pilgrims a day, who come for its 65-foot sculpture of Shiva, shown meditating on his spiritual home of Mt. Kailash. Water flows from his head, simulating the holy Ganges. By walking within the sculpture and paying Rs. 10, you can go on a simulated *yatra* (pilgrimage) that shows various sights holy to Shiva throughout India. ✉*Kemp Kids (aka Kemp Fort), Airport Rd., 567001* ☎*80/4152–6409* 🌐*www.kempkids.com* 🎫*Free* ⏲*24 hours a day.*

Fodor'sChoice ★

3 **Tipu's Palace.** Tipu Sultan built this palace for himself in 1789. Made of wood, it's a replica of his summer palace on Srirangapatnam (a river island near Mysore), sans the elaborate fresco painting inside but with the same teak pillars, which are still standing. Also inside is a small exhibit about Tipu and his times. Next door to the palace is the medium-size Venkataramanaswamy Temple, built by the Wodeyars in the 16th century. ✉*Albert Victor Rd., Chickpet* 🎫*Rs. 100* ⏲*Daily 8:30–5:30.*

Holy Trinity Church. Marking one end of M. G. Road (with Cubbon Park and its statue of Queen Victoria at the other), Holy Trinity Church held its first services in 1852, when the road was aptly named South Parade. Built for the use of the British soldiers and their families, it's been in continuous operation ever since, becoming part of the Church of South India after India's Independence. Inside this small, simple church with a tall bell tower and bright white walls are brass and marble plaques memorializing British soldiers and their relations who died in or on their way to India. "Sacred to the memory of George Staple Dobbie Esq. (Mysore Revenue Survey), who died from the effects of wounds inflicted by a tiger," reads one. ✉*M. G. Rd.* ☎*80/2558–4182.*

4 **Vidhana Soudha.** One of Bangalore's most beautiful buildings, Vidhana Soudha is a relatively recent addition to the city, built between 1954 and 1958 to house the state legislature and secretariat. This sprawling granite structure was designed in the Indo-Dravidian style, studded with pillars and carved ledges and topped with a central dome that's crowned, in turn, with a golden four-headed lion (originally the emblem of the great 3rd-century BC Buddhist king Ashoka and now the symbol of India). Unfortunately, the interior is not open to visitors. Facing the Vidhana Soudha head-on across the street is another of Bangalore's attractive public buildings, the pillared, redbrick High Court of Karnataka, built in 1885 as the seat of the then-British government. It's also closed to the public. ✉*Dr. Ambedkar Veedhi Rd., Raj Bhavan–Cubbon Park.*

WHERE TO EAT

Because Bangalore's many IT and outsourcing employees come from all over India—and all over the world—Chinese, American, Italian, and other "ethnic" food is easy to find. At the same time, there are many spots that Bangaloreans have been keeping popular for generations.

For the latest hot spots, check out city pages of the *Times of India*, the *Deccan Herald*, or the bimonthly *CityInfo* (*explocity.com*) magazine, available for free in many hotels and businesses. If you're spending some time in town, the *Times Food Guide*, published by the *Times of India*, is a good and opinionated guide to what's new, worthwhile, and timeless in the city's restaurant scene.

$$$$ **The Royal Afghan.** This posh poolside barbecue joint serves food from the North-West Frontier (part of modern-day Pakistan, Afghanistan, Mongolia, and Uzbekistan). Charcoal-grilled kababs are popular, along with the finely minced mutton with *paratha* bread. Other dishes such as tandoori *jhinga* (prawns), *sikandri raan* (leg of young lamb, marinated in a malt vinegar sauce), and *dal Bukhara* (lentils finished in rich cream sauce) make this a truly enjoyable dining experience. *The Windsor, 25 Sankey Rd., Golf Course 80/2226–9898 AE, DC, MC, V No lunch.*

$$$–$$$$ **Karavalli.** Made to resemble those traditional homes found along India's southwestern coast, Karavalli has dining tables on a shady terrace walled in by hedges and with a small pond, or in an adjoining cottage. The coconut-oriented menu features dishes from Goa, Kerala, and Mangalore; regional specialties include *kori gassi* (chicken simmered in coconut gravy) served with rice bread, a crab curry, and black pomfret fish pan-fried and then served in a banana leaf. *Taj Gateway Hotel, 66 Residency Rd., Downtown Bangalore 80/6660–4545 AE, DC, MC, V.*

$$$ **Jamavar.** Named for a luxurious kind of shawl made in Kashmir, this top-quality Indian restaurant, with handwoven carpets and elegant chandeliers, serves its guests regally. The dishes served—rack of lamb, tandoori jumbo prawns, *tandoori gobi* (cauliflower florets baked in a tandoor oven)—represent those served on the tables of former royal families from every corner of the country: the preparations are intensely flavorful and full of costly ingredients. *The Leela Palace, 23 Airport Rd., Kodihalli 80/2521–1234 Reservations essential AE, DC, MC, V.*

$$ **Olive Beach.** One of the most romantic restaurants in town, this former bungalow is an elegant but easygoing place for a drink as well as a meal, with white sand and pebbles beneath the tables outside, and wicker chairs and distressed wood used for furniture throughout. The menu hits most popular Italian classics, including pizzas, panini (one good option comes with goat cheese), as well as risottos and pasta dishes that use imported meats. Although the food is good, it does take second place to the glam surroundings. The crowd tends to be every bit as photogenic as the location, with businesspeople and socialites lunching by day; at dinner, especially close to Bangalore's 11 PM witching hour, the crowd gets younger and noisier, and the restaurant veers into nightclub territory. *16 Wood St., Ashok Nagar 80/4112–8400 www.olivebarandkitchen.com AE, DC, MC, V.*

$–$$ ✕ **Legend of Sikander.** It would be odd if a place named for the the Arabic rendering of Alexander the Great failed to have lots of Middle Eastern and Mughlai touches to its menu, and Sikander doesn't disappoint. The menu includes lots of kebabs and other North Indian fare, such as chicken biryani and *adana seek* (minced lamb with paprika), but there's also room for all-India classics like chicken tikka masala. In this large dining room, the metallic mosaics on the walls and the blue curtains on the windows are attractive and upbeat. As you dine, you can watch the chaos of the traffic four stories below from the large windows—it's certainly more entertaining from up here. At lunch, most diners head for the extensive and well-priced buffet, which includes a good mix of standards along a couple unusual items each day. Don't miss the addictive mini-samosas—or the homemade ice cream. ✉ *Garuda Mall, 4th fl., Magrath and Commissariat Rds., Ashok Nagar* ☎ *80/4125–2333* ▭ *AE, DC, MC, V.*

$–$$ ★ ✕ **Sunny's.** Small, elegant, and expensive, this place fits right in on the boutique-filled street named after the founder of United Breweries, Vittal Mallya, who used to brew his Kingfisher beer next door. Serving Western food in an open plan that makes it easy for diners to see each other, this is a typical Bangalore restaurant aimed at high-society types as well as expats and business delegations. Even if people-watching isn't your thing, the food still makes the place worth a visit. Best known for its French and Italian specialties—pasta (spaghetti carbonara or lamb lasanga), pizzas, and seasonal salads—Sunny's also serves some very good sandwiches. ✉ *Embassy Diamante, 34 Vittal Mallya Rd., off Lavelle Rd., Downtown Bangalore* ☎ *80/2224–3642* ▭ *AE, DC, MC, V.*

$ ★ ✕ **Angeethi.** On a hotel's rooftop terrace, this restaurant is a nostalgic, deliberately kitschy tribute to the many *dhabas* (roadside eateries) in the Punjab countryside: there are a thatched roof, a well, old Hindi film posters, and a lamppost. Especially worth ordering is anything tandoor (cooked in a traditional oven), such as the *murg malai* (chicken marinated in a tangy sauce), and the *Belliram Gosht* (goat meat in a sauce with whole coriander and other spices). At lunch there'a a well-priced North Indian buffet. Punjabi-style seafood—including pomfret and lobster—is available at dinner. ✉ *Museum Inn, 1 Museum Rd., Downtown Bangalore* ☎ *80/4111–3340* ▭ *AE, DC, MC, V.*

$ ✕ **Coconut Grove.** Specializing in the seafood- and coconut-heavy cuisine of Kerala, this palm-tree filled restaurant is a block south M. G. Road, across from one of the few bungalows remaining on busy Church Street. The restaurant's many large tables and easy-going atmosphere makes it good for groups and leisurely meals. *Thein elaner,* tender coconut water dressed up with mint and honey, is a good way to start off your meal. The fish specialties are a good bet, as is the *kozhi melago* (Chettinad-style chicken). Avoid the grisley pandy stew (Coorg-style pork stew), a rare misstep. For an accompaniment, be sure to get at least one order of *appams,* round, fluffy fried bread that's slightly sweet. The pineapple halwa, long simmered and cooked with ghee, is a rich way to draw the meal to a close. A streetside offshoot, Coco Grove, is popular for drinks and bar snacks. ✉ *86 Church St., Downtown Bangalore* ☎ *80/2559–6149* ▭ *AE, MC, V.*

$ ✕ **Nagarjuna Savoy.** Food from the state of Andhra Pradesh is the focus at this sit-down restaurant, an upscale sister restaurant to the more hectic Nagarjuna next door. Zesty and sweet chicken, mutton (goat), and *biryani* (fried rice and vegetables) are served in a bright room with brass-and-copper masks and framed prints of Indian folk art. One especially good dish is the *murgh maharaja,* a chicken dish whose name testifies to the richness of its sauce, made with pulverized cashews. ✉ *45/3 Residency Cross Rd., Downtown Bangalore* ☎ *80/4112–9897* 💳 *AE, DC, MC, V.*

$ ★ ✕ **Samarkand.** Dressed up like a fortress in the North-West Frontier, with fake torches on the rough-hewn walls and water served in copper tumblers, this is an excellent place for North Indian and middle Eastern food. Specialties include kebabs such as *murgh gilafee* (minced chicken flavored with cardamom and rolled in black pepper), *galawati kabab* (finely minced, very spicy lamb patties flavored with cumin), and other choices include standard curry dishes as well as the diet-busting *dal afghani* (long-cooked black lentils cooked with tomatoes, spices, butter, and cream) and *murgh khusk purdah* (chicken marinated in tandoori masala, grilled and then covered with a thick flour wrapping (the jokey name refers to the historical practice of some Moslem and Hindu wives being hidden from public view after marriage). ✉ *Gem Plaza, 66 Infantry Rd., Downtown Bangalore* ☎ *80/4111–3366* 💳 *AE, MC, V.*

¢ ✕ **Koshy's.** For a beer, a sandwich, fish-and-chips, or full-blown biriyani, this old-time café near busy M. G. Road is a good choice, and the tables of middle-aged and old men kibitzing through the day attests to its long role in Bangalore's history. With high ceilings and whirling fans, lots of smoke, and a dark, historic look, it has an air of permanence, and the waiters won't blink an eye if you hang out here for hours. The food may not win any prizes, but the experience (and maybe the coffee) just might. There is a separate air-conditioned dining section with an more upscale menu that's called the Jewel Box, but for the full Koshy experience, take a left as you enter and skip the a/c. ✉ *St. Marks Rd., Downtown Bangalore* ☎ *80/2291–5840* 💳 *AE, DC, MC, V.*

¢ ✕ **Mavalli Tiffin Rooms (MTR).** Come to this bustling Bangalore institution, established in 1924, for authentic vegetarian South Indian food. The furniture is plastic, the crowds are overwhelming at peak hours, and the system of assigning tables and ordering is chaos for a newcomer—but a better dosa would be hard to find in Bangalore, and the filter coffee (brewed, not instant) is superb. At lunch, only thalis (extensive multicourse combination platters) are served: come hungry. ✉ *Lalbagh Rd., Mavelli* ☎ *80/2222–0022* 💳 *No credit cards* ⏲ *Closed Mon.*

¢ ✕ **Nandhini.** This budget hotel's restaurant fills to the brim at lunch with area workers who mainly come for the thali, the traditional South Indian vegetarian meals that are served on banana leaves here. You can get silverware if you need it, but first try eating the rice and its accompaniments with your right hand, as you'll see the locals deftly doing. The many booths and mirrors on the wall give the place a faint resemblance to an American diner; the chain specializes in Andra Pradesh dishes, so good and spicy chicken and mutton dishes are also available. ✉ *72 St. Mark's Rd., Downtown Bangalore* ☎ *80/4123–3333* 💳 *AE, DC, MC, V.*

WHERE TO STAY

Although many hotels have been built in Bangalore since 2000, the continued business and outsourcing boom means that many of them are almost all full, especially on weekdays. If you want five-star luxury, expect to pay at or near full price.

$$$$ **Ista Hotel.** Natural materials are used extensively in the public areas of this sleek high-rise, which opened in mid-2006. Named for a Sanskrit word that means "sacred" or "welcoming," the hotel emphasizes comfort and service rather than show-stopping interiors. Rooms have blond-wood headboards, plasma TVs, and lots of glass and steel surfaces that create a functional and efficient mood. The all-day restaurant Lido, named for a movie theater that used to be at this location, serves an international menu around the stunning pool. **Pros:** great location near the start of M. G. Road, connected to a shopping center, everything is new. **Cons:** expensive, bathrooms are compact, might be too miminalist for some. ✉*1/1 Swami Vivekananda Rd. (Old Madras Rd.), Ulsoor, 560008* ☎*80/2554–9999* 🌐*www.istahotels.com* *143 rooms, 4 suites* *In-room: safe, refrigerator. In-hotel: 2 restaurants, room service, bar, pool, gym, laundry service, concierge, executive floor, no-smoking rooms* *AE, DC, MC, V.*

$$$$ ★ **The Leela Palace.** Opened in 2002, this huge luxury hotel is modeled in accordance with royal Mysore's hybrid architectural heritage and the magnificent sculptural wealth of the Vijayanagar Empire. Close to the airport and 5 km (3 mi) from downtown Bangalore, the Leela is a world unto itself, with a huge shopping gallery, an excellent Indian restaurant, a library bar with cigar lounge, and a nightclub disco. The interior is astounding: horse sculptures glaring down from huge pillars and the richly decorated ceilings are both in the style of the Vijayanagar empire (similar to the artifacts at Hampi and in the Srirangam temple in Trichy). Rooms are luxurious, with large Italian marble bathrooms, and overlook either the garden or the pool. **Pros:** extremely luxurious, close to airport, excellent service. **Cons:** extremely expensive, not within walking distance of main part of town. ✉*23 Airport Rd., Kodihalli, 560008* ☎*80/2521–1234, 800/426–3135 in U.S.* 🌐*www.theleela.com* *328 rooms, 29 suites* *In-room: safe, refrigerator, ethernet, Wi-Fi. In-hotel: 3 restaurants, room service, bar, pool, gym, spa, laundry service, concierge, executive floor, public Wi-Fi, airport shuttle, no-smoking rooms* *AE, DC, MC, V.*

$$$$ Fodor's Choice ★ **The Oberoi.** Slick, elegant, and well run, this hotel combines the lushness of a resort with the efficiency of a luxury business hotel. Looking like a movie set, the stunning lobby has a green marble floor, a central fountain, and a bank of windows overlooking an impressive landscaped garden with a fish-filled lotus pond. The spacious rooms, which are reached by hallways that open to the exterior of the hotel, have polished green-marble entryways and handsome brass-and-teak furnishings. All of them have private balconies that look out on garden. **Pros:** excellent service, great location at the start of M.G Road, beautiful, award-winning garden and surroundings, great restaurants. **Cons:** extremely expensive, may be a little overblown for some travelers.

9

✉37/39 M. G. Rd., Downtown Bangalore, 560001 ☎80/2558–5858 🌐www.oberoihotels.com 152 rooms, 9 suites In-room: safe, refrigerator, DVD, Wi-Fi. In-hotel: 3 restaurants, room service, bar, pool, gym, spa, laundry service, concierge, public Wi-Fi, airport shuttle, no-smoking rooms ▭AE, DC, MC, V.

$$$$ **The Park.** India's first boutique hotel, masterminded by designer Terence Conran, is done up in funky, vibrant shades, with different color schemes used on each floor. The slightly cramped lobby, filled with trancey music and oversized furniture seating businesspeople and wealthy tourists, is separated by silk curtains from the Monsoon, the Park's multicuisine restaurant. Rooms are crisp and modern, with modern art on the walls and lots of wood throughout. The staff, some of whom are dressed in black Nehru suits, are cheerful and fast. **Pros:** great location, great design, well trained and friendly staff. **Cons:** very expensive, lacks the grandeur of other hotels at this price. *✉14/7 M. G. Rd., Downtown Bangalore, 560042 ☎80/2559–4666 🌐www.theparkhotels.com 109 rooms, 5 suites In-room: safe, refrigerator, DVD, Wi-Fi. In-hotel: 2 restaurants, room service, 2 bars, pool, gym, spa, laundry service, concierge, executive floor, public Wi-Fi, no-smoking rooms ▭AE, DC, MC, V.*

$$$$ **Taj Gateway Hotel.** This Western-style Taj property is on a busy street, but it's pretty, well equipped, and quiet inside. The wide hallways are thickly carpeted, and the walls are decorated with some lovely prints throughout. Guest rooms have modern wood and wicker furniture and pale blue carpeting. With such a restful feel, it's no wonder that it attracts so many businesspeople. **Pros:** quiet, central location, high standards of service. **Cons:** very expensive, on a busy street. *✉66 Residency Rd., Downtown Bangalore, 560025 ☎80/6660–4545 🌐www.tajhotels.com 94 rooms, 4 suites In-room: safe, refrigerator, DVD, ethernet, Wi-Fi. In-hotel: 3 restaurants, room service, 3 bars, pool, gym, laundry service, concierge, executive floor, public Wi-Fi, airport shuttle, no-smoking rooms ▭AE, DC, MC, V.*

$$$$ **Taj Residency.** The large, white-marble lobby in this bougainvillea-accented high-rise bustles with VIPs, tourists, and businesspeople going about their day. Guest rooms are furnished with contemporary teak furniture and blue-and-green upholstery. Some of the rooms on upper floors have pretty views of Ulsoor Lake to the north; some "superior" rooms on the first floor have little patios and access to a small lawn that leads to the health club. The ground floor's pastry shop, Sugar & Spice, has tasty offerings—including good people-watching—and a small bookstore along with the expected cakes. **Pros:** great Taj service and central location. **Cons:** may seems stuffy to some, very expensive. *✉41/3 M. G. Rd., Downtown Bangalore, 560001 ☎80/6660–4444 or 80/6660–4444 🌐www.tajhotels.com 161 rooms, 5 suites In-room: safe (some), DVD, ethernet, Wi-Fi. In-hotel: 3 restaurants, room service, bar, pool, gym, spa, laundry service, concierge, executive floor, airport shuttle, no-smoking rooms ▭AE, DC, MC, V.*

$$$$ ★ **Taj West End.** Dating from 1887, the massive main building here was once a boardinghouse. Its Victorian Bangalore look (white walls, highly peaked "monkey roofs") continues throughout the exteriors of this

elegant hotel, where many of the guest rooms are located in smaller cottages and out-buildings among the 22 acres of trees, gardens, and ponds (the Bangalore Golf Club is adjacent). Guest rooms are elegantly contemporary, with wood floors and earth-tone color schemes, but many of them have colonial-but-not-fusty touches like brass lamps or extremely high ceilings. Blue Ginger, India's first Vietnamese restaurant, is one of the most excellent restaurants in town. **Pros:** beautiful surroundings and rooms, excellent service, peaceful. **Cons:** extremely expensive, no sights are within walking distance. ✉*23 Race Course Rd., 560001* ☎*80/6660–5660* 🌐*www.tajhotels.com* *117 rooms, 18 suites* *In-room: safe, kitchen (some), refrigerator, DVD, Wi-Fi. In-hotel: 3 restaurants, room service, bar, 2 tennis courts, 2 pools, gym, spa, no elevator, laundry service, concierge, executive floor, airport shuttle, no-smoking rooms* ▭*AE, DC, MC, V.*

$$$$ **The Windsor and Towers.** Bangalore's prettiest hotel has a striking white exterior with arched windows and wrought-iron ornaments, and it looks like a heritage building rather than one built in the 1980s. The Towers' lobby gleams with polished brass and a marble fountain sitting beneath a domed skylight paired with massive teak pillars: a suitable introduction to this even more opulent five-story wing. The handsome rooms in the original wing have modern furnishings, with tall ceilings and good-looking art on the walls. Modeled after Lal Bagh's, the hotel's multicuisine restaurants, the Raj Pavilion is bathed in natural light streaming through the glasshouse-like interior during the day. The Windsor can arrange golf dates on the city course, which is extremely close. **Pros:** prettiest hotel in town, lots of good restaurants, close to city golf course, in a nice-looking residential area. **Cons:** a bit of a drive to main business parts of town, very expensive. ✉*Windsor Sq., 25 Sankey Rd., Golf Course, 560052* ☎*80/2226–9898* 🌐*www.welcomgroup.com* *217 rooms, 23 suites* *In-room: safe, refrigerator, DVD (some), ethernet, Wi-Fi. In-hotel: 4 restaurants, room service, bar, pool, gym, spa, laundry service, concierge, executive floor, public Internet, public Wi-Fi, airport shuttle, parking (no-fee), no-smoking rooms* ▭*AE, DC, MC, V* *CP.*

$$$–$$$$ **Chancery Pavilion.** Across the street from the august Bangalore Club and close to many offices, this hotel, which opened in 2006, is in the right place to attract corporate guests. Interiors have lots of colorful abstract art on the walls, and the well-sized rooms are covered in light wood and tinted glass. With so many corporate clients nearby, some rooms are set up for long-term stays, with a kitchen and full desk areas. The lower level in back, which is attached to the lobby, contains the pool, restaurants, and the attractive nightclub, Amnesia. **Pros:** handy location, especially for business travelers, good-size rooms, 24-hour check-in and -out (days stayed here are measured in 24-hour increments). **Cons:** busy street, many sights and restaurants are a fair walk or short rickshaw ride away. ✉*Residency Rd., Downtown Bangalore, 560025* ☎*80/4141–4141* 🌐*www.chancerypavilion.com* *227 rooms, 7 suites* *In-room: safe, kitchen (some), refrigerator, DVD (some), ethernet, Wi-Fi (some). In-hotel: 2 restaurants, room service, 2 bars, pool, gym, spa, laundry service, concierge, executive floor, public Wi-Fi, airport shuttle, no-smoking rooms* ▭*AE, DC, MC, V.*

9

$$$ **The Chancery.** Aimed at business travelers, this large pale pink stucco hotel on swanky Lavelle Road is also a comfortable option for tourists. The lobby is bright and calm, with a shiny floor and lush plants. Comfortable rooms have wood floors, stone entryways, dark wooden furniture, ample wardrobe space, and some contemporary art on the walls. **Pros:** handy location close to M.G. Road and its stores and restaurants, good value, friendly service. **Cons:** rooms are a little generic. ✉ *10/6 Lavelle Rd., Downtown Bangalore* ☎ *80/2227–6767 or 80/4118–8888* 🌐 *www.chanceryhotel.net* *121 rooms, 7 suites* *In-room: safe, refrigerator, DVD (on request), Wi-Fi. In-hotel: 2 restaurants, room service, bar, gym, laundry service, concierge, executive floor, public Wi-Fi, airport shuttle, no-smoking rooms* *AE, DC, MC, V* *BP.*

$$$ **37th Crescent.** On a peaceful street near the Bangalore Golf Club, this boutique hotel gets lots of bookings from business travelers priced out of rooms in the five-stars around town. Opened in early 2006, the 37th Crescent aims for a post-modern look, with narrow rectangular fountain pools at the entrance, black-and-red ceiling panels, and elaborate and often shiny furniture in the lobby. Rooms are a good size, with laminate wood floors and brightly colored walls; in keeping with its no-nonsense clientiele, rooms have showers and not baths. If this hotel is full, the Goldfinch hotel, on the same block, has similar rooms at similar prices. **Pros:** pleasant, new surroundings, good-size rooms, peaceful location. **Cons:** street can sometimes be hard to find, no sights within walking distance, foreigner rack rate is significantly higher than Indian price. ✉ *37 Crescent Rd., High Grounds, 560001* ☎ *80/4037–3737* 🌐 *www.37thcrescent.in* *57 rooms, 3 suites* *In-room: safe, refrigerator, Wi-Fi. In-hotel: 3 restaurants, room service, bar, gym, laundry service, concierge, no-smoking rooms* *AE, DC, MC, V.*

$$ ★ **St. Mark's Hotel.** A short walk from Koshy's and about 2 km (1 mi) from the center of town, this seven-floor hotel, popular among business travelers, is a good value and has a friendly, efficient staff. The lobby is bright and glossy, with marble floors. Rooms have dusty-rose or light-green carpets, and come with coffee tables and flowery armchairs. The suites have separate living rooms and a generous amount of space. **Pros:** good value, good location, friendly staff. **Cons:** slightly fusty furnishings, not trendy, no pool. ✉ *4/1 St. Mark's Rd., Downtown Bangalore, 560001* ☎ *80/2227–9090 or 80/2248–3981* 🌐 *www.stmarkshotel.com* *88 rooms, 6 suites* *In-room: safe, refrigerator, Wi-Fi. In-hotel: restaurant, room service, bar, laundry service, gym, concierge, executive floor, public Wi-Fi, airport shuttle, no-smoking rooms* *AE, DC, MC, V* *BP.*

$$ **Shelton Grand.** Opened in the spring of 2007, this mid-range hotel has straightforward but pleasant rooms, with nice decorative touches like pale purple walls and floral fabric headboards. On busy Church Street, the Shelton is in a great location for sight-seeing and nightlife, although more sedate travelers might not find it quiet enough. **Pros:** great location in the heart of shopping and nightlife, everything's new. **Cons:** there may still be kinks to work out, location can be loud and busy. ✉ *73 M. G. Rd. (entrance on Church St.), 560001* ☎ *80/4043–0000*

www.sheltongrand.com *64 rooms, 6 suites* *In-room: refrigerator, DVD (on request), ethernet, Wi-Fi. In-hotel: 4 restaurants, room service, bar, laundry service, concierge, executive floor, public Internet, public Wi-Fi, airport shuttle* *AE, DC, MC, V* *BP.*

$–$$ Fodor'sChoice ★ **Villa Pottipati.** Restored by the Neemrama hotel group, which specializes in refurbishing old buildings, this heritage hotel is an attempt to conserve Bangalore's spectacular but fast-disappearing historic mansions and bungalows. High ceilings and antique wood furniture complement the beautiful European style rooms; many have small balconies or their own entrance to the porch outside in this 1880s building. A garden with jacaranda and gulmohur trees also help take you back in time, as do the gabled windows and four-poster beds. The neighborhood, Malleswaram, is not central to most typical destinations in Bangalore, but it is a traditional, attractive area that few travelers see. **Pros:** one of the most charming places to stay in the city, good value, personable service. **Cons:** not central, lacks the services of a bigger hotel. *142 8th Cross, 4th Main Rd., Malleswaram, 560003* *80/2336–0777, 80/4128–0832, or 80/4128–0833* *www.neemranahotels.com* *5 rooms, 3 suites* *In-room: safe, ethernet. In-hotel: restaurant, pool, no elevator, laundry service* *AE, DC, MC, V.*

¢ **Nilgiri's Nest.** On bustling Brigade Road in the heart of downtown Bangalore, this budget hotel is above Nilgiri's supermarket (founded in 1905 and perhaps the best supermarket in town). Rooms are a bit like dorms, with basic furnishings, tile floors, and bathrooms with showers without a separate enclosure. The rest of the hotel is little more than a small lobby with reception and a few couches. Head to the Nest if you want to save some cash, have only a short time in the city, are going to be out most of the day, or want to be within walking distance of pubs, restaurants, shops, and nightlife. Reserve at least a week in advance—if Nilgiri's is full, several other budget hotels are on the same stretch of Brigade. **Pros:** great location and price, large rooms, easy acces. **Cons:** rooms are institutional, low on atmosphere, hot water only available for four hours each day. *171 Brigade Rd., Downtown Bangalore, 560001* *80/2558–8401, 80/2558–8702, or 80/2558–8103* *80/2558–5348* *23 rooms* *In-room: no a/c (some). In-hotel: restaurant, room service, laundry service* *MC, V* *CP.*

NIGHTLIFE & THE ARTS

NIGHTLIFE

Since the early 1990s, Bangalore had been famous in India for its casual, upbeat pubs, and that reputation lingers even surviving a very stringently enforced closing time of 11 or 11:30. The variety of hangouts allow people (albeit mostly men) of all types and trades to meet over a drink (usually beer or whisky) and listen to music or watch TV (both of them often loud). One major group of pubs is centered around Church Street, parallel to M. G. Road.

Don't let the posh, modern style of the **I-Bar** (*The Park Hotel, 14/7 M. G. Rd., Downtown Bangalore* *80/2559–4666*) fool you; the vibe here is warm. The bar food is impressive, too. **Amoeba** (*22 Church*

St., Downtown Bangalore ☎*80/2559–4631*) combines 12 lanes of bowling with an arcade and restaurants.

Taking its name from the date the stone building was constructed, the stylish **Nineteen Twelve** (✉*40 St. Marks Rd., Downtown Bangalore* ☎*80/2299–7290*) attracts an upscale crowd for cocktails, chit-chat, and snacks. Open on one side to the Oberoi Hotel's garden, the regal, wood-filled **Polo Club** (✉*37–39 M. G. Rd., Downtown Bangalore* ☎*80/4135–8205*) feels very lush itself. **Taika** (✉*The Pavilion, Church St., Downtown Bangalore* ☎*80/4151–2828*), billed as a "spa lounge," also includes a restaurant, bar, and dance floor in a space full of candles and other vaguely spiritual touches.

Established in the 1980s, **Pub World** (✉*65 Residency Rd., Laxmi Plaza, Downtown Bangalore* ☎*80/2558–5206*) is still a nice, but somewhat loud, place to get a pint. It's divided into several different typical pubs, including one that channels the Old West. On weekends, the **Purple Haze** (✉*Opposite Konark Restaurant, 17/1 Residency Rd., Downtown Bangalore* ☎*80/2221–3758*) comes alive with hard rock, though it really isn't terribly quiet the rest of the week. **Dublin** (✉*The Windsor, 25 Sankey Rd., Golf Course* ☎*80/2226–9898*), made to resemble a classic Irish pub, serves cocktails and snacks. **Tavern at the Inn** (✉*Museum Inn, 1 Museum Rd., off M. G. Rd., Downtown Bangalore* ☎*80/4111–3339*) is an English-style pub in the day and a nightclub in the evening. **The Thirteenth Floor** (✉*13th Fl., Barton Centre, M. G. Rd., Downtown Bangalore* ☎*80/4178–3355*), a popular and tony nightclub, has an impressive open balcony on the 13th floor in the center of downtown that lets you enjoy the legendary Bangalore weather. A Rs. 500 cover, redeemable for food and drink, sometimes applies.

THE ARTS

Your best sources for information on cultural happenings are newspapers, especially the *Deccan Herald* and the local edition of the *Hindu*. Other sources are the *CityInfo* magazine (🌐*bangalore.explocity.com*, posters, Karnataka Tourism (🌐*www.karnatakatourism.org*) and the Events Bangalore Web site 🌐*www.eventsbangalore.net*.

The Bangalore Habba (festival), which occurs in early December, brings in dancers, musicians, and other artists for performances held throughout the city.

Shaped like a violin, the **Chowdiah Memorial Hall** (*CMH* ✉*Gayathri Devi Park Extension, Vyalikaval, Malleswaram* ☎*80/2344–5810*) hosts plays, dances, music performances, and film screenings. **Karnataka Chitrakala Parishath** (✉*Kumara Krupa Rd., Golf Course* ☎*80/2226–1816* 🌐*www.chitrakalaparishath.org*) is a fine-arts institution that also has an open-air theater for dance-and-music shows and puppet theater. Painting and photo exhibitions are frequent events. The **Ranga Shankara** (✉*36/2 8th Cross, J. P. Nagar* ☎*080/2659–2777* 🌐*www.rangashankara.org*) theater is used for plays in English, Kannada, Hindi, and other languages throughout the year.

The **Yavanika State Youth Center** (✉*Nrupathunga Rd., Raj Bhavan–Cubbon Park* ☎*80/2221–4911*) hosts free Indian classical music and dance performances and other cultural events most evenings.

On the outskirts of Bangalore, the **Nrityagram Dance Village** (✉*Hessaragatta, Bangalore Rural District, Bangalore North* ☎*80/8466-313 or 8466–314* 🌐*www.nrityagram.org*) is a dance institution founded by the late Odissi dancer Protima Gauri. Here you can watch students at work while sampling aspects of Karnataka folk culture. The premises, which include a guesthouse, are modeled on a Karnataka village, with granite, stone, mud, and thatch the primary building materials. Nrityagram is the only village of its kind in India devoted to the promotion and preservation of ancient classical-dance styles and two martial-art forms. For a taste of Indian mythology and cultural traditions, this is worth a visit. Accommodation is available at the Taj Kuteeram (🌐www.tajhotels.com) opposite the village.

SPORTS & THE OUTDOORS

GOLF

Designed by the British in 1876 and the second-oldest club in India, the **Bangalore Golf Club** (✉*2 Sankey Rd., Golf Course* ☎*80/2228–1876*) has an 18-hole course open to the public. Call ahead to reserve your game. You'll be allowed entry only if you carry your handicap card. Charges are Rs. 500 on weekdays and Rs. 800 on weekends. The **Karnataka Golf Association** (*KGA* ✉*Golf Ave., Airport Rd.* ☎*80/2529–8847* 🌐*www.kga.in*) runs a good golf course near the airport. You will need to carry your handicap card and a letter from your hotel, and the charges are Rs. 1,000 plus caddy fees.

HORSE RACING

The **Bangalore Turf Club** (✉*1 Race Course Rd.* ☎*80/2226–2391* 🌐*www.bangaloreraces.com*) goes into high gear from mid-May through the end of July, and November through March. Races take place every Saturday and Sunday afternoon (off-season races are only occasional).

MASSAGE & YOGA

Bangalore is a center for yoga, relaxation, and alternative health treatments. The **Angsana Oasis Spa & Resort** (✉*Main Doddaballapur Rd., Addievishwanathapura Village, Rajanukunte* ☎*80/2846–8892* 🌐*www.angsana.com*) offers Thai and ayurvedic massage in a lush resort northwest of Bangalore. You can either stay at the resort (Rs. 6,500 a double) or book a slot as a visitor. For stress management programs, ayurvedic treatments, yoga, and meditation, head to **AyurvedaGram Heritage Wellness Centre** (✉*Hemmandanahalli, Samethanahalli-Post, Whitefield* ☎*80/6565–1090* 🌐*www.ayurvedagram.com*). Among the packages are a day session (Rs. 1,460) that includes a vegetarian lunch and yoga, meditation, and *pranayama* (breathing exercises).

SHOPPING

M. G. Road is one of Bangalore's main shopping drags, with government shops and some giant silk emporiums. Brigade Road, which intersects with M. G. Road, is lined with flashy stores, foreign boutiques, and a number of multilevel shopping arcades. Commercial Street and the area around it date from the time of the Raj, when it supplied the British of the Cantonments with goods. It remains a narrow, eclectic shopping district, packed with storefronts selling suitcase locks, Kashmiri hats, precious jewelry, and clothing.

ANTIQUES & HANDICRAFTS

The state-run, fixed-price **Cauvery Arts Emporium** (☒*49 M. G. Rd., Downtown Bangalore* ☎*80/2558–1118*) sells all of Karnataka's craft products: sandalwood handicrafts, terra-cotta pots, carved rosewood furniture, silk, leather work, jute products, lacquered toys, *bidri* ware (decorative metalwork in black and silver tones), embossed bronze, soaps, perfumes, incense, and sachets. The **Central Cottage Industries Emporium** (☒*144 M. G. Rd., Downtown Bangalore* ☎*80/2558–4083 or 80/2558–4084*) is part of the nationwide government chain of fixed-price cottage-industry stores selling authentic crafts from all over India. It closes every day from 2 to 3. Downstairs is the state of Kerala's own government store, Kairali. Offering several floors of artifacts, pottery, apparel, leather, jewelry, and stationery, **The Bombay Store** (☒*99 EGK Prestige, M. G. Rd., Downtown Bangalore* ☎*80/2532–0014*) is a pleasant place to spend an hour or two hunting for gifts to take home. (Note this has no connection with the U.S. store of the same name.) Selling beautiful designer gifts and clothes, **Cinnamon** (☒*11 Walton Rd., off Lavelle Rd., Downtown Bangalore* ☎*80/2222–9794 or 80/2221–2426*) is an exclusive—and expensive—boutique. **Mysore Handicrafts Emporium** (☒*107 Commercial St., Downtown Bangalore* ☎*80/2558–6112*) showcases handicrafts from around Karnataka.

NEED A BREAK?

Two dueling coffee chains have blanketed Bangalore with outlets over the past five years. Barista (☒*St. Mark's Rd., Downtown Bangalore* 🌐*www.barista.co.in*) gets the nod over its main competitor, Café Coffee Day, based on taste, although both are equally good for people-watching. The Barista on M. G. Road is especially vibrant and busy, but if you want a retreat from the heat, head to the outlet on St. Mark's. It's in one of the old stone buildings adjoining the St. Mark's Cathedral grounds.

BOOKS

Bangalore has about a dozen large English-language bookstores. All have good bargains, but the best are on or near M. G. Road. The **Strand Book Stall** (☒*113 Manipal Centre, Dickenson Rd., Downtown Bangalore* ☎*80/2558–0000* 🌐*www.strandbookstall.com* ⏲*Closed Sun.*) has a wide selection of books, many at sale prices. It's a good place to stock up on bulky coffee-table books, since the Strand will also ship your purchases cheaply.

Gangaram's Gallery (✉ *72 M. G. Rd., Downtown Bangalore* ☎ *80/2558–8015*) is a four-story megastore that's especially strong in stationery and books about India. **Higginbotham's** (✉ *74 M. G. Rd., Downtown Bangalore* ☎ *80/2558–7359*) is a quiet bookstore that dates from the colonial era, as does its aging white facade. **Premier Bookshop** (✉ *46/1 Church St., Downtown Bangalore* ☎ *80/2558–8570* ⏲ *Closed Sun.*), a local legend, is a small store crammed to the ceiling with books. Ask the friendly staff, and the chances of finding what you want are very high.

Crossword (✉ *ACR Towers, Opp. Gateway Hotel, Residency Rd., Downtown Bangalore* ☎ *80/2558–2411* 🌐 *www.crosswordbookstores.com*), India's answer to Border's, stocks best-sellers, games, CDs, DVDs, and also has a large selection of books on Indian history and language.

Landmark (✉ *Forum Mall, Hosur Main Road, Koramangala* ☎ *2226–7777* 🌐 *www.landmarkonthenet.com*) has a large selection of magazines and DVDs as well as classics and best-sellers. The cookbook selection in this department store is probably the best in town.

Book World (✉ *44 Church St., Downtown Bangalore* ☎ *80/6599–1604*) has a large selection of used English-language books in good condition, and they'll buy as well as sell.

Blossom Book House (✉ *84/6 Church St., opposite Amoeba, Downtown Bangalore* ☎ *80/2532–0400* 🌐 *www.blossombookhouse.com*), one of the friendliest stores in town, devotes most of an upper floor to used books, including a fine children's selection, with new titles on the ground floor.

NEED A BREAK?

India Coffee House (✉ *78 M. G. Rd., Downtown Bangalore* ☎ *080/2226–6991*) is a Bangalore institution. Sit at one of the communal tables, wait for the turbaned waiter to swoop in, and grab your well-priced filter coffee. Some breakfast items and snacks, including dosa, are also available. **Soul Cafe** (✉ *65 Bluemoon Complex, M. G. Rd., Downtown Bangalore* ☎ *080/2558–9991*), with hanging chandeliers, dim lighting, and wood beams, is a restful place to get away from the craziness of M. G. Road. The primarily Continental dishes include snacks like chicken fingers and good sandwiches as well as more substantial dishes, including mutton pepper fry (goat meat in a spicy sauce). You can also smoke a *shisha* (hookah) at the tables outside.

HOUSEWARES

Indiana Crockery (✉ *97/1 M. G. Rd., Downtown Bangalore* ☎ *40/2559–4772*) is a friendly, helpful, jam-packed store for kitchen items and tableware.

SILKS

A number of giant silk emporiums on M. G. Road sell top-quality Karnataka silk products, including solid-color material by the meter and bright, ornately hand-blocked saris and scarves. **Deepam Silk International** (✉ *67 M. G. Rd., Downtown Bangalore* ☎ *80/2558–8760* 🌐 *www.deepam.com*) has been in business for decades. The stock is extensive, with lots of material from all over India, especially the South. **Karnataka Silk Industries Corporation Showroom** (✉ *44/45 Leo Complex, Residency Rd. Cross, off M. G. Rd., Downtown Bangalore* ☎ *80/2558–2118* ✉ *Gupta Market, K. G. Rd., Downtown Bangalore* ☎ *80/2226–2077* ⏲ *Closed Sun.*), a fixed-price government shop, sells silks that have come hot off the looms in Mysore. **Lakshmi Silk Creations** (✉ *144 M. G. Rd., below Central Cottage Industries Emporium, Downtown Bangalore* ☎ *80/2558–2129*) carries saris and material from Kanchipuram, a town famed for its silk, as well as from Mysore. **Nalli Silks Arcade** (✉ *21/24 M. G. Rd., Downtown Bangalore* ☎ *80/2558–3178*) sells silks of all kinds and some cotton clothing. **Vijayalakshmi Silks** (✉ *Blue Moon Complex, M. G. Rd., Downtown Bangalore* ☎ *80/2558–7395*) is a reliable option for silk textiles.

FOOD, WINE & LIQUOR

Nilgiri's (✉ *171 Brigade Rd., Downtown Bangalore* ☎ *80/2558–8401*) supermarket, one of the best groceries around, carries Indian snacks, pastries, freshly baked buns, and exotic fruit from a stand in front.

As with several other parts of India, Karnataka has had some new wineries emerge in recent years. Although their vintages are not yet as good as those from most of the world's major wine regions, they're getting better all the time. **Dewars Wine Store** (✉ *25 St. Mark's Rd., Downtown Bangalore* ☎ *80/2221–4945 or 2229–0244*), a Bangalore institution, carries local and imported wine as well as the Indians' favorite spirit: whiskey.

Foodworld Gourmet (✉ *Shariff Bhatia Towers, basement, 88 M. G. Rd., Downtown Bangalore* ☎ *80/4147–4789* 🌐 *www.gourmet-foodworld.in*) draws a mix of expats and wealthy Indians who come for the imported and prepared foods, hard-to-find meats and produce, and the good wine selection in the adjoining liquor store.

NEED A BREAK?

***Chaats*, streetside snacks that are one of India's tastiest contributions to world cuisine, combine sweet, sour, and salty flavors. Although some of the outdoor vendors can seem a little hygienically suspect, it would be a pity to visit India and miss out on the fun. In a hallway next to a Bata shoe store is Koshy's Outpost (✉ *Koshys Palace, 81 Brigade Rd., Downtown Bangalore* ☎ *80/2559–3823*), which bills itself as selling "Calcutta Chats." At this friendly indoor stall, there are no chairs, but what is available are lots of classic snacks, including *bhel puri* (crisp rice and potato mixed up in tamarind water) and samosa chat, in which the deep-fried and potato-filled pastries are first smashed and then drowned in coriander and tamarind chutney and curd (yogurt).**

SHOPPING AREAS & MALLS

For a time, it seemed as if a new mall was opening in Bangalore every month or so. Although that pace has slowed a little, development for these malls remains a big growth area. Weekends bring huge crowds of teenagers, families, expats, and curiosity-seekers to wander, socialize, snack, and maybe even buy something. If you'd rather not deal with people-watching on quite so grand a scale, save your mall trip for a weekday.

Commerical Street, to the north of M.G. Road, is full of shops selling clothes, leather goods and linens, and just about anything household-oriented. It's busy, loud, and hard to walk through, but it's classic Bangalore.

The Forum Mall (✉*21 Hosur Main Rd., Koramangala* ☎*80/2206–7676* ⏲*Daily 9:30* AM*–11* PM), the most popular and probably largest example of its kind in town, contains a multiscreen movie theater, lots of clothing stores, an Apple computer store, and multitude of restaurants, both fast-food and higher end. The two-story Landmark store is a good place for housewares, DVDs, stationery, and books. An emblem of the high-tech, tony neighborhood of Kormangala, the mall is about a 60-rupee auto-rickshaw ride from downtown.

The Garuda Mall (✉*Magrath and Commissariat Rds.Downtown Bangalore* ☎*80/6664–1100* 🌐*www.garudamall.net* ⏲*Daily 9:30* AM*–9:30* PM) has as its anchors the Westside and Shopper's Stop department stores. There's a large food court with some good options as well as a fun house, a movie theater, a FabIndia (for clothes and textiles), and a HiDesign store selling leather goods. Homestop, across the street from the mall, sells high-end housewares and linens.

EN ROUTE

If you're driving to Mysore and would like an eyeful of Karnataka's folk traditions, stop at the **Janapada Loka Folk Arts Museum,** 53 km (33 mi) southwest of Bangalore. Displays showcase puppets, masks, agricultural implements, household articles, and color photographs of tribal life. There are also occasional live performances by drummers, snake-charmers, and gypsy dancers. A simple, good restaurant is on site, serving rural Karnataka specialties like *ragi mudde* (soft-cooked balls of flour made from the local red-brown variety of millet). ✉*Bangalore-Mysore Hwy., near Ramnagaram* ☎*80/720–1143 local number, 80/2360–5033 city office in Bangalore for Karnataka Janapada Trust* 🌐*http://bangalorerural.nic.in* 🎫*Rs. 10* ⏲*Wed.–Mon. 9–1:30 and 2:30–5:30.*

MYSORE

140 km (87 mi) southwest of Bangalore, 1,177 km (730 mi) southeast of Mumbai, 473 km (293 mi) north of Chennai.

Once the capital of the princely state of Mysore, this palace-rich city of roughly 900,000 inhabitants remains the official residence of the former royal family. The maharajas accomplished much in the way of arts and culture, developing palaces, temples, and schools, and supporting the traditional Mysore school of painting, with its slightly cherubic Hindu images and abundance of gold leaf. When you witness the fruits of their patronage, you'll understand why Prince Jayachamaraja Wodeyar (father of the current erstwhile prince, Srikandatta Wodeyar) was appointed the first actual governor of Karnataka in 1956, when the state was formed. Mysore was known for its progressivism during his reign.

Nicknamed the City of Palaces, Mysore's main attraction, the Mysore Palace, can be explored in a few hours, and if you can manage a visit to the Lalitha Mahal Palace Hotel, the combination of the two will make your trip worthwhile. An evening visit to Brindavan Gardens is a nice way to experience the Indian fascination with kitschy but charming colored musical fountains.

Despite its opulent past, there's still not too much that's flashy or fancy about Mysore, at least not in the modern, commercial sense. There are relatively few places to wine and dine, and the streets are lined with far more dozing cows than boutiques. But the congenial climate and small-town surroundings, replete with leafy avenues, can make a trip to Mysore enchanting. Here you can admire (and buy) some of India's richest silks, woven with real gold, and other elements of an age-old spirit of elegance that endures. That elegance has been joined by the first glimmers of renewal, as more and more hi-tech companies have begun to open branches here, making it in some ways a satellite of Bangalore.

PALACE AREA

A GOOD WALK

Mysore is a small city, and its center is easy to walk around. Start your walk at the conveniently central **Mysore Palace** ❶. After you leave the palace, take a right and walk to Sayyaji Rao Road. At the second intersection, walk left toward the Jaganmohan Place and its **Sri Jayachamarajendra Art Gallery** ❹. When you're finished with the art, return to Sayyaji Rao and continue walking north to K. R. Circle. After crossing the circle, you'll reach Devaraja Market, filled with stalls selling produce, religious items, and household goods. When you've had your fill of shopping, jump in an auto-rickshaw and head to the **Zoological Garden** ❷ (the fare shouldn't be more than Rs. 20). After strolling through the gardens, take a taxi or auto-rickshaw to the top of **Chamundi Hill** ❸ for a beautiful panorama of Mysore. (It's at least 3 km [1.9 mi] from the zoo to the base of the hill, and the 1,000 steps are a killer). After admiring the view, walk down the hill's steps and catch a taxi, bus, or auto-rickshaw back to the city.

Numbers in the text correspond to numbers in the margin and on the Mysore map.

TIMING You'll need at least five hours for this walk, and most of the day if you make it to Chamundi Hill. Except between the zoo and Chamundi Hill, the distances are not long. You'll probably want about 90 minutes at the palace, an hour at the market, and two or three hours at the zoo. Note that the zoo is closed on Tuesday.

WHAT TO SEE

3 **Chamundi Hill.** Mysore looks its panoramic best from the top of this hill. Walking up its 1,000 steps is an excellent but tiring way to see it, but you can also take a taxi to the top and then walk down. At the 700th step, you'll pass a 16-foot stone **Nandi** (Shiva's holy bull). On the summit, the **Sri Chamundeswari Temple** is dedicated to the royal Wodeyar family's deity, the goddess Chamundi, an avatar of Parvati (Shiva's consort). In the middle of the parking lot stands a mandatory photo-op, the huge and gaudy **statue of Mahishasura,** the demon killed by the goddess Chamundi so that the region would be at peace; Mysore, originally called Mahishur, was named for him. The base of the temple dates from the 12th century; the ornately sculptured pyramidal *gopuram* (towering entrance) was built in the 1800s. Inside is an idol of Chamundi herself, believed to be made of solid gold. Tuesdays and Fridays, auspicious days, are the most crowded. Although the temple is technically free to enter, paying nothing usually means a wait in a very long line. Paying Rs. 100 or Rs. 20 for one of the special entry tickets means a much quicker trip to the goddess. Because the temple is a very popular religious and tourist site, the entire area surrounding the structure teems with beggars and peddlers. The temple's inner entrances are periodically staffed by aggressive priests hassling tourists into buying flower offerings and other blessings. To save some cash, don't accept items from anyone without asking how much it costs, and when collecting your shoes from the deposit spot, pay Rs. 1 or Rs. 2 a pair, rather than the inflated Rs. 100 or so that may be suggested. Also on the hill, the kitschy **Godly Museum** has gaudy paintings depicting eternal life and harmony. ✉*Southeast Mysore, 2½ km (1½ mi) south of Lalitha Mahal Palace Hotel* 🎫*Free* ⏲*Temple Fri. 7:30–2; Sat.–Thurs. 6–2, 3:30–6:30, 7:15–9; Godly Museum 6–11 and 4–9.*

1 ★ **Mysore Palace.** By far the most impressive structure in Mysore, the maharaja's palace (also called the Amba Vilas) is a massive edifice. On a 73-acre plot, the Mysore Palace took 15 years to rebuild after an earlier structure burned down during wedding festivities in 1897. One of the largest palaces in India, it was designed by the Irish architect Henry Irwin (1841–1922), who was famous for practicing in India, and especially for his work in the Indo-Saracenic style—a synthesis of Hindu, Gothic Victorian, and Islamic architecture. The main rooms and halls are a profusion of domes, arches, turrets, and colonnades, all lavishly carved, etched, or painted, with few surfaces spared. The halls and pavilions glitter with unabashed opulence: giant brass gates for grand elephant entrances; silver-plated doors encrusted with patterns and figures; richly carved teak ceilings; ivory gods and goddesses; a 616-pound solid-gold howdah (an elaborate seat, with a canopy and rails, placed on the back of a camel or elephant) in the first hallway you enter. The cavernous, octagonal **Kalyana Mantap** (Marriage Hall), where women sat behind screened balconies, exudes royal wealth, its turquoise-and-gold-painted cast-iron pillars soaring up to a translucent dome of Scottish stained glass with brilliantly colored peacocks and flowers. A massive brass chandelier from what's now the Czech Republic hangs far below, above a multicolor tile floor. The **Durbar,** where

Brindavan Gardens 6
Chamundi Hill 3
Government Silk Waving Factory 5
Mysore Palace 1
Sri Jayachamarajendra Art Gallery 4
Srirangapattana .. 7
Zoological Garden 2

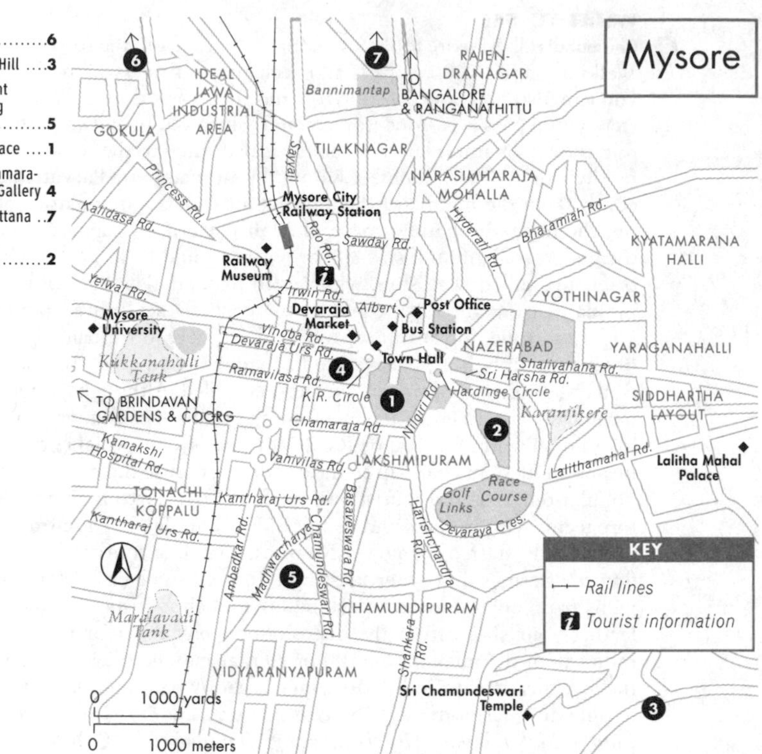

public gatherings were held, is elegant and impressive, with a painted ceiling, turquoise Indo-Saracenic arches, and floors of white Italian marble inlaid, along the edges, with semiprecious stones. The smaller hall nearby, used for private gatherings, is over-the-top baroque—sky-blue gold-leaf pillars, a stained-glass ceiling, a chandelier, finely carved wood on the ceiling, marquetry on the main doors, and inlaid ivory on the side doors.

Technically, the present-day titular maharaja is really a prince—the last maharaja died in 1974. He divides his time between a private wing at the rear of this palace, and in his palace in Bangalore. The **Residential Museum,** centered on a galleried courtyard, displays the prince's collection of Mysore paintings as well as artifacts illustrating royal life of the past. Although there are some beautiful things here, it's skippable if you're pressed for time.

On Sunday from 7 o- to 8 o- and on holidays, the palace is illuminated with thousands of tiny lights that turn it into a glittering statement of wealth. Negotiate the price for a guide (aim for Rs. 100–Rs. 150). Shoes and cameras are prohibited inside the palace—cameras have to be deposited in a stall near the entrance, and the shoes have to be left in lockers near the palace entrance. ✉ *Mirza Rd., 570001* *Palace Rs. 20, museum Rs. 20* ⏲ *Palace and museum daily 10–5:30.*

4 **Sri Jayachamarajendra Art Gallery.** Housed in the 150-year-old Jaganmohan Palace, this rundown museum displays paintings from various schools and periods of Indian art as well as beautiful antique inlaid wood, antique sandalwood and ivory carvings, and a variety of other decorative pieces. Some exhibits, such as those of dioramas using painted grains of rice, are truly esoteric, but there are lots of good gems among the clutter. The gallery has a solid selection of art by Raja Ravi Varma capturing beautiful portraits of Indian women. The musical instruments and games displayed on the top floor are interesting, but even better are the room's handpainted walls, fulls of lizards, bees, and other creatures. The service of a guide is free (and almost impossible to refuse), and all will expect a tip. No cameras are allowed. ✉*Jaganmohan Palace, Dewan's Rd., Devaraj Mohalla* ☎*821/242–3693* *Rs. 15* ⏲*Daily 8:30–5:30.*

DUSSEHRA IN MYSORE

For the ultimate palace experience, time your Mysore visit to coincide with the annual **Dussehra** festival (🌐 *www.mysoredasara.com*), held in September or October and commemorating the victory of Chamundi (a form of Durga) over the demon Mahishasura. For 10 days palaces and temples are lit up and cultural and sports events abound, culminating in a torchlight procession led by an elephant carrying the temple's idol, Chamundi, in a howdah of pure gold. Although some say the procession isn't as impressive as it was in the maharaja's time, it's still an amazing event.

2 **Sri Chamarajendra Zoological Garden.** This well-maintained 250-acre zoo was founded in 1892. Today it's populated by lions, tigers, giraffes, African elephants, hyenas, kangaroos, rhinos, peacocks, chimpanzees, and a variety of other animals from all over the world. One section is devoted entirely to reptiles and snakes. For Rs. 60 you can get a ride in a battery-operated vehicle, like a golf cart, that can shuttle you around the zoo. Another entertaining stop, the Karanji Nature Park, next to the zoo, has a large lake and a butterfly enclosure. ✉*Indiranagar* ☎*82/1252–0302 or 82/1244–0752* 🌐*www.mysorezoo.in* *Zoo Rs. 25, camera fee Rs. 10, video camera fee Rs. 150* ⏲*Wed.–Mon. 8:30–5:30.*

9

AROUND MYSORE

A GOOD TOUR

If you haven't had a chance to visit Chamundi Hill, get up early and make your pilgrimage. Then head down the mountain for a tour of the **Government Silk Weaving Factory** **5**, which opens at 10:30. After a break for shopping and lunch, finish with a trip to the **Brindavan Gardens** **6**, 19 km (12 mi) northwest of Mysore, in time for the evening fountain show before returning to Mysore for a late dinner. This leisurely day trip gives you some free time in the afternoon to have a relaxed lunch and shop for silks and handicrafts. Plan to spend at least an hour at each attraction and some time traveling between them; the gardens are about half an hour's drive away.

Alternatively, if you're feeling more adventurous, hire a taxi and set off for **Srirangapattana** ❼, a historic island on the Cauvery River. Spend the morning exploring the **Darya Daulat** (Tipu Sultan's summer palace), and the **Gumbaz** (mausoleum of Hyder Ali and Tipu Sultan). In the afternoon, head to **Ranganathittu Bird Sanctuary** and take a boat out on the Cauvery past nesting birds and crocodiles sunning themselves on the riverbank.

WHAT TO SEE

❻ **Brindavan Gardens.** Extending from the side of the Krishna Raja Sagar Dam, one of the largest in India, this vast, terraced garden is the pride of Mysore and a magnet for Indian tourists. The carefully manicured park is laced with long symmetrical paths and fountains. The profusion of fragrant flowers and the absence of cows and cars make it a peaceful place to stroll. At nightfall, scores flock to the far end of the gardens to see water spout into the air tinted by pulsing colored lights with a soundtrack of recorded pop-classical Indian music. To get here, hire a taxi for the roughly 30-minute ride or take Bus 303–304 from the city bus station. (Either way, you still need to set aside a half hour or so to walk to the end of the garden once you arrive.) ✉ *Krishnaraja Sagar Rd., 19 km (12 mi) northwest of Mysore* 🌐 *http://horticulture.kar.nic.in/brindavan.htm* 🎫 *Gardends Rs. 15, camera fee Rs. 50* ⏲ *Gardens daily 6:30 AM–9 PM; fountain Jan.–Sept., weekdays 7 PM–8 PM, weekends 7 PM–9 PM; Oct.–Dec., weekdays 6:30 PM–7:30 PM, weekends 6:30 PM–8:30 PM.*

★ **Darya Daulat** *(Wealth of the Sea)*. One of the few visual reminders of the brief Muslim rule of Mysore is set in a sunken garden on the island of Srirangapattana. Built in 1784 by Tipu Sultan as a summer palace to celebrate a victory over the British, it was later briefly occupied by Arthur Wellesley (the future Duke of Wellington, in charge of the forces that defeated Napoleon at Waterloo). Great green blinds protect the building from the daytime heat, and its interior is dim and cool. The walls are covered with a riot of frescoes dating from the late 18th century; the best-known depicts the Battle of Pollilur, one of the Anglo-Mysore skirmishes. Beautiful and flat-out fun to look at, these paintings also give you a glimpse into the history and spirit of 18th-century Mysore and the contest for power in south India. That contest was eventually won by the British in 1799 when the island fort was besieged and Tipu slain. ✉ *Srirangapattana, 1 km east of the fort on Srirangapattana Island and the Bangalore–Mysore Hwy., 571438* 🎫 *Rs. 100* ⏲ *Daily 9–5.*

❺ ★ **Government Silk Weaving Factory.** The late maharaja created this factory in 1932, both to ensure the finest hand-loomed silks for himself and his royal family and to arrange for some profitable exportation. Now run by the Karnataka Silk Industries Corporation, the slightly dilapidated factory continues to produce Mysore silks coveted by women throughout India. From spinning and soaking to weaving and dyeing, it's all done here, resulting in crêpe de Chine, chiffon, and other regal fabrics. Accompanied by a factory official, you can stroll through the numerous giant workrooms busy with whirring spooling machines and clanking mechanical looms, and witness the transformation of hundreds of hair-thin, colorless threads into a sari fit for a queen. Ask to see the work stations where threads of real gold are woven into elaborate *zari* (gold embroidered) borders—a distinctively South Indian style. Bring your wallet for a post-tour pilgrimage to the factory showroom. The silks aren't as sumptuous as those in, say, Kanchipuram, but they make nice souvenirs, and the prices are good. No cameras are allowed. ✉ *Mananthody Rd. 570008* ☎ *821/248–1803* 🌐 *www.ksicsilk.com* 🎫 *Free* ⏲ *Mon.–Sat. 10:30–12:30 and 2–2:30.*

Gumbaz. The attractive mausoleum of Hyder Ali, his wife Fatima, and his son Tipu Sultan stands on the eastern side of Srirangapattana island. After Tipu Sultan was slain in battle in 1799, the British accorded him a full state funeral. The mausoleum is an onion-dome structure with pillars of beautiful, pitch-black hornblende and an interior with stylized tiger stripes. Graves of other relations, including at least one of Tipu's wives and sons, are on the platform near the mausoleum itself. An exquisite palace once stood close to the gumbaz; it was razed to the ground and nothing remains on its site but gardens, trees, and fields. ✉ *Srirangapattana, 3 km (2 mi) east of the fort on Srirangapattana Island and the Bangalore–Mysore Hwy.* 🎫 *Free* ⏲ *Sat.–Thurs. 6 AM–6:30 PM.*

Ranganathittu Bird Sanctuary. This terrific little sanctuary in between rice paddies consists of tiny islands and river rocks in one of the most pastoral sections of the Cauvery. Pathways help you explore the sanctuary but to get a closer look at the birds (herons, spoonbills, and cormorants), you will have to hire a boat. Boat rides can be exciting; you might see crocodiles up close and personal as they sun themselves on the rocks. During the monsoon, rides are sometimes suspended due to flooding. On the grounds, a small restaurant provides snacks. ✉ *3 km (2 mi) from Srirangapattana* 🎫 *Sanctuary Rs. 75, camera fee Rs. 30, boats rides Rs. 100* ⏲ *Sat.–Thurs. 8:30–6:30; boats 8:30–1:30 and 2:30–6.*

WHERE TO EAT

Mysore has a relative dearth of sophisticated restaurants, although you can generally dine well in the hotels. For sampling straight up South Indian standards, the most accessible places are inside the budget hotels in and around Sri Harsha Road.

$–$$ ✕ **Lalitha Mahal Palace Hotel Restaurant.** Head to the maharaja's cavernous former ballroom for the experience and the surroundings—not for the often unmemorable food. In this baroque tour de force, the stained-glass domes and sky-blue walls are enhanced by ornate, white plaster moldings and pillars; it's like eating beneath an enormous Easter Egg. Although the restaurant is multicuisine, Indian dishes are the most reliable. Try the Mysore *thali* (a set meal with rice and many regional accompaniments) or the mutton *nariyal-ka gosht* (lamb cooked with coconut, red chilli, and curry). You'll hear live instrumental music (flute and sitar with tabla) at lunch and dinner. If you make a detour to the bar on your way out, you can even shoot some pool. ✉*Lalitha Mahal Palace Hotel, T. Narsipur Rd.* ☎*82/1247–0470 or 82/1247–0472* 💳*MC, V.*

$ ✕**Gardenia.** The Hotel Regaalis's cozy restaurant has a contemporary Indian look. North Indian fare represents the best choices, although there are Chinese and Continental options. The tandoori items are especially delicious: try the *murgh malai kebab* (tender, boneless chicken chunks seasoned with cream and spices) with some *kulcha* (Indian bread). ✉*Hotel Regaalis, 13–14 Vinoba Rd.* ☎*82/1242–6426 or 82/1242–7427* 💳*AE, DC MC, V.*

$ ✕**Dynasty.** In this narrow, somewhat dim hotel dining room you can get good kebabs, including a minced chicken version given a slow-burn hit of fenugreek. Continental and Indianized versions of Chinese dishes are also available, which helps keep the place a mainstay for both locals and tourists. Although the rooftop area is officially only open for breakfast and dinner, you may be able to induce a waiter to let you eat here for lunch as well. From here you can get good views of the clock tower and mosque next door and the gothic spires of St. Philomena, to the north. ✉*Palace Plaza Hotel, Sri Harsha Rd.* ☎*82/1241–7592* 💳*AE, DC, MC, V.*

$ ✕**Green Hotel Restaurant.** At this superb hotel restaurant you can choose to dine outdoors in comfortable wicker chairs, around tables dispersed throughout the gardens, or in a sunny, white, high-ceiling, glass-enclosed terrace surrounded by plants. Service is sometimes slow, so don't come here in a hurry. The excellent pan-Indian food includes green curries (the masala used includes ground chillies, coriander, and mint) that live up to the hotel's name. The vegetable *hariyali* (vegetables in a green gravy) is delicious, and kebabs are worthwhile as well. This is also a good quiet place to nurse a cool beer after dark. ✉*2270 Vinoba Rd.* ☎*821/251–2536 or 821/251–6139* 🌐*www.greenhotelindia.com* 💳*MC, V.*

¢–$ ✕**Mysore Memories.** This comfortable restaurant, decked out with banquettes along the wall and plaid tablecloths, serves primarily Indian specialties like *mutter methi malai* (peas in a cream and fenugreek gravy) and Mysore *koli saaru* (spicy chicken soup), and *bhendi-do-pyaza* (okra in an onion sauce). ✉*Kings Kourt Hotel, Jhansi Lakshmi Bai Rd.* ☎*821/242–1142* 💳*AE, DC, MC, V.*

¢ ✕**RRR.** Dishes are served on banana leaves in this busy diner-like restaurant, where the booths are communal and the food comes quickly. It's popular with families and area workers for its thalis, the rice-based combination meals, as well as for specialties of Andra Pradesh, including chicken and mutton (lamb) biryani. ✉*Gandhi Square, Sri Harsha Rd.* ☎*82/1244–1979* 💳*No credit cards.*

WHERE TO STAY

$$$ 🏨**Lalitha Mahal Palace Hotel.** Roughly 6 km (4 mi) from the Mysore railway station, this gleaming-white 1930s palace was built by the Maharaja to house the British Viceroy, who ruled India. The public areas are stunning, lavishly trimmed with ornate plaster moldings, huge pillars, and gorgeous domes; broad marble staircases rise majes-

tically up through the three floors, which are filled with old prints, a lion and tiger in glass cases, and other ultra-Raj paraphernalia. The rooms in the older section have appealing Victorian furnishings. Despite the grand surroundings, there are occasional missteps: the hot water and air-conditioning are not entirely reliable, and some rooms are distinctly musty. **Pros:** a stunning palace, ornate, romantic. **Cons:** some rooms run-down, service and looks not always as high as the price, some shop-owners on the premises are a little pushy. ✉ *T. Narsipur Rd., 570011* ☎ *821/247–0470 or 821/247–0471* 🌐 *www.lalithamahalpalace.com* *45 rooms, 10 suites* *In-hotel: restaurant, room service, bar, tennis court, pool, spa, laundry service, airport shuttle, no-smoking rooms* ▭ *MC, V.*

$$–$$$ **Hotel Metropole.** Run by the Royal Orchid group, this large white Raj building with egg-yolk-color trim has flower- and palm tree–filled grounds and a lobby with interesting touches, including a *sankheda jhula,* a swing meant for the bride and groom at Hindu weddings. Rooms have lots of wood, unfussy furnishings, including plain walls that nevertheless manage to evoke the building's colonial past (it was constructed in the 1920s for the Maharaja's foreign visitors). Every room has a balcony: those designated "royal" have similar furnishings but are larger. **Pros:** beautiful heritage building, good location near both train station and 1½ km (1 mi) from palace. **Cons:** service can be spotty, expensive for Mysore. ✉ *5 J. L. B. Rd., Chamarajapuram, 570005* ☎ *821/425–5566* 🌐 *www.royalorchidhotels.com* *25 rooms, 5 suites* *In-room: safe, refrigerator, DVD (some), Wi-Fi. In-house: 3 restaurants, room service, bar, pool, no elevator, laundry service, no-smoking rooms* ▭ *AE, DC, MC, V.*

$$–$$$ ★ **Hotel Regaalis.** Close to the railway station and about 1½ km (1 mi) from the Mysore Palace, this high-rise makes a handy home base. The large marble-floored lobby has luminous metallic ceilings, light-brown patterned furniture, and small bamboo trees throughout. With the excepion of the junior suites, all rooms have wood floors. Rooms on the top two floors, billed as "premier," have more modern furnishings, including fancier showers and clear sinks, but all the options here are worth taking. The cozy back lawn next to the pool is surrounded by high hedges that help to remove the hotel a bit from the busy road out front. **Pros:** good location, good looking, good-sized rooms. **Cons:** expensive for Mysore. ✉ *13–14 Vinoba Rd., 570005* ☎ *82/1242–6426 or 82/1242–7427* 🌐 *www.ushalexushotels.com* *82 rooms, 24 suites* *In-room: safe (some), refrigerator, Wi-Fi. In-hotel: 2 restaurants, room service, bar, pool, laundry service, concierge, no-smoking rooms* ▭ *AE, DC, MC, V.*

$$ **Royal Orchid Brindavan Garden.** After being vacant for a dozen years, this hotel re-opened under new management in July 2007. What was once yet another palace built in the late Victorian age by a maharaja for his British guests is now a bright white hotel that manages to be nostalgic (large open windows and terraces looking out over the garden, beautifully tiled floors) without being fusty. Rooms have large ceilings and four-poster beds; the King rooms are significantly bigger, with larger private balconies. The stunning Garden Café and

9

Elephant Bar are both semi-open, facing the gardens, the multicuisine restaurant C.K.'s is in a dramatic, round room, with doors that lead to great views of the waterfall in back. **Pros:** beautiful new rooms in a heritage building, great views. **Cons:** 30 minutes or so outside Mysore, a little expensive, not many restaurant options beyond the one in-house, can be a little awkward getting here through garden entrance. ✉*Brindavan Garden, Krishnaraja Sagar 571607* ☎*80/4127–6667 reservations, 99/45815–566* 🌐*www.royalorchidhotels.com* *24 rooms* *In-room: safe, refrigerator, DVD, Wi-Fi. In-hotel: 2 restaurants, room service, bar, pool, gym, spa, no elevator, laundry facilities* 💳*AE, DC, MC, V* *BP.*

$–$$ ★ **Green Hotel.** Formerly a house for two princesses, then later a film studio, the Green Hotel is now run by a British charity whose profits fund environmental projects. Airy, charming, and largely sea green inside, it feels like a Raj-era lodge. (Its Edwardian drawing rooms are equipped with chessboards.) Guest rooms have dark-wood furnishings, high, wood-beam ceilings, and in some cases kitschy film memorabilia; on the other hand, some rooms are small and have no closets or wardrobes, and there's no generator backup for electricity. You can choose from among the (fewer, more expensive) palace rooms in the old wing, or the less exciting garden rooms in the new wing. On Sunday the hotel hosts an organic-heavy "Green Bazaar." If saying "Green Hotel" stumps your auto-rickshaw or taxi driver, ask for "Premier Studio." **Pros:** beautiful, atmospheric, good restaurant. **Cons:** far from Mysore's center, no a/c, some rooms small. ✉*2270 Vinoba Rd., outside city center, past university, 570012* ☎*82/1425–5000 or 82/1425–5001* 🌐*www.greenhotelindia.com* *26 rooms, 5 suites* *In-room: no a/c, no TV, Wi-Fi. In-hotel: restaurant, room service, bar, public Internet, no elevator* 💳*MC, V* *BP.*

¢ ★ **Ginger Hotel.** If Ikea decided to open a hotel in India, it would probably look a lot like the Ginger, a stripped-down, budget-friendly chain owned by the same group as the luxury Taj hotels. With bright colors on the walls and dorm-style furniture, the reasonably sized rooms are comfortable and effiicent, although a few scuffs and nicks are starting to show. The small restaurant, open only at certain hours, serves just buffets, but the food's decent, and at these prices you can afford a few splurges elsewhere. **Pros:** good price, decent location, cheerful and modern service. **Cons:** not many frills, no bathtubs in bathroom, thin doors and walls mean that noise carrys. ✉*Nazerabad Moholla, Vasant Mahal Rd., 570010* ☎*82/1663–3333* 🌐*www.gingerhotels.com* *100 rooms* *In-room: refrigerator, Wi-Fi. In-hotel: restaurant, gym, laundry service, public Wi-Fi* 💳*AE, DC, MC, V.*

NIGHTLIFE & THE ARTS

Your best bet for a drink is a hotel bar or lounge. The **Lalitha Mahal Palace Hotel** (✉*T. Narsipur Rd.* ☎*821/247–4266 or 821/247–4268*) has a sophisticated bar, with Victorian furnishings and a casual vibe; if you don't stay here, it's worth stopping in for a drink just to see the majestic building. **Planet X** (✉*Maharana Prathap Singh Rd., near*

Mysore Race Club, Nazerabad ☎*82/1652–2100 or 82/1243–1043* ⊕*www.planetxonline.com*), an entertainment complex, finds room for go-karts, an arcade, golf, bowling, a restaurant, and what is probably straitlaced Mysore's only nightclub, Hookah, on its grounds. Themed along ancient Egyptian lines, with seated pharaohs on either side of the door, Hookah attracts a young, fun-loving crowd. The cover charge, which can be used to pay for food and drink, is Rs. 400 for couples, Rs. 200 for women, and Rs. 400 for men on weekends. Prices are slightly cheaper on weekdays.

To find out what's happening in Mysore, check with the Karnataka Department of Tourism (KDT) and look for posters and local newspapers around town. **Kalamandir Auditorium** (✉*Vinoba Rd.* ☎*821/241–5905* ⊕*www.rangayana.org*) hosts theater, dance, ballet, folk performances, and classical Indian music. The Rangayana theater festival is staged here every December. Admission to events is usually free or nominal. Classical, folk music, and dance performances are sometimes held in the **Jaganmohan Palace** (☎*821/242–3693*) or the Mysore Palace itself.

SPORTS & THE OUTDOORS

HORSE RACING

The **Mysore Race Club** (✉*11 Race Course Rd.* ☎*821/252–1675*) is a scene from August through October. Races are held approximately twice a week in the afternoon.

SHOPPING

9

Mysore is famous for its exquisite silks, fragrant jasmine, sandalwood products—oils, incense sticks, soaps, and carvings—and rosewood inlay work. The main shopping area is along **Sayaji Rao Road,** beginning at K. R. Circle in the center of town, with a plethora of silk emporiums, sweet stalls, and shops and hawkers of all kinds. In general, stores are open from 10 to 7, and many are closed on Sunday.

ANTIQUES & HANDICRAFTS

Cauvery Art and Crafts Emporium (✉*Sayaji Rao Rd., northwest of Devaraja Market* ☎*821/252–1258*) is the fixed-price government showroom for sandalwood carvings, handwoven cloth, rosewood figurines, brassware, and other Karnataka handicrafts. Devanraja Urs Road has stores of all sorts, including some crafts stores selling local sandalwood and rosewood products.

BOOKS

Ashok Book Centre (✉*396 Devaraja Market Building, Dhanwanthtri Rd.* ☎*82/1243–5553*) has a good selection of books on yoga, Mysore, and other tourist interests as well as lots of Indian fiction in English.

MARKETS

Devaraja Market (✉*Devaraja Urs Rd.*), bordering Sayaji Rao Road, is a riotous, old enclosed fruit, vegetable, and flower market where you can immerse yourself in the vibrant colors and smells of Karnataka's bounteous produce. Stacks of glittering glass bangles and mounds of brightly colored powders used for Hindu worship add to the entertainment value of this bazaar.

SILKS

Karnataka Silk Industries Corporation (*Government Silk Weaving Factory Complex* ✉*Mananthody Rd.* ☎*821/248–1803* 🌐*www.ksicsilk.com* ✉*Visveshwaraiah Bhavan, K. R. Circle* ☎*821/242–2658* ✉*Zoo Complex, Indiranagar* ☎*821/244–5502*), the state body that runs the Government Silk Weaving Factory, has several fixed-price showrooms where you can buy or just admire the profusion of silks created at the factory. The factory complex has a "seconds" showroom where a limited selection of silks with barely perceptible flaws is sold at up to 40% off.

SIDE TRIPS

RIVER/JUNGLE CAMPS

Karnataka's rivers teem with fish and crocodiles, and fishing expeditions are an important part of the state's tourist industry from December through March. The mammoth mahseer fish swim in the Cauvery River near Bhimeswari, about 100 km (60 mi) south of Bangalore and 75 km (46 mi) east of Mysore. Anglers fishing from *coracles* (round, basketlike boats) regularly hook mahseers weighing upwards of 50 pounds here, as well as smaller Carnatic carp, pink carp, and the good old catfish. The largest recorded catch was by an Englishman in 1992: 120 pounds. Catches can be weighed and photographed for proof but must be returned to the river—the fish are endangered.

A dense jungle belt rich with wildlife lies close to Mysore; there are several options for a few nights out in the wild without roughing it while taking part in such activities as trekking or white-water rafting.

WHERE TO STAY

$$$ **Cauvery Fishing Camps.** At the peaceful Bheemeshwari Fishing Camp on the bank of the Cauvery River you sleep overlooking the river in log huts or in twin-bed tents, both of which have attached bathrooms. The Indian buffet meals, included in the room price, are served in an open-air dining area around a campfire. For an additional fee of $65 a day, trained guides take you to the prime angling spots in Jeeps or coracle boats, but fishing equipment is not provided. Try to reserve several months in advance. There are two other camps that are roughly a 6-km (4-mi) trek along the riverbank and a little farther by dirt road close by—upstream at Doddamakkali and downstream at Galibore (there's white-water rafting at the latter). Facilities here are more rudimentary, and the camps are closer to the wild. **Pros:** great fishing, a fun way to experience India's nature. **Cons:** slightly expensive, somewhat hard to get to. *Reservations through Jungle Lodges & Resorts Ltd., back of Shrungar Shopping Centre, 2nd fl., near India Coffee House,*

M. G. Rd., Bangalore, 560001 ☎80/2559–7021, 80/2559–7024, or 80/2559–7025 ⊕www.junglelodges.com ⇨Tents and log huts ♿In-room: no a/c, no phone, no TV. In-hotel: water sports, no elevator ▭AE, DC, MC, V ♈AI.

$$ **K. Gudi Wilderness Camp.** The peaceful forests inside this wildlife sanctuary hold elephants, wild boar, porcupine, tigers, leopards, and *gaur* (a massive, bison-like beast that's the world's largest bovine). Activities at the camp include elephant rides, daytime safaris in a jeep to spot wildlife, and short guide-led hikes through the forest. Accommodation is in tents or log cabins, both of which have finished bathrooms and electricity in early morning and evening but no ceiling fans. (Rooms in the former maharaja's hunting lodge may also be available.) An added bonus is the very good home-style South Indian dishes served at mealtime. The best period to sight wildlife is November to June. **Pros:** easy way to experience India's wilderness, beautiful surroundings. **Cons:** somewhat hard to get to, slightly expensive. *Reservations through Jungle Lodges & Resorts Ltd., back of Shrungar Shopping Centre, 2nd fl., near India Coffee House, M. G. Rd., Bangalore, 560001 ☎80/2559–7021, 80/2559–7024, or 80/2559–7025 ⊕www.junglelodges.com ✉86 km (53 mi) southeast of Mysore, Bheemeshwari, Karnataka ☎80/2559–7021, 80/2559–7024, or 80/2559–7025 ⇨8 tents, 3 cabins, 4 rooms ♿In-room: no a/c, no phone, no TV. In-hotel: no elevator ▭AE, DC, MC, V ♈AI.*

COORG

Even in a state filled with beautiful landscapes, Coorg stands out for its lush rolling plantations and exciting wildlife. In the western part of Karnataka, and spanning about 4,100 square km (2,548 square mi), Coorg is a coffee and pepper growing area, so part of its charm is its easygoing plantation lifestyle. The Kodava people are extremely friendly and hospitable, and the food of the region has its own unique flavor because of all those local peppercorns and the special malt vinegar used in meat dishes. *Pandi* (pork) curry is a specialty—Coorg is one of the few places in India where pig makes any appearance in dining rooms. The weather is great year-round outside of the July and September portions of the monsoon periods, when it's wet, but not horrible.

Coorg is a trekker's dream; several established trails pass by dams and waterfalls, and, of course, plantations. Ask at your hotel to choose the most convenient trekking route. The main town is Madikeri (also known as Mercara), but you're better off staying in the forest or plantation areas. The National Park is one of the loveliest of its kind in the country. The Tibetan settlement at Bylakuppe and the elephant camp at Dubare are both worth a quick visit.

Nagarhole National Park (Rajiv Gandhi Memorial Park). The Karapur Forest of southwestern Karnataka has long provided elephants for India's now-defunct royalty—not to mention the world's zoos and circuses. Many years ago, an infamous practice called *khedda* (wild-elephant roundup) was common, pitting swarms of skilled tribes-

9

men against a herd of trumpeting elephants. Today, the kheddas have stopped, and instead you can watch wild elephants moving around the Nagarhole National Park, established in 1954 and spanning about 643 square km (400 square mi). From Kabini River Lodge you can join a fantastic game-viewing tour—inside your Jeep you might spot *dholes* (wild dogs), a massively muscular Indian *gaur* (wild ox), barking deer, *sambars* (reddish-brown wild deer), sloth bears, crocodiles, and families of elephants (mothers, calves, "aunt" elephants, and tuskers), and, if you're lucky, an elusive leopard or tiger. You can also glide around in a *coracle,* a round, basket-shaped boat that's slow and quiet enough to let you draw very close to the wild animals and abundant birds (more than 225 different species) without disturbing them. The best viewing times are early morning and evening from October through March. The area within and surrounding Nagarhole is home to tribal groups that include the Jenu Kurubas (traditionally honey gatherers) and Betta Kurubas, both of whom consider this area their historical home. ✉ *Within Coorg (Kodagu) and Mysore districts, 93 km (58 mi) southwest of Mysore, 08228* ☎ *82/7424–4221 or 82/2225–2041, park reservations 82/1248–0901* 🎟 *Park Rs. 200, video camera fee Rs. 300* ⏲ *Daily 6–6.*

The Tibetan refugee settlements at Bylekuppe. If you have time, visit these two settlements established in the 1960s and now with a population around 15,000. Here you can see monasteries as well as try Tibetan *momos* (dumplings) and *tsampa* (roasted ground barley). ✉ *87 km (54 mi) west of Mysore, 3 km (2 mi) from Kushalnagar.*

★ **The Dubare Elephant Camp.** Run by the Karnataka Forest Department, this is a great place to spend a day in close contact with these massive mammals. A sort of retirement home for old elephants and others that can't be easily introduced into the wild, camp residents are allowed to graze freely in the surrounding reserve forest. Mahouts round them up in the morning for their daily scrub-baths in the Cauvery and to check on pregnant and lactating cows (female elephants). Visitors are welcome to watch bathing and feeding routines. The animals also show off the commands they can recognize—many of them are ex-loggers and can lift and stack logs symmetrically. Admission for the all-day visit includes an elephant ride as well as refreshments at the century-old forest rest house. ✉ *15 km (9 mi) south of Kushalnagar* 📫 *Reservations through Jungle Lodges & Resorts Ltd., back of Shrungar Shopping Centre, 2nd fl., near India Coffee House, M. G. Rd., Bangalore 560001* ☎ *80/2559–7021, 80/2559–7024, or 80/2559–7025* 🌐 *www.junglelodges.com* 🎟 *Package Rs. 1,900.*

WHERE TO STAY

Many of Coorg's plantations are also run as B&B's. For more options, consult a travel agent or the KSTDC *(⇨Karnataka & Hyderabad Essentials).*

$$$$ 🏨 **Orange County Resort.** At this 300-acre coffee plantation 100 km (62 mi) from Mysore you can stay in luxurious country cottages and

indulge in trekking, fishing, swimming, and tours of the plantation. The ayurvedic spa here has an extensive list of pampering treatments. There are several types of cottages, some of which include living rooms and small private "splash" pools. **Pros:** secluded, elegant, beautiful. **Cons:** extremely expensive, somewhat difficult to get to. ✉*Near Karadigodu post office, Coorg district, Siddapur, 571253* ☎*80/4191–1044 reservations* 🌐*www.trailsindia.com* *50 cottages* *In-room: no a/c (some), refrigerator (some), no TV (some). In-hotel: restaurant, bar, pool, gym, spa, water sports, bicycles, no elevator, laundry service, airport shuttle* *AE, DC, MC, V* *FAP.*

$$ **Kabini River Lodge.** Once the hunting lodge of the viceroy and maharaja, this resort within Nagarhole National Park, 93 km (58 mi) southwest of Mysore, is a charming combination of comfort and rusticity. The cabins are surrounded by colorful flowering trees, and monkeys roam through the grounds. The peaceful surroundings allow for a languid daily routine. Long Jeep safaris or boat rides on the river are broken up by morning and afternoon tea on the veranda and hearty open-air meals (drinks are extra). **Pros:** surrounded by nature at its most beautiful, great place to see elephants without roughing it. **Cons:** somewhat expensive price for foreigners. *Reservations through Jungle Lodges & Resorts Ltd., back of Shrungar Shopping Centre, 2nd fl., near India Coffee House, M. G. Rd., Bangalore, 560001* ✉*Karapur* ☎*80/2559–7021 or 80/2559–7024 reservations* 🌐*www.junglelodges.com* *14 rooms, 6 cottages, 5 tents* *In-room: no a/c, no phone, no TV. In-hotel: restaurant, bar, no elevator* *AE, DC, MC, V* *AI.*

Fodor's Choice ★

¢ **Alath-Cad.** This coffee and pepper plantation 112 km (70 mi) from Mysore is quiet, beautiful, and lush. Most of the simply furnished, cozy rooms are inside the main house, a classic Coorg estate, with others in an outbuilding nearby. Within the 65 acres is a wonderful spot for a picnic, as well as a swimming hole in the river. The traditional dishes served here, especially the pork stew, are another highlight. **Pros:** beautiful surroundings, truly away from it all, great value in a homey place. **Cons:** a bit hard to get to, may be too isolated for some. ✉*Ammathi, 571211* ☎*82/7425–2190 or 82/7425–2589* 🌐*www.alathcadcoorg.com* *8 rooms, 1 suite, 1 cottage* *In-room: no a/c, no phone, no TV. In-hotel: restaurant, no elevator* *No credit cards* *BP.*

MANGALORE & KARWAR

MANGALORE

347 km (216 mi) west of Bangalore.

With a population of about 900,000, mellow Mangalore is a good place to sample Karnataka's largely untouched beaches, eat some delicious seafood, or jump on and off the scenic Konkan Railway, which runs north along the coast all the way to Mumbai. Once acclaimed as Karnataka's port city and pepper center, Mangalore has ceded the pepper honor to Kochi, in Kerala. Still a major port and a producer of iron ore and South India's ubiquitous red roof tiles, Mangalore retains has the low-pressure feel of a breezy seaside town, with many more bungalows and charming old buildings still standing in the town's center. Signs of its Portuguese past, including surnames such as D'Sousa and Cunha as well a large number of Roman Catholic churches and schools, are still visible.

Most travelers reach Mangalore from points north and south along the coast rather than from the Bangalore and other points west. Until east–west passenger train service is restored, an airplane is the best way to reach Mangalore from the interior of Karnataka. Although it's possible to make the trip via bus or car and driver, the roads over the Western Ghats are poor, making the route perilous, occasionally scary, and long (7–10 hours from Bangalore). But in compensaion, that trip takes you through beautiful plantations of coffee, pepper, and betel palms.

If you're in Mangalore, then a trip to pretty Malpe Beach is nearly mandatory. Near the end of this trip of about 2 hours and 70 km (44 mi), you'll pass the temple town of **Udupi,** once home of the 13th-century Sanskrit philosopher Madhwacharya. Of Udupi's three main temples, the primary one is devoted to Lord Krishna. With a *gopurum* (tower-like entrance) trimmed with gold, this large complex has multiple shrines spread throughout its interior, some of which have very old idols. Udupi, also known as Udipi, is famed for its "pure veg" restaurants—it's supposedly the birthplace of the masala dosa.

From the quiet yellow sands of Malpe Beach (5 km/3 mi west of Udupi), you may be able hire a boat to the rocky **St. Mary's Island,** where the 15th-century Portuguese explorer Vasco da Gama is believed to have landed before he stopped in northern Kerala, at Calicut, in 1498. St. Mary's is unpopulated and without food or water, so be sure to bring your own supplies. During the monsoon (July–Sept.), boats run less frequently and may be cancelled if the water is too turbulent. Whether or not the boats are running, you can take in the seaside surroundings by having some local prawns or ladyfish at the Paradise Isle Beach Resort, which faces the water.

If you don't want to venture too far, head 6 km (4 mi) north out of town to spend the morning exploring **Sultan's Battery** in Boloor, a stone fort built by Tipu Sultan in the 18th century to prevent enemy ships from entering the Gurpur River.

Lunch in Mangalore, and in the late afternoon, visit the beautiful, Mediterranean-style **St. Aloysius Church.** Inside are frescoes and oil paintings, done in 1900, that cover just about every inch of its interior. In keeping with its location in a Jesuit college, many of the scenes illustrate parables in the gospels. A kilometer away is the garden on Lighthouse Hill, from where there's a lovely view of the Arabian Sea. This is a perfect spot from which to watch the sunset.

Take some time after dinner to watch some **Yakshagana,** an ancient folk form of dance-drama performed in colorful costumes and greasepaint. Usually a night-long program performed in open fields (now often on stages), the Yakshagana involves robust dancing and mime; an inter-

CLOSE UP

The Rural Theatre of Yakshagana

When in Mangalore or Bangalore, don't miss an opportunity to watch a lively Yakshagana performance. Karnataka's own traveling rural theater form represents a unique blend of dance, music, narrative, stage techniques, and traditional costumes. Said to have originated more than five centuries ago, Yakshagana belongs to the coastal districts—Malnad, Uttar Kannada, and Dakshin Kannada—where troupes of actors travel from village to village, entertaining villagers who gather from miles around to watch them. Although often described as folk theater, it nonetheless has strong classical roots. The focus is typically Hindu mythology—performance begins with a *puja* (a ritual and offering) and is followed by enactment of scenes from the Hindu epics. The folk elements include the music, the language, the cross-dressing (there are no female actors), and the frequent appearance of mischief-makers and demons. Although the local language will be unfamiliar to you, it's still worthwhile to attend a performance for the sheer color and dynamism, the elaborate costumes, the make-up, the skilled and energetic performers, and the unmistakable humor. From the early 17th century, when a poet refashioned the entire *Ramayana* to suit the Yakshagana form, to the present day, when troupes perform nonclassical acts as well (anything from an original Kannada drama to a play based on Chekov), this living rural tradition has prospered and grown over the centuries. The best time to catch a yakshagana is between November and May; performances are few during the rainy season.

preter tells a story drawn customarily from mythology and sings to the accompaniment of drums and cymbals.

9

WHERE TO EAT & STAY

$$ ★ ✕ **Cardamom.** Named for a spice that's grown nearby and shows up in much of the regional cooking, this comfortable restaurant decorated with fishing paraphernalia is a good place to sample the local seafood specialties, which include almond-coated tiger prawns, *denji pulimunchi* (crab in a curry of red peppers and vinegar), and various takes on the thin ladyfish (*kane*). ✉ *Taj Manjarun, Old Port Rd.* ☎ *824/666–0420* ▭ *AE, DC, MC, V* ⏲ *No lunch.*

$ ✕ **Mangala.** The loud prints on the chairs and the tablecloths that have seen better days may make this cozy restaurant seem a little unpromising. But the groups of families that troop into this brightly lit dining room, especially on weekends, must know something. Run by the same company that owns the Moti Mahal restaurant chain, Mangala serves many Indian, Continental, and Chinese dishes, but it's the Indian food that's the thing, especially the local seafood dishes. The fish that's been marinated in a paste of garlic, ginger and other spices is especially memorable and addictive. ✉ *Moti Mahal Hotel, Falnir Rd.* ☎ *824/244–1411* ▭ *AE, DC, MC, V.*

$ **The Goldfinch.** Newly opened in the summer of 2007, the Goldfinch aims to bring a little boutique style to a somewhat conservative city. The small but comfortable lobby here is a portrait in white, with leather chairs and couchs and marble tables. Some rooms and hallway windows have views of nearby bungalows and other old Mangalore buildings. Rooms, each of them furnished slightly differently, include small couches next to the window, muted colors, flat-screen TVs, and wood or tile floors: those in the "executive" category come with an appreciable amount of extra space. **Pros:** handy location with small shopping mall in front, good value, stylish, brand-new rooms. **Cons:** far from water. ✉*236/2A1 Bunts Hostel Rd., 575003* ☎*824/4251300* 🌐*www.goldfinchhotels.com* *48 rooms, 12 suites* *In-room: safe, refrigerator, DVD (on request), Wi-Fi. In-hotel: restaurant, room service, bar, pool, gym, laundry service, executive floor, public Wi-Fi, airport shuttle* *AE, DC, MC, V* *BP.*

$ **Summer Sands Beach Resort.** About 10 km from Mangalore, this resort has 1,000 feet of beachfront on its 15 acres of palm-filled land. The villas, set in coconut groves, are cool and detached, and all accommodation is in cottage-style buildings. The Ullal beach is a treat—it's reasonably clean and quiet given that it's essentially a city beach. **Pros:** good beachfront location, relatively good deal. **Cons:** early checkout of 11 AM. ✉*Chota-Mangalore, Ullal, 574020* ☎*824/246–7690 to 92* 🌐*www.summer-sands.com* *44 rooms, 5 suites, 14 villas* *In-room: no a/c (some), no TV (some). In-hotel: 2 restaurants, pool, gym, spa, beachfront, no elevator, laundry service* *AE, DC, MC, V* *BP.*

$ Fodor'sChoice ★ **Taj Manjarun.** Although some rooms are showing their age, the excellent service and the prime location near the water still make this the best hotel in Mangalore. Rooms are attractive and cozy, with a good amount of space but without much character (if you can, spring for a sea view—they're worth the extra cost). There's a killer pool in back that's bordered by bamboo, the Cardamon restaurant serves some very good examples of local seafood, and the High Tide pub is a nice, quiet corner for a beer. Note that a top-to-bottom renovation is in the works and is due to finish up by early fall of 2008. **Pros:** very good hotel at a good price, great facilities, well-trained, helpful staff. **Cons:** somewhat dated interiors. ✉*Old Port Rd., 575001* ☎*824/666–0420* *824/666–0585* *82 rooms, 6 suites* *In-room: safe, refrigerator, Wi-Fi. In-hotel: 2 restaurants, room service, bar, pool, gym, laundry service, concierge, executive floor* *AE, DC, MC, V.*

¢ **Moti Mahal.** This large hotel is anchored by a sweeping central lobby that's open all the way up to the roof. The spacious rooms, a large courtyard and swimming pool in back, a very good Indian restaurant—all combined with hospitable staff—all make this a solid contender. However, some rooms can be musty, especially just after the rains, and they will all look a little severe and stripped-down to some (lots of tile and empty walls). Still, this comfortable spot has remained popular for a reason. **Pros:** good price, great location, lots of services. **Cons:** rooms are not fancy and some are a little run-down. ✉*Falnir Rd., 575001* ☎*824/244–1411 to 14 and 824/244–1416 to 20* 🌐*www.motimahalmangalore.com* *50 rooms, 40 suites* *In-room: refrigerator (some), Wi-Fi. In-hotel: 2 restaurants, room service, bar, pool, gym, spa, laundry service* *AE, DC, MC, V* *BP.*

KARWAR

262 km (163 mi) north of Mangalore; 100 km (62 mi) south of Panaji, Goa.

If you have time to explore the country north of Mangalore or are traveling on to Goa, stop at the tiny port town of Karwar, unremarkable in itself but across the water from Devbagh. Three kilometers (2 mi) away, this small island is the site for an attractive Jungle Lodges camp, set amid casuarina trees. Swimming and scuba diving are possible; one side of the island faces the sea and the other the mouth of the Kalinadi. **Dandeli Wildlife Sanctuary,** about two hours northeast of Karwar, is a pretty forest reserve set on the banks of the Kalinadi; it's home to crocodiles and waterbirds that can be spotted from coracles on the river.

WHERE TO STAY

$$ ★ **Devbagh Beach Resort.** A short boat ride from the tiny port town of Karwar can bring you to the small island that houses this all-inclusive resort, a fishing village, groups of mangroves and other trees, and long expanses of inviting beach. The tents and loghuts, inside a forest of deciduous trees, have fully furnished bathrooms and electricity, so very little roughing it is required. Activities, arranged around a stay of two days, include nature hikes, birdwatching, and a boat trip in search of the elusive local dolphins. Evening campfires, accompanied by freshly grilled fish and perhaps a cold Kingfisher are the prelude to the very good dinners, served in a gazebo. October to May is the best time to visit. **Pros:** beautiful beach and good swimming, restful and calm. **Cons:** frequent power outages can make for some hot nights, might be too slow for some travelers. *Reservations through Jungle Lodges & Resorts Ltd., back of Shrungar Shopping Centre, 2nd fl., near India Coffee House, M. G. Rd., Bangalore 560001 ✉ Devbagh, Karwar, 581301 ☎ 80/2559–7021, 80/2559–7024, or 80/2559–7025 www.junglelodges.com 8 log cabins, 4 tented cottages, 4 cottages In-room: no a/c (some), no phone, no TV. In-hotel: beachfront, water sports, no elevator AE, DC, MC, V AI.*

$$ **Kali Wilderness Camp.** At this peaceful resort in the Dandeli sanctuary, you can watch wildlife and go river rafting, trekking, fishing, and camping in the forest. The best time to visit is between October and June. You can either stay in rooms at the bungalow lodge or in tented cottages that each have their own hammock and area for small fires. **Pros:** loads of outdoor activities. **Cons:** out of the way. *Reservations through Jungle Lodges & Resorts Ltd., back of Shrungar Shopping Centre, 2nd fl., near India Coffee House, M. G. Rd., Bangalore, 560001 ☎ 80/2559–7021, 80/2559–7024, or 80/2559–7025 www.junglelodges.com ✉ 117 km (73 mi) northeast of Karwar, Dandeli 10 rooms, 8 tents In-room: no a/c, no phone, no TV. In-hotel: restaurant, no elevator AE, DC, MC, V AI.*

9

BELUR & HALEBID

Once flourishing cities of the 12th-century Hoysala dynasty, Belur and Halebid are now just small villages. Both, however, hold some of the finest examples of stone carving in South India, called "the signs of a very confident Hindu culture" by writer V. S. Naipaul.

Hassan, an otherwise unexceptional town, is the gateway to the temples at Belur and Halebid—it's about 35 km (22 mi) away from each of the two, forming a triangle. Lodging options in Belur and Halebid are few and far between, so you may want to base yourself in Hassan for a night or two.

To get the most out of the temples, hire a guide, at least for the first one you visit. The intricate carvings are hard to decipher without a firm basis in Hindu mythology. You must remove your shoes before entering the temples, so bring socks along on your visits; the stones can be painfully hot in the midday sun, particularly at Belur. If possible, bring a flashlight to see the temples' interior sculptures in full detail.

There's no easy way to reach Hassan, the main base for Belur and Halebid. The best way is to hire a car and driver from Mysore or Bangalore. If you don't mind crowds, take a KSTDC-run bus from the Mysore bus station: the ride takes three hours and leaves every half hour throughout the day. The KSTDC and various private companies also run tours of Belur and Halebid.

BELUR

192 km (120 mi) northwest of Mysore, 240 km (150 mi) west of Bangalore.

Surrounded by a lush tropical landscape, the old city of Belur is dusty and run-down, with only one vestige of its splendid past.

★ The **Chennakeshava Temple,** still a functioning temple dedicated to a Vishnu incarnate, stands almost as pristine as it did the day it was completed in 1119, 103 years after it was begun by the Hoysala king Vishnuvardhana. Legend claims that when Muslim conquerors came to Belur to destroy the temple, they were so awed by its magnificence that they left it alone.

Carved of soapstone, the temple is shaped like a star to allow maximum surface area for carving: a total of 32 corners. Now squat and flat on top, it may have once had a tower. From top to bottom, in row after row, as impossibly intricate carvings, are a profusion of humans and gods and goddesses in all their varied aspects and incarnations—scenes from the great Hindu epic, the *Ramayana,* as well as hunters, dancers, musicians, and beautiful women dressing and adorning themselves. In the center of the temple, the domed ceiling is supported by four pillars surmounted by sculptures of voluptuous women striking any number of graceful poses beneath the intricately pierced, scrolled, and scalloped stone canopies. The carving is so detailed that some of the stone bangles the women wear can be moved.

Although non-Hindus can't enter the inner sanctum, they can see in, and it's worth timing your visit to be there when it's open. To the left of the temple is a smaller prototype (without the ornate stonework), built as a study. To the south is a smaller shrine, the **Kappe Chennigaraya,** which is worth a good look, and so is the **Veera Narayana,** which has rows of very fine sculptures on its outer walls. ✉ *573115* 🎫 *Free, guide Rs. 150 for 2 people* ⏲ *Daily 8 AM–8:30 PM; Inner sanctums closed daily 10–11, 1–3, and 5–6.*

HALEBID

35 km (22 mi) northeast of Belur, 35 km (22 mi) north of Hassan.

Now just a tiny rural village, Halebid was once the capital of the Hindu Hoysala kingdom.

Fodor's Choice ★ Dedicated to Shiva, the **Hoysaleswara Temple** was begun by King Vishnuvardhana in 1121, after the one at Belur was complete. It was left unfinished after 190 years of labor because the Delhi sultanates' attacks on it leveled its pyramid-peak roof. Like the temple at Belur, this one has a star-shaped plan, but as a double-shrine temple, it has two of everything—one for the king and one for the queen. Moreover, the sculptors' virtuosity reached its peak here, leaving some 20,000 statues. The figures are carved in such detail that they appear to have been etched. You can see the taut fibers of the cord from which a drum hangs, feel the weight of the jewel beads dangling from a dancer's neck, almost hear the swinging of the bells around the arms of the elephant god Ganesh. At one time the temple also had 84 small statues hanging from the ceiling near pillars; all but 14 were seized by conquerors of one stripe or another.

The breathtaking friezes wrap all the way around the temple: first comes a row of elephants for stability, then a row of lordly lions for courage, then convoluting scrolls of swift horses, then a row of people in sexual poses. Indian philosophy has always merged the spiritual with the social and cultural. Consequently, religious monuments were also cultural centers. Temple sculptures from around the 8th century often depict images of musicians and dancers along with dieties; in about the 10th century, erotic themes were introduced as well. The inspiration for this was based on the tantric thought of congeniality between spirituality and sexuality. Sensual well-being was deemed an essential ingredient of social life. Following the invasion of Islamic rulers, this tendency was curbed.

Above the erotic scenes is more scrollwork as well as scenes from the religious epics that present philosophical ideas and mirror the living conditions of the time. The largest frieze is also the most exuberant: here the *apsaras* (celestial maidens) are clothed in jewels, with bracelets on each of their several arms. Behind the queen and the king's shrines (the one closest to the entrance) are giant sculptures of Nandi the bull, Shiva's vehicle, with beautifully smooth features and a polished belly that almost seems to breathe. A small museum next to the temple displays various statues and brass and copper figures excavated from the surrounding area. *Free; museum Rs. 2* *Temple daily sunrise–sunset; museum Sat.–Thurs. 10–5.*

About a half-mile down the road are three smaller and relatively unadorned **Jain temples,** their finely polished black pillars as reflective as mirrors. A few more yards down the same road is the **Kedareswara Temple,** which bears more exquisite carving. The lovely friezes are similar to those of the main temples at Belur and Halebid, and executed with equal finesse. Set on a low hill next to a lake, this is an attractive, peaceful spot in its own right. *Free; guide Rs. 150 for 2 people* *Daily sunrise–sunset.*

WHERE TO STAY

$$ **Hoysala Village Resorts.** There's not much charm in Hassan itself, so it makes sense to bypass it for this resort, 5 km (3 mi) from town and surrounded by sunflower fields. The rooms, inside cottages, are not luxurious, but they are pleasant, well lit, and big enough for a whole family. All rooms come with small outdoor patios. Calling or using a travel agent is likely to yield better rates than those on the Web site. **Pros:** appealing, good-looking rooms, resort atmosphere. **Cons:** Fairly expensive. *Belur Rd., Hassan, 573201* *81/7225–6764, 80/4191–1044 reservations* *www.trailsindia.com* *29 rooms, 4 suites* *In-room: no a/c (some). In-hotel: restaurant, bar, pool, no elevator, laundry service* *AE, MC, V* *AI.*

¢ **Hotel Mayura Shanthala.** The rooms are plain and straightforward, but this government-run tourist hotel, across the street from the Hoysaleswara temple, offers a location lots of fancier hotels would kill for. The grounds include a small garden, and the very basic restaurant serves ordinary South Indian and North Indian vegetarian fare. **Pros:** great location, very good value, pretty grounds. **Cons:** no frills, no a/c, slightly grimy walls. *Temple Rd., Halebid* *81/7727–3224* *4 rooms* *In-room: no a/c, no phone, no TV. In-hotel: restaurant, no elevator, laundry service* *No credit cards.*

¢ **Hotel Mayura Velapuri.** At this hotel run by the state government, the frills are low, but so is the price. A short walk down the street leading to the Chennakeshava temple, it's the perfect place to get the jump on the other tourists. **Pros:** cheap, great, handy location, friendly. **Cons:** institutional rooms with slightly dirty walls, no a/c or TVs. *Outside temple entrance, Belur* *8177/222–209* *12 rooms* *In-room: no a/c, no phone, no TV. In-hotel: restaurant, no elevator, laundry service* *No credit cards.*

SRAVANABELAGOLA

157 km (98 mi) west of Banglore, 42 km (26 mi) southeast of Hassan.

Often visited along with Belur and Halebid on the way to or from Bangalore or Mysore, the small town of Sravanabelagola is between two ★ hills, one of which has on its peak a **colossal monolithic statue.** Depicting the Jain saint Gomateshwara and carved in AD 981, this may be the largest monolithic statue in the world. Stark naked and towering 58-feet high, with 26-foot-wide shoulders, 10-foot feet, and other similarly massive endowments, Gomateshwara is at once imposing and soothing. Once every 12 years or so, thousands of devotees congregate here for the Mahamastakabhishekha, a ceremony in which the 1,000-year-old statue is anointed with milk, ghee, curds, saffron, and gold coins (the next ceremony will be in roughly 2018). You have to climb 600 big steps to see the statue, but the beauty of it paired with the panorama, dotted with ruined open-air temples and fields, is worth it. Another site worth a visit is the top of Chandragiri Hill, the facing peak, which has a complex of Jain temples (*bastis*) on its top. One of them, the Chandragupta Basti, has 600-year-old paintings. ✉ *84 km (52 mi) north of Mysore and 93 km (30½ mi) southeast of Hassan, 573135.*

HAMPI

Fodor'sChoice ★ The most awesome spectable in Karnataka, **Hampi** was once the capital of the massive Vijayanagar Empire. What's now little more than a large town holds the ruins of a vast city of stone temples, elephant stables, barracks, and palaces—from the late 14th century until the 17th, this was the center of the largest Hindu empire in South India. Today the ruins are interesting from an archaeological standpoint as well as for their sheer beauty—stone structures rise out a boulder-dotted landscape made all the more beautiful by the winding Tungabhadra River. To see this World Heritage site in its entirety, count on spending at least two full days here.

Legend has it that the city, which sprawls over 180 square km (70 square mi) in a rocky valley surrounded by rugged mountains, was founded by two brothers, Harihara and Bukka, in 1336. However, some of the buildings can be dated back 1,400 years. Hampi was a large, wealthy city of perhaps a half million people at its height. In 1565, however, a league of five neighboring Muslim powers conquered it, and it was during this time that the faces of the thousands of statues and sculptures on the numerous temples were broken off. Hampi was looted and burned for months, until it lay deserted and ruined.

Many people choose to explore the ruins by themselves, but you'll probably get more out of them if you hire one of the official guides who wait on the road leading into the still-thriving Hampi Bazaar. They charge about Rs. 500–Rs. 600 for a full day. The best time to visit Hampi is from November to March; the rest of the year it's too hot or too rainy. Be prepared to do quite a lot of walking; vehicles cannot access many of the best spots in Hampi.

Hampi is roughly divided into two section: the northern part has Hampi Bazaar and the Virupaksha Temple, and the southern zone contains remnants of the Royal Enclosure, where kings once lived. The distance from the Virupaksha temple to the Royal Enclosure is about 3 km (2 mi).

FINDING OUT MORE

The many monuments and places to explore in Hampi could fill their own guidebook. And so they have. One of the better, *Hampi*, by John M. Fritz and George Michel, is available in local shops. In addition, the unofficial guide to the area at *www.hampi.in* has very detailed maps and help for getting around and deciding on what to see.

In the center of Hampi's northern section is the enormous (and still-used) **Virupaksha Temple** (*Rs. 2 daily sunrise–sunset*), the home of hundreds of monkeys and a hangout for dozens of children intrigued by the sight of foreigners. The ancient temple—devoted to the patron deity of the Vijayanagar kings—has some old musical instruments and an interesting inverted pinhole image of its own tower cast on an inner wall. Outside the temple, the street called Hampi Bazaar was originally built for temple chariot processions; today it's also the center of life in the ruins—guides, money matters, and a cheap room for the night can all be arranged here. Half a kilometer south of the Virupaksha temple, two massive stone images of the elephant god Ganesha are ironically named sasivekalu and kadalekalu. The names, which mean "mustard seed" and "chickpea," are perhaps the Vijayanagar equivalent of nicknaming a fat man "Slim" or a bald man "Red." Make sure you see the monolithic sculpted image of the glaring man-lion Narasimha (a quarter-kilometer south of the Ganesha), and the small Shiva temple that houses a huge lingam half-submerged in water.

About 2 km (1 mi) east of the Virupaksha Temple is the stunning **Vittala Temple** (*Temple US$5, camera fee Rs. 25 daily sunrise–sunset*), possibly the most rewarding of all the Hampi sights. This temple dedicated to Vishnu has an intact stone chariot and halls with intricately carved "musical" pillars that sound tones when the stone is tapped. Near the Vittala is the King's Balance, where the king's weight was measured every year against gold. Climb **Matanga Hill,** 1 km (½ mi) southeast from the Virupaksha Temple at dawn or just before sunset for one of the best possible views of the ruins—from this hill close to the Virupaksha temple, you can see the spectacular ruins of the Achyutaraya temple complex, the Tungabhadra flowing through rocks and boulders, and the cream-color tower of the Virupaksha itself. There's a lovely little temple on top of this hill, but do not go up alone near sunrise or sunset—robberies and worse have been known to happen in this isolated spot.

In what's known as the Royal Enclosure area, a great stone platform, called the **Mahanavami Dibba** (House of Victory), is where the king used to watch proceedings at festival time. About 100 meters to the south is an excavated **bath,** said to have been used by the king. It's fed by a raised aqueduct, and has reducing steps of sharply carved green schist. About ¼ km northwest of the Mahanavami Dibba, is the intricately sculpted **Hazara Rama temple,** where the royals may have worshipped in private.

Hampi
Anjenadri Hill
Fort
ANEGONDI
Tungabhadra
River
VIRUPAPURGADDE
Vittala Temple Complex
King's balance
Virupaksha Temple Complex
HAMPI BAZAAR
Hampi Bazaar Street
Kodaridarama Temple
Hemakuta Hill Temples
Matanga Hill
Tiruvengalanatha Temple Complex
Kadalekalu Ganesha
Sasivekalu Ganesha
Narasimha Monolith
SACRED CENTRE
ISLAMIC QUARTER
Ahmad Khan's Mosque
TO HOSPET
Uddana Virabhadra Temple
Matanga Hill
Raghunatha Temple
URBAN CORE
Bukka's Gate
Lotus Mahal
Elephant Stables
Hazara Rama Temple
Madhava Temple Complex
ROYAL CENTRE
Mahanavami Dibba
Chandrashekhara Temple
Ganagitti Jain Temple
Queens' Bath
Bhima's Gate
Archaeological Museum
Patabhirama Temple Complex
0
1/2 mi
0
1/2 km
KAMALAPURA

Approximately ½ km north of the Hazara Rama temple is a walled complex called the Zenana Enclosure, said to have been the dwelling of the royal ladies and their entourage. The Lotus Mahal inside is one of the few intact buildings in Hampi. Just outside the enclosure are the towering **Elephant Stables,** once home to the 11 elephants of the royal guard. On the road to Kamalapur, just outside the royal enclosure is the **Queen's Bath.,** still elegant for all its current lack of water.

BEYOND HAMPI

Don't miss the chance to cross the river in a coracle and explore the ruins in the village of Anegundi, to the east of Hampi—its ruins are even older.

The **Archaeological Museum** (*Rs. 5 Sat.–Thurs. 10–5*) in the southern part of the ruins takes you through the (ongoing) excavation process and displays many of the weapons and cooking utensils found at Hampi, as well as some original temple statues. Snakes hide in the museum's gardens, so be careful where you walk.

WHERE TO EAT & STAY

There are no luxury hotels in Hampi, but what many of the rooming houses here lack in amenities and pampering, they make up in location and pleasantness. If you don't have a lot of luggage and are willing to play it by ear, it's not a bad idea to just walk around to see which guesthouse looks the best. (Avoid doing this in the high season of late December and January, when arriving without confirmed reservations isn't the safest bet.) Most of the guesthouses are very stripped down, and you'll want to have on hand your own towels, bedsheets, and toilet paper, and flashlight or candle. Basics can be bought in Hospet or in Hampi from one of the many backpacker-oriented stores.

Additional lodgings can be had at the other side of the river, reached via boat. The small town there, Virupapurgadde, consists of little more than one guesthouse after another. More isolated and less stringent in the rules about serving beer, the area has become the defacto base for fun-loving Israeli backpackers and others.

If you want more comfort, you can stay in Hospet, about 13 km (8 mi) from the ruins.

¢ ✕ **Mango Tree.** To get to this easy-going, beloved hangout, leave Hampi along the small road parallel to the river, keeping the water on your right. After about 1,000 feet, you'll reach a sign leading you through coconut trees to a terraced, open-air restaurant with beautiful river views. The food's not amazing, but the thali and the cashew curry are both good, and the banana-flavored lassis refreshing. No alcohol is served, which is the "official" policy in Hampi. ✉ *West of Hampi, along the river* ☎ *94/4876–5213* *No credit cards.*

$$$ **Hampi Boulders.** This striking resort is about 4 mi from Hampi, along the Tungabhadra River. The 13 rooms are spread over eight stone cottages, some of which are made to look like castles, and others of which

resemble local houses in nearby villages. It's a prime getaway that's become popular with nature-lovers, since its own 40 acres are next to a very large nature sanctuary. **Pros:** beautiful rooms made of local materials, exclusive, small. **Cons:** hard to get to, relatively far from Hampi, lacks the amenities of a city hotel, have to pay in cash. ✉ *Narayanpet, Bandi Harlapur, 509210* ☎ *08539/265939, 0924/2641551, or 0944/8034202* *6 rooms, 7 suites cottages* *In-room: no a/c (some), no phone, no TV. In-hotel: restaurant, pool, no elevator, laundry service, no-smoking rooms* *No credit cards* *FAP.*

¢ **Shanthi Guest House.** Roughly halfway along Virupapurgadde almost uninterrupted row of river-facing guesthouses, this house generally lives up to its name and gets lots of repeat customers. ("Shanti," as it's more commonly spelled, means inner peace, and it's a word often on the lips of the backpackers and other travelers staying in the area.) There are beautiful views of the rice fields and the river beyond, and although the rooms have concrete floors and few creature comforts beyond ceiling fans and mosquito net, the hammocks on each porch and the friendly surroundings make up for a lot. The restaurant, with a mix of basic Indian and common traveler dishes (fish-and-chips, pizza), is also decent and a great place to meet other travelers seeking their own shanti. Note: an unrelated Shanti guesthouse is in Hampi itself. **Pros:** very close to the action, super cheap (under $15). **Cons:** like most of the guesthouses in Virupapurgadde, it's very basic and isn't for everyone, six rooms have a shared bath, no running hot water (it can be bought for Rs. 10 a bucket). ✉ *Virupapurgadde, 583234* ☎ *83/9432-5352* *www.hampigh.blogspot.com* *30 rooms* *In-room: no a/c, no phone, no TV. In-hotel: restaurant, no elevator* *No credit cards.*

HYDERABAD

688 km (427 mi) northwest of Chennai, 562 km (349 mi) north of Bangalore, 771 km (442 mi) southeast of Mumbai.

It's too bad more tourists don't come to Hyderabad. On the rolling hills around the beautiful Hussain Sagar (Hussain Lake), the city's minarets pierce the clear blue sky. There's a lot to see and do in a visit of two or three days: you can shop for pearls and bangles, enjoy terrific food, and experience both Hindu and Islamic culture.

The capital of the large southeastern state of Andra Pradesh, Hyderabad was established in 1590. Some 80 years earlier, the governor of the Telengana region, Quli Qutab Shah declared independence from the Bahmani kingdom, and established himself 11 km (7 mi) from modern-day Hyderabad, at Golconda. Lack of water and epidemics of plague and cholera convinced Mohammad Quli, the fifth ruler after the founder Quli Qutab Shah, to venture beyond his fortress and to create a new city nearby on the Musi River. Quli named the new city Hyderabad—after his beloved queen Hyder Mahal, originally a Hindu village girl. At the center of the new city was built the Charminar, a great arch from which four roads fan out.

The city's grandness and wealth attracted the interest of Aurangzeb, the last great Mogul ruler. His armies besieged Golconda and captured it in 1687. When the Mogul empire began to fragment after the death of Aurangzeb, the viceroy, Asaf Jah I proclaimed himself *nizam* (ruler) in 1724. The wealth and influence of the new dynasty of nizams went beyond the imagination—Hyderabad became the most important Muslim city in India. In modern Hyderabad, software, outsourcing, and telecommunications now rule the city. These industries have joined the more traditional textile and jewelry trades, and the city has stolen some of the limelight from Bangalore for its technological growth—and its sprawl. Teeming with six million people, Hyderabad has a serious problem with moving people from Point A to B. If traffic is moving, prepare to hear the crunch of an accident; if it's gridlocked, prepare to breathe in some exhaust fumes. Consider it part of the adventure. Note that everyone uses the city name Hyderabad even when they're referring to its twin city, Secunderabad, to the north, on the other side of the lake. Secunderabad, once a British cantonment, is now of note only for its railway station, which receives many of Hyderabad's long-distance trains.

GETTING AROUND HYDERABAD

Most of Hyderabad's interesting sights are in the Old City, best navigated by walking or with short auto-rickshaw trips. The other area of interest is Golconda, 11 km (7 mi) outside the city. You'll probably want to take a car or auto-rickshaw to get there, but it's really best explored on foot. Stock up on water before tackling the fort. Don't bother with Hyderabad's newer, suburban-ish twin city, Secunderabad, built by the British in the early 1800s but with little to offer a casual visitor.

EXPLORING HYDERABAD

Numbers in the text correspond to numbers in the margin and on the Hyderabad map.

A GOOD TOUR

Make your first stop **Golconda Fort** ❶, the original stronghold of the Qutab Shahi kings that predates Hyderabad city. After taking an auto-rickshaw or car to the fort from Hyderabad, walk up a steep hill to the summer palace. It's easier to walk up before the high noon heat. From the fort, walk about 1 km (½ mi) over to the **Qutab Shahi Tombs** ❷, the palatial tombs of the Muslim rulers, which are also better seen and photographed before the sun is overhead. From here it's a 7-km (4½-mi) auto-rickshaw ride to the center of the Old Town, whose landmark is **Charminar** ❸, with its magnificent minarets. All around Charminar are bustling bazaars, including the Laad Bazaar, which has rows of shops selling glass and lacquer bangles, perfume, and Islamic prayer articles. Next to the Charminar (due south) is India's second-largest mosque, the **Mecca Masjid** ❹. The **Salar Jung Museum** ❺ is a little under 2 km (1 mi) north of Charminar but still on the south side of the Musi River. In the evening, you may want to return to Golconda Fort to attend the sound-and-light show. Alternately, stay in town and pay a visit to the **Sree Venkateswara Temple** ❻, better known as the Birla Mandir.

TIMING This route can be covered in one very long day, but it's better if you take two. Many sights are closed on Friday; some shops may also be closed because of the strong Muslim influence here. Non-Muslims should avoid visiting mosques on Friday or during early morning prayers.

WHAT TO SEE

❸ Fodor's Choice ★ **Charminar.** To get to the Charminar, cross over the Puranapol bridge to the Old City that lies south of the Musi River, passing the impressive Indo-Saracenic Osmania Hospital and High Court buildings that stand on either bank. Moving toward the heart of the Old City, you enter the Charkaman area between four (*char*) great gates (*kaman*). Within these gates you can find Hyderabad's famed pearl and bangle markets, and also the striking Charminar, an imposing granite edifice built by Mohammed Quli Qutab Shah in 1591 to appease the forces of evil and protect this new city from plague and epidemic. The arches, domes, and minarets show Islamic influence, while much of the ornamentation is Hindu in style. There's a Hindu temple at the base of the Charminar, right in the heart of the Muslim-dominated Old City. Climb a steep, dark spiral stairway to reach open verandas, from which you can see the rooftops and narrow streets of the Old City, the Mecca Masjid, the Unani, and Ayurvedic hospitals. Be careful, as there are gaps in the protective railing. ✉ *Charkaman center, Old City 500002* 🎫 *Charminar Rs. 100; video camera fee Rs. 25* ⏲ *Daily 9–5.*

❶ ★ **Golconda Fort.** If you clap at the gate of this fort, it echos clearly up to the summer palace, high on the hill just outside the city (about ½ km up). These are the ruins of what was once the state capital: the imposing fort with its well-planned water-supply system often sheltered whole communities under siege for months, and though tremendously worn by time and war, it tells vivid stories in crumbling stone. The fort only fell to one siege, but that siege was disastrous. In 1687, after eight months of bottling up the fort, Aurangzeb went through what is now called the Victory Gate and sent his troops storming in (a traitor from inside opened it for him). In the belief that there was hidden gold here, Aurangzeb ordered the roofs of all palaces ripped off. After Aurangzeb died, the fort was abandoned for the second time in favor of Hyderabad city, where the viceroy of the mughal empire set up shop in 1724 and declared himself ruler. So, 300 years later, little more than the great walls of the buildings stand at Golconda, amid the weeds and moss. Although hiring a guide isn't essential, it does help make sense of the structures here: try not to pay more than Rs. 200 or so. A very good, hour-long **sound-and-light show** is performed every night at the fort. It's narrated by Amitabh Bachchan (also known as "Big B"), one of the biggest Bollywood actors of all time. ✉ *Golconda, 6 km (4 mi) west of the city, 500028* ☎ *40/2351–3984* 🎫 *Fort Rs. 100; video camera fee Rs. 25, sound-and-light show Rs. 50* ⏲ *Fort daily 9–5; sound-and-light show in English Nov.–Feb., daily 6:30* PM*, Mar.–Oct., daily 7* PM.

9

CLOSE UP

A Walk in the Old City

To spend a morning in the Old City, the area around the Charminar, is to step back a century into an old and fascinating Muslim world. Along its narrow lanes, bangle sellers vie for space with prayer mat vendors, *attar* (perfume) merchants, *waraq* (silver leaf) makers, *naan* (tandoori bread) bakers, *Unani* doctors (who practice traditional Islamic medicine), hawkers of charms and spells, and outfitters of turbans and *sherwani* (a knee-length straight-cut coat, with a small round neck, worn by Muslim men).

The dull ring of the waraq maker's hammer against his layers of leather and silver mingles with the cries of the merchants and the bells of cycle taxis and cart drivers as you pass. If you ask for directions to any shop or landmark you may be told that it no longer exists, or that the people have gone away, or that you possibly mean some other shop or landmark. Don't be deterred: locals don't often deliberately mislead visitors; it's usually because they don't want to admit they don't know something, such as directions to a place, or because they may not recognize your pronunciation of a street or landmark's name. Ask a glass bangle seller for the whereabouts of a bidri or pearl shop, and he will tell you that there are no bidri or pearl shops in Hyderabad. Make sure you have a map and you've got your bearings, or you might find it difficult to find your way out again.

❹ **Mecca Masjid.** India's second-largest mosque after Delhi's, the Mecca Masjid is in the Charkaman area in the center of the old part of town. Non-Muslims are welcome except at prayer time, which includes all day Friday. Building the mosque, which can hold some 10,000 worshippers, took more than 70 years. Construction started during the Qutab Shahi period in 1614—reputedly with bricks made from earth brought from Mecca in 1618—and was completed in 1687, after the Mughals had overthrown Golconda. The nizams' tombs line the left side of the courtyard. In May 2007, an unknown party planted a pipe bomb here that killed nine people and injured many more gathered here for Friday prayers. Although the area and the mosque are generally safe, it makes sense to be up-to-date with current events before visiting. ✉ *Kishan Prasad Rd., southwest of Charminar, Old City* ☎ *No phone* 🎫 *Free* ⏲ *Sat.–Thurs. 9* AM*–sunset except during daily early-morning services.*

❷ **Qutab Shahi Tombs.** Each of the seven distinctive tombs of the Qutab Shahi dynasty has a square base surrounded by pointed arches. The seventh is unfinished because Shah Abdul Hassan was interrupted in the building of his tomb by Aurangzeb, who defeated him and captured the Golconda Fort. The gardenlike surroundings of the tombs make for a nice walk any time that the sun's not too fierce. ✉ *2 km (1 mi) north of Golconda Fort* ☎ *40/2351–3410* 🎫 *Walk-in entry Rs. 10, car with 5 persons including driver Rs. 100, camera fee Rs. 20, video camera fee Rs. 100* ⏲ *Sat.–Thurs. 9:30–5:30.*

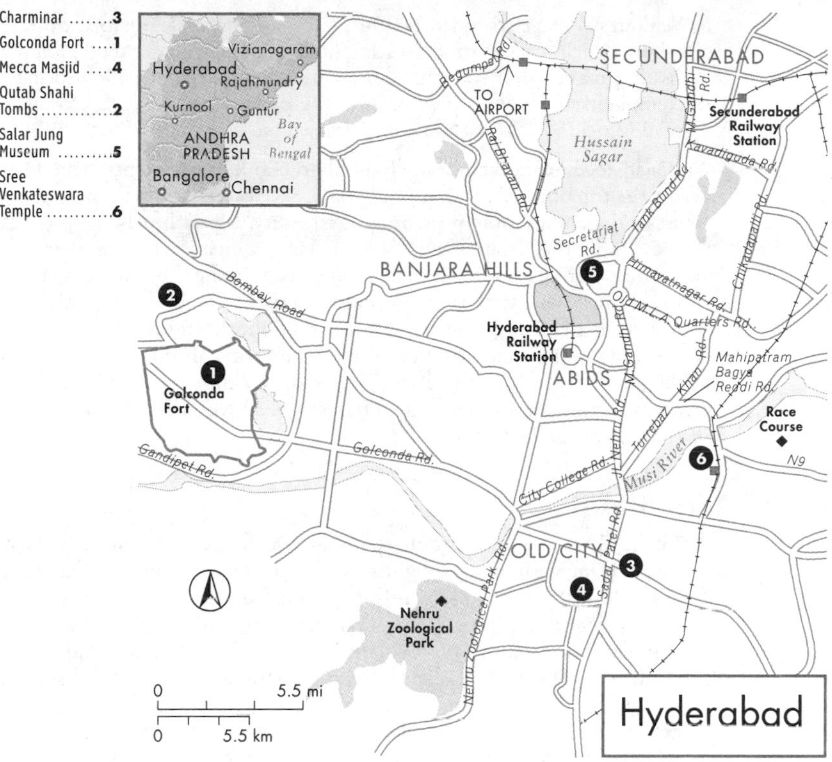

5 **Salar Jung Museum.** It's hard to believe that the riches in this collection all belonged to one man, Mir Yusuf Ali Khan Salar Jung III, who was prime ministare for a short time during the reign of Osman Ali Khan. Thirty-five thousand items, which constitute one of the world's largest private collections, are crammed into 35 rooms. The fantastic Chola bronzes, European glass, Chinese jade, jeweled weapons, miniatures, and finely woven shawls take some time to look through, but they're well worth it. A small cafeteria overlooking a garden is a nice place to take a break. No cameras are allowed. ✉ *C.L. Badari Malakpet, south of Musi River, Old City, 500012* ☎ *40/2452–3211* *Rs. 150* ⏲ *Sat.–Thurs. 10–5; ticket sales until 4:15.*

Fodor'sChoice ★

9

6 **Sree Venkateswara Temple.** Also known as the Birla Temple for the prominent industrialist family that built it, this awe-inspiring complex is made entirely of white marble from Rajasthan. Reached via steps and a path that winds among lots of stalls selling souvenirs, the temple stands tall on Kala Pahad ("Black Hill"). From the top, pilgrims and mere travelers alike can get a great view of the city and the lake. The temple was dedicated in 1976 to honor Lord Venkateswara, also known as Balaji, the same Vishnu avatar worshiped in the pilgrimage town of Tirupati. The image of the god here, inside the main tower, is itself on a grand scale, about 11 feet tall. Two separate shrines are dedicated

to Venkateswara's two consorts. On your way out, make a stop at the gift shop, which has lots of interesting (and shiny) jewelry and religious items that make good souvenirs. No cameras or bags are allowed in the temple itself. ✉*Steps near State Bank of Hyderabad, Kala Pahad* ☎*40/2323–5380* 🎫*Free* ⏲*Daily 7–noon and 2–9.*

Tank Bund Road. A showpiece of Hyderabad, Tank Bund is a promenade across the top of the dam that holds back the waters of Hussain Sagar (Hussain Lake), a dominant feature of the city. Many hotels are positioned so that their rooms overlook the lake, which is often used as a venue for sporting events. The road, which runs along the lake's eastern shore, is lined with statues of the state's native sons. A stunning sight from here is the 52-foot-high, 350-ton monolithic statue of Buddha, who stands in the southern part of the lake. You can take a boat out to the statue from Lumbini Park, or just sit by the water and eat ice cream watching the sun set as the Hyderabadis love to do. ✉*East side of Hussain Sagar Lake.*

WHERE TO EAT & STAY

$$$ ✕**Firdaus.** This airy restaurant—with high ceilings and lots of glass windows bringing in natural light—evokes the elegance of the nizams. *Punka* (old-fashioned fans) gently swaying from the ceiling, waiters dressed in *sherwanis* (long Nehru-style jackets), and live *ghazal* (classical Indian vocal music) performances on most nights help establish the ambience. The chef serves regal Hyderabadi cuisine. Typical dishes might include *achar gosht* (lamb cooked in pickled tomato masala paste) and *nizami handi* (vegetable and cottage-cheese curry) or *bagare baingan* (baby eggplant cooked in tamarind and nut sauce). The *rann-e-firdaus* (leg of lamb) is excellent. ✉*Taj Krishna, Rd. No. 1, Banjara Hills* ☎*40/6666–4242* ▭*AE, DC, MC, V.*

$ ✕**Southern Spice.** At this popular restaurant in Banjara Hills, the best things on the menu are local Andra specialties, such as lamb pulusu (in a very spicy curry sauce). That, combined with the good prices and friendly surroundings (lots of art on the walls), is what keeps the place popular with families in the area. One unusual side dish worth trying is ragi sankati, a stuffing-like mixture of millet and rice. No alcohol is served. ✉*8-2-350/3/2 Road No. 3, Banjara Hills* ☎*40/2335–3802 or 40/2335–3803* ▭*AE, DC, MC, V.*

¢–$ ✕**Chutneys.** Lively and very popular, this vegetarian restaurant in the upmarket Banjara Hills area serves good South Indian dishes in non-stuffy, bright surroundings that use lots of wood. It's a good place to try the local Andhra cuisine, which includes such dishes as the spicy *Guntur idlis,* steamed rice cakes topped with a red pepper–heavy powder. Dishes like this remind you that it makes sense to eat this type of food with either a glass of sweet *lassi* (a yogurt drink) or *raita* (seasoned yogurt). You can also order original dishes, including *dosas* that were custom-made for the popular Telugu actor Chiranjeevi: in this rendition, the crepelike dishes are steamed ("Japanese style") rather than fried, as they usually are. ✉*Shilpa Arcade, Rd. No. 3, Banjara Hills* ☎*40/2335–0569* ▭*MC, V.*

$$$$ **ITC Hotel Kakatiya Sheraton.** Aimed at wealthy business travelers, this imposing structure with a grand lobby makes a strong impression. Named after an old Hindu dynasty, the hotel doesn't seem especially Indian, opting instead for international five-star standards of comfort and elegance. The separate towers rooms have their own check-in, lounge, and other amenties to justify their higher cost. **Pros:** great service, beautiful facilities, separate "ladies-only" floor for woman travelers. **Cons:** expensive, not central to sight-seeing, business-oriented styling means it doesn't seem as if you're in India. ✉*Begumpet, 500016* ☎*40/2340–0132* 🌐*www.welcomgroup.com* *167 rooms, 21 suites* *In-room: safe, refrigerator, ethernet, Wi-Fi. In-hotel: 3 restaurants, room service, bar, pool, gym, spa, laundry service, concierge, executive floor, public Internet, public Wi-Fi, airport shuttle, parking (no fee), no-smoking rooms* *AE, DC, MC, V* *BP.*

$$$$ **Taj Deccan.** Designed to impress, the open lobby's lounge features bold relief work covering its towering walls. Rooms are furnished with the high standards of the Taj, with calm colors, plush carpets, and business-oriented amenities. **Pros:** good location in Banjara Hills, not as huge as the Taj Krishna across the street, high service standards. **Cons:** slightly bland, expensive, undergoing renovation in 2008. ✉*Rd. No. 1, Banjara Hills, 500034* ☎*40/6666–3939 or 40/2339–3939* 🌐*www.tajhotels.com* *151 rooms, 10 suites* *In-room: safe (some), refrigerator, ethernet, Wi-Fi. In-hotel: 2 restaurants, room service, bar, pool, gym, laundry service, concierge, executive floor, public Wi-Fi, airport shuttle, no-smoking rooms* *AE, DC, MC, V.*

$$$$ ★ **Taj Krishna.** A terraced high-rise with bougainvilleas spilling over the sides, this attractive, glitzy business hotel—the most expensive Taj in town—has a lobby and public areas with ornate French art as well as Moghul-inspired decorations. With 9 acres of property, the hotel is currently in the middle of an expansion that will add many more rooms and more conference space. Many of the sedately decorated rooms have views of Hussain Sagar Lake, and the service is extremely good throughout. The in-house restaurant, Firdaus, is one of the best places in the city to go for royal Hyderabadi cuisine. **Pros:** beautiful, great service, large size means many amenities. **Cons:** extremely expensive, even for a Taj, might be a little too opulent for all tastes. ✉*Rd. No. 1, Banjara Hills, 500034* ☎*40/6666–2323* 🌐*www.tajhotels.com* *246 rooms, 14 suites* *In-room: safe, refrigerator, ethernet, Wi-Fi. In-hotel: 4 restaurants, room service, bar, tennis courts, pool, gym, spa, laundry service, concierge, executive floor, public Internet, airport shuttle, no-smoking rooms* *AE, DC, MC, V.*

$$$–$$$$ **Hyderabad Marriott.** After a complete gutting and refurb, this impressive, gorgeous hotel re-opened in 2006 as one of the more striking establishments in town. An exterior with enormous hand-hewn sandstone elephants outside; a soaring, open lobby with fountains; a central elevator shaft with water flowing down on either side; and vivid carpeting throughout all work together to make it a business-hotel showstopper. The rooms are a generous size, with wood floors, bright colors for bedding and upholstery, and local arts and crafts (including saris) displayed on the walls. Although the pool is small, it's also

9

beautiful, with rocks along the side and small fountains in the corners. The Okra restaurant, open 24 hours a day, has chefs on duty who can make Asian-inspired dishes to order. Just 3 km (2 mi) from the airport and 4 km (2½ mi) from the Secunderabad railway station, the Marriott has stunning views over Hussain Sagar Lake. **Pros:** beautiful location and hotel, excellent service, impressive restaurants. **Cons:** extremely expensive, corporate feeling. ✉ *Tank Bund Rd., 500080* ☎ *40/2752–2999* 🌐 *www.marriott.com* *284 rooms, 13 suites* *In-room: safe, refrigerator, ethernet, Wi-Fi. In-hotel: 2 restaurants, room service, 2 bars, pool, gym, spa, laundry service, concierge, executive floor, public Wi-Fi, airport shuttle, no-smoking rooms* 💳 *AE, DC, MC, V.*

$$$–$$$$ **The Manohar.** Less than a kilometer from the airport, with soundproof windows to help reduce or eliminate the noise outside, this hotel is understandably popular with business travelers. In the lobby, calm music plays and the sofas and other surroundings are in burnt orange and other bright colors. Rooms have more sedate color schemes, with modern European furnishings, wood flooring, and plasma TVs. **Pros:** very handy to airport, classy looks. **Cons:** location makes the price much higher than it would otherwise deserve, some rooms aren't as carefully put together than they should be—have a look before checking in. ✉ *Airport Exit Rd., Begumpet, 500016* ☎ *40/6654–3456 or 40/6654–3333* 🌐 *www.hotelmanohar.com* *127 rooms, 8 suites* *In-room: safe, refrigerator, ethernet, Wi-Fi. In-hotel: 3 restaurants, room service, bar, pool, gym, laundry service, executive floor, public Internet, public Wi-Fi, airport shuttle, no-smoking rooms* 💳 *AE, DC, MC, V* *BP.*

$$$–$$$$ **Taj Banjara.** The third Banjara Hills Taj, a modern high-rise with its own small lake (and resident ducks), is a little bit north of the other two. The spacious lobby uses lots of marble, and it's as upbeat as the contemporary rooms, which use lots of bright colors in their bedding and furnishings. The lake-view rooms on the upper floors are especially nice; higher-priced Residency floors comes with breakfast, cocktails, and their own private lounge. **Pros:** pretty lake setting, nicely furnished rooms, upscale neighborhood. **Cons:** expensive, a short drive to sights. ✉ *Rd. No. 1, Banjara Hills, 500034* ☎ *40/6678–3176 or 40/6666–9999* 🌐 *www.tajhotels.com* *119 rooms, 3 suites* *In-room: safe, refrigerator, DVD (on request), Wi-Fi. In-hotel: 3 restaurants, room service, 2 bars, pool, laundry service, public Internet, public Wi-Fi, airport shuttle, no-smoking rooms* 💳 *AE, DC, MC, V.*

$$$ ★ **Central Court Hotel.** This mid-size, mid-range hotel has a good location in the middle of Hyderabad, rather than up in Banjara Hills like many luxury hotels. The somewhat small lobby is bright, with an open layout. Rooms are spacious and quiet, with tile floors and separate seating areas. The mattresses on the beds are rather thin, however, and the view may be of a messy construction site. The front desk can sometimes be a little overwhelmed, but the service here is otherwise mostly upbeat and efficient. Other pluses include the hotel restaurant Touch of Class, which serves very good Andra Pradesh food, and a free airport shuttle runs at certain times of the day. If you're trying to save some cash and are traveling alone, ask about the budget rooms, available only for sin-

gle occupancy. **Pros:** good (and central) location, good value, friendly staff. **Cons:** front desk can be a little disorganized, some rooms a little dated. ✉*Lakdi-ka-pool, 500004* ☎*40/2323–2323, 98/4932–3232 reservations* 🌐*www.thecentralcourt.com* *75 rooms, 1 suite* *In-room: refrigerator (some), Wi-Fi. In-hotel: 2 restaurants, room service, 2 bars, laundry service, airport shuttle* *AE, MC, V* *BP.*

$$$ **The Golkonda.** After an extensive renovation aimed at making it a five-star boutique hotel, the Golkonda has emerged with lots of slick touches, including attractively tiled bathrooms, shiny wood floors, softly lit sconces by the beds, and plasma TVs. Shaped like a triangle, with elevators at each corner, the building has a unique and vaguely Space-Age feel. Downstairs, the lobby is slightly small but still comfortable and well suited for hanging out or having a restorative from the heat outside. **Pros:** good downtown location, free Wi-Fi, nice new rooms. **Cons:** busy, traffic-filled neighborhood, recent renovations might mean not all the kinks have been worked out. ✉*Masab Tank, 500028* ☎*40/6611–0101* 🌐*www.thegolkondahotel.com* *133 rooms, 12 suites* *In-room: refrigerator, DVD (some), ethernet, Wi-Fi. In-hotel: 2 restaurants, room service, 2 bars, pool, gym, laundry service, concierge, executive floor, public Internet, public Wi-Fi, airport shuttle, no-smoking rooms* *AE, DC, MC, V* *BP.*

$$–$$$ **Green Park.** Three kilometers (2 mi) from the airport, the bustling Green Park hotel is an excellent value for business travelers. The lobby is done in marble, with soft music setting the tone; comfortable rooms are furnished in a modern, straightforward manner. The best rooms overlook the garden, but others have a view of little more than the overhanging roof. **Pros:** good value for business travelers, nice-looking hotel, free Wi-Fi. **Cons:** some rooms have views of little more than the overhanging roof, service can sometimes be a little spotty. ✉*Greenlands, Begumpet, 500016* ☎*40/2375–7575 or 40/6651–5151* 🌐*www.hotelgreenpark.com* *140 rooms, 6 suites* *In-room: safe (some), refrigerator (some), Wi-Fi. In-hotel: 2 restaurants, room service, 2 bars, gym, laundry service, executive floor, public Internet, public Wi-Fi, airport shuttle, no-smoking rooms* *AE, DC, MC, V* *BP.*

$ **Woodbridge.** The slightly small but brightly lit lobby and the rest of the furnishings here won't win any design awards, but the price is right, and rooms are clean and comfortable, with marble floors and primarily wood furniture. Rates here include a couple of items of laundry done per day—a nice bonus given Hyderabad's heat and dust. **Pros:** good value, handy location near most sights. **Cons:** very simply furnished rooms, lacks amenities of higher priced options. ✉*11-4-649C A.C. Guards, Lakdi-ka-pool, 500004* ☎*40/6666–6111* 🌐*www.woodbridgehyd.net* *60 rooms* *In-room: safe, refrigerator, Wi-Fi. In-hotel: restaurant, room service, laundry service, public Internet, airport shuttle, no-smoking rooms* *AE, MC, V* *BP.*

SHOPPING

Bidri Heritage (✉ *Opposite Meher Function Hall, Banjara Hills Road, Masab Tank* ☎ *40/2330–7552*) is a tiny, hole-in-the-wall place that does not take credit cards but offers a fascinating range of bidri artifacts and jewelry. **Kalanjali Arts & Crafts** (✉ *5-10-194 Hill Fort Rd., Saifabad* ☎ *40/2323–1147*) stocks traditional crafts, from wood carving to stoneware and paintings. **Krishna Pearls and Jewellers** (✉ *Taj Krishna, Rd. No. 1, Banjara Hills* ☎ *40/2339–5015 or 40/6656–4811* ✉ *Beside New Bharat Medical Hall, Before Masjid, 22-6-209 Pathergatti Rd.* ☎ *40/2441–7881 or 40/6614–7455* 🌐 *www.krishnapearls.com*) has a number of outlets in various luxury hotels, where the merchandise comes with pleasant, courteous service. Best of all, the prices are all as marked. **Mangatrai Pearls** (✉ *5-9-29/3 Liberty Cross Rd., opposite Hotel Shanbagh, Basheer Bagh* ☎ *40/6613–9999* ✉ *22-6-191 Pathergatti, near Charminar* ☎ *40/2341–1816 or 40/2341–1817* 🌐 *www.mangatrai.com*) offers both high-quality pearls and good service. **Sanchay** (✉ *Shops 21 and 22, Babukhan Estate, Basheer Bagh* ☎ *40/6666–9153*) has a fine selection hand-loomed silks. **Shafali** (✉ *72 Sarojini Devi Rd., Secunderabad* ☎ *40/2780–0908* 🌐 *www.shafalifabrics.com*) has a bold, distinctive range of caftans, nightdresses, linen, and shoulder bags in block printed cotton. **Shilparamam** (✉ *Jubilee Hills–High Tech City*) is a crafts village with rows of stalls managed by artisans displaying handicrafts from all over India; the Madhubani paintings are particularly good.

KARNATAKA & HYDERABAD ESSENTIALS

To research prices, get advice from other travelers, and book travel arrangements, visit www.fodors.com.

ADVENTURE SPORTS

To organize adventure sports trips or camps out in the wilds of Karnataka, it's best to find an agent who specializes in this sort of thing. Such agents can also arrange permits where necessary. Book several weeks in advance, as space and equipment can be limited and is usually much in demand.

Outlook Traveller's guidebook *Weekend Breaks from Bangalore* (Rs. 225) is a very handy guide for short trips. It's also includes good listings on adventure-sports organizations in the area.

Jungle Lodges & Resorts Ltd., the outdoor-activity branch of the Karnataka Department of Tourism (KDT), has rustic facilities in the state's protected wild areas. Professional guides can take you on jeep tours to wildlife-viewing spots or fish-rich rivers.

Contacts Jungle Lodges & Resorts Ltd. (✉ *Shrungar Shopping Centre, 2nd fl., near United Coffee House, M. G. Rd., Bangalore* ☎ *80/2559–7021, 80/2559–7024, or 80/2559–7025* 🌐 *www.junglelodges.com*). **Nature Admire** (☎ *080/4153–2333* 🌐 *www.natureadmire.com*).

Ozone (☎ *80/2356–1871* 🌐 *www.ozoneindia.com*).

AIR TRAVEL

Airlines & Contacts **Air India** (☎ *1407* 🌐 *www.indian-airlines.nic.in*). **IndiGO** (☎ *99/1038-3838, 800/180-3838 in India* 🌐 *www.goindigo.in*). **Jet Airways** (☎ *80/3989-3333 Karnataka, 40/3989-3333 Hyderabad* 🌐 *www.jetairways.com*). **Kingfisher** (☎ *80/4197-9797 or 12/4284-4700* 🌐 *www.flykingfisher.com*). **Paramount Airways** (☎ *44/4390-9090, 40/2790-4964 Hyderabad, 80/4115-4666 Bangalore* 🌐 *www.paramountairways.com*). **Simplifly Deccan** (☎ *080/3900-8888 or 984/577-7008 Karnataka, 040/3900-8888 or 984/967-7008 Hyderabad* 🌐 *www.flyairdeccan.net*). **Spice Jet** (☎ *987/180-3333, 800/180-3333 in India* 🌐 *www.spicejet.com*).

AIRPORTS & TRANSFERS

At this writing Bangalore's much-awaited new and massive airport is on track to open in the spring of 2008. From that time onward all flights are set to depart from the new airport, which is some 20 mi from downtown in an area called Devanahalli. However, some arrivals may still be landing at the old airport in the neighborhood of Kodahalli, about 4 mi from M. G. Road—confirm your airport with your airline in advance.

Although a special train is planned to transport passengers to and from the new airport and Bangalore's downtown, construction will not begin until the end of 2008 at the earliest. Until then, your best bet is to take a prepaid taxi.

Not having any intention of being left behind, Hyderabad is also set to open a new airport in 2008 at a location about 14 miles from town.

Airport Information **Bengaluru International Airport** (🌐 *www.bialairport.com*). **Hyderabad International Airport** (🌐 *www.newhyderabadairport.com*).

BUS TRAVEL

Local buses are frequent and cheap but also crowded and uncomfortable. On mornings and evenings you may see as many as 80 people stuffed into one bus.

Bangalore's main bus station is in the neighborhood of Subhash Nagar, more commonly called Majestic for a large movie theater in the area. From there Karnataka State Road Transport Corporation buses leave many times a day for Mysore. The journey takes from two to four hours, and the fare in the highest class of bus is Rs. 141.

Bus Information **Karnataka State Road Transport Corporation** (✉ *Subhash Nagar, Bangalore* 🌐 *www.ksrtc.in*).

MONEY

ATMS ATMs are easy to find throughout most parts of Bangalore and Hyderabad. If you're having a hard time finding an ATM in smaller towns, ask at your hotel.

CURRENCY EXCHANGE Most banks and Western-style hotels exchange foreign currency and cash traveler's checks. The main branches of the State Bank of India change currency and usually cash traveler's checks as well. Although banks will usually give you a better rate, Thomas Cook has better hours. The branches in both Bangalore and Hyderabad are open Monday through Saturday from 9:30 to 6.

Exchange Services (Bangalore) **Thomas Cook** (✉ *62/63, UG3, The Pavilion M. G. Rd., Bangalore* ☎ *80/2558–1337 or 80/2559–4168* 🌐 *www.thomascook.co.in*).

Exchange Services (Hyderabad) **Thomas Cook** (✉ *6-1-57 Nasir Arcade, Saifabad district* ☎ *40/2323–1988*)

TAXIS

Call the taxi companies a couple of hours before you think you'll need them, especially during the morning and evening rush.

Most call taxi drivers will also take you outside the city for a day trip, but be sure to be clear on the rate and all charges before having one pick you up. For multiday trips, it's usually better to work through a travel agency.

Contacts (Bangalore) **Cel Cabs** (☎ *80/2346–6666*). **Radio Taxis** (☎ *80/2332–0152*). **Garden City Taxi** (☎ *80/2343–7646 or 80/2343–4274*). **Spot Taxis** (☎ *80/2551–0000*).

Contacts (Hyderabad) **Cel Cabs** (☎ *40/2324–2526*). **Cosy Cabs** (✉ *1-10-179/208/1/8,Karan Apartments, ground floor, opposite Begumpet post office, Begumpet* ☎ *40/2776–2023 or 40/2776–0409*). **Orange Cabs** (☎ *40/5531–5555*).

TRAIN TRAVEL

Because India's train system is so immense, with lots of classes, options, and destinations, it makes sense to book important, time-sensitive trips through a travel agent.

The reservations offices at Bangalore City Railway Station and in Mysore are open Monday through Saturday 8–2 and 2:15–8, Sunday 8–2.

Hyderabad and Secunderabad are major rail centers. Some trains use either or both stations, but most long-distance trains use only Secunderabad. Leaving from Delhi's Nizamuddin station, the Rajdhani Express, takes 22 hours, while the less-expensive A.P. Express takes 26 hours, when it's running on time. From Mumbai, the Mumbai Hyderabad Husainsagar Express takes 14 hours; and from Chennai, the Charminar Express takes 14 hours.

The Hampi Express, train #6592, leaves for Hospet (the jumping-off point for Hampi) nightly from Bangalore at 9:30 PM; it arrives the next morning at 7:45. You can also reach Hospet directly from the north; trains run from Mumbai to Hubli, in Andhra Pradesh, and from there you can take a bus or train the 144 km (90 mi) to Hospet. Note that trains in this part of the country are very slow.

Several trains run between Bangalore and Mysore daily; the trip costs around Rs. 250. The super-fast, air-conditioned Shatabdi Express runs between Mysore and Chennai via Bangalore (Rs. 400 round-trip) every afternoon except Tuesday. The leg between Bangalore and Mysore takes two hours. The Chamundi Express, another option, takes three hours.

Mangalore is linked by train to Mumbai, Delhi, Kerala (Trivandrum and Ernakulam), and Chennai. The Konkan Railway runs between Mumbai and Mangalore, a run of 760 km (470 mi). Along the way its trains stop in Madgaon (Goa) and many other points along India's west coast. The Rajdhani Express train, for instance, leaves Mangalore at 6:20 in the morning on Tuesday and Thursday, reaching Karwar three hours later and Margao (in Goa) an hour later.

Train Information **Konkan Railway** (🌐 *www.konkanrailway.com*). **Southern Railway** (🌐 *www.srailway.com*).

TRAVEL AGENTS & TOURS

In Bangalore, the KSTDC is widely used for its car-hire service and its full- and half-day bus tours of major sights in Karnataka. Most tours are inexpensive and low on frills—the buses are aging—but they provide a concise, well-rounded look at what's important.

Bangalore Walks runs walking tours of Bangalore, including one that heads along M.G. Road to take in the remaining (and the merely remembered) signs of the city's Victorian past (Rs. 495). In deference to the area's potential heat and the inevitable traffic, the tour starts at 7 AM; it ends with breakfast in one of Bangalore's tallest buildings. Other tours, including a tree tour in Lal Bagh, are also available, as are personalized tours for groups of eight or more.

The most inexpensive tours in Hyderabad are organized by AP Tourist Development Corporation (⇨ Visitor Information). Tours include city sightseeing day tours, the Golconda sound-and-light show, and tours to other destinations, such as Nagarjunasagar, Hampi, Ajanta and Ellora caves, and Tirupati.

Skyway Tours, with bases in Bangalore and Mysore, is highly responsive and has good prices. Sri Sathya Sai Tourists is open 24 hours a day, 365 days a year.

Contacts **Ambassador Travel Services** (☎ *80/2845–0931 or 80/2845–0932 Bangalore* 🌐 *www.ambassadortours.in*). **Ashok Travels** (☎ *40/2326–1360 Hyderabad, 80/2225–4396 Bangalore* 🌐 *www.ashoktravels.com*). **Bangalore Walks** (☎ *098/4552–3660* 🌐 *www.bangalorewalks.com*). **Skyway International Travels** (☎ *80/2211–1401 Bangalore, 82/1244–4444 Mysore* 🌐 *www.skywaytour.com*). **Mercury Travels** (☎ *40/2781–2712 Hyderabad, 80/2559–1641 Bangalore*). **Sri Sathya Sai Tourists** (☎ *80/2664–1140 or 80/2654–1140 Bangalore, 82/1246–3733 Mysore* 🌐 *www.sathyasaitourist.com*).

VISITOR INFORMATION

For any stay longer than a couple days, the Eicher map of Bangalore (Rs. 200) is highly useful. It maps most landmarks, neighborhoods, and just about every street. The *Guide Map of Greater Hyderabad* (Rs. 295) performs a similar service for a city with some very confusing—or just nonexistent—street addresses. Both books are available at bookstores and larger magazine stalls.

The Bangalore branch of Karnataka Tourism that's handiest for most tourists is off of St. Mark's Road and open from 9 AM–8 PM daily. In addition to providing information on places throughout Karnataka, it can also book hotels, buses, and tours run by its parent organization, the Karnataka State Tourism Development Corporation (KSTDC). Skyway travel agency is in the same building on Papanna Lane. The Government of India Tourist offices have useful brochures on all of India; the Bangalore office is open weekdays 9:30–5 and Saturday 9–1, the one in Mysore is open Monday through Saturday 10–5:30. The Hyderabad office is open weekdays 9:30–6 and Saturday 9:30–1. All offices are often closed the second Saturday of each month.

For finding out about the latest goings-on in Hyderabad, the Channel 6 magazine (🌐 *www.channel6magazine.com*) is a good source. You can pick it up in major hotels and bookstores. Also handy is the number look-up service at ☎ 40/3999–9999.

Tourist Offices (Karnataka) Karnataka Tourism (✉ *Khanija Bhavan, #49, 2nd fl., Race Course Rd.* ☎ *80/2235–2828* 🌐 *www.karnatakatourism.org* ✉ *Karnataka Tourism House, 8 Papanna La., off of St. Mark's Rd.* ☎ *80/4132–9211*).

KSTDC (✉ *Railway Station, Bangalore* ☎ *80/2287–0068* 🌐 *www.kstdc.nic.in* ✉ *Bangalore airport* ☎ *80/2526–8012* ✉ *415 Raghavendra Compound, College Rd., Patel NagarHospet* ☎ *83/9422–1008*).

Government of India Tourist Office (✉ *Karnataka State Finance Corp. (KFC) Bldg., 48 Church St., Bangalore* ☎ *80/2558–5417* 🌐 *www.incredibleindia.org* ✉ *Old Exhibition Building, Irwin Rd., Mysore* ☎ *82/1242–2096*).

Tourist Offices (Andra Pradesh) Andhra Pradesh Travel & Tourism Development Corporation, Ltd. (*APTTDC* ✉ *Opp. BRK Bhavan, Tank Bund Rd., Hyderabad, 500063* ☎ *40/2345–0165, 040-23450444 tourist information center* 🌐 *www.aptourism.in*). **Government of India Tourist Office** (✉ *Netaji Bhawan, 2nd fl., Liberty Rd., Himayat Nagar* ☎ *40/2326–1360* 🌐 *www.incredibleindia.org*).

Kerala

A houseboat floating down the Kerala waterways

WORD OF MOUTH

"In Kerala we did the backwater trip with an overnight stay on the boat. I know many people have recommended only a day cruise, but I strongly disagree. Once the boat docks for the night, we did a little walk around the backwater village, and saw the local life. And the stars were incredible at night. Some of us woke up at 6 AM for the sunrise, and it was well worth it! A quick walk around the village before the breakfast was also very nice."

—CassieWithBag

www.fodors.com/forums

WELCOME TO KERALA

TOP REASONS TO GO

★ **Pleasures on the Harbor:** Snap a sunset photo of Fort Cochin's massive Chinese fishing nets and stroll to a local seafood joint to sample the day's catch.

★ **Ease Your Stress:** There's no place better than Kerala to get an ayurvedic oil massage. Let your tension melt away and your body kick back into equilibrium.

★ **A Night on the Backwaters:** Luxury houseboats come with hotel comforts, but the real attraction is the traditional village life you see drifting by.

★ **Beaches for Every Taste:** Relax along an isolated stretch of sand in North Kerala, go windsurfing on the island paradise of Lakshadweep, or party on Kovalam's Lighthouse Beach.

★ **Go Wild:** Watch bison, elephants, and wild boar from your balcony at the Lake Palace hotel inside the Lake Periyar Wildlife Sanctuary.

1 Kochi. This colonial port city is packed with historical homes, churches, mosques and a centuries-old synagogue where the city's small remaining population of Jews still worship.

2 Central Kerala. Central Kerala is blessed with natural beauty: beaches, the backwaters, stunning tea plantations, and cool mountain wildlife preserves. It's also a busy tourist destination with crowds in season.

3 Southern Kerala. The main attractions here are the beaches in and around Kovalam and the laid-back atmosphere. It also holds the capital city of Trivandrum.

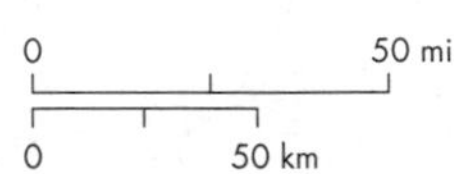

A converted house boat moves silently along the Kerala backwaters.

4 Northern Kerala. In this quiet area, you'll find long stretches of pristine sand and Bekal Fort, a 300-year-old beachfront fort that shouldn't be missed.

KARNATAKA
Calicut (Kozhikode)
Kottakkal
Malampuzha
TAMIL NADU
Cheruthuruthi
Guruvayur
Thrissur (Trichur)
2
47
Malayattur
Kaladi
Munnar
Kochi (Cochin)
Ernakulam
1
Painavu
Idukki
Kumarakom
Kottayam
Thekkady
Sabarimala
Lake Periyar Wildlife Sanctuary
Alappuzha (Alleppey)
47
Pathanamthitta
Kollam (Quilon)
Pon Mudi
3
Thiruvananthapuram (Trivandrum)
Kovalam

GETTING ORIENTED

The small state of Kerala is separated from the rest of the country by natural boundaries—the Arabian Sea to the west and the high Western Ghats to the east. The thickly forested and mountainous eastern edge can only be reached by road. Its hilly and fertile midlands are spotted with coconut farms and paddy (rice) fields; its coastal lowlands are famous for the beaches and backwaters. Although most people never venture beyond the central backwater resorts and the well-developed beach towns in the south, the north's long pristine beaches are also getting popular.

Tea harvesting

KERALA PLANNER

When to Go

Kerala's climate is sultry. Summers are hot, but winters are pleasant. For the best weather, visit during the relatively cool season, between October and February. This is also a good time to see some of the more interesting festivals. March, April, and May are hot and humid, though the hill stations of Thekkady and Munnar are still pleasant, even without air-conditioning. Heavy rains fall between June and mid-August, swallowing up most of the beaches and more than a few roads in low-lying areas. A second monsoon sweeps in in mid-October and lasts through December, bringing thunder, lightning, and afternoon showers. Crowds at this time are at a minimum and hotel rates are slashed. Monsoon season is also supposed to be the best time for ayurvedic treatments. Fall also brings the major harvest festival called Onam, during which snakeboat races are run.

Getting There & Around

Most international flights land in Trivandrum or Kochi. But the small Calicut airport also has flights coming from the Middle East and Sri Lanka. Kochi's international airport is about 40 km (25 mi) east of the city; abominable traffic can make it a two-hour trip. A taxi will cost about Rs. 500. The small airport in Trivandrum is 6 km (4 mi) west of the city center; taxis charge about Rs. 200 to get to the city and about Rs. 700 to reach Kovalam. Calicut's Karipur Airport is 23 km (14 mi) south of town; a cab will cost roughly Rs. 550.

Driving to Kerala is a good option. If you're coming from Tamil Nadu, the drive from Madurai along the Madurai–Kottayam Road is stunning. NH–17 runs along the coast from Mangalore south to Kochi, though it gets a little rough north of Calicut. Roads to the interior *ghats* (mountains) are often breathtaking: the landscape changes from the brilliant lime green of the rice fields to the rich, dark green of the tea plantations and jungle.

The most convenient way to get around Kerala is with a hired car and driver. The journey from Trivandrum to Kochi takes about five hours. Figure about Rs. 10 per km (½ mi) for a non-air-conditioned car and a halt charge of Rs. 150 per night. Shop around, and hire a car from a government-approved travel agency.

In Kochi, public ferries and private boats go between Fort Cochin, Willingdon Island, and Ernakulam throughout the day. Ernakulam's main boat jetty is south of the Taj Residency hotel. Boats leave for Fort Cochin roughly every half hour from 6 AM to 9 PM. There are frequent ferries to Mattancherry, and limited service to Embarkation Jetty, on Willingdon Island's eastern tip. Ferry rides cost only a few rupees.

In central Kerala boat cruises offer a fascinating look at the backwaters where people still live. Most houseboats are based in the Alleppey district. When booking an overnight stay on one, make sure it comes equipped with solar panels and air-conditioning or a fan, or you're in for a hot night. The going rate for a posh two-bedroom vessel with air-conditioning and meals included is roughly Rs. 14,000; a one-bedroom will run about Rs. 9,000.

Coconut & More Coconut

The Kerala table is eclectic, savory, and adventuresome. Rice is the staple, coconut milk and coconut oil are the two most important ingredients, and seafood is the star. In Fort Cochin, within the city of Kochi, you can buy a fish—just caught in one of the Chinese-style nets used in the region—have it fried at a nearby stall, and enjoy it alfresco. *Karimeen,* or pearl spot (a bony but tasty and tender white fish), is the favorite fish of central Kerala, found only in the backwaters.

Kerala's Christians are famous for their beef dishes, while the *moppillah* (Muslim cuisine of north Kerala) features a variety of breads, such as thin rice-flour *parathas* a local deep-fried eyelash bread. Also expect distinctive meat and fish dishes—rich beef or mutton stewed in coconut milk, bread stuffed with fried mussels, and savory *biriyanis* (rice dishes) with meat or fish. Vegetable dishes are plentiful—gourds, yam, mango, and bananas may be cooked or raw, in entrées and desserts. Grated coconut and *jaggery*—semi-refined palm sugar—are commonly used in sweets.

Kerala is known for *iddi appa,* or "string hoppers"—thin strands of dough formed into little nests that are steamed and served with coconut milk and sugar for breakfast or as an accompaniment to soups, stews, or curries. *Appam,* a slight variation on the theme, is a rice-flour pancake, thin and crispy on the edges with a spongy, raised center. Another specialty is *puttu,* a puddinglike dish made from fresh-grated coconut and rice flour, molded into a cylindrical shape and then steamed.

What It Costs In Rupees

	¢	$	$$	$$$	$$$$
Restaurants	under Rs. 100	Rs. 100–Rs. 300	Rs. 300–Rs. 500	Rs. 500–Rs. 700	over Rs. 700
Hotels	under Rs. 2,000	Rs. 2,000–Rs. 4,000	Rs. 4,000–Rs. 6,000	Rs. 6,000–Rs. 10,000	over Rs. 10,000

Restaurant prices are for an entrée plus bread or rice. Hotel prices are for a double room in high season, excluding a tax of up to 20%.

Planning Your Time

The most convenient way to tackle Kerala is with a car and driver, allowing for the maximum amount of flexibility. Spend at least a day in Kochi, soaking in the beauty and the cultural offerings. A four-day itinerary can also include two days of ayurvedic massages and great local food in the resort town of Kumarakom and an overnight houseboat cruise through inland waterways. Drive inland to Thekkady or Munnar and spend two days viewing the wildlife in Thekkady's Lake Periyar Wildlife Sanctuary (take the 4 PM boat cruise or a more adventurous jungle trek) and scenic Munnar, Kerala's Switzerland, with the added attractions of wild elephants and the Rajamala sanctuary. Some travelers arrive in Kerala by car from Madurai, in Tamil Nadu; if that's your plan, visit Idukki on your way west toward the coast. If beaches are your weakness, and you have the time, swing back through Kochi and take a boat or plane to Lakshadweep. Only about a third of these atolls off Kerala's coast are inhabited. Another option is to travel south from Thekkady to Trivandrum, Kerala's capital. Explore its sights and quiet lanes before heading for the mellow beaches, palm-fringed lagoons, and rocky coves near Kovalam. If you want to get away from the crowds, head for the rarely visited north to see the extraordinary Theyyam festivals of Kannur and the sweeping vistas of the fort at Bekal, near Kasargode.

Updated by Prashant Gopal

A CHARMING MYTH EXPLAINS the Creation of Kerala, the narrow state running 560 km (350 mi) along India's western coast. Parashurama, an avatar of Vishnu, performed a series of penances to atone for a grievous sin, and the god of the sea rewarded his devotion by reclaiming Kerala from the deep.

In 1956 the Malayalam-speaking states of Kochi and Travancore joined with the district of Malabar to form Kerala. The new Indian state became the first place in the world to adopt a communist government in a free election, an event that caused global speculation. Today this tropical enclave between the western mountains and the Arabian Sea is one of India's most progressive states, with a literacy rate of well over 90% and a life expectancy far higher than the Indian average. Even in the shabbiest backwater "toddy shop," where locals knock back glasses of potent coconut liquor, you'll find a copy of the day's newspaper. However, despite Kerala's very real accomplishments, unemployment remains endemic. Its citizens depends to a large degree on remittances (money sent from abroad). To be able to provide for their families back home, many Keralan men must leave to work in the Persian Gulf.

The Malayalis make up India's most highly educated population; many are conversant in English, Hindi, and Tamil, as well as Malayalam. In the nearly three millennia before the 1795 establishment of British rule, Phoenicians, Arabs, Jews, Chinese, and Europeans came in droves, attracted by the region's valuable cash crops: tea, rubber, cashews, teak, and spices—most notably black pepper and cardamom.

Since Independence, people have begun using the place names that were used prior to British colonization. The British had a strong presence in Kerala, so name changes are particularly germane here; hence Alleppey/Alappuzha, Calicut/Kozhikode, Cochin/Kochi, Quilon/Kollam, Trichur/Thrissur, and Trivandrum/Thiruvananthapuram. Official maps and tourist brochures reflect these changes but both the Anglicized and Malayalam names are still commonly used.

EXPLORING KERALA

Outside of the historic, spice-trading city of Kochi, attractions are rustic: quiet beaches spiked with palm trees line the west coast; the hilly eastern interior is heavily forested. Kochi is the anchor of low-lying central Kerala, a region dominated by lazy inland waterways, rice fields, and fishing boats; the backwater lifestyle is best experienced from the deck of a slow-moving boat. Farther inland, you'll find tranquil tea and spice plantations as well as two national parks. At Lake Periyar Wildlife Sanctuary, near Thekkady, you can observe creatures in their native habitat from the comfort of a boat. Rajamala National Park near Munnar is where you'll find the endangered *nilgiri tahr,* a shy but sweet-tempered mountain goat. The hills surrounding Thekkady and Munnar are lovely for trekking, rich in waterfalls and birdsong. Southern Kerala is best known for the beaches near Kovalam, which lie south of the stately capital city, Trivandrum (Thiruvanandapuram).

Undeveloped, conservative northern Kerala is the state's cultural heartland; you can witness some of the region's most spectacular festivals here. Kerala's Muslim community is concentrated in the north, and Christians in the central and southern regions. Many of Kerala's low-slung, modest temples restrict entry to Hindus only.

ABOUT THE RESTAURANTS

Eating out is a relatively new concept in Kerala; the older generation views restaurants with a great deal of suspicion and the act of dining outside the home as some sort of tragedy. Most restaurants, as a result, cater to visitors and are often attached to hotels. (The word hotel, in fact, is often synonymous with restaurant.) This doesn't mean that visitors are denied the opportunity to eat an outstanding, authentic meal in Kerala. On the contrary, you'll often find the best authentic food in the better hotels and resorts. The top independent restaurants are in the major cities of Kochi, Calicut, and Trivandrum, or the tourist hub of Kovalam.

ABOUT THE HOTELS

Many Kerala resorts make use of traditional regional architecture, from tribal-style huts to elaborate wooden manors. Heritage properties transplant or reassamble traditional teak wood homes, while other hotels are newly built in the old style, helping to support traditional carpentry.

In cities, most hotels have air-conditioning, but many resorts in less populated and cooler areas do not. Beach properties often rely on fan and sea breezes, and in the hilly interior, air-conditioning is usually unnecessary. Some buildings have no window screens, so if a cool and/or bug-free sleep is part of your plan, ask about both. Many resorts, even upscale establishments, don't have TVs in guest rooms. Outside of cities, power supply is tenuous. Most hotels have their own generators, but they take a few seconds to kick in. Don't be surprised if you're left in the darkness for a moment—it's unavoidable.

Some lodgings charge a 10% service fee, and the state government tacks on another 6%–16%, depending on the facilities. In luxury places, count on paying up to 25% in taxes. You may be able to offset such fees with off-season discounts—around 50% during the monsoon season, from June to August. On the other hand, many hotels charge higher-than-usual rates in peak season, from mid-December to mid-January.

KOCHI

1,380 km (860 mi) south of Mumbai.

Kochi, formerly and still commonly known as Cochin, is one of the west coast's largest and oldest ports. The streets behind the docks of the historic Fort Cochin and Mattancherry districts are lined with old merchant houses, godowns (warehouses), and open courtyards heaped with betel nuts, ginger, peppercorns, and tea. Throughout the

CLOSE UP

Ayurveda, Balance & Bliss

Ayurveda is everywhere in Kerala and much of the rest of India, in spas, beauty parlors, hospitals, pharmacies, nursing homes, and even supermarkets, who carry tons of soaps, shampoos, and other products with this or that herb. Most area hotels offer ayurvedic treatments, including packages (lasting from three days to one month) in which ayurvedic doctors, masseurs, and yoga and meditation instructors team up and attempt to optimize your physical and spiritual well-being. If an extended treatment sounds like ayurvedic overload, try a simple ayurvedic massage: a vigorous rubdown involving copious amounts of oil, a hard wooden table, and a masseur with hands like driftwood. A postsession application of an herbal powder removes most of the goo, leaving your skin feeling fresh. It's both invigorating and relaxing.

AYURVEDA'S DEEP ROOTS

Ayurveda may be trendy, but there's nothing new about it. This holistic belief system, which roughly means "knowledge of life" in Sanskrit, has been practiced for about 4,000 years. Over time it has become linked with Kerala, thanks to the region's tropical climate and its wealth of medicinal herbs. Its therapeutic powers are supposed to peak during the cool and wet monsoon season—a belief that has come as a blessing to the Kerala tourism department, which has used it successfully to attract off-season travelers.

Unlike other alternative medicines, which are sometimes used as replacements for conventional medicine, ayurveda is used in a complementary fashion. Its goal is to preserve a balance between the forces and principles thought to govern the body, mind, and soul. Doctors, who must complete more than five years of training, prescribe treatments based on their patient's constitution, and remedies usually take the form of medicated oils and herbal concoctions that are ingested, massaged into, or poured over the body. Oil, it's believed, has restorative powers, lubricating joints, rebuilding tissue, softening and hydrating skin and washing away toxins. The oils also decrease friction and spread heat evenly throughout the body.

RESTORING BALANCE

Resorts throughout Kerala offer ayurvedic packages, from three-day general health and rejuvenation programs to longer treatments tailored to specific ailments. Treatments for serious ailments, such as paralysis, can last as long as 41 days. But treatments for healthy people typically last no more than 15 days. Ayurveda is thought to be especially effective for rheumatoid arthritis, back pain, and repetitive strain injuries. The massage is also supposed to relieve stress and pain, slow the aging process, improve circulation, loosen muscles and improve sleep. Practitioners focus on the whole body rather than just on a specific ailment, and on prevention as well as healing. The idea is to bring the body back to its natural equilibrium.

Ayurvedic physicians believe that people are born with unique physical and psychological characteristics and their constitutions are made up of a combination of *doshas* (qualities): *vata* (air), *pitta* (fire) and *kapha* (earth). One or two doshas are typically dominant, but most people have a unique mix of all three. Each dosha is associated with a body and personality type and particular diseases. Vata people, who tend to have dry skin and thin frames, are prone to chronic diseases such as asthma and arthritis and nerve problems. People with strong pitta qualities have warm bodies and keen intelligence; they often can suffer from digestive and metabolic problems. And kaphas, who have cold skin and heavy, well-developed bodies, are prone to respiratory disease and weight gain.

Before prescribing treatments, ayurvedic doctors determine the patient's constitution by asking questions, observing and touching the body, and feeling the pulse. It's possible for patients with the same ailments to receive different herb and diet plans because of their unique constitutions. Treatments these days focus primarily on massage and *panchakarma* (detoxification), but ayurveda has a total of eight branches, including surgery, psychiatry, and reproductive medicine. The five detoxifying techniques of panchakarma are a lot less pleasant than having warm coconut oil rubbed into your back: they induced vomiting, enemas, laxatives, herbal nasal inhalation, and bloodletting. A course of panchakarma may also include massage, dietary prescriptions and sweat baths.

MODERN AYURVEDIC PRACTICE

The softer side of ayurveda—massage—is usually performed by two or more therapists who are the same sex as the patient. The massage is meant to release toxins by making a gentle circular motion with the forefinger at specific reflexology points (The body has 107 of them, according to ayurvedic principles). Masseurs rub the skin and pour heated oils and other liquids, sometimes including milk or buttermilk, over the head and body. The patient is asked to lie down or sit upright on a wooden board called a *droni*. Resorts have adapted the traditional techniques for modern, western clientele. A number of centers, for instance, use padded massage tables, which some tourists find more comfortable than the stiff board, especially those with low back pain. And some hotels have even started offering couples' massages.

The number of spas in Kerala has grown tremendously in recent years, all seeking to treat the hoards of tourists coming specifically for ayurvedic treatments. But not all spas are created equal. The Arya Vaidya Sala, a charitable institution founded in 1902 in Kottakkal (about two hours from Calicut) is considered to be the most authorative ayurvedic source. It addition to its clinic and hospital in Kottakkal, it has branches across the country.

In order to stop the growth of spas that fail to adhere to reasonable health and safety standards, the Indian government has created an accreditation system. "Green leaf" is the highest classification, followed by "olive leaf." A list of accredited spas is available at 🌐 keralatourism.org.

second millennium this ancient city exported spices, coffee, and coir (the fiber made from coconut husks), and imported culture and religion from Europe, China, and the Middle East. Today Kochi has a synagogue, several mosques, Portuguese Catholic churches, Hindu temples, and the United Church of South India (an amalgamation of several Protestant denominations).

HEAD FOR WATER

Traffic on land and the city's many bridges can be abominable. Private launches and small ferries zip through the waterways, making the journey as enjoyable as the destination.

EXPLORING KOCHI

The city is spread out over mainland, peninsula, and islands. Ernakulam, on the mainland 2 km (3 mi) from the harbor, is the commercial center and the one-time capital of the former state of Cochin. Willingdon Island, which was created by dredging the harbor, holds several luxury hotels as well as a navy base. The beautiful Bolghatty Island, north of Ernakulam, is a favorite picnic spot for locals. On it there's a government-run hotel in a colonial structure that was once used by the Dutch governor and later by the British Resident. The Fort Cochin district, Kochi's historic center, is at the northern tip of the Mattancherry peninsula. Houses here often recall Tudor manors; some have been converted to hotels, others remain in the hands of the venerable tea and trading companies. South of Fort Cochin, in the Mattancherry district, is where you'll find the city's dwindling Jewish community. Their small neighborhood, called Jew Town, is centered around the synagogue.

Numbers in the text correspond to numbers in the margin and on the Kochi map.

A GOOD TOUR

The sleepy, tree-lined streets of Fort Cochin are perfect for a leisurely stroll. Start at the **St. Francis Church** ❶, one of the earliest Indian churches to be built by Europeans. Portuguese explorer Vasco da Gama was once buried here. Continue northeast along Church Street, passing colonial bungalows, to Vasco da Gama Square and the famed **Chinese fishing nets** ❷. Follow River Road along the sea front past more colonial buildings. When you come to the end of the small Children's Park, take a right so that the edge of the park is on your right. At the park's far edge you'll hit tiny Princess Street—one of the first streets built in Fort Cochin, it's now crammed with shops, tour agencies, and modest European-style houses. The next major intersection is at Bastion Street. Take a left here and you'll soon see **Santa Cruz Cathedral** ❸ on your right. From here, hop in an auto-rickshaw to Mattancherry (a Rs. 30 trip) and visit the **Dutch Palace** ❹. When you exit, take a right and follow the road as it turns a corner. The **Pepper Exchange** is on your right. Step inside for a glimpse of local commerce in action. Turn right again and you'll reach the **Synagogue** ❺. In the afternoon browse in the antiques and spice shops that line Jew Town Road, or head back north to the jetty and catch a ferry to Ernakulam for shopping on Mahatma Gandhi (M.G.) Road.

TIMING You can see Fort Cochin and Mattancherry in half a day. Remember that all houses of worship close for a few hours around lunchtime. The Dutch Palace is closed on Friday, the synagogue is closed to visitors on Saturday, and many shops are closed on Sunday.

WHAT TO SEE

❷ **Chinese Fishing Nets.** The precarious-looking bamboo and wood structures hovering like cranes over the waterfront are Kochi's famous Chinese fishing nets. Although they've become identified with the city, they're used throughout central Kerala. Thought to have been introduced by Chinese traders in the 14th century, the nets and their catch are easily accessible from at Fort Cochin's Vasco da Gama Square. You can watch the fishermen haul up the nets around 6 AM, 11 AM, and 4 PM. They're particularly striking at sunset or at any time when viewed from the deck of a boat.

❹ **Dutch Palace.** Built by the Portuguese in the mid-16th century as a present for the Rajas of Cochin, this structure was added to by the Dutch when they took control of the area. The rajas, in turn, added some of India's best mythological murals—the entire story of the *Ramayana* is told on the walls in a series of bedchambers, which also have inviting window seats. In the ladies' ground-floor chamber, you can see a colorful, mildly erotic depiction of Lord Krishna with his female devotees. The coronation hall near the entrance holds portraits and some of the rajas artifacts, including a fantastic palanquin covered in red wool. The palace has rare, traditional Kerala flooring, which looks like polished black marble but is actually a mix of burned coconut shells, charcoal, lime, plant juices, and egg whites. ✉*Palace Rd., Mattancherry* ☎*No phone* *Rs. 2* ⊙*Sat.–Thurs. 10–5.*

NEED A BREAK?

A favorite hangout for artists and young tourists, Fort Cochin's Kashi Art Cafe (✉*Burgher St.* ☎*484/221-6769*) is about as funky as Kerala gets. The front room hosts rotating exhibitions, primarily of South Indian contemporary art, and light Continental fare and Western-style coffee is served in the garden café at the rear. The real treat is to experience this tiny little pocket of Kerala subculture.

10

❶ **St. Francis Church.** The Portuguese flag first appeared in Fort Cochin in 1500, and Vasco da Gama arrived in 1502. The following year, Afonso de Albuquerque came with half a dozen ships full of settlers—he built the fort, and five friars in the crowd built India's first European church, St. Francis, in 1510. Da Gama returned in 1524 as Portuguese viceroy of the Indies, died that same year, and was buried in this church. You can still visit his gravestone, but his remains were shipped back to Lisbon in 1538.

The church's history reflects the European struggle for colonial turf in India. It was a Catholic church until 1664, when it became a Dutch Reform church; it later became Anglican (1804–1947) and is now part

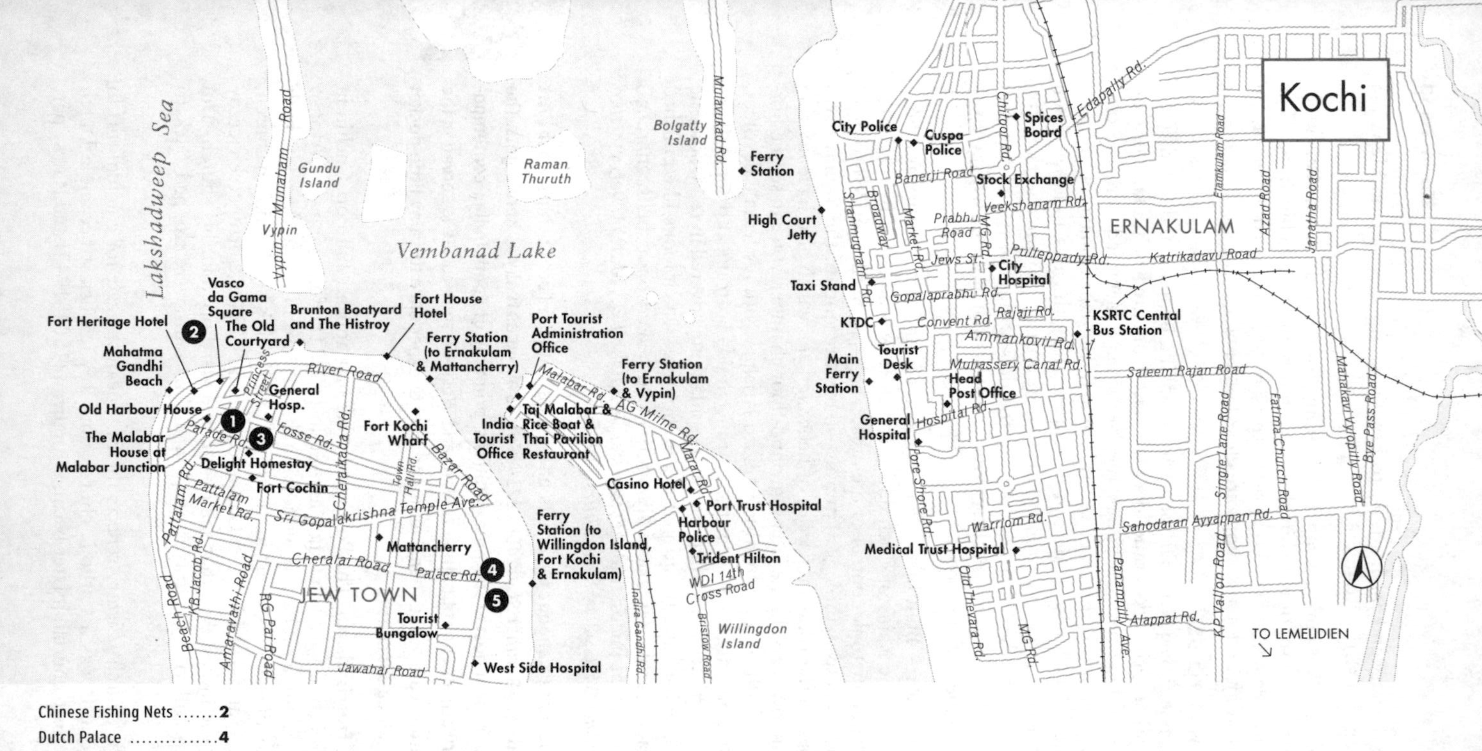

Chinese Fishing Nets 2
Dutch Palace 4
St. Francis Church 1
Santa Cruz Cathedral 3
Synagogue 5

of the Church of South India. Inside are beautifully engraved Dutch and Portuguese tombstones and the *doep boek,* a register of baptisms and marriages between 1751 and 1894 where you can view in photographic reproduction (the original is too fragile). ✉ *Church St., between Parade Rd. and Bastion St., Fort Cochin* ⏲ *Daily sunrise–sunset.*

3 **Santa Cruz Cathedral.** The interior of this cathedral is colorfully painted with scenes and decorations that some onlookers find gaudy, and others gorgeous. The cathedral's history dates from the 16th century, but the current structure was completed in 1904. ✉ *Parade and K. B. Jacob Rds., Fort Cochin* ⏲ *Daily sunrise–sunset.*

5 ★ **Synagogue.** The first migration of Jews to Kerala is thought to have taken place in the 6th century BC, followed by a much larger wave in the 1st century AD, when Jews fleeing Roman persecution in Jerusalem settled at Cranganore (on the coast about 26 km [16 mi] north of Kochi). In the 4th century, the local king promised the Jews perpetual protection, and the colony flourished, serving as a haven for Jews from the Middle East and, in later centuries, Europe. When the Portuguese leader Afonso de Albuquerque discovered the Jews near Cochin in the 16th century, however, he destroyed their community, having received permission from his king to "exterminate them one by one." Muslim anti-Semitism flared up as well. The Jews rebuilt in Mattancherry but were able to live without fear only after the less-belligerent Dutch took control in 1663.

This synagogue was built in 1568 and was considerably embellished in the mid-18th century by a wealthy trader, Ezekiel Rahabi. He had the clock tower built and the floor paved with 1,100 hand-painted, blue-and-white Chinese tiles—each one different. Like the facade, the interior is white with blue trim, embellished with hanging glass lamps from Belgium and a chandelier from Italy; look up at the ladies' gallery for an eye-pleasing row of colored lamps. Ask to see the 200-year-old Torah page, kept behind closed doors. The synagogue's most important relics—the impressive copper plates recording the 4th-century decree in which King Bhaskara Ravi Varma guaranteed the Jewish settlers domain over Cranganore—are no longer available for public viewing. You must remove your shoes before entering. ✉ *Synagogue La., Jew Town, Mattancherry* 🎫 *Rs. 2* ⏲ *Sun.–Fri. 10–noon and 3–5.*

OFF THE BEATEN PATH

Pepper Exchange. The New York Stock Exchange it's not, but the Pepper Exchange does allow a glimpse into the world of spice trading. Monitors in a small room display the going rate of pepper, and men sit by phones in cubicles that line the walls. When a bid comes in, the yelling and finger pointing starts. Then, just as suddenly, everyone goes back to reading the newspaper. You must obtain a visitor's pass from the secretary and remove your shoes before entering. The Pepper Exchange is between the Dutch Palace and the Synagogue. ✉ *Jew Town Rd., Mattancherry* ☎ *No phone* 🎫 *Free* ⏲ *Weekdays 9–4.*

WHERE TO EAT & STAY

As Kerala's premier city, Kochi offers the most options for dining out. Many top hotels open outdoor seafood grills in season (November to February), where you can pick from the day's catch and have it prepared as you like. Try *karimeen,* also known as the pearl spot, a bony but delicious fish found only in central Kerala, and keep an eye out for unusual Portuguese-influenced dishes. Lots of hotel restaurants feature live music, especially during peak season.

KOCHI BOAT TOURS

From Ernakulam's High Court or Sealord Jetty you can hire private boats, usually for about Rs. 500 an hour. The Kerala Tourism Development Corporation (KTDC) conducts two inexpensive boat tours of Kochi each day; the 3½-hour trips depart at 9 AM and 2 PM from the Sealord Jetty, opposite the Sealord Hotel, between the Main and High Court jetties.

Commercial Ernakulam hosts mainly business travelers, in addition to tourists. Accommodations on the islands are quieter and more scenic; friendly budget hotels and historic mansions are a specialty of Fort Cochin. Willingdon Island can feel a little deserted. However, the location is convenient, sandwiched as it is between Fort Cochin and the mainland Ernakulam district.

$$$ ★ ✕ **Rice Boat.** This perennial favorite of Kochi's well-to-do is shaped like a traditional wooden boat. Most tables overlook the waterfront. The menu focuses on seafood and Kerala specialties made with saltwater- and local freshwater fish grilled and cooked in traditional curries. Dishes also include imported seafood, including Norwegion salmon. The showpiece is an interactive kitchen where you can chat with the chef as he prepares your meal. ✉ *Taj Malabar Hotel, Malabar Rd., Willingdon Island* ☎ *484/266–6811* ▭ *AE, DC, MC, V* ⏲ *No lunch.*

$$–$$$ ★ ✕ **The History.** The intriguing, intensively researched menu draws on the myriad international influences on Kochi's history. Alongside traditional fare you'll find unusual dishes bearing the stamp of the Middle East, Portugal, the local Jewish community, or the days of the British Raj. The lofty, elegant dining room is windowed on all sides, and capped with a gabled wooden roof that's supported by massive wood beams—it looks like a ship has been overturned to form the ceiling. ✉ *Brunton Boatyard hotel, River Rd., Fort Cochin, 682001* ☎ *484/221–5461* ▭ *AE, DC, MC, V.*

$$ Fodor'sChoice ★ ✕ **Malabar Junction.** The mix of regional specialties and Mediterranean cuisine at this small, quirky restaurant with an open side facing a garden and swimming pool, isn't as crazy as it sounds—most dishes veer closer to one side or the other. A tasty red snapper fillet, for instance, is flavored with garlic and olives. If you're craving Western food, the pastas are excellent. Seafood is always fresh and perfectly cooked. Don't miss the chocolate-filled samosas in mango sauce, the restaurant's signature dessert. The restaurant has a large selection of Indian and foreign wines. ✉ *The Malabar House, 1/268–1/269 Parade Rd., Fort Cochin, 682001* ☎ *484/221–6666* ▭ *AE, MC, V.*

$ ★ ✕ **The Fort House.** Inside a budget hotel, this simple, open-air restaurant doesn't skimp on quality or authenticity. The menu is almost entirely seafood—chicken and specialty items (like lobster) must be ordered in advance. Every dish is cooked to order and presented in a clay vessel. The Prawns Kerala—fried—and the braised seerfish are terrific. If you agonize over oil, tell the chef in advance. ✉*2/6 A Calvathi Rd., Fort Cochin* ☎*484/221–7103 or 484/221–5221* ▭*MC, V.*

$ ✕ **The Springs.** The lunch buffet at the Avenue Regent's multicuisine restaurant is so popular that even visiting chefs pop in for a bite when they're in town. There's a variety of South Indian, North Indian, Mexican, Thai, Burmese, and Chinese specialties, but most people come for the hot, fresh, perfectly prepared appam—served with a mildly spicy coconut stew. ✉*Avenue Regent hotel, 39/206 M. G. Rd., Ernakulam* ☎*484/237–7977, 484/237–7688, or 484/237–7088.*

¢–$ ✕ **Pavilion.** In an out-of-the-way hotel south of Mattancherry, this plain-looking restaurant is a well-kept secret. Ignore the multicultural cuisine and go straight for a fish dish like the prawn curry or the *meen pollichathu,* spiced fish steamed in a banana leaf; it's so hot even Malayalees break a sweat. If you'd like it toned down, tell the chef beforehand. ✉*Hotel Abad, near intersection of Moulana Azad Rd. and Kochangadi Rd., Chullickal* ☎*484/222–8211* ▭*AE, DC, MC, V.*

¢ ✕ **Sree Krishna Inn.** Vegetarian meals and a pleasant, air-conditioned dining room draw in the business crowd to this handsome tile-roof building just off M. G. Road. The restaurant serves North and South Indian and Chinese dishes and snacks, as well as a large selection of ice creams. ✉*Warriam Rd., Ernakulam* ☎*484/236–6664* ▭*V.*

$$$$ Fodor'sChoice ★ **Brunton Boatyard.** Built in a combination of Dutch and Portuguese colonial styles, this elegant hotel is on the site of a former boatyard, facing the harbor's Chinese fishing nets. *Pankhas* (manually operated wooden fans) dangle from the open-air lobby's lofty ceiling. A gracefully bowing tree shades the grassy courtyard, which is surrounded by whitewashed arcades lined with terra-cotta tile. In the guest rooms, the four-poster beds are so high you need a footstool to climb in; the fixtures and furnishings are all antique in style, right down to the light switches. Most rooms have balconies from which to watch ships glide past in the harbor. **Pros:** all rooms and bathrooms are sea-facing, swanky hotel bar is one of the few in Kochi stocked with foreign liquor, great restaurants. **Cons:** pricey, doesn't offer no-smoking rooms. ✉*Calvetty Rd., Fort Cochin, 682001* ☎*484/221–5461* 🌐*www.cghearth.com* *26 rooms, 4 suites* *In-room: safe, refrigerator, Wi-Fi. In-hotel: restaurant, room service, bar, pool, no elevator, laundry service.* ▭*AE, DC, MC, V* *BP.*

$$$$ ★ **Le Meridien.** On 25 landscaped acres on the outskirts of Ernakulam, this imposing, green-tile-roofed complex houses a massive hotel and South India's largest convention center. The enormous marble lobby is appointed with wooden sculptures, a vintage Ford car, and a massive traditional lamp. A new 72-room tower, which opened in 2006, can only be accessed by motorboat. Rooms are spacious, with light-wood floors and modern furnishings, including LCD TVs. Views from deluxe rooms are often gorgeous, with manicured lawns in the foreground and

beyond to the tiered pool and the Chinese fishing nets. **Pros:** world-class amenities, plenty of entertainment options, including one of Kerala's few nightclubs. **Cons:** very expensive, several kilometers from anything worth seeing, tasteful decor lacks local flavor. ✉ *Kundannur Junction, NH–47 Bypass, Maradu, 682304* ☎ *484/270–5777* 🌐 *www.lemeridien.com/cochin* *223 rooms* *In-hotel: 4 restaurants, room service, bars, pool, gym, laundry service, no-smoking rooms.* 💳 *AE, DC, MC, V.*

$$$$ ★ **The Malabar House.** Luxurious but homey, this early-18th-century villa once housed European traders and bankers. A dramatic swimming pool, garnished with fallen frangipani, sits in the courtyard garden. Rooms are a mixture of regional-traditional and contemporary furnishings: yellow-and-red walls are offset by antique wooden furnishings. Somehow, the curious combinations of elements work. **Pros:** restaurant might be Kochi's best, deluxe rooms open into private garden. **Cons:** pricey, some standard rooms feel cramped. ✉ *1/268–1/269 Parade Rd., Fort Cochin 682001* ☎ *484/221–6666* 🌐 *www.malabarhouse.com* *11 rooms, 6 suites* *In-room: safe, refrigerator (some), Wi-Fi. In-hotel: restaurant, pool, no elevator, laundry service.* 💳 *AE, MC, V* *BP.*

$$$$ Fodor's Choice ★ **Taj Malabar.** Isolated at the tip of Willingdon Island, this grand hotel offers a heritage sensibility and style, and absolute luxury. The lobby has a stunning carved-wood ceiling and a similarly styled bar with a harbor view. The Heritage Wing dates to 1935, and its rooms are appointed with wood floors and Kerala-style furnishings. The newer Tower Wing reflects a similar style, with the addition of large, windowed bathrooms, so you can shower with a sea view. The top-notch ayurvedic spa is worth a visit. **Pros:** unmatched water views, spacious rooms, fantastic restaurants. **Cons:** isolated on an island where there's little to do, not cheap. ✉ *Malabar Rd., Willingdon Island, 682009* ☎ *484/266–6811* 🌐 *www.tajhotels.com* *87 rooms, 9 suites* *In-room: safe, refrigerator, Wi-Fi. In-hotel: 3 restaurants, room service, bar, pool, gym, laundry service.* 💳 *AE, DC, MC, V.*

$$$ ★ **Old Harbour Hotel.** Just opposite the Chinese fishing nets, this 300-year-old Dutch mansion, which opened in December 2006 after a two-year restoration, is a standout in Fort Cochin's ever-expanding field of boutique heritage hotels. Every brightly colored room is tastefully decorated with antique fixtures and contemporary Indian artwork, and most are spacious and filled with natural light. They also have views of either the fishing nets or a walled garden, where guests can dip in the elevated pool or read under a canopy of tall trees. The three cottages—beautifully designed with open-air showers bounded on one side by the garden's original Portuguese wall—are on the small side. Edgar, the proprietor, is brimming with tips about local sights, restaurants, and the history of the building and his hometown. **Pros:** restaurant serves very good Kerala delicacies, the nice-size standard rooms are a good value. **Cons:** still working out the kinks. ✉ *Tower Rd., 682001* ☎ *484/221–8006 or 484/221–8007* 🌐 *www.oldharbourhotel.com* *13 rooms, 3 cottages* *In-room: no phone, no TV, Wi-Fi. In-hotel: restaurant, pool, no elevator, airport shuttle.* 💳 *MC, V* *BP.*

$$$ Taj Residency. Standard rooms in this beautifully maintained downtown hotel are on the small side, and their bathrooms have showers rather than tubs. Opt for one of the large, sea-facing rooms, which have spectacular views. The North Indian restaurant features classical music performances every night. **Pros:** nice pool, rooms upgraded with new furniture and flooring at the end of 2006. **Cons:** basic, lacks Kerala charm, smallish rooms. ✉*Marine Dr., Ernakulam, 682011* ☎*484/237–1471* 🌐*www.tajhotels.com* *96 rooms, 12 suites* *In-room: safe, refrigerator, Wi-Fi. In-hotel: restaurant, room service, bar, laundry service, public Wi-Fi.* *AE, DC, MC, V* *CP.*

$$$ Trident Hilton. This tasteful and stylish hotel is outfitted for both business and leisure travelers. The low-rise, tile-roof building wraps around a central courtyard, so hallways are full of natural light. In the rooms, which face the pool or the garden, sand-color wood floors complement cream and teal color schemes. The staff is pleasant and helpful. **Pros:** bar, which overlooks the pool, stocks international liquor. **Cons:** Willingdon Island location is not ideal for sightseeing. ✉*Bristow Rd., Willingdon Island, 682003* ☎*484/266–9595* 🌐*www.trident-hilton.com* *76 rooms, 9 suites* *In-room: safe, DVD (some). In-hotel: restaurant, room service, bar, pool, gym, laundry service, public Wi-Fi.* *AE, DC, MC, V.*

$$ Casino Hotel. This modern hotel has rustic touches like coir carpeting in the hallways and tiny earthenware pots for bathroom amenities. Spacious, wood-floored rooms on the first floor have elegant interiors, with black marble bathrooms and wood-and-cane furniture; carpeted rooms on the third floor are not as well maintained, but have the best views of the leafy courtyard and swimming pool. The outdoor seafood restaurant, Fort Cochin, is immensely popular with locals. There's no menu: the day's catch is merely wheeled before you in a wooden cart, and your choice is cooked to order, whether you prefer it simply grilled or exquisitely spiced. Make sure you reserve a spot in advance to eat here. **Pros:** a relative bargain, quiet location, great restaurant. **Cons:** a bit far from the sites in Fort Cochin, location is a bit drab, no spa. ✉*K. P. K. Menon Rd., Willingdon Island, 682003* ☎*484/266–8221 or 484/266–8421* 🌐*www.cghearth.com* *66 rooms, 1 suite* *In-room: Wi-Fi. In-hotel: 2 restaurants, room service, bar, pool, laundry service.* *AE, DC, MC, V* *CP.*

10

$ Abad Atrium This impressively modern Western-style hotel is set back from M. G. Road, shielded from traffic noise by its sister establishment Abad Plaza. Abad Atrium caters mostly to business travelers, but in season it's popular with Indian tourists seeking luxury and value. Glass elevators shoot up and down the central atrium. Rooms are large, mostly carpeted, with high ceilings and full amenities. **Pros:** good value, rooftop swimming pool. **Cons:** smallish bathrooms, many rooms have views of a construction site. ✉*M. G. Rd., Ernakulam, 682035* ☎*484/238–1122 or 484/238–4380* 🌐*www.abadhotels.com* *48 rooms, 4 suites* *In-room: refrigerator, Wi-Fi. In-hotel: 3 restaurants, room service, pool, gym, laundry service.* *AE, DC, MC, V* *BP.*

$ **The Avenue Regent.** The spiffy marble lobby of this high-rise business hotel has art deco red bands around the ceiling molding and in the floor pattern. The rooms, which have wood flooring, are spacious and contemporary. Request a back-facing room for relative peace and quiet. **Pros:** good spot for shopping, clean, spacious rooms, in-room Internet access. **Cons:** noisy location, basic lobby lacks character, no room safes. ✉ *39/2026 M. G. Rd., Ernakulam, 682016* ☎ *484/237–7977, 484/237–7688* 📠 *484/237–5329* *49 rooms, 4 suites* *In-room: ethernet, Wi-Fi. In-hotel: 2 restaurants, bar, gym, laundry service, public Wi-Fi, no-smoking rooms.* 💳 *AE, DC, MC, V* *BP.*

$ **Fort Heritage.** Each room in this restored 17th-century Dutch mansion is slightly different from the next, though all are enormous and have towering wooden ceilings and period reproduction furniture. Upstairs rooms surround a common area with a giant wooden swing; a couple have balconies overlooking a courtyard. **Pros:** great location, good price, friendly atmosphere. **Cons:** ground-floor rooms open directly into the restaurant, no Internet access, no swimming pool. ✉ *1/283 Napier St., Fort Cochin, 682001* ☎📠 *484/221–5333 or 484/221–5455* 🌐 *www.fortheritage.com* *9 rooms, 3 suites* *In-room: safe, refrigerator. In-hotel: restaurant, room service, no elevator, laundry service.* 💳 *MC, V* *BP.*

$ **The Old Courtyard.** Slightly decrepit but still charming, this late-18th-century refurbished mansion in the heart of Fort Cochin has eight rooms overlooking a central courtyard. Suites are enormous, with wood floors and ceilings, antique furnishings, and tub baths. Some rooms have air-conditioning, others fans. **Pros:** restaurant menu has both Continental and Kerala options, great location, friendly staff. **Cons:** a little worn around the edges, basic accommodations without phones or Internet. ✉ *1/371 Princess St., Fort Cochin, 682001* ☎ *484/221–6302 or 484/221–5035* 🌐 *www.oldcourtyard.com* *6 rooms, 2 suites* *In-room: no a/c (some), no TV (some). In-hotel: restaurant, no elevator, laundry service.* 💳 *MC, V* *CP.*

¢ ★ **Delight.** This spotless homestay is wildly popular with budget travelers, in no small part because of the warm, knowledgeable, and extraordinarily helpful hosts who can arrange for great English-speaking taxi- and auto drivers. Their home, a centuries-old Portuguese mansion, is tucked away in a quiet corner of Fort Cochin. Guest rooms, in a newer wing of the house, are very large, clean, and simply furnished with ceiling fans. Be sure to reserve in advance. **Pros:** quiet location across from cricket field and a short walk from the Chinese Nets, great value. **Cons:** showers aren't separate so bathroom gets wet, limited number of rooms with a/c. ✉ *Parade Ground, Post Office Rd., Fort Cochin, 682001* ☎📠 *484/221–7658* 🌐 *www.delightfulhomestay.com* *7 rooms* *In room: no a/c (some), no phone, no TV. In-hotel: no elevator, laundry service, public Internet, airport shuttle.* 💳 *V* *CP.*

¢ **Raintree Lodge.** At the quiet end of busy Petercelle Street, this simply furnished hotel inside a 1700s Dutch building has earned raves for its reasonable rates and good-looking rooms, furnished with two-poster beds and other characterful wood furniture. All rooms have balconies, and there's an open-air terrace on the roof with pleasant views of the town around you. Although the Raintree has little else in the way of frills (you have to go down the road for a meal, for instance), the warmth of the owner and his staff keeps travelers happy and ready to return. Be sure to book ahead in high season. **Pros:** great location, atmospheric rooms. **Cons:** expensive for the limited facilities available, no restaurant. ✉ *1/618, Petercelli St., 682001* ☎ *484/395–1489* 🌐 *www.fortcochin.com* *5 rooms* *In-room: no phone, no TV. In-hotel: laundry service, no elevator.* *No credit cards.*

BEYOND KATHAKALI

Although Kathakali is by far the best known dance, some 50 other classical, folk, and tribal dances survive in Kerala. Many are unique to a particular caste or temple. The graceful, swaying movements of Mohiniyattam, a dance that lies somewhere between Kathakali and classical Bharata Natyam, are thought to mimic the movement of coconut palms.

THE ARTS

ART GALLERY

The former home of the Parishith Thampuran Museum now houses the **Kerala Lalita Kala Akademi Gallery** (✉ *D.H. Rd., Ernakulam* ☎ *484/236–7748* *Free* *Mon.–Sat. 11–6*). There's not much here by way of explanation, but the traditional tile-roof building is cool and airy, and the interesting collection features contemporary works by Indian artists.

DANCE

Dating back to the 17th century, Kathakali is an art form in which elaborately made-up and costumed dancers tell epic stories using stylized hand gestures. For centuries, Kathakali performances were the only after-dark entertainment in Kerala; shows began at sundown and lasted all night. Today, for the benefit of tourists, performances are often shortened to one or two hours. Many centers also offer the chance to watch dancers being made up, which can be as entertaining as the show.

Kathakali performances in the air-conditioned room of the **Cochin Cultural Centre** (✉ *K.B. Jacob Rd., Fort Cochin, near police station* ☎ *484/221–6911*) start at 6:30 PM, though you should arrive an hour before the show to see makeup being applied. Revered arts academy **Kerala Kalamandalam** (✉ *Cheruthuruthy, 29 km [18 mi] north of Trichur* ☎ *488/426–2418*) is credited with the revival of traditional arts in Kerala, providing training in Kathakali, Mohiniattam, and other native art forms. All-night Kathakali performances are staged here a few nights each year, and you're welcome to watch students in practice sessions that are held weekdays from 8:30 to noon and 3:30 to 5:30. **Kerala Kathakali Centre** (✉ *River Rd., near the bus stand, opposite Brunton Boatyard, Fort Cochin* ☎ *484/221–5827* 🌐 *www.kathakalicentre.com*) is a pleasant outdoor venue. Makeup starts at 5 PM and shows at 6:30 PM daily. Short-term courses in dance and music are offered here. At the **See India Foundation** (✉ *Kalthil Parambil La., Ernakulam* ☎ *484/237–6471*), the director provides lively explanations of the dance before every 6:45 PM show. Makeup starts at 6 PM.

MARTIAL ARTS

Kerala's dramatic, high-flying martial art, Kalarippayattu, may be the oldest in Asia. Some think it started in the 12th century, others think it began earlier, and still others say later. Some scholars believe that Buddhist monks from India introduced Kalarippayattu to China along with Buddhism. Participants learn both armed- and unarmed-combat techniques. One of the more unusual skills involves defending yourself against a knife-wielding attacker using only a piece of cloth. In peak season, many hotels stage performances. If you call in advance, ★ you can watch Kalarippayattu practitioners at the **E.N.S. Kalari Centre** (✉ *Nettoor neighborhood, Ernakulam* ☎ *484/270–0810*).

SHOPPING

The streets surrounding the synagogue in Mattancherry are crammed with stores that sell curios, and Fort Cochin's Princess Street has sprouted several small shops worth a browse. For saris, jewelry, handicrafts, and souvenirs, head to M.G. Road in Ernakulam. Be suspicious of the word "antique" in all stores, and bargain hard.

Cinnamon (✉ *1/658 Ridsdale Rd., Parade Ground, Fort Cochin* ☎ *484/221–7124 or 484/221–8124*) is a branch of the chic Bangalore boutique, and stocks stylish ethnic and modern housewares, silk scarves and purses, jewelry, and Indo-Western designer clothing. Cochin's upscale ladies buy the latest designer fineries at the pricey boutique **Glada** (✉ *Convent Rd., Ernakulam* ☎ *484/236–4952*). **Jayalakshmi** (✉ *M.G. Rd., near Rajaji Rd., Ernakulam* ☎ *484/408–9899*) houses a mind-blowing selection of saris, *lehangas* (long skirts with fitted blouses), and the like as well Indian and Western clothes for men and children.

KERALA CRAFTS

Look for cups, vases, spoons, and teapots carved from coconut shells and baskets, floor and table mats, and carpets handwoven from coir, coconut fiber, and sleeping mats and handbags made of resilient, pliable kova grass. Other goods include brass lamps, rosewood elephants, and lacquered wooden boxes with brass fittings—traditionally used to store the family jewels—and metal mirrors from Aranmula, northeast of Trivandrum. Cinnamon, cloves, cardamon, and other spices are also sold throughout Kerala.

The **Cochin Gallery** (✉ *6/116 Jew Town Rd., Mattancherry* ☎ *484/222–1225 or 484/221–0851*) carries jewelry, carpets, cushion covers, bronze figurines, and wooden boxes. Local hotels often get their antiques from **Crafter's** (✉ *6/141 Jew Town Rd., Mattancherry* ☎ *484/222–7652*). It's crammed with stone and wood carvings, pillars, and doors as well as such portable items as painted tiles, navigational equipment, and wooden boxes. **Fort Royal** (✉ *1/258 Napier St., Fort Cochin* ☎ *484/221–*

7832) is an expensive all-in-one shop with goods from all over India. You can find brocade work, marble inlay boxes, and Kashmiri carpets, plus local handicrafts and precious and semiprecious jewelry. **Indian Arts and Curios** (✉ *6/189 Jew Town Rd., Mattancherry* ☎ *484/222–8049*) is one of Kerala's oldest and most-reliable curio shops. **Kairali** (✉ *M. G. Rd., near Jose Junction, Ernakulam* ☎ *484/235–4507*) is a fixed-price government shop with a good selection of local handicrafts and curios. **Surabhi** (✉ *M. G. Rd., Ernakulam* ☎ *484/238–0144*) is run by the state's Handicrafts Cooperative Society. It has an impressive selection of local products.

Whether you're looking for a little information on Kerala or a little something to while away the hours, stop by **Idiom Books** (✉ *Jew Town Rd., Mattancherry* ☎ *484/222–5604* ✉ *1/348 Bastion St., near Princess St., Fort Cochin*), a small bookshop opposite the synagogue, or its branch in Fort Cochin. You can find an intriguing collection of recent Western and Indian fiction, as well as books on history, culture, cooking, and religion.

CENTRAL KERALA

Between Kochi and Quilon (Kollam), to the south, is the immense labyrinth of waterways called *kayals,* through which much of the life of the Malayalee has historically flowed. From the vastness of Vembanad Lake to quiet streams just large enough for a canoe, the backwaters have carried Kerala's largely coconut-based products from the village to the market for centuries, and continue to do so today. You can relax at some of Kerala's finest resorts, or briefly join the floating lifestyle by taking a boat cruise.

The terrain rises and the temperature drops as you move inland, up into the teak-forested hills of Thekkady and Munnar. Kerala's interior is elephant country—you'll find them roaming in Lake Periyar Wildlife Sanctuary and even appearing in the mists of Munnar's tea plantations.

KUMARAKOM

80 km (50 mi) south of Kochi.

Some of Kerala's finest resorts are hidden in this tiny, rapidly developing paradise on the shores of Vembanad Lake. Novelist Arundhati Roy's birthplace, Ayemenem (featured in her 1997 novel *The God of Small Things)* is close by. Birds abound in the backwaters, as well as in the sanctuary on the lake's eastern shore.

WHERE TO EAT & STAY

$ ✕**Lakshmi Hotel.** If you want a change of pace from your resort's dining room, the restaurant of this locally owned hotel offers reliable local fare along with North Indian specialties. Service is leisurely, but the food is freshly prepared and the air-conditioned dining room is clean and comfortable. The restaurant is known for its Karimeen fish wrapped

ON THE BACKWATERS

A **houseboat cruise** provides a window into traditional local life. Shaded by a woven bamboo canopy and fanned by cool breezes, you can drift past simple, tile-roof houses with canoes moored outside; tiny waterfront churches; and people washing themselves, their clothes, their dishes, and their children in the river. Women in bright pink and blue dresses stroll past green paddy fields, their waist-length hair unbound and smelling of coconut oil. Graceful palms are everywhere, as are village walls painted with political slogans and ads for computer training courses. Backwater trips can be designed to suit any time constraint or budget. Motorized or punted canoes squeeze into narrow canals, taking you to dreamy roadless villages, and big ferries ply the eight-hour Quilon–Alleppey route as if it were a major highway. Romantic houseboats give you the opportunity to stay overnight on the water; there's even an Oberoi luxury cruise ship offering every imaginable comfort. Any travel agent, hotel, or the Kerala Tourism Development Corporation (KTDC) (☎484/235–3234 🌐www.ktdc.com), can help you hire a private boat or plan a trip. Most cruises depart from Quilon, Alleppey, or Kumarakom. In addition, the Trident Hilton in Kochi can book you a stateroom on the *MV Vrinda*, an eight-bedroom luxury cruise ship.

in a banana leaf and its traditional vegetable thali, which includes 10 items for Rs. 60. ✉*Kottayam-Kumarakom Rd., Kumarakom North* ☎*481/252–3313* ▭*MC, V.*

$$$$ ★ **Coconut Lagoon.** This ground-breaking and much-imitated Vembanad Lake resort put Kerala's backwaters on the map. It's accessible only by boat, from one of two pick-up points along an adjoining river. The grounds are crisscrossed with canals and footbridges and dotted with white bungalows and two-story mansions that are a mixture of rustic and modern; the newer villa accommodations have their own plunge pools, and the open-air restaurant is reassembled from parts of an approximately 300-year-old Kerala home. The ayurvedic center is excellent, and the property also has its own *kalari*, a school for martial arts. Book well in advance. **Pros:** good restaurants, kid-friendly, staff naturalists can take guests on a tour of the local bird sanctuary and the hotel's small butterfly garden. **Cons:** the pricey two-story mansions have bathroom and bedrooms on different floors (opt for the one-level bungalow), can only be accessed by boat. ✉*Vembanad Lake, Kumarakom, 686563* ☎*481/252–4491* 🌐*www.cghearth.com* *42 rooms, 8 suites* *In-room: safe, no TV. In-hotel: 2 restaurants, pool, no elevator, children's programs (ages 8–15), laundry service.* ▭*AE, DC, MC, V* *MAP.*

$$$$ Fodor's Choice ★ **Kumarakom Lake Resort.** In the heritage section of this beautiful 25-acre lakefront property, palatial traditional villas, reassembled from old houses, are set around a network of canals. Each villa is outfitted with ornately carved wooden ceilings, colorful mural paintings and enormous garden bathrooms. The meandering pool villas are a modern take on the backwater lifestyle; you can step from your room directly into the curving, amoeba-like swimming pool. You can also relax by a

separate lakefront infinity pool, designed so the far edge seems to merge with the body of water on the horizon, or in the spacious ayurvedic center. **Pros:** amazing 250-meter (820-foot) meandering pool, gorgeous setting, large and varied buffet. **Cons:** pricey. ✉*Kumarakom North P.O., Kumarakom, 686563* ☎*481/252–4900* 🌐*www.klresort.com* *49 rooms, 2 suites* *In-room: safe, Wi-Fi. In-hotel: 2 restaurants, room service, bars, pools, gym, no elevator, laundry service.* *AE, MC, V* *BP.*

$$$$ **Taj Garden Retreat.** The main building of this tranquil, verdant resort is an 1891 plantation house, built by the son of an English missionary. Its large rooms open onto broad verandas, and overlook a small lagoon where you can canoe or pedal-boat. Guest quarters are in the main house, in freestanding cottages, or in stationary houseboats. The terrace is a lovely place to relax with a glass of lime juice. Vembanad Lake is a short boat ride away down a woodsy canal. Twelve of the cottages are new (2004) and have views of the lake. **Pros:** trees are populated by winged residents of the nearby bird sanctuary, nice pool-facing gym, plenty of activities for children. **Cons:** not as carefully maintained as other Taj properties—the central lake, for example, has a stagnant green tinge. ✉*Kumarakom, 686563* ☎*481/252–4377* 🌐*www.tajhotels.com* *28 rooms* *In-room: safe (some), Wi-Fi. In-hotel: restaurant, bar, pool, no elevator, laundry service.* *AE, DC, MC, V.*

$$$$ ★ **Radisson Plaza Resort and Spa.** The four-headed statue of a Kathakali dancer in the gleaming lobby, the boat-shaped check-in desk and the backwater setting all locate the property soundly in Kerala. But guests checked into this luxurious resort, which opened in 2006, can easily forget where they are as they indulge in the decidedly untraditional couple's massage or relax with a Havana stogie in the cigar bar. Cream-colored bungalows surround a man-made lake. The clean and modern rooms are fitted with fluffy, comfortable beds and quilts. **Pros:** enormous modern spa has both ayurvedic and Western treatments. **Cons:** room and massage rates among the highest in South India, look elsewhere if you want a Kerala experience. ✉*Karottukayal, Kumarokom, 686563* ☎*481/252–7272* 🌐*www.radisson.com/kumarakomin* *72 rooms* *In-room: safe, ethernet, Wi-Fi. In-hotel: 2 restaurants, room service, bar, pool, gym, spa, bicycles, concierge* *AE, MC, V* *BP.*

ALLEPPEY

35 km (22 mi) southwest of Kumarakom.

This coir-manufacturing city was once known as the Venice of India, though most residents have abandoned their canoes for cars. Alleppey (Alappuzha) is an important gateway to the backwaters—tour operators abound, and several resorts here are good alternatives to the pricier properties in Kumarakom.

On the second Saturday in August, throngs of supporters line the shore to watch the annual Nehru Cup Snake Boat Race, which starts with a water procession and concludes dramatically as the boats (propelled by as many as 100 rowers) vie for the trophy. Several snake-boat races take place in the area from mid-July to mid-September. Check with the Alleppey Tourism Development Cooperative (ATDC) for exact times and locations.

WHERE TO STAY

$$$ ★ **Marari Beach.** With a palm-fringed beach, an excellent ayurvedic center, and easy access to both Kochi and the backwaters, Marari packs a lot of Kerala into one bundle. Nestled between two fishing villages 17 km (10 mi) north of Alleppey, the 30-acre resort combines a warm, rustic feel with modern comforts. Brick paths lead through rows of deceptively modest thatch-roof cottages that are both extremely spacious and comfortable, with open-air bathrooms. Private gardens and side entrances add an air of seclusion. The main restaurant features live music. **Pros:** spacious rooms, friendly and professional staff, tennis courts. **Cons:** no TVs, pricey. ✉ *Mararikulam, 688549* ☎ *478/286–3801* 🌐 *www.cghearth.com* *59 rooms, 3 suites* *In room: no TV. In-hotel: restaurant, bars, tennis courts, pool, beachfront, bicycles, no elevator, laundry service, no-smoking rooms.* ▭ *AE, DC, MC, V* *BP.*

$$–$$$ **Punnamada Backwater Resort.** Small design details make this typical backwater resort sparkle. The traditional tile-roof buildings have ornate wooden carvings on the facades. Rooms have high ceilings, exposed wooden rafters, and decoratively tiled floors. Furnishings are done in antique style, including canopied beds and planter's chairs. The garden bathrooms are spacious. Four lakeview rooms with private patios are just steps from the water. **Pros:** beautiful lake views, relatively good value, major upgrade underway in late 2007 to add a spa and coffee shop. **Cons:** secluded location may be too quiet for some, no Internet in rooms. ✉ *Punnamada Jetty Rd., Alleppey, 688006* ☎ *477/223–3690 or 477/223–3692* 🌐 *www.punnamada.com* *25 rooms* *In-hotel: 2 restaurants, bar, pool, laundry service.* ▭ *MC, V* *BP.*

$$ **Kayaloram Heritage Lake Resort.** A common veranda surrounds each of the four buildings in this pleasant, small-scale heritage resort. Old wooden doors lead to the modestly furnished rooms which were renovated in 2006 to include better furniture and an additional window. All rooms have baths with open-air showers, and five have lake views. Food at the simple restaurant is freshly made to order. The property is just steps from the waterfront; boats pick you up in Alleppey. **Pros:** quiet, intimate environment. **Cons:** no TV, a/c is only at night. ✉ *Punnamada, Alleppey, 688011* ☎ *477/2232040 or 477/2231572* 🌐 *www.kayaloram.com* *12 rooms* *In-room: safe, no TV, Wi-Fi. In-hotel: restaurant, pool, no elevator, laundry service, some pets allowed.* ▭ *AE, DC, MC, V* *BP.*

¢–$ **Keraleeyam.** This quaint waterfront property specializes in ayurvedic treatments. Rooms in the heritage main building have air-conditioning but few windows; go for a simple thatched-roof non-air-conditioned cottage with a waterfront sit-out and watch the boats slip by from dawn to dusk. **Pros:** inexpensive, pretty location. **Cons:** very basic, spotty service, no television or Internet. ✉ *Thathampally, Alleppey, 688006* ☎ *477/223–1468 or 477/223–6950* 🌐 *www.keraleeyam.com* *14 rooms* *In-room: no a/c (some), no TV. In-hotel: restaurant, no elevator.* ▭ *MC, V* *BP.*

¢ **Palm Grove Lake Resort.** Simplicity rules the day at this coconut plantation hideaway near the starting point of the Nehru Cup Snake Boat Race. It consists of just four cottages, made entirely of bamboo—walls, ceilings, doors, and windows. Furnishings are basic but comfortable; bathrooms are attached to the room but have a partially open roof. The charm here is in the hammocks, the home-cooked food, the friendly staff, and the idyllic setting. Plans were underway to open two large, high-end rooms by the end of 2007; those rooms will have televisions, air-conditioning, refrigerators, intercoms, and luggage space, all for about Rs. 2,500. **Pros:** large, clean rooms. **Cons:** no a/c. ✉*Punnamada, Alleppey, 68006* ☎*477/223–5004 or 477/224–3474* 🖷*477/225–1138* *4 cottages* *In-room: no a/c, no TV. In-hotel: restaurant, no elevator, laundry service.* ▭*AE, MC, V.*

QUILON

71 km (44 mi) north of Trivandrum, 87 km (54 mi) south of Alleppey.

If you're coming up from Trivandrum, central Kerala starts here, with the peaceful waters of eight-armed Ashtamudi Lake. You can catch a ferry from Quilon (Kollam) in the morning and reach Alleppey eight hours later. The waterfront here is not nearly as developed as Vembanad Lake, and the few resorts are utterly peaceful and reasonably priced.

WHERE TO STAY

$$$ **Aquaserene.** The gorgeous lakeside setting will quickly help you forget the bumpy ride that got you here, on a barely paved road through a fishing village. Rooms are in individual heritage-style cottages, with semi-outdoor bathrooms and modern furnishing. Highlights here include a dip in the pool, within a lagoon, and the soaring wooden reception building. **Pros:** room rates typically include an early-morning fishing trip, guided village cycling tours, and a half-hour boat ride; many amentities for youngsters, including volleyball, table tennis and a children's park. **Cons:** a bit remote, pricey. ✉*South Paravoor, Quilon, 691391* ☎*474/251–2410 to 17* 🌐*www.aquasereneindia.com* *27 rooms, 1 suite* *In-hotel: restaurant, pool, no elevator, laundry service.* ▭*MC, V.*

$$ **Club Mahindra Backwater Retreat.** Ayurveda is the focus of this soothing resort on the shores of Ashtamudi Lake. Even without undergoing treatment, you can expect to find peace here, where Chinese fishing nets flicker like a mirage in the morning mists that rise off the silvery lake. Manicured lawns and well-kept hedges on the grounds are brightened by splashes of bougainvilla. A series of two-story white chalets lines the waterfront. Rooms are spacious and equipped with LCD televisions and DVD players, coffeemakers, and cane furniture; each has a balcony with a lake view. Home-style food in the open-air restaurant is made to order. After taking over the resort, Club Mahindra completely remodeled it in 2007 with hopes getting a five-star designation from the government. Because Mahindra club members have first dibs on

rooms, reserve at least 15 days in advance. **Pros:** plenty of activities for children, including clay modeling and video games. **Cons:** no gym, no bar. ✉ *Chavara South, Quilon, 691584* ☎ *476/288–2357, 476/288–2655, or 476/288–2310* 🌐 *www.clubmahindra.com* *22 rooms, 3 suites* *In-room: DVD. In-hotel: restaurant, room service, laundry service.* *MC, V* *BP.*

THEKKADY

130 km (81 mi) east of Kumarakom.

Due east of Kumarakom and Kottayam, this cool mountain town sits at 3,000 feet above sea level in the Cardamom Hills, midway between Kochi and the temple city of Madurai in Tamil Nadu. **■ TIP→ You don't need a room with air-conditioning here.**

★ Thekkady is the population center nearest the **Lake Periyar Wildlife Sanctuary,** one of India's best animal parks for spotting elephants, bison, wild boar, oxen, deer, and many species of birds. The best viewing period is October through May.

Lake Periyar, its many fingers winding around low-lying hills, is the heart of the 300-square-mi sanctuary. Forget exhausting treks or long safaris: here, you lounge in a motor launch as it drifts around bends and comes upon animals drinking at the shores. In dry season, when forest watering holes are empty, leopards and tigers also pad up to the water. A few words of advice: Indian children (and adults) love to scream and shout at wildlife sightings. On a quiet trip, elephants hardly notice the intrusion, although younger pachyderms will peer at you out of curiosity and then run squealing back to their elders when your boat comes too close. If you're brave-hearted, you can spend a night in a jungle lodge (if you go on a forest trek, look out for leeches on the ground, especially during the monsoon); if you're less adventurous you can commune with nature from the safety of a moated watchtower. Half-hour elephant rides are also available. For information about treks and the park, contact the Kerala Tourism Development Corporation (KTDC). ✉ *KTDC: Shanmugham Rd., Ernakulam, Kochi* ☎ *484/235–3234* 🌐 *www.ktdc.com* *Sanctuary Rs. 50, video-camera fee Rs. 100.*

WHERE TO STAY

$$$ **Hotel Lake Palace.** A ferry transports you to this former maharaja's hunting lodge on an island inside the Lake Periyar Wildlife Sanctuary. Six simple rooms, some with period furniture, look out through a palm-lined pathway and beyond to the lake and the preserve—you can spot animals from your balcony. Meals at the eclectic, fixed-menu restaurant are included. As the hotel is run by the state government, make reservations through the KTDC. **Pros:** the best lodge in Thekkady for watching wildlife. **Cons:** expensive, very basic accommodations. ✉ *Lake Periyar Wildlife Sanctuary, Thekkady, 685536* ☎ *486/232–2023* *KTDC, Shanmugham Rd., Ernakulam, Kochi, 682031* ☎ *484/235–3234* 🌐 *www.ktdc.com* *6 rooms* *In-room: no a/c,*

refrigerator. In-hotel: restaurant, room service, no elevator, laundry service, parking (fee). ▭*AE, DC, MC, V* 🍽*MAP.*

$$$ **Muthoot Cardamom County.** Views from this steeply pitched resort are gorgeous. The mid-size rooms are in individual or double whitewashed, red-tile-roof cottages with gabled ceilings. Each is has dark-wood furniture and terra-cotta floors. On the grounds there's a fishpond where you can catch your own dinner. **Pros:** great ayurvedic massage center with a well-trained doctor, large swimming pool. **Cons:** fills up with package tourists, can be noisy. ✉*Thekkady Rd., Thekkady, 685536* ☎*486/922–4501 to 03* 🌐*www.cardamomcounty.com* *42 rooms, 2 suites* *In-room: refrigerator. In-hotel: restaurant, pool, gym, bicycles, no elevator, laundry service.* ▭*AE, MC, V.*

$$$ ★ **Shalimar Spice Garden.** This rustic retreat is 20 bone-jarring minutes off the main road to Thekkady. Most guests come for ayurvedic treatment and yoga; the emphasis is on serenity and relaxation. A wooden bridge over a duck pond leads to the main building—a whitewashed, thatch-roof affair that houses a restaurant specializing in authentic Italian and Kerala food. The spotless white cottages are largely minimalist—perfectly executed—with only a colorful bedspread, a stained-glass window, or an ancient, dark-wood oar adding bits of contrast to each room. **Pros:** gorgeous setting, rooms include complimentary slippers and heaters. **Cons:** remote, rooms are somewhat small. ✉*Murikkady, 685535* ☎*486/922–2132 or 486/922–3232* 🌐*www.shalimarkerala.net* *10 rooms* *In-room: no TV. In-hotel: restaurant, pool, no elevator, laundry service, some pets allowed.* ▭*MC, V* 🍽*BP.*

$$$ **Spice Village.** Just outside the Lake Periyar Wildlife Sanctuary, this is Thekkady's finest resort. Its well-maintained thatch-roof cottages are built into a hillside. Lush plantings, including a spice garden, add fragrance and privacy. Interiors have knotty pine furnishings and trim, white walls, red-tile floors, and plaid upholstery and bedspreads. The restaurant serves Indian and Continental set meals. Jungle treks and Indian cooking classes are among the activities. **Pros:** plenty of activities, good location. **Cons:** expensive. ✉*Kummily Rd., Thekkady, 685536* ☎*486/922–2314 or 486/922–2315* 🌐*www.cghearth.com* *52 rooms* *In-room: no a/c, safe, no TV. In-hotel: 2 restaurants, bar, tennis court, pool, no elevator, laundry service.* ▭*AE, DC, MC, V* 🍽*BP.*

10

$$$ **Taj Garden Retreat.** On a former coffee plantation, this woodsy Taj property offers concrete cottages raised on stilts; balconies are nice touches, as is the thatch piled on the roofs. Rooms are modern and reliable—they're typically luxurious, as per the Taj standard. The restaurant serves excellent multicuisine food (Chinese, Continental, and regional Indian). **Pros:** good location and restaurant, cottages have private terraces. **Cons:** overpriced, no room service. ✉*Ambalambika Rd., Thekkady, 685536* ☎*486/922–2273, 486/922–2401 to 07* 🌐*www.tajhotels.com* *32 rooms* *In-room: no a/c, no phone, Wi-Fi. In-hotel: restaurant, bar, pool, bicycles, no elevator, laundry service.* ▭*AE, DC, MC, V.*

MUNNAR

100 km (62 mi) north of Thekkady, 130 km (80 mi) east of Kochi.

On the drive from Thekkady to Munnar, a good road winds through lofty forests as well as spice and tea plantations. The town of Munnar itself is small and unattractive. However, most of the land around it is owned by the Tata tea company and a few smaller concerns, resulting in a kind of unspoiled hill station, with hundreds of acres of tea, coffee, and cardamom plantations amid hills, lakes, streams, and waterfalls. During your visit you can tour these plantations; arrange trekking, rock-climbing, paragliding, and river trips; or just sit on your hotel balcony with a cup of tea, taking in the scenery.

Most lodgings can arrange a tea plantation tour, where you can walk through the steeply pitched, dense green hedges, and see how the leaf is processed. (Historically, the dregs of the batch get shipped to America, although this has been changing in recent years.) Cardamom plantations are just this side of heaven. The shade-loving spice needs plenty of forest cover, so a walk through a plantation feels like a stroll in the woods, complete with dappled sunlight, mountain streams, and birdsong. It's quite cool here, so you don't need to find a hotel with air-conditioning.

The **Rajamala National Park,** 15 km (9 mi) northwest of Munnar, is home to the endangered nilgiri tahr. You can get close to this endearingly tame mountain goat, pushed to the brink of extinction by its utter lack of suspicion toward human beings. Half the world's remaining population lives here. **■TIP→ The park is closed for 45 days during the calving season, roughly from January to February (check ahead of time).** ☎*4865/231–1587* *Rs. 200* *Daily 8–5.*

WHERE TO STAY

$$$ **Club Mahindra.** Set between a mountain peak and a tea plantation, this large, family-oriented resort has guest quarters in the main building or in hillside cottages. Rooms are spacious, with wood floors and furnishings; deluxe rooms also have entrancing views. Cottages are large—a one-bedroom can sleep four—yet still homey. The activity center offers everything from video games to rappelling, and the restaurant serves excellent North Indian food as well as other types of cuisine. **Pros:** clean, modern facilities, good value. **Cons:** no Internet in rooms, a bit noisy when tour groups roll in. ✉*Chinnakanal Village 22 km (14 mi) east of Munnar, 685618* ☎*486/824–9290* *www.clubmahindra.com* *103 rooms, 9 suites* *In-room: no a/c, refrigerator. In-hotel: restaurant, children's programs (all ages), laundry service.* *AE, DC, MC, V* *BP.*

$$$ **The Tall Trees.** You can hardly spot the wood-and-stone structures of this hushed, breezy resort on a 66-acre cardamom plantation. Getting around the hilly property is a workout—especially the hike to the skylight-topped restaurant—but the setting is phenomenal. The views are of trees, trees, trees. Standard double rooms are more pleasant than the narrow two-story deluxe rooms. Luxury cottages have spacious upstairs living rooms and balconies; spiral staircases lead to two bedrooms and bathrooms downstairs. Furnishings are of rustic cane and rubber wood. **Pros:** large rooms, hotel arranges lots of activities. **Cons:** tiring walk uphill to the restaurant, a lot to pay for relatively basic accommodations. *Box 40, Bison Valley Rd., Munnar, 685612 486/523–0641, 486/523–0593, or 486/523–2716 www.ttr.in 16 rooms, 3 suites In-room: no a/c, no TV. In-hotel: 2 restaurants, bicycles, no elevator, laundry service.* *MC, V MAP.*

$$–$$$ **Windermere Estate.** Plantation life can be pretty darn good, especially when you're not working in the fields and are instead made to feel like the guest of a planter. Guest quarters on this working cardamom, coffee, and vanilla plantation 5 km (2 mi) from Munnar are either in one of the five bedrooms of the main guesthouse, which has a communal balcony, or in an individual cottage. The hillside views are stunning, and the grounds are blessed with several streams and waterfalls, making for enchanting morning walks. **Pros:** service is warm and personalized. **Cons:** basic amenities, no bar. *Pothamedu Box 21, Munnar, 685612 486/523–0512, 484/242–5237 in Kochi for reservations www.windermeremunnar.com 15 rooms In-room: no a/c, no TV (some). In-hotel: bicycles, no elevator, laundry service.* *MC, V MAP.*

¢ **Siena Village.** Some of the rooms at this hotel capture the country-lodge feeling perfectly. Ignore the single-story standard rooms and opt for a split-level deluxe one. Their lower-level sitting areas have timber floors, comfy couches, and working fireplaces; balcony views are of the Anayirankal Dam (its name means "where the elephants come"). The semicircular restaurant also has panoramic vistas. **Pros:** outdoor buffet, musical performances, campfire during high season. **Cons:** basic rooms. *Chinnakanal 22 km (14 mi) east of Munnar, 685618 486/8249261 or 486/824–9461 www.thesienavillage.com 26 rooms, 2 suites In-room: no a/c. In-hotel: restaurant, room service, no elevator, children's programs (ages 6–12), laundry service, no-smoking rooms* *AE, DC, MC, V.*

LAKSHADWEEP

250 km (160 mi) off the coast of Kerala.

Of the 36 or so coral atolls that make up the isolated paradise of Lakshadweep, only about 10 are inhabited, and their population is devoutly Sunni Muslim. Tourism here is severely restricted to protect the fragile ecosystems and the traditional peoples. If you don't have an Indian passport, your visit will be limited to Agatti, Kadmat, or Bangaram Island, each of which has one resort property. (You need to obtain a government entry permit with passport details.)

Crystal waters and soft sands are Lakshadweep's main attraction; all resorts offer water sports, and there's even a scuba diving school on Kadmat Island.

Trips to Kadmat must be arranged through the **Society for the Promotion of Recreational Tourism and Sports** (*SPORTS Harbour Rd., Willingdon Island, Kochi 484/266–8387 or 484/266–8647 www.lakshadweep*

tourism.com). During the October-to-May tourist season, SPORTS offers packages involving overnight transport by ship from Kochi. One five-day package that takes tourists to three islands costs Rs. 4,000–Rs. 10,000 per person and includes room and board on the ship.

WHERE TO STAY

$$$$ ★ **Bangaram Island Resort.** This eco-friendly resort is Kerala's answer to the Maldives. The only people on this island are resort guests and staff. Construction is kept to a minimum—the restaurant is made entirely of bamboo and coconut leaves, allowing the white sands and turquoise water to steal the show. Accommodations are in simple, two- to four-bedroom, thatched cottages with terra-cotta floors and Western furnishings. Water sports, including kayaking, are the order of the day. Make reservations well in advance through the Casino Hotel in Kochi. **Pros:** quiet, exclusive beachfront. **Cons:** extremely expensive, no a/c. *Casino Hotel, K. P. K. Menon Rd., Willingdon Island, Kochi, 682003 ☎484/266–8221 www.cghearth.com 27 rooms, 3 suites In-room: no a/c, no TV. In-hotel: restaurant, bar, beachfront, diving, water sports, no elevator, laundry service. AE, DC, MC, V MAP.*

$$$ **Agatti Island Beach Resort.** A short drive from the airport, this modest resort offers a mid-range alternative (about half the price) to Bangaram Island. Rooms are in simply furnished, individual tile-roof cottages. Indulge in water sports or flop on a lounge chair beneath a thatch umbrella. Food and kayaking are included in the room rate. The hotel can arrange ship transportation during the season. **Pros:** a relative bargain. **Cons:** government does not permit liquor to be sold on the island. *✉Agatti Island ☎484/236–2232 19 rooms In-room: no a/c (some), no TV. In-hotel: restaurant, beachfront, diving, water sports, no elevator, laundry service. AE, MC, V MAP.*

SOUTHERN KERALA

The beaches near Kovalam are southern Kerala's main attraction—in fact, they're what brought Western tourists to the state in the first place, as the hippie scene from Goa moved down the coast. Parts of Kovalam are overdeveloped and full of touts selling cheap tie-dye clothes. There are, however, still some pleasant spots to relax within a few miles of the main beach. Just a half hour from Kovalam is Kerala's capital city of Trivandrum (Thiruvanandapuram), former home of the rajas of Travancore and now home to Kerala's primary international airport.

TRIVANDRUM

222 km (138 mi) south of Kochi, 253 km (157 mi) southwest of Thekkady.

Built on seven low hills and cleansed by ocean breezes, Kerala's capital is surprisingly calm and pleasant. Trivandrum's few sights and quiet lanes outside the town center make it an enjoyable place to spend the day.

The handsome **Padmanabhaswamy Temple,** dedicated to Vishnu, has a seven-story *gopuram* (entrance tower). The date of its original construction has been placed at 3000 BC; legend has it that it was built by 4,000 masons, 6,000 laborers, and 100 elephants over the course of six months. In the main courtyard there's intricate granite sculpture, supplemented by more stonework on the nearly 400 pillars supporting the temple corridors. The complex is technically open only to Hindus and keeps erratic hours, so call ahead to be assured of at least a glimpse. ✉*M. G. Rd. at Chali Bazaar* ☎*471/245–0233* ⏲*Daily sunrise–12:30 and 4:30–7:30.*

The 18th-century **Kuthiramalika (Puthenmalika) Palace Museum,** or Horse Palace, has carved rosewood ceilings and treasures of the royal family, including an ivory throne, weapons, paintings, and gifts from foreign dignitaries. Lifesize Kathakali figures stand in the dance room. Carved horses for which the palace is named line the eaves of an inner courtyard. Only one-third of the enormous compound is open to visitors; the entrance fee includes a knowledgeable guide, who will ask for some kind of tip at the end of the tour. Also note that you must remove your shoes upon entering. ✉*Next to Padmanabhaswamy Temple, East Fort* ☎*471/247–3952* *Palace Rs. 20, shoe-storage charge Rs. 1* ⏲*Tues.–Sun. 8:30–1 and 3:30–5:30.*

In an 80-acre park at the north end of M. G. Road are the many attractions of the **Museum and Art Gallery Complex.** Buy your ticket at the Natural History Museum, a musty collection of animal skeletons, dioramas, and stuffed birds. Head straight to the second floor to see an interesting model of a traditional *nalakettu* home (the traditional home of the Nairs, a warrior clan), complete with costumed figurines and a full explanation. The art museum's collection of local arts and crafts—including bronze and stone sculptures and musical instruments—is as noteworthy as the building itself, with its Cubist pattern of gables and its decorative interior. Memorabilia donated by the royal family, including a golden chariot used by the Maharaja of Travancore, is displayed in the tiny Sree Chitra Enclave. On the opposite side of the park, the Sree Chitra Art Gallery has an eclectic collection of paintings, including works of the Rajput, Mogul, and Tanjore schools; copies of the Ajanta and Sigirya frescoes; and works from China, Japan, Tibet, and Bali, along with canvases by modern Indian painters. ✉*Museum Rd.* ☎*471/231–8294* *Rs. 20* ⏲*Thurs.–Tues. 10–5, Wed. 1–5.*

OFF THE BEATEN PATH

Vijnana Kala Vedi Cultural Center. About 120 km (75 mi) north of Trivandrum, this institute, established by a French woman in 1977, is dedicated to preserving the arts and heritage of Kerala. People from all over the world come to study everything from singing to cooking to language with experienced masters in a simple village atmosphere. You can choose to give back by participating in a volunteer program to teach English in a local school. Short stays are available for $30 per night. A one-week stay is $200, all-inclusive; there are discounts for longer stays. ✉*Tarayil Mukku Junction, Aranmula, 689533* ☎*468/221–4483 or 468/231–0451* 🌐*www.vijnanakalavedi.org.*

WHERE TO EAT & STAY

$ ✕ **Orion.** Although it offers a variety of cuisines, this restaurant has acquired a reputation with locals for its traditional Indian dishes. The lunch-time South Indian buffet features such Kerala specialties as *elisseri* (pumpkin with red beans), *avial* (mixed vegetables in a mild coconut gravy), and fish curry. ✉*The Residency Tower, Press Rd.* ☎*471/233–1661* ▭*AE, DC, MC, V.*

$ ✕ **Swiss Bake House.** The graceful, two-story building—the former home of the antique-dealing Natesan family—is decorated with wood carvings and bronze artifacts. Come for the ambience: the food is only average. The attached café, however, serves yummy, Western-style pastries. ✉*Vellyambalam Junction* ☎*471/231–1720* ▭*MC, V.*

¢ ✕ **Azad.** The food won't disappoint, even if the interior isn't much to look at. Specialties include *biriani,* a flavorful rice cooked with chicken or mutton, and *kuthu paratha,* a Kerala Muslim delicacy of flat bread stuffed with minced fish. Azad has become a chain, but this, the original restaurant in East Fort, is probably the best. ✉*M. G. Rd., East Fort* ☎*471/247–0455* ▭*MC, V.*

¢ ✕ **Hotel Aryaas.** There's nothing fancy here—just simple, tasty, vegetarian food like *amma* (mom) would make. The air-conditioned restaurant is comfortable and clean, and menu options range from soups and salads to french fries. Opt for the traditional thali, a meal of rice and vegetable accompaniments—one extra-special thali comes with a whopping 18 dishes. ✉*Subramaniam Rd.* ☎*471/233–8999* ▭*No credit cards.*

$$ **Muthoot Plaza.** A roaring fountain encourages you to lounge ever deeper into the leather armchairs in the cream-tone marble lobby, where the Middle Eastern business clientele often gathers around the flat-screen TV. The carpeted rooms have high ceilings and bedside electric control panels. **Pros:** laptop provided in top-end rooms, breakfast buffet included. **Cons:** no pool. ✉*Punnen Rd., 695039* ☎*471/233–7733* *www.themuthootplaza.com* *53 rooms, 4 suites* *In-room: safe, Wi-Fi. In-hotel: restaurant, room service, bar, gym, laundry service.* ▭*AE, DC, MC, V* *BP.*

$–$$ **South Park.** At this writing, renovations are nearing completion at what is one of Trivandrum's premier hotels. Carpets in the large standard rooms have been replaced by wooden flooring, a foolproof way to get rid of the mustiness that plagues most Kerala hotels. Street-facing rooms can be noisy; opt for one at the back. **Pros:** good location, in-room Wi-Fi. **Cons:** large and impersonal, on a noisy street. ✉*Spencer Junction, M. G. Rd., 695034* ☎*471/233–3333* *www.thesouthpark.com* *62 rooms, 20 suites* *In-room: refrigerator, ethernet, Wi-Fi. In-hotel: 3 restaurants, room service, bar, laundry service.* ▭*AE, DC, MC, V* *BP.*

SHOPPING

Most shops are closed Sunday, and smaller shops occasionally shut down for a few hours at lunchtime on weekdays. For crafts from all over India, head to **The Craft Shop** (✉*G. A. K Rd., off M. G. Rd.* ☎*471/232–3335*). Weavers for Travancore's royal family sell traditional Kerala saris (made of plain white cotton) at **Karalkada** (✉*Kaithamukku Junc-*

tion ☎*471/247–2932*). **Natesan's** (✉*M. G. Rd.* ☎*471/233–1594*) is a respected art and antiques dealer. For Kerala handicrafts and souvenirs, hit the government emporium **SMSM** (✉*Statue Junction, off M. G. Rd.* ☎*471/233–1668*).

KOVALAM

16 km (10 mi) south of Trivandrum.

Kovalam's sandy beaches are lined with palm-fringed lagoons and rocky coves. Fishermen in *lungis* (colorful cloth wraps) drag in nets filled with the day's catch, then push their slender wooden boats out again with a Malayalam "Heave ho." Here you can spend the day loafing on warm sand or rocky outcroppings, watch the sun set, then sit back as the dim lights of distant fishing boats come on. In peak season, outdoor eateries spring up right on the beach—just point to the fish of your choice and specify how you'd like it prepared. ■ **TIP→ Be sure to find out how much it's going to cost—a little discreet bargaining might be in order.**

Overdevelopment had nearly ruined Kovalam, but it's experiencing something of a revival, with luxury hotels groups like the Leela coming to the area. The main beach, Lighthouse, has been cleaned up; the concrete promenade is lined with shops, restaurants, and budget hotels. It's well lit at night, allowing for a pleasant evening stroll as well as some semblance of nightlife. For peace and solitude, however, stick to the secluded beaches in villages to the north and south of Kovalam town.

OFF THE BEATEN PATH

Padmanabhapuram. Though it belongs to Kerala, this fantastic, 18th-century, carved-teak palace is actually across the border in neighboring Tamil Nadu, about a 1½-hour (63 km [39 mi]) drive south of Kovalam on National Highway 47. Once the home of the Travancore rajas (Travancore was the southernmost state, which was combined with Cochin and Malabar to form Kerala), it's one of the best-preserved examples of old wooden architecture in India.

WHERE TO EAT & STAY

$ ✕ **Hotel Rockholm Restaurant.** What might be Kovalam's best chef prepares excellent international and local dishes. Try the seasonal seafood dishes, such as fried mussels or prawns Kerala-style. You can eat indoors or on a terrace overlooking the ocean. ✉*Lighthouse Rd.* ☎*471/248–0607* ▭*AE, DC, MC, V.*

$$$$ **The Leela Kempinski Kovalam Beach Resort.** Once run by the government, the best-situated property in Kovalam recently completed a major renovation under the Kempinski Hotels group. The main block of exterior, designed by Mumbai-based architect Charles Correa, is built in tiers on a bluff overlooking the Arabian Sea. All rooms have balconies and at least a partial sea view; beachfront chalets also have tiny private compounds and windowed bathrooms. Views of the sunsets are spectacular here. In the "private club" wing, guests pay a premium for their own restaurant, spa, and swimming pool. **Pros:** spectacular views, exclusive beach area, good ayurvedic center. **Cons:** pricey, get-

ting to the bars and restaurants on Lighthouse Beach requires a bit of a walk. ✉*Kovalam, 695527* ☎*471/248–0101* 🌐*www.theleela.com* *178 rooms, 2 suites* *In-room: refrigerator, Wi-Fi. In-hotel: 3 restaurants, room service, bars, tennis court, pools, gym, laundry service.* *AE, DC, MC, V.*

$$$–$$$$ ★ **Surya Samudra Beach Garden.** Overlooking the sea, this rambling resort has an exquisite beach, lovely views, and a great deal of peace (loud noise isn't permitted). Most rooms are in restored wooden houses, each with an intricately carved facade, a domed wooden ceiling, open-air bathrooms, and understated decor. The handful of cottage rooms has interiors that blend modern and folk touches. An ayurvedic-spa complex was completed in 2005. **Pros:** great beach, some massive rooms, a don't-miss swimming pool cut out of rock with underwater sculptures. **Cons:** overpriced, no television, no activities for children. ✉*Pulinkudi, 10 km (6 mi) south of Kovalam, 695521* ☎*471/248–0413* 🌐*www.suryasamudra.com* *21 rooms, 4 suites* *In-room: no a/c (some), no TV, ethernet. In-hotel: restaurant, bar, pool, beachfront, no elevator, laundry service.* *AE, MC, V* *BP.*

$$–$$$ **Coconut Bay.** In an undeveloped area about 2 km (1 mi) south of Kovalam, this 3-acre property has a secluded beach and ayurvedic center. Rooms are in modern, redbrick tile-roof buildings with wooden ceilings, some with soaring ocean views. It's good value for the money, and usually booked well in advance by charter groups. **Pros:** large, comfortable beds. **Cons:** no bathtubs. ✉*Mulloor, 695521* ☎*471/248–0566, 471/248–0668, or 471/248–4566* 🌐*www.coconutbay.com* *27 rooms* *In-room: refrigerator. In-hotel: restaurant, pool, beachfront, water sports, no elevator, laundry service, airport shuttle* *MC, V* *BP.*

$$–$$$ **Lagoona Davina.** U.K. native Davina Taylor has created an intimate boutique resort in an out-of-this-world setting north of Kovalam. After a short drive from the airport, you're brought to a lagoon by boat. Thatched-roof guest quarters are small but attractive, with marble floors and hand painted with ethnic designs; most are steps from the water. If you don't feel like packing, just tell Davina your measurements and the colors you like, and she'll have clothes tailored for you. A personal room attendant is at your disposal throughout your stay. Ayurvedic massage, yoga, and Reiki (hands-on energy healing) are available. Davina prefers that her guests keep themselves occupied with things other than television, but TVs and DVD players are provided on request. **Pros:** gorgeous setting, waterfront swimming pool. **Cons:** no a/c. ✉*Pachalloor, 695027* ☎*471/238–0049 or 471/238–3608* 🌐*www.lagoonadavina.com* *18 rooms* *In-room: no a/c, no TV. In-hotel: restaurant, pool, no elevator, laundry service, airport shuttle, no kids under 16.* *MC, V.*

$$–$$$ **Manaltheeram.** Quieter and even closer to the water than its neighboring sister property, Somatheeram Beach Resort, Manaltheeram has rooms in simple, circular brick cottages that are neatly arrayed on ascending terraces. "Special" cottages have better sea views. **Pros:** quiet, exclusive beachfront, some restaurant tables set up on the beach. **Cons:** a little short on amenities. ✉*Chowara, 695501* ☎*471/226–*

6222 ⊕www.manaltheeram.com ⇆54 rooms ♨In-room: no TV. In-hotel: restaurant, room service, pool, beachfront, no elevator, laundry service. ▭AE, MC, V.

$$–$$$ **Somatheeram Ayurvedic Health Resort.** Stress-free Westerners in green robes roam the winding pathways of this popular ayurvedic beach resort. Lodging is in traditional wooden houses or simple brick cottages on 15 lush acres down by the sea. The grounds are a bit crowded with both people and cottages, but the setting is still pleasant. In 2006, the brothers who owned Somatheeram divided the resort into two, with one brother taking over the similar Somatheeram Beach Resort next door. The resorts share a restaurant. **Pros:** plenty of activities, including yoga and meditation. **Cons:** smallish, basic rooms. *✉Chowara, 695501 ☎471/226–6501 ⊕www.somatheeram.org ⇆46 rooms, 1 suite ♨In-room: no a/c, no TV. In-hotel: restaurant, beachfront, no elevator, laundry service. ▭AE, MC, V.*

$–$$$ **Nikki's Nest.** Most rooms in this retreat south of Kovalam have commanding sea views. Among bougainvillea, coconut palms, banana trees, orchids, and acacia are thatch-roof, circular cottages and traditional wooden houses. The cottage rooms are comfortable, spacious, and clean. The traditional *nalukettu* (quadrangular buildings) are beautifully maintained homes, with wooden rafters and dark-wood windows that open out completely. A well-lit path leads down to the crescent-shape beach. **Pros:** great hilltop beach views. **Cons:** uphill walk to the hotel from the beach. *✉Azhimala Shiva Temple Rd., Chowara, 695501 ☎471/226–8822 or 471/226–8821 ⊕www.nikkisnest.com ⇆37 rooms ♨In-room: no phone (some), no TV. In-hotel: 2 restaurants, pool, beachfront, no elevator, laundry service, no-smoking rooms. ▭MC, V ЮBP.*

$ **Beach & Lake.** Sandwiched between the roar of the Arabian Sea and the ripple of a backwater lagoon, this basic resort north of Kovalam is accessible only by boat. Ayurvedic treatments and plenty of quiet are the main draws. Midsize rooms in a whitewashed, one-story building are simply furnished and well maintained, with private sit-outs (patios) facing the lagoon. A two-minute walk gets you to the public beach. The resort added a new wing in 2006 holding six deluxe rooms with larger bedrooms and bathtubs. **Pros:** cheap, gorgeous views, friendly staff. **Cons:** can only be accessed by boat, basic accommodations, few eating options near the hotel. *✉Pozhikkara Beach, Pachalloor Village, 695527 ☎471/238–2086 ⊕www.beachandlakeresort.com ⇆11 rooms ♨In-room: no a/c (some), safe, Wi-Fi. In-hotel: restaurant, no elevator. ▭MC, V ЮBP.*

10

¢–$ **Ideal Ayurvedic Resort.** This small, homey resort south of Kovalam has specialized in ayurvedic treatment since 1997. Rooms in the marble-floor main building are simply furnished and spotless; some have balconies overlooking a coconut grove. There are also a few thatch-roof cottages, some with open-air bathrooms. The beach is a short walk away, but Ideal focuses more on Indian arts and culture than on fun in the sun; it offers study programs in yoga and ayurveda, among other healing treatments. At this writing, a major upgrade was underway that will add 14 rooms, a swimming pool, and a second ayurvedic center. **Pros:** friendly staff, little to distract guests from their treatment. **Cons:** few amenities, not on the beach. ✉*Just before Somatheeram, Chowara, 695501* ☎📠*471/226–8632* 🌐*www.idealayurvedicresort.com* *10 rooms, 5 suites* *In-room: no a/c, no TV. In-hotel: restaurant, no elevator, laundry service.* 💳*MC, V.*

¢ **Neelakanta.** This beachfront budget hotel is popular with foreigners. The low-rise building sits right on Kovalam's main drag. Private sea-facing balconies in every room let you see all the action—people strolling, sunbathing, and fishing—on Lighthouse Beach. Air-conditioned rooms are spacious, with high ceilings; all are simply furnished and clean. **Pros:** beach views. **Cons:** building looks a bit shabby. ✉*Lighthouse Beach, Kovalam Village, 695527* ☎*471/248–0321 or 471/248–6004* 🌐*www.hotelneelakantakovalam.com* *28 rooms, 6 suites* *In-room: no a/c (some). In-hotel: restaurant, no elevator, laundry service.* 💳*MC, V.*

NORTHERN KERALA

If Kerala is unspoiled India, then Malabar—as the northern part of the state was once known—is unspoiled Kerala. Arab traders landed here long before Vasco da Gama, and many trading families converted to Islam. Various conquerors built forts along spectacular stretches of coastline, and some of Kerala's most unique and colorful religious festivals take place in this region. With the exception of the hill station of Wyanad, tourism has yet to make in-roads into the northern part of Kerala. Resorts, cruises, and sunbathing are almost unheard of. Nothing you see here has been prepackaged for your convenience, making a visit to northern Kerala a bit more work—but highly rewarding.

CALICUT

146 km (91 mi) northwest of Kochi.

This city doesn't hold much excitement in itself, but Calicut (Kozhikode) has an airport and is a good base for exploring several interesting sights nearby, including the lushly forested Wyanad district to the northeast. The city's historical ties with the Middle East are clearly apparent due to the strong Arab presence.

In the town of Beypore, 10 km (6 mi) south of Calicut on the Beypore Road, is the **Tasara Center for Creative Weaving** (✉*Beypore North* ☎*495/241–4832*), where you can see weavers working on giant hand looms. Tasara also hosts programs for artists-in-residence. Call ahead to arrange a visit.

A group of local fishermen started the **Theeram Nature Conservation Society** when they discovered that the Olive Ridley turtles they'd been eating were an endangered species. The center and its small turtle hatchery are on the beach at Kolavippalam, near Payyoli, about 30 km (19 mi) north of Calicut and off National Highway 17. If you're lucky, you can catch female turtles arriving on the beach in November and December to lay their eggs, which hatch in January and February.

WHERE TO EAT & STAY

¢ ✕**Paragon.** It's not much to look at, but this Calicut stalwart serves up tasty food. The chicken *biriani* is excellent, as is the unusual fried shrimp dish that goes very well with parathas (local bread). ✉*Kannur Rd., Calicut* ☎*495/276–1020 or 495/276–7020* ▭*No credit cards.*

$$$ Fodor'sChoice ★ **Green Magic Nature Resort.** A true back-to-nature experience, this astonishing resort off the Wyanad Road 65 km (40 mi) northeast of Calicut has two extraordinary tree houses perched 90 feet above the forest floor. One tree house is accessed by a water-powered elevator, the other by a suspension bridge—to use either contraption requires a good deal of faith. If you suffer from vertigo, request one of the ground-level stone lodges. Everything here is constructed with indigenous materials, except for the modern bathrooms. Lighting is restricted to kerosene lamps, meals are served on banana leaves, and a resident elephant is available for treks. **Pros:** rare opportunity to sleep in a tree. **Cons:** expensive and basic. ✉*Vythiri, Wyanad District, 673576* ☎*471/233–0437, 471/233–1507 reservations through Tour India* 🌐*www.tourindiakerala.com* *10 rooms* ▭*MC, V* *In-room: no a/c, no phone, no TV. In-hotel: room service.* *MAP.*

$$ **Kadavu.** One of the first swank, world-class riverside resorts in the Calicut area, Kadavu signaled Malabar's foray into tourism. You enter the lobby under a traditional *mandapam,* a wood-frame canopy supported by pillars. A fountain spouts from the large lotus pool behind the lobby, which is flanked by the wings of the hotel. The courtyard opens onto an enormous swimming pool, from which steps descend to riverfront cottages. Rooms are large and have with bay windows; cottages also have balconies screened by coconut palms. Plans are underway to build another 138 rooms by 2008. **Pros:** stunning river views, good value. **Cons:** front-desk staff is less than proficient in English, 15-minute auto ride to Calicut. ✉*Off N.H. Bypass, Azhinjilam, Feroke, 18 km (11 mi) south of Calicut, 673632* ☎*483/283–0023 or 483/283–0027* 🌐*www.kadavuresorts.com* *61 rooms, 6 suites* *In-hotel: 3 restaurants, pool, gym, public Internet, laundry service.* ▭*AE, MC, V.*

$$ **Taj Residency.** Calicut's premier hotel is frequented by airline crews and wealthy Omanis, who come for lengthy treatments at the well-regarded ayurvedic center. A beautiful wooden ceiling with exposed beams caps the lobby, and rooms are large, with wooden floors and touches of wood trim. Some quarters have a leafy view; others overlook the pool. **Pros:** great pool. **Cons:** smallish rooms, unremarkable by Taj standards. ✉*P. T. Usha Rd., Calicut, 673032* ☎*495/276–5354* 🌐*www.tajhotels.com* *70 rooms, 4 suites* *In-room: refrigerator, Wi-Fi. In-hotel: restaurant, bar, pool, laundry service.* ▭*AE, DC, MC, V* *BP.*

$ **Fortune Hotel.** Slim wooden pillars encircle the pleasant lobby of this modern business hotel, and there's a beautiful terra-cotta-tile atrium decorated with a traditional brass lamp. The Yamaha piano is set to automatic, playing such hits as The Cars' "Drive." Rooms have large bathrooms and small balconies. **Pros:** rooftop pool affords nice city views, mid-size rooms are confortably furnished, great value. **Cons:** a little noisy, no Wi-Fi in rooms. ✉ *Kannur Rd., Calicut, 673006* ☎ *495/276–8888* 🌐 *www.fortunehotels.in* *60 rooms, 3 suites* *In-room: dial-up. In-hotel: 2 restaurants, bar, pool, gym, laundry service.* *AE, MC, V* *BP.*

KANNUR

92 km (57 mi) northwest of Calicut.

The Kannur district is the heartland of the Moppilahs (Kerala's Muslim community). It's also a center for the hand-loom industry as well as the manufacture of *beedis,* potent hand-rolled cigarettes made from tobacco sweepings. The town itself was for many years at the center of the maritime spice trade. The ruling Kolathiri rajas profited from the spice trade as did the European colonists. Today Kannur is a good hub for visiting several coastal sights—to the north and the south—including forts and undeveloped beaches. Come quick, though; massive development in the works at Bekal could change everything in five years.

★ A unique regional draw is the spectacular dance called **Theyyam.** More than an art form, it's a type of worship that is tribal in origin and thought and that predates Hinduism in Kerala. Theyyams aren't held in traditional temples, but rather in small shrines or family compounds. Dancers don elaborate costumes and terrifying makeup for the ritual dance, during which its believed they become possessed by the spirit of the deity they represent. These divine powers are thought to allow them to perform feats such as dancing with a 30-foot headdress, a flaming costume, or falling into a pile of burning embers. The ritual is accompanied by intense drumming, howling, and chanting. Theyyam season is from November to May.

In 1505 the Portuguese built **Fort St. Angelo,** with the consent of the ruling Kolathiri Raja, in order to protect their interests in the area. After passing into Dutch and then British hands, it's now maintained by the Archaeological Survey of India. There are still a few British cannons intact, and lovely views of the fishing activity in Moppillah Bay. ✉ *Off NH–17, 3 km (2 mi) north of Kannur* ☎ *No phone* *Free* *Daily 8–6.*

In 1839 Herman Gundert, a Protestant missionary from the Swiss Basel Mission, arrived in the town of Thalassery, south of Kannur. A prodigious scholar, Gundert pub-

FESTIVAL TIME

January's Tiruvatira features folk dancing and singing by young Malayali women. In Trichur (Thrissur), the Pooram and Vela festivals (March–April) are among Kerala's best known. Thrissur Pooram is an eight-day spectacle with parades of decked-up elephants, music, and fireworks. In the north, Kannur and Kasargode are known for the extraordinary Theyyam (November–May), a religious dance of tribal origin. The harvest festival, Onam (late August–early September), which lasts up to 10 days in some locations, is celebrated with floral displays and snake-boat racing.

lished some 50 books on Malabar in the 20 years he lived here, including the first English–Malayalam dictionary. His bungalow is now part of a college campus. The small **Gundert Memorial Church** next to the campus is a pretty blend of Kerala and European architecture. The walls beside the altar are decorated with paintings of medicinal herbs—one of Gundert's many interests. **■ TIP→ The church is only open during services.** ✉ *National Hwy., 20 km (12 mi) south of Kannur* ☎ *No phone* 🎫 *Free* ⏲ *Fri. 6:30–8 PM, Sunday 8–11 AM.*

The **Kanhirode Weaving Cooperative** is strewn with yarns of all colors, set out to dry after dyeing. You can watch the weavers at their giant, clackety-clacking looms, making bed sheets and upholstery for export as well as brightly colored saris. Cloth is available for purchase. ✉ *Off Kannur–Mysore Rd., 13 km (8 mi) east of Kannur, Kanhirode* ☎ *497/285–7865* 🌐 *www.weaveco.com* 🎫 *Free* ⏲ *Mon.–Sat. 9–5:30.*

The unusual **Sri Muthappan Temple** sits on the bank of the Valapattanam River at Parassini Kaduvu. It's devoted to Lord Shiva in the form of a tribal hunter, and it hosts Theyyam performances almost every day of the year. Though it's not as colorful as traditional outdoor festivals, you can at least get a taste of Theyyam. As Sri Muthappan is usually pictured with a hunting dog, friendly mutts roam the sanctuary, and offerings at the shrine take the form of bronze dog figurines. ✉ *Off NH–17, 18 km (11 mi) north of Kannur, Parassini* 🎫 *Free* ⏲ *Theyyams usually held 5:30 AM–8 AM and 6:30 PM–8 PM.*

The drive north from Kannur to Bekal, in the Kasargode district, is a dreamy trip through sleepy towns with nothing but coconut and rice fields in between. The largest fort in Kerala, **Bekal Fort,** covers more than over 40 seafront acres. The 300-year-old structure rises from a green lawn, and looks out over the Arabian Sea or distant coconut groves. You can easily spend a peaceful hour or two clambering around the ruins. The loudest noise you'll hear is the crashing of the waves against the ramparts. A massive resort development project is planned in the area, however, with grandiose plans to one day turn Bekal into a top Asian tourist destination. ✉ *NH–17, 72 km (45 mi) north of Kannur, Bekal* ☎ *467/227–2900* 🎫 *Rs. 100* ⏲ *Daily 9–5:30.*

10

WHERE TO EAT & STAY

¢ ✕ **Coachman's Inn.** Local well-to-do families often dine here at tables made more private by small dividers. The food is top notch though the restaurant is dark and drab. The naan here, garnished with black seseme seeds, is particularly good. Try also the fish *malabari* (cooked in a mild curry) or the justly popular butter chicken. ✉ *Kamala International, S. M. Rd., Kannur* ☎ *497/276–6910* 💳 *MC, V.*

$$$$ 🏨 **Ayisha Manzil.** A stay in this 200-year-old clifftop home built in 1862 may be the best way to experience what north Kerala is all about. People come here for the gorgeous sea views and the local food, cooked by host Faiza Moosa. Moosa's popular cookbook and 2004 cooking show, which airs often in the U.K., has brought her fame, and many guest choose to take her $75 cooking classes. Breakfast is served on the front terrace, overlooking the sea. The house manager can accompany

you on excursions in the area, or you can just hang out by the gorgeous brick-tile pool. Rooms are palatial, with high wood-beam ceilings and antique teak and rosewood furnishings. ■ **TIP→ Book a year in advance, as the six rooms fill up quickly. Pros:** great food, great views, meals and non-alcoholic drinks included in the room price. **Cons:** basic accommodations. ✉ *Court Rd., Thalassery, 670101* ☎ 📠 *490/234-1590* *6 rooms* *In-room: no a/c (some), no phone, no TV. In-hotel: pool, no elevator, laundry service.* 💳 *No credit cards* ⊙ *Closed April 30–July 31* *MAP.*

¢ **Mascot.** A terrific hillcrest location provides a Oceanside view. Standard rooms are clean and relatively spacious, with marble floors and plenty of windows; some with air-conditioning are a little smaller. Deluxe rooms are large and close to the water, with bay windows. A cliffside walkway leads to the large swimming pool and ayurvedic center. Payyambalam Beach is a 15-minute walk away. **Pros:** fantastic sea views from most rooms. **Cons:** the closest beach has been taken over by the navy. ✉ *Near Baby Beach, Burnassery, Kannur, 670013* ☎ *497/270-8445* 🌐 *www.mascotresort.com* *25 rooms* *In-room: no a/c (some). In-hotel: restaurant, pool, laundry service.* 💳 *MC, V.*

KERALA ESSENTIALS

To research prices, get advice from other travelers, and book travel arrangements, visit www.fodors.com.

AIR TRAVEL

Air India, Kingfisher Airlines and Jet Airways cover domestic routes; there are no flights within Kerala itself.

Airlines & Contacts Air India (☎ *484/238-1874 or 484/235-1295 international 484/237-1141 or 471/231-6870 domestic*). **Emirates** (☎ *471/408-4444*). **Gulf Air** (☎ *484/235-9242*). **Jet Airways** (☎ *484/229-3231 or 471/232-1018*). **Silk Air** (☎ *484/235-8127 or 471/231-4141*). **Sri Lankan Airlines** (☎ *484/236-1666 or 471/232-2309*).

AIRPORTS & TRANSFERS

Airport Information Calicut International Airport (☎ *483/271-0517*). **Kochi International Airport** (☎ *484/261-0115*). **Trivandrum International Airport** (☎ *471/250-1542 international information, 471/250-1537 domestic information*).

BOAT & FERRY TRAVEL

Private companies, the KTDC, and the Tourist Desk operate half-day backwater tours from Alleppey for around Rs. 100 to Rs. 400. The Alleppey Tourism Development Cooperative (ATDC) runs daily trips between Alleppey and Quilon (Rs. 300 for 8 hours). After Quilon, boats continue south to Trivandrum and Kovalam. Boats leave both Alleppey and Quilon at 10:30 AM.

Boat & Ferry Information ATDC (✉ *Komala Rd., Alleppey* ☎ *477/224-3462*). **KTDC** (✉ *Shanmugham Rd., Ernakulam, Kochi* ☎ *484/235-3234* 🌐 *www.ktdc.com*). **Tourist Desk** (✉ *Main Boat Jetty, Ernakulam, Kochi* ☎ *484/237-1761*).

MONEY

ATMS ATMs are now available in Kerala's major cities: Kochi, Trivandrum, and Calicut. Check for the Cirrus or Plus sign, as many local banks do not accept foreign cards. Look for international banks like ANZ Grindlays, HSBC, and Standard Chartered, as well as the Indian bank ICICI. Make sure your PIN is four digits.

CURRENCY EXCHANGE Most major hotels have exchange services. Thomas Cook offers good rates. The Bank of India and ANZ Grindlays cash traveler's checks and change money, as does any branch of the Bank of India. Traveler's checks sometimes get marginally higher rates than cash.

Exchange Services **Bank of India** (✉ *Shanmugham Rd., Ernakulam, Kochi* ☎ *484/235–3106*). **Thomas Cook** (✉ *M. G. Rd., Ernakulam, Kochi* ☎ *484/236–9729*).

TAXIS & AUTO-RICKSHAWS

Auto-rickshaws are a convenient and quick way to travel around town. In Trivandrum, figure Rs. 10 for the first 1½ kilometers and Rs. 4.50 per additional kilometer—other cities will be slightly less. Don't be alarmed if your driver doesn't use the meter—it usually doesn't work (whether because it was intentionally broken or not is difficult to say). Make sure to agree on a fare before you get in, and don't trust a driver for unbiased shopping recommendations.

Cabs are also a good option for destinations getting around Kochi. Fares will run about Rs. 100 an hour for a non-air-conditioned car. Most cabs have a Rs. 70 minimum. Ask at any tourist office about the latest legal rates. Taxis hired at your hotel will have a slightly higher rate but drivers are more likely to speak some English. Or you can grab a taxi at cab stands near the Sea Lord Jetty or at the intersection of M. G. Road and Club Road.

TRAIN TRAVEL

Rail journeys in Kerala can be scenic, and more comfortable than traveling by car. The KK Express—which travels from Kanya Kumari, at India's southern tip, all the way up to New Delhi—is a good train to take through Kerala, as is the Kerala Express. December is a major pilgrimage season, so you'll need to book tickets in advance. Check with KTDC for the latest schedules and fares, or try 🌐 www.indianrail.gov.in, and use a travel agent or your hotel's travel desk to make bookings, unless you don't mind standing in the unruly queue at the train station.

Train Information **Calicut Railway Station** (☎ *133*). **Ernakulam Junction** (☎ *131*). **Ernakulam Town Station** (☎ *484/235–3920*). **KTDC** (✉ *Shanmugham Rd., Ernakulam, Kochi* ☎ *484/235–3234* 🌐 *www.ktdc.com*). **Trivandrum Central Station** (☎ *132*).

TRAVEL AGENTS & TOURS

The KTDC has several inexpensive tours, including wildlife-spotting excursions to the Lake Periyar Wildlife Sanctuary and one- to two-week trips that follow a pilgrim trail through Kerala's sacred shrines. Sita Travels can help with bookings and arrange a car and driver. The

Great India Tour Company, one of Kerala's best travel agencies, has offices throughout South India. SATM Tours and Travel designs affordable packages around your interests. Trivandrum-based Tourindia created the houseboat phenomenon and offers unusual Kerala experiences. One intriguing two- to three-day trip—created by Tourindia and the forestry department—sends you deep into the jungle with a local guide, an armed escort, and a naturalist. Destination Holidays specializes in Kerala tours, and has a good reputation among budget operators for good service and local knowledge.

Contacts **Destination Holidays** (✉ *Pallath Bldgs., Kurisupally Rd., Ravipuram, Ernakulam* ☎ *484/235–6497 or 484/235–7316*). **Great India Tour Company** (✉ *Mullassery Towers, Vanross Junction, Trivandrum* ☎ *471/232–7627 or 471/301–1500* ✉ *Pithuru Smarana, 1st fl., Srikandath Rd., Ravipuram, Kochi* ☎ *484/231–7004*). **KTDC** (✉ *Shanmugham Rd., Ernakulam, Kochi* ☎ *484/235–3234* 🌐 *www.ktdc.com*). **Sita Travels** (✉ *Tharakan Building, M. G. Rd., Ernakulam, Kochi* ☎ *484/236–1101*). **Tourindia** (✉ *PB 136 M. G. Rd., Trivandrum* ☎ *471/233–0437 or 471/233–1507*). **Travelogics** (✉ *Warriam Rd., Kochi* ☎ *484/236–5765*).

VISITOR INFORMATION

Excellent brochures, maps, and pamphlets on all of Kerala's districts are available at any KTDC office. In Kochi, the office is open daily 8–7. Trivandrum's two KTDC offices—one in town and one at the airport—are open weekdays 10–5.

In Kochi, an alternative source of information is the Tourist Desk, a private, nonprofit organization that conducts moderately priced tours and provides clear, straightforward information about the state. In Kannur, the District Tourism Promotion Council is quite active. Central Kerala is well served by the ATDC. The Government of India Tourist Office—open weekdays 9–5:30 and Saturday 9–1—has its own vehicles, boats, lodgings, and tours.

Tourist Offices **ATDC** (✉ *Komala Rd., Alleppey* ☎ *477/224–3462*). **Government of India Tourist Office** (✉ *Malabar Rd., Willingdon Island, Kochi,* ☎ *484/266–8352*). **Kannur District Tourism Promotion Council** (✉ *Taluk Office Campus, Kannur* ☎ *497/270–6336*). **KTDC** (✉ *Shanmugham Rd., Ernakulam Kochi* ☎ *484/235–3234* ✉ *Museum Rd., Trivandrum* ☎ *471/232–2279* 🌐 *www.ktdc.com*). **Tourist Desk** (✉ *Main Boat Jetty, Ernakulam, Kochi* ☎ *484/237–1761*).

Tamil Nadu

A Bharatanatyam dancer in Tamil Nadu

WORD OF MOUTH

"Plenty of tourists [visit Tamil Nadu] every year, but it definitely doesn't get the movement or numbers of visitors of North India, where most first timers—and almost all tour groups—go. [All the same it] certainly has lots of attractions, history, variety, and a rich culture, and is surely a wonderful state to explore."

—Bonita

www.fodors.com/forums

WELCOME TO TAMIL NADU

Mahabalipuram temples

TOP REASONS TO GO

★ **Outstanding Temples—the Meenakshi, the Brihadiswara, and Rock Fort:** Tamil Nadu has some of the most magnificent and awe-inspiring temples in all of India.

★ **Getting Away From It All:** Without the tourist crowds of hotspots like Kerala and the Golden Triangle, Tamil Nadu remains a place where it's easy to be surrounded by locals instead.

★ **Sumptuous Silks:** Kanchipuram, Chennai, and other locations are central to India's silk and sari industry. Take along your bargaining skills if you want to bring some of these elegant handicrafts back home.

★ **Strolling the Streets of Pondicherry:** This former French colony town retains a distinct Gallic charm.

★ **South Indian Delicacies:** Filter coffee, *dosas, idlys,* and spicy Chettinad dishes are all wonderful ways to take in the culture of the South.

1 Chennai. The gateway to the south, India's fourth-largest city comes with all the traffic, noise, and spectacular growth that it implies. It's a good base camp for Tamil Nadu exploration, but its long history as a colonial powerhouse makes it worthy of exploration as well.

2 Mahabalipuram and Kanchipuram. Known for their masterful bas-relief sculptures and monumental temples, these two cities in northern Tamil Nadu are deservedly popular strongholds of traditional Tamil art and culture.

3 Pondicherry. With straight roads, colorful French colonial houses, and that certain *je ne sais quoi,* Pondicherry often seems like a small *ville* dropped onto the Bay of Bengal. Its laidback attitude and delicious restaurants make it a popular weekend escape with harried Chennai-ites as well as francophilic tourists.

4 Tiruchirappalli, Thanjavur, and Madurai. These ancient cities and their awe-inspiring temples are monumental reminders of the power, reach, and ambition of South India's early rulers. A long drive from Chennai, they can also be reached via air.

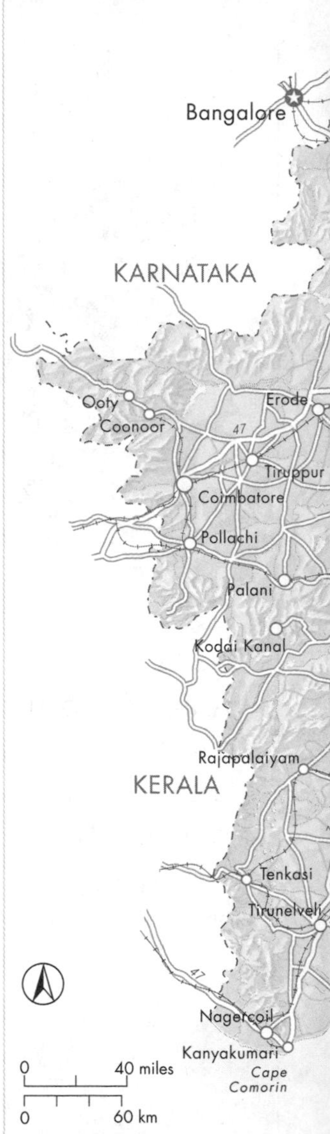

Riding through the streets of Tiruchirappalli

ANDRA PRADESH
Ambattur
Chennai
Vellore
Tambaram
Kanchipuram
Covelong Beach
Hosur
Mahabalipuram
Tiruvannamalai
Auroville
Viluppuram
Pondicherry
Yercaud
Cuddalore
Salem
Vriddhachalam
Neyvelli
Bay of Bengal
Chidambaram
Namakkal
Gangai-Konda-Solpuram
Kumbakonam
Tranquebar
Karur
Grand Anaicut
Swamimalai
Karaikal
Tiruchirappalli
Thanjavur
Nagapattinam
Velakani
Dindigul
Pudukkotai
Vedaranyam
Point Calimere
Madurai
Karaikkudi
Palk Strait
Manamadurai
Jaffna
Palk Bay
Ramanathapuram
Rameswaram
Talaimanner
Adam's Bridge
Coromandel Coast
Tuticorin
Palayankottai
Tiruchchendur
Gulf of Mannar
INDIAN OCEAN

GETTING ORIENTED

Tamil Nadu in many ways is South India. A state whose boundaries approximate the areas in which Tamil language, culture, and people predominate, the "land of the Tamils" runs about 805 km (500 mi) along the Bay of Bengal from north of Chennai to India's southernmost tip, Kanniyakumari. From Chennai, the base for many of the region's visitors, it's easy to reach nearby Kanchipuram and Mahabalpuram, as well as Pondicherry, farther south along the Coromandel Coast. Heading inland, the temple-blessed, ancient cities of Tiruchirappalli, Thanjavur, and Madurai form a sort of Tamil Nadu heartland.

Sri Ranganathaswamy Temple. Tiruchirapalli.

TAMIL NADU PLANNER

When to Go

Tamil Nadu's weather can be off-putting and draining, with high temperatures, high humidity, and impressive numbers of mosquitoes year-round in many areas. The best time to visit is between November and February, when the atmosphere remains relatively benign, and evenings might even be slightly cool. Winter is the time for temple festivals as well as the most important of Chennai's dance and music programs.

Summer, which begins around March, is even hotter. The state's single monsoon season (starting around October) cools things off, but it also brings torrential rains that can make roads impassable and travel difficult.

Upmarket hotels are being built at a quick pace, especially in Chennai, but room supply is still generally outnumbered by demand. To avoid a last-minute search and possible disappointments, make hotel reservations in advance—especially at the peak time of year.

Getting There & Around

Most travelers to Tamil Nadu fly into Chennai, Madurai, or Tiruchirappalli. Chennai's international airport is about 16 km (10 mi) from the center of town. From here you can get domestic flights to most major cities within India and to many smaller destinations in the south.

Travelers who can afford it often hire a car and driver for their stay in Tamil Nadu. Drivers know the major routes, and it can be a real convenience to have him with you for several days.

Chennai is linked to the north by National Highway 5 (NH–5), to the west by NH–4, and to the south by NH–45. Road and traffic conditions often make driving more time-consuming than the distance suggests, although major road improvements have made the drive to Bangalore, 334 km (207 mi) to the west, better than before.

From Chennai, the drives south to Kanchipuram, Mahabalipuram, and Pondicherry are short and simple, and make it easy to make side trips to DakshinaChitra and other interesting places along the way. The East Coast Road is more scenic than NH–45 and gets you to Mahabalipuram in one hour. The 50-km (31-mi) drive from Tiruchirappalli to Thanjavur crosses through rice fields interspersed with canals. And the daylong (10-hour) drive on NH–5 from Chennai to Madurai takes you through several villages.

For short trips of under four hours or so, taking a bus can be a good option. The low bus fares are hard to beat. However, the drawbacks—the lack of toilet facilities and the frequent lateness in schedules—mean that a bus trip isn't for everyone.

If you do choose to take a bus, head to the bus station and look for the nicest-looking buses headed for your destination. The cheapest buses tend to be old, with worn-out shocks and interiors, making for a very bumpy, long trip.

Trains can be a useful, albeit fairly time-consuming, way to get to the major cities of Tamil Nadu. The air-conditioned chair-car (rows of chairs, but no berths) service (Vaigai Express) from Chennai to Tiruchirappalli (6 hours) and Madurai (7½ hours) is a relaxing way to see the countryside. (Alternatively, the night trains to Madurai save you sightseeing time.)

See Essentials for contact info and more advice on getting around.

Visiting Tamil Nadu's Temples

If you're heading to Tamil Nadu, you're probably coming for the amazing temples. From a distance, it's the lofty *gopurams* (entrance towers) that stand out, most of them as brilliantly multicolored as a vivid cartoon. The pillared halls inside, called *mandapams,* often have friezes depicting myths of Hindu gods and goddesses, and sometimes tales of the temple's benefactors. South Indian temples are thronged daily with pilgrims and visitors, and they're as much social centers as places of worship. You'll see beggars, vendors selling religious items and souvenirs, groups of old men and women having a gossip, and families heading here for a day out. The larger, better-known temples are pilgrimage shrines or are visited mainly on special occasions, such as *Pongal* (a harvest festival held in January or February) and birthdays. The smaller temples and street shrines are part of daily life.

Hindus worship at their temples in a variety of ways. Some devotees withdraw to the inner sanctum for *puja,* or the act of showing reverence, which consists of *darshan* (visual communication with the image of the deity), making donations, and receiving blessings. Others worship a specific carved image in the mandapam frieze, and still others go to the sacred peepul tree and tie a ribbon around it. After puja, worshippers sit outside in the mandapam for a few minutes, absorbing their surrounding. In a temple courtyard, it's possible to see priests blessing livestock or a brand-new car.

Non-Hindus are usually free to explore these houses of worship, but they are typically barred from the inner sanctum. Be prepared to remove your shoes at the temple entrance.

What It Costs In Rupees

	¢	$	$$	$$$	$$$$
Restaurants	under Rs. 100	Rs. 100–Rs. 300	Rs. 300–Rs. 500	Rs. 500–Rs. 700	over Rs. 700
Hotels	under Rs. 2,000	Rs. 2,000–Rs. 4,000	Rs. 4,000–Rs. 6,000	Rs. 6,000–Rs. 10,000	over Rs. 10,000

Restaurant prices are for an entrée plus bread or rice. Hotel prices are for a double room in high season, excluding a tax of approximately 12.5%.

Planning Your Time

Because most of the temples in this chapter close in the middle of the day, it makes sense to get up early, see what you can, and then take a siesta or shopping break in preparation for more temple-going in early evening. By the same token, don't try to see too many and risk a case of temple overdose. It's often better to see a few and take your time rather than see a bunch of temples and have them all run together. The colorful bazaars, temples, and shopping in Chennai are worth one-to-two days' worth of your time. With a city this large, it's easy to waste the day getting from point A to B, so try to concentrate on one area of the city at a time, and try to avoid the evening rush hour if at all possible.

Mahabalipuram and its cave temples are a must-see, and they can be done as either a day trip or an overnight stay from a base in Chennai—if you do stay over, then the pilgrimage town of Kanchipuram and its 200 temples can be visited on the way back to Chennai.

If you're heading between Madurai and Chennai via car, Pondicherry is roughly mid-way, along the coast. With its Provincial-France-on-the-Indian-Ocean qualities, Pondicherry makes a good place to unwind and take a break from more rigorous sightseeing.

Updated by John Rambow

RUNNING ABOUT 800 KM (500 mi) along the Bay of Bengal, Tamil Nadu is the heartland of South India. From Tamil Nadu's coast, with its gorgeous, bright-green rice fields and coconut and banana trees, the land rises through the low-lying Eastern Ghats (mountains) up to tea, coffee, and spice plantations in the Nilgiri Hills, and finally to the higher Western Ghats.

A rich oral tradition, 2,000-year-old religious texts and literature, and Jain and Buddhist influences have made South Indian Hinduism a distinct, vibrant, evolving religion—one that pervades Tamils' lives, beliefs, philosophy, and behavior. The Tamils have survived incursions from North Indians and foreigners alike, but neither the Portuguese nor the French nor the British, who ruled Chennai (then Madras) for 300 years, made more than a superficial dent in the soul of Tamil culture. Majestic South Indian temples dominate the Tamil landscape, just as faith permeates Tamil life. A visit to at least a couple major temples is key to understanding this part of India.

EXPLORING TAMIL NADU

ABOUT THE RESTAURANTS

Many South Indians, especially Hindus, once preferred to eat only in their homes for reasons of hygiene and caste. The best restaurants were confined to the larger and fancier hotels, which catered to foreign travelers. But Chennai has become a more cosmopolitan city, and fine restaurants can now be found outside of high-end hotels. A 12.50% sales tax is levied on food and drink.

ABOUT THE HOTELS

Unless otherwise noted, all hotels have air-conditioning. Due to increasing commercial travel, reservations for rooms in Chennai are essential, especially between December and February. Tamil Nadu levies a "luxury tax" of 10%–12.5% on all rooms that cost more than Rs. 1,000 a night.

CHENNAI

The city that the British named Madras remains a major gateway to South India. In 1640 an East India Company agent Francis Day negotiated with the Raja of Chandragiri, the last Vijayanagar ruler, for a strip of land on the Coromandel coast; the British built a fortified factory there, called it Fort St. George after England's patron saint, and began what would become the modern city of today. From the time the British built their fort on that sliver of beach, the city has grown by absorbing the surrounding villages. Each area has developed distinctly, often along caste lines, from the Chettiars (South Indian groups of traders) of George Town to the civil servants and businessmen of Nungambakkam. At 4.4 million, Chennai is the fourth-largest city in India, and it continues to grow. Municipal boundaries expand; multistory apartments, office buildings, and malls replace bungalows; and new residential areas spring up along the Shore Road to Mahabalipuram.

IF YOU LIKE

SHOPPING

Indulge in browsing silver tribal jewelry, jute placemats, copies of Chola bronzes, Kanchipuram silks, *khadi* (hand-woven) shirts, carved wooden temple friezes, inlaid wooden boxes, contemporary artwork, and Thanjavur paintings on offer in the area. Chennai and Madurai have excellent shops, and nearly all major hotels have boutiques, most of which take credit cards and a few of which have fixed prices. Hotel stores tend to be expensive: shop around if you're buying a big-ticket item. Government-run craft emporiums have excellent selections, and the bazaars surrounding most large temples make for terrific shopping; bargaining is expected—and a duty if you don't want to grossly overpay. In the past, bazaars were the *only* places to shop for groceries, household goods, jewelry, fruit, electronics, and paper products; over time, though, supermarkets and malls have taken root in urban areas such as Chennai with a blossoming middle class.

SOUTH INDIAN FOOD

South Indian food comes as a surprise to many Westerners whose main experience with Indian food is with the heavy sauces and breads more common in the north. Start your day (or afternoon, or evening) with a filter coffee, also known as *decoction*, or "coffee by the yard." First, the thick, concentrated brew is mixed with hot milk, and then it's poured back and forth between two metal tumblers until frothy and cool enough to drink. It's delicious and one of the best cups of coffee in India.

A traditional Tamil meal is a balance of India's six tastes: sweet, sour, pungent, astringent, salty, and bitter. Rice is a basic ingredient, whether cooked or ground into flour. Tamil dishes can be hot or bland; those that are usually mild include *idlys*, cakes made of steamed rice and black gram batter (rice- and chickpea flour are soaked, ground into a batter, then steamed); plain *dosas*, crepes made of rice and black gram batter; *upma*, semolina and spices, often with vegetables; and *curd-rice*, yogurt mixed with rice at room temperature. The usually vegetarian *thali*, is a multicourse sampler on one platter.

PERFORMING ARTS

Partially through the efforts of Western scholars, Tamil Nadu's folk music and dance have received some attention since the 1950s and '60s. *Bharatanatyam* (literally "dance of India"), and Carnatic music are the best known of the traditional South Indian performing arts. Long-performed only by temple dancers, Bharatanatyam was revived in the 20th century by the classical Indian dancer Rukmini Devi. Widely performed during Chennai's December cultural festival, this is a highly stylized, dramatic dance featuring many of the *mudra* (meaningful hand gestures) that you see in Hindu statues.

Similar in composition to North Indian music, Carnatic song is nonetheless distinguished by its instruments and its vocal style, and it influence can be heard in many Tamil film scores.

Growth has made traffic nearly unbearable at times here, with increasing pollution and noise levels. Cars, buses, trucks, autorickshaws (or "autos," as they're popularly called), mopeds, bicycles, motorcycles, pedestrians, fruit carts, and cows all compete for space in the streets. (Traffic on the main streets, like Anna Salai, is regulated and moves along relatively smoothly.) The city's water supply is woefully inadequate—nonexistent in some areas. Tanker trucks bringing water around the city add to the congestion and pollution.

> **GETTING THE LAY OF THE LAND**
>
> For getting around town for any visit of more than just a few days, the Eicher company's very thorough street map of Chennai is invaluable. The book (Rs. 220) is available at most bookstores and many newsstands.

The rapid arrival of multinational corporations has changed the placid pace of life in Chennai, which in the old days was alive at 5 AM and asleep by 9 PM. Still, nothing seems to have shaken the city's spiritual essence. Chennai is a fascinating place; its cosmopolitan face contrasting sharply with its resolutely religious soul.

Just as the town itself has been renamed, so have many of its streets, very often to honor contemporary politicians. Many of the new names are not actually used that often, but here's a partial list, with the old name listed first (*salai* means street or road): Mount Road—Anna Salai; Chamier's Road—Muthuramalinga Road; Mowbray's Road—T. T. K. (Krishnamachari) Road; Edward Eliot's Road—Radhakrishnan Salai; North Beach Road—Rajaji Salai; Nungambakkam High Road—Mahatma Gandhi Salai; Poonamallee High Road—Periyar E. V. R. High Road; South Beach Road—Kamarajar Road. Also note that the Thyagaraja Nagar area, in the southern part of the city, is always referred to as T. Nagar, and Raja Annamalai Puram is always called R. A. Puram.

NORTHERN CHENNAI

The large commercial and administrative district of Northern Chennai has Fort St. George as its nerve center. All the commerce in this area is rooted in the early-colonial era—the neighborhood of George Town grew around the British-built fort to cater to its trading needs, and continues its historic business traditions in the present day.

Numbers in the text correspond to numbers in the margin and on the Chennai map.

A GOOD TOUR

The best way to explore Chennai is to start with its fort beginnings and then follow the city's expansion south. Some distances are short, but if the temperature is 100°F and the humidity is 80%, you won't feel like walking; when oppressive heat threatens, hire a car or jump in an auto-rickshaw. First head to **Fort St. George** ❷ for a visit to **St. Mary's Church** ❶ and the **Fort Museum**, walking by the **Tamil Nadu State Legisla-**

ture ❸. Head north ¼ mi to check out the **High Court ❹**, and then head to **George Town** for a stroll. Walk north along Armenian Street to the beautiful Armenian Church, which was built in 1629 and is no longer used for worship. As you wander, look up and you'll see evidence of second-story residences—many merchants still live in George Town. Complete your tour of George Town back at the High Court.

TIMING The ideal time to cover this route is Sunday morning, when the traffic and parking are most benign. The full tour should take three or four hours, including thorough tours of George Town and Fort St. George (90 minutes each) and some time by the High Court.

WHAT TO SEE

❷ ★ **Fort St. George.** As the first British fort in India, Fort St. George provided a protected trading post that allowed the British East India to gain a permanent foothold in the country and expand. The fort was founded in 1639 by Francis Day on a thin strip of sand leased from the Raja of Chandragiri. The Indian army and civil service, Colin Mackenzie's land survey, and the British archaeological, botanical, and zoological surveys of India were all conceived on this site. Complete with walls 20 feet thick, the fort is no longer a symbol of the Raj, or British India, as much as it is of the Tamil Nadu State Legislature, which now occupies a part of it. In fact, it's difficult to find historical buildings within the fort because of poor signage and certain areas being closed to the public. Head here on Sunday to avoid crowds at the security check you have to pass through to enter the fort. Once an exchange used by East India Company merchants, the **Fort Museum** contains everything from old uniforms and coins to palanquins and padlocks, and has some wonderful porcelain and portraits of heavy hitters during the Raj. ✉ *Entrance on Rajaji Salai* ☎ *442/567–1127 (Museum only)* ⏲ *Museum: Sat.–Thurs. 10–5* 🎟 *Fort free; museum Rs. 100, video camera Rs. 25.*

George Town. If you hate crowds, then George Town will be a nonstop nuisance. Walking—the only way to explore this teeming warren of congested streets—is often hard going. Before you venture into George Town, make sure you have a detailed map of this area, such as the one in the Eicher City Map, so you can wander with confidence (many streets have similar names). For the full experience, come in the morning, when the bustle is at its peak.

Originally called Black Town, this 2½-by-3-km (1½-by-2-mi) area was first settled by lower-caste artisans who provided textiles to the British traders. After Black Town burned in the British–French wars, the new town was laid out in a grid pattern, with different sections given over to different ethnicities and religions, with their own places of worship. The street names echo George Town's mercantile history; each area bears the cultural characteristics of the group—Portuguese, Scot, Armenian, or Jewish—who migrated there doing business with (or for) the East India Company. Another prominent group is the Chettiars, a collection of prominent merchants; you'll notice that many of the street names end in "chetti." Two competitive subcastes of the Chettiars long vied for mercantile power, first with the East India Company and then

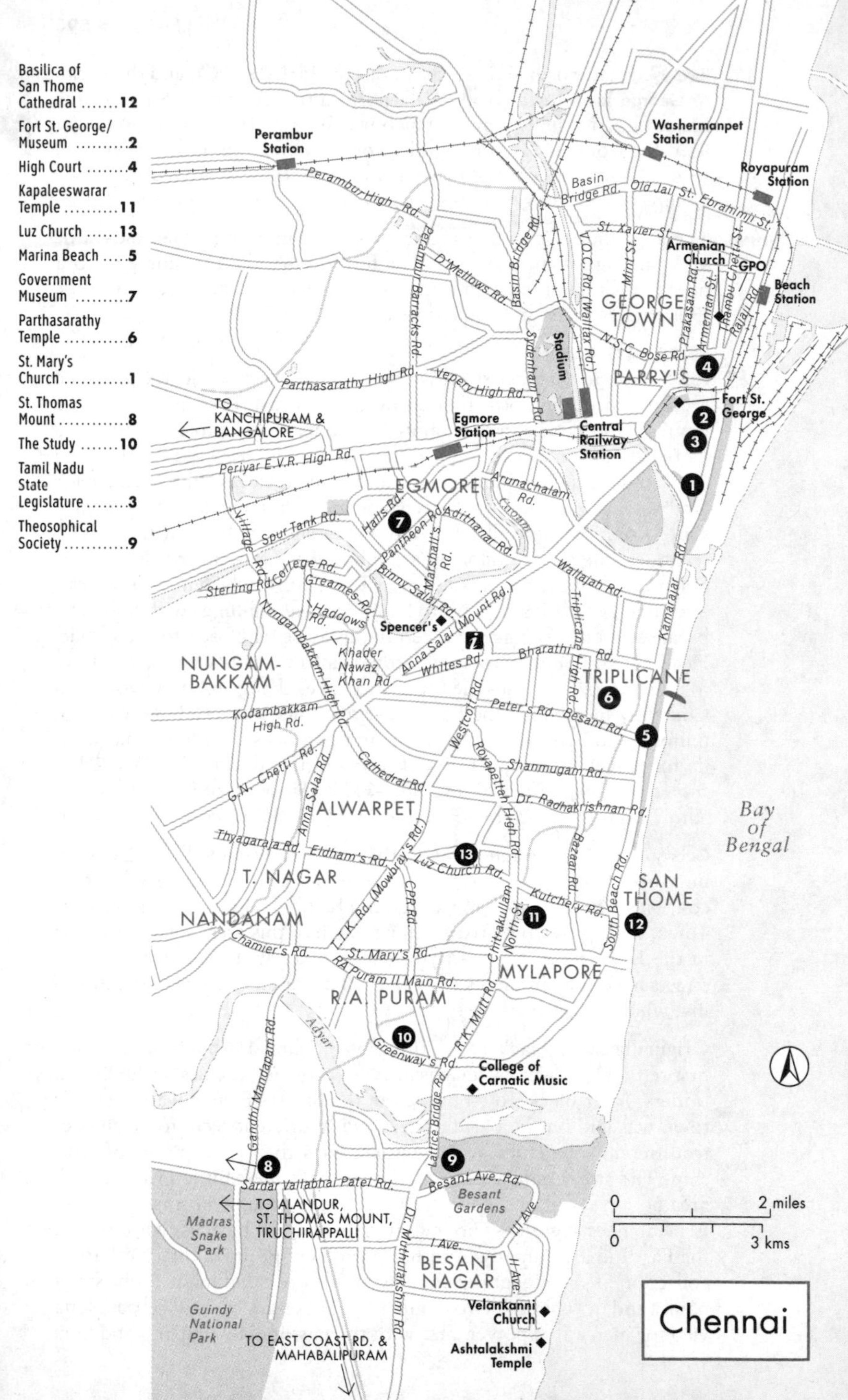

Basilica of San Thome Cathedral 12
Fort St. George/ Museum 2
High Court 4
Kapaleeswarar Temple 11
Luz Church 13
Marina Beach 5
Government Museum 7
Parthasarathy Temple 6
St. Mary's Church 1
St. Thomas Mount 8
The Study 10
Tamil Nadu State Legislature 3
Theosophical Society 9
Perambur Station
Washermanpet Station
Royapuram Station
Beach Station
Armenian Church
GPO
GEORGE TOWN
PARRY'S
Fort St. George
Stadium
Egmore Station
Central Railway Station
EGMORE
TO KANCHIPURAM & BANGALORE
Spencer's
NUNGAM-BAKKAM
TRIPLICANE
ALWARPET
T. NAGAR
NANDANAM
SAN THOME
MYLAPORE
R.A. PURAM
Bay of Bengal
College of Carnatic Music
Besant Gardens
TO ALANDUR, ST. THOMAS MOUNT, TIRUCHIRAPPALLI
Madras Snake Park
Guindy National Park
TO EAST COAST RD. & MAHABALIPURAM
BESANT NAGAR
Velankanni Church
Ashtalakshmi Temple
0 2 miles
0 3 kms
Chennai

with the merchants of the Raj. ✉ *Bordered by Basin Bridge Rd., Old Jail St., Ebrahim Sabib St., and Rajaji Rd., Parrys.*

4 **High Court.** This large judicial complex is an outstanding and over-the-top example of Indo-Saracenic architecture, a British style that combines Hindu, Islamic, and gothic elements. The court's red sandstone walls and minarets are covered with intricate ornamentation. (The tallest minaret was used as a lighthouse until the 1970s.) Inside is a labyrinth of corridors and courts, most of which are open for a look if a case or other proceeding is not being heard. Within the compound is a tomb in the shape of a pyramid; one of its two inscriptions is to the only son of Elihu Yale, governor of Fort St. George from 1687 to 1691. The child died in infancy and was buried in the High Court compound. ✉ *Entrance north of fort off N. S. C. Bose Rd., near intersection with Rajaji Salai, Parrys* ☎ *442/534–1773* *free* *Weekdays 10–5.*

1 ★ **St. Mary's Church.** Consecrated in 1680, this Anglican church is the oldest masonry structure in Fort St. George. The *punkahs* (pulley-operated ceiling fans) and some flags are gone, and the steeple has been replaced, but otherwise the building with its arcaded side aisles and bomb-proof roof has not changed. The wedding of governor Elihu Yale (of Yale University fame) was the first one performed here. Job Charnock, founder of Kolkata (then Calcutta), had his three daughters baptized here before the family moved to Bengal. The compound is paved with old tombstones including the oldest British tombstone in India, belonging to an Elizabeth Baker. ✉ *Fort St. George* *Free* *Daily 9:30–5; services Sunday 9* AM *and Fri. 1:30.*

3 **Tamil Nadu State Legislature.** This crowded, active seat of the state government occupies a large part of Fort St. George. The former house of Robert Clive (of the Battle of Plassey fame) is the "Pay Accounts" office. Other sections of the fort are under military control and closed to visitors. ✉ *Fort St. George.*

CENTRAL CHENNAI

As Chennai grew, the city moved south, expanding along the beach and inland to Egmore and Nungambakkam. The Chepauk district, home of Madras University and Chepauk Palace (now government offices), has some of India's best Indo-Saracenic buildings—a combination of Hindu, Muslim, and Victorian Gothic styles that makes a fitting display for a city with roots in all three cultures. Farther south along the beach is the Triplicane neighborhood, with the Parthasarathy Temple. Inland, toward the center of Chennai is Anna Salai, a major shopping and business district. North of Anna Salai is Egmore, bordered by the curves of the Cooum River and home to the National Museum and Art Gallery. Farther south across the Cooum is Nungambakkam, formerly a posh residential area of garden homes. It's now a mixture of expensive boutiques, hotels, and offices—only a few of the massive old houses with walled gardens remain.

Numbers in the text correspond to numbers in the margin and on the Chennai map.

A GOOD TOUR

It's easiest to cover this ground by hiring a car and driver for the day, but you can also take auto-rickshaws from point to point. Early in the morning, drive south on Rajaji Salai (Beach Road) from Fort St. George along the magnificent **Marina Beach** ❺, passing Indo-Saracenic government and university buildings on your right. Keep an eye out for the brick Ice House, near Besant Road: clipper ships from New England, which used ice as ballast, used to unload it here before it found its way into the drinks of the local nobility. It's now officially known as Vivekananda House for a swami that gave speeches here.

Farther south, beyond the contemporary political structures and the public swimming pool on the ocean side is the marina promenade: have your driver stop at its north end (just south of the pool), and take a stroll. Rejoin your driver back in the promenade parking lot and drive to the **Parthasarathy Temple** ❻. Later, take a side-trip to the Egmore neighborhood's **Government Museum** ❼ and its superb collection of South Indian bronze artifacts.

TIMING The marina walk and the temple will each take 30 minutes to an hour and the museum 1 to 2 hours, for a total of 3 to 4 hours.

WHAT TO SEE

❺ ★ **Marina Beach.** This beach is a favorite early-morning promenade and exercise spot. At 6 AM you can see fishing boats casting off and fitness-oriented folks jogging and performing calisthenics or yoga. In the evening, strollers mix with fishermen selling the day's catch. During holidays the beach turns into a carnival, complete with vendors and hand-driven carousels, and everyone comes out to mingle. One thing the beach isn't used for is swimming—the water is dirty and the undertow is dangerously strong. ✉*Kamarajar Rd., between Edward Eliot's Rd. and Cathedral Rd.*

❼ ★ **Government Museum.** This complex of six museums is best known for its superb collection of Pallava and Chola (8th- to 11th-century) bronze sculptures. One highlight is the many Chola Nataraj specimens—a detailed 2-foot statue of the dancing Shiva, surrounded by cosmic fire—but most of the bronzes are worth a look for their detailed craftsmanship and facial expressions. Other artwork from all over South India, including ancient Buddhist statues and Jain sculptures, are well represented. The grounds around the buildings also hold sculptures and other works in stone and metal. This includes some of Tipu Sultan's cannons, whose ends are made to look like a tiger's head. ✉*Pantheon Rd., Egmore* ☎*442/819–3238* 🌐*www.chennaimuseum.org* 🎟*Museum Rs. 250, camera fee Rs. 200, video-camera fee Rs. 500* ⏲*Sat.–Thurs. 9:30–5 (tickets sold until 4:30).*

❻ **Parthasarathy Temple.** Built by the Pallavas in the 8th century and rebuilt by the Vijayanagar kings in the 11th century, this Vishnu temple is dedicated to Krishna, the *sarathi* (charioteer) of Partha (Arjuna), and is probably the oldest temple in Chennai. Legend has it that on the eve of the great battle in the Pandava-Kaurava War, Krishna imparted to Arjuna the Bhagavad Gita (literally "Song of the Blessed Lord"), a religious and philosophic dialogue from the ancient epic, the *Mahabharata.* After passing under the colorful *gopuram* (temple gateway), you'll enter the courtyard, which has several carved shrines. The four streets surrounding the temple have stalls selling flowers, small idols, and other puja articles; musical instruments; and jewelry. ✉ *Off Triplicane High Rd.* ☎ *442/844–7042* 🎫 *Free* 🕙 *Daily 6–noon and 4–9.*

SOUTHERN CHENNAI

In the process of expanding ever southward, Chennai incorporated old areas like Mylapore ("Town of Peacocks"), which has a 13th-century temple, and in the 1930s developed some new areas like T. Nagar (its full name is Thyagaraja Nagar, but no one calls it that). More recently, Besant Nagar and Kalakshetra Colony were incorporated, both residential areas with broad, tree-lined streets and excellent shopping areas where it's relatively easy to get around—except at rush hour. (At one busy intersection in Adyar there's a restaurant called Hotel Traffic Jam. No doubt it's inspired many trapped passengers to pull over.)

Numbers in the text correspond to numbers in the margin and on the Chennai map.

A GOOD DRIVE

In the morning, hire a car and go to the cantonment, a military base and officers' training academy, to see **St. Thomas Mount** ❽. If you have a yen for reptiles, head back east to visit **Madras Snake Park,** in Guindy Park. Should you happen to be near while its open, head to the **Theosophical Society** ❾ and its impressively sylvan compound. Continue on to Krishnamurti's home, **The Study** ❿. From there, go to R.K. Mutt Road and head north to the **Kapaleeswarar Temple** ⓫, then turn right and continue to the end of Kutchery Road to see the **Basilica of San Thome Cathedral** ⓬. End with **Luz Church** ⓭, the oldest church in the city.

TIMING Allow five or six hours for this tour, as there's a lot of driving involved.

WHAT TO SEE

⓬ **Basilica of San Thome Cathedral.** It's commonly held that Thomas the
★ Apostle ("Doubting Thomas") lived his last years in South India, walking daily from his cave at Little Mount to the beach at Mylapore to preach. Before being captured by the French, Dutch, and then the English, San Thome was a Portuguese enclave, its name dating from the cathedral's inception in 1504. In the 1890s the cathedral was reconstructed as a neo-Gothic structure with a 180-foot-tall basilica. St. Thomas is believed to be entombed inside. ✉ *San Thome High Rd.* ☎ *442/498–5857* 🕙 *Daily 7 AM–9 PM.*

⓫ **Kapaleeswarar Temple.** Dating from the 16th century, this crowded Shiva
★ temple is one of the best examples of Dravidian architecture in India. Between mid-March and mid-April during the Arupathumoovar festi-

CLOSE UP

Early-Morning Art

For thousands if not millions of Hindu women across India, an important early-morning ritual is the drawing of intricate, usually symmetrical geometric patterns on the ground outside their front doors. Called *kolams* in Tamil Nadu, these ancient motifs continue to mark the beginning of a new day. Although the practice is not as universal in the cities as in the villages, it's still a widely upheld tradition in the south. People living in Chennai apartment blocks do not have a courtyard in which to draw their kolams, so they sometimes beat the system either by using paint or by buying rubber-and-plastic kolam stickers, which they affix on the landing outside their doors. And children delight in kolam rollers, perforated tubes that roll out designs on the floor when filled with powder.

Dawn is a special time of prayer and purification, and watching a village come to life at sunrise is a singular experience. The most visible aspect of this is the kolam—even an outsider on the street can watch this ritual being performed. First, the housewife sweeps the area outside the house clean with a stiff broom, then—especially in the villages and smaller towns—spreads a layer of cow dung and water on the ground to purify it. Using a white powder (usually made of ground rice, but sometimes limestone), she marks the ground with a series of dots that dictate how the pattern is to be drawn. After this, she pours out more of the powder swiftly between her thumb and fingers to form a delicate line pattern connecting or weaving around the dots. Some women are so skilled at this that they can draw more than one line at the same time using a single hand.

Apart from simply being an early-morning ritual, the using up of the rice is considered an offering to Lakshmi, goddess of wealth and prosperity. Kolams are meant to prevent poverty, welcome desirable guests, and protect the home from evil. At festivals, women pay extra attention to the ritual, making the kolams even larger and more complex than usual. There are also special kolams drawn for different life events. For instance, *thattil* (cradle kolams) are drawn for a baby's naming ceremony. Even though a new one will be drawn again the next day, a kolam is still a precious creation and a symbol that each day is unique.

val (commemorating the 63 Saivite saints, who were devoted to Shiva, also known as Saiva in Sanskrit), the temple streets are closed for 10 days to make room for processions of carts and idols around the complex. Kapaleeswarar is not a rarefied pilgrimage site, but a community gathering place for worship, very much a part of daily life.

Just inside the south entrance, under the gopuram, stands the shrine to Ganesh, a smooth black image of the elephant-headed god that's grown shiny from so many offerings. Worshippers break coconuts in front of and on Ganesh to ask his blessing for a new venture or just for a good day. The temple's large tank is full of hungry fish who have an easy life, devouring bread and other offerings from temple-goers.

Sometimes in the late afternoon, a priest talks to groups of widows in the *mandapam*, or courtyard. Farther on around the temple, to the left, you may see a man prostrate himself before the Nandi (the bull that is Shiva's vehicle), which guards the entrance to the inner sanctum. Continue around the building until you come to a mandapam with statues of the nine planets. It's auspicious to walk clockwise around these planets nine times, so join the procession. Several of the shrines set into the courtyard wall are accessible to non-Hindus. Photography is not allowed inside the temple. ⊠*Between Chitrukullan North St. and Kutchery Rd., Mylapore* ☎*442/464–1670* ⊙*Daily 4* AM*–12:30 and 4* PM*–10* PM.

13 **Luz Church.** Built in 1516, this little, cream-color Portuguese church is the oldest church in the city. It has its own large courtyard, a welcome enclave amid the chaos of narrow pedestrian lanes around it. The interior is mostly whitewashed, with an altar that seems to owe as much to Hindu as to Portuguese design. Legend surrounds the construction of the church: it's said to have been built by Portuguese sailors who claimed to see a mysterious light on the shore, which guided them safely to port. The church is located at the spot where the light disappeared. ⊠*156 Luz Church Rd., Mylapore* ☎*442/499–2568* ⊙*Daily sunrise–sunset.*

8 **St. Thomas Mount.** To get to this old church on a hill, drive to the cantonment and then climb the 135 granite steps, a route that takes in the Stations of the Cross along the way. A serene contrast to Chennai's traffic and crowded streets, the tiny church of Senhora da Expectação (Our Lady of Expectation), built in 1523, offers an aerial view nearly 90 meters (300 feet) above sea level. The interior, which is framed by a semicircular vaulted ceiling, includes two life-size dioramas, one of which memorializes the moment when Thomas the Apostle earned the epithet "Doubting Thomas." Legend has it that Thomas the Apostle ("Doubting Thomas") was martyred while praying here in AD 72. The stone cross set in the altar was excavated by the Portuguese, who built the church over it. The Mount gets very crowded on Sunday. ☎*442/234–2028* 🎟*Church free, camera fee Rs. 20* ⊙*Daily sunrise–8* PM.

10 **The Study.** "Discovered" as a boy by the theosophist C. W. Leadbeater while living on an island next to the Society's south Chennai headquarters, the thinker and religious teacher Krishnamurti would later break away from the Society to inspire others as an independent sage. Shortly before his death in 1986, he directed that the large house and gardens on this site become a place of learning and contemplation, open to anyone who wished to study his teachings in quiet and tranquil surroundings. Called simply "The Study," the center contains a complete library of Krishnamurti's writings, and other books on religion, philosophy, psychology, literature, and the arts. ⊠*Vasanta Vihar, 124/126 Greenways Rd., Bishop Garden* ☎*442/493–7803* 🌐*www.kfionline.org* 🎟*Free* ⊙*Tues.–Fri. 9:30–5:30; weekends 9:30–6:30.*

9 **Theosophical Society.** Although the Society's limited hours and hard-to-find location make it a bit of a feat to visit, this large compound of 270 acres is nevertheless a unique and scenic part of Chennai's history

that's worth the effort. Founded in 1875 in New York City, the Theosophical Society promotes beliefs that are an amalgamation of New Age, occult, and Hindu beliefs. In 1882, the Society moved to Chennai, where it remains. The Theosophical Society is widely renowned in India because of its president Annie Besant, who worked for India's independence from England in the years around World War I—many an Indian city has a Dr. Annie Besant Street as a result. In addition to the lush, tree-filled grounds, the Society also has a vast library containing many old religious and spiritual works. ✉*South side of Thiru Vi Ki Bridge, across from Malar Hosptial, Adyar* ☎*442/491–7198* 🌐*www.ts-adyar.org* 🎟*Free* ⏲*Mon.–Sat., 8:30–10 and 2–4; bookstore Mon.–Sat. 9:30–1 and 2:30–5:30.*

WHERE TO EAT

$$$–$$$$ ✕ **Dakshin.** Decorated with Thanjavur paintings, South Indian statues, and brass lanterns shaped like temple bells, this handsome restaurant serves regional dishes from the "South" (which is what Dakshin means). Meals are presented on banana leaves and set on shining thali trays as Indian musicians perform nightly. A couple of the best entrées include Tamil Nadu's *nandu puttu* (an addictive mixture of steamed crab and spices), or the *meen moilee* ("Malay"-style fish with coconut and ginger) from Kerala, but the extensive menu includes many good options. ✉*Welcomgroup Park Sheraton Hotel & Towers, 132 T. T. K. Rd., Alwarpet* ☎*442/499–4101* 💳*AE, DC, MC, V.*

$$$–$$$$ ✕ **Southern Aromas.** This small restaurant is a great place to go for South Indian nonvegetarian food, but watch out—the food can be very spicy. Wooden furniture with woven cane backing, traditional pillars and paintings, and an ornate tiled floor and ceiling constitute the old-fashioned Chettinad furnishings. One good dish is the *koli ghasi* (chicken simmered in rich chilli-and-coconut gravy). *Murungai ulli theeyal* (shallots and a long, thin fibrous green vegetable called a "drumstick" served with roasted spices and coconut) goes well with any of the several types of rice dishes on offer. If you want something mild, go for *appams* with stew or coconut milk. It's a good idea to make a reservation if it's Saturday night. ✉*The Residency Towers, 115 Sir Thyagaraja Rd., T. Nagar* ☎*442/815–6363* 💳*AE, DC, MC, V.*

$$$–$$$$ ✕ **Southern Spice.** Serving delicacies from the four southern states of Tamil Nadu, Andhra Pradesh, Kerala, and Karnataka, this luxurious restaurant is decorated with metal water jugs, linens with traditional patterns, and other pretty South Indian items. It's a good place to try the traditional Indian *thali,* a set combination lunch platter, and enjoy perfectly cooked *rasam* (a peppery soup), *sambar* (lentil stew), and *poriyals* (stir-fried spiced vegetables). ✉*Taj Coromandel, 37 M. G. Rd. (Nungambakkam High Rd.)* ☎*446/600–2827* 💳*AE, DC, MC, V.*

$$–$$$ ✕ **Raintree.** Outdoors, and among trees twinkling with white Christmas lights at night, this restaurant highlights a Bharatanatyam dance recital and/or an Indian flute performance with dinner. Along with the show you'll enjoy fiery, pepper-laden Chettinad cuisine served on a banana leaf on a copper plate. The *vathal kozhambu* (sun-ripened

berries cooked in a spicy sauce) and *meen varuval* (fish marinated in Chettinad spices, then deep fried) are good choices. So are the *appams* (rice pancakes with a soft middle and crisp edges) with coconut milk (extracted from fresh grated coconut). ✉ *Taj Connemara, 2 Binny Rd., Egmore* ☎ *446/600–0000* ▭ *AE, DC, MC, V* ⊙ *No lunch.*

$–$$ ★ ✕ **Annalakshmi.** Named after the goddess of food, this is one of the best places in the city to enjoy a quiet, laid-back vegetarian Indian meal. The restaurant is run by a charitable trust turning out homey food prepared by volunteers, and then served in a dining room full of religious sculpture and paintings. (Proceeds go to the trust, which funds medical, social, educational, and cultural causes). Try the amazing range of chutneys and ambrosia, a flavorful health drink that's nonalcoholic, like all the beverages served here. ✉ *804 Anna Salai, Mount Road* ☎ *442/852–5109* ▭ *AE, DC, MC, V* ⊙ *Closed Mon.*

$ ✕ **Casa Piccola.** This upstairs branch of a Bangalore chain of cafés has a few open-air tables for watching the shoppers and street traffic below, but there's also a (mercifully) air-conditioned interior for when the heat is unbearable. The eclectic menu here includes burgers, sandwiches, and pasta dishes as well as a few Indian classics. ✉ *11 Khader Nazaz Khan Rd., Nungambakkan* ☎ *446/450–0500* ▭ *MC, V.*

$ ★ ✕ **Somethin' Fishy.** The chef–owner of this comfortable restaurant in central Chennai worked for the Taj Coromandel and the ruler of Dubai before going on his own. Under an awning on the roof of a small hotel, the restaurant makes a nice change from the sometimes stuffy atmosphere of the other notable restaurants in town—and the food is often just a little better. The main ingredients for the seafood-heavy menu come from this port city's seafood markets—winners include beer-battered fish-and-chips (given a small *masala* kick), the crab cakes (made with very little filler), and a seafood risotto. The catch of the day options include such local varieties as emperor, seer, pomfret, and parrot fish. Because of Tamil Nadu licensing laws, no alcohol is served. ✉ *Inn Chennai, 578 Anna Salai, Mount Road* ☎ *444/554–4010* ▭ *MC, V* ⊙ *No lunch. Closed Mon.*

¢ ✕ **Hotel Saravana Bhavan.** This worldwide chain of Indian vegetarian restaurants provides snappy service as well as a long menu of solid dishes. Some branches include buffets, but most have table service (although the bill is usually paid at a counter near the entrance). This is a good place to try South Indian filter coffee as well as such classic South Indian items as dosas, idlys, and *vada* (savory, spicy doughnuts usually made from lentil flour). ✉ *77 Usman Rd., T. Nagar* ☎ *442/434–5577* 🌐 *www.saravanabhavan.com* ✉ *102 Sir Thiyagarata Rd., Pondy Bazaar* ☎ *442/815–4662* ✉ *Spencer Plaza, S-2, Phase I, 2nd fl., 769 Anna Salai, Mount Road* ▭ *MC, V.*

¢ ✕ **Komala's.** A South Indian McDonald's, Komala's began as a restaurant for Indian expats in Singapore. Now very popular in Chennai as well, it serves traditional favorites, such as *masala dosa* (wafer-thin rice and lentil pancakes with a spicy potato filling). The restaurant is a self-service cafeteria: pay at the counter, bring your receipt to the food area, collect a numbered placeholder, and then wait for the food to be delivered to your seat. It all happens more quickly than it takes to explain. ✉ *Near Parsn Complex, 3A Kodambakkam High Rd., Nungambakkam* ☎ *442/822–0074, 442/822–0075 or 442/822–0078* 🌐 *www.komalasweb.com* ▭ *MC, V.*

WHERE TO STAY

$$$$ **Chola Sheraton.** This establishment aims to combine boutique-hotel comfort with the options a larger business hotel provides. The rooms are comfortable and straightforward, with blond wood and the ability to adjust the lighting to different muted settings, turning your room into a nice retreat from the harsh sun outside. Close to the main drag of Anna Salai, the Chola Sheraton is central and about 2 km (1 mi) from downtown. It's also close to several good shopping areas and other attractions, including restaurants and the nightclub Sula. **Pros:** close to the action, pretty hotel, residential area. **Cons:** expensive, slightly bland furnishings, most attractions not walkable. ✉ *Cathedral Rd., Alwarpet, 600086* ☎ *442/811–0101* 🌐 *www.itcwelcomgroup.in* *46 rooms, 46 suites* *In-room: safe, refrigerator, DVD (some), Wi-Fi. In-hotel: 3 restaurants, room service, bar, pool, gym, laundry service, airport shuttle, parking (no fee).* ▭ *AE, DC, MC, V* *BP.*

$$$$ ★ **ITC Hotel Park Sheraton & Towers.** This modern hotel in south-central Chennai has everything the business traveler could possibly need. The Sheraton & Towers rooms and suites are geared for corporate luxury, with a conference room and such amenities as voice mail, Wi-Fi throughout the hotel, and a 24-hour business center. The hotel is expansive, expensive, quiet, and peopled with a courteous and efficient staff. There's also a ladies-only floor for single-women travelers. Its nightclub Dublin, one of the city's most exclusive, is jam-packed on weekends—its hefty annual membership fee is waived for hotel guests. **Pros:** beautiful, impressive hotel, women-only floor, business services. **Cons:** far from sights, very expensive, feels very corporate. ✉ *132 T.T.K. Rd., Alwarpet, 600018* ☎ *442/499–4101* 🌐 *www.itcwelcomgroup.in* *283 rooms, 37 suites* *In-room: safe, refrigerator, DVD, ethernet, Wi-Fi. In-hotel: 3 restaurants, bars, pool, gym, spa, laundry service, concierge, executive floor, airport shuttle, parking (no fee), no-smoking rooms.* ▭ *AE, DC, MC, V* *BP.*

$$$$ **Le Royal Meridien.** Memorable for a showy lobby with a soaring ceiling, this massive, lavish hotel is beautiful and extremely spacious. Near the airport, the Meridien is not exactly convenient to the center of town, but the 3½ acres of tropical, landscaped gardens, a curvy outdoor pool ringed with palm trees, and gracious service make it popular with tourists as well as business travelers. The multicuisine restaurant, Cilantro, is known for its very extensive buffets. **Pros:** close to the airport, beautiful pool, impressive hotel. **Cons:** very expensive, very far from sights, few non-hotel restaurants nearby. ✉ *1 G.S.T. Rd., St. Thomas Mount, 600016* ☎ *442/231–4343* 🌐 *www.leroyalmeridien-chennai.com* *217 rooms, 23 suites* *In-room: safe, refrigerator, Wi-Fi. In-hotel: 3 restaurants, room service, bars, pool, gym, laundry service, concierge, executive floor, airport shuttle, parking (no fee), no-smoking rooms.* ▭ *AE, DC, MC, V.*

$$$$ **Fodor's Choice** ★ **The Park.** Once the headquarters of Gemini Film Studio and a landmark building in the city's long film production history, this luxurious hotel is in a great location. Near the intersection of the Nungambakkam High Road, it's also near lots of shops and restaurants. The interior is showy and modern, with huge doors at the entrance, a soaring lobby divided up by bamboo, a beautiful pool on the roof, and Gemini and Bollywood movie posters in hallways and rooms. The Leather Bar, a tribute to the city's prosperous industry, is decorated accordingly, with leather accents, even on the floors. The nightclub, Pasha, admits hotel guests at no extra charge. **Pros:** great bars on-site, funky lobby, central location. **Cons:** very expensive, near a busy intersection, "superior" rooms come with a hefty surcharge. ✉ *601 Anna Salai, Nungambakkam, 600006* ☎ *444/214–4000* 🌐 *www.theparkhotels.com* *199 rooms, 15 suites* *In-room: safe, refrigerator, DVD, ethernet, Wi-Fi. In-hotel: 3 restaurants, room service, bar, pool, gym, spa, laundry service, airport shuttle, parking (no fee), no-smoking rooms.* *AE, DC, MC, V* *BP.*

$$$–$$$$ **Radisson GRT.** Inside this white, neocolonial hotel there's a charming garden and a wide porch for lounging. The rooms are spacious and furnished with classic wooden furniture. Service is extremely efficient, and the Wi-Fi here is free—a rarity in India. One of the house restaurants, the Great Kebab Factory, serves piles of kebabs—eat here only if you're really hungry. The hotel is 3 km (2 mi) from the airport, and therefore far from most sights. **Pros:** close to the airport, free Wi-Fi, great restaurant. **Cons:** fairly expensive, very far from sights, few non-hotel restaurants nearby. ✉ *531 G.S.T. Rd., St. Thomas Mount, 600016* ☎ *442/231–0101* 🌐 *www.grthotels.com* *94 rooms, 7 suites* *In-room: safe, refrigerator, Wi-Fi. In-hotel: 2 restaurants, room service, bar, pool, gym, spa, laundry service, concierge, airport shuttle, public Wi-Fi, parking (no fee).* *AE, DC, MC, V* *CP.*

$$$–$$$$ ★ **Taj Connemara.** Built as a *nawab's* (Muslim prince's) home in the 19th century, the Taj Connemara fills it generous hallways with period photographs. Despite the pull of the past, this historic luxury hotel holds a central location in modern Chennai, next door to Spencer Plaza and the rest of the bustle on Anna Salai. The marble-floored lobby is flanked by Hindu statues, temple friezes, and palm trees in copper pots; in the center is a lovely wrought-iron chandelier. Standard rooms include lots of wood and classic touches, but the pricier heritage rooms (in the old wing) have soaring ceilings, soft white lighting, and a desk area that overlooks the outdoor pool. The open-air Raintree restaurant offers classical Indian dance with dinner. **Pros:** beautiful heritage building, lots of wood and tall ceilings in good-sized rooms, close to Spencer Plaza. **Cons:** very expensive, near a busy intersection, occasional bad music in the bar. ✉ *2 Binny Rd., Egmore, 600002* ☎ *446/600–0000* 🌐 *www.tajhotels.com* *141 rooms, 9 suites* *In-room: safe (some), refrigerator, Wi-Fi. In-hotel: 3 restaurants, room service, bar, pool, gym, laundry service, airport shuttle.* *AE, DC, MC, V.*

$$$$ **Taj Coromandel.** An ornate marble fountain, enormous flower arrangements, lots of wood details, and plenty of lounge space tie together the giant lobby of this central hotel, where the emphasis is

on luxury and business services. Many of the elegant guest rooms—particularly those on the upper floors—have pretty city views, including palm trees. Entertainment centers with huge TVs and surround sound are also available in some rooms. **Pros:** magisterial lobby, great TVs in rooms, attentive service. **Cons:** very expensive, businessy feel, a little distant from sights. ✉ *37 M. G. Rd. (Nungambakkam High Rd.), 600034* ☎ *446/600–2827* 🌐 *www.tajhotels.com* *183 rooms, 22 suites* *In-room: safe, refrigerator, DVD (some), ethernet, Wi-Fi. In-hotel: 3 restaurants, room service, bar, pool, gym, spa, laundry services, concierge, airport shuttle, parking (no fee), no-smoking rooms.* *AE, DC, MC, V.*

$$$ **GRT Grand.** Soaring 31 meters (100 feet) high, an atrium lobby sets the scene at this efficient hotel in the central neighborhood of T. Nagar. Glass elevators take you up to well-equiped and well-designed rooms that get lots of light. The hotel is off of Anna Salai and a quick drive to many sights; Pondy Bazaar is about a 15 minute walk away. **Pros:** impressive lobby, great service, location that's great for shopping, cheerful, bright rooms. **Cons:** expensive, pool is underground, a bit of a corporate feel. ✉ *120 Sir Thyagaraja Rd., T. Nagar, 600017* ☎ *442/815–0500 or 44/2815–5500* 🌐 *www.grtgrand.com* *133 rooms, 7 suites* *In-room: safe, refrigerator, DVD (some), Wi-Fi. In-hotel: 3 restaurants, room service, bar, pool, gym, spa, concierge, executive floor, public Wi-Fi, airport shuttle, parking (no fee), no-smoking rooms.* *AE, DC, MC, V* *BP.*

$$$ **Fisherman's Cove.** The main building of this isolated Taj resort is colorful and whimsical. Its setting—the site of a former Dutch fort—is luxurious: there's a woodsy open-air lobby, a large pool with a swim-up bar, and an open-air seafood restaurant and bar right on the edge of the sea. (Unfortunately, the beach is rocky and not suitable for swimming.) At the water's edge, the round seaside cottages have porches and outdoor garden showers. The luxury cottages have spacious porches with hammocks where you can relax and catch a breeze. If you're taking a room in the main hotel building, keep in mind that seaview rooms are only about $25 more a night. The hotel is 28 km (17 mi) south of Chennai on the Shore Road to Mahabalipuram. **Pros:** beautiful location on the way to the Shore Temple, classic resort with seaside views and location, relaxing, luxurious rooms. **Cons:** no swimming here, too far from Chennai to visit the city easily, expensive. ✉ *Covelong Beach, Kanchipuram District 603112* ☎ *446/741–3333* 🌐 *www.tajhotels.com* *50 rooms, 38 cottages* *In-room: dial-up. In-hotel: 3 restaurants, 2 bars, tennis court, pool, gym, spa, beachfront, water sports, laundry service, public Internet, public Wi-Fi, airport shuttle.* *AE, DC, MC, V.*

$$$ **Raintree.** Not to be confused with the restaurant in the Taj Connemara, this luxury hotel, built in 2005, follows energy-saving and other environmentally sensitive procedures. The more expensive rooms have bamboo floors, and all are furnished in blond wood, cool colors, and crisp and minimal rather than busy patterns. The downstairs club Havana serves Cuban cigars as well as drinks, and the rooftop pool abuts the Above Sea Level restaurant. **Pros:** calm environment, new rooms, fun bars on-site. **Cons:** expensive for the size of the rooms,

earnest eco message not for everyone, rooms can seem a little bland. ✉*120 St. Mary's Rd., Alwarpet, 600018* ☎*444/225–2525* 🌐*www.raintreehotels.com* *100 rooms, 5 suites* *In-room: safe, Wi-Fi (some). In-hotel: 3 restaurants, room service, bars, gym, laundry service, airport shuttle, no-smoking rooms.* *AE, DC, MC, V* *BP.*

$$$ **Trident Hilton.** An exquisite brass lotus pond is a welcoming sight in this modern business hotel's small but attractive lobby, which also has an interior garden and waterfall. Indian fabrics decorate the spacious and elegant rooms, the best of which overlook the pool. The Trident's near the airport, 10 km (6 mi) outside the city. **Pros:** close to airport, beautiful pond, near business parks. **Cons:** expensive, very far from sights, not near non-hotel restaurants. ✉*1/24 G.S.T. Rd., Meenambakkam, 600027* ☎*442/234–4747* 🌐*www.trident-hilton.com* *162 rooms, 5 suites* *In-room: safe, refrigerator, DVD (some), Wi-Fi. In-hotel: restaurants, room service, bar, pool, gym, laundry service, concierge, airport shuttle, parking (no fee), no-smoking rooms.* *AE, DC, MC, V* *BP.*

$$ **The Residency Towers.** This sleek hotel is within walking distance of Pondy Bazaar. With standard floral or geometric carpets and gleaming wooden furniture rooms are both comfortable and modern. The Towers is well known for its popular bar and disco, Bike and Barrel, which is outfitted like an English pub. As a result weekends can be a little noisy, and in-house restaurants are often full. The hotel has one floor reserved exclusively for female guests. **Pros:** close to Pondy Bazaar, pleasant rooms, cool bar. **Cons:** a little pricey, bar can be loud on weekends, location not near most sight-seeing. ✉*Sir Thyagaraya Road, T. Nagar, 600017* ☎*442/815–6363* 🌐*www.theresidency.com* *156 rooms, 18 suites* *In-room: safe, kitchen (some), ethernet, Wi-Fi. In-hotel: 3 restaurants, room service, bar, pool, gym, spa, laundry service, public Wi-Fi, airport shuttle, parking (no fee), no-smoking rooms.* *AE, DC, MC, V* *BP.*

$ **Quality Inn Sabari.** With comfortable rooms and a good location in a residential area, the Quality Inn attracts lots of businesspeople from in and out of India. Some of the rooms have walls that are a little thin, but they're also quite comfortable and restful. The hotel's conference center across the street has a supermarket and pharmacy—two very handy amenities. **Pros:** great value in this pricey city, quiet location, easy to get to most parts of town, great supermarket across the street. **Cons:** small, poky restaurant, sights require a car or auto-rickshaw ride, thin walls in some rooms. ✉*29 Thirumalai Pillai Rd., T. Nagar, 600017* ☎*442/834–3030* 🌐*www.qualityinnsabari.com* *72 rooms* *In-room: safe, refrigerator, Wi-Fi. In-hotel: restaurant, room service, bar, laundry service, public Internet, airport shuttle, parking (no fee), no-smoking rooms.* *AE, DC, MC, V* *BP.*

$ **The Residency.** Making no pretense to overblown elegance or luxury this nine-story tower block is decorated with modest furnishings, in a relatively austere style—it's also a good value. Service is courteous and prompt; that, combined with the hotel's location and room rates, makes it very popular with Indian businessmen. Upper-floor corner rooms on two sides of the hotel have good views of Chennai. The 24-

hour coffee shop serves both Indian and Continental food. **Pros:** good value, hotel guests not just other Westerners, nice residential location. **Cons:** stripped-down, not fancy, no major sights in walking distance. ✉ *49 G.N. Chetty Rd., T. Nagar, 600017* ☎ *442/825–3434* 🌐 *www.theresidency.com* *101 rooms, 11 suites* *In-room: refrigerator, Wi-Fi. In-hotel: 3 restaurants, room service, bar, laundry service, airport shuttle.* ▭ *AE, DC, MC, V* 🍽 *BP.*

NIGHTLIFE & THE ARTS

A conservative and traditional Hindu city, Chennai has a nightlife that centers mainly around dance and musical events. It's a national center of classical Indian dance and Carnatic music (the classical music of South India; a song with improvised variations), December is the peak month for recitals, though there are performances in January and February, too. Because Tamil Nadu highly regulates alcohol, most bars and discos are usually open only until 11 PM and tend to be located inside large upmarket hotels.

DANCE

Dances from all over India are performed at DakshinaChitra, south of Chennai. See the Side Trips section. The **Kalakshetra Foundation** (✉ *Kalakshetra Rd., Thiruvanmiyur* ☎ *442/452–0836* 🌐 *www.kalakshetra.net*), founded by the famous dancer Rukmini Devi and now a government-run university, has music and dance classes where you can drop in and watch. **Kuchipudi Art Academy** (✉ *4 Greenways Rd., R.A. Puram* ☎ *442/493–7260* 🌐 *www.kuchipudi.com*) has classes in Kuchipudi dance.

MUSIC

The period from mid-December to mid-January is packed with hundreds of Carnatic music concerts and lectures. Concerts usually follow a set pattern: an initial *raga* (a melodic scale) is followed by variations and improvisation by both the soloist and the accompanying instrumentalists. See 🌐 www.artindia.net and local editions of newspapers, especially the *Hindu,* for performance listings.

BARS & DISCOS

Bike and Barrel (✉ *Sir Thyagaraja Rd., T. Nagar* ☎ *442/815–6363*), at the Residency Towers, is a very popular Brit-themed disco and bar for the wealthy, young, hot-to-trot locals. **Distil** (✉ *Taj Connemara, 2 Binny Rd., Egmore* ☎ *446/600–0000*), the Taj's pleasing and energetic bar, is a good place to meet for pre-dinner drinks.

Flame Le Club (✉ *Le Royal Meridien, 1 G.S.T. Rd., St. Thomas Mount* ☎ *442/231–4343*) disco is lit by electric torchlight. **Fort St. George** (✉ *Taj Coromandel, 37 M.G. Rd. [Nungambakkam High Rd.]* ☎ *446/600–2827*) is a classy bar that perfectly complements the Taj's business-class clientele. At the trendy Park Hotel, **The Leather Bar** (✉ *601 Anna Salai, Nungambakkam* ☎ *444/214–4000*) is a scene: it's all leather (even the floor), and it has a drawing room feel, with books and knickknacks on the shelves. **Pasha** (✉ *The Park, 601 Anna Salai, Nungambakkam* ☎ *444/214–4000*) is a fashionable lounge where DJ'd music spills out into the hotel lobby. **Zara's** (✉*74 Cathedral Rd., Alwarpet* ☎*442/811-4941*) serves cocktails, wine, and Spanish snacks. (Men aren't allowed to wear sandals here.)

COFFEE SHOPS

The coffee chains Barista and Café Coffee Day are scattered throughout the upscale areas of the city.

Mocha (✉*15 Khader Nawaz Khan Rd., Nungambakkam* ☎*444/231-7690*) café serves coffee, small dishes, and hookahs to groups of wealthy, young locals. The grounds, which include a lotus pond and lots of shade, make the place a great break from the dust and noise elsewhere.

SHOPPING

Khader Nawaz Khan Road, close to the city center in Nungambakkam, is a high-end shopping destination, with lots of boutiques and several coffee shops and restaurants for dropping once the shopping is through.

BAZAARS

Pondy Bazaar (✉*T. Nagar*), extending east along Thyagaraya Road from its start near Panagal Park, is a quintessentially Indian mixture of old- and new-style bazaars, with more than 30 stalls and stores selling stuffed animals, vegetables and fruit, silk saris, and jewelry. **Spencer's Plaza** (✉*768–769 Anna Salai, Mount Road*) is a large mazelike mall confusingly divided into "phases." Inside you can find leather goods, clothing, groceries, crockery, jewelry, and handicrafts as well as ATMs, travel agents, Internet cafés, and foreign exchange. There are also a large bookshop–home store, Landmark; a clothing chain, Pantaloons; and the Westside department store. The first floor holds an American Express office. The bazaars and the mall are open every day.

BOOKS

Higginbothams (✉*814 Anna Salai, Mount Road* ☎*442/851–3519*), in business since 1844, still operates its flagship from a big white store on Chennai's main drag. It has a good selection of books about South India, as well as Indian and Western fiction. **Landmark** (✉*Spencer Plaza, Phase 2, 768–769 Anna Salai, Mount Road* ☎*442/849–5995* 🌐*www.landmarkonthenet.com*) department store sells books, CDs and DVDs, stationery, luggage, housewares, and many other desirable items. **Oxford Bookstore** (✉*39/12 Haddows Rd., Nungambakkam* ☎*442/822–7714* 🌐*www.oxfordbookstore.com*) has a good selection of Indian and non-Indian literature, magazines, and art and travel books. There's also a nice tea bar with Internet access available.

CLOTHING AND ACCESSORIES

Cotton World (✉*Ambleside 1st fl., above Naturally Auroville, 8 Khader Nawaz Khan Rd., Nungambakkam* ☎*442/833–2074 or 442/833–3290*) is a good place for high-quality Western clothes. **Silkworm Boutique** (✉*30 Khader Nawaz Khan Rd., Nungambakkam* ☎*442/833–1991*) sells high-end saris, scarves, and other clothes for women.

Pantaloons (✉*Spencer Plaza, Phase II, 768–69 Anna Salai* ☎*44/2848–8533 or 44/2848–8534*) sells sporty and well-made men's, women's, and children's clothing.

Hidesign (✉*S120, 2nd floor, Phase III, Spencer Plaza, 768–69 Anna Salai* ☎*444/214–1487*) sells a wide selection of well-made wallets, purses, bags, and other leather goods in its boutique at the mall.

Co-optex (✉*350 Pantheon Rd., Egmore* ☎*442/819–3175 (office)* 🌐*www.cooptex.com*) may be a little run-down, and some of the prints can be a little *too* vivid, but this cooperative of textile makers has good prices and a large selection that make a visit worthwhile. It's a short walk from the Government Museum.

The giant **Nalli Chinnasami Chetty** (✉*9 Nageswaran Rd., Panagal Park, T. Nagar* ☎*442/434–4115 or 444/260–4567* 🌐*www.nallisilk.com*) store, better known as Nalli's, is famous for its Kanchipuram silk saris and vast assortment of silk fabrics, plus casual cotton clothes. It's a zoo, in the best possible way, and service is excellent. Another branch is around the corner, at 100 Usman Road. **Rasi** (✉*1 Sannadhi St., Mylapore* ☎*442/494–1906* 🌐*www. www.radhasilk.com*) carries fine Kanchipuram silks. **Shilpi** (✉*29 C.P. Ramaswamy Rd., Alwarpet* ☎*442/499–0918* ✉*Gee Gee Minar, College Rd., Nungambakkam* ☎*442/822–0186*) is a popular, chic boutique with well-designed ready-made clothes, including *salwars* (tunics), *kurtas* (shirts), skirts, and vests, as well as handloom fabrics and household furnishings. **Sundari Silks** (✉*38 North Usman Rd., T. Nagar* ☎*442/814–3093*) has Kanchipuram silks as well as silks and cottons from across India and a range of reasonably priced home furnishings.

JEWELRY

Many of Chennai's jewelry stores are concentrated near T. Nagar around Panagal Park, near Pondy Bazaar and the many silk and sari stores. The throng of spend-happy ladies here can make shopping into an Olympic event, especially before and during festivals.

G. R. Thanga Maligai (✉*136 Usman Rd., T. Nagar* ☎*442/434–5052 or 442/434–5052* 🌐*www.grtjewels.com*) is a city landmark for fine jewelry. A branch selling silver items is next door. **Prince Jewellery** (✉*41 Cathedral Rd., Alwarpet* ☎*442/811–7720 or 442/811–7730* 🌐*www.princejewellery.com*) specializes in modern and custom jewelry. More branches are in Spencer Plaza (Phase 1) and in Panagal Park (T. Nagar).

HOUSEWARES

Fabindia (✉*Ilford House, 3 Woods Rd., off Anna Salai, Mount Road* ☎*442/851–0395, 444/202–7015, or 444/216–8346* 🌐*www.fabindia.com*), in a beautifully restored heritage building, stocks tablecloths, cotton rugs, towels as well as clothes for men and women. **Evoluzione** (✉*3 Khader Nawaz Khan Rd., Nungambakkam* ☎*444/213–9800*) sells high-end, modernist vases, gift items, and furniture in a three-story boutique. A clothing annex is down the block at 30 Khader Nawaz Khan Road. **Naturally Auroville** (✉*Ambleside Ground Fl., 8 Khader*

Nawaz Khan Rd., Nungambakkam ☎*442/833–0517 to 18*) has stunning pottery, lamps and lampshades, incense, and other products from Auroville. **Arts & Teak** (✉*8 Harrington Rd., Chetpet* ☎*444/232–7887 or 444/232–7888*) sells jewelry and gift items as well as furniture, carpets, and other items for decorating the home.

HANDICRAFTS

The government-run **Central Cottage Industries Emporium** (✉*672 Anna Salai, Nandanam* ☎*442/433–0809*) stocks clothes, handicrafts, bronzes, hand-loomed fabrics and rugs, and jewelry from all over India. **Victoria Technical Institute (VTI)** (✉*765 Anna Salai, Mount Road* ☎*442/852–3141 or 442/852–3153* ⊙*Weekdays 9:30–6, Sat. 9:30–1:30*), in business since the beginning of the 20th century, has high-quality embroidery work, children's clothing, handicrafts, bronze and sandalwood items, metal lamps, wood carvings, and table linens. **Amethyst** (✉*14 Padmavathi Rd., off Lloyds Rd., Jeypore Colony, Gopalapuram* ☎*442/835–1143*) sells exclusive handicrafts, jewelry, and clothing displayed in a colonial building. There's also a café. **Contemporary Arts & Crafts** (✉*45 C.P. Ramaswamy Rd., Alwarpet* ☎*442/499–7069*) has an unusual range of pottery and metalcraft.

SIDE TRIPS

The Crocodile Bank and DakshinaChitra both make good stops on the way to or from Mahabalipuram, to the south.

MADRAS CROCODILE BANK

34 km (21 mi) south of Chennai.

★ Founded in 1976 by American conservationist Romulus Whitaker to protect India's dwindling crocodile population and to preserve the Irula (snake-catching) tribe's way of life, the Crocodile Bank has raised more than 6,000 crocodiles and related species. They're even shipped to other countries to support croc populations worldwide. The animals, which also include gharials and cute-looking turtles—are housed in sunken, open-air enclosures. Daily venom extractions from cobras, kraits, and vipers are not only an entertaining attraction (Rs. 5 additional), but also have helped the Irulas maintain their snake-catching culture. The venom is used to make anti-venom. ✉*East Coast Rd., Vendanemeli* ☎*442/747–2447* *www.madrascrocodilebank.org* *Rs. 20, camera fee Rs. 10, video-camera fee Rs. 75* ⊙*Tues.–Sun. 8–6.*

DAKSHINACHITRA

★ *29 km (18 mi) south of Chennai.*

The DakshinaChitra heritage center, "A Picture of the South," is a reconstructed village made to encapsulate major parts of South Indian culture. In a pretty, rural setting, open-air displays embody domestic Indian architecture from the 19th and 20th centuries. Many of these buildings were painstakingly moved and rebuilt here. Along the 19th-century streets stand tradesmen's houses, each typical of its professional group. Artisans employ traditional techniques to make exquisite pottery, baskets, and carved stone items, some of which are for sale. Authenticity and attention to detail rule here. The main hall of the Chettinad House hosts folk and classical dance performances, for which tickets can be reserved in advance. The restaurant serves South Indian dishes, and there are also several guesthouses with prices starting at Rs. 500. ✉ *East Coast Rd., Muttukadu, Chingelpet District 603118* ☎ *442/747–2603, 442/747–2783* 🌐 *www.dakshinachitra.net* 🎫 *Rs. 175* 🕒 *Wed.–Mon. 10–6.*

MAHABALIPURAM, KANCHIPURAM & PONDICHERRY

Mahabalipuram and Kanchipuram reflect the glorious pasts of three great dynasties: Pallava, Chola, and Vijayanagar. The Pallava capital Kanchipuram, a town of learning founded in the 4th century AD, became fertile ground for a vast number of temples. From the port at Mahabalipuram, the Pallavas began to trade with China and Indonesia, a tradition expanded by succeeding empires, Chola and Vijayanagar. Together, the three dynasties laid the foundations of Tamil history, language, and religion, and with each dynasty the temples became larger and more elaborate. When its port was abandoned in the ninth century, Mahabalipuram became a deserted historical site, so it's now largely a traveler's curiosity; Kanchipuram is still a major pilgrimage destination. Pondicherry, with its strong French influence, is cherished for being refreshingly different from any other place in India.

MAHABALIPURAM

59 km (37 mi) south of Chennai, 64 km (40 mi) southeast of Kanchipuram.

In the 8th century, the Pallava dynasty conducted a thriving maritime trade from this port city, sending emissaries to China, Southeast Asia, and Indonesia; carved stone is all that now remains of these dynamic businessmen, who ultimately ruled from the 6th to 9th centuries. The rock structures they left behind can be broken down into monolithic rock temples (*rathas*), cave temples, temples constructed from a conglomeration of materials, and bas-relief sculptures carved on large rocks.

It's a wonderful place to visit, especially between December and February, when the heat is under control. You can divide your time between exploring magnificent ancient temples and relaxing at a beach resort. In addition to the government shops, independent shops sell granite images and carvings reminiscent of the temples; many of these are remarkably well done. The sights are open all day, but the best times to visit are early morning and late afternoon.

Numbers in the text correspond to numbers in the margin and on the Mahabalipuram map.

Five Rathas 1
Krishna Mandapam........2
Mahishasuramardini Cave 3
Penance of Arjuna 4
Shore Temple 5
Tiger Cave 6
Tirukkalikundram 7

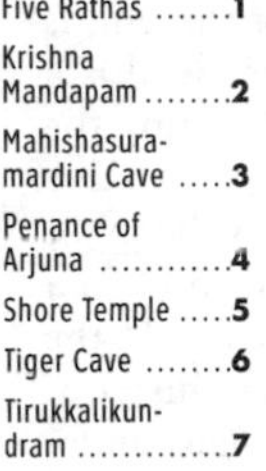

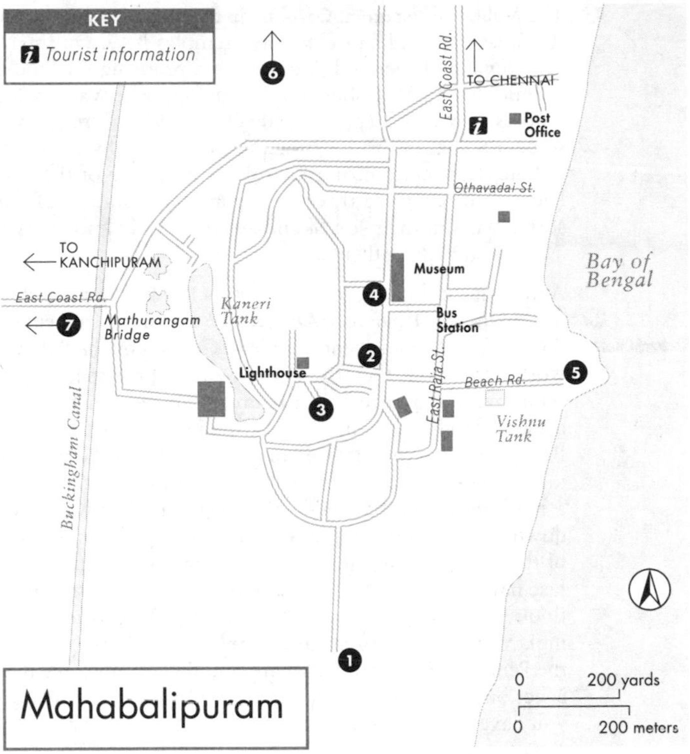
KEY
Tourist information
East Coast Rd.
TO CHENNAI
Post Office
Othavadai St.
TO KANCHIPURAM
Museum
Bay of Bengal
East Coast Rd.
Kaneri Tank
Mathurangam Bridge
Bus Station
Lighthouse
East Raja St.
Beach Rd.
Vishnu Tank
Buckingham Canal
0
200 yards
0
200 meters
Mahabalipuram

❶ The **Five Rathas** are also called the Pancha Pandava Rathas for the Five Pandava sons in the ancient Hindu epic *Mahabharata*. The Rathas, probably the most famous example of Pallava architecture, are carved out of five pieces of granite, and may have been "samples" created by a sculpting school based in Mahabalipuram. Each temple is distinctive, with its own elevation, plan, and exquisite detail. From north to south, they are the **Draupadi** (named for the wife of the Pandavas), dedicated to Durga, a warrior goddess; the **Arjuna** (named for the charioteer of the Bhagavad Gita, part of the *Mahabharata*), dedicated to the thunder god Indra; the **Bhima** (named for a Pandava son), the largest temple; the **Sahadeva** (named for a Pandava prince), part of which represents a Buddhist chapel; and the **Dharmaraja,** dedicated to Shiva. Three animal sculptures—an elephant, a lion, and the bull Nandi (the vehicles of Indra, Durga, and Shiva)—complete the display. Because all the temples are unfinished, it may be that the animal carvings were meant to have been moved to the appropriate Ratha. *Rs. 250, also allows same-day entry to Shore Temple* *Daily 9:30–6.*

❷ The bas-relief sculpture on the back wall of the **Krishna Mandapam** (a later cave temple) shows Krishna holding up the Govardhan mountain to protect his people from floods ordered by the thunder god Indra. There's also a naturalistic figure of a cow being milked. ✉ *W. Raja St.*

3 The **Mahishasuramardini Cave,** near the lighthouse on top of the hill, is the most outstanding of the cave temples here. On the right wall is a carved panel depicting Durga riding a prancing lion and defeating the buffalo demon Mahishasura. On the opposite wall, in contrast to this battle scene, is a deeply carved relief of Vishnu reclining on the great serpent Sesha. In this position, Vishnu is usually considered to be in a cosmic sleep, epitomizing his role as preserver of the universe. At the back of the cave are three cells containing statues of Shiva, his consort Uma, and their son Skanda—collectively known as Somaskanda, a common Pallava theme.

4 Fodor's Choice ★ A monumental bas-relief—29 meters (96 feet) long and 13 meters (43 feet) high—the **Penance of Arjuna,** also called the Descent of the Ganges, is carved on two adjacent boulders. Created by the Pallava dynasty, the work dates from the 7th century. Among the many figures depicted, both mythical and real, is a figure of Shiva with an ascetic Arjuna to his left, standing on one leg. The rendering illustrates a scene from the Bhagavad Gita, in which Arjuna asks Shiva for help defeating his enemies. An extensive but unfinished Pallava water canal system included a pool above the bas-relief; the idea was that water would cascade down a natural cleft in the rock from this pool, simulating the descent of the Ganges from the Himalayas. The entire, enormous project is a fascinating and vital combination of the mundane and the mythical (look for the starving cat at the bottom, who has renounced his mousing). More than a dozen **cave temples** are cut into the rock hill behind the Penance of Arjuna. Some are unfinished and some have been damaged, but nearly all are remarkable. Most are atop the granite hill, so you have to take a short hike to reach them. ✉ *Behind bus stand, W. Raja St.* 🎫 *Free.*

5 ★ Facing the Bay of Bengal, the **Shore Temple** has been subject for centuries to the vicissitudes of sun, sea, and sand, including the force of 2004's tsunami, which revealed additional sculptures that had been buried in the sand. Despite the ravages of time, the temple still retains many of the details it had when it was built by the Pallava king Rajasimha in the early 8th century. You enter the temple from the back, through a courtyard surrounded by a massive wall topped by reclining bulls and two Shiva towers. Inside one shrine, the calm image of Vishnu, lying in cosmic sleep on the sea with the serpent Sesha at his side, is still easy to make out. ✉ *On ocean, follow signs* 🎫 *Foreigners US$5, includes entry to Five Rathas* ⏲ *Daily 9:30–6.*

6 The **Tiger Cave,** which is actually two boulders set together, is in a shady grove near the ocean—it's a favorite picnic spot. Dedicated to Durga, the cave is distinguished by the crown of carved tiger heads around its temple. ✉ *Village of Saluvankuppam, 5 km (3 mi) north of Mahabalipuram.*

7 **Tirukkalikundram** *(Sacred Hill of Kites)* is the name of both a village and its temple, which has Dutch, English, and ancient Indian inscriptions. The ride here from Mahabalipuram takes you through rice fields. Pilgrims come to climb the 500 steps to the temple on the hilltop at noon,

in the hope that the two kites (hawks) will come to be fed by the Brahmin priests. ✉*15 km (9 mi) west of Mahabalipuram.*

WHERE TO EAT & STAY

Lodging in Mahabalipuram includes costly resorts with manicured grounds as well as guesthouses that cost under Rs. 500 a day. There's also an abundance of good, inexpensive restaurants serving mainly seafood. Located along the beach and on the main tourist drag of Othavadai Street, most of these places display their fish and seafood dinner choices. Choose what you want and how you want it prepared, agree on a price (a little bargaining might be in order), and then wait until it arrives with sides of rice and french fries.

$$–$$$ ✕ **The Wharf.** Under thatched roofs and overlooking the shore, the Wharf is an upscale version of the seaside shacks closer to town. Although there's a multicuisine menu, the focus is on seafood, with king prawns, kingfish, crab, and lobster cooked to order. With the grills and tandoor oven in plain sight, you can watch as the chef cooks your selection with the spices and method you indicate. ✉*GRT Temple Bay Resort, Kovalam Rd., Mahabalipuram* ☎*442/744–3636* ▭*AE, DC, MC, V.*

¢–$ ✕ **Sea Shore.** One of several more or less interchangeable shack restaurants in Mahabalipuram, this open-air eatery serves straightforward seafood and Continental dishes accompanied by peaceful views of fishing boats and the Shore Temple in the distance. If you want your dish to be spicy, be sure to let them know. ✉*Bottom of Othavadai St., near ocean, 30 Fisherman's Colony* ☎*442/744–2074 or 442/744–2047* ▭*No credit cards.*

¢–$ ✕ **Moonrakers.** One of the most popular restaurants in the backpacker part of town, this is the perfect place to soak in the laid-back Mahabalipuram mood. Dinner here is more comfortable than lunch (there's no air-conditioning) and is cooked to suit Western tastes. However, a request for "Indian-style" food usually yields good results as well. In addition to standard Indian and Western, the restaurant also serves solid seafood and European-style food at remarkably low prices—try the garlic prawns in butter sauce or the fried calamari. ✉*34 Othavadai St.* ☎*442/744–2115* 🌐*www.moonrakersrestaurant.com* ▭*No credit cards.*

$$$ ★ **GRT Temple Bay.** Facing a golden stretch of beach with the Shore Temple in view and within walking distance, the GRT has a beautiful (and practical) location. Built in 1957 and well-maintained on carefully manicured grounds, the hotel has rooms in a main building and in cottages with two doubles per unit. **Pros:** beautiful location, impressive restaurant and facilities, Shore Temple within walking distance. **Cons:** expensive given location, resort feel means you're isolated from town, no private beach and beach vendors can be a hassle. ✉*Kovalam Rd., Mamallapuram, 603104* ☎*442/744–3636* 🌐*www.grttemplebay.com* *70 rooms, 2 suites* *In-room: safe, refrigerator. In-hotel: 2 restaurants, room service, bar, pool, gym, spa, beachfront, laundry service, airport shuttle.* ▭*AE, DC, MC, V.*

¢ **Green Woods Beach Resort.** One of the better of the relatively barebones guesthouses in town, Green Woods lives up to its name, with the refurbished house's rooms surrounding potted plants, trees, and shrubs. Rooms have few amenities—you'll want to bring a top sheet, towel, and toiletries, or buy them on Othavadai Street. In return, you get a very good value, the beachfront a stone's throw away, and friendly, family-run management. **Pros:** quick walk to beach and all sights, homey, friendly staff, great value. **Cons:** rooms low on amenities, neighborhood can be busy, can be hard to find. ✉ *7 Othavadai Cross St., 603104* ☎ *411/424–3318 or 411/424–2212* ✉ *greenwoods_resort@yahoo.com* *13 rooms, 2 suites* *In-room: no a/c (some), no phone. In-hotel: restaurant, laundry facilities, airport shuttle.* ▭ *No credit cards* *CP or BP.*

¢ ★ **Ideal Beach Resort.** The grounds of this resort, run by Tamils from Sri Lanka, are restful and filled with shrubs, trees, sculptures, and even a cage of cheerful parakeets. Since the resort is a few miles out of town, it's most ideal for those more interested in the beach than ancient sculptures. Breakfast costs an additional Rs. 225 per person. **Pros:** beautiful grounds, great value, homey atmosphere. **Cons:** isolated and far from town, no other nearby dining options aside from hotel, breakfast overpriced. ✉ *East Coast Rd., Devaneri Village, 603104* ☎ *442/744–2240 or 442/744–2443* 🌐 *www.idealresort.com* *7 rooms, 2 suites, 36 cottages* *In-room: refrigerator, Wi-Fi. In-hotel: 3 restaurants, room service, bar, pool, spa, beachfront, no elevator, laundry service, airport shuttle.* ▭ *MC, V.*

¢ **Mamalla Heritage.** A happy medium between the more expensive beach resorts outside of town and the bare-bones backpacker spots, the Mamalla Beach resort is popular with Indian tourists as well as foreigners. Rooms are fairly large and comfortable; the buffet at the vegetarian restaurant Golden Palette is a good place for Indian classics, and at Rs. 95 it's also a good deal. **Pros:** great location, friendly staff, good restaurant. **Cons:** town can be loud and busy, furnishings feel a little plain, tour-group environment. ✉ *104 E. Raja St., 603104* ☎ *442/744–2060 or 442/744–2260* 🌐 *www.hotelmamallaheritage.com* *43 rooms* *In-room: safe, refrigerator. In-hotel: 2 restaurants, room service, bar, pool, laundry service.* ▭ *AE, MC, V* *CP.*

EN ROUTE

From October to March, thousands of waterbirds, egrets, pelicans, storks, and herons come to nest in the 73 acres that make up the **Vedanthangal Bird Sanctuary,** the oldest bird haven in India. The best times to see them are late afternoon and early morning in December and January. *For information contact the Wild Life Warden* *DMS Compound, 259 Anna Salai, 4th fl., Teynampet Chennai 600026* ✉ *65 km (40 mi) southwest of Mahabalipuram via Chengalpattu* ☎ *442/432–1471* 🌐 *www.forests.tn.nic.in* *Sanctuary Rs. 5, camera fee Rs. 25, video-camera fee Rs. 150* *Daily 6–6.*

KANCHIPURAM

76 km (47 mi) southwest of Chennai, 65 km (40 mi) north of Mahabalipuram.

The ride from Chennai to Kanchipuram passes by newly built factories for cell phones and cars as well as by rice and sugarcane fields, both of them next to the smooth national highway, NH–4. You'll also go through villages at very close range, with houses right on the roadside. Don't be surprised if you have to stop for goats crossing the road. The former capital of the ancient Pallavas, Kanchipuram holds the remains of three great dynasties—Pallava, Chola, and Vijayanagar—that for centuries weathered internal conflict and external trade but never northern invasion. The dynasties merely jostled each other, building ever greater shrines to their developing and intertwining sets of deities. Today, Kanchipuram, nicknamed the Golden City of 1,000 Temples (as well as "Kanchi"), is one of the seven holy pilgrimage sites for Hindus, with some temples to Vishnu and a majority devoted to Shiva. Through the diversity of building styles here, you can trace the development of Dravidian temple architecture from the 8th century to the present.

The temples covered below are some of the more famous of the nine major ones in Kanchi, but there are plenty of others to explore. All of them are generally open from 8:30 AM to 12:30 PM and then open again 4 to 8 PM. It's usually best to make an early start of it. Many of the temples have their own elephants (relating to the elephant-headed god Ganesh), who patiently stand by the main gopuram to bless anyone who makes a contribution (usually a one- or two-rupee piece). The elephant takes the money in its trunk, gives it to its minder, and then put its trunk on the blessee's head. It all makes for a fun and possibly beneficial photo-op.

The **Sri Ekambaranathar Temple** was originally built before the mid-9th century by the Pallavas, but its most significant feature, a massive, 200-foot gopuram with more than 10 stories of intricate sculptures, was a 16th-century addition by the Vijayanagar kings. The temple is dedicated to Shiva, who appears in the form of earth, one of Hinduism's five sacred elements. Inside the courtyard is a mango tree believed to be 3,500 years old; each of its four main branches is said to bear fruit with a different taste, representing the four Hindu Vedas (sacred texts). The temple's name may be a modification of Eka Amra Nathar (Lord of the Mango Tree). Of the original 1,000 pillars that once stood in the mandapam, fewer than 600 remain. The Ekambaranathar Temple is in the Saivite Brahmin section of Kanchipuram. On your way to the main entrance, notice the houses on either side of the dusty road, most augmented by open porches with raised sitting platforms. Many have *kolams* (rice-flour designs) in front of the entrance. These Brahmin houses epitomize the religious and cultural ambience of the temples; until fairly recently, Kanchipuram was a town whose people were segregated by caste. ✉ *Between W. and N. Mada Sts., northwest part of town* 🎫 *Free. camera fee Rs. 10, video-camera fee Rs. 20.*

★ Built mainly during the reign of King Rajasimha (700–728), **Kailasanatha Temple**—named for Kailasa, Shiva's Himalayan paradise—carried the development of Pallava temple architecture one step beyond what had come before. From the "dressed stone" (rocks formed into regular shapes) of the Shore Temple, the construction of Kailasanatha progressed to granite foundations and the more easily carved sandstone for the superstructure. The sculpted vimana (a tower over the inner sanctum) can trace its lineage in shape, design, and ornamentation to both the Shore Temple and the Dharmaraja Ratha. The cell-like structures surrounding the sanctum are similar in design to the Five Rathas: all have extensive sculptures of Shiva in various poses, symbolizing different aspects of his mythology. Lining the inner courtyard are 58 small meditation cells with remnants of multicolor 8th-century paintings on the wall. Less full of pilgrims than other temples in town, this quiet holy place is an exquisite place to contemplate some very fine stonework. ✉*Putleri St., 1½ km (1 mi) west of town center.*

TEMPLE TAGALONGS

When you visit the pilgrimage temples, be prepared for beggars as well as children beseeching you for candy, pens, and "foreign money for a school project." Some temples, especially the Ekambaranathar, have a large number of touts. They may attach themselves to your side and insist on serving as guides or demand a temple donation they pretend is mandatory. Some priests, too, are over-enthusiastic about getting foreigners blessed—and getting their cash. You'll be billed for all such services, whether you want them or not, so it pays to be on your guard.

In the heart of the old town, the **Kamakshi Amman Temple** is topped by a brilliant, gold-plated gopuram. Each February or March, the temple hosts a famous winter festival: deities from a number of temples are placed on wooden temple carts, called cars, and then pulled in a procession through the surrounding streets. Kamakshi is another name for Pavarti, Shiva's consort. ✉*Odai St.*

Built in the 8th century, **Vaikuntha Perumal Temple** *(Vishnu's paradise)* is a single structure whose principal parts make an integrated whole. The four-story vimana is square, with three shrines, each depicting Vishnu in a different pose. Two things make this temple unusual: a corridor for circumambulation of the shrines on the second and third floors, and its cloisters, with a colonnade of lion pillars and extensive sculptures bearing Pallava inscriptions. A bit removed from the crowds, the temple makes a good contrast to the more hectic options. ✉*1 km southwest of train station* 🎫*Temple free, camera fee Rs. 20.*

Fodor'sChoice ★ Also known as Varadaraja Perumal Temple (Bestower of Boons), the **Devarajaswamy Temple** is dedicated to Vishnu and is a favorite pilgrimage destination. Its exquisitely carved 96-pillar mandapam is one of the finest in India, and its decoration includes chains at the corners that have each been carved from one stone. The temple was originally built in the 11th century, but the 100-foot gopuram was restored by the

Vijayanagar kings 500 years later. ✉*3 km (2 mi) southeast of town; follow Gandhi Rd. until you see the temple, 631501* 🎫*Temple free, Mandapam Rs. 1, camera fee Rs. 5, video-camera fee Rs. 100.*

WHERE TO EAT & STAY

Accommodations in Kanchipuram are more for pilgrims than leisure travelers, and restaurants are basic. Although most travelers treat Kanchi as a day trip, staying for the night rather than moving on immediately to Chennai, Pondicherry, or Mahabalipuram is a good way to visit the temples during the non-prime hours of evening or early morning.

¢ ✕**Hotel Saravana Bhavan.** Service is excellent in this high-quality vegetarian restaurant that serves a large menu of tasty Indian items, including a basic *thali, vadai* (deep-fried, savory "doughnuts"), and good *masala dosas.* It's a good place for a cup of South Indian coffee or shakes and ice cream. One room is air-conditioned. ✉*Gandhi Rd.* ☎*442/722–2505* 🌐*www.saravanabhavan.com* 💳*MC, V.*

¢ 🏨**GRT Regency.** This basic, pleasant business hotel has nicely furnished, calm rooms that make for a good break from busy Kanchi outside. The restaurant Dakshin has a solid lunchtime buffet with fine renditions of South Indian and pan-Indian dishes, as well as Continental food. A roof garden gives a clear view of several temples in the distance and the bustle of the Gandhi Road silk stores below. **Pros:** good restaurant, great value, pleasant, business-oriented rooms, handy location. **Cons:** rooms lack character, streets outside can be busy, no pool. ✉*487 Gandhi Rd., 631502* ☎*442/722–5250* 🌐*www.grthotels.com* 🛏*32 rooms, 3 suites* 👍*In-room: safe, refrigerator (some), Wi-Fi. In-hotel: 2 restaurants, room service, bar, laundry service, airport shuttle, parking (no fee), no-smoking rooms.* 💳*AE, MC, V.*

¢ 🏨**Hotel Baboo Soorya.** In this well-located hotel with a big, open lobby, the rooms are basic, but they're also fairly large, and some come with small balconies. Located near the Kamatchi Amman Temple, the hotel is down a short driveway, which helps with street noise. **Pros:** super-cheap, friendly staff, handy location. **Cons:** rooms are plain and simple, not much atmosphere, no pool. ✉*85 E. Raja St.Kanchipuram, 631501* ☎*411/222–2258 or 411/222–2891* 🌐*www.hotelbaboosoorya.com* 🛏*36 rooms* 👍*In-room: no a/c (some). In-hotel: restaurant, room service, bar, laundry service, parking (no fee).* 💳*AE, MC, V.*

SHOPPING

Kanchipuram's silks and saris are famous throughout India for their brilliant colors and rich brocades of real gold and/or silver. More than 20,000 people work with silk alone in this city of weavers—entire families craft fabric in or near their homes, using age-old techniques. Many of the silk stores in town have "demo" looms to show how such intricate patterns are made. Shops here are open every day, and most will take credit cards. Silk is often more expensive in Kanchi than in Chennai, and energetic bargaining is a must. If you're interested in buying, do some homework in advance to know what sorts of prices are reasonable, and do your shopping at government-approved shops, many of which are on T.K. Nambi Street and Ghandhi Road.

PONDICHERRY

134 km (83 mi) south of Mahabalipuram, 160 km (100 mi) south of Chennai.

If you want to take the pace of life down a few notches, this quiet, unusual town is ideal. A former French holding, Pondicherry still retains the flavor of its colonizers, who left as recently as 1954. From the red *kepis* (caps) of the policemen to street names like Rue Romain Rolland, the French influence is deep-rooted and pervasive, and many of the local people still speak and study the language. A Union Territory, Pondicherry is not beholden to Tamil Nadu laws, and you'll notice that liquor, among other things, is cheaper and more easily available as a result. In many ways the city (now also known as Puducherry) is a slice of provincial France on Indian soil.

There's little in the way of sights here, but the grid of streets that make up the old part of town are a stroller's paradise. This is especially true of the section to the east of the canal, which separated the French quarter from the rest of the town. The streets are lined with tall white-washed villas swathed in bougainvillea, quaint churches and gardens, and little restaurants and cafés that serve French food and other dishes. Even if you don't enter the heritage buildings in the area, the sense of living history is palpable.

A stroll down coastal **Goubert Avenue** (also known as Beach Road) is quiet and pleasant, with minimal traffic. You'll find plenty of French tourists walking the beachfront in the evening, enjoying the feeling of holiday that manages to pervade Pondicherry throughout the year, even in the extreme heat of summer.

After your long walk in the hot sun, there are plenty of places to quench your thirst and soak in the flavors of France. Almost all the restaurants in this area are housed in colonial-style buildings with gardens and old-world cane furniture. As for the genuine, reasonably priced French food, plenty is to be had here. A visit to Pondicherry is incomplete without ordering bouillabaisse: the fish is local, and the soup rivals any you're likely to find in France.

While in the French quarter, make sure you see the round Douane (Customs) house on Goubert Avenue, and the samadhi (memorial) to Sri Aurobindo and the Mother *(⇨ Auroville)* in the ashram premises on Marine Street. The Church of Our Lady of the Immaculate Conception on Mission Street across the canal dates to 1791 and has a rich interior. The Sri Aurobindo Handmade Paper Factory on S. V. Patel Road is also worth a visit if you're interested in seeing traditional paper-making.

Auroville is an international project—a group of villages—and "experiment in international living" conceived by Mirra Alfassa, also known as the Mother and a companion of the mystic Sri Aurobindo. Once a freedom fighter, Sri Aurobindo moved to Pondicherry from Calcutta and founded an ashram here to propagate his ideas, a synthesis of yoga, philosophy, and spirituality. Inaugurated in 1968, Auroville attracts those in search of enlightenment without the trappings of traditional religion. With more than 1,300 residents from all over the world (primarily from the West), it is meant to reflect the unity of the human spirit. Auroville is not a tourist attraction, and its overseers say that visitors need to spend at least a few days here to understand the work being done. An exhibition at the visitor center (open from 9 AM to 5:30 PM) explains the concept behind the Auroville project, and depicts how its community is involved in a variety of environmentally friendly endeavors. They work with local villagers, introducing them to alternative technology and energy sources. Auroville has a handicrafts shop, a restaurant, and several guest houses. ✉ *10 km (6 mi) north of Pondicherry* 🌐 *www.auroville.org.*

Pondicherry Museum This museum near the park covers the area's ancient past, when it was a trading post with imperial Rome, as well as its more recent French Colonial past. Among the diverting items on display are French sculptures, portraits, furniture, pots used to hold Roman olive oil and wine, some impressive Chola bronzes, a palanquin, and a strange kind of carriage called a *pousse-pousse,* which a hapless servant had to push while its occupant steered. Cameras aren't allowed inside. (✉ *Ranga Pilai, St. Louis Str.* ☎ *413/222–3950* 🎟 *Rs. 2* ⏲ *Tues.–Sun. 9:40–1 and 2–5*)

WHERE TO EAT & STAY

There are several hotels that offer good rooms and facilities in Pondicherry, and a smattering of guesthouses in the colonial quarter preserve the French-colonial ambience. When it's time for lunch or dinner, head for the small restaurants near the waterfront and within the grid of French-named streets.

$ ✕ **Rendezvous.** This rooftop terrace restaurant is in the heart of the French quarter, overlooking a side street with whitewashed Mediterranean-style buildings. Open at 10:30 AM for breakfast, it's a good place to head for authentic bouillabaisse, seafood gumbo, and fresh, delicately flavored seafood. If the heat becomes too sweltering for eating outside, then head to an enclosed, air-conditioned area for some relief. There are also three spacious, homey guest rooms available. ✉ *30 Suffren St.* ☎ *413/233–9132* 🌐 *www.rendezvous-pondy.com* 💳 *AE, DC, MC, V* ⏲ *Closed Tues.*

¢–$ ✕ **Satsanga.** In a large pebbled garden, with an L-shaped covered area, the surroundings in this restaurant are perfect for the café-style menu served here: superb French food with a little Italian and Indian thrown in. Try the owner–chef Pierre Elouard's lemon chicken, or the crepes with honey if you're here for breakfast. The crowd, primarily French and other European tourists, is laid-back and upbeat. The restaurant is open for three meals daily, until 11 PM. ✉ *30 La Bourdonnais St.* ☎ *413/222–5867* 💳 *No credit cards.*

$–$$ 🏨 **Le Dupleix.** Although this cornerside luxury hotel was once an 18th-century villa and is named for a colonial governor, it's not a period piece. The common spaces have been updated with modern touches like exposed granite and stylish, slatted wooden tables and chairs for the courtyard's restaurant. Each of the rooms is different, with touches that might include a striking ceiling panel from a maharaja's palace, or an antique bed. All include large windows and soaring ceilings, but the cheaper rooms are a little small. Those staying here also have the use of the small pool at the Promenade, Dupleix's sister property. **Pros:** beautiful boutique surroundings, heritage building, super-high ceilings. **Cons:** cheap rooms are small, no pool on property, not much lobby to speak of. ✉ *Casserne St., 605001* ☎ *413/222–6999* 🌐 *www.sarovarhotels.com* *11 rooms, 3 suites* *In-room: safes, refrigerator, DVD, Wi-Fi. In-hotel: restaurant, room service, bar, laundry service, airport shuttle.* 💳 *AE, DC, MC, V.*

$ **Anandha Inn.** This multistory white structure is northwest of the French quarter, about a Rs. 20–Rs. 30 auto-rickshaw ride away. One of Pondy's contemporary hotels, with modern conveniences that can be hard to find closer to the beachfront, the Anandha attracts lots of tour groups and business travelers. The rooms in the back, away from the main road, are the quietest. **Pros:** lots of services for the same price as French quarter guest houses, efficient staff, good multicuisine restaurants. **Cons:** can be busy with tour groups, a little too far from the French quarter to walk there comfortably, modern hotel ambience isn't very "Pondy." ✉ *154 S. V. Patel Salai, 605001* ☎ *413/233–0711* 🌐 *www.anandhainn.com* *66 rooms, 4 suites* *In-room: safe, refrigerator, ethernet, dial-up, Wi-Fi. In-hotel: 2 restaurants, room service, bar, pool, gym, spa, laundry service, concierge, executive floor, public Wi-Fi, airport shuttle.* 💳 *AE, DC, MC, V* *BP.*

$ **Hotel de L'Orient.** Run by the meticulous Neemrana Group, this hotel is housed in a rambling French-colonial mansion on a French quarter street of antiques stores and curio shops. Rooms are nicely furnished with antiques and named after formerly French-occupied territories in the region; two of the cheaper rooms are in an annex. The restaurant serves very good Creole cuisine. Reserve several weeks in advance, since this is an extremely popular hotel. **Pros:** beautifully restored mansion, great location, boutique atmosphere. **Cons:** hard to get a reservation, more expensive than similar heritage properties, some rooms look out on restaurant area. ✉ *17 Rue Romain Rolland, 605001* ☎ *413/234–3067 to 68, 413/234–6589* 🌐 *www.neemranahotels.com* *14 rooms, 2 suites* *In-room: safe, kitchen (some). In-hotel: restaurant, bar, airport shuttle, laundry service, no elevator.* 💳 *AE, MC, V.*

$ **The Promenade.** Opened in late 2006, this modern hotel faces the sea near Pondy's Ghandi monument with a gleaming, crisp-white facade that blends in well with its colonial-French neighbors. Furnished with all the necessary boutique touches, including a small, sunken pool edging the sleek bar on the ground floor and a rooftop barbeque restaurant with mosaic floor, the interior trappings wouldn't seem out of place in Miami Beach. Soft leather touches turn up in the bar Risqué as well as in the elevators and bed headboards; the hotel is owned by the Indian leather maker Hidesign. The modernist, wood-filled rooms have large windows with large shutters and bright white walls—most have sea views, which cost extra. **Pros:** beautiful boutique hotel, great location across the street from the beach, stylish. **Cons:** fairly expensive, pool is small (albeit pretty), service still ironing out rough spots. ✉ *23 Goubert Ave., 605001* ☎ *413/222–7750 or 413/222–7757* 🌐 *www.sarovar*

hotels.com 33 rooms, 2 suites *In-room: safe, refrigerator, DVD (some), Wi-Fi. In-hotel: 2 restaurants, room service, bar, pool, gym, spa, beachfront, laundry service, parking (fee).* AE, DC, MC, V.

$ **Villa Helena.** One of the best places to stay in the French quarter, Villa Helena has a wonderful plant-filled courtyard. Rooms are decorated richly with red silk drapes, vintage Chinese prints, and antique furniture; the bathrooms are very spacious. Ceilings are high and tall, slatted windows look out onto the street. For breakfast you can get freshly baked croissants and coffee or tea served in the veranda as you lounge on cane furniture and admire the garden. The two suites are nearby in a separate, very private location—it's the next best thing to having your own apartment. **Pros:** big suites are a good value, great location, great price. **Cons:** lacks the service of a full-fledged hotel, no restaurant, small size means it's can be hard to get a reservation. *13 Lal Bahadur Shastri Rd., 605001 413/222–6789 413/222–7087 6 rooms, 2 suites In-room: no phone, no TV (some), WI-Fi. In-hotel: laundry service, no elevator. No credit cards BP.*

¢–$ **Coloniale Heritage.** Behind a gate on a quiet street that's nevertheless close to the beachfront, this old house has a lush garden in its courtyard. Popular with French tourists, the inn is relaxed and friendly. Rooms are furnished with antiques and old art, and two of them ("Les Jumelles") have their own balconies; the suite comes with its own private garden and veranda. **Pros:** quiet yet handy location, antique and pretty furnishings, garden courtyard picture-perfect, great deal. **Cons:** occasional loud phone ringing at night, no restaurant, limited service. *54 Romain Rolland St., 605001 413/222–4720 or 413/520–0334 www.colonialeheritage.com 5 rooms, 1 suite In-room: no phone, no TV. In-hotel: no elevator, laundry service. No credit cards. BP.*

¢–$ **Hotel de Pondichéry.** Inside a colonial mansion at the south end of the French quarter await spacious and nicely furnished rooms with high ceilings and a smattering of art on the walls. **Pros:** elegant mansion surroundings, spacious rooms are also nicely decorated, popular open-air garden courtyard restaurant a good place to meet other travelers. **Cons:** can be hard to get served at the restaurants, some rooms are showing their age and are a little dark. *38 Dumas St. 413/222–7409 or 413/233-9745 10 rooms In-room: Wi-Fi. In-hotel: 3 restaurants, bar, laundry service, no elevator.* MC, V.

¢ **Park Guesthouse.** This quiet guesthouse is meant for ashram members and devotees, though tourists are allowed to stay if there is room available when they arrive. Staying here means observing a rather institutional curfew (gates close at 10:30 PM) and abstaining from alcohol and smoking. **Pros:** one of the best locations in Pondicherry, on the water at the south end of the beach, super-cheap, interesting fellow guests. **Cons:** "can't drink, can't smoke" policy not for everyone, 10:30 curfew even less charming, no way to reserve in advance. *Goubert Ave. 413/223–3644 85 rooms In-room: no a/c (some), no phone, no TV. In-hotel: restaurant, bicycles, laundry service, no elevator, no-smoking rooms.* No credit cards.

SHOPPING

Many antique and curio shops are scattered throughout the French Quarter. In addition, Jawaharlal Nehru (J.N.) Street is chockablock with stores selling everything from clothing to sweets. Pondy is known for its handmade paper, and arts-and-crafts products from Auroville and the Aurobindo ashram.

La Boutique d'Auroville (✉ *38 J.N. St.* ☎ *413/233–7264* ⌚ *Tues.–Mon. 9:30–1 and 4–7:30*) sells lots of gifty items from Auroville, including fine pottery, stationery, and leather goods.

Splendour (✉ *16 Goubert Ave.* ☎ *413/233–6398 or 413/233–4382* ⌚ *Thurs.–Tues. 9:30–1 and 4–8:30*) is the sales outlet for Ashram products, from paper and candles to incense and potpourri.

Casablanca (✉ *165 Mission St.* ☎ *413/233–6495* 🌐 *www.hidesign.com* ⌚ *Daily 9–9:30*), owned by the Hidesign leather goods company and carrying a good selection of its bags and wallets, also sells upscale clothing and gift items from Auroville and elsewhere. The store is just off of J. N. Street.

Hidesign Outlet (✉ *31 J. N. St.* ☎ *413/222–0804* 🌐 *www.hidesign.com* ⌚ *Daily 9–9*) sells less-than-perfect, marked-down versions of its already attractively priced leather goods, many of which are made near Auroville.

TIRUCHIRAPPALLI, THANJAVUR & MADURAI

The history of Madurai and Trichy goes back to the 1st to 4th centuries BC, whereas Thanjavur came to prominence in the 10th century AD as the capital of the later Cholas. Tamil Nadu's "deep south" is a fascinating historical area ruled by various southern dynasties over a period stretching from the Sangam era—the beginning of recorded Tamil history and literature—until the 18th century, when South India was gradually subjugated by the British. The Pallavas, Pandyas, Cholas, Vijayanagars, Nayaks, and Marathas left an architectural legacy of forts, palaces, and, of course, fantastic temples.

TIRUCHIRAPPALLI

325 km (202 mi) southwest of Chennai.

The temple city of Tiruchirappalli (City of the Three-Headed Demon) was a pawn in the feudal wars of the Pallavas, Pandyas, and Cholas, which continued until the 10th century. After that, the Vijayanagar Empire reigned supreme. In the 18th century, Tiruchirappalli was at the center of the Carnatic wars between the British and French; between these two violent periods, there were periodic Muslim incursions. All of this international activity had an influence on South India's temple architecture, which reached its zenith in the Vijayanagar period under the Nayaks of Madurai, who built most of Tiruchirappalli. It was the Nayaks who built one of the largest temples in South India:

the Ranganathaswamy, on the island of Srirangam (8 km [5 mi] north of Tiruchirappalli).

Tiruchirappalli, also commonly known as Trichy, is spread out, with hotels centered in the southern cantonment (the old Raj military area). If you don't hire a car, auto-rickshaws are the best transportation here. The flat landscape to the north is dominated by the Rock Fort, near the bridge to Srirangam, which lies between the Cauvery River and its tributary, the Kolidam.

The military and architectural heart of Tiruchirappalli is its startling ★ **Rock Fort,** rising 272 feet above the city on the banks of the Cauvery River. Through an archway on the north side of the bustling China Bazaar, a short passage full of market stalls leads to the fort's 437 steps, cut into the rock. The steps lead first to a temple dedicated to Lord Vinayaka (the half-man, half-bird Garuda who is Vishnu's vehicle and who is prominent in *The Mahabharata*), and then to the summit. Along the way are various landings and shrines: an ancient temple dedicated to the elephant-head god Ganesh, a Shiva temple, and cave temples cut into the rock. (Non-Hindus are not permitted into any of the temples.) Finally, at the top, you're rewarded with a breathtaking view of Tiruchirappalli. To the north, the Srirangam temples rise dramatically out of fields and riverbeds. No photography of deities or of the temple interior is allowed. ✉ *2½ km (1½ mi) north of Trichy Cantonment* 🎫 *Fort Rs. 2, camera fee Rs. 20, video-camera fee Rs. 100* ⏲ *Daily 6–noon and 4–8.*

With outer walls that are more than 2 mi long and incorporating a village within it, ★ Srirangam's **Sri Ranganathaswamy Temple** *(Great Temple)* is the biggest temple in India. It was built by various rulers of the Vijayanagar Empire between the 13th and 18th centuries, with a few 20th-century additions. Dedicated to Vishnu, the single-sanctum temple has seven concentric walls and 22 gopurams. Non-Hindus aren't allowed into the inner sanctum, and photos can't be taken there either.

Just as the Pallavas had rampant lions, the Vijayanagar dynasty had rearing horses, magnificently displayed here in the Horse Court, the fourth courtyard of the Seshadgiri mandapam. At the time of the Festival of Vaikuntha Ekadasi (in honor of Vishnu's paradise), pilgrims can see the idol of Ranganatha brought into the mandapam from the inner sanctum under the golden dome. During the January Car Festival, Srirangam's magnificent temple carts—exceptional in their artisanship—are taken out for a series of processions. The temple's extensive and beautiful collection of precious gems is included in the cart display. An island of temples, Srirangam was also a center of religious philosophy and learning. The great Vaishnava Acharya Ramanuja taught and wrote in the Srirangam school at the end of the 11th century. ✉ *Srirangam, 8 km (5 mi) from Trichy* 🎫 *Temple free, camera fee Rs. 50, video-camera fee Rs. 100; Rs. 10 to climb wall for panoramic view* ⏲ *Daily 6–noon and 4–9.*

About 2½ km (1½ mi) east of the Great Temple, **Sri Jambukeswara Temple** is in some ways more impressive than its mammoth neighbor. The architecture of this temple, with five walls, seven gopurams, and a large central court, is among the finest Dravidian work still in existence. Courtyard pillars are remarkable for their rampant dragons, elaborate foliated brackets, and royal Nayak portraits. The temple is also known as **Thiruvanaikkaval** for a legendary elephant that worshipped the linga, the phallic stone that's Shiva's primary sign. In the temple's Mambukeswaram pagoda, the linga is submerged in water. Video cameras are not allowed. ✉*Srirangam* *Temple free, camera fee Rs. 20* *Daily 6–noon and 4–9.*

OFF THE BEATEN PATH

At Kallanai, 24 km (15 mi) east from Trichy is an impressive architectural feat, **The Grand Anaicut**, a dam still in use. Extending for 330 meters and 20 meters wide, this dam has a road that you can drive across. It was built by the Chola king Karikalan in the 1st century AD, with additions in the 19th century.

Two hours (90 km [56 mi]) south by road from Trichy is **Karaikudi**, the main town in the Chettinad district—home to the Chettiars, a prosperous community of traders. The baroque ancestral homes belonging to this community are famous for their size, rich furnishing, wooden pillars, and intricate tiled floors. If you want to take your time, stay at an early-20th-century planter's bungalow on the outskirts of Karaikudi, at the eight-room Bangala hotel ☎456/522–0221 www.thebangala.com. Rooms, which run Rs. 6,200 for double occupancy, with all meals included, are simply but elegantly furnished, and some have four-poster beds.

WHERE TO EAT & STAY

Trichy's hotels are concentrated in the cantonment area, also called Junction (for the Tiruchirappalli Junction Railway Station).

$–$$ ✕**Chembian.** This large, pleasant indoor restaurant is air-conditioned and serves Indian, Chinese, and Continental cuisines. A few good options include the *bagala bhath* (spiced rice and lentils), curd rice (spiced Indian yogurt and rice), or the chicken 65 (spicy hot fried chicken). The Hotel Sangam's other restaurant, Cascade, serves a similar menu but also includes some dosa specialties. ✉*Hotel Sangam, Collector's Office Rd.* ☎*431/241–4700* *AE, DC, MC, V.*

$$$ **Hotel Sangam.** This long, modern hotel is surrounded by a pleasant lawn and is about a 15-minute car trip from the airport. The spacious rooms, which get lots of sun, make use of lots of light-colored wood on the beds, and the bathrooms are full of marble. Go for a room overlooking the pool. The furnishings may include blue or green carpets and fabric headboards. **Pros:** beautiful plot of land, lots of services, very comfortable. **Cons:** expensive, far from the sights, slightly lacking in character. ✉*Collectors Office Rd., 620001* ☎*431/241–4700* *www.hotelsangam.com* *52 rooms, 4 suites* *In-room: safe, refrigerator, DVD (some), Wi-Fi (some). In-hotel: 2 restaurants, room service, bar, pool, gym, laundry service, parking (no fee), no-smoking rooms.* *AE, DC, MC, V* *BP.*

$ **Breeze Residency.** Rooms in this high-rise are spacious, with sturdy furniture and high-quality upholstery—the best ones offer a view of

Rock Fort. The hotel's bar, with a hilariously out-of-place Wild West theme, is worth a visit, and so is the house restaurant, Madras, which has more South Indian specialties than most tourist-oriented hotels. **Pros:** nice views, very good deal, memorable (but smoky) Wild West bar, good furnishings. **Cons:** not within walking distance to temples, tour groups can make it hard to get a reservation in high season, feels a little isolated from town. ✉*3/14 McDonald's Rd., 620001* ☎*431/241–4414* 🌐*www.breezehotel.com* *76 rooms, 8 suites* *In-room: safe (some), refrigerator (some), DVD (some), In-hotel: 2 restaurants, room service, bar, pool, gym, laundry service, airport shuttle, parking (no fee), no-smoking rooms.* 💳*AE, DC, MC, V* 🍽*BP.*

¢ **Femina Hotel.** Many rooms and hallways are a bit bare-bones and dated-looking, but the prices and the central location both count in this large hotel's favor. Rooms in the non-air-conditioned wing overlook banana trees and an old bungalow, and other options also have small verandas and stunning views of the Great Temple and St. Joseph's Church. Beer is available through room service, but only for drinking in your room. Woodlands restaurant serves Indian and Continental vegetarian cuisines. **Pros:** great views, well-priced rooms come in many varied sizes and classes, handy and good restaurants. **Cons:** many rooms are dated, hotel is a little far from the temples, large size and long hallways make it feel a little institutional. ✉*109 Williams Rd., 620001* ☎*431/241–4501* 📠*431/241–0615* *155 rooms, 10 suites* *In-room: no a/c (some), no phone (some), refrigerator (some). In-hotel: 2 restaurants, room service, pool, gym, laundry service* 💳*AE, DC, MC, V* 🍽*EP or BP.*

THANJAVUR

55 km (34 mi) east of Tiruchirappalli.

Nestled in the highly fertile delta of the Cauvery River, Thanjavur was the capital of the Cholas during their supremacy (907–1310). A fortuitous combination of flourishing agriculture, competent monarchs, and a long religious revival begun under the Pallavas in Kanchi culminated in the building of Thanjavur's Brihadiswara Temple. The two greatest Chola monarchs, Rajaraja I (985–1016) and his son Rajendra I (1012–44), consolidated their South Indian empire from coast to coast, including Kerala, and added Ceylon, the Maldives, and Srivijaya, in what is now Indonesia, to their holdings. As a result, active trade developed with Southeast Asia and China, fostering a two-way cultural exchange: Thanjavur paintings of the period show some Chinese influence, and in Java, Indian influence led to universal appreciation of the epic poem *The Ramayana.*

Although this soaring monument to Rajaraja's spirituality is dedicated ★ to Shiva, the sculptures on the gopuram of the **Brihadiswara Temple,** or Great Temple, depict Vishnu, and those inside are Buddhist. Until they were uncovered in 1970s, the more interesting Chola frescoes on the walls of the inner courtyard had been obscured by later Nayak paintings. Within a single courtyard, a serene, huge Nandi bull (second-largest in India, next to the bull in Mysore) and pillared halls point toward the 190-foot vimana, a pyramidal tower capped by a single 80-ton block of granite. It's theorized that the massive capstone was pulled to the top along an inclined plane that began in a village 6 km (4 mi) away. The delicate carving on the round granite cupola minimizes the capstone's size and provides a visual break from the massive pyramid. The temple's carefully planned and executed architecture make it a fine example of Dravidian artisanship; in fact, it's a UNESCO World Heritage Site. For the best experience, visit the temple early in the morning, before the crowds arrive and the temperature rises. ✉ *W. Main Rd. at S. Rampart St.* *Free* *Daily 6–12:30 and 4–9.*

★ **Thanjavur Palace** is the central building in the great fort built by Nayak and Maratha kings. It's hard to find your way around this dilapidated complex, much less imagine it in its prime, but visits to the Marata Durbar (audience) Hall and the **Art Gallery** (in Nayak Durbar Hall) are worth the effort. The art gallery has a magnificent collection of Chola bronzes, and the Marata Durbar Hall is beautiful and over-the-top, with primary-color stripes on the columns and ornate designs on the arches. Nearby is the seven-story bell tower, with impressive views of the temple and the rest of Thanjavur. The Royal Museum displays clothing, arms, and other regal memorabilia. Near the Durbar Hall is the **Saraswati Mahal Library,** with 46,000 rare palm-leaf and paper manuscripts in many languages. A small gallery there displays some of the more oddball and entertaining of the library's holdings (no cameras allowed), including some quaint books on nature and physiognomy. Bring lots of small bills to the palace, since many of the museums require separate admission and camera fees. To get here, look for the signboard on the side of the road. ✉ *Off E. Main St.* *Mahratta Durbar Hall and tower Rs. 50, camera fee Rs. 30, video-camera fee Rs. 100; Royal Museum Rs. 1, camera fee Rs. 30, video-camera fee Rs. 150; art gallery Rs. 20, camera or video-camera fee Rs. 30; library free* *Mahratta Durbar Hall, Royal Museum, and tower daily 10–5; art gallery daily 10–1 and 3–5:30; library Thurs.–Tues. 10–1 and 1:30–5:30.*

OFF THE BEATEN PATH

Gangaikondacholapuram. This capital city of the Cholas 75 km (47 mi) northeast of Thanjavur has a magnificent temple built by Rajendra I in the 11th century. Only the main portion of the original three parts of the temple remains—this temple is called the Brihadisvara, like the one in Thanjavur, but is no longer in use.

A little more than 100 km (62 mi) northeast of Thanjavur is the little ghost town of **Tranquebar,** where Dansborg fort is evidence of the Danish trading presence, dating from 1620. There's a small museum in the fort and you can easily while away half a day exploring the remains of colonial bungalows and the narrow streets of the town. In town is an eight-room Neemrana Group hotel, Bungalow on the Beach (Rs. 4,000–Rs. 5,000, ☎436/428–8065 www.neemranahotels.com), as well as budget rooms managed by the hotel. The Bungalow, on 24 King Street, has been restored to recall the age of Danish adventuring and trade on the Coromandel Coast.

WHERE TO EAT & STAY

Small vegetarian restaurants are easy to find in Thanjavur, especially along Gandhiji Road, the town's main drag.

$–$$ ✕ **Les Repas.** A pleasant, bright, and air-conditioned restaurant near the Great Temple, Les Repas serves a wide range of Indian, Continental, and Chinese dishes typical of the Western-tourist-oriented hotel restaurants in India. It's hardly memorable, but it is a good place to hole up when the heat and dust outdoors get to you. ✉ *Hotel Parisutham, 55 G.A. Canal Rd.* ☎ *436/223–1801 or 436/223–1844* ▭ *AE, DC, MC, V.*

$$$ **Hotel Sangam.** Built in the 1990s, this quiet hotel, a little away from the town, is set in a tranquil garden. The rooms and service are both very good and pleasant, although possibly not worth the high price charged for tourists. Since it's on the outskirts of Thanjavur, on the way to Trichy, it's a good place to stay if you're driving from place to place. **Pros:** nice-looking grounds away from the noise of Thanjavur, quiet rooms, good service. **Cons:** expensive for its small-town location, sights aren't within walking distance, tour groups can make it hard to make a reservation. ✉ *Trichy Rd., 613007* ☎ *436/223–9451* 🌐 *www.hotelsangam.com* *52 rooms, 2 suites* *In-room: safe, refrigerator. In-hotel: restaurant, room service, bar, pool, gym, laundry service, airport shuttle, parking (no fee).* ▭ *AE, DC, MC, V* 🍽 *BP.*

$$ **Hotel Parisutham.** With plants throughout, a marvelous pool, nice canal views, and comfortable, well-equipped rooms, the Parisutham attracts many tour groups. The grassy area in back, near the pool and the spa, is used for buffets with dance performances at night. **Pros:** unbeatable location (a five-minute walk from the Great Temple), friendly staff, pretty garden in back with impressive pool. **Cons:** can be hard to get a reservation because of tour groups, rack rate is high, canal can get a little pungent. ✉ *55 G.A. Canal Rd., 613001* ☎ *436/223–1801 or 436/223–1844* 🌐 *www.hotelparisutham.com* *48 rooms, 3 suites* *In-room: refrigerator. In-hotel: restaurant, room service, bar, pool, spa, laundry service, airport shuttle, no-smoking rooms.* ▭ *AE, DC, MC, V.*

$ ★ **Ideal River View Resort.** Set amid 45 acres of rice ("paddy") fields and semi-jungle, this resort's very comfortable and well-maintained cottages have balconies facing the peaceful Vennar River. Connected by road to Thanjavur and 10 km (6¼ mi) away from the Brihadiswara Temple, it's one of the best places to stay in the Thanjavur–Trichy area. Indian, Continental, Chinese, and Sri Lankan cuisine are served in the restaurant. **Pros:** beautiful location, price is a great bargain for what you get, quiet and scenic place to unwind after sightseeing. **Cons:** far from the sights, food is relatively expensive, might be too isolated for some people. ✉ *Vennar Bank, Palli Agraharam, 613003* ☎ *436/225–0533 or 436/225–0633* 🌐 *www.idealresort.com* *In-room: no TV, safe, Wi-Fi. In-hotel: restaurant, room service, bar, pool, spa, no elevator, laundry service, airport shuttle, parking (no fee).* ▭ *MC, V.*

SHOPPING

Poompuhar (✉*Ghandiji Rd.* ☎*452/234–0517* ⏲*Mon.–Sat. 10–8*) sells crafts collected from all over Tamil Nadu, including bronze lamps and woodwork.

MADURAI

191 km (118 mi) southwest of Thanjavur, 142 km (88 mi) south of Tiruchirappalli.

Once the capital of the Pandya dynasty, the second-largest city in Tamil Nadu supposedly got its name from the Tamil word for honey. According to legend, when King Kulasekhara Pandya first built Madurai more than 2,500 years ago, Shiva shook nectar from his locks to purify and bless the new city. Known as the Temple City, Madurai's old city, south of the Vaigai River, was laid out in accordance with ancient temple custom, with the great Meenakshi Temple at the center. Shops and stalls surround the Meenakshi on three concentric squares of streets that are used for religious processions almost every day.

Fodor'sChoice ★ The **Meenakshi Temple,** also called the Great Temple, has two sanctuaries, one to Meenakshi (the beautiful "fish-eyed" goddess), a form of Pavarti. The other sanctuary is to Shiva in the form of Sundareswar—Shiva married Meenakshi, daughter of a Pandya chief, in this form, and the temple's car festival celebrates this event each spring. During such festivals, idols are carried through the street in a huge, elaborately decorated temple cart.

One of the temple's high points is the Hall of a Thousand Pillars, built in approximately 1560 and adorned with 985 elaborately carved pillars. The **Temple Art Museum,** inside the Hall, houses many beautiful paintings and sculptures, although several have skimpy or inaccurate labels. One of the best of the many pillared halls is the one called Kambattadi Mandapam: it's outstanding for its excellent sculptures depicting the manifestations of Shiva.

The best way to appreciate this overwhelming site is to wander around the various crowded mandapams, observing the passionate worship that's going on. Every night in the main temple, around 9:30 PM, Shiva is carried to Meenakshi's bedroom, a procession that begins at the eastern gopuram. Non-Hindus are not allowed into the sanctum, and video cameras are not allowed altogether. ✉*Bordered by N, S, E, and W Chithirai Sts.* ☎*452/234–4360* 🌐*www.maduraimeenakshi.org* 🎫*Temple Rs. 10, camera fee Rs. 50, video-camera fee Rs. 250; museum Rs. 5, camera fee Rs. 25, video-camera fee Rs. 250* ⏲*Temple, daily 5 AM–12:30 PM and 4 PM–9:30 PM; museum, daily 7–5:30.*

Tirumala Nayak Mahal, an Indo-Saracenic palace, was built by Tirumala Nayak in 1636 and partially restored by Lord Napier, governor of Madras from 1866 to 1872. Although only a portion of the palace remains, what's still here is enough to give an idea of what it was like in its heyday, with Indo-Saracenic arches and cream-colored ceilings with intricate designs. One hall, once used for dances, contains

CLOSE UP

Penance Piercing

If you come across a hair-raising procession of men walking barechested through the streets with metal hooks piercing their bodies and arrows through their tongues, you've probably stumbled on the annual festival of Thaipusam. Celebrated by followers of Subramanya, granter of wishes and son of the god Shiva, the festival is associated with ritual bathing and acts of severe penance: pilgrims walk long distances, sometimes with their bodies hideously pierced, carrying the *kavadi* (ritual yoke) on their shoulders, to ask a favor, fulfill a vow of gratitude, and to repent for sins.

It's not uncommon to see men silenced by the metal rings that lock their lips, or drawing a small chariot attached to a hook set into their backs. One of the chief centers of pilgrimage for this festival—which can also involve walking across a pit filled with red-hot coals—is the Periyanayaki temple in Palani (a small town 120 km [75 mi] from Madurai). Here Thaipusam is celebrated for 10 days every year (the Hindu month of Thai is from mid-January to mid-February).

a museum of early sculptures. ✉*1½ km (1 mi) north of Meenakshi Temple* *Palace Rs. 50, camera fee Rs. 30, video-camera fee Rs. 100* ⏲*Daily 9–5.*

WHERE TO EAT & STAY

Decent restaurants are easy to find in sprawling Madurai, especially around the temple. There are plenty of places to stay on the west side of town, closer to the temple, but the more upscale hotels are across the river to the north.

$ ✕ **Surya.** As the Hotel Supreme's rooftop restaurant, Surya offers North and South Indian food for dinner, and thali lunches. Service is fast, and the temple views—especially at sunset—are impressive. ✉*110 W. Perumal Maistry St.* ☎*452/234–3151* ▭*MC, V.*

$$–$$$ **Taj Garden Retreat.** This hilltop hotel in a verdant, 62-acre setting has sweeping and distracting views of Madurai 6 km (4 mi) away. The rooms in the period bungalows retain a British-colonial appeal, with vintage etchings on the walls, wood everywhere, and airy verandas with beautiful views (the furnishing are a little dated but remain pleasant). Other rooms are modern, villa-style. The Taj Garden's restaurants include an outdoor barbecue. **Pros:** good for those who want a little calm and resort-time in between their temple-viewing, beautiful Raj details in the period rooms; amazing views. **Cons:** some rooms a little dated, hotel's very far from the sights, no non-resort restaurants at a convenient distance. ✉*Pasumalai Hill, 40 T.P.K. Rd., 625004* ☎*452/237–1601 or 452/237–1602* 🌐*www.tajhotels.com* *63 rooms* *In-room: safe (some), refrigerator, Wi-Fi (some). In-hotel: 2 restaurants, room service, bar, tennis court, pool, gym, spa, laundry service, parking (no fee), no-smoking rooms.* ▭*AE, DC, MC, V.*

Fodor's Choice ★

$ **Fortune Pandiyan Hotel.** Some famous personalities, including two former Indian presidents and a king of Nepal, have lodged in this five-story hotel. Rooms have wood beds and headboards and are decorated in yellows, creams, and other soft colors. The restaurant serves South Indian, Chinese, and Continental food. The hotel is 20 minutes from the airport and 10 minutes from the train station and Madurai's shops. **Pros:** good-looking rooms, decent price, comfortable, three acres of grounds. **Cons:** 4 km from the temple, hallways can feel a little cold, no in-room safes. ✉ *Race Course Rd., 625002* ☎ *452/435–6789* 🌐 *www.fortunehotels.in* *54 rooms, 3 suites* *In-room: refrigerator, Wi-Fi. In-hotel: restaurant, room service, bar, pool, gym, laundry service, airport shuttle, parking (no fee), no-smoking rooms.* ▭ *AE, DC, MC, V* *BP.*

$ **GRT Regency.** This hotel is preferred by business travelers. It is located about 4 km (2½ mi) away from the bustle of the city center and has a large, open atrium with a glass elevator. It's a good and comfortable place to stay, with attractive rooms. The spa Ayush has ayurvedic therapy available. **Pros:** very good price, nice-looking lobby, good value. **Cons:** some hallways are showing a bit of age, can be hard to get a reservation, dark bar is an after-thought. ✉ *38 Madakulam Main Rd., Palanganatham, 625003* ☎ *452/237–1155* *57 rooms* *In-room: Wi-Fi. In-hotel: restaurant, room service, bar, pool, spa, laundry service, public Wi-Fi, airport shuttle, parking (no fee).* ▭ *AE, DC, MC, V* *BP.*

$ **Hotel Germanus Days Inn.** At this Best Western, the comfortably furnished rooms and attentive staff make it a good place to recharge. **Pros:** a good price for modern conveniences, less than a mile to the Meenakshi Temple, calm and collected. **Cons:** not as many frills as pricier options, a little off the beaten track, somewhat cookie-cutter furnishings. ✉ *28 Bypass Rd., 625010* ☎ *452/435–6999 or 452/238–2001* 🌐 *www.hotelgermanus.com* *81 rooms, 4 suites* *In-room: safe (some), Wi-Fi. In-hotel: 2 restaurants, room service, bar, gym, laundry service, public Wi-Fi, airport shuttle, no-smoking rooms.* ▭ *AE, DC, MC, V* *BP.*

¢ **Hotel Park Plaza.** The rooms here are very basic, and along with the hallways, they can seem a little dark and dreary, but if you plan on spending most of your time seeking out temples rather than being pampered, then the Hotel Park Plaza makes a good base camp—it's a short walk from the temples. The Plaza will also throw in a free pickup from Madurai's airport or the train station. **Pros:** doubles start around Rs. 1500, an easy walk to the temples, free pickup from the train or airport. **Cons:** can be a little grim inside, street traffic is busy, not much luxury. ✉ *114 West Perumal Maistry St., 625001* ☎ *452/301–1111* 🌐 *www.hotelparkplaza.net* *52 rooms, 4 suites* *In-room: refrigerator (some), Wi-Fi. In-hotel: 2 restaurants, room service, bar, laundry service, airport shuttle.* ▭ *AE, DC, MC, V* *BP.*

SHOPPING

Shops full of carvings, textiles, and brasswork line the streets near Meenakshi Temple, particularly Town Hall Road and Masi Street. The **Handloom House** (✉ *E. Veli St.*) has great hand-loomed cottons. **Poompuhar** (✉ *12 West Veli St., opposite the railway station* ☎ *452/234–0517*) is convenient for an assortment of Tamil Nadu handicrafts under one roof.

TAMIL NADU ESSENTIALS

To research prices, get advice from other travelers, and book travel arrangements, visit www.fodors.com.

AIR TRAVEL

India has experienced a huge amount of growth in domestic air-flight in recent years, and new routes (and airlines) are popping up almost weekly. One important player in the South is Paramount Airlines, based in Chennai, which flies to many relatively smaller towns in and around Tamil Nadu. Air Deccan, based in Bangalore, often has the lowest-priced tickets, but because the company is infamous for canceling flights and being late, don't choose its flights if you have an important connection to make on arrival. Almost all Indian flights can be booked online.

Chennai International Airport is served by major international flights, and several international airlines have offices in the city.

Domestic Airlines

Air Deccan (☎ *984/037-7008 mobile, 443/900-8888* 🌐 *www.flyairdeccan.net*). **Air India** (✉ *19 Rukmani Lakshmipathi Rd. (Marshalls Rd.), Egmore, Chennai* ☎ *442/345-3301 or 442/345-3302* 🌐 *www.airindia.in*). **Jet Airways** (✉ *Thapar House, 43/44 Montieth Rd., Egmore, Chennai* ☎ *443/989-3333* 🌐 *www.jetairways.com*). **Kingfisher** (☎ *124/284-4700* 🌐 *www.flykingfisher.com*). **Paramount** (✉ *Chennai Airport* ☎ *442/256-1667 or 442/256-1670* 🌐 *www.paramountairways.com*).

International Airlines **Air France** (✉ *Level 1, 42 Kubers, Pantheon Rd., Egmore, Chennai* ☎ *442/819-9414, 442/256-0557 or 442/256-0558 airport* 🌐 *www.airfrance.com*). **Air India** (✉ *19 Rukmini Laxmipathy Rd. (Marshalls Rd.), Egmore* ☎ *442/857-8159 or 442/857-8165* 🌐 *www.airindia.com*). **British Airways** (☎ *98/4037-7470, 442/256-0952 or 442/256-0351 airport* 🌐 *www.britishairways.com*). **Lufthansa** (✉ *Opposite Spencer Plaza, 167 Anna Salai, Mount Road, Chennai* ☎ *443/021-3500* 🌐 *www.lufthansa.com*). **Singapore Airlines** (✉ *The Westminster, 108 Dr. Radhakrishnan Salai, Mylapore, Chennai* ☎ *442/847-2408 or 442/847-2402, 44/2256-0409 or 44/2256-0410 airport* 🌐 *www.singaporeair.com*).

AIRPORTS

Taxis are available at Chennai Airport through prepaid booths just past the baggage claim areas. To pay the least, head to the booth identified as being connected with the Governement of Tamil Nadu rather than those of travel agents. The ride will cost around Rs. 250–Rs. 300.

Trichy's airport is 8 km (5 mi) from the city center. A cab, prepaid at the airport, is your only option. For questions about airport locations or facilities, it's often easiest to contact your airline.

BIKE & CYCLE-RICKSHAW TRAVEL

Bicycles are available for rent in some smaller towns, such as Kanchipuram, and where the ground's not hilly it can be a fun way to travel small distances. Rental costs about Rs. 30 for the day. Be sure that you're issued a lock with your bike. You can also hitch a ride with a cycle-rickshaw in many temple cities and villages. A small, usually covered cart with a pedaling cycler in front, cycle-rickshaws are a leisurely, pleasant, and cheap way to travel. Cycle-rickshaws in Kanchipuram cost about Rs. 70–Rs. 100 for the day. In most bigger cities they are not restricted to smaller neighborhoods.

BUS TRAVEL

Most buses heading in and out of Chennai leave from the Moffusil bus stand, 10 km (6¼ mi) southwest of the main part of the city.

CARS & DRIVERS

When hiring a driver, be sure to get a price in advance that includes all the stops and all the days you will be staying overnight. Car travel by night can be dangerous—there are too many wild truck drivers around. Hire a car from a government-licensed operator *(⇨Travel Agents & Tours)*. For a driver with an air-conditioned car, the charge will be around Rs. 6–Rs. 10 per kilometer, with a "halt charge" of Rs. 150 per night. For limited travel in and around Chennai, Call Taxis (see Taxis) are another option. For such trips, a car and driver costs Rs. 100–Rs. 150 per hour. Autoriders is a 24-hour rental service with chauffeur-driven cars.

Cars & Drivers Autoriders (*✉426/784 Anna Salai, opposite YMCA, Mount Road, Chennai ☎442/433-0014 or 442/433-0057 ⊕www.autoriders.net*). **Bala Tourist Service** (*✉88A Kodambakkam High Rd., Chennai ☎442/413-5555 or 442/822-4444 ⊕www.bala.co.in*).

CONSULATES

The U.S. consulate is open weekdays 8:30–5:30. The U.K. consulate is open weekdays 9–1 and 1:30–3. Australia's hours are 9–5.

MAIL & SHIPPING

If you want to send mail abroad, the Chennai General Post Office (GPO) is the best place to do so; it's open every day but Sunday. There are also several international courier services scattered throughout the city. The most popular is Blue Dart, which is allied with DHL.

Post Offices Blue Dart (*⊕www.bluedart.com*).

Chennai General Post Office (GPO) (*✉Rajaji Salai, Chennai ☎442/526-7752 ⊕www.tamilnadupost.nic.in*).

MONEY

ATMS ATMs are easy to find in all the cities and towns covered in this chapter. ATMs that belong to international banks accept cards from abroad—those at State Bank of India machines or the like rarely do.

CURRENCY EXCHANGE Thomas Cook has a foreign-exchange office open daily 9:45 to 6. In other cities it's best to cash traveler's checks at your hotel.

Exchange Services Thomas Cook (*✉Ceebros Centre, 45 Montieth Rd., Chennai ☎442/855-3276 ⊕www.thomascook.co.in*).

TAXIS & AUTO-RICKSHAWS

In congested towns and cities, where many streets are not conducive to cars, auto-rickshaws can be the fastest and most economical way to get around. However, the rickshaw drivers of Chennai are famous throughout India for overcharging. It's often worth it to walk a block or so away from a luxury hotel or shopping mall to avoid the autos that loiter outside—they have no incentive to give a reasonable rate.

The set rate for an auto in Chennai is Rs. 14 for the first two kilometers and Rs. 7 for each additional kilometer, but it's unlikely that you'll be able to get off so cheaply. Drivers often claim that their meters don't work, so agree on a price before departure. Bargain hard, and be prepared to walk away from several rickshaws before finding one whose price you can accept. One tactic that might work is to offer to pay Rs. 10 or Rs. 20 over the meter reading. In any case, you don't have to tip on top of any fare you already agreed on.

With any kind of metered transit, it's wise to use a map to familiarize yourself with the shortest route to your destination. This is best done *before* you get into the taxi (or auto-rickshaw), but even with your driver staring at you in the rearview mirror, a little map work can help avoid overcharging. In smaller towns, which often have unmetered vehicles, *always* set the fare in advance.

Contacts Easy Call Taxi (✉ *Chennai* ☎ *442/620–9595*). **Sri Murugan Call Taxi** (✉ *Chennai* ☎ *442/486–4222*). **Zig Zag Cool Taxi** (✉ *Chennai* ☎ *442/474–9966*).

TRAVEL AGENTS & TOURS

Because many Indians still make travel plans through agents rather than online, there are multiple travel agents in just about every neighborhood in Chennai, and they will all be fine for something simple like buying plane tickets. If you are using an agent to rent a car and driver or something similar, be sure to get at least two quotes to make sure you're receiving a fair price. Call Taxis (see above) are a good option for day trips from Chennai to Kanchipuram or Mamallapuram: rates start around Rs. 100 an hour, with a "free" allotment of kilometers to travel built into the rate.

American Express shares an office with their money-changing services. Welcome Tours and Travels provides extremely efficient service and is open 24 hours a day throughout the year.

The Thomas Cook travel agency is open Monday through Saturday 10–8 and Sunday 10–6. Most major hotels also have travel desks where you can easily arrange a car and driver.

Contacts Akshaya India Tours and Travels (✉ *2/3, Kushkumar Rd., opposite NIIT, Nungambakkam, Chennai* ☎ *442/822–4617 to 18* 🌐 *www.akshayaindia.com*). **Ashok Travel and Tours** (✉ *29 Dr. P.V. Cherian Crescent, Ethiraj Salai, Egmore, Chennai* ☎ *442/828–1250 or 442/821–1782* 🌐 *www.attindiatourism.com*). **Moksha Tours** (✉ *G17 Eldorado Building, 112 Nungambakkam High Rd., Chennai* ☎ *444/302–1008* 🌐 *www.mokshatours.com*).

Thomas Cook (✉ *Spencer Plaza, A and B Phase I, 769 Anna Salai, Chennai* ☎ *442/849–2424* 🌐 *www.thomascook.co.in*). **TCI** (✉ *Heavitree, 47/23 Spurtank Rd., Chetpet, Chennai* ☎ *442/836–2556 or 442/836–2557* 🌐 *www.tcindia.com*). **Welcome Tours and Travels** (✉ *150 Anna Salai, near Spencer Plaza, Chennai* ☎ *442/846–0677 or 442/846–0908* 🌐 *www.allindiatours.com*).

TRAIN TRAVEL

Trains going south leave from Egmore Station. Check *www.southernrailway.org* or *www.indianrail.gov.in* for accurate schedules or look at Monday's *The Hindu*. Advance booking is always a good idea and especially important in the busy months of December and January.

VISITOR INFORMATION

The free magazine *CityInfo Chennai* (*www.explocity.com*), published bimonthly, is a good source for shopping, nightlife, events, and other listings. It's available in some stores and in many hotels and restaurants. The "In the City" section of the Friday edition of *The Hindu* lists cultural events for the coming week.

Within Chennai, the Government of India Tourist Office has offices opposite Spencer's and at the airport's domestic terminal, with knowledgeable staff and a very comprehensive computer database.

There's no tourist office in Kanchipuram, and the one in Mahabalpuram is often closed, so you may want to contact a Chennai tourist office before your trip. In addition to the main tourist office in Madurai, there are branches at the airport and the train station.

In Pondicherry, the very helpful Tourist Information Bureau of the Directorate of Tourism has maps of the area, including one with a detailed heritage walk.

Tourist Offices **Indiatourism** (*154 Anna Salai, Chennai* *442/846–0285 or 442/846–1459* *www.incredibleindia.org* *Weekdays 9–6, Sat. 9–1*)

Madurai (*1 W. Veli St.* *452/233–4757* *Weekdays 10–5:45*). **Pondicherry** (*40 Goubert Ave.* *413/233–9497 or 413/233–4575* *www.tourism.pon.nic.in* *Daily 8:45 AM–5:30 PM*). **Tamil Nadu Tourism Development Corporation** (*www.tamilnadutourism.org*). **Thanjavur** (*Hotel Tamilnadu complex, Gandhi Rd.* *436/223–0984* *weekdays 10–5:45*). **Tiruchirappalli** (*Hotel Tamilnadu complex, 1 Williams Rd.* *431/246–0136* *Daily 10–6*).

Orissa

Making traditional headdresses

WORD OF MOUTH

"[On my] third visit and having covered many destinations before, I wanted to see Orissa. I am glad I went; had some interesting conversations with folks and, of course, it does not see so many tourists, so the vibe is/was different."

—fuzzylogic

www.fodors.com/forums

WELCOME TO ORISSA

TOP REASONS TO GO

★ **Temple Carvings:** Dubbed the Temple City, Bhubaneswar, Orissa's capital, has multitude of temples showcasing a treasury of graceful carvings. These temples, especially with those in Konark and Puri, can keep you and your camera busy for days.

★ **Handicrafts:** Craft lovers take note: talented artisans seem to abound in the land of Orissa and each area champions a different type of craft passed down for generations.

★ **Beaches:** Gorgeous Puri's strip of sand has all the ingredients beach worshippers require. And then there is Gopalpur-on-Sea, too.

★ **Being Away from It All:** Orissa does not get a whole load of tourists—either Indian or foreign. Most of the time you will have beautiful stretches of landscape all to yourself.

1 Bhubaneswar. One of the few Indian cities that seems fairly well planned and organized, Bhubaneswar is easy to get around. In the midst of this young, modern city, ancient beehive-shape temples in every neighborhood provide a startling contrast. A short drive from Bhubaneswar is the ancient town of Dhauli where one of India's greatest kings, Emperor Ashoka, famously embraced Buddhism.

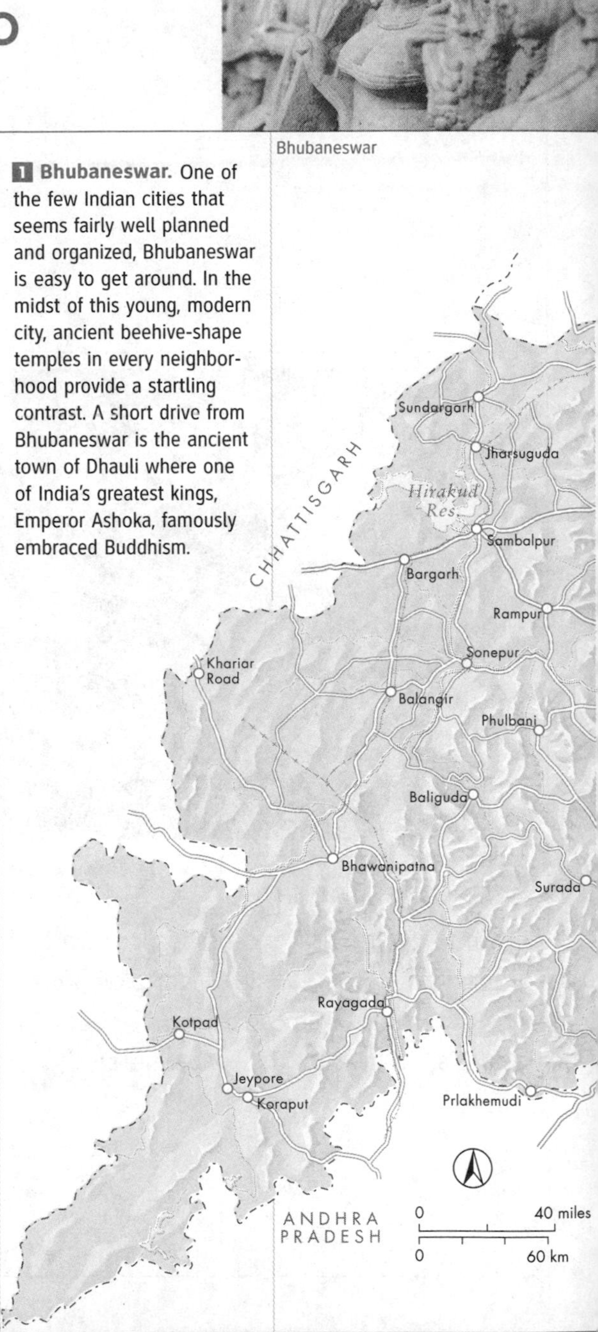

Konark Sun Temple

2 Puri. Serene, traditional Puri, on the Bay of Bengal, is a good jumping-off point for several stunning places in an easy day-trip radius of 50 to 70 km (about 30 to 45 mi). The unusual Chilika Lake, the splendid temple of Konark and the craft towns of Pipli and Raghorajpur can all be accessed from Puri effortlessly.

3 Gopalpur-on-Sea. This quiet beach town and fishing village, amidst casuarinas (coastal evergreens), swaying coconut palms, and sand dunes, is a bit farther south along the coast from Puri but must be accessed via Bhubaneswar on the NH–5 (which runs between Kolkata and Chennai) and should be planned as a side trip by itself.

GETTING ORIENTED

Orissa prides itself on being a rich realm of culture and the state has, indeed, a very sumptuous artistic legacy. Religion, dance, and art dominate its languid way of life, especially in the villages, where 87 percent of the population resides. The unique tribal culture of the Adivasis (the indigenous people), who live largely in the hilly northwest tracts of the state, is also a vital and colourful addition to Orissa's traditions.

Gadaba tribal woman wearing rings made up of coins celebrating the year of Indian independence in 1947

ORISSA PLANNER

When to Go

The ideal time to visit Orissa is October through March, when the temperature is around 77°F (25°C) during the day and the air is relatively dry. After March the heat starts building to 95°F (35°C) until the monsoon rains begin, in late May or early June. This cools things down a bit, but the rain can come down in buckets until mid-September, and during this time Orissa is prone to floods and cyclones. It is also sensible to avoid the standard holiday periods that Indian tourists flock to the area, such as the school holidays that occurs three times a year in summer from late April to early June; a few days before and after Diwali (in the fall); Durga Puja; and from late December to early January when mainly Bengali tourists flock to Orissa. The most exciting time in Puri is during July's Rath Yatra festival. It is also one of busiest times—Puri is swamped with pilgrims and finding accommodation in the town is tough; you are better off staying in Bhubaneswar and making a day trip to Puri. The classical dance festival at Konark is worth checking out.

Getting There & Around

If you choose to fly into Orissa you will be arriving at Bhubaneswar. Bhubaneswar is connected to Delhi, Mumbai, Kolkata, Hyderabad, and Bangalore by daily flights on several airlines. Biju Patnaik Airport, a small, decently efficient airport, is hardly 4 km (2½ mi) from the city center. There is a taxi stand outside. For Rs. 160 you can get into the city center. The "taxi-men" are reasonaby easy to deal with and are not that prone to cheating.

Trains from Delhi, Mumbai, Kolkata, and the South pull into Bhubaneswar's main railway station close to the city center. Auto-rickshaws can conveniently get you to your hotel. Puri is connected to Delhi and Kolkata by rail and you can use an auto-rickshaw to transfer to your hotel. The best way to see Orissa is by car, although there are good bus services linking Puri with Bhubaneswar. Road travel will offer a chance to wander through rather picturesque Oriya villages. Car agencies generally offer very reasonable prices in Orissa. A Bhubaneswar–Puri transfer will set you back no more than Rs. 850 or Rs. 950. Sightseeing around Puri to, say, Konark and Raghurajpur or to Chilka Lake, comes to a little over Rs. 1,000 for a 10-hour day. Allow your driver time for lunch, and give him Rs. 50 or so to have it, and remember to tip him at the end of the day—Rs. 100 or Rs. 150 is a decent amount (minus the lunch amount).

12

Awesome Architecture

The temples of Bhubaneswar, Konark, and Puri, built between the 7th and 15th centuries, bear elaborate and fascinating details; canonical texts governed their structural forms and proportions. The Orissan temple consists almost entirely of a spire that vaults upward among much-lower turrets. Supporting the tower is the cube-shape *deul* (shrine for the deity); next to the deul stands the *jagamohan* (porch), a meeting place for worshipers, usually square with a pyramidal roof. Sometimes one or two more halls—a *natmandir* (dancing hall) and a *bhogmandir* (hall of offerings)—are set in front of the porch. The architecture may seem heavy, but the sculptures on these temples are graceful, animated, often exuberantly erotic, and steeped in mythology. Most temples have a sacred tank in their yards in which worshippers bathe themselves for religious cleansing. Some temples are off-limits to non-Hindus.

Savory Seafood

Oriya cuisine is a cross between that of Bengal and cuisines of the deeper south. Like their Bengali neighbors, Orissans use mustard oil and mustard seeds in their cooking, but they also employ coconut, chillies, tamarind and curry leaves. Another Bengali touch: Orissans love bony hilsa and bekti. These fish are cooked up in watery gravy—*macher jhol*—and served steaming hot with rice. The semi-fresh water prawns found at Chilka Lake are enormous and you can sample them on the spot, fried hot and spicy in mustard oil on the beach. While seafood lovers will enjoy savoring all the aquatic treats, there is plenty of interesting vegetarian Oriya food to be sampled, too. Don't miss tasting yogurt eggplant or lemon rice and *bhindi* (okra) entrées.

What It Costs In Rupees

	¢	$	$$	$$$	$$$$
Restaurants	under Rs. 100	Rs. 100–Rs. 300	Rs. 300–Rs. 500	Rs. 500–Rs. 700	over Rs. 700
Hotels	under Rs. 2,000	Rs. 2,000–Rs. 4,000	Rs. 4,000–Rs. 6,000	Rs. 6,000–Rs. 10,000	over Rs. 10,000

Restaurant prices are for an entrée plus bread or rice. Hotel prices are for a double room in high season, excluding a tax of approximately 12.5%.

Planning Your Time

Orissa's main destinations are Bhubaneswar, Konark, and Puri—the Golden Temple Triangle. If you're short on time, you can see this special trio in two days, one devoted to Bhubaneswar and the other to Konark and Puri, with stops at Pipli, Raghurajpur, and Dhauli. A day extra will afford time to see sparkling, not-to-be-missed Chilka Lake with its unique geography and inhabitants. Or the Jain caves outside Bhubaneswar. Two days more will allow time to stop in at pretty Gopalpur-on-Sea, once a major British trading town.

Puri and Bhubaneswar are hardly 90 minutes apart along a narrow, somewhat crowded highway. But it will likely take much more than that to reach because you'll feel compelled to stop at the artisan towns along the way. At Pipli, the rows of shops in the main bazaar selling *birangi* (many-hued) appliqué items will occupy time and make inroads into your wallet. More interesting is the charming village of Raghurajpur where crafts are made in individual homes. You need just half an hour or less to take in the view from Dhauli, a peaceful mountain with a surrounding patchwork of fields and palm trees; this is where one of India's greatest kings adopted Buddhism.

If you have additional days you can use them for day trips from Bhubaneswar to Nandankanan Zoo, the Buddhist sites, the Jain caves, or Chilika Lake.

Updated by Vaihayasi Daniel

ORISSA IS A TANGIBLY RELIGIOUS PLACE. The state was once a center of Buddhist learning, but changes in ruling dynasties brought revolutions to spirituality, moving away from Buddhism, first to Jainism and then to Hinduism. Bhubaneswar, the capital, with its hundreds of temples; Puri, with its impressive Jagannath Temple, one of Hinduism's holiest shrines; and Konark, renowned for its extraordinary Sun Temple, are showcases for Orissa's distinctive sacred architecture, characterized by unusual shapes and fabulous, often erotic, sculptures. Buddhist history is preserved at Dhauli, where you can find an ancient Buddhist university's vast complex of ruins; this is where the legendary King Ashoka looked down from the hill at the carnage after a battle and experienced a conversion to Buddhism. The Jains have left a honeycomb of caves filled with sculptures to mark their era. Beyond these sites, you'll see signs of devotion everywhere: from village huts to taxis to hotels, the smiling, owl-eye face of Lord Jagannath, an avatar of Krishna and Orissa's main god, looks back at you. Oriyas are very dharmic (religious-minded) people.

The state, which lies along India's eastern seaboard, spans almost 156,000 square km (60,500 square mi) and is largely rural, with coastal plains, fields, and rivers; each village offers a postcard-perfect cameo of thatched huts, palms, and village ponds. Orissa is also known as Utkala ("land of arts and crafts"). In the towns or villages in the tropical countryside, striking crafts pop up everywhere, from superb hand-loomed silk and cotton fabrics to intricately detailed paintings and sculptures. It's also the home of 62 tribes, many of which still live in tiny villages scattered among beautiful hills and valleys, cleaving to their animist religion and a way of life—and mode of dress almost unchanged by the passing of centuries. (You can visit some tribes on organized excursions.) Thankfully Orissa remains uncharted territory for most tourist excursions, although its sights are captiviating.

Finally, Orissa has nature, and lots of it—from the miles of beaches where the rare Olive Ridley turtle nest to a remote and extremely alluring brackish-water lake drawing the uncommon Irrawaddy-species river dolphins and wintering birds from as far away as Siberia.

The infrastructure and facilities in this poor, mostly agrarian state are often quite basic, but definitely improving every day, so be patient and prepare to settle into a slower pace.

EXPLORING ORISSA

ABOUT THE RESTAURANTS

In Bhubaneswar and Orissa's other towns and resort areas, expect good food at low prices in unassuming restaurants (though Bhubaneswar does have a few more elegant eateries). Most restaurants are open from 7 to 10 for breakfast, noon to 3 for lunch, and 7:30 to 11 for dinner; hotels often have a 24-hour or all-day coffee shop. A few restaurants offer traditional Orissan items; watch for places serving *thalis* (sampler plates), which allow you to taste small portions of dishes in one go. And many offer Bengali food for the folks from Bengal who love to frequent this state.

12

ABOUT THE HOTELS

You don't come to Orissa for the hotels. As a rule, they're utilitarian, and service is far from snappy, with a few newer exceptions. Outside Bhubaneswar, a hot shower is a luxury; often, hot water is delivered in a bucket. Rates, however, are significantly lower than in more heavily traveled parts of India, and discounts are readily available outside high season (approximately December and January). The pricier hotels offer air-conditioning, currency exchange, and bathrooms with tubs. Some defensive-traveling tips: when you check into a hotel (other than a Trident or a Mayfair) in winter, ask that an extra blanket be sent to your room immediately, just in case; when you get to your room, check the hot water (if you have it)—sometimes it has to be turned on, and it's better to know sooner rather than when you're ready for your shower. Unless otherwise noted, hotels in this chapter have air-conditioning and private baths.

BHUBANESWAR & ENVIRONS

Although Bhubaneswar itself is a big, sprawling town full of government buildings, shops, traffic, and, of course, temples, the countryside to the south is lush with rice paddies so green they seem to glow, as well as coconut, mango, banana, and cashew trees, and tiny villages of thatch-roof mud huts clustered under tropical palms. Konark is 1½ hours south of the capital; a different road leads to Puri by way of Dhauli, Pipli, and Raghurajpur for a long day trip; an hour's drive south of Puri takes you to Satapada for a boat trip to where Chilika Lake joins the sea and dolphins cavort. Barkul, on Chilika's western shore, is 110 km (68 mi) south of Bhubaneswar; from Barkul it's a 60 km (37 mi) drive south to Gopalpur, or you can reach the beach town by a three-hour train from Bhubaneswar, then a taxi from Berhampur.

BHUBANESWAR

480 km (298 mi) southwest of Calcutta, 1,691 km (1,051 mi) northeast of Bombay, 1,225 km (761 mi) northeast of Madras.

Known as India's city of temples, Bhubaneswar once had some 7,000 religious shrines. Today only a fraction survives, but they still total around 500, in various stages of preservation. Unfortunately, the greatest and most vibrant of them, the gray, beautifully carved and proud Lingaraj, is off-limits to non-Hindus; you can see its huge tower from miles away, but the closest most foreign travelers will get to it is a viewing stand erected during the British Raj, when Lord Curzon, the British viceroy, paid a visit.

Admission is technically free at many of the temples except those under the care of the Archaelogy Survey of India. Temples are usually open from sunrise to sunset (entrance to the inner sanctums may be restricted for half an hour or so during offering times—early morning, around noon, and late afternoon). Upon entering any one of them, however, you may be harassed for money by the *panda* (priest), beggars, or an enterprising local, who will follow you around with a phony donation register scribbled with the names of foreign tourists and the amounts they've allegedly donated—with an extra zero tacked onto the end of each figure. The money is usually pocketed rather than used for the preservation of the temple, but it may be worth giving Rs. 10 or so just to avoid being tailed.

THE OLIVE RIDLEY TURTLE

Lepidochelys olivacea, commonly called the Olive Ridley turtle, is one of Orissa's rare species. These very small olive-and-yellow turtles with heart-shaped shells live in the Indian Ocean and crawl en masse onto Orissa's Gahirmath beach to lay their eggs. Some 130,000 turtles have nested on this beach in 2007. Trawling and oil excavation has upset their habis and the Indian government is looking at ways to protect this endangered animal.

Since Orissa isn't really on the way to or from any other prime tourist destination—the nearest major city to Bhubaneswar is Calcutta, at 480 km (298 mi), and the others are more than 1,000 km (621 mi) away—you'll probably want to get your money's worth out of a visit. Besides seeing Bhubaneswar's temples, there are other enjoyable ways to spend time while based in one of the town's good hotels. The textile and handicrafts shopping is excellent and there are interesting museums, a decent zoo, and several worthwhile day trips.

Bhubaneswar is divided in two by its rail line. On the southeastern side is Old Town, with higgledy-piggedly streets, most of them unpaved, winding between residential areas and the main temples. On the northwestern side is New Town, with wider streets and buildings spread out over a large area. There's no downtown, but Station Square, just west of the railway station, is a gathering spot for auto-rickshaws and taxis. Two main streets, Janpath and Sachivalaya Marg, run north–south through New Town; these are crossed by the east–west road Rajpath, which goes west from Station Square out to NH–5, the trunk road heading north to Calcutta and south to Hyderabad.

A GOOD TOUR

The major temples are within an area of less than 10 square km (4 square mi), so you can walk from one to another if it's not too hot. If it is, make an arrangement with a taxi or auto-rickshaw. Start with **Bindu Sagar,** where early-morning bathers seek blessings. From here a walk west brings you to the 8th-century **Vaital Temple.** On the opposite (east) side of Bindu Sagar is the 7th-century **Parasurameswara Temple.** About 1 km to the east is the 10th-century **Mukteswar Temple**; on the same grounds is the whitewashed **Kedar Gouri Temple.** Continue east for 700 yards to see the 11th-century **Rajarani Temple,** on manicured grounds. A little farther along Tankapani Road going east is a crossroads; turn right (south) and you'll come to wonderfully carved **Brahmeswar Temple.** You might want transport to travel the 3 km (2 mi) to the **Lingaraj Temple Complex;** to walk here, retrace your steps to the crossroads and turn left onto Tankapani, back down the way you came, but before Rajarani take another left that will bring you down to Puri Road. Cross over and head up the small, busy road lined with stalls to the temple. Afterward, hop a cycle- or auto-rickshaw for a quick lunch at Cooks' or Venus Inn, another to the nearby **Orissa State Museum,** then a taxi or an auto-rickshaw to the **Museum of Tribal Arts and Artefacts;** alternatively, spend the afternoon exploring the **Jain caves** or visiting **Nandankanan Zoological Park.**

TIMING It takes a full morning to see all the temples. Start by 8 AM at the latest so you won't have to hike around in the midday sun. Most of the temples take 15 to 20 minutes to explore, though you might want to spend more time browsing the stalls, checking out the goods sold by pilgrims at the Lingaraj Complex and generally soaking up the scene.

After lunch, spend at least an hour at the Orissa State Museum; from there it's a 10- or 15-minute ride by taxi or auto-rickshaw to the tribal museum, where you'll probably spend 45 minutes. Visiting the Jain caves, also about a 10-minute ride from most parts of town, should take two hours or so; Nandankanan is a 30-minute ride from town, and should also take about two hours. You can do this tour in a day, but it's a lot easier if you take your time and stretch it out over two days.

WHAT TO SEE

All temples are open daily from sunrise to sunset.

Bindu Sagar. Surrounded by a stone embankment, this, the largest sacred tank in Bhubaneswar (a square-ish man-made lake, more commonly seen next to South Indian temples), was the central point around which Bhubaneswar's multitude of temples was originally built. While standing at the banks of the tranquil tank you will be able to spot the ancient temples that surround it, especially the dignified, towering, saffron-flag-flying Lingaraj; it makes a great photograph. Pilgrims, believing that this tank is filled with water from every sacred stream and tank in India and can therefore wash away sins, come here to cleanse themselves. Once a year, Lingaraja, the main deity of that temple, is brought to Bindu Sagar to be washed. Bhubaneswar has its own chariot festival, like Puri (some time in April or May) that centers around this lake, when Chandrasekhar, a representative of Lingaraj's main god Shiva, king of the lingas, and deities Rukmuni and Basudev are taken on a chariot pulled by devotees to Rameswara Temple, 1½ km away. Near Lingara Temple.

Brahmeswar Temple. The exterior of this 11th-century temple, a ways south of the city center close to Rajarani Temple, is sumptuously carved with monkeys, swans, deer, figures of gods and goddesses, and religious scenes, as well as depictions of *shringar* (women at toilette). Over the entrance is a row of similar figures representing the nine planets, as opposed to eight planets depicted in earlier temples. Classical Odissi dance poses (Odissi is a classical dance form native to Orissa) can be quite easily identified in some of the friezes here; temples played a special role in the development of this 2,000-year-old dance form—the women who first performed Odissi did so for the gods in the inner sanctums of temples. Brahmeswar is one of the first Oriya temples to use iron beams. It is still a functioning temple but non-Hindus are allowed entry. If you're lucky, you'll be shown around by a priest who will explain their complicated symbolic significance. (He'll expect a small tip.) ✉ *off Tankapani Rd.*

Jain caves. About 8 km (5 mi) west of central Bhubaneswar are two twin granite hills, Khandagiri and Udayagiri, dotted with 33 rock-cut caves that were, in the 1st and 2nd century, converted and carved into accommodations for the ascetic members of a Jain monastery under the orders of the king of Kalinga, Kharvela. Kharvela did much to promote Jainism and details of his achievements are cataloged in the very famous Hathigumpha Inscription, found in the Hathigumpha (Elephant cave or Cave 14) in Udayagiri (it's written in Brahmi). There is excellent architecture at Khandagiri and Udaygiri, as well as carvings of everything from geese to athletes and elephants. Do especially see work in the Queen's Cave and the two-story Hathigumpha. Also here are remains of a hotel, lecture halls, prayer halls, and simple monks' lodgings (with rock cut beds that slope upwards to provide a pillow). Families of black-faced, fairly tame langurs rule these temples and are fascinating to watch. An India Tourism–trained guide *(⇨ Visitor Information in Orissa Essentials)* would be handy to have along on a half-day excursion. ✉ *Off Khandagiri Marg* ☎ *No phone* 🎫 *Rs. 100* ⏲ *Daily 8–6.*

Lingaraj Temple Complex. This giant and especially majestic 11th-century shrine is considered the ultimate in Orissan temple architecture by Hindu devotees and art historians alike and is one of the most prominent temples in this region. A world in itself, with some 100 smaller votive shrines, this Shiva temple sits in a huge walled compound that teems with activity and is a great illustration of the vibrancy of the Hindu faith. The temple's main deity is a granite Swayambhu *linga,* a symbol of Shiva. (Literally, linga means "self-established," indicating it was a stone that naturally occurred and was identified as a deity.) Lingaraj is partially a Vishnu temple, with idols of Vishnu within the inner sanctum as well. Linga are worshipped as Harihara, a combined Vishnu–Hindu deity. This is unusual, since traditionally temples are either Shaivite or Vaishnavite, but Lingaraj welcomes the whole pantheon of gods, showcasing harmony of the period in which the temple was built. Sadly, non-Hindus are barred the temple, and thus from experiencing the complex and intriguing rituals of this temple, like the daily ceremony of bathing the lingain milk and feeding it rice, curries, bananas, coconuts, sweets, and a *bhang* (marijuana beverage). From the small, raised platform 100 yards away, non-Hindus must strain to see the profuse exterior carvings, a high point of Hindu decorative art; alas, without binoculars, most of the details will elude you. Dating from about 1050, the temple originally consisted of only the porch and shrine; the dancing hall and hall of offerings were added about 100 years later. The *vimana* (curvilinear tower), built without mortar, soars to a height of 147 feet. Note that many enterprising locals have for years been posting themselves at the foot of the platform stairs with a phony guest register and demanding a donation; the money goes straight into their pockets.

Mukteswar Temple. Bhubaneswar's smallest and probably prettiest temple, built in the 9th century, is set in flowering gardens and tucked away in a quiet residential area. A couple of features in this temple signal the start of a new era in Orissa temple building, like a higher *jagamohan* (porch) roof. Its red sandstone body is encrusted with intricate carvings, from emaciated, crouching *sadhus* (Hindu holy men) to voluptuous, buxom women bedecked with jewels. Look out for monkeys that illustrate the folk tales from the famous Panchatantra around the windows in the jagamohan and impressive lions that jut out from its spire. On the left side of the entrance, statues of bearers grimace under the temple's monumental weight. The Mukteswar's most distinctive feature is its *torana,* a thick-pillared, arched gateway draped with carved strings of beads and ornamented with statues of smiling women in languorous positions. The semi-finished Siddeswara also exists in this compound and across the way stands the **Kedar Gouri Temple,** with its 8-foot-tall statue of Hanuman, the monkey god. (While here, pop over to the Raghunath Crafts Museum.) ✉ *Close to Lingaraj Templs.*

Museum of Tribal Arts and Artefacts. This small museum on a 12-acre campus run by the Tribal Research and Training Institute (watch for that name on the sign out front) provides a look into the lives of Orissa's 62 tribes. In five galleries painted with the white pictographs of the Saora tribe display about 2,000 artifacts (labeled in English), including hand-loomed clothing, some stunning jewelry, *dhokra* (a special metal casting whose effect is as if the object has been created out of wound metal wire) items, hunting weapons, agricultural implements, crafts, musical instruments, and photographs. Many of the items are still in use among the tribes, but some—like the Bonda's elaborate neck rings—are being phased out as the modern world seeps in. Out back are authentic huts from five tribes in which the artifacts were formerly displayed. ✉ *NH–5, off CRPF Square, between Priyardarshini Market and the Hanuman Temple* ☎ *674/246–1635* 💰 *Rs. 20* ⏲ *Mon.–Sat. 10–5; closed 2nd Sat. of month.*

Orissa State Museum. Innumerable treasures are hidden within this ill-maintained, poorly manned, and underlabeled sprawling complex, from the Mauryan-period Ashokan lion at the entrance to a room that is full of *patachitra* (Orissan paintings on silk or cotton cloth). You'll find an especially varied and interesting collection of sculptures dating back to the 3rd century BC, bronzes, coins, copperplate and stone inscriptions, armaments, musical instruments, handicrafts, Bronze Age tools, natural history exhibits (somewhat tattered and best avoided), and dioramas of tribal and jungle life. One room holds—on dusty open shelves—an amazing cache of more than 37,000 palm-leaf manuscripts in six languages, some with Orissan-style paintings; the oldest date back to the 16th century. There is a display of a king's throne room, which, though not that impressive (one would have imagined it to be more sumptuous), is intriguing. ✉ *Lewis Rd.* ☎ *674/243–1597* 💰 *Museum Rs. 50, camera fee Rs. 100* ⏲ *Tues.–Sun. 10–4:30;* PM.

CLOSE UP

Tribal Village Tours

Although most of Orissa's 62 tribes have been absorbed into mainstream life, others in tiny villages scattered over verdant hills and valleys, sometimes more than an hour's trek from any road, are remarkably untouched by modern life. A few of these villages are off-limits to outsiders, but most can be visited on a tour organized by one of several agencies in Bhubaneswar and Puri—an enlightening, amusing, sometimes worrying, but ultimately unforgettable experience. (Visiting on your own is not feasible.) The tour takes in parts of Jeypor, Rayagada, Baliguda.

Most of the tribes practice an agrarian lifestyle, growing paddy rice, vegetables, and fruits for their own use as well as to sell at colorful weekly markets where townsfolk and tribes from surrounding villages mix only briefly over business. There are markets most days of the week in different towns, and many villagers must walk for hours to reach them. Bonda women, whose villages are off-limits and who dress in magnificent drapings of perhaps a hundred strands of colored beads (some strung with coins), bring more of them to sell—and will let you take a photograph of them for Rs. 10 (in most of the villages the economic incentive is unnecessary and probably inadvisable).

In the villages you can see the utterly simple one- or two-room dirt-floor homes in which entire families live, eat, and sleep; the dormitories where young girls and boys get to know one another and play music; the flat stones arranged in a circle where the tribal councils meet; the totems and shrines of their animist religion; the mostly broken-down wells the government built and the ugly, poorly built houses it put up here and there amid the well-maintained thatched mud houses. You can watch the day's supply of rice being threshed in a small hand-woven apparatus or alcohol being made in jerry-rigged stills. With advance notice, your guide can arrange for traditional music-and-dance performances with drums, horns, and strings of bells.

Some people feel uneasy about coming into villages like a visitor at a human zoo, looking at people's clothing and jewelry and into their houses, taking photographs, and asking questions through the guide. But it helps when children gather around you as their parents either join them or peek back at you from doorways—they're as curious about you as you are about them. It's a precarious balance, though; the fear is that the more tourists who come, the more outside influence is likely to creep in. Certainly, in terms of authenticity, the sooner you make a visit, the better.

There are two basic options: You can travel from village to village, stopping at weekly markets along the way, then settle at night into the best available hotel in the area (which may be perfectly comfortable or may require fortitude and a sense of humor). Or you can choose to stay in the villages themselves, either in the tribal guest house or schoolhouse—usually a primitive shelter where you use your sleeping bag and look to nature for amenities—or in the tour company's tents. Because of the distances between villages, at least five days is recommended, which will cost $450 and includes hotel stays, travel, and food.

12

Parasurameswara Temple. Built in AD 650, this small and short Shiva temple near Bindu Sagar is the oldest temple in Bhubaneswar. It's a perfect and well-preserved example of the pre-10th-century Orissan style: a high spire that curves up to a point over the deul, or sanctum that houses the deity, and a pyramid-covered jagamohan where people sit and pray. The deul and jagamohan, two distinct features of this style of temple architecture, were seen in all Orissa temples after this. The facade is covered with exquisitely chiseled carvings, including one of Ganesh, the elephant god of wisdom and prosperity, that have outlasted damage from weather or invaders. Built about 200 years after a largely Buddhist Orissa had adopted Hinduism with new vigor, the temple asserts its symbols of Hinduism proudly. ✉*near Lingaraj Temple.*

★ **Rajarani Temple.** Standing calmly by itself in beautifully manicured and extensive gardens far back from the road, this 11th-century temple is perhaps the most harmoniously proportioned in town, and it is definitely the most peaceful. The king who created the Rajarani died before its finishing touch—a deity—was installed, leaving its inner sanctum godless. There are no aggressive priests here; instead, it has a strangely melancholy air about it. The carvings are lovely, with dragons tucked into cracks, couples in erotic poses, and smiling, beautiful women. *Rs. 100 ⏲Daily, sunrise to sunset ✉near Lingaraj Temple.*

Vaital Temple. This 8th-century, highly decorated, but rather small temple peeping at the Bindu Sagar is one of the area's earliest and is virtually hidden within its neighborhood of small whitewashed homes, cricket games, and modest shops. It's devoted to the tantric mother goddess Chamunda, who arose from fierce goddess Durga, an avatar of Parvati, the wife of Shiva. Chamunda is seated on a corpse, wearing a necklace of skulls, with a jackal and owl next to her. The two-story, barrel-shaped roof shows an influence of South Indian architecture. Bring a flashlight to see the carvings inside. *free ⏲Sunrise to sunset ✉near Lingaraj Temple.*

OFF THE BEATEN PATH

Nandankanan Zoological Park. Twenty kilometers (12 mi) north of Bhubaneswar and reachable by taxi, bus, or Orissa Tourism Development Corporation (OTDC) tour is this park carved out of Chandaka Forest. A lion safari leaves every 15 minutes on an open-air bus (but it won't go unless there are enough people; check in every hour). Other inhabitants of this semi-wild zoo and amusement park include leopards, striped hyenas, herons, and storks, crocodiles, rhinos, antelopes, bears, jaguars, and zebras. A tram crosses a lake to the Botanical Garden. You can also enjoy paddleboating, a toy train, and elephant rides here. ☎*674/246–6075* 🌐*www.nandankanan.org* *Zoo Rs. 100, camera fee Rs. 5, video-camera fee Rs. 500 ⏲Tues.–Sun. 8–5.*

Buddhist complex. On four hillsides between 85 and 100 km (53 and 62 mi) north of Bhubaneswar, excavations have revealed the ruins of a vast Buddhist university that flourished before the 7th century (perhaps as early as the 2nd) and continued until the 16th century. Separated by long stretches of idyllic green paddy fields and palm trees, the sites contain stone *stupas* (shrines), brick monasteries, and beautiful sculptures and bas reliefs, as well as some small museums with sculptures that were found on-site. The most extensive site is the scenic **Ratnagiri,** surrounded by the Brahmani and Birupa rivers and lush fields, the location of Stupa 1 which has a gorgeous, ornately carved doorway and an outer courtyard with seven interconnected closetlike stone chambers where monks meditated; carved panel fragments depict lovely scenes from the ancient Hindu epic *The Ramayana.* Look for decorative lotus-rhizome motifs (*patralatas*) that later became common at Hindu temple sites. The existence of sculpted figures from Vajrayana (or Tantric) Buddhism, of bodhisattvas (like Lokeshwara and Vajrapani, deities who protected Buddha) indicate that Ratnagiri may have had a role in the rise of a form of Buddhism that was the forerunner to Tibetan and Shingon Buddhism practiced by the Tibetans and the Japanese, respectively. A rather impressive, 10-foot statue of Buddha stands at Ratnagiri with a Pali inscription requesting devotees to serve humanity. **Udayagiri,** halfway between Ratnagiri and Lalitgiri, has a shrine with another beautiful stone doorway sculpted with *nagas,* guardian deities, and even ladies swinging on the branches of a tree. It also has a huge stupa. At **Lalitgiri** are the foundations of four brick monasteries; a *chaityagriha,* an amphitheater where performances were held; and a museum displaying colossal Buddha sculptures. All four sites at the Buddhist complex (the fourth and most recently excarated site is Langudi) would take a long day to explore; you'll need to bring along a knowledgeable guide just to find the sites(organize a trip through the tourist office in Bhubaneswar), and there's nowhere to eat—bring a picnic. ☎ *6725/240004* *Ratnagiri Rs. 100, Udaygiri free, Lalitgiri Rs. 100* ⏲ *Complex daily sunrise–sunset, Ratnagiri Sat.–Thurs. 10–5, Lalitgiri daily 7:30–5.*

WHERE TO EAT & STAY

$ ★ ✕ **Lemon Grass.** One of Bhubaneswar's most stylish restaurants, the Lemon Grass is decorated with elegant wood furniture, white etched pillars, statues set in the wall, and Chinese motifs and paper lanterns—there's a lot to look at in this 60-seat restaurant. The front of the restaurant is dominated by a red pagoda-style roof, the heads of some fearsome snow dragon, and a second giant dragon with a turtle riding piggyback. Aside from being eye candy, this restaurant serves a mix of Chinese, Indonesian, Thai, and Japanese. Opt for the fish steamed in a banana leaf or equally good the prawns *nanzin* (prawn cooked with corn in a chilly sauce). Javanese noodles (light noodles cooked with shallots and other vegetables) is one of several good dishes for vegetarians. ✉ *Mayfair hotel, 8-B Jaydev Vihar* ☎ *674/236–0101 to 20* ▭ *AE, DC, MC, V.*

$ ★ ✕ **Shanghai Express.** Inside an attractive room wrapped in frosted-glass windows etched with palm fronds, this Indo-Chinese restaurant serves big, crusty spring stuffed with chunks of prawns and shredded vegetables. Try the fabulous salt-and-pepper chicken: crispy fried nuggets tossed in a light sauce of peppercorns, ginger, garlic, soy sauce, and tender scallion bulbs, with a salty zing. Also good is the devil's chicken, cooked with ginger, red chilli, and spinach. If you don't like it hot, ask them to tone down the spices. ✉ *New Marrion hotel, 6 Janpath* ☎ *674/238–0850 to 674/238–0857* ▭ *AE, MC, V.*

¢–$ ✕ **Cooks' Restaurant.** This eatery in the heart of town—a bright and simple but pleasant room with a tile floor and brick walls—is upstairs from the clean, street-front open kitchen. Choose from a good selection of Indian, tandoori and Chinese dishes, including spring rolls, *paneer pasanda* (chunks of curdled cheese with a zesty stuffing and a thick tomato sauce), and a Cooks' Special, *murg tikka nawabi* (boneless chicken prepared either dry or with a masala sauce in a tandoori oven). ✉ *260 Bapuji Nagar* ☎ *674/253–0025 or 674/253–0035* ▭ *No credit cards.*

¢ ✕ **Dawat.** Once your eyes adjust to the darkness, you'll find yourself in a small, simple dining room with white stucco walls, terra-cotta-color tile floors, and glass-top tables. The larger room, behind it, is nicer and brighter, with mirrored walls. Universally praised by locals for its Chinese and decent, reasonably priced Indian fare (with a few Thai and Continental dishes thrown in), Dawat is always hopping with customers. Good choices include the ginger prawns and the vegetable *dopiaza,* a spicy mix of fresh vegetables cooked al dente. You can opt for some competently-cooked Oriya food as well; try the *dahi machli* (fish in yogurt sauce) or the santula (vegetables in coconut gravy). ✉ *620 Janpath, Sahid Nagar* ☎ *674/250–7087, 674/254–4027, or 674/309–0276* ▭ *MC, V.*

¢ ✕ **Venus Inn.** This popular midtown South Indian vegetarian restaurant offers a wide variety of *dosas* (stuffed crepes) and *uttappams* (rice-flour pancakes), along with paneer and vegetrarian dishes and some Chinese selections. Try the butter *rawa sada* dosa, a crunchy semolina dosa with a slightly salty-and-sweet grain filling, or the butter-and-coconut uttappam. A small, dark room filled with granite pedestal tables, this place is best suited for a quick, hearty lunch or a snack of ice cream or sweets when you're in the Market Building or the Janpath area shopping. Its popularity means you have to eat fast or the crowd will speed you along. ✉ *217 Bapuji Nagar* ☎ *674/253–1738 or 674/253–2685* ▭ *No credit cards.*

$$$ **Mayfair Lagoon.** In place of the nearby Trident's tranquility, this excellent resort offers lots of options for food and entertainment, plus a lovely jungle-landscaped man-made lagoon. Quirky, slightly over-the-top touches—planes parked in the garden, giant *raths* (chariots) running past the entrance, statues of tigers sitting at the lagoon, an in-house temple—give this enormous property a certain charm. Peace reigns, however, in the quiet, spacious, tastefully decorated and rather plush guest rooms, each with a private balcony. The best rooms overlook the lagoon, and from the "deluxe cottages" (suites) and the elegant two-bedroom villas you can lean over the rail and feed the ducks. The spa offers a full roster of services, and the gym has a wall of windows overlooking the gardens and beautiful pool. **Pros:** luxurious, palatial bathrooms, excellent, helpful attentive service. **Cons:** expensive. ✉ *8-B Jaydev Vihar, Bhubaneswar, 751013* ☎ *674/236–0101 to 20* 🌐 *www.mayfairhotels.com* *75 rooms, 9 suites* *In-room: safe, refrigerator, Wi-Fi. In-hotel: 5 restaurants, room service, bar, tennis court, gym, spa, laundry service, beachfront, public Internet, public Wi-Fi, no-smoking rooms.* ▭ *AE, DC, MC, V* *BP.*

Fodor's Choice ★

$$$ **Trident Hilton.** A tranquil, sophisticated property set among 14 acres of papaya, mango, banana, and coconut trees, 10 km (6 mi) from town, the Trident Hilton has the most expensive rooms in Bhubaneswar. The Spartan lobby reflects traditional Orissa ornamentation: at the center are huge brass temple bells suspended by 10-foot-long chains; the balcony, supported by beautifully carved sandstone columns, is guarded by six stone lions. The guest rooms combine Orissan art—such as the stone temple-style sculptures inset in the headboard above each bed—with touches that reflect the sensibility of the Thai designer who redid the rooms, imbuing them with Burmese teak parquet floors, beech cabinetry, oodles of cream marble, lush fabrics in teal blue and gold, and great mattresses and feather pillows. There's also a jogging track on site. **Pros:** lovely rooms, spacious public spaces. **Cons:** overpriced, public areas a bit non-descript. ✉ *C. B. 1, Nayapalli, Bhubaneswar, 751013* ☎ *674/230–1010* 🌐 *www.bhubaneswar.hilton.com* *62 rooms, 2 suites* *In-room: safe, refrigerator, Wi-Fi. In-hotel: 2 restaurants, room service, bar, tennis courts, pool, gym, spa, laundry service, concierge, no-smoking rooms.* *AE, DC, MC, V.*

$$ **Hotel Swosti.** This friendly 24-year-old hotel has efficient, courteous service. The building is on one of Bhubaneswar's main thoroughfares, close to the train station; for maximum quiet, ask for a room in the back. All the rooms are a good size, clean and relaxing, with plain, unremarkable contemporary furnishings, small sitting area, and big padded headboards; standard rooms have twin beds, and deluxe rooms have kings. Bathrooms are large but have showers. The Executive and Exclusive restaurants offer a wide variety of tasty food including plenty of seafood. All in all, Swosti is an old-fashioned, conventional, comfortable hotel complete patachitra paintings decorating the lobby. **Pros:** large rooms, delicious meals. **Cons:** noisy location, showers instead of bathtubs. ✉ *103 Janpath, Bhubaneswar, 751001* ☎ *674/253–5771 or 674/253–5779* 🌐 *www.swosti.com* *7 57 rooms57 rooms, 3 suites* *In-room: refrigerator. In-hotel: 2 restaurants, room service, bar, laundry service, public Internet.* *AE, MC, V.*

$$ **The New Marrion.** An unexceptional boxy exterior and a conventional and small lobby disguise some excellent, spacious, ultramodern rooms. Brown wall paneling, a profusion of geometric shapes, sparkling white tile floors, and wall televisions contribute to an air of cool sleekness in the guest rooms. Bathrooms have triangular sinks, square taps, and lots of shiny chrome and glass. Deluxe rooms have marble floors and king beds. The strongest point of this popular hotel is its rooms; public areas are less attractive and definitely short on class. There are also a great mosaic-tile pool, a pavilion with restaurants, a coffee bar, and a sweets shop. New Marrion has an interesting South Indian and Chinese restaurant attached. **Pros:** comfy rooms, jazzy decor, well located, good food. **Cons:** spotty service, public areas could be cleaner. ✉ *6 Janpath, Bhubaneswar, 751001* ☎ *674/238–0850 to 57* 🌐 *www.newmarrion.com* *56 rooms and 3 suites* *In-room: Wi-Fi, refrigerator, safe. In-hotel: 5 restaurants, room service, pool, gym, laundry service, public Internet.* *MC, V.*

¢ ★ **Ginger.** Part of the new Ginger budget-hotel chain launched by the Tata Group, which owns the Taj hotels, this motel, opened in 2006, is spic-and-span, with economically priced rooms in a functional environment. Like at other Ginger locations, the concept is well carried out here. Rooms are ultramodern, sleek, and minimalist, with Scandinavian-style furniture, bare blond-wood floors, and bright interiors that generate good taste but shy away from being cozy. Bathrooms are small and modern. Every room has Wi-Fi, a fridge, a coffeemaker, a phone, and flat-screen TV. The motel also has an ATM and an Internet café. A standard buffet, available for breakfast, lunch, and dinner, is served in the cafeteria-style dining area in the lobby. There's no room service, but you are welcome to order in food from outside. Its an ideal setup for young budget travelers. **Pros:** great value for money, tidy, convenient self check in. **Cons:** spartan, no bathtubs. ✉*Opposite Nalco Headquarters Jaidev Vihar Nayapalli, Bhubaneswar, 751013* ☎*674/230–3933* 🌐*www.gingerhotels.com* *101 rooms* *In-room: refrigerator, Wi-Fi. In-hotel: restaurant, laundry service, public Internet.* 💳*AE, MC, V.*

¢ **Royale Midtown.** This small, budget business hotel has a central location on the main drag and cheerful contemporary-style rooms with green-and-white-pinstripe bedspreads, green-and-orange cubist-patterned drapes, and framed prints of Orissa. Executive rooms are larger, with king beds, sofas, and coffeemakers. A good multicuisine restaurant and an attractive bar offer more space to hang out. Meetings are always going on, so expect traffic and noise during business hours. **Pros:** well-priced, practical. **Cons:** front desk grossly over-staffed and noisy. ✉*52–53 Janpath, Bhubaneswar, 751009* ☎*674/253–6138 to 41* 🌐*www.royalehotels.com* *48 rooms and 8 suites* *In-room: refrigerator. In-hotel: restaurant, room service, laundry service, public Internet.* 💳*AE, MC, V* *BP.*

NIGHTLIFE & THE ARTS

THE ARTS Odissi, the classical dance form native to Orissa, is perhaps the most lyrical style of Indian dance, flowing with graceful gestures and postures; it's performed, along with folk and tribal dances, during festivals throughout the state, notably in Konark. For information, contact the Orissa Department of Tourism. Cultural performances take place each Saturday evening at **Ekamra Haat** (✉*Next to the Exhibition Ground, Madhusudan Marg* ⏲*Daily 5 PM–9 PM*), a marketplace with 42 crafts shops plus 10 food stalls in a villagelike setting.

NIGHTLIFE **The Baron & the Baroness** (✉*Mayfair Lagoon hotel, 8-B Jaydev Vihar* ☎*674/236–0101*) has disco nights Saturday; other times it's a solid English pub, complete with a suit of armor and green leather banquettes. The **Bollywood 70** (✉*Crown Hotel, A1 [a] IRC Village, Nayapalli* ☎*674/255–5500*) restaurant shows 1970s Bollywood films nightly at 6:30. **Café Coffee Day** (✉*New Marrion hotel, 6 Janpath* ☎*674/238–0850*), the Indian version of Starbucks, with good coffees and desserts, has loudish music from a jukebox stuffed with tunes from everywhere. The bar **Landsdowne Road** (✉*New Marrion hotel, 6 Janpath* ☎*674/250–2328*) salutes cricket with a wall full of posters, gear, etc. The **Trident Hilton** (✉ *C. B. 1, Nayapalli* ☎ *674/230–1010*) has poolside barbecues with live Indian classical music nightly except at monsoon time. The multicuisine restaurant at the hotel **Sishmo** (✉ *86/ A-1 Gautam Nagar* ☎ *674/243–3600 to 05*) has a five-piece Hindi pop band at dinner Wednesday through Sunday.

SHOPPING

Shops are generally open daily from 8:30 or 9 AM until 8:30 or 9 PM. Capital Market, a street-long market where locals shop, across from the Market Building, is closed on Monday. The **Market Building,** actually a complex of interconnected buildings on Rajpath, with so-called towers (they're not) at the east and west end, has several good fabric and handicrafts shops.

Boyanika (✉ *Western Tower, Market Bldg.* ☎ *674/253–0232* ✉ *boyanika@satyam.net.in*), the Orissa State Handloom Weavers Co-operative Society shop, has lovely saris, bedcovers, and fabrics in various Orissan styles and textures. **Kalamandir** (✉ *Western Tower, Market Bldg.* ☎ *674/253–1133 or 674/253–0596* ⊕ *http://kalamandirorissa.com*) holds two attractive, well-lit floors of saris, shawls, and other stylish men's and women's clothing, plus fabric and bedcovers, from all over India; there's an annual sale in August. **Lalchand Jewellers** (✉ *Station Sq.* ☎ *674/253–4625 or 674/253–4888*) has a huge showroom including a wide selection of *tarkashi,* the silver-filigree work from Cuttack. **Mehers' Handloom** (✉ *Shriya Sq.* ☎ *674/250–2303 or 674/250–5341* ⊕ *www.mehersonline.com*), opened in 2000 by a family of master weavers from Sonepur, one of the great weaving villages of Orissa, has an attractive shop with hand-loomed traditional and *ikat* (woven from tie-dyed yarn where both the weft and the warp are matched) saris, fabrics, bedcovers, and other items, as well as fine pieces from all over India. **Odissika** (✉ *265 Lewis Rd.* ☎ *674/243–3314*) has a host of stone carvings, terra-cotta objects, dhokra bronze animals, and other authentic Orissan handicrafts.

Orissa Modern Art Gallery (✉ *A-17/8 Surya Nagar, near Gopabandhu Sq.* ☎ *674/240–4473* ✉ *omodernarts@hotmail.com*) sells exactly what its name implies, and proves there *is* indeed more to Orissan art than the 10 incarnations of Vishnu. **Priyadarshini** (✉ *Western Tower, Market Bldg.* ☎ *674/253–2140 or 674/253–0386* ✉ *Sahid Nagar* ☎ *674/254–6210* ✉ *Biju Patnaik airport* ☎ *674/253–4759*) sells very fine Orissan silk and cotton saris, mainly from Sambalpur. **Raghunath Crafts Museum** (✉ *By Kedar Gouri Temple* ☎ *674/259–2003* ⊕ *www.raghunathcrafts.com*) showcases small and giant sculptures by award-winning artist Raghunath Mohapatra, whose temple-esque works grace the headboards at the Trident. **Utkalika** (✉ *Eastern Tower, Market Bldg.* ☎ *674/253–0187*), a government fixed-price emporium, has a great selection of every type of Orissan handicraft.

CLOSE UP

Crafty Orissa

12

Orissa is renowned for its handicrafts. Foremost among them is the weaving of hand-loomed silk, *tussar* (raw) silk, and cotton fabrics and saris at centers like Sonepur, Sambalpur, and Cuttack, where you can find both simple designs and elaborate *ikats* (fabric) woven from tie-dyed yarn where both the weft and the warp are matched to produce soft-edged designs in the weave. Everywhere in Orissa you'll see superb stone sculptures inspired by temple architecture, statues crafted from soapstone that would be ideal souvenirs if it was not for their weight—though shops do arrange to ship larger pieces of sculpture.

Patachitra is the art of exquisitely detailed, fine-lined paintings on cotton, silk, or other cloth, usually illustrating stories from the ancient Hindu epics. *Talapatra* paintings or etchings are done on palm leaves treated so they're as hard as wooden slats. *Tarkashi*, a much-prized Orissan export for centuries, is the art of silver filigree, centered in Cuttack: jewelry, boats, temples, elephants, and other items are made by drawing silver through smaller and smaller holes to produce fine strands that are shaped into designs and soldered together. *Dhokra* is the art of casting animals, tribal figures, boats, bowls, and other items in brass using the lost-wax casting process; the object is then wrapped in rows of beeswax wires for a unique ribbed finish. Also look for items made from bell metal, lacquerware colorfully painted with folk designs, colorful appliqué work, and "golden grass" items made from swamp grasses. Serious shopping entails side trips to the beautiful, largely hidden Orissan villages that are home to master craftspeople. Most tour companies offer crafts tours of the best centers in the state.

Travelers are subject to grossly inflated prices, even in remote artisans' hamlets. Start bargaining (it's expected) at half the original price, and you may end up with a 30% to 40% "discount." In Pipli, competition drops the rate of initial inflation; here you'll need to bargain down only 5% to 10%. If you shy away from dickering, you can always buy good items at fixed prices at the government emporiums.

DHAULI

6 km (4 mi) southwest of Bhubaneswar.

It was from the top of a hill at Dhauli, off the Puri Road, that India's legendary king Ashok the Great in 272 BC looked down over the verdant countryside littered with bodies and a river of blood after his armies invaded what was then the kingdom of Kalinga, killing 150,000. Overcome with horror, Ashok underwent a transformation: he abandoned his drive to conquer and began to practice Buddhism, going on to incite a moral and spiritual revolution throughout Orissa and the rest of India. ★ **The site of Ashoka's conversion** is marked by the carving of an elephant emerging from a rock facing east—said to be the oldest rock-cut sculpture in India (3rd century BC)—that symbolizes the birth of the Buddha and the emergence of Buddhism. Carved in stone on the hillside (in Prakrit, using the Brahmi script), protected behind iron gratings, are the Ashokan edicts in which the once-ruthless warrior declared that all men were his children. He also asks his people to strive for purity of mind, tolerance toward all people, and kindness to animals. The rock was unearthed in 1837 by Britisher Markham Kittoe, a then-aspiring archaeologist.

Up the hill from the site of Ashoka's conversion is the **Shanti Stupa**, a Buddhist peace pagoda built jointly by Japanese and Indian groups in 1972. Visible from miles around, this striking white building, topped by a dome ringed with several umbrella-like protrusions (symbolizing Buddhist virtues), resembles a massive alien crustacean from a distance; close up you can examine the sculptural panel, tranquil Buddha figures and massive lions that encircle the stupa. The view from here—the Daya River curving through the green rice paddies and cashew trees—is lovely. Next door is a 13th-century Siva temple (rebuilt in 1972) that's worth a peek. ✉ *Off Puri Rd.*

PIPLI

16 km (10 mi) southeast of Bhubaneswar, 28 km (17 mi) north of Puri.

The little village of Pipli is famous throughout India for its brightly colored appliqué work that incorporates peacocks, elephants, parrots, trees, lotuses, jasmine, the sun, and Rahu (a naughty demon who gulps down the sun). Pipli has been producing this craft for centuries. Dozens of shops line both sides of the main street, crammed with piles of cheery beach umbrellas, lampshades, wall hangings, bags, and more, in patchworks of primary greens, yellows, blues, and reds with little circular bits of mirror inset for sparkle. All the shops offer pretty much the same traditional fare. In a few you'll see some attempts at modern design, and here and there you may catch an artisan at work.

RAGHURAJPUR

★ *16 km (10 mi) north of Puri, 44 km (27 mi) south of Bhubaneswar.*

Less than two hours' drive from Bhubaneswar, and just 20 minutes from Puri is the village of Raghurajpur, where every thatch-roof dwelling houses a family of artisans (*chitrakars*). Their skills in stone-and-wood carving, *talapatra* (palm-leaf paintings—very complicated and extremely intricate art that must be seen to believed), and patachitra (fine drawings on silk or cloth treated to get a leathery effect) are passed down from one generation to almost every member of the next generation. As you leave the main road and arrive at this idyllic village, several overly friendly escorts will offer to lead you to their house for "just a look," and the process of choosing the art you would like to purchase can get a bit rushed. Visit some of the homes your self-appointed guides take you to but don't feel pressured to buy. Take your time and wander the few streets and appreciate the murals that adorn the walls, done by some of the village's best artists, and absorb the simplicity of this unique hamlet with its quaint huts, palm groves, and village square. (Actually, Raghurajpur consists of 6 to 8 villages clumped together.)

If you're interested, the artisans will demonstrate their processes. In the technique of patachitra, for which the town is especially known, everything is done the old-fashioned way, from rubbing the silk or other cloth with tamarind-seed gum and stones to give it a parchmentlike texture to executing fine strokes of color with dyes made from plants and crushed stones. The subjects of the paintings are usually stories from the epics. They are created in all sizes and for all budgets and are a rare chance to buy very fine art at extremely reasonable prices. Some of the larger murals that illustrate, in fine cameos, tales from mythology or depictions of the Jagannath Rath Yatra can cost upward of Rs. 12,000 though there are paintings to be had for as little as Rs. 300. As is the case everywhere in India, the prices are raised for travelers, but you can bargain down to less than you'd pay anywhere else; expect to pay in rupees. Most artisans welcome customers daily from around 9 to 1 and 3 to 8 or later. An enterprising child will probably offer to arrange a dance for you—a memorable way to end a visit—or you can arrange one in advance. Call (☎675/227–4359, 675/222–6440, 675/227–4553, or 675/227–4485. Or you can get in touch by e-mail ✉ *chitrakara_raghurajpur@yahoo.com* or contact any of the artisans on the list 🌐 *http://craftrevivaltrust.org/Artisans/002408.htm*) to arrange a stay. You can stay overnight in a little house, built in 2004, to observe the creative process at length—or just enjoy the village life over the course of a typical day and night. For information, contact the OTDC (*See* the Orissa Essentials).

KONARK

64 km (40 mi) southeast of Bhubaneswar, 35 km (22 mi) northeast of Puri.

The sleepy town of Konark, 1½ hours from Bhubaneswar, is home to one of India's most fabulous, awe-inspiring temples—a World Heritage site. Visiting Orissa and not visiting Konark would be a sin, and the stately temple viewed at sunrise or sunset is profoundly beautiful. Konark's village exists for the temple, earning its income entirely from tourism via souvenir shops, food stalls, and basic restaurants. The beach, Chandrabhaga, is quiet, wide, and clean but not suitable for swimming because of the sharp currents; it offers an opportunity to see fishing folk in action at dusk. Nearby is the functioning 40-year-old Chandrabhaga lighthouse, open from 4 to 5.

Fodor'sChoice ★ Legend shrouds the towering sandstone **Sun Temple,** or Black Pagoda, so called because of the dark patina that has covered it over the centuries, though much of that black has now been cleaned off to reveal the stone's natural color. Built over 12 years by Ganga dynasty monarch King Narasimha (probably to enhance his prestige) in the 13th century, the Sun Temple takes the shape of the sun god Surya's chariot rising majestically from the sea. It's a wonder of architecture and engineering. Surya, according to Vedic texts, was considered the god of gods, the highest light. For centuries the temple lay, forgotten, virtually erased from the world, buried under tons of sand, and was only unearthed in the last century bit by bit. Its size alone astonishes. The word Konark is derived from *kona,* or "corner," and *ark,* or "sun." Today, only half the main temple and the audience hall remain to suggest the Sun Temple's original shape, but the complex once had a dancing hall, an audience hall, and a tremendous tower that soared to 227 feet. By 1869 the tower had fallen to ruin, and the audience hall had to be filled with stone slabs and sealed off to prevent its collapse. The temple's location near coastal sand is unique, but the briny air and the softness of the underlying dunes have taken their toll.

The Sun Temple was designed in the form of a chariot, with 24 wheels pulled by seven straining horses. Every last one of its surfaces is intricately carved with some of the most fantastic sculpture in India depicting the "carnival of life" from hunting to childbirth, images of war, dancers and musicians, and of course erotic pairings almost lyrically carved. Many panels also depict the range of graceful Odissi dance poses. Every structural feature is significant: the seven horses represent the seven days of the week, the 24 wheels are the 24 fortnights of the Indian year, and the eight spokes of each wheel are the eight *pahars,* eight segments of the 24 hour span which was the way ancients divided day and night.

Try to arrive between 7 and 8 AM, before the busloads of pilgrims and other tourists show up. If you cannot make it early then come with some water, a hat, comfortable footwear, and only a light bag—walking about in the hot sun for an hour plus is tiring business. The Archaeological Survey of India provides guides, but ask to see an identification badge, as many less-informed freelance guides are also eager to take you around. The going rate is Rs. 60 per person. A free museum (open daily 10–5) has sculptures found in the ruins. ✉ *Off Puri Rd. 725111* 🎫 *Rs. 100* 🕒 *Daily sunrise–sunset.*

The **Konark Dance Festival** (☎ *674/243–2217 Orissa Tourism Development Corporation [OTDC]*), held each December 1 through 5 in the evenings, features the best of Odissi and other dance forms on an outdoor stage with the illuminated Sun Temple as backdrop. If you can, bring something soft to cushion the hard, backless amphitheater seats—and mosquito repellent. OTDC runs special trips from Bhubaneswar or Puri and back during the festival for Rs. 125.

PURI

60 km (37 mi) south of Bhubaneswar, 35 km (22 mi) southwest of Konark.

The coastal town of Puri is heavily visited because it contains one of Hinduism's most sacred sites: the 12th-century **Jagannath Temple,** devoted to the Lord of the Universe. The interior of the temple complex, enclosed within high walls, is strictly off-limits to non-Hindus, probably due to numerous attacks by invaders through history; even the late Prime Minister Indira Gandhi was denied entrance on the eve of her death because she had married a non-Hindu. Hindus of non-Indian origin are occasionally admitted. The intricately sculpted main temple is 65 meters (213 feet) high, and, with its spire's crowning pennant, towers above its enclosure. Hordes of monkeys live in and around the lions and heads of demons carved in its beautiful beehive spire. The lively temple, undoubtedly one of India's most interesting, occupies 400,000 square feet and has about 6,000 pandas (priests). Devotees, monkeys, throngs of pilgrims, and priests populate the courtyards and flow around the sanctums. Its enormous kitchen feeds 10,000 people daily and 56 special types of food are offered to the gods after they are bathed and have their teeth brushed. Walk around the walls to see the four elaborately decorated gates. For a glimpse of the rest of the complex, pay a donation and, armed with binoculars, climb to the rooftop of the Raghunandan Library, across from the main temple entrance, called the Lion Gate, where pilgrims thrust their way in through the crowds of vendors.

Puri attracts even more crushing hordes than usual during the July Rath Yatra, or chariot festival, a 10-day festival involving processions of the painted and ceremonially dressed wooden temple deities—Lord Jagannath and his brother and sister—on elaborately decorated floatlike carts pulled by thousands of devotees to the sounds of cymbals, drums, and chanting. One of the most spectacular of India's temple fairs, it's also the only time non-Hindus get to see the statues, which are usually seated on their jeweled pedestals inside the temple.

In addition to the religious contingent, Puri is also a peaceful, pleasant beach and temple town with its very own laid-back rhythm attracting its share of modern hippies and backpackers drawn by the ethos of the international hippies who colonized the east end of the beach in the '60s. Today on this part of C. T. (Chakratirtha) Road you'll find many inexpensive lodgings and shops selling the cheapest tie-dye clothing, open-air garden restaurants, bar-restaurants with live music, and shops selling *bhang* (marijuana)—for religious purposes, of course.

Although Puri is still touted as a beach getaway, the sand is often littered with trash, and many of the hotels near the beach send their sewage directly into the sea, despite government efforts to curb the practice—in part, a reflection of Orissa's poverty. The Fisherman's Village, a thatch-roof community perhaps 10,000 strong of families of fishermen originally from Andra Pradesh, sits on the beach at the far eastern end of town and basically has no toilets; you do the math. It's still a pleasure to watch the sun rise and set over the same miles-long beach, to watch the little fishing boats with their one colorful sail cruise the waters, and to attend the nightly *aarti* (Hindu ceremony) on the main beach. But if you want to swim, rent a bike and head east for a few kilometers along the beach; eventually you'll come to clean sand (or just stay at Toshali Sands resort up the coast). Don't go alone if you're a woman—incidents have occurred involving locals—and be very conscious of potential rip tides.

There's quite a bit of shopping to be attempted right in Puri even if you do not get time to visit Raghurajpur. Head over to Priyadarshini on Chakratirtha Road to buy silk fabrics and to watch ikat weaving. Hand-loom saris and materials can purchased from any of the numerous hand-loom shops near the Jagannath Temple; try Orissa Handloom House (☎6752/222–054). Statues carved from sandstone of gods, goddesses, Nandi bulls, couples in erotic poses are available at Shreeram Handicrafts on Chakratirtha Road (☎6752/221–483). Some of the best patachitra and talapatra outside of Raghurajpur can found at Natraj Handicrafts Centre, Atharnala(☎9937/346–030).

WHERE TO EAT & STAY

$ ✕ **Wild Grass.** Puri has many garden restaurants, but in this charming garden—palm trees, flowering bushes, temple statues, terra-cotta lanterns—tables are set not only within a covered central area and under thatched open huts, but up on platforms in trees. You can get a good Orissan thali (platter) here, with specialties like grilled eggplant, tuna masala, the sugary tomato dish *khata,* and santula; but they need a little advance notice; call them the day before. Or go for the fresh seafood. Bengali dishes are also available but require advance notice. Be prepared to use the little bell on your table to summon the waiter—service is not fast. They offer a drop back to your hotel after your meal. ✉*VIP Rd.* ☎*6752/229–293* ▭*No credit cards.*

¢–$ ✕ **Peace.** This simple open-air restaurant, with a relaxed feel popular with foreigners, serves a heck of a grilled tuna at six or seven picnic tables under thatched huts in a tiny, handkerchief-size garden. In addition to other local fish and great grilled prawns, you can get pasta dishes, sandwiches (including peanut butter and banana on a toasted roll), soups, *pakoras* (deep-fried chick-pea-flour fritters), fries, and good breakfasts, such as delicious French toast with apples or bananas baked inside. The set menu includes main course, dal, rice, and a vegetable. ✉*Chakratirtha Rd.* ☎*No phone* ▭*No credit cards* ⊙*Closed mid-Aug.–Sept.*

$$$ ✕ **Hans Coco Palms.** At the end of Marine Drive on the beach, this self-contained resort on land that once belonged to royalty offers comfortable rooms with views of the ocean or the pool. The rooms are simply but attractively furnished in a contemporary style: a small sitting area with brightly cushioned wicker chairs, marble floors, decent-sized bathrooms with showers. The pool forms the central point of this 2-acre garden resort surrounded by abundant swaying coconut palms (as its name suggests). In your free time opt for a spot of yoga or an ayurvedic treatment. The terrace above the lobby is a great place to sunbathe. Continental, Indian, South Indian, and Oriya food is available at the Ocean Café. **Pros:** great location, restful don't-worry-be-happy vibe, excellent pool. **Cons:** over-priced. ✉*Swargdwar Beach, Puri 752001* ☎*6752/230–038 or 6752/230–951* 🖷*6752/230–165* 🌐*www.hanshotels.com* *36 rooms, 1 suite* *In-room: refrigerator, safe. In-hotel: restaurant, room service, bar, pool, gym, concierge, public Internet, laundry service.* ▭*AE, DC, MC, V* 🍽*BP.*

$$ ★ **Mayfair Beach Resort.** The best rooms in Puri are here, offering both style—teak floors with Persian-style rugs, elegant upholstery, carved headboards—and comfort, in the form of thick mattresses. Most rooms have balconies that look over rooftops to the sea. A flower-lined path leads to Mayfair's semiprivate beach. (They groom and staff it.) The resort is done in a vaguely New Mexican style, with burnt-orange stucco and lots of greenery. The outdoor patio restaurant with its wicker furniture is a pleasant place to relax over a drink. Neatly kept gardens and a pool that spills down right to the beach give the hotel a wonderful relaxing air. **Pros:** wonderful beach location, tranquil environment, luxurious extras. **Cons:** sprawling steps connect different parts of the resort. ✉ *Chakratirtha Rd., Puri, 752002* ☎ *6752/227–800* ⊕ *www.mayfairhotels.com* *34 rooms, 3 suites* *In room: refrigerator, safe. In-hotel: 2 restaurants, room service, bar, pool, spa, laundry service, public Internet, some pets allowed.* *AE, MC, V.*

$ **Toshali Sands.** If you've come to Puri for a peaceful beach vacation, this isolated 30-acre resort is for you. The virtually private beach, 8 km (5 mi) east of town, is a beautiful wide, clean strand backed by forest and a deer sanctuary. (It's a 20-minute walk from the hotel, or take a bike or a free jeep ride, available from the hotel.) Rooms, some in cottages strewn across a garden landscape others in a resort building, are simply decorated but comfortable. A shuttle service takes guests to and from town; on the premises you'll find good food (Chinese, Indian, Continental, Bengali, and excellent Oriya), a fine pool, a shopping arcade, ayurvedic center, daily yoga classes, and other activities. Arrangements can be made for boat rides on the river. **Pros:** very quiet, delicious food, attentive service, easy-going vibe. **Cons:** far from Puri town, beach 20 minutes away. ✉ *Ethnic Village Resort, Konark Marine Dr., 752002* ☎ *6752/250–571 to 74* ⊕ *www.toshalisands.com* *105 units* *In-room: refrigerator In-hotel: 2 restaurants, room service, bar, pool, gym, no elevator, laundry service, concierge, public Internet.* *AE, MC, V.*

¢ **Naren Palace Hotel.** This hotel, which opened in 2007, has large, clean, and comfortable rooms with mildly mismatched, but not unattractive, decor. Melon walls, peachy furnishing, and a small sofa done in a blue-black abstract decorate the space. Attached bathrooms are clean. The public areas, full of shiny gray marble, are well kept and cheerful, although in general, the modern block of a hotel lacks tangible character. There's a teensy-size pool out back and the public beach is close by. Indian and Western food is served in the hotel restaurant and if you step out of the hotel you have numerous meal choices very close by. **Pros:** centrally located, some rooms have a beach view, good value, tidy. **Cons:** lacking in the looks department. ✉ *Chakrathirtha Road, Puri, 752002* ☎ *6752/220–043 or 6752/220–047* *narenpalace@gmail.com* ⊕ *www.hotelpushpak.com/puri/naren/index.php* *22 rooms* *In-room: no a/c (some), refrigerator. In-hotel: restaurant, no elevator, public Internet.* *AE, MC, V.*

¢ **Z Hotel.** Probably the best, cleanest backpacker lodging in Puri, Z Hotel is in an airy 1916 bungalow called Amulya Bhavan owned once by the raja of Serampore (WestBengal), and surrounded by a quiet enclosed garden. Staying in this friendly rambling house is almost like a homestay. The 10 doubles, two singles, and six-bed women's dorm (great value at Rs. 100 a bunk) are spacious, very clean and bright, functionally furnished with white walls and tile floors. Only five rooms (doubles) have private baths; when the sun cooperates, there are solar-heated showers. Two doubles have balconies that let in even more light, but possibly more mosquitoes—a problem in Puri—but big white mosquito nets over the beds keep you safe at night. Book ahead; it's popular. **Pros:** historic bungalows, restaurant meals served by a superb seafood chef, extras include a library and welcoming sitting room. **Cons:** some rooms have shared baths, backpacker environment that may not appeal to some. ✉ *Chakratirtha Rd., Puri, 752002* ☎ *6752/222–554* 🌐 *www.zhotelindia.com* *12 rooms, 1 dormitory room* *In-room: no a/c, no phone, no TV. In-hotel: restaurant, public Internet.* 💳 *No credit cards.*

CHILIKA LAKE

★ *Barkul is 110 km (68 mi) south of Bhubaneswar, 60 km (37 mi) north of Gopalpur; Satapada is 50 km (31 mi) south of Puri; Rambha is 136 km (85 mi) south of Bhubaneswar, 45 km (28 mi) north of Gopalpur.*

From November through January, a visit to India's largest inland lake, covering 1,100 square km (425 square mi), is repaid with the sight of millions of birds, both residents and winter visitors. Siberian ducks and ibises are among the 150 species that have been cataloged here. A 10-km (6-mi), more than 1½-hour trip across this sparkling blue-green lake is a memorable, not-to-be-missed experience. The boats—a crude cross between a Kashmiri *shikhara* (graceful, simple flat-bottomed boat) and a Venetian gondola with noisy outboard motors—splutter past schools of dolphins, quaint fishing villages, remote island communities, two-huts-and-a-coconut-palm hamlets, tiny temples, fishing boats, prawn nets, coastal forest, and fishermen untangling their catch, eventually reaching a sandy beach, where the brackish lake joins the Bay of Bengal at its very narrow mouth.

To journey to the mouth of the lake you will need to catch a boat at Satapada and to go bird spotting, you'll need to take a boat at Barkul. OTDC (⇨ *Visitor Information in Orissa Essentials*) organizes excursion boats to take you out past the many islands that dot the lake to the best viewing area for birds, Nalabana Island, really a long stretch of reeds perfect for nesting, with enough of a sandbar for a watchtower. Private nonmotorized boats—one of the 300 fishing boats that ply the lake for mackerel, prawns, crabs, and bekti—can also take you to Nalabana, where you can climb the watchtower for a close-up view of the birds that form a solid ribbon on the reeds. You'll see the birds on an OTDC or a private motorized boat, but because of the sound of the motor you can't get too close without scattering the birds, so bring binoculars.

Private motorized boats (Rs. 750) will sail to the Bay of Bengal on a three-stop tour. The first stop is to see the swimming dolphin schools;

if you are very lucky you can catch them jumping in the air when two male dolphins skirmish. The next halt is at Kalijai Island for a look at its massively popular Vishnu shrine, with the full temple accoutrements of flower, sweets, and souvenir sellers. The final stop is the beach where eager fishermen will fry spicy seafood on the spot under makeshift thatched shelters or offer you coconut water. The ocean is one kilometer away.

One of Orissa's main rivers, the Mahanadi, empties into Chilika Lake. Silting caused the opening into the Bay of Bengal to close up and the lake was born. Some 225 species of fish inhabit the lake.

FLIPPER IN ORISSA

Chilika Lake is said to have about 124 Irrawaddy dolphins (a coastal dolphin). Because of their characteristic rolling movement, they're easy to spot in the water. Chilika is said to have about 125 such dolphins. The closest neighbors for these dolphins are the Ganga river water dolphins and Irrawaddy dolphins found at Sunderbans along the coast of West Bengal, but it's believed that they do not have interactions. This type of dolphin is facing extinction and Chilika has one of the highest populations.

The portion of the wetlands bordering Chilika have been demarcated into bird sanctuaries. The drive to Satapada, that takes you past ponds of flowering red and pink lotuses, prawn ponds, and charming rural communites, is delightful as well.

The OTDC runs day trips from Bhubaneswar to Barkul by bus (for larger groups; per head Rs. 160) and by hired car (Rs. 1,150) or from Bhubaneswar to Satapada by bus (for larger groups; Rs. 130 per head) and by hired car (Rs. 1,150), as well as from Puri to Satapada by bus (for larger groups; Rs. 110 per head) and by hired car (Rs. 750). It also has excursion boats (Rs. 100 to Rs. 160 per head or Rs. 1,500 to book the entire boat) that leave from Barkul, Rambha, Satapada, and Balugaon; at each of these locations you can get basic accommodations and tourist information from the OTDC offices, where the boats depart from. Dolphin Motor Boat Association, Satapada offers trips to Nalaban Bird Sanctuary (4 hours and Rs. 1,000). And also trips to the "dolphin point" and to the mouth of the lake. (3 hours and Rs. 700). Call 99/38518818 or 99/37618387. OTDC, Satapada 6752/262–077 and OTDC, Barkul 6756/220–488 Note of caution: pearls do not naturally occur in the Chilika Lake area. Do not get swindled into buying pearls just plucked from shells. They are plastic.

GOPALPUR-ON-SEA

178 km (111 mi) southwest of Bhubaneswar.

Gopalpur-on-Sea, a beach resort popular and often overrun with Bengalis holidaying from Kolkata (what Goa is to Mumbai folks), is a small fishing village with a few simple hotels scattered along the sand. The town has one main street, with a few shops for the locals and fast-food and seashell shops for tourists. The only trace of its past as a vital British seaport is a still-functioning lighthouse and the crumbling remains of European merchants' homes. Back in the Raj days when Britain did a lot of trade with Burma, Gopalpur-on Sea, with its umpteen warehouses, had a special prominence. Today it is more famous for cashew processing. The beach is long; you don't have to walk far to find solitude (though you might to find pristine sand). To get here, take a three-hour train ride from Bhubaneswar to Berhampur (164 km [102 mi] south of the city), then transfer to an auto-rickshaw (Rs. 80) for the 14-km (9-mi) ride southeast.

WHERE TO STAY

¢ **Green Park.** Here you'll find simple, clean rooms; those at the front of the building have a sea view, but it can be noisy. The hotel's big advantage over the other hotels in town is hot showers. Off-season, the restaurant only serves breakfast; in-season it's open for all meals. **Pros:** cheap, close to the beach. **Cons:** spartan facilities, sometimes noisy. ✉*Beach Rd., Gopalpur-on-Sea, 761002* ☎*680/224–3753* *19 rooms* *In-room: no a/c (some), no phone. In-hotel: room service, no elevator.* *No credit cards.*

¢ **Song of the Sea.** All the clean, simple rooms face the Bay of Bengal at this seafront hotel, built in 1996 by the family that runs it. The nicest rooms have balconies where you can watch the sun rise over the water and the colored sails of the fishing boats. Beams from the lighthouse sweep the place throughout the night—great for romantics, but not if you're a light sleeper (room 24 is *right* next to it). Hot water for bathing comes in a bucket. The dining room is big and cheerful, and there are lounge chairs on the lawn. **Pros:** homey atmosphere, lovely balconies views. **Cons:** bathrooms need updating. ✉*On the beach, Gopalpur-on-Sea, 761002* ☎*680/224–2347, 680/222–5056 at night* *In-room: no a/c (some), no phone. In-hotel: room service.* *No credit cards.*

ORISSA ESSENTIALS

To research prices, get advice from other travelers, and book travel arrangements, visit www.fodors.com.

AIR TRAVEL

Bhubaneswar's Biju Patnaik Airport is about 5 km (3 mi) from the center of town. Jet Lite, Kingfisher, Simplifly Deccan, Indigo, and Indian (Air India) fly into the city daily from Delhi, Mumbai, Kolkata, Hyderabad, and Bangalore.

Contacts Air India (☎*674/253–0533, 674/253–4472 at airport* *www.airindia.com*). **Indigo** (☎*99/1038–3838 02 or 1800/180–3838* *www.goindigo.in*). **Jet Lite** (☎*1800/223–020 or city code plus 3030–2020* *www.jetlite.com*). **Kingfisher** (☎*1/800/2333–131, 20/2729–3030 in Mumbai* *www.flykingfisher.com*). **Simplifly Deccan** (☎*city code plus 3900–8888* *www.airdeccan.net*).

AIRPORTS & TRANSFERS

The trip between Bhubaneswar's Biju Patnaik Airport and the city center takes 15 to 20 minutes. Most hotels provide free shuttle service if you give them your flight information in advance. White Ambassador and Tata Indica tourist taxis wait outside the terminal; fares are theoretically fixed, but be sure to agree on one before setting out. The fare to a central hotel should be around Rs. 140; to the outlying hotels, about Rs. 170.

If you're headed to Gopalpur on Sea or for a tribal village tour taking a flight to Visakhapatnam (Vizag) in Andhra Pradesh is equally or more convenient. The NH-5 connects Vizag with Gopalpur-on-Sea and the distance between Vizag and Gopalpur-on-Sea is 260 km (162 mi). Alternately take a train from Vizag to Berhampur (Brahmapur), Gopalpur-on-Sea's nearest rail head (about 5 hours like the daily Visakha Express or Howrah Mail). Rayagada, the destination of many tribal tours, is easily connected by train with Vizag, too (about 3 hours like the daily Dhanbad Express).

BUS TRAVEL TO & FROM ORISSA

Bhubaneswar's Baramunda bus station, where you can catch an overnight bus to Calcutta, is 5 km (3 mi) from the city center on the main highway heading toward Kolkata. Private luxury buses connect Bhubaneswar with Puri.

State buses are the most inexpensive way to travel within Orissa, but be prepared for extreme conditions: the buses are unreliable, and routes traverse only main roads, leaving you to walk 2 to 4 km (1 to 2½ mi) to get to villages. ORSTC run the state buses, ☎674/255–0695 in Bhubaneswar. Or try the private bus lines ☎674/255–0769 in Bhubaneswar.

CARS & DRIVERS

Car and driver is the best way to get around Orissa. Most hotel travel desks provide guests with cars and drivers, but the cost is often quite a bit higher than necessary. A good source (with better prices) is the OTDC (⇨ *Visitor Information*; Bhubaneswar Transport Unit ☎674/243–1515; Puri Transport Unit ☎6752/223–526). Its rates in Bhubaneswar or Puri for an Ambassador/Indica car are Rs. 504 (Rs. 720 for an air-conditioned car) for an eight-hour day covering 80 km (50 mi) or less; call ahead to confirm what the fare will be. Hiring a car in Bhubaneswar for a journey to Puri will set you back Rs. 700. You may be able to negotiate a better price with a taxi driver on your own, but remember that an English-speaking driver will be worth every extra penny. Be sure to specify which places you plan to visit and how long you plan to spend. The rate is roughly Rs. 4 per kilometer.

EMERGENCIES

In the event of a medical emergency, your first step should be to check with the hotel's front desk—they'll know what the best hospital is near their location. For ambulances in Bhubaneswar, try St. John's or Indian Red Cross. Puri also has ambulances you can call.

Medical Care **Ambulance (Puri)** (☎*675/240-2005*). **Capital Hospital** (✉*Unit 6, Bhubaneswar* ☎*674/240-1983*). **Kalinga Hospital** (✉*Nalco Chhak, Chandrasekharpur, north of the Trident hotel, Bhubaneswar* ☎*674/230-0997*). **Head Quarter Hospital** (✉*Grand Rd., Puri* ☎*675/222-3742*). **Indian Red Cross ambulance (Bhubaneshwar)** (☎*102*). **Municipal Hospital** (✉*Laxmi Bazar, Puri* ☎*675/222-3241*). **St. John's ambulance (Bhubaneshwar)** (☎*674/253-1485*).

MONEY

ATMS ATMs are all over. Finding either an HDFC, ICICI, or SBI ATM is not difficult and you can withdraw money against a MasterCard, Visa, and American Express (but not at SBI) at these ATMs.

To locate the nearest ICICI Bank ATM nearest to you check *www.icicibank.com*. To locate the nearest HDFC Bank ATM nearest you check *www.hdfcbank.com*. To locate the nearest SBI ATM near you check *www.sbi.co.in/atmlocator.jsp*.

CURRENCY EXCHANGE Most Western-style hotels will change money or traveler's checks for their guests. You can also cash traveler's checks at the main branches of the State Bank of India in Bhubaneswar (open weekdays 10–4, Saturday 10–1) and Puri.

Exchange Service **State Bank of India** (✉*Near Market Bldg., Rajpath, Bhubaneswar* ✉*VIP Rd., Puri*).

TAXIS & RICKSHAWS

Taxis and auto-rickshaws in Orissa have meters, but drivers never use them so you have to negotiate for every ride. Ask your hotel about the appropriate fare.

TRAIN TRAVEL

The Rajdhani Express is the fastest train between Delhi and Bhubaneswar, making the trip in 24 hours four days a week. Several slower trains travel from Puri to Bhubaneswar to Delhi, including the daily Purshottam Express, the Puri Express (four days a week), and the Neelachal Express (three days a week), which stops at Varanasi and Lucknow. From Bhubaneswar on the daily East Coast Express, it's seven hours north to Calcutta (Howrah station on the schedules) and 23 hours south to Hyderabad. The weekly Muzaffarpur–Yeshvantpur Express makes stops at Visakhapatnam (1 AM), Berhampur (also Brahmapur; nearest railhead to Gopalpur-on-Sea), Balugaon, and Bhubaneswar (4 AM). Every day but Sunday, the Jan Shatabdi Express makes an 8-hour run between Bhubaneswar and Kolkata.

Three days a week the Puri Express makes the 43-hour trip between Ahmedabad and Puri; links connect Puri with Visakhapatnam (8 hours) and the Orissan weaving town of Sambalpur (11½ hours). The fastest Chennai connections from Bhubaneswar are the daily Coromandel Express (20 hours) and the twice-weekly Chennai Express (21 hours). The Secunderabad Express to Chennai (22½ hours) continues on to Bangalore (8½ hours more) twice a week. The twice-weekly Ernakulam Express also connects with Chennai (22½ hours), continuing on to Kerala's Trivandrum, 3 hours farther down the line, and Ernakulam, 4½ hours more; the slower, twice-weekly Trivandrum Express makes the same stops. The Dhanbad Express connects daily Visakhapatnam and Rayagada (jumping off point for tribal tours). The Visakha Express and Howrah Mail daily connects Visakhapatnam with Berhampur (Brahmapur; closest railhead to Gopalpur-on-Sea.

TRANSPORTATION WITHIN ORISSA

Hiring a car and driver for a half or full day is not expensive, and is the most convenient way to get around Orissa in general and the towns in particular—you avoid having to haggle over fares with taxi or auto-rickshaw drivers, as well as the overcrowded conditions of the local buses. Auto-rickshaws are cheaper than taxis and usually slower (though quicker in heavy traffic). Apply the same fare rules as you would for taxis. For short distances within towns, cycle-rickshaws are easiest. A horde of cycle-rickshaws await you at the train stations. Always negotiate the fare with any taxi, auto-rickshaw, or cycle-rickshaw driver before you set off in order to avoid hassles or overcharging later. The OTDC arranges transport inexpensively to the main tourist spots. In a leisurely town like Puri, hire a bicycle or a motorbike for Rs. 150 per day at any of the shops on Chakratirtha Road.

TRAVEL AGENTS & TOURS

The Orissa Tourism Development Corporation (OTDC) offers several reasonably priced set or customized day tours and overnights anywhere in the region, using its own chain of inexpensive hotels.

A private tour guide can seriously enhance your sightseeing. The most knowledgeable and English-proficient guides are those trained by the India Tourism (the government of India's tourism division); you can hire one through the OTDC or India Tourism for about Rs. 280 per half-day and Rs. 400 for a full day (eight hours) for up to four people. Any of the agents below can organize vehicles or put together a tour package for you or a tribal tour.

Contacts **Discover Tours** (✉ *463 Lewis Rd., Bhubaneswar* ☎ *674/243-0477* 📠 *674/243-0828* 📧 *discovertours@yahoo.com* 🌐 *www.orissadiscover.com*). **Gandhara Tour and Travels** (✉ *Chakratirtha Rd., Puri* ☎ *6752/224-117* 📠 *6752/222-618* 🌐 *www.hotelgandhara.com/travels.htm*). **Heritage Tours and Treks** (✉ *Mayfair Beach Resort, Chakratirtha Rd., Puri* ☎ *675/222-3656* 📠 *675/222-4595* 📧 *heritagetours@hotmail.com, bubuno1@hotmail.com* 🌐 *www.heritagetoursorissa.com*). **Nabagunjara Travels** (✉ *Balighar, 10 Rathadandra Rd., Bhubaneswar* ☎ *674/243-1659 or 674/243-1759* 📠 *674/310-2899* 📧 *nabagunjara@hotmail.com* 🌐 *www.nabagunjaratravels.com*). **OTDC Puri** ✉ *Pantha Bhavan, Puri* ☎ *6752/222-562* 📠 *674/243-1053*. **OTDC Bhubaneshwar** (✉ *Panthanivas, Old Block, Lewis Rd., Bhubaneswar* ☎ *674/243-0764* 🌐 *www.panthanivas.com* 📧 *otdc@skycable.net*). **Swosti Travels** (✉ *Next to Swosti hotel, 103 Janpath, Bhubaneswar* ☎ *674/253-5773, 674/253-6228, or 674/253-4058* 📠 *674/253-5781* 🌐 *www.swosti.com*) **Toshali Tours and Travels** (✉ *Toshali Sands, Konark Marine Dr., Puri* ☎ *6752/250-571* 📠 *6752/250-899* 🌐 *www.toshalitours.com*). **Travel Link** (✉ *Triumph Residency hotel, 5-B Sahid Nagar, Bhubaneswar* ☎ *674/254-6591 to 94* 📠 *674/254-6595* 📧 *travlink@sancharnet.in*).

VISITOR INFORMATION

The OTDC is the best source of information on the state. All its offices are open Monday–Saturday from 10–5 (closed second Saturday of each month). India Tourism, the government of India's offices, are open weekdays 10–5.

Orissa Tourism Development Corporation (OTDC) (✉ *Panthanivas, Lewis Rd., Bhubaneswar 751014* ☎ *674/243—0764 or 674/243–1289* 🖷 *674/243–0887* ✉ *otdc@ortel.net or in Puri* ✉ *Pantha Bhavan, Puri* ☎ *6752/222–562*). This is the main OTDC number. OTDC has several departments that handle hotel bookings, transportation arrangements, festivals, and tour plans. They will redirect you the right department or offer you a local OTDC number in Puri or Satapada or elsewhere who can handle your query.

Government of Orissa Tourist Office (✉ *Tourist Office, Jayadev Marg, Bhubaneswar* ☎ *674/243–1299* ✉ *Tourist Office, VIP Chhak, Station Rd., Puri* ☎ *675/222–2664*). This tourist office offers general information about the sights of Bhubaneswar and Puri as well as Konark.

Tourist Information India Tourism (✉ *B-21 B. J. B. Nagar, Bhubaneswar 751014* ☎ *674/243–1299* ☎🖷 *674/243–2203* ✉ *Biju Patnaik Airport, Bhubaneswar* ☎ *No phone* 🌐 *www.tourismofindia.com* ✉ *itobbs@ori.nic.in*). **Orissa Tourism Development Corporation** (✉ *Head Office, Panthanivas, Lewis Rd., Bhubaneswar 751014* ☎ *674/243–0764* 🖷 *674/243–0887* ✉ *otdc@ortel.net* ✉ *Tourist Office, Jayadev Marg, Bhubaneswar* ☎ *674/243–1299* ✉ *Biju Patnaik Airport, Bhubaneswar* ☎ *674/240–4006* ✉ *Railway station, Bhubaneswar* ☎ *674/253–0715* ✉ *Tourist Office, Tourist Complex, Barkul* ☎ *675/622–0855* ✉ *Railway station, Berhampur* ☎ *680/228–0226* ✉ *Tourist Office, Yatrinivas, Konark* ☎ *675/823–6820 or 675/823–6821* ✉ *Tourist Office, VIP Chhak, Station Rd., Puri* ☎ *675/222–2664* ✉ *Railway station, Puri* ☎ *675/222–3536* 🌐 *www.orissatourism.gov.in*).

Kolkata (Calcutta)

Dancers at a Calcutta festival

WORD OF MOUTH

"The contrasts in Kolkata are amazing: the people in the parks and at the Victoria Memorial seemed like they were doing fine economically; some of the apartments in the neighborhood north of our hotel are undoubtedly very expensive; yet there are many extremely poor people on the streets all around and camped out under the causeway. And the electrical wires tangled above all the streets were remarkable."

—RCLCOLPB

www.fodors.com/forums

WELCOME TO KOLKATA (CALCUTTA)

TOP REASONS TO GO

★ **Eclectic Architecture:** The city is packed with gorgeous temples, mosques, universities, and colonial mansions and monuments.

★ **Walking City:** Kolkata is best seen on foot: take a walk across the Howrah Bridge or go for a wander through the giant Maidan park.

★ **Cultural Capital:** Catch a locally-produced English-language movie or play; for astonishing art, head to the Indian Museum, considered the country's best.

★ **Foodie's Paradise:** Kolkatans are proud of their food—especially their seafood—and for good reason. This is also the place to try Indian-Chinese food, originated a century ago by Chinese immigrants.

★ **Book Bargains:** You might just find a gem at one of the many bookstalls on College Street. Kolkata's book fair, in winter, is one of the largest in the world.

1 North Kolkata. This is the oldest part of the city. Its streets are narrow and crowded, but also vibrant and surprising. Here you'll find the College Street book stalls and the Marble Palace.

2 Central Kolkata. The bustling downtown is anchored by B.B.D. Bagh, where business and government buildings are concentrated. Many of the city's best shops and restaurants flank Park Street.

3 The Maidan. This very central park is not only a good place to see Kolkatans at play and sheep grazing, it's also where you'll see some of India's finest colonial buildings, including the Victoria Memorial across the street.

4 South Kolkata. The leafy residential neighborhood is home to the tony Tollygunge country club, the National Library, and Mother Teresa's hospice.

Dakshineshwar Kali Temple

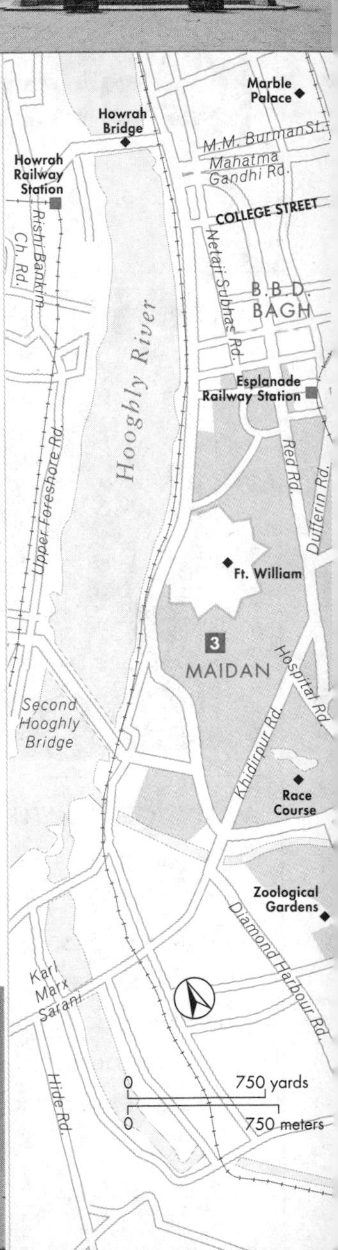

GETTING ORIENTED

On the eastern bank of the Hooghly River, Kolkata is the commercial hub of Northeastern India. In the southern part of West Bengal, Kolkata is about 45 mi west of Bangladesh and about 60 miles north of the Bay of Bengal. West Bengal borders Nepal to its northwest and the state of Assam and the country of Bhutan to its northeast; its western edge touches the state of Bihar, and Orissa is to its southwest.

Fower market

13

KOLKATA (CALCUTTA) PLANNER

When to Go

The hottest weather arrives in April and grows increasingly stifling through June, when the monsoon season begins. This runs through mid-September and cools Kolkata down, though the occasional downpour means you can expect a soaking or two. After the monsoon, it's festival time. The biggest of all festivals is the Durga Puja, which takes place over two weeks in September or October. Around December the mild winter sets in and lasts until March. This is the best time to visit, but as a result it's also the time that making advance reservations for hotels, trains, and airplanes is essential. If you visit around Christmas, you're likely to see such tangible signs of the season as Christmas lights and fruitcake-like puddings. The town of Shantiniketan has its major festival, the Poush Mela, around the same time.

Getting There & Around

Dum Dum Airport is 15 km (9 mi) north of the city. Outside the baggage claim–customs area, you can hire a taxi through the prepaid-taxi counter; the ride downtown takes at least 40 minutes and costs around Rs. 135 (a third of what you might be charged by the hustlers outside the terminal). The unreliable airport coach (Rs. 50), goes to most of the upscale hotels and to the city center.

Howrah Junction, which sees tremendous amounts of train traffic every day, is divided into the neighboring Old and New Howrah stations. Getting to central Kolkata by taxi from here takes 20 to 40 minutes, depending on traffic. Once you get downtown, it's usually best to hire a car and driver, which you can do from the travel agencies and rental agencies (⇨ *Kolkata Essentials*). Expect to pay Rs. 750 for five hours and 70 km (50 mi), with an hourly and per-kilometer rate beyond that. Hailing a plain old taxi can be cheaper. Take a cab to or from the area you're visiting, then walk or find a sturdy cycle rickshaw.

Auto-rickshaws are cheaper than taxis but are best avoided. The three-wheel menaces are often operated by unlicensed drivers and work much like buses, picking up passengers along fixed routes. Many taxi drivers are unfamiliar with the roads, so expect frequent stops for directions. Adding to the confusion is the haphazard way in which many streets have been renamed. As for buses, they're slow, creaking, and unbearably crowded during rush hours. They will cost you next to nothing but will set you back in terms of time and comfort.

Kolkata is the only city in the world to still have hand-pulled rickshaws: they're an efficient form of transportation for short distances. However, for many travelers, being carried around by a poor, barefooted man may be unsettling. Rickshaw fares fluctuate depending on the distance and the amount of traffic; negotiate ahead of time, using Rs. 20 per 10 minutes as a guide.

Kolkata's efficient metro system connects the airport with Tollygunge, a South Kolkata locality that's the southernmost stop on the route. Tickets cost Rs. 5–Rs. 10 and are available from machines and windows in every station.

Sweets & Street Food

Bengalis love to eat, and much of their street food is unique. Common dishes include *champ* (chicken or mutton cooked slowly in large, thick-cast open pans), *birianis* (rice-and-meat dishes), and tandoori items, none of which resembles dishes of the same name in other parts of India. From roadside vendors, the most popular item is the Calcutta roll, in which seasoned meats or vegetables and chutneys are wrapped in thick *parathas* (Indian breads) with onions and sometimes even eggs. Not to be missed either are Bengali sweet shops, whose products fill the life of every native.

Trinkets, Textiles & Touts

All of India tempts the shopper here: mammoth amounts of goods arrive in Kolkata from the rest of the subcontinent, especially crafts from Bangladesh and neighboring northeastern states. Prices are tantalizingly low. The irritants are touts, including the instant friends who approach you claiming they have nothing to sell and then start pushing you to buy their goods. Although roadside vendors' prices are negotiable, clerks at government emporiums, shops that sell branded goods, and most places with fixed-price tags may be put out if you try to bargain.

Some of the most interesting crafts in West Bengal are brightly painted terra-cotta figurines and bas-reliefs. *Dhokra* are cast figures made of clay and metal. Shells, bell metal, and soapstone are all used in popular Bengali trinkets and figurines. Kolkata's bazaars and shops sell all kinds of textiles, including embroideries. With its longtime traditions of literacy and cosmopolitanism, Kolkata is also a good place for English-language books.

What It Costs In Rupees

	¢	$	$$	$$$	$$$$
Restaurants	under Rs. 100	Rs. 100–Rs. 300	Rs. 300–Rs. 500	Rs. 500–Rs. 700	over Rs. 700
Hotels	under Rs. 2,000	Rs. 2,000–Rs. 4,000	Rs. 4,000–Rs. 6,000	Rs. 6,000–Rs. 10,000	over Rs. 10,000

Restaurant prices are for an entrée plus bread or rice. Hotel prices are for a double room in high season, excluding a tax of up to 20%.

Planning Your Time

You can see most of Kolkata's major sights comfortably in three days. Morning is a good time to hit the Maidan park and see Kolkatans playing sports and enjoying the outdoors before the afternoon sun forces them inside. The Victoria Memorial across from the park is a good place to escape the heat; its art exhibitions are fabulous. While you're in the neighborhood, be sure to see Fort William and the Eden Gardens. In the late afternoon, visit the peaceful South Park Street Cemetery (Don't get there too late; it closes around 5). Later, shop at New Market, and then join the locals for dinner, drinks, and dancing at the restaurants and hotel nightclubs on and around Park Street.

The next day, visit College Street and walk around the university area and the secondhand bookstalls. From College Street, you can walk to Nakhoda Mosque, the Marble Palace, and the Rabindra Bharati University Museum, with its Bengali-school paintings and Rabindranath Tagore memorabilia. For a dose of Hindu culture, take a cab to the Paresnath Temple. Continue on to Kumartuli to see artists create clay icons by the river. Another cab ride will take you to the Belur Math Shrine, then cross back to the Dakshineshwar Kali Temple.

If you have still have time in town, you can taxi down to Nirmal Hirday to visit the late Mother Teresa's first charitable home.

Updated by Prashant Gopal

NOTHING CAN PREPARE YOU FOR KOLKATA. As the birthplace of an empire and the home of the late Mother Teresa, as a playground for the rich and a haven for the destitute, as a wellspring of creative energy and a center for Marxist agitation, Kolkata dares people to make sense of it. Whether it shocks you or seduces you, Kolkata will impress itself upon you. To understand and learn from India today, a trip to Kolkata is vital. (Although the name was officially changed from Calcutta in 2001, both names are used more or less interchangeably.)

In 1690, Job Charnock, an agent for the British East India Company, leased the villages of Sutanati, Gobindpur, and Kalikutta and formed a trading post to supply his firm. Legend has it that Charnock had won the hearts of Bengalis when he married a local widow, thus saving her from *sati* (the custom that calls for a widow to throw herself on her husband's funeral pyre). However, new research has suggested that the story of Charnock founding Calcutta is more lore than fact and that the city existed before the British East India Company agent arrived here in 1690. Through Charnock's venture, the British gained a foothold in what had been the Sultanate of Delhi under the Moghuls, and the directors of the East India Company became Indian *zamindars* (landowners) for the first time. It was here, as traders and landowners, that British entrepreneurs and adventurers began what would amount to the conquest of India and the establishment of the British Raj. More than any other city in India, Kolkata is tied to the evolution and disintegration of the British presence.

Kolkata is the capital of the state of West Bengal, which borders Bangladesh (formerly East Bengal). The Bengali people—animated, garrulous, intellectual, spirited, argumentative, anarchic, imaginative, and creative—have dominated this city and made it an essential part of India for more than 150 years. Among the first to react to the intellectual and political stimuli of the West, the Bengali have produced many of India's most respected filmmakers, writers, scientists, musicians, dancers, and philosophers. Having embraced 19th-century European humanism, such Bengalis as the poet Rabindranath Tagore and others revived their indigenous culture and made the first organized efforts to oust the British. Emotions here ran high early on, and agitation in Bengal broke away from what would later be called Gandhian politics to choose terrorism—one reason the British moved their capital from Calcutta to Delhi in 1911.

Calcutta remained cosmopolitan and prosperous throughout the British period. But after Independence and Partition, in 1947, trouble began when the world's center of jute processing and distribution (Calcutta) was politically separated from its actual production center (the eastern Bengali hinterland). For Calcutta and the new East Pakistan, Partition was equivalent to separating the fingers of an industry from the thumb. Natural disasters—commonly cyclones and droughts, but also, as in 1937, earthquakes—had long sent millions from East Bengal (which later became East Pakistan) to Calcutta in search of shelter and sustenance; after Partition, a wave of 4 million political refugees from East Pakistan compounded and complicated the pressure. Conflict with

China and Pakistan created millions more throughout the 1960s, and Pakistan's 1971 military crackdown alone sent 10 million temporary refugees into the city from what would soon become Bangladesh. By the mid-1970s, Calcutta was widely seen as the ultimate urban disaster. Riddled with disease and squalor, plagued by garbage and decay, once the heart of the British Raj, the Paris of Asia, had quickly and dramatically collapsed.

Or had it? The city kept on growing, and these days, greater Kolkata's entire metropolitan district covers more than 426 square km (264 square mi) and has more than 12 million people. It now has two municipal corporation areas (Kolkata and the near suburb of Howrah), 32 municipalities, 62 nonmunicipal urban centers, and more than 500 villages. What the city has learned to accept, is that it has become marginalized in contemporary India's political and economic power structure. The people here have borne that acceptance with a slightly tired air of resignation and stoicism. A Marxist government has been ruling West Bengal since 1977 from the seat of power in Calcutta. But even this government has adapted to the new globalized economy, fusing Marx with market economics and talking less about agrarian reforms and more about the information-technology revolution. Today's traveler may actually notice more poverty in Mumbai than in the city more often associated with human strife. Kolkata remains open, smiling, and thoughtful: amid the difficulties there is dignity, and amid the crises there are ideas.

AMAZING FESTIVALS

The greatest Bengali festival of the year is the Durga Puja (Durga is an incarnation of Kali, Kolkata's patron goddess). The *pujas* (homage, literally, "worship") take place over several days in September or October. Colorful, handmade Hindu idols, sometimes more than 20 feet tall, are moved in large processions through the streets for several hours before reaching the river and being. The rites and processions blend tradition with innovation; some idols even commemorate people such as recent flood victims or the film star of the moment.

13

EXPLORING KOLKATA

Kolkata and Howrah (also written as Haora) straddle the Hooghly River, with Kolkata on the east side, and Howrah on the west. Across the Hooghly from Kolkata's old quarter, the Howrah district—which holds Kolkata's massive train station—is a constantly expanding suburb. On the eastern side of town is Salt Lake City, a planned, spotlessly clean, upscale residential community.

In Kolkata itself, the Howrah Bridge spills into Bara Bazaar, the vibrant wholesale-market area that anchors the city's commerce. North Kolkata includes Bara Bazaar and Kolkata University and extends to the distant neighborhood of Chitpur and the Jain Temple in Tala. The heart of Central Kolkata remains B.B.D. Bagh (Binoy Badel Dinesh Bagh, formerly Dalhousie Square), where commerce and government have been concentrated since British times. Central Kolkata also holds

CLOSE UP

Rickshaw Pullers

Kolkata is the last city on earth to use enormous Chinese-style rickshaws pulled by men on foot. The rickshaws were introduced in the 19th century by Chinese traders and the British made it a legal form of transportation in 1919. Kolkata has about 6,000 licensed rickshaw operators, but at least as many operate without licenses. The Communist government of West Bengal—concerned about its image as it positions Kolkata as a technology hub—placed a ban on the human-powered vehicles in late 2006. Government officials called the hand-pulled rickshaws "barbaric" and "inhuman" and vowed not to renew operators' licenses. But the rickshaw-puller union is fighting the move and remains skeptical of the government's offer to retrain pullers to be parking lot attendants. Many pullers say they would never want to use cycle-rickshaw wallahs, who use bicycles to transport their passengers. If you ever get the chance to pull a rickshaw, you will be surprised at how difficult it is, even when the rickshaw is empty.

the expansive Maidan park, the crowded bazaar at New Market, and the upmarket shops and restaurants on Park Street. At the south end of the Maidan are the Victoria Memorial and Kolkata's racecourse. South Kolkata has the Kali Temple and the late Mother Teresa's hospice in Kalighat and the National Library and zoo in Alipore, a posh residential community. To the east of the city is the Eastern Metropolitan Bypass (known to residents as "the bypass"), which links south Kolkata to the north. As people increasingly take the bypass (and as more affluent neighborhoods are built alongside and near it), destinations like Aquatica and Nicco Park have sprung up in the area.

Numbers in the text correspond to points of interest on the Kolkata map.

ABOUT THE RESTAURANTS

Eating out (and indeed eating in) is a favorite pastime in Kolkata. The city was the hub of happening restaurants and clubs in the 1960s—a culture that dwindled with the passing of years. However, after the liberalization of the economy and with the blessings of the open market (open to foreign goods and influences) Kolkata has experienced a vibrant restaurant culture since the mid-1990s. Restaurants here cater to a varied sensibility: Asian, Mexican, Italian, and, of course, Indian. The service is largely friendly, and many places are crowded enough, especially on weekends, to warrant reservations. Best of all, eating out in Kolkata is cheaper compared to cities like Delhi and Mumbai—and every bit as good in terms of quality. Restaurants are generally open daily 12:30 to 3 for lunch and 7:30 to 11 for dinner.

ABOUT THE HOTELS

Unless otherwise noted, hotels have air-conditioning, room TVs, and operate on the European meal plan (no meals included). Better hotels have foreign-exchange facilities, and most have rooms with bathrooms that have tubs. Some luxury hotels have exclusive floors with special privileges or facilities for the business traveler. Kolkata's top few hotels are fine establishments that meet international standards and then some. An exceptionally high luxury tax of approximately 20% is added to your bill.

NORTH KOLKATA

The streets in northern Kolkata are more crowded and narrower than those elsewhere in the city. This—the old village of Sutanuti—is where the Indians lived while the British spread their estates east and south of Fort William and Dalhousie Square (B. B. D. Bagh). The architecture reflects Italian and Dutch influences.

North Kolkata's attractions are somewhat scattered. You'll need to take taxis at least sporadically. The bazaar areas surrounding Mahatma Gandhi Road, universally known as M. G. Road, are at once intensely commercial and residential; tourists are only occasional, despite the fascinating sights and vibe. You may attract some curious stares, but anyone you stop and speak to is bound to be friendly and welcoming.

A GOOD TOUR

Start with a morning coffee at the Indian Coffee House on **College Street** ❶, then browse through the street's bookstalls. Walk west, crossing Chittaranjan Avenue, to the huge, sandstone **Nakhoda Mosque** ❷, and climb to the top floor for a great view of the bustle in the streets below. Walk back to Chittaranjan Avenue, turn left (north), then left after a few blocks on Muktaram Basu Street—halfway down the block on the left you'll see the **Marble Palace** ❸, a mélange of international architecture, statues, and furnishings. From the palace it's a short walk north to Tagore Street, where you turn left for the **Rabindra Bharati University Museum** ❹, in the poet's former home. Walking farther west on Tagore Street brings you to the Hooghly River, with the **Howrah Bridge** ❺ a block to the south. North and south of the Howrah Bridge along the waterfront is the wholesale flower market—before 7 AM. Also in this area is Strand Road, which heads south toward the Second Hooghly Bridge and, in the evening, makes for a delightful riverside stroll in that area. At sunset, both river and city look magical; Kolkata becomes a different town altogether.

A short taxi ride will bring you to the Jain **Paresnath Temple** ❻, perhaps one of the cleanest buildings in Kolkata. A 30-minute walk or quick cab ride farther north, near the river, is an area called **Kumartuli** ❼, where thousands of potters fashion clay images of gods and goddesses for Hindu festivals. The **Dakshineshwar Kali Temple** ❽, a major Hindu pilgrimage site, requires another taxi ride north. Cross the Second Hooghly Bridge (again, it's best to take a cab) to the suburb of Howrah and head south along Belur Road to the **Belur Math Shrine** ❾, headquarters of the Ramakrishna Mission. Return downtown by taxi.

TIMING This tour takes the better part of a day and can be very tiring; pack a lunch before you set off. The Marble Palace, Rabindra Bharati museum, Paresnath Temple, and Dakshineshwar Kali Temple each take 30 to 60 minutes to absorb. Try to sandwich your touring between the rush

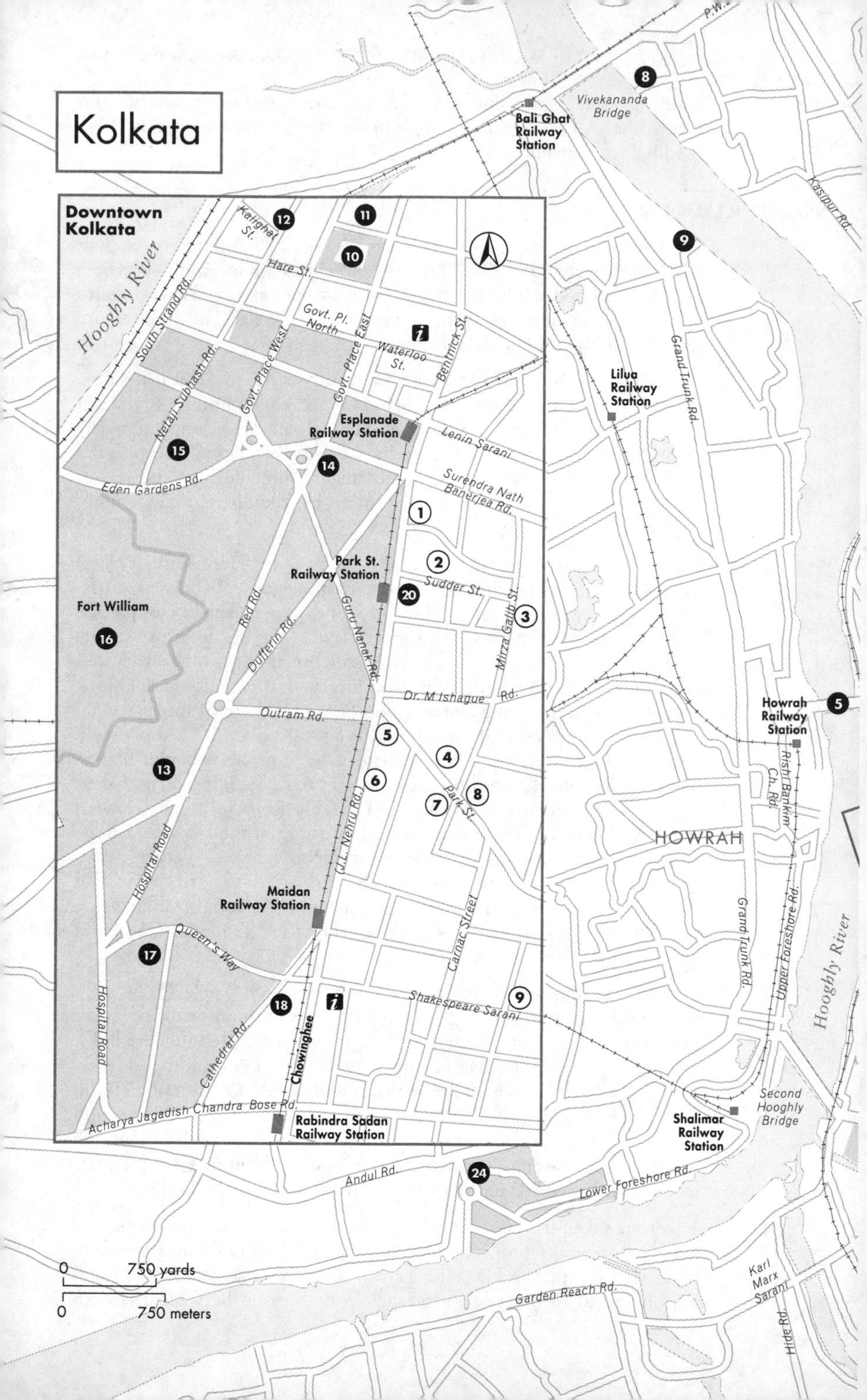

Kolkata
Downtown Kolkata
Kalighat St.
Hare St.
Hooghly River
South Strand Rd.
Netaji Subhash Rd.
Govt. Place West
Govt. Pl. North
Govt. Place East
Waterloo St.
Bentinck St.
Esplanade Railway Station
Lenin Sarani
Eden Gardens Rd.
Surendra Nath Banerjea Rd.
Park St. Railway Station
Sudder St.
Mirza Galib St.
Fort William
Red Rd.
Dufferin Rd.
Guru Nanak Rd.
Dr. M Ishague Rd.
Outram Rd.
(J.L. Nehru Rd.)
Park St.
Hospital Road
Maidan Railway Station
Carnac Street
Queen's Way
Shakespeare Sarani
Cathedral Rd.
Chowinghee
Acharya Jagadish Chandra Bose Rd.
Rabindra Sadan Railway Station
Andul Rd.
Lower Foreshore Rd.
Garden Reach Rd.
Karl Marx Sarani
Hide Rd.
Vivekananda Bridge
Bali Ghat Railway Station
Kasipur Rd.
Grand Trunk Rd.
Lilua Railway Station
Howrah Railway Station
Rishi Bankim Ch. Rd.
HOWRAH
Upper Foreshore Rd.
Hooghly River
Second Hooghly Bridge
Shalimar Railway Station
P.W.
0
750 yards
0
750 meters

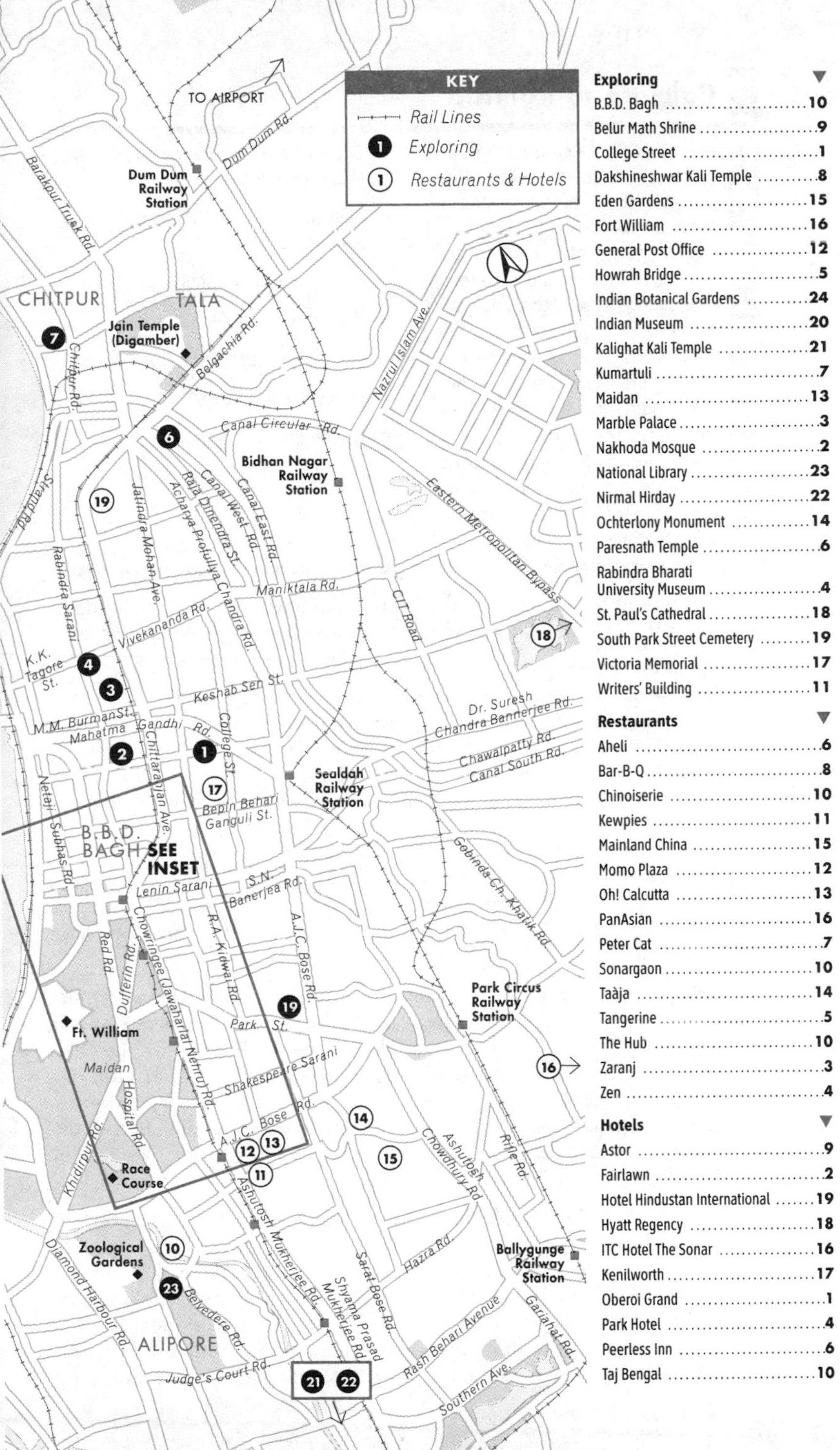
KEY
Rail Lines
Exploring
Restaurants & Hotels
TO AIRPORT
Dum Dum Rd.
Dum Dum Railway Station
Barakpur Trunk Rd.
CHITPUR
TALA
Jain Temple (Digamber)
Belgachia Rd.
Chitpur Rd.
Canal Circular Rd.
Bidhan Nagar Railway Station
Nazrul Islam Ave.
Eastern Metropolitan Bypass
Strand Rd.
Jatindra Mohan Ave.
Raja Dinendra St.
Acharya Profullya Chandra Rd.
Canal West Rd.
Canal East Rd.
Rabindra Sarani
Maniktala Rd.
CIT Road
Vivekananda Rd.
K.K. Tagore St.
Keshab Sen St.
M.M. Burman St.
Mahatma Gandhi Rd.
College St.
Dr. Suresh Chandra Bannerjee Rd.
Chawalpatty Rd.
Canal South Rd.
Chittaranjan Ave.
Sealdah Railway Station
Netaji Subhas Rd.
Bepin Behari Ganguli St.
B.B.D. BAGH SEE INSET
S.N. Banerjea Rd.
Lenin Sarani
Gobinda Ch. Khatik Rd.
Red Rd.
Dufferin Rd.
Chowringee (Jawaharlal Nehru) Rd.
R.A. Kidwai Rd.
A.J.C. Bose Rd.
Park Circus Railway Station
Ft. William
Park St.
Maidan
Hospital Rd.
Shakespeare Sarani
Khidirpur Rd.
A.J.C. Bose Rd.
Ashutosh Chowdhury Rd.
Rifle Rd.
Race Course
Ashutosh Mukherjee Rd.
Zoological Gardens
Hazra Rd.
Ballygunge Railway Station
Diamond Harbour Rd.
Belvedere Rd.
Sarat Bose Rd.
Shyama Prasad Mukherjee Rd.
Rash Behari Avenue
Gariahat Rd.
ALIPORE
Judge's Court Rd.
Southern Ave.
Exploring
B.B.D. Bagh 10
Belur Math Shrine 9
College Street 1
Dakshineshwar Kali Temple 8
Eden Gardens 15
Fort William 16
General Post Office 12
Howrah Bridge 5
Indian Botanical Gardens 24
Indian Museum 20
Kalighat Kali Temple 21
Kumartuli 7
Maidan 13
Marble Palace 3
Nakhoda Mosque 2
National Library 23
Nirmal Hirday 22
Ochterlony Monument 14
Paresnath Temple 6
Rabindra Bharati University Museum 4
St. Paul's Cathedral 18
South Park Street Cemetery 19
Victoria Memorial 17
Writers' Building 11
Restaurants
Aheli 6
Bar-B-Q 8
Chinoiserie 10
Kewpies 11
Mainland China 15
Momo Plaza 12
Oh! Calcutta 13
PanAsian 16
Peter Cat 7
Sonargaon 10
Taàja 14
Tangerine 5
The Hub 10
Zaranj 3
Zen 4
Hotels
Astor 9
Fairlawn 2
Hotel Hindustan International 19
Hyatt Regency 18
ITC Hotel The Sonar 16
Kenilworth 17
Oberoi Grand 1
Park Hotel 4
Peerless Inn 6
Taj Bengal 10

CLOSE UP

Calcutta to Kolkata

In early 2001, Calcutta's name was officially changed to Kolkata. This transformation, like similar ones in India, was supposed to contribute to ridding the city of its colonial past. But the two names are used interchangeably. Streets, too, have been renamed. Although some maps and street signs have only the new names, you're more likely to see just the old or both. Taxis and rickshaws use the names interchangeably, but old names are still favored, as most of the new names are ridiculously long and obscure. Here are a few of the most important name changes:

Chowringhee Road/Jawaharlal Nehru (J.L. Nehru) Road

Ballygunge Circular/Pramathesh Barua Sarani

Bowbazar/B.B. Ganguly Street

Harington Street/Ho Chi Minh Sarani

Lansdowne Road/Sarat Bose Road

Lower Circular Road/A.J.C. Bose Road

Rippon Street/Muzaffar Ahmed Street

Theatre Road/Shakespeare Sarani

hours, and remember that the Belur Math Shrine is closed from noon to 3:30 and the Nakhoda Mosque is off-limits during Friday prayer.

WHAT TO SEE

9 **Belur Math Shrine.** This is the headquarters of the Ramakrishna Mission, a reform movement inspired by Ramakrishna Paramahansa, who died in 1886. Having forsaken his privileged Brahmin heritage, Ramakrishna preached the unity of religious faiths and an adherence to altruistic values for all people. His disciple, Swami Vivekananda, established the mission in 1898. The Belur Math Shrine resembles a church, a temple, or a mosque, depending on where you're standing. Somber *aarti* (chants and hymns) are sung in the immense prayer hall every evening; visitors are more than welcome. ✉ *Belur Rd., Howrah, 2 km (1 mi) south of 2nd Hooghly Bridge (Vivekananda Setu)* ⏲ *Daily 6:30–noon and 3:30–7:30.*

1 **College Street.** Part of the animated area around Kolkata University, the sidewalks of College Street are stuffed with bookstalls where you just might discover a treasure. The neighborhood establishments here, like the classic but run-down **Indian Coffee House** (✉ *15 Bankin Chatterjee St., North Kolkata*), are crowded every night with students and intellectuals. Opposite the coffeehouse, a huge colonial building houses the university's **Presidency College,** arguably the most prestigious seat of learning in India. ✉ *North Kolkata.*

8 ★ **Dakshineshwar Kali Temple.** Far north along the Hooghly, this 19th-century complex with 13 temples is a major pilgrimage site for devotees of Shiva, Kali, Radha, and Krishna. The variety of temples makes this site a good introduction for the uninitiated to the Hindu deities. It was here that the 19th-century mystic Ramakrishna had the vision that led him to renounce his Brahmin caste and propound altruism and religious unity. His most famous disciple, Swami Vivekananda, went on to be a

major force in the intellectual and spiritual growth of Kolkata, and founded the Ramakrishna Mission, headquartered in the Belur Math Shrine. Ramakrishna's room here is a museum. ✉*P. W. D. Rd., near Second Hooghly Bridge (Vivekananda Setu)* *Free* *Daily dawn–10* PM.

BENGALI DISHES

Kolkata has a tradition of dining out that no other Indian city can rival. Ironically, Bengali food itself was noticeably long absent from the city's restaurants, but this has changed in recent years. Bengali cuisine is highly varied in flavor and has both vegetarian and nonvegetarian strands, with seafood figuring heavily. Two popular Bengali dishes are *macher jhol* (fish curry) and *chingri malai* curry (prawns cooked in coconut milk and spices). Note that Thursday in Kolkata is meatless—no red meat is served in most establishments.

13

6 **Howrah Bridge.** The Howrah train station almost dumps you onto this structure, and the bridge in turn puts you about 2 km (1 mi) north of Bara Bazaar in the heart of old Calcutta. Indeed, it seems more like a bazaar itself than a simple transport link between Howrah and Kolkata. Bordered by thin walkways, the bridge's eight lanes of chaotic traffic bear 2 million people each day in rickshaws, cars, scooters, bicycles, pushcarts, and animal-drawn carts. The web of girders stretches 1,500 feet over the Hooghly. A walk across the bridge provides terrific people watching.

7 **Kumartuli.** In this area, countless potters create the millions of clay images that serve as idols during Kolkata's Hindu festival season. ✉*Chitpur Rd., between Bidhan Sarani and Jatindra Mohan, North Kolkata.*

3 **Marble Palace.** One of the strangest buildings in Kolkata was the inspiration of Raja Rajendra Mullick Bahadur, a member of Bengal's landed gentry. Mullick built the palace in 1855, making lavish use of Italian marble. It's behind a lawn cluttered with sculptures of lions, the Buddha, Christopher Columbus, Jesus, the Virgin Mary, and Hindu gods. Near a small granite bungalow (where Mullick's descendants still live), a large pool houses some exotic birds with large headdresses. The palace has an interior courtyard, complete with a throne room where a peacock often struts around the seat of honor. The upstairs rooms are downright baroque: enormous mirrors and paintings cover the walls (including works by Reynolds, Rubens, and Murillo), gigantic chandeliers hang from the ceilings, and hundreds of statues and Far Eastern urns populate the rooms. The floors bear multicolored marble inlay on a giant scale, with a calico effect. Even the lamps are detailed creations, especially those on the staircases, where metal women are entwined in trees with a light bulb on each branch. Movie producers use the palace for shooting films. Make sure to tip your guide here. ✉*46 Muktaram Basu St., off Chittaranjan Ave., North Kolkata, 700007* ☎*33/2269–3310* *Free; you must obtain a pass from West Bengal Tourist Office 24 hrs in advance* *Tues., Wed., and Fri.–Sun. 10–4.*

Fodor's Choice ★

2 ★ **Nakhoda Mosque.** This massive red sandstone mosque, which can hold 10,000 worshippers, was built in 1926 as a copy of Akbar's tomb in Agra. Each floor has a prayer hall. The top floor has views of the streets below, which are crowded with stalls selling everything from paperback Korans to kebabs. ✉ *M. G. Rd. and Rabindra Sarani, North Kolkata* 🎫 *Free* ⏲ *Daily sunrise–8* PM.

6 ★ **Paresnath Temple.** Built in 1867 and dedicated to Sitalnathji, the 10th of the 24 *tirthankaras* ("perfect souls," or sages that have achieved Nirvana), this Jain temple is a flamboyant one, filled with inlaid-mirror pillars, stained-glass windows, floral-pattern marble floors, a gilded dome, and chandeliers from 19th-century Paris and Brussels. The garden holds blocks of glass mosaics depicting European figures and statues covered with silver paint. Paresnath is an unusual place of honor for the typically ascetic Jains. ✉ *Badridas Temple St., near Raja Dinendra St., North Kolkata* ⏲ *Daily sunrise–noon and 3–7.*

4 ★ **Rabindra Bharati University Museum.** Rabindranath Tagore's cheerful, lemon-yellow home opens onto tree-lined galleries on the second floor. Inside, the university fosters cultural activities and maintains a display of paintings by artists of the Bengali school. The nerve center of Calcutta's intellectual activity around the turn of the 20th century, Tagore's abode now holds memorabilia, including beautiful sepia photographs of the poet (quite fetching as a young man), his family, and his contemporaries. ✉ *6–4 Dwarkanath Tagore La., North Kolkata* ☎ *33/2269–5241 or 33/2218–1744* 🎫 *Rs. 100* ⏲ *Tues.–Sun. 10:30–5.*

CENTRAL KOLKATA & THE MAIDAN

The British first built Fort William in the middle of a dense jungle. When disagreements led the local Bengali ruler, Siraj ud-Daula, to attack and destroy it, the British response was a quick and decisive battle led by Robert Clive. Following the Battle of Plassey (some 160 km [100 mi] north of town), which transformed the British from traders into a ruling presence in 1757, the forest was cut down in order to provide a clear line for cannon fire in case of attack. It's really from the year 1757 that modern Kolkata traces its history, and from the impenetrable Fort William (completed in 1773) that the city began its explosive growth.

Starting about 1 km north of the fort, central Kolkata became the commercial and political heart of the city. It was here that the British conducted business, and here that they built their stately homes. The immense area cleared for British cannons is now Kolkata's 3-square-km (2-square-mi) park, the Maidan, and central Kolkata now goes beyond the Maidan to B. B. D. Bagh square and most of the commercial and residential areas to the east of the giant park.

A GOOD WALK

Around **B. B. D. Bagh** 10 are some of the finest examples of Victorian architecture in Kolkata. Most of the buildings are still offices (government or otherwise) and are most interesting from the outside, even when admission is permitted. On the north side of the square is the **Writers' Building** ⓫; in the southeast corner is St. Andrew's Church, built in 1818. West and one block north is the **General Post Office** ⓬, and to its left is the redbrick Collectorate, Kolkata's oldest public building. Two blocks south is St. John's Church, which holds Job Charnock's mausoleum. (If the church is locked, you can call the vicar, ☎33/2248–3439.) The High Court Building is on the next block south. Head east two blocks (until you're due south of B.B.D. Bagh) to see the Raj Bhavan, home of the governor of West Bengal.

Cross Lenin Sarani and you'll be in the **Maidan** ⓭, a place to escape street traffic and exhaust and to enjoy green grass. Walk down Government Place East and you'll come to a traffic circle dominated by the **Ochterlony Monument** ⓮. Veer southwest and go down Eden Gardens Road to the **Eden Gardens** ⓯, which have a photogenic Burmese pagoda. Next to that is the cricket stadium, where you can see India's most popular game played. If you walk along Strand Road toward the Hooghly from here, it's easy to arrange a brief, refreshing boat ride—boatmen are bound to approach you with offers of a "romantic" turn on the waters. Be careful: the boats are often as rickety as boatmen are dodgy; the going rate is about Rs. 100 for half an hour, though the money you pay will depend on how hard a bargain you can drive.

Continue 1½ km (1 mi) directly south of Eden Gardens to **Fort William** ⓰, the East India Company's main strategic defense in Calcutta. Red Road cuts south through the Maidan to the **Victoria Memorial** ⓱, which serves (somewhat ironically) as a postcard image of Kolkata. Inside is a compelling museum of the city's history as well as some Raj memorabilia. Two-hundred yards to the east along Queen's Way is **St. Paul's Cathedral** ⓲.

Queen's Way hits J.L. Nehru Road, usually known by its old name, **Chowringhee.** This is Kolkata's main drag—a wide boulevard bustling with pedestrians by day and a place for the homeless to stretch out by night. On the other side of Chowringhee, Queen's Road becomes Shakespeare Sarani, and after another 100 feet you can see Kolkata's government tourist office on the right. Farther north on Chowringhee, Park Street comes in at an angle. Park Street shares with Chowringhee the prestige of having high rents for shops, hotels, and restaurants, and, in fact, if you're wandering around hungry in the evening, this is the best street to prowl for a good restaurant. About 1½ km (1 mi) down the street to the east is the **South Park Street Cemetery** ⓳, with the graves of many British who changed the course of India and never made it back to dear old Blighty. Back on Chowringhee, shortly after the intersection with Park Street, is the **Indian Museum** ⓴, well worth dropping into for its collection of Indian antiquities. By now you may be in need of a little luxury, which you can find at the Oberoi Grand hotel, a Victorian oasis just 200 yards farther up the thoroughfare.

TIMING Two of the most interesting attractions on this route are the Victoria Memorial and the Indian Museum, for which you should allow at least an hour apiece; the entire walk should take approximately four hours. If you are touring in the hot season, April to July, avoid walking in the early afternoon.

CLOSE UP

Calcutta's Anglo-Indians

Calcutta, once the capital of British Raj, is home to the country's largest population of Anglo-Indians, a fast-vanishing group of native English-speakers who are of mixed European and Indian ancestry. Anglos thrived under the British, who set aside important government jobs for them, especially ones having to do with the railways. Many others were successful teachers, secretaries, nurses and singers. But after Independence many Anglo-Indians left for North America, England, and Australia, fearing hostility from other Indians who identified them with the former rulers.

The exodus continues, but the dwindling community works hard to maintain its identity. Younger generations marry outside the community and are gaining familiarity with the Bengali language and culture. But at home, they eat chicken *jalfrezi* (with tomatoes and green chillies) and other Anglo-Indian dishes, attend the community's churches and speak perfect English with little trace of an Indian accent. At Christmas, Anglo-Indians from around the world come to dance, sing, and party on the the narrow street that anchors Bow Barracks, a century-old neighborhood of Anglo-Indians behind Bowbazar Police Station in Central Calcutta. Among the most famous Anglo-Indians are singers Engelbert Humperdinck and Cliff Richard, who spent his early childhood in Calcutta.

WHAT TO SEE

10 ★ **B. B. D. Bagh.** The hub of all Kolkata, this square is still often referred to by its former name, Dalhousie Square. Once the administrative home of the East India Company, it later gave way to late-Victorian buildings used by the Colonial Civil Service and now houses the Indian government bureaucracy. Foot traffic is thick here. ✉ *East of Hooghly River, 2½ km (1½ mi) south of Howrah Bridge, Central Kolkata.*

★ **Chowringhee.** North Kolkata may be the city's intellectual heart, but in an age of business-friendly communist governments, the slick commercial area east of the Maidan is the city's spinal cord. Now technically called Jawaharlal (or J. L.) Nehru Road, Chowringhee runs along the east side of the Maidan, with shops, hotels, and old Victorian buildings lining the other side of the wide pavement. In the evening, hawkers do their best with potential shoppers, and at night, the homeless bed down. ✉ *Central Kolkata.*

15 **Eden Gardens.** These flower-speckled gardens in the northwest corner of the Maidan are often crowded, but you can still find relief from the busy streets. Don't miss the pagoda. ✉ *Eden Gardens Rd., Central Kolkata* 🎫 *Free* ⏲ *24 hrs.*

16 **Fort William.** The irregular heptagon south of the Eden Gardens is surrounded by a moat almost 50 feet wide. Begun in 1757 after Robert Clive's victory over Siraj ud-Daula at Plassey, Fort William was designed to prevent any future attacks. The fort's walls, as well as its barracks, stables, and Church of St. Peter, have survived to this day chiefly because the fort has, in fact, never been attacked. The Indian

government still uses the fort, but it's closed to the public. ✉ *Strand Rd., Central Kolkata.*

12 **General Post Office** *(GPO)*. Built in 1864 and still in use as Kolkata's main post office, this building's massive white Corinthian columns rest on the site of the original Fort William, where the British were attacked in 1756 and many officers were imprisoned by Siraj ud-Daula in the infamous "Black Hole of Calcutta," a tiny space that caused most of the group to suffocate. ✉ *Netaji Subhash Rd., near B. B.D. Bagh, Central Kolkata* ☎ *33/2242–1572* ⏲ *Weekdays 10–5:30.*

20 **Indian Museum.** India's oldest museum has one of the largest and most comprehensive collections in Asia, including one of the best natural-history collections in the world. It's known locally as *Jadu Ghar,* the "House of Magic." The archaeology section has representative antiquities from prehistoric times to the Moghul period, including relics from Mohenjo Daro and Harappa, the oldest excavated Indus Valley cities. The southern wing includes the Bharhut and Gandhara rooms (Indian art from the 2nd century BC to the 5th century AD), the Gupta and medieval galleries, and the Moghul gallery.

The Indian Museum also houses the world's largest collection of Indian coins; ask at the information desk for permission to see it. Gems and jewelry are on display. The art section on the first floor has a good collection of textiles, carpets, wood carving, papier-mâché figures, and terra-cotta pottery. A gallery on the third floor contains exquisite Persian and Indian miniature paintings, and banners from Tibetan monasteries. The anthropology section on the first floor is devoted to cultural anthropology, though the museum plans to establish India's first comprehensive exhibit on physical anthropology; some interesting specimens are an Egyptian mummy donated in 1880 by an English seaman, a fossilized 200-million-year-old tree trunk, the lower jaw of a 26-meter (84-foot) whale, and meteorites dating back 50,000 years. ✉ *27 J. L. Nehru Rd., Central Kolkata* ☎ *33/2286–1699* 🎫 *Rs. 10.* ⏲ *Tues.–Sun. 10–4:30.*

NEED A BREAK?

For breakfast or tea with sandwiches, try Flury's Tea Room (✉ *18 Park St., Central Kolkata* ☎ *33/2229-7664* ⏲ *Daily 7:30 AM–8 PM*). Kolkata's first Swiss confectioner opened in the 1920s and is now an institution. You can get a chicken or cheese omelet, beans on toast, and coffee for Rs. 200.

13 ★ **The Maidan.** Known as Kolkata's "green lung," the city's expansive park is dotted with some of its most significant attractions and is highly prized by its citizens, who turn out in the morning for sports and pony rides, and in the evening for snacks and carriage rides. The area came into existence when forests were cleared to give Fort William a clear line of fire. ✉ *Just south of B. B. D. Bagh to the northern border of Alipore, and from the Hooghly River to J. L. Nehru Rd. and the shops of Park St., Central Kolkata.*

14 **Ochterlony Monument.** On the north end of the Maidan stands a 148-foot pillar commemorating Sir David Ochterlony's military victories over the Nepalese in the border war of 1814–16. Built in 1828, the impres-

sive monument has a curious design: the base is Egyptian, the column is Syrian, and the cupola is Turkish. Now officially called the Shahid Minar (Martyr's Tower), it has been the site of many political rallies and student demonstrations during Calcutta's turbulent post-Independence history. ✉ *J. L. Nehru Rd., Central Kolkata.*

18 **St. Paul's Cathedral.** Completed in 1847, the cathedral now has a steeple modeled after the one at Canterbury; previous steeples were destroyed by earthquakes in 1897 and 1934. Florentine frescoes, the stained-glass western window, and a gold communion plate presented by Queen Victoria are prize possessions. Birds congregate in the interior eaves. ✉ *Cathedral Rd., east of Victoria Memorial, Central Kolkata* ☎ *33/2223–0127* ⏲ *Mon.–Sat. 9–noon and 3–6, Sun. 7–12:30 and 3–7.*

19 **South Park Street Cemetery.** The graves and memorials here form a repository of British imperial history. People who lived within the Raj from 1767 on are buried here, and in the records of their lives you can see the trials and triumphs of the building of an empire. ✉ *Park St. at Rawdon St., Central Kolkata* ☎ *No phone* ⏲ *Daily sunrise–sunset.*

17 **Victoria Memorial.** This massive, white marble monument was conceived in 1901 by Lord Curzon and built over a 20-year period. Designed in a mixture of Italian Renaissance and Saracenic styles, surrounded by extensive, carefully manicured gardens, and preceded by a typically sober statue of Victoria herself, it remains the single greatest symbol of the British Raj. Inside the building is an excellent museum of the history of Calcutta (there's a lot to read, but it will really sharpen your sense of the British-Bengali relationship) and various Raj-related exhibits, including Queen Victoria's writing desk and piano, Indian miniature paintings, watercolors, and Persian books. Cameras and electronic equipment must be left at the entrance. In the evenings there's a sound and light show, with narration in English, about Kolkata's history. ✉ *Queen's Way, Central Kolkata, 700071* ☎ *33/2223–1890* 🎟 *Monument Rs. 150, sound-and-light show Rs. 20* ⏲ *Tues.–Sun. 10–4:30; sound-and-light show Tues.–Sun. 7:15 (Oct.–Feb.) and 7:45 (Mar.–June).*

Fodor's Choice ★

11 **Writers' Building.** The original "writers" were the clerks of the British East India Company. Now a government office building, this dramatically baroque edifice is closed to the public. ✉ *North side of B.B.D. Bagh, Central Kolkata.*

SOUTH KOLKATA

Calcutta's rich and powerful moved consistently south as the city grew more and more crowded and unpleasant. Here you'll see an interesting mix of large colonial homes, modern hotels and businesses, open space, and crowded temple areas.

A GOOD TOUR

You can reach **Kalighat Kali Temple** ㉑ by metro, getting off at Kalighat Station and walking north on Murkaharji Road for about 2 km (1 mi)—or you can take a taxi for the trip through a variety of neighborhoods. **Nirmal Hirday** ㉒, where Mother Teresa lived, worked, and is buried, is just around the corner. The **National Library** ㉓ is a short taxi ride from either the temple or Nirmal Hirday and puts you near the Taj Bengal hotel, a restful place for a coffee break. To reach the **Indian Botanical Gardens** ㉔, across the river in Howrah, take another taxi (about 15 minutes) across the Second Hooghly Bridge (Vivekananda Setu).

TIMING Give yourself a full morning to cover this ground. Allow an hour and a half to arrive at and see Kalighat Kali Temple, another hour if you want to visit Nirmal Hirday, one of Mother Teresa's missions. You many want to skip the National Library unless you want to bundle it with an upscale rest stop (or a stay) at the Taj Bengal, and go straight to the Indian Botanical Gardens.

WHAT TO SEE

㉔ ★ **Indian Botanical Gardens.** Across the Second Hooghly Bridge (Vivekananda Setu) in Howrah are these massive botanical gardens, first opened in 1786. Darjeeling and Assam teas were developed here. The gardens' banyan tree has one of the largest canopies in the world, covering a mind-boggling 1,300 square feet. The gardens are so huge that you can even find a place to relax on Sunday, when locals turn out in droves to enjoy their day off. ✉ *Between Andul Rd. and Kurz Ave., Shibpur, Howrah* ☎ *33/2668–0554* 🎫 *Rs. 50* ⏲ *Daily 1 hr after sunrise–1 hr before sunset.*

㉑ ★ **Kalighat Kali Temple.** Built in 1809, the Kali is one of the most significant pilgrimage sites in India, with shrines to Shiva, Krishna, and Kali, the patron goddess of Kolkata. Human sacrifices were reputed to be commonly practiced here on special days during the 19th century, but only goats are slaughtered now, then offered to Kali with Ganges water and *bhang* (marijuana). The building rewards a close look: you'll see thin, multicolor layers of painted trim and swaths of tilework. Only Hindus are allowed in the inner sanctum, but the lanes and brilliant flower markets surrounding the temple are lovely in themselves. ✉ *Kalighat Rd., South Kolkata* ⏲ *Daily sunrise–sunset.*

㉓ **National Library.** Once the house of the lieutenant governor of Calcutta, this hefty neo-Renaissance building has miles of books and pleasant reading rooms. The rare-book section holds some significant works, adding to the importance of this 2-million-volume facility. There are no displays, but you can take a short walk through the grounds. ✉ *Belvedere Rd., near Taj Bengal hotel, Alipore, South Kolkata* ☎ *33/2479–1381 or 33/2479–138* ⏲ *Weekdays 9–8, weekends 9:30–6.*

㉒ **Nirmal Hirday** *(Pure Heart)*. Mother Teresa's first home for the dying is now one of 300 affiliated organizations worldwide that care for people in the most dire need. Learn more about Mother Teresa's work at the headquarters of the **Missionaries of Charity** (✉ *54A A.J.C. Bose Rd.,*

South Kolkata ☎*33/2464–4223*). It can be inspiring to see the joy among the people in one of the missionaries' homes or refuges. Mother Teresa is buried in this building—her home for 44 years. ✉*Next to Kali Temple, South Kolkata* ⏲*Fri.–Wed. 3–6.*

WHERE TO EAT

BENGALI

$$ Fodor'sChoice ★ ✕**Oh! Calcutta.** This large, upscale restaurant, hidden on the top floor of a mall, has been popular with locals since it opened in 2002 and is one of the best places to try authentic Bengali seafood. Surrounding the square tables are white walls sparsely decorated with old photographs and modern paintings, but the space feels inviting and homey rather than cold. Try the prawns cooked in coconut gravy and served in a coconut shell, or the boneless beckti fish in tangy mustard sauce. Either of them are good and memorable choices. ✉*Forum Mall, 10/3 Elgin Rd., South Kolkata* ☎*33/2283–7161* ✍*Reservations essential* 💳*AE, DC, V.*

$–$$ ✕**Kewpies.** The delicious *thalis* (combination platters) here are available in both vegetarian and nonvegetarian versions, the latter with assorted meats or fish. Either way, thalis come in a typically Bengali style: on cut banana leaves. You can also order the thalis' vegetable or meat portions à la carte. ✉*2 Elgin La., South Kolkata* ☎*33/2475–9880* ✍*Reservations essential* 💳*MC, V.*

$ ✕**Aheli.** Kolkata's first upscale Bengali restaurant still draws a crowd. Traditional Bengali delicacies, such as *macher sorse paturi* (fish cooked with mustard paste) and *chingri malai* curry (with prawns and coconut milk) are served in an intimate terra-cotta dining room. ✉*Peerless Inn, 12 J.L. Nehru Rd., Central Kolkata* ☎*33/2228–0301 or 33/2228–0302* 💳*AE, DC, MC, V.*

ECLECTIC

$$ ★ ✕**The Hub.** The 24-hour coffee shop of the Taj Bengal hotel has been dubbed Kolkata's "international food theater." The grand, spacious interior, with marble floors and a glass spiral staircase, matches that of the hotel lobby. Although the emphasis is on Italian food, you get a wide choice of cuisines. Try the homemade pasta or the rack of lamb in brown sauce, or the sumptuous, multicuisine champagne lunch buffets (Rs. 1,500), available on most Sundays. ✉*Taj Bengal, 34B Belvedere Rd., Alipore, South Kolkata* ☎*33/2223–3939* ✍*Reservations not accepted* 💳*AE, DC, MC, V.*

$$ Fodor'sChoice ★ ✕**Tangerine.** This is arguably the best place with a multicuisine menu in Kolkata. Small and cozy, with minimalist furniture and plate-glass windows overlooking a lake, this restaurant is peopled by friendly, helpful staff, and it serves great food. Don't-miss choices include prawn salad, fish-and-chips, lobster thermidor, and chilli crab. ✉*2–1 Outram St., Central Kolkata* ☎*33/2281–5450* ✍*Reservations essential* 💳*AE, MC, V.*

$ ★ ✕**Taaja.** This busy, split-level eatery whose name means "fresh," is one of the best Continental restaurants in Kolkata. Giving new meaning to the word "eclectic," the menu includes Greek, French, Italian, Spanish, and Hungarian food, and it offers dishes from the Caribbean and Far East as well. Paella, Cajun crab cakes, moussaka, and cannelloni are all good choices. ✉*29–1A Ballygunge Circular Rd., South Kolkata* ☎*33/2476–7334* *Reservations essential* ▭*MC, V.*

INDIAN

$$$ ★ ✕**Sonargaon.** The name means "golden village," and this North Indian restaurant is a tasteful replica of a rural home, complete with a courtyard, a well, dark wood on taupe stone, copper curios, and metal light fixtures. Popular dishes include *kakori* (minced lamb) kebab, *patthar ka ghosht* (mutton marinated with red chillies and masala and cooked on a marble stove), and chingri malai. ✉*Taj Bengal, 34B Belvedere Rd., Alipore, South Kolkata* ☎*33/2223–3939* *Reservations essential* ▭*AE, DC, MC, V.*

$$$ ✕**Zaranj.** Plush and well decorated with a fountain and ornate furniture, Zaranj is a relaxing dinner spot, both for its decor and its staff that never rushes diners. Choose from a large à la carte menu that specializes in North Indian and tandoori classics. The tasty *murgh nawabi* is a boneless chicken with yogurt and nuts, roasted over a charcoal grill. ✉*26 J. L. Nehru Rd., Central Kolkata* ☎*33/2249–0370* *Reservations essential* ▭*AE, DC, V.*

$ ★ ✕**Peter Cat.** Along with the nearby Mocambo restaurant, this is one of the city's oldest establishments, with an atmosphere that harkens back to its early days in the 1960s. The cello kebab here—a dish with *biriani*-style rice (flavored with saffron or turmeric), egg, butter, two mutton kebabs, and one chicken kebab—is one of the most popular dishes in Kolkata. The dining room is intimate, with white stucco walls, Tiffany-style lamps, and soft lighting; the menu is a mixture of good Continental and Indian dishes, especially tandoori fare. ✉*18 Park St., Central Kolkata* ☎*33/2229–8841* ▭*DC, MC, V.*

PAN-ASIAN

$$$$ Fodor'sChoice ★ ✕**Chinoiserie.** Consistently rated one of the best Chinese restaurants in India (no small honor these days), this place serves delicacies such as Peking duck, crispy spinach, and a highly unusual selection of corn dishes. Try the golden corn and broccoli in black pepper sauce or the potato corn *chilli mal-ha.* Unsurpassed food, a calm green-and-beige color scheme accented by old-world mirrors and paintings, and excellent Taj service make dining here a top experience. Reservations are advised on weekdays and crucial on weekends. ✉*Taj Bengal, 34B Belvedere Rd., Alipore, South Kolkata* ☎*33/2223–3939* *Reservations essential* ▭*AE, DC, MC, V.*

$$$$ ★ ✕**PanAsian.** This sleek, modern restaurant with massive ceilings is bathed in blacks and browns. As the name suggests, the menu here covers a broad variety of dishes from all over Asia. The menu's three

sections are divided into Japan, Mongolia, and Korea; Thailand; and China. Don't miss the Mongolian grill, the Thai curries, and the teppanyaki in the Japanese section. Try the green curry, which is authentically prepared by the restaurant's Thai chef. Reservations are advised on weekdays and essential on weekends at this favorite haunt of the expat community. ✉*ITC Hotel The Sonar, 1 Haldane Ave., Bypass and beyond* ☎*33/2345–4545* ▭*AE, DC, MC, V.*

$$$–$$$$ ✕**Zen.** Art deco meets postmodern in the sleek lines of this Southeast Asian restaurant, which serves cuisines from across the region. The Thai green curry and the Indonesian specialties, such as *soto ayam* (glass noodles) and *nasi gorang* (mixed fried rice) are rare finds in India. The grilled lobster with sweet-and-sour dip is an indulgence worth the price. ✉*Park Hotel, 17 Park St., Central Kolkata* ☎*33/2249–7336* ✍*Reservations essential* ▭*AE, DC, MC, V.*

$$ ✕**Mainland China.** Expect to find Kolkata's glamorous set populating this restaurant, part of a national chain. Though the dining room is large, grand mirrors give the illusion of even more space, and the furniture is minimalist but comfortable. The Szechuan menu is extensive. Opt for the seafood platter or the chicken in a hot garlic sauce. Attentive service helps make for a posh evening. ✉*3A Gurusaday Rd., South Kolkata* ☎*33/2283–7964* ▭*AE, DC, MC, V.*

¢–$ ✕**Bar-B-Q.** This local favorite serves Cantonese and Szechuan dishes in a setting that innovatively mixes Chinese and German-chalet style under a name that evokes neither of the two. Try the crisp fried chicken served with a mild sauce, the boneless chilli chicken, or the minced lamb cooked with cubes of tofu and hot garlic sauce. ✉*43 Park St., Central Kolkata* ☎*33/2229–2870* ✍*Reservations essential* ▭*AE, DC, MC, V.*

¢ ✕**Momo Plaza.** Kolkatans love Tibetan food, and the plain, no-nonsense Momo Plaza is an ideal place for a Tibetan snack if you're not stuck on having stylish surroundings. The chicken-stuffed *momos* (dumplings) come steamed or fried, and are served with a very hot red-chilli paste. They're accompanied by a light, watery spring-onion soup called *thukpa.* ✉*2A Suburban Hospital Rd., South Kolkata* ☎*33/2247–8250* ▭*No credit cards.*

WHERE TO STAY

$$$$ ★ **Hyatt Regency.** This sleek, tastefully designed business hotel is luxurious without being ostentatious. The rooms have wooden floors and bathrooms with Italian-marble floors, glass sinks, and sunken rain showers. La Cucina, the hotel's Italian restaurant, is spectacular, even by international standards. Suites here are modern, comfortable, and worth a splurge. The Presidential Suite, depending on the night, can cost as little as $500. Pros: close to the airport and the Salt Lake City tech hub, great restaurants, good spa with reasonably priced massages. Cons: expensive, 20-minute taxi ride to the center of town. ✉*JA-1 Sector 3, Salt Lake City, Bypass and beyond, 700098* ☎*33/2335–1234* 🌐*Kolkata.regency.hyatt.com* *222 rooms, 13 suites* *In-room: safe, refrigerator, ethernet. In-hotel: 6 restaurants, room service, bars, pool, gym, spa, laundry service, executive floor, no-smoking rooms.* ▭*AE, DC, MC, V.*

$$$$ ★ **ITC Hotel The Sonar.** Built around a 4-acre pond full of lotuses, and set in landscaped gardens, this hotel has a look inspired by the architecture in vogue when the Pala dynasty ruled Bengal. It's also one of the city's very best hotels. Although it's business-oriented, it works hard to create a resort atmosphere. Rooms are comfortable and modern (you can even watch TV from the bath) and the service is very attentive. Pros: guests-only spa has soothing water views, exclusive floor for female travelers. Cons: restaurants are good but pricey. *✉1 Haldane Ave., Bypass and beyond, 700046 ☎33/2345–4545 ⊕www.sheraton.com 231 rooms, 8 suites In-room: safe, refrigerator, Wi-Fi. In-hotel: 5 restaurants, room service, bar, tennis courts, pool, gym, spa, laundry service, no-smoking rooms. AE, DC, MC, V.*

$$$$ ★ **Park Hotel.** Inspired decoration has turned this place into one of the best hotels in Kolkata. Everything in the long, white building—right in the thick of things on Park Street—has been designed with care. The lobby sparkles with mirrors and cut-glass chandeliers amid rich wood and marble. Even the restaurants and café are creative, from their daring art-deco–meets-Zen style to the way they do simple tasks, such as serving cappuccino. Rooms are comfortable, if small. The bars and nightclub are very popular with both Indians and expats. Pros: great location, some of the hippest bars in town. Cons: front-desk staff is somewhat overwhelmed or downright unresponsive. *✉17 Park St., Central Kolkata, 700016 ☎33/2249–9000 ⊕www.theparkhotels.com 132 rooms, 17 suites In-room: safe, refrigerator, DVD (some), Wi-Fi. In-hotel: 3 restaurants, room service, bars, pool. AE, DC, MC, V.*

$$$$ Fodor's Choice ★ **Taj Bengal.** A fusion of traditional and modern India, this elegant hotel is on the fringe of the city center, overlooking the Maidan and the Victoria Memorial. Modern Indian art, artifacts (including terra-cotta reliefs), and antiques are showcased throughout the building. Rooms, which you access via quiet triangular atriums, are essentially Western, with Eastern accents and Indian prints. Service is truly outstanding. Ask for a pool-facing room, which provides a wonderful view of the memorial. Pros: gorgeous lobby with a well stocked tea lounge, very good location. Cons: some of the most expensive rooms in India, like many hotels in this class, the lobby is more impressive than the rooms. *✉34B Belvedere Rd., Alipore, South Kolkata, 700027 ☎33/6612–3939 ⊕www.tajhotels.com 216 rooms, 13 suites In-room: safe, refrigerator, Wi-Fi. In-hotel: 4 restaurants, bar, pool, gym. AE, DC, MC, V.*

$$$–$$$$ **Hotel Hindustan International.** You won't feel cramped inside this family-run hotel. Even the standard rooms are 220 square feet; they're clean and modern, though not particularly stylish. The best rooms overlook the pool, but many others have good views of Kolkata. The hotel also houses a popular nightclub, and at this writing, was preparing to open a new 300-seat coffee shop with a wine cellar. Pros: rates are usually less expensive than most of its five-star competitors. Cons: not as luxurious as most hotels in its class. *✉235–1 A. J. C. Bose Rd., South Kolkata, 700020 ☎33/4001–8000 ⊕www.hhihotels.com 176 rooms, 8 suites In-room: safe, refrigerator, Wi-Fi. In-hotel: 3 restaurants, room service, bars, pool, gym, spa. AE, DC, MC, V BP.*

$$$–$$$$ ★ **Oberoi Grand.** The height of elegance, this impeccably maintained Victorian landmark in the center of town has an off-white facade and a rich marble and dark-wood interior. Service is top-notch, and the restaurants are excellent. Guest rooms lack any sense of antiquity, but they're spacious, with wall-to-wall carpeting and modern bathrooms. The best rooms overlook the interior courtyard and pool. Pros: no-tipping policy, wonderful bar decorated with artifacts from the British Raj. Cons: faces a somewhat noisy street. *15 J.L. Nehru Rd., Central Kolkata, 700013 33/2249–2323 www.oberoihotels.com 204 rooms, 9 suites In-room: safe, refrigerator, DVD, Wi-Fi. In hotel: 3 restaurants, room service, laundry service, bar, pool, gym. AE, DC, MC, V.*

$$$ **Astor.** In this price category, this is one of the least expensive and most comfortable places around. The rooms are clean if somewhat small; and there are three restaurants, including a casual beer garden, ideal for whiling away a balmy evening and getting a bite to eat. Pros: good value. Cons: stale smell in the lobby. *15 Shakespeare Sarani, Central Kolkata, 700071 33/2282–7430 33/2287–7430 28 rooms, 7 suites In-room: refrigerator, Wi-Fi. In-hotel: 3 restaurants, bar, room service, no elevator. AE, MC, V CP.*

$$$ **Kenilworth.** Popular with repeat visitors to Kolkata, this hotel has two attractive wings and pretty gardens. Common rooms are filled with marble and cheerfully furnished; guest rooms are comfortable and spacious, with standard, anonymous furnishings. This hotel, which has a great downtown location and garden, gets a lot of business as a wedding venue. Pros: suites are a good value; digital safes in rooms. Cons: rooms look a bit dated, although a room renovation is planned by early 2008. *1–2 Little Russell St., Central Kolkata, 700071 33/2282–3939 www.kenilworthhotels.com 98 rooms, 7 suites In-room: safe, refrigerator, ethernet. In-hotel: 3 restaurants, room service, bar, laundry service, public Internet, no-smoking rooms. AE, DC, MC, V CP.*

$$$ **Peerless Inn.** On a crowded street near the Oberoi Grand and New Market, this hotel has somewhat cramped rooms and less-than-elegant furnishings, but its location and price make it popular. The presence of the Bengali restaurant Aheli is a bonus. Pros: lively tea lounge in the lobby is a good place to meet friends and make new ones. Cons: a bit noisy. *15 J.L. Nehru Rd., Central Kolkata, 700013 33/2228–0301 33/2228–6650 96 rooms, 24 suites In-room: refrigerator, ethernet, Wi-Fi. In-hotel: 3 restaurants, bar, gym, laundry facilities. AE, DC, MC, V BP.*

¢ ★ **Fairlawn.** If you want a taste of life in the Raj, stay in this Kolkata landmark that dates from 1801. A small hotel, the Fairlawn has memorabilia-cluttered walls, a winding staircase, and a great overall vibe. Waiters wear gloves, a gong sounds during mealtimes, and rooms have chintz bedspreads and old-fashioned bathtubs. Pros: wonderful old-world atmosphere. Cons: neighborhood is a little seedy. *13A Sudder St., Central Kolkata, 700013 33/2252–1510 www.fairlawnhotel.com 20 rooms In-hotel: restaurant, no elevator. MC, V FAP.*

NIGHTLIFE & THE ARTS

NIGHTLIFE

Nightlife became a Kolkata phenomenon in the 1990s—with the advent of discos, affluent young people began to hit the dance floors. Eating out, however, remains the nocturnal activity of choice, with 24-hour coffee shops at the top hotels doing a brisk business.

13

BARS & LOUNGES

The most attractive places to have a nightcap are the Oberoi Grand and the Taj Bengal. The pub at the Park Hotel sometimes offers decent beer on tap, making it a pleasant afternoon watering hole. The bar at the Fairlawn Hotel draws an interesting group and is a nice place to sit out and have a beer in a winter afternoon or summer evening. Bars stay open until 11 PM or midnight. Besides hotels, there aren't a lot of places to go to get a drink; most people either imbibe at a hotel bar or get a drink when they're out for dinner.

DISCOS

Kolkata's clubs are technically open only to members and hotel guests, but you can get in for either a cover charge or a smile, depending on the doorman. All clubs retain good DJs for a mixture of Indian pop and Western dance music.

Underground (✉ *Hotel Hindustan International, 235/1 A.J.C. Bose Rd., Central Kolkata* ☎ *33/2247–2394*) is a good choice, though the crowd gets rowdy as the evening wears on. **Big Ben** (✉ *Kenilworth Hotel, 1–2 Little Russell St., Central Kolkata* ☎ *33/2282–8394*) is an upscale pub where mid-career local professionals congregate. The barman may be the best in town. Kolkata's beautiful people are on display at the poolside bar, **Aqua** (✉ *Park Hotel, 17 Park St., Central Kolkata* ☎ *33/2249–9000*).

At **Fusion** (✉ *Golden Park Hotel, 13 Ho Chi Minh Sarani, Central Kolkata* ☎ *33/2288–3939*) you can dance into the wee hours. **Someplace Else** (✉ *Park Hotel, 17 Park St., Central Kolkata* ☎ *33/249–7336*) may well be the best pub in town, though drinks are expensive. You'll find good deals during happy hour, which takes place in the afternoon and early evening. The pub has a small dance floor but great music with varying themes for almost each night of the week. The dance floor at **Tantra** (✉ *Park Hotel, 17 Park St., Central Kolkata* ☎ *33/2249–7336*) is hot and the style is fantastic—cushions with embroidery and beadwork, jute items, *dhurries* (rugs), and silk hangings. If you're older than 30 you may feel a bit out of place.

THE ARTS

Kolkata has famously been India's deepest well of creative energy. Artists here live in the inspiring shadow of such pillars as poet Rabindranath Tagore and world-renowned film director Satyajit Ray. Happily, any anxiety about past accomplishments has not intimidated contemporary artists. To find out what's happening, check *Kolkata This Fortnight,* available from the West Bengal Tourist Office, and *CalCalling,* available in hotels. You can also check the listings pages of any English-language daily newspaper and the Web site ⊕ www.explocity.com.

ART GALLERIES

The **Academy of Fine Arts** (✉ *2 Cathedral Rd., Central Kolkata* ☎ *33/2223–4302*) has a permanent collection of paintings and manuscripts by Rabindranath Tagore. The **Birla Academy of Art and Culture** (✉ *108–109 Southern Ave., South Kolkata* ☎ *33/2466–2843*) has interesting displays of art old and new. Modern Indian art is frequently shown at **Galerie 88** (✉ *28B Shakespeare Sarani, Central Kolkata* ☎ *33/2290–2274* ⊕ *www.galerie88.in*).

FILM

Many movie theaters around New Market feature English-language films. Ask your hotel or the tourist office for information on current events; if they don't know what's on, they'll help you find out. English-language papers, including the *Hindustan Times,* the *Times* of India, the *Telegraph,* and the *Statesman* carry movie listings.

PERFORMING ARTS

Many auditoriums host regular performances of music, dance, and theater—the most Bengali of the performing arts. English-language plays are regularly staged by the **British Council** (☎ *33/2282–5370* ⊕ *www.britishcouncil.org*). Be sure to see what's happening at the **Academy of Fine Arts** (✉ *2 Cathedral Rd., Central Kolkata* ☎ *33/2223–4302* ⊕ *http://academyoffinearts.tripod.com*), and don't be intimidated if the offerings are in Bengali—you can still see some fascinating dramatizations of familiar stories by the likes of Shakespeare and Goethe. Bengali productions are often staged at **Kalamandir** (✉ *48 Shakespeare Sarani, Central Kolkata* ☎ *33/2247–9086*). Bengali dance and theater are often performed at **Rabindra Sadan** (✉ *Cathedral Rd., Central Kolkata* ☎ *33/2248–9917*).

SPORTS & THE OUTDOORS

Kolkata still puts class first when it comes to sports, with the result that you need to be a member's guest to enter the golf and racing clubs. Whether you want to watch or play, get cricket information from the **Calcutta Cricket and Football Club** (✉ *19–1 Gurusaday Rd., South Kolkata* ☎ *33/2461–5060*). The **Calcutta Polo Club** (✉ *31 J.L. Nehru Rd., Central Kolkata* ☎ *33/2282–2311*) has the polo schedules. The **Royal Calcutta Golf Club** (✉ *18 Golf Club Rd., South Kolkata* ☎ *33/2473–1288 or 33/473–1352*) caters to the elite. For horse-racing enthusiasts, the **Royal Calcutta Turf Club** (*RCTC* ✉ *11 Russell St., Central Kolkata* ☎ *33/2229–1104*) has an old-world air of sophistication.

SHOPPING

AUCTIONS

Kolkata's Sunday auctions take place along Russell Street. A trip to the oldest auction house, the **Russell Exchange** (✉*12C Russell St., Central Kolkata* ☎*33/2229–8974*) or any of its neighbors is invariably entertaining. Goods auctioned range from antiques and period furniture to crockery and cutlery.

BAZAARS & SHOPPING MALLS

Shopping in Kolkata bazaars is an adventure, and a test of your ability to shake off touts. In general, most shops are open six days a week, and closed Sunday. Hours tend to be 10:30 to 8.

East of Chitpur Road is **Bowbazar,** Kolkata's jewelry district, where you'll find a terrific collection of good-quality gold and silver plus beautifully designed and crafted stone settings. Prices are reasonable, and each shop has an astrologer to help you find the most auspicious stone for your stars. ✉*Near College St., parallel to Chittaranjan Ave. and bounded by Mahatma Gandhi Rd. and Vivekananda Rd., Calcutta Medical College, and Presidency College, North Kolkata.*

Part of the century-old **New Market,** officially Sir Stuart Hogg Market, houses about 2,500 stores under one roof, selling cotton saris, Bankura clay horses, Malda brassware, leather from Shantiniketan, silk from Murshidabad, *khadi* (handmade cotton) cloth, poultry, cheeses, nuts, and other foods. ✉*19 Lindsay St., off J. L. Nehru Rd., behind Oberoi Grand, Central Kolkata* ⏲*Weekdays 10:30–7, Sat. 10:30–2.*

Head up **Rabindra Sarani** from Lal Bazaar Road (near the West Bengal Tourist Office) and you'll soon enter an Islamic world. Women walk by in *burqas* (long, black, tent-shaped robes), their eyes barely visible behind veils. Men sit on elevated platforms selling Bengali *kurtas* (shirts) and pants, and colorful *lungis* and white *dhotis* (both are wraps) for men. Other vendors sell vials of perfume created from flowers. Rabindra Sarani is interesting all the way to Chitpur Road. ✉*North Kolkata* ⏲*Mon.–Sat. 10:30–8.*

Forum Mall (✉*3 Elgin Rd., South Kolkata* ☎*33/2283–6022*) has shops selling clothes, music, leather, toys, and lots more.

BOOKSTORES

Starmark at Emami Shoppers' City (✉*3 Lord Sinha Rd., Central Kolkata* ☎*33/282–2617 to 9*) is spacious and modern. It sells books and music under one roof. **Oxford Bookstore-Gallery** (✉*17 Park St., Central Kolkata* ☎*33/2229–7662*) has lots of books, from cooking, travel, and architecture to the very best fiction. Browse the Net here or have an iced lemon tea at the tea bar. **Seagull** (✉*31A SP Mukherjee Rd., South Kolkata* ☎*33/2476–5865*) has many titles and an eclectic selection. Exhibitions and seminars add to the mix.

CLOTHING & TEXTILES

Dakshinapan (✉*Near Dhakuria Bridge, South Kolkata*) houses government emporiums from all the states of India, making it an excellent place to eyeball a wide range of styles. Try the **Handloom House** (✉*2 Lindsay St., Central Kolkata* ☎*33/2249–9037*) for crafted textiles, mostly cottons. **Manjusha** (✉*7–1D Lindsay St., Central Kolkata* ☎*No phone*) sells all manner of textiles. **Monapali and Silk Route** (✉*15 Loudon St., Central Kolkata* ☎*33/2280–7106 or 2287–6103*) are co-managed designer boutiques with lovely collections of women's saris and *salwar kameez* (a two-piece outfit of long, loose-fitting tunic over loose pants tapered at the ankle) in cotton, satin, and silk. Designs are inspired by the Far East and enhanced with Indian motifs and artwork: batik, embroidery, and *zardozi* (gold threading). **Pantaloons** (✉*49–1 Gariahat Rd., South Kolkata* ☎*33/2461–8310*) sells shoes and clothes, many of them targeted at teens and twentysomethings. The innovative **Weavers Studio** (✉*5–1 Anil Moitra Rd., 1st fl., Ballygunj Pl., South Kolkata* ☎*33/2440–8937*) sells high-quality natural-dye and embroidered textiles. **Westside** (✉*22 Camac St., Central Kolkata* ☎*33/2281–7312*) offers casual wear.

CRAFTS

For curios in a hurry and at fixed prices, head to **Central Cottage Industries** (✉*7 J. L. Nehru Rd., Central Kolkata* ☎*33/2228–4139*).

On and around **Chitpur Road** (✉*Between Rabindra Sarani and Kosipore Rd., North Kolkata*) you'll see a mixture of potters and shops that make musical instruments.

Quaint little **Konark Collectables** (✉*Humayun Court, 20 Lindsay St., Central Kolkata* ☎*33/2249–7273*) has lots of handicrafts.

SIDE TRIPS

Escape Kolkata's traffic and enrich your Bengali experience with a trip to either of two peaceful havens to the west. Vishnupur is characterized by its centuries-old terra-cotta temples, built from the local red clay and all but alive with the epic scenes carved into their panels. Shantiniketan is home to the university founded by Rabindranath Tagore, a center for art, music, and Bengali heritage. Nearby Sriniketan is a center of batik, embroidery, and terra-cotta craftsmanship.

VISHNUPUR

152 km (94 mi) west of Kolkata (8 to 10 hours by road, overnight by train).

Set in a land of rich red soil, Vishnupur was the capital of the Hindu Malla kings from the 16th to 19th centuries, and they saw fit to convert its surroundings into some mind-blowing terra-cotta temples. Between its intricate, lifelike temple panels and old-world charm, Vishnupur is exquisite, an integral part of Bengal. The clay pottery created here—particularly the Bankura horse, named for the district—attracts thousands for its sheer beauty and color. It's a long trip from Kolkata, but Vishnupur is worth a detour for its exceptional carvings and figurines, immortalizing old Bengal at its artistic best.

Built out of the local red laterite soil, the temple town is scattered with monuments to the Malla rulers. Sights are spread out, so the easiest way to explore is to hire a cycle-rickshaw and ride through the maze of narrow streets. Be sure to see the Madan Gopal, Madan Mohan, Radhagobinda, Rasmancha, and Shyamrai temples, all built around the 16th century; each has a story to tell through its intricately carved figurines. Dalmadol is a cannon of pure iron. Pathar Darwaza ("Doorway of Stone") marked the entrance to the Malla fort. Vishnupur is a great place to buy souvenirs, especially terra-cotta toys, conch-shell handicrafts, jewelry, and silk. In August or September, local snake charmers demonstrate their age-old prowess at a snake festival called the *jhapan,* at which, among other activities, men throw cobras at each other to test their respective mettle.

WHERE TO STAY

¢ **Vishnupur Tourist Lodge.** The only decent place to stay here, this lodge is a modest and suburban place. Don't expect anything beyond the very basic. You can call the lodge, but it's easier to reserve a room through the West Bengal Tourist Office (☎33/2248–8271, 33/2248–5917, or 33/2248–5168) in Kolkata. *P.O. Vishnupur, Bankura ☎03244/252013 27 rooms In-room: no a/c (some). In-hotel: restaurant, no elevator.*

SHANTINIKETAN

210 km (130 mi) northwest of Kolkata (4 hours by train).

Nobel Laureate Rabindranath Tagore's dream became reality here: a university dedicated to the liberal arts. Today the art and music schools at **Vishva-bharati University,** part of the Shantiniketan university complex, are some of the best in the country. Designed in 1901 as a group of cottages in a green, idyllic setting, Shantiniketan embodies the Bengali artistic heritage. In accordance with Tagore's vision, some classes are still held outside, under the shade of huge trees, and stunning abstract sculptures reach toward the sky. A weekend retreat for many, Shantiniketan is almost a pilgrimage to Bengalis.

Within the university is the Rabindra Bhavan, a museum full of photographs, Tagore's personal belongings, and the poet's much-coveted Nobel Prize. The art school, Kala Bhavan, is decorated with frescoes and murals outside, and you can watch students at work inside. Sangeet Bhavan is the music school. Uttarayan, where Tagore lived, is a charming complex of five houses, ranging from mud hut to mansion, in a variety of architectural styles.

A few minutes' drive outside Shantiniketan, **Sriniketan** is a rural-development center helping locals fend for themselves by creating stunning handicrafts—colorful batiks; intricate embroidery on saris, scarves, and bags; and terra-cotta items, including jewelry. Here you'll find some of the most beautiful and exclusive craft items in Bengal.

A great time to visit Shantiniketan is during the town's biggest festival, **Poush Mela,** which is usually held December 22 to 25. The festival includes huge fairs where handicrafts and bric-a-brac are sold and performances of *bauls* (wandering minstrels) who sing their unique variety of folk songs.

WHERE TO STAY

¢ **Chhuti.** This sprawling hotel, built with an eye for detail, is one of the best in the vicinity, with a resortlike vibe and good food. Guest rooms and the air-conditioned cottages are spacious, clean, and refreshing, and the caring, experienced staff looks after all your needs. Pros: spacious rooms, good multicuisine food. Cons: few amenities. *241 Charupally, Jamboni, Bolpur 34/6325–2692 22 rooms In-room: no a/c (some). In-hotel: restaurant, no elevator. No credit cards.*

¢ **Mark Meadows.** More a resort than a mere rest stop, this is an ideal place to unwind. With its landscaped gardens, swimming pool, and fishing pond, it's also a great value. The rooms are cottage-style, clean, and tidy. Pros: beautiful location, good value, hotel organizes tribal and folk art performances. Cons: doesn't have no-smoking rooms, no in-room Internet access. *Santiniketan 33/2289–7154 or 094/3400–7777 33/2289–7154 32 rooms, 2 suites In-hotel: restaurant, pool, no elevator MC, V.*

KOLKATA ESSENTIALS

To research prices, get advice from other travelers, and book travel arrangements, visit www.fodors.com.

AIR TRAVEL

All international and domestic airlines use Dum Dum Airport, 15 km (9 mi) north of the city.

Airlines & Contacts **Indian Airlines** (*33/2211–0041 or 33/2483–7501*). **Jet Airways** (*011/3989–3333*).

Airport **Dum Dum Airport** (*33/2511–8787 or 33/2511–9720*).

CARS & DRIVERS

Contacts **Europcar Shaw Distributors** (*8–1 Sarat Bose Rd., South Kolkata 33/2475–8916*). **Hertz** (*New Kenilworth Hotel, ½ Little Russel St., Central Kolkata 33/3240–4000 or 33/3240–5000*). **Wenz** (*Oberoi Grand, Central Kolkata 33/2249–2323 Ext. 6247*).

CONSULATES

Contacts **U.S. Consulate** (*5–1 Ho Chi Minh Sarani, Central Kolkata 700071 33/2282–3611*).

MONEY

ATMS Locations **HSBC** (*31 B.B.D. Bagh, Central Kolkata 15 Gariahat Rd., South Kolkata 25A Shakespeare Sarani, Central Kolkata 33/2440–3930*). **Standard Chartered Grindlays Bank** (*19 N.S. Rd., Central Kolkata 41 Jawaharlal Nehru Rd., Central Kolkata 33/2288–9430*).

CURRENCY EXCHANGE Most of the legitimate currency exchange centers keep the same hours and offer the same services and rates. From them you can get far better rates than the hotels. Steer clear of the many cubbyholes with slapdash signs outside touting rates that seem too good to be true (they are); these are particularly prevalent in the New Market area.

BAD DRIVING

In response to the painful traffic situation, authorities have made many roads in Kolkata one-way, then the other way, then two ways at various times throughout the day and week.

13

Exchange Services American Express (✉ *21 Old Court House St., Central Kolkata* ☎ *33/2248–6281*). **ANZ Grindlays Bank** (✉ *19 Netaji Subhash Rd., Central Kolkata* ☎ *33/2230–8346*). **Bank of America** (✉ *8 India Exchange Pl., Central Kolkata* ☎ *33/2288–3409*). **Citibank** (✉ *Tata Center, 43 J.L. Nehru Rd., Central Kolkata* ☎ *33/2288–9897*). **State Bank of India** (✉ *33 J.L. Nehru Rd., Central Kolkata* ☎ *33/2240–2430*). **Thomas Cook** (✉ *Shakespeare Sarani, 19B, 1st floor Shakespeare Sarani at Theatre Rd. and Camac St., Central Kolkata* ☎ *33/2282–7567*).

TAXIS & AUTO-RICKSHAWS

Most Kolkatans rely on buses, trams, and the metro to get around, but you will probably rely on taxis, rickshaws, and your feet (the bus system is indecipherable, the slow, rickety trams are good only for an early-morning ride, and the metro is somewhat limited).

The base fare for Kolkata taxis is Rs. 20, and the meter should read about Rs. 30 after 5 km. The legal inflation factor, however, is 100%, and it changes periodically; so ask your hotel for the current inflation factor. If a driver refuses to turn the meter on, find another taxi. Traffic, unfortunately, plagues Kolkata, and it might bring your cab to a full stop amid humid air and diesel exhaust, so at rush hour you may just want to find a sweet shop and wait until it's over.

Auto-rickshaws are cheaper than taxis, but they're not as easy to find in the city center. At rush hour they can be more efficient (albeit dirtier) alternatives; taxis are liable to get stuck in traffic.

TOURS

These agencies can arrange a car and driver for local sightseeing or help make long-distance travel arrangements.

Contacts American Express (✉ *21 Old Court House St., Central Kolkata* ☎ *33/2248–6281*). **Ashok Travel and Tours** (✉ *Everest building 46 C J.L. Nehru Rd., Central Kolkata* ☎ *33/2288–0901 or 2288–5254*). **Mercury Travels** (✉ *46C J.L. Nehru Rd., Central Kolkata* ☎ *33/2249–2323* ✉ *Oberoi Grand, Central Kolkata* ☎ *33/249–2323*). **Thomas Cook** (✉ *Chitrakoot Bldg., 230A A.J.C. Bose Rd., South Kolkata* ☎ *33/2282–7567*).

WALKING TOURS The most interesting tours in Kolkata are the walks through various neighborhoods led by the Foundation for Conservation and Research of Urban Traditional Architecture (CRUTA).

Contact Foundation for Conservation and Research of Urban Traditional Architecture (✉ *67B Beadon St., North Kolkata 700006* ☎ *33/2554–6127*).

TELEPHONE NUMBERS

Phone numbers change with alarming frequency in Kolkata. Whenever you make a call and get a recorded message saying, "This telephone number does not exist," dial 1951 or 1952 or 197 to find out the new number. There are computerized as well as manual services.

TRAIN TRAVEL

The main reservation office at Howrah Junction has a foreign-tourist section upstairs, open daily 9–1 and 1:30–4; buy tickets here with either foreign currency or a valid encashment certificate for rupees. There are also ticket offices on the first floor of Old Howrah Station, the second floor of New Howrah Station, and in Kalighat. Sealdah Station is used exclusively by trains to and from northern destinations such as Darjeeling. Tickets are sold on the platform level.

Train Information **Howrah Junction** (✉ *1 block south of the west end of Howrah Bridge* ☎ *33/2660–3542 or 33/2660–7412* ✉ *6 Failie Pl., North Kolkata* ☎ *33/2660–2217* ✉ *14 Strand Rd., North Kolkata*). **Sealdah Station** (✉ *East end of Bepin Behari Ganguly St., North Kolkata* ☎ *33/2350–3535*).

VISITOR INFORMATION

The West Bengal Tourist Office is open Monday through Saturday 10 to 5. The regional Government of India Tourist Office is well equipped to help baffled travelers; it's open Monday–Saturday 9–6. The Kolkata Information Centre is also helpful. The West Bengal Tourist Office is in the heart of Kolkata's business hub, but people here will only be able to give you information about destinations within the state. The Government of India Tourist Office, near the city center, gives more of an overall picture (including the state). The staff is friendly to boot.

Tourist Offices **Kolkata Information Centre** (✉ *1/1 A. J.C. Bose Rd., Central Kolkata* ☎ *33/2223–2451*). **Government of India Tourist Office** (✉ *4 Shakespeare Sarani, Kolkata, Central Kolkata 700071* ☎ *33/2282–1475, 33/2282–7731, or 33/2282–5813*). **West Bengal Tourist Office** (✉ *3/2 B.B.D. Bagh E, Kolkata, Central Kolkata 700001* ☎ *33/2248–8271 to 73*).

Darjeeling & Sikkim

14

Buddhist monks during the Tibetan New Year celebration

WORD OF MOUTH

"I went to see Wes Anderson's movie *The Darjeeling Limited* yesterday. It was as weird and wonderful as the other films that he has made. But is there a Darjeeling Limited train in real life?"

—gard

"What there is, is the Darjeeling Himalayan Railway—absolutely marvelous—you can ride up a mountain, on the main street of Indian villages, behind a steam engine."

—thursdaysd

www.fodors.com/forums

WELCOME TO DARJEELING & SIKKIM

Buddhist monk in Sikkim

TOP REASONS TO GO

★ **Viewing Kanchenjunga and Everest:** Admire two of the highest peaks in the world and enjoy the regal magnificence of the Himalayas.

★ **Travel through Sikkim Countryside:** The beauty of this friendly, semi-tropical, mountainous land is memorable.

★ **Tea Garden Culture:** Sample some of the best teas in the world and sightsee in chai country.

★ **Kick Back, Relax, and Go Back in Time:** It was not for nothing that Darjeeling became a resort town. Its weather, languor, and Raj flavor are ideal ingredients for a peaceful interlude.

World Heritage toy train (b1889). Darjeeling.

Lachung

TIBET (CHINA)

Nathu La Pass

Changu Lake

BHUTAN

Kumai

1 Darjeeling. Sprawled across the top of several hillsides, this district is one of the most famous and distinctive in the world because of its key commodity—tea. Tea estates bring a special culture, landscape, and a style of life that has existed for generations.

2 East Sikkim. Gangtok and Rumtek are part of East Sikkim that extends right up to Nathu La pass on the sensitive Chinese border and also borders Bhutan. The road descending from China across the Nathu La pass was once part of the Silk Route. Bhutias, Lepchas, and Nepalis farm this countryside and in the upper and colder reaches yak tending is the chief occupation.

3 West Sikkim. Pelling and Pemayangtse, located next to each other at 6,800 feet, are principal destinations of West Sikkim. Pelling is the headquarters of this district and is rapidly growing into a resort town. West Sikkim is the gateway to some of the state's best trekking routes.

Solo trekking

GETTING ORIENTED

Darjeeling and tiny Sikkim together have a ringside seat to the eastern Himalayas. Sikkim is one of the smallest states of India and the least populated with just 540,00 people, while the Darjeeling district is home to 1.6 million people at last count. Both regions are racially and culturally diverse, Darjeeling more so where a mix of Nepalis, Tibetans, Bengalis and some Sikkimese (mainly Bhutias) live. Sikkim is a blend of Nepali and Sikkimese population and the Sikkimese have two ethnicities–Lepcha and Bhutia. There are various theories about the origin of both these groups–Lepchas are said to have migrated from Tibet centuries ago but have Burmese influences. Bhutias too hail originally from Tibet and became Sikkim's ruling class.

DARJEELING & SIKKIM PLANNER

When to Go

October through June is the opportune time to journey up to this part of the Himalayas. In December and January, Darjeeling, particularly, gets quite cold, and snow will hit the higher reaches of Sikkim. You will need to pack lots of warm wear. The monsoon season, when landslides occur, is not a great time to visit Sikkim. Navigating mountain roads are all the more difficult when they are wet and slippery.

Monasteries and Buddhism

Visits to the numerous and quite diverse colorful shrines to Buddhism that dot the countryside both in Darjeeling and Sikkim will add a special spiritual element to any journey to this part of India. It offers a peek into another culture that may have been unfamiliar before, full of radiating peace and harmony. It is easy to suffer monastery overload, so pick the few monasteries you would like to view with thought. Don't go over the top with the smaller ones; instead, conserve energy to the see finest. If you're skipping the countryside, make certain you include one monastery, even a simple one, on your itinerary.

Bargain Hunting

For such a small town, Darjeeling is a serious shopping center, with top-quality tea, Tibetan artifacts, jewelry, *thangkas* (silk-scroll paintings), antiques, statues, woolens, shawls, hats, Tibetan motif T-shirts, suede bags, masks, carpets, and brass jewelry and hand-loom items from the northeastern states of Mizoram and Manipur available in abundance. Look also for the finely-carved turquoise items that are quite reasonably priced and are said to originate in Tibet. Masks of all shapes, sizes, and ferocity are locally carved. Musical instruments, some exotically priced, are available in a few shops. There are even special stores to choose a kukri, an ornate Nepali dagger. Antiques—kettles, fantastically beautiful statues (of revered deity Tara who represents compassion and of *bodhisattvas* who are considered "the enlightened beings" in Buddhism), finely carved bowls—range from Rs. 1,000 to Rs. 25,000. Several shops will sew a Tibetan motif of your choice on a T-shirt while you watch. The Tibetan Refugee Center offers a small selection of beautifully woven carpets.

What It Costs In Rupees

	¢	$	$$	$$$	$$$$
Restaurants	under Rs. 100	Rs. 100–Rs. 300	Rs. 300–Rs. 500	Rs. 500–Rs. 700	over Rs. 700
Hotels	under Rs. 2,000	Rs. 2,000–Rs. 4,000	Rs. 4,000–Rs. 6,000	Rs. 6,000–Rs. 10,000	over Rs. 10,000

Restaurant prices are for an entrée plus bread or rice. Hotel prices are for a double room in high season, excluding a tax of up to 20%.

Getting Around the Darjeeling–Sikkim Circuit

To visit both Darjeeling and Sikkim, consider a clockwise tour of this region. The closest railhead for both is New Jalpaiguri (NJP) or Siliguri and the closest airport is at Bagdogra, 16 km from Siliguri. From the airport or the railway stations the drive to Darjeeling takes about three hours; to Gangtok about five.

Start with Darjeeling. At the airport or train station, hire a sturdy vehicle. You'll pay about Rs. 1,200 to Rs. 1,500 from Bagdogra to Darjeeling (88 km [55 mi]), possibly less from Siliguri. Better, but more expensive, is to have your hotel pick you up. Alternatively, the brave can buy a spot for Rs. 80 in a shared jeep, at Silguri taxi stand, which fits 9 passengers and takes mountain curves at breakneck speed. But do note that getting a taxi from the Bagdogra Airport or New Jalpaiguri to Siliguri will cost you about Rs. 250.

A half hour outside Siliguri, you'll find yourself deep in tea country. The most famous tea gardens are at higher altitudes, such as the Makaibari Estate and Castleton Estate, which makes the most expensive tea in the world. The road makes hairpin bends as it climbs, and about 30 km (19 mi) before Darjeeling is the town of Kurseong. As you approach Darjeeling, the track for Darjeling's historic Toy train weaves in and out of view, and you might pass one chugging feistily along. Just 8 km (5 mi) short of Darjeeling is Ghoom, site of the Yiga-Choling Tibetan monastery. Five km (3 mi) east of Ghoom, off the highway, is the region's highest point, Tiger Hill, at 2,520 meters (8,268 feet). Tourists flock here before dawn for spectacular views of the Kanchejunga and, on lucky days, Mt. Everest. Back on the road, you enter an amphitheater of towering snowy mountains and sweeping valleys.

After three days in Darjeeling, press on for Sikkim, ideally via Pelling 74 km (46 mi), about four hours northeast of Darjeeling. One pretty route descends through Darjeeling's densest tea gardens and tea villages to Jorethang. The road is narrow and bumpy, but this route is a rare glimpse at the underbelly of one of the world's wealthiest industries. Some of the villages with their little churches, temples, and clutch of houses on stilts make excellent pictures. Jorethang is a bustling border town. Beyond it, you'll be in the heart of Sikkim's mountainous but prosperous countryside.

Gangtok is 117 km (73 mi) from Pelling via Singtam, a six-hour drive through similar stunning semi-tropical and semi-mountainous vegetation and terrain.

Permits

Because of diplomatic tensions with Pakistan and China, which have occasionally escalated into war, India's northern borders have been sensitive for decades and remain heavily guarded. Movement is restricted in these regions, which means foreigners need permits to enter Sikkim. It's generally easiest to apply for a permit in advance through a travel agent or tour operator. Have two or three passport photographs and photocopies of your passport and your Indian visa handy. Once you have the permit, keep several photocopies of it with you, and make sure you have it stamped at checkposts. Remember not to take pictures of bridges, airports, or military installations in restricted areas.

See Permits under the Darjeeling-Sikkim Essentials at the end of this chapter.

B.Y.O.S. (Bring Your Own Sweater)

Hotels in Sikkim and Darjeeling are not centrally heated and you can't always count on space heaters or sufficient hot water; don't forget to pack lots of warm clothes. Also note: hotels here do not have elevators.

14

Updated by Vaihayasi Pande Daniel

THE TOWERING, DIGNIFIED HIMALAYAS, home to the planet's highest peaks, stretch in a glorious snowy arc across 2,400 km (1,491 mi), and six countries right from Pakistan to Bhutan. At its eastern end, where it begins to taper in width, it slices right past the district of Darjeeling and through the wee state of Sikkim, lending its wintery magnificence to their peaceful landscape. Mountains have always been symbols of calm and inspired awe, and those living in a land of mountains—especially mountains that command as much respect as the Himalayas—are considered blessed. It takes just a day to realize on a journey through Sikkim or Darjeeling that you are traveling in an earthly paradise—a Shambhala. Beauty in the form of hills, peaks, valleys, and waterfalls surrounds you and without a doubt this little region in a far corner of India is one of the prettiest in the world.

EXPLORING DARJEELING & SIKKIM

Splendor apart, a trip into the eastern Himalayas requires planning and a bit of research. Navigating hilly roads are always tough and slow going. Journeys must start early and end early and routes worked out in advance. If you plan to trek farther afield from Pelling or Gangtok, you will need to put yourself in touch with experienced tour coordinators. Timing is also very important: Sikkim's pretty rhododendron jungles will lack flowers if you choose the wrong time for a forest hike. Don't nurture hopes of seeing Kanchenjunga (let alone Everest) if you decide to venture to this neighborhood in the rainy season. Avoid being slack with your paperwork because extra permits are required to visit certain areas of Darjeeling and Sikkim. Weather can change drastically around here and hotel rooms have no central heating, so pack accordingly.

ABOUT THE RESTAURANTS

Both Darjeeling and Sikkim showcase some fine Chinese and Tibetan food cooked with quite some finesse. They're probably better quality than what you will find elsewhere in India. In Gangtok you can dig into some unusual Sikkimese food, with Indian, Nepali influences, that is big on greens (nettle and bamboo), *chhurpi* (yak cheese), *phitig* (glass noodles), and pork/beef dishes but includes dal and rice. Plenty of Indian food is available and runs to the usual (but not sub-standard) hodgepodge of dal makhnis, butter chickens, and navratan kormas. Continental food is dished out with some skill, too, especially in some of the traditional hotels and eateries. Dishes you've probably only heard about in Raj era novels, like steamed jam pudding and beef bolognaise can be sampled here. Most restaurants are reasonably priced and stay open post lunch so meals can be had throughout the day.

ABOUT THE HOTELS

While there is no shortage of hotels in either Sikkim or Darjeeling (the small town of Pelling alone has 80 hotels), the better hotels do get booked up quickly. Lodging in Darjeeling is more abundant in the backpacker category and there are fewer upmarket hotels. Sikkim has plenty of mid-range choices, but really just one top quality hotel. At this writing, fast-growing Gangtok is opening several luxury hotels.

The busy season is Christmas and New Year and during the school holidays of the Indian academic year (the only time kids get time off), which covers late April to early June, around Durga Puja, and Diwali depending on its date.

DARJEELING

Anyone with a yen for hill stations (a refuge in the hills) must see the "Queen of the Hills" in the far northwestern corner of West Bengal. Built during the British Raj as a health resort for soldiers, Darjeeling quickly became a center for the tea trade, apart from being a superb Himalayan spa resort where the British took refuge to escape the heat of the plains. Most of the graceful, old colonial buildings are a bit scruffy, but some still bear their regal stamp. Outside the pedestrianized town center, high-season traffic can impede an exploratory stroll; yet the town's old-world charm enchants even the most jaded travelers. In a few days here you can soak up the alpine scenery—dominated, in good weather, by far-off Mt. Kanchenjunga (28,208 feet), bargain in a local market, and trek on a nearby hillside. Fog engulfs the town from below at unpredictable intervals, but when it clears and the sun sparkles on snowy Kanchenjunga, third-highest mountain in the world (the name means "house of five treasures," in honor of its five summits), the effect is dazzling. Darjeeling, though in the state of West Bengal, shares more common history with neighboring Nepal and Sikkim. Once part of the kingdom of Sikkim, it was a small settlement until 1835 when it was leased by the king to the British who on medical grounds requested special permission to build a sanitarium (the British later brazenly annexed it). The sahibs went on to colonize it, planting tea plantations, setting up churches, clubs, mansions and bungalows, laying tracks for the Himalayan Railways, and bringing in Nepali labor. Soon the town sparkled as a popular resort and retreat for the British and Indian elite. Darjeeling also received a flood of Tibetan of refugees when China took over Tibet in 1950.

Long before you reach Darjeeling, as you ascend a winding road from the plains, you'll smell an invigorating blend of tea, wood smoke, verdant undergrowth, cedar, and wildflowers. The largely Nepali population, some of whose ancestors migrated centuries ago, has made its imprint more subtly than the Raj—even the simplest homes are embellished with brightly painted trim, small gardens, or flowerpots. And Nepali youths on every street corner play *chungi*—a kind of kickball with a ball made from a bunch of rubber bands.

Darjeeling taxis charge the earth for even small distances; Rs. 100 seems to be the starting point for any fare. Decide in advance the sights you want to see and plan taxi trips accordingly. The tea estate and Tibetan Refugee Self-Help Center are in the general direction of the zoo and the Himalayan Mountaineering Institute, so you can visit the tea estate on the way to the zoo and the HMI, and the Tibetan center on the way back to town. If you happen to find a good taxi driver, keep his cell number and call him for future use.

The weather in Darjeeling is delightful year-round, barring only the monsoon season, when rain and fog can make driving treacherous. You'll get the best views of Kanchenjunga between November and March. The town sometimes gets snow in December; bring heavy woolens in winter, light woolens in summer.

The pride of Darj, as it's affectionately called, is its main promenade, the **Mall** that encompasses the main square, the lively Chowrasta with its central statue of Bhanu Bhakta, and loops around Observatory Hill. Stroll about, duck into the antique shops, people-watch, and soak up the general air of well-being. There's always lots to see—well-dressed Nepali families, Tibetan matrons in full gear, Bengali tourists, monkey clans, and global backpackers all out for a stroll. If you're hungry after a long train journey, stop in a roadside café for a plate of steamed Tibetan *momos* (steamed dumplings) or opt for roasted corn-on-the-cob or popcorn masala. One clear days brilliant views of the mountains can be had from the Mall on the other side from the Chowrasta. You can wander off the Mall into some of the town's hilly cobblestoned lanes, sip chai (tea) at The House of Tea, or look at the old black-and-white photographs of Darjeeling at Das Studio, a photo shop. Nature lovers have plenty to admire right in town. Just be aware that many streets are one-way, so it can be confusing to get around.

A POET FOR THE PEOPLE

Nineteenth-century poet Bhanu Bhakta Acharya popularized the Nepali language by writing his poetry in Nepali rather than Sanskrit, the language of the elite and educated. One of his most important achievements was translating the Hindu epic *Ramayana* from Sanskrit into Nepali and into verse form so it was accessible to the masses. He continues to be revered among Nepalis today.

Most of Darjeeling's indoor sights are closed on Thursday.

The **Bengal Natural History Museum** (✉ *Meadowbank Rd.* ☎ *354/254–308* 🎫 *Rs. 5* ⏲ *Fri.–Wed. 10–4*) has an exhaustive collection of fauna including an extensive display of beetles and butterflies from the higher reaches of the eastern Himalayas and a curiously eccentric assortment of big-game trophies and pickled snakes.

Just north of the museum at one corner of the Mall, but *not* generally open to the public, is **Raj Bhavan,** the former home of Burdwan's maharaja, crowned by a shining blue dome. As photographs are not allowed, just stop and have a peek at this attractive building during a saunter around the Mall.

The clean, neatly laid-out and peaceful **Padmaja Naidu Zoo** (✉ *Off Jawahar Rd. W* ☎ *354/225–3709* 🎫 *Rs. 100* ⏲ *Fri.–Wed. 8:30–3:30*) is justly famous for its rare snow leopards, gorgeous clouded leopards, Siberian tigers, Tibetan wolves, Himalayan bears, shy red pandas, and other alpine animals that are not easy to see in other zoos.

On the walk to or from the zoo, take a picnic or just a detour up the hill—follow the sign for RIVER HILL DISTRICT MAGISTRATE'S OFFICE—to the recently renovated **Shrubbery Park,** a quiet beautifully manicured, neatly laid-out garden behind the Raj Bhavan with great views of Singla Valley and the Himalayas. Several cultural programs now take place here; for details check with the tourist office. Close by is the Hot Stimulating Café where you can stop for some hot *tomba* (beer) and snack on fresh momos.

Two minutes past the zoo (enter via zoo gates) is the **Himalayan Mountaineering Institute** (✉ *Off Jawahar Rd.* ☎ *354/225–0483 or 354/225–0487* 🌐 *www.himalayanmountaineeringinstitute.com* 🎫 *Rs. 10* ⏲ *Fri.–Wed. 8:30–3:30*), a training center with some public exhibits—photographs, autographs, equipment of famous mountaineers, costumes of hill folk—and a special section devoted to Everest expeditions. There is also a giant telescope Adolf Hitler presented to the king of Nepal. The institute was long directed by none other than Sherpa Tenzing Norgay, who accompanied Sir Edmund Hillary up Mt. Everest in 1953. Norgay's *samadhi,* or grave, is a few minutes from the Institute in a quiet spot. The Institute runs a variety of courses and has rock climbing enclosure for beginners at another location near the Tibetan refugee center.

14

Sacred sites also abound in Darjeeling. South of the town center, below the train station, the **Dhirdham Temple** was built in 1939 along the lines of the Pashupatinath Temple in Kathmandu and has a many-layered pagoda facade.

Both Buddhists and Hindus revere pine-covered **Observatory Hill,** above the Windamere hotel. The hill is topped by an unusual shrine blending Hindu and Buddhist styles, the **Mahakal Temple**; it's a steep climb up. Draped in strings of prayer flags and packed with worshippers milling in and out and ringing bells, this animated Shiva temple makes a colorful sight. A Buddhist monk and a Hindu priest conduct prayers together at the shrine that was once the site of a monastery. A *chorten* (memorial) housing the remains of a famous lama is also on the hill. The monkeys at the top can be quite aggressive, so walk with a group and don't carry food; but the monkeys antics at the temple can be fun to watch, especially if you're traveling with kids. Views are good from here; reach it in the morning or just before dusk.

There are several *gompas,* or Tibetan monasteries, nearby, including **Aloobari,** perched high up on Tenzing Norgay Road, 3 km from the center of town. Tibetan handicrafts are sold here.

The monastery **Bhutia Busti** houses the original *Bardo Thodol* (*Tibetan Book of The Dead*) and is a steep climb down, more than 1 km from Chowrasta. The oldest monastery in Darjeeling, it was once located on Observatory Hill but was destroyed in 1815 in a Nepali invasion. Although Bhutia Busti was rebuilt at its present location, it fell prey to the 1934 earthquake. The king of Sikkim provided funds to have it rebuilt.

Darjeeling's most celebrated house of worship, 8 km (5 mi) south of town in Ghoom, is the very large **Yiga-Choling** monastery, built in 1875, which houses the extremely sacred statue of Maitreya Buddha ("coming Buddha" or a Buddha awakening to enlightenment) image.

★ A ride on the narrow-gauge **Darjeeling Toy train** (now a World Heritage site) is a must providing a rare trip into the past. The engines run on coal, the carriages are narrow and tiny, and the tracks 1½ feet apart. Spraying its passengers with particles of coal, the little train moves ahead unhurriedly in a cloud of smoke and steam, tooting loudly at vehicles and people that grudgingly heed way, and edging closely past homes and shops, fields and forests. A journey to New Jalpaiguri is dramatic, but it takes about eight hours—the train is so slow that you can safely hop off and on as it moves along, and it stops to refuel almost every half hour. Consider going only up to Ghoom, perhaps to see the Yiga-Choling monastery—the toy train leaves Darjeeling every day at 9:15, stopping at Ghoom after one hour and continuing to New Jalpaiguri. (Grab a window seat on the right side of the train facing Ghoom.) Another good option is to ride one of the two-hour joy-ride trains (Rs. 250) departing three times daily at 8, 10:40, and 1:20. Buy the ticket in advance because during tourist seasons tickets sometimes sell out and ticket lines move slowly (budget about 15 minutes for this). The joy-ride train goes via the Batasia Loop where it weaves a figure eight at the war memorial, pauses within this garden for 10 minutes (a chance to take photographs of Kanchenjunga), and then heads to Ghoom (at 7,407 feet, one of the highest railway stations in the world). It halts for half an hour there and then makes the trip back. If you want to spend longer at the monastery, consider returning by taxi; but be warned it is a bit expensive (can be Rs. 300 or more) and sometimes taxis are difficult to locate. Your ticket covers entry into the small Ghoom railway museum, which is worth a visit if there is electricity (Darjeeling receives frequent power cuts). ☎ *354/225–2555 Darjeeling Himalayan Railway* ✉ *Darjeeling Railway Station, Hill Cart Rd.* 🌐 *www.dhr.in.*

Ghoom is a regular stop on the return journey from the **Tiger Hill** lookout point, where views of Kanchenjunga, the eastern Himalayas, and even Mt. Everest make it worth getting up well before sunrise. The fit and adventurous can walk back to Darjeeling on a quiet side road. If you're catching a flight from Bagdogra to Delhi or Kolkata and you're leaving Darjeeling early in the morning, consider leaving even earlier to stop at Tiger Hill on your way down.

On the way back from Tiger Hill, you can also ask your driver to stop at the serene **Japanese Peace Pagoda** for a lovely view of both the town and the mountains.

Overlooking the Mall on Birch Hill, **St. Andrew's Church,** built in 1843, still takes pride of place. You're welcome to attend the Sunday service. The Christmas carol service is a highlight of Darjeeling's holiday season.

THE RISE OF THE STEAM TRAMWAY

Until the Darjeeling Himalayan Railway came into existence Darjeeling could only be reached by tongas (horse-drawn carriages) on the Hill Cart Road that came up from the plains. The idea of starting a "steam tramway" was proposed in 1879 by the Eastern Bengal Railway Company and quickly accepted. By 1880 the tracks had been laid from Siliguri up to Kurseong and one year later the system was complete. Its 87-km (54-mi) track mostly hugged the Hill Cart Road and passed through 14 stations, 503 bridges, and across an unbelievable 177 unmanned railway crossings. The 12 steam engines left that run on this line date earlier than 1925. Windamere hotel in Darjeeling is the world headquarters of the Darjeeling Himalayan Railway Club, a group of Darjeeling toy-train enthusiasts. An entire steam train can be chartered for $685 per day. For more information, see *www.dhr.in.*

14

India is the world's largest producer of tea, generating about 850 million kilograms annually. Tea cultivation in Darjeeling began in 1841, when Chinese tea was introduced here by the British and Nepali labor was hired to pick leaves and maintain the estates. By the early 20th century, the Darjeeling area had some 117 tea gardens over some 42,000 acres. Today, Darjeeling black tea is one of the world's most prized varieties, and around 80,000 people are employed in these gardens. Some are temporary, earning about Rs. 53 per day during the plucking season.

To see how Darjeeling tea is processed, visit one of the closest gardens, the **Happy Valley Tea Estate,** 3 km (2 mi) outside town on the way to the zoo and the Tibetan refugee center. It's an easy walk downhill through tea bushes, but fairly strenuous on the way back up. In this dilapidated factory, tea is still made the orthodox way and some 1,000 kilograms are processed daily. Between Tuesday and Saturday from 8 to 4, an obliging employee can be an impromptu but effective guide (tip about Rs. 100) to the production process. Hours are bit variable around here, and the factory seems have a variety of unforeseen holidays. Tea production stops between December and March, when leaves are not picked, but you can still pop into the factory and hear the process explained. If you won't be going on to Sikkim, consider driving 27 km (17 mi) to the Sikkim border at Jorethang to see the heart of the tea country.

At the **Goomtee Tea Estate** at Mahanadi, near Kurseong, 30 km (19 mi) and about 90 minutes from Darjeeling, you can stay overnight in a century-old bungalow at the heart of the tranquil estate for $90 per night. Contact the **Mahanadi Tea Company** (☏*33/2247–1036* *www.darjeelingteas.com*) in Kolkata. As an alternative, you can visit Makaibari Tea Estate Guest House ⊕www.makaibari.com or Glenburn Tea Estate ⊕www.glenburnteaestate.com.

WHERE TO EAT & STAY

$ ✕ **Dekeva's.** Happily not much changes at this tiny family-run corner ★ café opposite the clock tower of the crumbling Capitol Cinema—the menu has been pratically the same for over a decade. It's a hot destination for pizza, momos (and other great Tibetan food), stir-fried noodles, excellent Chinese meals, and big, slurpy, garlicky soups, not to mention North Indian lassis. There are plenty of vegetarian options, and the laid-back atmosphere allows you to meet new people or just hang out with a book. ✉*51 Gandhi Rd., just east of Mall, below Dekeling Hotel* ☎*354/225–4159.*

$ ✕ **Glenary's.** Darjeeling's best independent restaurant is a popular meeting place for locals and travelers alike. Although stodgy and mildly seedy, Glenary's is an institution. All three floors have great views, and the top floor is particularly atmospheric in the evening and especially at dusk (reserve a booth near the window with a view of the valley). The kitchen serves tandoori, Chinese, and Western food with Indian beers and wines, and the downstairs pub has a range of cocktails. Most revered of all is the ground-floor tea service, established in 1938, with its classic desserts tasty cakes and alpine backdrop. (You can pack up some baked items or beef pickle to take away.) There's a convenient Internet café attached. ✉*Nehru Rd.* ☎*354/225–4122* ▭*V.*

$ ✕ **Lotus.** Its popularity with the locals means meals take a bit of time to be served at this well-frequented restaurant, and at lunch or dinner, it's often difficult to snag a table. The decor is functional but tidy and the Chinese food is well made. Pork dishes are recommended, but there are plenty of vegetarian choices, too. ✉*Laden La Rd.* ▭*No credit cards.*

$ ✕ **The Park.** Come here for hearty Mughlai and tandoori food, such as mutton curry, butter naan, and *palak paneer* (cubes of soft cottage cheese in creamed spinach). The butter chicken is recommended. Decor is simple: black leather chairs and glass-top tables without much of a view. The place fills up at lunchtime—a testament to its popularity—and a few Chinese dishes are available for those tired of North Indian food. Next door is its relatively new addition, Lemon Grass, a Thai restaurant, serving decent Thai specialities. ✉*41 Laden La Rd.* ☎*354/225–5270* ▭*No credit cards.*

¢ ✕ **Frank Ross Cafe.** This vegetarian café has an ambitious international menu: have a South Indian *dosa* (crisp, thin, delicious lentil and rice pancakes), a Mexican or Lebanese bite, or just a glass of fresh orange juice. A few minutes from the Mall, the homey dining room, done in green and white has wood floors, cane furniture, and marble tables and a few high stools in front of high counters. The dosas are rather good. So is the iced coffee. ✉*14 Nehru Rd.* ☎*354/225–8194.*

¢ ✕ **The House of Tea.** Goodricke Company teas—choose your flavor among teas sourced directly from some of the most famous Darjeeling tea gardens nearby with musical names like Barnsbeg, Badamtam,

TEA TIME

Soon after the British leased the area in 1839, Archibald Campbell, a member of the Bengal Medical Service attached to the British Army, was deputed to start a sanitarium in Darjeeling. In 1941, while experimenting with the kind of crops that grow in the Darjeeling area, he decided to plant some China tea seeds he had procured from Kolkata. The trial was successful and very soon tea cultivation began in the Darjeeling area. The initially the quality of tea was not terribly good, and it was obvious that though tea could thrive in Darjeeling, the strain needed a serious upgrade. The Horticultural Society of London hatched an elaborate plan to obtain better-quality tea plants from the interior of China, an area that was off-limits to Europeans at the time because of the Treaty of Nanking. Robert Fortune, a Scottish botanist, who spoke Mandarin, smuggled himself into China's interior disguised as local (complete with shaved head and ponytail) to covertly collect several varieties of plants including tea seedlings. He successfully sent 20,000 tea plants and even a few Chinese tea workers to Darjeeling. Over time, his efforts transformed Darjeeling into a source of premier, world-famous tea.

14

Margaret's Hope, Castleton and Thurbo—are served piping hot with homemade cookies at this little tea lounge overlooking the valley. It's a great place to catch your breath after meandering up and downhill through the bazaars. Buy a tin of Castleton tea, world's most expensive, or any other brand at this outlet. Scoops of ice cream also make a great post-hike treat. ✉ *11 Nehru Rd.* ☎ *354/225–4182.*

$$$ **Mayfair.** Once a summer palace of the Maharaja of Nazargunj, this smart resort, done in a cheerful sunny yellow, is downhill from the zoo road and has good views of the town (as opposed the mountains). The hotel's manicured garden (polished marble terraces with garden furniture), its swanky, well-stocked bar, and plush lounges all offer an appealing mix of coziness and luxury. Children will delight in a special play area and statues of geese and other animals to inspire Mother Goose–ish make-believe. The large elegant rooms are furnished with stylish, old-fashioned furniture, Tibetan rugs, and spacious sitting areas. Mayfair will open a branch in Gangtok in 2008. **Pros:** lovely garden environment, cheerful and luxurious. **Cons:** expensive, lacks a Kanchenjunga view. ✉ *The Mall, opposite the Raj Bhavan, 734101* ☎ *354/225–6476* 🌐 *www.mayfairhotels.com/darjeeling/index.asp* *31 rooms, 20 cottages* *In-room: no a/c, safe, refrigerator. In-hotel: restaurant, bar, no elevator, laundry service, public Internet.* *AE, DC, MC, V* *FAP.*

$$$ Fodor's Choice ★ **Windamere.** Set in heritage buildings dating back to the 1880s, this grande dame of the Raj is a justly famous landmark in the heart of Darjeeling. The drawing rooms and bar are packed with artifacts of British Darjeeling, and the verandas have magnificent views of the hills. High tea, served from 4 to 6, is a ceremony in itself and worth a trip even if you aren't staying here. The rooms, which combine Raj, art deco, chintz, and Tibetan furnishings, have fireplaces, heaters, hot-water bottles, and Victorian claw-foot bathtubs. The staff, skilled at serving

royals and film stars, once worked under the exacting eye of owner the late Mrs. Tenduf-La who is credited with turning Windamere into a Darjeeling institution during the 70-odd years she ran it. **Pros:** sumptuous breakfasts, ideal location. **Cons:** a little sniffy, room service only offers tea and coffee. ✉ *Observatory Hill, 734101* ☎ *354/225–4041 or 354/225–4042* 🌐 *www.windamerehotel.com* *39 rooms, 15 suites, 2 cottages* *In-room: no a/c, no TV (some). In-hotel: restaurant, bar, spa, no elevator, laundry service, public Internet.* 💳 *AE, MC, V* 🍽 *FAP.*

$$ ★ **The Elgin.** Rooms are decorative and classically elegant in this welcoming, centrally located Heritage Hotel with a pretty, white-and-green Raj exterior and manicured gardens. The delightfully regal lounges and public spaces take you back 60 years or more. In the rooms antique furniture, wood floors, Tibetan carpets, thick drapes in warm colors, and working fireplaces (in some rooms) add to the coziness. Bathrooms have modern conveniences and are in green marble. **Pros:** charming atmosphere, Victorian decor. **Cons:** No mountain views. ✉ *18 H.D. Lama Rd., 734101* ☎ *354/225–7227, 354/225–7226, or 354/225–4082* 🌐 *www.elginhotels.com* *22 rooms, 2 suites* *In-room: no a/c, no TV (some). In-hotel: restaurant, bar, no elevator, laundry service.* 💳 *AE, DC, MC, V* 🍽 *FAP.*

$ **Cedar Inn.** Nestled in majestic cedars high above the town center, this renovated Victorian Gothic resort is a serene retreat from the bustle, with free shuttle jeeps to take you to and fro. Wood, glass, and light predominate, and the rooms are bright, cozy, and elegant, with wood paneling, stripped-wood floors, and fabrics in soft neutral colors. Wake up in the morning to Kanchenjunga peeking through your window: Cedar's lodgings offer probably the best views of this magnificent peak in town. Each room is built on two levels, with a small sitting area, and some have fireplaces and bathtubs. Tasty Indian food is served at the restaurant and the sun deck and garden are good places to lounge. **Pros:** quiet mountaintop location, stunning vistas, good service. **Cons:** far from the town's main square, hot water in short supply. ✉ *Jalapahar Rd., 734101* ☎ *354/225–4446* 🌐 *www.cedarinndarjeeling.com* *29 rooms, 4 suites, some attic rooms* *In-room: no a/c. In-hotel: restaurant, bar, gym, no elevator, laundry service, public Internet.* 💳 *MC, V* 🍽 *CP.*

¢ **Dekeling.** You're welcomed as part of the family in this homey, lively second-story Tibetan hotel. The cheerful rooms have large windows, cedar paneling, and simple furnishings, including Tibetan wall hangings and, in some cases, stained-glass windows. Ask for an attic room with a view, an exceptional value. Solo travelers might enjoy the communal sitting room, and the "library" (a bookcase made up of guest donations with a great selection of paperbacks). For twice the money, you can also rent one of four lovely Tibetan suites at the owners' Dekeling Resort at Hawk's Nest, perched on a steep hill 2 km (1 mi) away. **Pros:** cozy, convenient meals in attached restaurant. **Cons:** no elevator and many steps up to lobby. ✉ *Above Dekeva's restaurant, 51 Gandhi Rd., 734101* ☎ *354/225–4159* 📠 *354/225–3298* 🌐 *www.dekeling.com* *22 rooms* *In-room: no a/c, no TV (some). In-hotel: restaurant, no elevator.* 💳 *MC, V.*

¢ **Mall Guest House.** This tiny, family-run guesthouse hugging the edge of the Mall is an excellent value for the money. It's cozy but simple, with a tiny, cute café (good music and ambience) where the owner rustles up just about anything you ask for. The rooms—with wood paneling, Tibetan carpets, plain furnishings, and a small sitting area—are comfortable and clean, with lovely views. Rooms with mountain views cost more. **Pros:** homey, well located, inexpensive room. **Cons:** completely basic, rooms are small. ✉*6/A Hermitage Mall Rd., 734101* ☎*354/641–9889* *plama@yahoo.com* *8 rooms* *In-room: no a/c, no phone. In-hotel: restaurant, no elevator.* *No credit cards.*

¢ **Sailung.** This charming Mall lodging is minutes from a spot called Viewpoint, near Observatory Hill, where people come to catch sunset *dekhos* (views) of Mt. Kanchenjunga. Occupying different levels in a pretty bungalow on the side of the hill, the rooms are simple but attractive, with red jute floor mats, walls lined with polished wood, cane furniture, neat bathrooms, and small veranda sitting areas. Inspect a few rooms for the best mountain view and opt for those that open out into the garden. There is an extra charge for heaters (Rs. 100). **Pros:** reasonably-priced, well located, Darjeeling-style sitting room. **Cons:** only a few rooms available, room are a tad small. ✉*Oakdane, East Mall, 22/1 B B Sarani, 734101* ☎*354/225–6289* *354/225–3577* *8 rooms* *In-room: no a/c. In-hotel: restaurant, no elevator.* *No credit cards.*

14

SHOPPING

Most of the best curio and handicraft shops, open every day but Sunday, are in the pedestrian-only area at Chowrasta and in the lanes descending from Chowratsa to the taxi stand and Capitol Cinema clock tower. A few are located on Laden La Road as well. (Expect some to be closed for a half hour at lunchtime). Prices are generally better, and service friendlier, than in large cities, but you still have to bargain. Shop around; you'll find the same item for sale at difference prices. At some of the stores, though the wares are attractive, the owners have tendency to size you up and offer service accordingly. On Laden La Road the posh Rink Mall has a multiplex cinema, a branch of the popular Big Bazar, a music store, a bookshop, a branch of the Café Coffee Day chain, and a Nathmulls tea lounge.

Established in 1890, **Habeeb Mullick and Son** (☎*354/225–4109*) is a local landmark specializing in fine gifts: handicrafts and curios, jewelry (particularly amber, turquoise, and moonstone), Kashmiri pashmina shawls, carpets, hand-carved wooden bowls from the northeastern state of Nagaland, and exquisite silver Buddhas. The shop gets crowded after dinner, so go early for personal attention, as the welcoming proprietor has plenty on offer beyond the packed displays. Head for the shop right next to Oxford book shop. Across the square from Habeeb Mullick, **Jolly Arts** (☎*354/225–4059*) offers silk thangka paintings, soft Tibetan shawls, and ritual silver, copper, gold-painted, and bronze *puja* objects used for worship. Service is friendly and attentive. A little farther down Nehru Road, beyond Glenary's **Asian Art**

Palace (☎*354/225–8103*) offers silver, turquoise, and brass jewelry, Nepali handicrafts, masks, and Tibetan curios. It has good service. At the Capitol Cinema clock tower, a few doors from Dekeva's, **Mandala** (☎*983/201–7071*) sells an interesting selection of silver jewelry, tea kettles, Buddhas, traditional beer mugs, and other Nepali and Tibetan handicrafts at rather reasonable prices.

Arts Crafts and Curios (☎*354/225–2872*) has a good selection of Tibetan artifacts. At the corner of Chowrasta and Nehru Road, Latif Badami at **Eastern Arts** (☎*354/52917*) lets you take your time browsing through ornate silver jewelry and lapis lazuli. Service is not particularly friendly. Clothing, bags, and other items crafted from Kashmiri leather and fur are the specialty at **Kashmir Arts** on Nehru Road.

The **Tibetan Refugee Self-Help Center** (✉*65 Gandhi Rd.*) is worth a taxi ride out of town to see the artisans (mostly elderly women) at work, dyeing, weaving, and spinning wool on old bicycle wheels—a great photo op. In some seasons cuddly Lhasa Apso puppies (for sale if you're not going abroad) scamper around in the yard. In addition to elegant sweaters (Rs. 850), pencil cases, woolens, brightly colored handwoven textiles (made into shirts, jackets, wallets, and backpacks), the store has a limited selection of beautiful carpet samples (Rs. 3,500 for an area rug about 5 feet by 4 feet). You can even bring your own design to be custom-made and shipped. The center, which started in 1959 to help Tibetan exiles, with just four people in two rooms, is open from 9 to 4 every day but Sunday (but its store remains open on Sunday); a good time to visit is around 11, when the workshop is humming. Next door, an interesting museum has black-and-white photographs charting the establishment of the center, the Tibet struggle, and the famous visitors.

Nathmull's (✉*Laden La Rd.* ☎*354/225–6437 or 354/225–2327* 🌐*www.nathmulltea.com*) has a vast selection of Darjeeling tea and an unusual variety of tea cozies and silver-plated tea services, but it's in a busy traffic area. To avoid the bustle, try the **Chowrasta Tea Store** (✉*The Mall* ☎*354/225–4059*) for a good selection of high-quality teas. No picnic is complete without a visit to **Chowrasta Stores** (✉*The Mall* ☎*354/225–4153*), an old-fashioned general store with everything from soup to nuts, including wine, Sikkim liqueurs, whiskey, chocolates, ice cream, cheese, cookies, toiletries, and so on. Just don't go around 3 PM or you'll have to fight the local schoolchildren for penny candy. Next door to Chowrasta Stores, with the same glass-cabinet displays and friendly service, **S. Lekhraj and Co.** (✉*The Mall* ☎*354/225–4275*) has all manner of "suitings and hosiery," from fun cotton T-shirts with Darjeeling designs to socks, underwear, and towels, to fabrics for on-site tailoring.

SIKKIM

It's not surprising that Lepchas, or Rongkup (Children of Rong), the first known inhabitants of Sikkim, gave their mountain home a name meaning "land of happiness." Sikkim is probably the least explored and most unspoiled part of India—far off the tourist path. Palden Thondup Namgyal, the last *chogyal* (king) to rule over Sikkim until it became India's 22nd state in 1975, was an avid conservationist who protected his Buddhist kingdom from development. And not that much has changed. As you cross the border into Sikkim, there's a sense of having entered another country; the state has a culture and lifestyle all its own. It is a friendly, welcoming land where the modern and traditional coexist in charming harmony.

Three distinct ethnic groups live in Sikkim. The Lepchas originally lived in seclusion in north Sikkim, where they developed a harmonious relationship with the environment to ensure their survival. Although most Lepchas converted to Buddhism, many still worship aspects of their physical surroundings: rainbows, clouds, rivers, and trees. Village priests preside over elaborate rituals, including animal sacrifices, to appease their animist deities.

Bhutias from Tibet came into Sikkim with the first Chogyal in the 17th century. Buddhism governs Bhutia life, with the monastery and the lama exerting tremendous influence over daily activities. Every village has its prayer flags and chortens (memorial stupas or shrines for relics), every home has an altar room, and most families have one relative in a monastery or convent. Buddhism works its way into weavings, handwoven rugs, thangka (silk-scroll) paintings, statues, and delicately carved *choktses* (low, colorfully carved wooden tables). In turn, the Bhutias' culture dominates Sikkim, right down to the women's national dress: the traditional *kho* or *bhoku,* the epitome of elegance, worn over a *wanju* (blouse), with the *pangden* (apron), the final colorful touch, restricted to married women and formal occasions. Today's best-known Bhutias are Bhaichung Bhutia, captain of the Indian soccer team, and Bollywood actor Danny Denzongpa.

Also sharing Sikkim are the Nepalese, now in the majority, who introduced terrace farming to the region. Although most Nepalese are Hindu, you'll see few Hindu temples in Sikkim, and their faith often incorporates Buddhist beliefs and practices (as it does in Nepal). The Nepalese are dominant in business, and theirs is the language most often heard in Sikkim; the present chief minister is a Nepali. In addition to these three groups, Sikkim has a small Tibetan community who tend to run restaurants and hotels.

Much of Sikkim is a continuous flow of hills and valleys, that are excellent for trekking and rafting. The state is famous for its wildflowers, particularly orchids and rhododendrons in spring. Trekking in Sikkim (March–May and September–December) means warm days and frigid nights. From Yuksom, in western Sikkim, you can trek closer to Mt. Kanchenjunga. Rafting on the Teesta and Rangeet rivers is best from October to December.

Because of Sikkim's sensitive border location, foreigners need an Inner Line Permit to visit. The best times to visit Sikkim are March through May and September through mid-November. June, July, and August bring monsoon rains, and December and January have cold snows. The peak period, when tourist services are taxed to the limit, is late September to early October, during the Hindu festival Durga Puja.

GANGTOK

94 km (58 mi) northeast of Darjeeling, 117 km (73 mi) northeast of Pelling, 114 km (71 mi) north of Siliguri.

Sikkim's capital is expanding fast across several valleys and ridges. With its pagoda-style roofs and tall buildings, not to mention its relative wealth, it has a different feel from other Indian hill stations.

If you're not planning a trip to nearby Rumtek, visit the 200-year-old **Enchey Monastery,** built in a pagoda style,in a grove of pines, and the pretty, whitewashed Do-Drul Chorten nearby, to get a taste of the Sikkimese Buddhist monastery—more colorful and modern than a Ladakhi gompa, but less cozy, with a metal roof and a stone, rather than wooden, floor. Some 90 monks of the Nyingma order preside over this monastery. You may be surprised to find monks in Sikkim that ride motorcycles, sport cell phones, and watch television.

Indian tourists swamp **Ganesh Tok,** a look-out point on the outskirts of town, for photo ops. On a clear day the views of the mountains and surrounding Sikkim are gorgeous.

The **Himalayan Zoological Park** (*Rs. 100, Rs 20 for vehicle Daily, 10* AM *to 4* PM) next door to Ganesh Tok in the Bulbulay area, houses snow leopards, musk deer, blue sheep, barking deer, red panda, and other Himalayan creatures. Despite being very spacious (205 hectares), the zoo does not have a large enough collection of animals to be that interesting but the alpine grounds are beautiful to stroll/trek through and offer wonderful views of the Kanchenjunga.

The main thoroughfare, M. G. Road, has a few shops selling colorful choktse tables (small carved writing desks), Buddhist items and interesting brassware—statues, prayer wheels, *dorjes* (ornaments signifying lightning), giant brass or copper oil lamp stands, brass tableware, and prayer bells. You might want to pick up a bottle of Sikkim's famous *paan* liqueur, sold for Rs. 70 in several shops on this road, or a *sonf* (aniseed) liqueur.

For shawls, masks, thankas (silk-scroll paintings), carpets, and choktse tables, try the sales emporium at the **Directorate of Handicrafts and Handloom** (*Zero Point, near Raj Bhavan 3592/202–926*), open 9:30 to 12:30 and 1 to 3 every day but Sunday

Once you escape city boundaries, you're surrounded by tropical forests rich with 600 species of orchids and 46 varieties of rhododendron. Waterfalls splash down mountains, powering prayer wheels. Tidy hamlets with cultivated terrace fields and prayer flags flapping in the breeze populate idyllic valleys. Sikkim's guardian deity, Mt. Kanchenjunga—the world's third-highest peak, at 28,208 feet—is still revered by all who live in its shadow.

The Tibetan border is a short 55 km (34 mi), or three hours, from Gangtok at Nathu La pass, one of the highest motorable roads in the world. Nathu La Pass—430 km (267 mi) from Lhasa—is off-limits to foreign nationals, but the gorgeous **Tsomgo Lake,** also called Changu Lake, 27 km (17 mi) short of Nathu La on the same road (the former Silk Route) is not. A drive up, along a narrow, not-too-smooth road to this lake takes you almost on a cross-country adventure up and down steep hills and valleys, past wee Sikkimese villages and numerous army settlements.

About 31 km (19 mi) out of Gangtok on the same road is the **Kyongnosla Waterfall** and the 31-square-km (12-square-mi) **Kyongnosla Alpine Sanctuary** (*Rs 50 Daily, sunrise to sunset*), famous for its red panda bear and other alpine animals as well as an abundance of wildflowers—especially rhododendrons from May to August. Nearby is a Shiva temple. The waterfall has a clutch of shops and teahouses where you can stop and warm yourself with a piping hot cup of chai.

As you climb higher the land gets somewhat more barren and the typical lush Sikkimese greenery of pines, ferns, orchids, and bamboo gives way to scrub, rocks, shrubs, mountain creeks, and dwarfed evergreens. Under green-roof shelters, medicinal herbs are cultivated. The settlements, with their rusty tin-sheet housing hold communities of yak and goat herders.

Tsomgo or **Changu Lake** is a calm high-altitude (12,400 feet) glacier lake with snowy mountainsides tapering right down to its shores. A stunning bright sapphire blue and one kilometer across, it spreads in oval formation like a lost jewel perched between the forlorn steep peaks in this remote, desolate region. *Tso* (lake) and *mgo* is derived from the Bhutia language and translates to mean "source of the lake." In winter it freezes up and at other times can be covered by dense, chilly, impenetrable fogs.

There's a scrappy, temporary settlement of souvenir stalls and tea stalls at Changu's shores. Locals here eke out an income by renting overdressed/decorated yaks for rides and offering costumes for tourists to try on.

The Nathu La Pass, closed since 1962, was re-opened in 2006 to allow traffic and trade to and from China. The British made strategic use of this pass in the 19th century, sending an expedition under the command of the famous "imperial adventurer" Sir Francis Younghusband up to Tibet through Nathu La with the aim of winning a toehold there and achieving a bit of one-upmanship in the Great Game rivalry that existed between the Russians and the British at the time. The Dalai Lama ironically traveled to India through this pass from an independent Tibet in 1956 for the 2,500th birthday of Lord Buddha, not knowing that he would be back in India two years later. Fleeing Tibetans used the pass to seek refuge in India.

Tourists require a special additional permit to visit Changu Lake. A travel agent can organize that with a little notice (*see* Sikkim & Darjeeling Essentials). Hiring a jeep (preferable on these mountain roads) will set you back approximately Rs. 2,000.

WHERE TO EAT & STAY

$ **✕Baker's Cafe.** Gangtok's trendiest café is sleek and modern, furnished in wood and green granite with wrought-iron tables and chairs. Serving burgers, pizza, and excellent cakes and pastries, it's a warm, lively place to kick back with a cup of coffee after hectic sightseeing. ✉*M. G. Marg, 737101* ☎*3592/220–195* ▭*No credit cards.*

$ ★ **✕Snow Lion.** This popular Chinese and Tibetan restaurant close to Paljor Stadium is within Tibet Hotel. Though its intricate Tibetan decor is housed inside a dark dining room, somehow Snow Lion remains welcoming. Sample the ginger rice, momos, minced chicken with flat noodles, stir-fried mushrooms, and pork fry. Indian food is also offered, but stick with the more tasty Chinese and Tibetan. Service is attentive and meals arrive quickly. ✉*Paljor Stadium Rd.* ☎*3592/222–523* ▭*No credit cards.*

$ **✕Tibet Kitchen.** This upstairs eatery near Hotel Tashi Delek has it in spades; it's simple, clean, authentic, friendly, cheap, and open for breakfast. Highlights are the *then-tuk* (flat-noodle soup), momos, and delicious Tibetan bread with honey; they also serve tasty Chinese food. You can sample home-brewed *chaang* (Tomba local beer) at the small bar. ✉*M. G. Marg* ☎*3592/221–153* ▭*No credit cards.*

$$ Fodor'sChoice ★ **Nor-Khill.** Built in 1932 as a royal guesthouse, Nor-Khill ("house of jewels") has a stately elegance, lovely landscaped gardens, and excellent views from its quiet ridge below the city. Traditional Sikkimese architecture is emphasized throughout, with colorful masks, etchings, antiques and local paintings—especially in the graceful main sitting room. The rooms are decorated with Sikkimese details, such as traditional carpets, choktses, and religious artwork; request a room with a view. Service is excellent and the atmosphere warm and welcoming. The small Shangrila Restaurant serves well-done Sikkimese, North Indian, Chinese, and Western food. The garden, under the shadow of the snowy mountains, shaded by gauzy tent umbrellas, is *the* place for a cup of Darjeeling tea, and the cozy, ornate bar provides an excellent spot to unwind at in the evenings. **Pros:** tasteful decor, fantastic views, good service. **Cons:** room service for only coffee and tea, little far from main square. ✉*Paljor Stadium Rd., 737101* ☎*3592/225–637 or 3592/200–170* 🌐*www.elginhotels.com* *25 rooms, 4 suites* *In-room: no a/c, hot water bottles. In-hotel: restaurant, bar, no elevator, laundry service, public Internet.* ▭*AE, MC, V* *FAP.*

$ **Chumbi Residency.** Built against a hillside, this modern, centrally located hotel is airy and bright, with oodles of white marble. The rooms, which look out over a ridge, are furnished in a pleasing Sikkimese style, with rich green carpets, royal maroon bedspreads—some with elaborate Sikkimese headboards—and wood furniture. Opt for the Jade rooms, which are spacious, very plush, and comfortable. The roomy, elegant suites are a good value. **Pros:** inviting public areas, reasonably priced. **Cons:** Busy, central area. ✉ *Tibet Rd., 737101* ☎ *3592/226–618 or 3592/226–619* 🌐 *www.sikkiminfo.net/chumbi* *26 rooms, 1 suite* *In-room: no a/c. In-hotel: restaurant, no elevator, laundry service.* *AE, MC, V.*

$ **Netuk House.** Staying at this traditional, small Sikkimese hotel is like living in a pleasant Gangtok home. Simple rooms are on the small side but are nevertheless attractive, with wood floors, tasteful Sikkimese furnishings, and a balcony for fresh air. The building, perched on a hill with a view of the valley, is in a quiet garden next to the owner's home. Prices include all meals, and home-style Sikkimese food is served. Call in advance to have a delicious Sikkimese meal here if you are not staying with them. **Pros:** warm, traditional environment; well-prepared food. **Cons:** no generator to combat power cuts, rooms on the small side. ✉ *Tibet Rd., 737101* ☎ *3592/202–374* *3592/226–778* *netukhouse@gmail.com or slg_netuk@sancharnet.in* *10 rooms* *In-room: no a/c, no TV. In-hotel: restaurant, no elevator.* *AE, DC, MC, V* *FAP.*

$ **Tashi Delek.** Don't be fooled by the drab facade: public areas in this modern hotel are bright and decorated in a sort of baroque-Sikkimese style. Conveniently located in the center of town near the taxi stand, traffic noise could be an issue. The guest rooms are simple in comparison and in need of maintenance, but they're pleasant, with carpets and solid wooden furniture. The suites have sitting rooms with Sikkimese decor. Ask for a mountain view, as many rooms have none. The menu at Dragon Hall's includes exotic seasonal greens such as ferns and stinging nettles and excellent Sikkimese *tomba* (millet beer), as well as Indian, Chinese, and Western food. Consider coming here for a Sikkimese meal (Rs. 350 per head) even if you are not staying with them, but they do require a day's notice. In season the rooftop garden is the nicest place in town to enjoy an afternoon meal or drink. **Pros:** good food, conveniently located. **Cons:** noise could be an issue, rooms and restaurant needs better maintenance. ✉ *M. G. Marg, 737101* ☎ *3592/202–991 or 3592/202–038* 🌐 *www.hoteltashidelek.com* *46 rooms, 6 suites* *In-room: no a/c. In-hotel: 2 restaurants, no elevator, laundry service, public Wi-Fi.* *AE, MC, V.*

¢ **Dho Tapu Guest House.** Located in the Deorali area, a few kilometers from the city center, this homey guesthouse in a modern block offers good value, especially for longer stays. The rooms are basic—carpets, dressing table, and clean, well-fitted bathrooms with showers—but comfortable. ✉ *1st fl., SNOD Shopping arcade, Deorali, 737102* ☎ *3592/281–501 or 3592/280–734* *3592/280124* *dhotapu@homail.com* *5 rooms, 3 suites* *In-room: no a/c. In-hotel: restaurant, public Internet.* *No credit cards.*

¢ **Himalayan Heights.** As its name suggests, this five-floor basic, gray facade hotel towers over Paljor Stadium Road. Spotlessly clean, the Heights has great views of Gangtok and the mountains—remember to opt for a top-floor room when booking. Guest rooms are equally clean, with simple, functional decor: small sitting area, Sikkimese pat-

14

tern headboards, and great balconies. Neat bathrooms, done in white tile, have showers. The rooftop café is a nice place to chill out. **Pros:** well-priced and tidy, lovely views. **Cons:** dull decor. ✉*Paljor Stadium Rd., 737101* ☎*3592/221–567 or 3592/221–568* 🌐*www.hotelhimalayanheights.com* *22 rooms* *In-room: no a/c. In-hotel: restaurant, laundry service.* ▭*MC, V.*

¢ **Hotel Tibet.** Owned by the Tibetan government in exile, this modest hotel is where the Dalai Lama stays when he visits, with warm Tibetan furnishings and touches. Guest rooms are plain, with wood floors (some with carpets), Tibetan-motif bedspreads, and clean bathrooms. Opt for the marginally more expensive valley-view rooms. **Pros:** traditional Tibetan touches, delicious food, good value. **Cons:** austere rooms. ✉*Paljor Stadium Rd., 737101* ☎*3592/202–253 or 3592/203–468* 🌐*www.sikkiminfo.net/hoteltibet* *40 rooms 1 suite* *In-room: no a/c. In-hotel: restaurant, no elevator, laundry service.* ▭*AE, MC, V.*

RUMTEK

24 km (15 mi) south of Gangtok.

The great **Rumtek Monastery,** a large, low-lying, multitier building an hour's drive south of Gangtok, is one of the most revered Tibetan Buddhist pilgrimage sites and Sikkim's most important monastery. It's the seat of the Karma Kagyu lineage or the Black Hat order of Tibetan Buddhist monks. Bring your passport, as police sometimes check your inner line permit at the entrance. There has been a shrine at Rumtek since the 16th century, but the monastery building is actually new and mildly gaudy, if impressive for its size and atmosphere. The drive here takes you past terraced fields, woods, and Himlayan peaks. A few minutes from Rumtek are two pleasant rural places to stay. ⏲ *10 AM to 5 PM* *Rs 5; donation inside appropriate.*

WHERE TO STAY

$ ★ **Bamboo Resort.** This eco-friendly mountain hideaway with a traditional ornate facade is tucked away in paddy fields about 1 km short of Rumtek in the village of Sajong. Access is by a steep bumpy road just off the main road; watch out for the hotel sign. Run by a hospitable Sikkimese/Swiss couple, the resort has a spartan but rather classy Sikkimese style; each room has a different bright-color scheme adorned with crisp linens, wood furniture, and cane items. The restaurant, complete with a wood-burning oven and an organic vegetable patch, serves Italian, Swiss, Sikkimese, and North Indian food. There's a children's play area, a meditation hall, a library, and a cozy lounge. **Pros:** warm home ambience, off-the-beaten-path authenticity. **Cons:** away from everything, doesn't accept credit cards. ✉*Sajong, 1 km from Rumtek, 737101* ☎*92325/13090, 3592/252–516 or 3592/286–649 in Gangtok* 🌐*www.sikkim.ch/bamboo-resort.html* *12 rooms* *In-room: no a/c, no phone, no TV. In-hotel: restaurant, spa, bicycles, laundry service, no elevator.* ▭*No credit cards* 🍽*FAP.*

$ **Shambhala Mountain Resort.** About one kilometer before Rumtek on the Gangtok–Rumtek Road, Shambhala is a spacious lodge whose lobby has a high ceiling, a flagstone floor, and blond-wood trimmings. The large rooms are immaculate, airy, and pleasing to the eye, with a continuing accent on wood—even the bathroom is lined with wood. Mandala-type designs adorn the wall. Each room has a little balcony. More intriguing are the four cottages a few furlongs from the hotel in the wilderness. Each cottage has a different style reflecting the types of homes found in Sikkim: Bhutia, Lepcha, and Nepali. The hotel can organize transport to Gangtok. **Pros:** lovely location, quiet solitary vibe. **Cons:** no backup generator, far from Gangtok. *Rumtek, 737135* *3592/252–240 or 3592/252–243* *16 rooms, 4 cottages* *In-room: no a/c, no phone, no TV. In-hotel: restaurant, bar, no elevator, laundry service.* *No credit cards.*

THE SIKKIM SPECIAL

To get a taste of the local brew, try *tomba* (also called *chaang),* which is served in a traditional bamboo or wood mug with a bamboo straw. Initially you receive a cupful of dryish, but strong-smelling fermented millets sprinkled with a few grains of rice. That's topped with steaming water and allowed to mull for a few minutes. The result? A milky-white beer that tastes a bit like sake but without the alcoholic wallop.

14

PELLING

117 km (73 mi) west of Gangtok.

After two or three days in and around Gangtok, you may want to travel toward Kanchenjunga by making a four- to five-hour trip to Pelling for the full Sikkim experience. As you head west, the scenery is stunning nearly every kilometer of the way: traditional Sikkim farms, orchards, terraced fields, and breathtaking mountain vistas.

★ Pelling is a tiny provincial town with just one sight: **Mt. Kanchenjunga.** People flock here to view the grand peak by dawn. Perched at a height, the town looks down on lakes, gorges, glaciers, forests, farmland, and the flat valley where the town of Yoksum marks the start of the Dzongri Trail.

On a lonely hilltop in the midst of a forest, peering down at Darjeeling and the swift Rangeet River, is the unforgettable serene 18th-century **Pemayangtse Monastery,** an important religious seat near Pelling. The monastery is a site of exquisite woodwork, statues and sculpture, lovely thangkas and murals, and Buddhist texts. This is Sikkim's finest monastery and is highly revered; each building here, surrounded by exuberantly flowering gardens, has carved ancient gateways, colorful trimming, classic Sikkimese style, and is wonderful to behold. The monastery, located at 8,460 feet, is run by some 100 monks, belonging to the mostly highly respected "pure monk" Nyigma order, hailing from Bhutia families. The head monk of this monastery was the only individual with the rights to crown the king of Sikkim. In days gone by, Pemayangste monks would journey to Mindoling Monastery in Tibet for higher learning. (*Pemayangtse* translates as "perfect sublime lotus.") Inside the shrine, where cameras and footwear are not allowed, exists a memorial to Lhatsun Chenpo who established this monastery and a collection of antique idols and sculpture. Most breathtaking is the extensive and detailed seven-tiered miniature representation of Sanghthokpalri, the mahagurus' heavenly palace, on the top floor, which will have a definite appeal for children. Crafted by one man—Dungzin Rimpoche—over five years, it incorporates pagodas, gardens, temples, fountains, animals, demons, Bodhisattvas, lamas, and bridges, all delicately modeled in this approximately 10-foot-by-10-foot glassed-in diorama. *Rs. 10 Daily 6:30–4.*

WHERE TO STAY

$ Fodor'sChoice ★ **Mount Pandim.** Perched on a hillside, quite close to the age-old Pemayangtse Monastery, this is one of the prettiest and best-located hotels in Sikkim. Once a summer haven of the Sikkim royal family, then a government-owned lodge, Mount Pandim was taken over by the Elgin hotel group and renovated in 2007. A grand view of Kanchenjunga filling your window is the stunning centerpiece of each room. The guest rooms are elegantly furnished with shining wood floors, silk bedspreads, drapes and cushions in dark green and red, snowy white linen, and Tibetan carpets; granite and wood-lined bathrooms complete the look. The hotel's Heritage is preserved in the lobby's main drawing room and dining room: period furniture, gilt-and-brown choktses, and Sikkimese portraiture project a warm, friendly ambience. Well-prepared meals—a mixture of Indian and Continental—are served. **Pros:** the garden is one more place to watch the Five Treasures of the Snow at dawn or dusk or under moonlight. **Cons:** no Internet services. *Pemayangtse 737113 3595/250–756 or 3595/250–353 www.elginhotels.com 24 rooms In-room: no a/c, hot water bottles. In-hotel: restaurant, bar, no elevator. AE, D, MC, V.*

$ **Norbu Ghang Resort.** This is really one of the few comfortable, cheery places to stay in Pelling. The hotel is built around a garden at the edge of a flat hilltop, with an envious view of Kanchenjunga. Rise at dawn, order a cup of coffee, and watch the revered peak turn an awesome array of hues until finally it glows pink. The rooms are simple, with red carpets, cheery Sikkim-print bedspreads and furnishings, and individual balconies; the cottages, with their own little porches, are even cozier. Norbu Ghang also runs a nearby lodge with rooms for Rs. 800. **Pros:** great vistas, peaceful. **Cons:** no back-up generator, bare-bones decor. *Pelling 737113 3595/250–566 or 3595/258–245 3595/258–271 norbugang@sify.com www.sikkiminfo.net/norbughang 35 rooms, 4 suites, 21 cottages In-room: no a/c. In-hotel: restaurant, bar, no elevator. MC, V.*

DARJEELING & SIKKIM ESSENTIALS

To research prices, get advice from other travelers, and book travel arrangements, visit www.fodors.com.

AIR TRAVEL

Flying is the quickest way to reach Bagdogra, but flight schedules can be thrown off, especially in winter, by variable weather in the mountains and stubborn winter fog in Delhi. Prepare for long delays on either end. It's crucial to double-check the flight schedule with the airline a few hours before departure. If a flight gets canceled overnight because of weather, the airline is sometimes liable to put you up for the night, put you on another day's flight, or give you a full refund depending on the fine print in your ticket.

The airport at Bagdogra, West Bengal, is about 90 km (56 mi) southeast of Darjeeling and 124 km (77 mi) south of Gangtok. Jet Airways, Kingfisher, Simplifly Deccan, and Indian Airlines fly daily from Kolkata and Delhi. Hire a car from Bagdogra to Darjeeling (a three-hour drive), or taxi the 15 km (9 mi) to New Jalpaiguri to catch the Toy train (⇨ *Train Travel*). For Sikkim, hop on one of the jeeps that make the four- to five-hour run from Bagdogra to Gangtok. Sikkim Tourism also runs a five-passenger helicopter between Bagdogra and Gangtok; it times its departure with the flights arriving in Bagdogra from Delhi and Kolkata, departing at 2 PM for Gangtok. The journey takes a half hour and costs Rs. 1,500 per head.

Carriers **Air India (formerly Indian Airlines)** (☎ *33/2511–9433 in Kolkata, 3592/223–354 in Gangtok, 354/225–4230 or 354/225–231 in Darjeeling, 353/251–1495 or 353/255–1666 in Bagdogra, 353/251–1495 in Siliguri* 🌐 *www.airindia.com*).

Jet Airways (☎ *33 33/2511–9894 in Kolkata, 353/243–5876, 353/243–5877, or 353/255–1588 in Bagdogra* 🌐 *www.jetairways.com*).

Sikkim Tourism Development Corporation (☎ *3592/222–634 in Gangtok, 3592/225–277 at Gangtok helipad, 353/2698–036 in Bagdogra, 353/253–1219 in Siliguri* 🌐 *www.sikkiminfo.net*).

AIRPORTS

Local airports can be useful for travel information after hours or on holidays, when airline offices have closed.

Airport Information **Bagdogra** (☎ *353/255–1431 or 353/255–1192*).

BUS TRAVEL

Bus fares are a tiny fraction of what it costs to travel by hired car, but non-air-conditioned (ordinary class, state-run) buses are not recommended. The handiwork of their drivers produces severe motion sickness, not to mention serious accidents, and they tend to make frequent stops and take unnecessary breaks. Air-conditioned deluxe buses are safer—opt for the most expensive category, such as a Volvo or picture-window coach with good suspension; check out the bus before buying a ticket, and travel only by day. Deluxe coaches usually depart from roughly the same stands as state buses, and seat reservations are usually not required; a travel agent or hotel can help you make arrangements.

14

CARS & DRIVERS

Most Himalayan drives involve endlessly winding, often bumpy, sometimes precarious roads on the edges of steep slopes. If you're prone to motion sickness, carry medication and eat light meals before and during your journey. Even more important, rent a heavy and powerful car. Jeeps (the Sumo or Qualis models) are sturdy but not that speedy; a solid sedan car such as a Hyundai, Innova, or Esteem moves faster. Do *not* take a Maruti van, as it's not heavy enough to be safe. Rates are higher in Darjeeling and Sikkim compared to elsewhere in India. Expect to pay as much as Rs. 13–Rs. 16 per kilometer for a non-air-conditioned diesel jeep, a bit more for a better car. If your driver will be staying with you the entire time, the daily tip you give the driver (over and above the initially agreed-upon charge) should cover his meal costs.

Night driving in the hills is extremely dangerous and must be avoided at all costs.

CELL PHONES

If you have a cell phone, purchase a calling card with roaming facilities in Kolkata, or Delhi before you go—just pop into an STD phone shop in the nearest market with your travel documents handy. Connectivity is decent in most places, except when traveling between towns in Sikkim and from Darjeeling to Siliguri. Don't expect to have connectivity at say Changu Lake and other such tiny spots.

EMERGENCIES

East–West Medical Centre, based in New Delhi, has an air ambulance for urgent evacuations from the remotest parts of India, Pakistan, Nepal, and Bhutan. The experienced staff in the 24-hour alarm center can recommend a network of medical centers, hospitals, and doctors throughout India.

Contacts **East-West Medical Centre** (✉ *38 Golf Links, New Delhi* ☎ *11/2629-3701, 11/2629-3702, 11/2462-3738, 11/2464-1494, 11/2469-9229, 11/2469-0429, or 11/2469-8865* *airambulance@eastwestrescue.com* *www.eastwestrescue.com*).

INTERNET, MAIL & SHIPPING

Internet café are all over Darjeeling; a couple dot Chowrasta. At Gangtok, Internet cafés are harder to find and often connections are poor.

The main post office in Darjeeling is opposite the new Rink Mall on Laden La Road. In Gangtok the main post office is at Paljor Stadium Road close to Tibet Hotel.

Internet Cafés **Komputech visio, Super market** (✉ *Denzong Cinema Rd., Sikkim* ☎ *03592/227-684*). **Glenary's** (✉ *Nehru Rd., Darjeeling* ☎ *354/225-4122*).

MONEY

ATMS ATMs are all over Darjeeling, Siliguri, and Bagdogra. Gangtok has several ATMs and even smaller Sikkim towns may have at least one. Finding either an HDFC, ICICI, or SBI ATM is not difficult and you can withdraw money against a Master Card, Visa, and Amex (not at SBI) at these ATMs.

CURRENCY EXCHANGE Try to carry American Express traveler's checks, as you might have a problem cashing Thomas Cook checks in smaller towns. Checks can sometimes be cashed at your hotel or a local bank; just note that most banks keep short hours, 10–2 weekdays and 10–noon on Saturday. There's a State Bank of India in just about every town. If you're curious about smaller towns, check the full list of branches on the bank's Web site.

Banks & Exchange Services **State Bank of India** (✉ *2 Laden La Rd., Darjeeling* ☎ *354/225–2788 or 354/225–3215* 🌐 *www.statebankofindia.com/branchlocator.jsp*).

PERMITS

You need an Inner Line Permit to enter the state of Sikkim and additional permits (Restricted Area or Protected Area Permits) to move closer to the China border. The Sikkim permit is good for 15 days, and you can get it within 24 hours at any Indian embassy or consulate overseas, the Sikkim Tourist Information Centres (⇨ Visitor Information) in Delhi, Kolkata, or Siliguri or—if you don't mind waiting a half hour—at the border post at Rongpo (the easiest method; keep Xeroxes and photographs handy). If you apply in advance, you must specify your date of entry into Sikkim. A 15-day extension is available in Gangtok from the Tashiling Secretariat (Home Department); one more 15-day extension brings you to the permitted total of 45 days. After that, you may not re-enter Sikkim within three months. No special permit is needed for Khecheopari Lake, Yuksom, Pelling (Pemayangtse), or Tashiling in western Sikkim, but for points beyond these, you need to travel with a government-recognized tour operator, and often in a group of at least four people. The tour company will take care of the paperwork. For further details about the kind of permits required check the Sikkim government's Web site: 🌐 *http://sikkim.nic.in/homedept/ilpfaqs.htm*

TRAIN TRAVEL

Overnight trains go from Kolkata's Sealdah Station to New Jalpaiguri—the most convenient being the daily Darjeeling Mail (has first a/c and second a/c rail accommodations) or otherwise the thrice-weekly Uttar Banga Express (second a/c accommodations only)—and from New Jalpaiguri station you can grab a taxi for the three- to four-hour drive to Darjeeling. Serious rail enthusiasts should board the famous Toy train for a stunning but very slow eight-hour journey up a series of hairpin turns through terraced fields. If you prefer not to spend eight hours covering 90 km (56 mi), you can always experience the Toy train as an excursion from Darjeeling.

Most people headed for Sikkim need to transfer from the train station to Siliguri bus stand, West Bengal. From here, shared jeeps (Rs. 130) can take you on to Gangtok, 114 km (71 mi) away, in four hours.

TRAVEL AGENTS & TOURS

Modern Tours and Travels offers treks in western Sikkim, with excellent food and service. Tashila Tours and Travels leads the way in rafting on the beautiful Teesta and Rangeet rivers. Tenzing Norgay Adventures is run by the sons of Norgay Tenzing, who climbed Mt. Everest with Sir Edmund Hillary. In addition to physical and cultural adventures in Sikkim, they lead expeditions to Nepal, Bhutan, and Tibet.

Contacts **Bayul Tours** (*Below C.P.W.D office, Bajra Cinema Hall Rd., Gangtok 3592/228-341 www.bayultours.com beyul@yahoo.co.uk or bayul@hotmail.com*).

Blue Sky Tours and Travels (*Lachung Khangsar, Tibet Rd., Gangtok 3592/225-113 or 3592/223-330 www.himalayantourismonline.com/home.htm*). **Club Side Tours** (*J P Sharma Rd., off Laden La Rd., Darjeeling 354/254-646 www.clubside.in*). **Modern Tours and Travels** (*Opposite Sikkim Tourist Information Centre, Traffic Point, M. G. Marg, Gangtok 3592/227-319 moderntourtreks@hotmail.com*). **Namgyal Treks and Tours** (*Tibet Rd., Gangtok 3592/203-701 www.namgyaltreks.net*). **Sikkim Taxi Owner Association** (*Near head post office, Gangtok 3592/232-391 or 98320/97331 ask for Pemba Bhutia: good driver but slightly expensive*). **Siniolchu Tours and Travels** (*Paljor Stadium Rd., Gangtok 3592/205-569*). **Tashila Tours and Travels** (*NH-31A, P.B. No. 70, Gangtok 3592/202-979 www.tashila.com/sikkim/index.html*). **Vinayak Travels** (*L. M. Moulik Complex, Hill Cart Rd., Siliguri 3593/253-1067 hotelvinayak@hotmail.com*)**Yak and Yeti Travels** (*Hotel Super View, Zero Point, Gangtok 94341/17418, 97332/14205, or 92335/22344 www.yaknyeti.com*). **Tenzing Norgay Adventures** (*1 D. B. Giri Rd., Darjeeling 354/225-3718 www.tenzing-norgay.com*).

VISITOR INFORMATION

Tourist Offices **Sikkim** (*14 Panchsheel Marg, Chanakyapuri, New Delhi 11/2611-5346 4/1 Middleton St., Kolkata 33/2281-5328 SNT Bus Compound, Tenzing Norgay Rd., Siliguri 353/251-2646, 353/255-1036 Bagdogra Airport M. G. Marg, Gangtok 3592/221-634 or 3592/227-720 or 03592/203423 Tourist Lodge, Rangpo 03592/240818*). **West Bengal** (*Silver Fir Bldg., The Mall, Darjeeling 354/225-5351 or 354/225-4214*).

India Essentials

PLANNING TOOLS, EXPERT INSIGHT, GREAT CONTACTS

There are planners and there are those who, excuse the pun, fly by the seat of their pants. We happily place ourselves among the planners. Our writers and editors try to anticipate all the issues you may face before and during any journey, and then they do their research. This section is the product of their efforts. Use it to get excited about your trip to India, to inform your travel planning, or to guide you on the road should the seat of your pants start to feel threadbare.

GETTING STARTED

We're really proud of our Web site: Fodors.com is a great place to begin any journey. Scan Travel Wire for suggested itineraries, travel deals, restaurant and hotel openings, and other up-to-the-minute info. Check out Booking to research prices and book plane tickets, hotel rooms, rental cars, and vacation packages. Head to Talk for on-the-ground pointers from travelers who frequent our message boards. You can also link to loads of other travel-related resources.

RESOURCES

ONLINE TRAVEL TOOLS

India is everywhere on the World Wide Web, so use it to help plan your trip. A good starting place is *www.incredibleindia.org*, the official Web site of India's Ministry of Tourism.

ALL ABOUT INDIA

The national newspaper *Indian Express* (*www.indianexpress.com*) is widely acclaimed for its investigative journalism and unique angles on national issues. A first of its kind in India, the local search engine (*www.onyomo.com*) went live in 2006 and was designed for locals who need to find restaurants, salons, cinemas, florists, etc. It's also good for tourists who want to explore the big metro areas without having to rely on the hotel's concierge. Looking for all the movie theaters close to your hotel in Mumbai? You can do that here. If you have a mobile phone you can also get contact information and directions sent via text messages. Rediff (*www.rediff.com*) dissects current events and pop culture across India.

Currency Conversion Google (*www.google.com*) does currency conversion. Just type in the amount you want to convert and an explanation of how you want it converted (e.g., "14 Swiss francs in dollars"), and then voilà. **Oanda.com** (*www.oanda.com*) also allows you to print out a handy table with the current day's conversion rates. **XE.com** (*www.xe.com*) is a good currency conversion Web site.

Safety Transportation Security Administration (*TSA; www.tsa.gov*).

Time Zones Timeanddate.com (*www.timeanddate.com/worldclock*) can help you figure out the correct time anywhere.

Weather Accuweather.com (*www.accuweather.com*) is an independent weather-forecasting service. **Weather.com** (*www.weather.com*) is the Web site for the Weather Channel.

Other Resources CIA World Factbook (*www.odci.gov/cia/publications/factbook/index.html*) has profiles of every country in the world. It's a good source if you need some quick facts and figures.

VISITOR INFORMATION

The America-based Indian tourism offices of the Indian government will send information such as brochures and CDs, but cannot help arrange any travel. It's better to call to request information—trying to get a response by e-mail usually doesn't work.

Contacts Ministry of Tourism (*800/953–9399 or 213/380–8855 www.incredibleindia.org*).

THINGS TO CONSIDER

GOVERNMENT ADVISORIES

As different countries have different world views, look at travel advisories from a range of governments to get more of a sense of what's going on out there. And be sure to parse the language carefully. For example, a warning to "avoid all travel" carries more weight than one urging you to "avoid nonessential travel," and both are much stronger than a plea to "exercise caution." A U.S. government travel warning is more permanent (though not necessarily more serious) than a so-called public announcement, which carries an expiration date.

The U.S. Department of State's Web site has more than just travel warnings and advisories. The consular information sheets issued for every country have general safety tips, entry requirements (though be sure to verify these with the country's embassy), and other useful details.

The U.S. Department of State generally does not list broad travel warnings for India because the majority of the country is safe for tourists. Still, there are a few unstable areas. Some terrorist groups operate in the state of Jammu and Kashmir, and the U.S. government advises tourists not to go there with the exception of the Ladakh region. Traveling close to the India–Pakistan border is also not recommended. The Indian government restricts travel to the Indian states of Mizoram, Manipur, Nagaland, Arunachal Pradesh, and Sikkim, and advanced permission from the Ministry of Home Affairs (MHA) is required to visit these places. Indian embassies and consulates abroad can also assit with obtaining permits, and an Indian travel agent or tour operator can help as well.

General Information & Warnings U.S. Department of State (*www.travel.state.gov*).

GEAR

India is full of beautiful, colorful, over-the-top fashions, but your visit here probably shouldn't include lots of fancy things from your own closet. Make it a point to buy Indian statement pieces during your travels if that's your thing, keeping the original contents of your suitcase simple: shirts made of plain cottons or cotton-synthetic blends and a couple of pairs of comfortable pants—all of which can be washed easily and worn again throughout your trip. Avoiding completely synthetic fabrics that don't breathe is key, since a majority of India is hot year-round, with temperatures topping 100 degrees or more in the summer months. Delicate fabrics just don't respond well to vigorous Indian laundering techniques and powerful detergents, let alone profuse amounts of sweat. Dry cleaning is available across every city and in all major hotels, but even if you think it's a safe bet, quality can vary significantly among dry cleaners, and they tend to use harsh chemicals.

Don't worry about looking too casual—India is not a dressy society. If an upscale function or fancy dinner at a big-city restaurant is on the itinerary, men can often get away with just a formal shirt and pants. Women can wear a simple dress or a dressier blouse with trousers and heels.

To top everything off, bring sunglasses, a bottle of high-SPF sunblock (the amount of protection among sunblocks sold in India is questionable) and two good pairs of footwear—sandals with rubber soles and lightweight walking shoes are smart options. Skip anything that's difficult to maneuver in, such as hiking boots—unless you'll be trekking in the north—since you'll often be required to remove your shoes to enter religious spots.

Most importantly, dress modestly, especially at sacred sights that call for the utmost respect. In those situations, long pants are appropriate for men; for women, stick to below-the-knee skirts, dresses, or neat pants. T-shirts are fine, but the male topless look should be left to wandering sadhus (Hindu ascetics). Women should always avoid wearing tight tank tops or tops that are sheer or have plunging necklines. It's not that Indian women never wear revealing clothing, but foreigners wearing such items often attract unwanted attention. If you must wear shorts, keep them on the long side, since only children can get away with short shorts. Avoid doing odd things like wearing a long Indian tunic as a dress or a sari blouse as a top. Bathing suits should be on the conservative side, but women should feel free to wear bikinis at beach resorts and large hotels that cater to a foreign clientele.

Things to keep handy at all times are toilet paper, moist towlettes, and hand sanitizer, especially on long train trips. Almost no public restroom—when you can find one—provides toilet paper or a way to thoroughly wash hands. In any case, there won't be any hand towels, so a handkerchief for drying your hands is also useful. Consider also carrying a money pouch or belt, a medical kit with basic first-aid, and a small flashlight. Good sanitary napkins are sold in India, but women should pack their own tampons unless they don't mind using ones without applicators, which are generally the only kind readily available in India.

If you visit in monsoon season, bring a collapsible umbrella. Instead of bringing your own rainboots, buy a cheap pair once you arrive. Locals call them gum shoes. In winter, bring a sweater or a light jacket for cool evenings, and if you plan to spend time in the Himalayas, bring a warm wardrobe. Plan to triple layer with long underwear, wool sweaters, and a lightweight, waterproof down coat. Bulky down parkas are advisable only for winter excursions or a climb into higher altitudes. A pair of lined Gore-Tex over-pants is indispensable when you're thrashing through wet underbrush.

Most adventure-travel firms supply sleeping bags for their clients. If you're roughing it on your own, choose a lightweight sleeping bag with an outer shell. You don't need a bag designed for an assault on a mountain peak unless that's the trip you've planned. A down bag guaranteed to keep you warm at 15°F (-9° C; a fairly low temperature in the Himalayan trekking season) is adequate. If you plan to take overnight trains, consider a sleeping-bag liner. On any outdoor adventure, long or short, assemble a day pack for your sweater, camera, moist towelettes, and plastic water bottle. Trekkers should also pack out their nonbiodegradable garbage and bury biodegradable refuse away from water sources. Use a trekking agency that carries kerosene for cooking.

PASSPORTS & VISAS

Unless you hold an Indian passport or are a citizen of Nepal or Bhutan, you need a visa to enter India. This applies to children and infants as well.

Info Indian Consulate General (*www.indiacgny.org*). **Indian Embasssy** (*www.indianembassy.org*). **Travisa** (*http://indiavisa.travisaoutsourcing.com*).

PASSPORTS

U.S. passports are valid for 10 years. You must apply in person if you're getting a passport for the first time; if your previous passport was lost, stolen, or damaged; or if your previous passport has expired and was issued more than 15 years ago or when you were under 16. All children under 18 must appear in person to apply for or renew a passport. Both parents must accompany any child under 14 (or send a notarized statement with their permission) and provide proof of their relationship to the child.

■ TIP→ Before your trip, make two copies of your passport's data page (one for someone at home and another for you to carry separately). Or scan the page and e-mail it to someone at home and/or yourself.

There are 13 regional passport offices, as well as 7,000 passport acceptance facilities in post offices, public libraries, and other governmental offices. If you're renewing a passport, you can do so by mail. Forms are available at passport acceptance facilities and online.

The cost to apply for a new passport is $97 for adults, $82 for children under 16; renewals are $67. Allow six weeks for processing, both for first-time passports and renewals. For an expediting fee of $60 you can reduce this time to about two weeks. If your trip is less than two weeks away, you can get a passport even more rapidly by going to a passport office with the necessary documentation. Private expediters can get things done in as little as 48 hours, but charge hefty fees for their services.

VISAS

A visa is essentially formal permission to enter a country. Following a world trend, the Indian Embassy started outsourcing the visa application process in October of 2007 to a company called Travisa Outsourcing, Inc. Consequently, at this writing the embassay and its consulates no longer handle visa issues, except on an emergency basis. Instead, you must go to Travisa's Web site to get the process started, which includes submitting an online application and submitting payment electronically. A standard, multiple-entry six-month tourist visa costs US$60, plus a US$13 service fee, for American citizens. Non-U.S. citizens pay different fees. If you're traveling on business or as a student or journalist, you require a different (and more expensive) visa.

Travisa has offices in Washington, New York, Chicago, San Francisco, and Houston, and you can submit your passport in person at those locations. However, the preferred method is by a trackable mail service such as FedEx. Refer to the Travisa Web site for detailed instructions. Your Indian visa should be processed within five days from the time Travisa receives your passport, but start the process at least two weeks before your departure to allow for glitches.

As far as the visa's validity goes, the clock starts ticking the day the government issues you one, not the day you arrive in India, so note the expiration date. You must enter and leave during the specified time period, and your passport must have a remaining validity of at least six months. If you need to extend your visa, go to the Foreigners' Regional Registration Office in one of the major cities. But beware—the Indian government makes it extremely difficult to extend a visa for any reason, and if you overstay your visa, you may be required to get clearance from India's Ministry of Home Affairs to leave the country. Punishment can range from heavy fines to actually being jailed. Bottom line—follow the visa rules and don't expect exceptions to be made, even if you think you have a good excuse.

U.S. Passport Information U.S. Department of State (☎ *877/487–2778* 🌐 *http://travel.state.gov/passport*).

U.S. Passport & Visa Expediters A. Briggs Passport & Visa Expeditors (☎ *800/806–0581 or 202/338–0111* 🌐 *www.abriggs.com*). **American Passport Express** (☎ *800/455–5166 or 800/841–6778* 🌐 *www.americanpassport.com*). **Passport Express** (☎ *800/362–8196* 🌐 *www.passportexpress.com*). **Travel Document Systems** (☎ *800/874–5100 or 202/638–3800* 🌐 *www.traveldocs.com*). **Travel the World Visas** (☎ *866/886–8472 or 301/495–7700* 🌐 *www.world-visa.com*).

GENERAL REQUIREMENTS FOR INDIA	
Passport	Must be valid for 6 months after date of arrival
Visa	Required for Americans ($60 plus $13 service fee)
Vaccinations	None required
Driving	International driver's license required; CDW is compulsory on car rentals and will be included in the quoted price
Departure Tax	None

SHOTS & MEDICATIONS

No vaccination certificate or inoculations are required to enter India from the United States, Canada, or the United Kingdom unless you're coming via Africa, in which case you'll need proof of inoculation against yellow fever. If you're coming from Africa, it's crucial to have proof of inoculation against yellow fever or you could be quarantined on arrival in dismal government facilities.

Ultimately you must decide what vaccinations are right for you before you travel to India. Talk to your doctor about vaccinations three months before departure. The Centers for Disease Control and Prevention post a list of recommended vaccinations for the Indian subcontinent on its Web site; these include hepatitis and typhoid fever.

In areas where malaria and dengue—both carried by mosquitoes—are prevalent, use mosquito nets, wear clothing that covers the body, apply repellent containing DEET, and use spray for flying insects in living and sleeping areas. On arrival in India, consider purchasing repellants that plug into the wall and release a mosquito-repelling scent. These are effective in keeping a room mosquito-free and can be found in any market. Also seriously consider taking antimalaria pills, as malaria is common even in the big cities. There's no vaccine to combat malaria and dengue.

You don't necessarily need to lug a medicine cabinet with you to India—practically every over-the-counter medication and medical supply under the sun is available in the big cities should you need them. While traveling in remote areas or in small towns, it's a good idea to have a medical kit containing a pain reliever, diarrhea medication, moist towelettes, antibacterial skin ointment and skin cleanser, antacids, adhesive bandages, and any prescriptions.

■TIP→ If you travel a lot internationally—particularly to developing nations—refer to the CDC's Health Information for International Travel (aka Traveler's Health Yellow Book). Info from it is posted on the CDC Web site (🌐 www.cdc.gov/travel/yb), or you can buy a copy from your local bookstore for $24.95.

For more information see Health under On the Ground in India.

Health Warnings National Centers for Disease Control & Prevention (*CDC ☎ 877/394–8747 international travelers' health line 🌐 www.cdc.gov/travel*). **World Health Organization** (*WHO 🌐 www.who.int*).

TRIP INSURANCE

What kind of coverage do you honestly need? Do you even need trip insurance at all? Take a deep breath and read on.

We believe that comprehensive trip insurance is especially valuable if you're booking a very expensive or complicated trip (particularly to an isolated region) or if you're booking far in advance. Who knows what could happen six months down the road? But whether or not you get insurance has more to do with how comfortable you are assuming all that risk yourself.

Comprehensive travel policies typically cover trip-cancellation and interruption, letting you cancel or cut your trip short because of a personal emergency, illness, or, in some cases, acts of terrorism in your destination. Such policies also cover evacuation and medical care. Some also cover you for trip delays because of bad weather or mechanical problems as well as for lost or delayed baggage. Another type of coverage to look for is financial default—that is, when your trip is disrupted because a tour operator, airline, or cruise line goes out of business. Generally you must buy this when you book your trip or shortly thereafter, and it's only available to you if your operator isn't on a list of excluded companies.

If you're going abroad, consider buying medical-only coverage at the very least. Neither Medicare nor some private insurers cover medical expenses

Trip Insurance Resources

INSURANCE COMPARISON SITES		
Insure My Trip.com	800/487-4722	www.insuremytrip.com
Square Mouth.com	800/240-0369	www.quotetravelinsurance.com
COMPREHENSIVE TRAVEL INSURERS		
Access America	866/807-3982	www.accessamerica.com
CSA Travel Protection	800/873-9855	www.csatravelprotection.com
HTH Worldwide	610/254-8700 or 888/243-2358	www.hthworldwide.com
Travelex Insurance	888/457-4602	www.travelex-insurance.com
Travel Guard International	715/345-0505 or 800/826-4919	www.travelguard.com
Travel Insured International	800/243-3174	www.travelinsured.com
MEDICAL-ONLY INSURERS		
International Medical Group	800/628-4664	www.imglobal.com
International SOS	215/942-8000 or 713/521-7611	www.internationalsos.com
Wallach & Company	800/237-6615 or 504/687-3166	www.wallach.com

anywhere outside of the United States (including time aboard a cruise ship, even if it leaves from a U.S. port). Medical-only policies typically reimburse you for medical care (excluding that related to pre-existing conditions) and hospitalization abroad, and provide for evacuation. You still have to pay the bills and await reimbursement from the insurer, though.

Expect comprehensive travel insurance policies to cost about 4% to 7% or 8% of the total price of your trip (it's more like 8%–12% if you're over age 70). A medical-only policy may or may not be cheaper than a comprehensive policy. Always read the fine print of your policy to make sure that you are covered for the risks that are of most concern to you. Compare several policies to make sure you're getting the best price and range of coverage available.

BOOKING YOUR TRIP

Unless your cousin is a travel agent, you're probably among the millions of people who make most of their travel arrangements online.

But have you ever wondered just what the differences are between an online travel agent (a Web site through which you make reservations instead of going directly to the airline, hotel, or car-rental company), a discounter (a firm that does a high volume of business with a hotel chain or airline and accordingly gets good prices), a wholesaler (one that makes cheap reservations in bulk and then re-sells them to people like you), and an aggregator (one that compares all the offerings so you don't have to)?

ONLINE

You really have to shop around. A travel wholesaler such as Hotels.com or Hotel-Club.net can be a source of good rates, as can discounters such as Hotwire or Priceline, particularly if you can bid for your hotel room or airfare. Indeed, such sites sometimes have deals that are unavailable elsewhere. They do, however, tend to work only with hotel chains (which makes them just plain useless for getting hotel reservations outside of major cities) or big airlines (so that often leaves out upstarts like jetBlue and some foreign carriers like Air India).

Also, with discounters and wholesalers you must generally prepay, and everything is nonrefundable. And before you fork over the dough, be sure to check the terms and conditions, so you know what a given company will do for you if there's a problem and what you'll have to deal with on your own.

Booking engines like Expedia, Travelocity, and Orbitz are actually travel agents, albeit high-volume, online ones. And airline travel packagers like American Airlines Vacations and Virgin Vacations—well, they're travel agents, too. But they may still not work with all the world's hotels.

An aggregator site will search many sites and pull the best prices for airfares, hotels, and rental cars from them. Most aggregators compare the major travel-booking sites such as Expedia, Travelocity, and Orbitz; some also look at airline Web sites, though rarely the sites of smaller budget airlines. Some aggregators also compare other travel products, including complex packages—a good thing, as you can sometimes get the best overall deal by booking an air-and-hotel package.

WITH A TRAVEL AGENT

If you use an agent—brick-and-mortar or virtual—you'll pay a fee for the service. And know that the service you get from some online agents isn't comprehensive. For example Expedia and Travelocity don't search for prices on budget airlines like jetBlue, Southwest, or small foreign carriers. That said, some agents (online or not) *do* have access to fares that are difficult to find otherwise, and the savings can more than make up for any surcharge.

A knowledgeable brick-and-mortar travel agent can be a godsend if you're booking a cruise, a package trip that's not available to you directly, an air pass, or a complicated itinerary. What's more, travel agents that specialize in a destination may have exclusive access to certain deals and insider information on things such as charter flights. Agents who specialize in types of travelers (senior citizens, gays and lesbians, naturists) or types of trips (cruises, luxury travel, safaris) can also be invaluable.

TIP→Remember that Expedia, Travelocity, and Orbitz are travel agents, not just booking engines. To resolve any problems

with a reservation made through these companies, contact them first.

Complain about the surcharges all you like, but when things don't work out the way you'd hoped, it's nice to have an agent to put things right.

Using a travel agent for a trip to India is often a good idea, especially for travel within the country itself. Booking a round-trip ticket to Delhi through a travel agent at this writing resulted in a savings of about $300 (fares usually start around $1,500 for a round-trip). However, the itinerary to Delhi included two flight changes and hours of waiting between flights—not so bad if you'll be gone for six weeks, impractical if you're staying just seven days. Travelers should still scour the Internet for deals to India, because the possibilities are endless. Choosing a travel agent that specializes in India will often result in lower fares. One drawback to booking with a traditional travel agent is they might still issue paper tickets, which means one more thing to keep track of.

Agent Resources American Society of Travel Agents (☎ *703/739–2782* 🌐 *www.travelsense.org*).

India Travel Agents Joy Travels (✉ *74–75 Scindia House, Connaught Pl., New Delhi, India 110001* ☎ *11/233–12768 or 12769* 🌐 *www.joy-travels.com*) **Travel Pros Inc.** (✉ *112 Highway 34, Matawan, NJ 07747* ☎ *732/727–4447* 🌐 *www.travelprosusa.com*) **RBS Tours and Travels** (✉ *Shop A-1, Hotel Connaught Place, 37 Shaheed Bhagat Singh Marg, New Delhi, India 110001* ☎ *11/233–64603 or 11/233–64592* 🌐 *www.rbstravels.com*).

ACCOMMODATIONS

Staying in India is can be a pleasure, regardless of whether you've paid top price at a national luxury chain or gone the no-frills route at a local hostel. For average accommodations somewhere in the middle, you often can expect to pay significantly less than what you'd pay at a comparable hotel in America, which makes getting the bill a pleasant surprise. Whether a room has plush carpets and chairs or a simple bed and table, most tend to be clean and neat.

The lodgings we list are the cream of the crop in each price category. We always list the facilities that are available, but we don't specify whether they cost extra. When pricing accommodations, always ask what's included and what costs extra. Properties are assigned price categories based on the range between their least and most expensive standard double rooms at high season, which in India is approximately September through March, excluding Christmas and New Year's. When you book a room at a hotel, however (especially an expensive hotel), ask for their best rate and push them to include breakfast and a station or airport pickup. Be a hard bargainer; consider asking them to knock the rate down further, even after they have given you a discount. You can always shop around and come back.

Try to secure all room reservations before arrival, especially during peak season and in the major cities and popular tourist destinations such as Mumbai, Delhi, Agra, Kerala, and Goa. But give yourself a little leeway to make plans upon arrival, especially if you have more than two weeks—a strong component of Indian culture is the relative unimportance of the concept of time, often making last-minute arrangements a breeze. This is especially true during monsoon season (June through August) when many hotels have vacancies and deep discounts. Indians vacation during school holidays in April, May, and early June; for a few days in October or November (for Diwali, or, in eastern India, Durga Puja); and for 10 days between Christmas and the New Year. Reservations are extra-difficult to secure during these times.

Room rates are extremely expensive in business-oriented cities like Bangalore,

Mumbai, Kolkata, Delhi, Hyderabad, and Chennai. Urban hotels rarely have off-season discounts, though some international chains have incentive programs for frequent guests. In other areas, hotels may be seeking guests, so you may be able to negotiate your price. When you reserve, ask about additional taxes and service charges, which increase the quoted room price. Do not agree to an airport pickup or breakfast without asking if these services involve extra costs. Airport pickups organized by luxury hotels are generally overpriced.

Delhi and Mumbai are in a financial league of their own when it comes to lodging, with Bangalore not far behind. For the rest of India, major cities such as Agra, Kolkata, Jaipur, Chennai, Pune, and Varanasi make up a second tier of prices. Costs elsewhere in India, especially in smaller towns and villages, tend to be much less expensive.

CATEGORY	COST
$$$$	over Rs. 10,000
$$$	Rs. 6,000–Rs. 10,000
$$	Rs. 4,000–Rs. 6,000
$	Rs. 2,000–Rs. 4,000
¢	under Rs. 2,000

All prices are in rupees for a standard double room in high season, based on the European Plan (EP) and excluding tax and service charges, which vary by region.

Most hotels and other lodgings require you to give your credit-card details before they will confirm your reservation. If you don't feel comfortable e-mailing this information, ask if you can fax it (some places even prefer faxes). However you book, get confirmation in writing and have a copy of it handy when you check in.

Be sure you understand the hotel's cancellation policy. Some places allow you to cancel without any kind of penalty—even if you prepaid to secure a discounted rate—if you cancel at least 24 hours in advance. Others require you to cancel a week in advance or penalize you the cost of one night. Most hotels allow children under a certain age to stay in their parents' room at no extra charge, but others charge for them as extra adults; find out the cutoff age for discounts.

Assume that hotels operate on the European Plan (EP, no meals) unless we specify that they use the Breakfast Plan (BP, with full breakfast), Continental Plan (CP, Continental breakfast), Full American Plan (FAP, all meals), Modified American Plan (MAP, breakfast and dinner) or are all-inclusive (AI, all meals and most activities).

GOVERNMENT LODGING

The national and state governments, the public works department, and the forestry department manage inexpensive accommodations throughout India. Most of these facilities are poorly maintained, and government employees and officials receive priority booking. Some states, however—particularly Madhya Pradesh, Maharashtra, and Kerala—run fairly competent hotels and often provide the best lodgings in remote destinations. For more information contact the tourist office in the capital of the state you plan to visit.

HERITAGE HOTELS

The Indian government has an excellent incentive program that encourages owners of traditional *havelis* (mansions), forts, and palaces to convert their properties into hotels or bring existing historic hotels up to government standards. (But do be careful where you stay, because government standards aren't always ideal for Westerners.) Many of these official Heritage Hotels—noted in reviews throughout this guide—are well outside large cities. Their architecture and style are authentically Indian, not Western. If this type of lodging appeals to you, contact one of the Indian tourist offices for more information. There are more than

60 such establishments in Rajasthan; about 15 in Gujarat; and a few in Madhya Pradesh, Himachal Pradesh, Kerala, and other states.

HOSTELS

Hostels offer bare bones lodging at low, low prices—often in shared dorm rooms with shared baths—to people of all ages, though the primary market is young travelers, especially students. Most hostels serve breakfast; dinner and/or shared cooking facilities may also be available. In some hostels you aren't allowed to be in your room during the day, and there may be a curfew at night. Nevertheless, hostels provide a sense of community, with public rooms where travelers often gather to share stories. Many hostels are affiliated with Hostelling International (HI), an umbrella group of hostel associations with some 4,500 member properties in more than 70 countries. Other hostels are completely independent and may be nothing more than a really cheap hotel.

Membership in any HI association, open to travelers of all ages, allows you to stay in HI-affiliated hostels at member rates. One-year membership is about $28 for adults; hostels charge about $10–$30 per night. Members have priority if the hostel is full; they're also eligible for discounts around the world, even on rail and bus travel in some countries.

Hostels in India are common in the big cities and a good option if you're on a tight budget. People of all ages and genders are usually welcomed, and many can accommodate you on a walk-up basis. You'll often find several types of sleeping options, including single rooms (which usually cost more) as well as shared ones. Some hostel rooms can be as good as those at inexpensive hotels, with air-conditioning and TVs.

Information Hostelling International—USA (☎ *301/495–1240* 🌐 *www.hiusa.org*). **Youth Hostels Association of India** (☎ *11/2611–0250* 🌐 *www.yhaindia.org*). **YWCA Hostels of Bombay International Center** (☎ *22/2202–5053* 🌐 *www.ywcaic.info*). **YWCA International Guest House, New Delhi** (☎ *11/2334–0294* 🌐 *www.ywcaindia.org*).

HOTELS

India's tourism department approves and classifies hotels based on a rating system of five stars (the fanciest) to no stars (no frills). The ratings are based on the number of facilities and on hotel and bedroom size. Hotels without pools or those that serve only vegetarian food or that don't have a 24-hour restaurant—including some historic, charming, comfortable properties—don't qualify for five-star status but are often just as luxurious as those that do. The rating system also fails to take service and other important intangibles into account. Although these ratings can be misleading, tour operators often use them, so ask what a star rating means when booking.

If a room you're taking looks a little dingy, chances are the staff will clean it again it for you. Make sure the door locks and that the bathroom's plumbing works.

If you opt for room service outside a luxury hotel, here are a few things to keep in mind: Tea or coffee usually comes premixed—ask to have a pot of tea or coffee with the milk, sugar, and tea bags or coffee powder brought separately. You can probably get food cooked according to your preferences, but you have to make the request. Ask for fruit juice without ice or sugar. Make sure the mineral water is sealed, and do not use water from flasks in the room.

Information Aman Resorts (🌐 *www.amanresorts.com*). **Clarks** (🌐 *www.hotelclarks.com*). **Indian Heritage Hotels Association** (🌐 *www.indianheritagehotels.com*). **Oberoi Hotels** (🌐 *www.oberoihotels.com*). **Taj Group** (☎ *866/969–1825 toll-free in U.S.* 🌐 *www.tajhotels.com*). **Welcomgroup** (🌐 *www.welcomgroup.com*).

AIRLINE TICKETS

Most domestic airline tickets are electronic; international tickets may be either electronic or paper. With an e-ticket the only thing you receive is an e-mailed receipt citing your itinerary and reservation and ticket numbers.

The greatest advantage of an e-ticket is that if you lose your receipt, you can simply print out another copy or ask the airline to do it for you at check-in. You usually pay a surcharge (up to $50) to get a paper ticket, if you can get one at all.

The sole advantage of a paper ticket is that it may be easier to endorse over to another airline if your flight is canceled and the airline with which you booked can't accommodate you on another flight.

TIP→ Discount air passes that let you travel economically in a country or region must often be purchased before you leave home. In some cases you can only get them through a travel agent.

Children under 12 and students ages 12 to 26 (with a valid ID) qualify for discounts on most domestic airlines. Groups are eligible for discounts, too. The Discover India pass of Indian Airlines (which merged with Air India in 2007, but at this writing, operates under its original name) allows for travel over 7, 15, or 21 days. At this writing, prices for the passes are in flux.

Jet Airways sells 7-day (US$375), 14-day (US$750), and 21-day (US$1,000) Visit India passes. The 7-day pass is for regional travel only.

Contact the airline directly or a travel agent to purchase the passes and get more information. A travel agent will be helpful with the Indian Airlines passes—at press time, it was difficult to contact Indian Airlines by phone, and Air India agents repeatedly said they could not help with the passes.

Air Pass Info Indian Airlines (Air India) (☎ *11/2460–3227 in India* 🌐 *www.airindia.com*). **Jet Airways** (☎ *11/3989–3333 in India, 877/835–9538 in North America* 🌐 *www.jetairways.com*).

HIRING A CAR & DRIVER

The bad news: renting a car and driving yourself around India isn't recommended. The rules and road conditions are probably like nothing you've ever experienced, so taking taxis or hiring a car and driver are the best choices. The good news: hiring a car and driver is affordable by Western standards, and even Indians use this option for weekend getaways. However, the price can add up for long trips, so be sure to establish terms, rates, and surcharges in advance. Drivers are usually paid by the company they work for, and every company has unique policies. It's not uncommon for you to pay for the whole trip in advance, or to pay for half at the front end while settling the balance at the end of the trip. In most cases, rates will include gasoline.

Shorter trips are generally priced by kilometer. Figure Rs. 6 to Rs. 10 per kilometer for a non-air-conditioned Ambassador—a hefty, roomy car designed by the British in the 1950s. Ambassadors are not as universal as they used to be, and now the most economic rates often get you a Maruti van or Uno. Neither is as comfortable as the Ambassador, as these are lighter cars that get bounced about on potholed roads. In some locations, a higher rate gets you a diesel Sumo jeep or an air-conditioned Cielo, Contessa, or Audi; still more cash gets you a Toyota, a minivan, or maybe even a Mercedes-Benz.

On longer trips one price usually covers a certain number of hours and kilometers; beyond that you pay extra. Expect to pay up to Rs. 1,000 a day to have a driver at your disposal—more if you're using an expensive hotel car. Add to this a "halt charge" of Rs. 100 to Rs. 200 per night for overnight trips. Some companies also charge a driver's fee for an eight-hour day.

Arrange a car and driver only through a reputable travel agency or licensed, government-approved operator or, for quite a bit more money, through your hotel. Be sure to discuss your itinerary up front. Roads in some areas—wildlife sanctuaries for example—require a jeep; better to iron out all the details than miss sights because you don't have the appropriate vehicle. On long journeys, decide in advance where and when you'll stop for tea or meal breaks. The daredevil road maneuvers that are the norm in India can be unsettling. Ask the driver to travel slowly, or have the operator inform the driver of your request.

If you must get behind the wheel yourself, start with Car Rental India or ask about other reliable local agencies when you get to India. Rates for international companies like Avis, for example, start at around $45 a day, and mileage is not unlimited. This is much more than you are likely to pay for a car and driver.

Your own driver's license is not acceptable in India—you need an International Driver's Permit. In North America you can get one of these from the American or Canadian automobile associations; in the United Kingdom, contact the Automobile Association or Royal Automobile Club.

Local Agency **Car Rental India** (☎ *11/2981–2200 to 2204 in Delhi* 🌐 *www.carrental-india.com)*.

VACATION PACKAGES

Packages *are not* guided excursions. Packages combine airfare, accommodations, and perhaps a rental car or other extras (theater tickets, guided excursions, boat trips, reserved entry to popular museums, transit passes), but they let you do your own thing. During busy periods packages may be your only option, as flights and rooms may be sold out otherwise.

Packages will definitely save you time. They can also save you money, particularly in peak seasons, but—and this is a really big "but"—you should price each part of the package separately to be sure. And be aware that prices advertised on Web sites and in newspapers rarely include service charges or taxes, which can up your costs by hundreds of dollars.

TIP→ Some packages and cruises are sold only through travel agents. Don't always assume that you can get the best deal by booking everything yourself.

Each year consumers are stranded or lose their money when packagers—even large ones with excellent reputations—go out of business. How can you protect yourself?

First, always pay with a credit card; if you have a problem, your credit-card company may help you resolve it. Second, buy trip insurance that covers default. Third, choose a company that belongs to the United States Tour Operators Association, whose members must set aside funds to cover defaults. Finally, choose a company that also participates in the Tour Operator Program of the American Society of Travel Agents (ASTA), which will act as mediator in any disputes.

A package tour to India can help tremendously when you have a short amount of time and want to pack in as much as possible. You'll save time by not having to arrange everything yourself or learn too much about the great Indian art of haggling, and you'll also know in advance what you're getting. The downside is that you'll often end up paying much more. Because tour companies assume, in general, that foreigners traveling to India expect Western standards of accommodation and dining, they'll often book you in the most expensive hotels and have you eating pricey meals. This approach often neglects a more authentic understanding of India, where independent travel and exploration can be very fulfilling—not to mention much cheaper—if you're willing to do a little research and branch out from the typical tourist spots.

Organizations **American Society of Travel Agents** (*ASTA ☎ 703/739–2782 or 800/965–2782 🌐 www.astanet.com*). **United States Tour Operators Association** (*USTOA ☎ 212/599–6599 🌐 www.ustoa.com*).

■ TIP→ Local tourism boards can provide information about lesser-known and small-niche operators that sell packages to only a few destinations.

GUIDED TOURS

Guided tours are a good option when you don't want to do it all yourself. You travel along with a group (sometimes large, sometimes small), stay in prebooked hotels, eat with your fellow travelers (the cost of meals sometimes included in the price of your tour, sometimes not), and follow a schedule.

A knowledgeable guide can take you places that you might never discover on your own, and you may be pushed to see more than you would have otherwise. Tours aren't for everyone, but they can be just the thing for trips to places where making travel arrangements is difficult or time-consuming (particularly when you don't speak the language).

Whenever you book a guided tour, find out what's included and what isn't. A "land-only" tour includes all your travel (by bus, in most cases) in the destination, but not necessarily your flights to and from or even within it. Also, in most cases prices in tour brochures don't include fees and taxes. And remember that you'll be expected to tip your guide (in cash) at the end of the tour.

The number of package tours to India is overwhelming. Quality and price vary greatly, but the ones listed here have proven track records. Overseas Adventure Travel offers a good, "classic" tour of India in which you'll visit points in Rajasthan as well as Agra, Khajuraho, and Varanasi. It's pricey, and clients tend to include older Americans who can afford a high standard of travel. Four Wheel Drive India is a Rajasthan-based tour company that provides several tour options like honeymoon and wildlife packages. The major advantage here is that if you don't see the exact tour you want, Four Wheel Drive can customize one for you and help coordinate every aspect, including international airfare. Compass Tours and Travel offers a dizzying array of options all over the sub-continent, from four-day jaunts in Goa to luxury tours of Rajasthan at all price points. Djoser offers a unique opportunity to travel with small groups of Europeans (mostly Dutch) and caters to a more independent-minded traveler. Their tours lack the cookie-cutter features of more mainstream tour companies).

Recommended Companies **Compass Tours and Travel** (*☎ 866/926–0200 or 609/926–9368 in the U.S. 🌐 www.compasstours-travel.com*). **Djoser** (*✉ 154 Woodgate La., Paoli, PA19301 ☎ 877/356–7376 🌐 www.djoserusa.com*). **Four Wheel Drive India** (*✉ 1-A Fateh Nagar, Surya Nagar, Taroon ki Koot, Tonk Rd., Jaipur, 302015 ☎ 141/272–2025 🌐 www.fourwheeldriveindia.com*). **Overseas Adventure Travel** (*✉ 347 Congress St., Boston, MA 02210 ☎ 800/493–6824 🌐 www.oattravel.com*).

SPECIAL-INTEREST TOURS

HIKING

Hiking and trekking in India's more rugged regions is probably the most popular specialized tour on the sub-continent. One World Trekking Adventure Travel, an independent travel company based in Colorado, specializes in small group treks to the Himalayas.

Contacts **One World Trekking Adventure Travel** (*✉ 1012 Blake Ave., Glenwood Springs, CO 81601 ☎ 970/945–2601 🌐 www.oneworldtrekking.com*).

TRANSPORTATION

The major international tourist hub is Delhi in the north. Mumbai (874 mi/1,407 km south) and Bangalore (1,280 mi/2,061 km south) have gained significant importance in business travel and also serve as good hubs depending on which part of India you plan to tackle. All the major cities are connected by a national highway system, air service, and trains.

Road travel is definitely an easy way to leisurely take in local color. Unfortunately most roads still have just two lanes and are in poor condition, and progress can be painstaking. However, that's changing as India continues to work on its modernization project, which has already produced the "Golden Quadrilateral," a four-lane highway similar to those in America that connects Delhi, Kolkata, Chennai, and Mumbai. The only region in which you are likely to experience major problems (besides run-of-the-mill congestion) might be near the Himalayas. There, distances of 100 mi or less can often take several hours, so it's important to plan for generous travel time. An onslaught of domestic airlines competing for business has made air travel throughout the sub-continent relatively hassle-free and convenient. It's the best option for those who are on a tight schedule, and typical problems associated with air travel—delays, lost baggage, etc.—don't seem to be any more predictable in India than in North America. However, many airports in India are much smaller than they need to be to handle current traffic effectively, so always be ready for a delayed flight.

The Indian train system is an intricate network shuttling millions of people across the country every day. It's very reliable, if run-down, and practically every point of interest in India has a train station nearby. Train travel is also likely to be the cheapest option for going long distances, making it perfect for travelers on a budget.

TRAVEL TIMES FROM DELHI

To	By Air	By Train
Agra	45 minutes	2½ hours
Jaipur	45 minutes	5 hours
Chandigarh	45 minutes	3–5 hours
Shimla	1 hour	12½ hours
Calcutta	2½ hours	17–24 hours
Mumbai	2 hours	16–22 hours
Goa	2 hours	35 hours
Bangalore	2½ hours	34–40 hours
Chennai	2½ hours	31–36 hours
Cochin	3 hours	38–49 hours

BY AIR

Flying to and within India has become easier in recent years with new international routes and the emergence of several new low-cost Indian domestic airlines. Flying from Delhi to Bangalore, for example, is as easy as flying between two major cities in America. Domestic tickets can generally be purchased through traditional travel agents, airline Web sites, travel Web sites, and even at Indian airports if you've decided to make a last-minute stop to somewhere you've missed.

Security in Indian airports, however, is typically tight, and procedures often require considerable time. People are routinely patted down, whether or not the metal detector goes off. Women are usually required to go into a separate dressing-room-like box to be patted down by female security, whereas men are checked out in the open. Because of what you might perceive as these extra-rigid procedures, it's a good idea to check in at least two hours before a flight within India.

Flying time to either Delhi or Mumbai is 16 hours from New York, 18 hours from Chicago, and 20 hours from Los Angeles.

Airlines & Airports Airline and Airport Links.com (*www.airlineandairportlinks.com*) has links to many of the world's airlines and airports.

Airline Security Issues Transportation Security Administration (*www.tsa.gov*) has answers for almost every question that might come up.

AIRPORTS

India's main international gateways are Indira Gandhi International Airport in Delhi (DEL), Chhatrapati Shivaji International Airport in Mumbai (BOM), and the new Bangalore International Airport in Bangalore (BLR), set to open in spring 2008. Unless you plan to spend most of your time in the south, Bangalore probably isn't the most convenient entry point for the typical tourist in India, although you might fly through there on a domestic flight. Delhi is best for all the major tourist spots in the north, and as a gateway to the Himalayas. Mumbai is more convenient for Goa and still farther points south, including Kerala. Both airport are reasonably close to the city centers and hotel options, and to the train stations if that's your next mode of travel.

The airports in Delhi and Bombay, which also accommodate domestic flights, are not yet like those in the U.S. or Europe—there are usually few shopping options or comfortable places to lounge, but the surroundings are getting better. The new international terminal being added to the Delhi airport is expected to be completed by 2010 to accommodate that year's Commonwealth Games. The new Bangalore International Airport will hopefully set a new standard for Indian airports, with large retail shops, bookstores, and restaurants planned to appease the city's ever-increasing number of business travelers. The airport experience at smaller domestic airports will probably continue to be no-frills compared to what's at home. If your flight is delayed while leaving India or while waiting for domestic flights, there's often little more you can do than wait and scrounge around for some tea or coffee.

Airport Information Bangalore International Airport (*www.bialairport.com*).

GROUND TRANSPORTATION

The best way to get to and from the major international airports is by taxi or auto-rickshaw (if you're feeling adventurous and don't have that much luggage). Your hotel can also arrange for a private pickup, in which case the driver will be holding a sign with your name on it at the exit point. Hotel pickups are considerably more expensive than any other option and vary greatly in price (expect a charge of at least Rs. 1,000 in big cities). All international passengers exit from the same place after retrieving luggage, and you'll immediately see countless drivers trying to drum up business.

As with almost every experience involving money in India, at some point negotiation skills will be needed to arrange transportion, and this issue usually starts at the airport. Rules of thumb for taking taxis and rickshaws vary greatly from city to city. For example, drivers in Delhi are known to laugh at your suggestion that they use the meters, while drivers in Mumbai tend to use the meters without exception. The general rule to follow is that no ride from an airport to any point in an Indian city should cost more than Rs. 500 if taking a taxi, Rs. 200 if taking a rickshaw. Even then, most rides in rickshaws—if the driver is being honest—should rarely cost more than Rs. 100. Be firm in negotiating, because drivers at airports assume a tourist will have no clue about what a ride should cost. Avoid the hassle by arranging a taxi at the prepaid, government-approved stands beyond immigration and customs.

Luggage room is ample in taxis in Delhi, but the cars used in Mumbai are older and smaller with considerably less room. Taxi drivers might try to charge you an extra fee (around Rs. 10) per bag, but again, this varies from city to city.

TRANSFERS BETWEEN AIRPORTS

The international airports in Delhi, Bombay, and Bangalore are also the domestic hubs. There are no companies with organized airport transfers—taxis and rickshaws are king. A transfer costs approximately Rs. 300 for a taxi and Rs. 100 for a rickshaw.

FLIGHTS

TO INDIA

International companies are constantly reevaluating their service to southern Asia. Call the air carriers listed below to confirm their flights and schedules, or work with a travel agent who's knowledgeable about the region. That said, you can get to India, usually with a stop in Europe, on several international carriers. Those offering daily direct flights include Continental Airlines (Newark to Delhi), American Airlines (Chicago to Delhi), and Air India (New York JFK, Newark, and Chicago to Bombay). Jet Airways flies daily from New York JFK to Delhi and Newark to Mumbai. Both flights are via Brussels.

WITHIN INDIA

India's domestic airline scene has boomed since the millennium, with several young air carriers adding low fares and their own brand of service to the mix of mainstays like Air India, Indian Airlines, and Jet Airways. Once considered the nation's default domestic airline, Indian Airlines actually merged with Air India in 2007, and at this writing, the company is to be known as Air India. However, flights continue to operate under the Indian Airlines name, which could cause some confusion.

The newer domestic airlines are ones you've probably never heard of, and each one has its pros and cons. Kingfisher is run by the same mogul who makes Kingfisher beer. The atmosphere is laid back, and the service is good. Simplify Deccan (also known as just Deccan), partially owned by Kingfisher, has some of the cheapest fares. They once had a well-earned reputation for being delayed or canceling flights outright, but since early 2007 they have been improving. Still, it's a good idea not to use them if you'll need to be back on the same day to catch your flight home. Jet Airways is probably the most expensive, but provides very good service—they also fly to North America. Air India and Indian Airlines are the government carriers. Prices tend to be too high, and they don't seem to be as progressive as the private airlines. Paramount, which is important for travel to Chennai and other points in the south, has a very good reputation and reliable service. Spice Jet wants to be considered the "fun" airline, with female flight attendants who wear short red skirts. You can get really good deals with them.

Airline Contacts **Air France** (☎ *800/237-2747* 🌐 *www.airfrance.com*). **Air India** (☎ *800/223-7776* 🌐 *www.airindia.com*). **American Airlines** (☎ *800/433-7300* 🌐 *www.aa.com*). **British Airways** (☎ *800/247-9297 in U.S., 124/412-0747 in India* 🌐 *www.britishairways.com*). **Continental Airlines** (☎ *800/523-3273 in U.S.* 🌐 *www.continental.com*). **Delta Airlines** (☎ *800/221-1212 for U.S. reservations, 800/241-4141 for international reservations* 🌐 *www.delta.com*). **Luftansa** (☎ *800/399-5838* 🌐 *www.lufthansa.com*). **Northwest Airlines** (☎ *800/225-2525* 🌐 *www.nwa.com*). **United Airlines** (☎ *800/864-8331 for U.S. reservations, 800/538-2929 for international reservations* 🌐 *www.united.com*).

Within India **Air India** (☎ *124/234-8888 in India, 800/625—6424, 800/223-7776 in U.S.* 🌐 *www.airindia.com*). **Jet Airways** (☎ *11/3989-3333 in India, 877/835-9538 in U.S.* 🌐 *www.jetairways.com*). **King Fisher Airlines** (☎ *22/6649-9393 in India, 866/435-9532 in U.S.* 🌐 *www.flykingfisher.com*). **Paramount Airways** (☎ *44/4343—4444* 🌐 *www.paramountairways.com*). **Simplify Deccan** (☎ *80/4114-8190 to 8199 in India* 🌐 *www.*

airdeccan.net). **Spice Jet** (☎ *987/180-3333 in India* 🌐 *www.spicejet.com*).

BY BUS

Bus travel isn't the most safe or comfortable way to travel in India, especially at night. Service in cities, especially in Delhi, is crowded and dangerous for women, with men literally hanging outside the bus (if they can manage to grab hold while the bus is still moving). The situation is a bit better in Mumbai, but a lack of published bus schedules and routes makes the city bus experience best left to locals or those who have time to figure it out. If you decide on bus travel between cities, try to take the most luxurious privately run air-conditioned coaches, such as Volvo buses, and have a local travel agent make the arrangements. Restroom arrangements for long-distance bus rides are either poor or nonexistent—buses make periodic pit stops for passengers answering the call of nature.

BY CAR

Travel by car in India isn't for the faint of heart, but if you can get over India's extremely different road philosophy, it can be an enjoyable, never-boring way to see the country and get from one city to the next. *Just remember to leave navigation up to the professionals: see Hiring a Car & Driver above.*

ROAD CONDITIONS

Roads in India may be wide and smooth in big cities, but they're usually narrow and terribly maintained in the countryside. Traffic in places like Delhi, Mumbai, and Bangalore is so erratic and abundant that it is hard to pin down local rush hours. Roads are filled with countless cars at all times of the day and even late at night, especially around the airports (international flights tend to arrive in the wee morning hours). Always expect some kind of traffic jam or other road drama if traveling by car.

Traffic is multifarious: you'll see slow-moving cyclists, bullock carts, cows, and even camels or elephants sharing the road with speeding, honking, quick-to-pass, ready-to-brake-for-animals vehicles of all shapes and sizes. Barring a few principal routes and highways built under the continuing modernization project, Indian roads are generally dilapidated and become worse during monsoon season. Speed limits, set according to road conditions, are frequently ignored. Road signs, when they exist, are often just in Hindi or the local language.

FROM DELHI

To	Distance in kilometers	Distance in miles
Agra	203	126
Jaipur	258	160
Chandigarh	238	148
Kolkata	1,461	908
Mumbai	1,407	874
Goa	1,912	1,188
Bangalore	2,061	1,281
Chennai	2,095	1,302
Cochin	2,065	1,283
Shimla	343	213

Because of India's British influence, newer sections of cities are filled with traffic circles. Older parts of the cities, however, are generally made up of extremely narrow streets. Old Delhi's streets tend to be one-way, although you won't be able to tell which way that is unless you simply look at the traffic. Locals drive fast when they can and show little regard for pedestrians.

In rural areas, two-way roads are often only one lane wide, so vehicles frequently dodge oncoming traffic for hours on end. Some roads also serve as innovative extensions to farms, with grain laid out to dry on the pavement or sisal rope strung over the route so that vehicles tramp the grain down. British-style left-side driving creates one more challenge to many motorists.

RULES OF THE ROAD

Hard copies of road regulations are difficult to come by in India. It's no wonder, since it seems as if Indians either ignore or genuinely aren't aware of road rules across the subcontinent. Take for instance speed limits. Rarely are they posted, and different states have different speed limits for cars traveling on the national highways. Any speed less than 100 km per hour is probably legal. Indians drive faster than that if not stifled by gridlock, and punishment for speeding is spotty at best. On the off chance that you're driving and you get stopped for speeding, you might have to pay a fine or a bribe depending on the officer's mood.

There are also laws requiring the use of seatbelts and laws against using your cell phone while driving. However, you'll be hard-pressed to find any local who wears his belt religiously or gets punished if he doesn't. People do seem to be more aware of restrictions on cell phone use, and talkers in cities like Delhi and Mumbai, especially foreigners, do get signaled out by the cops—it's best not to use your cell phone behind the wheel. The most serious offense—drunk driving—is taken very seriously and is punishable by jail time.

The Web site 🌐www.indiandrivingschools.com has a fairly comprehensive outline of basic Indian traffic regulations. Nevertheless, it's not too much of a stretch to characterize Indian roads as a free-for-all where traffic rules are theoretical at best.

BY TAXI & AUTO-RICKSHAW

Probably the best way to get around an Indian city is by taxi or motorized auto-rickshaw. The rickshaws, especially, are fast and cheap, if not as comfortable as an air-conditioned taxi.

Taxis and rickshaws are practically everywhere and are easy to flag down. One drawback is that most drivers don't speak English. If your driver can't understand your pronunciation of a landmark or hotel, pen and paper may do the trick. Bystanders are also often surprisingly helpful in getting from point A to B.

Most importantly, find out in advance the approximate fare for the distance you will be going—someone at your hotel can give you a ballpark figure. This is crucial, because even if your taxi or rickshaw has a meter, the driver might not use it. That is the standard practice in Delhi, where it's common for rickshaw drivers to quote foreigners outrageous fares and claim that the meter is "broken." Don't fight the system—just have an idea of a fair price before you get in, and expect that negotiation will usually be part of the game. A good rule of thumb is that no rickshaw ride should cost more than Rs. 100 (most are much less), and no taxi ride should cost more than Rs. 500. In Mumbai, drivers are good about using the meter and rate cards. Once you're at your destination, the card shows how much you should pay based on the figure displayed on the meter. If you think you're going to a place that may not have vehicles for the return journey (you will probably know for sure only when you reach your destination, unfortunately), then, when you arrive, negotiate a waiting fare and a return fare with the driver.

Remember that prepaid taxi and auto-rickshaw counters exist at airports and railway stations in major cities. You tell the clerk your destination and pay for it in advance. He may ask you how much luggage you have—paying an extra Rs. 5 is the norm for each large bag or suitcase. The clerk will give you a receipt, at which point you might have to stand in line for the taxi or rickshaw. The driver might also be standing next to you and escort you to his vehicle. Do not get waylaid by aggressive drivers who try to persuade you to come to them instead of going to the counter. They'll most certainly charge you more than the published rate at the counter. At your destination, do not pay the driver anything extra, even if he claims you gave the wrong destination to the counter clerk or gives other excuses.

Drivers supplement their incomes by offering to find you a hotel or to take you shopping at the "best" stores, which means they'll get a commission if you get a room or buy anything. The stores are usually very expensive, so if you don't want this kind of detour, you must be very firm. Finally, taxis close to luxury hotels are notorious for swindling customers who hire them outside the hotel. Establish beforehand, with the help of the doorman, that the taxi driver will follow his meter or rate card, or negotiate the fare in the presence of the doorman.

BY TRAIN

Traveling by train in India can be a fine experience if you plan it well. Trains connect the tiniest places across the subcontinent, and train journeys are a terrific way to see the real, off-the-beaten-track India. Traveling on second-class non-air-conditioned trains can be tough, but you'll get better views of the countryside, since the windows are wide open, not sealed, and don't have a smoky film on them, as they do in air-conditioned cars. On the other hand, air-conditioned trips are much more comfortable. Trains, especially on smaller routes, can often be late, so be prepared to cope with delays. Make an attempt to get off at stations when the train halts, and have a walk around to observe station life. Certain train routes are famous for their views and are historical routes established by the British—the narrow gauge toy trains, for example, that go to Darjeeling, Matheran, Ooty, and Shimla.

Like its international airports, India's railway stations are rather chaotic—though highly entertaining to observe. Hawkers sell everything from hot *puris* (deep-fried whole wheat bread) to boiled eggs and squeaky toys to hot coffee on a crude portable stove. Porters, also known as coolies, weave in and out, balancing unimaginable configurations of trunks and bags on their heads. Invariably, when one person sets out on a journey, five come to see him off. The platforms swirl with crowds and luggage. You need to be careful to hang on to your possessions and your bearings so you don't get bumped or swept away. Plan to be early, and keep your tickets safe. If the train is delayed or has not yet arrived, try to find a waiting room. Though usually drab and not very comfortable, these places are safe and might have attached bathrooms. Many large railway stations have restaurants or at least snack counters where you can take a break, too.

India's two luxury trains—Rajasthan's Palace on Wheels and Gujarat's Royal Orient, which travel in parts of Rajasthan and Gujarat—are destinations in themselves, offering sumptuous meals and luxury quarters as well as fine (albeit extremely busy) itineraries. Packages, which are very expensive, include food, coach tours in stations (after you disembark you're loaded onto a luxury bus for sightseeing), rail travel, and more. Palace on Wheels offers several tour packages starting at US$3,500 per person for double occupancy for a week or more. On the Royal Orient, prices range from US$200–US$350 per day depending on double or single occupancy. All prices are deeply discounted during the off season (March–October.) The Deccan Odyssey, another luxury train that started running in January 2004 from Mumbai along the coast to Karnataka, takes you to Ganapatiphule, Sindhudurg, Goa, Pune, Aurangabad, Ajanta, and Ellora. The seven-day journey costs between US$240 and US$700 per person per day depending on the type of accommodation you choose and the season. The Golden Chariot, set to begin service in early 2008, does a weeklong tour of Karnataka and nearby areas.

For regular train service, a one-way ticket can cost approximately Rs. 500 for air-conditioned first class, but prices vary greatly depending on where and how you're traveling. The Shatabdi and Rajdhani expresses are fast and have air-conditioned cars and reclining seats but only offer services between major cities. The next-fastest trains are called "mail" trains. "Passenger" trains, which usually offer only second-class accommodations, make numerous stops, and are crowded. Even on the best trains in this group, lavatories are less than pleasant and seats can be well worn. But traveling by first class air-conditioned makes for a leisurely and fairly grand journey and is well worth experiencing.

The Shatabdi Express and Taj Express travel between Delhi and Agra. Both leave early in the morning from Delhi; the Shatabdi takes about two hours, the Taj 2½. Each allows for a full day of sightseeing before returning to Delhi. There are also express trains connecting Delhi with Jaipur, Mumbai, and Kolkata. The Web site of the Indian Railway system has comprehensive schedules of every train running across India.

For long train rides, buy a yard-long chain with loops and a padlock to secure your luggage. (You might find a vendor on the platform at a large train station.) After you've locked your bag and stowed it in its place, loop the chain through its handle and attach it to a bar or hinge below the seat. Lock it once more and you won't have to mind your luggage. You can even step off the train to stretch your legs at interim stations, knowing your possessions are safe. Be sure to chain your luggage as soon as possible; a lot of small bag thefts take place during journey embarkation and disembarkation. Your journey will be more pleasant if you bring along packaged snacks, sandwiches, juice, and bottled water. Bigger trains provide meals as part of the ticket/tariff, and you can expect a number of the items on a food tray to be packaged.

Trains have numerous classes. The air-conditioned cars consist of first-class air-conditioned (also known as 1st a/c; lockable compartments with two or four sleeping berths), second-class air-conditioned (also known as 2nd a/c; two or four berths that convert to sleepers, but no lockable compartments), and third-class air-conditioned (also known as 3rd a/c; just like 2nd a/c but with six berths in each seating bay). Ordinary first-class are the non-air-conditioned lockable compartments with two or four sleeping berths. The a/c chair car (a/c chair class) is a comfortable way to go on day trips, with rows of two or three seats on each side. Seats are covered in either vinyl or cloth. Any of the previous classes are adequate, although 3rd AC can make for slightly cramped quarters. Sleeper class is the way many Indians who can afford to travel, especially on long-haul trips. The car is laid out just like the 3rd AC car without the air-conditioning. Finally there's second seating, the cheapest because no reservations are required. But it's not recommended for long distances—the car has an open-air plan with rows of padded or plain wood benches.

Whatever the class, remember to request an inside berth and not a "side" one along the corridor. Berths are in configurations of 4 or 6 in an open coupe arrangement on one side of a train car. On the other (corridor) side, berths are against the wall, in pairs of two; corridors run parallel past these "side" berths and bring in noise and traffic. The side berths also make for much smaller beds at nighttime.

You'll find two kinds of lavatories, the Western-style commode lavatory and the Indian-style toilet (essentially a hole over which you squat). Although it can be hard to get used to Indian-style facilities, they're actually more sanitary in the sense that there's no contact. Definitely bring enough toilet paper (and perhaps some hand sanitizer)—you won't find it on most trains.

In large cities, you can buy tickets with major credit cards. Elsewhere, expect to pay cash. Almost any local Indian travel agent can get train tickets for you.

You must reserve seats and sleeping berths in advance, even with a rail pass. If your plans are flexible, you can make reservations once you arrive in India. To save time, use a local travel agent (who may need to photocopy your passport); otherwise, head to the train station and prepare for long lines and waits. Large urban stations have a special counter for foreigners, where you can buy "tourist quota" tickets. (Every train reserves a few seats for tourists who haven't made reservations.) If you arrive early in the morning—around 8—getting a ticket shouldn't take you more than half an hour; however, in peak season, tourist quotas fill quickly, and you may have to change your dates altogether. When it's time to travel, arrive at the station at least half an hour before departure so you have enough time to find your seat. Sleeper and seat numbers are displayed on the platform and on each car, along with a list of passengers' names and seat assignments.

If you are not buying from the tourist quota and are booking during nonpeak season, booking through the Internet is a wonderful option. You can buy i-tickets, which must be printed out, at 🌐www.irctc.co.in. Don't confuse these with e-tickets, which are purchased online but then hand-delivered.

RAIL PASSES

A rail pass may cost more than individual tickets. In general, however, they are overpriced. You're not likely to save much money unless you plan on taking many long train journeys.

The Indian Railways Indrail Pass is available for 2nd-class to 1st-class air-conditioned trains and can be bought for 1 to 90 days.

Try to buy rail passes at least two months before your trip. Provide your agent with a complete itinerary to ensure seat confirmation. Every Government of India Tourist Office overseas has copies of the Tourist Railway Timetable, or you can consult Thomas Cook's International Railway Timetable. At any railway station you can find *Travel Links, Trains at a Glance,* and *Travel Hour,* all of which list plane and some train schedules.

To buy the Indrail Pass outside India, contact your travel agent or the Government of India Tourist Office. In India, you can buy the pass at railway offices in major cities; international airports; and government-recognized travel agents in Mumbai, Kolkata, Delhi, and Chennai. You must pay in U.S. dollars.

Luxury Train Contacts **Deccan Odyssey** (✉*Indian Holiday Pvt. Ltd., World Trade Center Bldg., New Delhi, 110001* ☎*11/2331–8383* 🌐*www.deccan-odyssey-india.com*). **Palace on Wheels** (*Palace on Wheels, Inc.* ✉*20 Wall St., Princeton, NJ 08540* ☎*609/683–5018 or 800/463–4299 toll free in U.S.* 🌐*www.palaceonwheels.net*). **Royal Orient** (*Gujarat State Tourism Development Corp.* ✉*A/6 State Emporia, Baba Kharak Singh Marg, New Delhi 110008* ☎*11/2374–4015* 🌐*www.gujarattourism.com*).

Train Information **Indian Railways** (🌐*www.indianrail.gov.in. To make online reservations, go to www.irctc.co.in*). **Indian Railways International Tourist Bureau** (✉*New Delhi Railway Station* ☎*11/2340–5156 or 11/2334–6804* ⏲*Mon.–Sat. 8–8, Sun. 8–2*).

ON THE GROUND

SIGHTSEEING

Religious monuments demand respect. With all of India's faiths, you must remove your shoes before entering a shrine, even if it appears to be in ruins (incidentally, this is also the case if you walk upon or close to a Christian church's altar in India). All religions require that you don't smoke, drink alcohol, or raise your voice on the premises. Some temples and mosques are off-limits to travelers who don't practice the faith, or to all women; don't try to bribe your way inside. Women visiting sacred places should dress modestly—no shorts and tank tops—and cover their heads before entering a Sikh temple or a mosque. Cameras and video cameras are sometimes prohibited inside houses of worship. On rare occasions, a Hindu or Muslim festival involves animal sacrifice, which may upset you or your child; do a little research on the festival rituals ahead of time.

Some Hindu and Jain temples don't allow any leather products inside their shrines, including wallets, purses, shoes, belts, and camera cases. Some temples also expect you to purify yourself by washing your hands and feet in a nearby tap or tank before you enter. In Sikh temples, don't point your feet toward the Holy Book or step over anyone sitting in prayer or meditation. Play it safe in both Hindu and Sikh temples: if you sit on the floor, sit cross-legged or with your feet tucked beneath you. In some shrines, the sexes are separated; look around (or follow instructions) and let the situation govern what you do. Step into the courtyards of mosques with your right foot first.

Many well-meaning travelers commit an unforgivable sacrilege when they visit a Buddhist monastery. You're welcome to spin any prayer wheel, but just as you must circumambulate the interior and exterior of a monastery, *stupa,* or *mani* wall in a clockwise direction, you must spin prayer wheels clockwise only. Inside the monastery, cushions and chairs are reserved for *lamas* (monks), so sit on the steps outside or on the floor. If you meet a *rimpoche* (head lama) or a respected monk, it's polite not to turn your back on him when you leave. Also remove your hat and lower your umbrella in the confines of a monastery and in the presence of a lama.

OUT ON THE TOWN

A night out in any of India's major cities can be as casual or as fancy as you want it to be. But you might find that even at top restaurants and formal functions, there aren't many stuffy rules or codes of behavior. Dress for a night out can range from jeans and a nice shirt to the most expensive suits and sparkling saris. With clubbing being so popular in Mumbai, women usually show up with flawless makeup and trendy name-brand or designer fashions, and the guys seem to pay just as much (or more) attention to their appearance.

Happy hours are becoming more common, and the young professional crowd often converges at hip bars in the early evening before dinner (especially in Mumbai, which has a much more vibrant nightlife than Delhi). Women smoking in public used to be somewhat taboo, but now the confident professional women of big cities will often think nothing of smoking while walking down the street. On the other hand, public displays of affection are still rare, so you won't see many couples holding hands, let alone going in for a full-on kiss.

DOING BUSINESS

Doing business in India has become more professional in a Western sense as the country's economy continues to grow and more and more international firms arrive. That mostly means that the concept of time (as in an Indian associate starting a

LOCAL DO'S & TABOOS

CUSTOMS OF THE COUNTRY

■ In India food and food-related hospitality is very important. Indians believe in showing their warmth by feeding a guest endless cups of tea, snacks, and meals. If you refuse to eat a meal or have a cup of tea you may offend your host. Indians also believe in offering food over and over again, essentially overstuffing the guest. So if you have had enough of something, be firm but polite in your refusals.

■ Higher-income households in the big cities are increasingly becoming more westernized, so you might not feel too out of place if you're invited to such a home. However, if you're invited to an extremely traditional Indian home, you'll observe certain customs. Men often sit separate from women. Sometimes, when the men entertain a foreign visitor (even a woman), the women of the house shy away or don't emerge; they may not speak English, or may be mildly xenophobic. Don't be surprised if the woman of the house serves you but doesn't join the gathering. Don't protest, and don't follow her into the kitchen—in orthodox Hindu homes the kitchen is frequently off-limits—just accept her behavior as the tradition of this particular home. In some homes, shoes are taken off before entering; here, too, inquire, or watch what the family does.

■ Numerous customs govern food and the partaking of meals. In many households, you arrive, sit and talk, and then have your meal; after you eat, the evening is over. Consequently, the meal might not start until 10 PM or later. When you eat in remote areas, you may not be given utensils; eat only with your right hand, as the left is considered unclean. (Left-handers can use utensils if available, though left-handedness in general is considered curious.) If you want a second helping or are buying openly displayed food, don't help yourself with your hands, which is considered polluting the food. Let your host or vendor serve you.

■ Indians have an entire set of rules on *jhuta* food, or food that has been touched to your plate, your hand, or your mouth. You do not touch your "food-contaminated" hand to a serving spoon or a pile of rotis or *papads* (lentil or rice wafers). At that time you must use your clean left hand to take a fresh serving. You do not touch the serving spoon to your plate. And take care to not mix serving spoons for vegetarian and nonvegetarian food. Do not take a spoon out from a meat dish and use it to serve yourself some rice, for instance. There may be others in the room who do not eat meat or food "contaminated" by meat. That said, a gracious host will not feel deeply offended if you're not aware of all these little rules.

GIFTS

■ If you visit someone's home for dinner or you're staying with an Indian family, it's a nice gesture to bring a gift from abroad. If there are youngsters in the home, bring something for them. Toys, cosmetics, perfume, and aftershaves are all good options, as is liquor if you're sure that your guests are drinkers—many Indians are not.

GREETINGS

■ People in India are not overly ceremonious on a day-to-day basis. The common greeting is a simple hello or *namaste* in Hindi. Beyond that, people tend to keep to themselves, especially in big cities like Delhi, and there's not really any body contact to speak of—no friendly hugs. However, you may see young men walking down the street holding hands with each other or with arms intertwined—this is an expression of friendship, not gayness. For safety's sake, foreign women are better off not making eye contact with or smiling at strange men on the street—it could be perceived as an invitation for more communication. When you're leaving, a simple goodbye or expression of thanks will do the trick. A firm handshake has become pretty common, especially in the business worlds of Delhi, Mumbai, and Bangalore.

meeting at the scheduled hour) has come to bear more importance. However, being significantly late to a meeting is still not considered a major offense: Indians in general don't take being on time for anything that seriously.

Indians aren't a very formal people when it comes to dress or greetings, and this carries over into the world of business. Rarely do Indians wear suits to meetings, though ties are now popular, and calling people by their first names is acceptable. Executives greet each other by shaking hands; occasionally, a woman executive may prefer not to do this. Business cards are de rigueur.

Indians are gracious hosts and will often foot the bill for business lunches or dinners. Unless he or she is invited, do not bring your spouse to a business dinner, but if you were to mention that you are traveling with a spouse your host will most likely suggest that he or she attend a meal.

LANGUAGE

Try to learn a little of the local language. You need not strive for fluency; even just mastering a few basic words and terms is bound to make chatting with the locals more rewarding.

Contrary to popular belief, English is not spoken by the majority of Indians. The country does function in English alongside Hindi, however, so barring rural areas, you aren't likely to experience too much of a language barrier, especially in cities and tourist hubs where command of English is superior. Hindi is the national language, but India isn't truly unified linguistically, and many Indians don't speak Hindi at all. Most states and countless smaller areas have their own unique tongues that bear no resemblance to the national language. For example, the languages of South India have completely different scripts and origins from those of the north—one reason why a command of both Hindi and English comes in handy.

ADDRESSES

Indian addresses are often haphazard. Building numbers may appear in postal addresses, but they aren't very useful, since they rarely appear on the buildings themselves. And in some towns and some residential areas, numbers do not even have a chronological order—house number 45/234 could be next to house 32/342. This makes neighborhood names and landmarks, which are often included in urban addresses, very important. Addresses for places in small villages may include the name of the nearest large town or big city. In India, postal codes play a big part in ensuring that a letter reaches its destination.

Common terms for the word "road" in local languages (India has many) include *marg, galli, rasta, salai, peth,* and *sarani.* Like many Indian cities, streets and roads have an older, British name and a newer, post-Independence name. Residents often refer to roads by their old names or use abbreviated versions of cumbersome names. In Mumbai, for instance, Netaji Subhash Chandra Marg is still called by its old, easy-to-remember name of Marine Drive and Jay Prakash Road is referred to as J.P. Road. Bombay and its post-Independence name, Mumbai, are used interchangeably, too.

BEGGARS & HAWKERS

It's easy to get upset by the number of beggars who beseech you for spare rupees, motioning from hand to mouth to indicate they have nothing to eat. Most disturbing are the children, as young as three years old, roaming in between cars on busy streets with no adult figure in sight. But know, too, that all these beggars could be part of a ring and may not be as destitute as they look. If you give a beggar money, a dozen more may immediately spring up, and you'll be forced to provide for all; it can also be difficult to get the first beggar, or the entire group, off your tail. Be firm and do not allow a beggar to tail you—a raised voice or mild threats usually work. If you're not firm, expect to be followed by a pack for a while—they do not give up easily.

If you want to contribute, seek out an established charity that's in a position to substantially help those in need. It also doesn't hurt to pass out small trinkets or candy to child beggars if you really can't stand the thought of ignoring them—but do it discreetly.

Hawkers and touts can also be a tremendous nuisance. If you're not interested in what a hawker is offering, give him a firm, polite no and ignore him after that. If he persists, tell him to clear off and employ some mock anger or else he will follow you for blocks. Do not encourage touts at all.

BUSINESS SERVICES & FACILITIES

Nearly every neighborhood or small town has small storefronts where photocopies can be made for a rupee or so a page. For professional services such as translating, business-class hotels are a good place to start.

CHILDREN IN INDIA

Bringing your kids to India may seem daunting, but children love it here. India is like a giant circus, with color, chaos, and a side show every minute. Kids are warmly welcomed everywhere except, perhaps, in the stuffiest of restaurants, and most Indians will bend over backward to help you with a child-related need. In fact, so much affection is lavished on children here—everyone wants to pick them up, pinch their cheeks, talk to them—that your little ones may even get perturbed.

However, there are a couple of thing to remember: Many diseases are prevalent in India that no longer exist elsewhere, so check with your pediatrician first and make sure your child's immunizations are current. It's easiest to bring an infant (who cannot yet crawl, and who is still dependent on breast-feeding or formula) or children who are a bit older and can walk on their own.

Something you might find strange is the fact that no one really uses car seats in India; even educated women think nothing of holding infants in their arms while sitting in the front seat of a moving vehicle (or on the back of a motorbike). So if you plan on getting a car and driver, don't expect to get a car seat—bring your own (don't expect, either, that seat belts will always work).

For general advice about traveling with children, consult *Fodor's FYI: Travel with Your Baby.*

FLYING

If your children are two or older, ask about children's airfares. As a general rule, infants under two not occupying a seat fly at greatly reduced fares or even for free. But if you want to guarantee a seat for an infant, you have to pay full fare. Consider flying during off-peak days and times; most airlines will grant an infant a seat without a ticket if there are available seats.

When booking, confirm carry-on allowances if you're traveling with infants. In general, for babies charged 10% to 50% of the adult fare you are allowed one carry-on bag and a collapsible stroller; if the flight is full, the stroller may have to be checked or you may be limited to less.

Experts agree that it's a good idea to use safety seats aloft for children weighing less than 40 pounds. Airlines set their own policies: if you use a safety seat, U.S. carriers usually require that the child be ticketed, even if he or she is young enough to ride free, because the seats must be strapped into regular seats. And even if you pay the full adult fare for the seat, it may be worth it, especially on longer trips. **Do check your airline's policy about using safety seats during takeoff and landing.** Safety seats are not allowed everywhere in the plane, so get your seat assignments as early as possible.

When reserving, request children's meals or a freestanding bassinet (not available at all airlines) if you need them. But note that bulkhead seats, where you must sit to use the bassinet, may lack an overhead bin or storage space on the floor.

FOOD

Almost all restaurants in India are kid-friendly, except perhaps the fanciest ones you'd find in top hotels. If your kid can't stand India's more exotic tastes, it's almost always possible to get pressed sandwiches like a grilled cheese and other familiarities like pizza. Nirula's is a well-known chain of family restaurants in Delhi and others points in the north, and they serve Indian as well as international fare like ice cream and pastries.

American fast-food is easily accessible in the larger cities. McDonald's seems to be everywhere, as well as Pizza Hut and Domino's Pizza (which will deliver to your hotel). KFC has a presence in South India. But in villages and smaller towns across the subcontinent, these safe bets are nonexistent. In that case, an order of plain bread such as *naan* may be just the ticket.

LODGING

As with restaurants, practically every hotel in India will gladly put up with children running around. Most allow children under a certain age to stay in their parents' room at no extra charge or for a nominal charge, but others charge for them as extra adults. Confirm the cutoff age for children's discounts. Only in the more upscale hotels will you find extra special accommodations like a cot or a crib. The same goes for structured children's programs: Oberoi and Taj hotels offer pretty reliable plans for kids with staff supervision, but programs vary from hotel to hotel, so you'll need to ask when making reservations. Most Oberoi hotels also have a library of kid-friendly DVDs. Beyond the luxury realm, however, there's nothing that kids will find particularly spectacular about the average Indian hotel, i.e., no over-the-top playgrounds. You're better off trying to impress them with the sights and the streets.

PRECAUTIONS

The precautions you take for yourself in India are the same ones you should take for your child. Make sure they have all their vaccinations, and consult a pediatrition about anti-malaria medication. Bring a mosquito repellant spray from home that you know to be safe for children. And only give them bottled water to help guard against stomach problems that could spoil a short trip.

SIGHTS & ATTRACTIONS

Places that are especially appealing to children are indicated by a rubber-duckie icon (🐤) in the margin.

SUPPLIES & EQUIPMENT

Sidewalks in Indian cities don't have much space for strollers, and often have cracks and holes. Be extra careful in Delhi and Mumbai as streets are crowded and cars unforgiving. **Pack all necessary medicines as well as rash creams, zinc oxide, sunscreen, diapers, and diaper wipes.** Clean bathrooms are hard to come by in both cities and the countryside, so **carry toilet paper and moist towelettes with you at all times.** Even more useful are hand sanitizers (make sure that any brand you buy is at least 60% alcohol to be effective). Your curious child may end up getting his hands dirty every so often and it's a good idea to clean up to avoid bacteria.

Although major brands of disposable diapers, as well as Nestlé instant baby cereals, are available in most cities, they can be hard to find. Powdered milk produced by such companies as Amul and Nestlé is readily available. Use those products instead of looking for fresh milk, which needs to be boiled properly. If you run out of formula, Lactogen is a reliable Indian brand. Bottled mineral water and packaged snacks—potato chips, cookies, chocolate bars, fruit juices, and soft drinks—are sold throughout India. Though not nutritious, such snacks are often preferable to food that may be spicy or not entirely hygienic. If you're heading out for a day of sightseeing, ask your hotel staff if they can pack a lunch for your child. A small hot pot or kettle can be useful for making instant soup or noodles, which are also available throughout India.

Pack cool, loose, easy-to-wash clothes. If you'll be taking any air-conditioned trains, bring a few pieces of warm clothing, as the cars get cold. Leggings help protect against mosquitoes in the evening, hats shade youthful faces from the sun, and rubber slippers or sandals are always practical. A few pairs of socks can come in handy. If you plan to travel by car **bring a portable car seat.** Choose accommodations that are air-conditioned or have rooms equipped with mosquito netting to protect your child from mosquito bites. **Pack plenty of insect repellent as well as a 3-square-foot piece of soft cloth netting** (available in fabric stores), which you can drape over a carriage or car seat to shield your child from insects. Pellet repellants that plug into the wall and release a mosquito-repelling scent are available in stores across India, and are effective in keeping a room mosquito-free. It's a good idea to purchase such a gizmo on arrival (try Good Knight or All Out). **Consult your pediatrician about having your child take antimalaria pills,** as malaria is common even in the big cities.

COMMUNICATIONS

INTERNET

High-speed Internet access is available almost everywhere in India at Internet cafés and hotels, and connection speeds often approach you're used to at home. Local Indian coffee chains, such as Café Coffee Day, and other hangout spots (as well as hotels) in the major cities sometimes offer wireless for a minimal charge, but it can be difficult to actually connect (the services aren't used that frequently). Rates at Internet cafés are very cheap (around Rs. 50 for an hour), so it's probably best to leave your computer at home unless you absolutely need it.

If you plan to bring a laptop to India, carry a spare battery and spare adapter. New batteries and replacement adapters may be expensive and hard to find. Never plug your computer into a socket before asking about surge protection—some hotels don't have built-in current stabilizers, and extreme electrical fluctuations can short your adapter or even destroy your computer.

Contacts Cybercafes (*www.cybercafes.com*) lists over 4,000 Internet cafés worldwide.

PHONES

The good news is that you can now make a direct-dial telephone call from virtually any point on earth. The bad news? You can't always do so cheaply. Calling from a hotel is almost always the most expensive option; hotels usually add huge surcharges to all calls, particularly international ones. In some countries you can phone from call centers or even the post office. Calling cards usually keep costs to a minimum, but only if you purchase them locally. And then there are mobile phones (*⇨ below*), which are sometimes more prevalent—particularly in the developing world—than landlines; as expensive as mobile phone calls can be, they are still usually a much cheaper option than calling from your hotel.

Using landline as well as mobile phones in India can be frustrating—sometimes the connections are great, sometimes they're lousy, and you'll almost always have to repeat youself at least once because connections just don't seem to be that crisp.

A few peculiarities to keep in mind: Indian businesses usually have a series of phone numbers instead of just one, because networks can get congested. If a number reads "562/331701 through 331708," for example, you can reach the establishment using any number between 331701 and 331708. Some of the numbers may be telefax numbers, so if you're trying to send a fax and someone answers, ask them to put the fax machine on. Homes may also have two phone lines.

Unfortunately there is no standard number of digits in landline phone numbers across the country. The norm, however, is ten digits, which includes a city code of two or three digits. Mobile phone numbers are always 10 digits and start with the number 9.

The country code for India is 91, after which you dial the city code, and then the phone number. Delhi's city code is 11, and Mumbai's is 22. Some city codes are three digits, such as the code for Amritsar, which is 183.

CALLING WITHIN INDIA

If you're calling long-distance within India to any of the landline numbers listed in this book, dial a zero, then the city code, then the phone number. You only have to dial a zero before a ten-digit mobile phone number—there is no city code. When calling from a mobile phone to another one in a different city, the call is considered long distance.

Aside from the quality of connections at times, the local telephone system is adequate for getting in touch when you need to. All phone numbers can be dialed directly from pretty much every public access phone, eliminating the need for an operator.

If you don't have a mobile phone, the easiest option is to make a call from one of the ubiquitous public call offices (PCOs), easily identifiable by their bright yellow signs. They're not really offices so much as open-air booths, and they're pretty much on every street corner in Indian cities and in small villages, too, as well as in airports and train stations. PCOs are equipped with ISD/STD capabilities, meaning you can make both international and long-distance domestic calls in addition to local ones. (ISD stands for international subscriber dialing, STD for subscriber trunk [direct distance] dialing.) You'll make a call from a regular telephone connected to a meter that keeps track of the time. Once you hang up, an attendant will give you a receipt with the meter reading and tell you how much you owe. Rates are on a per-minute basis, and there is no surcharge. At less than Rs. 10 per minute, domestic calls won't break the bank. It's much more expensive to call internationally, though, so inquire about current rates to different countries. Still, if you just want to call home quickly to tell a family member that you're safe, a PCO is extremely convenient and hassle-free. Try to avoid making calls from hotels. They often come with huge surcharges, and it's just as convenient to use the PCO down the street.

Directory assistance is spotty in India. The private company Just Dial (🌐www.justdial.com) is reliable and has numbers all over the country. One national number—3999–9999—can be called for assistance from anywhere in India.

CALLING OUTSIDE INDIA

International calls can be subject to long delays, but most hotels, airports, train stations, post offices and PCOs are connected to the International Subscriber Dialing (ISD) system. You just dial 00, followed by the country code, the area code, and the number. If calling from a public phone stall, you'll be handed a receipt with the number of minutes and an attendant will calculate how much you owe. Remember that hotels add an enormous surcharge to international calls and faxes; in addition, they sometimes charge a fee per call made on your calling card. Find out what the charges are before you dial. To avoid the surcharge, make your calls at a PCO (even then, the price will be around US$3 a minute to most places). There are no reduced-rate calling hours for international calls. Some Internet cafés are set up to let you use a Internet-based calling service such as Skype. This allows very inexpensive international rates.

The country code for the United States is 1.

Using an AT&T access code to reach an operator can be helpful if you absolutely must use your own calling card from home or want to have charges billed to your personal account. However, it's usually more trouble than it's worth, and calling cards bought locally are guaranteed to be cheaper. Some hotels might not let you use the access number, and surcharges are always involved.

Access Codes **AT&T USADirect** (☎ *000117*).

CALLING CARDS

Calling cards for use within India are fairly common. The Indian mobile service providers Airtel and Vodafone sell international prepaid calling cards that you can use to call domestically, too. International rates are less than Rs. 10 per minute. The cards work on mobile phones and landlines, including at PCOs, and can be bought at practically any stall or shop selling mobile services. Remember that there might be a surcharge for connecting with these cards on hotel phones.

MOBILE PHONES

If you have a multiband phone (some countries use different frequencies than what's used in the United States) and your service provider uses the world-standard GSM network (as do T-Mobile, Cingular, and Verizon), you can probably use your phone abroad. Roaming fees can be steep, however: 99¢ a minute is considered reasonable. And overseas you normally pay the toll charges for incoming calls. It's almost always cheaper to send a text message than to make a call, since text messages have a very low set fee (often less than 5¢).

If you just want to make local calls, consider buying a new SIM card (note that your provider may have to unlock your phone for you to use a different SIM card) and a prepaid service plan in the destination. You'll then have a local number and can make local calls at local rates. If your trip is extensive, you could also simply buy a new cell phone in your destination, as the initial cost will be offset over time.

■TIP→If you travel internationally frequently, save one of your old mobile phones or buy a cheap one on the Internet; ask your cell phone company to unlock it for you, and take it with you as a travel phone, buying a new SIM card with pay-as-you-go service in each destination.

Mobile phone technology is excellent in India, and whether you have your own phone or rent one, you'll likely be connected wherever you go because of extensive network coverage all over the country—even in small towns.

If you're based in Europe or another Asian country, your mobile phone will probably work in India. American mobile phones increasingly have international roaming capabilities, so inquire with your provider. But also confirm how much the provider charges per minute for international roaming, which is expensive unless you have a special plan.

If you are planning on staying several weeks, it may be worth your while (and the least hassle) to simply buy a phone along with a pre-paid local SIM card. In most cities there are mobile phone shops on just about every corner, and they often sell good-quality used phones as well as inexpensive new ones. You'll have to provide a copy of your passport, two passport-sized photos and your local address to register for a SIM card, and you'll usually be up and running with a phone number in less than 15 minutes. Renting a phone might also be a possibility at these shops, and luxury hotels often provide use of mobile phones for a fee, too.

You will have to pay a certain amount of rupees in advance to get talk time. Nonresidents do not have the option of "post-pay" plans. Rates are generally Rs. 1–Rs. 2 per minute. When you've run out of minutes, you can easily recharge your phone at a mobile service shop. Airtel and Vodafone are two of the country's largest mobile service providers.

Contacts Cellular Abroad (☎ *800/287–5072* *www.cellularabroad.com*) rents and sells GMS phones and sells SIM cards that work in many countries. **Mobal** (☎ *888/888–9162* *www.mobalrental.com*) rents mobiles and sells GSM phones (starting at $49) that will operate in 140 countries. Per-call rates vary throughout the world. **Planet Fone** (☎ *888/988–4777* *www.planetfone.com*) rents cell phones, but the per-minute rates are expensive.

CUSTOMS & DUTIES

You're always allowed to bring goods of a certain value back home without having to pay any duty or import tax. But there's a limit on the amount of tobacco and liquor you can bring back duty-free, and some countries have separate limits for perfumes; for exact figures, check with your customs department. The values of so-called "duty-free" goods are included in these amounts. When you shop abroad, save all your receipts, as customs inspectors may ask to see them as well as the items you purchased. If the total value of your goods is more than the duty-free limit, you'll have to pay a tax (most often a flat percentage) on the value of everything beyond that limit.

The customs process at the international gateways isn't difficult, although the line you have to wait in is likely to be long. If you're entering India with dutiable or valuable articles, you must mention this when you stop at customs. Officials may ask you to fill in a Tourist Baggage Re-Export Form (TBRE), as such articles must be taken with you when you leave India. You'll have to pay a duty on anything listed on the TBRE that you plan to leave in India. Depending on the attitude of the customs official, you may have to list your laptop computer, camera or video equipment, and mobile phone on a TBRE form. It's a good idea, though, not to go searching for forms or a customs official unless someone questions you.

Among other things, you may bring the following into India duty-free: personal effects (clothing and jewelry); a camera, a video camera, a laptop computer, a cell phone, 200 cigarettes or 50 cigars or 250 grams of tobacco, up to two liters of alcoholic liquors or wines, and gifts not exceeding a value of Rs. 8,000 (about US$200). You may *not* bring in illegal drugs, firearms, Indian currency, pornographic material, counterfeit or pirated goods or antiquities. Consult India's Central Board of Excise and Customs Web site for complete details.

LEAVING INDIA

Rupees aren't allowed out of India; you must exchange them before you depart, although you are unlikely to be questioned or searched for a few small bills you may have kept for a soda in the airport. Foreign-exchange facilities are usually in the same airport halls as the check-in counters but there's no access to these facilities once you pass through immigration. Tourists cannot take out more foreign currency then they brought in. There is no limit on gold jewelry.

All animal products, souvenirs, and trophies are subject to the Wildlife Protection Act of 1972. The export of ivory (unless you can prove it's antique) and the skins of protected species aren't allowed. Export of exotic birds, wildlife, orchids, and other flora and fauna is forbidden as well. Consult the regional deputy director for wildlife preservation or the chief wildlife wardens of the state governments in Mumbai, Kolkata, Delhi, or Chennai if you have questions.

In general, items more than 100 years old cannot be exported without a permit from the Archaeological Survey, which has offices in many cities, including Delhi, Mumbai, Kolkata, Bhubaneswar, Chennai, and Bangalore. Reputable shops will provide you with the necessary permit or help you get it.

Information in India **Central Board of Excise and Customs** (*www.customs.gov.in*).

U.S. Information **U.S. Customs and Border Protection** (*www.cbp.gov*).

EATING OUT

Indian culture definitely revolves around food, so there's no shortage of local restaurants and international chains serving foreign cuisines and fast food in big cities as well as regional Indian cuisine everywhere. There are also lots of little no-frills cafés and food stalls lining the streets where locals can pick up all kinds of snacks in between meals (although if you're staying in India for just a short time, you should probably take a cautious stance with its famous street food). India is also a haven for vegetarians with tons of "veg" restaurants, as they're called. Even non-veg places usually have delicious meatless options.

The restaurants we list are the cream of the crop in each price category. Properties indicated by an ✕ are lodging establishments whose restaurant warrants a special trip. Delhi and Mumbai are in a financial league of their own when it comes to restaurants with high prices—many other large cities, including Hyderabad, Kolkata, and Bangalore, aren't far behind. Restaurants outside of tourist and business areas, especially those in smaller towns, tend to be much less expensive.

For information on food-related health issues, see Health below.

MEALS & MEALTIMES

The Indian cuisine you may have been exposed to in Indian restaurants abroad is probably one percent of the variety of cuisine available in India. It's essential to travel across India cautiously but bravely, and enjoy as much of the food as possible. Indians love to feed guests and a food adventure is inevitable. The cuisine of India varies vastly from region to region. In the north you have Punjab's heavy, charcoal-roasted food and the Kashmiri meat dishes; in central India the food is lighter, and you also have the mustard-flavored fish of Bengal in the east and Tibetan and Chinese-influenced food in the northeast. In the west, there's the extravagant vegetarian cuisine of Gujarat and Rajasthan. Along the coast in the south—from the Konkan coast to Mangalore and down to Kerala—you'll find delicious fish and prawn curries. *Biryanis* and kebabs are native to Hyderbad in south-central India. And, of course, you have a zillion varieties of *dosas* (giant semolina or lentil-flour crepes filled with spicy potatoes), meat curries, fried fish, and light vegetarian dishes in Tamil Nadu, all the way south.

India does its own brand of Chinese very well. Don't miss out sampling one or two spicy, cilantro-flavored Indo-Chinese dishes—Manchurian dishes, for instance, are made with a deep-fried and battered ingredient such as cauliflower or chicken, which is then put into a sweet, chilli-heavy sauce. And British influence, still potent in some quarters, led to Anglo-Indian dishes such as mince cutlets, curry puffs, *kedgeree* (a soupy rice and fish dish), mulligatawny soup, and plum cake (available during the Christmas season).

A regular Indian meal consists of some rice or bread, served with spiced vegetables, meat, and lentils. Accessories to the meal can be *chaas* (a digestive drink), *lassi* (a sweet or salty yogurt drink), pickle, *papad* (a deep-fried or dry roasted wafer-like savory made from lentil or rice), chutney, *farsan* (a snack), and *raita* (spiced yogurt). A sweet, usually very sugary and milk-based, is the last course. At the end of the meal, as a digestive, *paan* (a stimulating concoction of sugar and various spices wrapped in the leaves of the betel pepper plant), *supari* (plain betel nut), cracked rock candy, or anise seed may be served.

Indian breakfasts are none too light and not that early. They can consist of any of the following: *idlis* (steamed rice and lentil cakes) with chutney, *rasam wada* (deep-fried lentil fritters served with a hot, spicy watery lentil curry), *dosas, jalebis* (deep-fried bright yellow flour fritters soaked in sugar syrup) served with milk, *upma* (light semolina, also known as farina, with vegetables), or *aloo poha* (spicy potatoes mixed with rice flakes).

A good portion of India is vegetarian for economic and religious reasons—meat is not part of a daily meal. Indians rarely eat beef and pork, except in certain regions or communities. Many Hindus consider the cow sacred and do not eat beef. Muslims do not touch pork as they consider it unclean. And many Hindus choose to eat only chicken and seafood and stay away from red meat. Jains are not only vegetarian but do not eat any vegetable grown under the ground—one reason may be that plucking up the root destroys life. As you travel through India, expect to encounter folks who don't eat meat on Tuesday or eat only fruits on Friday; much of India's religious and ethical life, indeed, revolves around food.

Lunches are early—not later than 1 PM. Restaurants in cities normally stay open until 11 PM or midnight, as Indians are known for starting dinner quite late (past 10 PM). In other areas, expect an earlier dinner in restaurants (finished by 9) unless you're staying in a luxury hotel. Coffee shops in urban luxury hotels are often open 24 hours.

Four o'clock is considered snack time, which means another round of elaborate savories and sweets served with tea. India is a major tea-drinking nation: *masala chai* (spiced tea) and ginger tea are extremely popular and are often consumed four to five times a day. But as you go south, coffee becomes equally important and is served boiling hot, creamy, and foamy (sort of like a triple expresso with cream and sugar).

Unless otherwise noted, the restaurants listed in this guide are open daily for lunch and dinner.

RESERVATIONS & DRESS

Regardless of where you are, it's a good idea to make a reservation if you can. In some places, it's expected. We only mention them specifically when reservations are essential (there's no other way you'll ever get a table) or when they are not accepted. For popular restaurants, book as far ahead as you can (often 30 days), and reconfirm as soon as you arrive. (Large parties should always call ahead to check the reservations policy.)

Very few restaurants require formal attire. By and large India is very casual about dress codes. However, certain clubs do not allow anyone—even in daylight hours—to wear shorts or men to wear sandals unless with Indian-style clothes. Reservations are also not required by most restaurants, except in the fanciest of upscale, big-city hotels.

WINES, BEER & SPIRITS

India produces many kinds of liquor, and exorboritant duties make imported spirits unaffordable to all but the most wealthy of its citizens. Its locally produced rums, vodka, and gin are adequate but generally unmemorable, although Old Monk rum is worth a try. Kingfisher beer is ubiquitous, refreshing, and bland. With every year more and more Indian wine is produced, and much of it is good, although not overly complex. Scotch whisky is by far the most popular kind of hard liquor in India: Director's Special is a mild and reliable brand.

Alcohol at luxury hotels is vastly marked up. Consider buying your own liquor and having it in your room—you can always call for a glass, bottled water, and soda. If you're a woman traveling alone, drinking in your room is probably a better option in any case.

Indian customs may appear prudish toward drinking—but open a bottle and you may find you're quite popular. According to proper Indian etiquette, alcohol is excluded from many occasions. When you visit someone's house you may not be offered a drink even in the evening, and the strongest beverage you may get is tea. At many weddings and at festival time alcohol may not be served. Women are infrequent drinkers, at least in public. However, don't be surprised if you encounter quite a few male teetotalers.

Dry days—when alcohol isn't available anywhere in the country—are observed on January 26, August 15, October 2, and on certain festival dates. Some states observe additional dry days; others prohibit everything but beer. Gujarat is always dry. As a foreigner you may apply to the Gujarat Tourism Development Corporation for a permit that allows you to buy alcohol in the state. The Government of India Tourist Office in Mumbai or Delhi (or even abroad) can also issue a three- to six-month liquor permit on your passport allowing you to carry liquor into Gujarat.

ELECTRICITY

Blackouts lasting anywhere from 30 minutes to 12 hours are a part of everyday Indian life, particularly in summer when the load is high. But if you're staying at a mid- to high-end hotel, there is no doubt a generator that can restore electricity within seconds. Storms can play havoc with electricity, and low-voltage electricity and surges are problems. Consider carrying a flashlight or packing a small hand-held fan if you plan on being in rural, rugged areas for any length of time.

WORD OF MOUTH

Was the service stellar or not up to snuff? Did the food give you shivers of delight or leave you cold? Did the prices and portions make you happy or sad? Rate restaurants and write your own reviews in Travel Ratings or start a discussion about your favorite places in Travel Talk on www.fodors.com. Your comments might even appear in our books. Yes, you, too, can be a correspondent!

The electrical current in India is 220 volts, 50 cycles alternating current (AC); most wall outlets take plugs with two round prongs.

Consider making a small investment in a universal adapter, which has several types of plugs in one lightweight, compact unit. Most laptops and mobile phone chargers are dual voltage (i.e., they operate equally well on 110 and 220 volts), so require only an adapter. These days the same is true of small appliances such as hair dryers. Always check labels and manufacturer instructions to be sure. Don't use 110-volt outlets marked FOR SHAVERS ONLY for high-wattage appliances such as hair-dryers.

Contacts Steve Kropla's Help for World Traveler's (*www.kropla.com*) has information on electrical and telephone plugs around the world. **Walkabout Travel Gear** (*www.walkabouttravelgear.com*) has a good coverage of electricity under "adapters."

EMERGENCIES

Delhi's 24-hour East-West Medical Center has a referral list of doctors, dentists, pharmacists, and lawyers throughout India. Its staffers can arrange treatment wherever you are in the country, and it's the only clinic in India recognized by most international insurance companies. It also provides air ambulances that can evacuate you from remote areas in the case of a medical emergency. Note: you must pay the center when you receive assistance—credit cards are accepted—and then apply for reimbursement by your insurance company later. It's necessary to get in touch with East-West first so that they can verify your policy details. This can take anywhere from a few hours to a day, depending on the day of the week and whether the details are in order; at that point East-West will organize payment.

For life-threatening conditions, go to Indraprastha Apollo Hospital, Delhi's premier private hospital, southeast of town. From there, you can call Meera Rescue, based in Delhi with branches in Bombay and Goa, if international evacuation is necessary. (Whatever happens, don't go to a government hospital. In a grave emergency, contact your embassy.) Meera Rescue is an extremely professional evacuation service recognized by international insurance companies; the company evacuates from anywhere in the country to hospitals in major cities, as well as overseas if necessary; it's open 24 hours. Like East-West, you must pay Meera and be reimbursed by your insurance company later.

FOREIGN EMBASSIES
United States ✉ *Shantipath, Chanakyapuri, New Delhi* ☎ *11/2419–8000* 🌐 *http://newdelhi.usembassy.gov.*

General Emergency Contacts **Indraprastha Apollo Hospital** (✉ *Delhi–Sarita Vihar, Delhi Mathura Rd.* ☎ *11/2692–5801 or 11/2692–5858* 🌐 *www.apollohospdelhi.com*). **East-West Medical Center** (✉ *38 Golf Links, New Delhi 110003* ☎ *11/2462–3738, 11/2469–9229, 11/2469–0429, or 11/2469–8865* 📠 *11/469–0428 or 11/463–2382* 🌐 *www.eastwestrescue.com*). **Meera Rescue** (✉ *112 Jor Bagh, New Delhi 110003* ☎ *11/2465–3100 or 11/2465–3170* 🌐 *www.meera-rescue.com*).

GAY & LESBIAN TRAVEL

Although India is a sexually conservative society, there's a growing awareness and acceptance of homosexuality in major cities. Still, gay and lesbian travelers should keep their sexual preference to themselves. Legally India does not accept homosexuality. No hotel will object to two people of the same sex sharing a room, but **don't display your affection in public.** Note that Indian men and boys commonly walk hand in hand as a sign of friendship. Mumbai now has a strong gay community and a few pubs and bars have gay nights. Other cities do as well, but such nights are usually not publicly advertised.

Gay- & Lesbian-Friendly Travel Agencies
Different Roads Travel (☎ *760/325–6964 or 800/429–8747 [Ext. 14]*). **Skylink Travel and Tour/Flying Dutchmen Travel** (☎ *707/546–9888 or 800/225–5759*); serving lesbian travelers.

HEALTH

The most common types of illnesses are caused by contaminated food and water. Especially in developing countries, drink only bottled, boiled, or purified water and drinks; don't drink from public fountains or use ice. You should even consider using bottled water to brush your teeth. Make sure food has been thoroughly cooked and is served to you fresh and hot; avoid vegetables and fruits that you haven't washed (in bottled or purified water) or peeled yourself. If you have problems, mild cases of traveler's diarrhea may respond to Imodium (known generically as loperamide) or Pepto-Bismol. Be sure to drink plenty of fluids; if you can't keep fluids down, seek medical help immediately.

Infectious diseases can be airborne or passed via mosquitoes and ticks and through direct or indirect physical contact with animals or people. Some, including Norwalk-like viruses that affect your digestive tract, can be passed along through contaminated food. If you are traveling in an area where malaria is prevalent, use a repellant containing DEET and take malaria-prevention medication before, during, and after your trip as directed by your physician. Condoms can help prevent most sexually transmitted diseases, but they aren't absolutely reliable and their quality varies from country to country. Speak with your physician and/or check the CDC or World Health Organization Web sites for health alerts, particularly if you're pregnant, traveling with children, or have a chronic illness.

For information on travel insurance, shots and medications, and medical-assistance companies see Shots & Medications under Things to Consider in Before You Go, above.

SPECIFIC ISSUES IN INDIA

The major health risk in India is traveler's diarrhea, caused by eating contaminated fruit or vegetables or drinking contaminated water, so it's important to watch what you eat. Avoid ice, uncooked food, and unpasteurized milk and milk products, and **drink only bottled water or water that has been boiled for 20 minutes.** Avoid tap water, ice, and drinks to which tap water has been added. **Turn down offers of "filtered" or "aquaguard" water;** it may have been filtered to take out particles but not purified to kill parasites. **When buying bottled water, make sure that the cap hasn't been tampered with.** Bottles are sometimes refilled with tap water. Soft drinks, in bottles or cans, and packaged fruit juices are safe, readily available options. And always **keep at least one bottle of water in your hotel room** for brushing your teeth as well as for drinking.

If your stomach does get upset, try to drink plenty of purified water or tea—ginger (*adrak*) tea is a good folk remedy. In severe cases, rehydrate yourself with a salt-sugar solution—½ teaspoon salt (*namak*) and 4 tablespoons sugar (*shakar*) per quart of water.

Avoid raw vegetables and fruit, even those that have been peeled unless it was cut and peeled by you. Make sure that all meats are thoroughly cooked. It's not necessary to go vegetarian, and to do so would mean missing out on some delicious dishes. Just choose restaurants with care, and eat hot foods while they're hot. A little bit of personal hygiene can also go a long way in preventing stomach upsets. Wash your hands before you eat anything, and carry moist towelettes. These are readily available in large cities.

Locally popular, worn-looking restaurants often serve the safest food. Such restaurants often can't afford refrigeration, so the cooks prepare food acquired that day—not always the case with the upscale places. Some hotel chefs buy in bulk and, thanks to temperamental electricity, a refrigerator may preserve more than just foodstuffs. That said, stomach upsets often are due more to the richness and spice of Indian cuisine as to the lack of hygiene. Many hotel restaurants cook Indian dishes with quite a bit of oil. If you have a sensitive stomach, order carefully and don't overdo things. Fried foods from street vendors often looks delicious, but inspect the oil: if it looks as old as the pot, it could be rancid.

Stomach issues are what tend to scare first-time visitors the most, and if you're only going to be in India for a short time, it makes sense to take as many precautions as possible so sickness won't cut into your vacation. However, if you're going to be in India for a longer period, try to acclimate yourself to things like street food, filtered water, ice, and the wonderful abundance of fresh-squeezed juices, because avoiding every single thing that could possibly make you sick in India is not only impractical, but limiting. Chances are that your body will simply adjust and become resistant to most stomach problems.

All Indian cities are heavily polluted, though serious efforts have been going on for years to reduce vehicle pollution. Regulations and devices were introduced in 1995, but quite a few vehicles still use leaded gas or diesel fuel. Mumbai and Delhi require their taxis to run on compressed natural gas, which has considerably reduced the smog. People with breathing problems, especially asthma, should **carry the appropriate respiratory remedies.** India's heat can dehydrate you, and dust can irritate your throat, so **drink plenty of liquids.** Dehydration will make you weak and more susceptible to other health problems. Seek air-conditioned areas when possible, and plan your day so you're visiting tourist sites in the early morning or late afternoon, when the sun is less strong.

If you travel into forested areas during or right after the monsoon, you may be fall victim to the disgusting but generally nondangerous plague of leeches, which lie in wait on damp land. Help protect yourself by covering your legs and carrying salt. Applying DEET and strong-smelling chemicals such as deodorant to your skin and pants will also help make your flesh less appealing. Don't wear sandals. If a leech clings to your clothing or skin, dab it with a pinch of salt and it will fall off. If itching persists, apply an antiseptic; infection is rare.

For bedbugs, buy a bar of Dettol soap (available throughout India) and use it when you bathe to relieve itching and discomfort. If you're staying in a dubious hotel, **check under the mattress** for bedbugs, cockroaches, and other unwanted critters. Use Flit, Finit, or one of the other readily available spray repellents on suspicious-looking furniture and in mosquito-infested rooms. Mosquito coils (*kachua*), which you must light, and Good Knight pellets, which are plugged into an outlet, are fairly effective at "smoking" mosquitoes away. On the road, **treat scratches, cuts, or blisters at once.** If you're trekking, save the bottle and cap from your first bottled water so you can refill it with water that you purify yourself.

Beware of overexposure even on overcast days. To avoid sunburn, **use a sunscreen** with a sun-protection factor of at least 24. To play it safe, **wear a wide-brimmed hat.** If you plan to travel above 10,000 feet, use zinc oxide, lip balm with sunblock, and sunglasses that block ultraviolet rays. When you're on snowy terrain, remember that UV rays reflect from below.

If you're up in the mountains, watch out for signs of altitude sickness, an adverse reaction to low oxygen pressure—it can be deadly. If your urine is bright yellow, you're not drinking enough water. To minimize high-altitude misery, **drink lots of water, eat foods high in carbohydrates, and cut back on salt.** Stop and rest immediately if you develop any of the following symptoms: nausea, loss of appetite, extreme headache or lightheadedness, unsteady feet, sleeplessness. If resting doesn't help, head for lower ground immediately.

OVER-THE-COUNTER REMEDIES

Buying over-the-counter medications is easy in India. In all cities and most towns, common remedies are abundant, and the pharmacies or "chemists"—which are also abundant—will carry a wide variety of both recognizable namebrands and Indian versions. If you're not sure what you need to make yourself feel better, shopkeepers can usually make good recommendations.

HOURS OF OPERATION

Most banks are open weekdays 10–2 and Saturday 10–noon, but ATMs are open around the clock in larger cities. International airports and some top hotels have 24-hour currency-exchange facilities, and the major American Express branches have extended hours for check-cashing. Post offices are generally open Monday–Saturday 10–5.

Gas stations are usually open daily from 6 AM–10 PM. In larger cities, some stay open 24 hours.

Most museums are closed on Monday. Site museums (adjoining archaeological monuments) are normally closed on Friday.

Pharmacies are usually open daily from 9:30–8, though in cities there are some 24-hour establishments. In some places you can also buy medicine from the 24-hour pharmacies at large hospitals. (Note that in India pharmacies are called "chemists.")

Outside the major metropolitan areas, many shopkeepers close their establishments for an afternoon siesta. Many stores are closed Sunday.

Bars and nightclubs in the big cities are usually done by 2 AM, although some local laws mandate much earlier closing times, such as 11.

HOLIDAYS

India's fixed national holidays are January 26 (Republic Day), August 15 (Independence Day), October 2 (Gandhi's birthday), and December 25 (Christmas). Endless festivals enliven—and shut down—different parts of the country throughout the year. Festivals often affect availability of travel connections or the time taken to reach the airport so look into the holidays that are coming up as you plan your itinerary.

MAIL

The Indian postal system is fairly reliable, and stamps can be bought in post offices and other various shops. Airmail letters and postcards take a week to 10 days to reach most destinations from India. Postal delays are caused by holiday rushes (during Diwali and the Christmas season) and strikes.

Airmail letters (weighing 10 grams) to Australia, New Zealand, United States, Canada, South Africa, or Europe cost Rs. 15; postcards cost Rs. 8. Aerograms to anywhere in the world are Rs. 8.50.

To receive mail in India, it's best to have something sent to your hotel or the address where you are staying. Inform your hotel that a package will be arriving in your name. You can also have letters or packages sent to an American Express office. Mail is held at these offices for 30 days before it's returned to the sender; it can also be forwarded for a nominal charge. To retrieve your mail, show your American Express card or American Express Travelers Checks plus one piece of identification, preferably a passport. This service is free to AmEx cardmembers and traveler's-check holders; others pay a fee.

SHIPPING PACKAGES

There are many options for shipping gifts home. Many stores—especially those that cater to tourists—ship items using courier services or other private methods. It's usually reliable and fast, but reconsider shipping anything special that you would absolutely hate to lose. You can send parcels home "surface air lifted," a special service provided by the Indian postal department that's cheaper than airmail. A letter or parcel of 250 grams or less costs Rs. 310 to the North America. Each additional 250 grams cost Rs. 65. Rates differ for other countries.

Express mail is known as "speed post" in India. There are speed-post centers all over the country; they're generally open daily 9–5. It costs Rs. 425 to send a letter or parcel of 250 grams or less to North America. Each additional 250 grams costs Rs. 100. Here, too, rates differ for other countries. You can send a package that weighs as much as 20 kilograms by speed post.

Private couriers and parcel companies—Airborne Express, Blue Dart, DHL, UPS, FedEx—operate in India as well. A letter sent through such a service takes about three working days to reach the

United States. Rates are much higher than speed-post rates—as much as $40 to send a simple envelope.

MONEY

A trip to India can be as luxurious and expensive—or as bare-bones and cheap—as you want it to be. The economy has really spiked since 2000, along with domestic travel and international foot traffic, and as a result, room rates at fancy urban hotels are comparable to those in New York, London, or Paris. You'll pay substantially more for everything in tourist spots and big cities compared with the rest of the country. Case in point: one popular tourist rest stop on the way to Agra charges Rs. 50 for its bottles of sodas. You could get at a food stall anywhere else for less than Rs. 20. In addition, many top hotels and some airlines charge foreigners U.S.-dollar prices that are substantially higher than the rupee prices paid by Indians. Thankfully, this tactic seems to be on the way out, though you will still pay a premium for everything at top hotels.

If you're willing to stay at modest hotels and eat where the locals do, you might find that the most expensive part of your trip turns out to be the international air fare ($1,000–$2,000, depending on when you go). It's possible to find good hotels for less than US$70 a night, and the cheapest run less than US$30. You could also conceivably eat every meal for less than US$2. Many merchants, even in big cities, still only accept cash. Always carry rupees as well as a credit card in your wallet. Although you can cash traveler's checks in big cities, it's rarely convenient to do so. Shopkeepers appreciate it when people pay with correct change or as close to it as possible. In fact they balk at giving change in general. The 1,000 rupee note should definitely not be used to pay for, say, something that costs Rs. 100, because merchants might not even have that much change on hand. Stick to denominations of Rs. 100 or less, and don't flaunt Rs. 500 and Rs. 1,000 notes.

A cup of tea from a stall costs about Rs. 2 (US5¢), but in top hotels it can cost more than Rs. 50 (US$1.25). A 650-ml bottle of beer costs about Rs. 75 (US$1.90) in a shop, Rs. 250 (US$6) without taxes in a top hotel. A 5-km (3-mi) taxi ride in Delhi is supposed to cost about Rs. 65 (US$1.60), though it rarely does because taxi drivers often do not want to use their meters and try to charge higher prices for tourists. Throughout this book, we quote admission fees for adults, which in India are usually the same as those for children.

ITEM	AVERAGE COST
Cup of Coffee	Rs. 5–Rs. 30, fancy Rs. 50
Glass of Wine	Rs. 200
Glass of Beer	Rs. 250 in a bar or hotel
Sandwich	Rs. 20–Rs. 50
Museum Admission	Rs. 200–Rs. 250 (foreign rates)

Prices throughout this guide are given for adults. Substantially reduced fees are almost always available for children, students, and senior citizens.

TIP→ Banks never have every foreign currency on hand, and it may take as long as a week to order. If you're planning to exchange funds before leaving home, don't wait till the last minute.

ATMS & BANKS

Your own bank will probably charge a fee for using ATMs abroad; the foreign bank you use may also charge a fee. Nevertheless, you'll usually get a better rate of exchange at an ATM than you will at a currency-exchange office or even when changing money in a bank. And extracting funds as you need them is a safer option than carrying around a large amount of cash.

TIP→ PIN numbers with more than four digits are not recognized at ATMs in many

countries. If yours has five or more, remember to change it before you leave.

There are only a few cash machines in smaller towns in India, but larger cities are dotted with ATMs. Look for ICICI, HDFC, or HSBC ATMs, which generally accept foreign cards. Other ATMs might only accept Indian cards, especially in smaller towns. If you know you'll be traveling to a rural area, it's crucial to have enough cash on hand.

If you think you'll need cash from your bank account or cash advances through your credit card, make sure that your bank and credit cards are programmed for ATM use in India before you leave home, and inform your bank that you'll be using your cards in India. All ATMs function in English, and most have security guards.

CREDIT CARDS

Throughout this guide, the following abbreviations are used: **AE,** American Express; **DC,** Diners Club; **MC,** MasterCard; and **V,** Visa.

It's a good idea to inform your credit-card company before you travel, especially if you're going abroad and don't travel internationally very often. Otherwise, the credit-card company might put a hold on your card owing to unusual activity—not a good thing halfway through your trip. Record all your credit-card numbers—as well as the phone numbers to call if your cards are lost or stolen—in a safe place, so you're prepared should something go wrong. Both MasterCard and Visa have general numbers you can call (collect if you're abroad) if your card is lost, but you're better off calling the number of your issuing bank, since MasterCard and Visa usually just transfer you to your bank; your bank's number is usually printed on your card.

If you plan to use your credit card for cash advances, you'll need to apply for a PIN at least two weeks before your trip. Although it's usually cheaper (and safer) to use a credit card abroad for large purchases (so you can cancel payments or be reimbursed if there's a problem), note that some credit-card companies *and* the banks that issue them add substantial percentages to all foreign transactions, whether they're in a foreign currency or not. Check on these fees before leaving home, so there won't be any surprises when you get the bill.

■ **TIP→ Before you charge something, ask the merchant whether or not he or she plans to do a dynamic currency conversion (DCC). In such a transaction the credit-card processor (shop, restaurant, or hotel, not Visa or MasterCard) converts the currency and charges you in dollars. In most cases you'll pay the merchant a 3% fee for this service in addition to any credit-card company and issuing-bank foreign-transaction surcharges.**

Dynamic currency conversion programs are becoming increasingly widespread. Merchants who participate in them are supposed to ask whether you want to be charged in dollars or the local currency, but they don't always do so. And even if they do offer you a choice, they may well avoid mentioning the additional surcharges. The good news is that you *do* have a choice. And if this practice really gets your goat, you can avoid it entirely thanks to American Express; with its cards, DCC simply isn't an option.

Credit cards are widely accepted in large Indian cities, especially at the retail chain stores and the upscale restaurants. Smaller merchants and street stalls, however, are likely to take only cash. It's a good idea to keep at least Rs. 1,000 (in small denominations) in your wallet at all times in the cities, along with your credit card, so you'll always have either option. In rural India, don't ever count on being able to pay with a credit card, and always have enough cash to see you through.

American Express is not widely accepted in India; neither is Diners Club, and Discover isn't accepted at all. In this book we use the following abbreviations: **AE,** American Express; **DC,** Diners Club; **MC,** MasterCard; **V,** Visa. Make sure you check with your credit-card company (or its Web site) to find out the number for reporting lost or stolen cards abroad.

Reporting Lost Cards American Express (☎ *800/528-4800 in the U.S. or 336/393-1111 collect from abroad* 🌐 *www.americanexpress.com*). **Diners Club** (☎ *800/234-6377 in the U.S. or 303/799-1504 collect from abroad* 🌐 *www.dinersclub.com*). **Discover** (☎ *800/347-2683 in the U.S. or 801/902-3100 collect from abroad* 🌐 *www.discovercard.com*). **MasterCard** (☎ *800/627-8372 in the U.S. or 636/722-7111 collect from abroad* 🌐 *www.mastercard.com*). **Visa** (☎ *800/847-2911 in the U.S. or 410/581-9994 collect from abroad* 🌐 *www.visa.com*).

CURRENCY & EXCHANGE

The units of Indian currency are the *rupee* and the *paisa*—100 paise equal one rupee. Paper money comes in denominations of 2 (quite rare), 5, 10, 20, 50, 100, 500, and 1,000 rupees. Coins are worth 5, 10, 20, 25, and 50 paise, 1 rupee, 2 rupees, and 5 rupees, but it's unlikely that you'll see anything less than 50 paise. At this writing, the rate of exchange is approximately US$1 to Rs. 40, so that a 500-rupee note is worth about $12.50.

India has strict rules against importing or exporting its currency. The currency-exchange booths at the international airports are always open for arriving and departing overseas flights. When you change money, remember to get a certain amount in small denominations (in 10's is best) to pay taxi drivers and such. Reject torn, frayed, taped, or soiled bills, as many merchants, hotels, and restaurants won't accept them, and it's a hassle to find a bank to get them exchanged.

WORST-CASE SCENARIO

All your money and credit cards have just been stolen. In these days of real-time transactions, this isn't a predicament that should destroy your vacation. First, report the theft of the credit cards. Then get any traveler's checks you were carrying replaced. This can usually be done almost immediately, provided that you kept a record of the serial numbers separate from the checks themselves. If you bank at a large international bank like Citibank or HSBC, go to the closest branch; if you know your account number, chances are you can get a new ATM card and withdraw money right away. **Western Union** (☎ *800/325-6000* 🌐 *www.westernunion.com*) sends money almost anywhere. Have someone back home order a transfer online, over the phone, or at one of the company's offices, which is the cheapest option. The U.S. State Department's **Overseas Citizens Services** (🌐 *www.travel.state.gov/travel* ☎ *202/501-4444*) can wire money to any U.S. consulate or embassy abroad for a fee of $30. Just have someone back home wire money or send a money order or cashier's check to the state department, which will then disburse the funds as soon as the next working day after it receives them.

Always change money from an authorized money-changer and insist on receiving an encashment slip. Some banks now charge a nominal fee for this slip, which you might need if you want to pay hotel bills or travel expenses in rupees, and again if you want to reconvert rupees into your own currency on departure from India. Don't be lured by illegal street hawkers who offer you a higher exchange rate.

For the most favorable rates, change money at banks. Although ATM transaction fees may be higher abroad than at home, ATM rates are excellent because they're based on wholesale rates offered only by major banks. India's state-run banks can take forever to cash traveler's checks. If you must use checks, save time and use an American Express office or the foreign-exchange service at your hotel. Rates will be slightly lower, but you'll save irritation and time. Rates are also unfavorable in airports, at train and bus stations, in restaurants, and in stores.

TIP→ Even if a currency-exchange booth has a sign promising no commission, rest assured that there's some kind of huge, hidden fee. (Oh... that's right. The sign didn't say no fee.). And as for rates, you're almost always better off getting foreign currency at an ATM or exchanging money at a bank.

TRAVELER'S CHECKS & CARDS

Some consider this the currency of the cave man, and it's true that fewer establishments accept traveler's checks these days. Nevertheless, they're a cheap and secure way to carry extra money, particularly on trips to urban areas. Both Citibank (under the Visa brand) and American Express issue traveler's checks in the United States, but Amex is better known and more widely accepted; you can also avoid hefty surcharges by cashing Amex checks at Amex offices. Whatever you do, keep track of all the serial numbers in case the checks are lost or stolen.

You can use traveler's checks in India, but in most cases, it's just not that convenient to cash them. Cash, then credit cards, are better options. You can only cash traveler's checks in big cities, and most merchants, whether urban or rural, don't accept them. Lost or stolen checks can usually be replaced within 24 hours. To ensure a speedy refund, buy your own traveler's checks—don't let someone else pay for them. The person who bought the checks should also make the call to request a refund. Don't leave traveler's checks in your hotel room, and keep the counterfoil with the check numbers separate from the checks.

Contacts American Express (☎ *888/412-6945 in the U.S., 801/945-9450 collect outside of the U.S. to add value or speak to customer service* 🌐 *www.americanexpress.com*).

RESTROOMS

When you need a restroom, ask for the "loo," or the toilet. Two types of toilets are available wherever you go in India. Traditional Indian toilets are holes in the ground—a squat variety with two steps to put your feet. There are also Western-style toilets, but the toilet seat, except in luxury hotels and better restaurants, may be messy. In many bathrooms you'll see a faucet, a small hand-held shower head, and/or a bucket with a beaker or other small vessel; Indians use these to rinse, bidet-style, after using the toilet. Hands are always washed elsewhere. Outside of hotels and some restaurants, clean public restrooms are hard to find, and are best avoided. On long road journeys finding any public restroom—let alone a clean one—is difficult. Always use the restroom before you set out and ration your fluid intake during a long journey. Be on the look out for a decent hotel or opt for the outdoors. Luxury hotels and fancier restaurants usually have clean bathrooms.

Nicer hotels and restaurants provide toilet paper, but you can't depend on this, as most Indians don't use the stuff (they use their left hand and running water to clean themselves, which is why this hand is considered unclean). And often soap and paper towels are not available for washing up afterwards. Keep toilet paper and towelettes with you at all times; it's readily available in pharmacies and grocery stores in large cities. Never throw anything in a toilet; India's septic systems can't handle it.

Find a Loo The Bathroom Diaries (🌐 *www.thebathroomdiaries.com*) is flush with unsanitized info on restrooms the world over—each one located, reviewed, and rated.

SAFETY

There are no generalizations that can be made regarding potential dangers for all tourists in India, but urban areas do have their particular crime patterns, and everyone is vulnerable. For example, Delhi is known to be dangerous for women at night and has more crime in general than other big cities in India. In Mumbai, however, women are relatively safe at all hours, with less crimes taking place, which is the main reason a reported rape there is almost always a big deal, but not so newsworthy in Delhi.

Scams for targeting foreigners abound. One of the more innocuous routines comes from the shoe shiners at Delhi's Connaught Place, who furtively sling mud at your feet and then point out how badly your shoes need to be cleaned. Just be cautious ever where you go, and know that in a country more popular than ever with tourists—and filled with locals vying for your business—you're always a potential target.

Theft in hotels is not common, but you should never leave money, traveler's checks, passports, or jewelry in plain sight. If your hotel has a safe, definitely use it, but if there's nothing to lock up valuables, you may wish to take them with you. Avoid wandering around late at night, especially in smaller towns where shutters close early, and avoid road journeys after dark. As anywhere, never leave suitcases unattended in airports or train stations.

India has no tourist police, except in Mumbai, and they patrol infrequently in orange jeeps. The most visible policemen are traffic cops, clad in white and khaki; they can usually help out, even with a nontraffic problem (though taxis are in their jurisdiction). Otherwise, look for a regular policeman, clad in khaki.

Avoid strangers who offer their services as guides or money changers, and do not agree to be taken anywhere with anyone. In crowds, be alert for pickpockets—wear a money belt, and/or keep your purse close to your body and securely closed. If you travel by train, don't accept food or beverages from a fellow passenger. Those who accept such generosity—and Indians are most commonly the victims—sometimes ingest drug-laced refreshment and are robbed once the drug takes effect. It's likely that you will be offered food on a train; Indians feel uncomfortable eating meals in front of another without sharing, but politely offer an excuse and refuse. In train stations, ignore touts who tell you that your hotel of choice is full or has closed; they hope to settle you into a place where they get a kickback for bringing in business. Do not agree to carry a parcel for anyone.

Women need to take extra precautions. If you're alone, don't travel late at night, especially in Delhi. Avoid seedy areas, touts volunteering their services, or over-friendly strangers and jostling crowds of men. Also, never get into a taxi or auto-rickshaw if a second man accompanies the driver. If you find yourself in a tricky situation—a taxi driver demanding a king's ransom, a hawker plaguing you, a stranger following you—head straight for a policeman or at least threaten to do so, which often works just as well. Don't hesitate to protest loudly if you're harassed.

Overnight trains are safe for women traveling alone provided they take the second-class air-conditioned category. You can't lock the door, but that's why it's safe—you're in a compartment packed with other people. Just remember to chain your luggage to the loops provided below your sleeping berth (luggage chains and locks are available at every major railway station). It's best to avoid general first-class or first-class air-conditioned trains, because on those you're locked in a room with three others—who will probably be male.

India is a conservative culture, and women here have fairly conservative manners. There are certain things even urban, sophisticated Indian women, young or old, are careful not to do, and these are best avoided by women tourists, too. Don't shake hands unless you are at a business meeting or with friends; you are not expected to. Wear appropriate clothes. Don't touch a man by way of a friendly gesture or vice-versa. Do not continuously look a man in the eye as you talk, and do not smile excessively. Do not sit next to the taxi driver or chauffeur in the front seat; sit at the rear. Avoid smoking publicly or drinking alcohol alone in public unless you are at a luxury hotel. Don't allow a man to buy you a meal or a drink or give a gift to you if you are alone. Definitely do not share your table or taxi with anyone. Do not invite anyone you do not know well enough to your hotel or your hotel room or let anyone even know the name of the hotel where you are staying if you are traveling alone (avoid having anything delivered to your hotel). And don't let on that you are traveling alone. (Most definitely shun crummy hotels if you are.)

If you're traveling alone, consider wearing a wedding ring to avoid harassment, and tell people you're meeting your husband later that day; Indians seldom understand why women would not be married in their twenties (unless they are widows). Do avoid long personal conversations on trains and in public places or with shopkeepers, hawkers, or unknown, excessively curious men; you may find it difficult to get rid of the person later. On trains and buses if you are suspicious of a fellow passenger's behavior or are being bothered, even in the middle of the night, make it public, raise a commotion, and attempt to call the conductor. If you're being bothered by someone, anywhere, make your displeasure known publicly and loudly and even complain to a passerby if a policeman is not nearby; create a ruckus. When reserving your train ticket, you can request a berth in one of the "ladies compartments" that exist on some long-distance trains.

TIP→ Distribute your cash, credit cards, IDs, and other valuables between a deep front pocket, an inside jacket or vest pocket, and a hidden money pouch. Don't reach for the money pouch once you're in public.

TAXES

Airport departure tax is Rs. 225 for non-Indians, and it's included in the price of your ticket. The tax is the same no matter which country you fly to.

VAT, or value-added tax, applies only to restaurant food, and it's 12.5%. If your hotel room costs more than Rs. 1,200 a night, you'll pay a service tax and possibly a luxury tax. Rates differ from state to state, but 10% is common.

TIME

There are no time changes from region to region in India. The entire country operates on Indian Standard Time, which is 5½ hours ahead of Greenwich Mean Time, 10½ hours ahead of Eastern Standard Time, 13½ hours ahead of Pacific Standard Time, 4½ hours behind Sydney time, and 7½ hours behind Auckland time. India does not observe daylight saving time.

TIPPING

It's true that much of India runs on tips, but you can get a skewed understanding of the system if you stay only in top hotels, where wealthy tourists and business people are a majority of the clientele. In those situations, hotel employees have come to appreciate modest tips. In smaller towns, however, tipping is less institutionalized and not expected in many instances. Always trust your instincts and reward good service accordingly wherever you are. Some guidelines:

Always tip in cash. You should leave 10% on any restaurant bill, 15% for exceptional service. At large luxury chains like Oberoi Hotels, tips to individuals are not encouraged, but they ask you to leave one tip at the end of your stay, which management then divides among staff. At other hotels, you won't go wrong if you tip your room valet Rs. 20 per night. Bellboys and bell captains should be paid Rs. 10 per bag. For room service, tip 10% of the bill. Tip the concierge about Rs. 10 if he gets you a taxi, or consider an Rs. 100 tip at the end of your stay if he has helped you in several situations. Train-station and airport porters should be paid Rs. 5–Rs. 10 per bag, depending on the weight. Set the rate before you let him take your bags (a sign may be posted with official rates). Taxi drivers don't expect tips unless they go through a great deal of trouble to reach your destination; in such a case Rs. 10–Rs. 15 is fair. Taxi drivers expect Rs. 5 per piece of luggage over and above the meter charge, but locals know this practice is not sanctioned in any other instance except with foreigners. If you hire a car and driver, tip the driver about Rs. 50–Rs. 100 per day, depending on the distance traveled and about Rs. 25 for each lunch or dinner; also give him a larger amount at the end of the journey if you have been using him for many days. Tip local guides 10% of the price of the tour.

TIPPING GUIDELINES FOR INDIA	
Bartender	10% percent of bill
Bellhop	Rs. 10 per bag
Hotel Concierge	Depends on level of service. At least Rs. 10 for getting a car or taxi.
Hotel Doorman	Rs. 5 if he opens car door
Room Valet	Rs. 20 a day
Hotel Room-Service Waiter	10% of bill
Porter at Airport or Train Station	Negotiate price before accepting service. Not more than Rs. 10 per bag
Skycap at Airport	Same as porter
Taxi Driver	None
Tour Guide	Depends on extent of tour. 10% of total price is acceptable
Valet Parking Attendant	Rs. 20
Waiter	10% at a regular restaurant. 15% at high-end and five star hotel restaurants. Make sure service has not been added to the bill.
Hired Driver	Rs. 50–Rs. 100 per day

INDEX

N

W

Y

Z

PHOTO CREDITS

Chapter 1: Experience India: 9, *Kevin Schafer/age fotostock*. 10 and 11 (right), *Dinodia Images/Alamy*. 11 (left), *James Cheadle/Alamy*. 13 (left), *Yadid Levy/age fotostock*. 13 (right), *R. Matina/age fotostock*. 15 (left), *INTERFOTO Pressebildagentur/Alamy*. 15 (right), *P. Narayan/age fotostock*. 16, *Dinodia Images/Alamy*. 17 (left), *Pictorial Press Ltd/Alamy*. 17 (right), *Walter Bibikow/age fotostock*. 18, *Dinodia/age fotostock*. 19, *David Noble Photography/Alamy*. 20, *Lebedinski Vladislav/Shutterstock*. 21 (left), *Manjari Sharma*. 21 (right), *Holger Mette/Shutterstock*. 28, *Eddie Gerald/Alamy*. 29 (left), *Johnny Stockshooter/age fotostock*. 29 (right), *James Cheadle/Alamy*. 30, *Images & Stories/Alamy*. **Chapter 2: Delhi:** 31, *Franck Guiziou/age fotostock*. 32, *Blaine Harrington/age fotostock*. 33, *Lee Marquis/Alamy*. **Chapter 3: North Central India:** 87, *Blaine Harrington/age fotostock*. 88, *Franck Guiziou/age fotostock*. 89 (top left), *Iconotec/Alamy*. 89 (bottom left), *Robert Preston/Alamy*. 89 (bottom right), *Blaine Harrington/age fotostock*. **Chapter 4: Rajasthan & Gujarat:** 157, *J.D. Heaton/age fotostock*. 158 and 159 (top), *Blaine Harrington/age fotostock*. 159 (bottom), *Picture Finders/age fotostock*. **Chapter 5: Uttarakhand:** 265, *Dinodia/age fotostock*. 266 (top), *Tolo Balaguer/age fotostock*. 266 (bottom), *P. Narayan/age fotostock*. 267, *Dhritiman Mukherjee/age fotostock*. **Chapter 6: Himachal Pradesh & Ladakh:** 287, *Angelo Cavalli/age fotostock*. 288, *Bruno Morandi/age fotostock*. 289 (top), *Salanderman/Shutterstock*. 289 (bottom), *Angelo Cavalli/age fotostock*. **Chapter 7: Mumbai & Maharashtra:** 341, *Dinodia/age fotostock*. 342, *Visual Arts Library (London)/Alamy*. 343 (top), *Dinodia/age fotostock*. 343 (bottom), *Neil McAllister/Alamy*. **Chapter 8: Goa:** 443, *Mediacolor's/Alamy*. 444 (top), *Jordi Camí/age fotostock*. 444 (bottom), *f1 online/Alamy*. 445 (top), *Jordi Camí/age fotostock*. 445 (bottom), *World Pictures/age fotostock*. **Chapter 9: Karnataka & Hyderabad:** 477, *P. Narayan/age fotostock*. 478 (top), *Nitish Naharas/Alamy*. 478 (bottom), *Mikhail Nekrasov/Shutterstock*. 479 (top), *Jens Storch/Alamy*. 479 (bottom), *Hornbil Images/Alamy*. **Chapter 10: Kerala:** 543, *Manjari Sharma*. 544 (top), *Jean Kugler/age fotostock*. 544 (bottom), *Maurice Joseph/Alamy*. 545 (top), *Stuart Pearce/age fotostock*. 545 (bottom), *Jean-Baptiste Rabouan/age fotostock*. **Chapter 11: Tamil Nadu:** 585, *Jean-Baptiste Rabouan/age fotostock*. 586, *Manjari Sharma*. 587 (top), *Larry Trupp/Alamy*. 587 (bottom), *P. Narayan/age fotostock*. **Chapter 12: Orissa:** 635, *Jean-Baptiste Rabouan/age fotostock*. 636, *Keren Su/China Span/Alamy*. 637 (top and bottom), *Maurice Joseph/Alamy*. **Chapter 13: Kolkata (Calcutta):** 667, *Tim Graham/Alamy*. 668 (top), *Luciano Mortula/Shutterstock*. 668 (bottom), *V. Muthuraman/SuperStock*. 669 (top), *Angelika Jakob/Bilderberg/Aurora Photos*. 669 (bottom), *Vittorio Sciosia/age fotostock*. **Chapter 14: Darjeeling & Sikkim:** 699 and 700, *Marcos Welsh/age fotostock*. 701 (top), *Dinodia/age fotostock*. 701 (bottom), *Richard Durnan/Aurora Photos*.

ABOUT OUR WRITERS

Harpreet Anand is a professional nomad with a passion for public health, travel, photography and writing; she wrote our Rajasthan chapter. When not gallivanting through remote parts of the world working on HIV/AIDS and reproductive health issues, she can be found globe-trotting with a camera in hand. She is most content when on the move and has lived in India, the United States, and is currently living and working on HIV/AIDS in southern Sudan.

The granddaughter of Estonian and Indian freedom fighters on both sides, **Vaihayasi Pande Daniel** was born in Montreal, grew up in Baltimore, and has lived in India since 1976. Peripatetic tendencies draw her all over India, and elsewhere, but she prefers Mumbai to any other place in the world. A managing editor at www.rediff.com and its New York–based newspaper, *India Abroad,* she has been writing on travel for 14 years. Vaihayasi's other passions include photography, cooking, and experimenting with all kinds of cuisines.

Barbara Floria has been a travel writer and photographer for 25 years, visiting 46 states and 26 countries. As the editor of *Vitality* magazine, an award-winning corporate health magazine, she has covered spas and spa-treatments worldwide. She has traveled in Haryana, Rajasthan and Uttar Pradesh, and spent several weeks in Goa during the monsoon for this Fodor's edition. She loves Indian people, food and history and hopes to live in this instructive country some day.

Prashant Gopal, who updated the Kerala and Kolkata chapters, writes about real estate for BusinessWeek.com in New York. Previously he covered real estate for The Record of Bergen County, N.J., and covered housing and development issues at the South Florida *Sun-Sentinel.* He has also worked for newspapers in Delaware and New Delhi. Gopal is a graduate of Bates College in Maine and the Columbia University Graduate School of Journalism.

Alison Granito is a freelance journalist who divides her time between New Delhi and New York. She has written about anything and everything from mergers and acquisitions in New York to Rajasthani folk music for magazines and newspapers on three continents. These days she can frequently be found with her nose in a good book on the way to wherever she's going next.

As a former staff writer for *The Indian Express*, journalist **Monica Mercer** covered countless stories in and around Mumbai and occasionally traveled for assignments like the 2004 International Film Festival of India in Goa. After surviving a motorcycle crash on the streets of New Delhi and a fanatical crowd of cricket fans in Lahore, Pakistan, Monica still loves to visit India—but now happily writes for an American newspaper.

A former Fodor's editor, **John Rambow** recently returned to New York from living two years in India, primarily in Bangalore. He is now editor of the travel blog gridskipper.com.